SMITHSONIAN CONTRIBUTIONS TO KNOWLEDGE

277

TABLES, DISTRIBUTION, AND VARIATIONS

OF THE

ATMOSPHERIC TEMPERATURE

IN THE

UNITED STATES,

AND SOME ADJACENT PARTS OF AMERICA.

COLLECTED BY THE SMITHSONIAN INSTITUTION, AND DISCUSSED UNDER THE DIRECTION OF

JOSEPH HENRY, SECRETARY.

BY

CHARLES A. SCHOTT,

ASSISTANT U. S. COAST SURVEY; MEMBER NAT. ACAD. OF SCIENCES; PHIL. SOCS. OF PHILADELPHIA AND WASHINGTON, AND OF ACADEMY OF SCIENCES OF CATANIA, SICILY.

WASHINGTON CITY:

PUBLISHED BY THE SMITHSONIAN INSTITUTION.

1876.

PHILADELPHIA:
COLLINS, PRINTER, 705 JAYNE STREET.

CONTENTS.

SECTION III.

Illustrations to Section III.

ADVERTISEMENT.

At the commencement of the operations of the Smithsonian Institution a system of meteorology was established, carried on by voluntary observers, which was continued for more than twenty years until it was transferred to the Signal Service of the United States Army in 1874 to be continued by means of the annual appropriations of Congress. This system included observations on the temperature, pressure, aqueous precipitation, moisture of the air, and winds.

The object now of the Smithsonian Institution is to render the results of these observations accessible to meteorologists by their reduction, discussion, and publication; but to give greater value to this work it has been thought advisable to incorporate in it all accessible and reliable meteorological observations that have been made in the United States since the early settlement of this country.

The first part of the general work, that on the aqueous precipitation, was published in 1872, that which relates to the winds is now in the press, and the other parts will follow in succession.

The present memoir relating to the temperatures contains the results of all observations to the end of the year 1870, from the following sources:—

1st. The registers of the Smithsonian Institution, embracing upwards of 300 folio volumes.

2d. The joint publications of the Institution and of the Patent Office and Department of Agriculture.

3d. All the publications and unpublished records of the meteorological system of the United States Army.

4th. The records of the United States Lake Survey under the Engineer Department of the United States Army.

5th. The records of the United States Coast Survey, under the Treasury Department.

6th. The volumes compiled by Dr. F. B. Hough from observations made under the direction of the Regents of the University of the State of New York.

7th. The records made in Pennsylvania under the direction of the Franklin Institute of Philadelphia.

8th. The transactions of various societies and periodical publications.

The first part of the work was the formation of an extended series of classified tables derived from the foregoing sources, and the second the deduction from these consolidated tables, of average temperatures. The first of these series, owing to its great bulk, must for the present remain in manuscript. It can, however, be consulted at any time at the Institution. The second series, which is given in the following pages, consisting of average temperatures, is sufficient to furnish all necessary information for the study of our climate as far as it depends upon temperature.

All the materials were placed in charge of Mr. Charles A. Schott, Assistant United States Coast Survey, to be reduced and discussed under his direction by trained computers, at the expense of the income of the Smithson fund. He was ably assisted by Mr. E. H. Courtenay, of the United States Coast Survey.

The character of Mr. Schott for scientific knowledge, sagacity, and skill in the line of investigation, and scrupulous accuracy as exhibited in the previous meteorological publications of the Institution, give assurance that the work here presented to the public is a valuable contribution to the knowledge of the climate of the United States.

JOSEPH HENRY,
Secretary Smithsonian Institution.

WASHINGTON, D. C.,
January, 1876.

SECTION I.

TABLES, DISTRIBUTION, AND VARIATIONS OF THE ATMOSPHERIC TEMPERATURE IN THE UNITED STATES,

AND SOME ADJACENT PARTS OF AMERICA.

GENERAL REMARKS.

THE laws of the distribution of winds, rain, and heat of a large portion of North America, embracing the normal or statical values as well as their variations with seasons and for longer periods of years, form part of those studies with whose results we are most directly concerned. Although this ground has been gone over many times and must continue to be cultivated, the continued accumulation of new materials enables the investigator gradually to present his results in a more precise form and to enter more fully into detail or local discussions. Whatever imperfections the available records may possess, their effect in the mean values will constantly diminish with the increase of reliable modern observations; moreover, they could not be dispensed with on account of inaccuracies, since they form the only material in our possession for the discussion of such subjects as possible changes in climate since the first settlement of the States. In the following work we shall therefore be chiefly occupied with the establishment of tabular results comparable among themselves, with obtaining mean or normal values or the so-called constants of temperature, as factors of the climate, and with the range of the fluctuations, daily, annual, and secular, also with the generalization of the results either in analytical or graphical form.

The advantages gained by an early discussion of observations beyond putting us in possession of results for immediate use are several; light is thrown on the reliability of the records, their sufficiency or insufficiency for our present or future wants, and the kind of results they are or are not capable of yielding, is indicated. Besides improvements in methods of observing and in instrumental means are likely to result, as well as incitements of the observer to renewed efforts.

Our earliest records of temperature, the results of which are given in the following tables, date about a quarter of a century after the invention of Fahrenheit's thermometer,[1] and with few exceptions all the observers in this country have made

[1] The following information is extracted from Gehler's Physikalisches Wörterbuch, Leipzig, 1839. * * * To Daniel G. Fahrenheit, of Dantzic (Prussia), is due the merit of having constructed,

use of his scale, in consequence of which all tabular quantities and results presented in this paper have reference to this graduation. For the sake of uniformity, records originally given in Réaumur or Centigrade scale have been converted into that of Fahrenheit, and however advisable otherwise it might have been to adopt the Centigrade scale, such a step was forbidden by the great labor and consequent expense which the conversion would have entailed.

---

on proper principles, thermometers upon which reliance could be placed; his earlier instruments were filled with alcohol, but about the year 1714 he used mercury for this purpose. According to his own account, he recognized three principal points, viz.: his so-called absolute zero, representing the extreme cold experienced by him in the severe winter of 1709 and erroneously supposed to indicate the greatest cold, the freezing point of water, and a point representing the heat of the human body; in practice, however, he made use of the freezing point as well as of the boiling point of water, with the fixity of which latter he became acquainted in 1714. Supposing the volume of mercury at the temperature represented by his zero point to be 11124 parts, he noticed an expansion of 32 parts at the temperature of freezing water, and of 212 parts at the temperature of boiling water, and accordingly adopted the numbers 32 and 212 to indicate these temperatures. Before Fahrenheit's instruments came into general use, Réaumur brought out his spirit thermometers graduated between the freezing and boiling points of water from 0 to 80, and shortly after, Celsius, about 1742, introduced the Centigrade division between the same points. The spirit thermometers used in the preceding century had arbitrary scales, and were not generally directly comparable. * * * Fahrenheit had already noticed the effect of a change in the atmospheric pressure on the position of the boiling point, but the proper allowance or reduction to a standard pressure was not satisfactorily ascertained in his time. It would seem that allowance was made for the expansion of the glass tube in the above-mentioned experiment, since the dilatation of mercury is nearly 0.0001 of its volume for 1° Fah. All of the thermometric scales mentioned are intended to measure equal increments of heat by equal increments in their scale readings, but for the purpose of comparison and discussion it is much to be desired that all should agree to use the same scale, the Centigrade scale being the one most likely to take the place of the others.

In connection with the cold indicated by the zero of Fahrenheit's scale it may be remarked as an *accidental* circumstance, that it may and has been taken *roughly* to be that of the mean annual temperature of the pole, hence the possibility of representing approximately the annual mean temperature in the latitude ϕ by the simple expression $81^\circ.5 \cos \phi$ *without* the addition of a constant.

TABULATION

OF

RESULTING MEAN TEMPERATURES

FROM

OBSERVATIONS EXTENDING OVER A SERIES OF YEARS, FROM THE EARLIEST TO NEARLY THE PRESENT TIME,

FOR

EACH MONTH, SEASON, AND THE YEAR,

PRINCIPALLY FOR

STATIONS IN NORTH AMERICA.

EXPLANATIONS AND REMARKS

ON THE

CONSOLIDATED TABLES OF RESULTING MEAN TEMPERATURES FOR EACH MONTH, SEASON, AND THE YEAR.

THAT part of the tables which refers to the United States is arranged in alphabetical order according to states and territories, and the names in each subdivision are given alphabetically. For all stations beyond the limits of the United States it was considered more advantageous to adopt a geographical arrangement, but the alphabetical sequence of stations under each geographical district is preserved.

The tables contain: The number and name of each station, its latitude and longitude, its elevation above the sea when known, its mean temperatures for each month, each season, and for the whole year, the beginning and ending of the series of observations, its actual extent, the observing hours, the name of the observer with references.

The geographical positions are given to the nearest minute of arc, as far as known, the longitudes are counted as usual west of Greenwich. The positions which became known through the operations of the United States Coast Survey are reliable, as well as those given upon the authorities of the United States Lake Survey, officers of the United States Army, directors of astronomical observatories, and, in general, all those positions which have been determined by direct astronomical observations and those connected with the General Land Office. Positions given on the authority of the observer, and these are by far the most numerous, are less trustworthy, since most of these were taken from State or county maps having no adequate astronomical basis. The results for longitude depending on the electric telegraph are of so recent date that but few maps have as yet incorporated them. Although no pains have been spared to render these geographical positions as trustworthy as possible, they are, in general, when taken from maps evidently in the given latitudes affected with a probable uncertainty of from $\pm 3'$ to $\pm 5'$ and in the given longitudes with a probable uncertainty of from $\pm 5'$ to $\pm 8'$. Fortunately for the immediate wants of the discussion of temperature a moderate approximation to the true position suffices. The elevations of the observing stations depend in all cases upon the statements of observers; these also no doubt require considerable improvement, as but few depend upon direct hypsometric measures or on measured differences of level from known railroad or canal levels; those depending on barometric observations can only be regarded as rough approximations. Heights near tide-water may be considered to be reliable.

Unless otherwise stated, the mean tabular values of the temperature, always expressed in degrees of the Fahrenheit scale, refer to the *observing hours* noted, and are consequently uncorrected for daily variation. In all cases where the observing hours were variable or were changed during the series, the results were referred either to those observing hours maintained for the longest period or to those susceptible of the greater accuracy, or else all were corrected for daily fluctuation. The means for correcting observed values, taken at stated epochs of the day and for any month, were furnished by the discussion of the daily variation, but the stations available for such discussions are comparatively so very few in number, and are almost wanting for the western part of the United States, that but a small portion of our results could be so corrected. If we had better and more complete materials for daily variation, it would undoubtedly have been preferable to correct all tabular results for this inequality, but in their absence it was deemed advisable to attempt no more than to present the results *in any one series* for a *uniform set* of hours of observation, correcting as stated in all cases where the observer has changed his times of observation; this gives us the advantage of effecting hereafter a more satisfactory reduction to the mean of twenty-four hours whenever we come into possession of new and, it is to be hoped, automatic registers.

Respecting the results obtained under the University System of the State of New York, the daily mean was directed[1] to be found by adding to the morning observation twice the afternoon observation, and twice the evening observation to that of next morning, and dividing their sum by six. This may be symbolically expressed by $\frac{1}{6}\{\odot_r + 3_a \text{ bis} + (\odot_s + 1^h) \text{ bis} + \odot_r\}$; the morning observation was to be taken a little before sunrise. The means given in the table were made out in accordance with this rule.[2]

With respect to the Smithsonian system of meteorological observations, the result of the three hours 7 A. M. 2 and 9 P. M. was found to approximate less closely to the true daily mean than the result obtained by adding twice the reading at 9 P. M. to the readings at 7 A. M. and 2 P. M. and dividing this sum by four. The latter rule was therefore adopted, and is symbolically indicated by $\frac{1}{4}\}7_m + 2_a + 9_a \text{ bis}\}$. In the column headed observing hours the symbols $\odot_r$ and $\odot_s$ stand for sunrise and sunset; the affixes m. and a. to any given hour indicate morning and afternoon respectively; N. and Mdt. stand for noon and midnight; M. and E. for morning and evening; Max. and Min. for mean from maximum and minimum readings;

---

[1] F. B. Hough, p. iv of the introduction to the results of meteorological observations made in obedience to instructions from the Regents of the University at sundry Academies in the State of New York, Albany, 1855.

[2] It should also be mentioned that for these Academy stations the monthly means are made up from the half-monthly means, there is therefore a slight inconsistency in the results for the months having an odd number of days (the first 15 days having been united into a mean for all months, excepting February). The October mean is most affected, less so May and March; the amount generally less than $0^\circ.1$ is small enough to be neglected.

"bis" attached to any hour indicates that the reading at this hour received double weight as explained above.

Respecting the corrections necessary to refer monthly and annual means depending on observations at certain hours to what they would have been had the observations been made hourly and continued day and night, the reader is referred to the discussion of the daily variation of the temperature. In this discussion it is shown that the mean of hourly observations represents the average temperature of the day within about 0°.01 Fah.

The following table of corrections for daily variation to means resulting from observations at certain hours was prepared directly from observations extending over a series of years at Toronto, Mohawk, New Haven, and Philadelphia; it is inserted here on account of its frequent application to our tabular results, either to refer them to the mean of the day or to a uniform set of hours, in which latter case the table can be made readily to apply. This table of corrections was found to answer well enough for the Eastern and Western States lying within the range of latitudes of the four stations; for Southern States and for the elevated western portion of the United States other less reliable corrections had to be supplied.

Table of corrections for daily variation of temperature, derived from observations made at Toronto, Mohawk, New Haven, and Philadelphia; for every hour and for various combinations of hours, in degrees of Fahrenheit.

Hours.	Jan.	Feb.	March.	April.	May.	June.	July.	August.	Sept.	Oct.	Nov.	Dec.	Year.
Mid't	+1.6°	+2.2°	+2.8°	+3.7°	+4.7°	+5.2°	+5.2°	+4.7°	+4.2°	+3.2°	+2.0°	+1.4°	+3.41°
1_m	+2.0	+2.7	+3.4	+4.6	+5.6	+6.3	+6.0	+5.4	+4.6	+3.8	+2.1	+1.8	+4.02
2_m	+2.2	+3.1	+3.9	+5.3	+6.4	+7.1	+6.7	+6.0	+5.2	+4.3	+2.5	+2.1	+4.57
3_m	+2.5	+3.6	+4.3	+5.7	+7.2	+7.8	+7.3	+6.5	+5.7	+4.7	+2.9	+2.4	+5.05
4_m	+2.7	+3.9	+4.7	+6.2	+7.8	+8.3	+7.8	+7.0	+6.2	+5.1	+3.2	+2.6	+5.46
5_m	+3.0	+4.2	+5.2	+6.5	+7.8	+8.1	+7.8	+7.2	+6.6	+5.4	+3.4	+2.8	+5.67
6_m	+3.0	+4.5	+5.4	+6.3	+6.4	+6.4	+6.3	+6.5	+6.4	+5.5	+3.5	+3.1	+5.27
7_m	+3.1	+4.6	+4.7	+4.7	+4.0	+3.8	+3.7	+4.5	+4.7	+4.6	+3.4	+3.1	+4.08
8_m	+2.8	+3.5	+2.7	+2.4	+1.5	+1.1	+1.1	+1.8	+2.2	+2.6	+2.4	+2.7	+2.24
9_m	+1.4	+1.3	+0.5	0.0	−0.9	−1.2	−1.2	−0.6	−0.2	+0.2	+0.7	+1.3	+0.11
10_m	−0.4	−0.9	−1.6	−2.0	−2.8	−3.2	−3.2	−2.8	−2.5	−2.1	−1.1	−0.5	−1.93
11_m	−1.9	−2.7	−3.2	−3.7	−4.4	−4.8	−4.9	−4.6	−4.4	−3.9	−2.6	−2.0	−3.60
Noon.	−3.2	−4.1	−4.5	−5.1	−5.7	−6.1	−6.2	−5.9	−5.7	−5.3	−3.8	−3.2	−4.91
1_a	−4.0	−5.1	−5.4	−6.2	−6.8	−7.1	−7.1	−6.9	−6.8	−6.2	−4.5	−4.0	−5.84
2_a	−4.5	−5.6	−6.1	−7.0	−7.5	−7.8	−7.6	−7.5	−7.4	−6.8	−4.8	−4.3	−6.42
3_a	−4.4	−5.7	−6.2	−7.2	−7.8	−8.1	−7.8	−7.8	−7.6	−6.7	−4.7	−4.1	−6.51
4_a	−3.8	−5.2	−5.8	−7.1	−7.8	−8.0	−7.5	−7.6	−7.4	−6.1	−3.8	−3.3	−6.12
5_a	−2.5	−3.9	−4.7	−6.3	−7.2	−7.2	−6.9	−6.8	−6.2	−4.4	−2.4	−2.0	−5.04
6_a	−1.5	−2.3	−2.9	−4.6	−5.5	−5.7	−5.4	−5.1	−4.0	−2.5	−1.3	−1.2	−3.51
7_a	−0.7	−1.2	−1.5	−2.2	−2.9	−3.3	−3.0	−2.5	−1.6	−1.0	−0.5	−0.6	−1.74
8_a	−0.1	−0.2	−0.4	−0.2	−0.2	−0.4	−0.2	+0.1	+0.3	+0.2	+0.1	−0.1	−0.09
9_a	+0.4	+0.5	+0.9	+1.2	+1.5	+1.6	+1.8	+1.7	+1.6	+1.1	+0.7	+0.3	+1.11
10_a	+0.9	+1.1	+1.5	+2.2	+2.7	+3.0	+3.1	+2.9	+2.7	+1.9	+1.1	+0.7	+1.99
11_a	+1.2	+1.7	+2.2	+3.0	+3.8	+4.3	+4.2	+3.8	+3.5	+2.6	+1.5	+1.0	+2.73
$\odot_r$	+3.0	+4.5	+5.3	+6.4	+7.8	+8.1	+7.8	+7.1	+6.5	+5.3	+3.4	+2.9	+5.68
$\odot_s$	−2.7	−3.0	−2.8	−2.8	−2.2	−1.5	−1.3	−2.4	−3.7	−3.7	−2.9	−2.7	−2.64
Max.	−4.5	−5.8	−6.2	−7.3	−7.9	−8.2	−7.8	−7.8	−7.7	−6.9	−4.9	−4.3	−6.62
Min.	+3.3	+4.6	+5.4	+6.5	+7.9	+8.4	+7.9	+7.2	+6.7	+5.6	+3.6	+3.2	+5.87
Max. & Min.	−0.6	−0.6	−0.4	−0.4	0.0	+0.1	+0.1	−0.3	−0.5	−0.6	−0.6	−0.6	−0.37
$\odot_r$ $\odot_s$	+0.2	+0.7	+1.3	+1.8	+2.8	+3.3	+3.2	+2.4	+1.4	+0.8	+0.2	+0.1	+1.52
$\odot_r$ 9_a	+1.7	+2.5	+3.1	+3.8	+4.6	+4.9	+4.8	+4.4	+4.0	+3.2	+2.1	+1.6	+3.39
6_m 1_a	−0.5	−0.3	0.0	0.0	−0.2	−0.3	−0.4	−0.2	−0.2	−0.4	−0.5	−0.4	−0.28
7_m 2_a	−0.7	−0.5	−0.7	−1.2	−1.7	−2.0	−2.0	−1.5	−1.3	−1.1	−0.7	−0.6	−1.17
7_m 9_a	+1.7	+2.6	+2.8	+3.0	+2.7	+2.7	+2.8	+3.1	+3.1	+2.9	+2.0	+1.7	+2.60
8_m 2_a	−0.8	−1.1	−1.7	−2.3	−3.0	−3.3	−3.3	−2.9	−2.6	−2.1	−1.2	−0.8	−2.09
8_m 7_a	+1.0	+1.2	+0.6	+0.1	−0.7	−1.1	−0.9	−0.4	+0.3	+0.8	+0.9	+1.1	+0.24
$\odot_r$ 9_m 3_a	0.0	0.0	−0.1	−0.3	−0.3	−0.4	−0.4	−0.4	−0.4	−0.4	−0.2	0.0	−0.24
$\odot_r$ N. $\odot_s$	−1.0	−0.9	−0.7	−0.5	0.0	+0.2	+0.1	−0.4	−1.0	−1.2	−1.1	−1.0	−0.62
$\odot_r$ 1_a 9_a	−0.2	0.0	+0.3	+0.5	+0.8	+0.9	+0.8	+0.6	+0.4	+0.1	−0.1	−0.3	+0.32
$\odot_r$ 1_a 10_a	0.0	+0.2	+0.5	+0.8	+1.2	+1.3	+1.3	+1.0	+0.8	+0.3	0.0	−0.1	+0.61
$\odot_r$ 2_a $\odot_s$	−1.4	−1.4	−1.2	−1.1	−0.6	−0.4	−0.4	−0.9	−1.5	−1.7	−1.4	−1.4	−1.13
$\odot_r$ 2_a 9_a	−0.4	−0.2	0.0	+0.2	+0.6	+0.6	+0.7	+0.4	+0.2	−0.1	−0.2	−0.4	+0.12
$\odot_r$ 3_a 9_a	−0.3	−0.2	0.0	+0.1	+0.5	+0.5	+0.6	+0.3	+0.2	−0.1	−0.2	−0.3	+0.09
6_m N. 6_a	−0.6	−0.6	−0.7	−1.1	−1.6	−1.8	−1.8	−1.5	−1.1	−0.8	−0.5	−0.4	−1.05
6_m 2_a 9_a	−0.4	−0.2	+0.1	+0.2	+0.1	+0.1	+0.2	+0.2	+0.2	−0.1	−0.2	−0.3	−0.01
6_m 2_a 10_a	−0.2	0.0	+0.3	+0.5	+0.5	+0.5	+0.6	+0.6	+0.6	+0.2	−0.1	−0.2	+0.28
7_m N. 6_a	−0.5	−0.6	−0.9	−1.7	−2.4	−2.7	−2.6	−2.2	−1.7	−1.1	−0.6	−0.4	−1.45
7_m 1_a 8_a	−0.3	−0.2	−0.4	−0.6	−1.0	−1.2	−1.2	−0.8	−0.6	−0.5	−0.3	−0.3	−0.62
7_m 1_a 9_a	−0.2	0.0	+0.1	−0.1	−0.4	−0.6	−0.5	−0.2	−0.2	−0.2	−0.1	−0.2	−0.22
7_m 2_a 5_a	−1.3	−1.6	−2.0	−2.9	−3.6	−3.7	−3.6	−3.3	−3.0	−2.2	−1.3	−1.1	−2.46
7_m 2_a 6_a	−1.0	−1.1	−1.4	−2.3	−3.0	−3.2	−3.1	−2.7	−2.3	−1.6	−0.9	−0.8	−1.95
7_m 2_a 7_a	−0.7	−0.7	−1.0	−1.5	−2.1	−2.4	−2.3	−1.8	−1.4	−1.1	−0.6	−0.6	−1.36
7_m 2_a 9_a	−0.3	−0.2	−0.2	−0.4	−0.7	−0.8	−0.7	−0.4	−0.4	−0.4	−0.2	−0.3	−0.41
7_m 3_a 9_a	−0.3	−0.2	−0.2	−0.4	−0.8	−0.9	−0.8	−0.5	−0.4	−0.3	−0.2	−0.2	−0.43
8_m 2_a 6_a	−1.1	−1.5	−2.1	−3.1	−3.8	−4.1	−4.0	−3.6	−3.1	−2.2	−1.2	−0.9	−2.56

Table of corrections for daily variation of temperature, etc.—Continued.

Hours.	Jan.	Feb.	March.	April.	May.	June.	July.	August.	Sept.	Oct.	Nov.	Dec.	Year.
$8_m\ 2_a\ 8_a$	−0.6°	−0.8°	−1.3°	−1.6°	−2.1°	−2.4°	−2.2°	−1.9°	−1.6°	−1.3°	−0.8°	−0.5°	−1.42°
$8_m\ 2_a\ 9_a$	−0.4	−0.5	−0.8	−1.1	−1.5	−1.7	−1.6	−1.3	−1.2	−1.0	−0.6	−0.4	−1.02
$8_m\ 2_a\ 10_a$	−0.3	−0.3	−0.6	−0.8	−1.1	−1.2	−1.1	−0.9	−0.8	−0.8	−0.4	−0.3	−0.73
9_m N. 9_a	−0.5	−0.8	−1.0	−1.3	−1.7	−1.9	−1.9	−1.6	−1.4	−1.3	−0.8	−0.5	−1.23
$9_m\ 3_a\ 9_a$	−0.9	−1.3	−1.6	−2.0	−2.4	−2.6	−2.4	−2.2	−2.0	−1.8	−1.1	−0.8	−1.76
$\odot_r\ 9_m\ 3_a\ 9_a$	+0.1	+0.2	+0.1	+0.1	+0.2	+0.1	+0.1	+0.1	+0.1	0.0	0.0	+0.1	+0.10
$\odot_r$ N. $2_a\ 6_a$	−1.6	−1.9	−2.1	−2.6	−2.7	−2.9	−2.8	−2.9	−2.6	−2.3	−1.6	−1.5	−2.29
$\odot_r$ N. $\odot_s\ 10_a$	−0.5	−0.4	−0.1	+0.2	+0.6	+0.9	+0.9	+0.4	−0.1	−0.4	−0.5	−0.6	+0.03
$\odot_r\ 2_a\ \odot_s\ 9_a$	−0.9	−0.9	−0.7	−0.5	−0.1	+0.1	+0.2	−0.3	−0.7	−1.0	−0.9	−0.9	−0.56
[1]	−0.9	−0.9	−0.6	−0.5	0.0	+0.3	+0.5	−0.2	−0.8	−1.1	−0.8	−0.7	−0.48
$3_m\ 9_m\ 3_a\ 9_a$	0.0	−0.1	−0.1	−0.1	0.0	0.0	0.0	0.0	−0.1	−0.2	−0.1	0.0	−0.06
$6_m\ 9_m\ 3_a\ 6_a$	−0.4	−0.5	−0.8	−1.4	−2.0	−2.1	−2.0	−1.7	−1.4	−0.9	−0.5	−0.2	−1.16
$6_m\ 9_m\ 3_a\ 9_a$	+0.1	+0.2	+0.1	+0.1	−0.2	−0.3	−0.2	−0.1	+0.1	0.0	0.0	+0.2	0.00
$7_m\ 2_a\ 9_a$ bis	−0.1	0.0	+0.1	0.0	−0.1	−0.2	−0.1	+0.1	+0.1	0.0	0.0	−0.1	−0.03

[1] For New York University System; derived from observations at Toronto and Mohawk.

Respecting the column headed References the following abbreviations were used:—

S. O.	for Smithsonian system of observations.
S. Coll.	for Smithsonian collection in general.
Sm. Con. to. Knowl.	for Smithsonian Contributions to Knowledge.
P. O. and S. I. Vol. I,	for Patent Office and Smithsonian Institution systems.
Ar. Met. Regs.	for Army Meteorological Registers.
MS. from S. G. O.	for Manuscript from Surgeon-General's Office.
Am. Alm	for American Almanac.
Agl. Rep.	for Agricultural Report.
Reg. Rep.	for Regents' Report.
N. Y. Univ. Syst.	for New York University System.

And various others whose meaning is sufficiently apparent

TABLES OF MEAN TEMPERATURE

FOR

EACH MONTH, SEASON, AND THE YEAR AT VARIOUS STATIONS, PRINCIPALLY IN NORTH AMERICA.

EXPRESSED IN DEGREES AND FRACTIONS OF THE FAHRENHEIT SCALE.

ICELAND.

Name of Station.	Lat.	Long.	Height.	Jan.	Feb.	March.	April.	May.	June.	July.	August.	Sept.	Oct.	Nov.	Dec.
1. Eya Fiord	65°42′	18°05′	..	25°.70	18°.50	20°.66	27°.50	36°.14	43°.52	46°.94	46°.94	43°.16	34°.34	25°.88	18°.32
2. Reikjavik	64 09	21 55	..	29.82	28.31	29.86	36.46	44.80	51.58	56.19	52.86	46.45	36.91	30.45	29.41

GREENLAND.

Name of Station.	Lat.	Long.	Height.	Jan.	Feb.	March.	April.	May.	June.	July.	August.	Sept.	Oct.	Nov.	Dec.
1. Friedrichsthal	60 05	44 50	..	19.62	18.72	22.10	27.50	..	..	..	..	..	32.45	35.15	29.75
2. Godthaab	64 10	52 10	..	12.38	12.56	15.60	22.01	32.16	39.09	41.92	40.84	35.65	29.84	21.94	17.49
3. Jacobshavn	69 12	50 58	..	0.05	− 2.20	5.90	16.92	31.77	40.32	45.27	41.67	34.25	26.37	11.52	4.55
4. Lichtenau	60 22	45 40	..	19.74	23.	27.63	32.43	39.27	43.09	45.37	41.09	39.70	35.58	26.13	22.4
5. Lichtenfels	63 00	51 20	..	11.59	13.05	17.71	24.03	32.47	38.73	43.07	40.39	34.77	28.60	21.20	13.93
6. Nye Hernhut	64 10	51 40	..	9.05	22.10	21.65	24.80	32.00	40.10	40.33	37.40	34.03	32.90	15.80	11.75
7. Omenak	70 41	52 00	..	− 6.25	− 8.95	− 1.30	13.77	29.97	38.75	43.02	40.55	32.90	22.55	13.77	− 0.17
8. Port Foulke[2]	78 18	73 00	0	−26.0	−24.9	−22.3	−11.0	+23.8	+33.9	+40.5	(+36.1)	+22.6	+7.6	+ 2.8	−12.8
9. Upernavik	72 47	56 03	..	−12.32	−18.40	− 9.85	+ 2.75	26.15	36.27	39.42	38.52	30.87	19.62	10.17	− 6.70
10. Van Rensselaer Harbor	78 37	70 53	0	−28.20	−26.45	−34.90	−10.35	+13.40	30.10	38.20	31.80	13.45	−3.60	−21.95	−31.15
11. Wolstenholme Sound	76 33	68 56	..	−25.07	−34.02	−17.47	− 3.74	25.82	39.73	40.52	33.67	26.76	11.32	−18.60	−27.05

BRITISH NORTH AMERICA.—ARCTIC REGION.

Name of Station.	Lat.	Long.	Height.	Jan.	Feb.	March.	April.	May.	June.	July.	August.	Sept.	Oct.	Nov.	Dec.
1. Arctic Ocean	74 41	101 22	..	−36.71	−41.12	−31.95	− 7.13	..	..	..	..	17.88	4.06	−20.18	−30.45
2. Assistance Bay	74 40	94 16	..	−29.00	−29.80	−22.40	− 3.20	12.50	34.30	37.80	..	21.30	1.50	− 6.70	−21.40
3. Batty Bay	73 12	91 10	..	−19.92	−18.19	−17.00	+ 2.14	..	..	..	..	22.59	8.53	−11.27	−15.45
4. Bay of Mercy	74 06	117 54	..	−35.59	−32.15	−26.91	− 1.38	10.24	31.50	36.72	33.25	22.34	− 1.15	−15.86	−23.04
5. Beechey Island	74 30	91 5[illegible]	..	−33.00	−25.44	−12.98	+ 1.85	18.92	36.77	39.40	34.25	20.50	10.78	+ 6.78	−23.89
6. Boothia Felix	69 59	92 01	..	−28.69	−32.02	−29.01	− 2.54	15.65	34.16	41.26	38.69	25.41	9.07	− 5.42	−22.43
7. Dealy Island	74 52	108 30	..	−36.13	−30.42	−19.17	− 2.47	16.09	33.04	36.42	33.01	18.80	−0.56	−12.07	−26.00
8. Disaster Bay	75 31	92 10	..	−36.38	−39.23	−29.87	+ 4.84	9.36	27.93	38.09	36.27	17.01	9.52	−17.20	−26.6
9. Fort Anderson	68 30	134 30	..	−38.05	−28.78	−24.80	+ 5.28	25.65	54.28	65.50	..	35.83	17.85	− 2.33	−31.23
10. Fort Confidence	66 54	118 49	500	−26.79	−19.48	−18.92	+ 4.36	27.68	46.69	52.90	45.20	37.66	22.12	− 1.71	−22.7
11. Griffith's Island	74 36	95 30	..	−31.90	−32.90	−25.70	− 7.00	23.00	35.00?	38.50?	36.30?	20.20	0.30	− 6.90	−22.20
12. Igloolik	69 21	81 53	..	−17.07	−20.41	−19.75	− 1.68	24.85	32.16	40.04	37.77	24.45	12.79	−19.37	−27.80
13. Melville Island	74 47	110 48	..	−30.09	−32.19	−18.10	− 8.37	16.66	36.24	42.41	32.68	22.54	−3.46	−20.60	−21.79
14. Northumberland Sound	76 52	97 00	..	−40.00	−28.57	−16.69	− 7.60	14.74	29.86	35.69	33.80	18.48	−0.40	− 5.64	−34.4
15. Peel River[4]	67 32	134 30	..	−24.45	−24.19	−13.88	+15.03	34.06	54.09	58.60	50.90	35.75	12.12	−11.84	−23.4
16. Port Kennedy	72 01	94 14	0	−34.4	−37.1	−18.2	− 2.8	+15.3	+35.3	+40.1	36.95	25.4	7.4	−11.7	−33.
17. Port Bowen	73 14	88 56	..	−28.91	−27.32	−28.38	− 6.50	17.65	36.12	37.29	35.77	25.88	10.85	− 5.00	−19.05
18. Port Leopold	73 31	90 18	..	−35.70	−35.20	−22.80	−10.10	..	..	..	..	..	9.70	−14.50	−36.40
19. Prince of Wales' Strait	72 47	117 34	..	−32.44	−37.67	−28.82	− 4.70	18.85	36.09	37.54	37.15	20.20	−0.23	−10.17	−23.3
20. Repulse Bay[6]	66 32	86 56	15	−29.32	−26.68	−28.10	− 3.95	17.88	31.38	41.46	..	28.57	12.56	+ 0.68	−19.2
21. Repulse Bay[7]	66 32	86 56	10	−32.4	−36.4	−16.9	+ 4.7	24.0	37.7	43.5	..	25.2	12.0	−19.8	−25.4

BRITISH NORTH AMERICA.—SOUTH OF LATITUDE 66° 30′.

Name of Station.	Lat.	Long.	Height.	Jan.	Feb.	March.	April.	May.	June.	July.	August.	Sept.	Oct.	Nov.	Dec.
1. Abbittibe	48 50	77 45	..	+ 2.21	− 2.91	14.16	21.74	30.65	64.58	71.35	61.08	50.40	37.35	23.51	+ 0.0
2. Athabasca Lake	58 43	111 48	700	−23.0	+ 4.8	+ 2.4	35.1	44.8	53.9	..	..	..	21.5	9.8	+ 0.4
3. Bedfont House	57 23	102 59	..	−19.0	−16.7	− 5.0	11.5	24.5	..	..	..	..	26.0	+ 1.5	−18.0
4. Caribou Castle	53 48	56 47	..	+ 0.33	10.67	15.56	35.98	42.59	55.29	51.79	..	..	34.49	24.05	10.0
5. Carlton House	52 51	106 13	1100	..	..	11.92	29.75	47.92	..	..	..	..	..	..	..
6. Cumberland House	53 57	102 20	900	− 5.	− 2.	6.	25.	50.	59.	70.	60.	48.	39.	11.	5.
7. Cumberland House	53 57	102 20	900	−13.2	− 1.1	12.1	35.0	50.0	58.8	61.8	56.2	47.0	36.9	13.0	3.2
8. Cumberland House	53 57	102 20	900	− 0.89	− 8.06	18.30	27.01	52.59	.	.	62.84	44.50	33.15	21.48	7.9
9. Edmondton House	53 40	112 45	1800	11.05	14.32	..	..	..	..	..	..	..	..	..	..
10. Fort à la Corne	53 10	104 30	.	..	..	..	..	..	..	..	..	..	..	19.95	1.4
11. Fort Chipewayan	58 43	111 15	700	− 8.76	− 4.01	+ 3.08	19.80	45.40	55.00	63.00	58.10	43.53	33.00	19.13	2.7

[1] Observations in "morning and evening," from October, 1796, to May, 1802, and from July, 1816, to June, 1821; from September, 1841, to June, 1845, at 10_m and 10_a.
[2] Value for August interpolated.
[3] Observations made every four hours.
[4] Fort McPherson.
[5] From 6 to 12 observations daily.
[6] Fort Hope.
[7] Fort Hope. The September and October observations, made at 8_m 8_a, have been referred to 8_m 2_a 8_a by means of the "Boothia Felix" table. Correction to scale at —35°= —4°.5; at 0° correction supposed 0, and a proportional amount between 0° and —35° applied.

ICELAND.

	Spring.	Summer.	Autumn.	Winter.	Year.	Series. Begins. Ends.	Extent yrs. mos.	Observing hours.	Observer.	References.
1	28°.10	45°.80	34°.46	20°.84	32°.30	....	2 0	......	Van Scheels.	Dove, Rep. Br. Assoc. 1847.
2	37.04	53.54	37.94	29.18	39.43	Jan. 1823; July, 1837	14 6	max. & min.	Thorstenson.	Dove, Rep. Br. Assoc. 1847.

GREENLAND.

	Spring.	Summer.	Autumn.	Winter.	Year.	Series. Begins. Ends.	Extent yrs. mos.	Observing hours.	Observer.	References.
1	..	..	..	22.70	..	....	0 7	......	....	Dove, Rep. Br. Assoc. 1847.
2	23.26	40.62	29.14	14.14	26.79	Oct. 1796; June, 1845	14 6	M. E.[1]	Bull, Muhlenpfort Bloch.	Dove, Rep. Br. Assoc. 1847.
3	18.20	42.42	24.05	0.80	21.37	Aug. 1842; July, 1846	4 0	M. N.	....	Dove, 1857.
4	33.11	43.18	33.80	21.72	32.95	July, 1841; Aug. 1843	2 0	......	....	Dove, Rep. Br. Assoc. 1847.
5	24.74	40.73	28.19	12.86	26.63	Jan. 1846; July, 1852	6 6	......	....	Dove, 1857.
6	26.15	39.28	27.58	14.30	26.83	July, 1842; June, 1843	1 0	......	Koegel.	Dove. Rep. Br. Assoc. 1848.
7	14.15	40.77	23.07	— 5.12	18.22	Aug. 1833; July, 1838	5 0	M. N.	....	Dove, 1857.
8	— 3.17	(36.83)	11.00	—21.23	(+5.86)	Sept. 1860; July, 1861	0 11	bi-hourly	Dr. I. I. Hayes.	Sm. Con. to Knowl. 1867.
9	+ 6.35	38.07	20.22	—12.47	13.04	Aug. 1833; July, 1838	5 0	M. N.	....	Dove, 1857.
10	—10.62	33.37	— 4.03	—28.60	— 2.47	Sept. 1853; Apr. 1855	1 8	hourly.	Dr. E. K. Kane.	Sm. Con. to Knowl. 1859.
11	+ 1.54	37.97	+ 6.49	—28.71	+ 4.32	Aug. 1849; July, 1850	1 0	[8]	Rae.	Richardson.

BRITISH NORTH AMERICA.—ARCTIC REGION.

	Spring.	Summer.	Autumn.	Winter.	Year.	Series. Begins. Ends.	Extent yrs. mos.	Observing hours.	Observer.	References.
1	..	..	+ 0.59	—36.09	..	Sept. 1853; Apr. 1854	0 8	......	Kellett.	"Voyage of Resolute."
2	— 4.37	..	+ 5.37	—26.73	..	Sept. 1850; July, 1851	0 11	tri-hourly.	Penny.	Sutherland.
3	..	..	+ 6.62	—17.85	..	....	0 8	......	....	Dove, 1857.
4	— 6.02	33.82	+ 1.78	—30.26	— 0.17	Sept. 1851; Apr. 1853	1 7	......	McClure.	Armstrong's Personal Narrative.
5	+ 2.60	36.81	12.69	—27.44	+ 6.16	....	1 0	tri-hourly.	....	Dove, 1857.
6	— 5.30	38.04	9.69	—27.71	+ 3.68	Oct. 1829; Mar. 1832	2 6	hourly.	Ross.	Ross.
7	— 1.03	34.16	+ 2.06	—30.85	+ 0.88	Sept. 1852; Aug. 1853	1 0	......	Kellett.	"Voyage of Resolute."
8	— 5.22	34.10	3.11	—34.07	— 0.52	....	1 0	......	....	Dove, 1857.
9	+ 2.04	..	17.12	—32.69	..	May, 1863; Apr. 1864	0 11	$7_m\ 2_a\ 9_a$ bis	M. M. McLeod.	S. O.
10	+ 4.37	48.26	19.36	—22.99	12.25	....	1 0	15 observations daily.	....	Dove, 1857.
11	— 3.23	36.60?	4.53	—29.00	+ 2.22	....	1 0	......	Austin.	"Voyage of Resolute."
12	+ 1.14	36.66	5.96	—21.76	+ 5.50	Sept. 1822; Aug. 1823	1 0	bi-hourly.	Parry.	Parry.
13	— 3.27	37.11	— 0.51	—28.02	+ 1.33	Sept. 1819; Aug. 1820	1 0	bi-hourly.	Parry.	Parry.
14	— 3.18	33.12	4.15	—34.35	— 0.07	....	1 0	......	....	Dove, 1857.
15	11.74	54.53	12.01	—24.04	13.56	Feb. 1863; Dec. 1865	2 7	$7_m\ 2_a\ 9_a$ [9]	A. Flett.	S. Coll. and S. O.
16	— 1.90	37.45	7.03	—35.03	1.89	Aug. 1858; Aug. 1859	1 1		Sir F. L. McClintock.	Sm. Con. to Knowl. 1862.
17	— 5.74	36.39	10.58	—25.09	4.03	Sept. 1824; Aug. 1825	1 0	bi-hourly.	Parry.	Parry.
18	..	..	..	—35.77	..	Oct. 1848; Apr. 1849	0 7	......	....	Belcher.
19	— 4.89	36.93	3.27	—31.16	+ 1.04	Aug. 1850; Aug. 1851	1 1	......	McClure.	"Voyage of Resolute."
20	— 4.72	..	13.94	—25.09	..	Sept. 1846; July, 1847	0 11	tri-hourly.	Rae.	Rae.
21	+ 3.93	..	+ 5.80	—31.40	..	Sept. 1853; July, 1854	0 11	$8_m\ 2_a\ 8_a$	Dr. J. Rae.	S. Coll.

BRITISH NORTH AMERICA.—SOUTH OF LATITUDE 66° 30′.

	Spring.	Summer.	Autumn.	Winter.	Year.	Series. Begins. Ends.	Extent yrs. mos.	Observing hours.	Observer.	References.
1	22.18	65.67	37.09	— 0.22	31.18	Sept. 1867; May, 1869	1 8	$7_m\ 2_a\ 9_a$ bis	J. Lockhart.	S. Coll. and S. O.
2	27.43	..	..	— 5.93	..	Oct. 1843; June, 1844	0 9	hourly	Richardson.	Blodget's Clim.
3	10.33	..	..	—17.90	..	Oct. 1795; May, 1796	0 8	......	Thompson.	S. Coll.
4	31.38	..	..	+ 7.00	..	Oct. 1777; July, 1778	0 10	[8]	....	Cartwright's Labrador.
5	29.86	..	..	..	..	1827	0 3	max. & min.	Richardson.	Franklin.
6	27.00	63.00	32.67	— 0.67	30.50	Oct. 1789; Sept. 1790	1 0	......	Thompson.	S. Coll.
7	32.37	58.93	32.30	— 3.70	29.98	Sept. 1819; Aug. 1820	1 0	......	....	Dove, Rep. Br. Assoc. 1847.
8	32.63	..	33.04	— 0.34	..	Aug. 1839; Sept. 1840	0 10	$8_m\ 8_a$ [9]	Lewis.	Richardson.
9	..	..	..	..	..	1827	0 2	max. & min.	Drummond.	Franklin.
10	..	..	..	..	..	1864	0 2	$7_m\ 2_a\ 9_a$ bis	....	S. O.
11	22.76	58.70	31.89	— 3.34	27.50	1825; 1839	3 6	$8_m\ 8_a$ [10]	Keith and Stewart.	Richardson.

[8] Observations made at daylight, warmest time of day, and after dark. [9] Corrected for daily variation by means of Dove's Toronto Table.

[10] The means for 1825–6 are derived from the daily extremes, those for 1838–39 from observations at $8_m\ 8_a$. They have been corrected for daily variation y means of the Toronto formula.

BRITISH NORTH AMERICA.—SOUTH OF LATITUDE 66° 30′.

Name of Station.	Lat.	Long.	Height.	Jan.	Feb.	March.	April.	May.	June.	July.	August.	Sept.	Oct.	Nov.	Dec.
12. Fort Churchill	58°50′	94°30′	20	—28.°	—20.°	12.°	20.°	38.°	50.°	58.°	50.°	42.°	28.°	5.°	—18.
13. Fort Churchill	58 50	94 30	20	—21.21	— 7.31	— 4.63	16.29	28.42	44.69	56.80	53.39	36.03	26.50	3.32	—14.
14. Fort Enterprise	64 28	113 06	850	—15.57	—25.88	—13.48	5.78	31.20	..	..	..	31.59	21.75	— 1.70	—30.
15. Fort Franklin	65 12	122 45	230	—22.34	—16.75	— 5.39	12.35	35.18	48.02	52.10	50.56	41.00	22.47	— 0.11	—10.
16. Fort Nascopie	54 25	65 22	..	—10.1	+ 1.7	8.0	17.4	31.0	43.3	..	..	..	28.8	15.8	— 2.
17. Fort Norman	64 30	125 00	200	—23.05	—12.93	— 9.48	14.28	47.68	..	..	..	..	..	..	..
18. Fort Prince of Wales	59	..	..	—25.6	—17.5	— 9.2	21.2	38.0	50.0	56.4	53.0	44.0	28.0	1.7	—15.
19. Fort Rae	62 46	109 01	..	—23.15	—23.15	— 2.68	18.64	41.53	..	..	..	..	23.65	+ 1.08	—17.
20. Fort Reliance	62 46	109 00	650	—25.01	—18.85	—10.47	8.23	36.03	..	..	..	..	..	13.44	—17.
21. Fort Resolution	61 10	113 50	500	..	—25.60	9.95	12.88	40.14	..	..	..	..	26.06	12.04	— 2.
22. Fort Simpson[3]	62 10	121 20	300	—13.46	—10.43	+ 4.47	25.94	47.89	63.50	60.81	53.16	[48.00]	23.20	7.52	— 9.
23. Fort Simpson	62 10	121 20	300	— 7.6	— 2.3	— 6.5	32.8	52.2	..	..	..	..	31.2	6.4	—18.
24. Fort Simpson	62 10	121 20	300	—18.13	—12.87	11.90	24.27	46.77	61.80	..	..	..	27.00	4.27	—14.
25. Fort Simpson	62 10	121 20	300	—15.43	— 9.98	+ 3.87	26.13	49.45	64.87	..	..	44.91	25.45	— 1.21	—15.
26. Hebron	58 20	63 30	..	— 5.24	— 5.31	4.62	16.83	33.01	36.61	43.57	49.10	38.84	29.43	23.58	5.
27. Hebron	58 20	63 30	..	— 5.03	— 0.04	9.93	21.76	32.69	41.41	47.41	48.04	39.89	29.59	19.36	3.
28. Isthmus Bay	53 47	56 30	..	8.55	7.10	24.79	27.76	36.14	45.59	..	..	..	..	..	11.
29. Kinogumissee	49 50	84 00	1000	3.27	10.70	11.21	33.29	42.30	62.28	64.25	61.35	48.47	38.37	22.85	11.
30. Little Whale River[5]	56 02	77 30	12	— 9.88	—12.05	14.63	20.45	33.08	37.95	50.83	47.20	[38.94]	32.13	17.15	— 2.
31. Moose Factory	51 15	80 45	30	— 7.28	— 4.95	9.05	25.53	39.33	52.56	59.12	56.67	45.83	36.20	21.70	4.
32. Moose Factory	51 15	80 45	30	—10.86	— 4.85	14.29	15.80	40.40	44.96	56.40	58.40	47.62	37.17	18.54	— 4.
33. Nain	57 10	61 50	..	—11.87	+ 3.87	6.35	27.50	37.17	43.47	50.45	51.80	44.82	33.12	23.00	6.
34. Nain	57 10	61 50	..	..	..	..	..	..	..	..	..	..	..	..	
35. Nain	57 10	61 50	..	— 4.33	— 3.21	8.74	19.21	31.66	37.44	44.03	51.01	41.04	26.03	24.71	7.
36. Nain	57 10	61 50	..	— 3.84	— 0.69	9.46	22.66	32.83	41.78	48.22	51.10	42.21	32.13	22.28	3.
37. Nain	57 10	61 50	..	0.95	3.51	7.52	29.97	36.23	42.53	50.18	50.99	44.98	33.98	26.51	6.
38. Norway House	53 50	98 00	..	— 7.13	— 2.36	7.58	27.40	44.62	54.99	63.55	61.13	46.40	31.09	12.48	1.
39. Okhak	57 45	63 20	..	2.15	1.95	8.25	29.0	38.25	44.65	51.65	52.0	44.45	31.15	22.4	8.
40. Okhak	57 45	63 20	..	— 5.33	— 2.04	11.28	23.92	33.14	43.00	49.46	51.31	41.90	30.33	21.99	4.
41. Oxford House	55 00	95 00	400	—22.06	— 1.90	8.57	28.62	38.01	..	..	..	..	17.53	13.29	—23.
42. Pelly Banks	62 45	130 45	1400	—21.95	—14.73	— 0.99	20.44	..	..	..	..	..	..	..	—13.
43. Red River Settlement	49 05	97 00	600	..	14.05	16.72	41.41	..	57.16	63.08	..	50.06	32.30	16.00	5.
44. Red River Settlement	49 05	97 00	653	— 1.79	— 1.09	18.25	33.38	51.62	62.82	67.50	64.62	54.91	40.93	18.79	— 0.
45. Rigolet	53 30	58 21	..	— 1.68	+ 1.57	20.36	27.05	33.95	42.36	..	..	..	..	22.35	3.
46. Rigolet	53 30	58 21	..	— 0.81	+ 2.87	13.43	26.62	34.69	41.66	51.69	50.96	41.70	32.18	21.84	4.
47. Rupert House	51 30	78 40	20	— 4.09	— 0.68	7.64	21.05	41.51	..	..	..	..	34.80	23.33	15.
48. Victoria	48 55	123 22	64	38.09	42.22	44.79	48.67	55.51	..	..	..	..	..	..	
49. Winnepeg	49 52	97 00	650	8.96	5.78	13.36	39.46	56.61	61.65	66.20	64.35	55.73	39.99	25.70	8.
50. Winowkupa	53	57	..	9.70	— 0.07	15.15	24.32	42.83	..	..	..	..	32.03	19.83	— 3.
51. Winter Island	66 10	83 10	..	—22.96	—24.97	—11.64	5.51	23.09	33.97	36.34	36.60	31.06	12.51	7.75	—12.
52. York Factory	57 00	92 26		— 5.12	— 6.60	4.77	19.21	33.53	47.67	59.99	54.85	41.90	33.43	25.17	3.

NEW FOUNDLAND.

Name of Station.	Lat.	Long.	Height.	Jan.	Feb.	March.	April.	May.	June.	July.	August.	Sept.	Oct.	Nov.	Dec.
1. St. John's[9]	47 34	52 40	140	23.34	20.86	24.20	33.38	39.26	48.00	56.10	57.86	52.96	44.44	33.96	25.
2. St. John's[10]	47 34	52 40	170	23.77	23.49	30.33	35.47	44.46	52.75	59.49	60.31	55.83	44.27	36.25	27.
3. St. John's	47 34	52 40	..	..	..	..	..	..	..	..	..	..	..	..	..

[1] Morning, afternoon, and evening.

[2] Corrected for daily variation by means of Dove's Toronto Table.

[3] Series much broken. Mean for September interpolated.

[4] Observations made at daylight, warmest time of day, and after dark.

[5] Value for September interpolated.

[6] Hours of Observation 7_m 8_m N. 4_a $5 \cdot 5_a$.

[7] Daily means derived from $\frac{7t_1 + 7t_2 + 10t_3}{24}$, t_1 t_2 t_3 representing the observations at the above hours; the instrument used was a Negretti ar Zambra maximum and minimum thermometer, tested at Kew.

BRITISH NORTH AMERICA.—SOUTH OF LATITUDE 66° 30′.

	Spring.	Summer.	Autumn.	Winter.	Year.	Series. Begins. Ends.	Extent yrs. mos.	Observing hours.	Observer.	References.
12	23°.33	52°.67	25°. 00	—22°.00	19°.75	1769	1 0	......	....	Dove, Rep. Br. Assoc. 1847.
13	13.36	51.63	21.95	—14.17	18.19	Feb. 1838; May, 1839	1 3	[1]	Harding.	Richardson.
14	7.83	..	17.21	—24.00	..	Sept. 1820; May, 1821	0 9	......	Franklin.	Richardson.
15	14.05	50.23	21.12	—16.66	17.18	Sept. 1825; May, 1827	1 9	18 times daily	Franklin.	Dove, Rep. Br. Assoc. 1847.
16	18.80	..	..	— 3.73	..	Oct. 1864; June, 1865	0 9	$7_m\ 2_a\ 9_a$	H. Connolly.	S. Coll.
17	17.49	..	..	..	..	1862	0 5	$7_m\ 2_a\ 9_a$ bis	A. Flett.	S. O.
18	16.67	53.13	24.57	—19.53	18.71	1768; 1769	1 0	......	Wales.	Williams' History of Vermont.
19	19.16	..	..	—21.40	..	Oct. 1859; May, 1863	1 5	$7_m\ 2_a\ 9_a$ bis	L. Clarke, Jr.	P. O. and S. I. Vol. 1, and S. O.
20	11-26	..	..	—20.31	..	Nov. 1833; Mar. 1835	1 0	15 times daily	Back.	Dove, Rep. Br. Assoc. 1847.
21	20.99	..	..	..	..	....	0 7	$8_m\ 8_a$[2]	....	Richardson.
22	26.10	59.16	[26.24]	—11.04	[25.12]	1837; 1840	2 6	$8_m\ 8_a$	McPherson.	Edin. N. Phil. Journ. Jan. 1841.
23	26.17	..	..	— 9.50	..	Oct. 1851; May, 1852	0 8	$8_m\ 2_a\ 8_a$	B. R. Ross.	S. Coll.
24	27.65	..	..	—15.16	..	Mar. 1856; Apr. 1859	2 1	max. & min.	B. R. Ross.	P. O. and S. I. Vol. 1.
25	26.48	..	23.05	—13.79	..	Sept. 1859; Apr. 1862	1 5	$7_m\ 2_a\ 9_a$ bis	B. R. Ross, A. Flett, W. W. Kirkby.	P. O. and S. I. Vol. 1, and S. O.
26	18.15	43.09	30.62	— 1.79	22.52	....	2 0	......	....	Dove, Rep. Br. Assoc. 1847.
27	21.46	45.62	29.61	— 0.41	24.07	Sept. 1842; Aug. 1848	6 0	$6_m\ 7_m$ N $6_a\ 7_a$[4]	....	Dove, 1857.
28	29.56	..	..	9.18	..	Dec. 1785; June, 1786	0 7		....	Cartwright's Labrador.
29	28.93	62.63	36.56	8.36	34.12	Sept. 1860; Apr. 1863	1 6	$7_m\ 2_a\ 9_a$ bis	T. Richards.	S. O.
30	22.72	45.33	[29.41]	— 8.03	[22.36]	Nov. 1861; Dec. 1862	1 1	"	W. Dickson.	S. O.
31	24.64	56.12	34.58	— 2.57	28.19	Sept. 1857; May, 1862	2 5	"	J. McKenzie.	P. O. and S. I. Vol. 1, and S. O.
32	23.50	53.25	34.44	— 6.75	26.11	Sept. 1858; Aug. 1859	1 0	$\odot_r\ 2_a\ 10_a$	J. McKenzie.	P. O. and S. I. Vol. 1.
33	23.67	48.57	33.65	— 0.40	26.37	Aug. 1777; Aug. 1780	3 1	8_m N. $4_a\ 8_a$	M. de la Trobe.	
34	23.90	48.38	33.44	0.60	26.58	....	..	......	....	Bridgewater Treatises.
35	19.87	44.16	30.59	+ 0.05	23.67	Sept. 1841; June, 1843	1 10	......	....	Dove.
36	21.65	47.03	32.21	— 0.38	25.13	Sept. 1841; July, 1852	9 6	[6]	....	Dove, 1857.
37	24.57	47.90	35.16	3.66	27.82	....	3 0	8_m N. $4_a\ 8_a$	....	Dove, Rep. Br. Assoc. 1847.
38	26.53	59.89	29.99	— 2.81	28.40	1841; 1847	7 0	max. & min.	Ross.	MS. in S. Coll.
39	25.17	49.43	32.67	4.18	27.86	1777; 1780	2 0	8_m N. $4_a\ 8_a$	....	Dove, Rep. Br. Assoc. 1847.
40	22.78	47.92	31.41	— 1.10	25.25	....	..	......	....	Dove, 1857.
41	25.07	..	..	—15.67	..	Oct. 1833; May, 1834	0 8	7_m N. 8_a[2]	....	Richardson.
42	..	..	..	[illegible]	..	Dec. 1848; Apr. 1849	0 5	⊙ 3 dusk[2]	Campbell.	Richardson.
43	..	..	32.79	..	..	1844	0 9	$\odot_r\ 9_m\ 3_a\ 9_a$	....	MS. in S. Coll.
44	34.42	64.98	38.21	— 1.11	34.12	June, 1855; Sept. 1861	4 4	$7_m\ 2_a\ 9_a$	D. Gunn.	P. O. and S. I. Vol. 1, and S. O.
45	27.12	..	..	+ 1.06	..	Nov. 1857; June, 1859	1 4	$\odot_r\ \odot_s$	H. Connolly.	P. O. and S. I. Vol. 1.
46	24.91	48.10	31.91	2.08	26.75	July, 1860; June, 1863	2 5	$7_m\ 2_a\ 9_a$ bis	H. Connolly.	S. O.
47	23.40	..	..	3.61	..	1839; 1840	0 8	$\odot_r\ 1.5_a\ \odot_s$[2]	....	Richardson.
48	49.66	..	..	..	..	1864	0 5	$8_m\ 3_a\ 10_a$[7]	Dr. D. Walker.	MS. in S. Coll.
49	36.48	64.07	40.47	7.66	37.17	Jan. 1869; Dec. 1870	1 3	$7_m\ 2_a\ 9_a$ bis	J. Stewart.	S. O.
50	27.43	..	..	1.93	..	Oct. 1865; May, 1866	0 8	"	H. Connolly.	S. O.
51	5.65	35.64	17.11	—20.29	9.53	Aug. 1821; July, 1822	1 0	bi-hourly	Parry.	Parry.
52	19.17	54.17	33.50	— 2.66	26.05	June, 1830; May, 1831	1 0	M. N. E.[8]	Charles.	Richardson.

NEW FOUNDLAND.

	Spring.	Summer.	Autumn.	Winter.	Year.	Series. Begins. Ends.	Extent yrs. mos.	Observing hours.	Observer.	References.
1	32.28	53.99	43.79	23.17	38.31	Jan. 1834; Dec. 1838	5 0	max. & min.	J. Templeman.	Printed Sheet.
2	36.75	57.52	45.45	25.07	41.20	Aug. 1849; Feb. 1869	7 1	......	G. R. Kennedy, J. Delaney & sons, E. M. J. Delaney, R. C. Caswell.	Sm. Coll., New Foundland Alm. 1862, P. O. and S. I. Vol. 1., and S. O.
3	..	..	..	..	40.80	1855; 1858	3 0	......	....	Trans. Nova Scotia Inst. Nat. Sci. Vol. 1.

[8] "The exact hours of morning and evening are not specified; they have been corrected by Dove's table on the supposition that the hours were $\odot_r$ and $\odot_s$."

[9] Colonial Secretary's Office.

[10] Observations made in several localities (for the most part at "Colonial Building"), and at various hours. They have been corrected for daily variation by means of the general table.

PROVINCE OF NOVA SCOTIA.

Name of Station.	Lat.	Long.	Height.	Jan.	Feb.	March.	April.	May.	June.	July.	August.	Sept.	Oct.	Nov.	Dec.
1. Albion Mines	45°34′	62°42′	120	19°.15	19°.42	27°.30	37°.43	48°.73	58°.63	66°.39	65°.54	56°.30	46°.47	35°.75	23°.98
2. Caledonia Coal Mine	46 12	59 57	60	19.27	19.70	24.23	32.77	41.42	54.15	60.55	64.15	57.03	45.67	36.22	24.88
3. Halifax	44 39	63 35	8	23.44	23.65	29.96	38.13	48.36	56.90	64.51	63.74	57.96	48.91	39.34	28.75
4. Halifax	44 39	63 35	..	..	..	..	..	..	..	..	..	..	..	..	..
5. Halifax[2]	44 39	63 35	..	23.75	24.50	29.00	38.50	47.75	56.25	62.00	63.25	57.25	46.50	39.00	26.25
6. Halifax	44 39	63 35	130	20.20	23.31	27.47	37.26	47.97	58.92	63.98	64.15	58.31	46.11	36.04	25.18
7. Windsor	44 59	64 07	200	26.84	29.01	36.33	48.96	61.05	70.47	75.82	75.02	66.68	54.26	40.61	32.12
8. Windsor	44 59	64 07	200	23.27	22.49	30.63	38.07	48.48	60.35	66.05	64.68	57.25	46.26	37.31	25.54
9. Wolfville	45 06	64 25	80	21.73	23.84	28.98	39.86	50.06	60.03	66.22	65.26	57.24	47.28	38.18	26.36

PRINCE EDWARD ISLAND.

Name of Station.	Lat.	Long.	Height.	Jan.	Feb.	March.	April.	May.	June.	July.	August.	Sept.	Oct.	Nov.	Dec.
1. Charlottetown	46 12	63 00	..	17.91	23.52	27.81	37.60	51.59	60.19	69.48	67 68	59.49	45.79	37.49	28.60

PROVINCE OF NEW BRUNSWICK.

Name of Station.	Lat.	Long.	Height.	Jan.	Feb.	March.	April.	May.	June.	July.	August.	Sept.	Oct.	Nov.	Dec.
1. Fredericton	45 57	66 40	..	17.	24.	33.	40.	37.	48.5	65.5	69.75	61.5	47.5	31.	13.5
2. St. John	45 22	66 04	135	18.21	21.97	27.81	36.35	46.33	54.49	59.27	59.01	54.80	44.53	35.59	22.96

PROVINCE OF QUEBEC (CANADA EAST).

Name of Station.	Lat.	Long.	Height.	Jan.	Feb.	March.	April.	May.	June.	July.	August.	Sept.	Oct.	Nov.	Dec.
1. Fort Coulonge	45 55	77 04	250	11.33	15.72	28.74	40.55	54.30	65.40	69.40	66.46	56.28	45.05	31.30	17.01
2. Island of St. Helen[5]	45 30	73 33	60	13.53	17.68	24.90	38.37	53.97	64.73	68.91	68.04	57.62	46.50	31.58	19.66
3. Montreal	45 31	73 33	60	14.66	18.13	28.43	41.94	58.06	68.12	78.89	69.67	60.23	47.43	33.83	18.96
4. Montreal	45 31	73 34	57	15.00	17.51	29.45	43.53	58.14	68.37	73.14	70.79	60.64	46.46	33.71	19.07
5. Montreal	45 31	73 33	..	14.52	16.20	28.63	41.84	58.99	71.01	74.46	73.12	62.42	47.05	33.97	19.29
6. Montreal	45 31	73 33	50	15.00	16.40	28.40	39.80	55.40	66.20	71.00	68.40	55.80	44.60	34.40	17.80
7. Montreal	45 31	73 33	118	12.29	17.27	27.05	40.76	55.59	67.01	70.98	68.32	60.21	47.66	35.50	19.65
8. Montreal	45 31	73 33	..	..	..	..	..	..	..	..	..	..	..	..	..
9. Nicolet	46 14	72 32	..	13.26	13.26	27.22	39.48	52.69	63.58	68.50	67.83	57.90	44.32	32.27	17.24
10. Quebec	46 49	71 12	..	10.	10.	22.	40.	52.	67.	69.	67.	51.	44.	36.	20.
11. Quebec	46 49	71 12	300	9.88	12.79	24.36	38.66	52.88	63.69	66.81	65.51	56.25	44.13	31.54	17.28
12. Quebec[6]	46 48	71 12	330	..	..	..	..	..	..	..	..	..	..	..	..
13. Quebec[6]	46 48	71 12	330	..	..	..	..	..	..	63.93	63.65	50.21	45.28	..	..
14. Quebec	46 49	71 12	..	10.98	14.83	28.38	39.40	53.58	65.27	71.29	70.77	57.50	43.70	34.32	12.64
15. Quebec	46 49	71 12	..	15.91	12.65	22.66	39.65	54.84	63.95	73.40	66.88	62.38	42.80	33.13	13.89
16. Quebec	46 49	71 12	..	..	..	..	..	..	..	..	..	..	..	..	..
17. St. Anne	47 24	70 05	175	11.05	18.35	25.18	36.23	..	..	..	..	..	..	..	22.00
18. St. Martin[8]	45 32	73 46	118	10.94	16.56	25.26	39.78	54.77	65.42	71.48	67.32	58.60	46.22	31.73	16.33
19. Sherbrook[9]	45 25	71 53	..	18.5	11.9	22.9	35.9	38.9	..	64.3	56.7	..	..	..	..
20. Stanbridge	45 08	73 00	222	14.68	16.90	25.43	39.81	54.32	64.07	68.32	65.71	56.87	44.18	33.15	19.27

[1] Observations for 1853–54, at 7_m 2_a 9_a.

[2] Results from three observations daily, at hours not stated.

[3] At the even hours. The values for 2_m and 4_m were interpolated from the readings at midn't and 6_m, and by means of a minimum thermometer.

[4] Corrected for daily variation by means of the general table.

[5] At the Barracks, R. A., opposite Montreal. During the first year, the observations were made bi-hourly, at the *even* hours; during the second, bi-hourly, at the *odd* hours.

[6] Cape Diamond.

PROVINCE OF NOVA SCOTIA.

	Spring.	Summer.	Autumn.	Winter.	Year.	Series. Begins.	Series. Ends.	Extent yrs.	Extent mos.	Observing hours.	Observer.	References.
1	37°.82	63°.52	46°.17	20°.85	42°.09	1843;	1854	11	1	$\odot_r\ 9_m\ 3_a\ 9_a$[1]	H. Poole.	MS. in S. Coll.
2	32.81	59.62	46.31	21.28	40.00	Jan. 1867;	Dec. 1869	3	0	max. & min.	H. Poole.	Trans. Nova Scotia Inst. Nat. Sci. Vol. II.
3	38.82	61.72	48.74	25.28	43.64	Oct. 1845;	Feb. 1861	10	6	$6_m\ 3_a\ 8_a$	Generd, C. Harrison.	Dove; Board of Trade First Paper; P. O. and S. I. Vol. I, and S. O.
4	..	..	..	..	43.65	1860;	1863	4	0	......	....	Trans. Nova Scotia Inst. Nat. Sci. Vol. I.
5	38.42	60.50	47.58	24.83	42.83	Jan. 1863;	Dec. 1866	4	0	......	Colonel Myers.	Trans. Nova Scotia Inst. Nat. Sci. Vols. I and II.
6	37.57	62.35	46.82	22.90	42.41	Jan. 1867;	Dec. 1869	3	0	bi-hourly[3]	F. Allison.	Trans. Nova Scotia Inst. Nat. Sci. Vol. II.
7	48.78	73.77	53.85	29.32	51.43	Jan. 1794;	Dec. 1811	17	4	......	....	S. Coll.
8	39.06	63.69	46.94	23.77	43.36	May, 1867;	June, 1863	3	5	$7_m\ 2_a\ 9_a$	Profs. J. D. Everett, H. How, and J. M. Hensley.	P. O. and S. I. Vol. I, and S. O.
9	39.63	63.84	47.57	23.98	43.75	Sept. 1855;	Dec. 1870	11	6	[4]	A. P. S. Stuart, C. F. Hartt, D. F. Higgins.	P. O. and S. I. Vol. I, and S. O.

PRINCE EDWARD ISLAND.

	Spring.	Summer.	Autumn.	Winter.	Year.	Series. Begins.	Series. Ends.	Extent yrs.	Extent mos.	Observing hours.	Observer.	References.
1	39.00	65.78	47.59	23.34	43.93	....		1	0	......	....	Dove, 1857.

PROVINCE OF NEW BRUNSWICK.

	Spring.	Summer.	Autumn.	Winter.	Year.	Series. Begins.	Series. Ends.	Extent yrs.	Extent mos.	Observing hours.	Observer.	References.
1	36.67	61.25	46.67	18.17	40.69	....		1	0	......	....	Dove, Rep. Br. Assoc. 1848.
2	36.83	57.59	44.97	21.05	40.11	Dec. 1863;	Dec. 1870	7	0	$6_m\ 2_a\ 10_a$	G. Murdoch.	S. O.

PROVINCE OF QUEBEC (CANADA EAST).

	Spring.	Summer.	Autumn.	Winter.	Year.	Series. Begins.	Series. Ends.	Extent yrs.	Extent mos.	Observing hours.	Observer.	References.
1	41.20	67.09	44.21	14.69	41.80	Jan. 1824;	Dec. 1831	8	0	$\odot_r$ N. $\odot_s$	Severight.	S. Coll.
2	39.08	67.23	45.23	16.96	42.12	Aug. 1839;	July, 1841	2	0	......	J. S. McCord.	Printed Report, Montreal, 1842.
3	42.81	72.23	47.16	17.25	44.86	1826;	1840	15	0	max. & min.	J. S. McCord.	Drake.
4	43.71	70.77	46.94	17.19	44.65	Jan. 1826;	Dec. 1852	27	0	$7_m\ 3_a$	W. S. Kakel.	Hall's MS. Phil. Mag.
5	43.15	72.86	47.81	16.67	45.12	Jan. 1845;	Dec. 1853	9	0	$8_m\ 1_a\ 6_a$	L. A. H. Latour.	MS. in S. Coll.
6	41.20	68.53	44.93	16.40	42.77	Jan. 1846;	Dec. 1850	5	0	......	Dr. Bethune.	S. Coll.
7	41.13	68.77	47.79	16.40	43.52	Sept. 1855;	June, 1863	6	5	$7_m\ 2_a\ 9_a$	Dr. A. Hall.	P. O. and S. I. Vol. I, and S. O.
8	..	..	..	..	41.45	1857;	1861	4	0	......	....	Trans. Nova Scotia Inst. Nat. Sci. Vol. I.
9	39.80	66.64	44.83	14.59	41.46	Jan. 1838;	Dec. 1846	9	0	$6_m\ 3_a$	Desanniers.	S. Coll.
10	38.00	67.67	43.67	13.33	40.67	1743;	1744	1	0	......	Gautier.	Sill. Journal.
11	38.63	65.34	43.97	13.32	40.31	Jan. 1809;	Dec. 1818	10	0	......	Dr. Sparks.	S. Coll.
12	..	..	..	..	37.19	1828;	1836	9	0	[7]	Watt.	"
13	..	..	..	..	..	1829		0	4	......	....	"
14	40.45	69.11	45.17	12.82	41.89	1845;	1847	2	0	......	....	Dove, 1853.
15	39.05	68.08	46.10	14.15	41.85	....		..		......	....	Bouchette.
16	38.84	68.00	46.04	14.18	41.76	....		..		......	....	Bridgewater Treatises.
17	..	..	..	17.13	..	Dec. 1866;	Apr. 1867	0	5	$7_m\ 2_a\ 9_{a\ bis}$	J. O'Donohue.	S. O.
18	39.94	68.07	45.52	14.61	42.03	Jan. 1851;	Jan. 1862	10	1	$7_m\ 2_a\ 9_a$	Dr. C. Smallwood.	S. Coll., P. O. and S. I. Vol. I, and S. O.
19	32.57	..	..	..	..	1836		0	7	$\odot_r\ 1_a\ 9_a$	Z. Thompson.	S. Coll.
20	39.85	66.03	44.73	16.95	41.89	Mar. 1856;	Dec. 1870	11	4	$7_m\ 2_a\ 9_{a\ bis}$	J. C. Baker, A. H. I. Gilmour.	P. O. and S. I. Vol. I, and S. O.

7 Hours of observation $6_m\ 9_m$ N. $3_a\ 6_a\ 9_a$.—Captain Lefroy, in the "Canadian Journal" for November, 1852, notes a diminution of 2°.5 in the mean annual temperature, resulting from the last five years of this series, when compared with that for the first four years. It appears to be due to a change in the hours of observation.

8 Observations for 4 years 6 months of this series were made at $6_m\ 2_a\ 10_a$. They were referred to $7_m\ 2_a\ 9_a$ by means of the general table.

9 Observations for the first five months at "Hatley," a few miles to the southwest of "Sherbrook."

PROVINCE OF ONTARIO (CANADA WEST).

Name of Station.	Lat.	Long.	Height.	Jan.	Feb.	March.	April.	May.	June.	July.	August.	Sept.	Oct.	Nov.	Dec.
1. Ancaster	43°15′	80°07′	..	27°.50	25°.45	33°.79	43°.80	54°.60	63°.20	68°.73	66°.42	59°.01	47°.34	37°.64	30°.23
2. Brantford	43 08	80 14	..	27.00	25.87	35.88	51.50	61.75	72.62	78.75	75.38	63.13	49.00	37.44	28.22
3. Clifton[1]	43 05	79 06	..	..	26.60	36.57	39.27	50.89	68.61	73.83	70.69	60.30	47.98	39.50	28.60
4. Fort William	48 23	89 22	660	5.70	8.22	22.72	31.42	48.87	58.73	62.19	58.84	48.16	41.88	23.43	18.16
5. Hamilton	43 15	79 57	300	26.43	26.29	33.73	43.68	55.60	66.47	72.46	70.44	61.86	49.65	39.84	29.93
6. Kingston	44 13	76 29	300	16.0	20.5	32.0	48.0	56.0	63.0	68.5	68.0	62.5	46.0	32.5	26.5
7. Kingston	44 13	76 29	..	18.99	9.88	27.01	40.01	58.01	65.99	70.00	67.01	59.99	49.01	36.99	25.99
8. Kingston	44 13	76 29	..	..	..	..	..	..	..	..	..	..	..	..	..
9. Kingston	44 13	76 29	294	..	..	..	..	..	..	..	..	..	..	..	..
10. Kingston	44 13	76 29	294	20.98	23.14	34.00	40.20	59.62	63.49	66.26	68.53	59.07	48.09	38.34	19.07
11. Lake Temiscamingue	47 19	79 31	630	9.23	18.44	24.41	39.04	49.35	62.75	67.28	65.58	53.39	40.83	25.97	17.68
12. Michipicoten	47 56	85 06	660	10.63	16.66	26.09	34.66	51.88	55.00	57.03	60.04	49.67	44.92	29.01	22.38
13. Michipicoten	47 56	85 06	660	8.72	12.62	23.84	39.00	52.30	59.00	70.01	64.68	57.11	46.32	32.33	22.21
14. Michipicoten[3]	47 56	85 06	660	5.79	6.09	16.62	36.05	42.12	[55.52]	59.03	60.80	51.00	42.82	29.62	14.69
15. Niagara	43 09	79 06	270	..	27.05	30.81	43.57	49.67	61.80	..	..	..	51.17	38.47	34.60
16. Penetangushene	44 48	80 00	600	22.50	21.23	30.82	37.48	55.09	67.85	73.15	68.72	54.93	48.83	37.85	24.38
17. Toronto	43 39	79 23	342	22.24	19.17	29.41	40.44	..	..	..	..	..	..	34.75	26.01
18. Toronto[5]	43 39	79 23	342	23.13	23.03	29.57	41.09	51.52	61.60	67.30	66.06	58.17	45.80	36.73	26.05

ALABAMA.

Name of Station.	Lat.	Long.	Height.	Jan.	Feb.	March.	April.	May.	June.	July.	August.	Sept.	Oct.	Nov.	Dec.
1. Ashville	33 50	86 19	..	32.75	51.13	42.46	49.73	63.50	70.93	72.63	74.33	67.46	60.56	46.27	45.70
2. Auburn	32 36	85 31	821	42.98	49.50	53.01	64.35	71.36	77.66	80.08	79.12	76.48	62.88	56.65	48.96
3. Bon Secour[6]	30 18	87 46	..	50.45	56.17	62.73	..	..	..	80.10	79.03	78.49	..	58.51	54.17
4. Cahawba	32 19	87 11	160	..	..	..	..	..	..	82.25	80.56	75.39	57.41	57.48	..
5. Carlowville	32 05	87 08	400	46.98	52.89	58.02	63.47	71.86	78.58	81.82	80.42	74.54	64.98	54.32	48.76
6. Coatopa[7]	32 40	88 15	350	..	49.98	53.13	60.55	71.45	76.23	80.35	79.84	74.10	66.70	53.03	43.78
7. Elyton, near	33 30	86 54	..	..	46.00	50.03	59.29	70.19	76.59	81.21	79.34	72.79	63.57	49.78	40.08
8. Eric	32 45	87 31	..	52.21	57.20	66.54	66.74	76.20	81.38	84.78	82.72	76.99	67.02	55.32	54.30
9. Erie	32 45	87 31	..	45.62	51.86	58.92	63.92	73.83	75.70	80.81	81.51	75.19	64.80	53.20	47.24
10. Eutaw[8]	32 50	88 00	..	41.27	52.22	58.04	65.68	73.58	79.93	82.40	80.69	73.73	61.84	50.47	45.20
11. Florence	34 47	87 41	..	45.5	42.8	63.0	63.5	70.0	77.3	77.0	78.7	72.6	59.0	56.5	44.3
12. Fort Morgan[9]	30 14	88 01	20	55.29	50.34	56.16	65.11	74.97	80.01	82.18	81.38	76.96	70.94	60.86	56.84
13. Fort Morgan	30 14	88 01	20	58.96	55.50	63.61	69.33	71.04	80.86	85.34	86.64	82.95	71.83	60.93	55.84
14. Greene Springs	32 50	87 46	500	43.60	49.49	56.01	62.75	70.79	76.99	79.58	78.77	73.09	61.90	52.07	45.77
15. Greensboro[11]	32 43	87 40	350	45.39	50.47	56.16	61.90	70.31	76.92	79.31	78.28	72.22	61.97	52.60	47.21
16. Huntsville	34 45	86 40	600	42.06	42.59	51.34	61.30	67.25	74.23	76.39	76.24	70.15	59.50	49.74	41.81
17. Mobile	30 41	88 02	15	51.3	53.7	59.4	67.1	74.1	77.8	79.8	79.4	76.1	65.7	57.0	52.3
18. Mobile	30 41	88 02	15	55.25	55.57	65.64	70.00	76.37	82.17	82.41	82.76	77.59	67.95	59.92	54.32
19. Monroe	32 23	86 40	..	..	56.99	62.97	71.97	73.00	75.98	78.98	79.99	..	61.99	..	..
20. Monroeville	31 32	87 28	150	47.91	56.40	62.78	65.59	73.50	78.31	79.99	80.15	76.13	69.46	56.38	52.73
21. Montgomery	32 23	86 18	162	46.98	52.73	60.88	63.80	75.49	77.62	..	..	73.40	61.40	50.19	50.18
22. Moulton	34 29	87 23	643	41.66	47.47	52.63	61.46	68.49	74.17	77.20	76.48	70.19	56.95	48.33	42.93
23. Mount Airy	32 20	86 52	..	47.73	..	60.96	..	..	78.91	82.45	85.85	77.80	66.22	54.69	..
24. Mt. Vernon Arsenal	31 05	88 02	200	49.98	54.20	60.09	66.60	74.05	78.48	80.15	79.85	76.17	66.03	56.84	51.37
25. Newbern	32 38	87 37	..	..	..	..	..	..	..	..	..	..	..	51.89	47.94
26. Opelika, near	32 38	85 25	..	45.77	50.70	56.88	62.84	68.96	77.74	80.18	78.41	74.81	62.31	52.08	46.93
27. Orville	32 20	87 20	200	..	..	..	..	..	..	..	..	..	61.97	56.45	45.00

[1] Near Niagara Falls. This series has been formed by combining the observations at "Clifton" with those at "Suspension Bridge, N. Y." They were made at various hours, and have been corrected for daily variation by means of the general table.

[2] Corrected for daily variation by means of Dove's Toronto table.

[3] Value for June interpolated.

[4] "The readings were recorded regularly at 8_m N. 5_a 8_a. When the highest or lowest temperature for the day occurred at other periods it was registered."

[5] Magnetic and Meteorological Observatory, in the grounds of the University of Toronto. The hours of observation for 1840 are not known, but the results can differ little from the true mean of the day; from January, 1841, to June, 1842, the observations were taken bi-hourly; from July 1, 1842, to June 30, 1848, hourly. Afterwards, to the end of 1852, the observing hours were irregular; not less than six readings were taken daily, and some hourly and bi-hourly. From January, 1853, to the end of the series, the observations were taken regularly at 6_m 8_m 2_a 4_a 10_a and M., "excepting on Sundays Christmas day, and Good Friday, when the instruments were read at 6_m 2_a only. These latter readings, though recorded in the daily register, are no

PROVINCE OF ONTARIO (CANADA WEST).

	Spring.	Summer.	Autumn.	Winter.	Year.	Series. Begins. Ends.	Extent yrs. mos.	Observing hours.	Observer.	References.
1	44°.06	66°.12	48°.00	27°.73	46°.48	Jan. 1835; Dec. 1845	11 0	$9_m\ 9_a$	Craigie.	S. Coll.
2	49.71	75.58	49.86	27.03	50.54	Nov. 1836; Dec. 1844	8 2	......	McDougal.	" "
3	42.24	71.04	49.26	..	..	May, 1867; Dec. 1870	1 6	......	W. M. Jones.	S. O.
4	34.34	59.92	37.82	10.69	35.69	....	..	$8_m\ 8_a$ [2]	....	Richardson.
5	44.34	69.79	50.45	27.55	48.03	Jan. 1846; Dec. 1859	13 6	$9_m\ 9_a$	Dr. W. Craigie.	Can. Journ. Feb. 1854, and P. O. and S. I. Vol. I.
6	45.33	66.50	47.00	21.00	44.96	July, 1843; Feb. 1845	1 8	......	Smith.	MS. in S. Coll.
7	41.68	67.67	48.66	18.29	44.07	....	1 0	......	....	Dove, 1857.
8	..	..	..	..	42.77	1856; 1858	3 0	......	....	Trans. Nova Scotia Inst. Nat. Sci. Vol. I.
9	..	..	..	..	44.56	1856; 1861	6 0	$9.5_m\ 3.5_a$	J. Williamson.	S. Coll.
10	44.61	66.09	48.50	21.06	45.07	Jan. 1859; Dec. 1860	2 0	"	"	" "
11	37.60	65.20	40.06	15.12	39.50	....	..	$\odot_r$ N. $\odot_s$ [2]	Severight.	Richardson.
12	37.54	57.36	41.20	16.56	38.16	....	..	$8_m\ 8_a$	Keith.	"
13	38.38	64.56	45.25	14.52	40.68	1847	1 0	$8_m\ 2_a$	Swanston.	Regent's Report.
14	31.60	[58.45]	41.15	8.86	[35.01]	Nov. 1860; Mar. 1866	1 5	$7_m\ 2_a\ 9_a$ bis	C. Rankin.	S. O.
15	41.35	..	..	..	..	Feb. 1861; June, 1863	0 10	$7_m\ 1_a\ 9_a$	H. Phillipps.	S. O.
16	41.13	69.91	47.20	22.70	45.24	May, 1825; Apr. 1826	1 0	max. & min.[4]	Todd.	Franklin's Second Journey.
17	..	..	..	22.47	..	Jan. 1831; Dec. 1839	4 0	......	Dade.	Up. Can. Med. Journ.
18	40.73	64.99	46.90	24.07	44.17	Jan. 1840; Dec. 1870	31 0	......	....	....

ALABAMA.

	Spring.	Summer.	Autumn.	Winter.	Year.	Series. Begins. Ends.	Extent yrs. mos.	Observing hours.	Observer.	References.
1	51.90	72.63	58.10	43.19	56.45	1857	1 0	......	T. M. Barker.	P. O. and S. I. Vol. I.
2	62.91	78.95	65.34	47.15	63.59	Jan. 1855; Jan. 1858	3 0	$7_m\ 2_a\ 9_a$	Prof. J. Darby.	" " " "
3	..	..	..	53.60	..	Nov. 1866; Sept. 1868	1 0	$7_m\ 2_a\ 9_a$ bis	W. J. Vankirk.	S. O.
4	..	..	63.43	..	..	1859	0 5	$7_m\ 2_a\ 9_a$	Dr. M. Troy.	P. O. and S. I. Vol. I.
5	64.45	80.27	64.61	49.54	64.72	June, 1856; Dec. 1870	7 2	$7_m\ 2_a\ 9_a$ bis	Dr. H. L. Alison.	P. O. and S. I. Vol. I, and S. O.
6	61.71	78.81	64.61	..	..	Aug. 1859; Dec. 1870	1 0	"	Rev. S. U. Smith, Dr. S. K. Jennings.	" " " " "
7	59.84	79.05	62.05	..	..	1870	0 11	"	E. B. Shields.	S. O.
8	69.83	82.96	66.44	54.57	68.45	May, 1824; June, 1825	1 2	6_m N. 4_a	Osborn.	S. Coll.
9	65.56	79.34	64.40	48.24	64.38	1849; 1852	3 8	$\odot_r\ 9_m\ 3_a\ 9_a$	Jennings and Osborn.	" "
10	65.77	81.01	62.01	46.23	63.75	1850; 1853	2 2	"	A. Winchell.	" "
11	65.50	77.67	62.70	44.20	62.52	1849	1 0	......	B. R. Gifford.	" "
12	65.41	81.19	69.59	54.16	67.59	Jan. 1835; Dec. 1867	2 10	[10]	Assistant Surgeon.	Ar. Met. Reg. 1855, and MS. from S. G. O.
13	67.99	84.28	71.90	56.77	70.24	1848; 1850	..	hourly.	Officers of U. S. C. S.	S. Coll.
14	63.18	78.45	62.35	46.29	62.57	Jan. 1854; Dec. 1870	10 0	$7_m\ 2_a\ 9_a$ bis	H. Tutwiler and J. W. A. Wright.	P. O. and S. I. Vol. I, and S.
15	62.79	78.17	62.26	47.69	62.73	June, 1856; Jan. 1870	6 6	"	R. B. Waller, Dr. S. K. Jennings.	" " " " "
16	59.96	75.62	59.80	42.15	59.38	1829; 1842	13 0	......	Allan.	Drake.
17	66.87	79.00	66.27	52.43	66.14	....	10 0	......	....	Patent Office Report.
18	70.67	82.45	68.49	55.05	69.16	Apr. 1840; Feb. 1870	3 4	$7_m\ 2_a\ 9_a$	Dr. S. B. North, L. B. Taylor.	Am. Alm. 1842 and foll., and S. O.
19	69.31	78.32	..	..	..	....	0	"	....	Dove, 1857.
20	67.29	79.48	67.32	52.35	66.61	1849; 1853	3 11	$\odot_r\ 9_m\ 3_a\ 9_a$	Cumming.	S. Coll.
21	66.72	..	61.66	49.96	..	Mar. 1849; Apr. 1861	1 5	[10]	Swan & J. A. Shepherd	" "
22	60.86	75.95	58.49	44.02	59.83	Mar. 1859; Dec. 1869	3 8	$7_m\ 2_a\ 9_a$ bis	A. J. Harris, A. D. Hunt, T. M. Peters, J. Shackelford.	P. O. and S. I. Vol. I, and S. O.
23	..	82.40	66.24	..	..	1850; 1851	0 8	$\odot_r\ 9_m\ 3_a\ 9_a$	Percivall.	S. Coll.
24	66.91	79.49	66.35	51.85	66.15	Aug. 1840; Nov. 1860	19 4	[10]	Assistant Surgeon.	Ar. Met. Regs. 1855, and 1860, and MS. from S. G. O.
25	..	..	..	..	..	1850	0 2	$\odot_r\ 9_m\ 3_a\ 9_a$	A. Winchell.	S. Coll.
26	62.89	78.78	63.07	47.80	63.13	Mar. 1867; Dec. 1869	2 7	$7_m\ 2_a\ 9_a$ bis	E. B. & J. H. Shields.	S. O.
27		..	..	..	..	1859	0 3	$7_m\ 2_a\ 9_a$	Dr. S. K. Jennings.	P. O. and S. I. Vol. I.

ncluded in the hourly means of the month." From 1841 to 1863, inclusive, the observations have been corrected for daily variation, but since the correction to the mean of any one month amounts, in maximo, to only about $\pm$°.1, and for the year to but + °.02, it has been omitted from 1864–1870. The luties of the observatory are carried on by the director, G. T. Kingston, A.M., assisted by Messrs. Walker, Menzies, Stewart, and Davidson.

[6] Observations in 1867–68 at Fish River, or Bolivar, 5 miles N.W. of Bon Secour. [7] Observations in August, 1859, at Livingston, 5 miles to the S.

[8] Observations in 1853 at $7_m\ 2_a\ 9_a$. No correction for change of hours has been applied. [9] Observations in 1867 at Fort Gaines some miles to the west.

[10] Observations at various hours; they have been referred to the mean of the day, making use of the "Fort Morgan table."

[11] Observations from January, 1868, to October, 1869, inclusive, "6 miles east of Havana;" and from November, 1869, to January, 1870, inclusive, 'near Greensboro." All the stations are within a radius of a few miles, and have about the same elevation.

ALABAMA.—Continued.

Name of Station.	Lat.	Long.	Height.	Jan.	Feb.	March.	April.	May.	June.	July.	August.	Sept.	Oct.	Nov.	Dec.
28. Prairie Bluff	32°08′	87°32	..	46°.15	58°.05	57°.48	65°.08	71°.33	80°.93	81°.98	81°.43	76°.00	65°.70	57°.65	..
29. Selma	32 25	87 01	200	49.69	50.71	57.43	62.83	74.02	77.99	80.66	79.18	73.77	64.70	54.91	48°.2
30. Springhill	30 41	88 07	157	53.46	53.21	60.74	73.34	87.07	88.95	91.26	88.09	82.81	71.38	64.67	55.7
31. Springhill College	30 41	88 07	157	..	..	..	..	..	77.54	..	..	..	..	..	..
32. Tuscaloosa[1]	33 12	87 39	245	46.11	41.88	52.90	..	..	77.47	81.53	83.27	78.00	64.23	51.06	44.9
33 Tuskegee	32 25	85 46	..	..	..	59.16	58.70	63.74	73.67	..	..	..	..	..	..
34. Wewokaville	33 18	86 12	..	44.21	47.20	..	..	..	..	..	82.80	76.20	..	..	..
35. Yorkville	33 24	88 18	..	..	..	..	..	.	..	..	86.29	79.93	68.45	55.06	..

ALASKA.

Name of Station.	Lat.	Long.	Height.	Jan.	Feb.	March.	April.	May.	June.	July.	August.	Sept.	Oct.	Nov.	Dec.
1. Fort Kadiak	57 48	152 21	..	33.06	26.51	33.99	38.72	44.11	49.21	56.03	55.71	52.13	45.02	38.03	32.2
2. Fort Kenai[2]	60 33	151 18	..	..	..	..	..	..	..	59.59	60.18	..	..	..	..
3. Fort St. Michael	63 28	161 52	..	— 2.57	21.37	20.12	25.75	39.28	50.27	52.15	54.55	..	32.47	4.23	1.6
4. Fort Tongass	54 46	130 30	20	33.96	36.28	38.52	44.87	50.28	56.42	58.71	59.09	53.12	48.81	41.05	38.0
5. Fort Wrangel	56 28	132 23	..	25.01	32.38	31.81	43.80	50.54	55.99	58.25	58.26	51.83	45.07	37.63	36.0
6. Fort Yukon	66 34	145 18	..	—26.85	—26.44	—11.16	12.66	41.24	53.49	65.75	59.90	38.66	21.60	— 8.28	—18.4
7. Fort Yukon	66 34	145 18	412	—29.5	—11.6	+ 0.6	..	+41.3	..	..	..	..	..	..	..
8. Illoolook[4]	53 54	166 24	..	29.82	31.80	30.79	35.72	41.28	46.21	50.60	51.91	43.66	36.72	32.90	29.6
9. Illoolook	53 54	166 24	..	32.45	32.22	30.65	32.45	37.17	43.02	47.73	53.15	49.32	40.10	29.75	31.5
10. Illoolook	53 54	166 24	..	35.1	34.0	28.5	35.7	..	..	..	..	..	39.0	35.3	30.3
11. Kotzebue Sound	..	163 00	..	..	..	..	..	..	..	52.33	43.	34.04	..	..	..
12. Kotzebue Sound	66 58	165 07	15	—12.01	—15.49	— 6.00	14.49	29.99	38.77	50.04	43.94	38.39	25.00	1.10	5.2
13. Nulato	64 42	157 55	..	—17.70	—12.60	+14.87	26.40	46.47	..	..	..	..	..	..	— 9.3
14. Point Clarence	60 35	165 00	..	—11.06	+ 0.74	+ 4.59	11.50	32.83	40.41	51.91	44.91	40.68	22.62	0.63	0.2
15. Point Providence[6]	64 14	173 03	..	20.50	16.00	6.26	21.49	29.50	38.14	..	..	..	25.49	17.51	3.7
16. St. Paul's Island	57 15	170 00	40	30.52	24.68	30.79	32.63	38.28	44.89	..	..	..	..	33.53	29.3
17. Sitka	57 03	135 20	20	35.73	36.32	39.70	42.85	48.80	54.95	58.53	59.02	53.87	46.49	40.82	34.6
18. Sitka	57 03	135 20	20	29.57	30.67	34.02	39.89	46.00	52.47	55.08	55.10	50.05	44.03	37.69	35.6
19. Sitka[7]	57 03	135 20	20	30.39	31.69	34.32	39.58	45.84	50.60	54.24	54.43	50.59	43.85	37.27	31.
20. Sitka	57 03	135 20	20	34.96	36.76	38.04	43.67	47.37	53.82	56.86	57.34	53.34	48.20	40.81	35.
21. Unalaklik	63 51	160 44	..	—10.40	..	..	..	..	..	..	..	..	..	6.47	3.

ARIZONA.

Name of Station.	Lat.	Long.	Height.	Jan.	Feb.	March.	April.	May.	June.	July.	August.	Sept.	Oct.	Nov.	Dec.
1. Camp Bowie	32 10	109 50	..	44.31	48.68	54.95	62.41	70.66	79.68	78.23	77.09	75.01	66.78	55.63	48.
2. Camp Colorado	34 08	114 18	..	54.08	58.83	64.66	71.26	79.23	86.96	92.23	91.06	83.70	72.11	63.84	51.
3. Camp Crittenden	31 43	110 35	..	42.13	45.00	51.87	61.89	69.41	79.25	77.36	74.53	73.30	61.33	53.64	42.
4. Camp Date Creek[8]	34 18	112 40	3726	43.52	47.35	51.73	61.49	70.38	81.16	83.69	81.66	76.41	63.48	53.21	45.
5. Camp El Dorado	35 45	114 50	..	52.92	53.20	..	74.85	80.34	88.78	94.17	..	..	..	..	..
6. Camp Goodwin	32 52	109 51	..	44.63	49.84	56.27	65.47	74.83	82.91	87.06	83.52	79.58	69.00	55.08	46.
7. Camp Grant[9]	32 54	110 40	..	47.12	51.49	57.77	66.25	76.62	85.55	87.53	83.69	79.18	70.34	58.24	48.
8. Camp Hualpai[10]	34 15	114	..	37.02	..	..	59.40	64.26	71.81	73.76	71.36	..	..	48.47	35.
9. Camp Lincoln	34 52	111 35	..	..	..	..	..	..	64.40	..	77.38	72.68	63.69	53.69	.
10. Camp Lowell Tucson	32 13	110 53	..	49.16	50.89	58.77	67.11	76.58	85.54	87.04	83.98	80.77	72.19	61.41	50.
11. Camp McDowell	33 46	111 36	..	50.36	53.95	59.04	69.69	78.89	88.60	92.42	89.58	83.83	73.22	60.90	52.
12. Camp Reno	33 56	111 20	..	47.85	50.91	62.48	68.48	78.85	89.56	91.35	88.11	85.42	71.38	61.20	48.
13. Camp Skull Valley	34 45	112 30	5000	42.16	39.03	42.37	57.83	..	..	..	..	..	..	..	.

[1] University of Alabama.

[2] Formerly Fort Nicholas.

[3] "Observations in summer at 6_m 6_a; in winter as early as the thermometer could be read in the morning, and as late in the evening.—Dove's corre tions for these hours at Toronto have been applied."

[4] Old style. The difference in the calendars is 12 days, but the Russians carrying their time *eastward* and we *westward*, one day must be subtract thus making our account 11 days nominally in advance of the Russian. The Observations for 1866–67, and probably for the other years of the series, w made 8_m N. 8_a.

ALABAMA.—Continued.

	Spring.	Summer.	Autumn.	Winter.	Year.	Series. Begins.	Series. Ends.	Extent yrs. mos.	Observing hours.	Observer.	References.
28	64°.63	81°.45	66°.45	..	..	1867		0 11	$7_m\ 2_a\ 9_a$ bis	W. Henderson, R. M. Reynolds.	S. O.
29	64.76	79.28	64.46	49°.54	64°.51	Apr. 1858;	Dec. 1870	1 11	$7_m\ 2_a\ 9_a$	Dr. S. K. Jennings, C. F. Fahs, R. B. Deans.	P. O. and S. I. Vol. I, and S. O.
30	73.72	89.43	72.95	54.12	72.56	1841		1 0	9_m N. $3_a\ 9_a$	Fabre.	Printed Journal.
31	..	..	..	..	..	1866		0 1	$6_m\ 2_a$	A. Cornette.	S. O.
32	..	80.76	64.43	44.30	..	Jan. 1854;	Mar. 1855	0 11	$7_m\ 2_a\ 9_a$	Prof. M. Tuomey, and G. Benagh.	P. O. and S. I. Vol. I.
33	60.53	..	..	..	..	1842		0 4	7_m	Jennings.	Regents' Report.
34	..	..	..	..	..	Aug. 1849;	Feb. 1854	0 4	$7_m\ 2_a\ 9_a$	B. T. Holley.	S. Coll.
35	..	..	67.81	..	..	1854		0 4	$8_m\ 2_a\ 8_a$	Dr. J. W. Payne.	P. O. and S. I. Vol. I.

ALASKA.

	Spring.	Summer.	Autumn.	Winter.	Year.	Series. Begins.	Series. Ends.	Extent yrs. mos.	Observing hours.	Observer.	References.
1	38.94	53.65	45.06	30.62	42.07	Apr. 1869;	Aug. 1870	1 5	$7_m\ 2_a\ 9_a$	Assistant Surgeon.	MS. from S. G. O.
2	..	..	..	..	..	1870		0 2	"	" "	" "
3	28.38	52.32	..	6.60	..	Oct. 1865;	Aug. 1866	0 11	$7_m\ 2_a\ 9_a$ bis	H. M. Bannister, J. M. Bean.	S. O.
4	44.56	58.07	47.66	36.10	46.60	June, 1868;	Sept. 1870	2 4	$7_m\ 2_a\ 9_a$	Assistant Surgeon.	MS. from S. G. O.
5	42.05	57.50	44.84	31.15	43.89	May, 1868;	Sept. 1870	1 10	"	" "	" "
6	14.25	59.71	17.33	—23.91	16.84	....		..	[3]	....	Richardson.
7	..	..	..	..	..	1861		0 4	$7_m\ 2_a\ 9_a$	R. Kennicott.	S. Coll.
8	35.93	49.57	37.76	30.42	38.42	Oct. 1827;	Mar. 1867	7 1	M. N. E.	Bishop Veniaminsnoff, I. Shayatnikoff	Ex. Doc. (H.) No. 177 40th Cong. 2d Sess.
9	33.42	47.97	39.72	32.07	38.30	....		2 0	$8_m\ 1_a\ 9_a$[5]	....	Dove, 1857.
10	..	..	..	33.13	..	Oct. 1867;	Apr. 1868	0 7	$7_m\ 2_a\ 9_a$	Dr. P. Panshin.	U. S. Coast Survey.
11	..	..	..	..	..	1826;	1827	0 3	max. & min.	Beechey.	Dove, Rep. Br. Assoc. 1848.
12	12.83	44.25	21.50	— 7.42	17.79	....		1 0	hourly.	....	Dove, 1857.
13	29.25	..	..	—13.21	..	Dec. 1866;	May, 1867	0 6	$9_m\ 1_a\ 8_a$	W. H. Dall.	S. O.
14	16.31	45.74	21.31	— 3.34	20.01	July, 1850;	June, 1852	2 0	hourly.	....	Dove, 1857.
15	10.08			[illegible]	[illegible]	[illegible]		0 9		....	" "
16	33.90	..	..	28.14	..	Nov. 1869;	Dec. 1870	0 10	$7_m\ 2_a\ 9_a$	Assistant Surgeon, C. Bryant.	MS. from S. G. O. and U.S.C.S.
17	43.78	57.50	47.06	35.55	45.97	1833;	1842	9 9	9_m N. $3_a\ 9_a$	Wrangel, Veniamisnoff, Cygnaeus.	Dove, 1853.
18	39.97	54.22	43.92	32.05	42.54	Mar. 1842;	1848	5 6	hourly.	....	" "
19	39.91	53.09	43.90	31.28	42.05	May, 1847;	Sept. 1867	16 11	"	....	Annales de L'Observatoire Physique Central de Russie, and Ex. Doc. (H.) No. 177, 40th Cong. 2d Sess.
20	43.03	56.01	47.45	35.71	45.55	Nov. 1867;	Dec. 1870	3 2	$7_m\ 2_a\ 9_a$	Assistant Surgeon, C. Bryant.	MS. from S. G. O. and S. O.
21	..	..	..	..	..	Nov. 1866;	Jan. 1867	0 3	9_m N. 8_a	F. Westdaht.	S. O.

ARIZONA.

	Spring.	Summer.	Autumn.	Winter.	Year.	Series. Begins.	Series. Ends.	Extent yrs. mos.	Observing hours.	Observer.	References.
1	62.67	78.33	65.81	47.20	63.50	Aug. 1867;	Dec. 1870	3 5	$7_m\ 2_a\ 9_a$	Assistant Surgeon.	MS. from S. G. O.
2	71.72	90.08	73.22	54.96	72.50	Jan. 1869;	Dec. 1870	2 0	"	" "	" "
3	61.06	77.05	62.76	43.08	60.99	Apr. 1868;	Dec. 1870	2 8	"	" "	" "
4	61.20	82.17	64.37	45.53	63.32	May, 1867;	Dec. 1870	3 8	"	" "	" "
5	..	..	..	..	..	1867		0 6	"	" "	" "
6	65.52	84.50	67.89	46.85	66.19	Jan. 1866;	May, 1870	3 10	"	" "	" "
7	66.88	85.59	69.25	48.93	67.66	Dec. 1860;	Dec. 1870	4 10	"	" "	" "
8	..	72.31	..	..	..	1870		0 8	"	" "	" "
9	..	..	63.35	..	..	1868		0 5	"	" "	" "
10	67.49	85.52	71.46	50.24	68.68	Nov. 1866;	Dec. 1870	4 0	"	" "	" "
11	69.21	90.20	72.65	52.27	71.08	Sept. 1866;	Dec. 1870	4 3	"	" "	" "
12	69.94	89.67	72.67	48.98	70.31	Jan. 1869;	Feb. 1870	1 2	"	" "	" "
13	..	..	..	..	..	1867		0 4	"	" "	" "

[5] Corrected for daily variation. [6] In Siberia.

[7] Old style. The observations were taken at the Magnetic and Meteorological Observatory on Japonski Island. From May, 1847, to March, 1849, and for 1862 they were made hourly; from June, 1849, to Dec. 1856, 17 observations were taken daily, hourly, from 6_m to 10_a; for the years 1857–1861, and 1863–64, 19 observations were taken each day, hourly, from 4_m to 10_a. The observing hours in 1867 not stated, but the corrections to them must be very small. The series has been corrected for daily variation by means of the Sitka table by Schott.

[8] In 1867–68 called "Camp McPherson." [9] Formerly "Fort Breckenridge." [10] Also called "Fort Tollgate."

ARIZONA.—Continued.

Name of Station.	Lat.	Long.	Height.	Jan.	Feb.	March.	April.	May.	June.	July.	August.	Sept.	Oct.	Nov.	Dec.
14. Camp Verde	34°32′	111°54′	..	44°.57	48°.49	53°.45	61°.63	71°.55	80°.80	87°.31	79°.56	75°.71	62°.13	51°.53	41°.64
15. Camp Wallen	31 31	110 11	..	44.88	46.53	54.14	60.64	67.53	77.42	78.72	74.92	71.69	63.61	52.30	48.54
16. Camp Willow Grove	35 34	113 27	..	36.58	38.70	44.01	51.24	59.35	71.15	76.02	73.16	68.99	57.99	44.06	41.49
17. Fort Buchanan	31 40	110 55	5330	39.69	44.62	50.84	59.37	67.83	77.29	75.30	75.79	72.57	62.55	48.54	40.29
18. Fort Canby[1]	35 43	109 10	6500	24.04	31.29	39.50	47.30	54.58	67.22	70.51	67.69	58.64	47.36	37.57	26.37
19. Fort Mojavé	35 06	114 35	604	52.23	56.42	64.06	73.67	80.38	90.02	94.51	93.25	84.15	74.84	61.73	53.50
20. Fort Whipple	34 27	112 20	5700	35.40	39.20	42.29	52.39	66.34	72.09	73.63	70.98	64.73	55.85	44.94	35.43
21. Tubac	31 40	111 00	3000	51.14	55.56	..	..	..	..	..	..	81.15	72.38	57.99	56.68

ARKANSAS.

Name of Station.	Lat.	Long.	Height.	Jan.	Feb.	March.	April.	May.	June.	July.	August.	Sept.	Oct.	Nov.	Dec.
1. Camden	33 32	92 48	..	..	..	..	..	..	..	..	..	..	..	57.16	..
2. Fayetteville	36 02	94 12	1350	..	..	..	..	..	..	..	..	..	61.15	51.80	34.85
3. Flippin's Barrens[2]	36 20	92 23	1000	40.63	43.13	52.66	64.30	71 24	75.70	82.48	77.95	..	..	43.28	25.71
4. Fort Smith	35 23	94 29	460	38.17	44.33	50.92	62.35	69.10	76.32	80.23	78.88	72.76	60.43	48.77	39.15
5. Fort Wayne	36 25	94 38	..	40.90	51.73	55.88	62.86	67.80	75.89	77.37	76.92	68.58	60.19	44.28	38.53
6. Helena, near	34 36	90 36	..	41.17	44.87	53.89	61.76	69.02	75.25	80.92	80.14	72.67	58.32	52.54	43.23
7. Jacksonport	35 40	91 15	..	..	..	..	..	..	..	81.90	79.17	..	..	..	..
8. Little Rock	34 40	92 12	..	39.81	49.62	49.64	62.58	70.07	81.61	80.82	82.27	75.71	66.20	50.97	43.20
9. Springhill	33 34	93 35	..	48.75	51.55	60.75	71.15	76.70	..	..	..	..	62.50	60.83	..
10. Washington, near	33 44	93 41	660	42.96	47.60	53.84	63.06	69.87	76.32	79.87	78.37	72.42	60.60	50.59	43.28

CALIFORNIA.

Name of Station.	Lat.	Long.	Height.	Jan.	Feb.	March.	April.	May.	June.	July.	August.	Sept.	Oct.	Nov.	Dec.
1. Alcatraz Island	37 49	122 25	..	53.18	54.82	54.69	55.49	55.94	56.61	57.77	57.80	59.40	60.31	58.99	55.18
2. Angel Island[4]	37 51	122 26	30	50.58	53.04	55.15	58.10	60.13	61.51	63.91	63.14	62.71	61.05	58.27	52.66
3. Auburn	38 53	121 04	1176	..	..	..	65.70	60.40	..	..	90.39	81.53	81.65	60.97	55.16
4. Benicia Barracks[5]	38 03	122 09	64	47.43	50.94	53.93	58.34	60.92	66.47	67.78	66.75	66.18	63.32	55.27	47.88
5. Cahto	39 15	123 17	2000	49.03	49.28	47.25	53.70	59.18	65.45	76.08	72.75	65.35	60.07	54.08	45.72
6. Camp Babbitt	36 22	119 17	..	47.91	51.77	55.87	64.96	74.30	75.32	82.02	81.00	..	64.50	50.65	48.59
7. Camp Bidwell	41 50	120 10	4680	30.42	32.66	38.95	48.22	57.17	66.36	73.87	73.14	63.04	50.41	41,48	33.82
8. Camp Cady	34 58	116 32	3000	46.13	51.04	58.76	70.08	76.78	88.31	92.72	88.90	79.75	64.17	51.92	42.94
9. Camp Far West	39 07	121 18	175	45.33	48.45	51.29	59.20	67.00	71.66	75.53	76.29	69.34	65.35	52.30	44.85
10. Camp Gaston	41 01	123 34	..	44.33	45.57	50.22	56.12	62.48	67.86	73.96	72.37	66.10	57.67	50.43	46.21
11. Camp Independence	36 50	118 11	4800	37.87	41.29	48.07	57.50	65.42	76.14	81.01	79.61	71.72	59.16	48.07	38.97
12. Camp Lincoln	41 50	124 05	..	45.70	46.49	48.03	54.92	58.11	57.75	62.02	58.82	58.35	55.47	51.54	49.33
13. Camp Union	38 32	121 30	54	46.80	47.77	53.45	62.45	70.24	73.10	76.69	74.09	70.29	63.50	51.39	49.68
14. Camp Wright	39 48	123 17	..	40.41	44.34	47.59	55.22	63.03	70.15	77.73	76.11	67.67	59.03	49.62	42.69
15. Chico	39 43	121 48	150	47.83	50.88	51.30	60.13	67.40	76.30	85.78	81.55	71.70	62.65	53.68	45.44
16. Clayton	37 56	121 55	76	50.78	52.33	49.78	57.10	..	..	..	..	..	..	..	..
17. Crescent City	41 45	124 12	12	42.93	...	..	..	..	..	..	..	..	..	..	..
18. Downieville	39 33	120 49	2200	..	..	..	..	..	..	..	70.13	59.30	50.80	42.38	36.19
19. Drum Barracks	33 47	118 17	32	55.29	55.34	56.35	61.12	63.93	68.16	72.83	74.68	70.82	66.91	61.39	56.02
20. Folsom	38 40	121 10	..	..	..	55.03	58.57	63.64	68.70	80.50	77.54	74.80	62.82	..	..
21. Fort Bragg	39 56	123 55	..	47.69	47.17	49.11	50.19	54.36	57.98	59.64	57.34	57.81	54.13	49.56	49.27
22. Fort Crook	41 07	121 29	3390	29.59	34.41	40.76	49.05	56.91	64.85	72.36	71.64	63.19	50.91	41.49	33.52
23. Fort Humboldt[7]	40 45	124 10	50	47.29	47.55	49.22	51.84	55.00	58.20	58.09	58.15	57.67	54.05	51.25	46.17
24. Fort Jones[7]	41 36	122 52	2570	32.19	38.13	44.75	52.09	57.62	67.45	73.38	72.52	65.68	51.27	40.09	31.92
25. Fort Miller[7]	37 00	119 40	402	47.61	53.09	57.80	64.70	70.70	82.86	88.53	85.71	77.46	67.86	54.92	47.47

[1] Old Fort Defiance. The observations previous to 1855, were taken at $\odot_r\ 9_m\ 3_a\ 9_a$, and have been referred to $7_m\ 2_a\ 9_a$ by means of the general table.

[2] Observations in 1859 at Yellville, some miles to the southwest.

[3] Observations at various hours; they have been corrected for daily variation by means of the general table.

[4] Also called Camp Reynolds.

ARIZONA.—Continued.

	Spring.	Summer.	Autumn.	Winter.	Year.	Series. Begins.	Series. Ends.	Extent yrs. mos.	Observing hours.	Observer.	References.
14	62°.21	82°.56	63°.12	44°.90	63°.20	Dec. 1868;	Dec. 1870	2 1	$7_m\ 2_a\ 9_a$	Assistant Surgeon.	MS. from S. G. O.
15	60.77	77.02	62.53	46.65	61.74	Nov. 1866;	Sept. 1869	2 10	"	" "	" "
16	51.53	73.44	57.01	38.92	55.23	Feb. 1868;	Sept. 1869	1 8	"	" "	" "
17	59.35	76.13	61.22	41.53	59.56	Aug. 1857;	June, 1861	3 11	"	" "	Ar. Met. Reg. 1860, and MS. from S. G. O.
18	47.13	68.47	47.86	27.23	47.67	Dec. 1851;	Nov. 1863	8 11	"	" "	Ar. Met. Regs. 1855 and 1860, and MS. from S. G. O.
19	72.70	92.59	73.57	54.05	73.23	June, 1859;	Dec. 1870	6 5	"	" "	Ar. Met. Reg. 1860, and MS. from S. G. O.
20	53.67	72.23	55.17	36.68	54.44	Jan. 1865;	Dec. 1870	4 9	"	" "	MS. from S. G. O.
21	..	..	70.51	54.46	..	Sept. 1867;	Feb. 1868	0 6	"	" "	" "

ARKANSAS.

	Spring.	Summer.	Autumn.	Winter.	Year.	Series. Begins.	Series. Ends.	Extent yrs. mos.	Observing hours.	Observer.	References.
1	..	..	..	..	..	1855		0 1	$7_m\ 2_a\ 9_a$	J. J. McElrath.	P. O. and S. I. Vol. I.
2	..	..	..	..	..	1870		0 3	$7_m\ 2_a\ 9_a$ bis	C. L. McClung.	S. O.
3	62.73	78.71	..	36.49	..	Nov. 1859;	Aug. 1860	0 10	"	W. B. Flippin.	" "
4	60.79	78.48	60.65	40.55	60.12	Jan. 1840;	Dec. 1870	19 3	[5]	Assistant Surgeon, Dr. Shumard, F. Springer.	Ar. Met. Regs. 1851, 1855, 1860, S. Coll., S. O. and MS. from S. G. O.
5	62.18	76.73	57.68	43.72	60.08	1840		1 0	$7_m\ 2_a\ 9_a$	Assistant Surgeon.	Ar. Met. Reg. 1851.
6	61.56	78.77	61.18	43.09	61.15	Dec. 1865;	Dec. 1870	3 2	$7_m\ 2_a\ 9_a$ bis	O. F. Russell.	S. O.
7	..	..	..	..	..	1859		0 2	$7_m\ 2_a\ 9_a$	Dr. G. A. Martin.	P. O. and S. I. Vol. I.
8	60.76	81.57	64.29	44.21	62.71	Jan. 1840;	Dec. 1867	2 1	"	Anthony and Dr. W. J. Goulding.	Am. Alm. 1842, Ar. Met. Reg. 1851 and S. Coll.
9	69.53	..	..	..	..	Oct. 1859;	May, 1860	0 7	$7_m\ 3_a$	P. F. Finley.	P. O. and S. I. Vol. I, and S. O.
10	62.26	78.19	61.20	44.61	61.56	Jan. 1840;	Dec. 1870	22 1	[7]	Dr. N. D. Smith, Assis. Surg., H. Bishop, and Dr. A. P. Moore.	S. Con. to Know. 1860, S. O. MS. from S. G. O.

CALIFORNIA.

	Spring.	Summer.	Autumn.	Winter.	Year.	Series. Begins.	Series. Ends.	Extent yrs. mos.	Observing hours.	Observer.	References.
1	55.37	57.39	59.57	54.39	56.68	Feb. 1860;	Dec. 1870	8 6	$7_m\ 2_a\ 9_a$	Assistant Surgeon.	MS. from S. G. O.
2	57.79	62.85	60.68	52.09	58.35	Dec. 1867;	Dec. 1870	3 1	"	" "	" " "
3	..	..	74.72	..	..	Aug. 1859;	May, 1860	0 7	2_a	R. Gordon.	P. O. and S. I. Vol. I, and S. O.
4	57.73	67.00	61.59	48.75	58.77	Nov. 1849;	Dec. 1870	15 7	$7_m\ 2_a\ 9_a$	Assistant Surgeon.	Ar. Met. Regs. 1855 and 1860 and MS. from S. G. O.
5	53.38	71.43	59.83	48.01	58.16	Dec. 1869;	Dec. 1870	1 1	$7_m\ 2_a\ 9_a$ bis	Dr. Thornton and daughter.	S. O.
6	65.04	79.45	..	49.42	..	Nov. 1863;	Feb. 1866	1 8	$7_m\ 2_a\ 9_a$	Assistant Surgeon.	MS. from S. G. O.
7	48.11	71.12	51.64	32.30	50.79	Nov. 1863;	Dec. 1870	4 9	"	" "	" " "
8	68.54	89.98	65.28	46.70	67.63	Jan. 1868;	Dec. 1870	3 0	"	" "	" " "
9	59.16	74.49	62.33	46.21	60.55	Jan. 1850;	Mar. 1852	1 11	$\odot_r\ 9_m\ 3_a\ 9_a$	" "	Ar. Met. Reg. 1855.
10	56.27	71.40	58.07	45.37	57.78	Sept. 1861;	Dec. 1870	8 8	$7_m\ 2_a\ 9_a$	" "	MS. from S. G. O.
11	57.00	78.92	59.65	39.38	58.74	Nov. 1862;	Dec. 1870	5 5	"	" "	" " "
12	53.69	59.53	55.12	47.17	53.88	Sept. 1866;	May, 1869	2 8	"	" "	" " "
13	62.05	74.63	61.73	48.08	61.62	Apr. 1864;	Aug. 1865	1 4	"	" "	" " "
14	55.28	74.66	58.77	42.48	57.80	Aug. 1864;	Dec. 1870	6 0	"	" "	" " "
15	59.61	81.21	62.68	48.05	62.89	Nov. 1869;	Dec. 1870	1 2	$7_m\ 2_a\ 9_a$ bis	W. F. Cheney.	S. O.
16	..	..	..	..	..	1870		0 4	"	C. L. McClung.	" "
17	..	..	..	..	..	1860		0 1	"	R. B. Randall.	" "
18	..	..	50.83	..	..	Nov. 1859;	Dec. 1860	0 7	"	Dr. T. R. Kibbe.	P. O. and S. I. Vol. I, and S. O.
19	60.47	71.89	66.37	55.55	63.57	May, 1864;	Dec. 1870	5 11	$7_m\ 2_a\ 9_a$	Assistant Surgeon.	MS. from S. G. O.
20	59.08	75.58	..	..	..	1861		0 8	[6]	S. V. Blakeslee.	S. O.
21	51.22	58.32	53.83	48.04	52.85	Dec. 1860;	Sept. 1864	3 4	$7_m\ 2_a\ 9_a$	Assistant Surgeon.	MS. from S. G. O.
22	48.91	69.62	51.86	32.51	50.72	Jan. 1858;	Apr. 1869	10 4	"	" "	Ar. Met. Reg. 1860 and MS. from S. G. O.
23	52.02	58.15	54.32	47.00	52.87	Jan. 1854;	Dec. 1869	11 9	"	" "	Ar. Met. Regs. 1855 and 1860, and MS. from S. G. O.
24	51.49	71.12	52.35	34.08	52.26	Jan. 1853;	June, 1858	5 0	"	" "	Ar. Met. Regs. 1855 and 1860.
25	64.40	85.70	66.75	49.39	66.56	Aug. 1851;	Aug. 1864	7 6	"	" "	Ar. Met. Regs. 1855 and 1860, and MS. from S. G. O.

[5] Observations prior to 1855 at $\odot_r\ 9_m\ 3_a\ 9_a$; a correction was applied, making use of the Key West Table, to refer them to $7_m\ 2_a\ 9_a$. The *annual* mean is not affected by this change of hours.

[6] Observing hours irregular; corrected for daily variation.

[7] Observations previous to 1855 at $\odot_r\ 9_m\ 3_a\ 9_a$, referred to $7_m\ 2_a\ 9_a$.

CALIFORNIA.—Continued.

Name of Station.	Lat.	Long.	Height.	Jan.	Feb.	March.	April.	May.	June.	July.	August.	Sept.	Oct.	Nov.	Dec.
26. Fort Point[1]	37°48′	122°29′	27	50°.59	51°.81	53°.15	55°.52	57°.61	58°.93	59.86	58°.84	59°.31	58°.36	56°.44	52°.22
27. Fort Reading[2]	40 28	122 13	674	44.31	49.78	55.83	59.31	65.47	77.69	82.96	80.16	72.61	64.52	52.30	43.10
28. Fort Ross	38 33	123 15	..	47.18	48.04	49.95	51.26	55.32	56.90	57.82	58.39	55.97	53.42	50.90	48.91
29. Fort Tejon	34 53	118 55	3240	43.61	46.34	50.10	54.98	60.01	71.49	76.62	75.61	68.35	58.75	48.49	42.05
30. Fort Ter-Waw	41 30	123 52	..	43.72	47.84	49.15	51.70	54.35	59.63	59.79	60.92	59.92	54.91	50.41	45.11
31. Fort Yuma[3]	32 46	114 44	200	56.20	60.97	66.62	74.02	79.57	89.55	94.25	92.42	87.25	75.65	64.08	56.72
32. Indian Valley	40 07	120 50	3280	..	..	..	..	..	..	..	..	..	..	50.65	39.20
33. Los Angeles	34 03	118 15	457	58.83	55.12	58.33	..	..	73.05	75.01	..	..	..	..	60.87
34. Mare Island, Naval Hospital	38 06	122 15	30	48.46	52.43	57.00	..	..	..	71.28	69.60	66.35	64.45	63.08	51.20
35. Marsh Ranche	37 53	121 42	..	42.25	..	52.15	57.38	64.35	73.38	80.95	79.37	..	..	55.38	53.25
36. Marysville	39 09	121 34	80	45.39	51.03	54.23	60.08	66.29	72.71	77.64	74.84	72.97	63.90	54.07	45.46
37. Meadow Valley[4]	39 56	121 02	3700	32.54	35.14	41.09	47.01	53.04	60.59	66.97	64.71	59.08	50.15	40.57	33.72
38. Monterey[5]	36 37	121 52	40	50.04	50.35	52.13	54.56	57.05	58.67	60.05	60.47	59.95	57.94	54.01	50.14
39. Murphy's	38 08	120 28	2200	38.19	42.98	48.92	54.13	55.50	62.48	75.73	76.93	64.58	55.60	..	42.95
40. New San Diego	32 43	117 10	10	54.59	56.01	57.30	60.86	66.38	67.57	68.71	70.90	68.18	65.16	60.89	53.30
41. Paradise City	37 36	121 04	125	44.98	45.12	..	..	..	..	..	..	..	..	..	..
42. Point San José	37 48	122 26	..	51.61	55.11	55.33	58.78	55.96	..	..	59.12	60.76	59.01	56.36	50.83
43. Presidio[6]	37 47	122 28	150	49.69	51.01	52.34	54.52	55.37	56.91	57.62	57.87	59.13	58.01	54.70	50.25
44. Rancho de Jurupa	34 02	117 27	1000	53.31	53.89	56.89	64.42	63.56	71.83	76.22	74.51	74.07	66.90	56.52	52.37
45. Rancho del Chino	33 59	117 44	1000	55.43	56.82	56.57	60.75	63.75	68.76	72.54	72.63	70.06	68.58	60.39	53.61
46. Sacramento	38 34	121 26	52	46.39	50.52	54.44	59.42	63.65	70.05	72.79	70.74	68.82	62.85	53.49	46.85
47. San Benito	36 08	121 02	140	46.46	46.77	53.84	56.80	59.58	65.61	68.27	67.00	..	62.26	54.97	54.47
48. San Diego	32 42	117 14	150	53.55	54.60	57.11	60.72	62.59	66.68	70.32	72.02	69.38	65.16	59.04	54.11
49. San Francisco	37 48	122 25	130	48.81	50.81	53.24	55.24	56.40	57.90	57.98	58.24	59.73	58.82	54.89	50.66
50. San Joaquin	33 38	117 48	..	49.3	57.4	56.6	65.5	74.9	88.5	..	82.9	78.1	67.1	56.6	49.7
51. San Luis Rey	33 13	117 20	20	52.01	50.74	54.33	..	..	..	70.64	73.71	73.50	65.53	58.50	50.60
52. Santa Barbara	34 24	119 43	20	..	..	58.38	64.05	63.33	67.54	66.63	70.33	67.00	..	..	..
53. Santa Catilina Island	33 26	118 30	..	..	58.96	58.74	..	..	..	..	..	..	..	..	..
54. Santa Clara[9]	37 20	121 54	100	48.95	52.53	56.13	..	..	..	..	..	63.29	61.67	53.33	46.26
55. Silver Creek	40 00	120 40	3700	..	35.48	..	..	..	..	..	..	62.00	51.55	38.48	33.95
56. Sonoma	38 18	122 27	100	50.96	52.84	53.04	57.47	..	..	..	..	..	..	53.81	49.16
57. Stockton[10]	37 57	121 15	..	44.95	50.51	55.17	59.04	64.92	68.89	71.99	70.34	67.93	62.66	58.63	49.19
58. Stony Point	38 40	122 50	500	..	..	..	..	..	..	68.50	..	68.25	..	..	..
59. Union Ranche	39 25	121 30	..	45.37	47.70	53.37	58.57	63.80	74.80	81.29	79.21	73.53	63.65	52.77	46.45
60. Vacaville	38 21	121 58	175	50.49	52.69	54.71	60.81	65.68	72.15	74.73	72.23	73.80	68.58	61.00	48.03
61. Visalia	36 22	119 16	2500	44.82	51.27	50.48	59.22	68.50	75.40	84.85	82.08	70.73	59.98	50.30	40.05
62. Watsonville	36 56	121 43	45	52.99	54.59	55.87	58.57	60.38	62.40	66.39	65.52	..	60.15	56.08	49.57
63. Yerba Buena Island	37 48	122 22	..	51.97	52.17	53.95	55.85	57.27	58.38	61.80	60.79	61.17	61.02	57.49	50.46

COLORADO.

Name of Station.	Lat.	Long.	Height.	Jan.	Feb.	March.	April.	May.	June.	July.	August.	Sept.	Oct.	Nov.	Dec.
1. Central City[11]	39 52	105 31	..	24.05	..	..	38.53	49.27	62.73	67.90	..	56.33	..	35.83	37.30
2. Denver	39 45	105 01	5250	26.57	32.75	31.85	46.90	60.28	67.13	72.68	67.70	61.26	48.78	39.22	22.45
3. Fort Garland[12]	37 32	105 40	8365	18.46	23.37	33.63	42.75	52.41	62.23	66.61	64.34	55.61	43.97	30.88	20.05

[1] Observations of one series, two years and four months, at $7_m\ 2_a\ 9_a$, were referred to 6_m N. 6_a and combined with the other series.

[2] Observations for one year and two months at $7_m\ 2_a\ 9_a$, referred to $\odot_r\ 9_m\ 3_a\ 9_a$.

[3] Observations previous to 1855 at $\odot_r\ 9_m\ 3_a\ 9_a$, referred to $7_m\ 2_a\ 9_a$

[4] Observations for four months in morning and evening; assumed to be at $\odot_r$ and $\odot_s$, and referred to $7_m\ 2_a\ 9_{a\ bis}$.

[5] Observations for four years and one month at $\odot_r\ 9_m\ 3_a\ 9_a$, referred to $7_m\ 2_a\ 9_{a\ bis}$.

[6] Observations prior to 1855 at $\odot_r\ 9_m\ 3_a\ 9_a$; a correction was applied, making use of the Key West Table, to refer them to $7_m\ 2_a\ 9_a$. The annua mean is not affected by this change of hours.

CALIFORNIA.—Continued.

	Spring.	Summer.	Autumn.	Winter.	Year.	Series. Begins.	Series. Ends.	Extent yrs. mos.	Observing hours.	Observer.	References.
26	55°.43	59°.21	58°.04	51°.54	56°.05	Jan. 1860;	Dec. 1870	10 11	6_m N. 6_a	Assistant Surgeon, F. P. Thompson, W. Knapp, H. E. Uhrlandt.	MS. from S. G. O. and U. S. Coast Survey.
27	60.20	80.27	63.14	45.73	62.34	Apr. 1852;	Mar. 1856	3 10	$\odot_r\ 9_m\ 3_a\ 9_a$	Assistant Surgeon.	Ar. Met. Regs. 1855 and 1860.
28	52.18	57.70	53.43	48.04	52.84	Jan. 1837;	Dec. 1840	4 0	$7_m\ 2_a\ 6_a$	" "	Dove, S. Coll.; and Ar. Met. Reg. 1855.
29	55.03	74.57	58.53	44.00	58.03	Mar. 1855;	Aug. 1864	6 9	$7_m\ 2_a\ 9_a$	" "	Ar. Met. Reg. 1860, and MS. from S. G. O.
30	51.73	60.11	55.08	45.56	53.12	Apr. 1859;	Oct. 1861	2 3	"	" "	" " " "
31	73.40	92.07	75.66	57.96	74.77	Dec. 1850;	Dec. 1870	14 11	"	" "	Ar. Met. Regs. 1855 and 1860, and MS. from S. G. O.
32	..	..	..	..	..	1870		0 2	$7_m\ 2_a\ 9_{a\ bis}$	M. E. Pulsifer.	S. O.
33	..	..	..	58.27	..	June, 1847;	Mar. 1848	0 6	$\odot_r\ 9_m\ 3_a\ 9_a$	Assistant Surgeon.	Ar. Met. Reg. 1855.
34	..	..	64.63	50.70	..	Jan. 1868;	Sept. 1870	1 0	"	J. M. Brown, W. E. Taylor.	S. O.
35	57.96	77.90	..	..	..	May, 1867;	May, 1868	0 10	$7_m\ 2_a\ 9_{a\ bis}$	F. M. Rogers.	" "
36	60.20	75.06	63.65	47.29	61.55	May, 1857;	Aug. 1863	3 0	"	W. C. Belcher.	P. O. and S. I. Vol. 1, and S. O.
37	47.05	64.09	49.93	33.80	48.72	Jan. 1860;	June, 1866	3 11	"	J. H. Whitlock and M. D. Smith.	S. O.
38	54.58	59.73	57.30	50.18	55.45	May, 1847;	Dec. 1870	12 5	"	Assistant Surgeon, and Dr. C. A. Canfield.	Ar. Met. Reg. 1855, MS. from S. G. O., P. O. and S. I. Vol. 1, S. O.
39	52.85	71.71	..	41.37	..	Mar. 1868;	Mar. 1869	1 0	"	E. Cutting.	S. O.
40	61.51	69.06	64.74	54.63	62.49	Dec. 1864;	Dec. 1870	1 9	$7_m\ 2_a\ 9_a$	Assistant Surgeon.	MS. from S. G. O.
41	..	..	..	..	..	1869		0 2	$7_m\ 2_a\ 9_{a\ bis}$	J. W. A. Wright.	S. O.
42	56.69	..	58.71	52.52	..	Oct. 1865;	Dec. 1870	1 6	$7_m\ 2_a\ 9_a$	Assistant Surgeon.	MS. from S. G. O.
43	54.08	57.47	57.28	50.32	54.79	Oct. 1847;	Dec. 1870	19 0	"	" "	Ar. Met. Regs. 1855 and 1860, MS. from S. G. O. and S.O.
44	61.62	74.19	65.83	53.19	63.71	Oct. 1852;	Mar. 1854	1 6	$\odot_r\ 9_m\ 3_a\ 9_a$	" "	Ar. Met. Reg. 1855.
45	60.36	71.31	66.34	55.29	63.32	July, 1851;	Aug. 1852	1 2	"	" "	" " " "
46	59.17	71.19	61.72	47.92	60.00	July, 1849;	Mar. 1867	14 0	[7]	Assist. Surgeon, Drs. F. W. Hatch and T. M. Logan.	Ar. Met. Reg. 1855, MS. from S. G. O., Am. Alm., P. O. and S. I. Vol. 1., and S. O.
47	[illegible]	[illegible]	..	[illegible]	..	May, 1861;	July, 1863	1 9	$7_m\ 2_a\ 7_{a\ bis}$	Dr. C. A. Canfield.	S. O.
48	60.14	69.67	64.53	54.09	62.11	July, 1849;	Dec. 1870	20 10	[8]	Assistant Surgeon, A Cassidy, and W. Knapp.	Ar. Met. Regs. 1855 and 1860, MS. from S. G. O., and U. S. Coast Survey.
49	54.96	58.04	57.81	50.09	55.23	Jan. 1854;	Sept. 1868	11 2	$7_m\ 2_a\ 9_{a\ bis}$	Drs. H. Gibbons and W. O. Ayres.	P. O. and S. I. Vol. 1. and S. O.
50	65.67	..	67.27	52.13	..	....		1 5	......	....	Pat. Off. Rep.
51	..	..	65.84	51.12	..	July, 1850;	Mar. 1851	0 9	$\odot_r\ 9_m\ 3_a\ 9_a$	Assistant Surgeon.	Ar. Met. Reg. 1855.
52	61.92	68.17	..	..	..	1864		0 7	$7_m\ 2_a\ 9_{a\ bis}$	Dr. W. W. Hays.	S. O.
53	..	..	..	..	..	1864		0 2	$7_m\ 2_a\ 9_a$	Assistant Surgeon.	MS. from S. G. O.
54	..	..	59.43	49.25	..	Sept. 1859;	Mar. 1861	0 7	"	Prof. O. S Frambes.	P. O. and S. I. Vol. 1, and S. O.
55	..	..	50.68	..	..	Sept. 1862;	Feb. 1863	0 5	$7_m\ 2_a\ 9_{a\ bis}$	M. D. Smith.	S. O.
56	..	..	..	50.99	..	Nov. 1850;	Apr. 1851	0 6	$\odot_r\ 9_m\ 3_a\ 9_a$	Assistant Surgeon.	Ar. Met. Reg. 1855.
57	59.71	70.41	63.07	48.22	60.35	Jan. 1854;	June, 1867	1 11	[7]	Dr. R. K. Reid, W. M. Trivett, Assis. Surg.	P. O. and S. I. Vol. 1, S. O., and MS. from S. G. O.
58	..	..	..	..	..	1869		0 2	$7_m\ 2_a\ 9_{a\ bis}$	Dr. Thornton.	S. O.
59	58.58	78.43	63.32	46.51	61.71	Mar. 1858;	Jan. 1863	3 7	"	J. Slaven, W. L. and E. S. Dunkum.	P. O. and S. I. Vol. 1, and S. O.
60	60.40	73.04	67.79	50.40	62.91	Feb. 1869;	Apr. 1870	1 3	"	Prof. J. C. Simmons.	S. O.
61	59.40	80.78	60.34	45.38	61.47	1870		1 0	"	J. W. Blake.	" "
62	58.27	64.77	..	52.38	..	Jan. 1869;	Dec. 1870	1 10	"	Dr. A. J. Compton.	" "
63	55.69	60.32	59.89	51.53	56.86	Feb. 1869;	Dec. 1870	1 10	$7_m\ 2_a\ 9_a$	Assistant Surgeon.	MS. from S. G. O.

COLORADO.

	Spring.	Summer.	Autumn.	Winter.	Year.	Series. Begins.	Series. Ends.	Extent yrs. mos.	Observing hours.	Observer.	References.
1	..	..	..	..	..	Apr. 1861;	Jan. 1862	0 8	$7_m\ 2_a\ 9_a$	Dr. W. T. Ellis.	S. O.
2	46.34	69.17	49.75	27.26	48.13	Jan. 1859;	Dec. 1870	1 6	$7_m\ 2_a\ 9_{a\ bis}$	D. C. Collier, W. N. Byers, F. J. Stanton, S. T. Sopris.	P. O. and S. I. Vol. 1, and S. O.
3	42.93	64.39	43.49	20.63	42.86	Sept. 1852;	Dec. 1870	15 3	$7_m\ 2_a\ 9_a$	Assistant Surgeon.	Ar. Met. Regs. 1855 and 1860, and MS. from S. G. O.

7 Observing hours irregular; corrected for daily variation.

8 Observing hours irregular; corrected for daily variation, making use of the Key West Table.

9 University of the Pacific.

10 State Insane Asylum, except for three months of 1863 when the observations were taken at Camp Stamford Stockton.

11 Observations for April and May, 1861, were made at Mountain City, a few miles to the southeast.

12 Observations from September, 1852, to July, 1858, were made at old Fort Massachusetts, a few miles east of Fort Garland.

COLORADO.—Continued.

Name of Station.	Lat.	Long.	Height.	Jan.	Feb.	March.	April.	May.	June.	July.	August.	Sept.	Oct.	Nov.	Dec.
4. Fort Lyon[1]	38°08′	102°50′	4000	26°.01	33°.65	39°.68	49°.72	64°.74	74°.80	79°.65	76°.13	64°.33	49°.08	39°.08	27°.3
5. Fort Morgan	40 15	103 46	4500	19.78	33.67	30.52	47.20	58.25	71.00	78.99	79.85	70.65	57.41	..	29.3
6. Fort Reynolds	38 15	104 12	..	32.26	36.23	41.67	51.73	63.13	72.50	78.79	73.94	64.38	50.98	39.78	27.0
7. Fort Sedgwick	40 58	102 23	3600	26.23	31.60	34.65	46.25	59.49	70.88	78.81	72.21	60.62	49.62	40.20	28.5
8. Golden City	39 44	105 18	5240	..	..	..	49.77	61.00	67.57	73.33	74.73	65.80	..	..	..
9. Montgomery	39 00	106 00	..	17.86	24.45	19.78	29.75	41.28	..	..	..	..	..	..	19.5

CONNECTICUT.

Name of Station.	Lat.	Long.	Height.	Jan.	Feb.	March.	April.	May.	June.	July.	August.	Sept.	Oct.	Nov.	Dec.
1. Brookfield	41 27	73 24	100	33.10	30.79	31.85	45.24	57.23	68.32	72.40	70.46	63.54	50.85	40.24	30.8
2. Canton	41 52	72 55	750	27.87	25.11	29.63	40.57	54.15	58.93	68.79	64.03	59.67	50.24	39.10	29.5
3. Colebrook	42 00	73 03	1210	20.89	23.31	28.76	43.12	53.84	64.55	69.38	67.13	59.40	47.30	36.61	24.6
4. Columbia	41 41	72 18	..	25.88	28.87	33.94	45.76	56.52	65.87	70.62	68.87	61.73	51.13	40.65	29.2
5. Farmington, near[2]	41 42	72 50	..	42.09	49.07	56.33	62.58	69.10	77.52	81.37	78.25	71.17	63.44	50.17	42.4
6. Fort Trumbull	41 21	72 05	23	30.48	31.68	37.42	47.78	57.71	67.40	72.61	71.58	64.69	54.07	43.88	33.2
7. Georgetown	41 15	73 25	300	16.28	..	27.41	46.03	50.63	64.79	71.45	66.30	61.53	50.02	40.10	27.8
8. Goshen[3]	41 48	72 07	561	26.55	26.12	34.00	45.92	56.11	65.26	70.53	69.06	60.89	49.95	39.89	29.0
9. Hartford	41 46	72 41	60	29.11	29.32	37.71	48.30	57.66	66.87	72.14	70.25	62.58	51.39	41.12	31.2
10. Knight Hospital	41 18	72 55	..	32.08	..	..	..	60.35	65.76	75.68	75.77	65.52	56.80	49.24	35.9
11. Litchfield	41 45	73 12	800	24.02	26.19	32.92	38.88	51.45	62.58	68.06	64.39	58.48	49.44	35.52	25.0
12. Lynde Point Lt. Ho.	41 16	72 20	10	26.96	28.82	33.43	44.09	54.33	63.31	71.10	69.56	63.14	53.59	42.71	30.7
13. Middletown	41 33	72 39	175	26.23	28.93	33.86	45.66	56.24	66.34	70.96	68.97	61.43	50.80	38.95	28.6
14. New Haven	41 18	72 57	45	26.46	28.08	36.03	46.96	57.28	66.96	71.69	70.24	62.49	51.06	40.28	30.4
15. New London	41 21	72 07	90	28.42	29.75	36.32	45.47	56.28	66.28	71.79	69.17	63.27	52.87	42.68	32.3
16. North Colebrook	42 01	73 06	..	..	..	..	..	52.48	63.35	66.96	..	..	..	..	..
17. North Greenwich	41 04	73 40	300	..	..	..	..	..	..	..	..	..	..	..	29.5
18. Norwich	41 32	72 04	50	24.65	28.21	30.65	45.15	55.51	67.47	73.87	69.92	64.43	51.25	41.32	30.6
19. Plymouth	41 40	73 04	..	26.10	26.29	27.98	41.70	56.42	62.18	68.83	67.80	57.85	48.74	38.97	25.9
20. Pomfret	41 51	71 56	587	22.89	28.07	30.99	43.30	53.77	63.17	68.12	65.82	58.88	48.46	42.36	26.2
21. Salisbury	41 59	73 25	737	24.65	25.28	34.65	44.44	56.32	65.87	70.44	68.06	60.09	50.18	39.23	27.5
22. Sharon	41 52	73 28	200	24.90	26.15	34.42	45.64	57.65	65.96	70.11	68.00	61.14	49.96	39.29	28.7
23. Southington	41 35	72 54	..	..	..	..	49.48	59.11	70.93	73.82	71.94	63.83	52.90	41.04	30.1
24. Wallingford	41 27	72 50	133	24.42	27.85	34.79	44.72	54.99	65.77	69.76	67.36	60.49	50.82	39.28	28.4
25. Warren Centre	41 44	73 20	..	21.70	20.66	35.31	41.21	52.41	64.31	67.67	67.34	58.41	48.32	45.46	27.2
26. Waterbury	41 33	73 02	363	24.52	27.55	33.62	44.93	54.26	64.78	70.92	69.05	60.32	45.22	38.01	24.6
27. West Cornwall	41 53	73 22	1000	24.00	22.41	38.23	41.10	56.70	64.83	71.17	67.17	59.70	51.01	38.35	21.9
28. Windsor	41 55	72 39	..	..	..	31.00	..	..	66.34	..	70.00	..	..	..	..

DAKOTA.

Name of Station.	Lat.	Long.	Height.	Jan.	Feb.	March.	April.	May.	June.	July.	August.	Sept.	Oct.	Nov.	Dec.
1. Fort Abercrombie	46 27	96 21	..	4.53	8.44	17.41	39.37	59.20	69.73	73.33	69.75	58.88	44.39	28.17	10.8
2. Fort Buford	48 01	103 58	1900	8.07	13.28	18.15	45.61	57.47	67.84	72.77	67.94	55.93	42.25	29.39	13.9
3. Fort Dakota	43 30	96 45	..	17.25	17.65	22.65	41.55	58.55	..	..	..	53.90	44.13	28.32	15.4
4. Fort Pierre	44 23	100 20	1456	7.33	23.20	33.21	47.60	61.08	71.52	78.28	70.51	62.56	52.52	30.96	11.3
5. Fort Randall	43 01	98 37	1245	18.70	22.80	23.45	45.26	61.12	71.61	78.06	74.17	63.48	49.31	34.39	21.2
6. Fort Ransom	46 35	97 47	..	6.98	10.20	16.42	43.73	59.07	65.62	70.34	65.27	57.41	39.16	28.03	13.9
7. Fort Rice	46 32	100 33	..	13.23	16.29	26.12	45.37	59.14	68.15	74.76	67.14	54.28	40.45	29.11	17.6
8. Fort Stevenson[6]	47 36	101 10	..	5.23	11.79	22.51	44.96	58.08	69.33	77.41	69.76	57.18	44.23	31.87	13.0
9. Fort Sully	44 50	100 35	..	16.65	20.57	23.25	44.98	60.14	69.21	76.82	72.09	60.62	45.85	35.42	24.5
10. Fort Totten	47 56	99 16	..	—0.52	7.41	13.47	46.19	59.22	67.52	69.59	65.82	58.67	38.33	27.57	12.4
11. Fort Wadsworth	45 13	97 10	..	5.21	9.43	10.96	40.22	55.33	65.17	70.39	67.27	58.99	43.45	30.40	12.9
12. Yankton Indian Agency[7]	42 52	98 24	1900	17.66	27.30	37.68	50.89	61.86	71.29	74.30	74.43	58.58	51.24	32.98	20.4

[1] Observations from January, 1861, to May, 1862, were made at Fort Wise or old Fort Lyon, some miles to the southeast of the present fort.

[2] The observations were made six miles S. of Farmington.

[3] The observations are stated to have been made in Windham Co. as indicated by the given position and height, but perhaps a mistake of 1° in Lon has been made.

[4] The observations were made at variable hours, the means being corrected for daily variation.

COLORADO.—Continued.

	Spring.	Summer.	Autumn.	Winter.	Year.	Series. Begins.	Ends.	Extent yrs. mos.	Observing hours.	Observer.	References.
4	51°.38	76°.86	50°.83	29°.01	52°.02	Jan. 1861;	Dec. 1870	5 5	$7_m\ 2_a\ 9_a$	Assistant Surgeon.	MS. from S. G. O.
5	45.32	76.61	..	27.59	..	Dec. 1866;	Apr. 1868	1 3	"	" "	" " "
6	52.18	75.08	51.71	31.85	52.70	May, 1868;	Dec. 1870	2 8	"	" "	" " "
7	46.80	73.97	50.15	28.78	49.92	Apr. 1867;	Dec. 1870	3 6	"	" "	" " "
8	..	71.88	..	..	..	May, 1860;	Apr. 1867	0 6	"	M. L. Blunt, J. McDonald, E.L. Berthoud	S. O.
9	30.27	..	..	20.63	..	Dec. 1863;	May, 1864	0 6	$7_m\ 2_a\ 9_a$ bis	J. Luttrell.	" "

CONNECTICUT.

	Spring.	Summer.	Autumn.	Winter.	Year.	Series. Begins.	Ends.	Extent yrs. mos.	Observing hours.	Observer.	References.
1	44.77	70.39	51.54	31.57	49.57	Oct. 1868;	Dec. 1870	2 2	$7_m\ 2_a\ 9_a$ bis	S. W. Roe.	S. O.
2	41.45	63.92	49.67	27.50	45.63	Dec. 1861;	July, 1863	1 7	"	J. Case.	" "
3	41.91	67.02	47.77	22.96	44.91	Sept. 1860;	Nov. 1870	9 9	"	C. Rockwell.	" "
4	45.41	68.45	51.17	28.00	48.26	Dec. 1856;	Dec. 1870	13 8	"	W. H. Yeomans.	P. O. and S. I. Vol. 1, and S. O.
5	62.67	79.05	61.59	44.55	61.96	May, 1838;	Apr. 1841	3 0	3_a	Smith.	Pat. Off. Rep. 1851.
6	47.64	70.53	54.21	31.81	51.05	Jan. 1833;	Dec. 1870	23 8	$7_m\ 2_a\ 9_a$	Rev. E. Dewhurst and Assistant Surgeon.	Ar. Met. Regs. 1840, '51, & '55, MS. from S. G. O., and S. O.
7	41.36	67.51	50.55	..	..	Mar. 1856;	Jan. 1857	0 11	"	A. B. Hull.	P. O. and S. I. Vol. 1.
8	45.34	68.28	50.24	27.24	47.78	Jan. 1829;	Dec. 1850	22 0	$\odot_r$ N.	Clark.	MS. in S. Coll.
9	47.89	69.75	51.70	29.89	49.81	Oct. 1806;	July, 1852	16 7	$9_m\ 3_a$	Rev. A. Flint and Hoadley.	Med. and Agr. Reg. Bost. Vol. 1, 1806–7, and MS. in S. Coll.
10	..	72.40	57.19	..	..	May, 1863;	Jan. 1864	0 9	$7_m\ 2_a\ 9_a$	....	MS. from S. G. O.
11	41.08	65.01	47.81	25.10	44.75	Jan. 1850;	Dec. 1852	3 0	......	Hendrick.	Regent's Rep.
12	43.95	67.99	53.15	28.84	48.48	Jan. 1854;	May, 1861	6 10	$7_m\ 2_a\ 9_a$	J. Rankin.	P. O. and S. I. Vol. 1, and S. O.
13	45.25	68.76	50.39	27.94	48.09	1849;	Dec. 1870	14 8	$7_m\ 2_a\ 9_a$ bis	Cutter and Prof. J. Johnston.	S. Coll., P. O. and S. I. Vol. 1, and S. O.
14	46.76	69.63	51.28	28.32	49.00	July, 1778;	Oct. 1865	86 0	[4]	Various observers.	Trans. Con. Acad. Vol. 1, Part 1, New Haven, 1866.
15	46.02	69.08	52.94	30.17	49.55	Mar. 1849;	Nov. 1858	9 2	$7_m\ 2_a\ 9_a$	Rev. T. Edwards.	S. Coll., & P. O. & S. I. Vol. 1.
16	..	..	..	..	..	1849		0 3	$\odot_r\ 9_m\ 3_a\ 9_a$	Cobb.	S. Coll.
17	..	..	..	..	..	1870		0 1	$7_m\ 2_a\ 9_a$ bis	W. P. Alcott.	S. O.
18	43.77	70.42	52.33	27.85	48.59	Mar. 1856;	Feb. 1858	[illegible]	$7_m\ 2_a\ 9_a$	[illegible]	P. O. and S. I. Vol. 1.
19	42.03	66.27	48.52	26.12	45.74	June, 1862;	May, 1864	2 0	$7_m\ 2_a\ 9_a$ bis	D. W. Learned.	S. O.
20	42.69	65.70	49.90	25.75	46.01	Mar. 1853;	Apr. 1869	16 0	"	Rev. D. Hunt.	S. Coll., P. O. and S. I. Vol. 1, and S. O.
21	45.14	68.12	49.83	25.82	47.23	Jan. 1844;	Dec. 1854	11 0	$\odot_r\ 9_m\ 3_a\ 9_a$	Dr. O. Plumb.	S. Coll., & P. O. & S. I. Vol. 1.
22	45.90	68.02	50.13	26.59	47.66	Jan. 1816;	Dec. 1836	20 11	6_m N. 6_a	Gov. Smith.	MS. in S. Coll.
23	..	72.23	52.59	..	..	1870		0 9	$7_m\ 2_a\ 9_a$ bis	L. Andrews.	S. O.
24	44.83	67.63	50.20	26.89	47.39	Apr. 1856;	July, 1862	6 4	$7_m\ 2_a\ 9_a$	B. F. Harrison.	P. O. and S. I. Vol. 1, and S. O.
25	42.98	66.44	50.73	23.20	45.84	1849		1 0	......	Hendrick.	Regent's Rep.
26	44.27	68.25	47.85	25.57	46.49	Jan. 1867;	Aug. 1869	2 4	[6]	Rev. R. C. Williams.	S. O.
27	45.34	67.72	49.69	22.77	46.38	1854		1 0	$7_m\ 2_a\ 9_a$	Z. L. Gold.	P. O. and S. I. Vol. 1.
28	..	..	..	..	..	1850;	1852	0 3	$\odot_r\ 9_m\ 3_a\ 9_a$	Phelps.	S. Coll.

DAKOTA.

	Spring.	Summer.	Autumn.	Winter.	Year.	Series. Begins.	Ends.	Extent yrs. mos.	Observing hours.	Observer.	References.
1	38.66	70.94	43.81	7.95	40.34	Feb. 1859;	Dec. 1870	10 1	$7_m\ 2_a\ 9_a$	Assistant Surgeon.	Ar. Met. Reg. 1860, and MS. from S. G. O.
2	40.41	69.52	42.52	11.76	41.05	Sept. 1866;	Dec. 1870	4 2	"	" "	MS. from S. G. O.
3	40.92	..	42.12	16.78	..	Sept. 1866;	May, 1869	0 10	"	" "	" " "
4	47.30	73.44	48.68	13.96	45.84	Jan. 1854;	May, 1857	2 5	"	F. Behman, Assistant Surgeon.	P. O. and S. I. Vol. 1, Ar. Met. Reg. 1860.
5	43.28	74.61	49.06	20.93	46.97	Nov. 1856;	Dec. 1870	12 8	"	Assistant Surgeon.	Ar. Met. Reg. 1860, and MS. from S. G. O.
6	39.74	67.08	41.53	10.38	39.68	Dec. 1868;	Dec. 1870	2 1	"	" "	" " " "
7	43.54	70.02	41.28	15.72	42.64	July, 1868;	Dec. 1870	2 3	"	" "	" " " "
8	41.85	72.17	44.43	10.01	42.11	Sept. 1866;	Dec. 1870	2 11	"	" "	" " " "
9	42.79	72.71	47.30	20.59	45.85	Jan. 1866;	Dec. 1870	2 7	"	" "	" " " "
10	39.63	67.64	41.52	6.46	38.81	Aug. 1869;	Dec. 1870	1 5	"	" "	" " " "
11	35.50	67.61	44.28	9.18	39.14	Sept. 1866;	Dec. 1870	3 3	"	" "	" " " "
12	50.14	73.34	47.60	21.80	48.22	Nov. 1859;	Dec. 1862	1 11	$7_m\ 2_a\ 9_a$ bis	F. Norvell, H. G. Williams, G. M. Lamson.	P. O. and S. I. Vol. 1, and S. O.

[5] There were from three to seventeen observations daily, between 6_m and 10_a; corrected for daily variation by means of the New Haven Table. Thermometer tested.

[6] Observations prior to August, 1867, at Fort Berthold, a few miles to the southwest.

[7] Also called "Greenwood." Observations in 1862, at Yankton, to the east.

Name of Station.	Lat.	Long.	Height.	Jan.	Feb.	March.	April.	May.	June	July.	August.	Sept.	Oct.	Nov.	Dec.
DELAWARE.															
1. Dover	39°10′	75°30′	40	..	..	..	..	..	..	..	76°.80	67°.48	58°.19	46°.28	35°.60
2. Fort Delaware[1]	39 35	75 34	10	32°.26	33°.80	40°.08	51°.59	63°.44	72°.25	77°.61	75.84	69.60	57.32	45.90	36.62
3. Georgetown	38 43	75 22	..	44.00	33.65	45.06	56.15	61.02	77.36	78.64	76.78	71.49	60.13	46.54	43.90
4. Milford	38 55	75 25	20	40.87	34.58	42.74	54.97	62.17	74.68	77.74	75.62	66.12	51.81	41.22	38.20
5. Newark	39 38	75 47	120	28.61	32.95	36.74	48.68	59.53	69.47	74.71	73.26	64.63	52.58	44.14	36.57
6. Wilmington	39 44	75 33	..	..	..	..	..	..	..	..	..	..	..	..	..
7. Wilmington	39 44	75 33	115	27.62	32.16	42.10	51.89	64.24	71.91	74.78	74.00	66.46	51.40	43.06	35.36
DISTRICT OF COLUMBIA.															
1. Georgetown	38 55	77 04	..	33.85	36.29	45.63	53.36	64.85	72.66	76.33	76.31	69.13	59.40	46.97	37.18
2. Washington	38 53	77 02	30	27.27	40.29	42.84	53.25	62.97	72.36	75.01	76.01	68.63	53.69	42.41	33.98
3. Washington	38 54	77 02	30	41.4	36.5	45.7	60.2	71.4	75.2	79.9	79.7	70.3	56 5	43.3	39.5
4. Washington	38 54	77 02	75	34.09	36.82	45.36	55.70	66.26	74.44	78.26	76.28	67.76	56.70	44.83	37.41
5. Washington	38 55	77 02	110	35.3	37.	46.5	54.0	61.7	76.	74.8	76.5	68.0	53.5	47.5	41.7
6. Washington	38 53	77 01	80	27.21	37.71	44.45	56.51	64.76	69.59	77.88	75.53	66.11	55.61	40.83	31.57
7. Washington	38 53	77 01	80	35.10	35.41	46.08	52.31	60.45	73.32	75.40	72.02	68.07	48.80	43.73	35.70
8. Washington	38 54	77 03	110	36.0	36.4	44.8	58.0	68.8	75.9	78.3	77.0	70.1	57.6	47.9	40.1
9. Washington	38 53	77 02	40	31.96	35.65	43.27	52.63	64.17	74.06	78.50	74.60	67.93	55.45	51.01	35.77
10. Washington	38 54	77 03	110	32.43	34.40	40.49	51.75	61.81	70.93	75.89	74.28	67.47	54.67	44.35	34.23
11. Washington	38 54	77 03	110	37.19	34.65	41.79	51.88	61.79	72.67	78.28	76.23	68.78	54.75	44.21	34.87
FLORIDA.															
1. Belair	30 23	84 17	70	52.25	59.18	61.08	66.22	75.73	79.88	82.08	81.29	77.70	69.43	58.83	58.48
2. Cedar Keys[6]	29 07	83 03	35	56.33	58.47	64.37	68.68	75.88	79.84	82.03	81.27	79.40	71.96	63.73	58.82
3. Chattahoochie Ars.	30 42	84 50	180	..	..	..	..	71.68	79.40	83.10	79.68	..	..	..	..
4. Fairview (near Palatka)	29 36	81 37	152	58.37	56.96	61.97	67.76	73.81	78.88	81.99	80.91	76.65	70.89	61.76	55.57
5. Fernandina	30 40	81 28	25	50.96	57.60	61.27	65.58	71.73	77.60	79.87	85.89	76.96	71.56	65.47	53.89
6. Fort Barrancas[7]	30 21	87 18	20	52.71	55.27	61.26	68.47	75.51	80.59	82.20	82.00	78.41	69.55	60.79	55.13
7. Fort Brooke	27 57	82 26	20	60.99	63.00	66.87	71.88	76.64	79.58	80.96	80.63	79.42	73.86	67.29	61.99
8. Fort Dallas[8]	25 48	80 13	20	66.10	66.16	70.30	74.97	74.40	80.99	82.17	82.48	80.59	77.91	73.45	69.37
9. Fort Deynaud	26 45	81 30	..	60.04	64.41	67.79	71.98	76.96	79.53	79.76	80.51	80.14	71.95	71.52	64.75
10. Fort Fanning	29 35	82 56	50	58.52	57.97	67.04	70.72	76.26	79.32	82.05	82.40	80.55	72.16	60.55	54.93
11. Fort Gamble	30 20	84 00	50	55.54	60.71	69.06	71.27	75.42	80.04	79.79	79.74	79.06	68.25	60.04	55.82
12. Fort Hamer	27 30	82 30	20	..	..	..	..	77.55	80.34	80.96	83.64	82.24	..	..	..
13. Fort Heiloman	29 48	82 05	25	56.32	56.45	63.33	70.68	75.65	81.88	80.25	79.71	77.07	71.57	59.57	51.94
14. Fort Henderson	30 51	82 09	25	55.64	58.27	64.46	70.52	76.26	82.03	80.16	79.76	77.54	69.85	59.94	51.20
15. Fort Jefferson	24 38	82 52	11	70.96	70.67	73.22	74.43	79.59	83.31	84.79	84.62	83.86	80.12	74.84	71.71
16. Fort King	29 12	82 12	50	58.41	58.13	64.38	71.41	76.59	79.90	80.80	80.59	78.21	70.56	63.18	58.55
17. Fort Marion[9] (St. Augustine)	29 54	81 19	25	56.79	59.85	63.25	68.75	74.06	79.32	80.91	80.86	79.04	72.57	64.10	58.12
18. Fort Meade	27 45	81 47	80	58.40	63.23	69.02	69.89	76.69	78.24	79.76	80.03	79.18	73.81	68.48	60.15
19. Fort Micanopy	29 35	82 31	78	60.36	60.29	67.43	72.05	76.92	79.38	80.22	79.42	77.95	70.52	60.96	55.94
20. Fort Myers	26 40	81 56	50	62.86	66.08	69.85	73.26	79.20	80.96	82.38	82.89	81.24	76.43	72.53	65.75
21. Fort Pierce	27 28	80 18	30	62.45	64.80	69.05	73.13	77.36	79.80	82.61	83.02	81.43	75.07	69.57	65.72
22. Fort Russell[10]	29 15	82 15	50	61.40	56.30	69.70	71.64	76.10	79.30	84.44	83.76	78.48	68.79	61.23	57.56
23. Fort Shannon	29 34	81 48	25	58.00	59.00	64.69	71.64	76.43	79.37	81.66	80.38	79.09	71.07	61.89	58.63

[1] Observations in 1854, at ⊙$_r$ 9_m 3_a 9_a; they were referred to 7_m 2_a 9_a by means of the general table. The observations of 1866 and 1867 were combined with those made at Delaware City.

[2] The observations have been corrected for daily variation. The series is much broken and many of the monthly means are imperfect, so that the results afford only a tolerable approximation to the truth. [3] Corrected for daily variation by means of the general table.

[4] The observations were made bi-hourly, at 0.2^h A. M., 2.2^h A. M., and so on.

[5] The observations were made tri-hourly at Mid., 3 A. M., 6 A. M., and so on. [6] Also called Atsuna Otie.

	Spring.	Summer.	Autumn.	Winter.	Year.	Series. Begins.	Ends.	Extent yrs. mos.	Observing hours.	Observer.	References.
						DELAWARE.					
1	..	..	57°.32	..	..	1870		0 5	$7_m\ 2_a\ 9_a$ bis	J. H. Bateman.	S. O.
2	51°.70	75°.23	57.61	34°.23	54°.69	Feb. 1825;	Sept. 1870	18 10	$7_m\ 2_a\ 9_a$	Assistant Surgeon, J. M. Vanhekle.	Ar. Met. Regs. 1855 and 1860, MS. from S. G. O., and S. O.
3	54.08	77.59	59.39	40.52	57.89	July, 1857;	Dec. 1858	1 6	$8_m\ 1_a\ 6_a$	Dr. D. W. Mauld.	P. O. and S. I. Vol. 1.
4	53.29	76.01	53.05	37.88	55.06	Dec. 1857;	Dec. 1870	2 2	$7_m\ 2_a\ 9_a$ bis	A. C. Whittier, W. R. Phillips, R. A. Martin.	P. O. and S. I. Vol. 1, and S. O.
5	48.32	72.48	53.78	32.71	51.82	July, 1847;	Feb. 1858	4 3	[2]	E. E. Norton, Crawford, and others.	P. O. & S. I. Vol. 1, and S. Coll.
6	..	..	..	..	51.30	Aug. 1834;	July, 1835	1 0	......	....	Am. Almanac.
7	52.74	73.56	53.64	31.71	52.91	Jan. 1864;	Oct. 1865	1 10	$7_m\ 2_a\ 9_a$ bis	Dr. U. D. Hedges.	S. O.
						DISTRICT OF COLUMBIA.					
1	54.61	75.10	58.50	35.77	56.00	Dec. 1859;	Feb. 1863	3 1	$7_m\ 2_a\ 9_a$ bis	Rev. C. B. Mackee.	P. O. and S. I. Vol. 1, and S. O.
2	53.02	74.46	54.91	33.85	54.06	Jan. 1820;	Dec. 1821	2 0	[3]	J. Q. Adams, J. Meigs.	Col. Force's Rec., and MS. in S. Coll.
3	59.10	78.27	56.70	39.13	58.30	Apr. 1823;	Dec. 1824	1 6	$7_m\ 9_m$ N. 4_a	Jules de Wallenstein.	Trans. Am. Phil. Soc. Vol. 2, 1825.
4	55.77	76.33	56.43	36.11	56.16	Jan. 1823;	Dec. 1834	12 3	$7_m\ 2_a\ 9_a$	Assist. Surgeon, Rev. R. Little.	Ar. Met. Reg. 1855.
5	54.1	75.8	56.3	38.0	56.0	Jan. 1828;	Dec. 1829	2 0	max. & min.	....	From J. Elliot's Hist. Sketches of the 10 miles square.
6	55.24	74.33	54.18	32.16	53.98	July, 1838;	Dec. 1840	2 6	$3_m\ 9_m\ 3_a\ 9_a$	Lieut. J. M. Gilliss, U. S. N.	Pub. Doc. 2d Sess. 28th Con. Vol. x, 1845.
7	52.95	73.58	53.53	35.40	53.87	Jan. 1841;	June, 1842	1 1	[4]	" " "	" " " " "
8	57.20	77.07	58.53	37.50	57.58	Jan. 1846;	Dec. 1849	4 0	$9_m\ 3_a\ 9_a$	U. S. Naval Obs'y.	Am. Alm. 1848 and foll.
9	53.36	75.72	58.13	34.46	55.42	Aug. 1850;	Dec. 1859	8 10	$7_m\ 2_a\ 9_a$	Smithsonian Inst.	S. Coll., P. O. and S. I. Vol. 1.
10	51.35	73.70	55.50	33.69	53.56	Jan. 1862;	Dec. 1870	9 0	[5]	Prof. J. R. Eastman.	U. S. Naval Obs'y.
11	51.82	75.73	55.91	35.57	54.76	Jan. 1868;	Dec. 1870	3 0	max. & min.	" " " "	" " "
						FLORIDA.					
1	67.68	81.08	68.65	56.64	68.51	Oct. 1856;	May, 1861	3 10	$7_m\ 2_a\ 9_a$	B. F. Whitner.	P. O. and S. I. Vol. 1, and S. O.
2	69.64	81.05	71.70	57.87	70.06	Aug. 1851;	July, 1867	11 4	"	Judge A. Steele, Assistant Surgeon, and W. C. Andrass.	Ar. Met. Reg. 1855, P. O. and S. I. Vol. 1, S. Coll., and S. O.
3	..	80.73	..	..	..	May, 1869;	Aug. 1870	0 4	$7_m\ 2_a\ 9_a$ bis	M. Martin.	S. O.
4	67.85	80.59	69.77	56.97	68.79	Feb. 1869;	Nov. 1870	1 6	"	G. D. Robinson, and W. M. L. Fiske.	" "
5	66.19	81.12	71.33	54.15	68.20	July, 1863;	July, 1867	1 6	$7_m\ 2_a\ 9_a$	H. M. Corey.	MS. from S. G. O., and S. O.
6	68.41	81.60	69.58	54.37	68.49	Jan. 1822;	Dec. 1860	20 2	"	Assistant Surgeon.	Ar. Met. Regs. 1855 and 1860, and MS. from S. G. O.
7	71.80	80.39	73.52	61.99	71.92	Jan. 1825;	July, 1869	27 11	"	" "	" " "
8	73.22	81.88	77.32	67.21	74.91	Feb. 1839;	Oct. 1870	6 11	"	Assist. Surg., W. H. Hunt.	Ar. Met. Regs. 1855 and 1860, and S. O.
9	72.24	79.93	74.54	63.07	72.45	Feb. 1855;	Apr. 1858	2 5	"	Assistant Surgeon.	Ar. Met. Reg. 1860.
10	71.34	81.26	71.09	57.14	70.21	Oct. 1840;	Jan. 1843	2 4	"	" "	Ar. Met. Reg. 1855.
11	71.92	79.86	69.12	57.36	69.57	Jan. 1840;	Dec. 1842	2 3	"	" "	" " "
12	..	81.65	..	..	..	1850		0 5	☉r $9_m\ 3_a\ 9_a$	" "	Ar. Met. Reg. 1850.
13	69.89	80.61	69.40	54.90	68.70	Jan. 1838;	May, 1841	2 7	$7_m\ 2_a\ 9_a$	" "	Ar. Met. Reg. 1855.
14	70.41	80.65	69.11	55.04	68.80	Oct. 1838;	Dec. 1839	1 0	"	" "	" " "
15	75.75	84.24	79.61	71.11	77.68	Feb. 1861;	Dec. 1870	8 1	"	....	MS. from S. G. O.
16	70.79	80.43	70.65	58.36	70.06	Oct. 1832;	Feb. 1843	6 1	"	Assistant Surgeon.	Ar. Met. Reg. 1855.
17	68.69	80.36	71.90	58.25	69.80	Oct. 1824;	Oct. 1870	25 4	"	Assist. Surg., Dr. P. B. Mauran, and G. W. Atwood.	Ar. Met. Reg. 1855, P. O. and S. I. Vol. 1, MS. from S.G.O., and S. O.
18	71.87	79.34	73.82	60.59	71.41	May, 1851;	Nov. 1854	3 7	☉r $9_m\ 3_a\ 9_a$	Assistant Surgeon.	Ar. Met. Reg. 1855.
19	72.13	79.67	69.81	58.86	70.12	July, 1838;	Dec. 1842	4 5	$7_m\ 2_a\ 9_a$	" "	" " "
20	74.10	82.08	76.73	64.90	74.45	Jan. 1851;	June, 1858	7 6	"	" "	Ar. Met. Regs. 1855 and 1860.
21	73.18	81.81	75.36	64.32	73.67	Jan. 1840;	May, 1858	8 4	"	" "	" " " "
22	72.48	82.50	69.50	58.42	70.72	July, 1838;	June, 1842	1 10	"	" "	Ar. Met. Reg. 1855.
23	70.92	80.47	70.68	58.54	70.15	Jan. 1838;	Jan. 1850	4 5	"	" "	" " "

[7] The first seven years of this series were observed at Cantonment Clinch, three miles from Pensacola and fourteen miles from Fort Barrancas.

[8] The observations were made at Fort Lauderdale from Jan. to Sept. 1839, and from July to Sept. 1840. This post is a few miles N. of Fort Dallas and the same distance from the sea.

[9] The observations composing this series were made at Fort Marion and St. Augustine; principally at Fort Marion.

[10] The observations composing this series were made at Forts Russell, Harley, and Wheelock, the same position being given for all.

FLORIDA.—Continued.

Name of Station.	Lat.	Long.	Height.	Jan.	Feb.	March.	April.	May.	June.	July.	August.	Sept.	Oct.	Nov.	Dec.
24. Fort Wacohootee	29°28′	82°25′	50	59°.13	55°.58	67°.21	69°.67	72°.00	75°.00	80°.00	78°.00	77°.00	65°.67	59°.33	56°.33
25. Fort Wacassassa	29 30	82 45	45	58.53	57.59	66.93	70.50	74.13	77.32	79.66	79.56	78.62	69.74	59.63	56.58
26. Gainesville	29 38	82 20	184	53.96	58.73	61.21	67.18	73.97	78.13	79.37	78.35	76.40	68.65	61.11	57.56
27. Gordon	29 52	82 21	..	53.07	61.48	66.00	72.90	73.95	79.23	81.73	81.20	79.75	70.38	63.50	55.94
28. Hibernia	30 04	81 42	15	59.85	..	..	..	..	..	..	..	..	..	..	59.47
29. Jacksonville	30 20	81 39	20	55.51	57.27	62.76	69.45	75.59	79.53	81.73	81.69	78.67	69.78	61.67	54.09
30. Key West	24 33	81 48	10	70.04	70.68	73.79	76.29	80.20	82.15	83.31	83.52	82.53	79.12	75.59	72.83
31. Key West	24 33	81 48	10	69.18	70.51	72.70	75.65	79.21	82.66	83.84	83.54	82.29	78.70	74.66	71.63
32. Key West	24 33	81 48	10	64.92	71.18	76.09	77.62	82.25	83.54	85.09	84.99	..	80.30	..	70.93
33. Knox Hill[2]	30 40	85 58	148	48.66	55.40	62.52	66.31	75.34	77.93	79.26	79.58	77.23	67.96	59.72	55.12
34. Lake City[3]	30 12	82 38	185	56.15	56.94	62.51	68.98	75.27	80.73	79.82	80.28	77.94	69.12	59.35	59.18
35. Manatee	27 30	81 45	6	66.64	63.08	66.57	70.80	76.78	82.74	82.73	83.40	80.60	75.30	65.98	63.45
36. Micanopy	29 30	82 18	78	55.23	61.45	67.22	69.42	75.99	80.70	80.79	80.14	77.31	71.87	60.05	60.32
37. Mosquito Inlet (12 miles N. W. of)	29 12	81 02	10	..	..	..	..	..	..	78.12	79.89	77.20	73.88	62.80	54.18
38. Newport	30 10	84 15	..	..	..	..	..	73.36	77.15	79.37	79.51	75.36	67.38	56.83	48.90
39. New Smyrna	29 00	80 56	20	62.27	63.64	67.57	73.14	74.88	78.91	80.04	78.94	78.29	72.06	67.15	63.49
40. Ocala	29 11	82 09	..	61.89	62.73	63.18	67.17	72.86	79.62	81.13	82.35	79.24	69.40	59.73	57.45
41. Orange Grove	27 28	82 35	10	..	..	..	67.08	75.89	79.89	81.38	81.81	80.00	74.99	..	..
42. Pensacola	30 25	87 13	..	56.17	57.87	64.51	68.67	76.49	80.69	84.92	83.57	78.90	71.00	61.29	57.84
43. Picolata	29 57	81 36	25	61.21	56.80	64.30	72.60	73.46	78.60	81.70	80.50	77.88	70.67	61.04	57.86
44. Port Orange	29 04	80 57	..	59.17	59.07	63.99	68.76	74.83	78.40	82.01	81.37	79.41	72.96	64.34	58.48
45. Seville	30 29	84 07	..	51.32	51.54	58.55	59.60	69.36	75.90	76.40	73.15	71.61	62.78	55.19	49.25
46. Warrington[4]	30 21	87 17	12	53.02	57.10	63.19	69.12	75.74	81.16	83.84	82.90	78.97	70.30	61.58	56.51
47. White Springs	30 24	82 56	..	..	..	..	..	..	80.13	84.20	..	..	..	..	..

GEORGIA.

Name of Station.	Lat.	Long.	Height.	Jan.	Feb.	March.	April.	May.	June.	July.	August.	Sept.	Oct.	Nov.	Dec.
1. Athens	33 58	83 25	850	44.58	45.99	53.63	61.43	68.40	75.09	76.33	75.81	71.60	59.39	51.31	47.61
2. Atlanta	33 45	84 24	1050	40.90	43.45	51.14	58.01	65.65	71.71	77.50	75.40	68.86	57.55	48.92	41.22
3. Augusta[5]	33 29	81 51	150	47.06	49.86	55.85	63.92	72.97	79.13	81.30	78.04	74.56	63.66	49.68	43.53
4. Augusta Arsenal	33 28	81 53	350	47.20	50.57	55.67	65.10	72.28	79.12	82.16	79.85	73.95	63.68	53.85	46.68
5. Berne	30 50	81 50	25	52.03	49.25	54.08	61.15	70.83	75.97	79.64	77.40	71.93	63.56	52.96	47.73
6. Boston	30 42	83 50	..	47.45	54.35	..	..	..	..	..	..	..	..	..	..
7. Brunswick	31 05	81 30	..	51.3	56.0	59.3	66.7	75.3	75.0	82.0	82.0	80.0	68.0	58.3	52.3
8. Catawba	32 40	84 52	..	..	..	..	..	..	82.0	..	..	..	..	..	..
9. Clarksville	34 40	83 31	1632	40.40	45.97	48.93	55.33	..	70.93	72.82	72.45	65.86	55.05	46.01	44.42
10. Columbus	32 29	84 59	..	..	..	..	62.92	..	..	..	..	..	..	..	..
11. Culloden	32 51	84 06	825	46.17	52.33	59.70	64.36	73.89	77.73	79.63	76.97	72.27	64.01	55.84	48.76
12. Cuthbert	31 44	84 50	..	..	..	..	..	..	79.60	83.78	79.10	..	..	..	..
13. Dalton	34 47	85 00	775	39.90	44.87	49.30	..	..	..	..	..	..	..	..	..
14. Factory Mills	33 40	84 46	..	..	..	47.96	54.97	..	..	..	..	..	..	..	..
15. Griffin	33 03	84 15	..	..	..	..	60.26	..	..	..	..	..	..	..	..
16. Hillsborough	33 10	83 38	566	48.82	44.47	55.36	62.81	71.89	77.65	..	..	74.13	59.41	50.48	51.77
17. La Grange	33 02	85 01	..	47.87	..	..	..	..	..	..	..	..	..	..	..
18. Macon	32 50	83 40	..	44.60	47.63	59.73	62.38	70.85	..	..	..	..	..	..	..
19. Macon (Lewis High School)	32 47	83 47	1300	50.95	48.03	54.45	63.70	68.70	78.09	80.88	80.10	..	..	50.23	42.75
20. Macon	32 50	83 38	339	49.83	49.05	55.15	61.95	67.03	..	..	..	..	..	..	42.48
21. Milledgeville	33 05	83 12	577	..	..	60.68	65.12	72.39	80.16	77.19	81.07	74.15	59.47	57.90	48.95

1 Corrected for daily variation by the Key West table.
2 Also called Orange Hill.
3 Also called Alligator.
4 This series is composed of observations made at the Navy Yard and U. S. Naval Hospital.

FLORIDA.—Continued.

	Spring.	Summer.	Autumn.	Winter.	Year.	Series. Begins.	Series. Ends.	Extent yrs. mos.	Observing hours.	Observer.	References.
24	69°.63	77°.67	67°.33	57°.01	67°.91	Jan. 1841;	Mar. 1842	1 3	$\odot_r\ 2_a\ 9_a$	Assistant Surgeon.	Ar. Met. Reg. 1855.
25	70.52	78.85	69.33	57.57	69.07	Oct. 1840;	Dec. 1842	2 3	$7_m\ 2_a\ 9_a$	" "	" " "
26	67.45	78.62	68.72	56.75	67.89	Feb. 1856;	Feb. 1861	4 9	"	J. B. Bailey.	P. O. and S. I. Vol. 1, and S. O.
27	70.95	80.72	71.21	56.83	69.93	Apr. 1866;	Jan. 1868	1 3	$7_m\ 2_a\ 9_a$ bis	H. B. Scott.	S. O.
28	..	..	..	..	..	Dec. 1857;	Jan. 1858	0 2	$7_m\ 2_a\ 9_a$	F. L. Batchelder.	P. O. and S. I. Vol. 1.
29	69.27	80.98	70.04	55.62	68.98	Feb. 1839;	Dec. 1870	12 4	$7_m\ 2_a\ 9_a$ bis	Dr. A. S. Baldwin.	MS. in S. Coll., P. O. and S. I. Vol. 1, and S. O.
30	76.76	82.99	79.08	71.18	77.50	1823;	1836	9 0	$\odot_r\ 2_a\ 10_a$ max. & min.	Whitehead.	Manuscript.
31	75.85	83.35	78.55	70.44	77.05	Jan. 1830;	Dec. 1870	26 6	[1]	Assist. Surg., Coll'tor of Customs, J. and W. A. Whitehead, W. C. Dennis, A. Gordon, G. T. Ferguson, J. G. Oltmanns.	Ar. Met. Regs. 1855 and 1860, MS. from S. G. O., Am. Alm. 1835, and foll., MS. in S. Coll., P. O. and S. I. Vol. 1, and S. O.
32	78.65	84.54	..	69.01	..	June, 1851;	May, 1852	0 10	hourly.	U. S. Coast Survey.	Manuscript.
33	68.06	78.92	68.30	53.06	67.09	July, 1851;	Dec. 1855	4 5	[1]	J. Newton.	S. Coll., P. O. & S. I. Vol. 1.
34	68.92	80.28	68.80	57.42	68.85	Mar. 1857;	Jan. 1869	4 0	$7_m\ 2_a\ 9_a$	E. R. Ives.	P. O. and S. I. Vol. 1, and S. O.
35	71.38	82.96	73.96	64.39	73.17	Jan. 1869;	July, 1870	1 7	$7_m\ 2_a\ 9_a$ bis	B. A. Coachman.	S. O.
36	70.88	80.54	69.74	59.00	70.04	June, 1858;	Dec. 1859	1 7	$7_m\ 2_a\ 9_a$	Dr. J. B. Bean.	P. O. and S. I. Vol. 1.
37	..	..	71.29	..	..	1870		0 6	$7_m\ 2_a\ 9_a$ bis	S. N. Chamberlin.	S. O.
38	..	78.68	66.52	..	..	1870		0 8	"	C. Bucher.	" "
39	71.86	79.30	72.50	63.13	71.70	Jan. 1840;	Oct. 1853	3 0	$7_m\ 2_a\ 9_a$	Assistant Surgeon.	Ar. Met. Reg. 1855.
40	67.74	81.03	69.46	60.69	69.73	Jan. 1869;	Sept. 1870	1 5	$7_m\ 2_a\ 9_a$ bis	E. Barker.	S. O.
41	..	81.03	..	..	..	1870		0 7	"	W. J. Clark.	" "
42	69.89	83.06	70.40	57.29	70.16	Aug. 1849;	Dec. 1852	3 5	$\odot_r$ N. $\odot_s$	Pearson.	Manuscript.
43	70.12	80.27	69.86	58.62	69.72	Sept. 1840;	Sept. 1841	1 1	$\odot_r\ 2_a\ 9_a$	Assistant Surgeon.	Ar. Met. Reg. 1855.
44	69.19	80.59	72.24	58.91	70.23	Jan. 1867;	Apr. 1870	2 10	$7_m\ 2_a\ 9_a$ bis	Dr. and Mrs. J. W. Hawks.	S. O.
45	62.50	75.15	63.19	50.70	62.89	1859		0 9	7_m	L. Gibbon.	P. O. and S. I. Vol. 1.
46	69.35	82.63	70.28	55.54	69.45	Oct. 1849;	Dec. 1860	10 9	[1]	J. Pearson, W. Johnson and others.	S. Coll., P. O. and S. I, Vol. 1.
47	..	..	..	..	..	1870		0 2	$7_m\ 2_a\ 9_a$ bis	R. W. Adams.	S. O.

GEORGIA.

	Spring.	Summer.	Autumn.	Winter.	Year.	Series. Begins.	Series. Ends.	Extent yrs. mos.	Observing hours.	Observer.	References.
1	61.15	75.74	60.77	46.06	60.93	Jan. 1845;	Sept. 1859	6 6	[5]	McCoy, Prof. J. D. Easter.	Southern Cultivator, and P. O. and S. I. Vol. 1.
2	58.27	74.87	58.44	41.86	58.36	Jan. 1859;	Dec. 1870	5 2	$7_m\ 2_a\ 9_a$ bis	Dr. J. G. Westmoreland, Assist. Surg., F. Deckner & son.	P. O. and S. I. Vol. 1, S. O., and MS. from S. G. O.
3	64.25	79.49	62.63	46.82	63.30	Jan. 1839;	July, 1868	7 5	[6]	Drs. M. and S. H. Holbrook, W. H. Dougherty, W. Haines, S. Elliott.	Am. Alm., P. O. and S. I. Vol. 1, and S. O.
4	64.35	80.38	63.83	48.15	64.18	Jan. 1826;	Dec. 1870	21 7	$7_m\ 2_a\ 9_a$	Assistant Surgeon.	Ar. Met. Reg. 1855, and MS. from S. G. O.
5	62.02	77.67	62.82	49.67	63.04	June, 1869;	Dec. 1870	1 7	$7_m\ 2_a\ 9_a$ bis	H. L. Hillyer.	S. O.
6	..	..	..	..	..	1861		0 2	"	W. Blewett.	" "
7	67.10	79.67	68.77	53.20	67.18	June, 1838;	May, 1839	1 0	$8_m\ 2_a\ 6_a$	J. Bancroft.	Am. Alm.
8	..	..	..	..	..	1853		0 1	$7_m\ 2_a\ 9_a$	Shields.	S. Coll.
9	..	72.07	55.64	43.60	..	June, 1847;	Apr. 1861	2 3	[5]	Campbell and J. Vanburen.	Pat. Off. Rep., S. O., and P. O. and S. I. Vol. 1.
10	..	..	..	..	..	1870		0 1	$7_m\ 2_a\ 9_a$ bis	N. J. Fogarty.	S. O.
11	65.98	78.11	64.04	49.09	64.31	May, 1852;	June, 1854	2 2	[5]	Prof. J. Darby.	S. Coll., & P. O. & S. I. Vol. 1.
12	..	80.83	..	..	..	1860		0 3	$7_m\ 2_a\ 9_a$ bis	C. C. Seavey.	S. O.
13	..	..	..	..	..	1861		0 3	"	Dr. J. R. McAfie.	" "
14	..	..	..	..	..	1857		0 2	$7_m\ 2_a\ 9_a$	F. T. Simpson.	P. O. and S. I. Vol. 1.
15	..	..	..	..	..	1851		0 1	$\odot_r\ 2_a\ 9_a$	....	S. Coll.
16	63.35	..	61.34	48.35	..	Sept. 1857;	June, 1858	0 10	$7_m\ 2_a\ 9_a$	E. S. Glover.	P. O. and S. I. Vol. 1.
17	..	..	..	..	..	1855		0 1	$\odot_r$ N. $\odot_s$	....	" " "
18	64.32	..	..	..	..	1868		0 5	$7_m\ 2_a\ 9_a$ bis	J. A. Rockwell.	S. O.
19	62.28	79.69	..	47.24	..	Nov. 1868;	Aug. 1869	0 10	"	Misses S. G. Whiting, and S. M. Proctor.	" "
20	61.38	..	..	47.12	..	Dec. 1868;	May, 1869	0 6	"	J. F. Adams.	" "
21	66.06	79.47	63.84	..	..	Oct. 1843;	Dec. 1849	1 1	$\odot_r\ 9_m\ 3_a\ 9_a$	J. R. Catting & Jacobs.	MS. in S. Coll. and S. Coll.

[5] Corrected for daily variation.

[6] Observations of 1839 and for four months of 1868 at Summerville, about one mile south of Augusta.

GEORGIA.—Continued.

Name of Station.	Lat.	Long.	Height.	Jan.	Feb.	March.	April.	May.	June.	July.	August.	Sept.	Oct.	Nov.	Dec.
22. Oglethorpe B'ks	32°05′	81°07′	40	52°.03	54°.05	58°.76	66°.89	75°.60	80°.31	82°.67	81°.43	77°.49	67°.26	57°.85	50°.9…
23. Penfield	33 38	83 09	724	47.59	45.93	50.74	61.21	69.02	76.85	80.25	78.58	71.02	62.22	50.06	42.4…
24. Perry	32 28	83 43	280	42.64	53.50	63.08	64.35	73.67	78.99	81.37	78.57	74.57	67.55	53.26	50.6…
25. Powelton	33 25	82 50	620	..	..	..	..	74.55	76.71	79.72	75.80	72.33	..	52.17	..
26. Quitman (ten miles S. W. of)	30 40	83 40	..	..	..	..	..	..	..	..	..	..	..	..	49.2…
27. Richmond Hill	33 26	81 53	275	..	..	..	..	..	..	82.70	..	..	..	..	..
28. St. Mary's	30 44	81 34	15	..	..	..	..	72.38	77.39	80.55	80.38	76.48	69.56	57.97	49.1…
29. Savannah	32 05	81 06	42	51.29	54.31	59.73	66.97	74.47	79.38	81.67	80.77	75.90	66.71	57.83	52.0…
30. Sparta	33 15	82 54	550	43.66	48.89	54.08	61.50	71.33	76.08	80.18	78.28	73.49	61.95	52.90	46.3…
31. The Rock[1]	32 52	84 23	833	42.87	47.95	55.68	63.59	70.35	77.34	78.63	74.80	72.49	61.50	51.62	44.0…
32. Thomson	33 29	82 25	..	..	49.78	57.98	63.65	74.34	..	..	..	..	..	..	54.2…
33. Thornhill	31 37	81 11	10	..	..	..	..	..	79.47	79.57	82.13	76.06	69.10	..	..
34. Whitemarsh Island	32 00	81 00	18	48.20	53.16	57.64	64.59	72.86	77.85	80.12	79.60	75.09	65.59	57.56	51.7…
35. Zebulon	33 06	84 21	..	43.85	51.77	56.09	61.88	71.75	79.86	81.68	78.48	72.06	66.64	53.69	48.9…

IDAHO.

Name of Station.	Lat.	Long.	Height.	Jan.	Feb.	March.	April.	May.	June.	July.	August.	Sept.	Oct.	Nov.	Dec.
1. Camp Connor	..	..	..	11.38	12.51	..	..	..	..	..	..	..	..	..	20.0…
2. Cantonment Loring[2]	43 04	112 27	4700	24.31	24.06	25.23	42.71	..	..	..	63.39	59.62	47.97	34.67	22.5…
3. Chelemta Depot	48 42	116 19	1796	..	..	..	..	..	..	..	71.6	58.1	49.1	40.1	..
4. Fort Boisé	43 40	116 00	..	26.50	32.89	40.90	52.56	62.62	70.68	78.38	76.05	63.75	52.84	42.33	30.0…
5. Fort Lapwai	46 18	116 54	..	29.78	36.09	41.36	53.70	63.89	70.26	77.59	72.86	62.40	51.27	41.62	33.4…
6. Lapwai[3]	46 18	116 54	2000	31.83	38.50	42.75	52.75	57.50	68.87	70.13	72.00	64.00	48.13	41.50	40.4…

ILLINOIS.

Name of Station.	Lat.	Long.	Height.	Jan.	Feb.	March.	April.	May.	June.	July.	August.	Sept.	Oct.	Nov.	Dec.
1. Albion	38 24	88 04	..	..	..	..	40.81	..	..	..	..	..	..	..	..
2. Alto[4]	41 45	89 00	..	19.53	24.05	30.85	45.77	56.57	68.45	73.17	68.70	59.90	47.37	35.85	23.5…
3. Alton	38 53	90 14	650	34.05	33.66	41.13	48.01	62.30	73.93	76.53	75.69	66.65	51.10	43.84	28.3…
4. Andalusia[5]	41 25	90 45	686	23.17	25.83	36.14	47.64	58.95	69.78	75.82	72.17	63.57	51.57	38.24	26.0…
5. Athens	39 57	89 45	800	31.16	29.78	39.25	47.29	60.14	70.11	73.16	71.36	62.78	51.42	42.98	26.2…
6. Athens[6]	39 57	89 45	800	25.12	29.24	39.08	52.17	63.00	72.01	77.68	75.36	68.56	55.40	40.49	29.8…
7. Augusta[7]	40 12	90 58	500	25.52	29.08	38.28	50.94	61.77	70.56	75.19	72.75	65.27	52.49	40.23	28.4…
8. Aurora	41 46	88 17	696	21.26	24.08	34.90	46.23	57.14	67.72	73.29	68.29	58.81	49.55	41.37	23.1…
9. Batavia[8]	41 52	88 16	636	21.17	27.41	36.83	43.87	58.25	67.75	73.58	70.28	62.71	48.23	33.42	24.2…
10. Belleville	38 29	89 58	600	30.88	31.38	45.03	56.03	70.72	75.03	79.81	79.27	70.83	59.84	46.43	40.2…
11. Belvidere	42 16	88 48	810	19.54	21.98	31.57	44.84	58.16	66.29	73.09	68.14	60.01	44.89	34.03	21.8…
12. Brighton	39 00	90 13	..	27.64	31.72	38.07	45.47	63.54	74.55	81.87	76.99	67.63	56.76	37.37	32.4…
13. Bruce[9]	41 09	88 50	550	..	..	..	..	59.25	63.30	..	..	...	..	43.56	15.6…
14. Carthage	40 23	91 17	..	24.53	30.10	42.64	46.65	66.97	70.25	79.14	75.56	66.11	52.59	39.07	24.8…
15. Centralia	38 31	89 08	..	27.53	37.40	..	..	..	..	..	..	..	..	..	..
16. Channahon	41 26	88 12	630	..	..	36.50	50.97	58.20	70.70	..	..	..	..	..	..
17. Charleston	39 30	88 10	..	27.93	29.45	35.31	53.31	64.96	71.39	77.18	71.21	67.35	54.13	41.31	26.2…
18. Chicago[10]	41 54	87 38	600	23.01	24.96	32.01	45.31	53.34	61.59	70.34	68.34	60.19	48.41	36.36	26.3…
19. Clinton	40 09	88 57	430	20.72	25.75	35.41	52.65	..	..	..	..	..	..	..	19.9…
20. Coloma (near)	38 14	89 16	405	29.15	32.55	37.57	51.48	59.67	70.60	75.72	72.60	64.23	51.24	42.59	30.9…
21. Decatur	39 51	88 57	685	27.53	28.38	34.45	52.85	65.23	72.05	77.98	71.75	67.20	49.65	38.99	28.2…

[1] The results previous to 1854 are defective on account of frequent blanks in the record. In 1856 and 1859 the observations were made at Thomasto… about three miles N. E. of The Rock.

[2] Old Fort Hall.

[3] Observations assumed to have been taken at or in the vicinity of the Fort.

[4] Also called Rochelle.

[5] Observations previous to 1866 were made at Edgington, about one mile to the west of Andalusia.

GEORGIA.—Continued.

	Spring.	Summer.	Autumn.	Winter.	Year.	Series. Begins.	Series. Ends.	Extent yrs.	Extent mos.	Observing hours.	Observer.	References.
22	67°.08	81°.46	67°.53	52°.35	67°.11	Jan. 1832;	Dec. 1870	12	4	$7_m\ 2_a\ 9_a$	Assistant Surgeon.	Ar. Met. Reg. 1855 and MS. from S. G. O.
23	60.32	78.56	61.10	45.33	61.33	1852;	Dec. 1870	2	7	$7_m\ 2_a\ 9_a$ bis	Prof. S. P. Sanford and Willis.	S. O. and S. Coll.
24	67.03	79.64	65.13	48.93	65.18	Apr. 1851;	1853	2	3	$\odot_r\ 9_m\ 3_a\ 9_a$	Cooper.	S. Coll.
25	..	77.41	..	..	..	1852		0	6	"	Pendleton.	" "
26	..	..	..	..	..	1870		0	1	$7_m\ 2_a\ 9_a$ bis	J. L. Cutler.	S. O.
27	..	..	..	..	..	1854		0	1	$7_m\ 2_a\ 9_a$	W. Schley, Jr.	P. O. and S. I. Vol. 1.
28	..	79.44	68.00	..	..	1870		0	8	$7_m\ 2_a\ 9_a$ bis	E. Barker.	S. O.
29	67.06	80.61	66.81	52.56	66.76	Jan. 1819;	Oct. 1859	26	1	$7_m\ 2_a\ 7_a$	A. G. Pemler, Dr. J. F. Posey, and Williams.	Am. Alm. 1838 and foll. especially 1856, MS. in S. Coll., and P. O. and S. I. Vol. 1.
30	62.30	78.18	62.78	46.30	62.39	1850;	Apr. 1861	9	0	$7_m\ 2_a\ 9_a$	Dr. E. M. Pendleton.	P. O. and S. I. Vol. 1, S. O., and S. Coll.
31	63.21	76.92	61.87	44.97	61.74	May, 1839;	Dec. 1859	7	5	"	Dr. J. Anderson.	MS. in S. Coll., P. O. and S. I. Vol. 1.
32	65.32	..	..	..	..	Dec. 1858;	May, 1859	0	5	"	....	P. O. and S. I. Vol. 1.
33	..	80.39	..	..	..	1849		0	5	$\odot_r\ 9_m\ 3_a\ 9_a$	Grant.	S. Coll.
34	65.03	79.19	66.08	51.03	65.33	Apr. 1849;	Apr. 1861	11	9	$7_m\ 2_a\ 9_a$	R. T. Gibson.	P. O. and S. I. Vol. 1, S. O., and S. Coll.
35	63.24	80.01	64.13	48.20	63.90	Jan. 1856;	Mar. 1857	2	9	"	Mrs. J. T. Arnold.	P. O. and S. I. Vol. 1.

IDAHO.

	Spring.	Summer.	Autumn.	Winter.	Year.	Series. Begins.	Series. Ends.	Extent yrs.	Extent mos.	Observing hours.	Observer.	References.
1	..	..	..	14.64	..	Dec. 1864;	Feb. 1865	0	3	$7_m\ 2_a\ 9_a$	Assistant Surgeon.	MS. from S. G. O.
2	..	..	47.42	23.62	..	Aug. 1849;	Apr. 1850	0	9	$\odot_r\ 9_m\ 3_a\ 9_a$	" "	Ar. Met. Reg. 1855.
3	..	..	49.10	..	..	1860		0	4	$7_m\ 2_a\ 9_a$	....	Rep. of N. W. Bound Com.
4	52.03	75.04	52.97	29.81	52.46	Feb. 1864;	Dec. 1870	5	10	"	Assistant Surgeon.	MS. from S. G. O.
5	52.98	73.57	51.76	33.11	52.86	Jan. 1864;	Dec. 1870	5	11	"	Spalding.	MS. from S. G. O.
6	51.00	70.33	51.21	36.91	52.36	1837;	1841	2	2	......	"	Wilkes.

ILLINOIS.

	Spring.	Summer.	Autumn.	Winter.	Year.	Series. Begins.	Series. Ends.	Extent yrs.	Extent mos.	Observing hours.	Observer.	References.
1	..	..	..	..	..	1857		0	1	$7_m\ 2_a$	E. P. Thompson.	P. O. and S. I. Vol. 1.
2	44.40	70.11	47.71	22.39	46.15	July, 1866;	Dec. 1870	4	2	$7_m\ 2_a\ 9_a$ bis	Dr. Carey.	S. O.
3	50.48	75.38	53.86	32.01	52.93	May, 1849;	Dec. 1851	1	6	$\odot_r\ 9_m\ 3_a\ 9_a$	Johnson.	MS. in S. Coll.
4	47.58	72.59	51.13	25.00	49.07	Mar. 1857;	Dec. 1870	9	1	$7_m\ 2_a\ 9_a$ bis	Dr. E. H. Bowman.	P. O. and S. I. Vol. 1, and S. O.
5	48.89	71.51	52.39	29.06	50.47	1847,	1850	3	3	$\odot_r\ 9_m\ 3_a\ \odot_s$	Prof. J. Hall.	Pat. Off. Rep.
6	51.42	75.02	54.82	28.06	52.33	Jan. 1851;	Dec. 1858	7	11	$7_m\ 2_a\ 9_a$	" " "	S. Coll., P. O. and S. I. Vol. 1.
7	50.33	72.83	52.66	27.67	50.87	Aug. 1833;	Dec. 1870	26	9	$7_m\ 2_a\ 9_a$ bis	Dr. S. B. Mead.	MS. in S. Coll.
8	46.09	69.77	49.91	22.84	47.15	Oct. 1857;	Dec. 1870	7	4	"	A. J. Babcock, Dr. A. Spaulding and wife.	P. O. and S. I. Vol. 1, and S. O.
9	46.32	70.54	48.12	24.28	47.31	Jan. 1854;	July, 1861	3	8	$7_m\ 2_a\ 9_a$	Prof. W. Coffin, T. Mead, and F. Crandon.	" " " " "
10	57.26	78.04	59.03	34.18	57.13	May, 1860;	Dec. 1862	2	1	$7_m\ 2_a\ 9_a$ bis	N. T. Baker, J. J. R. Patrick.	S. O.
11	44.86	69.17	46.31	21.11	45.36	Apr. 1868;	Dec. 1870	2	9	"	G. B. Moss.	" "
12	49.03	77.80	53.92	30.62	52.84	June, 1856;	Feb. 1859	2	9	$7_m\ 2_a\ 9_a$	Rev. W. V. Eldridge.	S. Coll., P. O. and S. I. Vol. 1.
13	..	..	..	..	..	Nov. 1859;	June, 1860	0	4	"	Dr. G. O. Smith.	P. O. and S. I. Vol. 1, and S. O.
14	52.09	74.98	52.59	26.51	51.54	Aug. 1858;	Dec. 1859	1	2	$7_m\ 1_a\ 7_a$	Mrs. E. M. A. Belle.	P. O. and S. I. Vol. 1.
15	..	..	..	..	..	1865		0	2	$7_m\ 2_a\ 9_a$ bis	H. A. Schauber.	S. O.
16	48.56	..	..	..	..	1861		0	4	"	I. Fitch.	" "
17	51.19	73.26	54.26	27.89	51.65	Apr. 1870;	Dec. 1870	0	9	"	C. Gramesby.	" "
18	43.55	66.76	48.32	24.78	45.85	July, 1832;	Dec. 1870	17	3	"	Assist. Surg., S. Meacham, S. Brooks, I. I. Langguth, and others.	Rec. of Mech. Inst. and S. O.
19	..	..	..	22.14	..	Dec. 1864;	May, 1866	0	5	$7_m\ 9_a$	C. N. Moore.	S. O.
20	49.57	72.97	52.69	30.89	51.53	June, 1865;	Nov. 1870	5	5	$7_m\ 2_a\ 9_a$ bis	W. C. Spencer.	" "
21	50.84	73.93	51.95	28.06	51.19	Oct. 1869;	Dec. 1870	1	3	"	T. Dudley.	" "

6 Observations previous to Feb. 1853, at other hours; they were referred to $7_m\ 2_a\ 9_a$.

7 Observations previous to April, 1853, at $\odot_r\ 9_m\ 3_a\ 9_a$; they were referred to $7_m\ 2_a\ 9_a$ bis.

8 Observations at three stations within a radius of a few miles.

9 Also called High Open Prairie.

10 Observations previous to 1844 were made at Fort Dearborn.

ILLINOIS.—Continued.

Name of Station.	Lat.	Long.	Height.	Jan.	Feb.	March.	April.	May.	June.	July.	August.	Sept.	Oct.	Nov.	Dec.
22. Edgar Co. (near S. W. corn.)	39°30′	88°56′	..	33°.42	17°.25	35°.42	44°.37	53°.61	..	..	..	..	..	..	..
23. Effingham	39 07	88 32	592	30.73	..	..	..	62.73	73°.40	77°.45	79°.65	..	..	..	..
24. Elgin	42 03	88 16	777	23.01	20.62	36.85	45.13	56.99	66.26	70.26	69.40	59°.91	48°.63	34°.59	22°.11
25. Elmira	41 10	89 50	..	20.76	26.92	33.53	48.72	61.15	70.52	75.26	70.96	62.94	48.76	38.01	23.35
26. Evanston (N. W. University)	42 03	87 39	618	23.49	25.86	34.32	45.63	55.89	66.15	70.20	70.43	66.75	49.63	39.78	23.89
27. Farm Ridge	41 13	88 53	600	20.90	26.05	40.00	46.73	62.43	66.10	69.48	68.13	59.08	49.86	31.50	18.73
28. Fort Armstrong	41 30	90 40	528	22.80	24.68	37.83	51.06	62.67	71.39	76.48	74.48	62.98	52.26	39.02	27.16
29. Fremont Centre	42 18	88 06	736	19.73	23.43	33.93	36.56	53.41	67.61	75.22	71.56	65.82	49.45	30.28	32.24
30. Galesburg (Univrs.)	40 55	90 24	795	21.41	26.10	33.22	49.01	59.63	70.41	74.06	71.75	63.69	49.93	38.75	26.40
31. Golconda	37 23	88 30	..	35.05	41.29	45.34	58.31	65.89	75.18	81.76	80.59	72.07	58.97	46.17	36.31
32. Granville	41 14	89 15	..	..	..	..	..	55.56	..	..	..	..	..	..	..
33. Havana	40 18	90 05	475	..	..	..	..	..	..	..	..	66.15	52.28	41.04	25.85
34. Hennepin	41 15	89 20	..	26.85	28.90	32.85	54.78	67.75	74.83	80.45	74.28	67.93	53.73	41.45	25.90
35. Highland[1]	38 44	89 40	620	32.77	35.18	44.52	57.50	67.62	75.54	79.55	77.97	70.88	55.95	42.98	34.44
36. Hillsborough	39 12	89 26	..	..	25.39	39.40	..	..	..	..	..	..	..	..	..
37. Hoyleton	38 26	89 17	480	25.70	..	..	49.03	62.27	73.63	79.30	75.65	68.48	48.75	42.25	28.85
38. Jacksonville[2]	39 45	90 12	676	28.99	24.27	41.48	55.18	61.69	75.13	74.45	72.52	65.53	54.97	44.89	34.76
39. Joliet	41 30	88 05	..	29.39	31.57	..	52.79	56.07	..	73.35	68.65	..	40.75	..	..
40. King's Mill	42 05	88 33	..	26.78	24.20	26.78	42.48	53.23	63.15	68.90	69.08	..	.	.	..
41. Lawn	40 59	89 38	..	..	..	27.25	49.78	..	..	..	..	..	..	..	..
42. Lebanon	38 35	89 49	500	30.37	35.09	43.63	55.40	65.20	73.95	75.75	77.32	69.25	57.40	46.28	39.88
43. Lee Centre	41 45	89 17	..	..	..	..	..	..	..	..	..	..	..	33.98	20.55
44. Loami	39 40	89 51	675	26.13	30.36	32.47	52.27	58.90	71.68	76.18	74.34	64.57	51.09	40.36	25.68
45. Louisville	38 45	88 30	..	33.71	34.39	38.48	55.00	66.25	73.16	78.67	76.14	67.15	50.59	42.34	31.34
46. Magnolia (near)	41 15	89 15	300	15.93	25.78	34.98	47.29	35.72	71.61	85.10	66.40	..	..	41.65	25.95
47. Manchester	39 31	90 34	683	26.41	30.65	38.55	52.04	62.90	71.88	76.11	73.72	66.00	53.56	40.47	29.58
48. Manlius	41 24	88 36	..	..	..	..	..	..	..	..	..	..	..	33.90	..
49. Marengo	42 14	88 34	842	19.42	23.81	33,14	43.78	55.36	67.37	72.16	68.29	60.39	48.89	33.78	26.05
50. Mattoon	39 29	88 23	740	30.00	28.85	34.73	53.18	66.80	73.48	78.42	75.52	67.77	51.48	40.87	30.34
51. Meeker's Store	37 24	89 20	487	36.80	34.25	47.55	55.40	..	..	73.17	76.85	67.72	58.22	46.63	44.63
52. Milford	41 33	88 40	..	17.72	29.28	39.69	49.04	58.80	68.76	76.71	73.93	58.22	57.06	36.90	26.90
53. Mound City	37 06	89 12	..	44.75	41.63	47.18	..	..	..	..	..	77.37	..	48.75	46.66
54. Mount Sterling	39 58	90 47	..	26.04	30.46	36.68	52.92	62.99	73.54	80.03	74.87	65.52	53.27	42.18	28.53
55. Monroe	42 08	87 55	600	29.49	30.21	34.25	43.06	53.17	68.67	70.96	68.07	61.11	49.35	43.56	22.06
56. Murrayville	39 35	90 14	683	..	..	..	51.30	65.14	74.87	72.08	74.37	73.84	54.97	..	..
57. Nachusa Nursery	41 50	89 23	..	..	27.41	..	47.53	54.89	66.00	71.43	..	..	..	..	..
58. Naperville	41 46	88 06	..	22.35	24.53	..	..	..	..	74.99	72.21	60.29	47.51	..	17.00
59. Olney	38 44	88 03	..	..	..	..	..	..	..	..	..	63.13	54.88	..	..
60. Oquawka	40 55	90 59	..	..	..	..	..	..	..	79.83	72.93	68.30	55.43	43.35	27.95
61. Orchard Farm	40 36	89 45	..	24.35	30.55	37.87	49.52	61.71	68.87	72.33	71.94	63.28	50.58	37.29	29.46
62. Osceola	41 12	89 46	..	22 69	28.53	39.14	50.78	61.64	70.13	74.55	73.60	64.55	54.70	33.95	20.23
63. Ottawa	41 20	88 47	500	23.48	26.70	35.62	45.78	59.82	69.98	74.55	71.63	63.91	52.49	37.26	25.79
64. Pana	39 23	89 05	735	29.23	30.75	36.28	54.24	66.18	71.60	76.76	74.85	66.55	50.12	39.67	28.91
65. Paris	39 37	87 41	600	..	..	..	..	..	..	..	..	63.48	..	..	..
66. Pekin	40 35	89 38	..	21.62	26.04	36.58	49.00	60.74	70.53	74.77	71.43	65.43	50.63	37.78	24.52
67. Peoria	40 43	89 30	512	25.06	28.67	37.98	51.05	62.87	72.14	77.11	74.12	66.37	52.63	39.81	28.47
68. Pleasant Ridge Nursery	41 15	89 36	550	22.75	28.42	32.96	47.98	59.31	69.52	73.66	70.29	62.13	48.13	39.34	25.99
69. Quincy	39 55	91 25	650	..	31.88	37.55	45.09	62.62	73.29	79.30	72.88	68.38	55.45	43.58	28.45
70. Ridge Farm	39 53	87 38	3120	..	..	..	..	59.75	69.35	81.19	69.43	60.88	50.80	..	..
71. Riley	42 11	88 35	760	17.54	22.87	31.88	43.53	55.71	65.60	70.04	67.82	60.08	46.54	33.56	21.93
72. Rock Island Arsenal	41 32	90 31	528	22.49	25.88	33.24	49.24	60.96	72.92	77.54	75.89	63.94	51.26	39.89	24.49
73. Rushville	40 05	90 39	..	..	..	..	..	..	72.00	79.13	..	..	..	..	..
74. Sandwich	41 40	88 35	575	21.12	25.59	33.94	43.18	58.61	68.31	72.73	70.27	62.23	48.46	36.45	22.39
75. South Pass[3] (near)	37 28	89 14	650	36.98	38.23	43.66	56.15	66.35	75.66	76.84	79.70	73.35	51.80	43.13	37.62
76. Springfield	39 48	89 40	550	24.85	29.67	35.81	48.98	60.31	71.21	77.25	73.59	64.06	42.41	40.34	28.33

[1] Observations after 1860 made at $7_m\ 2_a\ 9_a$, were referred to $6_m\ 9_m$ N. 3_a.

ILLINOIS.—Continued.

	Spring.	Summer.	Autumn.	Winter.	Year.	Series. Begins. Ends.	Extent yrs. mos.	Observing hours.	Observer.	References.
22	44°.47	..	..	..	..	1858	0 5	$\odot_r$	J. W. Brown.	P. O. and S. I. Vol. 1.
23	..	76°.83	..	..	..	May, 1869; Jan. 1870	0 5	$7_m\ 2_a\ 9_{a\ bis}$	W. Thompson.	S. O.
24	46.32	68.64	47°.71	21°.91	46°.15	Jan. 1858; July, 1862	4 0	"	J. B. Newcomb.	P. O. and S. I. Vol. 1, and S. O.
25	47.80	72.25	49.90	23.68	48.41	May, 1862; Aug. 1870	5 10	"	O. A. Blanchard.	S. O.
26	45.28	68.93	52.05	24.41	47.67	Feb. 1858; Dec. 1870	4 1	"	C. E. Smith, J. H. Gill, O. Marcy, and others.	P. O. and S. I. Vol. 1, and S. O.
27	49.72	67.90	46.81	21.89	46.58	Feb. 1860; Dec. 1860	0 10	"	E. Baldwin.	S. O.
28	50.52	74.12	51.42	24.88	50.23	Jan. 1824; Dec. 1835	11 6	$7_m\ 2_a\ 9_a$	Assistant Surgeon.	Ar. Met. Reg. 1855.
29	41.30	71.46	48.52	25.13	46.60	Jan. 1857; Mar. 1858	1 3	"	I. H. Smith.	P. O. and S. I. Vol. 1.
30	47.29	72.07	50.79	24.64	48.70	Feb. 1861; Dec. 1870	9 7	$7_m\ 1_a\ 9_a$	W. Livingstone.	S. O.
31	56.51	79.18	59.07	37.55	58.08	Jan. 1866; Sept. 1870	4 9	$7_m\ 2_a\ 9_{a\ bis}$	W. V. Eldridge.	" "
32	..	..	..	..	..	1857	0 1	$7_m\ 2_a\ 9_a$	J. L. Jenkins.	P. O. and S. I. Vol. 1.
33	..	..	53.16	..	..	1870	0 4	"	J. Cochrane.	S. O.
34	51.79	76.52	54.37	27.22	52.48	1870	1 0	"	E. Osborn.	" "
35	56.55	77.69	56.60	34.13	56.24	Jan. 1841; Mar. 1864	15 1	$6_m\ 9_m$ N. 3_a	Dr. Ryhiner, A. F. Bandelier.	MS. in S. Coll. and S. O.
36	..	..	..	..	..	1858	0 2	$7_m\ 2_a\ 9_a$	J. S. Titcomb.	P. O. and S. I. Vol. 1.
37	..	76.19	53.16	..	..	Apr. 1854; June, 1866	1 0	$7_m\ 2_a\ 7_{a\ bis}$	J. Ellsworth, O. J. Marsh.	S. O.
38	52.78	74.03	55.13	29.34	52.82	Apr. 1849; Mar. 1862	2 11	"	T. Dudley and Coffin.	P. O. and S. I. Vol. 1, S. O., and S. Coll.
39	..	..	..	..	..	Oct. 1843; July, 1845	0 8	$\odot_r\ 9_m\ 3_a\ 9_a$	Dr. M. K. Brownson.	MS. in S. Coll.
40	40.83	67.04	..	..	..	1869	0 8	$7_m\ 2_a\ 9_{a\ bis}$	Dr. A. Spaulding and wife.	S. O.
41	..	..	..	..	..	1867	0 2	"	A. H. Thompson.	" "
42	54.74	75.67	57.64	35.11	55.79	Nov. 1859; June, 1862	1 8	"	N. E. Cobleigh.	P. O. and S. I. Vol. 1, and S. O.
43	..	..	..	..	..	1860	0 2	"	E. D. Strauss.	S. O.
44	47.88	74.07	52.01	27.39	50.34	Jan. 1866; Sept. 1869	2 9	"	T. Dudley.	" "
45	53.24	75.99	53.36	33.15	53.93	Mar. 1869; Dec. 1870	1 10	"	Dr. D. H. Chase.	" "
46	39.33	74.37	..	22.55	..	Nov. 1866; Aug. 1868	1 4	"	H. A. Smith.	" "
47	51.16	73.90	53.34	28.88	51.82	July, 1854; Dec. 1870	15 6	$7_m\ 1_a\ 9_a$	J. Grant & daughter.	P. O. and S. I. Vol. 1, and S. O.
48	..	..	..	..	..	1860	0 1	$7_m\ 2_a\ 9_{a\ bis}$	[illegible]	S. O.
49	44.09	69.27	47.69	23.09	46.04	Apr. 1856; Mar. 1869	5 6	"	O. P. & J. S. Rogers.	" "
50	51.57	75.81	53.37	29.73	52.62	Aug. 1869; Dec. 1870	1 5	"	Dr. W. E. Henry.	" "
51	..	..	57.52	38.56	..	Mar. 1861; Feb. 1862	0 10	"	R. Meeker.	" "
52	49.18	73.13	50.73	24.63	49.42	1854	1 0	......	Hendrick.	Regents' Rep.
53	..	..	..	44.35	..	Sept. 1862; Mar. 1863	0 6	$7_m\ 2_a\ 9_a$	....	MS. from S. G. O.
54	50.86	76.15	53.66	28.34	52.25	Jan. 1866; Dec. 1870	4 11	$7_m\ 2_a\ 9_{a\ bis}$	Rev. A. Duncan.	S. O.
55	43.49	69.23	51.34	27.25	47.83	1849; 1850	1 5	$\odot_r\ 9_m\ 3_a\ 9_a$	Main.	S. Coll.
56	..	73.77	..	..	..	1865	0 7	$7_m\ 1_a\ 9_a$	J. Grant & daughter.	S. O.
57	..	..	..	..	..	Apr. 1863; May, 1867	0 7	$7_m\ 2_a\ 9_{a\ bis}$	J. T. Little.	" "
58	..	..	..	21.29	..	July, 1859; Feb. 1860	0 7	$7_m\ 2_a\ 9_a$	M. S. & L. Ellsworth.	P. O. and S. I. Vol. 1. and S. O.
59	..	..	..	..	..	1860	0 2	$7_m\ 2_a\ 9_{a\ bis}$	H. A. Brickenstein.	S. O.
60	..	..	55.69	..	..	1870	0 6	"	H. N. Patterson.	" "
61	49.70	71.05	50.38	28.12	49.81	Jan. 1860; Mar. 1864	4 0	"	J. H. Riblet.	" "
62	50.52	72.76	51.07	23.82	49.54	Jan. 1860; May, 1861	1 5	"	Dr. J. S. Pashley.	" "
63	47.07	72.05	51.22	25.32	48.92	1852: Nov. 1870	18 9	"	Dr. J. O. Harris, Mrs. E. A. Merwin, and Meacham.	P. O. and S. I. Vol. 1, S. O., S. Coll.
64	52.23	74.40	52.11	29.63	52.09	June, 1869; Dec. 1870	1 7	"	Dr. T. Finley.	S. O.
65	..	..	..	..	..	1868	0 1	"	C. Lee.	" "
66	48.77	72.24	51.28	24.06	49.09	Jan. 1855; Oct. 1865	6 10	"	J. H. Riblet.	MS. in S. Coll., P. O. and S. I. Vol. 1, and S. O.
67	50.63	74.46	52.94	27.40	51.36	Jan. 1856; Dec. 1870	14 9	"	Dr. F. Brendel, M. A. Breed.	P. O. and S. I. Vol. 1, and S. O.
68	46.75	71.16	49.87	25.72	48.37	July, 1863; July, 1870	7 1	"	V. Aldrich.	S. O.
69	48.42	75.16	55.80	..	..	Feb. 1850; Dec. 1870	0 11	"	F. J. Hearne and Giddings.	S. O. and S. Coll.
70	..	73.32	..	..	..	1868	0 6	"	B. C. Williams.	S. O.
71	43.71	67.82	46.73	20.78	44.76	Apr. 1856; Dec. 1870	12 0	"	E. Babcock, J. W. James.	" "
72	47.81	75.45	51.70	24.29	49.81.	Feb. 1866; Dec. 1870	4 6	$7_m\ 2_a\ 9_a$	....	MS. from S. G. O.
73	..	..	..	..	..	1833	0 2	......	Mead.	S. Coll.
74	45.24	70.44	49.05	23.03	46.94	Dec. 1858; Apr. 1870	11 2	$7_m\ 2_a\ 9_{a\ bis}$	Dr. N. E. Ballou.	P. O. and S. I. Vol. 1, and S. O.
75	55.39	77.40	56.09	37.61	56.62	Dec. 1857; Feb. 1870	3 11	"	H. C. Freeman and wife, F. Baker, and S. C. Spaulding.	MS. in S. Coll., P. O. and S. I. Vol. 1, and S. O.
76	48.37	74.02	48.94	27.62	49.74	Jan. 1865; Aug. 1870	5 7	"	G. M. Brinkerhoff.	S. O.

[2] Observations previous to 1861 at other hours; they were referred to $7_m\ 2_a\ 9_{a\ bis}$.

[3] Observations for 1862–3–4 are not very reliable.

ILLINOIS.—Continued.

Name of Station.	Lat.	Long.	Height.	Jan.	Feb.	March.	April.	May.	June.	July.	August.	Sept.	Oct.	Nov.	Dec.
77. Upper Alton[1]	38°57′	90°04′	650	29°.43	34°.39	43°.47	52°.02	63°.53	73°.16	76°.65	75°.05	67°.87	53°.59	40°.70	31°.39
78. Upper Alton	38 57	90 04	650	26.05	27.14	32.64	52.64	63.97	71.73	77.84	73.36	67.39	53.64	40.86	30.81
79. Vandalia	38 58	89 05	..	..	..	..	..	..	78.61	75.57	..	..	..	..	..
80. Wapella	44 14	88 58	..	..	27.78	47.10	..	..	..	..	..	..	..	..	..
81. Warsaw (near)	40 21	91 23	550	25.36	29.23	37.45	50.15	61.78	70.50	74.67	72.88	65.57	51.67	37.48	29.14
82. Waterloo	38 20	90 10	..	25.86	37.26	44.52	53.41	64.74	79.47	82.79	80.45	70.79	59.32	45.78	31.36
83. Waukegan	42 21	87 55	646	..	..	35.90	41.72	51.08	..	..	..	..	..	..	..
84. Waverly	39 36	89 58	680	26.26	30.81	39.33	50.62	63.61	70.84	74.35	73.35	67.74	50.40	39.72	29.38
85. Waynesville	40 16	89 07	..	29.89	24.27	43.05	51.66	57.36	72.21	75.54	73.21	65.98	53.48	33.78	31.50
86. West Salem	38 30	88 00	..	27.97	34.22	44.43	54.49	67.11	74.26	78.80	75.14	68.55	57.18	42.36	33.98
87. West Urbana	40 09	88 17	550	24.27	27.97	39.63	47.11	60.48	70.34	76.74	74.23	66.06	51.96	38.41	29.94
88. Wheaton	41 49	88 06	682	28.49	21.41	36.22	51.70	56.09	68.17	72.04	70.62	61.39	49.10	36.11	24.97
89. Willow Creek Nursery	41 45	88 56	1040	18.70	26.75	..	..	..	..	70.93	69.43	60.83	..	37.25	..
90. Winnebago	42 17	89 12	900	19.19	21.80	31.83	44.67	57.69	67.13	71.59	68.94	60.81	47.04	34.60	21.02
91. Woodstock	42 18	88 24	..	..	28.60	40.13	47.11	63.02	67.78	72.85	70.13	60.66	49.11	..	..
92. Wyanet (four miles N. W. of)	41 30	89 45	..	21.72	26.76	33.16	49.03	59.11	60.11	75.09	71.20	62.91	50.43	39.68	24.09
93. York Neck.	40 05	91 33	..	23.90	33.35	38.55	49.00	62.90	72.05	73.25	72.30	70.15	52.00	41.30	25.65

INDIANA.

Name of Station.	Lat.	Long.	Height.	Jan.	Feb.	March.	April.	May.	June.	July.	August.	Sept.	Oct.	Nov.	Dec.
1. Annapolis	39 52	87 12	3090	..	..	..	..	..	..	..	..	..	55.38	39.23	24.88
2. Anoma	38 45	85 33	..	..	38.42	40.51	53.57	60.42	73.33	74.39	..	..	54.51	51.79	25.29
3. Aurora	39 04	84 55	509	28.95	33.79	40.59	52.90	62.44	73.36	79.04	74.42	67.45	52.67	41.59	29.90
4. Balbac	40 30	85 00	1000	24.27	21.15	32.35	55.05	..	..	..	..	..	..	..	..
5. Bloomingdale (Friends' Acad.)	39 48	87 00	600	24.23	33.20	..	..	65.75	74.90	79.58	72.88	..	..	..	..
6. Bloomington	39 12	86 33	771	35.71	35.22	41.30	48.97	60.88	70.68	80.15	71.49	52.06	51.23	41.44	27.48
7. Cadiz[3] (one mile S. of)	39 55	85 20	1060	23.85	27.96	35.56	47.19	57.93	65.70	70.33	67.71	60.03	47.31	37.08	27.17
8. Cannelton	37 58	86 45	400	30.39	38.17	44.04	54.00	64.20	72.55	75.47	73.61	66.80	56.10	45.50	37.48
9. Columbia City	41 10	85 25	..	23.61	27.33	32.98	48.38	56.32	71.27	75.30	70.29	62.65	50.29	39.77	27.23
10. Evansville	38 00	87 30	390	32.45	38.84	44.24	51.60	63.56	73.70	79.00	76.39	70.69	57.59	43.10	42.63
11. Farmers' Institute	40 20	86 57	..	..	..	..	..	60.97	71.23	69.08	68.40	70.15	50.10	..	..
12. Fort Wayne	41 05	85 04	..	..	..	..	..	58.10	70.34	..	..	..	..	..	25.23
13. Greencastle	39 39	86 49	..	24.50	35.00	41.55	..	61.91	69.43	..	..	..	..	..	..
14. Green Mount	39 52	84 58	..	33.38	35.05	..	..	..	..	..	..	..	..	..	..
15. Harveysburg	39 59	87 16	3090	26.25	28.15	33.44	51.26	61.54	72.09	75.37	73.22	65.63	43.48	37.45	30.98
16. Indianapolis	39 47	86 09	698	26.45	30.87	37.64	49.94	60.45	71.73	74.58	71.60	64.63	50.43	40.82	28.80
17. Jalapa	40 40	85 48	..	34.58	33.95	32.05	..	56.13	67.20	78.76	68.53	59.46	49.31	42.09	27.49
18. Jeffersonville	38 19	85 42	400	48.	45.	45.	59.	69.	80.	79.	82.	70.	60.	53.	37.
19. Kendallville	41 21	85 14	975	..	31.46	40.47	50.48	60.12	71.77	78.95	75.70	66.67	..	..	..
20. Kentland	40 47	87 22	725	31.00	31.89	31.28	46.98	57.00	65.84	71.32	73.25	63.88	44.03	34.60	27.50
21. Laconia[4]	38 05	86 03	..	35.18	34.05	39.80	56.05	65.40	71.95	76.75	75.55	67.83	51.64	42.67	33.52
22. Lafayette	40 25	86 52	620	29.73	32.38	31.35	47.58	61.18	69.80	71.20	74.25	..	..	..	30.70
23. Laporte	41 37	86 43	550	28.19	26.40	36.25	47.27	61.26	68.69	72.99	70.73	64.67	48.84	40.90	26.49
24. Laporte	41 37	86 43	550	25.0	28.0	36.0	40.0	50.0	60.0	64.0	65.0	54.0	45.0	34.0	20.0
25. Lo	41 13	85 10	..	..	..	..	..	55.29	..	..	..	..	..	..	..
26. Logansport	40 45	86 19	600	24.15	30.36	37.97	49.98	60.84	70.59	77.50	73.58	64.48	52.03	38.02	28.40
27. Madison	38 45	85 20	450	32.87	31.53	43.53	55.82	62.87	71.11	80.08	75.31	69.56	56.27	39.24	37.33

[1] Observations at $6_m\ 2_a\ 6_a$, from Nov. 1, 1851, to May, 1853, subsequently at $7_m\ 2_a\ 9_a$; no correction for change of hours has been applied.

[2] Observations previous to 1857 were made at irregular hours; the series has been corrected for daily variation.

ILLINOIS.—Continued.

	Spring.	Summer.	Autumn.	Winter.	Year.	Series. Begins. Ends.	Extent yrs.mos.	Observing hours.	Observer.	References.
7	53°.01	74°.95	54°.05	31°.74	53°.44	1849; 1854	4 4	$\odot_r\ 9_m\ 3_a\ 9_a$	James.	S. Coll.
8	49.75	74.31	53.96	28.00	51.51	Jan. 1854; Apr. 1864	5 5	$7_m\ 2_a\ 9_a$	Dr. L. James and Anna C. Trifle.	P. O. and S. I. Vol. 1, and S. O.
9	..	..	..	..	..	1865	0 2	$7_m\ 2_a\ 9_a$ bis	J. A. Sanborn.	S. O.
0	..	..	..	..	..	1868	0 2	"	T. L. Groff.	" "
1	49.79	72.68	51.57	27.91	50.49	May, 1840; Dec. 1870	9 10	[2]	Ben. Whitaker.	MS. in S. Coll., P. O. and S. I. Vol. 1, and S. O.
2	54.22	80.91	58.63	31.49	56.31	Mar. 1865; Dec. 1870	3 0	$7_m\ 2_a\ 9_a$ bis	H. Künster, F. Sum, Dr. C. Jozelle.	S. O.
3	42.90	..	..	..	..	1849	0 3	$\odot_r\ 9_m\ 3_a\ 9_a$	Joslyn.	S. Coll.
4	51.19	72.85	52.62	28.82	51.37	Apr. 1862; Dec. 1865	3 5	$7_m\ 2_a\ 9_a$ bis	T. Dudley.	S. O.
5	50.69	73.65	51.08	28.55	50.99	Jan. 1858; Mar. 1859	1 3	$7_m\ 2_a\ 9_a$	J. E. Cantril.	P. O. and S. I. Vol. 1.
6	55.34	76.07	56.03	32.06	54.87	Feb. 1856; Oct. 1860	4 5	"	H. A. Titze.	P. O. and S. I. Vol. 1, and S. O.
7	49.07	73.77	52.14	27.39	50.59	Apr. 1857; Dec. 1859	2 9	"	Dr. J. Twain.	P. O. and S. I. Vol. 1.
8	48.00	70.28	48.87	24.96	48.03	Dec. 1857; Dec. 1861	2 7	$7_m\ 2_a\ 9_a$ bis	Prof. G. H. Collier.	P. O. and S. I. Vol. 1, and S. O.
9	..	..	..	..	..	Jan. 1860; Nov. 1861	0 9	"	E. E. Bacon.	S. O.
0	44.73	69.22	47.48	20.67	45.53	Jan. 1858; Dec. 1870	12 9	"	J. W. Tolman and daughter.	P. O. and S. I, Vol. 1, and S. O.
1	50.09	70.25	..	..	..	Sept. 1859; Apr. 1861	1 0	"	G. R. Bassett.	" " " " " "
2	47.10	68.80	51.01	24.19	47.77	June, 1864; Dec. 1870	6 4	"	E. S. Phelps and daughter.	S. O.
3	50.15	72.53	54.48	27.63	51.20	Jan. 1864; Dec. 1870	2 0	......	V. P. Gay.	MS. in S. Coll.

INDIANA

	Spring.	Summer.	Autumn.	Winter.	Year.	Series. Begins. Ends.	Extent yrs.mos.	Observing hours.	Observer.	References.
1	..	..	..	..	..	1870	0 3	$7_m\ 2_a\ 9_a$ bis	R. S. Robertson.	S. O.
2	51.50	..	..	..	..	1849; 1850	0 10	$\odot_r\ 9_m\ 3_a\ 9_a$	Thomson.	S. Coll.
3	51.98	75.61	53.90	30.88	53.09	Jan. 1859; Dec. 1870	5 9	$7_m\ 2_a\ 9_a$ bis	G. Sutton.	P. O. and S. I. Vol. 1, and S. O.
4	..	..	..	..	..	1866	0 4	"	Miriam Griest.	S. O.
5	..	75.79	..	..	..	Feb. 1864; July, 1865	0 8	"	W. H. and Mary A Hobbs.	" "
6	50.38	74.11	48.24	32.80	51.38	Mar. 1868; Sept. 1869	1 3	"	C. M. Dodd & others.	" "
7	46.89	67.91	48.14	26.33	47.32	Dec. 1854; Mar. 1865	9 7	"	W. Dawson and T. B. Redding.	S. Coll. and S. O.
8	54.08	73.88	56.13	35.35	54.86	Jan. 1857; Apr. 1869	3 4	"	H. Smith, Jr., and P. Smith.	P. O. and S. I. Vol. 1, and S. O.
9	45.89	72.29	50.90	26.06	48.79	Sept. 1865; Dec. 1870	5 0	"	Dr. F. McCoy and daughter, Dr. W. J. Maxwell.	S. O.
0	53.13	76.36	57.13	37.97	56.15	Mar. 1857; Sept. 1858	1 7	$7_m\ 2_a\ 9_a$	J. F. Crisp.	P. O. and S. I. Vol. 1.
1	..	69.57	..	..	..	1865	0 6	$7_m\ 2_a\ 9_a$ bis	I. E. Windle.	S. O.
2	..	..	..	..	..	May, 1849; Dec. 1870	0 3	"	R. S. Robertson and Huestes.	S. O. and S. Coll.
3	..	..	..	..	..	1843; 1854	0 5	$7_m\ 2_a\ 9_a$	Profs. C. J. Downey and J. Tingley.	Newspaper slip, P. O. and S. I. Vol. 1, and S. Coll.
4	..	..	..	..	..	1860	0 2	$7_m\ 2_a\ 9_a$ bis	J. Haines.	S. O.
5	48.75	73.56	48.85	28.46	49.91	Feb. 1869; Sept. 1870	1 6	"	B. C. Williams.	" "
6	49.34	72.64	51.96	28.71	50.66	Jan. 1864; Dec. 1870	6 5	"	W. W. Butterfield and others.	" "
7	..	71.50	50.29	32.01	..	June, 1868; June, 1869	1 0	"	Dr. A. C. Irwin.	" "
8	57.67	80.33	61.00	43.33	60.58	1819	1 0	$7_m\ 2_a\ 9_a$	....	Rep. Brit. Assoc. 1847.
9	50.36	75.47	..	..	..	1854	0 8	"	J. Knauer and W. B. Coventing.	P. O. and S. I. Vol. 1.
0	45.09	70.14	47.50	30.13	48.22	Feb. 1869; Dec. 1870	0 11	$7_m\ 2_a\ 9_a$ bis	D. Spitler.	S. O.
1	53.75	74.75	54.05	34.25	54.20	July, 1869; Dec. 1870	1 6	"	A. Crozier.	" "
2	46.70	71.75	..	30.94	..	May, 1854; Jan. 1870	0 11	"	A. H. Bixby and J. W. Newton.	P. O. and S. I. Vol. 1, and S. O.
3	48.26	70.80	51.47	27.03	49.39	1849; Dec. 1870	2 6	"	F. G. Andrew and Newkirk.	S. O. and S. Coll.
4	42.00	63.00	44.33	24.33	43.41	1851	1 0	......	Reid.	Pat. Off. Rep.
5	..	..	..	..	..	1861	0 1	9_a	Dr. W. W. Spratt.	S. O.
6	49.60	73.89	51.51	27.64	50.66	July, 1854; June, 1863	5 2	$7_m\ 2_a\ 9_a$ bis	E. L. Berthaud, C. B. Laselle, I. Bartlett, and T. B. Helen.	MS. in S. Coll. and S. O.
7	54.07	75.50	55.02	33.91	54.63	Nov. 1854; July, 1866	2 10	"	C. Barnes, and Rev. S. Collins.	P. O. and S. I. Vol. 1, and S. O.

[3] Observations after February, 1863, were made at *Newcastle* very near *Cadiz*.

[4] Also called *Tobacco Landing*.

Name of Station.	Lat.	Long.	Height.	Jan.	Feb.	March.	April.	May.	June.	July.	August.	Sept.	Oct.	Nov.	Dec.
INDIANA.—Continued.															
28. Merom	39°05′	87°30′	..	28°.54	33°.87	38°.20	51°.76	62°.03	72°.29	78°.93	76°.44	64°.99	52°.93	43°.16	30°.5
29. Michigan City	41 42	86 49	622	24.28	29.30	36.05	44.63	56.46	67.48	72.95	70.80	63.72	47.87	35.69	27.6
30. Milton	39 47	85 06	800	30.20	29.31	38.53	52.61	62.24	71.13	75.52	73.13	67.80	50.26	42.09	31.5
31. Mishawaka[1]	41 39	86 08	..	..	..	..	43.84	63.21	64.97	73.31	70.72	62.27	51.11	43.72	..
32. Mount Carmel	39 25	84 52	900	31.18	30.83	36.00	51.85	65.13	70.77	76.31	75.98	67.74	50.14	38.85	29.8
33. Mount Hope[2]	39 47	85 33	800	31.88	29.75	38.09	50.28	61.63	69.97	75.32	74.44	66.45	49.29	40.51	28.1
34. Muncie	40 12	85 20	1000	25.54	30.73	35.70	49.08	60.32	70.75	75.16	70.71	62.27	49.03	40.17	29.3
35. New Albany	38 19	85 50	353	26.85	39.56	40.03	51.46	61.98	71.76	76.90	73.06	68.61	51.57	43.72	35.4
36. New Harmony	38 10	87 54	350	34.11	41.53	52.56	56.04	67.64	76.36	78.85	75.50	65.65	55.72	43.27	37.3
37. New Harmony	38 10	87 54	350	31.32	36.29	43.77	55.26	65.53	73.20	78.53	76.04	68.92	54.44	44.25	35.1
38. Newport	39 57	84 54	..	..	..	..	..	..	..	..	..	..	48.08	43.28	..
39. Pennville	40 20	85 00	1000	19.80	31.45	42.50	51.88	63.35	70.24	71.83	70.19	..	..	..	21.1
40. Rensselaer	40 56	87 05	725	22.99	28.00	34.91	47.39	59.24	70.73	75.02	71.70	65.24	47.49	36.98	24.6
41. Richmond[3]	39 50	84 51	850	26.25	31.04	39.45	50.01	60.59	70.08	73.85	71.44	65.88	52.20	39.48	30.1
42. Rockville (one mile N. of)	39 47	87 10	1100	25.90	28.50	36.40	50.40	60.30	67.40	74.70	71.50	65.90	50.90	40.50	28.9
43. Rockville	39 46	87 10	1100	25.59	29.15	36.65	52.13	62.88	68.00	72.20	72.05	63.68	46.43	40.10	27.6
44. South Bend	41 39	86 12	600	21.14	29.14	35.38	46.99	61.07	68.93	72.47	71.34	62.60	47.81	38.74	29.7
45. Spiceland	39 51	85 26	1025	25.57	30.62	36.69	50.36	60.28	70.55	74.74	71.29	64.36	49.47	40.13	29.2
46. Vevay	38 45	85 05	525	29.38	35.76	43.47	56.13	63.78	74.62	79.09	75.51	69.35	53.89	42.90	32.3
47. Warsaw	41 14	85 52	..	..	..	..	..	..	..	..	..	..	..	..	29.9
INDIAN TERRITORY.															
1. Armstrong Acad.[5]	34 07	96 12	..	47.36	46.56	53.22	63.02	69.90	77.08	80.72	82.56	74.24	66.17	53.19	42.1
2. Baptist Mission	35 00	97 00	..	..	..	..	..	..	..	..	..	..	..	47.75	38.5
3. Caney[6]	..	..	..	..	..	53.42	64.83	70.05	76.40	82.23	76.03	68.97	55.90	43.23	..
4. Fort Arbuckle	34 29	97 17	1000	38.09	45.14	53.35	61.33	69.95	77.12	82.29	81.24	73.76	61.61	49.65	39.0
5. Fort Gibson	35 48	95 20	560	38.81	41.83	51.50	62.53	69.21	76.33	80.84	80.22	73.43	61.29	49.61	40.1
6. Fort Sill	34 45	98 38	..	..	..	..	62.83	73.21	77.23	82.14	78.64	74.99	56.17	46.97	..
7. Fort Towson	34 00	95 12	300	42.96	45.91	53.31	63.85	69.53	76.67	80.56	79.53	72.36	60.84	50.08	42.3
8. Fort Washita	34 11	96 38	645	41.69	47.30	54.01	63.27	70.39	76.72	81.21	80.97	74.80	62.64	51.62	41.6
9. Good Water Mission	33	95 25	..	..	..	..	..	..	83.60	94.43	..	..	..	..	..
10. Lee's Creek	35 30	94 30	..	..	..	48.70	..	..	..	..	..	..	..	..	..
IOWA.															
1. Algona	43 05	94 15	1500	11.69	17.93	26.60	42.15	58.15	67.51	71.62	68.47	59.64	44.51	31.59	19.5
2. Algona (ten miles S. W. of)	42 55	94 17	1500	10.82	16.04	21.10	41.70	55.20	66.79	72.58	67.28	56.12	44.75	31.98	17.9
3. Ames (six miles N. of)	42 07	93 35	790	..	..	26.40	..	..	..	..	..	62.63	..	..	..
4. Atalissa	41 31	91 08	..	..	25.19	24.13	44.98	50.08	..	..	..	..	..	..	..
5. Bangor	42 10	93 09	..	26.58	..	35.03	50.35	62.88	..	73.68	71.90	61.95	..	..	..
6. Bellevue	42 15	90 25	..	16.98	22.53	34.38	43.96	58.26	68.49	73.44	69.51	61.41	49.21	33.64	20.1

[1] This series includes observations in Sept. Oct. and Nov. 1858, and May, 1859, at *Notre Dame*, about three and half miles N. W. of *Mishawaka*.

[2] Observations in Feb. March, April, and May, 1868, were made at *Carthage*, about one and half miles S. E. of *Mount Hope*.

[3] Observations from May to August, 1849, both inclusive, were made at *Walnut Hills*, about one and half miles N. W. of *Richmond*.

INDIANA.—Continued.

	Spring.	Summer.	Autumn.	Winter.	Year.	Series. Begins. Ends.	Extent yrs. mos.	Observing hours.	Observer.	References.
28	50°.66	75°.89	53°.69	30°.98	52°.81	June, 1866; Dec. 1870	4 3	$7_m\ 2_a\ 9_a$ bis	T. Holmes, and B. F. McHenry.	S. O.
29	45.71	70.41	49.09	27.06	48.07	Jan. 1857; Sept. 1860	2 9	$7_m\ 2_a\ 9_a$	C. S. Woodward, W. Woodbridge, and H. Blake.	P. O. and S. I. Vol. I, and MS. from U. S. Lake Survey.
30	51.13	73.26	53.38	30.34	52.03	Jan. 1853; Dec. 1855	3 0	"	Dr. V. Kersey.	P. O. & S. I. Vol. I, and S. Coll.
31	..	69.67	52.37	..	..	Sept. 1858; Oct. 1859	0 10	"	G. C. Meinfield, and T. Vagnier.	P. O. and S. I. Vol. I.
32	50.99	74.35	52.24	30.62	52.05	June, 1869; Dec. 1870	1 7	$7_m\ 2_a\ 9_a$ bis	J. A. Applegate and daughter.	S. O.
33	50.00	73.24	52.08	29.94	51.32	Feb. 1868; Dec. 1870	2 6	"	C. M. Hobbs and D. Deem.	" "
34	48.37	72.21	50.49	28.55	49.90	Oct. 1863; May, 1870	4 7	"	E. J. Rice and Dr. G. W. H. Kemper.	" "
35	51.16	73.91	54.63	33.94	53.41	Apr. 1856; Mar. 1869	4 3	"	C. Barnes, and D. E. L. Crozier.	S. O. and P. O. and S. I. Vol. I.
36	58.75	76.90	54.88	37.67	57.05	1826; 1828	2 5	......	Troost.	Dove, 1857.
37	54.85	75.92	55.87	34.25	55.22	1850; Dec. 1870	19 5	$7_m\ 2_a\ 9_a$ bis	J. Chapell Smith.	P. O. and S. I. Vol. I, S. O., and S. Coll.
38	..	..	..	..	..	Nov. 1851; Nov. 1853	1 3	$7_m\ 2_a\ 9_a$	Roberts.	S. Coll.
39	52.58	70.75	..	24.13	..	May, 1864; Aug. 1865	0 1	$7_m\ 2_a\ 9_a$ bis	Miriam Griest.	S. O.
40	47.18	72.48	49.90	25.22	48.70	July, 1864; Oct. 1870	3 11	"	Dr. J. H. Loughridge.	" "
41	50.02	71.79	52.52	29.16	50.87	1849; Aug. 1868	12 3	[4]	W. W. Austin, J. Moore, J. Haines, E. W. Rambo, J. Valentine.	P. O. and S. I. Vol. I, S. O., & S. Coll.
42	49.03	71.20	52.43	27.77	50.11	Jan. 1862; Dec. 1866	5 0	......	H. H. Anderson.	MS. in S. Coll.
43	50.55	70.75	50.07	27.46	49.71	Jan. 1860; Dec. 1864	1 4	$7_m\ 2_a\ 9_a$ bis	H. H. and Mary A. Anderson.	S. O.
44	47.81	70.91	49.72	26.67	48.78	May, 1862; June, 1865	3 0	"	J. H. Dayton, R. Burroughs.	" "
45	49.11	72.10	51.33	28.47	50.37	May, 1863; Dec. 1870	7 8	"	W. Dawson.	" "
46	54.46	76.41	55.38	32.48	54.68	Aug. 1864; Dec. 1870	5 11	"	C. G. Boerner.	" "
47	..	..	..	..	..	1870	0 1	"	G. R. Thralls.	" "

INDIAN TERRITORY.

	Spring.	Summer.	Autumn.	Winter.	Year.	Series. Begins. Ends.	Extent yrs. mos.	Observing hours.	Observer.	References.
1	62.05	80.12	64.53	45.35	63.01	1850; 1853	2 5	$\odot_r\ 9_m\ 3_a\ 9_a$	Brown.	S. Coll.
2	..	..	..	..	..	1860	0 2	$7_m\ 2_a\ 9_a$ bis	H. F. Buckner.	S. O.
3	62.77	78.22	56.03	..	..	1860	0 9	$7_m\ 2_a\ 9_a$	J. B. Hitchcock.	" "
4	61.54	80.22	61.67	40.76	61.05	Oct. 1850; Aug. 1870	12 2	[4]	Assistant Surgeon.	Ar. Met. Regs. 1855 and 1860, and MS. from S. G. O.
5	61.08	79.13	61.44	40.25	60.48	July, 1827; June, 1857	29 10	[4]	" "	Ar. Met. Regs. 1855 and 1860, and S. Coll.
6	..	79.34	59.38	..	..	1870	0 8	$7_m\ 2_a\ 9_a$	" "	MS. from S. G. O.
7	62.23	78.92	61.09	43.74	61.50	Jan. 1832; Apr. 1854	18 3	[4]	" "	Ar. Met. Reg. 1855.
8	62.56	79.63	63.02	43.53	62.18	Jan. 1843; Mar. 1861	16 3	[4]	" "	Ar. Met. Regs. 1855 and 1860, and MS. from S. G. O.
9	..	..	..	..	..	1860	0 2	$7_m\ 2_a\ 9_a$ bis	S. McBeth.	S. O.
10	..	..	..	..	..	1861	0 1	$7_m\ 2_a\ 9_a$	J. B. Hitchcock.	" "

IOWA.

	Spring.	Summer.	Autumn.	Winter.	Year.	Series. Begins. Ends.	Extent yrs. mos.	Observing hours.	Observer.	References.
1	42.30	69.20	45.25	16.39	43.29	June, 1861; Dec. 1870	7 8	$7_m\ 2_a\ 9_a$ bis	Dr. F. McCoy and daughter, and J. H. Warren.	S. O.
2	39.33	68.88	44.28	14.93	41.86	Sept. 1866; Aug. 1870	3 10	"	P. Dorweiler.	" "
3	..	..	..	..	..	Sept. 1869; Mar. 1870	0 2	"	J. M. Cotton.	" "
4	39.73	..	..	..	..	1867	0 4	"	B. Carpenter.	" "
5	49.42	..	..	..	..	Aug. 1861; July, 1862	0 7	"	J. M. Gidley.	" "
6	45.53	70.48	48.09	19.89	46.00	Jan. 1856; Aug. 1860	4 6	"	J. C. Tory.	P. O. and S. I, Vol. I. and S. O.

[4] Observations corrected for daily variation by means of the general table.

[5] Observations at $7_m\ 2_a\ 9_a$ after March, 1853. No correction for change of hours has been applied.

[6] Also called "Eh-yoh-hee."

IOWA.—Continued.

Name of Station.	Lat.	Long.	Height.	Jan.	Feb.	March.	April.	May.	June.	July.	August.	Sept.	Oct.	Nov.	Dec.
7. Booneshoro . . .	42°04′	93°55′	1160	15°.64	21°.94	31°.68	44°.62	62°.44	67°.70	76°.45	65°.82	59°.47	44°.68	35°.26	23°.29
8. Border Plains . .	42 24	94 05	..	18.47	20.09	35.54	41.93	57.84	69.89	76.05	72.37	64.57	51.25	34.10	20.20
9. Bowen's Prairie .	42 16	91 09	800	20.92	23.93	29.41	47.44	60.84	69.15	72.22	69.47	60.85	45.27	34.68	21.19
10. Burlington . . .	40 49	91 07	600	25.91	30.39	45.93	47.65	65.02	68.63	78.59	74.24	63.66	50.60	41.23	24.48
11. Brookside[1] . . .	42 25	92 00	..	15.32	19.92	27.65	45.50	58.99	68.33	73.54	69.38	61.39	46.36	33.77	19.08
12. Ceres	42 49	91 12	825	13.75	18.44	28.90	44.01	56.55	68.67	71.55	69.54	63.41	50.69	38.19	20.49
13. Clarinda	40 44	95 02	..	23.48	24.03	..	..	..	..	..	..	..	..	..	25.88
14. Clinton (or Lyons[2])	41 50	90 10	630	20.69	24.20	32.19	47.45	58.65	68.79	73.74	71.43	63.46	49.33	36.81	25.06
15. Council Bluffs . .	41 16	95 51	1327	18.43	27.14	37.26	52.37	62.90	73.77	76.24	76.44	65.93	52.00	36.45	20.60
16. Dakota	42 43	94 12	..	7.07	16.59	23.64	38.32	51.29	67.90	70.62	70.32	60.53	49.33	36.73	19.23
17. Davenport . . .	41 30	90 39	737	19.18	24.09	32.21	46.30	59.07	69.60	74.21	70.98	62.88	48.38	37.12	23.98
18. Des Moines City[3] .	41 36	93 38	780	23.51	26.67	35.59	54.47	59.92	67.91	76.27	71.23	62.32	46.57	36.88	26.00
19. Dubuque	42 30	90 40	680	20.31	23.62	33.57	48.02	60.40	70.14	74.22	70.76	63.18	48.76	35.55	23.71
20. Fairfield	41 01	91 57	940	21.0	23.0	35.0	61.0	68.0	69.0	75.0	72.0	70.0	52.0	33.0	20.0
21. Fairfield	41 01	91 57	940	23.28	25.56	38.43	47.14	59.49	71.08	77.07	72.32	64.40	52.47	35.38	26.24
22. Fayette Village . .	42 51	91 51	1000	..	23.35	38.78	46.80	61.48	66.55	69.85	66.68	57.85	45.94	33.06	11.26
23. Forrestville . . .	42 40	91 32	..	14.12	19.66	32.45	46.76	57.66	65.27	70.72	68.32	58.45	49.32	33.53	21.73
24. Fort Atkinson . .	43 09	92 00	700	20.95	20.12	29.43	49.73	58.38	64.77	72.47	68.57	61.30	45.40	31.02	20.14
25. Fort Croghan . .	41 21	95 23	1250	24.90	13.78	12.86	48.63	58.22	68.25	73.77	69.46	63.80	..	..	..
26. Fort Dodge . . .	42 31	94 12	944	15.66	21.70	27.07	42.49	58.15	71.13	76.36	71.62	62.61	51.44	33.43	19.56
27. Fort Madison[4] . .	40 37	91 28	600	23.12	27.56	37.56	49.85	62.57	72.81	77.58	73.81	65.59	52.28	38.65	25.70
28. Franklin	42 45	92 11	..	15.64	21.22	33.03	43.82	57.35	69.68	73.33	69.29	61.59	50.74	32.93	20.25
29. Grant City . . .	42 15	94 53	..	17.70	22.92	25.42	46.97	62.74	69.62	75.46	71.49	62.90	44.48	34.02	22.34
30. Guttenberg . . .	42 46	91 09	690	14.06	20.82	27.74	43.33	56.34	66.37	71.25	65.94	57.56	44.94	33.95	19.22
31. Guttenberg (near) .	42 46	91 14	800	15.87	20.64	25.88	44.80	59.33	68.55	66.28	69 90	64.98	46.56	34.92	16.77
32. Harris Grove[5] . .	41 39	95 47	900	18.19	26.74	30.67	45.76	58.55	66.83	74.13	69.30	60.48	49.79	37.54	24.44
33. Hesper	43 30	91 46	720	13.23	19.90	26.80	..	..	..	69.38	67.35	56.88	49.00	30.40	17.50
34. Independence . .	42 29	91 57	850	15.38	21.82	27.31	45.61	59.01	68.57	73.72	69.15	61.19	46.15	35.20	20.35
35. Iowa City . . .	41 37	91 30	621	19.94	23.32	32.50	47.35	58.84	68.90	73.64	71.22	63.86	49.00	35.99	24.80
36. Iowa Falls[6] . . .	42 32	93 21	..	15.56	21.99	26.68	45.20	59.67	70.05	74.66	70.80	63.31	47.89	34.65	20.65
37. Keokuk	40 25	91 21	600	26.53	32.37	39.09	50.37	60.82	73.13	76.43	74.74	67.41	55.60	39.13	29.21
38. Lizard	42 30	94 25	..	..	24.63	..	..	..	..	..	..	..	..	..	..
39. Manchester . . .	42 29	91 38	925	19.40	14.98	25.55	46.90	56.00	63.73	71.55	63.13	61.00	47.66	35.43	17.27
40. Maquoketa . . .	42 04	90 41	..	..	26.42	34.94	..	..	..	..	..	..	..	..	..
41. Marble Rock . .	42 58	92 52	..	..	..	..	..	..	70.00	71.08	70.90	61.60	52.28	40.63	20.75
42. Mineral Ridge . .	42 11	93 55	1200	20.23	25.93	28.20	45.20	..	..	71.65	74.32	63.28	41.83	31.23	25.78
43. Monticello . . .	42 15	91 15	880	16.26	22.47	29.53	46.62	58.80	68.14	73.48	69.03	60.63	46.52	35.03	19.91
44. Mount Vernon . .	41 58	91 28	..	17.63	22.25	30.40	46.95	58.57	68.34	73.11	69.48	61.76	47.89	34.99	20.98
45. Muscatine . . .	41 26	91 05	586	20.69	24.76	34.58	48.25	58.25	67.09	71.22	68.94	62.12	49.09	35.21	23.52
46. Mount Pleasant .	42 57	91 37	..	19.41	28.68	33.56	46.08	62.75	72.10	76.93	72.87	66.71	46.58	33.85	22.72
47. Newton	41 42	93 03	1400	20.15	..	..	..	..	..	..	71.23	60.45	40.80	30.63	22.65
48. North Union (near)[7]	42 58	91 50	1250	19.95	22.89	27.52	49.24	63.74	69.99	74.69	71.26	64.39	45.64	35.14	20.92
49. Onowa City . . .	42 02	96 09	1000	..	28.33	31.23	44.05	59.00	72.65	74.48	71.33	68.03	..	..	..
50. Osage	43 17	92 49	..	9.58	17.20	..	45.80	57.75	67.78	76.29	66.50	55.96	49.50	..	19.10
51. Pella	41 30	92 55	730	17.35	22.36	32.33	49.78	59.92	69.58	74.07	71.19	63.83	49.90	33.01	22.16
52. Pleasant Plain . .	41 07	91 55	950	20.08	24.94	35.50	46.76	61.49	71.07	74.75	72.10	64.47	49.79	35.09	24.16
53. Poultney	42 40	91 21	..	12.62	16.57	31.41	48.05	60.32	67.29	71.78	69.69	63.12	47.16	33.77	20.99
54. Quasqueton . . .	42 23	91 23	888	13.06	16.38	28.51	51.30	61.02	70.70	74.97	71.39	65.77	50.03	33.66	22.03
55. Rockford . . .	43 03	92 56	..	7.38	18.28	37.63	..	..	..	..	67.48	54.35	46.98	34.03	18.90
56. Rolfe	42 50	94 28	..	12.17	17.57	29.01	43.13	60.97	68.12	75.19	69.39	56.45	42.44	29.49	18.44
57. Rossville	43 10	91 21	1400	22.17	18.27	36.92	40.40	55.51	66.05	72.32	71.11	59.40	46.64	31.29	19.66
58. Sac City	42 25	95 00	900	..	..	..	49.64	63.77	..	..	..	..	48.54	39.14	22.00
59. Sioux City . . .	42 35	96 27	1258	16.67	19.29	32.85	43.27	56.99	69.17	71.72	70.13	62.16	47.32	29.10	24.05
60. St. Mary's . . .	41 00	95 45	1200	17.01	32.41	..	..	..	..	..	..	..	..	41.60	31.00

[1] Also called *Byron*. [2] Observations in 1857–58 were made at *Camanche*, about three miles southwest from *Clinton*.
[3] Observations previous to 1865 were made at *Fort Des Moines*, about two miles east of *Des Moines City*.

IOWA.—Continued.

	Spring.	Summer.	Autumn.	Winter.	Year.	Series. Begins.	Series. Ends.	Extent yrs. mos.	Observing hours.	Observer.	References.
7	46°.25	69°.99	46°.47	20°.29	45°.75	Nov. 1867;	Dec. 1870	2 6	$7_m\ 2_a\ 9_a$ bis	E. Babcock.	S. O.
8	45.10	72.77	49.97	19.59	46.86	July, 1856;	Sept. 1859	3 3	$7_m\ 2_a\ 9_a$	W. K. Goss.	P. O. and S. I. Vol. I.
9	45.90	79.28	46.93	22.01	46.28	Feb. 1853;	Dec. 1870	3 3	$7_m\ 2_a\ 9_a$ bis	S. Woodworth, Bidwell, and Farwell.	S. O. and S. Coll.
10	52.87	73.82	51.83	26.93	51.36	Feb. 1859;	May, 1868	1 9	“	J. M. Corse, and L. P. Love.	P. O. and S. I. Vol. I, and S. O.
11	44.05	70.42	47.17	18.11	44.94	Apr. 1862;	Dec. 1870	8 3	“	A. C. Wheaton.	S. O.
12	43.15	69.92	50.76	17.56	45.35	May, 1865;	May, 1868	3 1	“	J. M. Hagensick.	“ “
13	..	..	..	24.46	..	Jan. 1865;	Feb. 1866	0 3	“	Dr. S. H. Kridelbaugh.	“ “
14	46.10	71.32	49.87	23.32	47.65	Apr. 1856;	Dec. 1870	10 5	“	N. H. Parker.	P. O. and S. I. Vol. I, and S. O.
15	50.84	75.48	51.46	22.06	49.96	Jan. 1820;	Dec. 1825	6 0	$7_m\ 2_a\ 9_a$	Assistant Surgeon.	Army Register.
16	37.75	69.61	48.86	14.30	42.63	Apr. 1867;	Mar. 1868	1 0	$7_m\ 2_a\ 9_a$ bis	W. O. Atkinson.	S. O.
17	45.86	71.60	49.46	22.42	47.33	Apr. 1858;	Dec. 1870	9 3	“	A. J. Finley, W. P. Dunwoody, J. Chamberlain, D. S. Sheldon.	P. O. and S. I. Vol. I, and S. O.
18	49.99	71.80	48.59	25.39	48.94	Oct. 1843;	June, 1867	3 10	“	J. A. Nash, & Assist. Surg.	Ar. Met. Reg. 1855, and S. O.
19	47.33	71.71	49.16	22.55	47.69	Jan. 1851;	Dec. 1870	18 10	“	Asa Horr.	MS. in S. Coll., S. O., P. O. and S. I. Vol. I, and S. Coll.
20	54.67	72.00	51.67	21.33	49.92	1855		1 0	......	Dr. J. M. Schaffer.	P. O. and S. I. Vol. I.
21	48.35	73.49	50.79	25.03	49.41	Apr. 1856;	Dec. 1859	3 7	$7_m\ 2_a\ 9_a$	“ “ “	“ “ “ “
22	49.02	67.69	45.62	..	..	Oct. 1859;	Nov. 1860	1 1	$7_m\ 2_a\ 9_a$ bis	J. M. McKenzie.	P. O. and S. I. Vol. I, and S. O.
23	45.62	68.10	47.10	18.51	44.83	June, 1859;	Apr. 1863	3 2	“	D. Sheldon.	“ “ “ “ “
24	45.85	68.60	45.91	20.40	45.19	Jan. 1842;	May, 1846	4 5	$\odot_r\ 9_m\ 3_a\ 9_a$	Assistant Surgeon.	Ar. Met. Reg. 1855.
25	39.90	70.49	..	..	..	Jan. 1843;	Oct. 1843	0 9	“	“ “	“ “ “
26	42.57	73.04	49.16	18.97	45.94	Aug. 1851;	Mar. 1869	4 1	$7_m\ 2_a\ 9_a$ bis	Assistant Surgeon and C. N. Jorgenson.	Ar. Met. Reg. 1855, and S. O.
27	49.99	74.73	52.17	25.46	50.59	Mar. 1848;	Dec. 1870	21 10	6_m N. 7_a	D. McCready.	MS. in S. Coll., S. O., and P. O. and S. I. Vol. I.
28	44.73	70.77	48.42	19.04	45.74	May, 1856;	Apr. 1862	4 4	$7_m\ 2_a\ 9_a$	D. and Mrs. C. Beal.	P. O. and S. I. Vol. I, and S. O.
29	45.04	72.19	47.13	20.99	46.34	Jan. 1869;	Dec. 1870	1 11	$7_m\ 2_a\ 9_a$ bis	E. Miller and wife.	S. O.
30	42.47	67.85	45.48	18.03	43.46	July, 1866;	Dec. 1870	4 6	“	J. P. Dickinson.	“ “
31	43.34	68.24	48.82	17.76	44.54	Aug. 1864;	Mar. 1866	1 7	“	P. Dorweiler.	“ “
32	44.99	70.09	49.27	23.12	46.87	May, 1866;	Dec. 1870	4 5	“	J. T. Stern.	“ “
33	..	..	45.43	16.88	..	July, 1860;	Mar. 1861	0 9	“	H. B. Williams.	“ “
34	43.98	70.48	47.51	19.18	45.29	Nov. 1861;	Dec. 1870	7 4	“	D. S. Deering.	“ “
35	46.23	71.25	49.62	22.69	47.45	May, 1856;	Dec. 1870	11 6	“	Prof. T. S. Parvin, H. H. Fairall, Dr. W. Reynolds.	Printed Slip, S. Coll., P. O. & S. I. Vol. I, and S. O.
36	43.85	71.86	48.62	19.40	45.93	Nov. 1863;	Dec. 1870	6 9	“	N. Townsend.	S. O.
37	50.09	74.77	54.05	29.37	52.07	1851;	Jan. 1855	2 5	$\odot_r\ 9_m\ 3_a\ 9_a$	Dr. and Mrs. J. E. Ball.	P. O. & S. I. Vol. I, & S. Coll.
38	..	..	..	..	..	1869		0 1	$7_m\ 2_a\ 9_a$ bis	J. J. Bruce.	S. O.
39	42.82	66.14	48.03	17.22	43.55	Sept. 1865;	Nov. 1866	1 3	“	A. Mead.	“ “
40	..	..	..	..	..	1857		0 2	$\odot_r$ N. 10_a	E. F. Hobart.	P. O. and S. I. Vol. I.
41	..	70.66	51.50	..	..	1867		0 7	$7_m\ 2_a\ 9_a$ bis	H. Wadey.	S. O.
42	..	..	45.45	23.98	..	Apr. 1869;	Mar. 1870	0 10	“	A. L. Sullivan.	“ “
43	44.98	70.22	47.39	19.55	45.54	July, 1864;	Dec. 1870	6 2	“	C. Mead.	“ “
44	45.31	70.31	48.21	20.29	46.03	Oct. 1856;	Dec. 1870	10 1	“	Profs. B. W. Smith and A. Collier.	P. O. and S. I. Vol. I. and S. O.
45	47.03	69.08	48.81	22.99	46.98	Jan. 1839;	Nov. 1870	27 6	“	T. S. Parvin.	Am. Alm. 1839 and foll., MS. in S. Coll., P. O. and S. I. Vol. I, and S. O.
46	47.46	73.97	49.05	23.60	48.52	Dec. 1863;	Sept. 1864	0 10	“	Rev. E. L. Briggs and daughter.	S. O.
47	..	..	43.96	..	..	Aug. 1869;	Jan. 1870	0 6	“	A. Failer.	“ “
48	46.83	71.98	48.39	21.25	47.11	Jan. 1869;	Dec. 1870	2 0	“	F. McClintock.	“ “
49	44.76	72.82	..	..	..	1864		0 8	“	Dr. R. Stebbins.	“ “
50	..	70.19	..	15.29	..	Apr. 1866;	Feb. 1867	0 10	“	A. Bush and F. Marsh.	“ “
51	47.34	71.61	48.91	20.62	47.12	Jan. 1852;	Mar. 1856	4 3	$7_m\ 2_a\ 9_a$	E. H. A. Scheeper.	P. O. and S. I. Vol. I, and MS. in S. Coll.
52	47.92	72.64	49.78	23.06	48.35	Jan. 1856;	Sept. 1865	9 6	$7_m\ 2_a\ 9_a$ bis	T. McConnell.	P. O. and S. I. Vol. I, and S. O.
53	46.59	69.59	48.02	16.73	45.23	July, 1853;	June, 1859	3 4	$7_m\ 2_a$ a9	Rev. B. F. Odell.	P. O. & S. I. Vol. I, & S. Coll.
54	46.94	72.35	49.82	17.16	46.57	Dec. 1853;	June, 1856	2 4	“	Dr. E. C. Bidwell.	“ “ “ “ “
55	..	..	45.12	14.85	..	1868		0 8	$7_m\ 2_a\ 9_a$ bis	H. Wadey.	S. O.
56	44.37	70.90	42.79	16.06	43.53	Feb. 1868;	Jan. 1870	2 0	“	O. J. Strong.	“ “
57	44.28	69.83	45.78	20.03	44.98	Nov. 1857;	Dec. 1859	2 0	$7_m\ 2_a\ 9_a$	C. D. Beeman.	P. O. and S. I. Vol. I.
58	..	..	..	..	..	1870		0 5	$7_m\ 2_a\ 9_a$ bis	D. B. Nelson.	S. O.
59	44.37	70.34	46.19	20.00	45.22	Aug. 1857;	Mar. 1863	3 6	“	Dr. J. J. Saville and A. J. Millard.	MS. from S. G. O., S. O., and P. O. and S. I. Vol. I.
60	..	..	..	26.81		Nov. 1853;	Feb. 1854	0 4	$7_m\ 2_a\ 9_a$	D. E. Read.	P. O. & S. I. Vol. I, & S. Coll.

[4] Four miles northwest from town on the Bluff Prairie.

[5] Also called *Logan*.

[6] Also called *Spring Grove*.

[7] The observations in 1870 were made at *West Union*, two miles west of *North Union*.

IOWA.—Continued.

Name of Station.	Lat.	Long.	Height.	Jan.	Feb.	March.	April.	May.	June.	July.	August.	Sept.	Oct.	Nov.	Dec.
61. Vawter's Grove[1]	41°18′	94°34′	1500	17°.02	24°.87	29°.46	46°.16	59°.53	69°.96	75°.87	70°.56	60°.29	48°.79	36°.60	22°.88
62. Vernon Springs	43 20	92 12	..	..	17.83	28.15	50.61	57.36	64.48	70.00	69.85	61.28	47.05	29.05	23.63
63. Vinton	42 10	92 02	607	..	..	..	..	60.68	66.65	72.68	73.43	61.70	41.30	31.43	23.58
64. Waukon	43 16	91 29	..	15.00	19.90	25.83	45.85	59.13	65.58	..	68.20	58.28	36.95	28.76	17.70
65. Washington	41 17	91 45	..	..	..	..	..	..	..	..	74.25	68.22	..	..	..
66. Waterloo	42 31	92 24	666	17.46	21.76	28.48	45.24	58.17	67.46	72.68	68.56	60.75	47.29	35.99	20.67
67. Webster City	42 28	93 49	1500	18.10	24.28	26.28	49.76	63.75	69.93	75.28	66.65	62.95	47.48	32.56	21.15
68. Whiteboro	41 40	95 44	..	8.48	22.43	39.93	42.23	62.25	69.55	80.20	65.90	53.38	48.05	33.55	20.19
69. Woodbine	41 45	95 42	..	20.24	25.98	28.03	47.57	61.21	67.22	72.81	69.96	61.13	43.47	36.21	23.04
70. Woodlands, The	43 00	93 00	..	19.24	22.38	25.68	49.09	61.97	69.27	73.58	68.37	62.01	46.00	34.67	23.52

KANSAS.

Name of Station.	Lat.	Long.	Height.	Jan.	Feb.	March.	April.	May.	June.	July.	August.	Sept.	Oct.	Nov.	Dec.
1. Atchison	39 34	95 08	1000	23.61	30.15	35.40	51.80	62.28	72.40	77.76	74.41	66.80	53.08	41.07	27.41
2. Avon[2]	38 12	95 35	775	..	..	..	58.43	61.20	70.28	..	..	..	..	..	..
3. Baxter Springs	37 01	94 44	..	33.26	38.46	46.85	57.20	69.33	76.43	82.65	79.75	71.75	58.49	47.04	34.84
4. Burlingame	38 45	95 45	..	30.22	32.47	45.90	52.72	64.65	73.37	78.68	75.10	67.86	55.69	40.15	27.04
5. Council City	38 42	95 50	..	35.70	29.58	35.23	41.59	55.78	72.05	80.38	74.51	..	..	..	..
6. Council Grove	38 40	96 30	1480	28.27	34.70	38.99	52.99	63.94	73.03	79.22	76.72	67.49	55.77	44.77	30.72
7. Crawfordsville (ne'r)	37 31	94 55	..	31.93	40.58	43.58	..	66.88	69.83	75.04	77.85	..	45.53	42.95	31.45
8. Douglas	37 33	97 01	..	..	..	..	..	..	..	..	74.34	66.77	56.30	45.87	30.91
9. Douner's Station	38 48	99 51	..	..	32.63	45.56	49.06	64.53	..	..	..	..	57.17	44.27	40.04
10. Emporia	38 25	96 12	..	..	..	..	..	65.98	..	..	..	..	..	..	..
11. Fort Atkinson (Ark. Riv.)	37 47	100 14	2330	33.43	35.18	44.61	55.15	64.81	73.02	79.21	79.13	70.73	56.98	36.24	27.52
12. Fort Dodge	37 30	100 00	..	30.89	38.38	44.00	53.95	66.83	73.13	82.63	76.96	67.50	55.56	44.81	34.14
13. Fort Harker[3]	38 44	98 15	..	26.93	34.55	32.64	54.24	64.91	73.70	79.33	72.47	63.32	56.23	43.53	24.79
14. Fort Hays	38 59	99 20	2107	30.28	36.43	41.16	51.91	66.07	75.60	81.74	78.22	67.88	52.51	43.94	32.45
15. Fort Larned	38 10	98 57	1932	28.03	35.97	36.09	53.57	65.97	75.22	79.85	77.10	69.56	56.10	43.32	31.03
16. Fort Leavenworth[4]	39 21	94 54	896	27.43	31.29	41.62	54.76	64.69	72.70	77.94	75.09	67.51	54.79	40.76	29.33
17. Fort Riley (Kans. Riv.)	39 03	96 35	1300	25.28	32.63	41.81	55.15	66.73	75.83	81.69	78.45	71.02	56.30	41.69	28.78
18. Fort Scott	37 45	94 45	1000	32.73	34.98	43.13	55.72	65.44	72.11	77.22	75.53	68.62	55.28	41.92	31.09
19. Gardner	38 47	95 00	800	..	27.15	42.15	58.58	70.50	78.53	80.64	78.68	70.66	59.60	41.38	33.18
20. Holton	39 27	95 48	1172	24.87	32.04	40.02	52.07	64.05	74.14	80.78	75.45	65.35	51.90	40.42	29.00
21. Junction City	39 02	96 51	..	..	..	..	47.93	67.03	76.73	..	..	..	..	..	..
22. Lawrence	38 58	95 12	850	30.44	33.19	43.70	52.57	64.03	72.96	78.98	75.52	66.85	52.15	40.24	31.30
23. Leavenworth City[5]	39 15	94 52	896	26.09	29.67	38.77	52.25	61.59	71.97	77.21	73.54	64.48	52.38	39.19	30.32
24. Lecompton	39 03	95 09	825	24.35	35.69	50.13	58.25	..	..	79.94	78.16	69.29	57.59	43.83	25.07
25. Le Roy	38 03	95 37	..	30.95	36.63	35.95	54.74	63.05	70.05	79.00	81.73	67.13	48.44	39.78	31.65
26. Manhattan[6]	39 13	96 39	1000	26.85	31.20	40.68	51.55	63.62	73.95	79.63	75.85	67.08	53.82	40.67	29.72
27. Mapleton	38 04	94 51	..	38.88	..	..	..	63.17	76.22	82.93	79.74	70.87	..	..	37.19
28. Moneka	38 19	94 49	..	..	..	..	..	70.55	72.09	82.76	69.40	68.87	..	..	..
29. Mountain City	..	..	..	20.80	30.40	32.07	..	..	..	..	55.48	49.65	39.85	31.10	27.53
30. Neosho Falls	38 03	95 31	..	29.54	35.11	42.89	55.62	65.57	73.98	79.13	77.98	69.39	52.23	41.85	27.90
31. Olatha	38 53	94 51	..	24.84	32.29	37.17	50.73	61.16	71.89	77.48	74.12	65.41	52.30	40.71	27.16
32. Paola (three and a half miles N. W. of)	37 36	94 57	875	30.45	35.65	38.50	56.55	65.28	71.10	77.60	76.47	66.51	51.24	42.09	30.09
33. Topeka	39 03	95 39	..	..	23.81	48.13	53.69	62.23	75.24	..	..	..	..	..	..
34. Williamstown	39 03	95 20	915	..	..	..	..	..	..	..	73.85	68.90	57.10	45.88	29.65
35. Wyandotte City	39 08	94 40	707	32.05	36.10	48.53	..	..	..	..	76.82	68.91	54.89	45.92	21.71

[1] Also called *Fontanelle*. [2] Also called "near Burlington." [3] Also called Ellsworth.

[4] Observations in April, 1858, at Cayuga, about five miles northwest of Fort Leavenworth, are included in this series.

IOWA.—Continued.

	Spring.	Summer.	Autumn.	Winter.	Year.	Series. Begins.	Ends.	Extent yrs. mos.	Observing hours.	Observer.	References.
51	45°.05	72°.13	48°.56	21°.59	46°.83	May, 1866;	Dec. 1870	4 8	$7_m\ 2_a\ 9_a$ bis	A. F. Bryant.	S. O.
52	45.37	68.11	45.79	..	..	Apr. 1861;	June, 1863	1 1	"	G. Marshall.	" "
53	..	70.92	40.81	..	..	1869		0 8	"	J. Wood.	" "
54	43.60	..	41.33	17.53	..	Apr. 1869;	Dec. 1870	1 3	"	E. M. Hancock.	" "
55	..	..	..	..	..	1861		0 2	"	....	" "
56	43.96	69.57	48.01	19.96	45.38	Jan. 1863;	Aug. 1870	6 5	"	L. H. Doyle.	" "
57	46.60	70.62	47.66	21.18	46.51	1870		0 9	"	C. L. Croft.	" "
58	48.14	71.88	44.99	17.03	45.51	Dec. 1867;	Nov. 1868	1 0	"	D. R. Witter.	" "
59	45.60	70.00	46.94	23.09	46.41	Jan. 1869;	Dec. 1870	1 9	"	" " "	" "
60	45.58	70.41	47.56	21.71	46.31	Jan. 1869;	Dec. 1870	2 0	"	H. Wadey.	" "

KANSAS.

	Spring.	Summer.	Autumn.	Winter.	Year.	Series. Begins.	Ends.	Extent yrs. mos.	Observing hours.	Observer.	References.
1	49.83	74.86	53.65	27.06	51.35	May, 1865;	Dec. 1870	5 2	$7_m\ 2_a\ 9_a$ bis	Dr. H. B. Horn and daughter.	S. O.
2	..	..	..	..	..	1866		0 3	"	A. Crocker.	" "
3	57.79	79.61	59.09	35.52	58.00	July, 1867;	Dec. 1870	3 6	"	Messrs. Ingraham & Hyland.	" "
4	54.42	75.72	54.57	29.91	53.66	Jan. 1858;	Mar. 1861	3 3	"	E. and L. Fish.	P. O. and S. I. Vol. 1, and S. O.
5	44.20	75.65	...	..	..	Feb. 1857;	Jan. 1858	0 8	$7_m\ 2_a\ 9_a$	E. Fish.	P. O. and S. I. Vol. 1.
6	51.97	76.32	56.01	31.23	53.88	Apr. 1865;	Dec. 1870	5 9	$7_m\ 2_a\ 9_a$ bis	Dr. A. Woodworth.	S. O.
7	..	74.24	..	34.65	..	June, 1869;	May, 1870	0 10	"	P. Daniels.	" "
8	..	..	56.31	..	..	1870		0 5	"	Dr. W. W. Lamb.	" "
9	53.05	..	..	..	..	Oct. 1867;	May, 1868	0 7	$7_m\ 2_a\ 9_a$	....	MS. from S. G. O.
10	..	..	..	..	..	1862		0 1	$7_m\ 2_a\ 9_a$ bis	C. F. Oakfield.	S. O.
11	54.86	77.12	54.65	32.04	54.67	Nov. 1850;	Sept. 1853	2 11	$\odot_r\ 9_m\ 3_a\ 9_a$	Assistant Surgeon.	Ar. Met. Reg. 1855.
12	54.93	77.57	55.96	34.47	55.73	Nov. 1867;	Dec. 1870	3 2	$7_m\ 2_a\ 9_a$	....	MS. from S. G. O.
13	50.60	75.17	54.36	28.76	52.22	Nov. 1866;	Dec. 1870	1 6	"	....	" " "
14	53.05	78.52	54.78	33.05	54.85	Aug. 1867;	Dec. 1870	3 5	"	....	" " "
15	51.88	77.39	56.33.	31.68	54.32	Sept. 1860;	Dec. 1870	9 9	"	......	" " "
16	53.69	75.24	54.35	29.35	53.16	Jan. 1830;	Dec. 1870	39 11	"	Assistant Surgeon.	MS. from S. G. O. and Ar. Met. Regs. 1855 and 1860.
17	54.56	78.66	56.34	28.90	54.62	Nov. 1853;	Dec. 1870	16 10	"	Assist. Surg., T. R. Drew, E. E. Lee, J. H. Prince, and J. Schaffer.	Ar. Met. Regs. 1855 and 1860, MS. from S. G. O. and S.O.
18	54.76	74.95	55.27	32.93	54.48	Jan. 1843;	Mar. 1853	10 3	$\odot_r\ 9_m\ 3_a\ 9_a$	Assistant Surgeon.	Ar. Met. Reg. 1855.
19	57.08	79.28	57.21	..	..	Apr. 1860;	Feb. 1862	1 3	$7_m\ 2_a\ 9_a$ bis	G. F. Merriam, J. Scott, J. S. Gardner.	S. O.
20	52.05	76.79	52.56	28.63	52.51	May, 1867;	Dec. 1870	3 8	"	Dr. J. Walters, W. H. Gilman.	P. O. and S. I. Vol. 1, and S. O.
21	..	..	..	..	..	1862		0 3	"	Dr. E. W. Seymour.	S. O.
22	53.43	75.82	53.08	31.64	53.49	July, 1857;	Dec. 1870	7 9	"	G. W. Brown, W. J. R. Blackburn, W. G. Soule, A. W. Fuller, G. W. Hollingsworth, Prof. F. H. Snow.	P. O. and S. I. Vol. 1, and S. O.
23	50.87	74.24	52.02	28.69	51.45	Nov. 1857;	Dec. 1870	7 6	"	H. D. McCarty, M. Shaw, Dr. J. Stayman, F. B. Stowell.	" " " " "
24	..	..	56.90	28.37	..	July, 1859;	Feb. 1861	1 1	"	Dr. W. T. Ellis.	" " " " "
25	51.25	76.93	51.78	33.08	53.26	Jan. 1867;	Apr. 1870	1 9	"	J. G. Shoemaker.	S. O.
26	51.95	76.48	53.86	29.26	52.89	Mar. 1857;	Dec. 1870	11 10	"	I. T. Goodnow, Rev. N. O. Preston, H. L. Denison, B. F. Mudge and wife.	P. O. and S. I. Vol. 1, and S. O.
27	..	79.63	..	..	..	Dec. 1857;	Sept. 1858	0 7	$7_m\ 2_a\ 9_a$	Dr. S. O. Himoe.	P. O. and S. I. Vol. 1.
28	..	74.75	..	..	..	1859		0 5	$7_m\ 2_a$	J. O. Wattles.	" " " "
29	..	..	40.20	26.24	..	Aug. 1860;	Mar. 1861	0 8	$7_m\ 2_a\ 9_a$ bis	Dr. W. T. Ellis.	S. O.
30	54.69	77.03	54.49	30.85	54.27	Mar. 1859;	Apr. 1870	3 9	"	B. F. Goss, Mrs. E. W. Groesbeck.	P. O. and S. I. Vol. 1, and S. O.
31	49.69	74.50	52.81	28.10	51.27	May, 1864;	Dec. 1870	6 7	"	W. Beckwith.	S. O.
32	53.44	75.06	53.28	32.06	53.46	May, 1869;	Dec. 1870	1 8	"	L. D. Walrad.	" "
33	54.68	..	..	..	..	1858		0 5	$7_m\ 2_a\ 9_a$	F. W. Giles.	P. O. and S. I. Vol. 1.
34	..	..	57.29	..	..	1870		0 5	$7_m\ 2_a\ 9_a$ bis	J. M. Cotton & wife.	S. O.
35	..	..	56.57	29.95	..	Aug. 1859;	Mar. 1860	0 8	"	J. H. Millar.	P.O. and S. I. Vol. 1, and S. O.

[5] This series includes observations made at the Leavenworth City High School in April, May, October, November, and December, 1868.

[6] Observations after 1864 were made at Manhattan College, about one mile southeast of Manhattan.

KENTUCKY.

Name of Station.	Lat.	Long.	Height.	Jan.	Feb.	March.	April.	May.	June.	July.	August.	Sept.	Oct.	Nov.	Dec.
1. Arcadia	37°34′	84°42′	900	36°.00	36°.18	40°.53	56°.25	67°.08	73°.15	74°.95	66°.45	65°.80	53°.21	42°.87	35°.5
2. Ballardsville	38 25	85 22	461	30.60	33.23	40.65	56.20	64.61	75.24	78.14	76.21	69.57	58.32	44.54	34.5
3. Bardstown (St. Jos. Coll.)	37 51	85 32	..	37.13	37.07	46.74	55.50	65.38	74.04	76.59	73.75	66.82	55.38	44.48	37.5
4. Beech Fork	37 45	85 12	..	..	..	..	..	..	72.28	77.13	75.50	64.23	55.10	39.88	31.2
5. Bowling Green	37 01	86 31	450	35.12	40.09	48.70	55.63	65.51	73.36	77.85	76.15	70.18	56.30	44.77	38.0
6. Chilesburg	38 04	84 18	900	31.30	36.41	42.68	54.36	61.30	70.36	76.28	72.94	67.42	53.49	43.54	33.7
7. Clinton	36 40	89 07	..	40.27	39.96	42.68	54.92	65.69	74.48	82.33	73.50	65.55	54.74	43.40	32.3
8. Danville	37 40	84 48	900	35.49	39.47	45.51	57.14	66.20	74.41	77.25	75.07	70.42	57.04	47.33	38.5
9. Lexington	38 07	84 32	950	..	..	..	..	..	69.85	74.98	72.67	68.54	51.15	47.59	..
10. Lebanon	37 37	85 17	717	..	..	..	54.59	64.18	..	77.24	73.35	..	49.70	46.28	..
11. London	37 08	84 08	1100	34.38	..	44.70	..	..	75.30	75.80	72.58	..	..	44.18	..
12. Louisville	38 18	85 50	450	36.37	37.22	47.09	54.50	65.54	70.72	75.94	75.23	69.08	55.42	42.88	38.4
13. Maysville	38 44	83 41	630	34.43	36.73	..	..	..	..	..	..	..	51.56	46.17	37.0
14. Millersburg	38 23	84 09	804	29.61	33.27	42.72	52.45	63.91	73.61	76.85	75.39	66.80	55.61	45.23	36.8
15. Newport Barracks	39 06	84 29	500	31.91	35.46	43.47	53.89	64.10	73.00	77.16	75.01	68.50	55.53	44.25	35.0
16. Nicholasville	37 56	84 38	940	35.78	38.03	42.67	54.35	63.77	70.21	73.54	74.57	68.81	57.05	44.39	40.9
17. Nolin	37 34	85 54	..	..	..	..	57.21	65.39	..	..	..	..	..	..	..
18. Ohio River[1]	39 04	84 40	812	..	..	..	..	60.10	75.45	72.22	73.95	66.60	..	..	..
19. Paris	38 15	84 17	810	27.83	34.70	41.17	51.39	62.06	70.76	75.62	71.88	64.54	53.14	41.49	34.8
20. Pleasant Valley M'ls	38 10	83 49	..	..	..	..	..	..	..	..	73.18	66.73	47.18	46.59	..
21. Prospect Hill	38 40	83 33	700	36.18	35.60	44.16	51.16	61.01	72.69	72.85	73.57	64.74	52.26	46.65	35.7
22. Springdale	38 07	85 44	570	32.08	36.23	43.39	54.01	62.39	70.35	74.43	72.48	66.89	53.29	43.73	35.1
23. Taylor Barracks	..	..	..	..	..	..	..	..	..	..	..	..	65.91	47.10	32.5
24. Taylorsville	38 02	85 25	600	..	..	..	..	63.75	74.85	80.35	..	..	..	..	..

LOUISIANA.

Name of Station.	Lat.	Long.	Height.	Jan.	Feb.	March.	April.	May.	June.	July.	August.	Sept.	Oct.	Nov.	Dec.
1. Baton Rouge	30 26	91 11	41	53.06	55.31	61.89	69.08	75.74	80.73	81.90	81.45	77.39	67.47	59.52	54.2
2. Benton	32 30	93 45	..	47.85	51.23	58.66	64.55	71.94	80.14	82.41	81.19	75.63	63.78	55.79	49.8
3. Black River Plant'n	31 30	91 46	108	49.05	57.74	61.47	64.46	74.44	79.33	81.77	82.23	75.21	66.45	53.27	52.2
4. Camp Lawrence	30 26	91 18	41	..	..	..	..	..	..	..	80.00	74.64	..	..	..
5. Camp Salubrity	31 40	93 15	80	53.75	60.00	60.50	70.50	73.00	80.00	85.75	80.59	75.51	65.25	57.75	49.7
6. Cheneyville (near)	31 00	92 18	..	..	..	59.10	67.10	75.55	79.10	81.18	81.60	79.33	..	..	..
7. Collins	30 30	90 20	20	..	..	..	..	..	..	..	..	..	..	59.73	49.7
8. Fort Jackson[2]	29 21	89 27	0	58.82	58.86	62.54	72.02	77.08	82.76	82.95	81.84	80.32	72.65	63.71	58.7
9. Fort Jessup	31 35	93 25	80	50.64	52.71	59.16	67.87	73.80	80.32	82.33	81.43	76.13	65.96	56.67	50.2
10. Fort Pike	30 10	89 38	10	55.18	56.72	62.82	70.64	77.06	82.31	83.54	83.22	79.31	70.67	62.84	55.6
11. Fort Sabine	29 45	93 50	10	51.60	43.82	59.12	70.26	..	79.05	79.53	78.35	72.39	71.37	64.62	53.8
12. Fort Wood	30 09	89 47	20	54.89	56.56	60.30	71.11	78.11	81.50	82.96	82.34	79.04	68.84	62.40	55.1
13. Jackson	30 51	91 09	100	47.6	49.4	56.6	65.4	70.8	78.7	81.7	79.9	75.1	67.4	50.0	48.4
14. Monroe	32 31	92 07	100	39.3	49.7	68.4	70.5	75.7	80.4	82.45	80.0	72.1	57.7	48.1	42.6
15. New Orleans	29 56	90 03	25	56.75	58.39	66.58	72.41	77.26	81.78	82.22	82.12	79.42	69.71	58.71	52.2
16. New Orleans	29 56	90 03	25	54.75	57.90	63.69	68.67	75.76	80.69	82.13	80.43	78.84	69.48	61.07	55.3
17. New Orleans	29 56	90 03	25	56.6	54.4	61.5	67.4	73.8	78.5	80.0	79.5	77.3	69.3	57.6	56.4
18. New Orleans	29 56	90 03	25	59.0	56.0	66.5	67.0	74.0	79.3	78.7	81.0	78.4	66.7	63.6	57.3
19. New Orleans	29 56	90 03	25	55.4	60.8	61.3	71.5	78.3	82.6	84.6	83.7	78.8	67.8	61.6	56.6
20. Petite Coquille	..	..	..	..	..	..	68.00	69.80	74.25	..	..	..	..	..	..
21. Rapides	31 08	92 20	76	53.5	54.0	62.2	67.1	73.2	79.3	80.5	80.5	75.6	66.5	57.5	51.9
22. St. Francisville	30 49	91 22	80	..	..	..	..	..	..	..	..	..	..	..	50.8
23. Trinity[5] (near)	31 37	91 47	68	38.14	53.16	61.59	61.27	72.79	82.92	84.57	81.66	..	66.65	..	50.9
24. Vidalia Plantation	31 35	91 30	200	..	..	..	67.73	72.85	..	..	..	..	..	..	..
25. West Feliciana	30 40	91 20	96	50.6	54.6	59.3	65.9	72.5	77.7	79.7	78.6	75.5	66.6	56.7	51.7

[1] Eight miles above Cincinnati.

[2] Observations corrected for daily variation. The value of this series is much impaired on account of great irregularity in the hours of observation.

KENTUCKY.

	Spring.	Summer.	Autumn.	Winter.	Year.	Series. Begins. Ends.	Extent yrs. mos.	Observing hours.	Observer.	References.
1	54°.62	71°.52	53°.96	35°.91	54°.00	July, 1840; Dec. 1870	1 7	$7_m\ 2_a\ 9_a$ bis	Rev. J. A. Sheperd and H. Shriver.	MS. in S. Coll. and S. O.
2	53.82	76.53	57.48	32.78	55.15	May, 1853; Jan. 1862	3 7	"	Dr. J. Swain.	P. O. and S. I. Vol. 1, S. O., & S. Coll.
3	55.87	74.79	55.56	37.26	55.87	Jan. 1858; Oct. 1861	2 9	"	J. H. Lünemann and T. H. Miles.	P. O. and S. I. Vol. 1, and S. O.
4	..	74.97	53.07	..	..	1860	0 7	"	Dr. C. D. Chase.	S. O.
5	56.61	75.79	57.08	37.74	56.81	1849; Oct. 1855	4 4	$\odot_r\ 9_m\ 3_a\ 9_a$	Younglove and F. C. Herrick.	P. O. & S. I. Vol. 1, and S. Coll.
6	52.78	73.19	54.82	33.83	53.65	Mar. 1865; Dec. 1870	5 9	$7_m\ 2_a\ 9_a$ bis	Dr. S. D. Martin.	S. O.
7	54.43	76.77	54.56	37.51	55.82	May, 1868; May, 1869	1 1	"	Rev. T. H. Cleland.	" "
8	56.28	75.58	58.56	37.84	57.07	Feb. 1853; Dec. 1870	12 7	"	Prof. O. Beatty.	P. O. and S. I. Vol. 1, S. O., and S. Coll.
9	..	72.50	55.76	..	..	Aug. 1859; July, 1869	0 6	"	Rev. S. R. Williams and N. Williams.	P. O. and S. I. Vol. 1, and S. O.
10	..	..	..	..	..	1843	0 6	$\odot_r\ 9_m\ 3_a\ 9_a$	Thebaud.	Manuscript.
11	..	74.56	..	..	..	June, 1865; Mar. 1866	0 6	$7_m\ 2_a\ 9_a$ bis	W. S. Doak.	S. O.
12	55.71	73.96	55.79	37.34	55.70	1851; Feb. 1870	4 6	"	Rev. S. R. Williams, E. N. Woodruff, S. Manly, and C. B. Blackburn.	P. O. and S. I. Vol. 1, S.O., and S. Coll.
13	..	..	..	36.06	..	1852; 1853	0 7	$7_m\ 2_a\ 9_a$	Berthoud.	S. Coll.
14	53.03	75.28	55.88	33.25	54.36	June, 1853; Apr. 1862	4 10	$7_m\ 2_a\ 9_a$ bis	Rev. J. Miller, Rev. G. S. Savage.	P. O. and S. I. Vol. 1, S. O., and S. Coll.
15	53.82	75.06	56.09	34.14	54.78	July, 1847; Dec. 1870	23 0	$7_m\ 2_a\ 9_a$	Assistant Surgeon.	Ar. Met. Regs. 1855 and 1860, and MS. from S. G. O.
16	53.60	72.77	56.75	38.24	55.34	Jan. 1861; June, 1863	2 3	$7_m\ 2_a\ 9_a$ bis	J. McD. Matthews.	S. O.
17	..	..	..	..	..	1858	0 2	$7_m\ 2_a\ 9_a$	J. Grinnell.	P. O. and S. I. Vol. 1.
18	..	73.87	..	..	..	1861	0 5	$7_m\ 2_a\ 9_a$ bis	M. G. Williams.	S. O.
19	51.54	72.75	53.06	32.45	52.45	Jan. 1856; Dec. 1859	4 0	$7_m\ 2_a\ 9_a$	Dr. L. G. Ray.	P. O. and S. I. Vol. 1.
20	..	..	53.50	..	..	1850	0 4	"	Bixby.	S. Coll.
21	52.11	73.04	54.55	35.83	53.88	1849; 1851	1 9	$\odot_r\ 9_m\ 3_a\ 9_a$ [2]	Beatty.	" "
22	53.26	72.42	54.64	34.50	53.71	July, 1841; Dec. 1870	27 8		Mrs. L. Young.	P. O. and S. I. Vol. 1, MS. in S. Coll., and S. O.
23	..	..	..	..	..	1870	0 3	$7_m\ 2_a\ 9_a$	....	MS. from S. G. O.
24	..	..	..	..	..	1866	0 3	$7_m\ 2_a\ 9_a$ bis	H. C. Mathis.	S. O.

LOUISIANA.

	Spring.	Summer.	Autumn.	Winter.	Year.	Series. Begins. Ends.	Extent yrs. mos.	Observing hours.	Observer.	References.
1	68.90	81.36	68.13	54.20	68.15	Jan. 1822; Dec. 1860	28 0	$7_m\ 2_a\ 9_a$	Assistant Surgeon.	Ar. Met. Regs. 1855 and 1860, and MS. from S. G. O.
2	65.05	81.25	65.07	49.65	65.25	May, 1867; Nov. 1870	2 11	$7_m\ 2_a\ 9_a$ bis	J. H. Carter.	S. O.
3	66.79	81.11	64.98	53.01	66.47	Oct. 1856; May, 1859	2 7	$7_m\ 2_a\ 9_a$	Dr. A. R. Kilpatrick.	P. O. and S. I. Vol. 1.
4	..	..	..	..	..	1858	0 2	"	Assistant Surgeon.	Ar. Met. Reg. 1860.
5	68.00	82.11	66.17	54.50	67.70	July, 1844; June, 1845	1 0	$\odot_r\ 9_m\ 3_a\ 9_a$	" "	Ar. Met. Reg. 1860.
6	67.25	80.63	..	..	..	1870	0 7	$7_m\ 2_a\ 9_a$ bis	R. S. Jackson.	S. O.
7	..	..	..	..	..	1870	0 2	"	H. C. Collins.	" "
8	70.55	82.52	72.23	58.81	71.03	Jan. 1822; Mar. 1835	4 10	$7_m\ 2_a\ 9_a$	Assistant Surgeon.	Ar. Met. Reg. 1855.
9	66.94	81.36	66.25	51.19	66.44	Jan. 1823; Dec. 1845	22 11	"	" "	" " "
10	70.17	83.02	70.94	55.86	70.00	Oct. 1824; Dec. 1870	15 8	"	" "	Ar. Met. Reg. 1855 and MS. from S. G. O.
11	..	78.98	69.46	49.75	..	July, 1837; June, 1838	0 11	"	" "	Ar. Met. Reg. 1855.
12	69.84	82.27	70.09	55.55	69.44	July, 1832; Apr. 1846	6 2	"	" "	" " "
13	64.27	80.10	64.17	48.47	64.25	1839; 1841	3 0	$\odot_r\ 2_a\ \odot_s$	Carpenter.	Sill. Journal.
14	71.53	80.95	59.30	43.87	63.91	1808; 1819	10 0	"	....	Dr. Barton.
15	72.08	82.04	69.28	55.80	69.80	....	3 0	$8_m\ 2_a\ 8_a$ [4]	....	Rep. Brit. Assoc. 1847.
16	69.37	81.08	69.80	56.00	69.06	Jan. 1826; Dec. 1870	32 9		Assist. Surg., D. T. Lillie, Dr. E. H. Barton, J. Harrison, E. L. Ranlett.	Ar. Met. Regs. 1855 and 1860, MS. from S. G. O., Am. Alm. 1842, and foll., Printed Slip in S. Coll., P. O. and S. I. Vol. 1, and S. O., and MS.
17	67.57	79.33	68.07	55.80	67.69	1833; 1850	18 0	......	....	Barton's Rep. 1851.
18	69.17	79.67	69.57	57.43	68.96	1849	1 0	......	....	Rep. of Board of Health, 1850.
19	70.37	83.63	69.40	57.60	70.25	1807; 1810	3 0	......	....	Barton's Rep. 1851.
20	..	..	..	..	..	1820	0 3	$\odot_r\ \odot_s$	Dr. E. H. Belle.	S. Coll.
21	67.50	80.10	66.53	53.13	66.81	1833; 1850	10 0	$\odot_r\ 2_a\ \odot_s$	Voorhies.	Barton's Rep. 1851.
22	..	..	..	..	..	1856	0 1	$\odot_r\ 1_a\ 9_a$	B. R. Gifford.	P. O. and S. I. Vol. 1.
23	65.22	83.05	..	47.43	..	Dec. 1856; Oct. 1860	1 1	$7_m\ 2_a\ 9_a$	Dr. E. Merrill.	P. O. and S. I. Vol. 1, and S. O.
24	..	..	..	..	..	1867	0 2	$7_m\ 2_a\ 9_a$ bis	Rev. A. K. Teele.	S. O.
25	65.90	78.67	66.27	52.30	65.78	1820; 1833	13 0	$\odot_r\ 2_a\ \odot_s$	Barton.	Barton's Rep. 1851.

[3] Previous to July, 1831, the observations were made at Fort St. Philip, one mile N. W. of Fort Jackson.

[4] Corrected for daily variation by the Fort Morgan Table.

[5] In 1860, the observations were made at Moss Grove Plantation, near Trinity.

MAINE.

Name of Station.	Lat.	Long.	Height.	Jan.	Feb.	March.	April.	May.	June.	July.	August.	Sept.	Oct.	Nov.	Dec.
1. Augusta	44°19′	69°47′	..	19°.87	27°.00	32°.20	38°.67	50°.30	65°.61	68°.65	65°.86	60°.39	50°.50	42°.55	21°.58
2. Bangor	44 49	68 46	40	21.87	17.57	33.27	41.01	53.92	62.73	66.76	64.51	..	..	35.37	21.07
3. Bath	43 55	69 49	50	23.22	23.32	31.65	41.86	52.37	61.32	68.71	66.06	59.23	47.74	35.90	25.10
4. Belfast	44 26	69 00	..	15.58	20.49	28.74	41.25	54.21	62.88	68.34	65.70	58.43	46.38	36.08	19.95
5. Bethel	44 20	70 51	650	14.10	18.68	26.63	38.40	49.62	61.80	67.27	63.97	56.57	47.12	33.23	22.68
6. Biddeford	43 30	70 27	45	21.70	25.01	33.22	42.89	53.96	67.02	71.22	69.77	60.56	49.78	38.49	25.63
7. Blue Hill	44 25	68 34	50	..	..	..	..	..	..	67.05	..	..	..	..	..
8. Brunswick	43 54	69 57	74	20.10	22.93	31.54	42.56	52.69	62.29	67.44	65.60	58.28	47.78	36.71	24.86
9. Bucksport	44 40	68 48	90	24.57	28.12	34.85	44.15	55.86	60.73	74.08	71.27	63.59	52.65	40.69	26.36
10. Carmel	44 47	69 00	175	13.59	14.48	26.90	39.32	54.83	64.32	72.35	64.04	55.03	45.27	33.91	18.33
11. Castine	44 23	68 47	50	21.41	22.30	30.38	41.43	50.53	59.43	64.82	64.66	58.39	48.44	38.06	25.57
12. Cornish	43 44	70 51	784	18.47	21.16	28.32	40.58	52.53	63.51	68.56	66.05	58.20	45.92	34.53	21.77
13. Dennysville	44 53	67 14	..	19.13	20.06	29.06	39.66	50.42	59.84	65.67	63.87	56.67	46.69	35.76	23.20
14. Dexter	45 02	69 18	650	14.53	21.15	27.21	39.34	52.51	62.12	66.99	66.76	58.74	46.25	34.94	21.21
15. East Exeter (or Exeter)	45 00	69 10	190	18.84	19.99	30.73	42.15	..	62.22	67.30	66.67	57.58	..	..	..
16. Eastport	44 54	66 59	40	20.0	22.7	28.8	39.5	48.2	55.5	63.8	63.7	56.2	46.1	35.7	24.5
17. East Wilton	44 36	70 14	..	..	..	..	..	..	..	..	..	..	..	37.05	..
18. Fort Fairfield	46 46	67 49	415	15.16	13.10	24.40	35.90	47.70	57.05	62.83	64.70	49.13	39.92	29.15	12.53
19. Fort Kent	47 15	68 35	575	10.76	11.26	23.26	35.08	46.78	59.00	62.51	63.45	51.18	39.58	27.52	10.86
20. Fort Preble	43 39	70 14	31	22.54	24.61	32.62	43.22	52.84	63.31	68.57	66.64	59.66	49.14	38.01	26.88
21. Fort Sullivan	44 54	66 59	70	22.06	23.23	30.57	40.11	48.67	56.24	61.99	62.23	57.14	47.73	37.27	25.56
22. Foxcraft	45 12	69 13	..	..	..	31.83	..	53.70	59.78	66.70	65.64	55.03	47.70	..	..
23. Fryeburg	44 00	71 04	..	11.18	15.93	23.75	45.08	53.61	..	..	..	..	..	..	..
24. Gardiner	44 14	69 48	76	17.94	20.72	29.49	41.24	52.69	63.06	68.64	66.47	58.07	46.58	35.31	22.14
25. Hampden	44 43	68 50	180	8.88	21.00	29.64	43.78	51.88	62.29	63.21	67.67	56.75	44.12	30.30	21.64
26. Hancock Barracks (Houlton)	46 07	67 49	620	14.87	16.68	27.09	39.43	51.18	61.15	66.09	64.73	56.16	43.71	30.99	18.60
27. Hiram	43 51	70 52	400	17.01	18.39	28.23	39.26	51.45	61.33	67.17	64.11	56.29	44.54	33.17	20.91
28. Houlton	46 07	67 49	..	..	..	..	36.17	48.21	61.25	67.79	66.74	..	..	..	..
29. Kennebec Arsenal	44 19	69 46	..	22.95	15.51	28.40	40.74	52.54	64.59	69.47	65.49	58.91	47.02	37.25	25.98
30. Lee	45 25	68 18	..	13.08	21.62	27.71	41.85	50.20	64.14	66.92	65.34	56.23	45.16	35.69	22.45
31. Linneus	46 04	67 58	..	17.20	..	..	..	..	..	..	63.90	..	..	..	..
32. Lisbon[2]	44 04	70 07	130	18.46	22.67	29.23	41.55	54.08	63.53	68.92	67.24	58.21	47.62	37.63	22.66
33. Newcastle	44 07	69 36	88	..	..	..	..	..	..	..	..	..	44.06	..	..
34. North Bridgeton	44 02	70 48	300	14.05	22.83	28.00	38.55	51.62	61.85	70.57	65.65	58.17	47.77	34.25	23.05
35. Oldtown[3]	44 58	68 40	137	16.24	17.17	25.07	37.38	48.97	58.75	66.79	63.88	55.49	45.07	32.49	18.32
36. Oxford[4]	44 08	70 33	182	19.06	18.15	28.48	40.35	52.54	64.44	68.94	65.87	56.71	44.63	33.81	20.72
37. Patten	46 00	68 27	..	..	..	22.90	35.23	..	..	65.21	..	52.63	42.90	38.35	..
38. Pembroke	44 55	67 09	40	19.23	19.00	32.70	40.50	54.15	58.58	..	62.50	56.78	..	..	..
39. Perry	45 00	67 05	100	19.76	23.17	28.82	38.89	49.11	57.59	63.29	61.55	55.67	46.21	35.62	24.11
40. Portland	43 39	70 15	87	19.26	21.46	29.72	40.05	50.58	60.27	66.30	64.68	57.45	45.39	34.41	23.85
41. Portland[5]	43 39	70 15	50	19.46	21.25	29.89	40.12	50.32	60.31	66.28	64.59	57.66	46.27	35.54	24.35
42. Prospect	44 28	68 46	207	..	..	30.93	40.02	..	..	..	..	..	..	..	..
43. Rumford	44 30	70 37	600	..	24.75	24.77	39.60	51.85	66.38	66.00	67.35	54.43	46.15	37.55	21.75
44. Saco	43 31	70 26	69	21.08	21.29	31.21	43.69	54.28	65.06	70.31	68.44	60.92	47.18	37.18	25.34
45. South Thomaston	44 04	69 08	50	22.96	24.96	29.49	39.12	50.90	63.37	66.74	63.84	56.51	48.63	37.05	21.03
46. Standish	43 45	70 37	280	19.89	22.18	27.71	41.51	52.84	65.18	69.97	67.33	59.49	44.74	35.24	22.28
47. Steuben	44 31	67 58	50	19.10	21.34	28.52	38.66	48.74	58.57	63.73	62.30	55.65	45.42	35.81	22.75
48. Surry	44 30	68 30	50	..	..	..	..	..	66.15	..	68.53	60.20	50.15	38.28	26.43
49. Topsham	43 54	69 57	60	16.59	25.23	31.49	37.27	47.92	..	67.82	..	..	37.56	35.58	19.21
50. Vassalboro	44 27	69 42	..	17.84	19.01	29.35	40.57	54.06	62.18	64.92	66.64	56.28	46.53	36.83	21.10
51. West Waterville	44 33	69 46	250	18.18	21.89	29.77	42.10	53.20	65.10	69.91	67.09	59.20	46.15	35.14	22.78
52. Williamsburg	45 21	69 06	..	13.94	16.68	24.33	38.29	50.33	61.55	66.93	63.59	50.57	45.05	32.72	17.80
53. Windham	43 46	70 28	..	16.43	20.70	30.86	38.52	57.89	64.01	68.93	67.28	59.14	47.45	34.56	25.63

[1] Hours of observation 7_m 1_a 6_a. Observations corrected for daily variation by means of the general table.

[2] Observations from Dec. 1865, to May, 1867, at Webster, about three miles east of Lisbon.

[3] The observations for 1870 were made at Orono, about three miles southeast of Oldtown.

MAINE.

	Spring.	Summer.	Autumn.	Winter.	Year.	Series. Begins. Ends.	Extent yrs. mos.	Observing hours.	Observer.	References.
1	40°.39	66°.71	51°.15	22°.82	45°.27	Nov. 1849; Mar. 1864	1 2	$6_m\ 2_a\ 9_a$	G. E. Brackett and others.	Pat. Off. Rep. 1851 and S. O.
2	42.73	64.67	..	20.17	..	1843; June, 1860	1 2	$7_m\ 2_a\ 9_a$	Young.	S. O. and Manuscript.
3	41.96	65.36	47.62	23.88	44.71	Jan. 1832; July, 1842	10 7	$\odot_r\ 2_a\ \odot_s$	John Hayden.	Am. Alm. 1842 and S. Coll.
4	41.40	65.64	46.96	18.67	43.17	July, 1859; June, 1866	4 3	7_m N. 6_a	G. E. Brackett.	P. O. and S. I. Vol. 1, MS. in S. Coll., and S. O.
5	38.22	64.35	45.64	18.49	41.68	Jan. 1861; Feb. 1862	1 2	$7_m\ 2_a\ 9_a$ bis	A. G. Gaines.	S. O.
6	43.36	69.33	49.61	24.11	46.60	Jan. 1848; June, 1852	4 5	$\odot_r\ 1\frac{1}{2}_a\ \odot_s$	J. G. Garland.	Am. Alm. 1850.
7	..	..	..	..	..	1864	0 1	$7_m\ 2_a\ 9_a$ bis	H. H. Osgood.	S. O.
8	42.26	65.11	47.59	22.63	44.40	Jan. 1807; Dec. 1859	51 3	1	Prof. P. Cleaveland.	Sm. Con. to Knowl.
9	44.95	68.69	52.31	26.35	48.07	Jan. 1849; Feb. 1853	4 2	$9_m\ 3_a$	R. Buck.	S. Coll.
10	40.35	66.90	44.74	15.47	41.87	Jan. 1852; Jan. 1857	4 10	$7_m\ 2_a\ 9_a$	J. J. Bell.	P. O. and S. I. Vol. 1, & S. Coll.
11	40.78	62.97	48.30	23.09	43.79	Jan. 1810; Dec. 1849	40 0	......	Judge Nelson.	S. Coll.
12	40.48	66.04	46.22	20.47	43.30	Jan. 1856; Dec. 1870	14 10	$7_m\ 2_a\ 9_a$ bis	G. W. Guptill, S. West.	P. O. and S. I. Vol. 1, and S. O.
13	39.71	63.13	46.37	20.80	42.50	Jan. 1816; Dec. 1855	40 0	max. & min.	T. Lincoln.	S. Coll.
14	39.69	65.29	46.64	18.96	42.65	June, 1860; June, 1863	3 0	$7_m\ 2_a\ 9_a$ bis	B. F. Wilbur.	S. O.
15	..	65.40	..	..	..	Jan. 1858; Sept. 1861	1 0	$7_m\ 2_a\ 9_a$	S. Gilman, J. B. Wilson.	P. O. and S. I. Vol. 1, and S. O.
16	38.83	61.00	46.00	22.40	42.06	Jan. 1833; Dec. 1834	2 0	......	....	Am. Alm. 1836.
17	..	..	..	..	..	1861	0 1	$7_m\ 2_a\ 9_a$ bis	H. Reynolds.	S. O.
18	36.00	61.53	39.40	13.60	37.63	Jan. 1842; Aug. 1843	1 8	$\odot_r\ 9_m\ 3_a\ 9_a$	Assistant Surgeon.	Ar. Met. Reg. 1855.
19	35.04	61.65	39.43	10.96	36.77	Jan. 1842; Aug. 1845	3 0	"	" "	" " "
20	42.89	66.17	48.94	24.68	45.67	Jan. 1824; Dec. 1870	26 2	$7_m\ 2_a\ 9_a$	" "	Ar. Met. Reg. 1855, and MS. from S. G. O.
21	39.78	60.15	47.38	23.62	42.73	Jan. 1822; Dec. 1870	23 9	$\odot_r\ 9_m\ 3_a\ 9_a$	" "	" " " "
22	..	64.04	..	..	..	June, 1863; Mar. 1864	0 7	$7_m\ 2_a\ 9_a$ bis	M. Pitman.	S. O.
23	40.81	..	..	..	..	1856	0 5	$7_m\ 2_a$	Dr. E. B. Barrows.	P. O. and S. I. Vol. 1.
24	41.14	66.06	46.65	20.27	43.53	Jan. 1837; Dec. 1870	30 11	$7_m\ 2_a\ 9_a$ bis	R. H. and F. Gardiner.	P. O. and S. I. Vol. 1, S. Coll., and S. O.
25	41.77	64.39	43.72	17.17	41.76	Aug. 1843; July, 1844	1 0	$\odot_r\ 9_m\ 3_a\ 9_a$	J. Herrick.	Am. Alm. 1846.
26	39.23	63.99	43.62	16.72	40.89	Jan. 1829; Dec. 1870	18 5	$7_m\ 2_a\ 9_a$	Assit. Surg., C. H. Fernald.	Ar. Met. Regs. 1855 and S. O.
27	39.65	64.20	44.67	18.77	41.82	Jan. 1831; 1864	34 0	max. & min.	G. [illegible]	M[illegible] S. Coll.
28	..	65.26	..	[illegible]		[illegible]	0 5	$\odot_r\ 9_m\ 3_a\ 9_a$	M. Welch.	S. Coll.
29	[illegible]	[illegible]	47.73	21.48	44.07	May, 1857; Aug. 1858	1 4	$7_m\ 2_a\ 9_a$	Assistant Surgeon.	Ar. Met. Reg. 1860.
30	39.92	65.47	45.69	19.05	42.53	June, 1864; Sept. 1867	2 11	$7_m\ 2_a\ 9_a$ bis	E. Pitman, B. H. Towle.	S. O.
31	..	..	..	..	..	Aug. 1863; Jan. 1864	0 2	$7_m\ 2_a\ 9_a$	A. G. Young and daughter.	" "
32	41.62	66.56	47.82	21.26	44.32	Apr. 1859; Dec. 1870	8 5	$7_m\ 2_a\ 9_a$ bis	A. P. Moore, A. Robinson.	P. O. and S. I, Vol. 1. and S. O.
33	..	..	..	..	..	1859	0 1	$7_m\ 2_a\ 9_a$	C. L. Nichols.	P. O. and S. I. Vol. 1.
34	39.39	66.02	46.73	19.98	43.03	1861	1 0	$7_m\ 2_a\ 9_a$ bis	Dr. M. Gould.	S. O.
35	37.14	63.14	44.35	17.24	40.47	Jan. 1849; Dec. 1870	6 5	$\odot_r\ 9_m\ 3_a\ 9_a$	Rev. S. H. Merrill, M. C. Fernald.	P. O. and S. I, Vol. 1, S. O, and Manuscript.
36	40.46	66.42	45.05	19.31	42.81	Feb. 1860; Dec. 1870	4 0	$7_m\ 2_a\ 9_a$ bis	H. D. Smith, G. W. Verrill, Jr.	S. O.
37	..	..	44.63	..	..	1849; 1850	0 6	$\odot_r\ 9_m\ 3_a\ 9_a$	S. Eveleth.	S. Coll.
38	42.45	..	..	..	..	1862	0 8	$7_m\ 2_a\ 9_a$ bis	E. Dewhurst.	S. O.
39	38.94	60.81	45.83	22.35	41.98	July, 1849; July, 1865	14 1	$7_m\ 2_a\ 9_a$	W. D. Dana.	P. O. and S. I. Vol. 1, S. O., and Manuscript.
40	40.12	63.75	45.75	21.52	42.78	1815; 1852	35 6	$\odot_r$ N. 8_a	Moody.	Manuscript.
41	40.11	63.73	46.49	21.69	43.00	Jan. 1820; Dec. 1859	37 3	"	Becket, H. Willis.	P. O. and S. I. Vol. 1, and S. Coll.
42	..	..	..	..	..	1867	0 2	$7_m\ 2_a\ 9_a$ bis	V. G. Eaton.	S. O.
43	38.74	66.58	46.04	..	..	Oct. 1866; Apr. 1869	1 2	"	W. Pettingill.	" "
44	43.06	67.94	48.43	22.57	45.50	July, 1843; June, 1848	5 0	$7_m\ 2_a\ 7_a$	J. M. Batchelder.	Am. Alm. 1845 and foll.
45	39.84	64.65	47.40	22.98	43.72	1849; 1855	2 2	$\odot_r\ 9_m\ 3_a\ 9_a$	J. Bartlett.	P. O. & S. I. Vol. 1, & S. Coll.
46	40.69	67.49	46.49	21.45	44.03	May, 1865; Jan. 1870	4 0	$7_m\ 2_a\ 9_a$ bis	J. P. Moulton.	S. O.
47	38.64	61.53	45.63	21.06	41.72	Aug. 1854; Apr. 1870	15 6	"	J. D. Parker.	P. O. and S. I. Vol. 1. and S. O.
48	..	..	49.54	..	..	1870	0 6	"	O. H. & L. S. Tupp.	S. O.
49	38.89	..	..	20.34	..	Nov. 1859; Dec. 1861	1 4	"	W. Johnson.	P. O. and S. I. Vol. 1, and S. O.
50	41.33	64.58	46.55	19.32	42.94	Aug. 1859; July, 1863	3 5	"	J. Van Blascom.	" " " " "
51	41.69	67.37	46.83	20.95	44.21	Dec. 1863; Dec. 1870	7 1	"	B. F. Wilbur.	S. O.
52	37.65	64.02	42.78	16.14	40.15	June, 1863; Dec. 1870	4 0	"	E. and H. W. Pitman.	" "
53	42.42	66.74	47.05	20.92	44.28	1849; Feb. 1856	4 0	$7_m\ 2_a\ 9_a$	S. A. Eveleth.	P. O. & S. I. Vol. 1, & S. Coll.

[4] The observations for 1860–61 were made at Norway, about three miles northeast of Oxford.

[5] Observations from Jan. 1820, to Dec. 1852, probably included in the preceding series.

MARYLAND.

Name of Station.	Lat.	Long.	Height.	Jan.	Feb.	March.	April.	May.	June.	July.	August.	Sept.	Oct.	Nov.	Dec.
1. Agricultural College	38°59′	76°57′	..	34°.69	39°.29	46°.37	55°.82	61°.62	73°.35	72°.73	75°.22	70°.67	61°.57	47°.25	40°.55
2. Annapolis	38 58	76 30	20	33.85	36.19	41.85	52.41	62.73	73.45	77.83	75.85	69.14	56.87	46.59	37.80
3. Baltimore	39 17	76 37	80	32.52	33.67	41.45	50.84	62.38	70.34	75.61	74.28	66.58	54.29	44.35	35.15
4. Baltimore	39 17	76 37	80	33.10	34.30	42.40	53.00	63.20	71.60	76.60	74.50	67.70	55.80	45.00	37.80
5. Bladensburg	38 57	76 56	75	31.23	33.62	40.63	51.54	62.32	71.66	75.75	74.25	63.56	54.31	43.43	33.84
6. Calvert College (New Windsor)	39 31	77 06	..	30.16	34.95	41.67	..	..	..	75.12	..	..	..	..	37.38
7. Catonsville[2] (St. Timothy's Hall)	39 17	76 42	500	27.14	27.63	34.75	48.47	56.94	68.79	74.64	69.02	66.36	53.24	44.39	31.14
8. Chestertown (Wash. Coll.)	39 13	76 04	85	30.20	33.56	41.10	50.98	63.51	71.45	75.81	74.67	69.00	56.35	45.75	36.04
9. Cumberland	39 39	78 45	..	27.75	28.43	35.14	45.38	55.62	66.89	69.52	67.14	59.22	46.91	38.25	29.83
10. Elkton	39 38	75 50	40	..	..	..	..	..	..	70.7	..	..	..	..	32.0
11. Emmettsburg[3]	39 43	77 20	498	29.75	31.15	36.74	49.56	58.35	69.05	74.14	71.93	64.14	50.93	42.01	30.34
12. Eyrie House (Mt. Savage)	39 42	78 52	1818	30.6	26.3	40.2	51.9	61.6	64.2	69.5	70.7	65.4	51.7	44.3	32.9
13. Fallston	39 30	76 24	300	..	..	..	..	..	..	..	..	68.70	58.20	46.63	35.08
14. Fort McHenry	39 16	76 35	36	33.00	34.57	42.27	53.22	63.54	72.56	77.35	75.34	68.65	56.75	45.71	35.93
15. Fort Severn	38 59	76 29	20	33.34	34.84	42.96	54.24	64.82	73.06	78.22	76.17	69.02	57.73	46.90	36.81
16. Fort Washington	38 42	77 04	60	36.24	38.57	46.19	56.22	67.56	76.02	79.93	76.97	69.57	59.13	47.03	37.58
17. Frederick City	39 24	77 24	274	31.47	33.69	40.32	50.67	62.31	71.76	76.30	72.15	65.96	53.72	44.60	34.16
18. Hagerstown	39 39	77 43	..	..	..	..	..	..	71.45	..	..	..	..	..	..
19. Isthmus	38 45	76 15	..	..	..	..	54.6	..	..	78.4	77.8	..	58.2	..	40.2
20. Leitersburg	39 42	77 30	..	28.46	32.72	41.45	48.39	60.81	69.19	73.06	71.58	63.58	52.93	39.98	31.03
21. Leonardtown	38 17	76 37	..	39.10	38.19	49.92	52.09	64.25	72.07	75.44	74.41	69.61	51.71	44.25	37.44
22. Nottingham	38 42	76 43	..	..	31.38	46.52	..	..	..	..	..	..	..	..	..
23. Port Deposit	39 37	76 06	..	..	..	..	..	..	74.21	78.27	..	..	..	..	..
24. Ridge	38 06	76 21	..	26.12	43.28	41.83	49.90	65.51	78.72	84.12	..	73.14	59.25	48.29	34.60
25. St. Mary's City	38 10	76 28	45	35.24	36.85	42.72	53.89	61.89	72.64	76.14	78.00	70.50	57.84	47.23	38.88
26. Schellman Hills (near Sykesville)	39 25	77 00	700	30.65	32.13	40.28	50.35	62.19	69.85	73.28	71.20	65.13	53.81	43.34	33.55
27. Union Bridge	39 34	76 10	400	..	..	..	..	65.50	..	..	..	..	..	..	..
28. Woodlawn	39 39	76 04	..	30.51	32.44	38.97	51.57	59.74	71.28	75.24	72.25	66.77	53.11	43.47	32.30
29. Woodstock	39 19	76 51	400	..	..	..	..	..	..	..	..	..	..	..	32.17

MASSACHUSETTS.

Name of Station.	Lat.	Long.	Height.	Jan.	Feb.	March.	April.	May.	June.	July.	August.	Sept.	Oct.	Nov.	Dec.
1. Amherst (College)	42 22	72 34	267	22.99	23.31	33.02	44.77	55.72	65.07	69.94	67.73	59.45	47.33	37.19	26.14
2. Amherst (College)	42 22	72 34	267	22.91	24.82	31.57	44.28	56.01	65.29	69.90	67.21	59.76	48.68	38.55	26.01
3. Andover	42 38	71 10	..	24.54	25.64	33.27	45.27	55.95	66.57	70.66	69.97	61.28	49.21	37.44	29.85
4. Baldwinsville	42 37	72 04	847	17.97	24.24	29.25	42.19	55.55	63.60	68.19	67.62	59.36	42.82	37.84	24.04
5. Barnstable	41 42	70 19	20	30.23	27.93	..	..	..	..	..	..	..	..	..	..
6. Bird Island	42 21	71 01	..	31.90	..	41.00	..	..	..	68.90	69.80	..	56.31	47.56	40.85
7. Boston	42 21	71 03	82	26.38	27.91	35.36	45.64	55.83	65.53	71.49	69.01	62.20	51.04	39.87	29.96
8. Bradford	42 46	71 05	..	25.42	30.26	32.16	46.98	57.92	64.91	75.49	70.74	61.07	54.59	42.68	36.95
9. Bridgewater	42 02	71 00	150	24.41	26.70	34.39	43.97	52.33	64.22	69.52	65.29	61.36	49.96	40.46	29.31
10. Byfield	42 44	70 56	..	..	..	..	43.18	53.97	..	..	..	..	..	..	..
11. Cambridge	42 23	71 07	60	28.99	31.18	37.09	47.99	58.66	67.26	72.92	70.91	62.01	51.57	41.12	30.91
12. Cambridge	42 23	71 07	60	28.0	30.7	36.5	48.5	58.5	68.5	73.7	72.5	64.0	50.7	37.0	31.5
13. Cambridge	42 23	71 07	60	22.50	23.90	32.90	45.10	54.40	66.10	69.60	69.40	60.00	50.10	40.20	29.04

[1] Corrected for daily variation by means of the general table.

[2] Previous to 1865 the observations were made at Oakland, about five miles S. E. of Catonsville.

MARYLAND.

	Spring.	Summer.	Autumn.	Winter.	Year.	Series. Begins. Ends.	Extent yrs. mos.	Observing hours.	Observer.	References.
1	54°.60	73°.77	59°.83	38°.18	56°.60	Feb. 1861; July, 1862	1 2	$7_m\ 2_a\ 9_a$ bis	Dr. M. Jones.	S. O.
2	52.33	75.71	57.53	35.95	55.38	Nov. 1855; Dec. 1870	13 10	"	Dr. A. Zumbrock, & W. R. Goodman.	P. O. and S. I. Vol. 1, and S. O.
3	51.56	73.41	55.07	33.78	53.46	Jan. 1817; Aug. 1859	18 9	1	L. Brantz, Dr. Edmondson, Prof. N. M. Meyer, and A. Zumbrock.	Printed Journ. in S. Coll., P. O. and S. I. Vol. 1, S. Coll., and printed record.
4	52.87	74.23	56.17	35.07	54.58	....	22 0	......	....	Pat. Off. Rep.
5	51.50	73.89	53.77	32.90	53.02	Dec. 1854; Aug. 1865	9 4	$7_m\ 2_a\ 9_a$ bis	B. O. Lowndes	P. O. and S. I. Vol. 1, and S. O.
6	..	..	..	34.16	..	1852; 1853	0 5	$\odot_r\ 9_m\ 3_a\ 9_a$	Nelson.	S. Coll.
7	46.72	70.82	54.66	28.64	50.21	Dec. 1857; Feb. 1868	3 0	$7_m\ 2_a\ 9_a$ bis	G. S. Grape, E. L. Raulett, F. Reed, P. Tabb, and L. R. Cofran.	P. O. and S. I. Vol. 1, and S. O.
8	51.86	73.98	57.03	33.27	54.04	June, 1855; July, 1864	3 8	"	Prof. J. R. Dutton & others.	" " " " "
9	45.38	67.85	48.13	28.67	47.51	Jan. 1859; Dec. 1870	11 5	7_m	....	MS. in S. Coll.
10	..	..	..	..	..	Dec. 1843; July, 1849	0 2	$\odot_r\ 9_m\ 3_a\ 9_a$	F. Finch.	Manuscript.
11	48.22	71.71	52.36	30.41	50.67	Nov. 1866; Dec. 1870	4 2	$7_m\ 2_a\ 9_a$ bis	E. Smith, and P. C. H. Jourdan.	S. O.
12	51.23	68.13	53.80	29.93	50.77	Jan. 1846; Sept. 1846	0 9	$\odot_r\ 3_a\ 11_a$	T. C. Atkinson.	MS. in S. Coll.
13	..	..	57.84	..	..	1870	0 4	$7_m\ 2_a\ 9_a$ bis	G. G. Curtis.	S. O.
14	53.01	75.08	57.04	34.50	54.91	Jan. 1831; Dec. 1870	36 0	$7_m\ 2_a\ 9_a$	Assistant Surgeon.	Ar. Met. Regs. 1855 and 1860, MS. from S. G. O., and MS. in S. Coll.
15	54.01	75.82	57.88	35.00	55.68	Jan. 1822; July, 1845	7 5	"	" "	Ar. Met. Reg. 1855.
16	56.66	77.64	58.58	37.46	57.58	Jan. 1824; Sept. 1870	15 6	"	" "	Ar. Met. Reg. 1855, and MS. from S. G. O.
17	51.10	73.40	54.76	33.11	53.09	1851; June, 1870	15 6	$7_m\ 2_a\ 9_a$ bis	H. E. & J. K. Henshaw, H. M. Baer, and Jones.	P. O. and S. I. Vol. 1, S. O., and S. Coll.
18	..	..	..	..	..	1852	0 1	$\odot_r\ 9_m\ 3_a\ 9_a$	Carter.	S. Coll.
19	..	..	..	..	..	Apr. 1843; July, 1845	0 6	"	R. Banning.	Manuscript.
20	50.22	71.28	52.16	30.74	51.10	Oct. 1851; June, 1862	4 7	$7_m\ 2_a\ 9_a$ bis	J. E. Bell.	P. O. and S. I. Vol. 1, S. O., and S. Coll.
21	55.42	73.97	55.19	38.24	55.71	Jan. 1858; Sept. 1859	1 0	$7_m\ 2_a\ 9_a$	Dr. A. McWilliams.	P. O. and S. I. Vol. 1.
22	..	..	..	..	..	1849	0 2	$\odot_r\ 9_m\ 3_a\ 9_a$	Dalrymple.	S. Coll.
23	..	..	..	..	..	1850	0 2	"	Thorpe.	" "
24	52.41	..	60.23	34.67	..	May, 1856; June, 1867	1 1	$7_m\ 2_a\ 9_a$	T. G. Stagg.	P. O. and S. I. Vol. 1.
25	52.83	75.59	58.52	36.99	55.98	Dec. 1859; Feb. 1870	6 8	$7_m\ 2_a\ 9_a$ bis	Rev. J. Stephenson.	P. O. and S. I. Vol. 1, and S. O.
26	50.94	71.44	54.09	32.11	52.15	Jan. 1846; Dec. 1865	19 8	"	Miss H. M. Baer.	P. O. and S. I. Vol. 1, MS. in S. Coll., and S. O.
27	..	..	..	..	..	1864	0 1	"	W. Gillingham.	S. O.
28	50.09	72.92	54.45	31.75	52.30	Mar. 1865; Dec. 1870	5 9	"	J. O. McCormick.	" "
29	..	..	..	..	..	1870	0 1	"	A. X. Valente.	" "

MASSACHUSETTS.

	Spring.	Summer.	Autumn.	Winter.	Year.	Series. Begins. Ends.	Extent yrs. mos.	Observing hours.	Observer.	References.
1	44.17	67.58	47.99	24.15	45.97	Jan. 1836; Dec. 1853	17 6	......	Prof. E. S. Snell.	MS., Ag'l. Rep., and S. Coll.
2	43.95	67.47	49.00	24.58	46.25	Jan. 1854; Dec. 1870	16 11	$7_m\ 2_a\ 9_a$ bis	" " " "	P. O. and S. I. Vol. 1, and S. O.
3	44.83	69.07	49.31	26.68	47.47	Jan. 1798; Dec. 1808	11 0	$\odot_r$ max.	French.	Mem. Am. Acad.
4	42.33	66.47	46.67	22.08	44.39	Mar. 1863; Sept. 1865	2 3	$7_m\ 2_a\ 9_a$ bis	Rev. E. Dewhurst.	S. O.
5	..	..	..	..	..	1854	0 2	$7_m\ 2_a\ 9_a$	R. R. Gifford.	P. O. and S. I. Vol. 1.
6	..	..	..	..	..	1843; 1844	0 9	6_m N. 6_a	Clark.	Manuscript.
7	45.61	68.68	51.04	28.08	48.35	Feb. 1806; Apr. 1858	38 5	[4]	J. P. Hall, and R. T. Paine.	Med. and Agr. Reg. Bost. Vol. 1, 1806–7, Sill. Journ., MS. in S. Coll., P. O. and S. I. Vol. 1, and Memoirs Americaines.
8	45.69	70.38	52.78	30.88	49.93	1772	1 0	6_m N. 6_a	Williams.	Phil. Soc. Trans.
9	43.56	66.34	50.59	26.81	46.83	Apr. 1856; June, 1861	3 4	[4]	L. A. Darling and others.	P. O. and S. I. Vol. 1, and S. O.
10	..	..	..	..	..	1851	0 2	$\odot_r\ 9_m\ 3_a\ 9_a$	Root.	S. Coll.
11	47.91	70.36	51.57	30.36	50.05	Jan. 1742; Dec. 1773	32 0	......	Winthrop.	Am. Alm. 1837, p. 176.
12	47.83	71.57	50.57	30.07	50.01	July, 1780; Dec. 1783	3 0	......	Rev. E. Wigglesworth.	Mems. Am. Acad.
13	44.13	68.37	50.10	25.15	46.94	Jan. 1784; Dec. 1788	5 0	......	Williams.	Am. Alm. 1837, p. 176.

[3] The observations were partly made at Mount St. Mary's College, about one mile S. W. of Emmettsburg.

[4] Observations corrected for daily variation by means of the general table.

MASSACHUSETTS.—Continued.

Name of Station.	Lat.	Long.	Height.	Jan.	Feb.	March.	April.	May.	June.	July.	August.	Sept.	Oct.	Nov.	Dec.
14. Cambridge	42°23′	71°07′	60	25°.25	26°.28	34°.39	44°.40	56°.01	66°.74	71°.86	69°.82	61°.89	50°.18	39°.28	29°.3
15. Canton	42 10	71 08	90	22.67	32.26	..	..	..	..	..	..	..	..	39.02	28.6
16. Chelsea	42 25	71 00	40	24.05	28.48	35.91	44.34	58.24	68.27	71.57	68.90	62.83	54.63	40.57	29.3
17. Clinton	42 25	71 42	..	22.95	30.93	33.60	..	56.30	65.18	67.63	69.20	57.75	48.58	..	..
18. Concord	42 29	71 22	..	25.1	29.0	30.1	42.6	..	..	..	..	..	..	..	..
19. Danvers	42 35	70 58	..	25.19	28.34	..	..	..	..	..	..	..	..	..	28.9
20. Deerfield	42 32	72 36	..	22.24	22.29	30.28	42.97	55.38	65.77	70.28	68.20	60.43	45.57	37.35	26.6
21. Duxbury	42 02	70 41	..	..	..	..	..	53.16	66.33	71.12	..	..	..	..	..
22. East Douglas	42 05	71 42	..	..	..	38.98	48.61	52.47	71.34	71.15	69.70	..	..	..	..
23. Fall River	41 43	71 09	200	..	..	..	..	..	..	..	..	..	..	42.48	34.3
24. Falmouth	41 33	70 37	20	..	..	30.48	..	..	..	..	..	..	..	..	..
25. Fitchburg	42 35	71 50	484	23.80	31.35	35.80	44.82	54.25	66.05	70.47	67.65	61.57	52.82	39.95	25.8
26. Fort Independence	42 22	71 02	50	26.85	27.72	35.00	45.34	56.23	64.30	71.66	69.46	62.89	52.76	41.64	31.2
27. Fort Sewall	42 30	70 50	..	21.81	28.01	38.02	48.62	55.17	58.17	..	..	59.54	43.40	41.43	31.3
28. Fort Warren	42 19	70 55	..	27.83	27.99	33.14	44.49	53.93	65.19	70.88	69.96	62.33	51.64	41.59	30.0
29. Framingham	42 19	71 26	150	22.76	24.16	32.89	44.43	55.09	65.56	69.01	67.17	59.06	47.81	36.97	24.6
30. Georgetown	42 43	71 00	225	22.57	25.68	32.57	44.94	52.21	65.26	68.71	68.52	60.33	47.02	38.35	26.4
31. Grafton	42 13	71 41	..	20.40	31.07	32.75	42.15	51.62	62.95	..	..	..	..	..	..
32. Harwich	41 41	70 04	..	..	..	..	..	..	63.83	70.50	70.50	63.66	..	..	..
33. Hinsdale	42 27	73 08	1360	24.13	21.15	23.87	42.08	53.65	64.76	69.59	66.27	58.54	43.08	33.00	23.1
34. Ipswich	42 41	70 50	50	30.0	30.0	38.0	48.0	56.5	68.0	70.5	70.0	63.5	51.6	39.0	37.0
35. Kingston	42 00	70 48	65	28.05	28.65	31.47	43.53	51.89	64.02	70.12	67.98	61.97	51.16	41.87	31.1
36. Lawrence	42 42	71 10	143	23.21	25.65	31.23	42.19	53.21	64.26	69.13	67.86	59.83	47.98	38.41	26.3
37. Lenox	42 20	73 18	1000	22.77	16.77	29.92	37.24	51.51	63.27	64.92	64.36	54.62	42.86	32.79	21.9
38. Leominster	42 31	71 44	..	29.5	..	..	..	..	..	..	..	..	..	..	..
39. Lowell	42 38	71 19	..	24.26	25.10	34.26	44.11	56.00	66.56	73.50	70.46	62.69	50.19	40.10	29.1
40. Lunenburgh	42 35	71 43	450	25.06	26.11	33.79	44.71	55.71	66.37	71.07	65.69	61.13	50.16	39.60	28.3
41. Lynn	42 28	70 57	..	17.14	19.97	24.47	44.03	56.90	66.42	71.25	67.86	62.18	50.68	39.51	36.0
42. Medfield	42 11	71 18	..	23.81	26.10	34.53	43.69	54.48	64.69	68.92	68.09	59.21	49.17	38.56	29.6
43. Mendon	42 06	71 34	..	24.35	24.10	32.03	44.00	54.44	64.53	70.47	67.70	59.93	48.53	38.78	27.0
44. Milton	42 16	70 44	115	27.00	27.59	32.34	44.89	54.44	65.61	70.70	69.32	61.13	50.20	39.15	28.8
45. Nantucket	41 17	70 06	30	32.19	33.62	37.75	45.15	54.39	64.71	71.09	69.88	64.37	55.38	45.22	38.5
46. Nantucket	41 17	70 06	30	32.07	31.98	36.56	44.59	52.76	63.17	70.10	68.84	64.13	55.36	45.63	36.5
47. New Bedford	41 39	70 56	90	28.79	29.44	35.50	44.66	54.24	63.50	69.12	68.23	62.05	52.29	42.48	32.4
48. Newbury	42 47	70 54	25	23.30	25.80	32.63	45.07	53.49	66.26	70.59	67.40	57.29	46.62	38.11	27.2
49. Newburyport	42 48	70 52	46	23.14	23.54	30.79	42.99	53.57	64.02	70.10	65.95	61.41	49.59	38.88	28.0
50. North Attleboro'	41 59	71 20	175	23.01	27.19	32.40	45.29	57.31	69.02	73.44	67.39	63.07	51.15	40.47	28.5
51. North Billerica	42 35	71 17	135	24.62	27.13	31.57	45.21	54.71	67.20	72.10	69.07	61.25	48.55	38.01	26.5
52. Northampton	42 19	72 38	100	..	..	40.23	48.25	59.53	..	72.89	71.03	60.99	51.87	..	24.5
53. Pittsfield	42 27	73 15	1084	..	23.30	28.20	34.41	..	64.42	67.28	64.32	57.33	49.11	31.10	26.
54. Plainfield	42 31	72 56	..	..	25.85	23.23	..	..	..	..	..	..	..	..	..
55. Princeton	42 28	71 53	1113	20.24	17.61	25.58	41.18	52.83	62.85	69.46	64.38	58.73	49.16	37.45	24.4
56. Richmond	42 23	73 22	1100	21.80	24.17	30.83	44.01	57.83	68.18	71.57	68.70	62.22	49.55	36.03	25.6
57. Roxbury	42 21	71 04	82	..	..	40.94	47.88	53.23	70.47	72.23	71.27	63.40	52.90	48.17	..
58. Salem	42 31	70 53	75	25.59	27.85	35.56	46.16	56.86	67.22	72.41	70.60	63.00	51.36	39.82	30.
59. Sandwich	41 45	70 30	20	26.23	29.73	37.48	45.01	53.78	61.42	69.16	70.29	59.40	50.92	43.43	32.
60. Southwick	42 03	72 46	265	21.05	..	32.60	41.77	60.88	69.44	..	..	54.35	..	36.32	24.
61. Springfield	42 06	72 35	199	24.37	26.21	34.25	46.37	58.77	69.93	73.28	70.99	61.82	50.43	39.90	28.
62. Taunton	41 54	71 06	..	..	22.78	30.43	..	62.69	69.90	77.13	69.47	63.40	54.27	43.20	29.
63. Topsfield	42 39	70 56	..	25.27	27.21	33.52	44.75	54.30	64.90	69.91	68.32	60.53	48.87	40.49	28.
64. Warwick	42 41	72 20	..	18.20	20.00	27.80	43.60	..	63.85	69.30	69.05	59.10	47.30	35.50	27.

[1] Observations corrected for daily variation by means of the general table.

MASSACHUSETTS.—Continued.

	Spring.	Summer.	Autumn.	Winter.	Year.	Series. Begins.	Series. Ends.	Extent yrs.	Extent mos.	Observing hours.	Observer.	References.
14	44°.93	69°.47	50°.45	26°.96	47°.95	Jan. 1790;	Dec. 1870	48	5	$7_m\ 2_a\ 9_a$	Profs. Farrar, Bond, and others.	Am. Almanac 1837, MS. in S. Coll., Am. Almanac 1843 and foll. especially 1854, and S. O.
15	..	..	..	27.86	..	Dec. 1856;	Jan. 1858	0	6	"	D. H. Ellis.	P. O. and S. I. Vol. 1.
16	46.16	69.58	52.68	27.30	48.93	Jan. 1861;	June, 1865	3	4	$\odot_r\ 9_m\ 3_a\ 9_a$	W. F. Patton, J. L. Fox, and J. Beale, Surgeons.	MS. in S. Coll. and S. O.
17	..	67.34	..	..	..	May, 1860;	Mar. 1861	0	9	$7_m\ 2_a\ 9_a$ bis	Dr. G. M. Morse.	S. O.
18	..	..	..	..	..	1806		0	4	$\odot_r\ 2_a^1$	Dr. I. Hurd.	Med. and Agr. Reg. Bost. Vol. 1, 1806–7.
19	..	..	..	27.49	..	Dec. 1858;	Feb. 1859	0	3	$7_m\ 2_a\ 9_a$	A. W. Mack.	P. O. and S. I. Vol. 1.
20	42.88	68.08	47.78	23.71	45.61	Apr. 1806;	Nov. 1818	3	4	1	E. Hoyt and Hitchcock.	Med. and Agr. Reg. Bost. Vol 1, 1806–7, and Sill. Journ.
21	..	..	..	..	..	1849		0	3	$\odot_r\ 9_m\ 3_a\ 9_a$	Ritchie.	S. Coll.
22	46.69	70.73	..	..	..	1849		0	6	"	Rice.	" "
23	..	..	..	..	..	1861		0	2	$7_m\ 2_a\ 9_a$ bis	C. C. Terry.	S. O.
24	..	..	..	..	..	1863		0	1	"	Dr. N. Barrows.	" "
25	44.96	68.06	51.45	27.01	47.87	Jan. 1861;	Nov. 1861	0	11	"	G. Raymond.	" "
26	45.52	68.47	52.43	28.60	48.76	Jan. 1824;	Dec. 1870	26	7	$7_m\ 2_a\ 9_a$	Assistant Surgeon.	Ar. Met. Regs. 1855 and 1860, and MS. from S. G. O.
27	47.27	..	48.12	27.05	..	Sept. 1864;	June, 1865	0	10	"	....	MS. from S. G. O.
28	43.85	68.68	51.85	28.63	48.25	Oct. 1862;	Dec. 1870	7	8	"	....	" " "
29	44.14	67.25	47.95	23.86	45.80	1843;	1852	5	10	$\odot_r\ 9_m\ 3_a\ 9_a$	Hyde.	S. Coll.
30	43.24	67.50	48.57	24.90	46.05	Feb. 1865;	Dec. 1870	4	2	$7_m\ 2_a\ 9_a$ bis	H. M. Nelson.	S. O.
31	42.17	..	..	..	..	1861		0	6	"	Rev. H. W. Scandlin.	" "
32	..	68.28	..	..	..	1847;	1848	0	8	$\odot_r$ N. $\odot_s$	Brooks.	Pat.Off. Rep. 1851.
33	39.87	66.87	44.87	22.82	43.61	July, 1868;	Dec. 1870	2	3	$7_m\ 2_a\ 9_a$ bis	Rev. E. Dewhurst.	S. O.
34	47.50	69.50	51.37	32.33	50.18	....		3	0	......	....	Rep. Brit. Asso. 1847.
35	42.30	67.37	51.67	29.28	47.65	July, 1866;	Dec. 1870	4	6	$7_m\ 2_a\ 9_a$ bis	G. S. Newcomb.	S. O.
36	42.21	67.08	48.74	25.06	45.77	Jan. 1856;	Dec. 1870	14	0	"	J. Fallon.	P. O. and S. I. Vol. 1, and S. O.
37	39.56	64.18	43.42	20.49	41.91	Jan. 1837;	Dec. 1838	2	0	......	Metcalf.	Rep. Brit. Asso. 1847.
38	..	..	..	..	..	1806		0	1	$\odot_r\ 2_a^1$	A. Bigelow.	Med. and Agr. Journ. Bost. Vol. 1, 1806–7.
39	44.79	70.17	50.99	26.18	48.03	Jan. 1846;	Dec. 1852	7	0	$7_m\ 2_a$	R. and J. R. Moor.	Am. Alm. 1848 and foll.
40	44.74	67.71	50.30	26.52	47.32	Jan. 1838;	Dec. 1870	33	0	$7_m\ 2_a\ 9_a$	G. A. Cunningham.	S. Coll. and S. O.
41	41.80	68.51	50.79	24.37	46.37	1849;	1853	1	7	$\odot_r\ 9_m\ 3_a\ 9_a$	Batcheder.	S. Coll.
42	44.23	67.23	48.98	26.53	46.74	Jan. 1821;	Dec. 1832	12	0	$\odot_r\ 2_a\ 9_a$	Sanders.	Am. Alm. 1834.
43	43.49	67.57	49.08	25.15	46.32	Jan. 1833;	Dec. 1870	35	0	$7_m\ 2_a\ 9_a$ bis	Dr. J. G. Metcalf.	Am. Alm. 1843 and foll., MS. in S. Coll., P. O. and S. I. Vol. 1, and S. O.
44	43.89	68.54	50.16	27.81	47.60	Jan. 1867;	Dec. 1870	3	8	"	A. K. Teele.	S. O.
45	45.76	68.56	54.99	34.78	51.02	Jan. 1827;	Dec. 1853	9	3	......	W. Mitchell.	MS. in S. Coll.
46	44.64	67.37	55.04	33.54	50.15	Jan. 1854;	Mar. 1861	6	3	$7_m\ 2_a\ 9_a$	" "	P.O. and S. I. Vol. 1, and S. O.
47	44.80	66.95	52.27	30.21	48.56	Oct. 1812;	Dec. 1870	58	1	$\odot_r\ 2_a\ \odot_s\ 10_a$	S. Rodman and E. T. Tucker.	Sill Journ., MS. in S. Coll., P. O. and S. I. Vol. 1, S. Coll., and S. O.
48	43.73	68.08	47.34	25.43	46.15	May, 1864;	Dec. 1870	5	5	$7_m\ 2_a\ 9_a$ bis	J. H. Caldwell.	S. O.
49	42.45	66.69	49.96	24.91	46.00	Mar. 1806;	Sept. 1868	6	1	1	Dr. H. C. Perkins.	Med. and Agr. Journ. Boston Vol. 1, 1806–7, P. O. and S. I, Vol. 1, S. Coll., and MS.
50	45.00	69.95	51.56	26.25	48.19	1850;	Mar. 1857	7	2	$7_m\ 2_a\ 9_a$	H. Rice.	P. O. and S. I. Vol. 1, & S. Coll.
51	43.83	69.46	49.27	26.10	47.16	Feb. 1866;	Dec. 1870	4	11	$7_m\ 2_a\ 9_a$ bis	Rev. E. Nason.	S. O.
52	49.34	..	..	..	..	1844;	1845	0	8	6_m N. 6_a	Plant.	Manuscript.
53	..	65.34	45.85	..	..	1851;	1853	1	3	$6_m\ 2_a\ 10_a$	Benjamin.	Manuscript and S. Coll.
54	..	..	..	..	..	1857		0	2	$7_m\ 9_m$ N. 9_a	F. Shaw.	P. O. and S. I. Vol. 1.
55	39.86	65.56	48.45	20.77	43.66	Nov. 1853;	Dec. 1857	3	8	$7_m\ 2_a\ 9_a$	J. Brooks.	P. O. & S. I. Vol. 1, & S. Coll.
56	44.22	69.48	49.27	23.86	46.71	1851;	Dec. 1870	14	10	"	W. Bacon.	S. O., S. Coll., and P. O. and S. I. Vol. 1.
57	47.35	71.32	54.82	..	..	1849		0	9	$\odot_r\ 9_m\ 3_a\ 9_a$	Kent.	S. Coll.
58	46.19	70.08	51.39	27.97	48.91	Jan. 1786;	Dec. 1828	43	0	8_m N. $\odot_s\ 10_a$	Dr. Holyoke.	Am. Alm. 1834, 1837.
59	45.42	66.96	51.25	29.38	48.25	May, 1863;	Apr. 1865	1	11	$7_m\ 2_a\ 9_a$ bis	Dr. N. Barrows.	S. O.
60	45.08	..	..	..	..	1849;	1851	1	0	$\odot_r\ 9_m\ 3_a\ 9_a$	Holcomb.	S. Coll.
61	46.46	71.40	50.72	26.24	48.71	Jan. 1848;	Dec. 1866	9	11	1	L. C. Allin, F. A. Brewer, J. Weatherhead.	P. O. and S. I. Vol. 1, S. O., Manuscript, and S. Coll.
62	..	72.17	53.62	..	..	May, 1854;	Mar. 1856	0	10	$7_m\ 2_a\ 9_a$	A. Schlegel.	P. O. and S. I. Vol. 1.
63	44.19	67.71	49.96	26.93	47.20	Apr. 1860;	Dec. 1870	9	9	$7_m\ 2_a\ 9_a$ bis	N. B. Brown, J. H. Caldwell, and A. M. Merriam.	S. O.
64	..	67.40	47.30	21.93	..	June, 1806;	Sept. 1807	1	3	$\odot_r\ 2_a^1$	....	Med. and Agr. Reg. Bost. Vol. 1, 1806–7.

MASSACHUSETTS.—Continued.

Name of Station.	Lat.	Long.	Height.	Jan.	Feb.	March.	April.	May.	June	July.	August.	Sept.	Oct.	Nov.	Dec.
65. Watertown Arsenal[1]	42°21′	71°11′	100	25°.85	25°.86	33°.14	45°.75	55°.59	66°.02	71°.61	70°.19	61°.83	49°.42	37°.78	28°.27
66. West Denis . . .	41 40	70 11	25	..	..	..	..	..	..	..	..	60.77	50.50	..	..
67. Westfield . . .	42 06	72 45	180	26.64	29.39	37.55	47.90	60.98	68.04	74.39	69.35	60.39	51.25	38.95	32.04
68. Westfield . . .	42 06	72 45	180	22.48	25.48	32.91	45.16	55.92	64.59	69.58	66.94	59.57	48.55	38.31	27.22
69. West Stockbridge .	42 16	73 22	..	..	19.51	..	..	..	69.72	..	..	..	..	..	..
70. Weymouth . . .	42 12	70 56	150	22.06	33.90	33.09	42.51	53.98	63.99	69.78	66.46	60.99	51.00	40.15	29.29
71. Williamstown (Will. Coll.)	42 43	73 13	686	21.63	22.92	30.93	43.60	55.78	65.56	69.66	66.52	58.81	46.92	36.34	25.28
72. Wood's Hole . .	41 32	70 40	25	30.58	28.80	37.05	44.54	55.59	66.84	70.99	69.95	64.84	53.82	43.62	36.48
73. Worcester (State Lun. As.)	42 16	71 49	528	23.74	25.60	33.10	45.75	56.18	65.84	70.94	67.71	60.89	49.74	39.26	27.67

MICHIGAN.

Name of Station.	Lat.	Long.	Height.	Jan.	Feb.	March.	April.	May.	June	July.	August.	Sept.	Oct.	Nov.	Dec.
1. Adrian	41 58	84 11	1240	23.80	22.03	28.03	46.65	58.10	67.18	..	..	..	..	..	..
2. Ann Harbor . .	42 19	83 44	891	21.39	20.74	30.75	47.85	58.61	68.89	72.07	69.72	63.05	50.49	37.86	26.77
3. Battle Creek . .	42 22	85 15	750	24.45	25.98	34.19	44.55	58.19	69.79	73.89	71.44	63.46	49.61	38.21	28.35
4. Benzonia . . .	44 37	86 08	620	22.18	21.40	28.63	44.63	59.18	..	..	..	..	..	39.05	27.98
5. Brooklyn . . .	42 06	83 36	1020	19.8	25.9	36.4	..	..	..	..	..	..	..	..	..
6. Carp Lake Mine[4] .	46 52	89 54	1440	15.23	21.85	22.98	36.50	..	..	68.53	67.88	53.03	41.98	29.84	15.50
7. Central Mine . .	47 00	88 54	1177	14.24	12.01	21.51	34.02	48.18	58.93	64.58	60.63	52.80	39.79	29.08	17.26
8. Clinton	42 05	84 00	750	25.15	32.52	39.52	44.08	56.79	..	..	..	54.31	43.67	40.73	26.28
9. Coldwater . . .	41 59	85 02	..	26.71	26.38	27.96	46.32	57.75	65.44	72.52	68.08	60.94	45.75	35.63	34.35
10. Cooper[5]	42 25	85 38	690	21.21	24.46	30.42	45.09	54.55	67.97	73.80	69.90	62.86	49.00	34.58	28.22
11. Copper Falls Mine .	47 26	88 22	1250	8.15	6.85	18.05	31.85	46.70	56.70	65.85	61.35	50.40	42.00	28.90	17.60
12. Dearbornville . .	42 20	83 18	..	24.99	21.26	33.79	43.42	54.73	64.82	69.95	65.32	58.00	51.76	35.01	24.26
13. Detroit	42 20	83 03	597	25.84	25.89	34.11	46.18	56.09	65.43	69.60	69.11	58.51	49.85	38.14	28.09
14. Eagle River . .	47 25	88 26	627	10.93	11.13	18.93	38.63	49.50	61.46	68.16	61.08	54.61	47.21	29.63	17.85
15. Eureka Valley . .	47 06	88 51	800	17.57	19.59	23.98	35.73	51.25	59.08	66.80	64.78	50.18	40.68	29.33	21.80
16. Flint	43 02	83 42	..	22.85	19.68	33.15	48.07	59.80	66.90	74.12	70.93	64.39	49.06	36.92	25.03
17. Forestville . . .	43 38	82 39	600	..	..	..	..	..	66.8	70.1	..	..	..	..	..
18. Fort Brady . . .	46 30	84 28	600	16.73	15.89	24.77	38.39	49.67	59.57	65.50	63.10	54.75	43.88	32.60	21.44
19. Fort Gratiot . . .	42 59	82 29	598	25.42	25.39	32.72	44.30	54.26	63.79	69.81	67.95	60.01	48.78	38.28	27.19
20. Fort Mackinac . .	45 51	84 40	728	19.10	17.27	25.69	37.32	48.18	57.72	64.90	64.17	55.30	45.32	34.14	23.14
21. Fort Wayne . . .	42 20	83 05	..	34.21	29.91	..	..	59.83	64.96	74.32	75.10	65.46	53.49	36.92	35.90
22. Fort Wilkins . .	47 28	88 02	630	23.40	21.40	28.93	38.07	48.42	56.68	63.55	62.17	55.79	42.91	30.17	20.55
23. Grand Haven . .	43 05	86 15	588	25.80	25.53	32.98	45.25	56.08	65.40	70.12	70.27	60.38	49.83	38.00	28.73
24. Grand Rapids . .	43 00	85 42	780	23.29	24.71	30.94	45.63	57.49	67.28	73.59	68.38	61.07	47.79	36.79	25.86
25. Holland	42 49	86 08	..	24.71	26.51	32.10	44.31	54.58	66.01	70.48	65.82	58.15	47.70	37.78	28.24
26. Homestead . . .	44 36	86 02	..	21.50	23.47	25.65	41.47	51.65	65.64	67.13	62.09	59.76	46.29	37.62	25.65
27. Jackson	42 17	84 27	..	..	25.77	..	..	..	..	..	..	..	..	..	..
28. Lake George . .	46 15	85 00	..	..	..	..	..	49.79	..	66.15	66.69	54.21	..	..	..
29. Lansing (State Agr. Coll.)	42 46	84 36	895	23.61	25.36	32.50	46.59	56.51	67.20	70.65	67.43	59.88	45.72	37.29	25.90
30. Laphamsville . .	43 00	85 30	650	28.90	32.65	39.33	43.87	54.38	64.10	69.50	66.24	64.26	49.59	35.23	26.14
31. Litchfield . . .	42 05	84 46	1040	21.35	24.37	29.16	44.63	55.74	67.22	72.74	67.45	59.95	47.12	36.18	23.34
32. Macon	42 05	83 52	..	..	..	..	..	..	..	..	..	..	..	..	23.13
33. Manchester . . .	42 11	84 06	..	..	..	..	..	58.08	70.98	66.60	66.65	..	..	..	..

[1] Observations after 1844 were made at West Newton, about two miles West of Watertown Arsenal, by J. H. Bixby.

[2] Observations corrected for daily variation by means of the general table.

[3] The names of the observers from 1839 to 1859 are not given.

MASSACHUSETTS.—Continued.

	Spring.	Summer.	Autumn.	Winter.	Year.	Series. Begins. Ends.	Extent yrs. mos.	Observing hours.	Observer.	References.
65	44°.83	69°.27	49°.68	26°.66	47.°61	Jan. 1837; Dec. 1870	10 0	[2]	Assist. Surg., and J. H. Bixby.	Ar. Met. Reg. 1855, and S. O.
66	..	..	..	..	..	1864	0 2	$7_m\ 2_a\ 9_a$ bis	E. Tappan.	S. O.
67	48.81	70.59	50.20	29.36	49.74	....	2 0	......	....	Dove, 1857.
68	44.66	67.04	48.81	25.06	46.39	Nov. 1824; May, 1866	12 11	[2]	Rev. E. Davis.	P. O. and S. I. Vol. I, S. O., Sill. Journ., and Manuscript.
69	..	..	..	..	..	June, 1849; Feb. 1855	0 2	$7_m\ 2_a\ 9_a$	....	P. O. & S. I. Vol. I, & S. Coll.
70	43.19	66.74	50.71	28.42	47.27	May, 1856; Jan. 1859	1 9	[2]	Dr. N. O. Tinell.	P. O. and S. I. Vol. I.
71	43.44	67.25	47.36	23.28	45.33	Jan. 1816; Dec. 1870	36 8	$7_m\ 2_a\ 9_a$	Profs. C. Dewey and E. Kellogg, A. Hopkins and others.	MS. communicated to S. I. by E. W. Morley, P. O. and S. I. Vol. I, and S. O.
72	45.73	69.26	54.09	31.95	50.26	Aug. 1852; Apr. 1855	1 10	"	R. R. Gifford.	P. O. & S. I. Vol. I, & S. Coll.
73	45.01	68.16	49.96	25.67	47.20	Jan. 1839; Dec. 1870	31 9	[2]	H. C. Prentiss, F. H. Rice, J. Draper.[3]	Am. Alm. 1842 and foll., P. O. and S. I. Vol. I, S. O., and Rep. Brit. Assoc. 1847.

MICHIGAN.

	Spring.	Summer.	Autumn.	Winter.	Year.	Series. Begins. Ends.	Extent yrs. mos.	Observing hours.	Observer.	References.
1	44.26	..	..	..	..	1870	0 6	$7_m\ 2_a\ 9_a$ bis	....	S. O.
2	45.74	70.23	50.47	22.97	47.35	June, 1852; Dec. 1870	4 10	$7_m\ 2_a\ 9_a$	L. Woodruff, Prof. N. C. Winchell & wife.	P. O. and S. I. Vol. I, S. O., & S. Coll.
3	45.64	71.71	50.43	26.26	48.51	Mar. 1849; Dec. 1859	10 9	"	D. W. M. Campbell.	P. O. & S. I. Vol. I, & S. Coll.
4	44.15	..	..	23.85	..	1870	0 7	$7_m\ 2_a\ 9_a$ bis	W. Wilson.	S. O.
5	..	..	..	..	..	Mar. 1853; Mar. 1854	0 4	$7_m\ 2_a\ 9_a$	Dr. M. K. Taylor.	P. O. and S. I. Vol. I.
6	..	..	41.62	17.53	..	July, 1864; Apr. 1865	0 10	$7_m\ 2_a\ 9_a$ bis	Dr. E. Ellis.	S. O.
7	34.57	61.38	40.56	14.50	37.75	May, 1867; Dec. 1870	3 7	"	G. H. Whittlesey.	" "
8	46.80	..	46.24	27.98	..	1850; 1852	0 11	$\odot_r\ 9_m\ 3_a\ 9_a$	Wainwright.	S. Coll.
9	44.01	68.68	47.44	29.15	47.32	July, 1868; Dec. 1870	2 6	$7_m\ 2_a\ 9_a$ bis	N. L. Southworth.	S. O.
10	43.35	70.56	48.81	24.63	46.84	June, 1854; Mar. 1867	7 1	"	Mrs. O. C. Walker & Dr. M. Chase.	P. O. and S. I. Vol. I, and S. O.
11	32.20	61.30	40.43	10.87	36.20	Dec. 1855; Aug. 1857	1 9	$7_m\ 2_a\ 9_a$	C. S. Whittlesey.	MS. in S. Coll. and P. O. and S. I. Vol. I.
12	43.98	66.70	48.26	23.50	45.61	1836; 1839	3 9	"	Assistant Surgeon.	Army Register.
13	45.46	68.05	48.82	26.61	47.24	Apr. 1836; Dec. 1867	30 3	[6]	Various observers.	Ar. Met. Regs. 1855, S. Coll., U. S. Lake Survey, MS. and Rep. of 1867 and 1868, P. O. and S. I. Vol. I, and S. O.
14	35.69	63.57	43.82	13.30	39.09	Dec. 1855; Dec. 1856	1 1	$7_m\ 2_a\ 9_a$	Mrs. M. A. Goff.	P. O. and S. I. Vol. I.
15	36.99	63.55	40.06	19.65	40.06	Jan. 1862; Feb. 1864	1 5	$7_m\ 2_a\ 9_a$ bis	W. Van Orden.	S. O.
16	47.01	70.65	50.12	22.52	47.58	Jan. 1854; Dec. 1855	2 0	$7_m\ 2_a\ 9_a$	Drs. D. Clark and M. Miles.	P. O. and S. I. Vol. I.
17	..	..	..	..	..	1858	0 2	$6_m\ 9_m\ 3_a\ 6_a$	C. N. Turnbull.	MS. from U. S. Lake Survey.
18	37.61	62.72	43.74	18.02	40.52	Jan. 1823; Dec. 1870	32 1	$7_m\ 2_a\ 9_a$	Assistant Surgeon.	Ar. Met. Regs. 1855 and 1860, and MS. from S. G. O.
19	43.76	67.18	49.02	26.00	46.49	Apr. 1830; Aug. 1859	17 5	"	Assist. Surg. & Lieut. C. N. Turnbull.	P. O. and S. I. Vol. I, Ar. Met. Reg. 1855, and U. S. Lake Survey, and MS.
20	37.06	62.26	44.92	19.84	41.02	Sept. 1825; Apr. 1861	27 6	"	Assistant Surgeon.	Ar. Met. Regs. 1855 and 1860, and MS. from S. G. O.
21	..	71.46	51.96	33.34	..	May, 1862; Feb. 1863	0 10	"	....	MS. from S. G. O.
22	38.47	60.80	42.96	21.78	41.00	June, 1844; June, 1846	2 1	$\odot_r\ 9_m\ 3_a\ 9_a$	Assistant Surgeon.	Ar. Met. Reg. 1855.
23	44.77	68.60	49.40	26.69	47.36	Sept. 1859; July, 1863	3 11	$7_m\ 2_a\ 9_a$	H. Squier.	U. S. Lake Survey, Rep. of 1867.
24	44.69	69.75	48.55	24.62	46.90	1849; Dec. 1870	11 3	$7_m\ 2_a\ 9_a$ bis	A. O. Courrier, L. H. Strong, E. A. Strong, & Dr. E. S. Holmes.	P. O. and S. I. Vol. I, S.O., and S. Coll.
25	43.66	67.44	47.88	26.49	46.37	June, 1856; Dec. 1870	8 3	"	L. H. Streng.	P. O. and S. I, Vol. I. and S. O.
26	39.59	64.95	47.89	23.54	43.99	Jan. 1865; Feb. 1870	2 9	"	G. E. Steele.	S. O.
27	..	..	..	..	..	1865	0 1	"	Dr. F. M. Reasner.	" "
28	..	..	..	..	..	1859	0 4	......	Capt. A. W. Whipple, and E. Perrault.	P. O. and S. I. Vol. I.
29	45.20	68.43	47.63	24.96	46.55	Dec. 1858; Dec. 1870	7 3	$7_m\ 2_a\ 9_a$ bis	J. C. Holmes, C. Abbe, and R. C. Kedzie.	" " " "
30	45.86	66.61	49.69	29.23	47.85	Dec. 1850; Nov. 1851	1 0	......	Wetmore.	Pat. Off. Rep.
31	43.18	69.14	47.75	23.02	45.77	July, 1866; Dec. 1870	4 6	$7_m\ 2_a\ 9_a$ bis	R. Bullard.	S. O.
32	..	..	..	..	..	1870	0 1	"	D. Howell.	" "
33	..	68.08	..	..	..	1865	0 4	"	Dr. F. M. Reasner.	" "

[4] The observations in 1864 were made at Garlick, about two miles east of Carp Lake Mine.

[5] The observations in 1866–7 were made at Kalamazoo, about five miles west of Cooper.

[6] Observations corrected for daily variation.

MICHIGAN.—Continued.

Name of Station.	Lat.	Long.	Height.	Jan.	Feb.	March.	April.	May.	June.	July.	August.	Sept.	Oct.	Nov.	Dec.
34. Marquette . . .	46°32′	87°35′	710	18°.65	17°.92	25°.74	37°.72	49°.22	59°.89	65°.08	64°.72	56°.66	45°.00	32°.73	22°.13
35. Mill Point . . .	43 06	86 10	..	20.62	22.70	29.57	42.93	50.82	62.71	65.82	64.78	56.07	47.15	34.01	26.37
36. Monroe[1]	41 56	83 27	551	25.60	23.85	35.19	46.78	57.35	68.19	73.04	70.55	61.11	49.47	38.83	28.03
37. Muskegon . . .	43 15	86 16	..	29.79	27.92	32.60	50.22	63.35	67.48	76.44	73.47	67.93	46.69	38.37	29.83
38. Newark	42 30	86 00	..	..	..	..	46.62	..	..	..	..	..	..	..	..
39. New Buffalo . .	41 50	86 46	661	29.14	24.94	38.09	46.34	58.01	67.38	71.19	68.77	61.57	50.22	38.12	28.64
40. Northport[2] . . .	45 08	85 40	592	22.54	22.08	26.21	39.23	50.00	60.40	68.20	64.18	58.78	47.09	36.75	25.77
41. Old Mission . . .	44 45	85 30	600	..	..	..	..	50.88	57.85	67.23	66.40	63.15	39.18	..	..
42. Ontonagon . . .	46 53	89 30	620	16.41	15.57	21.80	36.91	48.26	59.49	64.89	63.50	55.98	43.79	33.25	20.46
43. Otsego	42 30	85 42	..	27.95	31.03	34.99	45.53	54.34	65.31	70.32	67.35	61.99	47.45	40.83	30.83
44. Pennsylvania Mine .	47 20	88 15	1200	22.09	17.70	19.35	34.30	48.03	..	..	..	..	..	..	..
45. Pleasanton . . .	44 29	86 10	750	21.79	20.40	25.56	40.05	55.16	60.92	66.51	63.69	58.44	39.41	30.47	25.75
46. Pontiac	42 40	83 21	927	21.49	26.28	34.09	45.28	57.47	68.24	68.81	68.20	56.98	44.87	36.77	25.55
47. Portage Lake[3] . .	47 10	88 37	670	10.9	14.2	26.7	36.8	46.8	62.4	..	62.4	..	..	..	..
48. Port Huron . . .	42 58	82 27	606	29.08	24.39	35.62	43.28	52.89	64.85	71.90	68.80	63.63	49.32	35.07	31.26
49. Redford Centre .	42 25	83 20	650	..	..	..	..	..	67.80	69.70	69.95	..	..	..	..
50. Romeo	42 44	83 02	714	13.23	14.86	24.83	45.79	54.23	68.46	72.68	66.79	59.87	49.94	35.80	22.30
51. St. James . . .	45 44	85 00	596	20.36	15.48	24.64	39.04	50.35	59.65	66.53	66.55	59.60	47.87	35.48	24.76
52. St. Mary's River .	46 20	84 10	585	..	..	..	..	..	55.59	..	..	..	..	..	..
53. Saginaw	43 27	84 00	650	..	..	37.19	41.39	53.30	60.57	..	..	..	..	..	..
54. Saugatuck . . .	42 40	86 12	..	23.03	22.31	31.91	49.35	55.57	65.22	75.04	72.09	68.00	54.56	41.93	29.89
55. Sault de St. Marie .	46 29	84 29	600	19.45	18.55	27.90	40.45	49.90	60.70	64.90	62.90	55.60	42.60	30.70	22.95
56. Sugar Island . .	46 29	84 20	574	20.05	21.73	28.22	33.48	..	..	..	..	..	..	32.60	22.79
57. Tawas City . . .	44 16	83 31	583	21.56	23.67	30.20	39.80	50.75	62.03	67.49	66.68	58.88	48.06	36.89	25.91
58. Thunder Bay Island	45 02	83 17	610	23.29	22.67	27.72	37.14	47.02	57.12	64.19	65.26	58.29	46.73	36.41	26.71
59. Woodmere Cem'ry (near Detroit) .	42 20	83 03	562	22.68	23.43	30.30	48.69	60.98	68.36	72.98	70.99	66.00	53.04	38.33	27.00
60. Ypsilanti	42 15	83 40	750	24.42	26.73	34.19	44.56	58.16	65.30	70.03	68.95	58.81	48.62	37.61	28.10

MINNESOTA.

Name of Station.	Lat.	Long.	Height.	Jan.	Feb.	March.	April.	May.	June.	July.	August.	Sept.	Oct.	Nov.	Dec.
1. Afton	44 53	92 50	950	11.78	14.77	20.17	42.88	56.09	66.12	70.23	66.05	59.86	42.53	32.43	14.99
2. Alexandria . . .	45 52	95 22	1225	..	..	..	..	..	..	..	..	..	..	..	12.48
3. Beaver Bay . . .	47 12	91 18	1270	12.87	14.37	22.36	36.22	47.02	55.92	62.03	61.62	52.76	41.56	30.96	16.32
4. Beaver River Valley	47 11	91 25	950	..	..	31.18	..	51.33	61.08	63.13	59.90	48.95	..	..	..
5. Bowles' Creek . .	44 55	92 55	650	9.80	..	..	..	..	..	..	..	..	..	.	..
6. Buchanan . . .	47 33	92 00	..	22.12	10.50	30.32	37.72	49.85	..	..	..	..	..	..	25.44
7. Burlington . . .	47 01	91 42	645	17.57	14.25	29.86	34.86	47.09	55.91	62.52	62.04	54.38	41.63	28.69	13.34
8. Cass Lake . . .	47 30	94 31	1450	13.12	4.28	..	..	..	..	60.31	60.94	43.98	..	..	3.61
9. Chatfield	43 50	92 14	900	14.98	20.63	32.65	46.17	56.48	64.91	71.27	69.26	57.24	46.48	33.82	12.31
10. Clearwater Lake .	45 12	94 06	975	..	..	..	..	..	..	..	65.31	..	..	..	..
11. Danville	..	..	..	5.03	13.47	35.17	38.54	..	67.36	..	..	..	..	..	..
12. Fond du Lac . .	46 48	92 03	660	14.97	20.27	30.05	33.80	48.09	61.53	63.91	..	..	43.56	37.93	12.19
13. Forest City . . .	45 11	94 30	..	10.18	15.60	27.87	43.36	57.06	66.40	69.08	66.89	57.83	44.79	30.21	15.47
14. Fort Ridgeley . .	44 30	94 45	1230	10.70	14.80	25.89	43.69	59.31	68.72	73.52	69.62	60.85	47.37	31.24	16.05
15. Fort Ripley (Gaines)	46 10	94 24	1130	7.41	11.89	23.98	40.82	54.80	65.97	70.50	66.18	56.52	44.77	28.26	11.08
16. Fort Snelling . .	44 53	93 10	820	13.23	17.25	29.96	46.05	59.35	68.92	74.04	70.19	59.31	47.27	31.78	16.90
17. Grand Portage . .	47 50	89 50	[4]	..	..	..	..	46.73	54.20	59.45	59.15	50.15	..	..	..
18. Hastings	44 44	92 54	..	..	..	..	..	..	70.50	69.72	68.55	59.07	46.32	30.23	21.80
19. Hazlewood (or "Oomahoo")	..	..	..	5.92	9.43	20.48	40.15	55.81	68.18	72.93	69.03	56.93	47.20	29.33	17.54
20. Hennepin Co. . .	45 00	93 20	..	11.6	23.0	24.1	41.3	58.0	67.1	66.5	67.2	67.3	47.7	38.4	9.3
21. Itasca	45 16	93 32	856	3.85	17.12	27.32	44.77	50.15	69.60	67.25	..	..	..	29.85	14.95
22. Kandotta . . .	45 45	94 55	..	8.25	11.75	..	..	..	..	..	..	..	..	..	..
23. Koniska	45 10	94 10	..	12.01	13.17	25.21	43.38	57.12	63.15	68.24	62.58	57.58	40.07	30.40	16.86

[1] This series includes observations made in December at Brest, about five miles northeast of Monroe.

[2] This series includes observations made in March, 1862, at Grand Traverse Lt. Ho., about five miles northeast of Northport.

MICHIGAN.—Continued.

	Spring.	Summer.	Autumn.	Winter.	Year.	Series. Begins. Ends.	Extent yrs.mos.	Observing hours.	Observer.	References.
34	37°.56	63°.23	44°.80	19°.57	41°.29	Sept. 1857; Dec. 1867	10 4	$7_m\ 2_a\ 9_a$	H. S. & F. M. Bacon, P. White, and G. H. Baker.	U. S. Lake Survey, Rep. of 1867-8, P. O. and S. I. Vol. 1, and S. O.
35	41.11	64.44	45.74	23.23	43.63	July, 1860; June, 1862	2 0	$7_m\ 2_a\ 9_a$ bis	L. M. S. Smith.	S. O.
36	46.44	70.59	49.80	25.83	48.17	Jan. 1849; Dec. 1870	11 9	"	J. Lane, H. J. and F. E. Whelpley and others.	U. S. Lake Survey, Rep. of 1867-8, P. O. and S. I. Vol. 1., S. O., and S. Coll.
37	48.72	72.46	51.00	29.18	50.34	Oct. 1868; Aug. 1870	1 10	"	H. A. Pattison.	S. O.
38	..	..	..	..	..	1856	0 1	$7_m\ 2_a\ 9_a$	L. H. Streng.	P. O. and S. I. Vol. 1.
39	47.48	69.11	49.97	27.57	48.53	Jan. 1858; May, 1862	2 10	$7_m\ 1_a\ 9_a$	J. B. Crosby.	P. O. and S. I. Vol. 1. and S. O.
40	38.48	64.26	47.54	23.46	43.43	Mar. 1862; Dec. 1870	4 8	$7_m\ 2_a\ 9_a$ bis	Rev. G. N. Smith, & H. R. Shetterly.	S. O.
41	..	63.83	..	..	..	1869	0 6	"	C. P. Avery.	" "
42	35.66	62.63	44.34	17.48	40.03	Aug. 1859; Dec. 1870	11 5	"	H. Shelby, H. B. Smith, & Dr. E. Ellis.	U. S. Lake Survey, Rep. of 1867 and 1868, and S. O.
43	44.95	67.66	50.09	29.94	48.16	Apr. 1867; Sept. 1870	3 6	"	Dr. M. Chase & wife.	S. O.
44	33.89	..	..	..	..	1869	0 5	"	R. H. Griffith.	" "
45	40.26	63.71	42.77	22.65	42.35	Mar. 1869; Aug. 1870	1 6	"	J. D. Millard.	" "
46	45.61	68.42	46.21	24.44	46.17	Mar. 1864; Aug. 1865	1 6	"	J. A. Weeks.	" "
47	36.77	..	..	..	..	Jan. 1854; Aug. 1862	0 7	$\odot_r$ N. $\odot_s$	C. H. Palmer and J. B. Minick.	MS. in S. Coll. and S. O.
48	43.93	68.52	49.34	28.24	47.51	May, 1857; July, 1859	2 1	$7_m\ 2_a\ 9_a$	J. Allen.	P. O. and S. I. Vol. 1.
49	..	69.15	..	..	..	1861	0 3	$7_m\ 2_a\ 9_a$ bis	Dr. C. S. Smith.	S. O.
50	41.62	69.31	48.54	16.80	44.07	Jan. 1856; Mar. 1857	1 2	$7_m\ 1_a\ 9_a$	D. S. L. Andrews.	P. O. and S. I. Vol. 1.
51	38.01	64.24	47.65	20.20	42.53	Sept. 1852; May, 1856	3 3	$7_m\ 2_a\ 9_a$	J. J. Strong.	" " " "
52	..	..	..	..	..	1859	0 1	......	....	" " " "
53	43.96	..	..	..	..	1849	0 4	$\odot_r\ 9_m\ 3_a\ 9_a$	Birney.	S. Coll.
54	45.61	70.78	54.83	25.08	49.08	Feb. 1854; May, 1856	2 1	$7_m\ 2_a\ 9_a$	L. H. Streng.	P. O. and S. I. Vol. 1.
55	39.42	62.83	42.97	20.32	41.38	Sept. 1823; June, 1825	1 10	"	Col. Cutler.	MS. in S. Coll.
56	..	..	..	21.52	..	Nov. 1863; Apr. 1868	0 11	$7_m\ 2_a\ 9_a$ bis	J. W. Church and J. W. Paxton.	MS. from U. S. Lake Survey, and S. O.
57	40.25	65.40	47.94	23.71	44.33	Sept. 1858; Dec. 1867	9 4	$7_m\ 2_a\ 9_a$	J. Oliver and C. H. Whittemore.	U. S. Lake Survey, Rep. of 1867–68.
58	37.29	62.19	47.14	24.22	42.71	Aug. 1858; Dec. 1870	9 0	"	J. W. Paxton & others.	Survey of N. and N. W. Lakes, Rep. of 1867, MS, and S. O.
59	46.66	70.78	52.46	24.37	48.57	Feb. 1870; Dec. 1870	0 11	$7_m\ 2_a\ 9_a$ bis	F. W. Higgins.	S. O.
60	45.64	68.09	48.35	26.42	47.13	Jan. 1859; Sept. 1864	4 11	"	C. S. Woodward.	P. O. and S. I. Vol. 1, and S. O.

MINNESOTA.

	Spring.	Summer.	Autumn.	Winter.	Year.	Series. Begins. Ends.	Extent yrs.mos.	Observing hours.	Observer.	References.
1	39.71	67.47	44.94	13.85	41.49	Apr. 1865; July 1870	3 5	$7_m\ 2_a\ 9_a$ bis	Dr. B. F. Babcock & wife.	S. O.
2	..	..	..	..	..	1868	0 1	"	S. Bloomfield.	" "
3	35.20	59.86	41.76	14.52	37.84	Nov. 858; Dec. 1870	10 11	"	T. Clarke, and C. Wieland.	P. O. and S. I. Vol. 1, and S. O.
4	..	61.37	..	..	..	1860	0 6	"	H. Wieland.	S. O.
5	..	..	..	..	..	1866	0 1	"	A. Stouffer.	" "
6	39.30	..	..	19.35	..	Dec. 1857; May, 1858	0 6	7_m N. $3_a\ 9_a$	S. Walsh.	P. O. and S. I. Vol. 1.
7	37.27	60.16	41.57	15.05	38.51	Jan. 1858; Sept. 1860	2 8	$7_m\ 2_a\ 9_a$	A. A. Hibberd.	P. O. and S. I. Vol. 1, and S. O.
8	..	..	..	7.00	..	1852; 1853	0 6	$\odot_r\ 9_m\ 3_a\ 9_a$	Barnard.	S. Coll.
9	45.10	68.48	45.85	15.97	43.85	May, 1859; May, 1861	1 9	$7_m\ 2_a\ 9_a$ bis	T. F. Thickstun.	P. O. and S. I. Vol. 1, & S. O.
10	..	..	..	..	..	1868	0 1	"	S. Bloomfield.	S. O.
11	..	..	..	..	..	1868	0 5	"	T. A. Kellett.	" "
12	37.31	..	..	15.81	..	1849; 1850	0 11	$\odot_r\ 9_m\ 3_a\ 9_a$	Holt.	S. Coll.
13	42.76	67.46	44.28	13.75	42.06	June, 1858; May, 1866	5 10	$7_m\ 2_a\ 9_a$ bis	A. C. & H. L. Smith.	P. O. and S. I. Vol. 1, and S. O.
14	42.96	70.62	46.49	13.85	43.48	July, 1853; Apr. 1867	13 4	$7_m\ 2_a\ 9_a$	Assistant Surgeon.	Ar. Met. Regs. 1855 and 1860, and MS. from S. C. O.
15	39.87	67.55	43.18	10.13	40.18	July, 1849; Dec. 1870	19 6	"	" "	" " " "
16	45.12	71.05	46.12	15.79	44.52	Oct. 1819; Dec. 1870	42 2	"	" "	" " " "
17	..	57.60	..	..	..	1867	0 5	$7_m\ 2_a\ 9_a$ bis	R. Bardon.	S. O.
18	..	69.59	45.21	..	..	1861	0 7	"	T. F. Thickstun.	" "
19	38.81	70.05	44.49	10.96	41.08	Aug. 1860; July, 1862	1 10	"	S. R. Riggs and A. W. Higgins.	" "
20	41.13	66.93	51.13	14.63	43.46	Dec. 1864; Dec. 1865	1 1	4_m N. 8_a	J. B. Clough.	Graphical Rec. in S. Coll.
21	40.75	..	..	11.97	..	Nov. 1860; Mar. 1863	0 10	$7_m\ 2_a\ 9_a$ bis	O. H. Kelly.	S. O.
22	..	..	..	..	..	1859	0 2	$7_m\ 2_a\ 6_a$	A. Whitefield.	P. O. and S. I. Vol. 1.
23	41.90	64.66	42.68	14.01	40.81	Jan. 1869; Dec. 1870	1 9	$7_m\ 2_a\ 9_a$ bis	T. M. and Mary H. Young.	S. O.

[3] This series includes observations made in August, 1862, at Houghton, about four miles southwest of Portage Lake.

[4] Altitude 12½ feet above Lake Superior.

MINNESOTA.—Continued.

Name of Station.	Lat.	Long.	Height.	Jan.	Feb.	March.	April.	May.	June.	July.	August.	Sept.	Oct.	Nov.	Dec.
24. Lac qui parle[1]	45°00′	95°30′	946	8°.85	13°.26	26°.48	42°.78	56°.25	66°.32	72°.14	68°.28	57°.13	45°.79	28°.05	13°.2
25. Lake Winibigoshish	47 30	94 40	..	—8.83	6.67	24.57	..	51.19	..	..	..	..	..	24.03	2.4
26. Litchfield	45 12	94 45	..	..	..	..	..	..	..	71.48	63.89	62.65	46.53	38.24	17.7
27. Madelia	44 00	94 30	..	12.18	14.10	18.86	45.62	62.16	69.24	73.84	69.47	64.76	43.34	32.29	20.0
28. Manketo	44 08	94 02	[2]	..	..	..	..	..	..	..	69.58	..	..	..	..
29. Minneapolis	44 58	93 15	856	9.89	14.58	21.47	41.94	56.96	67.10	71.25	66.68	58.92	44.71	32.35	14.1
30. New Ulm	44 19	94 30	821	11.25	16.52	22.79	43.50	59.34	69.58	74.73	70.67	62.29	47.49	34.65	16.1
31. Pembina	48 58	97 02	900	7.84	18.54	18.19	36.73	52.78	66.85	74.47	69.93	..	..	..	..
32. Princeton	45 34	93 38	..	8.96	13.33	31.54	36.47	56.32	67.28	73.88	67.98	58.65	45.36	27.39	12.3
33. Red Lake	48 30	95 30	..	..	..	..	38.37	..	..	..	..	..	..	..	..
34. Red Wing	44 33	92 30	800	9.25	17.90	16.75	40.26	46.70	68.10	71.17	72.87	..	..	33.05	10.8
35. St. Anthony's Falls	45 00	93 15	820	5.09	19.00	30.72	45.62	57.31	64.33	73.61	70.40	58.75	51.63	38.78	25.2
36. St. Cloud	45 39	94 12	..	8.72	8.57	21.58	34.58	58.88	69.00	68.88	66.11	52.43	..	..	..
37. St. Joseph	48 55	98 00	..	—1.18	6.33	20.62	43.16	52.28	65.77	68.30	66.63	54.68	45.19	25.01	13.3
38. St. Paul	44 56	93 05	800	11.37	16.94	23.06	43.04	57.47	66.65	70.64	66.81	58.30	44.09	32.55	16.9
39. Sandy Lake	45 46	93 01	1300	13.93	17.08	29.68	38.23	50.15	60.94	67.69	65.47	58.10	43.36	22.83	9.7
40. Sauk Centre	45 43	94 56	1125	12.80	..	..	..	..	..	..	..	..	..	..	..
41. Sections 17 & 22[3]	45 43	95 30	..	7.90	10.38	28.43	41.39	60.90	..	..	..	..	..	..	11.0
42. Sibley	44 30	94 12	..	8.89	13.37	19.54	41.87	58.24	68.13	72.79	68.36	59.68	45.33	32.89	15.0
43. Stillwater	45 04	92 45	756	..	..	..	..	..	..	..	..	..	..	28.34	..
44. Tamarack[4]	44 58	93 38	..	11.98	21.88	26.90	46.18	57.00	70.92	..	..	..	..	..	20.1
45. Travers des Sioux	44 21	94 00	1500	..	..	..	43.02	..	..	72.57	..	..	..	..	..
46. Wabashaw	44 30	92 15	850	21.58	11.29	35.80	..	56.64	70.47	72.16	71.76	..	..	..	25.8
47. White Bear Lake	45 37	95 30	..	2.73	..	19.20	..	..	..	..	..	..	..	..	3.6
48. White Earth	47 40	96 20	1670	3.50	10.35	21.43	..	..	..	..	..	56.83	33.88	23.75	13.7
49. Zapham	46 10	96 00	850	15.95	5.04	..	..	..	67.01	69.86	..	..	..	24.02	15.2

MISSISSIPPI.

Name of Station.	Lat.	Long.	Height.	Jan.	Feb.	March.	April.	May.	June.	July.	August.	Sept.	Oct.	Nov.	Dec.
1. Academus, P. H.	32	89	..	..	52.48	58.62	..	75.65	..	..	..	..	..	..	..
2. Bay of St. Louis	30 20	89 18	20	..	..	..	68.80	78.76	78.92	82.23	81.48	77.80	..	..	..
3. Brookhaven[5] (near)	31 34	90 24	430	48.96	51.07	58.14	64.36	70.75	77.25	80.23	79.93	73.32	62.76	54.30	46.2
4. Clinton	32 20	90 20	..	..	..	..	..	..	..	..	..	..	..	..	43.9
5. Columbus	33 31	88 28	227	43.29	47.83	53.59	62.66	70.28	77.21	80.27	79.21	73.52	60.81	52.15	45.3
6. Early Grove	35 00	90 00	484	..	..	..	..	..	..	..	..	..	..	..	36.8
7. East Pascagoula	30 20	88 33	10	..	..	..	..	76.96	81.95	83.93	83.78	80.04	69.95	60.94	..
8. Enterprise[6]	32 12	88 50	285	50.88	51.50	54.60	62.63	73.83	79.25	85.50	84.00	75.63	65.88	54.26	40.8
9. Fayette	31 43	91 07	..	45.55	55.93	51.93	61.98	67.93	74.67	75.34	75.65	73.10	59.18	51.77	46.6
10. Garlandsville	32 14	89 06	..	48.54	49.53	61.11	69.69	77.71	83.00	85.63	87.10	82.77	69.97	56.05	49.3
11. Grenada	33 48	89 50	..	44.41	47.57	54.38	62.54	67.36	76.11	80.31	79.34	73.70	62.54	55.44	46.8
12. Hernando	34 48	90 00	275	..	..	..	..	..	..	..	..	..	59.18	56.87	35.4
13. Holly Springs	34 45	89 25	..	..	55.02	60.87	62.83	70.46	79.15	81.91	80.65	73.63	62.50	..	..
14. Jackson	32 29	90 12	350	46.86	52.60	58.64	62.06	71.25	75.95	79.57	80.43	75.09	63.43	55.41	48.4
15. Kingston	31 24	91 26	..	48.64	59.67	55.33	..	..	..	..	..	..	64.31	..	50.2
16. Lake Washington	33 00	91 06	..	...	50.18	62.19	63.35	72.90	77.33	81.73	81.27	..	..	..	..
17. Marion C. H.	32 25	89 46	168	48.15	48.67	55.50	63.97	72.65	79.00	79.33	82.10	74.48	60.48	55.38	49.2
18. Monticello	31 34	90 04	600	48.53	51.63	..	..	..	81.85	83.95	79.95	73.05	62.80	52.95	47.2
19. Natchez	31 34	91 27	264	48.89	52.35	58.59	65.80	72.07	78.62	80.89	79.93	75.73	64.94	55.70	50.0
20. Natchez[7]	31 34	91 27	264	51.68	53.21	60.49	69.25	74.05	80.23	81.76	80.97	76.86	66.10	57.29	50.2
21. Oxford	34 23	89 29	300	36.03	39.05	48.30	67.03	73.54	76.06	79.24	..	74.63	61.94	54.64	42.7
22. Pass Christian	30 20	89 12	20	..	..	..	..	..	83.20	84.00	80.90	79.34	68.20	..	..
23. Paulding	32 02	89 03	215	47.84	53.48	59.57	66.32	74.75	80.42	81.91	81.55	76.73	69.03	56.01	50.9
24. Philadelphia	32 48	89 06	550	45.20	49.20	51.90	60.73	70.48	73.98	79.23	79.28	74.45	64.43	52.60	42.3
25. Port Gibson	31 59	91 00	..	38.05	53.77	56.69	56.60	..	..	..	81.03	72.86	64.41	54.16	46.6
26. Salem	31	89	..	..	..	..	76.13	81.79	..	..	..	..	..	..	..
27. Ship Island	30 12	88 57	15	58.40	56.91	67.27	70.48	..	..	..	86.70	..	74.40	66.20	64.8
28. Vicksburg	32 23	90 50	350	48.01	52.75	58.79	65.27	73.30	79.94	81.41	80.21	76.20	64.77	55.66	50.5
29. Westville	31 52	89 54	..	..	..	..	..	77.85	..	87.95	83.95	78.34	63.98	62.25	44.8

[1] Also called Hazelwood. [2] Altitude 50 feet above low water in Minnesota River. [3] Township 126 N., Range 38 W.

[4] The observations in 1864 were made on the North Arm of Lake Minnetonka, one mile west of Tamarack.

MINNESOTA.—Continued.

	Spring.	Summer.	Autumn.	Winter.	Year.	Series. Begins.	Series. Ends.	Extent yrs. mos.	Observing hours.	Observer.	References.
24	41°.84	58°.91	43°.66	11°.80	41°.55	Feb. 1844;	Dec. 1859	6 5	$7_m\ 2_a\ 9_a$	Rev. S. R. Riggs.	P. O. and S. I. Vol. 1, MS. in S. Coll., and S. Coll.
25	..	..	..	0.10	..	Nov. 1856;	May, 1857	0 6	"	Rev. B. F. Odell.	P. O. and S. I. Vol. 1.
26	..	..	49.14	..	..	1870		0 6	$7_m\ 2_a\ 9_a$ bis	H. L. Wadsworth.	S. O.
27	42.21	70.85	46.80	15.45	43.83	Jan. 1869;	Dec. 1870	2 0	"	W. W. Murphy.	" "
28	..	..	..	..	..	1864		0 1	"	W. Kilgore.	" "
29	40.12	68.34	45.33	12.87	41.67	Nov. 1864;	Dec. 1870	6 2	"	W. Cheney.	" "
30	41.88	71.66	48.14	14.63	44.08	Feb. 1864;	Dec. 1870	6 11	"	C. Roos.	" "
31	35.90	70.42	..	..	..	1851;	1853	0 9	$\odot_r\ 9_m\ 3_a\ 9_a$	Cavilur.	S. Coll.
32	41.44	69.71	43.80	11.55	41.63	Oct. 1856;	Aug. 1860	3 9	$7_m\ 2_a\ 9_a$ bis	O. E. Garrison and S. M. Byers.	P. O. and S. I. Vol. 1, and S. O.
33	..	..	..	..	..	1853		0 1	$\odot_r\ 9_m\ 3_a\ 9_a$	Spencer.	S. Coll.
34	34.57	70.71	..	12.67	..	Nov. 1855;	Aug. 1867	0 11	$7_m\ 2_a\ 9_a$ bis	Rev. J. Brooks and A. M. Stephens.	P. O. and S. I. Vol. 1, and S. O.
35	44.55	69.45	49.72	16.44	45.04	Mar. 1853;	Nov. 1854	1 8	$7_m\ 2_a\ 9_a$	Dr. C. L. Anderson.	P. O. & S. I. Vol. 1, and S. Coll.
36	38.35	68.00	..	..	..	May, 1860;	Feb. 1869	1 2	$7_m\ 2_a\ 9_a$ bis	O. E. Garrison.	S. O.
37	38.69	66.90	41.63	6.17	38.35	Jan. 1854;	Feb. 1855	0 11	$7_m\ 2_a\ 9_a$	Rev. D. B. Spencer, A. A. Kellum.	P. O. and S. I. Vol. 1.
38	41.29	68.03	44.98	15.09	42.32	June, 1862;	Dec. 1870	8 5	$7_m\ 2_a\ 9_a$ bis	Rev. A. B. Patterson & J. W. Heimstreet.	S. O.
39	39.35	64.70	41.43	13.57	39.76	1850;	1852	1 10	$\odot_r\ 9_m\ 3_a\ 9_a$	Holt and others.	S. Coll.
40	..	..	..	..	..	1869		0 1	$7_m\ 2_a\ 9_a$ bis	S. Bloomfield.	S. O.
41	43.57	..	..	9.77	..	Apr. 1861;	May, 1862	0 8	"	O. E. Garrison.	" "
42	39.88	69.76	45.97	12.42	42.01	May, 1865;	Dec. 1870	5 7	"	C. W. & C. E. Woodbury.	" "
43	..	..	..	..	..	1858		0 1	$7_m\ 2_a\ 9_a$	A Van Vorhes.	P. O. and S. I. Vol. 1.
44	43.36	..	..	18.01	..	Apr. 1863;	June, 1864	0 9	$7_m\ 2_a\ 9_a$ bis	Mary A. Grave.	S. O.
45	..	..	..	..	..	1849;	1851	0 2	$\odot_r\ 9_m\ 3_a\ 9_a$	Hopkins.	S. Coll.
46	..	71.46	..	19.57	..	Dec. 1857;	Aug. 1858	0 8	$7_m\ 2_a\ 9_a$	Rev. I. Z. Hillier.	P. O. and S. I. Vol. 1.
47	..	..	..	..	..	Dec. 1860;	Mar. 1861	0 3	$\odot_r$ N. $\odot_s$	O. E. Garrison.	S. O.
48	..	..	38.15	9.21	..	Sept. 1869;	Mar. 1870	0 7	$7_m\ 2_a\ 9_a$ bis	Dr. D. Pyle.	" "
49	..	..	..	12.07	..	Nov. 1857;	Dec. 1858	0 8	$7_m\ 2_a\ 9_a$	E. M. Wright, S Locke, and F. McMullin.	P. O. and S. I. Vol. 1.

MISSISSIPPI.

	Spring.	Summer.	Autumn.	Winter.	Year.	Series. Begins.	Series. Ends.	Extent yrs. mos.	Observing hours.	Observer.	References.
1	..	..	..	..	..	1853		0 3	$\odot_r\ 9_m\ 3_a\ 9_a$	Robinson.	S. Coll.
2	..	80.88	..	..	..	July, 1833;	Sept. 1835	1 0	$7_m\ 2_a\ 9_a$	Assistant Surgeon.	Ar. Met. Reg. 1855.
3	64.42	79.14	63.46	48.74	63.94	Jan. 1868;	Dec. 1870	3 0	$7_m\ 2_a\ 9_a$ bis	T. J. R. and Mrs. W. E. A. Keenan.	S. O.
4	..	..	..	..	..	1870		0 1	"	R. S. Jackson.	" "
5	62.18	78.90	62.16	45.50	62.19	Jan. 1855;	Dec. 1870	15 9	"	J. S. Lull.	P. O. and S. I. Vol. 1, and S. O.
6	..	..	..	..	..	1870		0 1	"	W. M. Abernethy.	S. O.
7	..	83.22	70.31	..	..	Aug. 1848;	Aug. 1853	1 11	$\odot_r\ 9_m\ 3_a\ 9_a$	Assistant Surgeon.	Ar. Met. Reg. 1855.
8	63.69	82.92	65.26	47.73	64.90	1870		0 11	$7_m\ 2_a\ 9_a$ bis	E. S. Robinson.	S. O.
9	60.61	75.22	61.35	49.38	61.64	Nov. 1866;	Dec. 1870	1 2	"	Rev. T. H. Cleveland.	" "
10	69.50	85.24	69.60	49.14	68.37	Jan. 1854;	May, 1855	1 4	$7_m\ 2_a\ 9_a$	Rev. E. S. Robinson.	P. O. and S. I. Vol. 1.
11	61.43	78.59	63.89	46.28	62.55	Mar. 1853;	Dec. 1870	4 3	$7_m\ 2_a\ 9_a$ bis	A. Moore & Waddell.	S. Coll., S. O., MS. from S. G. O.
12	..	..	..	..	..	1859		0 3	$7_m\ 2_a\ 9_a$	Dr. W. M. Johnston.	P. O. and S. I. Vol. 1.
13	64.72	80.57	..	..	..	Aug. 1867;	Sept. 1868	0 10	"	....	MS. from S. G. O.
14	63.98	78.65	64.64	49.30	64.14	1849;	Dec. 1855	4 2	$\odot_r\ 9_m\ 3_a\ 9_a$	A. R. Green, and Hatch & Co.	S. Coll., P. O. and S. I. Vol. 1.
15	..	..	..	52.85	..	Oct. 1866;	Mar. 1867	0 5	$7_m\ 2_a\ 9_a$ bis	J. E. Smith.	S. O.
16	66.15	80.11	..	..	..	1854		0 7	$7_m\ 2_a\ 9_a$	Rev. J. A. Shepherd.	P. O. and S. I. Vol. 1.
17	64.04	80.14	63.45	48.69	64.08	Mar. 1868;	Mar. 1870	1 5	$7_m\ 2_a\ 9_a$ bis	Dr. T. W. Florer.	S. O.
18	..	81.92	62.93	49.13	..	June, 1860;	Feb. 1861	0 9	"	Prof. J. R. Cribbs.	" "
19	65.49	79.81	65.46	50.43	65.30	Feb. 1799;	May, 1870	15 5	"	W. Dunbar, J. E. Smith, & R. McCary.	MS. in S. Coll., Phil. Trans. 1809, P. O. and S. I. Vol. 1, MS. from S. G. O., & S. O.
20	67.93	80.99	66.75	51.71	66.84	Jan. 1836;	June, 1851	14 3	6_m N. 6_a	Dr. H. Tooley.	MS. in S. Coll.
21	62.96	..	63.74	39.29	..	Sept. 1854;	June, 1856	1 9	$7_m\ 2_a\ 9_a$	Prof. L. Harper.	P. O. and S. I. Vol. 1.
22	..	82.70	..	..	..	July, 1843;	July, 1860	0 11	$\odot_r\ 9_m\ 3_a\ 9_a$	Rev. J. A. Shepherd and Assist. Surg.	MS. in S. Coll., Ar. Met. Reg. 1855.
23	66.88	81.29	67.26	50.75	66.55	Feb. 1858;	July, 1869	2 9	$7_m\ 2_a\ 9_a$	Rev. E. L. Robinson.	P. O. and S. I. Vol. 1, and S. O.
24	61.04	77.50	63.83	45.58	61.99	Feb. 1870;	Dec. 1870	0 10	$7_m\ 2_a\ 9_a$ bis	Ida S. and Lucy A. Bowden.	S. O.
25	..	..	63.81	46.15	..	Aug. 1855;	Apr. 1857	0 11	$7_m\ 2_a\ 9_a$	Prof. J. B. Elliott.	P. O. and S. I. Vol. 1.
26	..	..	..	..	..	1849		0 2	$\odot_r\ 9_m\ 3_a\ 9_a$	Moore.	S. Coll.
27	..	..	..	60.04	..	Aug. 1867;	Apr. 1868	0 8	$7_m\ 2_a\ 9_a$	....	MS. from S. G. O.
28	65.79	80.52	65.54	50.45	65.57	Dec. 1840;	May, 1870	8 11	"	N. Hatch.	Am. Alm. 1843 & fol., MS. from S. G. O., P. O. & S. I. Vol. 1, & S. Coll.
29	..	..	68.19	..	..	Dec. 1859;	May, 1860	0 7	"	J. R. Cribbs.	P. O. and S. I. Vol. 1, and S. O.

[5] In 1868, the observations were made two miles southwest, and afterwards two miles east of Brookhaven.

[6] Also called Fellowship.

[7] The temperature recorded at 6 P. M., is probably too high, being nearly as high as at noon.

MISSOURI.

Name of Station.	Lat.	Long.	Height.	Jan.	Feb.	March.	April.	May.	June.	July.	August.	Sept.	Oct.	Nov.	Dec.
1. Allentown	38° 29′	90° 45′	..	27°.77	34°.36	40°.15	53°.15	62°.19	70°.44	75°.01	72°.37	64°.42	51°.04	42°.58	30°.64
2. Athens[1]	40 30	91 45	482	27.89	35.13	42.36	51.16	61.74	72.29	80 30	78.00	75.40	54.35	46.30	28.42
3. Bolivar	37 35	93 30	1000	36.45	37.85	41.25	57.63	66.23	72.05	78.10	81.10	68.75	53.00	47.60	34.17
4. Brunswick	39 24	93 05	..	40.25	42.50	47.00	63.50	67.50	73.00	81.00	77.50	70.00	55.50	41.25	47.25
5. Canton	40 07	91 34	..	18.75	28.83	..	48.48	56.79	75.75	79.33	77.60	..	..	..	..
6. Cape Girardeau	37 20	89 34	..	34.30	35.14	38.29	46.06	60.23	70.74	76.03	74.58	69.46	57.24	42.13	38.72
7. Carrollton	39 20	93 28	..	..	..	14.10	50.10	..	..	..	..	..	..	..	..
8. Cassville	36 41	93 56	..	36.00	42.60	49.94	58.70	66.04	75.09	80.65	76.74	67.61	57.87	46.66	32.59
9. Corning	40 17	95 33	[2]	..	..	..	54.43	..	..	..	71.40	67.55	54.53	42.60	26.87
10. Dundee	38 30	91 10	536	28.50	33.80	38.70	51.20	71.75	74.95	81.40	79.65	..	..	..	..
11. East Prairie	36 50	89 20	..	36.37	39.89	46.29	56.32	64.24	71.46	78.42	76.38	67.33	53.50	42.52	33.84
12. Easton	39 46	94 42	..	24.17	29.27	42.22	53.96	68.15	75.78	76.42	74.54	67.11	53.14	41.94	21.95
13. Edinburg	40 06	93 50	..	17.80	..	..	..	..	..	..	..	..	..	41.63	29.12
14. Hannibal	39 44	91 23	..	23.16	37.30	43.35	52.41	61.79	73.40	82.13	83.20	69.30	53.19	43.15	33.80
15. Harrisonville	38 38	94 25	..	26.55	33.57	37.65	52.96	63.64	72.19	77.08	74.11	67.11	53.00	41.87	28.57
16. Hematite	38 11	90 37	475	37.23	38.29	41.17	55.28	66.41	73.00	79.85	76.15	66.73	53.88	44.21	32.37
17. Hermitage	37 56	93 15	..	28.30	33.43	42.37	51.32	62.62	70.91	77.59	73.96	65.86	51.07	41.37	31.53
18. Hornersville	36 05	90 05	..	38.00	46.49	53.99	63.11	74.28	78.95	83.23	79.53	73.88	61.80	48.50	42.39
19. Jefferson Barracks	38 28	90 15	472	32.47	35.34	45.26	57.03	66.83	74.63	78.90	76.92	68.47	56.35	43.27	34.06
20. Jefferson City	38 35	92 16	650	30.18	35.01	41.34	53.33	66.50	73.49	80.79	76.41	65.39	52.74	42.78	30.27
21. Kansas City	39 05	94 40	710	31.90	38.53	41.00	57.05	66.48	72.38	78.85	74.23	67.68	55.35	45.05	29.28
22. Keysterville	39 27	93 03	..	..	..	..	..	62.37	69.45	74.88	77.25	..	44.80	..	..
23. Laborville	38 33	90 43	..	29.08	38.50	40.38	52.18	66.90	74.90	..	..	..	..	..	33.78
24. Oregon	39 59	95 09	1100	23.67	31.83	31.82	50.66	62.94	72.05	78.32	74.06	64.99	53.09	41.48	28.98
25. Palmyra, St. Paul's Coll.	39 47	91 37	..	..	..	..	39.90	57.00	71.99	76.87	71.69	67.42	58.20	36.90	23.22
26. Paris (near)	39 30	92 00	700	25.91	34.49	43.83	55.08	64.07	71.92	71.33	72.95	64.05	53.14	43.56	28.46
27. Rhineland	38 42	91 46	[4]	..	38.13	46.60	55.78	67.70	..	..	..	..	..	43.15	22.45
28. Rocheport	38 55	92 38	..	..	..	38.55	60.99	66.44	81.26	..	..	..	..	..	..
29. Rolla (3½ mil. W. of)	37 58	91 44	950	32.20	35.97	43.95	52.16	62.68	70.60	77.77	74.51	66.95	52.73	43.04	33.18
30. Springfield	37 12	93 12	..	38.86	30.80	48.50	54.74	..	..	74.16	70.88	71.07	53.57	40.89	40.11
31. St. Joseph	39 45	94 53	..	33.14	35.42	38.52	56.36	63.53	70.99	77.14	76.09	67.09	50.88	35.38	34.39
32. St. Louis[5]	38 37	90 12	481	31.06	34.59	43.40	56.33	65.55	74.17	78.13	76.05	68.55	55.16	43.94	33.05
33. Stockton	37 43	93 48	800	..	42.44	52.68	63.45	72.53	..	85.90	75.79	68.24	52.75	46.87	26.39
34. Tower Grove	38 36	90 20	500	27.87	33.11	42.12	54.03	63.48	70.35	75.09	75.59	67.03	53.65	41.60	37.96
35. Union	38 25	91 07	616	27.67	34.74	37.59	56.73	61.21	73.07	79.28	72.20	61.63	54.23	44.68	33.62
36. Warrensburg	38 45	93 40	600	33.88	33.43	38.10	53.85	65.23	71.90	80.99	77.22	64.98	56.08	41.93	25.93
37. Warrenton	38 50	91 15	[6]	30.79	33.90	43.12	55.64	64.24	72.87	77.69	75.37	66.27	53.33	41.35	31.64
38. Wyaconda Prairie	40 12	91 37	..	23.76	28.59	36.33	48.81	63.83	71.44	76.82	72.99	67.24	49.82	38.57	26.57

MONTANA.

Name of Station.	Lat.	Long.	Height.	Jan.	Feb.	March.	April.	May.	June.	July.	August.	Sept.	Oct.	Nov.	Dec.
1. Baton City	..	..	..	..	27.88	..	..	..	..	..	..	..	..	..	..
2. Camp Baker	..	..	..	..	..	..	..	..	..	..	..	..	39.12	..	..
3. Camp Cook	47 48	109 38	..	15.20	21.76	25.24	47.64	60.28	68.62	72.36	71.48	56.31	47.75	35.37	21.09
4. Cantonment Stevens	46 16	114 00	3412	13.3	31.2	39.4	48.3	56.3	64.2	71.9	72.6	56.7	45.9	34.1	30.2
5. Deer Lodge City	46 26	112 32	4240	20.63	25.00	26.80	43.43	54.00	61.83	65.41	58.52	50.72	37.02	33.50	21.05
6. Fort Benton.	47 50	110 39	2730	19.43	29.67	23.13	52.91	58.05	71.65	77.60	64.19	62.20	48.15	35.81	26.33
7. Fort C. F. Smith	45 20	107 56	..	18.43	26.62	25.47	48.43	55.29	68.52	73.03	77.80	61.38	53.88	45.35	31.39
8. Fort Ellis	45 32	111 12	4800	23.26	29.48	28.43	44.00	58.20	65.60	69.65	64.64	54.61	43.23	35.97	25.44
9. Fort Shaw	47 30	111 42	6000	18.26	30.63	31.63	48.05	55.98	66.12	71.10	65-28	57.21	47.33	38.67	27.33
10. Port Union	48 03	104 00	2000	12.29	21.44	28.54	50.87	53.78	65.84	..	67.50	56.80	45.30	26.20	..
11. Helena City	46 37	112 00	4150	11.21	20.96	21.98	37.95	41.35	56.80	78.05	76.00	57.70	48.18	40.95	25.30
12. Missoula	46 45	113 45	3300	..	..	..	..	..	..	..	..	..	..	36.63	20.45

[1] This series is considered not very reliable.

[2] Altitude 25 feet above high water in Missouri River.

[3] Observations corrected for daily variation.

MISSOURI.

	Spring.	Summer.	Autumn.	Winter.	Year.	Series Begins.	Series Ends.	Extent yrs. mos.	Observing hours.	Observer.	References.
1	51°.83	72°.61	52°.68	30°.92	52°.01	Apr. 1864;	Dec. 1870	6 2	$7_m\ 2_a\ 9_a$ bis	A. Fendler.	S. O.
2	51.75	76.86	58.68	30.48	54.44	Mar. 1863;	July, 1866	2 4	"	J. T. Caldwell.	" "
3	55.04	77.08	56.45	36.16	56.18	Dec. 1868;	Jan. 1870	1 2	"	J. A. Race.	" "
4	59.33	77.17	55.58	43.33	58.85	1845		1 0	$8_m\ 2_a$	Blue.	Pat. Off. Rep.
5	..	77.56	..	..	..	May, 1867;	Apr. 1868	0 7	$7_m\ 2_a\ 9_a$ bis	G. P. Ray.	S. O.
6	48.19	73.78	56.28	36.05	53.58	Oct. 1856;	Jan. 1858	1 0	$\odot_r\ 9_m\ 3_a\ 9_a$	Rev. J. Knoud.	P. O. and S. I. Vol. 1.
7	..	..	..	..	..	1860		0 2	$\odot_r\ \odot_s$	O. J. Kerby.	S. O.
8	58.23	77.49	57.38	37.06	57.54	Aug. 1859;	June, 1861	1 7	$7_m\ 2_a\ 9_a$ bis	M. S. Wyzick.	P. O. and S. I. Vol. 1, and S. O.
9	..	..	..	54.89	..	1870		0 6	"	H. Martin.	S. O.
10	53.88	78.67	..	..	..	1860		0 8	"	S. S. Bailey.	" "
11	55.62	75.42	54.45	36.70	55.55	Jan. 1868;	Dec. 1870	3 0	[4]	A. Miller.	" "
12	54.78	75.58	54.06	25.13	52.39	Sept. 1864;	Nov. 1866	1 8	$7_m\ 2_a\ 9_a$ bis	P. B. Sibley.	" "
13	..	..	..	..	..	Nov. 1866;	Jan. 1867	0 3	"	J. E. Vertrees.	" "
14	52.52	79.58	55.21	31.42	54.68	Mar. 1853;	Nov. 1854	1 5	"	O. H. P. Lear.	P. O. and S. I. Vol. 1, and S. O.
15	51.42	74.46	53.99	29.56	52.36	June, 1863;	Sept. 1870	7 2	"	J. Christian.	S. O.
16	54.29	76.33	54.94	35.96	55.38	Apr. 1868;	Dec. 1870	2 9	"	J. M. Smith.	" "
17	52.10	74.15	52.77	31.09	52.53	Sept. 1867;	Dec. 1869	2 3	"	Dr. W. and Miss Isabella Moore.	" "
18	63.79	80.57	61.39	42.29	62.01	Jan. 1860;	Apr. 1861	1 2	"	W. Horner.	" "
19	56.37	76.82	56.03	33.96	55.79	Jan. 1827;	July, 1862	32 11	$7_m\ 2_a\ 9_a$	Assistant Surgeon.	Ar. Met. Regs. 1855 and 1860, and MS. from S. G. O.
20	53.72	76.90	53.64	31.82	54.02	Feb. 1868;	Dec. 1870	2 8	$7_m\ 2_a\ 9_a$ bis	N. De Wyl.	S. O.
21	54.84	75.15	56.03	33.24	54.82	Feb. 1870;	Dec. 1870	0 11	"	S. W. Salisbury.	" "
22	..	73.86	..	..	..	1869		0 5	"	C. Veatch.	" "
23	53.15	..	..	33.79	..	Dec. 1863;	June, 1864	0 7	"	W. Meier.	" "
24	48.47	74.81	53.19	28.16	51.16	Jan. 1867;	Dec. 1870	3 11	"	W. Kaucher.	" "
25	..	73.52	54.17	..	..	June, 1856;	Sept. 1857	1 1	$\odot_r\ 9_m\ 3_a\ 9_a$	G. P. Comings.	P. O. and S. I. Vol. 1.
26	54.33	72.07	53.58	29.62	52.40	Aug. 1859;	Jan. 1862	1 11	$7_m\ 2_a\ 9_a$ bis	W. F. Maxey.	P. O. and S. I. Vol. 1, and S. O.
27	56.69	..	..	..	..	Nov. 1859;	May, 1860	0 6	"	C. Vogel.	" " " " "
28	55.33	..	..	..	..	1856		0 4	$7_m\ 2_a\ 9_a$	Dr. C. Q. Chandler.	P. O. and S. I. Vol. 1.
29	52.93	74.29	54.24	33.78	53.81	May, 1867;	Dec. 1870	3 8	$7_m\ 2_a\ 9_a$ bis	H. Ruggles.	S. O.
30	..	..	55.18	36.59	..	July, 1857;	Apr. 1858	0 10	$\odot_r\ 9_m\ 3_a\ 9_a$	J. A. Stephens.	P. O. and S. I. Vol. 1.
31	52.80	74.74	51.12	34.32	53.24	May, 1857;	Aug. 1870	2 1	$7_m\ 2_a\ 9_a$ bis	F. B. Neeley and H. Bullard.	P. O. and S. I. Vol. 1, and S. O.
32	55.09	76.12	55.88	32.90	55.00	Jan. 1830;	Dec. 1870	41 0	[5]	Drs. G. Engelmann, A. Wislizenus, B. B. Brown, A. Fendler, J. H. Lüneman, and others.	Ar. Met. Regs. 1855 and 1860, MS. in S. Coll., St. Louis Med. & Surg. Journ., Trans. St. Louis Acad. Sci., S. O. P. O. and S. I. Vol. 1, and Sill Journ.
33	62.89	..	55.95	..	..	Aug. 1859;	Feb. 1861	1 0	$7_m\ 2_a\ 9_a$ bis	W. Wells.	P. O. and S. I, Vol. 1, and S. O.
34	53.21	73.68	54.09	32.98	53.49	Jan. 1861;	Jan. 1864	2 5	"	A. Fendler.	S. O.
35	51.84	74.85	53.51	32.01	53.05	Mar. 1866;	June, 1867	1 4	"	Dr. W., and Miss I. Moore.	" "
36	52.39	76.70	54.33	31.08	53.63	July, 1868;	Aug. 1869	1 2	"	J. E. Pollock.	" "
37	54.33	75.31	53.65	32.11	53.85	Oct. 1859;	July, 1863	3 11	"	M. A. Tidswell and M. F. Hamacker.	P. O. and S. I. Vol. 1, and S. O.
38	49.66	73.75	51.88	26.31	50.40	Mar. 1862;	Dec. 1868	5 2	"	G. P. Ray.	S. O.

MONTANA.

	Spring.	Summer.	Autumn.	Winter.	Year.	Series Begins.	Series Ends.	Extent yrs. mos.	Observing hours.	Observer.	References.
1	..	..	..	..	..	1868		0 1	$7_m\ 2_a\ 9_a$ bis	Dr. H. M. Lehman.	S. O.
2	..	..	..	..	..	1870		0 1	$7_m\ 2_a\ 9_a$	Assistant Surgeon.	MS. from S. G. O.
3	44.39	70.82	46.48	19.35	45.26	Sept. 1866;	Sept. 1869	2 10	"	" "	" " "
4	48.00	69.57	45.57	24.90	47.01	1853;	1854	1 0	......	Burr.	Blodget's Climatology.
5	41.41	61.92	40.41	22.23	41.49	Jan. 1869;	Dec. 1870	2 0	$7_m\ 2_a\ 9_a$ bis	G. Stuart.	S. O.
6	44.70	71.15	48.72	25.14	47.43	Nov. 1869;	Dec. 1870	1 2	$7_m\ 2_a\ 9_a$	Assistant Surgeon.	MS. from S. G. O.
7	43.06	73.12	53.54	25.48	48.80	Sept. 1866;	June, 1868	1 10	"	" "	" " "
8	43.54	66.63	44.60	26.06	45.21	Aug. 1868;	Dec. 1870	2 5	"	" "	" " "
9	45.22	67.50	47.74	25.41	46.47	Sept. 1867;	Dec. 1870	3 4	"	" "	" " "
10	44.40	..	42.77	..	..	Jan. 1854;	Jan. 1858	0 11	"	E. T. Denig, F. G. Riter.	P. O. and S. I. Vol. 1.
11	33.76	70.28	48.94	19.16	43.04	Jan. 1866;	Mar. 1868	1 7	$7_m\ 2_a\ 9_a$ bis	A. C. Wheaton.	S. O.
12	..	..	..	..	..	1870		0 2	"	J. M. Minnesinger.	" "

[4] Altitude 300 feet above Missouri River.

[5] This series includes observations at the St. Louis Arsenal, from Jan. 1843, to Dec. 1856.

[6] Altitude 825 feet above the Gulf.

NEBRASKA.

Name of Station.	Lat.	Long.	Height.	Jan.	Feb.	March.	April.	May.	June.	July.	August.	Sept.	Oct.	Nov.	Dec.
1. Bellevue	41°08′	95°55′	..	21°.80	26°.84	37°.05	48°.81	61°.79	71°.05	76°.02	72°.65	65°.10	50°.42	37°.65	25°.20
2. Brownville	40 24	95 40	..	28.02	26.92	42.89	..	64.18	74.51	79.56	76.53	66.97	53.89	32.70	24.67
3. Dakota	42 25	96 25	1090	17.11	24.35	35.56	44.76	63.32	68.20	74.32	73.99	..	50.59	36.35	22.42
4. Decatur	42 00	96 16	[1]	..	..	30.95	46.98	60.15	66.18	71.60	..	..	..	..	..
5. De Sota	41 31	96 05	1100	17.29	24.18	28.11	46.63	60.66	70.06	75.11	70.69	60.67	48.20	36.05	23.26
6. Fontanelle	41 32	96 27	1000[2]	16.90	22.74	29.85	45.90	59.78	71.16	72.77	71.61	61.81	45.23	33.65	23.44
7. Fort Calhoun[3]	41 30	96 02	1327	18.95	26.64	36.90	51.74	64.16	74.15	76.34	76.20	65.48	52.77	37.33	22.06
8. Fort Childs	40 40	99 41	..	7.71	17.50	..	..	..	..	..	..	..	..	..	..
9. Fort Kearney[4]	40 38	98 57	2360	19.99	25.57	34.70	46.92	57.96	69.89	75.01	72.34	62.57	50.51	34.71	20.17
10. Fort McPherson	41 00	100 30	..	28.72	34.14	37.03	49.66	63.45	71.63	79.97	74.68	63.88	51.64	40.94	30.82
11. Glendale, near	40 55	96 05	1010	16.56	23.65	29.91	46.82	59.03	68.94	75.87	71.99	59.95	48.14	34.95	23.41
12. Ionia	42 41	96 50	2500	..	..	..	..	..	..	..	73.03	..	..	..	..
13. Lincoln	40 50	96 45	1647	..	..	..	51.16	..	..	..	..	..	..	..	..
14. Nebraska City	40 41	95 51	1005	..	..	..	..	64.07	71.45	78.88	74.95	63.23	51.53	39.39	16.03
15. Nebraska City	40 41	95 51	1225	25.83	29.81	36.31	53.92	63.50	72.06	77.78	72.48	64.43	50.32	37.95	25.28
16. New Castle	42 37	96 47	800	..	..	..	..	..	70.80	78.15	68.15	62.48	..	36.00	29.20
17. Nursery Hill	40 40	96 13	1266	21.63	29.45	32.05	45.70	63.38	..	..	..	..	..	..	..
18. Omaha[5]	41 15	95 56	1300	20.07	28.23	33.41	48.42	63.37	72.11	76.99	73.67	64.10	49.59	39.60	21.79
19. Omaha Agency[6]	42 07	96 22	..	21.54	27.81	34.37	48.60	63.99	70.47	78.19	72.76	62.73	51.20	38.78	26.85
20. Peru	40 29	95 45	1000	27.70	30.35	33.18	..	..	69.94	..	..	..	..	..	..
21. Richland[7]	41 22	96 16	1350	17.26	23.82	31.63	45.91	61.77	70.87	75.08	72.42	62.86	49.02	35.09	21.41
22. Rock Bluff	40 56	95 50	1100	..	28.20	..	..	..	..	..	..	..	55.70	36.57	22.13

NEVADA.

Name of Station.	Lat.	Long.	Height.	Jan.	Feb.	March.	April.	May.	June.	July.	August.	Sept.	Oct.	Nov.	Dec.
1. Camp Halleck	40 42	115 30	5600	24.49	28.57	37.03	46.23	53.09	63.95	69.73	69.19	58.82	47.34	38.65	29.46
2. Camp McDermit	41 58	117 40	4700	27.59	31.23	36.07	46.17	54.68	64.46	73.52	72.61	62.09	49.90	40.38	29.24
3. Camp McGarry	41 40	119 00	6000	21.82	27.25	27.65	39.47	46.77	54.38	63.77	66.23	56.65	47.56	38.02	26.44
4. Camp Winfield Scott	41 34	117 30	..	28.11	29.81	35.36	48.71	56.11	67.55	77.78	76.92	63.63	51.31	36.71	36.31
5. Fort Churchill	39 17	119 19	4284	32.08	35.57	43.84	52.55	60.95	70.75	78.37	76.41	67.61	53.00	42.47	35.99
6. Fort Ruby	40 01	115 35	5922	27.44	29.86	37.46	45.45	58.08	64.89	72.65	73.82	62.72	51.21	40.57	32.46
7. Star City	40 30	118 10	7500	..	..	..	..	..	..	..	..	..	49.73	43.18	20.65

NEW HAMPSHIRE.

Name of Station.	Lat.	Long.	Height.	Jan.	Feb.	March.	April.	May.	June.	July.	August.	Sept.	Oct.	Nov.	Dec.
1. Charlestown	43 15	72 23	..	..	..	..	41.97	..	..	69.96	68.11	..	45.67	..	26.51
2. Claremont	43 24	72 21	536	18.35	22.47	30.79	43.51	54.96	65.27	69.21	66.56	58.48	46.53	37.11	23.68
3. Concord	43 12	71 29	374	20.84	22.73	31.49	43.21	56.17	65.86	69.91	66.80	59.15	48.82	37.96	24.87
4. Contoocooksville	43 15	71 42	450	..	..	..	..	..	..	..	..	..	..	39.83	28.88
5. Dover	43 13	70 54	150	24.00	23.60	31.80	42.70	53.70	63.90	70.40	64.70	58.80	46.40	35.50	25.20
6. Dublin	42 54	72 03	1869	18.52	21.58	27.70	36.99	49.14	63.18	67.15	64.18	57.37	45.44	33.67	21.14
7. Dunbarton	43 06	71 35	750	27.74	24.78	30.08	42.60	54.54	66.44	72.84	70.25	61.20	48.89	36.65	26.38
8. Epping	43 03	71 05	..	..	..	..	..	..	..	..	..	..	..	..	..
9. Exeter	42 59	71 00	[8]	19.89	21.20	31.41	40.85	54.47	63.81	69.89	67.82	59.00	49.22	38.06	25.33
10. Farmington	43 22	71 07	300	22.20	..	..	..	..	..	..	..	..	..	..	..
11. Farmouth[9]	43 51	71 19	450	23.98	22.15	26.41	43.19	55.50	69.09	71.32	68.20	57.99	45.38	33.13	24.00
12. Fort Constitution	43 04	70 42	40	24.89	26.26	34.37	43.26	53.50	62.34	67.06	65.06	59.12	49.64	38.89	28.74
13. Francestown	42 59	71 48	..	18.58	24.29	30.08	42.00	53.50	64.09	69.32	68.15	59.45	47.09	38.19	29.46
14. Great Falls[10]	43 15	70 55	250	21.32	20.25	31.96	41.73	56.83	64.78	75.50	68.90	60.98	51.01	38.16	22.13
15. Hanover (Dartmouth Coll.)	43 42	72 17	530	16.24	15.[illegible]7	26.15	37.66	52.53	61.69	65.68	63.34	55.55	44.30	32.31	17.08
16. Hanover[11]	43 42	72 17	530	17.62	18.89	29.10	40.10	53.40	62.70	67.15	65.60	56.33	44.18	33.76	20.99
17. Keene	42 56	72 16	..	..	..	..	41.20	54.60	..	68.79	70.40	..	44.80	31.20	25.50

[1] 35 feet above Missouri River. [2] 1025 feet in 1868–69. [3] Old Council Bluffs.

[4] Observations for 1849–54 at ☉r, 9_m 3_a 9_a; they were referred to 7_m 2_a 9_a by means of the general table.

[5] Observations from Jan. 1859 to July, 1860, at "Pioneer Grove," near Omaha, to the northwest, at an elevation of 1400 feet. Observations for Nov and Dec. 1868, at an elevation of 900 feet; for 1869–70 at "Omaha Barracks."

NEBRASKA.

	Spring.	Summer.	Autumn.	Winter.	Year.	Series. Begins. Ends.	Extent yrs. mos.	Observing hours.	Observer.	References.
1	49°.22	73°.24	51°.06	24°.61	49°.53	June, 1857; Dec. 1870	12 4	$7_{m}\,2_{a}\,9_{a}$ bis	W. Hamilton and E. E. Caldwell.	P. O. and S. I. Vol. 1. and S. O.
2	..	76.87	51.19	26.54	..	May, 1858; Oct. 1859	1 2	$7_{m}\,2_{a}\,9_{a}$	C. B. Smith.	P. O. and S. I. Vol. 1.
3	47.88	72.17	..	21.29	..	Oct. 1867; Aug. 1869	1 7	$7_{m}\,2_{a}\,9_{a}$ bis	H. H. Brown.	S. O.
4	46.03	..	..	..	..	1869	0 5	"	Dr. S. C. Case.	" "
5	45.13	71.95	48.31	21.58	46.74	Apr. 1867; Dec. 1870	3 8	"	C. Seltz.	" "
6	45.18	71.85	46.90	21.03	46.24	Jan. 1859; Nov. 1869	2 8	"	J. Evans, H. Gibson.	P. O. and S. I. Vol. 1, and S. O.
7	50.93	75.56	51.86	22.55	50.23	Jan. 1820; Dec. 1826	7 0	$7_{m}\,2_{a}\,9_{a}$	Assistant Surgeon.	Ar. Met. Reg. 1855.
8	..	..	..	..	..	1849	0 2	$\odot_{r}\,9_{m}\,3_{a}\,9_{a}$	" "	S. Coll.
9	46.53	72.41	49.26	21.91	47.53	Jan. 1849; Jan. 1868	15 11	$7_{m}\,2_{a}\,9_{a}$	" "	Ar. Met. Regs. 1855 and 1860, and MS. from S. G. O.
10	50.05	75.43	52.15	31.23	52.21	Nov. 1866; Dec. 1870	3 5	"	" "	MS. from S. G. O.
11	45.25	72.27	47.68	21.21	46.60	Aug. 1861; Oct. 1869	4 0	$7_{m}\,2_{a}\,9_{a}$ bis	Dr. A. L. & J. E. Child.	S. O.
12	..	..	..	..	..	1865	0 1	"	L. T. Hill.	" "
13	..	..	..	..	..	1870	0 1	"	Dr. G. A. Goodrich.	" "
14	..	75.09	51.38	..	..	1859	0 8	$7_{m}\,2_{a}\,9_{a}$	E. E. Mason.	P. O. and S. I. Vol. 1.
15	51.24	74.11	50.90	26.97	50.81	July, 1868; Dec. 1870	2 3	$7_{m}\,2_{a}\,9_{a}$ bis	P. Zahner.	S. O.
16	..	72.37	..	..	..	1870	0 6	"	L. H. Smith.	" "
17	47.04	..	..	..	..	1865	0 5	"	R. O. Thompson.	" "
18	48.40	74.26	51.10	23.36	49.28	June, 1858; Dec. 1870	4 0	$7_{m}\,2_{a}\,9_{a}$	J. T. Allan, W. N. Byers, Assis. Surg., J. G. Rain, C. B. Wells.	P. O. and S. I. Vol. 1, S. O., and MS. from S. G. O.
19	48.99	73.81	50.90	25.40	49.77	Aug. 1867; Dec. 1870	3 1	$7_{m}\,2_{a}\,9_{a}$ bis	W. Hamilton.	S. O.
20	..	..	..	..	..	June, 1867; June, 1869	0 5	"	J. M. McKenzie.	" "
21	46.44	72.79	48.99	20.83	47.26	June, 1858; Mar. 1870	11 3	"	J. S. & A. M. J. Bowen.	P. O. and S. I. Vol. 1, and S. O.
22	..	..	..	..	..	Oct. 1860; Feb. 1861	0 4	$7_{m}\,2_{a}\,9_{a}$	H. C. Pardee.	S. O.

NEVADA.

	Spring.	Summer.	Autumn.	Winter.	Year.	Series. Begins. Ends.	Extent yrs. mos.	Observing hours.	Observer.	References.
1	45.45	67.62	48.27	27.51	47.21	Oct. 1867; Dec. 1870	3 2	$7_{m}\,2_{a}\,9_{a}$	Assistant Surgeon.	MS. from S. G. O.
2	45.64	70.20	50.79	29.35	49.00	Dec. 1865; Dec. 1870	4 8	"	" "	" " "
3	37.96	61.46	47.41	[illegible]	[illegible]	[illegible] 1865; Nov. 1868	2 10	"	" "	" " "
4	40.73	74.08	50.55	31.41	50.69	Dec. 1866; July, 1870	3 6	"	" "	" " "
5	52.45	75.18	54.36	34.55	54.13	Oct. 1860; May, 1869	7 10	"	" "	" " "
6	47.00	70.45	51.50	29.92	49.72	Jan. 1863; Oct. 1868	5 3	"	" "	" " "
7	..	..	..	..	..	1865	0 3	$7_{m}\,2_{a}\,9_{a}$ bis	R. C. Johnson.	S. O.

NEW HAMPSHIRE.

	Spring.	Summer.	Autumn.	Winter.	Year.	Series. Begins. Ends.	Extent yrs. mos.	Observing hours.	Observer.	References.
1	..	..	..	..	..	1843; 1844	0 5	......	....	Manuscript.
2	43.09	67.01	47.37	21.50	44.74	Sept. 1857; Nov. 1868	9 7	$7_{m}\,2_{a}\,9_{a}$ bis	F. A. Freeman, A. Chase, & S. O. Mead.	P. O. and S. I. Vol. 1, and S. O.
3	43.62	67.52	48.64	22.81	45.65	Jan. 1828; May, 1870	22 2	$7_{m}\,2_{a}\,9_{a}$	J. C. Knox, J. Farmer, Dr. Prescott, H. E. Sawyer, J. T. Wheeler.	P. O. & S. I. Vol. 1, S. O., S. Coll., and Am. Alm. 1837 & foll.
4	..	..	..	..	..	1870	0 2	$7_{m}\,2_{a}\,9_{a}$ bis	E. D. Couch.	S. O.
5	42.73	66.33	46.90	24.27	45.06	Jan. 1833; July, 1843	10 7	$\odot_{r}\,1_{a}\,10_{a}$	A. A. Tufts.	Am. Alm. 1836–7 and foll.
6	37.94	64.84	45.49	20.41	42.17	Jan. 1849; Aug. 1853	4 8	$\odot_{r}\,9_{m}\,3_{a}\,9_{a}$	Leonard.	S. Coll.
7	42.41	69.84	48.91	26.30	46.87	Mar. 1868; Dec. 1870	2 10	$7_{m}\,2_{a}\,9_{a}$ bis	A. Colby.	S. O.
8	..	.	..	..	44.76	1833; 1834	2 0	......	Plummer.	Am. Alm.
9	42.24	67.17	48.76	22.14	45.08	1849; May, 1863	6 11	$7_{m}\,2_{a}\,9_{a}$ bis	Rev. S. W. Leonard, E. Nason.	S. O. and S. Coll.
10	..	..	..	..	..	1861	0 1	......	L. Bell.	S. O.
11	41.70	69.54	45.50	23.38	45.03	Feb. 1867; Dec. 1870	1 4	$7_{m}\,2_{a}\,9_{a}$ bis	A. Brewster.	" "
12	43.71	64.82	49.22	26.63	46.09	Jan. 1822; Sept. 1853	25 2	$7_{m}\,2_{a}\,9_{a}$	Assistant Surgeon.	Ar. Met. Reg. 1855.
13	41.86	67.19	48.24	24.11	45.35	Mar. 1853; May, 1858	2 3	"	A. H. Bixby, Dr. M. N. Root, & Sawyer.	P. O. & S. I. Vol. 1, & S. Coll.
14	43.15	69.73	50.05	21.23	46.13	1853; Jan. 1857	1 2	"	G. B. & H. E. Sawyer, Titcomb.	" " " "
15	38.78	63.57	44.05	16.26	40.67	Nov. 1834; Dec. 1854	4 0	$\odot_{r}\,1\tfrac{1}{2}_{a}\,9\tfrac{1}{2}_{a}$	Prof. I. Young, A. A. Young.	P. O. and S. I. Vol. 1, Am. Alm. 1837 and foll.
16	40.87	65.15	44.76	19.17	42.49	1835; 1854	20 0	"	Young.	Manuscript.
17	..	..	..	..	..	1843	0 7	$\odot_{r}\,9_{m}\,3_{a}\,9_{a}$	Whalock.	" "

[6] Observations for 1867 at "Blackbird Hills," a few miles to the southwest of the mission.

[7] Also known as "Elkhorn City."

[8] Nason gives altitude 125 feet above river bed.

[9] Also called *Tamworth*.

[10] This series is composed of observations at Great Falls by H. E. Sawyer, and at Salmon Falls, about two miles southeast of Great Falls, by G. B. Sawyer.

[11] Observations from January, 1835, to December, 1837, probably included in preceding series.

NEW HAMPSHIRE.—Continued.

Name of Station.	Lat.	Long.	Height.	Jan.	Feb.	March.	April.	May.	June.	July.	August.	Sept.	Oct.	Nov.	Dec.
18. Littleton[1]	44°20′	71°49′	..	17°.57	18°.40	24°.44	38°.62	52°.84	58°.91	66°.60	65°.81	55°.58	46°.60	33°.90	15°.0
19. Londonderry	42 53	71 20	300	22.64	24.38	31.89	43.48	56.21	66.36	71.69	68.41	61.09	50.61	38.87	26.9
20. London Ridge	43 20	71 25	475	23.70	30.77	38.45	49.18	62.23	67.20	74.08	72.85	70.25	..	42.28	33.0
21. Manchester	42 59	71 28	300	23.84	26.38	34.06	45.01	64.34	67.54	72.94	69.67	62.11	51.09	40.22	27.4
22. Mason	42 45	71 45	..	29.10	31.70	30.15	43.60	..	66.10	68.80	67.90	..	..	..	26.2
23. Mt. Washington	44 16	71 18	6285	..	..	..	..	..	43.58	49.39	47.68	..	..	..	..
24. North Barnstead[3]	43 22	71 15	..	21.65	24.74	31.03	43.27	54.49	64.04	69.00	68.12	60.86	48.29	38.77	25.4
25. Portsmouth	43 05	70 46	12	25.45	27.75	30.85	47.15	57.10	65.80	69.65	68.15	60.35	48.80	34.80	26.2
26. Portsmouth	43 05	70 46	38	21.62	27.48	36.00	43.07	53.00	63.96	69.37	67.64	59.64	47.63	36.36	26.3
27. Salisbury	43 23	71 45	..	18.83	20.32	31.42	42.15	..		..	..	61.55	47.43	36.27	27.3
28. Shelburne	44 23	71 14	700	16.32	19.26	27.44	39.80	52.07	62.91	69.36	64.18	55.46	43.78	33.35	20.2
29. Stratford	44 40	71 39	1000	13.27	17.17	24.92	37.37	50.84	61.36	65.21	62.27	54.46	42.21	31.37	16.0
30. Wakefield	43 34	71 07	..	28.00	28.80	39.25	49.80	61.20	73.40	79.40	77.20	67.60	52.80	44.20	31.8
31. West Enfield	43 38	72 07	..	20.10	20.11	27.25	39.07	51.77	63.86	68.73	65.48	58.26	45.58	31.86	19.5
32. Whitefield	44 23	71 39	1332	22.50	16.35	24.18	43.65	53.23	64.48	67.61	62.42	57.68	43.43	31.36	21.7

NEW JERSEY.

Name of Station.	Lat.	Long.	Height.	Jan.	Feb.	March.	April.	May.	June.	July.	August.	Sept.	Oct.	Nov.	Dec.
1. Bloomfield[5]	40 48	74 12	120	28.58	30.58	36.01	47.36	57.60	69.16	73.99	71.01	64.60	54.19	43.65	33.6
2. Branchburg Township[6]	40 36	74 44	..	27.35	34.40	33.78	..	59.78	75.25	76.40	72.30	64.40	51.68	48.00	30.8
3. Burlington	40 04	74 51	60	28.87	31.39	39.10	49.85	60.17	70.09	74.57	71.36	65.54	54.43	44.46	33.3
4. Chester[7]	40 00	74 57	..	27.79	31.22	38.29	50.01	59.62	69.82	74.98	72.61	65.34	52.20	42.83	31.9
5. Dover	40 54	74 34	619	26.99	28.31	35.59	46.59	54.92	66.65	72.70	69.94	62.57	52.62	43.77	29.6
6. Elwood	39 34	74 42	..	26.08	23.91	39.80	46.40	56.23	67.90	76.85	72.48	65.88	51.55	43.08	28.7
7. Freehold	40 15	74 16	..	30.35	31.62	39.32	46.48	57.13	68.14	72.34	71.01	64.03	53.98	42.93	34.3
8. Greenwich	39 24	75 20	30	30.97	33.94	39.68	51.53	60.43	71.00	75.74	73.02	66.73	53.71	44.19	34.5
9. Haddonfield	39 53	75 02	50	29.61	31.94	38.31	50.54	59.41	70.06	74.66	72.19	65.47	52.23	42.98	32.5
10. Lambertsville	40 23	74 57	96	29.55	29.85	37.90	48.86	60.20	70.16	75.09	72.14	64.40	51.60	42.30	32.5
11. Lesser Cross Roads	40 41	74 39	..	36.13	31.73	..	..	..	.	..	..	..	..	39.88	33.4
12. Long Branch	40 18	73 58	10	..	..	..	..	..	..	..	..	..	..	..	35.4
13. Middletown	40 24	74 07	50	34.80	35.48	41.81	53.10	61.47	66.83	71.93	72.23	66.40	57.37	45.73	34.8
14. Moorestown	39 58	74 57	104	29.18	..	46.41	62.17	68.03	74.74	72.69	65.16	..	..	..	32.7
15. Mount Holly	39 59	74 48	30	29.60	33.51	39.67	50.98	60.35	69.03	73.03	71.65	65.31	54.37	44.59	34.5
16. Navesink Highlands	40 24	73 59	111	29.50	36.45	38.20	47.88	54.23	67.23	70.30	..	..	..	..	..
17. Newark	40 44	74 10	35	31.63	25.90	34.45	45.62	56.31	66.01	70.51	69.04	60.71	49.86	39.92	29.0
18. Newark	40 44	74 10	35	29.36	30.65	37.40	48.28	57.91	67.51	72.93	70.61	63.60	52.31	43.22	32.2
19. New Brunswick	40 30	74 27	90	27.12	29.46	35.67	50.11	58.36	68.30	74.07	71.09	63.66	51.90	41.99	30.9
20. Newfield	39 40	74 50	125	35.18	31.49	36.97	48.78	59.73	72.83	77.45	73.43	65.87	55.42	41.94	32.6
21. New Germantown	40 41	74 45	320	32.59	30.63	32.88	49.87	58.89	70.11	73.06	71.62	64.41	50.54	39.09	29.5
22. New Stone	40 40	75 00	..	..	..	..	..	59.05	71.50	73.30	73.65	..	..	..	..
23. Newton	41 04	74 45	659	28.71	28.71	30.83	47.34	55.96	64.78	69.40	..	..	..	..	..
24. Paterson	40 56	74 10	60	26.58	29.45	35.69	49.11	58.77	69.49	74.37	70.97	64.77	51.27	41.66	30.5
25. Rio Grande	39 01	74 53	13	37.92	36.03	36.17	47.95	57.47	70.54	76.37	73.92	67.44	53.19	42.78	35.1
26. Scaville	39 11	74 45	18	26.26	37.35	40.17	51.16	53.38	70.98	76.72	74.48	69.69	53.54	44.48	28.3
27. Sergeantsville	40 27	74 57	..	28.54	31.39	38.65	43.02	60.42	69.61	74.86	76.45	71.17	62.83	43.46	36.6
28. South Orange	41 45	74 15	..	..	..	..	..	..	..	..	..	64.47	54.57	42.35	31.6
29. Trenton	40 14	74 45	60	31.80	33.11	39.24	52.08	60.05	70.55	75.21	73.33	66.22	54.20	44.29	33.0
30. Vineland	39 29	75 01	119	33.51	31.23	37.83	49.53	59.77	72.99	78.60	74.70	66.41	53.12	42.57	31.7
31. Woodstown	39 39	75 19	30	..	..	..	..	..	..	..	..	..	45.33	47.84	31.9

[1] This series is composed of observations at Littleton, by R. C. Whiting, and at North Littleton, about one mile north of Littleton, by R. Smith.
[2] The observing hours were $\odot_r$ 2_a. The observations were corrected for daily variation by means of the general table.
[3] Also called *Barnstead*. [4] Observations corrected for daily variation by means of the general table.
[5] The observations in March, 1849, were made at Belleville, about three miles northeast of Bloomfield.

NEW HAMPSHIRE.—Continued.

	Spring.	Summer.	Autumn.	Winter.	Year.	Series. Begins.	Series. Ends.	Extent yrs. mos.	Observing hours.	Observer.	References.
18	38°.63	63°.77	45°.36	17°.02	41°.20	Mar. 1863;	July, 1864	1 5	$7_m\ 2_a\ 9_a$ bis	R. C. Whiting, R. Smith.	S. O.
19	43.86	68.82	50.19	24.64	46.88	Mar. 1849;	Feb. 1857	5 10	$7_m\ 2_a\ 9_a$	R. C. Mack.	P. O. and S. I. Vol. 1, & MS.
20	49.95	71.38	..	29.17	..	Jan. 1862;	Feb. 1863	1 0	$7_m\ 2_a\ 9_a$ bis	D. I. S. French.	S. O.
21	47.80	70.02	51.14	25.90	48.72	Jan. 1845;	Mar. 1860	14 1	$\odot_r\ 2_a\ \odot_s$	S. N. Bell.	P. O. & S. I. Vol. 1, S. Coll., & S. O.
22	..	67.60	..	29.00		Jan. 1806;	June, 1807	0 10	[8]	....	Med. and Agr. Reg. Bost. Vol. 1, 1806-7.
23	..	46.88	..	..	..	1853;	1859	0 3	$7_m\ 2_a\ 9_a$	J. S. Hall, Noyes.	P. O. & S. I. Vol. 1, & Print. Reg.
24	42.93	67.05	49.31	23.94	45.81	Feb. 1860;	Dec. 1868	8 8	$7_m\ 2_a\ 9_a$ bis	C. H. Pittman.	S. O.
25	45.03	67.87	47.98	26.47	46.84	Feb. 1806;	Sept. 1807	1 5	[8]	C. Peirce.	Med. and Agr. Reg. Bost. Vol. 1, 1806-7.
26	44.02	66.99	47.88	25.15	46.01	Jan. 1839;	July, 1868	9 11	$\odot_r\ 9_m\ 3_a\ 9_a$	J. Hatch, Surg. Delaney and Chase.	MS. in S. Coll. and S. O.
27	..	..	48.42	22.15	..	Nov. 1861;	Oct. 1870	0 8	$7_m\ 2_a\ 9_a$ bis [4]	E. D. Couch.	S. O.
28	39.77	65.48	44.20	18.60	42.01	Dec. 1856;	May, 1869	6 9		F. Odell.	P. O. and S. I. Vol. 1, and S. O.
29	37.71	62.95	42.68	15.50	39.71	Aug. 1855;	Dec. 1870	13 4	$7_m\ 2_a\ 9_a$ bis	W. B. C., B. G. & B. Brown, A. Wiggin.	" " " "
30	50.08	76.67	54.87	29.53	52.79	1846;	1850	5 0	N.	Dow.	Manuscript.
31	39.36	66.02	45.23	19.91	42.63	Sept. 1856;	Dec. 1858	2 3	$7_m\ 2_a\ 9_a$	N. Purmort.	P. O. and S. I. Vol. 1.
32	40.35	64.84	44.16	20.19	42.39	June, 1869;	Dec. 1870	1 7	$7_m\ 2_a\ 9_a$ bis	L. D. Kidder.	S. O.

NEW JERSEY.

	Spring.	Summer.	Autumn.	Winter.	Year.	Series. Begins.	Series. Ends.	Extent yrs. mos.	Observing hours.	Observer.	References.
1	46.99	71.39	54.15	30.94	50.87	Mar. 1849;	Dec. 1862	10 7	$7_m\ 2_a\ 9_a$	R. L. Cooke, and Merrick.	P. O. and S. I. Vol. 1, S. O., & S. Coll.
2	..	74.65	54.69	30.87	..	Nov. 1866;	Oct. 1870	1 1	$7_m\ 2_a\ 9_a$ bis	J. Fleming, and W. T. Kerr.	S. O.
3	49.71	72.01	54.81	31.22	51.94	Mar. 1849;	Mar. 1868	13 3	"	Rev. A. Frost, Dr. E. R. Schmidt, and J. C. Deacon.[6]	P. O. and S. I. Vol. 1, S.O., and S. Coll.
4	[illegible]	[illegible]	[illegible]	[illegible]	[illegible]	May, 1863;	Dec. 1870	7 3	"	I. S. and T. J. Beans.[7]	S. O.
5	45.70	69.76	52.99	28.32	49.19	Oct. 1866;	Jan. 1869	2 4	"	H. Shriver.	" "
6	47.48	72.41	53.50	26.23	49.91	Mar. 1868;	Nov. 1868	0 9	"	J. S. Tritts.	" "
7	47.64	70.50	53.65	32.09	50.97	Jan. 1857;	Feb. 1862	5 0	"	O. R. Willis.	P. O. and S. I, Vol. 1. and S. O.
8	50.55	73.25	54.88	33.14	52.95	Jan. 1864;	Dec. 1870	7 0	"	Rebecca C. Sheppard.	S. O.
9	49.42	72.30	53.56	31.38	51.67	Jan. 1864;	Dec. 1870	6 9	"	J. S. Lippincott, S. Wood, & J. Boadle.	" "
10	48.99	72.46	52.77	30.66	51.22	Jan. 1843;	Dec. 1859	17 0	$7_m\ 2_a\ 9_a$	L. H. Parson.	Am. Alm. 1845 & foll., MS. in S. Coll., & P. O. & S. I. Vol. 1.
11	..	..	..	33.75	..	Oct. 1869;	Feb. 1870	0 4	$7_m\ 2_a\ 9_a$ bis	J. Fleming.	S. O.
12	..	..	..	..	..	1861		0 1	"	H. A. Stokes.	" "
13	52.13	70.33	56.50	35.03	53.50	June, 1831;	Mar. 1849	3 2	$7_m\ 2_a\ 9_a$	Colb and Jenkins.	Sill. Journ. and S. Coll.
14	58.87	70.86	..	..	..	July, 1849;	Aug. 1868	0 10	$7_m\ 2_a\ 9_a$ bis	Miss E. E. Thornton & J. W. Lippincott.	P. O. and S. I. Vol. 1, S. O., and S. Coll.
15	50.33	71.24	54.76	32.56	52.22	Jan. 1861;	Mar. 1868	7 1	"	Dr. M. J. Rhees.	S. O.
16	46.77	..	..	..	..	1861		0 7	"	Prof. L. Harper.	" "
17	45.46	68.52	50.16	28.86	48.25	1829;	1850	22 0	$\odot_r$ N. [8]	....	Pat. Off. Rep. 1851.
18	47.86	70.35	53.04	30.75	50.50	May, 1843;	Dec. 1870	24 5		W. A. Whitehead.	MS. in S. Coll., printed slip, P. O. and S. I, Vol. 1, & S. O.
19	48.05	71.15	52.52	29.17	50.22	Mar. 1863;	May, 1870	6 1	$7_m\ 2_a\ 9_a$ bis	G. W. Thompson, G. H. Cook, E. H. Bogardus, & J. E. Hasbrouck.	S. O.
20	48.49	74.57	54.41	33.09	52.64	Oct. 1867;	July, 1870	2 10	"	E. D. Couch.	" "
21	47.21	71.60	51.35	30.94	50.27	Oct. 1868;	Dec. 1870	2 2	"	A. B. Noll.	" "
22	..	72.82	..	..	..	1867		0 4	"	J. Fleming.	" "
23	44.71	..	..	..	..	1869		0 7	"	Dr. T. Ryerson.	" "
24	47.86	71.61	52.57	28.85	50.22	Oct. 1863;	Dec. 1870	6 8	"	W. Brooks.	" "
25	47.20	73.61	54.47	36.36	52.91	Apr. 1868;	Dec. 1870	2 5	"	Mrs. J. R. Palmer.	" "
26	48.24	74.06	55.90	30.66	52.21	Jan. 1865;	Apr. 1868	2 0	"	B. Cole.	" "
27	47.36	73.64	59.15	32.18	53.08	Jan. 1857;	Mar. 1858	1 3	$7_m\ 2_a\ 9_a$	J. T. Sergeant.	P. O. and S. I. Vol. 1.
28	..	..	53.80	..	..	1870		0 4	$7_m\ 2_a\ 9_a$ bis [8]	Dr. W. J. Chandler.	S. O.
29	50.46	73.03	54.90	32.66	52.76	Jan. 1840;	Dec. 1870	11 0		Dr. F. A. Ewing, and E. R. Cook.	Am. Alm. 1842 and S. O.
30	49.04	75.43	54.03	32.17	52.67	Aug. 1867;	Dec. 1870	3 5	$7_m\ 2_a\ 9_a$ bis	Dr. J. Ingram.	S. O.
31	..	..	..	..	..	1859		0 3	$7_m\ 2_a\ 9_a$	G. Watson.	P. O. and S. I. Vol. 1.

[6] The observations composing this series were made at Branchburg Township, Mechanicsville, and Beadington, all within a radius of about three miles.

[7] The observations previous to 1865 were made at the junction of the Delaware and Rancocus Rivers, about four miles northwest of Chester.

[8] Observations corrected for daily variation by means of the general table.

NEW MEXICO.

Name of Station.	Lat.	Long.	Height.	Jan.	Feb.	March.	April.	May.	June.	July.	August.	Sept.	Oct.	Nov.	Dec.
1. Abiquin	36°15′	106°30′	6500	..	..	..	..	..	..	74°.06	70°.87	64°.86	53°.28	..	..
2. Albuquerque[1]	35 06	106 38	5032	32°.77	38°.19	47°.09	56°.07	65°.92	74°.24	78.36	76.22	68.80	56.88	43°.29	33°.39
3. Camp Cimarron	..	..	..	..	..	..	..	..	69.99	70.98	74.47	67.01	..	..	..
4. Camp Plummer	36 18	106 42	..	16.67	18.10	25.64	42.40	50.05	62.18	66.87	..	..	47.10	29.44	30.37
5. Camp Rio Mimbres	32 32	107 56	..	..	..	45.08	59.03	66.32	..	..	..	..	..	..	..
6. Cantonment Burgwin[2]	36 26	105 30	7900	21.81	28.97	37.55	45.92	54.45	65.48	68.52	64.62	56.32	46.72	32.18	20.89
7. Cebolleta	35 15	107 20	6200	32.90	35.93	44.50	51.36	61.65	72.52	77.45	75.65	68.45	59.06	41.03	30.49
8. Doña Ana	32 26	106 48	4000	..	..	..	..	69.89	78.94	82.22	81.50	..	..	..	..
9. El Paso	31 44	106 32	3830	45.75	49.25	60.36	74.31	77.92	87.36	88.53	87.06	85.22	70.00	..	38.37
10. Fort Bascom	35 24	103 50	..	36.21	45.41	53.25	61.26	75.03	77.83	81.23	81.83	77.43	60.74	54.27	41.66
11. Fort Bayard	32 46	108 30	4450	36.38	39.56	43.97	51.67	58.49	69.25	71.13	69.91	66.61	57.87	45.86	38.68
12. Fort Conrad	33 47	106 48	4576	36.26	41.99	51.31	60.87	66.70	74.21	79.06	77.04	69.99	58.20	43.60	38.40
13. Fort Craig[3]	33 36	107 00	4576	38.03	44.00	53.19	61.30	71.09	79.30	81.89	79.12	72.24	60.30	47.09	36.84
14. Fort Cummings	32 32	107 40	..	46.80	49.14	54.94	64.30	72.40	77.88	81.08	78.42	76.52	66.60	59.83	46.66
15. Fort Fauntleroy[4]	35 29	108 23	..	24.06	..	..	49.50	62.19	70.48	74.17	71.66	61.08	51.54	36.66	32.46
16. Fort Fillmore[5]	32 14	106 42	3937	43.57	48.10	55.42	63.90	72.30	81.78	82.95	81.65	76.33	65.82	51.18	43.67
17. Fort Lowell	36 39	106 40	..	19.91	20.95	33.65	41.07	..	..	..	61.93	54.69	44.25	31.19	20.44
18. Fort McRae	33 18	107 03	4500	38.53	40.41	49.47	61.70	72.13	78.53	81.37	78.03	73.80	61.43	48.59	38.73
19. Fort Selden	32 23	106 55	..	44.12	48.06	55.45	63.55	72.89	81.53	82.57	80.27	74.77	63.54	51.89	43.10
20. Fort Stanton	33 29	105 38	..	34.61	38.10	44.52	52.15	61.06	68.39	69.40	67.74	61.38	51.97	41.56	35.24
21. Fort Sumner	34 25	104 08	..	39.27	40.76	47.68	56.44	68.54	77.67	78.78	78.07	71.92	59.56	47.26	39.65
22. Fort Thorn[5]	32 40	107 09	4500	37.56	41.98	51.03	61.19	68.33	77.84	80.88	77.14	69.38	58.24	44.83	36.66
23. Fort Union[5]	35 54	104 57	6670	32.03	35.43	40.82	49.08	58.83	66.49	69.87	67.46	61.55	51.35	41.56	33.03
24. Fort Webster	32 43	108 10	6350	35.96	40.48	46.20	53.10	59.44	70.11	75.15	69.89	63.08	53.85	43.62	42.82
25. Fort West	33 00	108 39	..	..	..	53.22	57.64	67.56	77.34	77.44	77.05	..	45.80	..	..
26. Fort Wingate	35 30	107 45	..	30.14	36.57	43.48	50.47	60.58	69.43	73.80	70.87	64.19	54.63	41.05	31.68
27. Laguna	35 03	107 14	6000	38.91	46.24	..	..	..	..	..	..	..	57.43	46.38	40.10
28. Las Vegas	35 35	105 16	6418	33.36	31.20	37.23	47.07	56.41	67.82	71.41	73.01	66.47	48.88	32.98	21.73
29. Los Pinos	34 51	106 39	5000	33.07	39.78	50.49	56.18	67.20	75.96	79.72	76.45	60.53	55.83	41.31	33.16
30. Rayado	36 27	104 55	6000	..	..	..	..	61.62	71.48	..	..	..	..	..	..
31. Santa Fé[6]	35 41	106 02	6846	28.38	33.21	40.73	50.27	59.17	69.36	72.13	70.01	63.79	51.79	38.44	29.25
32. Socorro	34 05	106 50	4560	37.60	38.05	48.74	57.31	65.69	76.46	79.60	80.48	73.61	60.38	42.60	33.30

NEW YORK.

Name of Station.	Lat.	Long.	Height.	Jan.	Feb.	March.	April.	May.	June.	July.	August.	Sept.	Oct.	Nov.	Dec.
1. Adirondack	44 00	74 05	..	..	..	24.49	33.79	48.03	57.87	64.18	60.65	..	..	..	..
2. Albany	42 39	73 44	130	25.00	26.00	34.00	48.50	59.25	66.25	73.50	71.50	62.50	49.75	38.16	27.00
3. Albany	42 39	73 44	130	22.90	26.75	32.11	49.02	60.32	68.67	71.26	72.06	64.01	51.33	41.47	29.34
4. Albany	42 39	73 44	130	22.49	26.46	34.44	47.71	59.23	69.87	74.08	70.99	62.88	49.94	37.46	28.31
5. Albany (Academy)	42 39	73 44	130	24.37	24.72	35.03	47.74	60.06	68.13	72.24	70.17	61.38	49.48	39.16	28.40
6. Albany	42 39	73 44	130	24.14	28.94	34.35	44.00	56.31	66.60	71.78	67.75	59.44	51.42	39.09	27.75
7. Albany (Dudley Observatory)	42 40	73 45	..	21.71	23.33	30.43	45.22	58.08	69.31	74.36	70.50	61.49	47.68	37.59	25.54
8. Albany	42 39	73 45	75	23.38	28.00	38.50	56.80	..	..	72.65	72.90	70.26	50.78	44.35	37.10
9. Albany	42 39	73 44	130	23.29	24.88	33.68	46.87	59.06	68.26	72.90	70.13	61.26	48.97	38.44	27.60
10. Albion	43 14	78 14	505	32.85	31.34	40.26	48.48	58.71	67.08	72.26	70.81	62.35	53.76	42.47	34.80
11. Albion	43 14	78 14	505	31.80	29.21	35.46	43.17	56.32	69.05	73.14	70.90	62.77	50.04	43.37	30.47
12. Alexander	42 53	78 18	..	..	..	..	..	58.37	66.21	71.45	..	..	..	..	..
13. Alfred	42 15	77 50	..	17.19	24.44	29.40	..	..	..	..	..	..	..	..	..
14. Amenia	41 50	73 33	540	21.79	20.12	35.56	41.54	56.66	66.55	67.88	67.86	57.76	46.99	45.15	28.24
15. Angelica	42 18	78 03	1500	16.59	20.84	26.09	41.74	54.12	65.56	71.28	65.63	60.05	46.23	35.42	25.15
16. Auburn	42 55	76 35	650	24.37	25.08	33.51	45.26	54.84	64.47	69.38	68.23	59.45	48.23	37.75	29.54
17. Auburn	42 55	76 35	650	24.39	25.38	32.77	44.98	60.33	68.73	72.38	72.29	63.86	50.42	38.74	28.79
18. Auburn	42 55	76 35	650	23.65	24.44	32.92	44.81	55.98	65.58	70.75	68.97	59.75	47.83	37.33	29.55
19. Baldwinsville	43 09	76 20	..	22.62	24.69	30.39	42.09	53.75	64.17	68.79	66.03	59.08	47.29	37.72	26.76

[1] Observations for four years, Sept. 1849, to Dec. 1854, $\odot_r\ 9_m\ 3_a\ 9_a$; they were referred to $7_m\ 2_a\ 9_a$.

[2] Observations for May and June, 1850, at Taos. For seven months of the series, the observing hours were $\odot_r\ 9_m\ 3_a\ 9_a$; a correction was applied to refer them to $7_m\ 2_a\ 9_a$.

[3] Observations for nine months of 1854, at $\odot_r\ 9_m\ 3_a\ 9_a$; referred to $7_m\ 2_a\ 9_a$.

[4] Also known as Fort Lyon.

[5] Observations prior to 1855, at $\odot_r\ 9_m\ 3_a\ 9_a$; referred to $7_m\ 2_a\ 9_a$.

[6] From January, 1855, to September, 1867, inclusive, the observations were made at Fort Marcy, about one mile from Santa Fé. Previous to 1855, the observing hours were $\odot_r\ 9_m\ 3_a\ 9_a$; they have been referred to $7_m\ 2_a\ 9_a$.

NEW MEXICO.

	Spring.	Summer.	Autumn.	Winter.	Year.	Series. Begins.	Ends.	Extent yrs.	mos.	Observing hours.	Observer.	References.
1	..	..	..	..	..	1851		0	4	$\odot_r\ 9_m\ 3_a\ 9_a$	Assistant Surgeon.	Ar. Met. Reg. 1855.
2	56°.36	76°.27	56°.32	34°.78	55°.93	Sept. 1849;	July, 1867	14	5	$7_m\ 2_a\ 9_a$	" "	Ar. Met. Regs. 1855 and 1860, and MS. from S. G. O.
3	..	71.81	..	..	..	1868		0	4	"	" "	MS. from S. G. O.
4	39.36	..	..	21.71	..	Oct. 1867;	July, 1868	0	10	"	" "	" " "
5	56.81	..	..	..	..	1864		0	3	"	" "	" " "
6	45.97	66.21	45.07	23.89	45.29	May, 1850;	Apr. 1860	5	11	"	" "	Ar. Met. Regs. 1855 and 1860, and MS. from S. G. O.
7	52.50	75.21	56.18	33.11	54.25	Dec. 1849;	Sept. 1851	1	10	$\odot_r\ 9_m\ 3_a\ 9_a$	" "	Ar. Met. Reg. 1855.
8	..	80.89	..	..	..	1851		0	4	"	" "	" " "
9	70.86	87.65	..	44.46	..	Aug. 1850;	Aug. 1851	1	0	"	" "	" " "
10	63.18	80.30	64.15	41.09	62.18	Feb. 1864;	Oct. 1870	3	10	$7_m\ 2_a\ 9_a$	" "	MS. from S. G. O.
11	51.38	70.10	56.78	38.21	54.12	Mar. 1867;	Dec. 1870	3	10	"	" "	" " "
12	59.63	76.77	57.26	38.88	58.14	Oct. 1851;	Mar. 1854	2	6	$\odot_r\ 9_m\ 3_a\ 9_a$	" "	Ar. Met. Reg. 1855.
13	61.86	80.10	59.88	39.62	60.37	Apr. 1854;	Dec. 1870	13	10	$7_m\ 2_a\ 9_a$	" "	Ar. Met. Regs. 1855 and 1860, and MS. from S. G. O.
14	63.88	79.13	67.65	47.53	64.55	Mar. 1869;	Nov. 1870	1	9	"	" "	MS. from S. G. O.
15	..	72.10	49.76	..	..	Oct. 1860;	Sept. 1861	0	10	"	" "	" " "
16	63.87	82.13	64.44	45.11	63.89	Sept. 1851;	May, 1861	9	8	"	" "	Ar. Met. Regs. 1855 and 1860, and MS. from S. G. O.
17	..	..	43.38	20.43	..	Aug. 1868;	Apr. 1869	0	9	"	" "	MS. from S. G. O.
18	61.10	79.31	61.27	39.22	60.23	Mar. 1864;	Dec. 1870	3	1	"	" "	" " "
19	63.96	81.46	63.40	45.09	63.48	Nov. 1865;	Dec. 1870	4	8	"	" "	" " "
20	52.58	68.51	51.64	35.98	52.18	Aug. 1855;	Dec. 1870	9	11	"	" "	Ar. Met. Reg. 1860, and MS. from S. G. O.
21	57.55	78.17	59.58	39.89	58.80	Apr. 1864;	July, 1869	5	0	"	" "	MS. from S. G. O.
22	60.18	78.62	57.48	38.73	58.75	Jan. 1854;	Jan. 1859	5	0	"	" "	Ar. Met. Regs. 1855 and 1860.
23	49.58	67.94	51.49	33.50	50.63	Aug. 1851;	Dec. 1870	17	3	"	" "	Ar. Met. Regs. 1855 and 1860, and MS. from S. G. O.
24	52.91	71.72	53.52	39.75	54.48	Feb. 1852;	Dec. 1853	1	11	$\odot_r\ 9_m\ 3_a\ 9_a$	" "	Ar. Met. Reg. 1855.
25	59.47	77.28	..	..	..	1863		0	7	$7_m\ 2_a\ 9_a$	" "	MS. from S. G. O.
26	51.51	71.37	53.29	32.80	52-24	Nov. 1862;	Dec. 1870	7	7	"	" "	" " "
27	..	..	..	41.75	..	Oct. 1851;	Feb. 1852	0	5	$\odot_r\ 9_m\ 3_a\ 9_a$	" "	Ar. Met. Reg. 1855.
28	46.90	70.75	49.44	28.76	48.96	Jan. 1850;	July, 1851	1	7	"	" "	" " "
29	57.96	77.38	52.56	35.34	55.81	Jan. 1863;	May, 1866	2	9	$7_m\ 2_a\ 9_a$	" "	MS. from S. G. O.
30	..	..	..	..	..	1851		0	2	$\odot_r\ 9_m\ 3_a\ 9_a$	" "	Ar. Met. Reg. 1855.
31	50.06	70.50	51.34	30.28	50.54	Jan. 1849;	Dec. 1870	18	6	$7_m\ 2_a\ 9_a$	" "	Ar. Met. Regs. 1855 and 1860, and MS. from S. G. O.
32	57.25	78.85	58.86	36.32	57.82	Nov. 1849;	Aug. 1851	1	9	$\odot_r\ 9_m\ 3_a\ 9_a$	" "	Ar. Met. Reg. 1855.

NEW YORK.

	Spring.	Summer.	Autumn.	Winter.	Year.	Series. Begins.	Ends.	Extent yrs.	mos.	Observing hours.	Observer.	References.
1	35.44	60.90	..	..	..	1852		0	6	$6_m\ 2_a\ 10_a$	....	MS. in S. Coll.
2	47.25	70.42	50.14	26.00	48.45	Jan. 1795;	Dec. 1796	1	11	max. & min.	De Witt.	" " "
3	47.15	70.66	52.27	26.33	49.10	Jan. 1813;	Dec. 1814	2	0	$7_m\ 3_a\ 9_a$	Dr. Eyhts.	" " "
4	47.13	71.65	50.09	25.75	48.65	Jan. 1820;	Dec. 1825	6	0	$7_m\ 2_a\ 9_a$	Dr. Beach.	" " "
5	47.61	70.18	50.01	25.83	48.41	Jan. 1826;	Dec. 1849	24	0	[7]	Various observers.	N. Y. Univ. Syst. 1855.
6	44.89	68.71	49.98	26 94	47.63	Jan. 1850;	Dec. 1852	3	0	$6_m\ 2_a\ 10_a$	....	MS. in S. Coll.
7	44.58	71.39	48.92	23.53	47.10	Jan. 1862;	Dec. 1870	9	0	$8_m\ 7_a$	Various observers.	Annals of the Dudley Observ'y Vol. 2.
8	..	..	55.13	29.49	..	Jan. 1865;	Apr. 1866	1	1	$7_m\ 2_a\ 9_a$ bis	H. M. Paine.	S. O.
9	46.54	70.43	49.56	25.26	47.95	Jan. 1795;	Dec. 1870	45	11	[8]	Various observers.	Consolidated series.
10	49.15	70.05	52.86	33.00	51.26	1845;	1848	....		......	McHarf.	Dove.
11	44.98	71.03	52.06	30.49	49.64	1849;	1853	2	8	$\odot_r\ 9_m\ 3_a\ 9_a$[9]	Munger.	MS. in S. Coll.
12	..	..	..	..	..	1851		0	3	$6_m\ 2_a\ \odot_s$	....	" " "
13	..	..	..	..	..	1852		0	3	$6_m\ 2_a\ 10_a$	....	" " "
14	44.59	67.43	49.97	23.38	46.34	Jan. 1849;	July, 1850	1	1	[7]	A. Winchell.	N. Y. Univ. Syst. 1855.
15	40.65	67.49	47.23	20.86	44.06	May, 1854;	Dec. 1870	3	4	$7_m\ 2_a\ 9_a$	Dr. E. M. Alba, C. P. Arnold.	P. O. and S. I. Vol. 1, and S. O.
16	44.54	67.36	48.48	26.33	46.68	Jan. 1827;	Dec. 1849	22	0	[7]	Various observers.	N. Y. Univ. Syst. 1855.
17	46.03	71.13	51.01	26.19	48.59	Jan. 1860;	Dec. 1865	6	0	$7_m\ 2_a\ 9_a$ bis	J. B. Dill.	S. O.
18	44.57	68.43	48.30	25.88	46.80	Jan. 1827;	Dec. 1865	28	0	[8]	Various observers.	Consolidated series.
19	42.08	66.33	48.03	24.69	45.28	1849;	May, 1867	16	0	[8]	J. Bowman.	MS. in S. Coll., P. O. and S. I. Vol. 1, and S. O.

[7] Daily means computed by the formula $\frac{a + 2b + 2c + a'}{6}$ where a represents an observation a little before sunrise, b one at 3_a, c one at one hour after sunset, and a' the morning observation on the following day. The results thus obtained appear, on the average, to be about 0°.5 too high.

[8] Corrected for daily variation by means of the general table.

[9] Observations at $9_m\ 3_a\ 9_a$ in May, June, September, October, 1850, and March, 1851; subsequently at $7_m\ 2_a$.

NEW YORK.—Continued.

NAME OF STATION.	Lat.	Long.	Height.	Jan.	Feb.	March.	April.	May.	June.	July.	August.	Sept.	Oct.	Nov.	Dec.
20. Barnesville	42°38′	74°26′	1200	..	..	30°.48	47°.28	60°.20	72°.68	..	..	..	..	..	..
21. Beaver Brook	41 30	74 37	700	..	..	24.95	44.62	59.28	68.14	76°.00	71°.17	65°.15	53°.43	38°.66	24°.32
22. Belleville (Union Acad.)	43 47	76 06	300	23°.73	22°.92	32.64	48.18	56.50	64.68	69.59	66.13	60.04	48.98	37.77	25.93
23. Bellport	40 44	72 52	15	31.12	30.70	37.29	45.01	54.35	64.32	69.17	68.58	62.10	53.14	42.54	33.63
24. Beverly	41 22	73 56	180	24.79	27.94	35.25	46.89	57.55	66.87	72.37	69.05	62.34	50.76	41.09	29.06
25. Blackwell's Island[3]	40 45	73 58	29	22.31	30.64	33.67	46.99	56.20	68.48	74.66	72.24	66.95	54.13	43.95	35.06
26. Bloomingdale	40 49	73 58	..	32.77	28.86	40.77	51.95	60.88	69.44	74.22	74.04	69.26	53.45	47.40	33.93
27. Bridgewater	42 52	75 17	1286	20.64	21.89	29.88	42.29	52.98	59.58	66.64	62.90	55.44	44.66	31.42	23.68
28. Brooklyn	40 41	73 58	125	..	..	..	..	..	74.03	77.03	74.60	65.94	57.81	46.26	35.38
29. Buffalo	42 53	78 53	623	23.41	21.13	35.49	40.69	55.29	67.44	71.55	69.99	59.89	48.75	37.22	22.85
30. Buffalo Barracks	42 53	78 52	660	27.00	24.62	30.85	44.10	52.96	64.16	68.35	68.51	61.87	45.55	35.53	29.55
31. Buffalo	42 53	78 52	569	24.36	26.39	31.37	43.63	53.59	65.04	69.58	68.58	61.19	49.51	40.13	28.40
32. Buffalo	42 53	78 52	600	24.75	26.52	32.61	43.08	53.06	64.30	70.34	68.56	61.78	49.96	39.25	28.48
33. Buffalo	42 53	78 52	600	24.72	27.49	32.05	43.12	53.19	63.79	69.65	68.43	60.94	48.91	38.75	28.09
34. Caldwell	43 24	73 43	300	..	..	..	..	..	..	74.03	70.48	62.63	49.35	..	..
35. Cambridge (Washington Co. Acad.)	43 00	73 25	500	22.44	21.45	32.69	44.19	55.99	64.82	68.88	66.09	58.29	46.76	36.56	26.21
36. Canajoharie (Acad.)	42 51	74 42	284	20.97	19.61	30.46	47.29	58.33	64.06	70.34	67.36	58.69	49.06	37.87	25.26
37. Canandaigua (Aca.)	42 55	77 16	590	23.34	21.09	31.84	45.94	55.92	65.70	69.49	66.80	57.32	47.85	36.14	26.68
38. Canton	44 36	75 11	304	17.94	14.44	26.04	42.65	57.18	67.20	72.50	68.89	60.42	48.74	36.48	21.15
39. Cazenovia (Acad.)[4]	42 55	75 51	1260	21.43	22.21	29.85	42.87	53.09	61.99	66.71	64.61	57.66	45.84	35.63	24.69
40. Champion	43 57	75 41	..	11.35	24.30	..	..	..	..	..	..	..	..	..	..
41. Charlotte[5]	43 15	77 37	273	25.47	27.88	32.93	44.57	54.69	66.33	70.65	69.76	62.22	50.68	40.83	29.23
42. Chatham	42 24	73 36	..	25.57	23.52	30.40	45.05	56.90	68.71	72.00	69.36	61.24	48.19	45.57	20.56
43. Cherry Valley Acad.	42 48	74 45	1335	22.03	21.66	30.30	43.64	53.84	63.48	67.68	65.58	57.82	45.81	34.36	25.34
44. Clinton (Hamilton Coll.)	43 03	75 24	1127	21.78	24.25	30.28	43.70	56.55	65.84	72.46	69.39	61.54	49.75	37.92	28.44
45. Clockville	43 00	75 48	1300	..	24.63	28.25	40.33	49.47	66.90	..	..	..	..	..	..
46. Clyde (near)	43 05	76 54	400	23.82	27.35	30.96	44.77	53.65	63.61	66.77	65.25	59.47	50.62	37.38	31.95
47. Constableville	43 33	75 27	..	..	..	..	..	..	62.04	68.85	64.89	60.74	..	..	..
48. Constantia	43 15	76 02	424	..	..	..	..	..	..	..	..	62.87	..	..	..
49. Cooperstown	42 42	74 57	1300	27.80	19.48	24.73	46.50	58.63	71.88	73.35	69.13	60.65	46.22	34.83	26.06
50. Cuba	42 12	78 18	1502	18.10	22.48	28.02	40.41	51.21	62.60	63.52	63.22	55.12	40.19	32.61	23.58
51. Dansville	42 35	77 44	714	28.82	31.53	32.35	46.87	52.20	65.22	68.95	68.01	60.80	52.12	37.50	34.03
52. Delhi (Delaware Acad.)	42 16	74 58	1384	22.82	28.58	33.59	39.49	55.30	68.05	68.95	64.69	55.86	45.92	37.01	31.45
53. Depauville (1 mile north of)	44 06	76 06	350	19.24	20.76	29.20	42.82	53.10	64.85	69.57	66.49	60.32	46.36	35.96	23.72
54. East Hampton (Clin. Acad.)	40 58	72 28	16	30.13	30.75	36.36	44.43	53.18	62.80	69.68	68.51	62.54	52.13	42.27	33.45
55. Eden (Brown Cottage)	42 30	79 07	700	13.25	32.05	25.99	41.70	54.07	63.75	72.47	68.26	62.60	48.63	36.30	34.55
56. Ellisburg	43 47	76 08	250	23.74	22.82	33.42	48.65	57.49	64.73	69.73	66.94	61.34	48.72	38.39	26.53
57. Elmira	42 05	76 50	860	19.50	26.66	32.15	39.85	56.09	62.80	67.81	64.29	58.55	51.02	33.90	32.86
58. Fairfield Academy	43 05	74 55	1185	19.73	19.73	29.85	42.57	53.91	62.53	66.39	65.79	57.53	46.02	34.50	23.98
59. Falconer	42 05	79 10	..	23.44	27.90	32.01	..	..	..	..	..	..	..	..	..
60. Fishkill Landing	41 30	73 59	42	25.15	27.51	34.86	47.47	58.77	68.45	73.49	70.48	63.49	52.79	41.15	30.08
61. Flatbush (Erasmus Hall)[6]	40 39	73 58	54	30.47	31.57	38.38	48.41	58.36	67.51	73.32	71.34	64.48	53.68	43.94	34.31
62. Flushing[7]	40 46	73 48	..	32.57	29.12	33.80	49.65	62.38	72.55	76.73	74.13	66.10	55.50	41.98	31.09
63. Fordham (St. John's Coll.)	40 54	73 50	147	21.35	32.81	37.11	..	..	..	75.42	..	65.21	53.15	44.35	30.16
64. Fort Ann	43 22	73 28	1430	34.55	36.05	45.31	56.49	60:37	76.53	78.18	75.10	60.84	45.45	42.68	29.98
65. Fort Columbus	40 42	74 01	23	29.87	30.53	37.96	48.47	59.43	69.46	75.09	73.38	65.96	54.57	43.64	33.50
66. Fort Edward	43 13	73 33	175	25.31	21.00	33.13	45.45	57.79	69.96	70.74	67.57	60.85	49.09	36.06	27.60

[1] Corrected for daily variation by means of the general table.

[2] Daily means computed by the formula $\frac{a + 2b + 2c + a'}{6}$ where a represents an observation a little before sunrise, b one at 3_a, c one at one hour after sunset, and a' the morning observation on the following day. The results thus obtained appear, on the average, to be about 0°.5 too high.

[3] New York, Penitentiary Hospital.

NEW YORK.—Continued.

	Spring.	Summer.	Autumn.	Winter.	Year.	Series. Begins. Ends.	Extent yrs. mos.	Observing hours.	Observer.	References.
20	45°.99	..	..	..	..	1870	0 4	$7_m\ 2_a\ 9_a$ bis	G. S. France.	S. O.
21	42.95	71°.77	52°.41	..	..	1854	0 10	[1]	C. S. Woodard.	P. O. and S. I. Vol. I.
22	45.77	66.80	48.93	24°.19	46°.42	Jan. 1830; Dec. 1844	9 0	[2]	Various observers.	N. Y. Univ. Syst. 1855.
23	45.55	67.36	52.59	31.82	49.33	Aug. 1857; June, 1862	4 11	$7_m\ 2_a\ 9_a$ bis	H. W. Titus.	S. O.
24	46.56	69.43	51.40	27.26	48.66	1851; Dec. 1870	17 3	[1]	T. B. Arden.	MS. in S. Coll., P. O. and S. I. Vol. 1, and S. O.
25	45.62	71.79	55.01	29.34	50.44	Jan. 1856; Nov. 1857	1 11	$7_m\ 2_a\ 9_a$	Dr. W. W. Sanger.	P. O. and S. I. Vol. I.
26	51.20	72.57	56.70	31.85	53.08	1846	1 0	$\odot_r\ 2_a\ \odot_s$	Earle.	Dove.
27	41.72	63.04	43.84	22.07	42.67	Jan. 1833; Dec. 1837	4 0	[2]	Various observers.	N. Y. Univ. Syst. 1855.
28	..	75.22	56.67	..	..	Aug. 1849; Dec. 1870	0 9	$7_m\ 2_a\ 9_a$ bis	Bea & son, J. P. Mailler.	MS. in S. Coll. and S. O.
29	43.82	69.66	48.62	22.46	46.14	Jan. 1831; Dec. 1832	2 0	[2]	Various observers.	N. Y. Univ. Syst. 1855.
30	42.64	67.01	47.65	27.06	46.09	July, 1841; Aug. 1845	4 7	$\odot_r\ 9_m\ 3_a\ 9_a$	Assistant Surgeon.	Ar. Met. Reg. 1855.
31	42.86	67.73	50.28	26.38	46.81	July, 1859; Dec. 1867	8 6	$7_m\ 2_a\ 9_a$	E. Dorr.	U. S. Lake Survey, 1855.
32	42.92	67.73	50.33	26.58	46.89	Jan. 1854; Dec. 1870	12 7	[1]	W. Ives, E. O. Salisbury.	Climate copy of Buffalo 1867, P. O. and S. I. Vol. 1, and S. O.
33	42.79	67.29	49.53	26.77	46.59	Jan. 1831; Dec. 1870	27 8	[1]	Various observers.	Consolidated series.
34	..	..	..	..	..	1870	0 4	$7_m\ 2_a\ 9_a$ bis	A. M. Strong.	S. O.
35	44.29	66.60	47.20	23.37	45.36	Jan. 1827; Dec. 1841	14 0	[2]	Various observers.	N. Y. Univ. Syst. 1855.
36	45.36	67.25	48.54	21.95	45.77	Jan. 1830; Dec. 1835	3 0	[2]	" "	" " " " "
37	44.57	67.33	47.10	23.70	45.68	Jan. 1829; Dec. 1838	10 0	[2]	H. Howe.	" " " " "
38	41.96	69.53	48.55	17.84	44.47	Aug. 1853; Aug. 1858	3 10	$7_m\ 2_a\ 9_a$	E. W. Johnson.	P. O. and S. I. Vol. 1, & S. Coll.
39	41.94	64.44	46.38	22.78	43.88	Jan. 1830; Dec. 1870	27 7	[2]	Various observers.	N. Y. Univ. Syst. 1855, P. O. and S. I. Vol. 1, and S. O.
40	..	..	..	..	..	1844	0 2	{ $7_m\ 9_m$ N. $4_a\ 7_a\ 9_a$	Dr. F. B. Hough.	MS. in S. Coll.
41	44.06	68.91	51.24	27.53	47.93	July, 1859; Dec. 1867	8 6	$7_m\ 2_a\ 9_a$	A. Mulligan.	U. S. Lake Survey, Rep. 1867, and MS.
42	44.12	70.02	51.67	23.22	47.26	1849; 1854	1 11	[1]	C. T. Chase.	P. O. & S. I. Vol. 1, and S. Coll.
43	42.59	65.58	46.00	23.01	44.30	Jan. 1827; Dec. 1845	15 0	[2]	Various observers.	N. Y. Univ. Syst. 1855.
44	43.51	69.23	49.74	24.82	46.82	Jan. 1852; Mar. 1865	6 10	$7_m\ 2_a\ 9_a$ bis	Prof. O. Root, Dr. H. M. [illegible]	P. O. and S. I. Vol. I, MS. in S. Coll., and S. O.
45	39.35	[illegible]	[illegible]	[illegible]	[illegible]	1850	0 5	$\odot_r\ 9_m\ 3_a\ 9_a$	Chapman.	S. Coll.
46	43.13	65.21	49.16	27.71	46.30	Jan. 1861; June, 1862	1 6	$7_m\ 2_a\ 9_a$ bis	M. Mackie.	S. O.
47	..	65.26	..	..	..	1851; 1853	0 4	$\odot_r\ 9_m\ 3_a\ 9_a$	Fairchild.	S. Coll.
48	..	..	..	..	..	1861	0 1	$7_m\ 2_a\ 9_a$ bis	S. Clark.	S. O.
49	43.29	71.45	47.23	24.45	46.61	Oct. 1869; Dec. 1870	1 3	"	G. Pomeroy Keese.	" "
50	39.88	63.11	42.64	21.39	41.76	1840; 1841	2 0	$10_m\ 10_a$	Fallcott.	Regents' Report.
51	43.81	67.39	50.14	31.46	48.20	Jan. 1861; Dec. 1863	0 10	$7_m\ 2_a\ 9_a$ bis	J. J. Brown.	S. O.
52	42.79	67.23	46.26	27.62	45.98	Jan. 1828; Dec. 1852	3 0	[2]	S. C. Johnson, D. Shepard.	N. Y. Univ. Syst. 1855, and MS. in S. Coll.
53	41.71	66.97	47.55	21.24	44.37	Feb. 1865; Dec. 1870	5 11	$7_m\ 2_a\ 9_a$ bis	H. Haas.	S. O.
54	44.66	67.00	52.31	31.44	48.85	Jan. 1827; Dec. 1843	17 0	[2]	Various observers.	N. Y. Univ. Syst. 1855.
55	40.59	68.16	49.18	26.62	46.14	Mar. 1856; Dec. 1857	1 1	$7_m\ 2_a\ 9_a$	S. & A. S. Landon.	P. O. and S. I. Vol. I.
56	46.52	67.13	49.48	24.36	46.87	....	10 0	[2]	....	Dove, 1857.
57	42.70	64.97	47.82	26.34	45.46	Jan. 1852; Oct. 1852	0 10	$6_m\ 2_a\ 10_a$	Various observers.	MS. in S. Coll.
58	42.11	64.90	46.02	21.15	43.54	Jan. 1827; Dec. 1849	20 10	[2]	" "	N. Y. Univ. Syst. 1855, and MS. in S. Coll.
59	..	..	..	..	..	1854	0 3	$7_m\ 2_a\ 9_a$	L. A. Langdon.	P. O. and S. I. Vol. I.
60	47.03	70.81	52.48	27.58	49.47	Jan. 1854; Oct. 1866	10 5	$7_m\ 2_a\ 9_a$ bis	W. H. Denning, W. Harkness.	MS. in S. Coll., P. O. and S. I. Vol. I. and S. O.
61	48.38	70.72	54.03	32.12	51.31	Jan. 1826; Dec. 1870	39 9	[3]	Various observers.	N. Y. Univ. Syst. 1855, MS. in S. Coll., P. O. and S. I. Vol. I, and S. O.
62	48.61	74.47	54.53	30.93	52.13	July, 1855; Dec. 1870	1 0	$7_m\ 2_a\ 9_a$	" "	P. O. and S. I. Vol. 1, and MS. from S. G. O.
63	..	..	54.24	28.11	..	Feb. 1856; Mar. 1862	1 0	$7_m\ 2_a\ 9_a$ bis	J. Aubier, Prof. J. Monroe.	P. O. and S. I. Vol. 1, and S. O.
64	54.06	76.60	49.66	33.53	53.46	Nov. 1863; May, 1866	2 0	"	P. A. McMoore.	S. O.
65	48.62	72.64	54.72	31.30	51.82	Oct. 1821; Dec. 1870	48 8	$7_m\ 2_a\ 9_a$	Assistant Surgeon.	Ar. Met. Reg. and MS. from S. G. O.
66	45.46	69.42	48.67	24.64	47.05	Nov. 1857; May, 1870	2 2	"	Prof. S. Tias, J. S. Cooley.	P. O. and S. I. Vol. I, and S. O.

[4] Observations after 1849, at $7_m\ 2_a\ 9_a$; they were referred to the New York Academy system by means of the general table.

[5] Observations previous to June, 1860, at $6_m\ 9_m\ 3_a\ 6_a$; referred to $7_m\ 2_a\ 9_a$.

[6] Observations after 1849, at $7_m\ 2_a\ 9_a$; referred to the New York Academy System.

[7] Observations at Flushing, Willett's Point and Fort Schuyler combined.

NEW YORK.—Continued.

Name of Station.	Lat.	Long.	Height.	Jan.	Feb.	March.	April.	May.	June.	July.	August.	Sept.	Oct.	Nov.	Dec.
67. Fort Hamilton	40°36′	74°02′	25	30°.06	30°.79	37°.41	47°.59	58°.11	68°.43	73°.97	73°.17	66°.43	55°.02	44°.52	33°.7
68. Fort Niagara	43 15	79 05	263	26.71	26.98	33.34	43.32	54.59	65.12	70.53	69.56	61.62	50.49	39.75	29.1
69. Fort Ontario	43 34	76 12	295	24.21	23.26	30.94	42.87	51.76	62.23	69.57	68.28	61.56	48.49	38.55	26.7
70. Fort Porter	42 50	78 55	660	24.32	25.58	30.90	41.26	52.26	66.09	72.03	70.16	62.92	50.83	39.37	27.7
71. Fort Wood	40 42	74 11	..	30.42	26.57	36.36	45.09	55.72	67.45	73.34	71.67	63.78	55.44	42.02	32.2
72. Fredonia (Acad.)	42 26	79 21	715	28.37	27.75	35.16	45.85	56.67	65.23	70.66	68.47	61.01	50.93	39.71	31.0
73. Friendship	42 12	78 10	1536	15.75	29.72	27.71	43.05	47.95	65.90	66.18	65.23	56.93	45.65	38.07	22.5
74. Gaines (Academy)	43 16	78 15	427	25.37	28.38	34.46	46.54	54.48	62.99	71.76	66.48	59.83	47.69	35.25	28.4
75. Geneva	42 53	77 00	567	21.10	24.87	31.61	43.82	54.09	65.78	71.89	68.09	61.51	49.91	39.34	28.7
76. Germantown	42 05	73 52	..	20.62	25.15	34.12	45.62	55.06	68.76	73.19	65.30	61.10	51.45	40.70	25.8
77. Glasco	42 00	74 00	150	31.93	26.28	30.20	48.25	55.20	71.75	72.95	69.20	61.35	50.00	38.58	28.2
78. Goshen (Farmer's Hall)	41 23	74 20	425	25.66	26.31	36.51	47.42	56.22	64.73	68.70	67.64	59.76	48.81	38.79	28.0
79. Gouverneur	44 20	75 27	400	17.23	18.17	28.56	42.89	54.81	64.11	69.70	66.71	56.67	45.59	33.73	20.9
80. Greenville (Acad.)	42 24	74 02	..	30.27	27.48	33.78	40.18	62.51	66.78	68.88	68.72	61.73	51.26	36.96	28.1
81. Hamilton (Acad.)	42 48	75 29	1127	22.91	22.95	31.80	45.43	54.97	63.08	67.36	65.86	58.28	45.88	35.64	26.3
82. Hamilton	42 48	75 29	1127	21.32	26.60	31.52	40.79	55.20	62.06	67.75	65.14	58.71	49.48	35.76	25.5
83. Hartwick (Sem.)	42 37	75 00	1100	24.27	25.22	33.89	44.42	56.48	65.08	68.25	66.72	58.75	48.46	38.11	28.1
84. Havana	42 30	73 30	1041	25.13	..	..	..	..	..	..	..	..	..	..	..
85. Henrietta	43 03	77 39	600	29.70	28.48	38.44	48.31	58.70	64.95	69.76	66.57	60.07	51.31	39.48	30.7
86. Hermitage	42 45	78 16	1500	23.26	23.44	26.74	39.40	50.74	60.57	64.49	64.31	56.31	46.62	35.46	26.6
87. Homer (Courtland Acad.)	42 38	76 11	1096	22.90	22.51	31.12	42.40	53.93	61.67	65.92	64.22	56.45	46.53	35.81	26.9
88. Houseville	43 40	75 32	900	20.92	21.40	28.37	38.89	51.56	64.97	69.16	65.18	57.79	46.81	34.28	20.2
89. Hudson (Acad.)	42 14	73 47	150	25.19	25.78	34.85	47.61	58.93	67.62	71.53	70.06	61.91	50.33	38.92	28.5
90. Huntingdon	40 52	73 27	50	26.	29.	24.	49.	63.	65.	75.	71.	69.	54.	42.	31.
91. Ithaca (Acad.)	42 25	76 30	417	27.78	27.78	34.90	46.73	57.82	65.42	70.78	68.68	60.35	49.20	38.97	31.0
92. Jamaica (Union Hall)	40 42	73 48	30	29.42	29.34	37.64	47.25	56.96	65.71	71.23	70.58	62.79	51.85	41.72	32.5
93. Jamestown	42 06	79 16	1364	20.20	24.58	32.68	43.38	57.16	65.98	68.67	66.26	60.94	48.39	36.62	29.2
94. Jericho	40 47	71 33	..	..	..	..	44.11	..	..	..	..	..	..	..	..
95. Johnstown (Acad.)	42 59	74 22	[2]250	21.27	22.14	31.68	43.50	55.89	64.76	68.89	67.70	58.16	46.73	34.97	24.8
96. Kinderhook (Aca.)	42 22	73 23	125	22.90	23.32	33.74	46.30	57.26	65.44	70.15	68.47	60.30	47.54	38.28	25.2
97. Kingston (Acad.)	41 55	74 00	188	26.66	27.31	37.20	49.37	59.53	67.22	72.76	70.93	62.29	50.54	41.02	30.9
98. La Fargeville	44 12	76 00	..	26.00	32.67	32.67	42.67	58.00	65.00	72.00	66.33	62.00	51.33	32.67	24.0
99. Lansingburgh (Acad.)	42 45	73 40	30	22.67	24.83	34.34	47.00	58.67	67.48	71.68	69.89	61.89	49.96	38.21	26.6
100. Ledyard (Cayuga Acad.)	42 43	76 42	447	28.70	28.18	36.91	46.59	56.55	66.15	72.27	70.71	62.96	50.53	40.60	29.8
101. Leroy	42 57	78 03	..	..	..	..	41.87	56.90	71.50	77.20	..	..	..	..	..
102. Lewiston (S. High School)	43 09	79 04	280	27.23	26.92	34.80	46.32	56.91	64.80	71.56	69.94	61.88	50.10	39.70	29.9
103. Leyden	43 34	75 22	1312	22.76	16.01	25.58	40.25	52.73	57.82	66.33	61.35	59.05	39.74	28.53	23.5
104. Liberty	41 45	74 46	1474	18.19	20.13	26.71	39.95	51.59	62.62	68.79	64.34	56.63	47.84	33.95	26.3
105. Lima	42 53	77 40	..	22.63	30.75	..	..	..	..	..	..	..	..	..	..
106. Lisle	42 21	76 02	..	..	..	..	..	53.39	..	..	..	..	..	..	..
107. Little Genesee	42 00	78 15	1500	22.13	23.58	28.65	43.26	52.38	65.44	68.97	64.97	58.50	45.27	35.58	24.4
108. Lockport[4]	43 09	78 44	..	24.2	27.6	33.2	40.4	53.7	66.3	68.8	66.7	59.6	49.9	43.9	34.4
109. Lodi[5]	42 36	76 50	1000	23.43	24.09	30.19	42.02	56.57	67.49	72.25	68.36	62.18	49.37	37.05	26.4
110. Lowville (Acad.)	43 47	75 30	847	19.75	21.49	29.78	43.70	54.59	62.61	67.91	64.84	57.43	45.80	34.45	23.4
111. Ludlowville	42 33	76 35	600	28.40	27.63	26.83	45.90	55.85	66.68	70.73	69.28	..	..	..	..
112. Luzerne	43 18	73 50	500	..	..	..	..	..	..	..	..	..	..	35.33	24.1
113. Lyons	43 04	77 02	..	24.90	26.22	31.80	42.64	54.73	63.06	67.12	66.39	57.94	49.67	38.04	28.9
114. McGrawville	42 34	76 11	1450	9.23	30.52	25.65	35.72	51.98	61.16	70.01	64.66	59.43	46.48	35.46	32.0
115. Madison Barracks[6]	43 57	76 04	262	21.79	23.81	32.89	44.35	54.56	64.49	69.08	68.96	60.62	49.49	37.88	25.8
116. Madrid	44 43	75 09	280	16.73	18.06	29.62	40.39	56.53	66.62	72.34	69.18	59.06	46.49	35.10	22.1

[1] Daily means computed by the formula $\frac{a + 2b + 2c + a'}{6}$ where a represents an observation a little before sunrise, b one at 3_a, c one at one hour aft sunset, and a' the morning observation on the following day. The results thus obtained appear, on the average, to be about 0°.5 too high.

NEW YORK.—Continued.

	Spring.	Summer.	Autumn.	Winter.	Year.	Series. Begins.	Ends.	Extent yrs. mos.	Observing hours.	Observer.	References.
67	47°.70	71°.86	55°.32	31°.53	51°.60	Jan. 1843;	Dec. 1870	27 2	$7_m\ 2_a\ 9_a$	Assistant Surgeon.	Ar. Met. Reg. and MS. from S. G. O.
68	43.75	68.40	50.62	27.62	47.60	Jan. 1829;	Dec. 1867	22 3	"	L. Leffman, Assistant Surgeon.	Ar. Met. Reg. 1855, and U. S. Lake Survey, Rep. of 1867–8.
69	41.86	65.69	49.53	24.74	45.71	Jan. 1843;	Dec. 1870	11 1	$\odot_r\ 9_m\ 3_a\ 9_a$	Assistant Surgeon.	Ar. Met. Regs. 1855–60.
70	41.47	69.43	51.04	25.89	46.96	Jan. 1849;	Dec. 1870	8 9	$7_m\ 2_a\ 9_a$	Hosmer.	MS. from S. G. O. and S. Coll.
71	45.72	70.82	53.75	29.74	50.01	1837;	1838	2 0	"	Assistant Surgeon.	Army Register.
72	45.89	68.12	50.55	29.06	48.41	Mar. 1829;	Feb. 1864	20 9	[1]	Various observers.	N. Y. Univ. Syst. 1855, MS. in S. Coll., and S. O.
73	39.57	65.77	46.88	22.66	43.72	Nov. 1866;	Nov. 1867	0 11	$7_m\ 2_a\ 9_a$ bis	G. W. Fries.	S. O.
74	45.16	67.08	47.59	27.40	46.81	Jan. 1839;	Dec. 1842	4 0	[1]	Various observers.	N. Y. Univ. Syst. 1855.
75	43.17	68.59	50.25	24.92	46.73	Feb. 1852;	Aug. 1868	6 3	$7_m\ 2_a\ 9_a$ bis	" "	P. O. and S. I. Vol. 1, MS. in S. Coll., and S. O.
76	44.93	69.08	51.08	23.86	47.24	May, 1866;	May, 1868	2 0	"	S. W. Roe.	S. O.
77	44.55	71.30	49.98	28.83	48.66	Jan. 1870;	Dec. 1870	0 11	"	D. B. Hendricks.	" "
78	46.72	67.02	49.12	26.66	47.38	Jan. 1835;	Dec. 1849	11 0	[1]	Various observers.	N. Y. Univ. Syst. 1855.
79	42.09	66.84	45.33	18.78	43.26	Jan. 1831;	Dec. 1870	28 8	$7_m\ 2_a\ 9_a$ bis	" "	N. Y. Univ. Syst. 1855 and P. O. and S. I. Vol. 1, and S. O.
80	45.49	68.13	49.98	28.63	48.06	1826		1 0	[1]	E. B. Wheeler.	N. Y. Univ. Syst. 1855.
81	44.07	65.43	46.60	24.07	45.04	Jan. 1827;	Dec. 1849	18 0	"	Various observers.	" " " "
82	42.50	64.98	47.98	24.49	44.99	Sept. 1850;	Dec. 1852	2 4	$6_m\ 2_a\ 10_a$	" "	Manuscript.
83	44.93	66.68	48.44	25.89	46.49	Jan. 1826;	Dec. 1850	16 0	[1]	" "	N. Y. Univ. Syst. 1855.
84	..	..	..	..	..	1860		0 1	$7_m\ 2_a\ 9_a$ bis	E. C. Frost.	S. O.
85	48.48	67.09	50.29	29.65	48.88	Jan. 1835;	June, 1862	5 6	[1]	J. S. Whitaker, E. D. Ransom, A. S. Wadsworth.	N. Y. Univ. Syst. 1855, & S. O.
86	38.96	63.12	46.13	24.45	43.16	Nov. 1860;	Aug. 1864	3 10	$7_m\ 2_a\ 9_a$ bis	A. A. Hibberd.	S. O.
87	42.48	63.94	46.26	24.12	44.20	Feb. 1829;	Feb. 1856	21 8	[1]	Various observers.	N. Y. Univ. Syst. 1855, P. O. & S. I. Vol. 1, & MS. in S. Coll.
88	39.61	66.44	46.29	20.85	43.30	1849;	Oct. 1870	9 4	$7_m\ 2_a\ 9_a$ bis	W. D. Yale.	P. O. and S. I. Vol. 1, S. O., & S. Coll.
89	47.13	69.74	50.39	26.50	48.44	Jan. 1827;	Jan. 1870	19 9	[1]	Various observers.	N. Y. Univ. Syst. 1855, MS. in S. Coll. and S. O.
90	45.33	70.33	55.00	28.67	49.84	Sept. 1821;	Aug. 1822	1 0	......	....	Sketch of Long Island.
91	46.48	68.29	49.51	28.86	48.29	Jan. 1827;	Dec. 1852	20 10	[1]	Various observers.	N. Y. Univ. Syst. 1855, and MS. in S. Coll.
92	47.28	69.17	52.12	30.42	49.75	Jan. 1826;	Dec. 1850	25 0	[1]	" "	N. Y. Univ. Syst. 1855.
93	44.41	66.97	48.65	24.69	46.18	Jan. 1852;	Mar. 1866	3 4	$7_m\ 2_a\ 9_a$ bis	Dr. S. W. Roe & others.	MS. in S. Coll. and S. O.
94	..	..	..	..	..	1849		0 1	......	Wills.	S. Coll.
95	43.69	67.12	46.62	22.75	45.04	Jan. 1828;	Dec. 1845	16 0	[1]	Various observers.	N. Y. Univ. Syst. 1855.
96	45.77	68.02	48.71	23.82	46.58	Jan. 1830;	Dec. 1846	17 0	[1]	T. Metcalf.	" " " "
97	48.70	70.30	51.28	28.29	49.64	Sept. 1828;	Nov. 1869	19 10	[1]	Various observers.	N. Y. Univ. Syst. 1855, and S. O.
98	44.45	67.78	48.67	27.56	47.11	1851		1 0	$\odot_r$ N. $\odot_s$	Rothers	Pat. Off. Rep.
99	46.67	69.68	50.02	24.71	47.77	Jan. 1826;	Dec. 1852	23 0	[1]	Various observers.	N. Y. Univ. Syst. 1855, and Reg. Rep.
100	46.68	69.71	51.36	28.89	49.16	Jan. 1830;	Dec. 1850	13 0	[1]	" "	N. Y. Univ. Syst. 1855.
101	..	..	..	..	..	1854		0 4	$7_m\ 2_a$	L. F. Munger.	P. O. and S. I. Vol. 1.
102	46.01	68.77	50.56	28.03	48.34	May, 1830;	Dec. 1849	18 8	[1]	Various observers.	N. Y. Univ. Syst. 1855.
103	39.52	61.83	42.44	20.76	41.14	Mar. 1869;	July, 1870	1 2	$7_m\ 2_a\ 9_a$ bis	C. Collins Merriam.	S. O.
104	39.42	65.25	46.14	21.55	43.09	Jan. 1852;	Apr. 1856	2 3	[3]	Various observers.	P. O. & S. I. Vol. 1, & MS. in S. Coll.
105	..	..	..	..	..	1861		0 2	$7_m\ 2_a\ 9_a$ bis	Prof. S. A. Lattimer.	S. O.
106	..	..	..	..	..	1849		0 1	$\odot_r\ 7_m\ 3_a\ 9_a$	Mitchell.	S. Coll.
107	41.43	66.46	46.45	23.39	44.43	Feb. 1866;	Dec. 1870	4 11	$7_m\ 2_a\ 9_a$ bis	D. Edwards.	S. O.
108	42.43	67.27	51.13	28.73	47.39	Nov. 1848;	Dec. 1870	4 6	[3]	J. G. Trevor, Giddings, B. W. Clark.	MS. in S. Coll. and S. O.
109	42.93	69.37	49.53	24.65	46.62	1849;	Jan. 1858	8 8	$7_m\ 2_a\ 9_a$	J. Lefferts.	P. O. & S. I. Vol. 1, & S. Coll.
110	42.69	65.12	45.89	21.55	43.81	Jan. 1827;	Dec. 1857	24 3	[1]	Various observers.	N. Y. Univ. Syst. 1855, MS. in S. Coll, & P. O. & S. I. Vol. 1.
111	42.86	68.90	..	..	..	1869		0 8	$7_m\ 2_a\ 9_a$ bis	C. P. Murphy.	S. O.
112	..	..	..	..	..	1870		0 2	"	A. M. Strong.	" "
113	43.06	65.52	48.55	26.67	45.95	Jan. 1861;	Aug. 1862	2 8	"	E. W. Sylvester.	" "
114	37.78	65.28	47.12	23.94	43.53	Sept. 1856;	Sept. 1857	0 11	$7_m\ 2_a\ 9_a$	J. M. Smith.	P. O. and S. I. Vol. 1.
115	43.93	67.51	49.33	23.82	46.15	Jan. 1824;	Dec. 1870	18 3	[3]	Assistant Surgeon.	Ar. Met. Reg.
116	42.18	69.38	46.88	18.97	44.35	Jan. 1849;	Jan. 1859	5 7	$7_m\ 2_a\ 9_a$	E. A. Dayton.	P. O. and S. I. Vol. 1, & S. Coll.

[2] Altitude 688 feet, according to Regents' Report.

[3] Corrected for daily variation by means of the general table.

[4] Series approximately corrected for daily variation; observations often interrupted and hours of observation changed.

[5] Also called *Townsendville* and *Covert*.

[6] Observations previous to 1829 not very reliable.

NEW YORK.—Continued.

Name of Station.	Lat.	Long.	Height.	Jan.	Feb.	March.	April.	May.	June.	July.	August.	Sept.	Oct.	Nov.	Dec.
117. Malone (Franklin Acad.)	44°50′	74°18′	703	18°.24	24°.48	31°.42	45°.07	53°.01	60°.22	66°.90	[illegible]5°.45	55°.17	46°.92	32°.85	21°.22
118. Marathon	42 25	76 02	1200	..	..	25.53	..	56.73	59.43	69.62	..	..	..	..	..
119. Martinsburgh	43 43	75 28	..	..	..	..	50.30	55.60	64.93	..	..	..	..	..	..
120. Mexico (Acad.)	43 27	76 14	331	21.90	23.39	30.88	41.93	52.23	62.84	66.89	65.86	58.63	46.40	34.78	25.95
121. Middlebury (Aca.)	42 48	78 08	800	26.27	26.28	33.96	45.59	56.00	63.89	68.75	66.91	59.14	48.00	37.22	29.17
122. Milo	42 39	77 01	868	28.53	21.25	25.43	44.38	55.14	66.12	68.74	67.09	61.24	45.96	35.44	27.71
123. Millville (Acad.)	43 10	78 20	600	26.00	26.36	32.28	45.55	54.69	63.23	68.24	67.73	59.50	46.63	37.76	28.99
124. Minaville	42 54	74 15	..	20.44	16.93	25.70	42.40	57.02	68.64	73.52	69.92	61.28	46.67	34.08	20.92
125. Mohawk	43 00	75 02	435	20.87	22.69	28.04	42.33	54.89	64.59	69.64	67.73	58.77	47.93	36.87	23.12
126. Montgomery (Aca.)	41 32	74 13	300	25.36	27.02	36.63	47.63	58.36	65 98	72.34	70.31	62.51	49.23	39.47	29.03
127. Moriches[2]	40 47	72 48	13	30.81	33.49	38.39	49.14	58.45	69.07	74.40	72.86	66.60	54.27	44.24	34.10
128. Morley	44 40	75 00	..	18.87	19.58	25.01	..	..	68.05	71.17	68.70	56.33	42.20	38.33	17.59
129. Morrisania (Fairmount Inst.)	40 50	73 54	150	24.93	28.72	32.27	46.00	57.82	70.39	75.77	74.75	67.31	55.51	43.24	37.49
130. Mt. Pleasant (Aca.)	41 03	73 52	125	27.96	29.39	38.04	48.34	57.87	67.68	71.40	71.12	62.49	50.63	40.29	30.24
131. Newark Valley	44 20	76 30	..	24.14	20.69	27.05	41.77	54.65	65.52	70.80	66.45	58.74	45.22	35.03	26.43
132. Newburgh (Acad.)	41 31	74 00	74	28.29	27.60	36.13	48.27	59.02	68.21	72.75	71.05	64.20	52.52	42.03	29.81
133. New York	40 42	74 01	56	25.25	27.27	38.75	49.32	65.97	80.37	81.05	80.82	67.10	54.27	40.10	36.50
134. New York	40 42	74 01	56	30.20	30.80	38.50	49.10	59.60	69.10	74.90	73.30	65.90	54.30	43.50	33.90
135. New York (D. & D. Inst.)	40 50	73 56	25	30.52	31.04	37.49	48.45	58.85	69.74	75.04	73.07	65.54	53.69	44.38	34.23
136. New York (U. S. Nav. Hosp.)	40 41	73 57	56	29.61	31.39	37.91	48.70	58.68	70.43	75.07	73.20	65.31	53.94	44.42	33.11
137. New York[3]	40 45	73 58	42	28.83	31.86	37.28	49.29	58.74	70.15	75.30	73.39	65.49	53.50	43.47	31.92
138. New York[4]	40 45	73 58	42	29.78	31.41	37.63	48.78	58.76	69.69	75.06	73.28	65.59	53.71	46.25	33.16
139. Nichols	42 01	76 28	800	24.22	26.10	32.52	44.14	55.79	65.47	69.81	67.13	59.65	47.89	37.86	28.23
140. North Argyle	43 18	73 30	290	..	..	..	44.30	60.30	65.70	70.98	68.90	..	..	..	..
141. North Granville (Acad.)	43 23	73 17	250	20.67	20.09	31.29	43.63	56.15	66.50	70.82	68.28	58.72	47.70	35.89	24.79
142. North Hammond	44 23	75 45	..	19.18	19.56	27.12	42.10	56.62	68.70	73.19	69.77	62.28	49.53	36.18	22.01
143. North Nassau	42 32	73 38	..	23.98	27.90	36.48	43.95	..	65.50	70.19	65.13	57.69	46.65	39.45	22.73
144. North Salem (Aca.)	41 20	73 34	361	26.55	26.07	35.55	46.12	56.70	66.07	71.71	69.00	60.65	49.67	39.11	28.69
145. North Volney	43 20	76 28	..	27.34	21.10	29.62	42.20	58.54	67.00	72.31	68.36	61.54	47.54	35.87	25.92
146. Oaklands	42 53	74 31	480	28.49	27.69	36.32	37.68	53.37	68.00	72.80	68.50	60.65	49.28	45.40	28.95
147. Ogdensburgh (Acad.)	44 40	75 28	232	20.08	20.20	30.51	40.05	52.95	64.45	68.68	67.92	57.65	48.51	39.36	22.88
148. Oneida	43 04	75 38	500	23.33	24.32	30.45	44.66	55.70	65.37	70.14	67.69	60.77	48.39	37.82	27.12
149. Onondaga (Acad.)	42 56	76 08	1260	25.28	25.67	33.81	45.97	58.01	65.49	68.91	68.05	59.75	48.26	36.54	29.12
150. Oswego	43 25	76 34	232	24.12	25.43	31.32	42.10	52.88	63.15	69.57	68.10	61.28	49.74	40.40	28.05
151. Ovid (Seneca Coll. Inst.)	42 41	76 52	800	20.33	25.25	26.35	41.53	53.26	65.08	72.70	68.78	61.77	47.85	38.61	29.08
152. Oxford (Acad.)	42 23	75 40	961	22.90	23.59	31.98	43.98	55.33	63.44	67.98	65.81	58.18	46.58	35.59	26.09
153. Oyster Bay (Acad.)	40 52	73 32	50	27.48	34.14	38.94	49.31	57.58	67.17	72.57	70.30	64.02	54.00	43.27	33.96
154. Palermo	43 20	76 16	327	20.84	21.99	28.01	42.23	53.76	64.40	69.19	66.72	58.74	46.65	36.10	24.55
155. Palmyra	43 04	77 13	466	23.85	25.06	34.92	45.78	57.78	67.00	69.46	67.26	60.04	48.00	39.63	29.17
156. Penn Yan	42 42	77 04	740	25.60	25.54	33.40	44.16	55.28	64.42	69.22	66.81	59.48	47.88	38.22	28.44
157. Perry City	42 27	76 47	800	..	..	..	..	..	..	..	..	63.95	..	..	..
158. Plainville	43 00	76 16	..	33.86	32.55	28.76	37.07	53.97	62.71	..	66.94	60.04	..	..	..
159. Plattsburgh (Acad. and Barracks[6])	44 41	73 26	186	18.68	19.54	28.51	41.52	54.76	64.34	68.73	66.90	59.01	46.09	35.45	23.15
160. Pompey (Acad.)	42 52	76 02	1300	21.43	21.75	29.28	40.80	52.33	61.65	65.95	64.29	55.55	44.46	32.71	24.07

[1] Daily means computed by the formula $\frac{a + 2b + 2c + a'}{6}$ where a represents an observation a little before sunrise, b one at 3_a, c one at one hour after sunset, and a' the morning observation on the following day. The results thus obtained appear, on the average, to be about 0°.5 too high.

[2] Also called *Brookhaven.*

NEW YORK.—Continued.

	Spring.	Summer.	Autumn.	Winter.	Year.	Series. Begins. Ends.	Extent yrs. mos.	Observing hours.	Observer.	References.
117	43°.17	64°.19	44°.98	21°.31	43°.41	Jan. 1839; Dec. 1842	3 0	[1]	Various observers.	N. Y. Univ. Syst. 1855.
118	..	..	..	..	..	1863	0 4	$7_m\ 2_a\ 9_a$ bis	L. Swift.	S. O.
119	..	..	..	..	..	1844		$\left\{ \begin{array}{l} 7_m\ 9_m\ N. \\ 4_a\ 7_a\ 9_a \end{array} \right.$	Dr. F. B. Hough.	MS. in S. Coll.
120	41.68	65.20	46.60	23.75	44.31	Jan. 1837; Jan. 1857	14 11	[1]	Various observers.	N. Y. Univ. Syst. 1855, MS. in S. Coll., & P. O. & S. I. Vol. I.
121	45.18	66.52	48.12	27.24	46.77	Jan. 1826; Dec. 1848	19 0		" "	N. Y. Univ. Syst. 1855.
122	41.65	67.32	47.55	25.83	45.59	May, 1869; Dec. 1870	1 8	$7_m\ 2_a\ 9_a$ bis	G. D. Baker.	S. O.
123	44.17	66.40	47.96	27.12	46.41	Jan. 1840; Dec. 1847	8 0	[1]	Various observers.	N. Y. Univ. Syst. 1855.
124	41.71	70.69	47.34	19.43	44.80	July, 1867; Dec. 1870	3 6	$7_m\ 2_a\ 9_a$ bis	J. W. Bussing.	S. O.
125	41.75	67.32	47.86	22.23	44.79	June, 1860; Mar. 1869	6 3	hourly.	J. Lewis, M.D.	S. Coll.
126	47.54	69.54	50.40	27.14	48.66	Jan. 1828; Dec. 1842	13 0	[1]	Various observers.	N. Y. Univ. Syst. 1855.
127	48.66	72.11	55.04	32.80	52.15	Mar. 1864; Dec. 1870	6 9	$7_m\ 2_a\ 9_a$ bis	E.A. Smith & daughter.	S. O.
128	..	69.31	45.62	18.68	..	1849; 1850	0 10	$\odot_r\ 9_m\ 3_a\ 9_a$	....	S. Coll.
129	45.36	73.64	55.35	30.38	51.18	Jan. 1856; Jan. 1858	1 7	$7_m\ 2_a\ 9_a$	J. S. Norton, J. Zaepffel.	P. O. and S. I. Vol. I.
130	48.08	70.07	51.14	29.20	49.62	Jan. 1831; July, 1849	13 1	[1]	Various observers.	N.Y. Univ. Syst. 1855, & S. Coll.
131	41.16	67.59	46.33	23.75	44.71	Mar. 1868; Dec. 1870	2 7	$7_m\ 2_a\ 9_a$ bis	Rev. S. Johnson.	S. O.
132	47.81	70.67	52.92	28.57	49.99	Jan. 1828; Dec. 1870	27 1	[1]	Various observers.	N. Y. Univ. Syst. 1855, MS. in S. Coll., and S. O.
133	51.35	80.75	53.82	29.67	53.90	May, 1782; June, 1784	2 2	......	De La Lerve.	Cotté.
134	49.07	72.43	54.57	31.63	51.92	....	30 0	......	....	Pat. Off. Rep.
135	48.26	72.62	54.54	31.93	51.83	Jan. 1844; Dec. 1870	21 8	$7_m\ 2_a\ 9_a$ bis	Prof. O. W. Morris.	MS. in S. Coll., P. O. and S. I. Vol. I, and S. O.
136	48.43	72.90	54.56	31.37	51.81	1849; Sept. 1870	12 0	$\odot_r\ 9_m\ 3_a\ 9_a$	T. L. Smith.	S. O.
137	48.44	72.95	54.15	30.87	51.60	Jan. 1854; June, 1870	8 7	$7_m\ 2_a\ 9_a$ bis	Various observers.	P. O. and S. I, Vol. I, and S. O.
138	48.39	72.68	55.18	31.45	51.92	Jan. 1844; Dec. 1870	21 11	[5]	" "	Consolidated series.
139	44.15	67.47	48.47	26.18	46.57	Jan. 1857; Dec. 1870	14 0	$7_m\ 2_a\ 9_a$ bis	R. Howell.	MS. in S. Coll., P. O. and S. I. Vol. I, and S. O.
140	..	68.53	..	..	..	1864	0 5	"	G. M. Hunt.	S. O.
141	43.69	68.53	47.44	21.85	45.38	Jan. 1835; Dec. 1849	14 0	[1]	J. C. Parker, E. T. Mack.	N. Y. Univ. Syst. 1855.
142	41.95	70.55	49.33	20.25	45.52	June, 1866; Dec. 1870	4 7	$7_m\ 2_a\ 9_a$ bis	C. A. Wooster.	S. O.
143	..	66.94	47.93	24.87	..	1850; 1851	1 4	$\odot_r\ 9_m\ 3_a\ 9_a$	Ball.	S. Coll.
144	46.12	68.93	49.81	27.10	47.99	Jan. 1829; Jan. 1857	22 11	[1]	Various observers.	N. Y. Univ. Syst. 1855, P. O. and S. I. Vol. I, MS. in S. Coll.
145	43.45	69.22	48.32	24.79	46.45	Mar. 1868; Dec. 1870	2 4	$7_m\ 2_a\ 9_a$ bis	J. M. Patrick.	S. O.
146	42.46	69.77	51.78	28.38	48.10	1849; 1850	2 0	......	....	Observations, N. Y. State Agr. Society, 1850 (p. 43).
147	41.17	67.02	48.51	21.05	44.44	Jan. 1838; Dec. 185[illegible]	3 8	[1]	Prof. J. H. Coffin, Griest.	N. Y. Univ. Syst. 1855, MS. in S. Coll.
148	43.60	67.73	48.99	24.92	46.31	Jan. 1862; Dec. 1870	8 9	$7_m\ 2_a\ 9_a$ bis	Dr. S. Spooner.	S. O.
149	45.93	67.48	48.18	26.69	47.07	Jan. 1826; Dec. 1844	16 0	[1]	Various observers.	N. Y. Univ. Syst. 1855.
150	42.10	66.94	50.47	25.87	46.35	July, 1849; Dec. 1870	18 7	$7_m\ 2_a\ 9_a$ bis	J. S. Hart, W. S. Malcom.	P. O. and S. I. Vol. I, S.O., and S. Coll.
151	40.38	68.85	49.41	24.89	45.88	Nov. 1855; Jan. 1858	2 3	$7_m\ 2_a\ 9_a$	J. W. Chickering.	P. O. and S. I. Vol. I.
152	43.76	65.74	46.78	24.19	45.12	Jan. 1828; Dec. 1852	21 8	[1]	Various observers.	N. Y. Univ. Syst. 1855, and MS. in S. Coll.
153	48.61	70.01	53.76	31.86	51.06	Jan. 1834; Dec. 1837	2 0	[1]	G. B. Docharty, N. H. Wells.	N. Y. Univ. Syst. 1855.
154	41.33	66.77	47.16	22.46	44.43	Jan. 1860; Dec. 1870	10 11	$7_m\ 2_a\ 9_a$ bis	E. B. Bartlett.	S. O.
155	46.16	67.91	49.22	26.03	47.33	Jan. 1835; Sept. 1865	2, 7	"	J. F. Cogswell, S. Hyde.	N. Y. Univ. Syst. 1855, S. O., and S. Coll.
156	44.28	66.82	48.53	26.53	46.54	Jan. 1829; Dec. 1859	31 0	$\odot_r\ 2_a\ \odot_s$	Dr. H. P. Sartwell.	Reg. Rep., MS. in S. Coll., & P. O. and S. I. Vol. I.
157	..	..	..	..	..	1869	0 1	$7_m\ 2_a\ 9_a$ bis	C. P. Murphy.	S. O.
158	39.93	..	..	..	..	Aug. 1856; June, 1857	0 8	$7_m\ 2_a\ 9_a$	J. H. Norton.	P. O. and S. I. Vol. I.
159	41.60	66.66	46.85	20.46	43.89	Jan. 1839; Dec. 1870	15 9	$\odot_r\ 9_m\ 3_a\ 9_a$	Various observers.	Ar. Met. Reg., MS. from S. G. O., N. Y. Univ. Syst. 1855, P. O. and S. I. Vol. I, and MS. in S. Coll.
160	40.80	63.96	44.24	22.42	42.85	Jan. 1826; Jan. 1858	21 1	[1]	" "	N.Y. Univ. Syst. 1855, MS. in S. Coll., & P. O. & S. I. Vol. I.

[3] The observations for this series were made at *Columbia College*, *Lewis M. Rutherfurd's Observatory*, *Rutgers Female College*, *St. Francis Xavier's College*, *No. 232 Fifth Avenue*, and one other location, not given.

[4] This series is composed of the three preceding series, corrected for daily variation.

[5] Corrected for daily variation by means of the general table.

[6] The observations for this series were made at various hours, $\odot_r\ 9_a\ 3_a\ 9_a$ predominating. They were referred to $\odot_r\ 9_a\ 3_a\ 9_a$ by means of the general table.

NEW YORK.—Continued.

Name of Station.	Lat.	Long.	Height.	Jan.	Feb.	March.	April.	May.	June.	July.	August.	Sept.	Oct.	Nov.	Dec.
161. Pompey Hill	42°52′	76°09′	1737	..	..	..	..	50°.07	65°.55	69°.82	..	..	..	..	..
162. Potsdam (St. Lawr. Acad.)	44 40	75 01	394	18°.41	18°.78	29°.96	43°.75	55.03	63.96	68.39	66°.75	57°.37	44°.99	33°.72	22°.11
163. Poughkeepsie (Dutchess Acad.)	41 40	73 55	..	26.29	27.27	36.26	49.92	59.81	68.39	73.60	72.24	64.01	52.01	41.51	30.78
164. Poughkeepsie	41 42	73 56	..	..	..	39.14	..	55.83	..	75.27	..	..	..	..	..
165. Prattsburgh (Franklin Acad.)	42 34	77 20	1494	24.47	24.61	32.99	46.15	52.88	61.28	66.77	65.86	57.47	45.93	35.21	28.19
166. Red Hook (Acad.)	41 58	73 52	..	24.66	26.06	35.83	49.14	58.00	66.98	71.88	68.64	61.61	50.41	39.59	27.58
167. Rochester	43 08	77 40	506	25.49	25.91	32.73	45.21	56.23	65.63	70.38	68.10	60.43	48.53	38.09	27.97
168. Rockland (Female Inst.)	41 09	74 00	81	..	34.75	37.10	51.78	59.55	..	..	..	..	..	..	..
169. Rouse's Point	44 59	73 22	117	18.02	18.91	29.21	40.23	54.66	64.63	68.89	66.81	57.59	46.45	36.53	21.74
170. Sackett's Harbor	43 55	76 07	266	21.14	24.14	30.36	43.64	54.37	65.20	70.06	70.26	61.56	50.07	40.77	25.87
171. Sag Harbor	41 00	72 18	40	31.00	31.88	33.69	45.97	56.79	68.40	73.73	70.86	65.41	55.55	44.73	34.38
172. Salem (Wash. Ac.)	43 09	73 20	..	22.42	22.75	32.57	45.65	57.03	65.94	69.29	69.55	60.06	46.63	38.55	28.31
173. Saratoga	43 04	73 47	960	19.74	29.66	29.70	41.41	56.17	64.68	72.30	69.90	60.83	47.31	37.96	26.29
174. Schenectady (Ac.)	42 47	73 57	300	22.09	21.79	30.43	44.58	59.05	66.67	70.15	68.09	59.84	47.09	37.54	29.22
175. Seneca Falls	42 54	76 50	463	25.72	28.54	32.31	42.69	55.58	66.21	71.08	68.51	61.17	51.76	33.31	23.89
176. Sennett	42 57	76 32	..	..	..	..	40.07	..	..	..	..	..	..	..	..
177. Sherburne	42 40	75 31	..	..	..	36.50	46.65	54.70	65.98	64.95	65.80	65.48	..	..	..
178. Sing Sing	41 09	73 52	125	32.34	34.20	38.68	46.53	59.31	70.35	74.40	70.54	64.95	51.14	46.97	32.24
179. Skaneateles	42 55	76 26	932	23.55	27.06	30.02	43.07	53.41	63.09	67.88	65.18	60.72	47.27	37.18	26.25
180. Sloansville	42 41	74 31	..	27.97	24.95	24.25	42.18	55.00	..	..	..	..	..	..	..
181. Smithville	43 52	76 06	300	21.38	21.01	28.60	42.08	52.40	63.57	70.71	67.70	60.04	47.59	40.14	22.61
182. Somerville	44 10	75 00	412	18.51	22.81	26.87	40.80	54.41	67.66	71.98	68.49	60.20	48.54	37.16	18.04
183. South Alabama	43 03	78 25	..	..	..	..	..	..	..	..	..	..	..	34.57	33.61
184. South Edmeston	42 40	75 19	..	23.13	26.77	31.40	44.88	54.79	66.57	70.25	67.29	54.09	50.66	41.78	23.12
185. South Hartford	43 18	73 25	500	20.81	24.41	32.09	47.80	59.11	70.52	74.85	71.94	63.45	50.25	38.96	25.52
186. South Trenton	43 13	75 15	835	19.10	21.08	25.97	39.01	51.66	66.06	69.29	65.38	60.39	45.27	34.28	22.90
187. Spencertown (Ac.)	42 19	73 41	750	18.31	24.42	28.14	43.54	53.00	64.47	72.54	67.11	60.74	48.55	37.14	25.09
188. Springville (Acad.)	42 30	78 42	500	24.88	25.95	30.75	45.45	53.14	61.62	67.51	64.18	57.61	46.23	37.50	28.41
189. Stapleton (Stat. Isl.)	40 39	74 04	50	27.13	25.00	..	..	..	..	..	..	..	57.00	45.05	30.50
190. Suffern	41 07	74 08	..	..	..	33.88	..	..	..	..	..	..	..	..	..
191. Syracuse (Acad.)	43 02	76 14	407	24.15	26.62	32.25	42.41	55.50	65.58	70.82	68.60	61.38	50.44	36.36	29.95
192. Theresa	44 12	75 48	365	15.59	20.17	27.09	41.92	54.68	64.20	68.51	67.46	58.96	45.23	35.38	23.94
193. Throgg's Neck	40 48	73 47	44	28.41	30.34	34.95	47.71	57.39	68.59	73.72	72.05	65.82	53.00	42.89	31.11
194. Troy (Rensselaer Inst.)	42 44	73 41	58	22.16	25.31	33.85	44.92	57.26	68.01	73.80	71.06	61.69	50.63	39.76	26.71
195. Union Springs	42 48	76 14	400	..	..	..	..	..	..	..	65.22	..	..	..	..
196. Utica	43 05	75 13	473	23.28	24.28	32.43	45.20	56.68	64.67	69.28	67.57	59.58	48.58	36.83	26.56
197. Wales	42 46	78 34	..	..	..	..	..	49.84	..	..	..	..	..	..	..
198. Wampsville	43 07	75 48	500	21.72	24.32	30.31	42.66	55.98	64.61	70.29	66.42	59.45	47.87	38.05	25.57
199. Warsaw	42 44	78 10	..	..	..	38.73	45.73	54.85	..	..	..	..	..	..	..
200. Waterbury	42 30	76 45	800	25.40	22.73	24.41	43.46	54.89	65.51	69.36	65.93	58.93	44.13	33.14	25.22
201. Waterford	42 47	73 43	70	21.97	24.63	31.08	44.89	56.36	66.37	71.31	68.63	62.05	49.71	38.30	25.95
202. Watertown	43 58	75 54	268	12.87	19.12	25.71	46.05	54.31	64.84	72.79	67.64	62.93	48.43	35.76	17.69
203. Waterville	42 54	75 25	1223	25.04	26.03	29.76	39.27	49.81	66.37	69.91	67.28	57.35	44.99	44.17	24.29
204. Watervliet Arsenal	42 43	73 50	50	23.27	23.84	34.02	45.98	59.08	68.62	74.00	71.14	62.00	49.50	38.95	27.26
205. Waverly	42 22	78 59	1300	..	30.00	..	..	..	..	..	..	..	..	..	..
206. Wellsville	42 07	78 00	1480	21.47	26.93	29.51	39.74	50.23	63.57	71.19	65.59	59.63	46.20	37.14	34.20
207. West Day	43 20	74 08	1200	..	..	29.10	42.60	51.90	68.80	70.30	67.00	59.40	50.00	..	..
208. West Point (Military Acad.)	41 24	73 57	167	28.68	29.60	37.85	49.27	60.68	69.64	74.51	72.57	65.10	54.26	42.96	32.49
209. White Plains	41 02	73 46	..	27.51	29.65	34.40	47.56	57.00	67.38	70.92	69.97	63.04	52.28	42.81	31.05
210. Whitestown (Oneida Inst. of Science, and Ind.)	43 08	75 20	824	19.68	20.85	29.12	43.74	56.48	64.53	71.41	65.99	58.50	47.09	34.57	23.97
211. Wilson	43 17	78 50	250	26.55	26.88	31.06	42.61	54.56	64.16	71.38	70.51	60.47	48.93	38.60	29.82
212. Youngsville	41 47	74 55	1000	15.08	31.28	29.48	37.22	52.16	61.34	68.36	66.02	57.56	44.96	36.50	24.26

[1] Daily means computed by the formula $\frac{a + 2b + 2c + a'}{6}$ where a represents an observation a little before sunrise, b one at 3_a, c one at one hour after sunset, and a' the morning observation on the following day. The results thus obtained appear, on the average, to be about 0°.5 too high.

NEW YORK.—Continued.

	Spring.	Summer.	Autumn.	Winter.	Year.	Series. Begins. Ends.	Extent yrs.	Extent mos.	Observing hours.	Observer.	References.
61	..	..	..	..	..	1856	0	3	$7_m\ 2_a\ 9_a$	J. F. Kendall.	P. O. and S. I. Vol. I.
62	42°.91	66°.37	45°.36	19°.77	43°.60	Jan. 1828; Dec. 1848	21	0	1	Various observers.	N. Y. Univ. Syst. 1855.
63	48.66	71.41	52.51	28.11	50.17	Feb. 1828; Apr. 1870	18	0	1	" "	" " " " "
64	..	..	..	..	..	1849	0	3	$7_m\ 9\frac{1}{2}_m\ 3_a\ 9_a$	Warring.	S. Coll.
65	44.01	64.64	46.20	25.76	45.15	Jan. 1829; Dec. 1846	10	0	1	Various observers.	N. Y. Univ. Syst. 1855.
66	47.66	69.17	50.54	26.10	48.37	Jan. 1830; Dec. 1842	12	0	1	" "	" " " " "
67	44.72	68.04	49.02	26.46	47.06	Jan. 1830; Dec. 1870	38	9	2	" "	P. O. and S. I. Vol. I, S. O., MS. in S. Coll, Reg. Rep., & N. Y. Univ. Syst. 1855.
68	49.48	..	..	..	..	1869	0	4	$7_m\ 2_a\ 9_a$ bis [2]	C. De La Verny.	S. O.
69	41.37	66.78	46.86	19.56	43.64	Mar. 1845; Sept. 1862	8	6		John Bratt.	MS. in S. Coll. & MS. from S. G. O.
70	42.79	68.51	50.80	23.72	46.45	Aug. 1849; Dec. 1867	8	10	$7_m\ 2_a\ 9_a$	H. Metcalf, Platt.	U. S. Lake Survey, Rep. of 1867–68 and S. Coll.
71	45.48	71.00	55.23	32.42	51.03	Oct. 1849; Dec. 1858	9	1	"	E. N. Byram.	P. O. and S. I. Vol. I, & S. Coll.
72	45.08	68.26	48.41	24.49	46.56	Jan. 1828; Dec. 1847	10	0	1	Various observers.	N. Y. Univ. Syst. 1855.
73	42.43	68.96	48.70	25.23	46.33	Dec. 1856; Jan. 1858	1	2	$7_m\ 2_a\ 9_a$	W. H. Riker.	P. O. and S. I. Vol. I.
74	44.69	68.30	48.16	24.37	46.38	Jan. 1829; Dec. 1864	4	0	1	Various observers.	N. Y. Univ. Syst. 1855, & S. O.
75	43.53	68.60	48.75	26.05	46.73	1849; July, 1864	4	11	$7_m\ 2_a\ 9_a$ bis	P. Cowing, Fairchild.	S. Coll. and S. O.
76	..	..	..	..	..	1857	0	1	$7_m\ 2_a\ 9_a$	H. B. Fellows.	P. O. and S. I. Vol. I.
77	45.95	65.58	..	..	..	1865	0	7	$7_m\ 2_a\ 9_a$ bis	Rev. J. R. Haswell.	S. O.
78	48.17	71.76	54.35	32.93	51.80	Mar. 1849; 1852	2	8	$\odot_r\ 9_m\ 3_a\ 9_a$	Mannic.	S. Coll.
79	42.17	65.38	48.39	25.62	45.39	Jan. 1861; Dec. 1867	5	11	$7_m\ 2_a\ 9_a$ bis	W. M. Beauchamp.	S. O.
80	40.48	..	..	..	..	May, 1868; Jan. 1870	0	5	"	G. W. Potter.	" "
81	41.03	67.33	49.26	21.67	44.82	Mar. 1849; May, 1856	4	2	$7_m\ 2_a\ 9_a$	J. E. Breed.	MS. in S. Coll., and P. O. and S. I. Vol. I.
82	40.69	69.38	48.63	19.79	44.62	1849; 1852	3	1	$\odot_r\ 9_m\ 3_a\ 9_a$	Hough.	S. Coll. and Reg. Rep.
83	..	..	..	..	..	1852	0	2	"	Bemis.	S. Coll.
84	43.69	68.04	48.84	24.34	46.23	1850; 1853	1	11	"	Beardsley.	" "
85	46.33	72.44	50.89	23.58	48.31	Aug. 1863; Dec. 1870	7	2	$7_m\ 2_a\ 9_a$ bis	G. M. Ingalsbe.	S. O.
86	[illegible]	[illegible]	[illegible]	[illegible]	[illegible]	[illegible]	3	9		Capt. J. Barrows.	
87	41.56	68.04	48.81	22.61	45.25	July, 1854; June, 1861	4	0	$7_m\ 2_a\ 9_a$	Various observers.	P. O. and S. I. Vol. I, S. O., and MS. in S. Coll.
88	43.11	64.44	47.11	26.41	45.27	Jan. 1830; Dec. 1850	7	0	1	" "	N. Y. Univ. Syst. 1855.
89	..	..	..	27.54	..	Oct. 1867; Feb. 1868	0	5	$7_m\ 2_a\ 9_a$ bis	S. L. Hillier.	S. O.
90	..	..	..	..	..	1863	0	1	"	J. H. Warren.	" "
91	43.39	68.33	49.39	26.91	47.00	Jan. 1843; Dec. 1852	3	5	$6_m\ 2_a\ 10_a$	L. W. Conkey, Drumore.	N. Y. Univ. Syst. 1855 and S. Coll.
92	41.23	66.72	46.52	19.90	43.59	Mar. 1861; Feb. 1866	4	9	$7_m\ 1_a\ 9_a$	S. O. Gregory.	S. O.
93	46.68	71.15	53.90	29.95	50.50	Dec. 1863; Dec. 1870	6	6	$7_m\ 2_a\ 9_a$ bis	F. Morris.	" "
94	45.34	70.96	50.69	24.73	47.93	Jan. 1854; Dec. 1868	6	3	"	Various observers.	P. O. and S. I. Vol. I, and S. O.
95	..	..	..	..	..	1861	0	1	"	J. S. Allen.	S. O.
96	44.77	67.17	48.33	24.71	46.25	Jan. 1826; Dec. 1870	27	2	1	Various observers.	N. Y. Univ. Syst. 1855, S. Coll., Am. Alm. 1843, Reg. Rep., S. O., and P. O. and S. I. Vol. I.
7	..	..	..	..	..	1854	0	1	7_m	Carpenter.	S. O.
8	42.98	67.11	48.46	23.87	45.60	Jan. 1854; Dec. 1861	6	10	$7_m\ 2_a\ 9_a$ bis	Dr. S. Spooner.	P. O. and S. I. Vol. I, and S. O.
9	46.44	..	..	..	..	1865	0	3	"	J. P. Morse.	S. O.
0	40.92	66.93	45.40	24.45	44.43	Jan. 1869; Oct. 1870	1	9	"	D. Trowbridge.	" "
1	44.11	68.77	50.02	24.18	46.77	Jan. 1856; May, 1863	6	3	"	J. C. House.	P. O. and S. I. Vol. I, and S. O.
2	42.02	68.42	49.04	16.56	44.01	1856	1	0	$7_m\ 2_a\ 9_a$	Dr. P. O. Williams.	P. O. and S. I. Vol. I.
3	39.61	67.85	48.84	25.12	45.35	1849; 1851	1	7	$\odot_r\ 9_m\ 3_a\ 9_a$	Lower.	S. Coll.
4	46.36	71.25	50.15	24.79	48.14	Jan. 1824; Dec. 1854	30	9	$7_m\ 2_a\ 9_a$	Assistant Surgeon.	Ar. Met. Reg. 1855.
5	..	..	..	..	..	1861	0	1	"	W. Flint, J. Curtiss.	S. O.
6	39.83	66.78	47.66	27.53	45.45	Jan. 1857; Apr. 1858	1	2	"	H. M. Sheerar.	P. O. and S. I. Vol. I.
7	41.20	68.70	..	..	..	1858	0	8	$\odot_r$ N. $\odot_s$	J. M. Young.	MS. in S. Coll.
8	49.27	72.24	54.11	30.26	51.47	Jan. 1824; Dec. 1870	46	5	$7_m\ 2_a\ 9_a$	Assistant Surgeon.	Ar. Met. Reg. 1855, and MS. from S. G. O.
9	46.32	69.42	52.71	29.40	49.46	Jan. 1854; Dec. 1870	8	9	$7_m\ 2_a\ 9_a$ bis	Prof. O. R. Willis, Jenkins.	S. O. and S. Coll.
0	43.11	67.31	46.72	21.50	44.66	Jan. 1834; Dec. 1840	7	0	1	Various observers.	N. Y. Univ. Syst. 1855.
1	42.74	68.68	49.33	27.75	47.13	Jan. 1860; Dec. 1864	4	3	$7_m\ 2_a\ 9_a$ bis	Dr. E. S. Holmes.	S. O.
2	39.62	65.24	46.34	23.54	43.69	....	3	0	$6_m\ 1_a\ 9_a$	J. Hamam.	" "

[2] Corrected for daily variation by means of the general table.

NORTH CAROLINA.

Name of Station.	Lat.	Long.	Height.	Jan.	Feb.	March.	April.	May.	June.	July.	August.	Sept.	Oct.	Nov.	Dec.
1. Asheville . . .	35°33′	82°30′	2200	39.°02	37°.41	43°.96	53°.10	60°.75	68°.38	72°.40	70°.90	65°.95	53°.07	43°.77	37°.3
2. Attaway Hill . .	35 25	80 00	850	38.53	41.80	46.76	56.75	63.66	73.64	77.42	75.84	69.18	56.95	44.92	38.9
3. Beaufort	34 43	76 39	20	47.04	47.54	51.68	56.23	67.72	74.09	78.02	83.42	74.60	62.84	56.52	50.1
4. Bethmont . . .	36	79	..	39.34	35.34	42.36	50.14	59.17	66.50	71.80	71.80	65.00	49.50	48.50	42.7
5. Chapel Hill (Univ. of N. C.)	35 58	78 54	..	40.40	44.96	49.84	59.31	67.39	75.79	78.38	76.22	70.84	59.70	50.84	43.4
6. Davidson College .	35 30	80 44	850	43.74	41.42	48.01	58.30	66.56	73.92	77.57	80.33	64.24	57.23	45.46	43.2
7. Fort Johnston . .	33 55	78 01	20	49.10	50.58	56.39	64.26	73.04	79.09	81.64	80.25	76.09	67.13	59.29	52.2
8. Fort Macon . . .	34 42	76 40	20	44.72	43.95	49.97	59.97	68.95	77.29	80.02	79.74	74.84	64.58	56.56	48.0
9. Gaston (or Green Plains)	36 28	77 38	..	36.82	42.06	47.91	54.38	65.70	74.18	77.92	76.07	68.40	57.51	47.28	40.0
10. Goldsboro' . . .	35 25	77 51	102	41.38	47.60	50.20	60.16	68.67	76.96	81.19	78.38	72.66	61.78	50.45	43.7
11. Jackson	36 20	77 25	..	41.06	46.52	52.83	58.50	69.68	76.49	79.31	..	..	60.74	49.01	25.9
12. Kenansville (Webster Inst.)	34 58	77 50	60	46.35	42.78	48.56	57.46	66.67	74.78	78.66	78.34	68.75	56.84	47.03	39.5
13. Lake Scuppernong .	35 50	76 18	25	41.23	44.69	50.87	54.74	68.35	72.75	78.50	74.47	68.54	61.10	51.29	45.7
14. Marlborough . .	35 36	77 30	..	48.11	40.96	49.77	62.33	68.19	77.01	..	79.09	..	..	..	..
15. Morgantown . .	35 49	81 32	1135	38.79	38.29	50.51	54.62	66.24	72.73	80.04	..	..	..	..	50.7
16. Mount Olive . .	35 14	77 55	100	..	..	..	..	..	..	81.28	80.08	69.33	56.33	..	..
17. Murfreesboro' . .	36 26	77 01	..	40.74	44.95	49.21	57.02	66.46	75.60	77.34	76.45	68.61	58.22	49.15	42.6
18. Oxford	36 22	78 29	..	38.87	42.56	46.59	57.50	65.61	74.80	79.97	74.96	69.99	55.53	46.57	37.7
19. Raleigh	35 48	78 38	317	37.84	43.82	47.28	58.15	65.33	75.52	79.75	76.44	72.10	58.09	49.18	38.7
20. Rutherfordton . .	35 24	81 48	800	..	..	..	..	..	76.96	74.35	76.55	69.85	56.61	52.07	42.2
21. Scuppernong . .	35 50	76 18	20	..	48.11	53.00	60.89	68.87	73.43	79.15	76.22	71.65	..	..	..
22. Statesville . . .	35 49	80 46	..	34.81	39.37	43.76	54.67	61.76	71.09	77.14	74.60	64.62	53.66	41.34	30.1
23. Thornbury . . .	36 20	77 21	..	41.47	39.80	49.28	59.22	69.72	75.13	79.53	..	..	..	46.72	37.7
24. Trinity College . .	35 45	79 40	400	40.40	43.90	46.63	57.23	63.73	..	..	..	..	..	..	..
25. Warrenton . . .	36 24	78 02	..	42.00	39.40	41.63	55.00	64.95	73.57	78.35	74.40	67.43	59.71	48.56	37.8
26. Westminster . . .	36 02	79 52	..	..	..	.	..	..	73.85	78.42	73.55	..	..	..	..
27. Wilson	35 45	77 47	105	..	43.98	51.08	63.50	66.73	..	81.33	75.18	73.55	59.95	51.00	41.8

OHIO.

Name of Station.	Lat.	Long.	Height.	Jan.	Feb.	March.	April.	May.	June.	July.	August.	Sept.	Oct.	Nov.	Dec.
1. Athens	39 20	82 02	750	23.62	34.00	43.95	50.37	64.29	71.61	75.71	71.74	64.69	55.18	40.79	30.3
2. Austinburgh[1] . .	41 48	80 54	816	22.33	26.23	30.33	43.67	56.06	67.01	72.55	69.75	64.67	50.11	38.57	34.2
3. Avon	41 27	82 04	840	31.10	33.42	45.76	45.72	62.14	64.72	72.92	70.38	62.05	47.17	40.74	31.3
4. Bellefontaine . .	40 23	83 42	1031	24.89	25.05	36.61	48.89	61.12	71.38	75.80	70.65	64.45	51.93	39.28	28.8
5. Bethel	39 00	84 00	555	26.89	32.50	38.27	50.77	59.18	69.25	74.14	70.48	63.36	49.23	39.76	30.5
6. Bowling Green . .	41 24	83 38	700	28.97	29.28	35.85	48.91	58.76	69.14	74.43	70.80	62.89	51.09	40.44	32.0
7. Brecksville . . .	41 22	81 40	800	24.43	32.83	..	..	..	..	..	..	..	48.62	42.41	21.9
8. Carthagena . . .	40 28	84 33	..	..	..	..	..	..	..	..	..	70.79	55.85	43.48	28.5
9. Chilicothe . . .	39 18	82 52	..	40.0	40.0	41.0	57.0	69.0	77.0	77.0	80.0	70.0	56.0	59.0	39.0
10. Cincinnati . . .	39 06	84 30	540	33.50	33.15	42.94	55.35	63.33	70.86	75.47	73.25	65.46	52.30	41.71	33.0
11. Cincinnati (Woodward Coll.)	39 06	84 30	540	32.91	35.35	43.15	54.81	64.42	72.64	77.75	75.33	67.82	54.22	43.59	34.5
12. Cincinnati . . .	39 06	84 30	540	33.70	33.40	42.90	55.20	63.60	70.90	75.60	73.20	65.20	52.40	41.60	33.7
13. Cincinnati . . .	39 06	84 30	540	33.79	37.98	45.66	57.11	65.96	73.23	77.32	75.50	68.79	53.39	45.37	35.8
14. Cincinnati . . .	39 06	84 30	[2]	30.76	34.87	41.24	54.15	63.44	72.64	77.21	74.96	67.59	53.41	42.57	33.6
15. Cleveland . . .	41 30	81 42	643	25.94	28.31	34.85	47.03	56.96	67.94	71.73	69.36	63.08	51.35	40.58	30.7
16. Clifton	39 44	83 57	..	..	..	..	..	..	..	..	74.55	..	..	..	..
17. College Hill (Farmer's Coll.)	39 19	84 35	800	29.88	33.31	42.07	53.41	62.38	70.26	74.06	72.18	65.49	53.42	42.11	31.7

[1] Observations previous to 1862 were made at Jefferson, about five miles southeast of Austinburgh.
[2] Observations corrected for daily variation by means of the general table.

NORTH CAROLINA.

	Spring.	Summer.	Autumn.	Winter.	Year.	Series. Begins. Ends.	Extent yrs. mos.	Observing hours.	Observer.	References.
1	52°.60	70°.56	54°.26	37°.91	53°.83	Aug. 1857; Dec. 1870	4 5	7_m 2_a 9_a bis	W. W. McDowell, E. J. Krow, and E. J. Aston.	S. O. and P. O. and S. I. Vol. I.
2	55.72	75.63	57.02	39.77	57.04	Apr. 1861; Dec. 1870	4 7	"	F. J. Kron.	S. O.
3	58.54	78.51	64.65	48.24	62.48	June, 1863; Dec. 1864	1 4	7_m 2_a 9_a	....	MS. from S. G. O.
4	50.56	70.03	54.33	39.14	53.52	1850	1 0	$\odot_r$	Bingham.	Pat. Off. Rep. 1851.
5	58.85	76.80	60.46	42.92	59.76	Jan. 1820; May, 1870	20 0	7_m 2_a 9_a bis	Caldwell, Prof. J. Phillips, D. S. Patrick.	Rep. Brit. Assoc. 1847, Am. Alm. 1847 and foll., Dove, MS. in S. Coll., and S. O.
6	57.62	77.27	55.64	42.79	58.33	Nov. 1857; Dec. 1859	1 10	7_m 2_a 9_a	Prof. W. C. Kerr.	P. O. and S. I. Vol. I.
7	64.56	80.33	67.50	50.66	65.76	Jan. 1822; July, 1845	15 10	"	Assistant Surgeon.	Ar. Met. Reg. 1855.
8	59.63	79.02	65.33	45.59	62.39	Oct. 1833; Aug. 1849	5 3	"	" "	" " "
9	56.00	76.06	57.73	39.65	57.36	Oct. 1856; Mar. 1861	4 6	"	Dr. G. F. Moore.	P. O. and S. I. Vol. I, and S. O.
10	59.68	78.84	61.63	44.24	61.10	Jan. 1856; Dec. 1870	6 5	7_m 2_a 9_a bis	Prof. D. Morrelle and Prof. E. W. Adams.	" " " " " "
11	60.34	..	..	37.83	..	1852; 1854	2 0	7_m 2_a 9_a	Gnald.	S. Coll.
12	57.56	77.26	57.54	42.89	58.81	Jan. 1860; May, 1870	3 0	7_m 2_a 9_a bis	Prof. N. B. Webster, and J. N. Sprunt.	S. O.
13	57.99	75.24	60.31	43.90	59.36	1849; 1853	3 0	$\odot_r$ 9_m 3_a 9_a	Shepherd.	S. Coll.
14	60.10	..	..	..	..	1858	0 7	7_m 2_a 9_a	....	P. O. and S. I. Vol. I.
15	57.12	..	..	42.62	..	Dec. 1867; July, 1868	0 8	"	....	MS. from S. G. O.
16	..	..	..	..	..	1869	0 4	7_m 2_a 9_a bis	E. D. Pearsall.	S. O.
17	57.56	76.46	58.66	42.77	58.86	Oct. 1856; Apr. 1861	4 3	7_m 2_a 9_a	Rev. N. McDowell.	P. O. and S. I. Vol. I, and S. O.
18	56.57	76.58	57.36	39.72	57.56	July, 1866; Dec. 1870	4 1	7_m 2_a 9_a bis	J. H. Mill and Dr. W. R. Hicks.	S. O.
19	56.92	77.24	59.79	40.14	58.52	Aug. 1866; June, 1869	2 11	"	F. P. Brewer.	" "
20	..	75.95	59.51	..	..	1849	0 7	$\odot_r$ 9_m 3_a 9_a	Galloway.	S. Coll.
21	60.92	76.27	..	..	..	1853	0 8	7_m 2_a 9_a	Hardison.	" "
22	53.40	74.28	53.21	34.78	53.92	June, 1866; Dec. 1870	4 0	7_m 2_a 9_a bis	Col. T. P. Allison.	S. O.
23	59.41	..	..	39.66	..	Jan. 1854; Apr. 1855	1 1	7_m 2_a 9_a	Rev. T. Fitzgerald & Prof. D. Morrelle.	P. O. and S. I. Vol. I.
24	55.86	..	..	..	..	Jan. 1861; May, 1869	0 5	7_m 2_a 9_a bis	O. W. Carr, E. D. Pearsall, & others.	S. O.
25	53.86	75.44	58.57	39.76	56.91	Aug. 1857; Dec. 1870	1 2	"	Dr. W. M. Johnston and H. A. Foote.	P. O. and S. I. Vol. I, and S. O.
26	..	75.27	..	..	..	1843	0 3	$\odot_r$ N. $\odot_s$	J. Watkins.	S. Coll.
27	60.44	..	61.50	..	..	1866	0 10	7_m 2_a 9_a bis	E. W. Adams.	S. O.

OHIO.

	Spring.	Summer.	Autumn.	Winter.	Year.	Series. Begins. Ends.	Extent yrs. mos.	Observing hours.	Observer.	References.
1	52.87	73.02	53.55	29.32	52.19	1849; 1852	1 8	$\odot_r$ 9_m 3_a 9_a	Mathew.	S. Coll. and MS.
2	43.35	69.77	51.12	27.59	47.96	Mar. 1856; Dec. 1867	5 7	7_m 2_a 9_a bis	J. D. Herrick, J. G. Dale, G. S. S. Griffing, and E. D. Winchester.	P. O. and S. I. Vol. I, and S. O.
3	51.21	69.34	49.99	31.94	50.62	Nov. 1858; Dec. 1859	1 2	7_m 2_a 9_a	Rev. L. T. Ward.	P. O. and S. I. Vol. I.
4	48.87	72.61	51.89	26.25	49.91	Dec. 1855; Dec. 1870	3 7	"	J. Shaw, W. Barringer.	P. O. and S. I, Vol. I. and S. O.
5	49.41	71.29	50.78	29.98	50.37	Feb. 1860; Dec. 1870	9 4	7_m 2_a 9_a bis	G. W. Crane.	S. O.
6	47.84	71.46	51.47	30.10	50.22	July, 1857; Dec. 1870	10 3	"	Dr. W. R. Peck, J. Clarke.	P. O. and S. I. Vol. I, MS. in S. Coll., and S. O.
7	..	..	..	26.41	..	Oct. 1859; Feb. 1861	0 5	"	Rev. S. L. Hillier, L. L. Willis.	P. O. and S. I. Vol. I. and S. O.
8	..	..	56.71	..	..	1870	0 4	"	R. Müller.	S. O.
9	55.67	78.00	61.67	39.67	58.75	1819	1 0	7_m 2_a 9_a	....	Rep. Brit. Asso. 1847.
10	53.87	73.19	53.16	33.25	53.37	1806; 1813	8 0	......	Mansfield and Drake.	Drake.
11	54.13	75.24	55.21	34.28	54.72	Jan. 1819; Dec. 1870	36 8	[2]	Prof. Ray, G. H. Phillips, and others.	MS. in S. Coll., Blodget's Clim. Drake, View of Cinn., P. O. and S. I. Vol. I, and S. O.
12	53.90	73.23	53.07	33.60	53.45	1835; 1848	14 0	......	....	Drake.[3]
13	56.24	75.35	55.83	35.86	55.85	1843; 1853	9 0	max. & min.	Lea.	Warder Hort. Reg.
14	52.94	74.94	54.52	33.08	53.87	Jan. 1860; Dec. 1870	10 1	7_m 2_a 9_a bis	G. W. Harper.[4]	S. O.
15	46.28	69.68	51.67	28.32	48.99	1850; Dec. 1870	17 1	[2]	G. A. & Mrs. Hyde, B. A. Stanard, and Wade.	U. S. Lake Survey, MS. & Rep. of 1867–8, P. O. and S. I. Vol. I, S. O., and S. Coll.
16	..	..	..	..	..	1870	0 1	[2]	....	S. O.
17	52.62	72.17	53.67	31.65	52.53	Jan. 1814; Dec. 1870	47 10	$\odot_r$ N. $\odot_s$	Jackson, Profs. R. S. Bosworth & J. H. Wilson, L. D. Tuckerman & J. W. Hammitt.	P. O. and S. I. Vol. I, S. O., and S. Coll.

[3] As quoted by Dove.

[4] Altitude given as 305 feet above low-water in the Ohio River.

OHIO.—Continued.

Name of Station.	Lat.	Long.	Height.	Jan.	Feb.	March.	April.	May.	June.	July.	August.	Sept.	Oct.	Nov.	Dec.
18. Columbus[1]	39°57′	82°59′	834	30°.94	36°.44	42°.26	53°.12	65°.30	70°.98	77°.64	74°.69	60°.72	49°.80	42°.34	35°.28
19. Coshocton	40 18	81 53	765	29.38	29.88	..	..	..	..	..	..	..	54.32	40.55	36.20
20. Croton	40 13	82 38	..	28.55	32.56	37.08	50.68	60.15	68.30	72.25	71.71	62.95	51.20	37.78	31.84
21. Cuyahoga Falls	41 10	81 33	..	18.40	..	..	52.70	..	73.53	..	..	..	..	40.13	25.55
22. Dayton (Cooper Sem.)	39 44	84 08	860	27.36	30.80	29.00	55.23	59.55	72.76	74.64	70.69	64.11	55.01	42.44	..
23. East Cleveland	41 31	81 40	683	27.71	28.67	34.89	48.00	53.45	63.41	67.13	66.44	61.95	48.02	37.81	32.05
24. East Fairfield[3]	40 47	80 45	1152	25.45	29.94	35.06	48.73	56.99	66.50	70.35	68.97	62.59	49.67	40.18	29.89
25. Eaton	39 44	84 35	1400	23.95	30.15	36.10	49.50	60.10	73.40	71.50	..	64.70	50.45	40.80	30.08
26. Edgerton	41 29	84 45	831	..	..	33.65	..	..	..	73.25	..	61.58	..	..	..
27. Edinburg	41 09	81 10	520	34.06	22.11	33.57	41.94	55.23	68.17	72.71	68.90	63.80	51.69	35.52	35.23
28. Elmwood	40 05	82 00	900	..	..	..	..	..	71.14	77.01	73.39	66.98	54.75	41.43	30.55
29. Fort Washington	..	..	..	40.17	42.12	50.90	60.16	..	75.90	79.17	80.90	72.18	58.14	53.19	38.11
30. Freedom	41 16	81 12	1100	27.32	26.39	34.55	46.68	62.19	68.51	72.71	70.30	61.13	49.29	39.77	30.95
31. Fremont	41 22	83 07	..	..	..	..	..	..	..	..	..	..	..	..	33.10
32. Gallipolis	38 50	82 05	600	29.78	35.11	41.44	53.91	61.87	70.65	75.72	72.79	68.98	53.84	43.57	34.68
33. Gambier (Kenyon Coll.)[4]	40 24	82 23	1000	29.94	28.23	36.61	46.10	61.54	69.85	73.55	68.59	62.99	49.54	41.34	28.41
34. Garretsville	41 18	81 08	900	..	..	..	..	..	..	69.73	70.20	62.67	..	38.55	35.18
35. Germantown[5]	39 36	84 20	720	22.57	30.11	35.69	53.46	61.28	70.17	76.36	72.01	67.09	52.56	40.41	27.99
36. Gilmore	40 18	81 20	1180	33.30	32.93	31.78	50.28	62.55	69.99	74.91	73.85	..	44.53	..	34.28
37. Granville	40 03	82 30	995	26.23	27.84	34.76	47.06	55.44	63.93	67.17	65.56	58.33	46.15	36.75	29.74
38. Hillsboro'	39 10	83 27	1150	29.07	31.59	38.24	51.32	60.46	68.29	72.88	70.16	63.81	50.79	40.33	30.90
39. Hiram	41 20	81 10	1290	22.59	27.57	33.37	44.32	54.92	68.03	72.63	67.66	62.74	51.00	36.58	31.28
40. Hudson (W. Reserve Coll.)	41 16	81 27	1137	28.40	30.45	38.63	48.76	57.72	65.94	70.91	69.51	62.05	49.68	37.09	29.91
41. Huron	41 25	82 34	..	..	30.50	40.35	47.02	57.39	69.33	..	..	..	..	..	..
42. Iberia	40 44	82 47	1160	..	..	..	..	..	..	..	..	63.09	47.65	44.88	..
43. Jackson (Jackson C.)	39 02	82 32	700	33.21	34.16	40.73	52.37	62.14	70.74	75.19	72.25	66.62	51.87	43.61	31.33
44. Jackson (Monroe C.)	39 40	80 56	540	34.80	31.80	40.73	52.18	63.23	70.96	76.88	69.59	64.96	51.51	40.33	34.20
45. Jacksonburg	39 30	84 20	1152	33.36	32.90	35.54	51.76	61.29	69.49	77.02	74.62	66.45	51.85	41.31	29.69
46. Keene	40 23	81 53	1000	28.97	34.17	40.40	48.41	60.77	69.89	74.38	72.47	66.06	51.06	43.62	29.84
47. Kelley's Island	41 36	82 43	587	26.60	28.71	33.69	45.33	57.37	68.21	73.56	72.22	65.22	52.76	41.73	30.26
48. Kenton	40 40	83 33	1562	30.00	33.41	36.63	48.06	54.96	72.14	79.73	74.50	67.01	52.29	40.21	31.24
49. Kingston	39 26	82 49	692	26.94	33.62	39.34	53.37	59.57	70.44	74.28	70.84	66.71	51.45	42.09	30.54
50. Lafayette	40 50	84 10	..	20.02	33.70	..	..	..	..	..	..	..	..	..	..
51. Lancaster	39 42	82 31	926	31.02	..	..	51.93	60.44	73.53	75.07	71.72	64.01	51.02	39.17	37.58
52. Lebanon	39 26	84 09	828	34.66	34.25	42.77	54.38	62.76	70.46	73.50	71.15	65.12	52.10	49.89	28.01
53. Lewisville	40 12	82 58	760	..	..	..	..	..	..	..	66.44	61.22	..	..	..
54. Little Mountain	41 38	81 16	[6]	25.53	27.94	29.79	46.26	55.75	65.74	69.83	69.57	62.66	49.73	41.44	28.15
55. Madison[7]	41 48	81 06	620	26.54	27.43	34.23	45.32	55.64	65.43	70.41	68.26	62.07	50.42	39.19	30.86
56. Mansfield	40 48	82 30	900	25.41	33.12	41.70	..	..	61.06	72.92	75.23	..	52.16	39.01	28.23
57. Margaretta	41 27	82 46	850	27.54	27.67	33.43	46.89	58.88	68.37	75.28	71.81	64.18	49.61	39.35	29.63
58. Marietta[8]	39 28	81 26	670	31.12	33.94	41.60	52.68	61.67	69.28	73.12	71.47	64.60	52.03	41.93	33.45
59. Marion	40 37	83 07	1077	24.82	28.12	34.72	48.86	57.23	67.66	72.81	68.90	62.96	48.56	38.49	27.68
60. Martin's Ferry	40 10	80 45	..	27.59	35.18	34.98	50.41	54.58	71.93	..	..	..	..	..	..
61. Montville (or Medina)	41 07	81 52	1255	29.45	29.24	36.42	45.84	57.19	65.57	70.07	68.85	62.30	50.94	38.27	31.38
62. Mount Auburn Inst.[9]	39 07	84 31	[10]	31.20	33.48	38.11	54.55	63.42	73.16	77.46	76.19	70.50	56.19	42.92	34.87

[1] The observations composing this series were made at the State Library and Camp Dennison.

[2] Observations corrected for daily variation by means of the general table.

[3] Also called Elk Run.

[4] Observations previous to 1869 were made at Mount Vernon, about five miles west of Gambier.

[5] Observations in Jan. and Febr. were made at Franklin, about six miles southeast of Germantown.

[6] Altitude 600 feet above Lake Erie.

OHIO.—Continued.

	Spring.	Summer.	Autumn.	Winter.	Year.	Series. Begins.	Series. Ends.	Extent yrs. mos.	Observing hours.	Observer.	References.
18	53°.56	74°.44	50°.95	34°.22	53°.29	Apr. 1843;	May, 1865	3 0	2	T. Kennedy, J. Greiner, and others.	MS. from S. G. O. and S. Coll.
19	..	..	..	31.82	..	Oct. 1861;	Feb. 1862	0 5	$7_m\ 2_a\ 9_a$ bis	T. H. Johnson.	S. O.
20	49.30	70.75	50.64	30.98	50.42	Mar. 1860;	Mar. 1863	2 11	"	M. Sperry.	" "
21	..	..	..	..	..	Nov. 1864;	June, 1865	0 5	"	D. M. Rankin.	" "
22	47.93	72.70	53.85	..	..	Jan. 1845;	Nov. 1858	1 11	$7_m\ 2_a\ 9_a$	M. G. Williams, Dr. J. C. Fisher, L. Groneweg, and others.	MS. in S. Coll., P. O. and S. I. Vol. 1.
23	45.45	65.66	49.26	29.48	47.46	Jan. 1840;	July, 1866	9 11	2	Mrs. M. A. Pillsbury.	S. Coll. and S. O.
24	46.93	68.61	50.81	28.43	48.69	Sept. 1859;	May, 1867	6 9	$7_m\ 2_a\ 9_a$ bis	S. B. McMillan.	P. O. and S. I, Vol. 1, and S. O.
25	48.57	..	51.98	28.06	..	Dec. 1863;	July, 1865	1 1	"	Ollilippa Larsh.	S. O.
26	..	..	..	..	..	July, 1869;	Mar. 1870	0 3	"	A. B. Knight.	" "
27	43.58	69.93	50.34	30.47	48.58	Mar. 1857;	Dec. 1858	1 9	$7_m\ 2_a\ 9_a$	S. Sanford.	P. O. and S. I. Vol. 1.
28	..	73.85	54.39	..	..	1870		0 7	$7_m\ 2_a\ 9_a$ bis	C. A. Stillwell.	S. O.
29	..	78.66	61.17	40.13	..	June, 1790;	Apr. 1791	0 11	3_a	Turner.	Phil. Trans.
30	47.81	70.51	50.06	28.22	49.15	May, 1859;	May, 1862	1 11	$7_m\ 2_a\ 9_a$ bis	H. M. and W. Davidson, Jr.	P. O. and S. I. Vol. 1, and S. O.
31	..	..	..	..	..	1852		0 1	$\odot_r\ 1_a\ 9_a$	....	S. Coll.
32	52.41	73.05	55.46	33.19	53.53	Mar. 1854;	Dec. 1870	7 8	$7_m\ 2_a\ 9_a$ bis	Dr. G. W. Livesay, A. P. Rogers.	P. O. and S. I. Vol. 1, and S. O.
33	48.08	70.66	51.29	28.86	49.72	1852;	Nov. 1870	2 6	$7_m\ 2_a\ 9_a$ bis	F.A. Benton, C.A. Stillwell, & F. K. Dunn.	P. O. and S. I. Vol. 1, S.O., and S. Coll.
34	..	..	..	..	..	1861		0 5	"	W. Peirce.	S. O.
35	50.14	72.85	53.35	26.89	50.81	Jan. 1854;	Feb. 1857	3 2	$7_m\ 2_a\ 9_a$	L. Groneweg, J. S. Binkerd, and Dr. L. Schenck.	P. O. and S. I. Vol. 1.
36	48.20	72.92	..	33.50	..	Jan. 1869;	Aug. 1870	1 2	$7_m\ 2_a\ 9_a$ bis	S. M. Moore.	S. O.
37	45.75	65.55	47.08	27.94	46.58	Jan. 1837;	Feb. 1857	19 10	2	Dr. Richards, Prof. S. N. Sanford, & Carter.	MS. in S. Coll., P. O. & S. I. Vol. 1.
38	50.01	70.44	51.64	30.52	50.65	Jan. 1836;	Dec. 1870	32 4	2	J. McD. Mathews & C. C. Simms.	" " " " "
39	44.20	69.44	50.11	27.15	47.73	Sept. 1855;	Oct. 1860	3 9	$7_m\ 2_a\ 9_a$	Rev. S. S. Hillier, S. M. Luther.	P. O. and S. I. Vol. 1, & S. O.
40	48.37	68.79	49.61	29.59	49.09	Mar. 1838;	June, 1863	9 5	2	Prof. E. Loomis, Prof. C. A. Young, E. W. Childs, and others.	Newspaper slips in S. Coll., P. O. & S. I. Vol. 1, and S. O.
41	48.25	..	..	..	..	1854		0 5	7_m N. 5_a	E. W. West.	P. O. and S. I. Vol. 1.
42	..	..	51.87	..	..	1859		0 3	$7_m\ 2_a\ 9_a$	S. T. Boyd.	" " " "
43	51.75	72.73	54.03	32.90	52.85	1849;	June, 1858	6 7	2	G. L. Crookham, & M. Gilmore.	S. Coll. and P. O. and S. I. Vol. 1.
44	52.05	72.48	52.27	33.60	52.60	Jan. 1858;	Dec. 1859	2 0	$7_m\ 2_a\ 9_a$	E. D. Johnson.	P. O. and S. I. Vol. 1.
45	49.53	73.71	53.20	31.98	52.11	May, 1868;	Dec. 1870	2 8	$7_m\ 2_a\ 9_a$ bis	Dr. J. B. Ousley.	S. O.
46	49.86	72.25	53.58	30.99	51.67	1849;	1854	3 5	$\odot_r\ 9_m\ 3_a\ 9_a$	Bidwell and Spooner.	P. O. & S. I. Vol. 1, & S. Coll.
47	45.46	71.33	53.24	28.52	49.64	Apr. 1859;	Dec. 1870	11 9	$7_m\ 2_a\ 9_a$ bis	G. C. Huntington.	Printed slip in S. Coll. & S. O.
48	46.55	75.46	53.17	31.55	51.68	Apr. 1862;	Dec. 1870	4 10	"	Dr. C. H. Smith.	S. O.
49	50.76	71.85	53.42	30.37	51.60	Nov. 1863;	Dec. 1867	3 7	"	Prof. J. Haywood.	" "
50	..	..	..	..	..	1867		0 2	"	S. Knoble.	" "
51	..	73.44	51.40	..	..	Apr. 1843;	Jan. 1859	1 10	$7_m\ 2_a\ 9_a$	M. Z. Kreider, L. M. Dayton, and H. W. Jæger.	MS. in S. Coll., P. O. and S. I. Vol. 1.
52	53.30	71.70	55.70	32.31	53.25	Jan. 1845;	Mar. 1850	3 0	$\odot_r\ 9_m\ 3_a\ 9_a$	J. C. Hatfield.	S. Coll.
53	..	..	..	..	..	1852		0 2	"	Bidwell.	" "
54	43.93	68.38	51.28	27.21	47.70	Jan. 1867;	Dec. 1870	3 5	$7_m\ 2_a\ 9_a$ bis	E. J. Ferris.	S. O.
55	45.06	68.03	50.56	28.28	47.98	Dec. 1854;	Feb. 1863	8 0	"	Mrs. A. C. King, Rev. S. L. Atkins.	P. O. and S. I. Vol. 1, and S. O.
56	..	69.74	..	28.92	..	June, 1851;	Mar. 1852	0 9	$\odot_r\ 9_m\ 3_a\ 9_a$	Benton.	S. Coll.
57	46.40	71.82	51.05	28.28	49.39	Jan. 1868;	Dec. 1870	3 0	$7_m\ 2_a\ 9_a$ bis	T. Neill.	S. O.
58	51.98	71.29	52.85	32.84	52.24	June, 1818;	Dec. 1870	49 10	2	J. Wood, Dr. S. P. Hildreth, Dr. G. O. Hildreth, D. P. Adams, and W. H. Fuller.	Sm. Cont. to Knowl. 1868, MS. in S. Coll., and S. O.
59	46.94	69.79	50.00	26.87	48.40	Feb. 1865;	Dec. 1870	5 11	$7_m\ 2_a\ 9_a$ bis	Dr. H. A. Johnson & Kate E. Johnson.	S. O.
60	46.66	..	..	..	..	Jan. 1867;	Apr. 1869	0 10	"	C. R. and Martha B. Shreeve.	" "
61	46.48	68.16	50.50	30.02	48.79	Feb. 1857;	Feb. 1863	6 1	"	Rev. L. F. Ward, W. P. Clark.	P.O. and S. I. Vol. 1, and S. O.
62	52.03	75.60	56.54	33.18	54.34	Oct. 1855;	Dec. 1870	5 4	"	E. Hannaford, Prof. S. A. Norton & others.	" " " " "

[7] Observations in part of 1855 and 1856 were made at Arcola and Unionville in Lat. 41°50′, Long. 81°00′. Possibly these are different names for the same locality.

[8] This series includes observations in 1860–61 at Harmar, about one and a half miles west of Marietta.

[9] Observations previous to 1861 were made at Cheviot, about three miles north of Mount Vernon Institute.

[10] Altitude 470 feet above low-water in the Ohio River.

OHIO.—Continued.

Name of Station.	Lat.	Long.	Height.	Jan.	Feb.	March.	April.	May.	June.	July.	August.	Sept.	Oct.	Nov.	Dec.
63. Mount Tabor	40°15′	83°40′	1094	33°.91	35°.37	39°.66	..	..	..	..	..	63°.14	53°.41	48°.70	29°.67
64. Mount Union	40 54	81 27	..	32.60	26.31	..	48°.50	61°.28	..	..	..	..	49.99	43.39	30.18
65. Newark	40 04	82 22	825	26.07	30.04	37.13	49.91	56.22	65°.45	70°.00	69°.90	61.22	52.32	38.51	32.26
66. New Athens (Franklin Coll.)	40 16	81 04	..	..	..	.	..	..	65.3	75.3	..	..	46.8	..	32.4
67. New Birmingham[1]	40 10	81 37	..	24.38	29.07	35.24	48.76	57.32	66.20	72.19	68.51	61.90	47.22	36.94	31.02
68. New Concord	40 03	81 44	..	33.68	32.25	38.21	..	62.37	73.32	73.48	71.95	64.01	52.01	47.17	30.52
69. New Holland[2] (1½ miles S. W. of)	39 30	83 09	..	30.21	30.71	38.23	54.66	68.38	..	..	..	..	51.95	43.38	34.85
70. New Lisbon	40 50	80 50	961	26.20	29.45	35.76	48.93	59.70	69.92	74.55	71.04	63.58	50.51	40.31	31.08
71. New Westfield	41 24	83 46	692	..	32.90	..	50.00	59.88	66.95	77.20	76.58	66.85	53.50	38.78	34.15
72. Nicholasville	..	..	..	..	..	..	..	..	..	..	..	..	..	46.23	..
73. North Bass Island	41 42	82 46	587	28.08	27.28	31.68	47.27	62.13	68.53	73.38	73.53	68.10	51.93	39.60	30.86
74. North Bend	39 08	84 42	800	32.55	34.48	41.09	54.17	63.66	69.98	73.88	73.56	65.92	56.04	41.95	31.29
75. North Fairfield	41 10	82 36	660	28.32	29.32	34.10	48.89	58.10	68.69	74.18	72.10	65.95	51.08	40.79	28.74
76. Northwood (or Geneva Hall)	40 30	83 45	1170	32.79	31.08	39.11	32.11	57.23	71.15	76.55	71.29	..	49.93	36.09	30.50
77. Norton	41 04	81 37	1200	..	..	34.40	48.30	51.12	69.03	66.30	..	..	..	..	..
78. Norwalk	41 16	82 36	..	25.29	29.34	35.02	47.70	55.95	66.66	70.64	68.78	61.64	50.67	40.31	30.35
79. Oberlin	41 20	82 12	800	24.88	28.14	34.97	46.30	58.10	69.34	72.20	70.31	64.53	50.75	39.49	29.55
80. Oxford	39 30	84 44	950	26.36	31.40	38.33	50.67	60.67	71.44	76.24	73.41	66.58	51.32	40.53	29.24
81. Pennsville	39 35	81 50	555	..	..	..	..	..	72.20	75.75	72.65	66.03	55.88	..	29.60
82. Perrysburg	41 35	83 36	..	25.60	26.90	36.55	50.58	61.16	72.18	77.68	71.80	67.34	54.03	40.55	31.10
83. Portsmouth	38 42	82 53	537	33.07	36.17	44.71	54.29	64.74	72.29	75.59	74.51	65.37	57.70	44.61	36.76
84. Prospect Hill	38 40	83 33	700	36.18	35.60	44.16	51.16	61.01	72.69	72.85	73.57	64.74	52.26	46.65	35.70
85. Republic	41 09	83 00	873	..	..	..	..	..	..	..	..	62.18	51.43	..	..
86. Ripley (Brown Co.)	38 44	83 39	[4]574	35.16	35.62	43.38	56.76	63.77	73.28	76.83	74.54	64.22	54.92	42.51	34.87
87. Ripley (Huron Co.)	41 05	82 36	965	22.58	30.57	36.07	46.92	56.20	70.49	72.29	71.99	66.27	49.71	43.88	30.53
88. Rockport[5]	41 30	81 50	665	32.26	34.01	41.08	50.34	62.27	67.28	72.98	72.45	64.39	53.95	44.04	34.87
89. Saint Clairsville	40 08	80 55	600	30.77	30.91	38.27	40.39	50.30	59.43	72.54	71.77	57.38	45.31	42.40	28.01
90. Salem	40 56	80 54	950	31.83	29.35	34.30	52.45	64.35	70.05	75.33	74.10	64.45	51.63	38.93	26.90
91. Savannah	41 02	82 24	1098	25.17	28.54	35.94	48.60	59.27	68.41	73.88	71.22	64.38	51.23	38.22	29.72
92. Saybrook	41 52	80 52	650	21.32	26.87	33.90	47.73	55.75	67.18	69.36	68.69	63.93	48.44	40.01	31.50
93. Seville	41 00	81 47	1075	26.86	33.60	35.43	48.72	53.02	67.65	69.75	63.45	63.10	53.60	38.80	34.98
94. Sidney	40 18	84 09	..	18.38	39.75	35.20	40.33	56.08	67.81	74.22	70.50	64.22	53.50	38.96	21.15
95. Smithville	40.52	81 50	934	20.55	27.20	..	48.43	58.93	66.98	71.80	72.73	63.09	45.98	40.88	27.93
96. Springfield	39 54	83 46	..	38.90	..	..	52.80	66.78	72.35	77.90	..	68.65	..	..	..
97. Steubenville	40 25	80 41	670	29.76	31.95	39.53	51.54	61.91	70.77	74.94	72.09	64.79	51.87	40.91	31.95
98. Tarlton	39 37	82 45	..	30.93	35.96	41.61	46.07	58.71	64.73	69.71	64.23	64.47	49.55	38.67	30.13
99. Toledo[6]	41 40	83 33	604	26.92	29.72	35.71	46.77	58.22	68.45	72.35	69.79	62.44	50.48	39.58	30.01
100. Troy	40 03	84 11	1103	29.24	32.81	40.48	50.69	63.91	70.92	74.70	73.48	63.98	52.23	40.38	30.53
101. Twinsburg	41 22	81 30	1050	..	..	..	..	..	..	68.73	68.33	58.63	52.23	..	..
102. Urbana (Univ.)	40 06	83 43	1015	25.75	29.26	37.13	49.79	61.29	69.55	74.14	71.10	64.58	50.79	39.56	30.14
103. Welchfield	41 23	81 12	1205	26.63	27.40	34.68	44.97	57.57	66.41	71.21	69.70	61.90	48.93	37.83	30.75
104. Wellington	41 13	82 12	875	..	33.13	..	..	62.88	67.20	73.10	..	..	..	..	..
105. West Barre	41 30	84 00	..	..	..	..	..	..	74.54	69.85	..	..	..	..	..
106. West Bedford	40 18	82 01	876	14.83	38.41	33.56	..	..	..	..	..	62.48	54.62	41.83	23.99
107. Westerville	40 04	82 46	..	28.70	31.31	38.77	50.84	60.37	68.89	73.56	70.45	63.82	50.27	40.20	31.74
108. West Union	38 48	83 21	..	30.23	..	..	..	..	..	..	..	..	..	..	..
109. Williamsport (Monroe Co.)	39 45	80 45	..	27.00	35.10	37.05	49.70	..	..	..	..	..	..	39.20	27.35
110. Windham	41 17	81 06	..	32.36	27.42	37.02	43.56	57.09	65.37	70.80	68.12	62.24	49.64	37.61	32.50
111. Wooster	40 51	81 59	872	24.05	29.31	34.85	49.75	59.32	71.31	75.47	72.65	66.36	50.38	39.73	29.36
112. Yankeetown	40 00	84 32	700	..	..	..	..	..	69.60	..	76.40	..	..	..	..
113. Yellow Spring	39 49	83 49	..	..	..	..	..	..	..	..	..	..	47.80	37.75	..
114. Zanesfield	40 22	83 36	..	..	..	..	..	61.25	..	..	..	..	..	..	..
115. Zanesville	39 58	81 59	700	31.89	35.10	35.30	56.20	64.20	71.69	77.25	73.67	69.48	52.40	45.31	32.64

[1] Also called Milnersville.

[2] Also called Williamsport.

[3] Observations corrected for daily variation by means of the general table.

[4] Altitude 130 feet above low-water in the Ohio River

OHIO.—Continued.

	Spring.	Summer.	Autumn.	Winter.	Year.	Series. Begins. Ends.	Extent yrs. mos.	Observing hours.	Observer.	References.
63	..	..	55°.08	32°.98	..	1849; 1850	0 7	$\odot_r\ 9_m\ 3_a\ 9_a$	Lapham.	S. Coll.
64	..	..	..	29.70	..	Dec. 1857; May, 1860	1 2	$7_m\ 2_a\ 9_a$ bis	N. Anthony.	P. O. and S. I. Vol. 1, and S. O.
65	47°.75	68°.45	50.68	29.46	49°.09	Jan. 1855; Aug. 1863	3 9	"	L. M. Dayton & J. Dille.	" " " " "
66	..	..	..	..	..	July, 1843; June, 1844	0 4	$\odot_r\ 9_m\ 3_a\ 9_a$	J. P. Mason.	MS. in S. Coll.
67	47.11	68.97	48.69	28.16	48.23	May, 1862; Aug. 1870	6 3	$7_m\ 2_a\ 9_a$ bis	Rev. D. Thompson.	S. O.
68	..	72.92	54.40	32.15	..	May, 1849; Mar. 1850	0 11	$\odot_r\ 9_m\ 3_a\ 9_a$	Irvine.	S. Coll.
69	53.76	..	..	31.92	..	Oct. 1867; Oct. 1870	1 2	$7_m\ 2_a\ 9_a$ bis	J. R. Wilkinson.	S. O.
70	48.13	71.84	51.47	28.91	50.09	Jan. 1855; Mar. 1870	13 4	"	J. F. Benner and W. R. Smiley.	MS. in S. Coll., P. O. and S. I. Vol. 1, and S. O.
71	..	73.58	53.04	..	..	Apr. 1862; Feb. 1863	0 10	"	A. E. Jerome.	S. O.
72	..	..	..	..	..	1861	0 1	"	....	" "
73	47.03	71.81	53.21	28.74	50.20	June, 1869; Dec. 1870	1 7	"	Dr. G. R. Morton.	" "
74	52.97	72.47	54.64	32.77	53.21	Oct. 1859; Jan. 1869	3 8	"	A. A. & R. B. Warder.	P. O. and S. I. Vol. 1, and S. O.
75	47.03	71.66	52.61	28.79	50.02	Feb. 1867; Dec. 1870	3 11	"	O. Burras.	S. O.
76	42.82	73.00	..	31.46	..	1852; Mar. 1861	1 10	$7_m\ 2_a\ 9_a$	Rev. R. Shields, and J. C. Smith.	P. O. and S. I. Vol. 1, S. O., & S. Coll.
77	44.61	..	..	..	..	1861	0 5	$7_m\ 2_a\ 9_a$ bis	A. S. Steever.	S. O.
78	46.22	68.69	50.87	28.33	48.53	Oct. 1854; Dec. 1868	8 1	"	Rev. A. Newton and G. A. Hyde.	P. O. and S. I. Vol. 1, and S. O.
79	46.46	70.62	51.59	27.52	49.05	1849; Dec. 1870	8 5	$7_m\ 2_a\ 9_a$	Profs. J. H. Fairchild, G. N. Allen, and L. Herrick.	P. O. and S. I. Vol. 1, S. O., and S. Coll.
80	49.89	73.70	52.81	29.00	51.35	Jan. 1864; Dec. 1870	6 9	$7_m\ 2_a\ 9_a$ bis	Prof. O. N. Stoddard.	S. O.
81	..	73.53	..	..	..	1870	0 6	"	J. T. Bingman.	" "
82	49.43	73.89	53.97	27.87	51.29	Mar. 1854; Apr. 1858	4 1	$7_m\ 2_a\ 9_a$	F. & D. K. Hollenbeck.	P. O. and S. I. Vol. 1.
83	54.58	74.13	55.89	35.33	54.98	Feb. 1824; Aug. 1865	29 9	8	Dr. G. B. Hempstead, G. H. Poe, Dr. D. B. Cotton, & L. Engelbrecht.	MS. in S. Coll., S. O., P. O. and S. I. Vol. 1, and Drake.
84	52.11	73.04	54.55	35.83	53.88	Mar. 1849; Jan. 1851	1 9	$\odot_r\ 9_m\ 3_a\ 9_a$	Beatly.	S. Coll.
85	..	..	..	..	..	1851	0 2	"	Dorsay.	" "
86	54.64	74.88	53.88	35.22	54.66	Oct. 1857; Dec. 1867	5 4	$7_m\ 2_a\ 9_a$ bis	J. Ammon.	P. O. and S. I. Vol. 1, and S. O.
87	46.48	71.39	53.29	27.09	49.79	Apr. 1867; Dec. 1870	2 8	"	Mrs. M. M. Marsh.	S. O.
88	51.23	70.90	54.13	33.71	52.49	Mar. 1855; Dec. 1863	5 0	"	Prof. G. M. Barber, E. Colbrunn.	P. O. and S. I. Vol. 1, and S. O.
89	42.99	67.91	48.36	29.90	47.29	Nov. 1849; Oct. 1851	2 0	$\odot_r\ 2_a$	Tenin.	Pat. Off. Rep.
90	50.37	73.16	51.67	29.36	51.14	1870	1 0	$7_m\ 2_a\ 9_a$ bis	J. E. Pollock.	S. O.
91	47.94	71.17	51.28	27.81	49.55	Mar. 1854; July, 1863	9 1	"	Dr. J. Ingram.	P. O. and S. I. Vol. 1, and S. O.
92	45.79	68.41	50.79	26.56	47.89	Feb. 1862; Apr. 1866	2 5	"	Rev. L. S. Atkins, J. B. Fraser.	S. O.
93	45.72	66.95	51.83	31.81	49.08	Jan. 1861; Dec. 1862	1 4	"	L. F. Ward.	" "
94	43.87	70.84	52.23	26.43	48.34	Sept. 1856; Aug. 1857	1 0	$7_m\ 2_a\ 9_a$	J. Shaw.	P. O. and S. I. Vol. 1.
95	..	70.50	49.98	25.23	..	Oct. 1864; Sept. 1865	1 1	$7_m\ 2_a\ 9_a$ bis	J. H. Myers, and W. Hoover.	S. O.
96	..	..	..	..	..	Jan. 1869; Sept. 1870	0 6	"	J. H. Henan and G. P. Hachenberg.	" "
97	50.99	72.60	52.52	31.22	51.83	Dec. 1830; Dec. 1870	39 11	6_m N. 6_a	R. Marsh & J. B. Doyle.	MS. in S. Coll. and S. O.
98	48.80	66.22	50.90	32.34	49.56	Dec. 1850; Nov. 1851	1 0	$\odot_r$	Julien.	Pat. Off. Rep.
99	46.90	70.20	50.83	28.88	49.20	June, 1856; June, 1870	13 10	$7_m\ 2_a\ 9_a$ bis	Dr. J. B. Trembley, H. Bennett, & Miss S. E. Bennett.	P. O. and S. I. Vol. 1, and S. O.
00	51.69	73.03	52.20	30.86	51.95	Jan. 1859; May, 1863	4 3	"	C. L. McClurg.	" " " " " "
01	..	..	..	..	..	1860	0 4	"	N. A. Chapman.	S. O.
02	49.40	71.60	51.64	28.38	50.26	1852; Dec. 1870	17 1	"	M. G. Williams.	S. O., P. O. and S. I. Vol. 1, and S. Coll.
03	45.74	69.11	49.55	28.26	48.17	Mar. 1857; Mar. 1866	9 0	"	B. F. Abell.	P. O. and S. I. Vol. 1, and S. O.
04	..	..	..	..	..	1863	0 4	"	L. F. Ward.	S. O.
05	..	..	..	..	..	1853	0 2	$7_m\ 2_a\ 9_a$	Taft.	S. Coll.
06	..	..	52.98	25.74	..	Sept. 1856; Mar. 1857	0 7	"	H. D. McCarty.	P. O. and S. I. Vol. 1.
07	49.99	70.97	51.43	30.58	50.74	Jan. 1858; Dec. 1870	11 7	$7_m\ 2_a\ 9_a$ bis	Prof. J. Haywood.	P. O. and S. I. Vol. 1, and S. O.
08	..	..	..	..	..	1861	0 1	"	Rev. W. Lundeen.	S. O.
09	..	..	..	29.82	..	Nov. 1860; Apr. 1861	0 6	"	Dr. W. W. Spratt.	" "
10	45.89	68.10	49.83	30.76	48.64	Mar. 1857; Dec. 1859	2 10	$7_m\ 2_a\ 9_a$	S. W. Treat.	P. O. and S. I. Vol. 1.
11	47.97	73.14	52.16	27.57	50.21	July, 1849; Aug. 1870	6 3	$7_m\ 2_a\ 9_a$ bis	M. Winger and wife and Par-dee.	S. O. and S. Coll.
12	..	..	..	..	..	1854	0 2	$7_m\ 2_a\ 9_a$	A. Jaque.	P. O. and S. I. Vol. 1.
13	..	..	..	..	..	1843	0 2	$\odot_r\ 9_m\ 3_a\ 9_a$	Phelps.	Manuscript.
14	..	..	..	..	..	1854	0 1	$7_m\ 2_a\ 9_a$	J. F. Lukins.	P. O. and S. I. Vol. 1.
15	51.90	74.20	55.73	33.21	53.76	Jan. 1819; Nov. 1859	3 11	"	W. Peters, Dr. J. G. F. Holston, & L. M. Dayton.	MS. in S. Coll., P. O. and S. I. Vol. 1.

[b] This series includes observations in March, 1855, at Berea, about six miles southwest of Rockport.

[c] Observations previous to 1860 were made at Collingwood, about five miles northwest of Toledo.

OREGON.

Name of Station.	Lat.	Long.	Height.	Jan.	Feb.	March.	April.	May.	June.	July.	August.	Sept.	Oct.	Nov.	Dec.
1. Albany (near)	44°35′	122°50′	600	32°.02	39°.48	37°.93	52°.28	59°.55	..	67°.83	71°.20	62°.73	..	..	..
2. Astoria[1]	46 11	123 48	52	38.44	38.78	44.24	48.75	53.16	57°.50	60.29	60.77	58.30	52°.69	46°.23	40°.8
3. Auburn	44 35	118 06	3350	52.04	..	..	..	..	..	71.48	70.38	..	..	..	31.2
4. Block-House	44 25	123 30	..	39.38	42.83	44.49	46.83	52.13	58.58	60.59	61.78	59.31	52.19	44.91	40.5
5. Camp Harney	43 00	119 00	..	22.74	28.25	36.89	48.55	56.92	67.34	74.27	70.96	62.05	51.17	40.42	29.6
6. Camp Logan	44 16	119 14	5600	..	..	..	43.41	49.08	56.61	66.53	66.53	57.71	49.04	45.52	..
7. Camp Lyons	42 43	116 52	5500	14.87	27.19	41.82	49.23	52.52	61.29	72.25	72.69	58.31	51.56	41.85	34.1
8. Camp Three Forks	42 15	116 54	..	22.78	29.89	37.11	43.78	53.08	63.08	71.00	71.23	61.65	52.61	41.70	31.1
9. Camp Warner	42 28	119 42	..	25.08	30.38	34.17	42.40	49.79	59.15	67.62	66.61	57.23	48.32	38.25	30.2
10. Camp Watson	44 22	119 48	..	23.38	28.05	36.10	43.65	49.56	57.39	62.95	66.14	56.60	43.99	37.66	33.2
11. Corvallis	44 32	123 04	..	31.57	37.59	36.32	50.60	..	56.85	64.07	66.10	..	46.92	..	42.8
12. Eola	44 57	122 54	500	36.40	39.05	39.40	46.79	51.86	58.47	67.45	68.64	58.19	49.32	42.07	33.2
13. Fort Dalles[2]	45 33	120 50	350	31.59	38.21	45.93	53.51	61.34	67.29	73.79	72.62	63.87	54.44	42.52	33.6
14. Fort Hoskins	45 06	123 26	..	38.74	41.61	44.96	50.35	55.05	60.43	63.55	64.19	59.78	52.29	45.08	40.3
15. Fort Klamath	42 40	121 50	4200	22.78	25.21	34.06	38.81	44.60	52.26	60.92	58.77	47.98	40.65	34.60	24.9
16. Fort Lane	42 20	122 46	2000	39.29	43.52	51.78	52.45	60.23	68.66	74.55	73.09	..	60.43	40.39	32.7
17. Fort Orford[2]	42 44	124 29	50	48.73	48.17	49.95	51.13	55.06	58.66	59.57	60.92	59.19	55.82	50.42	48.7
18. Fort Stevens	46 12	123 57	..	38.28	40.76	43.41	48.95	53.58	58.70	62.89	61.37	58.18	53.59	48.90	42.5
19. Fort Umpqua	43 42	124 10	8	44.17	46.22	48.12	50.69	54.48	59.47	59.93	59.72	58.91	54.10	49.57	45.5
20. Fort Yamhill	45 21	123 15	..	37.12	39.62	43.55	47.81	53.42	56.97	60.92	61.23	58.14	51.21	43.52	38.1
21. Oregon City	45 20	122 18	200	38.60	42.00	45.20	55.90	60.90	66.30	72.27	71.63	60.20	55.80	47.23	38.9
22. Portland[3]	45 30	122 36	45	40.65	40.73	42.20	51.65	56.50	65.61	69.47	68.09	62.98	53.18	48.40	39.3
23. Salem	44 56	122 45	120	41.3	49.2	46.5	49.5	58.4	64.5	67.1	69.3	65.2	70.5	58.2	50.3
24. Salem	44 56	122 45	120	..	..	..	..	..	..	..	..	..	49.48	..	..
25. Willamette Univ.	45 22	122 23	120	39.50	..	..	..	52.23	..		..	..	..	..	..

PENNSYLVANIA.

Name of Station.	Lat.	Long.	Height.	Jan.	Feb.	March.	April.	May.	June.	July.	August.	Sept.	Oct.	Nov.	Dec.
1. Abington	41 31	75 46	1183	23.93	26.11	31.97	45.31	55.15	65.95	69.98	67.12	60.78	47.39	37.90	27.4
2. Allegheny Arsenal	40 29	79 59	704	28.89	31.67	38.84	50.36	61.49	69.90	73.58	71.59	64.15	51.45	40.38	32.0
3. Allegheny City	40 28	80 03	..	..	..	..	51.66	..	..	..	..	..	..	..	..
4. Allegheny Tunnel	40 30	78 36	2161	29.67	..	34.92	47.14	57.54	68.67	70.59	71.31	..	..	..	..
5. Altoona	40 32	78 24	1208	..	..	33.03	46.28	..	..	..	..	..	46.49	42.27	29.4
6. Ashland	40 48	76 20	1005	..	27.23	31.88	50.75	58.01	..	..	..	..	..	..	..
7. Avondell	40 27	77 22	515	27.15	25.97	35.32	45.98	57.51	68.28	73.79	70.42	61.98	49.69	41.22	26.3
8. Beaver	40 43	80 20	..	29.89	27.79	..	54.52	62.35	72.56	74.42	72.10	59.63	53.14	38.87	29.8
9. Beaver Seminary	40 43	80 23	..	32.11	30.48	37.89	48.74	60.18	67.76	74.56	71.54	62.81	50.02	40.76	31.9
10. Bedford	40 01	78 30	..	27.77	30.68	37.90	49.90	60.52	70.97	74.12	72.19	63.64	52.18	40.13	31.4
11. Berwick	41 05	76 15	583	25.21	31.29	39.36	47.63	59.76	68.60	73.00	71.05	62.08	51.94	40.94	30.9
12. Bethlehem	40 43	75 20	300	31.81	34.25	38.53	48.31	58.59	69.82	73.63	69.54	61.34	51.39	45.66	33.0
13. Blairsville	40 27	79 15	1010	22.7	28.2	34.3	42.1	52.4	54.9	64.8	66.0	52.8	47.7	40.2	28.0
14. Blooming Grove	41 23	75 09	..	21.81	23.63	29.25	43.99	52.96	64.61	68.66	64.58	59.23	44.78	35.60	24.6
15. Brookville	41 12	79 08	..	..	..	..	..	59.55	68.57	75.30	72.00	64.77	..	..	..
16. Brownsville	40 02	79 52	..	35.33	30.90	..	54.03	68.40	74.88	80.55	77.00	70.38	58.55	41.66	34.2
17. Buffalo Township	40 44	79 40	1000	..	..	..	47.80	63.03	65.13	69.08	..	..	..	..	..
18. Bustleton	40 05	75 01	..	28.25	..	..	..	..	..	..	..	..	..	..	..
19. Butler	40 54	79 50	850	28.48	32.92	39.92	49.71	60.78	71.06	74.82	71.81	64.08	54.63	41.96	30.7
20. Byberry	40 06	74 58	70	27.04	33.68	38.07	48.85	61.78	69.17	74.57	73.36	66.08	56.78	44.35	34.4
21. Canonsburg (Jefferson Coll.)	40 17	80 11	850	27.95	31.67	38.41	48.77	59.49	67.74	71.80	70.13	63.73	51.97	39.89	31.2
22. Carlisle (Barracks)	40 12	77 11	600	28.10	30.17	37.31	50.16	61.25	71.00	75.04	72.54	65.42	52.39	39.15	31.2
23. Carpenter	41 37	76 51	..	..	..	..	..	51.05	60.95	66.28	66.00	59.73	..	..	..

[1] Observations in 1850 and 1851 at $\odot_r$ 9_a 3_a 9_a, referred to 6_m N. 6_a.

[2] Observations previous to 1855 at $\odot_r$ 9_m 3_a 9_a, referred to 7_m 2_a 9_a.

OREGON.

	Spring.	Summer.	Autumn.	Winter.	Year.	Series. Begins. Ends.	Extent yrs. mos.	Observing hours.	Observer.	References.
1	49°.92	..	..	..	..	Jan. 1867; Jan. 1868	0 9	$7_m\ 2_a\ 9_a$ bis	S. M. W. Hindman.	S. O.
2	48.72	59°.52	52°.41	39°.35	50°.00	Aug. 1850; Dec. 1870	18 3	6_m N. 6_a	Assistant Surgeon, L. Wilson.	Ar. Met. Reg. 1855, and U. S. Coast Survey.
3	..	..	..	..	..	Dec. 1863; Aug. 1864	0 4	$7_m\ 2_a\ 9_a$ bis	R. B. Imside.	S. O.
4	47.82	60.32	52.14	40.91	50.30	Mar. 1858; Dec. 1862	4 3	$7_m\ 2_a\ 9_a$	Assistant Surgeon.	Ar. Met. Reg. 1860, and MS. from S. G. O.
5	47.45	70.86	51.21	26.86	49.10	Jan. 1868; Dec. 1870	3 0	"	" "	MS. from S. G. O.
6	..	63.22	50.76	..	..	Nov. 1867; Oct. 1868	0 8	"	" "	" " "
7	47.86	68.74	50.57	25.40	48.14	Oct. 1867; Sept. 1868	1 0	"	" "	" " "
8	44.66	68.44	51.99	27.93	48.25	Jan. 1868; Dec. 1869	2 0	"	" "	" " "
9	42.12	64.46	47.93	28.57	45.77	Jan. 1868; Dec. 1870	3 0	"	" "	" " "
10	43.10	62.16	46.08	28.22	44.89	Apr. 1867; Apr. 1869	2 1	"	" "	" " "
11	..	62.34	..	37.35	..	June, 1866; Feb. 1868	1 1	$7_m\ 2_a\ 9_a$ bis	A. D. Barnard.	S. O.
12	46.02	64.85	49.86	36.22	49.24	1870	1 0	"	T. Pearce.	" "
13	53.59	71.23	53.61	34.50	53.23	Sept. 1850; Mar. 1866	13 2	$7_m\ 2_a\ 9_a$	Assistant Surgeon.	Ar. Met. Regs. 1855 and 1860, and MS. from S. G. O.
14	50.12	62.72	52.38	40.25	51.37	Nov. 1856; Mar. 1865	8 0	"	" "	Ar. Met. Reg. 1860, and MS. from S. G. O.
15	39.16	57.32	41.08	24.32	40.47	Dec. 1863; Mar. 1866	2 4	"	" "	MS. from S. G. O.
16	54.82	72.10	..	38.50	..	Jan. 1855; Oct. 1856	1 6	"	" "	Ar. Met. Reg. 1860.
17	52.05	59.72	55.14	48.56	53.87	June, 1852; July, 1856	3 0	"	" "	Ar. Met. Regs. 1855 and 1860.
18	48.65	6[illegible].99	53.56	40.54	50.93	Nov. 1865; Sept. 1868	2 8	"	" "	MS. from S. G. O.
19	51.10	59.71	54.19	45.30	52.57	Aug. 1856; May, 1862	5 10	"	" "	Ar. Met. Reg. 1860 and MS. from S. G. O.
20	48.26	59.71	50.96	38.30	49.31	Oct. 1856; Apr. 1866	9 5	"	" "	" " " "
21	54.00	70.07	54.41	39.84	54.58	Jan. 1849; Dec. 1851	2 11	$\odot_r\ 2_a\ \odot_s$	Assistant Surgeon, G. M. Atkinson.	Ar. Met. Reg. 1855, and S. Coll.
22	50.12	67.72	54.85	40.23	53.23	Apr. 1858; Dec. 1870	2 0	$7_m\ 2_a\ 9_a$ bis	G. H. Stibbins, J. S. Reed, S. W. Gilliland.	P. O. and S. I. Vol. 1, and S. O.
23	51.47	66.97	64.63	46.93	57.50	Oct. 1856; Sept. 1857	1 0	......	....	Newspaper slip and P. O. and S. I. Vol. 1.
24	..	..	..	..	..	1863	0 1	$7_m\ 2_a\ 9_a$ bis	P. L. Willis.	S. O.
25	..	..	..	..	..	May 1861; Jan. 1864	[illegible]		T. H. Crawford.	" "

PENNSYLVANIA.

	Spring.	Summer.	Autumn.	Winter.	Year.	Series. Begins. Ends.	Extent yrs. mos.	Observing hours.	Observer.	References.
1	44.14	67.68	48.69	25.81	46.58	Jan. 1864; Dec. 1870	7 0	$\odot_r$ N. $\odot_s$	R. Sisson.	Table in S. Coll. and S. O.
2	50.23	71.69	51.99	30.87	51.19	Jan. 1825; Apr. 1867	33 2	$7_m\ 2_a\ 9_a$	Assistant Surgeon.	Ar. Met. Regs. 1855–60 and MS. from S. G. O.
3	..	..	..	..	..	1849	0 1	$\odot_r\ 9_m\ 3_a\ 9_a$	Stewart.	S. Coll.
4	46.53	70.19	..	..	..	1853	0 7	$7_m\ 2_a\ 9_a$	Seabrook.	" "
5	..	..	..	..	..	Oct. 1859; Apr. 1863	0 5	$7_m\ 2_a\ 9_a$ bis	W. R. Boyers, T. H. Savery.	P. O. and S. I. Vol. 1, and S. O.
6	46.68	..	..	..	..	1870	0 4	"	W. E. Honeyman.	S. O.
7	46.27	70.83	50.96	26.48	48.64	June, 1867; Apr. 1869	1 11	"	W. E. Baker.	" "
8	..	73.03	50.55	29.16	..	1839; 1840	1 2	$7_m\ 2_a\ 9_a$	W. Allison.	Journ. Frank. Inst.
9	48.94	71.29	51.20	31.52	50.74	Oct. 1867; Dec. 1870	3 3	$7_m\ 2_a\ 9_a$ bis	Rev. R. T. Taylor.	S. O.
10	49.44	72.43	51.98	29.96	50.95	1839; Dec. 1861	11 8	$7_m\ 2_a\ 9_a$	S. Brown, King, and Rev. H. Heckerman.	P. O. and S. I. Vol. 1, S. O. Journ. Frank. Inst., & S. Coll.
11	48.92	70.88	51.65	29.14	50.15	Jan. 1856; Jan. 1865	6 0	$7_m\ 2_a\ 9_a$ bis	J. Eggert.	P. O. and S. I. Vol. 1, and S. O.
12	48.48	71.00	52.80	33.04	51.33	1849; 1851	2 3	$\odot_r\ 9_m\ 3_a\ 9_a$	Kluge.	S. Coll.
13	42.93	61.90	46.90	26.30	44.51	Oct. 1861; Jan. 1865	3 0	$7_m\ 2_a\ 9_a$ bis	W. R. Boyers.	S. O.
14	42.07	65.95	46.54	23.35	44.48	May, 1865; Dec. 1870	5 6	"	J. Gratwohl.	" "
15	..	71.96	..	..	..	1854	0 5	6_m N. 6_a	D. S. Dearing.	P. O. and S. I. Vol. 1.
16	..	77.48	56.86	33.49	..	Nov. 1869; Dec. 1870	1 1	$7_m\ 2_a\ 9_a$ bis	Dr. J. A. Hubbs.	S. O.
17	..	..	..	..	..	1860	0 4	"	J. H. Baird.	" "
18	..	..	..	..	..	1854	0 1	$7_m\ 2_a\ 9_a$	J. C. Martindale.	P. O. and S. I. Vol. 1.
19	50.14	72.56	53.56	30.72	51.75	1839; 1851	5 5	"	Michling.	Journ. Frank. Inst. and MS.
20	49.57	72.37	55.74	31.72	52.35	1852; Dec. 1863	5 11	"	J. Comley and others.	P. O. & S. I. Vol. 1, S. Coll., & S. O.
21	48.89	69.89	51.86	30.28	50.23	1839; Dec. 1870	18 8	$7_m\ 2_a\ 9_a$ bis	Various observers.	P. O. and S. I. Vol. 1., Journal Franklin Institute, and S. Coll.
22	49.57	72.86	52.32	29.85	51.15	July, 1839; Dec. 1870	29 5	$7_m\ 2_a\ 9_a$	Assist. Surg., H. Duffield, W. C. Wilson, H. W. Cook.	Ar. Met. Reg., 1855, MS. from S. G. O, P. O. & S. I. Vol. 1, and S. Coll.
23	..	64.41	..	..	..	1862	0 5	$7_m\ 2_a\ 9_a$ bis	E. L. McNutt.	S. O.

[3] Observations for ten months, of 1858 and 1859, at 6_m N. 6_a, referred to $7_m\ 2_a\ 9_a$ bis.

PENNSYLVANIA.—Continued.

Name of Station.	Lat.	Long.	Height.	Jan.	Feb.	March.	April.	May.	June.	July.	August.	Sept.	Oct.	Nov.	Dec.
24. Catawissa	40°58′	76°30′	..	..	..	..	..	..	68°.68	71°.28	..	60°.98	..	39°.88	..
25. Ceres	42 00	78 25	1440	23°.36	23°.55	32°.34	42°.84	56°.06	64.63	68.55	66°.62	59.01	45°.76	36.19	27°.08
26. Chambersburg	39 56	77 40	618	29.47	35.22	43.95	50.23	61.49	72.04	76.18	73.91	66.33	54.27	40.45	33.29
27. Chester (U. S. Gen. Hosp.)	39 51	75 21	..	33.86	36.21	39.91	50.35	..	..	..	..	..	..	..	38.06
28. Chromedale (or Lima)	39 55	75 25	196	29.77	31.58	38.55	47.86	59.35	69.53	74.36	70.48	63.76	53.10	43.30	33.53
29. Dyberry	41 38	75 18	..	20.13	22.36	29.15	43.37	50.76	65.14	67.16	62.54	58.21	43.98	35.19	30.58
30. Easton	40 43	75 16	340	24.29	27.13	35.81	47.56	58.69	69.33	74.43	69.64	63.56	50.72	40.36	30.37
31. Ephrata	40 11	76 11	..	29.60	31.78	37.18	51.65	59.90	72.26	77.33	72.63	67.88	54.30	44.11	32.43
32. Fallsington	40 12	74 48	30	30.14	32.15	38.28	49.56	59.60	69.20	73.65	72.28	65.20	53.80	43.30	32.87
33. Fayette Tannery (2 miles east of Connellsville)	40 02	79 32	..	28.41	30.46	36.65	49.29	57.91	67.62	72.42	69.67	63.29	49.97	40.59	31.27
34. Fleming[2]	40 55	77 53	780	24.05	28.38	35.89	47.66	58.06	67.60	71.97	67.77	61.08	49.64	38.74	29.73
35. Fountain Dale	39 44	77 18	..	35.12	32.88	36.21	49.57	59.93	69.87	74.99	71.88	63.73	50.17	40.23	30.48
36. Frankford Arsenal	40 00	75 04	30	32.36	31.86	40.73	51.04	60.73	69.43	75.44	73.01	66.11	53.96	42.41	33.71
37. Franklin	41 24	79 50	980	26.68	24.26	31.92	44.68	57.76	66.91	73.98	68.52	60.75	47.13	37.26	27.48
38. Freeport	40 41	79 41	1000	..	..	..	..	..	..	79.60	77.27	71.83	57.19	40.37	..
39. Fort Mifflin	39 52	75 13	20	32.54	31.97	40.46	50.66	61.64	71.63	76.55	74.02	68.41	55.82	45.69	34.69
40. Germantown	40 01	75 10	100	29.26	31.66	38.72	51.33	61.59	71.55	75.16	72.82	65.25	52.14	41.11	31.69
41. Gettysburg	39 49	77 15	624	27.82	30.76	38.86	49.87	60.76	69.79	73.79	71.28	63.38	50.18	40.00	31.06
42. Greencastle	39 47	77 44	650	..	..	..	..	..	..	80.90	77.77	70.50	..	..	..
43. Hamlinton	41 25	75 26	..	32.38	26.20	29.23	47.38	59.82	73.50	..	70.35	60.75	45.31	36.13	30.73
44. Harrisburg	40 16	76 53	375	30.67	32.18	40.23	51.78	63.27	73.28	78.63	74.92	67.37	54.48	44.28	33.68
45. Haverford College	40 00	75 21	400	31.42	33.41	39.08	50.82	61.50	70.81	76.54	73.62	67.60	55.46	44.35	31.65
46. Hazleton	40 58	76 00	1850	..	..	..	..	..	..	..	..	..	..	..	25.95
47. Hollidaysburg	40 28	78 23	1200	29.23	32.19	37.71	47.86	59.49	72.50	73.42	70.28	62.99	49.34	45.00	29.66
48. Honesdale	41 36	75 24	..	..	20.22	..	..	..	..	69.71	..	..	..	..	..
49. Huntingdon	40 31	78 01	734	26.35	31.59	40.98	49.81	60.76	73.02	74.41	72.89	64.68	50.58	39.75	30.71
50. Indiana	40 40	79 08	1320	27.03	31.76	36.89	50.01	62.12	67.94	72.70	68.22	60.59	56.04	42.52	29.62
51. Johnstown	40 20	78 53	1200	32.92	26.95	33.77	44.44	55.51	65.62	71.55	68.09	59.52	47.78	37.00	29.23
52. Lancaster	40 03	76 21	350	30.42	33.32	41.10	51.89	60.33	70.12	73.54	71.93	64.37	52.60	41.65	32.21
53. Lancaster Colliery	40 48	76 35	920	26.15	30.19	37.37	43.25	56.22	65.45	69.84	66.33	59.34	49.24	39.43	30.90
54. Latrobe	40 20	79 21	569	..	..	..	..	56.25	..	..	..	..	..	..	..
55. Lehigh University (S. Bethlehem)	40 38	75 22	320	23.40	19.75	35.83	42.85	55.58	68.26	73.47	70.41	61.79	49.44	41.65	26.45
56. Lewisburg Univ.	40 58	76 55	..	23.42	26.58	34.56	47.58	57.84	69.05	73.14	68.91	61.68	48.86	38.73	28.17
57. Lewistown	40 35	77 37	..	29.91	36.21	41.38	56.89	67.23	68.25	75.43	72.71	65.35	58.20	..	..
58. Linden	41 14	77 11	..	27.22	30.39	40.23	44.85	..	..	..	..	..	..	34.91	..
59. Manchester	40 32	80 03	750	34.54	37.24	40.95	45.04	58.63	70.59	75.18	71.80	62.54	50.24	45.01	32.03
60. Meadville	41 39	80 09	1088	23.25	28.45	31.89	46.31	57.43	68.77	72.22	68.09	62.42	51.09	38.76	29.84
61. Mercersburg	39 50	77 55	..	34.28	30.78	41.41	54.80	65.44	69.74	74.94	75.15	67.43	54.09	41.03	33.05
62. Mifflintown	40 32	77 28	..	26.28	32.70	41.30	52.66	60.24	70.40	71.43	69.92	61.90	53.82	38.01	30.81
63. Milford	41 18	74 50	..	..	..	..	..	..	..	68.17	67.40	..	..	..	..
64. Mooreland	40 00	75 11	250	27.81	30.80	37.48	50.22	58.00	68.92	72.96	70.87	64.62	51.65	42.04	31.28
65. Morrisville	40 13	74 52	30	30.48	29.61	38.23	50.43	62.20	70.85	74.66	71.90	65.37	53.70	42.50	31.27
66. Moss Grove	41 40	79 51	1400	24.20	25.87	30.38	44.37	57.88	68.31	72.02	69.14	60.76	48.71	38.67	26.05
67. Mount Joy	40 06	76 31	..	31.33	32.27	40.53	51.95	62.79	73.03	77.26	73.74	67.04	54.92	43.79	33.53
68. Murrysville	40 26	79 41	1000	26.74	26.47	39.84	44.63	58.04	69.40	71.89	69.88	61.80	51.30	36.39	35.72
69. Nazareth	40 43	75 21	530	24.80	27.98	36.74	47.64	59.10	68.45	72.61	69.32	61.90	49.86	40.81	30.53
70. New Castle	41 02	80 21	..	27.20	30.09	34.77	49.96	59.32	70.41	74.40	70.85	64.11	52.14	41.40	28.71
71. Newtown	40 15	74 57	..	30.76	30.40	39.09	49.31	59.46	68.60	73.94	71.55	63.17	51.33	39.74	31.37

[1] Observations were made at very irregular hours. They were corrected for daily variation by means of the general table.

[2] Observations in 1839–40–41, and from Dec. 1858, to June, 1859, a period of three years four months, were made at Bellefontaine, about four miles east of Flemming.

PENNSYLVANIA.—Continued.

	Spring.	Summer.	Autumn.	Winter.	Year.	Series. Begins.	Series. Ends.	Extent yrs. mos.	Observing hours.	Observer.	References.
24	..	..	..	..	..	1870		0 4	$7_m\ 2_a\ 9_a$ bis	A. Curtis.	S. O.
25	43°.75	66°.60	46°.99	24°.66	45°.50	Jan. 1835;	Mar. 1854	9 9	[1]	H. C. King, R. P. Stevens.	P. O. and S. I. Vol. 1, Rec. in S. Coll.
26	51.89	74.04	53.68	32.66	53.07	July, 1858;	Apr. 1862	2 6	$7_m\ 2_a\ 9_a$ bis	W. Heyser.	P. O. and S. I, Vol. 1. and S. O.
27	..	..	..	36.04	..	Dec. 1863;	Apr. 1864	0 5	$7_m\ 2_a\ 9_a$	....	MS. from S. G. O.
28	48.59	71.46	53.39	31.63	51.27	Jan. 1849;	Feb. 1859	9 9	“	J. Edwards.	P. O. and S. I. Vol. 1, and printed slip.
29	41.09	64.95	45.79	24.36	44.05	Jan. 1865;	Dec. 1870	5 7	$7_m\ 2_a\ 9_a$ bis	T. Day.	S. O.
30	47.35	71.13	51.55	27.26	49.32	Jan. 1855;	Dec. 1859	5 0	$7_m\ 2_a\ 9_a$	S. J. Coffin, G. R. Houghton.	P. O. and S. I. Vol. 1.
31	49.58	74.07	55.43	31.27	52.59	Nov. 1855;	Dec. 1870	4 9	$7_m\ 2_a\ 9_a$ bis	W. H. Speras.	S. O.
32	49.15	71.71	54.10	31.72	51.67	Jan. 1860;	Dec. 1870	11 0	“	E. Hanse.	“ “
33	47.95	69.90	51.28	30.05	49.80	Jan. 1862;	Dec. 1870	8 11	$7_m\ 2_a\ 9_a$ bis [3]	J. Taylor.	“ “
34	47.20	69.11	49.82	27.39	48.38	Jan. 1839;	June, 1867	14 0		S. Brugger, J. I. Burrell, Atkins, Harris, Livingstone.	P. O. and S. I. Vol. 1, S. O., & Journ. Frank. Inst.
35	48.57	72.25	51.38	32.83	51.26	Dec. 1867;	Dec. 1870	2 10	$7_m\ 2_a\ 9_a$ bis [4]	S. C. Walker.	S. O.
36	50.83	72.63	54.16	32.64	52.57	Jan. 1836;	Dec. 1843	8 0		Maj. Mordecai.	Blodget's Climatology.
37	44.79	69.80	48.38	26.14	47.28	Oct. 1867;	Dec. 1870	3 2	$7_m\ 2_a\ 9_a$ bis	Rev. M. A. Tolman.	S. O.
38	..	..	56.46	..	..	1854		0 6	$7_m\ 2_a\ 9_a$	A. D. Weir.	P. O. and S. I. Vol. 1.
39	50.92	74.07	56.64	33.07	53.67	Jan. 1822;	Oct. 1853	11 2	$\odot_r\ 9_m\ 3_a\ 9_a$	Assistant Surgeon.	Ar. Met. Reg. 1855.
40	50.55	73.18	52.83	30.87	51.86	June, 1819;	Dec. 1870	17 1	$7_m\ 2_a\ 9_a$ bis	Haines, C. J. Wister, Jr., T. Meechan.	S. Coll. and S. O.
41	49.83	71.62	51.19	29.88	50.63	Jan. 1839;	Feb. 1865	24 2	[3]	Prof. M. Jacobs.	P. O. and S. I. Vol. 1, MS. in S. Coll., and S. O.
42	..	..	..	..	..	1870		0 3	$7_m\ 2_a\ 9_a$	S. W. Rhode.	S. O.
43	45.48	..	47.40	29.77	..	Sept. 1869;	Aug. 1870	0 11	$7_m\ 2_a\ 9_a$ bis	J. D. Stoker.	“ “
44	51.76	75.61	55.38	32.18	53.73	Jan. 1840;	July, 1870	29 3	“	J. Heisely, W. O. Hickok, Dr. W. H. Egle, R. A. Martin.	P. O. and S. I. Vol. 1, MS. in S. Coll., and S. O.
45	50.47	73.66	55.80	32.16	53.02	Jan. 1854;	June, 1863	8 2	$7_m\ 2_a$	Dr. P. Swift.	P. O. and S. I. Vol. 1. and S. O.
46	..	..	..	..	..	1870		0 1	$7_m\ 2_a\ 9_a$ bis	J. Haworth.	S. O.
47	48.35	72.07	52.44	30.36	50.81	1853		1 0	$7_m\ 2_a\ 9_a$	Lowrie.	S. Coll.
48	..	..	..	..	..	1839;	1840	0 2	“	Richardson.	Journ. Frank. Inst.
49	50.52	73.44	51.67	29.55	51.29	1840;	1841	1 11	“	Miller.	“ “ “
50	49.67	69.62	53.05	29.47	50.45	1839;	Aug. 1858	3 11	“	White, Pector.	Journ. Frank. Inst., P. O. and S. I. Vol. 1, and S. Coll.
51	44.57	68.42	48.10	29.70	47.70	Feb. 1868;	Dec. 1870	2 11	$7_m\ 2_a\ 9_a$ bis	D. Peelor.	S. O.
52	51.11	71.86	52.87	31.98	51.96	Jan. 1839;	1850	6 5	$7_m\ 2_a\ 9_a$	Winchell, Atler.	Journ. Frank. Inst., S. Coll. & Dove, 1853.
53	45.61	67.21	49.34	29.08	47.81	Nov. 1856;	Dec. 1859	3 2	“	P. Friel.	MS. in S. Coll., and P. O. and S. I. Vol. 1.
54	..	..	..	..	..	1861		0 1	$7_m\ 2_a\ 9_a$ bis	W. R. Boyers.	S. O.
55	44.75	70.71	50.96	23.20	47.41	June, 1867;	Nov. 1868	1 6	“	Prof. A. M. Mayer, N. C. Tooker.	“ “
56	46.66	70.37	49.76	26.06	48.21	Jan. 1856;	Dec. 1870	10 9	“	Prof. C. S. James.	P. O. and S. I. Vol. 1, and S. O.
57	55.17	72.13	..	..	..	1839		0 10	$7_m\ 2_a\ 9_a$	Culbertson.	Journ. Frank. Inst.
58	..	..	..	..	..	Nov. 1858;	Apr. 1859	0 5	$7_m\ 1_a\ 9_a$	J. Barrett.	P. O. and S. I. Vol. 1.
59	48.21	72.52	52.60	34.60	51.98	Mar. 1849;	Apr. 1851	2 2	$\odot_r\ 9_m\ 3_a\ 9_a$	Marks.	S. Coll.
60	45.21	69.69	50.76	27.18	48.21	1839;	Sept. 1858	5 9	$7_m\ 2_a\ 9_a$	T. F. Thickstun, Shippen, Williams.	P. O. and S. I. Vol. 1, S. Coll., and Journ. Frank. Inst.
61	55.88	73.28	54.18	32.70	53.51	1842;	1847	2 2	$\odot_r\ 2_m\ 9_a$	Green.	Manuscript.
62	51.40	70.58	51.24	29.93	50.79	1839;	1841	2 10	$7_m\ 2_a\ 9_a$	Benkird.	Journ. Frank. Inst.
63	..	..	..	..	..	1839		0 2	$7_m\ 2_a\ 7_a$	Ball.	“ “ “
64	48.57	70.92	52.77	29.96	50.55	June, 1864;	Dec. 1870	6 7	$7_m\ 2_a\ 9_a$ bis	Anna Spencer.	S. O.
65	50.29	72.47	58.86	30.45	51.77	Jan. 1790;	Dec. 1859	67 10	$\odot_r\ 2_a\ 10_a$	Pierce, E. Hance.	MS. in S. Coll., P. O. and S. I. Vol. 1.
66	44.21	69.82	49.38	25.37	47.20	Feb. 1852;	Feb. 1857	4 10	$7_m\ 2_a\ 9_a$	F. Schreiner.	P. O. and S. I. Vol. 1, & S. Coll.
67	51.76	74.68	55.25	32.38	53.52	Mar. 1857;	Nov. 1870	12 11	$7_m\ 2_a\ 9_a$ bis	Dr. J. R. Hoffer, Miss M. E. Hoffer.	S. O.
68	47.50	70.39	49.83	29.64	49.34	Apr. 1857;	Mar. 1868	2 4	$7_m\ 2_a\ 9_a$	T. H. & F. L. Stewart.	“ “
69	47.83	70.13	50.86	27.77	49.15	Jan. 1787;	Oct. 1866	14 5	$7_m\ 2_a\ 9_a$ bis	C. J. Reichel and others.	MS. in S. Coll., S. O., P. O. and S. I. Vol. 1.
70	48.02	71.89	52.55	28.67	50.28	Jan. 1866;	Dec. 1870	5 0	“	E. M. McConnell.	S. O.
71	49.29	71.36	51.41	30.84	50.73	Feb. 1837;	Mar. 1843	6 2	$7_m\ 2_a\ 9_a$	L. H. Parsons.	MS. in S. Coll. and Journ. Frank. Inst.

[3] Observations corrected for daily variation.

[4] Observations made hourly, or else corrected for daily variation.

PENNSYLVANIA.—Continued.

Name of Station.	Lat.	Long.	Height.	Jan.	Feb.	March.	April.	May.	June.	July.	August.	Sept.	Oct.	Nov.	Dec.
72. Norristown . .	40°08′	75°19′	153	30°.90	32°.46	39°.33	48°.26	59°.27	68°.56	73°.82	71°.89	64°.10	53°.77	43°.53	33.°40
73. Northumberland .	40 55	76 49	..	24.40	30.97	40.23	52.37	61.22	69.24	73.30	71.01	62.74	50.89	38.84	30.64
74. Oil City	41 26	79 43	..	25.94	..	..	..	..	..	..	..	..	46.19	39.43	31.57
75. Oxford	39 47	75 59	575	..	..	..	..	61.35	73.55	73.30	71.38	70.63	..	..	..
76. Oakland Observ. .	40 26	80 02	1026	25.80	31.17	39.81	46.51	60.43	70.23	74.27	71.70	65.73	53.75	42.68	28.84
77. Paradise[1] . . .	40 00	76 08	..	26.21	26.63	33.12	42.29	67.92	77.50	81.96	78.25	71.58	58.88	37.58	29.46
78. Pennsville . . .	41 00	78 38	1400	21.10	23.56	30.17	43.42	52.83	65.32	69.14	65.70	58.97	44.74	34.71	23.97
79. Philadelphia[2] . .	39 56	75 10	36	33.5	40.0	50.0	62.0	75.0	81.0	87.5	85.0	80.5	64.0	54.7	49.5
80. Philadelphia . .	39 56	75 10	36	32.14	35.45	40.38	51.05	60.05	69.64	74.08	73.03	64.03	54.61	43.89	34.68
81. Philadelphia . .	39 56	75 10	36	33.3	33.4	41.2	52.9	62.1	71.9	76.4	75.6	68.1	57.1	43.7	34.9
82. Philadelphia[2] . .	39 56	75 10	36	32.7	36.1	45.6	57.2	68.1	78.9	82.2	80.7	73.4	64.1	47.6	37.1
83. Philadelphia . .	39 56	75 10	36	30.7	29.7	38.9	49.2	60.7	68.3	73.8	70.2	63.4	53.2	44.5	33.9
84. Philadelphia . .	39 56	75 10	36	30.1	29.4	38.8	49.4	61.2	69.7	73.9	71.1	63.6	51.7	41.5	30.7
85. Philadelphia[3] . .	39 56	75 10	36	30.8	29.4	38.1	51.1	62.9	71.5	75.2	72.4	65.9	53.9	42.3	31.2
86. Philadelphia (Girard Coll.)	39 58	75 10	114	33.7	31.6	39.8	50.6	58.9	68.8	72.8	71.5	64.1	51.3	40.7	32.6
87. Philadelphia[4] . .	39 56	75 10	36	31.32	32.57	40.19	50.66	61.48	71.04	76.02	73.45	65.64	53.99	43.68	33.64
88. Philadelphia[6] (Nav. Hosp.)	39 56	75 10	36	30.79	32.71	40.10	48.57	61.26	69.62	74.83	72.86	65.18	54.45	43.29	33.26
89. Phoenixville . .	40 07	75 32	120	33.20	33.68	35.11	50.45	58.59	70.03	..	..	..	..	..	..
90. Pittsburg . . .	40 27	79 59	840	29.68	31.81	38.47	49.92	60.64	70.12	75.73	71.38	65.84	52.88	43.38	33.44
91. Pocopson . . .	39 54	75 40	218	28.80	31.14	38.12	49.02	60.06	70.47	75.86	73.64	66.20	53.18	42.85	32.15
92. Port Carbon . .	40 43	76 06	..	28.95	26.05	37.25	45.38	57.50	71.13	71.94	70.44	58.77	47.87	40.65	29.98
93. Pottsville . . .	40 41	76 12	..	31.86	26.18	34.87	49.30	59.26	65.35	74.65	68.00	61.90	51.08	42.14	29.46
94. Plymouth Meeting	40 06	75 16	..	35.84	29.69	36.29	48.63	58.72	70.27	75.41	72.62	65.19	51.38	41.15	31.94
95. Punxatawney . .	40 59	79 00	..	..	..	..	..	..	..	..	..	58.13	42.07	34.42	..
96. Randolph . . .	41 38	80 00	1720	21.90	20.89	33.02	43.23	57.95	68.15	74.10	68.89	65.11	51.65	35.13	28.18
97. Reading . . .	40 20	75 55	269	29.53	31.40	37.76	51.29	59.79	69.32	74.44	71.37	63.74	53.11	42.62	31.84
98. Rose Cottage . .	41 07	79 09	..	26.66	30.61	36.74	51.04	..	..	61.18	64.82	56.93	51.25	..	25.14
99. Salem	41 25	75 25	1600	..	..	..	45.08	53.55	67.02	68.20	65.98	62.05	50.54	39.61	29.54
100. Shamokin . . .	40 48	76 35	700	31.01	32.44	38.96	47.26	60.06	68.52	70.73	71.24	64.92	54.65	41.53	34.89
101. Shirleysburg . .	40 17	77 43	640	30.87	34.08	39.97	52.12	63.13	75.22	75.56	73.59	65.83	49.02	..	..
102. Silver Lake . .	41 55	76 01	..	16.83	27.10	35.56	48.43	58.39	65.00	71.55	71.16	59.16	51.20	38.16	22.40
103. Silver Spring . .	40 05	76 40	..	28.36	30.02	38.69	49.12	60.18	69.94	74.00	71.35	63.16	50.00	41.82	32.21
104. Sewickleyville .	40 34	80 10	656	27.12	32.25	36.33	47.92	53.42	68.27	67.25	69.20	61.40	48.36	37.52	29.55
105. Somerset . . .	40 02	79 05	2195	25.43	27.46	34.37	45.53	55.49	64.83	67.28	65.72	58.82	47.30	37.90	28.69
106. Stevensville . .	41 45	76 35	300	18.88	32.83		..	..	67.50	72.73	62.50	59.80	49.48	40.33	26.75
107. St. Mary's . . .	41 25	78 45	..	..	27.20	40.02	48.28	57.62	..	75.12	..	..	..	..	..
108. St. Vincent's College	40 14	79 29	922	32.23	34.62	39.04	48.85	58.42	68.82	70.77	70.60	63.27	54.25	39.65	36.38
109. Smithport . . .	41 54	78 33	..	33.51	29.83	32.52	45.34	54.13	62.72	67.00	64.05	55.11	48.40	32.20	25.03
110. Sugar Grove . .	42 00	79 24	1450	22.35	24.09	31.48	41.33	56.00	..	..	..	..	..	..	..
111. Susquehanna Depot	41 56	75 40	800	..	..	..	..	..	68.18	76.90	..	..	..	..	..
112. Tamaqua . . .	40 49	76 00	700	..	..	30.48	47.85	59.55	69.85	..	..	61.50	..	..	..
113. Tarentum . . .	40 37	79 46	950	28.64	32.75	39.20	46.23	60.19	68.44	72.81	70.22	62.73	50.84	39.19	34.37
114. Tioga	41 54	77 11	1000	23.30	25.26	31.99	45.40	55.56	67.07	71.86	68.33	62.56	46.66	36.70	26.76
115. Towanda (Susq. Coll. Inst.) . .	41 47	76 30	840	26.15	33.32	..	49.57	54.57	68.05	..	69.00	63.37	..	..	..
116. Troy Hill . . .	40 28	80 07	937	16.40	20.72	28.35	..	..	..	..	..	..	48.50	46.18	33.85
117. Turtle Creek Valley	40 28	79 38	960	..	..	..	..	..	..	71.23	..	..	..	..	..
118. Warrior's Mark .	40 41	78 09	..	..	..	35.22	44.70	58.00	67.20	74.13	..	..	..	..	..

[1] The observations from May to October, both inclusive, appear to be about 5° too high. Probably due to a bad exposure of the thermometer during those months.

[2] These observations evidently require a negative correction of about 6°.

[3] The greater part of this series is probably included in the preceding six.

PENNSYLVANIA.—Continued.

	Spring.	Summer.	Autumn.	Winter.	Year.	Series. Begins.	Ends.	Extent yrs.	mos.	Observing hours.	Observer.	References.
2	48°.95	71°.42	53°.80	32°.25	51°.61	Aug. 1843;	July, 1863	13	10	$7_m\ 2_a\ 9_a$ bis	Rev. J. C. Ralston, Rev. J. Grier, L. E. Corson.	P. O. and S. I. Vol. 1, S. Coll., Blodget's Climatology, and S. O.
3	51.27	71.18	50.82	28.67	50.49	1839;	1841	3	0	$7_m\ 2_a\ 9_a$	Huston.	Journ. Frank. Inst.
4	..	..	..	..	..	Oct. 1863;	Jan. 1864	0	4	$7_m\ 2_a\ 9_a$ bis	I. A. Weeks.	S. O.
5	..	72.74	..	..	..	1865		0	5	"	D. H. Duffield.	" "
6	48.92	72.07	54.05	28.60	50.91	1849;	1854	2	5	$7_m\ 2_a\ 7_a$	Wilson.	S. Coll.
7	47.78	79.24	56.01	27.43	52.61	Jan. 1835;	Dec. 1858	24	0	......	J. Frantz.	MS. in S. Coll., P. O. and S. I. Vol. 1.
8	42.14	66.72	46.14	22.88	44.47	July, 1864;	Dec. 1870	6	6	$7_m\ 2_a\ 9_a$ bis	E. Fenton.	S. O.
9	62.3	84.5	66.4	41.0	63.6	Oct. 1748;	Sept. 1749	1	0	......	Bertram Kalin, travels in N. A.	Blodget's Climatology.
30	50.49	72.25	54.18	34.09	52.75	Jan. 1758;	Dec. 1777	13	0	......	....	Trans. Am. Phil. Soc. 1839.
1	52.1	74.6	56.3	33.9	54.2	Jan. 1798;	Dec. 1804	7	0	......	Dr. J. R. Coxe.	Blodget's Climatology.
2	57.0	80.6	61.7	35.3	58.6	Jan. 1807;	Dec. 1826	20	0	......	James Young.	Darby's U. S.
3	49.6	70.8	53.7	31.4	51.4	Jan. 1829;	Dec. 1838	10	0	......	Dr. Thomas Hewson.	Trans. Am. Phil. Soc. 1839.
4	49.8	71.6	52.3	30.0	50.9	Jan. 1831;	July, 1839	8	7	......	....	Journ. Frank. Inst.
5	50.7	73.0	54.0	30.5	52.1	....		57	0	......	....	P. O. Report.
6	49.77	71.03	52.03	32.63	51.36	June, 1840;	June, 1845	5	1	hourly.	A. D. Bache.	Observations at the Magnetic & Meteorological Observatory, Washington, 1847, Vol. 3.
7	50.78	73.50	54.44	32.51	52.81	Feb. 1831;	Dec. 1870	39	10	[5]	J. A. Kirkpatrick and daughter, A. D. Bache, Dr. Conrad, and others.	Same as above, Journ. Frank. Inst. 1861 to 1869, Blodget's Climatology, S. O., S. Coll., and Dove.
8	49.98	72.44	54.31	32.25	52.25	Apr. 1843;	Dec. 1864	8	4	$\odot_r\ 9_m\ 3_a\ 9_a$	Surgeons of the Hosp.	MS. in S. Coll.
9	48.05	..	..	..	..	1869		0	6	$7_m\ 2_a\ 9_a$ bis	Dr. J. L. Coffinan.	S. O.
40	49.68	72.41	54.03	31.64	51.94	1839;	Dec. 1870	12	3	[6]	Various observers.	Journ. Frank. Inst., S. O., P. O. and S. I. Vol. 1, & S. Coll.
1	49.07	73.32	54.08	30.70	51.79	Jan. 1853;	Dec. 1870	17	9	$7_m\ 2_a\ 9_a$ bis	F. Darlington.	P. O. and S. I. Vol. 1, S.O., and S. Coll.
2	46.71	71.17	49.10	28.33	48.83	1839;	1840	1	4	$7_m\ 2_a\ 9_a$	Hewes.	Journ. Frank. Inst.
3	47.81	69.33	51.71	29.17	49.50	1839;	July, 1858	2	0	"	Dr. A. Heger, Rev. B. R. Smyser, D. Washburn, Porter.	Journ. Frank. Inst., P. O. and S. I. Vol. 1.
4	47.88	72.77	52.57	32.49	51.43	Feb. 1868;	Dec. 1870	2	11	$7_m\ 2_a\ 9_a$ bis	M. H. Corson.	S. O.
5	..	..	44.87	..	..	1839		0	3	$7_m\ 2_a\ 9_a$	Smith.	Journ. Frank. Inst.
6	44.73	70.38	50.63	23.66	47.35	Aug. 1851;	Feb. 1856	3	5	"	O. T. Hobbs.	P. O. & S. I. Vol. 1, & S. Coll.
7	49.61	71.71	53.16	30.92	51.35	1839;	Dec. 1870	6	8	$7_m\ 2_a\ 9_a$ bis	J. H. Raser, Engleman.	Journ. Frank. Inst., P. O. and & S. I. Vol. 1, and S. O.
8	..	..	..	27.47	..	1839;	1840	0	11	$7_m\ 2_a\ 9_a$	Gaskel.	Journ. Frank. Inst.
9	..	67.07	50.73	..	..	Apr. 1869;	Dec. 1870	0	10	$7_m\ 2_a\ 9_a$ bis	J. D. Stoker.	S. O.
50	48.76	70.16	53.70	32.78	51.35	Mar. 1860;	Jan. 1863	2	10	"	P. Friel.	" "
1	51.74	74.79	..	..	..	1853		0	10	$7_m\ 2_a\ 9_a$	Brewster.	S. Coll.
2	47.46	69.24	49.51	22.11	47.08	1839;	1841	2	9	"	Rose.	Journ. Frank. Inst.
3	49.33	71.76	51.66	30.20	50.74	Mar. 1863;	May, 1869	4	7	$7_m\ 2_a\ 9_a$ bis	H. I. Burckart.	S. O.
4	45.89	68.24	49.09	29.64	48.22	Oct. 1859;	Jan. 1862	1	4	"	J. A. Travelli, G. H. Tracy.	P. O. and S. I. Vol. 1, and S. O.
5	45.13	65.94	48.01	27.19	46.57	Dec. 1839;	Dec. 1861	15	7	$7_m\ 2_a\ 9_a$	G. Mowry, Dr. F. Chorpenning.	Journ. Frank. Inst., S. Coll., P. O. and S. I. Vol. 1, and S. O.
6	..	67.58	49.87	26.15	..	June, 1866;	Feb. 1867	0	9	$7_m\ 2_a\ 9_a$ bis	I. R. Dutton.	S. O.
7	48.64	..	..	..	..	1849		0	5	$\odot_r\ 9_m\ 3_a\ 9_a$	Stokes.	S. Coll.
8	48.77	70.06	52.39	34.41	51.41	Jan. 1851;	June, 1862	1	6	$7_m\ 2_a\ 9_a$ bis	Prof. R. Müller.	S. O.
9	44.00	64.59	45.24	29.46	45.82	1839;	1841	2	8	$7_m\ 2_a\ 9_a$	Chadwick.	Journ. Frank. Inst.
0	42.94	..	..	..	..	1854		0	5	"	W. O. Blodget.	P. O. and S. I. Vol. 1.
1	..	..	..	..	..	1863		0	2	$7_m\ 2_a\ 9_a$ bis	H. H. Atwater.	S. O.
2	45.96	..	..	..	..	1870		0	5	"	J. Haworth.	" "
3	48.54	70.49	50.92	31.92	50.47	Sept. 1856;	Mar. 1860	3	3	$7_m\ 2_a\ 9_a$	J. H. Baird.	P. O. and S. I. Vol. 1, and S. O.
4	44.32	69.09	48.64	25.11	46.79	July, 1863;	Dec. 1870	7	0	$7_m\ 2_a\ 9_a$ bis	E. T. Bentley.	S. O.
5	..	..	..	..	..	1861		0	7	"	S. J. Coffin.	" "
6	..	..	..	23.66	..	Jan. 1856;	Dec. 1863	0	6	"	V. Scriba, Prof. R. Müller.	P. O. and S. I. Vol. 1, and S. O.
7	..	..	..	..	..	1867		0	1	"	F. L. Stewart.	S. O.
8	45.97	..	..	..	..	1854		0	5	$7_m\ 2_a\ 9_a$	J. R. Lowrie.	P. O. and S. I. Vol. 1.

[4] This series includes the preceding one.

[5] Observations corrected for daily variation.

[6] This series was not combined with the preceding one because the record appears defective. It gives the temperature at 9 P. M. lower than at sunrise, which is contrary to experience at other stations.

PENNSYLVANIA.—Continued.

Name of Station.	Lat.	Long.	Height.	Jan.	Feb.	March.	April.	May.	June.	July.	August.	Sept.	Oct.	Nov.	Dec.
119. Westchester	39°58′	75°35′	541	29°.99	32°.14	37°.66	48°.70	59°.54	69°.10	74°.21	71°.06	63°.40	53°.69	43°.10	32°.[illegible]
120. Westtown	39 57	75 34	550	33.87	29.33	40.64	48.47	56.41	73.61	74.31	71.07	63.52	56.05	39.71	35.9
121. Whitchall	40 40	75 32	450	27.42	29.69	36.33	48.35	59.15	68.19	73.62	71.20	63.68	52.05	41.28	31.1
122. Worthington	40 52	79 37	1050	29.27	30.95	39.41	47.70	59.86	65.93	69.21	68.88	61.07	50.88	40.13	29.8
123. Williamsport	41 15	77 04	533	35.35	29.56	..	48.03	60.05	67.30	..	..	..	..	..	..
124. Youngsville	41 50	79 20	1185	23.15	25.42	32.50	41.63	..	..	..	..	..	..	..	..

RHODE ISLAND.

Name of Station.	Lat.	Long.	Height.	Jan.	Feb.	March.	April.	May.	June.	July.	August.	Sept.	Oct.	Nov.	Dec.
1. Acquidneset	41 40	71 26	30	18.61	14.78	30.66	51.01	..	..	..	..	..	..	..	..
2. Fort Adams	41 29	71 20	40	30.23	30.53	35.89	45.45	55.48	65.98	72.18	71.54	63.89	53.97	42.94	33.6
3. Fort Wolcott	41 30	71 20	20	29.49	30.48	37.24	46.02	55.54	64.52	70.41	69.59	63.22	54.30	43.03	34.2
4. Little Compton	41 31	71 11	..	..	..	..	..	61.44	..	67.96	..	..	..	..	..
5. Newport	41 30	71 19	25	29.93	29.40	36.14	44.51	53.88	64.70	70.14	69.52	63.43	53.55	43.27	34.1
6. Newport	41 30	71 19	25	28.59	30.50	33.58	44.44	53.25	63.80	68.61	67.79	63.39	51.27	41.26	31.0
7. North Scituate	41 50	71 34	300	24.33	25.71	34.07	42.20	56.95	66.38	68.70	63.42	60.09	47.02	39.31	26.0
8. Providence	41 50	71 24	155	25.84	27.01	34.43	45.64	55.75	63.85	70.93	69.08	61.73	50.85	40.45	29.3
9. Smithfield	41 57	71 28	..	24.2	..	30.0	44.9	52.9	63.3	67.9	68.9	61.0	50.9	38.8	29.1

SOUTH CAROLINA.

Name of Station.	Lat.	Long.	Height.	Jan.	Feb.	March.	April.	May.	June.	July.	August.	Sept.	Oct.	Nov.	Dec.
1. Abbeville[3]	34 12	82 17	500	46.41	48.92	54.89	62.61	69.99	77.55	79.43	78.67	74.31	60.95	54.33	46.5
2. Aiken	33 32	81 33	565	44.15	47.83	53.22	61.49	69.25	76.08	78.80	77.19	72.23	61.80	51.84	45.4
3. All Saints	33 40	79 17	20	45.69	49.46	53.66	62.66	70.43	76.70	79.85	79.08	74.77	64.07	55.47	49.3
4. Beaufort	32 26	80 41	14	44.44	50.17	56.57	61.05	69.78	76.98	81.97	83.05	..	66.85	57.68	50.7
5. Black Oak	33 19	80 00	..	50.56	51.50	58.66	69.76	77.63	81.57	83.40	79.41	73.77	66.33	..	51.6
6. Bluffton	32 14	80 51	..	55.98	53.08	57.25	64.20	73.35	78.90	83.33	82.33	77.30	70.80	60.30	48.2
7. Camden	34 15	80 31	240	42.71	47.28	53.37	61.73	70.60	78.32	80.64	78.99	73.56	60.94	52.28	45.4
8. Charleston	32 47	79 56	20	49.33	53.71	58.43	65.16	72.87	78.94	80.22	79.48	74.19	65.34	57.35	51.3
9. Charleston	32 47	79 56	20	50.40	51.70	58.30	65.00	72.80	78.50	81.30	80.30	76.10	67.20	59.00	51.2
10. Columbia	34 02	80 57	315	43.71	44.61	53.99	62.02	69.85	76.75	78.78	78.14	73.48	60.55	54.35	48.1
11. Edgefield	33 47	81 51	..	22.99	..	..	..	..	..	..	..	..	..	..	..
12. Edisto Island	32 34	80 18	23	38.72	49.98	53.11	65.25	71.62	79.82	..	80.79	74.48	65.55	59.61	51.0
13. Evergreen	34 22	82 46	..	47.08	45.85	52.10	65.35	..	..	..	..	..	..	..	..
14. Fort Mill	35 02	80 52	..	..	..	47.28	60.80	69.78	74.45	..	..	70.73	..	..	..
15. Fort Moultrie	32 45	79 51	25	50.28	52.40	58.19	65.21	73.26	79.44	81.94	81.30	76.92	67.77	59.50	52.6
16. Gowdysville	34 55	81 30	600	47.20	44.35	51.11	63.07	70.07	76.67	82.43	82.24	73.15	59.60	49.94	42.6
17. Greenville	34 52	82 18	..	49.0	50.4	53.9	64.8	70.8	75.1	76.2	76.6	71.3	57.6	52.0	46.5
18. Hilton Head	32 14	80 43	15	45.43	52.24	58.58	67.12	73.14	79.16	83.75	83.58	78.17	67.57	57.02	52.4
19. Morris Island	32 42	79 52	15	..	51.40	55.65	61.56	72.00	..	..	..	..	..	..	49.9
20. Mount Pleasant	32 47	79 55	20	..	57.63	54.17	..	..	..	..	..	..	..	..	..
21. Nightingale Hall	..	..	..	43.33	47.00	60.17	69.33	74.83	79.50	78.00	80.17	76.50	..	..	..
22. Orangeburg	33 30	80 48	..	50.37	52.43	57.02	63.79	71.17	77.37	82.91	81.06	74.96	63.89	56.31	51.5
23. Richmond Hill	33 38	82 00	..	..	..	..	..	..	..	82.70	..	..	..	..	..
24. Robertville	32 36	81 12	50	50.0	47.0	46.0	60.5	70.0	75.0	79.3	76.3	76.5	62.5	54.5	42.5
25. St. Johns	33 10	79 50	50	46.19	51.34	55.84	62.17	69.89	75.36	78.28	77.48	72.41	64.48	54.26	49.4
26. Wilkinson	35 00	81 27	..	38.50	38.48	52.60	57.85	68.30	..	81.58	77.45	71.72	61.12	52.77	..

[1] Observations corrected for daily variation.

[2] Corrected for daily variation by means of the New Haven table.

PENNSYLVANIA.—Continued.

	Spring.	Summer.	Autumn.	Winter.	Year.	Series. Begins. Ends.	Extent yrs. mos.	Observing hours.	Observer.	References.
119	48°.63	71°.46	53°.40	31°.63	51°.28	July, 1843; Dec. 1870	16 6	[1]	E. W. Beans, T. H. Aldrich, J. C. Green and others.	P. O. and S. I. Vol. 1, MS. in S. Coll., and S. O.
120	48.51	73.00	53.09	33.06	51.91	July, 1857; Mar. 1859	1 9	$7_m\ 2_a\ 9_a$	S. Alsop.	P. O. and S. I. Vol. 1.
121	47.94	71.00	52.34	29.41	50.17	Jan. 1856; Dec. 1870	14 10	$\odot_r$ N. $\odot_s$	E. Kohler.	P. O. and S. I. Vol. 1, and S. O.
122	48.99	68.01	50.69	30.02	49.43	Jan. 1859; July, 1862	3 6	$7_m\ 2_a\ 9_a$ bis	S. Scott.	" " " " " "
123	..	..	..	..	..	May, 1864; Feb. 1870	0 7	"	H. C. Moyer.	S. O.
124	..	..	..	..	..	1854	0 4	$7_m\ 2_a\ 9_a$	Dr. A. P. Blodget.	P. O. and S. I. Vol. 1.

RHODE ISLAND.

	Spring.	Summer.	Autumn.	Winter.	Year.	Series. Begins. Ends.	Extent yrs. mos.	Observing hours.	Observer.	References.
1	..	..	..	..	..	1856	0 4	$7_m\ 2_a\ 9_a$	E. G. Arnold.	P. O. and S. I. Vol. 1.
2	45.61	69.90	53.60	31.46	50.14	Jan. 1842; Dec. 1870	19 2	"	Assistant Surgeon.	Ar. Met. Regs. 1855 and 1860, and MS. from S. G. O.
3	46.27	68.17	53.52	31.42	49.84	Jan. 1822; Dec. 1835	14 0	"	" "	Ar. Met. Reg. 1855.
4	..	..	..	..	..	1849; 1850	0 2	$\odot_r\ 9_m\ 3_a\ 9_a$	Bailey.	S. Coll.
5	44.84	68.12	53.42	31.16	49.39	1817; 1856	40 0	......	Taylor.	Printed Journal.
6	43.76	66.73	51.97	30.03	48.12	Sept. 1865; Dec. 1870	5 4	$7_m\ 2_a\ 9_a$ bis	W. H. Crandall, W. A. Barber.	S. O.
7	44.41	66.17	48.81	25.35	46.18	Jan. 1853; June, 1854	1 6	$7_m\ 2_a\ 9_a$	H. C. Sheldon.	P. O. and S. I. Vol. 1, & S. Coll.
8	45.27	67.95	51.01	27.41	47.91	Dec. 1831; Apr. 1867	34 8	[2]	A. Caswell, H. C. Sheldon.	Sm. Cont. to Knowl. 1860, and S. O.
9	42.60	66.70	50.23	..	..	July, 1806; Oct. 1807	1 2	$\odot_r\ 2_a$	....	Med. and Agr. Reg. Boston, 1806–7.

SOUTH CAROLINA.

	Spring.	Summer.	Autumn.	Winter.	Year.	Series. Begins. Ends.	Extent yrs. mos.	Observing hours.	Observer.	References.
1	62.50	78.55	63.20	47.29	62.88	July, 1838; 1851	2 10	[4]	Th. Parker, & Barratt.	Am. Alm. 1840 and S. Coll.
2	61.32	77.36	61.95	45.82	61.61	Jan. 1853; Dec. 1860	8 8	$7_m\ 2_a\ 9_a$ bis	H. W. Ravenal, J. H. Cornish, & Newton.	P. O. and S. I. Vol. 1, S. Coll., S. O. and MS. from S. G. O.
3	62.25	78.54	64.77	48.16	63.43	Oct. 1854; Apr. 1861	6 5	$7_m\ 2_a\ 9_a$	Rev. A. Glennie.	P. O. and S. I. Vol. 1, and S. O.
4	62.47	80.67	..	48.47	..	July, 1863; Mar. 1865	1 5	$7_m\ 2_a\ 9_a$ bis	Dr. M. M. Marsh.	S. O.
5	68.68	81.46	..	51.25	..	1844; 1845	1 8	7_m N. $4_a\ 6_a\ 9_a$	Ferguson.	Manuscript.
6	64.93	81.52	69.47	52.44	67.09	1870	1 0	$7_m\ 2_a\ 9_a$ bis	J. S. J. Guerard.	S. O.
7	61.90	79.32	62.26	45.16	62.16	Jan. 1838; Apr. 1869	9 9	$7_m\ 2_a\ 9_a$	Dr. M. Holbrook, C. McRae, T. Carpenter, J. A. Young.	Am. Alm. 1840, S. O., P. O. and S. I. Vol. 1, and S. Coll.
8	65.49	79.55	65.63	51.46	65.53	Jan. 1738; Oct. 1861	24 8	[4]	Drs. J. L. Dawson, Lining, Chalmers, and Johnson, and John Ryan.	Am. Alm. 1842 and foll., Print. slips, P. O. and S. I. Vol. 1, Phil. Trans., 1748, MS. in Coll., and S. O.
9	65.37	80.03	67.43	51.10	65.98	....	20 0	......	....	Pat. Off. Rep.
10	61.95	77.89	62.79	45.48	62.03	Feb. 1836; Nov. 1859	4 11	$7_m\ 2_a\ 9_a$	Dr. E. H. Barton and others.	P. O. and S. I. Vol. 1, Rep. Brit. Assoc. 1847, Printed Journ. Pat. Off. Rep.
11	..	..	..	..	..	1857	0 1	$\odot_r\ \odot_s$	....	P. O. and S. I. Vol. 1.
12	63.33	..	66.55	46.57	..	Feb. 1856; Jan. 1857	0 11	$7_m\ 2_a\ 9_a$	E. A. and Dr. E. N. Fuller.	" " " "
13	..	..	..	..	..	1870	0 4	$7_m\ 2_a\ 9_a$ bis	E. J. Earle.	S. O.
14	59.29	..	..	..	..	Sept. 1869; June, 1870	0 5	"	R. A. Spring, Jr.	" "
15	65.55	80.89	68.06	51.78	66.57	Jan. 1823; Dec. 1860	32 11	$7_m\ 2_a\ 9_a$	Assistant Surgeon.	Ar. Met. Regs. 1855 and 1860.
16	61.42	80.45	60.90	44.74	61.88	Mar. 1869; Dec. 1870	1 9	$7_m\ 2_a\ 9_a$ bis	C. Petty.	S. O.
17	63.17	75.97	60.30	48.63	62.02	Mar. 1839; Nov. 1845	2 2	$\odot_r$ max. $\odot_s$	Major E. Earle.	MS. in S. Coll.
18	66.28	82.16	67.59	50.04	66.52	Apr. 1862; June, 1865	3 11	$7_m\ 2_a\ 9_a$	Capt. J. R. Suter, & Maj. J. W. Albert.	MS. from S. G. O., and S. O.
19	63.07	..	..	..	..	Dec. 1863; May, 1864	0 5	"	....	MS. from S. G. O.
20	..	..	..	..	..	1857	0 2	$8_m\ 2_a\ 9_a$	Dr. E. N. Fuller.	P. O. and S. I. Vol. 1.
21	68.11	79.22	..	..	..	1849	0 9	$\odot_r\ 2_a\ \odot_s$	Kelly.	Pat. Off. Rep.
22	63.99	80.45	65.05	51.46	65.24	Aug. 1849; Mar. 1851	1 8	$\odot_r\ 9_m\ 3_a\ 9_a$	Elliott.	S. Coll.
23	..	..	..	..	..	1854	0 1	$7_m\ 2_a\ 9_a$	....	" "
24	58.83	76.87	64.50	46.50	61.68	1843	1 0	max. & min.	Smith.	Newspaper slip in S. Coll.
25	62.63	77.04	63.72	49.00	63.10	Mar. 1846; Mar. 1861	13 11	$\odot_r\ 2_a\ 9_a$	W. H. and T. P. Ravenal.	Black Oak Agr. Soc., Printed Journ., Pamph. in S. Coll., P. O. & S. I. Vol. 1, and S. O.
26	59.58	..	61.87	..	..	Sept. 1867; Nov. 1868	1 1	$7_m\ 2_a\ 9_a$ bis	C. Petty.	S. O.

[3] Observations after 1839 were made at Barratsville, about three miles southwest of Abbeville.

[4] Observations corrected for daily variation by means of the general table.

TENNESSEE.

Name of Station.	Lat.	Long.	Height.	Jan.	Feb.	March.	April.	May.	June.	July.	August.	Sept.	Oct.	Nov.	Dec.
1. Alexandria	36°06′	86°06′	..	29°.87	..	..	..	..	..	..	..	..	..	44°.72	35°.91
2. Austin[1]	36 12	86 20	2000	36.60	42°.82	49°.59	57°.23	67°.22	75°.04	78°.07	76°.52	69°.55	60°.09	44.73	39.69
3. Chattanooga	35 02	85 21	..	.	..	..	57.65	..	..	..	..	..	..	..	..
4. Clearmont	35 44	86 02	1000	..	..	..	..	..	70.43	75.78	75.03	68.23	58.30	47.15	36.28
5. Dixon's Springs	36 20	86 08	..	34.68	40.91	49.44	58.13	67.98	76.75	79.90	73.62	69.59	62.84	44.46	44.08
6. Dover	36 29	87 55	..	39.03	41.08	48.76	57.38	64.48	70.25	74.42	73.41	66.65	55.76	47.54	42.09
7. Elisabethton	36 18	82 12	1500	38.52	38.93	45.37	55.23	62.90	70.47	75.80	74.84	66.97	54.20	42.02	34.27
8. Fayetteville	35 12	86 38	..	44.40	45.24	56.59	61.19	68.64	76.76	78.51	79.45	70.21	57.96	50.74	42.66
9. Franklin	35 55	86 53	..	..	..	..	..	..	..	77.08	76.88	74.90	60.65	50.47	45.82
10. Fort Humboldt	35 51	88 56	..	..	..	..	60.99	73.87	77.52	83.66	81.77	77.63	62.92	50.30	37.16
11. Friendship	35 50	89 25	..	..	..	..	70.13	68.90	72.49	78.17	..	..	..	..	..
12. Gallatin	36 21	86 30	..	47.0	48.0	46.0	60.0	67.0	75.0	76.0	75.0	71.0	..	54.0	..
13. Glenwood Cottage	36 28	87 20	481	36.44	40.63	47.36	57.17	64.59	71.67	75.87	74.29	68.70	56.11	46.68	38.83
14. Greenville (Tusculum Coll.)	36 05	82 50	..	36.10	39.97	43.80	55.52	63.53	71.55	76.76	74.82	66.79	..	42.98	35.38
15. Knoxville East Tennessee University	35 56	83 56	1000	36.90	40.79	46.93	56.92	63.56	71.20	77.67	75.33	74.31	56.93	44.63	35.76
16. La Grange	35 08	89 15	480	40.92	48.20	54.97	60.69	71.10	76.28	82.44	79.40	74.39	63.77	50.33	37.50
17. Lookout Mountain	35 00	85 27	1626	40.69	43.76	47.95	58.24	66.53	74.41	79.46	78.00	70.81	59.15	49.23	38.86
18. Memphis	35 08	90 04	262	40.19	44.75	52.72	59.89	69.97	77.40	81.39	79.79	71.75	59.14	50.06	41.41
19. Nashville	36 09	86 49	533	37.66	42.22	49.77	61.81	67.96	73.18	79.26	76.53	69.61	57.31	45.35	39.12
20. Nashville	36 09	86 49	533	35.63	38.74	50.27	56.14	66.77	75.79	77.63	78.97	70.19	..	49.80	39.94
21. Pomona	36 00	85 00	2200	36.03	40.45	45.98	59.08	65.93	71.65	78.15	74.33	66.38	55.22	45.91	34.83
22. Trenton	35 57	89 02	..	43.95	45.23	47.65	60.63	68.49	74.09	79.65	79.31	71.69	58.29	46.27	41.88
23. University Place	35 12	86 00	2000	39.02	42.17	47.91	61.33	67.18	72.33	78.58	73.23	66.53	55.95	43.35	36.18
24. Walnut Grove	36 00	82 53	1350	..	..	..	..	..	..	80.66	72.86	..	..	43.40	..
25. Winchester	35 12	86 15	..	38.98	41.60	..	..	..	..	..	..	..	..	..	37.90

TEXAS.

Name of Station.	Lat.	Long.	Height.	Jan.	Feb.	March.	April.	May.	June.	July.	August.	Sept.	Oct.	Nov.	Dec.
1. Anahuac	29 47	94 54	..	..	..	60.35	69.12	74.97	80.37	84.65	80.60	78.80	..	..	..
2. Aransas Canal	27 47	97 08	[2]	..	..	..	..	..	..	..	..	..	..	62.00	..
3. Austin	30 17	97 44	650	49.46	54.10	60.14	67.31	74.05	79.71	82.61	82.72	76.83	66.22	57.59	49.92
4. Blue Branch[3]	30 27	97 26	600	52.53	54.06	59.51	65.17	71.81	78.03	79.86	81.50	76.22	65.53	62.70	46.73
5. Bluff Settlement	30 00	97 00	180	..	..	..	..	..	80.68	82.17	82.49	80.31	71.52	61.87	48.98
6. Bonham	33 40	96 13	435	..	..	..	..	..	..	..	..	..	63.01	60.08	35.48
7. Buffalo Springs	33 30	98 14	1800	39.48	48.68	..	..	..	..	..	..	..	..	55.70	54.14
8. Burkeville	31 00	93 38	..	47.49	50.98	56.98	66.32	73.35	82.90	86.10	79.33	75.63	62.40	54.68	43.87
9. Camp Colorado	31 55	99 17	..	42.98	52.05	59.25	64.75	74.53	82.81	86.31	83.28	75.25	65.40	52.21	44.09
10. Camp Concordia	31 46	106 21	3600	47.04	50.95	61.92	67.45	71.97	86.81	83.09	80.30	78.67	69.26	57.04	49.96
11. Camp Cooper	31 01	99 00	..	..	51.14	56.11	55.59	74.74	83.39	87.10	81.53	74.27	62.77	..	..
12. Camp Hudson	29 42	101 10	..	49.34	56.75	64.36	71.34	79.30	83.98	87.23	84.36	78.51	71.18	57.32	49.39
13. Camp Moore	..	..	..	46.00	48.70	62.13	64.05	70.61	..	..	..	..	..	..	..
14. Camp Stockton	30 20	102 30	..	46.54	51.43	59.44	68.20	79.81	82.51	84.33	80.75	74.69	65.15	56.07	44.07
15. Camp Verde	30 00	99 10	1400	47.39	52.72	58.43	64.45	73.70	82.00	82.07	81.20	72.71	66.60	53.99	46.09
16. Cedar Grove Plantation	29 08	95 42	60	53.09	54.78	62.90	69.58	74.77	80.21	81.84	81.10	78.33	70.11	59.19	58.11
17. Chapel Hill	30 10	96 20	542	53.38	63.23	..	..	74.38	78.73	80.23	78.95	..	..	..	..
18. Clarkeville	33 35	95 02	..	..	..	..	..	..	78.74	83.98	82.24	78.97	69.67	59.74	45.40
19. Clinton	29 04	97 23	..	54.81	57.23	61.35	67.64	75.11	80 64	81.49	81.60	77.44	67.39	63.78	49.69
20. Corpus Christi	27 47	97 27	20	50.05	55.11	64.75	69.87	77.92	82.00	82.46	83.11	81.20	72.36	65.42	56.93
21. Cross Roads	30 33	97 46	672	..	53.45	62.03	70.55	75.53	85.55	89.60	..	78.63	70.33	57.11	41.61
22. Dallas[4]	32 44	96 45	..	42.02	53.34	60.24	62.22	72.72	75.01	80.55	81.03	79.04	67.46	58.37	43.78

[1] The observations previous to 1861 were made at Cumberland University at Lebanon, very near Austin.

[2] Altitude given as 15 feet above the Gulf.

TENNESSEE.

	Spring.	Summer.	Autumn.	Winter.	Year.	Series. Begins. Ends.	Extent yrs. mos.	Observing hours.	Observer.	References.
1	..	..	..	..	..	1851; 1852	0 3	$\odot_r\ 9_m\ 3_a\ 9_a$	Sawyer.	S. Coll.
2	58°.01	76°.54	58°.12	39°.70	58°.09	1850; Oct. 1870	6 0	$7_m\ 2_a\ 9_{a\ bis}$	Prof. A. P. Stewart and others.	P. O. and S. I. Vol. 1, S. O., & S. Coll.
3	..	..	..	..	..	1864	0 1	"	G. H. Blaker.	S. O.
4	..	73.75	57.89	..	..	1870	0 7	"	T. P. Wright.	" "
5	58.52	76.76	58.96	39.89	58.53	Feb. 1852; Jan. 1853	1 0	$\odot_r\ 9_m\ 3_a\ 9_a$	Sawyer.	S. Coll.
6	56.87	72.69	56.65	40.73	56.74	1846; 1850	4 5	"	Favel.	Manuscript.
7	54.50	73.70	54.40	37.24	54.96	Jan. 1868; Dec. 1870	3 0	$7_m\ 2_a\ 9_{a\ bis}$	C. H. Lewis.	S. O.
8	62.14	78.24	59.64	44.10	61.03	Mar. 1849; Feb. 1851	2 0	$\odot_r\ 9_m\ 3_a\ 9_a$	McWelly.	S. Coll.
9	..	..	62.01	..	..	1867	0 6	$7_m\ 2_a\ 9_{a\ bis}$	J. M. Parker.	S. O.
10	..	80.98	63.62	..	..	1870	0 9	$7_m\ 2_a\ 9_a$	....	MS. from S. G. O.
11	..	..	..	..	..	1855	0 4	"	Dr. R. T. Turner.	P. O. and S. I. Vol. 1.
12	57.67	75.33	..	..	..	1819	0 10	"	....	Rep. Brit. Asso. 1847.
13	56.37	73.94	57.16	38.63	56.53	Mar. 1851; Dec. 1870	19 8	$7_m\ 2_a\ 9_{a\ bis}$	Prof. W. M. Stewart.	P. O. and S. I. Vol. 1, S. O., and S. Coll.
14	54.28	74.38	..	37.15	..	July, 1843; Dec. 1870	2 4	"	S. S. & W. S. Doak.	S. O. and Manuscript.
15	55.80	74.73	58.62	37.82	56.74	1843; Dec. 1870	6 4	"	Prof. G. Cooke and others.	P. O. and S. I. Vol. 1, S. O., S. Coll., and MS.
16	62.25	79.37	62.83	42.21	61.66	Apr. 1858; Dec. 1870	1 1	"	J. R. Blake, and Dr. W. E. Franklin.	P. O. and S. I. Vol. 1, and S. O.
17	57.57	77.29	59.73	41.10	58.92	June, 1866; Dec. 1870	4 5	"	E. F. Williams & Rev. C. F. P. Bancroft.	S. O.
18	60.86	79.53	60.32	42.12	60.71	1849; Mar. 1870	11 3	"	Various observers.	Met. Rep. Memphis, 1857, P. O. and S. I. Vol. 1, S. O., and S. Coll.
19	59.85	76.32	57.42	39.67	58.32	Jan. 1834; Dec. 1844	6 7	......	Prof. J. Hamilton.	Am. Alm. 1836 and foll.
20	57.73	77.46	..	38.10	..	1849; Feb. 1868	2 2	$\odot_r\ 9_m\ 3_a\ 9_a$	Rothrock, F. H. French, and Dr. J. W. Parker.	S. O. and S. Coll.
21	57.00	74.71	55.84	37.10	56.16	Oct. 1859; May, 1861	1 7	$7_m\ 2_a\ 9_{a\ bis}$	J. W. Dodge and son.	P. O. and S. I. Vol. 1, and S. O.
22	58.92	77.68	58.75	43.69	59.76	Feb. 1869; Oct. 1870	1 9	"	W. T. Grigsby.	S. O.
23	58.81	74.71	55.28	39.12	56.98	Dec. 1859; Mar. 1861	1 4	"	C. R. Barney.	P. O. and S. I. Vol. 1, and S. O.
24	..	..	..	[illegible]	[illegible]	1856	[illegible]	$7_m\ 2_a\ 9_a$	J. B. [illegible]	P. O. and S. I. Vol. 1.
25	..	..	..	39.49	..	Dec. 1859; Feb. 1860	0 3	$7_m\ 2_a\ 9_{a\ bis}$	S. W. Houghton.	P. O. and S. I. Vol. 1. and S. O.

TEXAS.

	Spring.	Summer.	Autumn.	Winter.	Year.	Series. Begins. Ends.	Extent yrs. mos.	Observing hours.	Observer.	References.
1	68.15	81.87	..	..	..	1831	0 7	......	....	Dove.
2	..	..	..	..	..	1860	0 1	$7_m\ 2_a\ 9_{a\ bis}$	F. Koler.	S. O.
3	67.17	81.68	66.88	51.16	66.72	1852; Dec. 1870	19 0	"	J. Van Nostrand, Dr. S. V. Jennings, and S. Palm.	MS. from S. G. O., S. Coll., P. O. & S. I. Vol. 1, & S. O.
4	65.50	79.80	68.15	51.11	66.14	Jan. 1869; Dec. 1870	2 0	"	F. H. Wade, and W. H. Good.	S. O.
5	..	81.78*	71.23	..	..	1870	0 7	"	J. Fietsam.	" "
6	..	..	..	..	..	1859	0 3	$7_m\ 2_a\ 9_a$	Prof. J. Sias.	P. O. and S. I. Vol. 1.
7	..	..	..	47.43	..	Nov. 1867; Feb. 1868	0 4	"	....	MS. from S. G. O.
8	65.55	82.78	64.24	47.45	65.00	Nov. 1859; Apr. 1861	1 6	$7_m\ 2_a\ 9_{a\ bis}$	Dr. N. P. West.	P. O. and S. I. Vol. 1, and S. O.
9	66.18	84.13	64.29	46.37	65.24	Nov. 1856; Jan. 1861	4 2	$7_m\ 2_a\ 9_a$	Assistant Surgeon.	Ar. Met. Reg. 1860, and MS. from S. G. O.
10	67.11	83.40	68.32	49.32	67.04	Apr. 1868; Mar. 1869	1 0	"	....	MS. from S. G. O.
11	62.15	84.01	..	..	..	Feb. 1857; Oct. 1859	1 2	"	Assistant Surgeon.	Ar. Met. Reg. 1860.
12	71.67	85.19	69.00	51.83	69.42	May, 1858; Dec. 1861	2 10	"	" "	Ar. Met. Reg. 1860, and MS. from S. G. O.
13	65.60	..	..	..	..	1857	0 5	"	" "	Ar. Met. Reg. 1860.
14	69.15	82.53	65.30	47.35	66.08	Jan. 1860; Dec. 1870	2 3	"	" "	Ar. Met. Reg. 1860 and MS. from S. G. O.
15	65.53	81.76	64.43	48.73	65.11	Nov. 1856; Feb. 1869	4 4	"	" "	" " " "
16	69.08	81.05	69.21	55.33	68.67	Mar. 1867; May, 1869	2 2	$7_m\ 2_a\ 9_{a\ bis}$	H. Stevens, and J. B. Boshwick.	S. O.
17	..	79.30	..	..	..	May, 1866; Feb. 1867	0 6	"	Dr. W. Gantt.	" "
18	..	81.65	69.46	..	..	1870	0 7	"	J. Anderson.	" "
19	68.03	81.24	69.54	53.91	68.18	Jan. 1869; Dec. 1870	1 10	"	Dr. A. C. White.	" "
20	70.85	82.52	72.99	54.03	70.10	Nov. 1845; Mar. 1856	3 5	$\odot_r\ 9_m\ 3_a\ 9_a$	Assistant Surgeon.	Ar. Met. Regs. 1855 and 1860.
21	69.37	..	68.69	..	..	Nov. 1859; Nov. 1860	0 11	$7_m\ 2_a\ 9_{a\ bis}$	F. S. Wade.	P. O. and S. I. Vol. 1, and S. O.
22	65.06	78.86	68.29	46.38	64.65	July, 1851; Dec. 1859	1 5	$\odot_r$ N. $\odot_s$	J. M. Crockett, W. A. Ferris.	P. O. and S. I. Vol. 1, and MS. in S. Coll.

[3] Also called Mine Creek and Sandy Fly.

[4] The observations, except for October, November, and December, 1859, were made at Ferris Plantation, about five miles east of Dallas.

TEXAS.—Continued.

Name of Station.	Lat.	Long.	Height.	Jan.	Feb.	March.	April.	May.	June.	July.	August.	Sept.	Oct.	Nov.	Dec.
23. Fort Belknap	33°08′	98°46′	1600	40°.29	47°.79	56°.13	65°.67	72°.45	80°.27	85°.18	84°.42	78°.45	66°.64	50°.78	43°.73
24. Fort Bliss[1]	31 47	106 30	3830	44.22	49.52	57.64	64.75	74.48	81.46	83.03	80.49	74.93	65.09	54.55	52.10
25. Fort Brown	25 50	97 37	50	60.08	63.89	68.66	74.62	79.99	83.17	84.74	84.53	80.83	74.43	68.79	61.98
26. Fort Chadbourne	31 58	100 15	2120	41.94	48.57	57.05	64.56	71.86	78.62	82.83	81.23	73.78	63.52	51.86	43.95
27. Fort Clark	29 17	100 25	1000	49.56	54.94	62.82	70.53	77.51	81.73	83.89	83.70	78.32	69.51	60.43	51.33
28. Fort Croghan	30 40	98 25	1000	49.29	52.21	60.38	65.66	71.54	78.34	81.06	82.56	77.53	67.30	56.10	46.89
29. Fort Davis	30 40	104 07	4700	43.99	49.63	56.87	65.64	73.69	76.25	75.71	75.01	69.69	61.34	53.40	44.50
30. Fort Duncan	28 39	100 30	1460	51.96	58.65	66.08	75.78	81.36	85.76	86.66	87.02	81.68	73.05	61.60	53.47
31. Fort Ewell	28 10	99 00	200	52.92	57.56	67.10	74.06	78.42	82.70	84.37	83.84	80.57	72.44	64.77	56.89
32. Fort Gates	31 26	97 52	1000	48.80	50.90	59.18	63.67	71.53	78.94	82.92	85.10	79.18	67.25	56.97	45.81
33. Fort Graham	32 00	97 21	900	47.95	52.14	58.09	64.06	72.59	79.45	83.14	84.70	77.46	67.64	55.49	46.48
34. Fort Griffin	..	..	..	42.27	48.09	50.33	64.58	73.32	77.23	82.89	83.72	76.10	..	58.03	38.19
35. Fort Houston	31 42	95 44	..	65.20	60.50	68.70	72.70	85.50	80.10	84.20	81.40	83.50	72.30	62.30	60.00
36. Fort Inge	29 10	99 50	845	50.41	57.93	63.32	69.49	77.61	82.09	84.32	84.33	79.75	68.93	59.15	51.42
37. Fort Lancaster	30 46	101 48	2350	44.84	53.57	60.99	66.54	75.77	82.64	85.12	83.61	76.28	66.17	52.52	44.94
38. Fort Lincoln	29 22	99 35	900	51.77	59.02	63.32	66.81	73.23	78.33	82.27	82.52	79.76	70.00	55.64	53.79
39. Fort McIntosh	27 35	99 48	806	54.82	61.33	69.18	76.46	82.50	84.99	86.97	87.50	82.73	73.82	64.74	55.61
40. Fort McKavett	30 48	100 08	2060	44.63	50.31	57.68	66.09	73.23	77.24	80.34	80.16	73.78	65.41	53.26	47.11
41. Fort Martin Scott	30 10	99 05	1300	46.18	52.45	57.61	62.48	68.50	75.48	77.26	78.14	72.95	62.04	52.41	43.10
42. Fort Mason	30 40	99 15	1200	48.05	54.65	59.06	68.62	75.20	80.47	83.61	82.75	75.97	67.74	55.67	49.89
43. Fort Merrill	28 10	98 00	150	55.02	57.31	68.96	73.65	80.39	82.78	83.39	84.52	80.68	73.26	63.67	57.18
44. Fort Polk	26 00	97 30	15	66.74	..	..	..	..	..	81.25	81.11	81.01	74.36	72.24	62.21
45. Fort Quitmann	30 45	105 00	3710	40.20	47.75	56.23	61.03	73.93	83.35	82.02	80.88	74.75	63.96	52.69	38.58
46. Fort Richardson	33 15	98 01	..	46.44	51.12	56.03	66.24	73.70	81.73	84.53	81.17	75.33	63.14	54.68	42.49
47. Fort Terrett	30 20	100 11	1320	44.43	45.98	56.91	66.35	72.83	75.96	78.21	78.77	73.35	65.09	56.23	49.59
48. Fort Worth	32 42	97 18	1100	45.58	48.78	56.30	62.56	70.48	77 44	80.99	82.87	76.54	66.22	53.36	43.38
49. Galveston	29 18	94 47	30	51.55	56.36	63.93	68.55	75.56	81.92	84.42	84.86	79.94	70.72	62.11	52.62
50. Gilmer (3 miles west of)	32 40	94 59	950	45.84	50.97	59.34	65.97	72.37	80.01	83.30	82.34	75.73	63.56	56.26	46.95
51. Goliad	28 35	97 30	50	58.64	58.83	63.57	69.82	77.66	79.96	83.33	84.42	79.76	68.97	60.49	58.58
52. Gonzales	29 32	97 32	150	59.2	58.0	67.8	68.8	78.1	80.6	84.4	84.0	82.4	75.1	65.6	56.7
53. Helena	28 58	97 56	600	48.94	63.47	65.78	..	..	..	..	..	..	..	..	..
54. Houston	29 44	95 28	..	53.69	55.19	63.74	68.64	73.62	78.61	79.58	76.18	73.35	69.98	64.34	50.23
55. Huntsville	30 41	95 40	..	54.64	58.76	65.06	65.67	73.34	82.85	82.23	84.38	79.04	69.03	60.64	54.11
56. Indianola	28 32	96 31	..	..	..	..	..	..	..	85.26	85.75	82.46	..	..	..
57. Jefferson	32 44	94 20	..	62.28	56.65	55.27	66.91	76.42	79.71	84.12	82.56	76.96	63.65	53.49	44.32
58. Larissa	32 01	95 19	755	51.07	52.92	60.15	65.28	73.84	80.39	83.06	84.21	76.56	67.35	56.01	45.38
59. Lavaca	28 37	96 37	17	53.08	56.55	60.93	66.53	74.79	80.25	82.39	83.34	77.08	65.54	66.23	51.38
60. Lockhart	29 55	97 44	..	51.78	55.80	59.58	67.98	75.58	82.10	82.03	81.82	..	..	..	..
61. New Braunfels[3]	29 42	98 15	720	48.50	55.24	63.02	69.34	78.06	82.78	84.90	86.24	79.53	69.38	58.96	50.86
62. Northern tier of counties	..	..	..	..	51.45	58.27	59.27	72.50	78.24	80.92	..	..	..	..	..
63. Oakland	29 35	97 00	..	..	..	..	69.96	76.07	79.85	82.59	81.69	80.37	71.39	63.12	49.58
64. Palestine	31 45	95 40	480	50.73	54.20	57.73	67.55	75.25	..	..	..	..	67.50	63.38	47.42
65. Pine Oak	30 00	97 09	..	38.59	49.46	57.13	70.01	71.83	79.28	81.57	84.22	75.39	66.59	55.66	49.32
66. Plantation Hill[4]	32 20	99 45	1100	42.93	49.31	58.02	66.39	71.93	76.47	80.73	81.50	74.43	63.59	53.26	46.26
67. Ringgold Barracks	26 25	99 00	521	57.25	63.59	70.04	76.56	82.07	85.95	86.42	86.35	82.01	75.00	66.04	58.94
68. Round Top	30 03	96 44	..	52.68	58.13	63.04	69.13	76.97	83.81	86.74	85.05	78.91	68.41	60.91	47.70
69. San Antonio	29 25	98 25	600	49.76	57.39	63.51	70.03	77.90	82.07	84.47	84.64	80.19	73.06	61.44	51.07
70. Sisterdale	29 59	98 43	1000	45.07	57.25	59.86	66.69	77.65	83.52	84.91	86.05	76.32	63.06	58.95	39.00
71. Turner's Point	32 30	96 08	..	..	53.33	..	..	..	..	..	..	..	..	..	..
72. Union Hill[5]	30 14	96 31	540	49.99	56.41	59.77	65.27	71.93	77.11	81.20	80.61	77.43	69.49	56.71	47.86
73. Waco	31 35	97 08	..	45.86	50.01	60.79	65.55	73.63	82.58	84.87	83.24	77.89	63.30	54.35	52.58
74. Washington	30 19	96 15	..	49.62	57.50	62.26	64.36	75.64	80.20	82.72	84.02	77.90	69.23	60.71	48.27
75. Webberville (Parson's Sem.)	30 14	97 34	394	..	59.56	64.88	69.89	79.60	83.18	84.58	85.81	78.65	66.44	..	..

[1] The observations in 1865, except for December, were made at Franklin, about two miles northwest of Fort Bliss.

[2] Observations corrected for daily variation by means of the general table.

TEXAS.—Continued.

	Spring.	Summer.	Autumn.	Winter.	Year.	Series. Begins.	Series. Ends.	Extent yrs.	Extent mos.	Observing hours.	Observer.	References.
23	64°.75	83°.29	65°.29	43°.94	64°.32	July, 1851;	Dec. 1858	7	1	$7_m\ 2_a\ 9_a$	Assistant Surgeon.	Ar. Met. Regs. 1855 and 1860.
24	65.62	81.66	64.86	48.61	65.19	July, 1854;	Dec. 1870	10	4	"	" "	Ar. Met. Reg. 1860, MS. from S. G. O.
25	74.42	84.15	74.68	61.98	73.81	Nov. 1846;	Dec. 1870	13	5	"	" "	Ar. Met. Regs. 1855 and 1860, and MS. from S. G. O.
26	64.49	80.89	63.05	44.82	63.31	May, 1852;	Mar. 1861	8	10	"	" "	" " " "
27	70.29	83.11	69.42	51.94	68.69	Aug. 1852;	Dec. 1870	10	1	"	" "	" " " "
28	65.86	80.65	66.98	49.46	65.74	June, 1849;	Aug. 1853	4	3	$\odot_r\ 9_m\ 3_a\ 9_a$	" "	Ar. Met. Reg. 1855.
29	65.40	75.66	61.48	46.04	62.14	Nov. 1854;	Dec. 1870	7	10	$7_m\ 2_a\ 9_a$	" "	Ar. Met. Reg. 1860 & MS. from S. G. O.
30	74.41	86.48	72.11	54.69	71.92	Oct. 1849;	Mar. 1861	10	5	"	" "	Ar. Met. Regs. 1855 and 1860, and MS. from S. G. O.
31	73.19	83.64	72.59	55.79	71.30	Sept. 1852;	Sept. 1854	2	1	$\odot_r\ 9_m\ 3_a\ 9_a$	" "	Ar. Met. Reg. 1855.
32	64.79	82.32	67.80	48.50	65.85	Oct. 1849;	Jan. 1852	2	4	"	" "	" " "
33	64.91	82.43	66.86	48.86	65.77	Mar. 1850;	Aug. 1853	3	6	"	" "	" " "
34	62.74	81.28	..	42.85	..	Aug. 1869;	Dec. 1870	1	2	$7_m\ 2_a\ 9_a$	....	MS. from S. G. O.
35	75.63	81.90	72.70	61.90	73.03	1842		1	0	......	....	Rep. Brit. Assoc. 1847.
36	70.14	83.58	69.28	53.25	69.06	Sept. 1849;	Jan. 1868	7	9	$7_m\ 2_a\ 9_a$	Assistant Surgeon.	Ar. Met. Regs. 1855 and 1860, and MS. from S. G. O.
37	67.77	83.79	64.99	47.78	66.08	May, 1856;	Feb. 1861	4	10	"	" "	Ar. Met. Reg. 1860, and MS. from S. G. O.
38	67.79	81.04	68.47	54.86	68.04	Aug. 1849;	July, 1852	2	3	"	" "	Ar. Met. Reg. 1855.
39	76.05	86.49	73.76	57.25	73.39	July, 1849;	Dec. 1870	10	10	"	" "	Ar. Met. Regs. 1855 and 1860, and MS. from S. G. O.
40	65.67	79.25	64.15	47.35	64.10	Apr. 1852;	Aug. 1870	7	5	"	" "	" " " "
41	62.86	76.96	62.47	47.24	62.38	Aug. 1849;	Mar. 1852	2	7	$\odot_r\ 9_m\ 3_a\ 9_a$	" "	Ar. Met. Reg. 1855.
42	67.63	82.28	66.46	50.86	66.81	Apr. 1852;	Feb. 1861	5	9	$7_m\ 2_a\ 9_a$	" "	Ar. Met. Regs. 1855 and 1860, and MS. from S. G. O.
43	74.33	83.56	72.54	56.50	71.73	Apr. 1851;	Nov. 1855	3	5	"	" "	Ar. Met. Reg. 1855 and 1860.
44	..	..	..	75.87	..	July, 1849;	Jan. 1850	0	7	$\odot_r\ 9_m\ 3_a\ 9_a$	" "	Ar. Met. Reg. 1855.
45	63.73	82.08	63.80	42.18	62.95	Jan. 1859;	Dec. 1870	3	1	$7_m\ 2_a\ 9_a$	" "	Ar. Met. Reg. 1860, and MS. from S. G. O.
46	65.32	82.48	64.38	46.68	64.72	Apr. 1868;	June, 1870	2	3	"	....	MS. from S. G. O.
47	[illegible]	[illegible]	[illegible]	[illegible]	[illegible]	[illegible]	[illegible]	1	[illegible]	$\odot_r\ 9_m\ 3_a\ 9_a$	Assistant Surgeon.	Ar. Met. Reg. 1855.
48	63.11	80.43	65.37	45.91	63.71	Nov. 1849;	Aug. 1853	3	10	"	" "	" " "
49	69.35	83.73	70.92	53.51	69.38	Sept. 1851;	Apr. 1870	3	1	[5]	U. S. Coast Survey.	MS. from S. G. O. & MS. in S. Coll.
50	65.89	81.88	65.18	47.92	65.22	July, 1859;	Dec. 1870	5	0	$7_m\ 2_a\ 9_a$ bis	J. M. Glasco.	P. O. and S. I. Vol. 1, and S. O.
51	70.35	82.57	69.74	58.68	70.34	Dec. 1832;	Dec. 1858	2	2	$7_m\ 2_a\ 9_a$	J. C. Brightman.	P. O. and S. I. Vol. 1, & MS.
52	71.57	83.00	74.37	57.97	71.73	Feb. 1848;	June, 1850	2	4	max. & min.	C. D. Bennett.	MS. in S. Coll.
53	..	..	..	..	..	1857		0	3	$7_m\ 2_a\ 9_a$	J. C. Brightman.	P. O. and S. I. Vol. 1.
54	68.67	78.12	69.22	53.04	67.26	May, 1867;	Dec. 1870	2	2	$7_m\ 2_a\ 9_a$ bis	Miss E. Baxter.	S. O.
55	68.02	83.15	69.57	55.84	69.15	1849;	Mar. 1854	2	5	$\odot_r$ N. $\odot_s$	T. Gibbs and Browne.	P. O. and S. I. Vol. 1, & S. Coll.
56	..	..	..	..	..	1868		0	3	$7_m\ 2_a\ 9_a$	....	MS. from S. G. O.
57	66.20	82.13	64.70	54.42	66.86	July, 1869;	Dec. 1870	1	6	"	....	" " "
58	66.42	82.55	66.64	49.79	66.35	Jan. 1858;	Dec. 1859	2	0	"	F. L. Yoakum.	P. O. and S. I. Vol. 1.
59	67.42	81.99	69.62	53.67	68.17	Feb. 1869;	Aug. 1870	1	7	$7_m\ 2_a\ 9_a$ bis	L. D. Heaton.	S. O.
60	67.71	81.98	..	..	..	July, 1869;	Aug. 1870	0	10	"	L. Woodruff.	" "
61	70.14	84.64	69.29	51.53	68.90	July, 1850;	Dec. 1859	9	1	$7_m\ 2_a\ 9_a$	Prof. L. C. Ervendburg.	P. O. & S. I. Vol. 1, and S. Coll.
62	63.35	..	..	..	..	1859		0	6	$\odot_r\ 7_m\ 2_a\ 7_a\ 9_a$	....	P. O. and S. I. Vol. 1.
63	..	81.38	71.63	..	..	1870		0	9	$7_m\ 2_a\ 9_a$ bis	F. Simpson.	S. O.
64	66.84	..	..	50.78	..	Oct. 1869;	Dec. 1870	0	10	"	N. S. Brooks.	" "
65	66.32	81.69	65.88	45.79	64.92	1856		1	0	$\odot_r$ N. $\odot_s$	Dr. W. H. Gantt.	P. O. and S. I. Vol. 1.
66	65.45	79.57	63.76	46.16	63.73	Dec. 1851;	Mar. 1854	2	4	$\odot_r\ 9_m\ 3_a\ 9_a$	Assistant Surgeon.	Ar. Met. Reg. 1855.
67	76.22	86.24	74.35	59.93	74.19	Oct. 1849;	Dec. 1870	10	5	$7_m\ 2_a\ 9_a$	" "	Ar. Met. Regs. 1855 and 1860, and MS. from S. G. O.
68	69.71	85.20	69.41	52.84	69.29	Jan. 1859;	Apr. 1861	2	4	$7_m\ 2_a\ 9_a$ bis	B. Schumann.	P. O. and S. I. Vol. 1, and S. O.
69	70.48	83.73	71.56	52.74	69.63	Jan. 1846;	Dec. 1870	8	7	$7_m\ 2_a\ 9_a$	Assistant Surgeon and F. Peterson.	Ar. Met. Regs. 1855 and 1860, MS. from S. G. O., & S. O.
70	68.07	84.83	66.11	47.11	66.53	1859		1	0	"	E. Kapp.	P. O. and S. I. Vol. 1.
71	..	..	..	..	..	1861		0	1	"	J. T. Rayel.	S. O.
72	65.66	79.64	67.88	51.42	66.15	Jan. 1857;	Aug. 1867	3	6	$7_m\ 2_a\ 9_a$ bis	Dr. W. H. Gantt, and W. Rutherford.	P. O. and S. I. Vol. 1, and S. O.
73	66.66	83.56	65.18	49.48	66.22	Apr. 1867;	Apr. 1869	2	0	"	Dr. E. Merrill.	S. O.
74	67.42	82.31	69.28	51.80	67.70	Dec. 1856;	Dec. 1859	2	8	$7_m\ 2_a\ 9_a$	B. H. Rucker.	P. O. and S. I. Vol. 1.
75	71.46	84.52	..	..	..	Feb. 1859;	Apr. 1861	1	0	"	E. W. Yellowby.	P. O. and S. I. Vol. 1, and S. O.

[3] Formerly called New Wied.

[4] Also called Phantom Hill.

[5] The observations in July and August, 1867, were made at Long Point, about two miles northeast of Union Hill.

UTAH.

Name of Station.	Lat.	Long.	Height.	Jan.	Feb.	March.	April.	May.	June.	July.	August.	Sept.	Oct.	Nov.	Dec.
1. Camp Douglas	40°47′	111°52′	4800	28°.71	31°.99	38°.82	48°.78	60°.32	69°.06	75°.90	75°.49	64°.67	54°.34	42.°77	31°.9
2. Coalville	41 00	111 00	5630	..	27.75	32.15	..	54.83	64.26	70.99	68.39	59.69	45.52	38.11	19.5
3. Fort Crittenden[1]	40 12	112 06	4860	19.42	28.61	37.79	48.47	59.38	72.96	76.33	72.71	61.01	48.30	36.80	24.5
4. Great Salt Lake City[2]	40 46	111 54	4260	25.86	32.98	40.70	48.73	60.35	69.21	76.56	74.94	64.10	55.05	41.54	32.3
5. Heberville[3]	40 32	111 16	..	34.41	39.67	48.55	56.53	75.43	82.58	84.83	84.29	74.12	62.65	54.95	38.4
6. St. Mary's	40 42	111 00	6200	..	26.05	28.00	36.70	54.70	61.00	70.70	70.67	59.25	46.75	38.85	19.4
7. Wanship	40 40	111 20	6200	19.69	25.61	30.33	37.10	51.83	59.91	70.18	69.97	61.44	50.32	38.35	31.0

VERMONT.

Name of Station.	Lat.	Long.	Height.	Jan.	Feb.	March.	April.	May.	June.	July.	August.	Sept.	Oct.	Nov.	Dec.
1. Barnet	44 18	72 05	952	10.91	25.87	25.54	45.42	52.75	66.43	72.78	64.70	..	..	36.63	8.7
2. Bradford	44 01	72 10	..	22.95	13.70	26.06	..	..	..	..	..	..	..	..	..
3. Brandon	43 49	73 03	460	19.29	21.95	28.57	41.91	54.75	64.01	68.67	65.87	58.43	46.27	36.28	23.4
4. Brattleboro	42 50	72 31	359	24.78	26.05	33.89	41.29	52.51	67.58	71.49	66.77	60.85	47.79	43.51	21.2
5. Brookfield	44 02	72 36	1000	..	15.95	17.60	37.65	52.63	..	..	..	..	..	..	..
6. Burlington	44 28	73 12	346	14.4	18.9	28.5	39.5	56.3	66.6	68.2	67.6	57.1	45.2	33.5	24.7
7. Burlington	44 28	73 12	346	20.02	20.04	28.39	41.76	54.68	64.21	68.52	67.24	58.76	47.16	35.85	22.8
8. Calais	44 22	72 25	..	17.23	18.81	24.77	36.12	48.51	..	63.59	..	53.60	..	..	..
9. Castleton	43 38	73 09	490	22.65	19.48	29.03	42.60	53.34	67.76	73.44	70.25	60.10	48.38	37.45	24.6
10. Craftsbury	44 40	72 23	1100	13.51	16.62	24.57	37.60	50.72	60.97	65.27	62.15	54.70	42.49	31.71	18.3
11. Fairfax	44 39	73 00	..	..	..	..	..	..	66.77	..	..	..	..	..	..
12. Fayetteville	42 57	72 36	350	18.4	19.9	31.0	44.0	56.2	63.5	67.5	66.1	57.4	46.7	34.9	24.1
13. Ferrisburg	44 11	73 14	..	26.08	18.83	24.70	46.33	56.28	68.45	72.88	78.50	62.69	46.48	33.84	24.7
14. Grafton	43 12	72 34	..	..	..	..	40.60	51.66	..	..	..	..	..	..	..
15. Luxenburg	44 28	71 44	1124	15.68	17.52	26.32	37.77	51.84	63.96	67.52	64.55	55.64	44.55	32.24	19.3
16. Middlebury	44 02	73 10	398	18.51	21.30	29.84	42.82	54.52	65.78	69.80	66.01	58.91	46.93	37.15	23.2
17. Montpelier[4]	44 17	72 36	540	22.85	17.86	24.77	38.86	50.66	60.67	67.40	63.98	57.49	46.40	38.94	23.2
18. Newbury	44 06	72 07	420	17.58	19.04	29.08	41.81	53.87	64.70	69.15	67.06	57.60	45.68	35.38	21.1
19. New Fane	42 58	72 35	..	18.88	19.29	30.67	43.27	54.45	64.49	67.28	66.53	56.90	46.89	35.58	24.4
20. Newport	43 57	72 18	750	15.54	22.29	25.73	42.38	53.22	64.95	71.11	65.55	57.85	47.44	34.67	25.6
21. Norwich[5]	43 45	72 21	..	6.61	27.17	24.43	42.05	51.59	65.50	69.71	68.12	65.40	44.63	32.28	20.7
22. Randolph	43 55	72 36	700	17.19	19.65	25.64	40.37	52.79	65.07	69.59	64.98	57.45	44.32	34.08	20.2
23. Rupert	43 15	73 11	750	21.55	25.45	31.73	43.20	58.51	67.96	72.74	70.79	62.63	50.13	38.79	25.7
24. Rutland	43 37	72 57	500	18.0	18.5	32.0	41.0	50.0	64.0	67.5	67.5	57.0	41.0	37.0	30.0
25. Rutland	43 37	72 57	500	27.75	30.13	34.65	43.38	..	..	..	67.30	55.00	47.33	39.70	26.9
26. St. Johnsbury	44 27	72 02	540	15.61	16.82	27.16	37.64	52.99	62.16	64.15	63.62	55.16	43.61	33.05	17.4
27. Shelburn	44 23	73 11	150	9.51	21.06	24.97	41.63	53.22	64.71	71.62	65.04	58.09	45.05	35.11	22.2
28. Springfield	43 18	72 25	300	16.19	21.19	29.24	39.38	53.33	62.00	66.08	66.37	58.67	48.37	37.56	22.8
29. West Charlotte	44 20	73 15	90	25.69	22.80	26.56	44.54	55.71	68.48	75.02	71.04	63.43	47.77	35.40	25.2
30. Williamstown	44 08	72 34	1000	15.34	15.72	25.45	37.93	50.12	59.45	64.04	61.36	52.98	41.79	30.08	18.0
31. Wilmington	42 53	72 50	1200	11.95	26.43	..	..	52.28	64.97	70.33	60.03	56.60	45.50	36.75	21.7
32. Windsor	43 29	72 25	..	22.7	25.7	29.6	37.7	57.2	66.7	68.3	63.7	61.1	47.8	35.0	23.6
33. Woodstock	43 36	72 31	650	16.44	14.95	23.52	38.78	52.13	62.59	68.07	62.91	55.81	41.85	31.08	19.6

[1] Observations previous to March, 1861, were made at old Camp Floyd.

[2] Observations prior to 1861 at various hours; they have been referred to $7_m\ 2_a\ 9_{a\ bis}$, by means of the general table.

[3] Also known as St. George. The series is unreliable; when compared with other stations the results are shown to be much too high; probably due improper exposure of the instrument, or defective scale.

UTAH.

	Spring.	Summer.	Autumn.	Winter.	Year.	Series. Begins. Ends.	Extent yrs. mos.	Observing hours.	Observer.	References.
1	49°.31	73°.48	53°.93	30°.87	51°.90	Dec. 1862; Dec. 1870	7 9	$7_m\ 2_a\ 9_a$	Assistant Surgeon.	MS. from S. G. O.
2	..	67.88	47.77	..	..	May, 1869; Dec. 1870	1 5	$7_m\ 2_a\ 9_a$ bis	T. Bullock.	S. O.
3	48.55	74.00	48.70	24.19	48.86	July, 1858; July, 1861	3 0	$7_m\ 2_a\ 9_a$	Assistant Surgeon.	Ar. Met. Reg. 1860, and MS. from S. G. O.
4	49.93	73.57	53.56	30.38	51.86	Jan. 1850; Aug. 1870	9 0	$7_m\ 2_a\ 9_a$ bis	H. E. & W. W. Phelps, and others.	Ar. Met. Reg. 1855, P. O. and S. I. Vol. 1, and S. O.
5	60.17	83.90	63.91	37.50	61.37	Jan. 1861; June, 1870	2 2	"	H. Pearce and C. Johnson.	S. O.
6	39.80	67.46	48.28	..	..	June, 1865; Aug. 1867	2 0	$7_m\ 2_a\ 9_a$	T. Bullock.	S. Coll.
7	39.75	66.69	50.04	25.46	45.48	June, 1866; Mar. 1869	2 4	$7_m\ 2_a\ 9_a$ bis	" "	S. O.

VERMONT.

	Spring.	Summer.	Autumn.	Winter.	Year.	Series. Begins. Ends.	Extent yrs. mos.	Observing hours.	Observer.	References.
1	41.24	67.97	..	15.16	..	Apr. 1866; Mar. 1869	1 3	$7_m\ 2_a\ 9_a$ bis	Dr. B. F. Eaton.	S. O.
2	..	..	..	..	..	1858	0 3	$7_m\ 2_a\ 9_a$	L. W. Bliss.	P. O. and S. I. Vol. 1.
3	41.74	66.18	46.99	21.56	44.12	Oct. 1852; June, 1869	13 10	$7_m\ 2_a\ 9_a$ bis	D. and H. Buckland.	P. O. and S. I. Vol. 1, S. O., and S. Coll.
4	42.56	68.61	50.72	24.03	46.48	Mar. 1849; Sept. 1851	1 6	$\odot_r\ 9_m\ 3_a\ 9_a$	Frost.	S. Coll.
5	35.96	..	..	..	..	1863	0 4	$7_m\ 2_a\ 9_a$ bis	T. F. Pollard.	S. O.
6	41.43	67.47	45.27	19.33	43.37	1803; 1808	6 0	......	Sanders.	Tompson's Hist. Vermont.
7	41.61	66.66	47.26	20.97	44.12	Jan. 1828; Nov. 1864	29 6	$\odot_r\ 1_a\ 9_a$	Prof. Z. Thompson, and M. K. Petty.	MS. in S. Coll., S. O., P. O. and S. I. Vol. 1.
8	36.47	..	..	..	..	Feb. 1861; Sept. 1864	1 2	$7_m\ 2_a\ 9_a$ bis	J. K. Toby.	S. O.
9	41.66	70.48	48.64	22.27	45.76	1851; Dec. 1870	4 3	"	D. Underwood and R. G. Williams.	P. O. and S. I. Vol. 1, S. O., & S. Coll.
10	37.63	62.80	42.97	16.16	39.89	Jan. 1854; Dec. 1870	16 4	"	C. A. J. Marsh, J. A. Paddock, and E. P. Wild.	P. O. and S. I. Vol. 1, and S. O.
11	..	..	..	..	..	1854	0 1	$7_m\ 2_a\ 9_a$	Prof. S. H. Peabody.	P. O. and S. I. Vol. 1.
12	43.73	65.79	46.33	20.80	44.14	May, 1826; Dec. 1834	8 8	$\odot_r\ 2_a\ 9_a$	Gen. M. Field.	Am. Journ. Sci. and MS. in S. Coll.
13	42.44	73.28	47.67	23.22	46.65	May, 1869; Dec. 1870	1 8	$7_m\ 2_a\ 9_a$ bis	D. C. & M. E. Barto.	S. O.
14	..	..	..	..	..	1843	0 2	$\odot_r\ 9_m\ 3_a\ 9_a$	Peabody.	S. Coll.
15	38.64	65.34	44.15	17.52	41.41	1848; Dec. 1870	19 0	$7_m\ 2_a\ 9_a$ bis	H. A. Cutting	S. O. and S. Coll.
16	42.39	67.20	47.66	21.01	44.57	1849; Dec. 1870	10 1	"	H. A. Shelden and Parker.	" " "
17	38.10	64.02	47.61	21.32	42.76	May, 1849; May, 1863	2 5	$\odot_r$ N. $\odot_s$	B. J. Wheeler, Dr. M. M. Marsh, and Thompson.	P. O. and S. I. Vol. 1, S. O., and S. Coll.
18	41.59	66.97	46.22	19.26	43.51	May, 1835; Dec. 1854	18 5	6_m N. 6_a	D. Johnson.	Dove, Regents' Report.
19	42.80	66.10	46.46	20.88	44.06	....	6 0	$\odot_r\ 2_a\ 9_a$	....	Dove, 1857.
20	40.44	67.20	46.65	21.15	43.86	Nov. 1856; Nov. 1870	2 1	$7_m\ 2_a\ 9_a$ bis	L. W. Bliss, and J. M. Currier.	P. O. and S. I. Vol. 1, and S. O.
21	39.36	67.78	47.44	18.17	43.19	Mar. 1856; Sept. 1869	1 8	$7_m\ 2_a\ 9_a$	Prof. A. Jackmann, and Dr. B. F. Eaton.	" " " " " "
22	39.60	66.55	45.28	19.02	42.61	1850; Dec. 1870	5 8	$7_m\ 2_a\ 9_a$ bis	C. S. Paine, E. Bethel, and Manly.	S. O. and S. Coll.
23	44.48	70.50	50.52	24.25	47.44	Jan. 1857; Mar. 1863	5 6	"	J. Parker.	P. O. and S. I. Vol. 1, and S. O.
24	41.00	66.33	45.00	22.17	43.62	1789	1 0	......	Williams.	Williams's Hist. of Vermont.
25	..	..	47.34	28.29	..	Aug. 1863; Apr. 1864	0 9	$7_m\ 2_a\ 9_a$ bis	S. O. Mead.	S. O.
26	39.26	63.31	43.94	16.62	40.78	Jan. 1853; Jan. 1861	5 2	$7_m\ 2_a\ 9_a$	J. K. Colby and F. Fairbanks.	P. O. & S. I. Vol. 1, & S. Coll.
27	39.94	67.12	46.08	17.61	42.69	Mar. 1856; Dec. 1857	1 10	"	G. Bliss.	P. O. and S. I. Vol. 1.
28	40.65	64.82	48.20	20.08	43.44	Dec. 1860; Nov. 1863	2 4	$7_m\ 2_a\ 9_a$ bis	J. W. Chickering.	S. O.
29	42.27	71.51	48.87	24.57	46.81	May, 1868; Dec. 1870	2 8	"	M. E. Wing.	" "
30	37.83	61.62	41.62	16.37	39.36	Feb. 1829; Dec. 1841	12 9	$\odot_r\ 1_a\ 9_a$	Paine.	MS. in S. Coll.
31	..	65.11	46.28	20.03	..	May, 1866; Feb. 1867	0 10	$7_m\ 2_a\ 9_a$ bis	J. B. Perry.	S. O.
32	41.50	66.23	47.97	24.00	44.92	1806	1 0	$\odot_r\ 2_a$[6]	B. Towler.	Med. and Agr. Reg. Bost. Vol. 1, 1806–7.
33	38.14	64.52	42.91	17.01	40.65	Mar. 1857; Dec. 1870	3 0	$7_m\ 2_a\ 9_a$ bis	C. Marsh, H. Doton, and L. A. Miller.	P. O. and S. I. Vol. 1, & S. O.

[4] The observations previous to 1863 were made at East Montpelier, about three miles east of Montpelier.

[5] Observations in Sept. 1869 at Hartford, about one and a half miles southeast of Norwich.

[6] Observations corrected for daily variation.

VIRGINIA.

Name of Station.	Lat.	Long.	Height.	Jan.	Feb.	March.	April.	May.	June.	July.	August.	Sept.	Oct.	Nov.	Dec.
1. Alexandria . . .	38°48′	77°02′	56	32°.65	34°.05	41°.26	52°.53	63°.47	74°.94	78°.59	76°.19	67°.76	54°.50	46°.35	35°.98
2. Ashland (Randolph Macon Coll.) . .	37 45	77 30	221	42.85	..	..	..	..	..	..	..	..	..	..	..
3. Bellona Arsenal .	37 33	77 32	120	38.73	41.97	50.31	58.36	67.79	76.58	79.19	77.90	70.57	60.08	50.59	43.43
4. Berryville . . .	39 08	77 58	575	21.86	32.22	35.24	43.59	57.81	72.78	75.41	72.05	65.99	54.45	42.78	36.14
5. Cape Charles Light.	37 07	75 54	20	36.05	33.20	39.70	52.85	60.48	70.05	76.00	76.75	74.00	63.28	51.83	38.03
6. Charlottesville . .	38 01	78 26	150	38.87	39.01	48.05	53.26	63.71	73.11	77.87	76.77	66.33	57.34	48.11	36.60
7. Christiansburgh .	37 05	80 23	2000	37.73	43.68	..	52.55	63.78	67.55	..	..	..	..	47.26	38.56
8. Cottage Home . .	37 10	76 50	..	43.05	40.88	48.76	57.52	66.53	76.74	82.04	79.31	72.49	58.49	47.72	39.42
9. Crichton's Store[1] .	36 40	77 46	500	39.31	42.29	49.39	59.25	68.03	75.35	80.45	77.89	71.48	59.52	49.61	41.32
10. Fredericksburg . .	38 18	77 27	600	42.02	53.80	56.14	53.05	64.10	75.30	75.07	74.28	66.11	55.39	49.52	36.84
11. Fortress Monroe .	37 00	76 19	8	42.41	41.81	49.90	55.99	66.13	74.62	78.73	77.86	72.44	61.90	51.41	41.10
12. Garysville . . .	37 18	77 16	..	21.92	32.10	43.84	58.33	65.33	76.50	80.50	70.33	61.00	53.00	47.00	37.00
13. Glasgow Station (near)	37 36	78 57	..	30.06	37.92	44.15	53.81	62.07	71.18	78.49	75.14	69.03	57.95	48.08	35.68
14. Hampton . . .	37 02	76 21	5	44.24	42.51	43.60	54.92	64.35	75.94	80.24	77.69	70.50	58.42	46.72	40.72
15. Harper's Ferry (heights, near) .	39 20	77 44	..	..	..	..	..	..	..	..	..	..	54.73	42.48	..
16. Heathville . . .	37 52	76 26	..	..	..	44.77	52.41	61.72	..	..	..	..	..	..	..
17. Hewlett's Station (near)	37 52	77 45	..	..	..	..	59.13	60.98	74.38	74.58	70.18	..	..	..	..
18. Lewinsville . . .	38 56	77 12	180	38.62	40.97	50.38	52.67	65.35	72.85	76.76	73.76	66.82	56.69	42.41	41.67
19. Lexington[3] . . .	37 44	79 24	1000	38.41	39.31	44.19	54.22	63.74	72.51	78.71	76.04	66.52	53.29	42.05	34.85
20. Longwood . . .	37 30	79 31	800	24.22	46.43	41.72	..	..	..	..	..	..	..	..	..
21. Lynchburg . . .	37 22	79 07	575	..	42.94	51.09	57.30	68.63	75.43	83.80	80.37	..	..	..	..
22. Lynchburg (six miles west of) . . .	37 22	79 12	800	39.57	40.42	46.30	55.88	63.18	71.63	78.28	76.09	68.77	57.88	48.76	39.35
23. Madison C. H. . .	38 22	78 17	500	..	..	..	..	66.13	..	..	..	..	..	..	..
24. Meadow Dale . .	38 23	79 35	..	28.52	34.36	34.59	42.43	54.80	65.05	67.02	66.05	59.93	50.19	37.17	37.64
25. Mechanicsville . .	38 50	78 00	..	36.68	33.73	38.50	51.98	62.63	70.83	76.10	74.10	65.35	55.63	39.80	33.88
26. Montross	38 07	76 46	200	34.02	38.91	44.49	50.98	62.99	72.83	76.08	73.85	67.51	52.46	44.59	37.88
27. Mossy Creek . .	38 25	79 02	..	28.78	34.35	37.73	49.59	59.99	72.34	..	..	63.70	44.59	39.29	33.13
28. Mount Solon . .	38 17	79 02	..	38.05	37.49	46.33	54.19	61.39	71.24	76.73	73.85	69.85	55.93	..	33.86
29. Mount View . .	38 00	78 30	521	36.21	40.12	48.77	54.82	66.29	70.61	74.26	73.22	64.57	53.49	46.63	34.54
30. Mulberry Hill . .	36 50	76 50	100	45.13	43.25	45.26	56.74	65.21	76.58	81.49	..	68.30	54.28	42.20	43.80
31. Newark (near) . .	38 00	78 10	..	..	..	..	..	..	..	..	..	..	..	..	..
32. Norfolk	36 51	76 17	20	43.73	48.44	55.72	62.01	71.00	76.73	80.21	77.09	74.09	65.54	59.58	47.35
33. Norfolk	36 51	76 17	20	40.50	41.00	47.50	56.10	65.90	74.20	78.30	77.10	71.40	61.70	51.20	43.20
34. Paddystown . . .	39 28	78 55	..	30.42	..	..	..	..	..	..	..	..	..	35.01	36.95
35. Peachlawn[4] . . .	38 19	77 27	350	37.18	37.33	46.23	52.67	64.46	72.42	76.48	76.05	68.16	57.90	47.10	36.95
36. Piedmont . . .	38 40	78 00	900	38.43	33.43	38.23	52.53	62.08	71.08	76.75	73.13	66.08	56.70	41.12	34.55
37. Portsmouth[5] . . .	36 50	76 18	25	40.10	43.91	48.79	56.65	64.83	75.32	79.08	77.11	71.36	60.14	50.42	43.23
38. Powhatan Hill . .	38 13	77 12	100	41.69	37.18	43.75	53.89	63.92	74.25	79.60	76.85	70.53	56.26	45.50	35.92
39. Prince Edward C. H.	37 10	78 21	..	37.21	41.63	47.09	53.42	63.46	70.48	75.46	72.61	65.10	56.71	49.26	39.63
40. Prospect Hill Farm	37 25	75 52	40	43.18	40.64	42.05	52.63	61.98	72.16	78.03	75.72	70.03	57.53	47.07	38.88
41. Richmond . . .	37 32	77 26	172	37.21	42.79	48.68	54.87	65.97	74.10	77.50	75.08	67.85	58.98	47.27	40.10
42. Rose Hill . . .	38 00	76 57	250	34.71	35.17	45.51	52.24	62.87	75.37	76.77	76.90	..	57.74	50.10	45.42
43. Rougemont . . .	38 05	78 21	450	29.72	39.19	44.82	53.35	63.34	74.11	79.18	76.05	69.43	58.58	45.44	40.89
44. Ruthven[6] . . .	37 21	77 33	..	36.07	38.18	50.41	52.85	63.63	74.86	76.49	74.78	69.77	55.60	44.31	38.64
45. Smithfield . . .	36 57	76 38	100	35.89	39.28	45.53	55.94	64.09	73.85	77.26	75.03	68.72	58.07	47.74	39.43
46. Snowville . . .	37 00	80 00	1800	34.30	36.45	41.06	49.35	58.15	66.45	71.77	69.30	62.55	48.30	38.91	32.34
47. Staunton	38 09	79 04	1387	41.04	37.68	39.98	52.04	61.22	71.39	74.83	74.58	64.66	51.65	42.49	33.95
48. Stribling Springs .	38 17	79 12	1639	28.43	32.08	41.17	45.16	..	..	..	..	59.05	49.71	33.70	34.59
49. The Plains (near) .	38 50	77 51	..	..	..	46.60	50.71	..	..	..	..	..	..	..	..
50. The Shades . . .	39 00	78 00	..	..	..	..	..	..	..	..	..	63.55	..	..	..
51. Vienna[7]	38 57	77 19	400	37.40	32.08	40.00	54.73	65.33	75.35	77.05	72.50	65.33	..	41.35	31.48

[1] This series is of very little value on account of great irregularity in the hours of observation.

[2] Observations corrected for daily variation by means of the general table.

[3] The observations, except the first three months of 1861, were made at Tribrook Farm, about three miles northeast of Lexington, by W. H. Ruffner.

[4] Also called Hartwood or Falmouth.

VIRGINIA.

	Spring.	Summer.	Autumn.	Winter.	Year.	Series. Begins.	Ends.	Extent yrs. mos.	Observing hours.	Observer.	References.
1	52°.42	76°.57	56°.20	34°.23	54°.86	Oct. 1849;	Feb. 1864	6 8	$7_m\ 2_a\ 9_a$	B. Hallowell and others.	P. O. and S. I. Vol. I, MS. from S. G. O., and S. Coll.
2	..	..	..	..	..	1865		0 1	$7_m\ 2_a\ 9_a$ bis	Prof. R. M. Smith.	S. O.
3	58.82	77.89	60.41	41.38	59.62	Jan. 1824;	Sept. 1833	7 10	$7_m\ 2_a\ 9_a$	Assistant Surgeon.	Ar. Met. Reg. 1855.
4	45.55	73.41	54.41	30.07	50.86	Jan. 1856;	Dec. 1857	1 11	"	Dr. R. and Miss E. Kownslar.	P. O. and S. I. Vol. I.
5	51.01	74.27	63.04	35.76	56.02	Mar. 1867;	Feb. 1868	1 0	$7_m\ 2_a\ 9_a$ bis	J. G. Potts (Prison Keeper).	S. O.
6	55.01	75.92	57.26	38.16	56.59	July, 1837;	Dec. 1852	2 11	$7_m\ 2_a\ 9_a$	Meriwether.	Am. Alm. 1839 and S. Coll.
7	..	..	..	39.99	..	1850;	1853	0 9	$\odot_r\ 9_m\ 3_a\ 9_a$	Chevalier and Hogan.	S. Coll.
8	57.60	79.36	59.57	41.12	59.41	May, 1867;	Dec. 1870	3 7	$7_m\ 2_a\ 9_a$ bis	B. W. Jones.	S. O.
9	58.89	77.90	60.20	40.97	59.49	Jan. 1854;	Jan. 1861	7 1		R. F. Astrop.	Rec. in S. Coll. and S. O.
10	57.76	74.88	57.01	44.22	58.47	Mar. 1849;	Apr. 1860	1 3	$\odot_r\ 9_m\ 3_a\ 9_a$	C. H. Robey and Wellford.	S. O. and S. Coll.
11	57.34	77.07	61.92	41.77	59.52	Jan. 1825;	Dec. 1870	45 5	$7_m\ 2_a\ 9_a$	Assistant Surgeon.	Ar. Met. Regs. 1855 and 1860, and MS. from S. G. O.
12	55.83	75.78	53.67	30.34	53.91	1856		1 0	$\odot_r\ 2_a\ \odot_s$	Dr. T. F. Beckwith.	P. O. and S. I. Vol. I.
13	53.34	74.94	58.35	34.55	55.30	Oct. 1866;	Sept. 1868	2 0	......	R. J. Davis.	S. O.
14	54.29	77.96	58.55	42.49	58.32	Jan. 1869;	Dec. 1870	2 0	$7_m\ 2_a\ 9_a$ bis	J. M. Sherman.	" "
15	..	..	..	..	..	1860		0 2	"	L. J. Bell and wife.	" "
16	52.97	..	..	..	..	1849		0 3	$\odot_r\ 9_m\ 3_a\ 9_a$	Miller.	S. Coll.
17	..	73.05	..	..	..	1867		0 5	$7_m\ 2_a\ 9_a$ bis	J. F. Adams.	S. O.
18	56.13	74.46	55.31	40.42	56.58	June, 1858;	Oct. 1859	1 5	$7_m\ 2_a\ 9_a$	Rev. C. B. Mackee.	P. O. and S. I. Vol. I.
19	54.05	75.75	53.95	37.52	55.32	Jan. 1861;	Dec. 1870	2 8	$7_m\ 2_a\ 9_a$ bis	W. K. Park and W. H. Ruffner.	S. O.
20	..	..	..	..	..	1857		0 3	$7_m\ 2_a\ 9_a$	T. J. Wickline.	P. O. and S. I. Vol. I.
21	59.01	79.87	..	..	..	1854		0 7	"	A. Nettleton.	" " " "
22	55.12	75.33	58.47	39.78	57.18	Oct. 1866;	Dec. 1870	3 9	$7_m\ 2_a\ 9_a$ bis	C. J. Merriwether.	S. O.
23	..	..	..	..	..	[illegible]		0 1	$\odot_r\ 9_m\ 3_a\ 9_a$	Gilman.	S. Coll.
24	43.94	66.04	49.10	33.51	48.15	Jan. 1857;	Feb. 1859	2 2	$7_m\ 2_a\ 9_a$	J. and J. B. Slaven.	P. O. and S. I. Vol. I.
25	51.04	73.68	53.59	34.76	53.27	Nov. 1869;	Dec. 1870	1 2	$7_m\ 2_a\ 9_a$ bis	W. A. Martin.	S. O.
26	52.82	74.25	54.85	36.94	54.72	Dec. 1856;	Oct. 1859	2 6	$7_m\ 2_a\ 9_a$	H. H. Fountleroy and E. E. Spence.	P. O. and S. I. Vol. I.
27	49.10	..	49.19	32.09	..	Apr. 1853;	May, 1858	1 8	"	J. Hotchkiss.	P. O. and S. I. Vol. I, & S. Coll.
28	53.97	73.94	..	36.47	..	Apr. 1856;	Apr. 1869	1 10	$7_m\ 2_a\ 9_a$ bis	Dr. J. T. Clarke.	P. O. and S. I. Vol. I, and S. O.
29	56.63	72.70	54.89	36.96	55.29	Feb. 1859;	Apr. 1861	2 2	"	J. R. Abell.	" " " " "
30	55.74	..	54.93	44.06	..	Jan. 1869;	July, 1870	1 6	"	R. Binford.	S. O.
31	..	..	..	..	59.75	1823;	1828	6 0	......	Watson.	Am. Alm.
32	62.91	78.01	66.40	46.51	63.46	1822		1 0	$7_m\ 2_a\ 9_a$	....	Long's Expedition to St. Peter's River, Vol. 2.
33	56.50	76.53	61.43	41.57	59.01	....		25 0	......	....	Pat. Off. Rep.
34	..	..	..	..	..	1852;	1853	0 3	$\odot_r\ 9_m\ 3_a\ 9_a$	Webster.	S. Coll.
35	54.45	74.98	57.72	37.15	56.08	Jan. 1858;	Mar. 1861	3 3	$7_m\ 2_a\ 9_a$ bis	A. Van Doren.	P. O. and S. I. Vol. I, and S. O.
36	50.95	73.65	54.63	35.47	53.68	Nov. 1869;	Dec. 1870	1 2	"	F. Williams.	S. O.
37	56.76	77.17	60.64	42.41	59.24	Apr. 1843;	Sept. 1870	12 1	"	Various observers.	S. Coll., P. O. and S. I. Vol. I, and S. O.
38	53.85	76.90	57.43	38.26	56.61	Feb. 1868;	Dec. 1870	2 10	"	C. T. Taylor.	S. O.
39	54.66	72.85	57.02	39.49	56.01	1849;	1852	2 8	$\odot_r\ 9_m\ 3_a\ 9_a$	Metteaur.	S. Coll.
40	52.22	75.30	58.21	40.90	56.66	Apr. 1868;	Dec. 1870	2 9	$7_m\ 2_a\ 9_a$ bis	C. R. Moore.	S. O.
41	56.51	75.56	58.03	40.03	57.53	Jan. 1824;	Feb. 1860	7 2	$\odot_r$ N. $\odot_s$	Chevalier, D. Turner, and J. Applyard.	Darby's View of the U. S. pp. 4 and 11, S. O., and S. Coll.
42	53.54	76.35	..	38.43	..	Jan. 1857;	Aug. 1858	1 1	$7_m\ 2_a\ 9_a$	G. U. Upshaw.	P. O. and S. I. Vol. I.
43	53.84	76.45	57.82	36.60	56.18	Feb. 1853;	Mar. 1861	5 6	$7_m\ 2_a\ 9_a$ bis	A. Nettleton and G. C. Dickinson.	P. O. & S. I. Vol. I, S. Coll., & S. O.
44	55.63	75.38	56.56	37.63	56.30	Aug. 1856;	May, 1859	2 4	$7_m\ 2_a\ 9_a$	J. C. Ruffin.	P. O. and S. I. Vol. I.
45	55.19	75.38	58.18	38.20	56.74	July, 1854;	Mar. 1861	6 8	"	Dr. J. R. Purdie.	P. O. and S. I. Vol. I, and S. O.
46	49.52	69.17	49.92	34.36	50.74	Sept. 1867;	June, 1870	2 10	$7_m\ 2_a\ 9_a$ bis	Dr. J. W. Stalnacker.	S. O.
47	51.08	73.60	52.93	37.56	53.79	Sept. 1868;	Dec. 1870	2 3	"	J. C. Covell.	" "
48	..	..	47.49	31.70	..	Sept. 1858;	Apr. 1859	0 8	$7_m\ 2_a\ 9_a$	J. Hotchkiss.	P. O. and S. I. Vol. I.
49	..	..	..	..	..	Apr. 1859;	Apr. 1860	0 3	$7_m\ 2_a\ 9_a$ bis	J. Rickett.	P. O. and S. I. Vol. I, and S. O.
50	..	..	..	..	..	1870		0 1	"	L. E. Payne.	S. O.
51	53.35	74.97	..	33.65	..	1870		0 11	"	J. B. Bowman and Lilly Thrift.	" "

5 This series is composed of observations made at Gosport Navy Yard, the United States Naval Hospital, and Portsmouth proper.

6 This series is not at all reliable.

7 The observations in Jan., Feb., June, July, Nov., and Dec. were made at Fairfax Co. Ho., about three miles southeast of Vienna.

VIRGINIA.—Continued.

Name of Station.	Lat.	Long.	Height.	Jan.	Feb.	March.	April.	May.	June.	July.	August.	Sept.	Oct.	Nov.	Dec.
52. Vienna (near)	38°55′	77°15′	400	40°.58	35°.90	40°.18	54°.75	64°.35	72°.85	76°.83	75°.27	68°.29	54°.07	44°.08	36°.61
53. Washington and Lee University	37 44	79 24	1075	..	..	..	..	..	..	..	..	66.00	53.88	40.20	31.25
54. Westwood	37 33	77 27	..	38.20	42.17	50.00	56.29	65.83	73.30	76.69	74.83	69.11	57.05	50.14	36.86
55. Wytheville[1]	36 55	81 03	2257	36.31	35.29	42.10	52.26	59.70	66.88	72.98	71.14	63.47	51.78	40.20	33.18
56. Williamsburg[2]	37 18	76 40	100	41.43	43.68	47.88	57.59	64.00	72.48	76.49	75.26	68.72	59.41	47.28	42.65
57. Winchester	39 10	78 09	..	31.37	34.37	42.44	51.85	64.38	72.99	..	..	67.99	54.62	43.68	34.68
58. Woodlawn (near Mt. Vernon)	38 40	77 10	150	..	..	..	..	..	..	..	..	..	..	44.45	32.95

WASHINGTON TERRITORY.

Name of Station.	Lat.	Long.	Height.	Jan.	Feb.	March.	April.	May.	June.	July.	August.	Sept.	Oct.	Nov.	Dec.
1. Camp Simiahmoo	49 01	122 47	11	36.63	37.56	42.86	47.34	53.76	60.80	62.27	60.84	56.17	48.47	40.20	35.70
2. Camp Steele[5]	48 28	123 01	150	37.96	40.38	43.12	49.07	54.95	59.74	61.85	61.03	57.07	50.74	45.51	40.90
3. Cape Disappointment	46 17	124 03	30	41.24	42.65	44.96	51.32	56.33	60.52	62.43	61.23	59.12	54.70	51.43	47.16
4. Cathlamet, near	46 15	123 12	40	..	..	40.05	48.44	52.95	59.18	64.95	64.45	..	..	..	35.36
5. Fort Bellingham	48 45	122 30	88	37.78	39.60	44.68	50.27	55.91	61.13	62.11	62.21	58.03	50.16	44.50	39.81
6. Fort Cascades	45 39	121 50	..	36.81	41.51	45.12	50.38	55.31	63.48	65.52	66.91	61.37	53.22	43.54	34.73
7. Fort Chehalis	46 54	124 07	..	43.25	45.19	46.16	48.26	51.26	..	..	65.68	62.28	56.17	48.24	44.21
8. Fort Colville[6]	48 42	118 02	1963	19.12	26.79	33.20	46.44	55.77	64.75	69.87	66.49	55.37	42.81	32.81	26.10
9. Fort George	46 18	123 00	..	36.13	42.42	44.79	48.67	53.92	59.59	61.42	62.67	59.54	56.13	47.59	39.67
10. Fort Simcoe	46 30	120 40	..	30.31	31.81	40.71	52.99	60.99	67.85	71.99	72.70	64.49	50.18	38.99	32.71
11. Fort Steilacoom[7]	47 11	122 34	250	37.36	39.92	42.94	48.85	55.81	61.14	64.57	64.54	59.09	51.88	44.51	39.06
12. Fort Townshend[8]	48 07	122 45	135	39.14	41.36	43.12	42.56	53.58	59.63	..	..	..	..	..	41.41
13. Fort Vancouver	45 40	122 30	50	37.48	43.67	44.58	46.00	48.98	62.77	66.03	66.08	61.13	55.14	43.08	42.94
14. Fort Vancouver	45 40	122 30	50	36.34	37.17	45.76	50.22	58.43	58.72	61.76	63.05	61.10	50.44	39.03	36.54
15. Fort Vancouver[8]	45 40	122 30	50	36.96	40.41	44.87	51.92	58.63	63.04	67.68	66.93	61.21	52.86	44.89	37.54
16. Fort Walla-Walla	46 03	118 20	..	31.35	37.18	42.54	52.38	62.28	70.50	77.01	75.01	65.25	54.54	41.80	33.76
17. Koos-Koos-Kee	46 30	122 37	..	31.59	37.58	44.84	52.85	57.80	69.40	70.47	72.72	68.47	48.96	42.40	41.52
18. Lake Washington	47 36	122 20	..	..	..	41.25	50.88	55.53	62.80	68.95	66.10	..	..	..	..
19. Nee-ah Bay	48 22	124 37	40	38.81	38.84	39.81	44.33	50.43	55.11	57.00	57.33	52.97	51.25	45.39	40.39
20. Port Townshend	48 07	122 45	8	29.63	40.78	..	48.95	53.28	58.48	61.20	59.85	55.68	47.88	45.55	39.80
21. Sinyakwateen Depot	48 25	117 18	1894	..	..	..	46.9	55.3	62.7	70.7	68.8	..	..	..	..
22. Tatoosh Island Light-house	48 23	124 44	90	41.94	41.86	44.13	50.12	53.49	57.72	61.39	59.58	56.50	52.82	49.31	44.75
23. Walla-Walla	46 05	118 54	930	34.85	..	..	..	..	..	..	..	..	..	42.33	37.20

WEST VIRGINIA.

Name of Station.	Lat.	Long.	Height.	Jan.	Feb.	March.	April.	May.	June.	July.	August.	Sept.	Oct.	Nov.	Dec.
1. Ashland[10]	38 34	82 10	600	33.25	45.87	51.00	56.75	65.81	73.43	76.91	75.01	69.97	56.45	44.72	36.98
2. Ashland	38 34	82 10	600	30.96	37.15	40.83	53.89	63.10	70.57	76.31	74.58	70.25	53.97	43.56	35.71
3. Ashland	38 30	82 15	600	35.14	37.43	42.54	53.89	61.05	71.49	74.72	72.36	68.79	52.18	42.98	37.60
4. Buffalo	38 36	81 56	500	27.97	38.09	47.61	51.25	65.13	69.72	75.75	71.70	66.15	59.30	41.93	35.63
5. Buffalo	38 36	81 56	..	..	..	..	..	66.85	81.58	81.82	80.14	..	..	..	..
6. Burning Springs	38 56	81 21	..	31.94	31.36	51.83	..	..	..	..	..	..	..	..	..
7. Capon Bridge[11]	39 16	78 29	..	..	38.96	38.87	43.39	59.94	..	..	..	..	..	..	..
8. Crack Whip	39 02	78 33	1720	23.31	31.48	34.63	45.41	55.87	68.47	70.54	66.27	60.00	50.38	40.27	28.31
9. Cross Creek[12]	40 16	80 33	..	27.58	31.59	41.77	48.85	65.47	66.49	71.38	70.01	61.15	46.73	36.63	31.19

[1] The observations from Feb. 1868, to Dec. 1870, were made by J. A. Brown, near Wytheville, the position being Lat. 36°57′, Long. 81°06′, Alt. 2400.

[2] The observations from July, 1777, to Aug. 1778, both inclusive, were made at William and Mary College, and are the means of daily extremes between 8 A. M. and 4 P. M.; the hours of observation were assumed to be 8_m 3_a, and the corresponding correction applied.

[3] Observations corrected for daily variation by means of the general table.

[4] Bihourly, 6_m to 10_a, from July, 1857, to Oct. 1858; hourly in Jan. Feb. March, 1859; hourly, 6_m to 10_a in April, 1859, and at 7_m 2_a 9_a for remaining 16 months of series. A small correction has been applied to the results for 7_m 2_a 9_a, the rest are assumed to represent very nearly the true mean of the day.

VIRGINIA.—Continued.

	Spring.	Summer.	Autumn.	Winter.	Year.	Series. Begins. Ends.	Extent yrs. mos.	Observing hours.	Observer.	References.
52	53°.09	74°.98	55°.48	37°.70	55°.31	Aug. 1869; Dec. 1870	1 5	$7_m 2_a 9_a$ bis	H. C. Williams.	S. O.
53	..	..	53.36	..	..	1870	0 4	"	Prof. J. L. Campbell.	" "
54	57.37	74.94	58.77	39.08	57.54	Jan. 1859; Feb. 1852	2 2	"	C. J. Merriwether.	P. O. and S. I. Vol. 1, and S. O.
55	51.35	70.33	51.82	34.93	52.11	May, 1860; Dec. 1870	4 8	"	H. Shriver, W. D. Roedel, and J. A. Brown.	S. O.
56	56.49	74.74	58.47	42.59	58.07	Jan. 1760; Aug. 1778	9 2	8	Farquier & Madison.	Jefferson's Notes on Va., Cotté, and Phil. Soc. Trans.
57	52.89	..	55.43	33.47	..	Sept. 1851; Dec. 1859	6 7	$7_m 2_a 9_a$	Prof. J. W. Marvin.	P. O. & S. I. Vol. 1, and S. Coll.
58	..	..	..	..	..	1870	0 2	$7_m 2_a 9_a$ bis	C. Gillingham.	S. O.

WASHINGTON TERRITORY.

	Spring.	Summer.	Autumn.	Winter.	Year.	Series. Begins. Ends.	Extent yrs. mos.	Observing hours.	Observer.	References.
1	47.99	61.30	48.28	36.63	48.55	July, 1857; June, 1860	3 0	4	Assistant Surgeon.	Rep. of N. W. Bound. Com. and MS. from S. G. O.
2	49.05	60.87	51.11	39.75	50.19	Feb. 1860; Dec. 1870	10 0	$7_m 2_a 9_a$	" "	MS. from S. G. O.
3	50.87	61.39	55.08	43.68	52.76	July, 1864; Apr. 1869	4 4	"	" "	Med. and Surg. Reporter, Feb. 13, 1869, & MS. from S. G. O.
4	47.15	62.86	..	..	..	1870	0 7	$7_m 2_a 9_a$ bis	C. McCall.	S. O.
5	50.29	60.82	50.90	39.06	50.52	Mar. 1857; July, 1859	2 5	$7_m 2_a 9_a$	Assistant Surgeon.	Ar. Met. Reg. 1860.
6	50.27	65.30	52.71	37.68	51.49	May, 1858; May, 1861	3 1	"	" "	Ar. Met. Reg. 1860 and MS. from S. G. O.
7	48.56	..	55.56	44.22	..	Aug. 1860; May, 1861	0 10	"	" "	MS. from S. G. O.
8	45.14	67.04	43.66	24.00	44.96	Nov. 1859; Dec. 1870	9 1	"	" "	Rep. of N. W. Bound. Com. and MS. from S. G. O.
9	49.13	61.23	54.42	39.41	51.05	June, 1821; Mar. 1824	2 0	6_m N. 6_a	Scouler.	Edinburgh Journ. of Sci. Vol. VI.
10	51.56	70.85	51.22	31.61	51.31	Apr. 1857; Apr. 1859	2 1	$7_m 2_a 9_a$	Assistant Surgeon.	Ar. Met. Reg. 1860.
11	49.20	63.42	51.83	38.78	50.81	Nov. 1849; Mar. 1868	17 7	"	" "	Ar. Met. Regs. 1855 and 1860 and MS. from S. G. O.
12	46.42	..	..	40.64	..	Jan. 1859; May, 1861	1 [illegible]	"	" "	Ar. Met. Reg. 1860, and MS. from S. G. O.
13	[illegible]	[illegible]	53.12	41.36	51.49	Nov. 1832; Oct. 1833	1 0	M. N.	....	Sill. Journal.
14	51.47	61.18	50.19	36.68	49.88	Oct.; Mar.	1 6	$7_m 1_a$	Parker.	Dove.
15	51.81	65.88	52.99	38.30	52.24	June, 1841; July, 1868	17 5	$7_m 2_a 9_a$	McLaughlin, Assistant Surgeon.	Wilkes, Ar. Met. Regs. 1855 & 1860, and MS. from S. G. O.
16	52.40	74.17	53.86	34.10	53.63	Jan. 1857; May, 1867	8 10	"	Assistant Surgeon.	Ar. Met. Reg. 1860, and MS. from S. G. O.
17	51.83	70.86	53.28	36.90	53.22	....	2 0	$\odot_r 2_a \odot_s 9_a$	....	Dove, 1857.
18	49.22	65.95	..	..	..	1870	0 6	$7_m 2_a 9_a$ bis	J. E. Whilworth.	S. O.
19	44.86	56.48	49.87	39.35	47.64	June, 1862; Mar. 1867	3 11	"	J. G. Swan.	" "
20	..	59.84	49.70	36.74	..	Sept. 1867; Aug. 1868	0 11	"	S. S. Bentley.	" "
21	..	67.40	..	..	..	1860	0 5	$7_m 2_a 9_a$	....	Rep. of N. W. Bound Com.
22	49.25	59.56	52.88	42.85	51.13	Apr. 1869; Dec. 1870	1 9	$7_m 2_a 9_a$ bis	A. Sampson.	S. O.
23	..	..	..	..	..	Nov. 1869; Jan. 1870	0 3	"	A. H. Simmons.	" "

WEST VIRGINIA.

	Spring.	Summer.	Autumn.	Winter.	Year.	Series. Begins. Ends.	Extent yrs. mos.	Observing hours.	Observer.	References.
1	57.85	75.12	57.05	38.70	57.18	1851—1854	2 8	$\odot_r 9_m 3_a 9_a$	Prof. G. R. Rossiter, S. Couch.	MS. in S. Coll.
2	52.61	73.82	55.93	34.61	54.24	Jan. 1854; Jan. 1858	3 2	$7_m 2_a 9_a$	" " "	P. O. and S. I. Vol. 1.
3	52.49	72.86	54.65	36.72	54.18	Feb. 1865; July, 1870	4 6	$7_m 2_a 9_a$ bis	C. L. Roffe.	S. O.
4	54.66	72.39	55.79	33.90	54.19	1852	1 0	$\odot_r 9_m 3_a 9_a$	Prof. G. R. Rossiter.	MS. in S. Coll.
5	..	81.18	..	..	..	1858	0 4	$7_m 2_a 9_a$	W. R. Boyers.	P. O. and S. I. Vol. 1.
6	..	..	..	..	..	1868	0 3	$7_m 2_a 9_a$ bis	R. H. Boliven	S. O.
7	47.40	..	..	..	..	1857	0 4	$7_m 2_a 9_a$	Dr. J. J. T. Offutt.	P. O. and S. I. Vol. 1.
8	45.30	68.43	50.22	27.70	47.91	Jan. 1856; May, 1861	2 6	"	D. H. Ellis.	P. O. and S. I, Vol. 1, & S. O.
9	52.03	69.29	48.17	30.12	49.90	Nov. 1858; June, 1860	1 8	"	B. D. Sanders.	" " " " "

5 Also known as "Camp Pickett" and "San Juan Island."

6 The earlier observations were made at Colville Depot, some miles to the southeast, and for five months of 1860 at Harney Depot.

7 Observations previous to 1855 at $\odot_r 9_m 3_a 9_a$; they were referred to $7_m 2_a 9_a$.

8 For additional observation in this vicinity, see "Port Townshend."

9 Observations for four months, in 1841, at $6_m 2_a 6_a$, and for four years and one month, from Dec. 1849, to Dec. 1854, at $\odot_r 9_m 3_a 9_a$; they were referred $7_m 2_a 9_a$.

10 Observations at $7_m 2_a 9_a$ after Jan. 1853.

11 Observations in March and May imperfect.

12 Also known as "Trout Run Valley" and Wardenville.

WEST VIRGINIA.—Continued.

Name of Station.	Lat.	Long.	Height.	Jan.	Feb.	March.	April.	May.	June.	July.	August.	Sept.	Oct.	Nov.	Dec.
10. Grafton	39°21′	79°56′	..	28°.77	37°.03	40°.33	54°.45	61°.20	..	76°.89	76°.40	70°.49	56°.86	46°.91	35°.1
11. Holiday's Cove	40 22	80 37	..	..	..	..	..	..	..	..	76.98	63.76	54.36	..	..
12. Kanawah[1]	38 53	81 25	..	33.83	40.66	44.90	55.39	62.84	69°.79	72.79	71.62	64.19	56.27	43.49	35.4
13. Kanawah	38 53	81 25	..	22.00	38.05	42.34	52.42	63.39	71.57	76.87	72.80	65.55	56.61	42.05	31.3
14. Lewisburgh	37 49	80 28	2000	29.03	37.21	44.07	48.00	62.37	66.48	71.51	68.60	61.42	51.63	39.73	33.1
15. Lewisburgh[2]	37 49	80 28	2000	33.18	39.48	47.18	53.37	66.76	72.62	78.47	74.24	68.62	57.08	44.48	36.4
16. Lewisburgh	37 49	80 28	2000	30.64	34.12	40.79	51.59	62.98	69.35	74.05	71.95	64.03	52.01	41.68	33.4
17. New Creek Depot	39 25	79 00	..	..	38.99	40.87	..	..	..	..	74.20	..	..	..	..
18. N. R. Mills	39 20	78 29	..	33.5	34.7	53.5	57.3	..	..	..	..	..	..	..	..
19. Peach Grove Lodge	39 15	81 00	1100	20.19	26.08	31.76	53.86	61.24	71.60	76.88	70.69	..	..	..	..
20. Point Pleasant	38 51	82 09	480	32.32	37.79	48.79	44.64	73.50	72.13	..	..	..	..	38.36	39.8
21. Poplar Grove[3]	38 20	81 30	720	34.92	38.98	44.28	52.88	64.15	70.35	75.76	72.70	65.82	55.05	43.75	37.9
22. Romney	39 20	78 42	573	29.26	30.68	44.03	50.42	58.69	70.54	76.61	72.74	65.82	52.73	42.81	29.0
23. Salem	39 20	80 01	1100	..	36.93	47.72	..	..	..	74.81	..	69.51	54.39	..	..
24. Sistersville	39 34	80 56	540	..	..	..	..	57.13	69.16	73.08	..	65.45	50.51	38.78	38.3
25. Weston	39 00	80 22	..	28.87	33.63	35.95	..	..	69.85	..	..	..	..	42.98	40.1
26. White Day	39 30	79 55	..	38.27	36.94	39.94	..	63.81	72.67	81.65	77.71	67.73	54.35	45.19	33.2
27. Wheeling	40 05	80 43	600	31.43	32.90	42.37	51.40	..	..	..	..	..	..	42.15	28.6
28. Wirt Court House[4]	39 05	81 26	..	28.29	33.69	37.67	47.49	60.25	72.58	75.62	72.41	63.84	53.88	38.76	35.0

WISCONSIN.

Name of Station.	Lat.	Long.	Height.	Jan.	Feb.	March.	April.	May.	June.	July.	August.	Sept.	Oct.	Nov.	Dec.
1. Appleton (Lawrence University)	44 18	88 31	800	17.99	20.79	30.67	42.34	54.58	65.77	70.73	65.94	59.32	47.07	33.52	21.6
2. Aztalan	43 04	88 55	808	26.82	29.60	35.97	43.28	56.40	68.06	71.29	69.56	62.63	48.37	35.84	20.3
3. Baraboo	43 29	89 54	920	18.87	23.03	29.94	44.51	57.58	69.62	73.17	69.15	62.50	49.27	34.58	22.1
4. Bay City (or Ashland)	46 36	91 00	610	13.94	12.27	23.45	33.02	45.20	56.58	65.08	60.90	53.48	39.38	26.40	15.9
5. Bayfield	46 50	90 57	..	13.44	15.08	23.68	38.59	49.65	60.15	67.84	63.59	54.70	41.59	30.25	18.2
6. Bellefontaine	43 30	89 15	750	18.47	22.21	33.24	45.42	57.97	68.79	72.58	70.75	61.74	48.71	34.08	21.3
7. Beloit College	42 30	89 11	750	19.77	23.64	32.05	45.37	57.44	68.39	72.38	69.33	61.76	48.50	34.99	23.0
8. Bloomfield	42 35	88 32	600	18.38	23.54	30.79	43.90	55.66	66.22	71.30	67.83	60.45	46.12	35.53	22.2
9. Ceresco	43 50	88 57	917	17.15	8.71	30.78	48.87	59.90	..	73.20	70.80	60.80	51.39	31.60	..
10. Dartford	43 45	89 16	850	17.05	20.32	30.69	44.24	52.55	67.25	68.45	69.13	61.37	49.15	34.25	28.5
11. Delafield (or Summit)	43 04	88 34	900	22.59	24.51	33.43	44.28	56.03	64.14	69.41	68.30	60.82	48.94	35.74	22.5
12. Delavan	42 39	88 42	957	15.69	23.01	27.57	44.65	52.33	67.29	68.84	66.34	60.54	47.06	36.37	19.9
13. Edgerton	42 38	89 00	1700	18.94	22.54	30.94	46.41	61.15	68.22	74.24	70.06	61.76	47.65	37.05	22.4
14. Embarrass[5]	44 25	89 00	..	15.19	20.78	26.71	40.58	54.41	65.19	69.95	65.32	58.09	44.56	32.54	18.7
15. Emerald Grove	42 39	88 54	1005	23.92	26.48	34.60	42.50	55.43	67.39	70.51	68.57	61.05	48.07	34.48	19.1
16. Fort Crawford	43 03	91 14	642	19.47	21.72	34.59	51.02	59.78	69.89	75.58	72.19	61.64	48.98	35.18	22.6
17. Fort Howard	44 33	88 09	620	18.83	20.10	31.19	43.20	55.87	66.27	71.57	67.93	57.28	46.75	34.24	21.1
18. Fort Winnebago	43 33	89 35	770	19.56	18.53	32.64	47.33	57.07	65.97	71.26	67.48	57.92	47.25	32.12	21.3
19. Galesville (Univ.)	44 07	91 29	775	21.00	..	..	..	..	69.48	..	69.68	..	..	..	..
20. Green Bay	44 29	88 00	732	15.19	23.00	27.14	39.77	54.46	66.36	69.85	68.09	60.46	45.85	35.98	17.6
21. Greenfield	44 00	90 45	750	..	..	..	..	63.28	68.28	70.55	66.30	63.78	49.08	37.18	19.4
22. Green Lake	43 45	89 00	670	24.57	27.22	32.13	40.37	50.42	67.48	69.35	67.33	60.90	49.16	37.11	20.3
23. Holland	43 36	87 58	670	15.01	23.49	27.17	43.58	56.20	63.93	69.91	67.67	60.58	44.61	35.22	23.0
24. Janesville	42 41	89 00	780	18.30	20.60	31.26	45.57	57.42	68.82	72.36	70.11	62.23	48.11	34.43	23.6
25. Kenosha	42 35	87 56	600	23.86	26.07	33.06	40.96	52.40	63.43	70.51	68.50	60.94	49.71	36.46	26.[illegible]
26. Lake Mills	43 06	89 02	..	12.50	21.50	26.81	..	..	..	..	..	..	..	..	..
27. Lebanon	44 28	88 54	900	..	..	..	..	..	67.85	72.20	..	..	..	..	..
28. Lowell	43 20	88 54	..	5.95	25.84	27.05	33.86	53.03	63.04	69.72	66.81	62.54	47.80	29.83	29.6
29. Madison (Wisconsin University)	43 05	89 24	1088	17.65	21.19	30.00	43.88	56.54	66.81	71.82	68.70	62.46	48.46	33.67	23.6
30. Manitowoc	44 07	87 46	658	21.76	23.92	31.31	41.72	51.91	62.04	67.91	65.95	58.64	46.95	36.21	25.4
31. Menasha	44 13	88 34	..	26.77	14.50	35.00	..	..	..	..	..	..	47.09	29.91	28.0
32. Milwaukee	43 04	88 00	604	21.39	25.22	32.81	43.36	52.95	63.60	69.86	67.61	60.99	48.78	37.10	25.3

[1] The morning and evening observations were probably taken at $\odot_r$ and $\odot_s$.

[2] Observations at 7_m 2_a 9_a after Jan. 1853, except for March, May, June, July, and Oct. 1853, at 7_m 2_a.

WEST VIRGINIA.—Continued.

	Spring.	Summer.	Autumn.	Winter.	Year.	Series. Begins.	Series. Ends.	Extent yrs. mos.	Observing hours.	Observer.	References.
10	51°.99	..	58°.09	33°.66	..	Jan. 1867;	Feb. 1868	1 1	$7_m\ 2_a\ 9_a$ bis	Dr. W. H. Sharp.	S. O.
11	..	..	..	..	..	1858		0 3	$7_m\ 2_a\ 9_a$	R. B. Sanders.	P. O. and S. I. Vol. 1.
12	54.38	71°.40	54.65	36.66	54°.27	Jan. 1829;	Jan. 1843	7 10	M. N. E.	D. Ruffner.	MS. in S. Coll.
13	52.72	73.75	54.74	30.45	52.91	Jan. 1856;	July, 1859	2 8	$7_m\ 2_a\ 9_a$	D. L. Ruffner, W. C. Reynolds.	P. O. and S. I. Vol. 1.
14	51.48	68.86	50.93	33.13	51.10	Apr. 1851;	Mar. 1853	2 0	9_m	Patton.	MS. in S. Coll.
15	55.77	75.11	56.73	36.37	55.99	1851—1854		3 9	$9_m\ 3_a$	" "	" " "
16	51.79	71.78	52.57	32.75	52.22	Jan. 1854;	Mar. 1861	7 1	$7_m\ 2_a\ 9_a$	Dr. T. Patton, Dr. J. W. Stalnaker.	P. O. and S. I. Vol. 1, and S. O.
17	..	..	..	..	..	1854		0 3	"	M. McDonald.	P. O. and S. I. Vol. 1.
18	..	..	..	..	..	1868		0 4	2_a	S. J. Stump.	S. O.
19	48.95	73.06	..	..	..	1856		0 8	$7_m\ 2_a\ 9_a$	W. C. Quincy.	P. O. and S. I. Vol. 1.
20	55.64	..	..	36.65	..	Nov. 1858;	June, 1859	0 8	"	W. R. Boyers.	" " " "
21	53.77	72.94	54.87	37.29	54.72	June, 1856;	Jan. 1861	4 4	"	J. E. Kendall.	P. O. and S. I. Vol. 1, and S. O.
22	51.05	73.30	53.79	29.65	51.95	May, 1866;	Sept. 1870	3 1	$7_m\ 2_a\ 9_a$ bis	W. H. McDowell.	S. O.
23	..	..	..	..	..	July, 1857;	Mar. 1858	0 5	$7_m\ 2_a\ 9_a$	J. C. Wells.	P. O. and S. I. Vol. 1.
24	..	..	51.58	..	..	1857		0 7	"	E. D. Johnson.	" " " "
25	..	..	..	34.21	..	Nov. 1865;	Mar. 1870	0 6	$7_m\ 2_a\ 9_a$ bis	B. Owen.	S. O.
26	..	77.34	55.76	36.14	..	May, 1868;	Mar. 1869	0 11	"	Dr. W. A. Sharp.	" "
27	..	..	..	31.01	..	Nov. 1859;	Apr. 1860	0 6	$7_m\ 2_a\ 9_a$	G. P. Lockwood.	P. O. and S. I. Vol. 1, and S. O.
28	48.47	73.54	52.16	32.33	51.62	May, 1856;	Dec. 1858	2 8	"	Dr. J. W. Hoff.	P. O. and S. I. Vol. 1.

WISCONSIN.

	Spring.	Summer.	Autumn.	Winter.	Year.	Series. Begins.	Series. Ends.	Extent yrs. mos.	Observing hours.	Observer.	References.
1	42.53	67.48	46.64	20.15	44.20	Jan. 1856;	May, 1870	8 4	$7_m\ 2_a\ 9_a$ bis	Prof. R. Z. Mason & others.	P. O. and S. I. Vol. 1. and S. O.
2	45.22	69.64	48.95	25.60	47.35	1850;	1851	1 11	$\odot_r\ 9_m\ 3_a\ 9_a$	Brayton.	S. Coll.
3	44.01	70.65	48.78	21.35	46.20	1850;	Dec. 1870	7 6	$7_m\ 2_a\ 9_a$ bis	M. C. Waite, & Mills.	S. O. and S. Coll.
4	33.89	60.85	39.75	14.04	37.13	July, 1856;	Apr. 1866	6 11	"	Dr. E. Ellis.	P. O. and S. I. Vol. 1, and S. O.
5	37.31	63.86	42.18	15.58	39.73	Sept. 1858;	Dec. 1870	3 6	"	J. H. [illegible] and A. Tate.	" " " "
6	[illegible]	[illegible]	48.18	20.87	46.27	1850;	1853	3 0	$\odot_r\ 9_m\ 3_a\ 9_a$	Gay.	S. Coll.
7	44.95	70.03	48.42	22.16	46.39	Jan. 1850;	July, 1867	17 5	$7_m\ 2_a\ 9_a$ bis	Prof. W. Porter and others.	P. O. and S. I. Vol. 1, S. O., & S. Coll.
8	43.45	68.45	47.37	21.37	45.16	May, 1863;	Dec. 1870	6 4	"	W. H. Whiting.	S. O.
9	46.52	..	47.93	..	..	Mar. 1854;	May, 1855	0 11	$7_m\ 2_a\ 9_a$	Miss M. E. Baker.	P. O. and S. I. Vol. 1.
10	42.49	68.28	48.26	21.97	45.25	Mar. 1861;	Apr. 1862	1 1	$7_m\ 2_a\ 9_a$ bis	M. H. Powers.	S. O.
11	44.58	67.28	48.50	23.20	45.89	Jan. 1845;	June, 1863	10 2	$\odot_r$ N. $\odot_s$	E. W. Spencer and others.	MS. in S. Coll., S. O., P. O. and S. I. Vol. 1.
12	41.52	67.49	47.99	19.55	44.14	Sept. 1864;	Dec. 1867	3 3	$7_m\ 2_a\ 9_a$ bis	L. Eddy.	S. O.
13	46.17	70.84	48.82	21.30	46.78	July, 1867;	Dec. 1870	3 6	"	W. J. Shintz.	" "
14	40.57	66.82	45.06	18.25	42.67	Oct. 1856;	Dec. 1870	8 10	"	J. E. & E. E. Breed.	P. O. and S. I. Vol. 1, and S. O.
15	44.18	68.82	47.87	23.20	46.02	Mar. 1849;	1853	4 3	$\odot_r\ 9_m\ 3_a\ 9_a$	Densmore.	S. Coll.
16	48.46	72.55	48.60	21.29	47.73	Jan. 1822;	Aug. 1845	18 5	$7_m\ 2_a\ 9_a$	Assistant Surgeon.	Ar. Met. Reg. 1855.
17	43.42	68.59	46.09	20.03	44.53	Jan. 1822;	May, 1852	21 5	"	" "	" " "
18	45.68	68.24	45.76	19.81	44.87	Jan. 1829;	Aug. 1845	15 3	"	" "	" " "
19	..	..	..	..	..	June, 1867;	Jan. 1868	0 3	$7_m\ 2_a\ 9_a$ bis	W. Gale.	S. O.
20	40.46	68.10	47.43	18.62	43.65	May, 1858;	Sept. 1865	3 0	"	D. Underwood and F. Deckner.	P. O. and S. I. Vol. 1, and S. O.
21	..	68.38	50.01	..	..	1870		0 8	"	G. Pegler.	S. O.
22	40.97	68.05	49.06	24.05	45.53	Jan. 1850;	Mar. 1852	2 2	$\odot_r\ 2_a$	F. C. Pomeroy.	Am. Alm. 1852 and S. Coll.
23	42.32	67.17	46.80	20.52	44.20	Oct. 1868;	Dec. 1870	2 2	$7_m\ 2_a\ 9_a$ bis	J. DeLyser.	S. O.
24	44.75	70.43	48.25	20.84	46.07	Jan. 1853;	July, 1862	8 6	$7_m\ 2_a\ 9_a$	J. F. Willard and others.	P. O. and S. I. Vol. 1, S. O., and S. Coll.
25	42.14	67.48	49.04	25.54	46.05	1850;	June, 1863	9 9	"	Rev. J. and Dr. G. Gridley.	" " " "
26	..	..	..	..	..	1861		0 3	7_m	J. Atwood.	S. O.
27	..	..	..	..	..	1864		0 2	$7_m\ 2_a\ 9_a$ bis	J. C. Hicks.	" "
28	37.98	66.52	46.72	20.49	42.93	1857		1 0	......	N. C. Daniels.	Am. Alm. 1859.
29	43.47	69.11	48.20	20.84	45.40	Jan. 1853;	Dec. 1870	9 3	$7_m\ 2_a\ 9_a$ bis	Various observers.	P. O. and S. I. Vol. 1, S. O., and S. Coll.
30	41.65	65.30	47.27	23.72	44.48	Oct. 1851;	Dec. 1870	19 3	"	J. Lilps.	P. O. and S. I. Vol. 1, and S. O.
31	..	..	..	23.11	..	Oct. 1859;	Mar. 1858	0 6	$7_m\ 2_a\ 9_a$	Col. D. Underwood.	P. O. and S. I. Vol. 1.
32	43.04	67.02	48.96	24.00	45.75	Jan. 1837;	Dec. 1870	26 7	$7_m\ 2_a\ 9_a$ bis	Dr. I. A. Lapham and others.	S. Coll., Am. Alm. 1852 and foll., P. O. and S. I. Vol. 1, and S. O.

[3] Also known as "Kanawah Salines." [4] Also known as "Elizabethtown."

[5] The observations previous to 1864 were made by J. E. Breed at New London, about four miles south of Embarrass.

WISCONSIN.—Continued.

Name of Station.	Lat.	Long.	Height.	Jan.	Feb.	March.	April.	May.	June.	July.	August.	Sept.	Oct.	Nov.	Dec.
33. Mosinee	44°48′	89°46′	750	13°.24	17°.67	25°.38	45°.33	58°.60	66°.20	67°.80	62°.08	59°.13	44°.00	31°.75	16°.75
34. Mt. Morris	44 06	89 20	..	..	..	34.91	42.02	..	..	..	..	..	..	..	..
35. New Danemore	44 17	90 38	..	20.60	17.80	36.41	41.09	55.68	67.55	71.16	66.43	58.04	46.04	30.00	18.50
36. New Holstein	43 58	88 12	..	16.38	..	..	..	..	..	..	..	..	..	..	31.90
37. New Lisbon	43 52	90 17	..	16.51	20.56	28.21	45.12	57.70	68.03	72.93	67.48	60.50	45.46	34.92	20.74
38. New Richmond	45 06	92 42	..	..	..	..	40.17	..	..	..	..	..	..	..	..
39. Norway[1]	42 50	88 10	753	9.75	20.54	27.37	47.11	56.96	71.14	74.56	68.58	60.21	50.01	34.48	16.22
40. Pardeeville	43 29	89 14	..	..	..	..	..	..	..	..	..	..	46.59	35.92	15.10
41. Parfreyville (or Rural)	44 15	89 05	910	13.83	21.57	26.75	44.61	57.27	69.70	70.23	67.80	61.30	50.76	36.22	30.90
42. Platteville	42 45	90 37	800	17.22	21.21	33.25	46.43	60.58	70.74	76.51	73.03	63.42	49.96	33.61	20.68
43. Plymouth	43 45	88 06	870	16.54	19.94	25.75	40.54	51.39	64.67	69.95	65.72	58.34	44.08	34.82	20.77
44. Prescott	44 46	92 55	800	4.23	14.50	35.00	..	..	..	..	..	..	47.09	29.91	28.06
45. Racine	42 43	87 54	660	19.33	20.74	29.56	39.39	50.44	66.73	69.89	63.35	58.00	50.52	36.91	26.00
46. Ripon College	43 48	88 33	..	17.33	17.75	25.90	46.07	54.50	67.44	74.55	64.35	..	..	39.68	22.10
47. Rocky Run	43 26	89 19	..	16.90	21.60	29.33	45.01	57.40	67.49	71.00	68.33	60.06	46.55	34.64	21.17
48. St. Croix Falls	45 27	92 47	660	21.60	11.01	33.10	..	..	..	..	..	..	..	..	25.30
49. Southport	42 30	87 30	..	28.27	29.06	..	41.52	50.71	64.78	69.48	77.61	62.89	50.59	47.37	21.47
50. Springdale	43 31	89 16	..	19.63	23.53	38.80	46.45	58.65	65.45	69.53	..	..	..	..	..
51. Sturgeon Bay	44 52	87 30	35	14.91	17.80	26.30	44.46	57.91	67.85	70.18	66.63	62.80	50.59	38.30	24.70
52. Superior	46 44	92 13	680	11.56	14.17	22.22	36.76	47.03	57.53	64.52	63.70	53.01	43.15	30.38	13.74
53. Waterford	42 48	88 18	..	17.50	26.04	30.32	46.30	53.62	66.75	..	..	..	..	32.13	21.13
54. Watertown	43 13	88 45	840	26.59	..	..	..	..	71.60	74.11	70.86	58.82	52.36	31.08	24.79
55. Waukesha	43 00	88 20	812	18.47	19.48	32.58	45.88	53.89	68.38	72.78	68.18	62.05	49.31	33.01	24.30
56. Waupaca	44 21	89 10	900	17.24	22.06	28.73	43.98	56.53	69.27	72.57	68.68	60.05	46.45	36.06	22.15
57. Wausau	44 58	89 43	..	14.97	22.42	25.42	40.03	58.29	65.03	76.62	67.39	57.52	43.82	33.26	14.99
58. Weyauwega	44 20	89 02	870	15.72	18.83	27.54	44.25	56.82	67.70	70.33	66.51	62.75	44.78	32.56	23.42

WYOMING.

Name of Station.	Lat.	Long.	Height.	Jan.	Feb.	March.	April.	May.	June.	July.	August.	Sept.	Oct.	Nov.	Dec.
1. Camp Scott	41 18	110 32	..	18.38	26.98	34.52	42.24	46.50	53.54	..	..	..	..	..	21.20
2. Camp Stanbaugh	..	..	..	..	..	..	..	..	..	..	..	..	..	..	13.73
3. Deer Creek Agency	42 49	106 00	5000	..	..	..	..	..	..	..	..	..	..	32.14	18.32
4. Fort Bridger	41 20	110 23	6656	18.88	22.89	27.73	38.44	50.09	59.12	65.44	64.37	53.86	42.26	31.56	20.66
5. Fort D. A. Russell	41 12	104 50	..	28.57	30.60	24.54	36.14	48.60	58.86	68.70	63.64	55.50	42.98	38.69	23.32
6. Fort Fetterman	42 45	105 37	..	28.11	..	27.08	41.92	54.41	62.35	71.23	66.32	55.29	41.46	35.05	23.32
7. Fort F. Steele	41 45	107 10	..	23.24	24.16	28.58	40.84	53.54	63.47	69.45	66.16	56.87	44.00	36.78	20.05
8. Fort Halleck	41 34	106 50	7800	21.16	23.72	29.12	37.09	51.76	62.11	65.79	68.90	54.95	41.78	33.45	21.50
9. Fort Laramie	42 12	104 31	4472	28.43	31.83	37.26	46.94	56.60	68.34	75.93	73.49	62.07	49.68	36.42	27.68
10. Fort P. Kearney	44 30	106 50	6000	14.88	25.44	23.57	42.75	53.60	69.24	76.33	74.66	62.60	47.11	36.64	29.09
11. Fort Sanders	41 13	105 38	7161	20.60	25.26	28.85	38.61	47.15	57.26	66.20	62.07	53.04	44.16	35.49	23.93
12. Fort Thompson	42 48	108 56	..	10.67	..	..	..	..	..	..	..	..	..	..	..
13. Gilbert's Trading P'st	42 28	108 40	7400	7.57	..	..	..	..	..	..	..	..	..	..	9.23
14. Sweetwater Bridge	42 30	107 25	7000	..	..	29.80	41.88	53.93	..	..	..	..	..	..	..

MEXICO.

Name of Station.	Lat.	Long.	Height.	Jan.	Feb.	March.	April.	May.	June.	July.	August.	Sept.	Oct.	Nov.	Dec.
1. Bar of Tabasco	18 34	92 40	10	..	..	77.83	..	80.80	..	..	81.93	81.20	77.90	..	72.48
2. Cordova	18 45	96 51	860	65.03	67.13	70.51	73.12	74.86	73.37	72.31	73.05	71.83	70.29	66.74	65.65
3. Frontera	18 32	92 40	12	72.28	76.00	77.72	79.84	81.28	81.84	80.62	81.30	81.58	..	..	71.65
4. Gulf of Mexico	..	..	..	74.66	71.06	75.74	80.24	82.58	84.01	84.01	79.34	80.78	80.60	75.01	74.66
5. Matamoras	25 49	97 38	55	64.95	65.89	70.48	76.00	81.33	83.47	85.72	85.73	82.55	77.06	71.32	62.02
6. Mazatlan	23 15	106 29	..	71.15	72.25	69.85	75.20	81.60	87.60	83.00	85.25	84.40	84.65	79.90	75.05
7. Mexico City	19 27	99 05	7665	58.39	57.30	61.84	64.00	67.07	64.72	62.79	63.02	62.06	60.83	56.82	54.36

[1] This series includes observations in Sept. Oct. and Nov. 1861, at Caldwell's Prairie, about four miles southwest of Norway.

WISCONSIN.—Continued.

	Spring.	Summer.	Autumn.	Winter.	Year.	Series. Begins. Ends.	Extent yrs. mos.	Observing hours.	Observer.	References.
33	43°.10	65°.36	44°.96	15°.89	42°.33	Jan. 1859; Dec. 1870	1 2	$7_m\ 2_a\ 9_a$ bis	Dr. J. S. Pashley and J. O. Donoghue.	P. O. and S. I. Vol. 1, and S. O.
34	..	..	..	..	..	1858	0 2	$7_m\ 2_a\ 9_a$	....	P. O. and S. I. Vol. 1.
35	44.39	68.38	44.69	18.97	44.11	Jan. 1858; June, 1859	1 3	6_m N. 6_a	E. Haeuser.	" " " "
36	..	..	..	..	..	Dec. 1864; Jan. 1865	0 2	$7_m\ 2_a\ 9_a$ bis	F. Hatchez.	S. O.
37	43.68	69.48	46.96	19.27	44.85	Mar. 1867; June, 1870	2 10	"	J. L. Dungen.	" "
38	..	..	..	..	..	1866	0 1	"	C. Scribner.	" "
39	43.81	71.43	48.23	15.50	44.74	Mar. 1856; Nov. 1861	1 4	$7_m\ 2_a\ 9_a$	J. E. Himoe and S. Armstrong.	P. O. and S. I. Vol. 1, and S. O.
40	..	..	..	..	..	1859	0 1	"	S. Armstrong.	P. O. and S. I. Vol. 1.
41	42.88	69.24	49.43	22.10	45.91	May, 1860; Apr. 1865	1 1	$7_m\ 2_a\ 9_a$ bis	R. H. Struthers, and J. C. Hicks.	S. O.
42	46.75	73.43	49.00	19.70	47.22	Sept. 1851; Dec. 1859	9 4	$7_m\ 2_a\ 9_a$	Dr. J. L. Pickard.	P. O. and S. I. Vol. 1, & S. Coll.
43	39.23	66.78	45.75	19.08	42.71	Jan. 1865; Feb. 1870	4 10	$7_m\ 2_a\ 9_a$ bis	G. Moeller.	S. O.
44	..	..	..	15.60	..	Oct. 1857; Mar. 1858	0 6	$7_m\ 2_a\ 9_a$	Rev. S. L. Hillier.	P. O. and S. I. Vol. 1.
45	39.80	66.66	48.48	22.02	44.24	Nov. 1855; Jan. 1861	1 11	"	E. Seymour, J. W. Durham, and H. W. Phelps.	P. O. and S. I. Vol. 1, and S. O.
46	42.16	68.78	..	19.06	..	Nov. 1865; Aug. 1866	0 10	$7_m\ 2_a\ 9_a$ bis	Prof. W. H. Ward.	S. O.
47	43.91	68.94	47.08	19.89	44.96	Aug. 1859; Dec. 1870	10 11	"	W. W. Curtis.	P. O. and S. I. Vol. 1, & S. O.
48	..	..	..	19.30	..	Dec. 1857; Mar. 1858	0 4	$7_m\ 2_a\ 9_a$	M. T. W. Chandler & W. M. Blanding.	P. O. and S. I. Vol. 1.
49	..	70.62	53.62	26.27	..	1849; 1850	0 11	⊙$_r$ $9_m\ 3_a\ 9_a$	Gridley.	S. Coll.
50	47.97	..	..	..	..	1860	0 7	$7_m\ 2_a\ 9_a$ bis	S. Armstrong.	S. O.
51	42.89	68.22	50.56	19.14	45.20	1870	0 11	"	R. M. Wright.	" "
52	35.34	61.92	42.18	13.16	38.15	June, 1855; Dec. 1867	10 0	$7_m\ 2_a\ 9_a$	G. R. Stuntz, E. H. Bly, W. H. Newton, W. Mann.	U. S. Lake Survey, Rep. of 1867–68, P. O. & S. I. Vol. 1, and S. O.
53	43.41	..	..	21.56	..	Nov. 1860; Apr. 1863	0 10	$7_m\ 2_a\ 9_a$ bis	S. Armstrong.	S. O.
54	..	72.19	47.42	..	..	1852; 1853	0 8	⊙$_r$ $9_m\ 3_a\ 9_a$	Ayres.	S. Coll.
55	44.12	69.78	48.12	20.75	45.69	Mar. 1856; Mar. 1859	2 9	$7_m\ 2_a\ 9_a$	Prof. S. A. Bean, Dr. L. C. Lyle.	P. O. and S. I. Vol. 1.
56	43.08	70.17	47.52	20.48	45.31	Dec. 1863; Dec. 1870	7 5	$7_m\ 2_a\ 9_a$ bis	H. C. Mead, C. D. Webster.	S. O.
57	41.25	69.68	44.87	17.46	43.31	Nov. 1858; Dec. 1859	1 2	$7_m\ 2_a\ 9_a$	Dr. W. A. Gordon.	P. O. and S. I. Vol. 1.
58	42.87	68.18	46.70	19.32	44.27	June, 1860; May, 1867	4 7	$7_m\ 2_a\ 9_a$ bis	Various observers.	S. O.

WYOMING.

	Spring.	Summer.	Autumn.	Winter.	Year.	Series. Begins. Ends.	Extent yrs. mos.	Observing hours.	Observer.	References.
1	41.09	..	..	22.19	..	Dec. 1857; June, 1858	0 7	$7_m\ 2_a\ 9_a$	Assistant Surgeon.	Ar. Met. Reg. 1860.
2	..	..	..	..	..	1870	0 1	"	" "	MS. from S. G. O.
3	..	..	..	..	..	1859	0 2	"	Maj. T. S. Twiss.	P. O. and S. I. Vol. 1.
4	38.75	62.98	42.56	20.81	41.27	July, 1858; Dec. 1870	10 6	"	Assistant Surgeon.	Ar. Met. Reg. 1860, and MS. from S. G. O.
5	36.43	63.73	45.72	27.50	43.35	Dec. 1869; Dec. 1870	1 1	"	" "	MS. from S. G. O.
6	41.14	66.63	43.93	..	..	Nov. 1868; Dec. 1870	1 9	"	" "	" " "
7	40.99	66.36	45.88	22.48	43.93	Jan. 1869; Dec. 1870	2 0	"	" "	" " "
8	39.32	65.60	43.39	22.13	42.61	Sept. 1862; Nov. 1866	3 3	"	" "	" " "
9	46.93	72.59	49.39	29.31	49.56	Sept. 1849; Dec. 1870	17 9	"	" "	Ar. Met. Regs. 1855 and 1860, and MS. from S. G. O.
10	39.97	73.41	48.78	23.14	46.33	Jan. 1867; July, 1868	1 7	"	" "	MS. from S. G. O.
11	38.20	61.84	44.23	23.26	41.88	Sept. 1866; Dec. 1870	3 8	"	" "	" " "
12	..	..	..	..	..	1858	0 1	"	W. H. Wagner.	P. O. and S. I. Vol. 1.
13	..	..	..	..	..	Dec. 1858; Jan. 1859	0 2	"	C. H. Miller.	" " " " "
14	41.87	..	..	..	..	1864	0 3	$7_m\ 2_a\ 9_a$ bis	A. F. Ziegler.	S. O.

MEXICO.

	Spring.	Summer.	Autumn.	Winter.	Year.	Series. Begins. Ends.	Extent yrs. mos.	Observing hours.	Observer.	References.
1	..	..	..	..	..	Dec. 1862; Oct. 1863	0 6	$7_m\ 2_a\ 9_a$ bis	C. Lazlo.	S. O.
2	72.83	72.91	69.62	65.94	70.32	Jan. 1858; Dec. 1864	6 0	9_m N. $3_a\ 6_a\ 9_a$	J. A. Hieto.	P. O. and S. I. Vol. 1, and S. O.
3	79.61	81.25	..	73.31	..	Dec. 1863; July, 1865	1 3	$7_m\ 2_a\ 9_a$ bis	C. Lazlo.	S. O.
4	79.52	82.45	78.80	73.46	78.56	Aug. 1838; July, 1839	1 0	......	Bevard.	Dove.
5	75.94	84.97	76.98	64.29	75.54	1830; 1851	9 2	[2]	Dr. J. L. Berlandier.	Manuscript.
6	75.55	85.28	82.98	72.82	79.16	1868	1 0	⊙$_r$ N.	....	S. O.
7	64.30	63.51	59.90	56.68	61.10	Apr. 1769; Nov. 1856	3 11	[3]	Alzate, Burkhardt, Berard, L. C. Ervendberg.	Cotté, Blodget's Climatology, Rep. Brit. Assoc. 1847, P. O. and S. I. Vol. 1.

[2] The observations were made at $6_m\ 8_m\ 9_m\ 10_m\ 1_a\ 2_a\ 3_a\ 4_a\ 6_a\ 8_a$.

[3] Corrected for daily variation by the Gulf table.

MEXICO.—Continued.

Name of Station.	Lat.	Long.	Height.	Jan.	Feb.	March.	April.	May.	June.	July.	August.	Sept.	Oct.	Nov.	Dec.
8. Mexico City	19°27′	99°05′	7665	..	..	..	65°.50	65°.70	66°.10	62°.60	60°.40	61°.50	57°.90	56°.70	..
9. Minatitlan	17 59	94 30	45	..	..	78°.29	81.58	82.72	80.31	78.59	78.25	77.35	77.91	72.15	72°.73
10. Mirador	19 15	96 40	3600	61°.78	64°.08	67.85	70.46	73.51	72.27	70.96	71.55	70.59	68.67	64.68	62.54
11. San Juan Bautista	17 47	92 46	40	..	73.67	..	..	..	..	80.77	..	..	..	72.85	..
12. Tuxpan	20 45	97 17	12	..	..	..	..	..	..	..	..	78.93	75.93	73.38	69.90
13. Veta Grand	22 50	102 25	8030	49.06	51.35	57.65	60.13	63.37	63.52	60.31	59.49	58.62	58.37	55.44	52.00
14. Vera Cruz	19 12	96 09	26	69.98	71.60	73.40	77.18	80.42	81.86	81.50	82.40	80.96	78.44	75.38	71.06
15. Vera Cruz	19 12	96 09	26	..	..	..	..	..	..	..	..	..	..	..	..
16. Vera Cruz	19 12	96 09	26	73.10	73.31	76.90	77.43	81.79	80.33	81.17	81.61	80.66	79.93	74.58	71.77
COSTA RICA.															
1. Heredia	10 00	84 00	3837	69.98	69.75	71.11	71.73	71.78	69.80	69.13	70.57	68.54	67.69	69.44	70.39
2. Port of Limon	10 00	83 03	..	77.4	77.2	76.5	..	81.9	80.6	79.7	79.8	..	80.1	78.1	78.8
3. San José	9 54	84 06	3772	68.34	69.25	70.45	72.10	72.49	71.90	68.21	67.40	68.15	68.19	67.57	67.36
GUATEMALA.															
1. Guatemala	14 35	90 30	4961	62.74	64.39	66.49	68.96	68.55	68.14	66.83	66.86	66.73	66.64	64.72	64.02
HONDURAS.															
1. Belize	17 29	88 12	..	75.	78.	78.	80.	81.	82.	82.	82.	82.	81.	79.75	75.
2. Belize	17 29	88 12	..	75.15	77.94	79.55	79.49	81.90	83.67	82.74	83.12	82.55	80.81	78.13	74.91
3. Truxillo	15 54	86 00	80	..	..	..	..	..	..	82.75	81.85	..	80.27	77.24	74.08
NICARAGUA.															
1. Leon	12 20	86 30	180	..	..	..	..	..	..	80.46	..	..	..	..	..
2. Nicaragua (Virgin Bay)	11 24	85 39	..	..	..	77.25	..	..	..	..	..	..	..	..	..
BAHAMA ISLANDS.															
1. Nassau (New Providence)	25 05	77 21	80	74.31	73.81	77.21	78.46	80.18	82.74	85.23	85.53	84.32	80.94	76.39	75.98
2. Nassau (New Providence)	25 05	77 21	80	69.	73.	76.	78.	79.	83.	87.	88.	87.	80.	74.	70.
3. Salt Cay	21 00	71 15	20	74.55	..	..	..	..	..	..	..	..	..	..	..
4. Turk's Island	21 29	71 05	15	76.94	75.12	75.05	76.02	79.40	80.31	82.34	83.44	83.40	82.42	80.14	77.53
BERMUDA ISLANDS.															
1. Bermuda (R. N. Hospital, Centre Signal Station)	32 23	64 40	..	61.88	61.04	61.83	64.09	69.65	73.99	78.24	80.05	78.09	73.10	67.21	64.33
2. St. George	32 23	64 43	123	61.5	62.7	62.2	60.7	70.7	75.1	74.2	80.0	77.0	72.4	69.7	64.8

MEXICO.—Continued.

	Spring.	Summer.	Autumn.	Winter.	Year.	Series. Begins. Ends.	Extent yrs. mos.	Observing hours.	Observer.	References.
8	..	63°.03	58°.70	..	..	1769	0 8	......	Alzate.	Blodget's Climatology.
9	80°.86	79.05	75.80	..	..	May, 1858; May, 1859	0 11	$7_m\ 3_a$	C. Lazlo.	P. O. and S. I. Vol. 1.
0	70.61	71.59	67.98	62°.80	68°.25	Jan. 1854; Dec. 1870	16 0	$7_m\ 2_a\ 9_a$ bis	C. Sartorius.	P.O. and S. I. Vol. 1, and S. O.
1	..	..	..	..	..	Feb. 1861; Nov. 1862	0 3	"	C. Lazlo.	S. O.
2	..	..	76.08	..	..	1867	0 4	"	B. Crowther.	" "
3	60.38	61.11	57.48	50.80	57.44	1839; 1840	2 0	$8\frac{1}{2}_m\ 4\frac{1}{2}_a$	Burkhardt.	Rep. Brit. Assoc. 1847.
4	77.00	81.92	78.26	70.88	77.02	1791; 1803	13 0	......	Orta.	" " " "
5	77.90	81.50	78.62	71.96	77.72	....	....	......	....	Bridgewater Treatise.
6	78.71	81.04	78.39	72.73	77.72	June, 1847; Aug. 1859	3 7	[1]	Assist. Surg., Dr. G. Berendt.	Army Reg., P. O. and S. I. Vol. 1.

COSTA RICA.

	Spring.	Summer.	Autumn.	Winter.	Year.	Series. Begins. Ends.	Extent yrs. mos.	Observing hours.	Observer.	References.
1	71.54	69.83	68.56	70.04	69.99	1868	1 0	$7_m\ 2_a\ 7_a$	Señor Rohrmoser.	S. O.
2	..	80.03	..	77.80	..	Oct. 1865; Aug. 1866	0 10	"	Philip Valentin.	MS. in S. Coll.
3	71.68	69.17	67.97	68.32	69.28	Jan. 1861; June, 1861	4 1	$7_m\ 2_a\ 9_a$ bis	C. M. Raotte, Dr. A. Frantzius.	S. O.

GUATEMALA.

	Spring.	Summer.	Autumn.	Winter.	Year.	Series. Begins. Ends.	Extent yrs. mos.	Observing hours.	Observer.	References.
1	68.00	67.28	66.03	63.72	66.26	Jan. 1845; Dec. 1859	4 0	[1]	Bailly & A. Canndas.	Rep. Brit. Assoc. 1847, P. O. and S. I. Vol. 1.

HONDURAS.

	Spring.	Summer.	Autumn.	Winter.	Year.	Series. Begins. Ends.	Extent yrs. mos.	Observing hours.	Observer.	References.
1	79.67	82.00	80.92	76.00	79.65	....	1 0	......		Martin's Brit. Colonies p. 138.
2	80.31	83.18	80.59	76.00	80.00	1863	1 0	max. & min.	S. Cockburn.	S. Coll.
3	..	..	..	..	..	1854	0 5	$9_m\ 3_a$	E. Purdot.	P. O. and S. I. Vol. 1.

NICARAGUA.

	Spring.	Summer.	Autumn.	Winter.	Year.	Series. Begins. Ends.	Extent yrs. mos.	Observing hours.	Observer.	References.
1	..	..	..	..	..	1849	0 1	$\odot_r\ 9_a\ 3_a$	Squier.	S. Coll.
2	..	..	..	..	..	1865	0 1	$7_m\ 2_a\ 6_a$	F. M. Rogers.	S. O.

BAHAMA ISLANDS.

	Spring.	Summer.	Autumn.	Winter.	Year.	Series. Begins. Ends.	Extent yrs. mos.	Observing hours.	Observer.	References.
1	78.62	84.50	80.55	74.70	79.59	Jan. 1841; Aug. 1859	3 11	[1]	J. C. Lees, Chief Justice, and A. M. Smith.	Printed Journ. in S. Coll., P. O. and S. I. Vol. 1.
2	77.67	86.00	80.33	70.67	78.67	....	1 0	......	....	Martin's Brit. Colonies p. 105.
3	..	..	..	..	..	1861	0 1	$7_m\ 2_a\ 9_a$ bis	S. S. Garland.	S. O.
4	76.82	82.03	81.99	76.53	79.34	Feb. 1844; Dec. 1868	2 9	[1]	J. Arthur, J. B. Hayne, J. C. Crisson, A. G. Carothers (U. S. Consul).	MS. in S. Coll., P. O. and S. I. Vol. 1, and S. O.

BERMUDA ISLANDS.

	Spring.	Summer.	Autumn.	Winter.	Year.	Series. Begins. Ends.	Extent yrs. mos.	Observing hours.	Observer.	References.
1	65.19	77.43	72.80	62.42	69.46	Jan. 1836; Dec. 1859	12 9	[1]	Capt. Page, R. E., S. L. D. Wells, Assist. Surg. R. N., Serg't 56th, Reg. Signal Director, and Hartshorn.	Pamphlet by Sir W. Reid, Gov., MS. in S. Coll., Bermuda Royal Gazette, and Board of Trade.
2	64.53	76.43	73.03	63.00	69.25	Jan. 1856; Dec. 1859	2 5	$\{3\frac{1}{2}_m\ 9\frac{1}{2}_m$ / $3\frac{1}{2}_a\ 9\frac{1}{2}_a$	R. E. Met. Obs'y.	Bermuda Royal Gazette.

[1] Corrected for daily variation by the Gulf table.

CARIBBEAN ISLANDS.

Name of Station.	Lat.	Long.	Height.	Jan.	Feb.	March.	April.	May.	June.	July.	August.	Sept.	Oct.	Nov.	Dec.
1. Antigua	17°08′	61°48′	..	76°.80	75°.90	76°.40	77°.50	79°.40	80°.10	80°.10	81°.70	80°.60	80°.30	84°.30	79°.4
2. Antigua	17 08	61 48	..	..	..	..	..	..	..	..	..	..	..	..	..
3. Barbadoes	13 04	59 37	..	76.11	..	..	..	79.77	80.40	80.05	80.63	79.58	79.72	79.86	76.7
4. Barbadoes	13 04	59 37	..	78.04	78.04	79.16	78.23	79.64	78.10	79.01	78.49	82.11	82.25	81.87	79.3
5. Guadeloupe	15 59	61 25	..	76.14	75.33	76.53	78.30	79.79	81.07	80.98	81.72	81.64	80.37	79.27	77.5
6. Roseau (Dominica Island)	15 18	61 22	..	76.0	74.0	77.0	77.0	79.0	81.0	81.0	80.0	80.0	80.0	75.0	..
7. St. Bartholomew	17 53	63 00	..	79.05	78.69	79.99	80.06	79.86	79.59	83.30	81.01	79.18	80.17	79.48	79.3
8. St. Christopher	17 30	62 45	..	78.02	78.13	80.09	80.32	81.46	83.28	84.19	83.89	83.48	82.40	81.27	78.7
9. St. Thomas	18 21	64 56	..	80.78	79.43	81.55	81.32	82.85	83.57	82.22	82.58	82.22	83.48	82.94	81.3
10. St. Thomas	18 21	64 56	..	79.30	79.02	78.21	80.67	80.67	82.65	82.76	82.87	83.69	82.06	81.54	81.3
11. St. Vincent	13 10	61 15	..	79.80	79.12	79.51	80.92	81.99	81.94	81.95	82.60	82.87	82.48	81.85	80.1
12. Santa Cruz	17 45	64 40	..	76.0	77.5	74.0	76.0	..	..	.	..	..	..	..	75.7
13. Sombrero Island	18 37	63 27	45	75.55	74.92	75.50	77.41	79.37	80.16	81.05	81.62	81.53	81.68	79.35	76.7
14. Tortola	18 27	64 40	860	77.35	77.00	76.09	78.39	78.56	80.79	80.44	81.96	81.00	80.95	80.02	79.8
15. Trinidad (Port of Spain)	10 39	61 38	16	76.82	76.95	78.14	78.28	78.66	78.75	..	..	..	..	..	..
16. Trinidad	10 39	61 38	16	78.13	78.14	..	..	..	..	..	..	..	80.13	79.57	75.9
17. Trinidad	10 38	61 34	..	76.50	76.50	77.50	78.50	77.50	78.00	79.00	79.50	79.00	78.50	79.00	76.5

CUBA.

Name of Station.	Lat.	Long.	Height.	Jan.	Feb.	March.	April.	May.	June.	July.	August.	Sept.	Oct.	Nov.	Dec.
1. Havana	23 09	82 23	..	74.60	75.51	78.80	80.69	82.62	84.96	87.57	86.90	86.67	83.07	80.91	73.[illegible]
2. Havana	23 09	82 23	..	65.34	70.04	72.05	75.43	79.66	83.68	85.23	83.62	80.60	78.44	72.79	69.9
3. Havana	23 09	82 23	50	69.98	71.96	75.74	78.98	82.58	83.12	83.30	83.84	82.04	79.52	75.56	71.7
4. Havana	23 09	82 23	..	71.38	74.03	74.08	76.62	77.97	81.01	81.46	81.57	80.38	78.85	75.13	73.5
5. Havana	23 09	82 23	..	73.33	75.39	77.97	79.12	82.02	84.02	85.89	85.37	83.13	80.47	79.54	72.4
6. Havana	23 09	82 23	..	..	..	..	..	..	..	..	..	..	..	..	..
7. Havana (College of Belen)	23 09	82 23	..	72.90	74.19	76.46	78.94	81.23	83.57	84.26	83.99	83.02	80.40	75.77	73.8
8. Matanzas	23 02	81 40	50	73.53	72.10	75.76	80.23	80.75	82.09	81.58	82.12	82.15	78.79	77.71	74.6
9. San Fernando	22 22	80 09	554	69.90	71.40	73.20	74.60	77.90	78.90	80.50	79.60	78.60	75.90	72.90	67.9
10. Ubajay	23 00	82 00	290	64.50	67.50	66.88	70.00	76.13	82.25	83.63	83.25	79.63	76.50	69.25	62.3

JAMAICA.

Name of Station.	Lat.	Long.	Height.	Jan.	Feb.	March.	April.	May.	June.	July.	August.	Sept.	Oct.	Nov.	Dec.
1. San Antonio	18 10	76 30	..	75.60	74.60	74.75	75.10	77.25	79.45	79.75	79.40	80.40	79.45	78.70	75.4
2. Up Park Camp	17 59	76 56	225	78.95	79.65	81.15	..	..	..	..	..	..	82.38	82.26	82.9
3. Up Park Camp	17 59	76 56	225	78.	78.	82.	83.	81.	82.	83.	82.	82.	80.	79.	78.
4. Kingston	18 00	76 47	50	75.73	76.00	75.87	78.08	80.27	80.60	81.67	81.00	80.73	79.80	78.73	76.7

SAN DOMINGO.

Name of Station.	Lat.	Long.	Height.	Jan.	Feb.	March.	April.	May.	June.	July.	August.	Sept.	Oct.	Nov.	Dec.
1. San Domingo	18 29	70 00	..	85.17	84.04	85.17	86.00	85.50	82.06	78.69	77.00	78.69	78.69	77.83	78.[illegible]
2. Tivoli (Hayti)	18 35	70 00	..	69.08	68.90	71.60	73.40	72.50	78.08	77.90	77.00	77.00	74.71	73.58	70.8

PORTO RICO.

Name of Station.	Lat.	Long.	Height.	Jan.	Feb.	March.	April.	May.	June.	July.	August.	Sept.	Oct.	Nov.	Dec.
1. Estate San Isidro	18 25	66 12	..	76.43	75.14	75.40	76.90	..	..	..	..	..	..	..	..
2. Ponce	17 56	66 35	23	..	78.5	..	..	..	..	..	..	..	..	..	..
3. Porto Rico	18 29	66 13	..	77.33	78.83	75.33	80.33	81.33	84.00	87.33	89.33	83.67	81.33	79.67	78.[illegible]

GUIANA (BRITISH).

Name of Station.	Lat.	Long.	Height.	Jan.	Feb.	March.	April.	May.	June.	July.	August.	Sept.	Oct.	Nov.	Dec.
1. Demerara	6 45	58 02	36	..	..	..	..	..	..	81.8	..	..	..	..	..
2. Demerara	6 45	58 02	..	79.5	81.0	81.0	80.5	82.0	79.0	82.0	83.0	82.0	81.0	81.0	76.5
3. Georgetown	6 49	58 12	..	77.5	77.8	79.1	79.5	79.7	79.4	..	..	..	..	..	..

CARIBBEAN ISLANDS.

	Spring.	Summer.	Autumn.	Winter.	Year.	Series. Begins. Ends.	Extent yrs. mos.	Observing hours.	Observer.	References.
1	77°.77	80°.63	81°.73	77°.37	79°.38	Dec. 1833; Nov. 1834	1 0	......	....	Martin's Brit. Colonies, p. 80.
2	..	..	..	..	79.68	1836	1 0	......	....	" " " "
3	..	80.36	79.72	..	..	May, 1841; Jan. 1842	0 9	[1]	Lawson.	Rep. Brit. Assoc. 1847.
4	79.01	78.53	82.08	78.48	79.52	1844	1 0	$\odot_r$ 9_a	R. Young.	Dove.
5	78.21	81.26	80.43	76.32	79.05	1849; 1851	3 0	max. & min.	....	Rep. Brit. Assoc. 1847.
6	77.67	80.67	78.33	..	..	....	0 11	......	....	Martin's Brit. Colonies, p. 75.
7	79.97	81.30	79.61	79.02	79.97	May, 1786; Apr. 1787	1 0	6_m N. 2_a 6_a	Fahlberg.	Rep. Brit. Assoc. 1847.
8	80.62	83.79	82.38	78.29	81.27	....	1 3	max. & min.	....	" " " "
9	81.91	82.79	82.88	80.51	82.02	1840; 1846	1 11	......	Knox.	Dove, 1853.
10	79.85	82.76	82.43	79.87	81.23	1833	1 0	6_m 7_m 4_a 8_a	Schonburgh.	Rep. Brit. Assoc. 1847.
11	80.81	82.16	82.40	79.70	81.27	1824; 1832	8 0	......	....	" " " "
12	..	..	..	76.40	..	Dec. 1836; Apr. 1837	0 5	{ $6\frac{1}{2}_m$ 9_m N. { 3_a 6_a 9_a	Rev. Dr. Tuckerman.	Am. Alm. 1839.
13	77.43	80.94	80.85	75.75	78.74	Feb. 1863; Oct. 1865	1 10	7_m 2_a $9_{a\,bis}$	A. A. Julien.	S. O.
14	77.68	81.06	80.66	78.07	79.37	1831; 1833	3 0	6_m 2_a 6_a	Schonburgh.	Rep. Brit. Assoc. 1847.
15	78.36	..	..	..	..	....	.....	......	Deville.	Dove, 1853.
16	..	..	..	77.40	..	Oct. 1856; Feb. 1857	0 5	7_m 2_a 9_a	Geological surveyors.	P. O. and S. I. Vol. I.
17	77.83	78.83	78.83	76.50	78.00	....	1 0	max. & min.	....	Martin's Brit. Colonies, p. 26.

CUBA.

	Spring.	Summer.	Autumn.	Winter.	Year.	Series. Begins. Ends.	Extent yrs. mos.	Observing hours.	Observer.	References.
1	80.70	86.48	83.55	74.46	81.30	1794	1 0	......	....	Dove, 1853.
2	75.71	84.18	77.28	68.44	76.40	1800; 1807	4 0	......	....	" "
3	79.10	83.42	79.04	71.24	78.20	1810; 1812	3 0	......	Humboldt.	" "
4	76.22	81.35	78.12	72.98	77.17	1825; 1831	7 0	......	....	Rep. Brit. Assoc. 1847.
5	79.70	85.09	81.05	73.73	79.89	Jan. 1842; Oct. 1849	1 3	8_m 2_a 8_a	Gibbs and Pocy.	MS. in S. Coll. & Print. Journ.
6	78.98	83.30	78.98	71.24	78.08	....	.....	......	....	Bridgewater Treatise.
7	78.88	83.94	79.73	73.66	79.05	Jan. 1859; Nov. 1870	11 3	[2]	Various observers.	Printed Records of Observa.
8	78.91	81.93	79.55	73.43	78.46	1832; 1835	2 0	$\odot_r$ 2_a $\odot_s$	Mallory.	Sill. Journ.
9	75.23	79.67	75.80	69.73	75.11	Jan. 1839; June, 1840	1 0	8_m N. $\odot_s$	Blake.	" "
10	71.00	83.04	75.13	64.79	73.49	1831; 1833	3 0	6_m 2_a 6_a	Schonburgh.	Rep. Brit. Assoc. 1847.

JAMAICA.

	Spring.	Summer.	Autumn.	Winter.	Year.	Series. Begins. Ends.	Extent yrs. mos.	Observing hours.	Observer.	References.
1	75.70	79.53	79.52	75.20	77.49	1819; 1820	2 0	$\odot_r$ N.	Arnold.	Rep. Brit. Assoc. 1847.
2	..	..	..	80.51	..	Oct. 1855; Mar. 1856	0 6	$9\frac{1}{2}_m$ $3\frac{1}{2}_a$	Col. W. B. Marlow, and J. G. Lawkins.	P. O. and S. I. Vol. I.
3	82.00	82.33	80.33	78.00	80.67	....	.....	......	From Sir J. McGregor's Office, Military Medical Dep.	Martin's Brit. Colonies, p. 5.
4	78.07	81.09	79.75	76.16	78.77	1832	1 0	......	....	Martin's Brit. Colonies, p. 57.

SAN DOMINGO.

	Spring.	Summer.	Autumn.	Winter.	Year.	Series. Begins. Ends.	Extent yrs. mos.	Observing hours.	Observer.	References.
1	85.56	79.25	78.40	82.63	81.46	May, 1782; Apr. 1783	1 0	......	....	Rep. Brit. Assoc. 1847.
2	72.50	77.66	75.10	69.62	73.72	1779	1 0	......	....	" " " "

PORTO RICO.

	Spring.	Summer.	Autumn.	Winter.	Year.	Series. Begins. Ends.	Extent yrs. mos.	Observing hours.	Observer.	References.
1	..	..	..	..	..	1868	0 4	7_m 2_a 8_a	G. Latimer.	S. O.
2	..	..	..	..	..	1844	0 1	$\odot_r$ 9_m 3_a 9_a	W. A. Mitchell.	MS. in S. Coll.
3	79.00	86.89	81.56	78.05	81.37	....	5 0	7_m N. 5_a	Vertez.	Rep. Brit. Assoc. 1847.

GUIANA (BRITISH).

	Spring.	Summer.	Autumn.	Winter.	Year.	Series. Begins. Ends.	Extent yrs. mos.	Observing hours.	Observer.	References.
1	..	..	..	..	..	1843	0 1	3_m 9_m 3_a 9_a	D. Blair.	MS. in S. Coll.
2	81.17	81.33	81.33	79.00	80.71	....	1 6	......	....	Rep. Brit. Assoc. 1847.
3	79.43	..	..	..	..	1854	0 6	max. & min.	J. P. Dawes.	MS. in S. Coll.

[1] Means of 18 daily observations.

[2] The observing hours were 6_m 8_m 10_m N. 2_a 4_a 6_a 8_a 10_a.

GUIANA (DUTCH).

Name of Station.	Lat.	Long.	Height.	Jan.	Feb.	March.	April.	May.	June.	July.	August.	Sept.	Oct.	Nov.	Dec.
1. Catharina Sophia	5°48′	56°47′	..	79°.18	79°.99	80°.42	80°.40	80°.22	79°.75	80°.14	81°.45	81°.42	82°.19	80°.60	79°.39
2. Commervine	5 38	54 42	..	78.26	77.18	77.00	78.08	78.26	78.08	77.90	78.08	78.26	79.16	78.80	78.80
3. Guanabacoa	5 05	..	..	71.00	72.76	78.33	76.00	78.67	79.33	81.33	82.00	80.67	79.33	72.00	70.33
4. Paramaribo	5 44	55 13	..	78.24	78.01	78.94	79.16	79.88	79.52	80.02	82.00	83.44	83.28	81.46	79.66
5. Rio Berbice	6 29	57 30	..	78.44	78.62	79.88	80.24	80.78	82.22	83.12	84.38	83.84	84.20	82.76	80.24
6. Rustenburg	6 00	55 00	..	77.24	77.56	78.19	78.24	77.93	77.40	77.81	79.61	80.17	80.76	79.06	78.04

NEW GRANADA.

Name of Station.	Lat.	Long.	Height.	Jan.	Feb.	March.	April.	May.	June.	July.	August.	Sept.	Oct.	Nov.	Dec.
1. Aspinwall	9 21	79 54	6	78.82	78.85	79.13	79.98	79.98	79.43	78.96	79.26	78.91	78.64	78.57	78.98
2. Barbacoas	8 30	79 00	65	..	..	..	..	..	78.74	..	..	..	..	..	..
3. Bogota	4 36	74 14	8863	..	..	..	..	..	60.07	..	..	..	..	..	..
4. Bogota	4 36	74 14	8863	..	..	..	..	..	..	..	..	..	..	..	..
5. Chagres	9 21	79 59	..	..	79.7	80.6	..	..	..	..	..	..	..	..	..
6. Manzanilla Island	9 21	79 57	..	..	..	..	..	78.53	77.22	78.66	77.82	77.84	79.82	..	..
7. Panama	8 57	79 30	..	..	..	..	81.9	..	..	..	..	..	..	..	..
8. Rio Hacha	11 28	73 00	..	81.32	81.83	84.25	81.50	84.30	84.38	..	..	..	..	..	81.70

VENEZUELA.

Name of Station.	Lat.	Long.	Height.	Jan.	Feb.	March.	April.	May.	June.	July.	August.	Sept.	Oct.	Nov.	Dec.
1. Caracas	10 31	66 55	2900	69.72	69.98	70.25	71.66	73.04	72.30	73.63	73.07	72.73	73.00	72.39	69.44
2. Cumana	10 30	64 15	..	80.35	80.51	81.95	83.84	84.54	83.10	83.28	81.50	..	..	83.21	80.83
3. Cumana	10 30	64 15	..	..	..	..	..	..	..	..	..	..	..	..	..
4. Curaçoa	12 06	69 20	..	77.90	78.62	78.62	80.24	80.96	81.86	..	..	..	..	81.14	72.68
5. Colonia Tovar	10 26	67 20	6500	60.65	62.85	62.76	63.36	63.92	61.05	60.50	61.57	61.49	61.51	60.77	61.26
6. Colonia Tovar	10 26	67 20	6500	61.51	62.64	64.06	64.89	64.89	65.34	65.75	65.75	66.01	64.62	64.62	63.05
7. La Guayra	10 37	67 00	..	76.59	76.51	77.42	78.45	79.42	79.78	79.30	80.70	81.12	80.69	79.64	76.81
8. Maracaybo	10 43	71 52	..	81.20	83.36	82.83	86.35	85.93	86.60	86.66	86.91	86.42	84.99	83.91	81.87
9. Puerto Cabello	10 28	68 17	..	..	79.2	..	..	..	81.4	..	82.2	82.2	81.3	..	79.3

BRAZIL.

Name of Station.	Lat.	Long.	Height.	Jan.	Feb.	March.	April.	May.	June.	July.	August.	Sept.	Oct.	Nov.	Dec.
1. Gongo Soco	—19 59	43 30	3360	71.07	71.25	70.20	68.65	65.75	60.20	59.52	63.81	61.67	70.60	72.19	72.20
2. Para	— 1 28	48 29	20	80.00	78.90	78.90	79.30	80.60	81.10	81.60	81.50	81.10	81.20	81.90	81.50
3. Parnambuco	— 8 10	34 57	..	79.59	81.19	81.80	78.30	78.22	76.44	75.38	75.03	76.33	81.06	82.93	81.09
4. Rio de Janeiro	—22 54	43 09	..	80.13	80.04	77.95	75.47	70.68	68.68	67.15	69.96	70.48	72.82	74.39	77.27
5. Rio de Janeiro	—22 54	43 09	..	82.83	83.95	81.18	77.77	74.48	71.73	71.99	73.38	74.63	76.49	77.16	80.56
6. Rio de Janeiro	—22 54	43 09	..	..	..	..	..	..	71.86	71.49	68.92	69.72	69.99	..	..

BUENOS AYRES.

Name of Station.	Lat.	Long.	Height.	Jan.	Feb.	March.	April.	May.	June.	July.	August.	Sept.	Oct.	Nov.	Dec.
1. Buenos Ayres	—34 37	58 24	..	73.57	75.71	73.31	64.77	55.41	53.41	52.55	51.83	54.64	58.91	68.43	70.91
2. Buenos Ayres	—34 37	58 24	..	..	..	..	..	..	..	..	..	..	..	..	..

CHILI.

Name of Station.	Lat.	Long.	Height.	Jan.	Feb.	March.	April.	May.	June.	July.	August.	Sept.	Oct.	Nov.	Dec.
1. Chanarcillo	—27 28	70 28	3860	66.49	66.94	65.93	..	..	..	..	..	..	..	62.44	65.13
2. Rio de Condon	..	..	..	..	..	..	63.74	61.34	56.48	52.70	52.51	55.75	58.10	..	..
3. Talcahuana	—36 34	72 57	..	..	..	..	64.72	59.90	56.84	52.15	51.44	51.62	55.04	..	..
4. Valdivia	—39 50	73 10	..	61.47	60.80	55.17	51.57	50.67	48.87	43.47	48.20	45.11	48.26	49.95	57.42
5. Valparaiso	—33 02	71 40	..	..	65.50	62.75	62.45	59.05	54.98	57.72	57.77	59.50	61.50	63.62	64.75
6. Valparaiso	—33 02	71 40	..	..	..	..	..	..	54.09	54.34	53.26	..	..	..	..

GUIANA (DUTCH).

	Spring.	Summer.	Autumn.	Winter.	Year.	Series. Begins.	Ends.	Extent yrs. mos.	Observing hours.	Observer.	References.
1	80°.35	80°.45	81°.40	79°.52	80°.43	Feb. 1856;	Dec. 1859	3 9	$6_m\ 2_a\ 6_a$	C. T. Hering.	P. O. and S. I. Vol. I.
2	77.78	78.02	78.74	78.08	78.15	1843;	1844	2 0	......	....	Rep. Brit. Assoc. 1847.
3	77.67	80.89	77.33	71.36	76.81	July, 1819;	June, 1820	1 0	6_m N. 9_a	....	" " " "
4	79.33	80.51	82.73	78.64	80.30	Jan. 1833;	Feb. 1835	2 0	$7_m\ 2_a\ 7_a$	Dieperink.	" " " "
5	80.30	83.24	83.60	79.10	81.56	1772		1 0	$7_m\ 3_a\ 7_a$	Massé.	" " " "
6	78.12	78.27	80.00	77.61	78.50	May, 1861;	Dec. 1865	3 7	$7_m\ 2_a\ 6_a$	C. T. Hering.	S. O.

NEW GRANADA.

	Spring.	Summer.	Autumn.	Winter.	Year.	Series. Begins.	Ends.	Extent yrs. mos.	Observing hours.	Observer.	References.
1	79.70	79.22	78.71	78.88	79.13	Oct. 1862;	Dec. 1868	5 10	$7_m\ 2_a\ 9_a$ bis	Drs. W. T. White, & J. P. Kluge.	S. O.
2	..	..	..	..	..	1852		0 1	......	Bertherd.	Manuscript.
3	..	..	..	..	..	1857		0 1	$10_m\ 4_a\ 10_a$	Dr. E. Wricoschea.	P. O. and S. I. Vol. I.
4	59.54	59.54	58.10	59.18	59.09	....		1 4	......	....	Kaemptz.
5	..	..	..	..	..	1850		0 2	$6_m\ 9_m$ N. $3_a\ 6_a$	A. Fendler.	MS. in S. Coll.
6	..	77.90	..	..	..	1851		0 6	$\odot_r\ 9_m\ 3_a\ 9_a$	....	S. Coll.
7	..	..	..	..	..	1849		0 1	$9_m\ 3_a$	Major Emory.	Am. Acad. Trans.
8	83.35	..	..	81.62	..	Dec. 1822;	June, 1823	0 7	$7_m\ 3_a$	Wright.	Rep. Brit. Assoc. 1847.

VENEZUELA.

	Spring.	Summer.	Autumn.	Winter.	Year.	Series. Begins.	Ends.	Extent yrs. mos.	Observing hours.	Observer.	References.
1	71.65	73.00	72.71	69.71	71.77	July, 1841;	Aug. 1848	1 2	max. & min.	Graham & A. Fendler.	Dove, 1853, P. O. & S. I. Vol. I.
2	83.44	82.63	..	80.56	..	Nov. 1799;	Aug. 1800	0 10	......	Don Rubio.	Rep. Brit. Assoc. 1847.
3	83.66	82.04	80.24	80.24	81.86	....		.....	......	....	Bridgewater Treatise.
4	79.94	..	..	76.40	..	....		0 8	5_m N. 9_a	Dorfel.	Rep. Brit. Assoc. 1847.
5	63.35	61.04	61.26	61.59	61.81	Apr. 1854;	Nov. 1856	1 6	$\odot_r 9_m$ N. $3_a \odot_s$	A. Fendler	MS. in S. Coll., P. O. and S. I. Vol. I.
6	[illegible]	[illegible]	[illegible]	[illegible]	[illegible]	[illegible]		[illegible]	[illegible]	[illegible]	Dove, 1853.
7	78.43	79.93	80.48	76.64	78.87	Sept. 1834;	Aug. 1837	3 0	$6_m\ 11_m\ 4_a\ 9_a$	Halle.	" "
8	85.04	86.72	85.11	82.14	84.75	Sept. 1823;	Aug. 1824	1 0	$7_m\ 3_a$	Wright.	Rep. Brit. Assoc. 1847.
9	..	..	..	..	..	June, 1843;	Feb. 1844	0 6	$\odot_r\ 9_m\ 3_a\ 9_a$	F. Litchfield, U. S. Consul.	MS. in S. Coll.

BRAZIL.

	Spring.	Summer.	Autumn.	Winter.	Year.	Series. Begins.	Ends.	Extent yrs. mos.	Observing hours.	Observer.	References.
1	68.20	61.18	68.15	71.51	67.26	....		.....	{ $6_m\ 9_m$ N. 4_a / $6_a\ 8_a\ 12_a$	....	Rep. Brit. Assoc. 1847.
2	79.60	81.40	81.40	80.13	80.63	Dec. 1844;	May, 1849	4 6	......	Deweg.	Blodget's Climatology.
3	79.44	75.62	80.11	80.62	78.95	1842		1 0	......	Loudon.	Dove, 1853.
4	74.70	68.60	72.56	79.15	73.75	1782;	1788	7 0	trihourly.	Dorta.	Rep. Brit. Assoc. 1847
5	77.81	72.37	76.09	82.45	77.18	Jan. 1832;	Dec. 1843	12 0	N.	Gardner.	Sill. Journ.
6	..	70.76	..	..	..	....		0 5	bihourly.	King.	Dove, 1853.

BUENOS AYRES.

	Spring.	Summer.	Autumn.	Winter.	Year.	Series. Begins.	Ends.	Extent yrs. mos.	Observing hours.	Observer.	References.
1	64.50	52.60	60.66	73.40	62.79	Jan. 1822;	June, 1823	1 6	......	....	Dove, 1853.
2	64.58	52.52	59.36	73.04	63.12	....		1 4	......	....	Kaemptz.

CHILI.

	Spring.	Summer.	Autumn.	Winter.	Year.	Series. Begins.	Ends.	Extent yrs. mos.	Observing hours.	Observer.	References.
1	..	..	..	66.19	..	Nov. 1858;	Mar. 1859	0 5	{ $6_m\ 9_m$ N. / $3_a\ 6_a\ 9_a$	E. B. Dorsey.	P. O. and S. I. Vol. I.
2	..	53.90	..	..	..	1827		0 7	......	....	Dove, 1853.
3	..	53.48	..	..	..	1828		0 7	......	....	" "
4	52.47	46.85	47.77	59.90	51.75	Apr. 1851;	Mar. 1852	1 0	$6_m\ 7_a$	....	Dove.
5	61.42	56.82	61.54	..	..	1853;	1854	1 6	$9\frac{1}{2}_m\ 3\frac{1}{2}_a$	MacKey.	Board of Trade.
6	..	53.90	..	..	..	....		0 3	bihourly.	King.	Dove.

NOTE.—The heading of the seasons corresponds to those existing at the time in the *northern* hemisphere; for stations in south latitude they would be the opposite ones.

ECUADOR.

Name of Station.	Lat.	Long.	Height.	Jan.	Feb.	March.	April.	May.	June.	July.	August.	Sept.	Oct.	Nov.	Dec.
1. Antisana	—0°27′	78°28′	13455	43°.11	41°.11	41°.99	42°.60	41°.92	40°.08	37°.31	37°.41	39°.27	41°.02	41°.95	42°.42
2. Quito	—0 14	78 45	8970	58.24	60.98	60.04	59.86	60.62	59.00	59.18	60.94	61.34	59.95	60.53	..
3. Quito	—0 14	78 45	8970	..	..	..	..	..	..	..	..	..	..	..	..

FALKLAND ISLANDS.

Name of Station.	Lat.	Long.	Height.	Jan.	Feb.	March.	April.	May.	June.	July.	August.	Sept.	Oct.	Nov.	Dec.
1. Falkland Islands (Cape Oxford)	—52 00	61 00	...	56.00	54.00	51.61	48.65	46.64	43.50	37.41	38.64	45.75	47.51	47.20	49.87
2. Falkland Islands (Byron Sound)	—51 25	59 59	...	..	..	..	..	..	..	..	..	..	..	..	..
3. Port Egmont	—51 20	60 00	...	54.10	54.21	51.60	48.63	46.63	43.48	37.47	38.62	45.73	47.50	47.19	49.87

PATAGONIA.

Name of Station.	Lat.	Long.	Height.	Jan.	Feb.	March.	April.	May.	June.	July.	August.	Sept.	Oct.	Nov.	Dec.
1. Cape Horn	—56 08	67 00	...	..	..	40.01	35.69	..	35.42	..	..	36.68	..	..	43.34
2. Port Famine (Tierra del Fuego)	—53 38	70 58	...	..	47.80	45.09	38.94	37.55	33.75	33.40	35.13	..	..	..	..
3. Port Famine (Tierra del Fuego)	—53 38	70 58	...	51.10	49.37	41.22	35.47	32.97	33.03	33.25	..	..	..	..	..

PARAGUAY.

Name of Station.	Lat.	Long.	Height.	Jan.	Feb.	March.	April.	May.	June.	July.	August.	Sept.	Oct.	Nov.	Dec.
1. Asuncion	—25 16	57 45	...	82.35	81.73	79.43	75.34	71.24	..	66.69	67.67	..	..	..	84.54

PERU.

Name of Station.	Lat.	Long.	Height.	Jan.	Feb.	March.	April.	May.	June.	July.	August.	Sept.	Oct.	Nov.	Dec.
1. Callao	—12 03	77 13	...	73.94	..	69.80	..	66.56	64.76	..	61.70	..	..	68.36	71.96
2. Jauja	—12 00	75 15	10000	59.37	..	..	..	..	..	..	..	..	..	..	..
3. Lima	—12 03	77 08	530	78.08	79.88	80.06	77.36	77.90	68.36	68.54	67.28	66.20	69.26	71.96	74.84

URUGUAY.

Name of Station.	Lat.	Long.	Height.	Jan.	Feb.	March.	April.	May.	June.	July.	August.	Sept.	Oct.	Nov.	Dec.
1. Montevideo	—34 54	56 13	...	80.	77.	74.	72.	58.	56.	57.	59.	58.	66.	70.	75.

ECUADOR.

	Spring.	Summer.	Autumn.	Winter.	Year.	Series. Begins.	Ends.	Extent yrs. mos.	Observing hours.	Observer.	References.
1	42.17	38.27	40.75	42.21	40.85	Dec. 1845;	Dec. 1846	1 1	......	Anguire.	Dove, 1853.
2	60.17	59.71	60.61	..	..	1825;	1828	2 6	......	Hallarn.	Rep. Brit. Assoc. 1847.
3	60.26	60.08	63.50	59.72	60.89	....		2 3	......	....	Kaemptz.

FALKLAND ISLANDS.

	Spring.	Summer.	Autumn.	Winter.	Year.	Series. Begins.	Ends.	Extent yrs. mos.	Observing hours.	Observer.	References.
1	48.97	39.85	46.82	53.29	47.23	....		1 0	......	....	Rep. Brit. Assoc. 1847.
2	48.46	39.56	46.58	53.06	46.94	....		.....	......	....	Bridgewater Treatise.
3	48.95	39.86	46.81	52.73	47.09	....		1 0	N.	Friquinet.	Rep. Brit. Assoc. 1847.

PATAGONIA.

	Spring.	Summer.	Autumn.	Winter.	Year.	Series. Begins.	Ends.	Extent yrs. mos.	Observing hours.	Observer.	References.
1	..	..	..	..	..	....		.....	......	....	Rep. Brit. Assoc. 1847.
2	40.53	34.09	..	..	..	1828		0 7	bihourly.	King.	Dove, 1853.
3	36.55	..	..	..	..	....		.....	$6_m\ 9_m$ N. $3_a\ 6_a$	....	Rep. Brit. Assoc. 1847.

PARAGUAY.

	Spring.	Summer.	Autumn.	Winter.	Year.	Series. Begins.	Ends.	Extent yrs. mos.	Observing hours.	Observer.	References.
1	75.34	..	..	82.87	..	Dec. 1853;	1854	0 8	8_m N. $4_a\ 9_a$	Hopkins.	S. Coll.

PERU.

	Spring.	Summer.	Autumn.	Winter.	Year.	Series. Begins.	Ends.	Extent yrs. mos.	Observing hours.	Observer.	References.
1	..	..	..	..	..	....		.....	......	....	Rep. Brit. Assoc. 1847.
2	..	..	..	..	..	1861		0 1	$9_m\ 2_a\ 9_a$	G. H. Brown.	S. O.
3	78.44	68.06	69.14	77.60	73.31	1799;	1800	2 0	N.	Uranne.	Rep. Brit. Assoc. 1847.

URUGUAY.

	Spring.	Summer.	Autumn.	Winter.	Year.	Series. Begins.	Ends.	Extent yrs. mos.	Observing hours.	Observer.	References.
1	68.00	57.33	64.67	77.33	66.83	....		1 0	......	Friquinet.	Rep. Brit. Assoc. 1847.

NOTE.—The heading of the seasons corresponds to those existing at the time in the *northern* hemisphere; for stations in south latitude they would be the opposite ones.

GRAPHICAL REPRESENTATION

OF THE PRECEDING

TABULAR RESULTS BY ISOTHERMAL CHARTS.

EXPLANATION

OF

THE ISOTHERMAL CHARTS ACCOMPANYING THIS PAPER.

The three accompanying charts have been constructed to show the distribution of the atmospheric temperature within the limits of the United States, on the average during the year, and for the winter and summer seasons.

The great value of the graphical method consists in its capacity of bringing into a connected view the result of a large mass of apparently disconnected figures, and thus presenting their relations to the eye. In the present case, these relations depend on the geographical and hypsometrical features of the country.

The results brought out in these tables form the basis of the charts. They are laid down by means of curves connecting places of equal temperature. These curves may be conceived as forming the intersections of the earth's surface by a series of thermal surfaces of equal temperature one above the other and for equal differences of temperature. The difference, here adopted, is 4° Fah., and is the same for all the charts. During the winter season the decrease of temperature between the southern and northern limits of the United States is greater than during the summer season, hence a greater number of curves appear on the chart showing the distribution of temperature in the winter than on that for the year, and the chart for the distribution in summer has the least number of curves. The limiting curves are as follows: For the cold season 4° to 72° Fah., for the yearly average 36° to 76° Fah., and for the warm season 56° to 88° Fah.

From the above designation of the isothermals it follows that each curve must be continuous no matter how tortuous its course may be, that is, it cannot abruptly come to an end; of this instructive examples are presented on the chart for the year by the curve of 48° Fah., and on the chart for the summer by the curve of 68° Fah. The construction of the curves for the yearly distribution was found slightly more troublesome than those for either of the other charts, owing to the way in which the mean temperature results, from the monthly means, are influenced by the annual variation. Some difficulty was experienced in tracing out the summer curves for the western part of California, owing to the well-known exceptional and remarkable distribution of its temperature, of which more will be said further on.

The want of a reliable hypsometric chart of the United States was seriously felt, not one only on which the existence of hills and mountains should be *correctly* indicated as regards position, but one, on which the actual elevations are indicated by contour lines. A rough hypsometric chart of the latter description was constructed by me to aid in the tracing out of the thermal curves, but the latter are not what they might be, respecting accuracy in detail, were we in possession of an elaborate hypsometric chart.

On each chart was plotted the mean temperature for the respective period, corrected for daily variation, if necessary, for all the available stations within the area of the chart. On the east of the Mississippi all series extending over five years or more were given to the nearest tenth of a degree of Fahrenheit, those of less than five years' duration were set down to the nearest whole degree.

The decimal point marked the position of the place. For stations west of the Mississippi the limit of 3° was adopted instead of 5°. The curves were constructed with due regard to the elevations of the ground, producing a resemblance, for short distances, of the thermal curves to contour lines of equal elevation. The isothermals thus constructed are *not reduced* to the *sea level* for the following reasons. In the first place, we desire a knowledge of the true distribution of the temperature near the surface to which we are actually exposed and which affects agricultural and other pursuits, and not of any artificial distribution under special, qualified conditions such as the reduction to the sea level; in fact we might as well correct also for propinquity to the sea, for prevailing wind, for proximity of table-land or large lakes, nature of the soil, and a variety of other disturbing causes, which process would finally bring about a close conformity of the isothermals with parallels of latitude, and would represent what has been called the solar climate. Moreover, we do not possess the precise data for such a reduction; thus to experience a diminution of 1° Fah. in the atmospheric temperature, near the surface, the average values vary between 250 and 500 feet of rise, and at elevations beyond a mile, the change in altitude must be greater for the same difference in temperature. Besides, the law is different in the different seasons. It is proper to connect the decrease of temperature in altitude with the decrease of pressure to which it is supposed proportional (when starting from the absolute zero of temperature), a fall of 1° of temperature corresponds approximately to a decrease in pressure of nearly 0.25 inch, the barometric column indicating about 29 inches, and to 0.35 inch nearly for pressure at and below 27 inches.

On the other hand, if the meteorological stations were sufficiently numerous and equally distributed in area, the isothermal curves drawn among them would themselves furnish the best means of ascertaining the separate effects on the climate (temperature) of the various modifying elements of elevation, slope, surface condition (wooded or barren), and many other circumstances.

If we review the indications presented by each chart separately and notice only the leading characteristic features of the distribution of temperature, we may conveniently divide the area of the United States into two parts, viz.: that east of the 100th meridian, of comparatively small elevation, generally below 1000 feet and only exceptionally rising to 4000, and that west of this meridian, with an elevation generally above 4000 feet, and not unfrequently attaining the altitude of 10,000 feet and above.

When referring to the isothermal curves in the description of the charts, those referring to the yearly period will simply be designated as "isothermals," those referring to the winter as "isocheimals," and those referring to the summer as "isotherals."

As already pointed out, the position of the isothermal curves is intimately connected with the hypsometric features of the country, and this direct dependence has consequently been made the basis of the above division, greater or less elevation constituting the principal cause of their deflections. This appears, for instance, conspicuously in the isothermal of 52°, depending on the direction of the Apalachian range, and in the isothermal of 44°, depending on the directions of the Rocky Mountains, the Cascade range, and the Sierra Nevada.

In the *eastern* part of the United States, the distribution of heat appears normal, as indicated by the isothermals between 44° and 68° which follow, with no great departures, parallels of latitude; in the *western* part, on the contrary, it is altogether more irregular, and the pure solar climate is apparently subverted, the distribution of temperature on the Pacific shore being governed by a system almost at right angles to that in the eastern part, and possessing an *intermediate* system of distribution at the head of the Gulf of California.

In the *winter* months, the proximity of the Gulf stream to the Atlantic sea-board has the effect of *elevating* the temperature in the vicinity of the ocean, the amount being 0° in Florida, about 4° in North Carolina, and about 8° or 10° in Massachusetts; in the *summer* months, the effect is reversed, as shown by the isotherals curving southwards; this is due to the cold current running southwards between the coast and the gulf stream, and the depression produced would be still greater but for the circumstance of the prevalence of *westerly* winds which carry the heated air to seaward. The depressing effect, however, in amount, is less than one-half that given for the opposite season. It would appear that in summer nearly the whole of Florida enjoys an almost equal temperature, barely rising above 80° Fah.; with this we connect the fact that in Florida summer constitutes the rainy season.

On the yearly average the vicinity of the Atlantic is apparently without any direct effect on the temperature of the coast.

Passing now to the influence of the great lakes we shall find it similar, viz.: a *warming* effect in *winter*, rising to about 10°, and a *cooling* effect in *summer*, depressing about 5°, whereas, during the year the presence or absence of this body of water would seem to be of no particular consequence as regards mean temperature.

The coldest region is in northern Minnesota and northeastern Dakota, the isocheimal of 4° appearing along the low elevations near Red Lake in Minnesota. It is near these regions that the extremely cold waves, which occasionally sweep over the eastern and southern states during the winter appear to enter the United States.

In the western part of the country we recognize as the most remarkable feature, the great uniformity of the distribution of temperature along the Pacific coast as exhibited in the isothermal of 52°, skirting the coast for about 650 miles between San Francisco and the northwestern part of Washington Territory; the same feature is indicated by the direction of the isocheimals, approximating to parallelism with that of the coast and again in the isotheral of 60°. The direct influence of the Pacific Ocean on the climate of the western states (west of 100° longitude) is heightened by the presence of a cool current running southward close along the coast. The presence of the cool ocean, together with the prevailing westerly winds, sweeping the air which had been resting over the ocean across a great portion of the country, thus impresses the chief character on the climate, viz.: a comparatively high and uniformly distributed *winter* temperature, which is even felt beyond the Rocky Mountains in central Montana, to which latent heat is carried by the moist winds, as clearly exhibited in my Rain Chart[1] for the winter season. With the high winter temperature, we associate the fact of comparatively great precipitation. Secondly, we are impressed with the comparatively low *summer* temperature over the Pacific States; in fact the coldest place in the whole United States, at this season, excepting only the high mountain ranges and peaks, is just outside the Golden Gate, Bay of San Francisco, where we encounter the isotheral of 56°, which appears nowhere else during this season. To exhibit the contrast more forcibly, we have in the corresponding season and latitude on the Atlantic side (near the mouth of Chesapeake Bay, a temperature higher by as much as 18°. With this low summer temperature we connect the fact of but little precipitation.

In *winter* this contrast between the two (opposite) coasts is of the opposite kind, the isocheimal of 52°, off the Golden Gate, corresponding to the isocheimal of 42°, off the mouth of the Chesapeake, a temperature *lower* by 10°. Finally, we notice the extraordinary difference in the range of the mean temperature at the extreme seasons, this being nearly 4° on the Pacific, and nearly 33° on the Atlantic.

We next notice the greater accumulation of heat in valleys than in the plains, the most remarkable instance being that of the Joaquin Valley and its northern prolongation, the Sacramento Valley. This feature is most apparent in the *summer* season, when these valleys seem to become reservoirs of heat, and when their sloping sides are most exposed to insolation. The mean summer temperature in the central part of San Joaquin Valley rises above 84°, when on the sea-coast, close by, it is below 60°. Other instances of this kind are presented on the chart for the summer temperature, by the heated plains of the Columbia River, by the region along the Colorado and Gila Rivers, and, to return to the eastern portion of the country, by the lower valley of the Rio Grande, where the temperature reaches 84°, by the Hudson Valley, and lastly by that of the St. Lawrence.

The hottest region in the United States is along the lower course of the Colorado and Gila Rivers, where we meet with the isotheral of 88°.

It is needless to follow out, in further detail, the various features presented by the charts, since they address themselves sufficiently to the eye, nor has it been deemed necessary to construct isothermal charts for the intermediate seasons of spring and autumn, which, being periods of transition, cannot present features as striking as those exhibited by the extreme seasons.

The total number of results from series plotted on the charts and from which the isothermal curves were constructed are 1300 nearly for the year, 1450 nearly for the winter, and 1500 nearly for the summer. For the base chart, the Smithsonian Institution is indebted to Prof. Francis A. Walker, Superintendent U. S. Census.

---

[1] Tables and Results of the Precipitation, in Rain and Snow, in the United States. Smithsonian Contributions to Knowledge, No. 222; Washington, May, 1872.

DISCUSSION

OF THE

DAILY FLUCTUATION OF THE ATMOSPHERIC TEMPERATURE,

WITH

TABLES OF HOURLY VALUES AND OF HOURLY DIFFERENCES FROM THE DAILY MEAN,

FOR

EACH MONTH AND THE YEAR,

AT VARIOUS PLACES IN NORTH AMERICA.

SECTION II.

DISCUSSION OF THE DAILY FLUCTUATION OF THE ATMOSPHERIC TEMPERATURE,

WITH

TABLES OF HOURLY VALUES AND OF HOURLY DIFFERENCES FROM THE DAILY MEAN, FOR EACH MONTH AND THE YEAR,

AT VARIOUS PLACES IN NORTH AMERICA.

The Daily Fluctuation of the Temperature.—The daily variation of the temperature, due to the change in the sun's altitude, and dependent upon the length of the day or time of insolation, is principally affected by the amount of aqueous vapor suspended in the atmosphere, by the serenity or cloudiness of the sky, and by the elevation of the ground. As an accumulative effect, the greatest heat will occur some time after the sun has reached its greatest altitude, and the greatest cold some time after its greatest depression. Even in midwinter, in the high latitudes of the Arctic Regions and in the continued absence of the sun, this periodic fluctuation is still perceptible, which may be accounted for by the progress of waves of heat and by its transfer from more southern and still partly insolated regions. In midsummer, when the sun remains above the horizon, the range of the daily fluctuation in the Arctic Regions is very small owing to the small variation in the sun's altitude. As an instance of a small daily fluctuation in a low latitude, Key West near the northern tropic may be cited; here the great humidity of the air tends to confine the daily amplitude within narrow limits. As an example of the opposite effect or of an excessive daily variation, Albuquerque in the valley of the Rio Grande may be cited; it is due to the dryness of the air and the great altitude of the place.

For the investigation of the daily fluctuation hourly observations are quite sufficient, but they should be continued for several years, whenever it is desirable to bring out reliable values of the average daily amplitude for each month. It is in these investigations that the want of self-registering instruments or thermographs is most felt. Our records of temperatures, continued regularly during day and night, even for a single year, are very scanty, and there are but three stations where the observations continue over a sufficiently long period; these are Toronto, Canada, and Mohawk, New York, with full hourly records extending over six years at each place, and Sitka, Alaska, with records over more than twice this period. To Dr.

James Lewis, of Mohawk, is due the merit of having early brought into operation a thermograph of his own invention.

The collection of monthly values for daily fluctuation comprises the results from bihourly, hourly, and semi-hourly observations at 18 stations, see first table accompanying this section of the paper. They are arranged according to latitude. From these the second series of tables is derived as follows: For each month separately, the daily mean temperature t is subtracted from the observed temperature at any hour, and the difference is set down; a positive sign thus indicates a higher, and a negative sign a lower temperature than that of the day. These tables of differences would furnish the true diurnal fluctuation, if the effect of the annual fluctuation was fully eliminated, and if the daily mean was accurately known. The amount of the annual fluctuation in one day is generally small when compared with the daily fluctuation, and corrections for it need only be applied in extreme cases, as for instance in the Arctic Regions, where the daily range is small in comparison with the annual range; at Van Rensselaer harbor and Port Kennedy the maximum effect for 24 hours amounts to a little more than half a degree (Fah.), on account of which the maximum correction for midnight and the hour preceding it would be one-fourth of a degree, and proportionally less for the intermediate hours. This correction is greatest in April and October, and insensible in July and January.

These tables of hourly differences furnish at once the means of correcting any irregularly observed series, and the mean temperature thus corrected will be the same as that found from an unbroken and regular series of hourly observations. The chief value of these tables lies in this application, and in any special case we have only to select the table for that locality where the thermal conditions may be supposed the same, or at least most nearly resembling those at the locality for which the interpolation or reduction is to be made. For the purpose of facilitating this application, a series of mean values for certain selected combinations of hours is added to each table—these require some further explanation.

These combinations refer to those observing hours from which most probably the nearest approximation to the mean temperature of the day may readily be deduced, not only for the entire year, but also for each month and for any locality, and apply to the cases of record limited to two, three, and four entries a day. The tabular corrections to the selected four hour combination specially, become serviceable for self-registering instruments, when with the least labor (reading off the trace or punctures at those four hours) we wish to obtain a reliable daily mean short of the tedious process of operating on 24 equidistant records.

About the year 1815, Prof. C. Dewey examined[1] the hours 7 A. M., 2 and 9 P. M., adopted by the Manheim[2] Meteorological Society, with reference to their applicability to our climate, and in 1816 and 1817 instituted a short series of hourly observations at Williamstown which proved the fitness of these hours for observation in the United States. These results he communicated to Secretary Calhoun,

---

[1] Annual Report of the Board of Regents of the Smithsonian Institution for the year 1857, p. 310; also annual report for 1860, p. 413.

[2] In Baden, Germany.

and the hours 7, 2, 9 were, in consequence, adopted for the system of meteorological observations at the military posts of the United States, organized in 1819 under the direction of the surgeon-general of the United States Army. Although these hours were at one time abandoned (between 1841 and 1854, when the epochs a little before sunrise, 3 and 9 P. M. were substituted), they were re-established in 1855, mainly through the exertions of Dr. Coolidge, U. S. A. The convenience and satisfactory character of the results of these hours, also led to their adoption in the meteorological observations undertaken conjointly by the United States Patent Office and the Smithsonian Institution in 1854, and they have since been adhered to by the latter Institution. The recognition of the fact that the results by the three hours 7, 2, 9 can be greatly improved by taking one-fourth of the ordinates at 7, 2, and twice 9 in the place of one-third of the ordinates at 7, 2, 9, appears also to be due to Dr. Dewey.

From the present collection of results it appears that the homonymous hours, 10, 10, give differences of less than $\pm$ 0°.5 in the annual mean, that the triplets, 6, 2, 9, and equidistant hours, 6, 2, 10, are of nearly equal value, and but slightly superior to the preceding pair of hours, the former combination producing a higher, the latter a lower mean than the true value of twenty-four equidistant observations, but deviating less than 0°.4. The combination 7, 2, 9, produces a result nearly 0°.5 in excess, whereas the modification 7, 2, 9 (*bis*) diminishes this difference to nearly 0°.1 with a change of signs for different stations. The four-hour combination 3, 9, 3, 9, adopted by the Royal Society, is the best of all, being generally less than 0°.1 above the true daily mean. In the following table of differences from the daily mean, of the average temperature observed at 7, 2, 9, the sign + indicates an excess, the sign — a defect of the latter average. The *first* line for each station answers to the combination $\frac{1}{3}$ (7, 2, 9), the *second* to the modification $\frac{1}{4}$ [7, 2, 9 (*bis*)].

STATION.	Jan.	Feb.	March.	April.	May.	June.	July.	August.	Sept.	Oct.	Nov.	Dec.	Year.
Van Rensselaer harb. $\phi=78°.6$	0.0° 0.0	+0.5° +0.5	+0.5° +0.1	+0.8° +0.5	+0.8° +0.5	+0.7° +0.5	0.0° —0.2	+0.4° +0.2	+0.4° 0.0	—0.1° —0.3	—0.2° —0.3	+0.1° —0.1	+0.3° +0.1
Fort Kennedy. $\phi=72°.0$	0.0 +0.1	+0.3 +0.2	+0.4 —0.1	+0.4 —0.2	+0.7 0.0	+0.7 0.0	+0.4 +0.2	+0.3 +0.2	+0.2 +0.2	+0.1 0.0	0.0 —0.2	—0.1 —0.1	+0.3 0.0
Sitka (13 yrs.). $\phi=57°.1$	+0.23 +0.06	+0.14 —0.13	+0.11 —0.33	+0.44 —0.12	+0.72 +0.07	+0.69 +0.12	+0.69 +0.12	+0.40 —0.13	+0.27 —0.16	+0.27 —0.04	+0.21 +0.03	+0.12 —0.01	+0.36 —0.04
Thunder Bay Isl. $\phi=45°.0$	+0.5 +0.4	+0.6 +0.3	+0.5 +0.1	+0.6 +0.2	+0.6 +0.1	+0.9 +0.2	+0.9 +0.3	+0.7 +0.1	+0.3 —0.1	+0.4 0.0	+0.3 +0.2	+0.3 +0.2	+0.52 +0.15
Toronto. $\phi=43°.6$	+0.42 +0.28	+0.03 —0.13	+0.12 —0.19	+0.38 —0.17	+0.81 +0.04	+0.72 —0.07	+1.01 —0.02	+0.48 —0.35	+0.37 —0.12	+0.32 —0.08	+0.29 +0.10	+0.19 +0.10	+0.44 —0.05
Mohawk. $\phi=43°.0$	+0.28 +0.14	+0.33 +0.29	+0.14 +0.16	+0.13 +0.09	+0.28 +0.14	+0.50 +0.24	+0.29 —0.05	+0.19 —0.07	+0.15 —0.10	+0.21 +0.05	+0.09 —0.05	+0.29 +0.18	+0.24 +0.08
Amherst. $\phi=42°.4$	+0.52 +0.01	+0.33 +0.18	+0.62 0.00	+0.89 +0.23	+0.96 +0.30	+0.93 +0.20	+0.87 —0.11	+0.59 +0.04	+0.78 +0.07	+0.52 +0.12	+0.31 +0.03	+0.55 +0.24	+0.65 +0.11
New Haven. $\phi=41°.3$	+0.28 —0.06	+0.21 —0.15	+0.30 —0.19	+0.36 —0.23	+0.88 +0.10	+1.11 +0.38	+0.83 +0.21	+0.64 +0.07	+0.53 —0.02	+0.45 —0.03	+0.34 +0.01	+0.37 +0.02	+0.53 +0.01
Frankford Arsen'l $\phi=40°.0$	+0.29 —0.21	+0.39 —0.08	+0.37 —0.07	+0.30 —0.25	+0.79 +0.14	+1.00 +0.09	+1.02 +0.11	+0.78 —0.14	+0.65 —0.35	+0.75 —0.09	+0.34 —0.32	+0.52 —0.01	+0.59 —0.11
Philadelphia. $\phi=40°.0$	+0.28 +0.17	+0.22 +0.09	+0.03 —0.24	+0.59 +0.23	+0.67 +0.20	+0.85 +0.25	+0.68 +0.15	+0.53 +0.04	+0.40 —0.19	+0.39 —0.03	+0.28 +0.02	+0.37 +0.27	+0.44 +0.08
Fort Morgan. $\phi=30°.2$	0.0 0.0	0.0 —0.1	—0.1 0.0	+0.6 +0.4	+0.5 +0.4	+0.3 0.0	+0.5 +0.2	+0.2 —0.2	+0.2 +0.1	+0.3 +0.3	+0.1 +0.1	+0.1 +0.1	+0.3 +0.1
Key West. $\phi=24°.6$	—0.02 —0.16	—0.21 —0.28	—0.02 —0.29	+0.09 —0.17	+0.24 —0.15	—0.05 —0.40	+0.21 —0.11	+0.09 —0.08	+0.09 —0.07	+0.10 —0.06	—0.09 —0.17	—0.28 —0.29	+0.01 —0.19

With the exception of Key West, where the proximity of the gulf stream produces an anomaly, the combination $\frac{1}{4}$ (7, 2, 9 (*bis*)) is superior to the simple mean for the three hours, and, in general, the results at the different stations are sufficiently accordant to permit monthly average values of differences to be taken; omitting, therefore, the first three stations and the last station, we find the following mean values applicable to most localities in the United States between latitudes 30° and 45° and east of the Mississippi.

Table of average differences, in temperature, of the mean derived from the observations at 7, 2, 9, also as deduced from 7, 2, 9 (*bis*), from the true daily mean; + in excess, — in defect of the true value. Expressed in degrees of the Fahrenheit scale.

COMBINATION.	Jan.	Feb.	March.	April.	May.	June.	July.	August.	Sept.	Oct.	Nov.	Dec.	Year.
Hours: 7, 2, 9 7, 2, 9 (bis)	+0.32° +0.09	+0.26° +0.06	+0.25° —0.05	+0.48° +0.06	+0.69° +0.18	+0.79° +0.16	+0.76° +0.10	+0.68° —0.06	+0.42° —0.09	+0.42° +0.03	+0.26° +0.01	+0.34° +0.14	+0.47° +0.05

In order to make use of the values of this table, *as corrections* to means derived from observations at these hours, the *sign is to be reversed.*

The above tabular values are derived from more than 22 years of hourly observations made at eight stations. The assumption that the average of *hourly* observations equals the daily average, is so nearly correct as to require no further consideration; thus at Thunder Bay Island, Mich., the mean of 24 observations taken at the full hours is 42°.84, the mean of 24 observations taken at the intermediate half hours is 42°.83, which is also the mean of the 48 semi-hourly observations.

Times of Sunrise and Sunset in different Latitudes and for every tenth day in each month.—We meet frequently, particularly in the older meteorological observations, with records taken at the times of sunrise and sunset; this practice, now generally superseded by better selected fixed epochs, still obliges us to resort to tables of times of sunrise and sunset, with the day of the month and the latitude as arguments, whenever we aim at a careful reduction of the recorded temperatures.

In computing such a table for various latitudes and to answer for any year, the deduced times can only be more or less close approximations on account of the small variations, in different years, in the sun's declination, in its distance, and in the equation of time, on the same nominal day. Fortunately a few minutes of error with a tendency to cancel itself for long series, are of little moment in the meteorological record. The tabular quantities will generally be found correct within 2 or 3 minutes, excepting in the higher latitudes, where this limit may occasionally be slightly exceeded.

The times were computed by the formulæ

$$\cos t = \frac{\cos \zeta - \sin \phi \sin \delta}{\cos \phi \cos \delta} \quad \text{and} \quad \zeta = 90° + r - \pi + s + d = 90°51' \text{nearly.}$$

where ϕ = latitude, δ = sun's declination, ζ = sun's zenith distance, t = hour angle,

r = refraction in horizon, s = sun's semidiameter, π = sun's horizontal parallax, d = dip of horizon.

The apparent time was changed to mean time by application of the equation of time (E).

The value of δ may vary in different years, for the same nominal day, by $\pm$ 9′ nearly, from its average amount; the value of s hardly varies as much as $\pm$ 0′.5; the variations in E for the same nominal day amount to less than $\pm \frac{1}{4}$ of a minute, and the maximum half-daily change is of the same amount. The use of the value of δ for the meridian of Washington instead of any other meridian within the limits of the United States, cannot occasion an error as great as that previously noted for δ. The changes in the horizontal refraction due to extremes of temperature (and atmospheric pressure) may amount, at most, to about $\pm$ 8′ from the mean state, assumed at 35′ (temp. 50° Fah.; pressure 30 inch.). The value of ζ was taken as constant, δ was taken from the ephemeris for the times of sunrise and set for those parts of the year where the use of the meridional value would introduce a notable defect. Both, δ and E, refer to average years.

15 February, 1875.

Time of Sunrise.

Latitude.

Date.	23°	24°	25°	26°	27°	28°	29°	30°	31°	32°	33°	34°	35°
Jan. 1	6h 42m	6h 44m	6h 46m	6h 48m	6h 50m	6h 52m	6h 54m	6h 56m	6h 58m	7h 00m	7h 03m	7h 05m	7h 08m
11	6 43	6 45	6 47	6 49	6 51	6 53	6 55	6 57	6 59	7 01	7 04	7 09	7 08
21	6 44	6 45	6 47	6 49	6 50	6 52	6 54	6 56	6 58	7 00	7 01	7 03	7 05
Feb. 1	6 40	6 41	6 43	6 44	6 46	6 47	6 48	6 50	6 52	6 54	6 56	6 57	6 59
11	6 35	6 36	6 38	6 39	6 40	6 41	6 42	6 44	6 45	6 47	6 49	6 50	6 51
21	6 28	6 29	6 30	6 31	6 32	6 33	6 33	6 34	6 35	6 36	6 37	6 39	6 40
Mar. 1	6 22	6 22	6 23	6 24	6 25	6 25	6 26	6 27	6 28	6 28	6 29	6 29	6 30
11	6 12	6 12	6 12	6 13	6 13	6 13	6 13	6 14	6 14	6 15	6 15	6 16	6 16
21	6 02	6 02	6 02	6 02	6 02	6 02	6 02	6 02	6 02	6 02	6 01	6 01	6 01
Apr. 1	5 53	5 53	5 52	5 52	5 51	5 51	5 50	5 49	5 49	5 48	5 48	5 47	5 47
11	5 44	5 43	5 42	5 41	5 40	5 39	5 38	5 37	5 36	5 35	5 35	5 34	5 33
21	5 35	5 34	5 33	5 32	5 30	5 29	5 28	5 27	5 26	5 24	5 23	5 22	5 21
May 1	5 27	5 25	5 24	5 23	5 21	5 20	5 19	5 17	5 15	5 13	5 12	5 11	5 09
11	5 21	5 19	5 17	5 15	5 14	5 12	5 10	5 09	5 07	5 05	5 03	5 01	4 59
21	5 16	5 14	5 12	5 10	5 08	5 07	5 05	5 03	5 00	4 58	4 55	4 53	4 52
June 1	5 13	5 11	5 09	5 07	5 05	5 03	5 01	4 58	4 55	4 53	4 50	4 48	4 46
11	5 13	5 11	5 09	5 07	5 05	5 03	5 01	4 58	4 55	4 52	4 49	4 47	4 44
21	5 14	5 12	5 10	5 07	5 05	5 03	5 01	4 59	4 56	4 54	4 51	4 48	4 45
July 1	5 17	5 15	5 13	5 11	5 09	5 07	5 05	5 02	4 59	4 56	4 54	4 51	4 48
11	5 21	5 19	5 17	5 15	5 13	5 11	5 09	5 06	5 04	5 02	4 59	4 57	4 54
21	5 25	5 23	5 21	5 19	5 18	5 16	5 14	5 12	5 10	5 07	5 05	5 02	5 00
Aug. 1	5 30	5 28	5 26	5 25	5 24	5 22	5 20	5 18	5 16	5 14	5 12	5 11	5 09
11	5 34	5 32	5 31	5 30	5 29	5 27	5 26	5 25	5 23	5 21	5 19	5 17	5 16
21	5 38	5 37	5 36	5 35	5 34	5 32	5 31	5 30	5 29	5 28	5 27	5 25	5 24
Sept. 1	5 42	5 42	5 41	5 40	5 39	5 38	5 37	5 36	5 35	5 34	5 33	5 32	5 32
11	5 46	5 45	5 45	5 44	5 44	5 43	5 42	5 42	5 42	5 41	5 41	5 40	5 40
21	5 48	5 48	5 48	5 48	5 48	5 48	5 47	5 47	5 47	5 47	5 47	5 47	5 47
Oct. 1	5 52	5 52	5 52	5 53	5 53	5 53	5 53	5 54	5 54	5 54	5 55	5 55	5 55
11	5 55	5 55	5 56	5 57	5 58	5 58	5 59	6 00	6 01	6 01	6 02	6 02	6 03
21	6 00	6 01	6 02	6 03	6 03	6 04	6 05	6 06	6 08	6 09	6 10	6 11	6 12
Nov. 1	6 05	6 06	6 08	6 09	6 10	6 11	6 12	6 14	6 16	6 17	6 19	6 21	6 22
11	6 11	6 12	6 14	6 15	6 17	6 18	6 20	6 22	6 23	6 25	6 27	6 29	6 31
21	6 17	6 19	6 21	6 23	6 24	6 26	6 28	6 30	6 32	6 34	6 36	6 38	6 40
Dec. 1	6 24	6 26	6 28	6 30	6 32	6 34	6 36	6 38	6 40	6 43	6 45	6 47	6 50
11	6 32	6 34	6 36	6 38	6 40	6 42	6 44	6 46	6 49	6 51	6 53	6 56	6 59
21	6 37	6 39	6 41	6 43	6 46	6 48	6 50	6 53	6 55	6 58	7 01	7 03	7 05

Time of Sunrise.—Continued.

Latitude.

Date.	36°	37°	38°	39°	40°	41°	42°	43°	44°	45°	46°	47°	48°
Jan. 1	7h 10m	7h 13m	7h 16m	7h 19m	7h 22m	7h 25m	7h 29m	7h 32m	7h 35m	7h 39m	7h 43m	7h 47m	7h 51m
11	7 10	7 13	7 16	7 18	7 21	7 24	7 27	7 30	7 33	7 36	7 40	7 43	7 47
21	7 07	7 10	7 12	7 15	7 18	7 20	7 23	7 25	7 28	7 31	7 34	7 37	7 41
Feb. 1	7 01	7 03	7 05	7 07	7 09	7 11	7 13	7 15	7 18	7 20	7 23	7 25	7 28
11	6 52	6 54	6 55	6 57	6 58	7 00	7 01	7 03	7 05	7 07	7 09	7 12	7 14
21	6 41	6 43	6 44	6 45	6 46	6 47	6 49	6 50	6 51	6 52	6 53	6 55	6 57
Mar. 1	6 31	6 32	6 33	6 33	6 34	6 35	6 36	6 37	6 38	6 39	6 40	6 41	6 42
11	6 16	6 16	6 17	6 17	6 17	6 17	6 18	6 18	6 19	6 19	6 20	6 20	6 21
21	6 01	6 01	6 01	6 01	6 01	6 01	6 01	6 00	6 00	6 00	6 00	6 00	6 00
Apr. 1	5 46	5 46	5 45	5 45	5 44	5 44	5 43	5 43	5 42	5 41	5 41	5 40	5 39
11	5 33	5 32	5 31	5 30	5 29	5 28	5 26	5 25	5 24	5 23	5 22	5 21	5 19
21	5 20	5 19	5 17	5 16	5 14	5 13	5 11	5 10	5 08	5 06	5 04	5 02	5 00
May 1	5 07	5 05	5 03	5 01	5 00	4 58	4 56	4 54	4 51	4 49	4 46	4 44	4 41
11	4 57	4 55	4 52	4 50	4 48	4 45	4 43	4 41	4 38	4 36	4 33	4 30	4 27
21	4 49	4 47	4 44	4 42	4 39	4 36	4 33	4 30	4 27	4 24	4 20	4 17	4 13
June 1	4 43	4 40	4 38	4 35	4 32	4 29	4 25	4 22	4 18	4 15	4 11	4 07	4 03
11	4 41	4 38	4 35	4 33	4 30	4 27	4 23	4 19	4 15	4 12	4 08	4 03	3 59
21	4 42	4 39	4 36	4 33	4 30	4 27	4 23	4 19	4 15	4 12	4 08	4 03	3 58
July 1	4 45	4 42	4 39	4 36	4 34	4 31	4 27	4 23	4 19	4 16	4 12	4 08	4 04
11	4 51	4 48	4 45	4 42	4 40	4 37	4 34	4 30	4 27	4 23	4 19	4 15	4 11
21	4 58	4 55	4 53	4 50	4 48	4 45	4 42	4 39	4 36	4 33	4 29	4 25	4 22
Aug. 1	5 06	5 04	5 02	5 00	4 58	4 55	4 52	4 50	4 47	4 45	4 42	4 39	4 36
11	5 14	5 12	5 10	5 09	5 07	5 [illegible]	5 [illegible]	5 [illegible]	4 [illegible]	4 [illegible]	4 53	4 50	4 47
21	5 23	5 22	5 20	5 19	5 17	5 15	5 13	5 12	5 10	5 08	5 06	5 04	5 02
Sept. 1	5 31	5 30	5 29	5 28	5 27	5 26	5 25	5 24	5 23	5 22	5 21	5 20	5 18
11	5 39	5 39	5 38	5 37	5 37	5 36	5 35	5 35	5 34	5 34	5 33	5 32	5 31
21	5 47	5 47	5 46	5 46	5 46	5 46	5 45	5 45	5 45	5 45	5 45	5 44	5 44
Oct. 1	5 55	5 56	5 56	5 57	5 57	5 57	5 58	5 58	5 59	5 59	5 59	5 59	6 00
11	6 03	6 04	6 05	6 06	6 07	6 07	6 08	6 09	6 10	6 11	6 12	6 13	6 14
21	6 13	6 15	6 16	6 17	6 18	6 20	6 21	6 22	6 23	6 24	6 25	6 27	6 28
Nov. 1	6 24	6 25	6 26	6 28	6 29	6 31	6 33	6 35	6 37	6 39	6 41	6 43	6 45
11	6 33	6 35	6 37	6 39	6 41	6 43	6 45	6 48	6 50	6 52	6 55	6 58	7 01
21	6 42	6 45	6 47	6 50	6 52	6 55	6 57	7 00	7 03	7 06	7 10	7 13	7 17
Dec. 1	6 52	6 55	6 57	7 00	7 02	7 05	7 08	7 12	7 15	7 18	7 22	7 25	7 29
11	7 01	7 04	7 07	7 09	7 12	7 15	7 18	7 22	7 25	7 29	7 33	7 37	7 41
21	7 08	7 1[illegible]	7 13	7 16	7 19	7 23	7 26	7 30	7 33	7 36	7 40	7 44	7 48

Time of Sunrise.—Continued.

Latitude.

Date.	49°	50°	51°	52°	53°	54°	55°	56°	57°	58°	59°	60°
Jan. 1	$7^h 55^m$	$8^h 00^m$	$8^h 05^m$	$8^h 10^m$	$8^h 15^m$	$8^h 20^m$	$8^h 25^m$	$8^h 31^m$	$8^h 38^m$	$8^h 46^m$	$8^h 54^m$	$9^h 03^m$
11	7 51	7 55	8 00	8 04	8 09	8 14	8 19	8 25	8 31	8 38	8 45	8 53
21	7 44	7 48	7 52	7 56	8 00	8 04	8 09	8 14	8 20	8 26	8 32	8 38
Feb. 1	7 31	7 34	7 38	7 41	7 45	7 48	7 51	7 55	7 59	8 04	8 09	8 14
11	7 16	7 19	7 21	7 24	7 26	7 29	7 32	7 35	7 39	7 42	7 45	7 49
21	6 58	7 00	7 01	7 03	7 04	7 06	7 08	7 10	7 13	7 16	7 19	7 22
Mar. 1	6 43	6 44	6 45	6 46	6 47	6 49	6 50	6 51	6 53	6 55	6 57	6 59
11	6 21	6 22	6 22	6 23	6 24	6 25	6 25	6 26	6 26	6 27	6 27	6 28
21	6 00	6 00	6 00	6 00	5 59	5 59	5 59	5 59	5 59	5 59	5 59	5 59
Apr. 1	5 38	5 37	5 36	5 35	5 34	5 33	5 32	5 31	5 29	5 28	5 27	5 25
11	5 18	5 16	5 15	5 13	5 11	5 09	5 07	5 05	5 03	5 01	4 58	4 55
21	4 57	4 55	4 53	4 50	4 48	4 46	4 43	4 40	4 36	4 33	4 30	4 26
May 1	4 39	4 36	4 33	4 30	4 27	4 23	4 20	4 16	4 12	4 07	4 03	3 58
11	4 24	4 20	4 16	4 12	4 08	4 04	3 59	3 54	3 48	3 43	3 38	3 32
21	4 10	4 06	4 01	3 56	3 52	3 47	3 42	3 36	3 30	3 23	3 16	3 08
June 1	3 59	3 55	3 50	3 45	3 40	3 34	3 28	3 21	3 14	3 06	2 57	2 47
11	3 55	3 50	3 44	3 38	3 32	3 26	3 20	3 13	3 05	2 56	2 47	2 37
21	3 54	3 49	3 43	3 37	3 31	3 25	3 19	3 12	3 04	2 55	2 45	2 34
July 1	3 59	3 54	3 48	3 42	3 36	3 30	3 24	3 17	3 09	3 00	2 50	2 40
11	4 07	4 03	3 58	3 53	3 47	3 42	3 36	3 29	3 22	3 14	3 05	2 55
21	4 18	4 14	4 09	4 04	3 59	3 54	3 49	3 43	3 37	3 30	3 23	3 15
Aug. 1	4 32	4 28	4 24	4 20	4 16	4 12	4 08	4 03	3 58	3 52	3 46	3 40
11	4 45	4 43	4 40	4 36	4 33	4 29	4 25	4 21	4 17	4 12	4 08	4 03
21	5 00	4 58	4 55	4 53	4 50	4 48	4 45	4 42	4 39	4 35	4 32	4 28
Sept. 1	5 17	5 15	5 13	5 11	5 09	5 08	5 06	5 04	5 02	4 59	4 57	4 54
11	5 31	5 30	5 29	5 28	5 26	5 25	5 24	5 23	5 22	5 20	5 19	5 17
21	5 44	5 44	5 44	5 44	5 43	5 43	5 43	5 43	5 43	5 43	5 42	5 42
Oct. 1	6 00	6 00	6 01	6 01	6 02	6 02	6 02	6 03	6 03	6 04	6 04	6 05
11	6 15	6 16	6 17	6 18	6 19	6 20	6 22	6 23	6 25	6 26	6 28	6 30
21	6 30	6 32	6 34	6 36	6 38	6 40	6 42	6 44	6 46	6 49	6 52	6 55
Nov. 1	6 47	6 50	6 53	6 55	6 58	7 01	7 04	7 07	7 11	7 15	7 19	7 23
11	7 04	7 07	7 10	7 14	7 17	7 20	7 24	7 28	7 33	7 38	7 43	7 48
21	7 20	7 24	7 28	7 32	7 36	7 40	7 45	7 50	7 56	8 02	8 08	8 14
Dec. 1	7 32	7 36	7 41	7 46	7 51	7 56	8 01	8 07	8 13	8 20	8 27	8 35
11	7 45	7 49	7 54	7 59	8 04	8 09	8 15	8 22	8 29	8 37	8 45	8 53
21	7 52	7 57	8 02	8 08	8 13	8 19	8 24	8 30	8 37	8 45	8 54	9 03

Time of Sunset.

Latitude.

DATE.	23°	24°	25°	26°	27°	28°	29°	30°	31°	32°	33°	34°	35°
Jan. 1	5h 26m	5h 24m	5h 22m	5h 20m	5h 18m	5h 16m	5h 14m	5h 12m	5h 09m	5h 07m	5h 05m	5h 02m	5h 00m
11	5 34	5 32	5 30	5 28	5 26	5 24	5 22	5 20	5 18	5 16	5 14	5 11	5 09
21	5 40	5 39	5 37	5 35	5 34	5 32	5 30	5 28	5 26	5 24	5 22	5 20	5 19
Feb. 1	5 48	5 47	5 45	5 43	5 42	5 40	5 39	5 38	5 36	5 34	5 32	5 30	5 29
11	5 55	5 54	5 52	5 51	5 50	5 48	5 47	5 46	5 45	5 43	5 42	5 40	5 39
21	6 00	5 59	5 58	5 57	5 56	5 55	5 54	5 54	5 53	5 52	5 51	5 49	5 48
Mar. 1	6 04	6 03	6 03	6 02	6 02	6 02	6 01	6 00	6 00	5 59	5 58	5 57	5 56
11	6 08	6 08	6 08	6 07	6 07	6 07	6 06	6 06	6 05	6 05	6 04	6 04	6 04
21	6 12	6 12	6 12	6 12	6 12	6 12	6 12	6 12	6 12	6 12	6 13	6 13	6 13
Apr. 1	6 15	6 16	6 17	6 18	6 18	6 18	6 19	6 19	6 20	6 21	6 21	6 22	6 22
11	6 19	6 20	6 21	6 21	6 22	6 23	6 24	6 25	6 25	6 26	6 27	6 28	6 29
21	6 24	6 25	6 26	6 27	6 28	6 29	6 30	6 31	6 33	6 34	6 35	6 37	6 38
May 1	6 28	6 30	6 31	6 32	6 33	6 35	6 36	6 38	6 39	6 41	6 43	6 44	6 46
11	6 32	6 34	6 35	6 36	6 38	6 40	6 42	6 44	6 46	6 48	6 50	6 52	6 53
21	6 36	6 38	6 40	6 42	6 44	6 46	6 48	6 50	6 52	6 55	6 57	6 59	7 01
June 1	6 41	6 43	6 45	6 47	6 49	6 51	6 54	6 56	6 58	7 01	7 03	7 06	7 08
11	6 45	6 47	6 49	6 51	6 53	6 55	6 58	7 00	7 02	7 05	7 08	7 11	7 14
21	6 48	6 50	6 52	6 54	6 57	6 59	7 01	7 03	7 05	7 08	7 11	7 14	7 17
July 1	6 49	6 51	6 53	6 55	6 57	6 59	7 02	7 04	7 06	7 09	7 12	7 15	7 18
11	6 49	6 51	6 53	6 55	6 57	6 59	7 02	7 04	7 07	7 09	7 12	7 14	7 16
21	6 47	6 48	6 50	6 52	6 54	6 56	6 58	7 00	7 03	7 05	7 08	7 10	7 12
Aug. 1	6 41	6 43	6 45	6 46	6 48	6 50	6 51	6 53	6 55	6 57	6 59	7 01	7 03
11	6 36	6 37	6 38	6 39	[illegible]	6 41	6 43	6 43	6 47	6 48	6 50	6 52	6 54
21	6 28	6 29	6 30	6 31	6 32	6 33	6 34	6 36	6 37	6 39	6 40	6 41	6 42
Sept. 1	6 18	6 19	6 20	6 20	6 21	6 22	6 23	6 24	6 24	6 25	6 26	6 27	6 28
11	6 08	6 09	6 09	6 10	6 10	6 10	6 11	6 12	6 12	6 13	6 13	6 14	6 14
21	5 58	5 58	5 58	5 58	5 58	5 58	5 59	5 59	5 59	5 59	5 59	5 59	5 59
Oct. 1	5 48	5 48	5 48	5 47	5 47	5 47	5 46	5 46	5 46	5 46	5 45	5 45	5 45
11	5 39	5 38	5 37	5 37	5 36	5 35	5 35	5 34	5 34	5 33	5 32	5 32	5 31
21	5 30	5 29	5 28	5 28	5 27	5 26	5 25	5 24	5 22	5 21	5 20	5 19	5 18
Nov. 1	5 23	5 22	5 20	5 19	5 18	5 16	5 15	5 14	5 12	5 11	5 09	5 08	5 06
11	5 17	5 16	5 14	5 12	5 11	5 09	5 08	5 06	5 04	5 02	5 00	4 58	4 57
21	5 15	5 14	5 12	5 10	5 08	5 06	5 04	5 02	5 00	4 58	4 56	4 54	4 52
Dec. 1	5 14	5 12	5 10	5 08	5 06	5 04	5 02	5 00	4 58	4 55	4 53	4 50	4 48
11	5 16	5 14	5 12	5 10	5 08	5 06	5 04	5 02	5 00	4 57	4 54	4 51	4 49
21	5 21	5 19	5 16	5 14	5 12	5 10	5 07	5 05	5 03	5 00	4 58	4 55	4 53

Time of Sunset.—Continued.

Latitude.

Date.	36°	37°	38°	39°	40°	41°	42°	43°	44°	45°	46°	47°	48°
Jan. 1	4h 57m	4h 54m	4h 51m	4h 48m	4h 46m	4h 43m	4h 40m	4h 36m	4h 33m	4h 29m	4h 25m	4h 21m	4h 17m
11	5 06	5 04	5 01	4 59	4 56	4 53	4 50	4 47	4 44	4 41	4 37	4 34	4 30
21	5 16	5 14	5 11	5 08	5 06	5 03	5 01	4 58	4 56	4 53	4 50	4 47	4 43
Feb. 1	5 27	5 25	5 23	5 21	5 19	5 16	5 14	5 12	5 10	5 08	5 05	5 03	5 00
11	5 39	5 37	5 35	5 33	5 32	5 31	5 29	5 27	5 25	5 23	5 21	5 18	5 16
21	5 47	5 46	5 45	5 44	5 43	5 41	5 40	5 39	5 37	5 36	5 35	5 34	5 33
Mar. 1	5 56	5 55	5 55	5 54	5 53	5 52	5 51	5 50	5 49	5 48	5 47	5 46	5 45
11	6 04	6 03	6 03	6 03	6 03	6 02	6 02	6 02	6 01	6 01	6 01	6 00	6 00
21	6 13	6 13	6 13	6 13	6 13	6 13	6 13	6 14	6 14	6 14	6 14	6 14	6 15
Apr. 1	6 22	6 23	6 23	6 24	6 24	6 25	6 26	6 26	6 27	6 28	6 29	6 29	6 30
11	6 30	6 31	6 32	6 33	6 34	6 35	6 36	6 37	6 38	6 40	6 42	6 43	6 45
21	6 40	6 41	6 43	6 44	6 45	6 47	6 48	6 50	6 52	6 54	6 56	6 58	7 00
May 1	6 47	6 49	6 51	6 53	6 55	6 57	6 59	7 01	7 03	7 06	7 08	7 11	7 14
11	6 55	6 57	6 59	7 01	7 04	7 06	7 09	7 12	7 14	7 17	7 20	7 23	7 27
21	7 04	7 06	7 09	7 11	7 14	7 16	7 19	7 22	7 25	7 28	7 32	7 36	7 40
June 1	7 10	7 13	7 16	7 19	7 22	7 25	7 29	7 32	7 35	7 39	7 43	7 47	7 51
11	7 16	7 19	7 22	7 25	7 28	7 31	7 35	7 38	7 42	7 46	7 50	7 55	7 59
21	7 20	7 23	7 26	7 29	7 32	7 35	7 39	7 43	7 46	7 50	7 55	7 59	8 04
July 1	7 20	7 23	7 26	7 29	7 32	7 36	7 39	7 43	7 47	7 50	7 55	7 59	8 03
11	7 18	7 21	7 24	7 27	7 30	7 33	7 37	7 40	7 43	7 47	7 51	7 55	7 59
21	7 14	7 17	7 19	7 21	7 24	7 27	7 30	7 33	7 36	7 39	7 42	7 46	7 50
Aug. 1	7 05	7 07	7 09	7 12	7 14	7 17	7 19	7 22	7 24	7 27	7 30	7 33	7 36
11	6 55	6 57	6 58	7 00	7 02	7 04	7 07	7 09	7 12	7 14	7 16	7 19	7 21
21	6 43	6 44	6 46	6 47	6 49	6 50	6 52	6 54	6 55	6 57	6 59	7 01	7 03
Sept. 1	6 29	6 30	6 31	6 32	6 33	6 34	6 35	6 36	6 37	6 38	6 39	6 41	6 42
11	6 14	6 15	6 15	6 16	6 16	6 17	6 17	6 18	6 19	6 20	6 20	6 21	6 22
21	5 59	5 59	5 59	5 59	5 59	5 59	5 59	6 00	6 00	6 00	6 00	6 00	6 01
Oct. 1	5 44	5 44	5 44	5 43	5 43	5 43	5 42	5 42	5 41	5 41	5 41	5 40	5 40
11	5 30	5 29	5 29	5 28	5 27	5 27	5 26	5 25	5 24	5 23	5 22	5 21	5 20
21	5 17	5 16	5 15	5 14	5 12	5 11	5 09	5 08	5 07	5 06	5 04	5 02	5 01
Nov. 1	5 04	5 03	5 01	5 00	4 59	4 57	4 55	4 53	4 51	4 49	4 47	4 45	4 43
11	4 55	4 53	4 51	4 49	4 47	4 45	4 43	4 40	4 38	4 36	4 33	4 30	4 27
21	4 50	4 47	4 45	4 42	4 40	4 37	4 34	4 32	4 29	4 26	4 23	4 19	4 16
Dec. 1	4 45	4 43	4 41	4 38	4 36	4 33	4 30	4 27	4 24	4 20	4 16	4 13	4 09
11	4 46	4 43	4 41	4 38	4 36	4 33	4 29	4 26	4 23	4 19	4 15	4 11	4 07
21	4 50	4 47	4 44	4 42	4 39	4 36	4 32	4 29	4 26	4 22	4 18	4 14	4 10

Time of Sunset.—Continued.

Latitude.

Date.	49°	50°	51°	52°	53°	54°	55°	56°	57°	58°	59°	60°
Jan. 1	4h 13m	4h 08m	4h 03m	3h 58m	3h 53m	3h 48m	3h 43m	3h 37m	3h 30m	3h 22m	3h 14m	3h 05m
11	4 26	4 22	4 17	4 12	4 08	4 03	3 58	3 52	3 46	3 39	3 32	3 24
21	4 40	4 36	4 32	4 28	4 24	4 20	4 15	4 10	4 04	3 59	3 53	3 46
Feb. 1	4 58	4 55	4 51	4 48	4 45	4 41	4 38	4 34	4 29	4 25	4 20	4 15
11	5 14	5 12	5 10	5 07	5 04	5 02	4 59	4 56	4 53	4 50	4 46	4 42
21	5 31	5 30	5 28	5 26	5 24	5 22	5 20	5 18	5 16	5 13	5 10	5 07
Mar. 1	5 44	5 43	5 41	5 39	5 38	5 37	5 36	5 35	5 34	5 32	5 30	5 28
11	5 59	5 59	5 58	5 58	5 57	5 56	5 56	5 55	5 55	5 54	5 53	5 52
21	6 15	6 15	6 15	6 15	6 15	6 16	6 16	6 16	6 16	6 17	6 17	6 17
Apr. 1	6 31	6 32	6 33	6 34	6 35	6 36	6 37	6 38	6 39	6 40	6 42	6 44
11	6 46	6 47	6 48	6 50	6 52	6 54	6 56	6 58	7 00	7 02	7 04	7 07
21	7 02	7 04	7 06	7 09	7 11	7 14	7 17	7 20	7 23	7 26	7 30	7 34
May 1	7 16	7 18	7 21	7 24	7 28	7 31	7 35	7 39	7 43	7 48	7 53	7 58
11	7 30	7 34	7 38	7 42	7 46	7 50	7 54	7 59	8 04	8 10	8 16	8 22
21	7 43	7 47	7 52	7 57	8 02	8 06	8 11	8 17	8 23	8 30	8 38	8 46
June 1	7 55	7 59	8 04	8 09	8 14	8 20	8 26	8 32	8 39	8 48	8 57	9 07
11	8 03	8 08	8 14	8 20	8 26	8 32	8 38	8 45	8 53	9 01	9 10	9 21
21	8 08	8 13	8 19	8 25	8 31	8 37	8 43	8 50	8 58	9 07	9 17	9 28
July 1	8 07	8 12	8 18	8 24	8 30	8 36	8 42	8 49	8 57	9 05	9 15	9 26
11	8 03	8 07	8 12	8 17	8 23	8 28	8 34	8 40	8 47	8 55	9 04	9 14
21	7 54	7 58	8 02	8 07	8 12	8 17	8 22	8 28	8 34	8 41	8 48	8 56
Aug. 1	7 39	7 43	7 47	7 51	7 55	7 59	8 03	8 08	8 13	8 19	8 25	8 31
11	7 24	7 26	7 29	7 33	7 36	7 40	7 43	7 47	7 51	7 55	7 59	8 04
21	7 05	7 07	7 09	7 12	7 14	7 17	7 20	7 23	7 27	7 30	7 33	7 37
Sept. 1	6 44	6 45	6 46	6 48	6 49	6 51	6 53	6 55	6 57	7 00	7 02	7 05
11	6 22	6 23	6 23	6 24	6 25	6 26	6 27	6 28	6 29	6 31	6 33	6 35
21	6 01	6 01	6 01	6 01	6 01	6 02	6 02	6 02	6 02	6 03	6 03	6 03
Oct. 1	5 39	5 39	5 38	5 38	5 37	5 37	5 37	5 37	5 36	5 36	5 35	5 34
11	5 19	5 18	5 16	5 15	5 14	5 12	5 11	5 10	5 08	5 06	5 05	5 03
21	4 59	4 58	4 56	4 54	4 52	4 50	4 48	4 46	4 43	4 41	4 38	4 35
Nov. 1	4 40	4 38	4 35	4 32	4 30	4 27	4 24	4 21	4 17	4 13	4 09	4 05
11	4 24	4 21	4 18	4 14	4 10	4 07	4 04	4 00	3 56	3 51	3 46	3 40
21	4 12	4 09	4 05	4 01	3 57	3 53	3 48	3 43	3 38	3 32	3 26	3 19
Dec. 1	4 06	4 02	3 57	3 52	3 47	3 42	3 37	3 32	3 26	3 19	3 11	3 03
11	4 03	3 59	3 54	3 49	3 44	3 39	3 33	3 27	3 20	3 12	3 04	2 55
21	4 06	4 01	3 56	3 50	3 45	3 39	3 34	3 28	3 21	3 13	3 04	2 55

TABLES

OF

BI-HOURLY, HOURLY, AND SEMI-HOURLY MEAN TEMPERATURES,

FOR

EACH MONTH AND THE YEAR,

AT VARIOUS PLACES IN NORTH AMERICA.

TABLES OF MEAN TEMPERATURES AT DIFFERENT HOURS OF THE DAY, FOR EACH MONTH AND THE YEAR.

INDEX TO STATIONS.

[Arranged according to latitudes.]

Hour.	Jan.	Feb.	Mar.	April.	May.	June.	July.	Aug.	Sept.	Oct.	Nov.	Dec.	Year.

HOURLY MEANS OF TEMPERATURE (Fah. scale).

Van Rensselaer Harbor, North Greenland.[1] Lat. 78° 37′. Long. 70° 53′ W. of G.

Near sea level. Dr. E. K. Kane. Sept. 1853, to Jan. 1855, inclusive.

Hour.	Jan.	Feb.	Mar.	April.	May.	June.	July.	Aug.	Sept.	Oct.	Nov.	Dec.	Year.
Mdn't	—28°.3	—33°.6	—38°.4	—11°.4	+10°.2	+28°.2	+36°.9	+29°.8	+10°.7	—4°.7	—22°.6	—31.°4	—4°.5
1	28.3	34.3	38.8	12.2	9.0	27.0	36.6	29.2	11.2	3.5	21.3	31.5	—4.7
2	28.5	34.3	38.6	12.2	9.3	27.1	36.7	29.5	11.3	3.5	21.3	31.3	—4.6
3	28.6	34.1	38.8	12.6	10.0	27.2	36.8	29.5	11.5	3.5	21.3	31.6	—4.6
4	28.7	33.5	39.0	12.1	10.6	27.6	36.8	29.8	11.4	3.4	21.3	31.8	—4.4
5	28.7	34.2	38.9	11.2	11.8	28.8	36.9	29.7	11.4	3.3	22.0	30.9	—4.2
6	28.7	33.6	38.7	10.6	12.7	29.5	37.6	30.3	12.0	3.3	22.2	30.8	—3.8
7	29.0	33.2	38.0	9.5	13.5	30.4	37.8	31.0	13.0	3.2	22.0	31.0	—3.3
8	28.5	32.9	37.6	8.4	14.4	31.6	38.4	31.9	14.4	3.2	22.2	31.0	—2.7
9	28.6	32.6	36.3	6.8	14.4	30.8	39.4	33.0	15.2	2.9	22.0	30.7	—2.2
10	28.3	32.1	35.7	6.1	15.1	31.0	39.6	33.9	15.8	2.7	22.1	30.6	—1.8
11	27.8	32.4	34.5	5.1	15.3	31.4	40.0	34.0	16.2	2.8	21.6	30.5	—1.5
Noon	27.3	31.8	34.0	4.5	15.9	32.2	40.0	34.2	16.4	3.0	21.4	30.0	—1.1
1	27.5	31.3	33.6	4.0	16.1	32.3	39.8	34.2	16.5	3.0	21.7	30.1	—1.0
2	27.6	31.3	33.2	3.2	16.4	32.2	39.7	34.2	16.1	3.2	21.8	30.4	—1.0
3	28.1	31.4	33.8	3.1	16.5	31.9	39.7	33.8	15.6	3.1	21.8	30.8	—1.2
4	28.3	31.5	34.9	3.4	16.7	31.6	39.6	33.3	15.0	3.3	21.9	31.1	—1.5
5	28.0	31.8	35.6	3.5	16.2	31.4	38.9	33.0	14.4	3.5	21.8	31.2	—1.8
6	28.0	31.7	36.2	4.4	15.3	31.2	38.5	32.5	13.9	3.9	22.0	31.3	—2.1
7	27.9	31.6	36.7	5.8	14.5	30.8	38.2	32.1	13.1	4.5	22.2	31.9	—2.6
8	28.1	31.8	37.6	6.7	13.6	30.6	37.7	31.7	12.6	4.6	22.3	31.8	—3.0
9	28.1	32.2	37.7	8.1	12.8	29.9	37.2	31.5	12.2	4.6	22.8	31.7	—3.4
10	28.0	33.3	38.0	9.6	11.7	29.5	36.7	30.8	11.8	4.6	22.5	31.7	—3.9
11	—28.6	—33.3	—38.2	—10.3	+10.7	+28.6	+36.8	+30.4	+11.1	—4.6	—22.7	—31.6	—4.3
Mean	—28.2	—32.7	—36.8	— 7.7	+13.4	+30.1	+38.2	+31.8	+13.4	—3.6	—22.0	—31.1	—2.9

BI-HOURLY MEANS OF TEMPERATURE.

Port Foulke, North Greenland.[2] Lat. 78° 18′. Long. 73° 00′ W. of G.

Near sea level. Dr. I. I. Hayes. Sept. 1860, to July, 1861, inclusive.

Hour.	Jan.	Feb.	Mar.	April.	May.	June.	July.	Aug.[3]	Sept.	Oct.	Nov.	Dec.	Year.
Mdn't	—26.2	—25.8	—24.8	—13.5	+21.1	+33.0	+39.4	+30.4	+21.5	+6.9	+2.5	—12.1	+4.37
2	—26.6	—27.0	—25.3	—14.0	+20.0	+32.2	+39.5	+30.7	+22.0	+6.7	+2.1	—11.4	+4.08
4	—26.2	—27.2	—26.0	—14.4	+21.9	+33.7	+39.8	+31.0	+22.3	+6.8	+2.0	—12.7	+4.24
6	—26.7	—26.0	—25.4	—13.1	+23.1	+34.6	+40.2	+31.3	+22.4	+6.6	+2.9	—12.9	+4.75
8	—25.7	—24.2	—23.1	—11.5	+25.4	+35.1	+41.7	+32.2	+22.6	+7.1	+2.8	—13.3	+5.73
10	—25.4	—24.2	—22.4	—10.9	+26.2	+36.3	+42.5	+32.6	+22.7	+7.8	+3.0	—12.7	+6.29
Noon	—25.2	—24.0	—20.7	— 9.6	+26.7	+36.8	+42.3	+32.7	+23.2	+8.5	+3.2	—12.6	+6.78
2	—25.9	—23.0	—17.0	— 8.7	+26.4	+37.4	+43.7	+33.6	+23.5	+8.8	+3.3	—12.5	+7.46
4	—26.2	—24.1	—18.5	— 9.7	+26.1	+36.9	+43.4	+33.4	+23.4	+8.7	+3.6	—11.6	+7.12
6	—26.2	—24.5	—20.8	—10.8	+25.8	+36.3	+42.4	+32.6	+22.8	+8.3	+3.9	—12.8	+6.42
8	—25.9	—24.7	—21.9	—11.4	+23.9	+35.3	+41.6	+32.1	+22.6	+8.1	+3.5	—12.7	+5.88
10	—26.3	—24.6	—23.3	—13.0	+22.3	+33.9	+41.3	+31.8	+22.3	+7.2	+3.4	—13.4	+5.13
Mean	—26.05	—24.95	—22.44	—11.72	+24.08	+35.13	+41.49	+32.04	+22.59	+7.62	+3.01	—12.56	+5.69

N. B. The above numbers are corrected for error of scale of thermometers, but are not changed for the effect of the annual fluctuation, which in Feb. is zero and in May 0.4 (its maximum amount) at midnight; see table on p. 183 of Sm. Cont's, No. 196.

[1] Smithsonian Contributions to Knowledge; Washington, 1859.

[2] Smithsonian Contributions to Knowledge, No. 196; Washington, 1867.

[3] The August values are interpolated, means of July and Sept. values.

BI-HOURLY MEANS OF TEMPERATURE.

Port Kennedy, North Somerset.[1] Lat. 72° 01′. Long. 94° 14′ W. of G.

Near sea level. Sir F. L. McClintock. Aug. 1858, to Aug. 1859, inclusive.

Hour.	Jan.	Feb.	Mar.	Apr.	May.	June.	July.	Aug.	Sept.	Oct.	Nov.	Dec.	Year.
Mdn't	—34°.6	—37°.6	—21°.1	—6°.1	+11°.4	+31°.1	+37°.0	+35°.9	+24°.7	+6°.4	—13°.0	—34°.0	0°.00
2	—34.6	—37.7	—21.5	—5.7	11.0	30.2	36.5	35.6	24.5	6.9	—12.0	—33.2	0.00
4	—35.1	—37.3	—21.5	—4.7	13.3	33.3	37.2	35.6	24.2	7.4	—11.6	—33.1	+0.64
6	—34.8	—37.3	—22.0	—4.1	14.3	35.0	39.2	36.0	24.1	7.0	—11.0	—33.3	+1.09
8	—34.8	—37.0	—19.9	—2.6	16.5	38.1	41.3	36.8	24.7	7.2	—10.8	—34.0	+2.12
10	—34.4	—36.9	—15.2	—0.6	17.6	39.8	42.9	37.6	25.5	8.1	—10.5	—33.4	+3.37
Noon	—34.1	—36.3	—12.4	+1.0	18.8	39.8	43.5	38.1	26.5	8.9	—10.7	—33.5	+4.13
2	—34.4	—36.3	—12.5	+1.4	19.0	38.5	42.3	38.2	27.0	8.4	—11.5	—33.4	+3.89
4	—34.1	—36.8	—14.2	+0.3	18.2	36.9	42.0	38.0	26.8	7.4	—12.0	—33.8	+3.22
6	—33.7	—37.3	—18.9	—2.2	16.5	35.4	41.1	37.7	26.4	7.2	—12.3	—33.9	+2.18
8	—33.9	—37.1	—19.7	—4.4	14.3	33.9	40.0	37.2	25.6	7.1	—12.6	—34.0	+1.37
10	—33.9	—37.0	—20.0	—5.8	+12.6	+32.0	+38.6	+36.7	+25.4	+7.0	—12.7	—34.1	+0.73
Mean	—34.4	—37.1	—18.2	—2.8	+15.3	+35.3	+40.1	+36.9	+25.4	+7.4	—11.7	—33.6	+1.89

Means corrected for error of scale.

HOURLY MEANS BETWEEN 4 A. M. AND 10 P. M.

Sitka, Alaska Ter'y. Lat. 57° 03′. Long. 135° 20′ W. of G.

Alt. 20 ft. 1857 to 1864, inclusive. Magnetical and meteorological observatory at Japonski Island.

(Annales de l'observatoire, physique central de Russie.)

Hour.	Jan.	Feb.	Mar.	Apr.	May.	June.	July.	Aug.	Sept.	Oct.	Nov.	Dec.	Year.
Mdn't	..	..	..	..	..	..	..	..	..	..	..	..	[39.80]
1	..	..	..	..	..	..	..	..	..	..	..	..	[39.57]
2	..	..	..	..	..	..	..	..	..	..	..	..	[39.40]
3	..	..	..	..	..	..	..	..	..	..	..	..	[39.30]
4	29.89	28.76	32.61	35.41	40.45	45.97	50.24	50.71	47.41	41.99	36.95	31.46	39.32
5	29.93	28.69	32.35	35.67	41.04	47.03	50.97	50.97	47.54	42.08	36.88	31.30	39.54
6	29.95	28.58	32.35	36.31	42.61	48.69	52.15	51.51	47.75	42.12	36.63	31.32	40.00
7	29.89	28.38	33.12	38.03	44.46	49.86	53.69	53.08	48.76	42.28	36.68	31.25	40.79
8	29.84	28.76	34.67	39.89	46.13	52.04	55.17	54.59	50.24	42.96	36.74	31.28	41.86
9	30.16	29.93	36.59	41.52	47.84	53.71	56.88	56.20	51.82	44.03	37.42	31.44	43.13
10	30.89	31.59	38.11	42.98	49.23	55.06	58.07	57.58	53.33	45.07	38.27	31.98	44.35
11	31.82	33.23	39.33	44.12	50.38	56.16	59.00	58.77	54.68	45.99	39.06	32.69	45.42
Noon	32.63	33.71	39.83	44.60	50.83	57.22	59.76	59.56	55.60	46.75	39.94	33.44	46.16
1	32.71	34.00	40.17	45.23	51.06	57.22	60.03	59.54	55.87	46.75	40.05	33.57	46.35
2	32.67	33.93	39.98	44.53	50.83	56.84	59.80	59.33	55.56	46.66	39.85	33.37	46.11
3	32.13	33.45	39.51	44.19	50.22	56.39	59.52	58.81	55.13	46.21	39.29	32.87	45.66
4	31.39	32.71	38.91	43.32	49.57	55.75	58.39	58.10	54.38	45.50	38.70	32.42	44.93
5	30.85	31.66	37.69	42.32	48.55	54.95	57.42	57.06	53.41	44.67	38.11	32.02	44.06
6	30.56	30.92	36.31	41.02	47.27	53.67	56.25	55.78	52.11	43.92	37.80	31.77	43.11
7	30.22	30.34	35.10	39.51	45.83	52.25	55.06	54.59	50.94	43.34	37.51	31.73	42.20
8	30.20	29.97	34.38	38.27	44.24	50.58	53.80	53.44	50.09	43.00	37.44	31.64	41.42
9	30.02	29.67	33.96	37.75	43.02	49.26	52.70	52.81	49.55	42.66	37.28	31.51	40.85
10	29.84	29.66	33.61	36.95	42.14	48.24	51.98	52.29	49.17	42.51	37.11	31.53	40.42
11	..	..	..	..	..	..	..	..	..	..	..	..	[40.08]
Means[2]	30.61	30.58	35.59	39.59	45.38	51.37	54.76	54.60	50.99	43.73	37.78	31.94	42.24

[1] Smithsonian Contributions to Knowledge, No. 146; Washington, 1862.

[2] The temperatures for the 5 hours, 11 to 3, were obtained by a graphical process, and the above means were taken from 24 values. The reckoning being in old style and easterly, *our* months begin and end 11 days earlier than those to which the above numbers correspond. The original record is given in Reaumur's scale, it is here converted in Fahrenheit's scale. Interpolated values for 4 and 5 A. M., January, 1861, —0°.63 and —0°.53 (Reaumur).

HOURLY MEANS OF TEMPERATURE.

Island of St. Helen, opposite Montreal. Lat. 45° 30′. Long. 73° 33′ W. of G.

Alt. 60 ft. J. S. McCord. Printed Report, Montreal, 1842.

Observations at the *even* hours from Aug. 1839, to July, inclusive, 1840.
" " " " *odd* " " " 1840, " " " 1841.

Hour.	Jan.	Feb.	Mar.	Apr.	May.	June.	July.	Aug.	Sept.	Oct.	Nov.	Dec.	Year.
Mdn't	7°.00	19°.56	26°.00	39°.75	52°.06	59°.13	66°.00	62°.40	53°.81	45°.48	29°.03	21°.74	40°.16
1	17.53	12.91	18.12	31.35	46.48	60.53	62.35	64.66	52.61	42.17	31.60	15.03	37.94
2	5.74	18.15	24.22	37.90	49.66	56.96	63.22	61.01	53.36	44.30	28.80	22.42	38.81
3	17.66	11.80	17.32	29.33	44.82	59.98	60.62	63.70	52.33	41.09	31.18	14.12	36.99
4	5.22	17.48	22.75	35.18	49.66	57.20	62.82	60.06	52.10	43.47	28.58	22.04	38.05
5	17.09	10.57	15.66	27.93	44.77	58.78	59.66	63.25	52.10	40.25	30.68	13.62	36.19
6	4.56	16.94	22.09	36.71	50.00	58.83	64.93	60.41	53.11	43.48	29.03	22.10	38.51
7	16.98	9.30	15.43	30.63	47.77	60.36	64.38	67.59	54.06	41.09	30.75	13.85	37.68
8	5.00	17.62	24.01	38.83	53.55	63.50	69.79	63.61	55.51	45.79	29.61	22.50	40.78
9	17.80	10.53	19.54	33.76	50.83	65.10	67.20	70.27	56.80	43.93	32.13	14.77	40.22
10	8.31	21.65	27.34	43.06	57.58	66.13	73.24	68.14	59.18	49.30	30.80	23.21	43.94
11	20.04	14.69	25.01	36.95	54.12	68.50	70.63	73.30	59.73	47.43	34.11	16.40	43.41
Noon	10.92	24.34	31.54	47.28	63.71	69.55	75.85	72.03	63.13	52.53	32.26	24.64	47.32
1	20.45	19.32	29.91	39.40	57.11	71.05	73.50	76.30	62.65	50.11	36.25	18.29	46.19
2	12.17	26.27	33.80	48.26	65.37	72.10	77.75	74.33	64.30	55.27	32.76	25.96	49.03
3	21.32	20.60	31.53	40.80	57.79	72.01	75.43	77.03	64.18	50.50	35.98	18.69	47.15
4	11.98	24.44	33.27	48.06	64.96	71.38	77.90	74.12	64.40	53.93	32.91	26.64	48.66
5	19.59	18.64	28.98	40.10	57.95	71.26	73.95	75.16	63.36	47.85	33.95	17.35	45.67
6	9.87	22.34	30.74	46.15	60.48	69.40	75.79	72.03	60.50	51.10	31.43	24.72	46.21
7	19.56	15.75	24.90	37.40	54.83	68.25	70.30	71.14	58.15	45.70	33.20	16.61	42.98
8	9.00	21.43	28.54	43.08	58.22	65.48	71.06	67.10	57.60	48.56	30.36	23.40	43.65
9	19.62	15.48	23.25	34.03	50.72	63.50	66.25	68.11	56.21	44.38	32.63	16.62	40.90
10	7.93	20.62	27.61	41.63	54.74	61.91	67.75	64.41	55.31	46.89	29.21	22.53	41.71
11	18.35	14.28	20.82	32.41	48.91	61.53	64.03	66.59	54.51	42.33	31.28	15.69	39.22
Ev. h. 1839–40	8.14	20.90	27.65	42.15	56.66	64.29	70.50	66.63	57.69	48.34	30.39	23.49	43.07
Odd h. 1849–41	18.83	14.48	22.54	34.50	51.34	65.07	67.35	69.75	57.22	44.73	32.81	15.92	41.21

SEMI-HOURLY MEANS OF TEMPERATURE.

Thunder Bay Island, Lake Huron, Mich. Lat. 45° 2′. Long. 83° 17′ W. of G.

Alt. 610 ft. [and 40 above Lake Huron]. Observer: J. J. Malden. Dec. 1863, to Dec. 1865. Report, N. and N. W. Lake Survey, for 1867.

Hour.	Jan.	Feb.	Mar.	Apr.	May.	June.	July.	Aug.	Sept.	Oct.	Nov.	Dec.	Year.
Mdn't	19.4	21.4	25.3	34.5	43.1	54.3	60.8	62.9	57.7	43.0	36.8	24.6	40.3
0 30	19.0	21.5	24.6	34.0	42.4	53.9	60.1	62.6	58.0	43.2	36.6	24.4	40.0
1	18.7	21.1	24.3	33.6	42.1	53.7	59.7	62.4	57.8	43.0	36.4	24.3	39.8
1 30	18.3	20.8	24.1	33.4	41.8	53.3	59.2	62.1	57.7	42.8	36.3	24.2	39.5
2	18.0	20.7	23.8	33.0	41.5	53.0	58.8	61.8	57.5	42.6	36.2	24.1	39.2
2 30	17.8	20.5	23.6	32.8	41.4	52.7	58.5	61.7	57.3	42.5	36.1	24.0	39.1
3	17.7	20.4	23.5	32.7	41.3	52.5	58.2	61.5	57.2	42.5	36.0	23.8	38.9
3 30	17.7	20.4	23.6	32.8	41.2	52.7	58.2	61.5	57.1	42.4	36.0	23.9	38.9
4	17.8	20.5	23.7	32.9	41.3	52.8	58.3	61.4	57.0	42.4	35.9	24.0	39.0
4 30	17.9	20.5	23.8	33.0	41.4	52.8	58.4	61.4	56.8	42.3	35.9	24.0	39.0
5	18.0	20.7	23.9	33.1	41.6	53.2	58.6	61.4	56.8	42.3	35.9	24.1	39.1
5 30	18.1	20.8	24.0	33.4	42.3	53.7	59.1	61.6	56.9	42.4	36.0	24.2	39.3
6	18.2	20.9	24.2	33.8	43.2	54.6	59.9	61.9	56.9	42.5	36.0	24.3	39.7
6 30	18.3	21.0	24.6	34.5	43.9	55.9	61.1	62.7	57.3	42.6	36.0	24.3	40.1
7	18.3	21.2	25.0	35.4	45.0	56.9	62.7	63.7	57.8	42.9	36.0	24.3	40.8
7 30	18.4	21.4	25.5	36.3	46.0	58.1	63.4	65.0	58.6	43.3	36.1	24.5	41.4
8	18.8	21.7	26.5	37.2	46.9	59.2	64.5	66.2	59.5	43.7	36.3	24.7	42.1
8 30	19.1	22.1	27.4	38.0	47.6	60.1	65.6	67.3	60.1	44.3	36.6	24.8	42.7
9	19.4	22.7	28.0	38.7	48.2	60.7	66.5	68.2	61.0	45.0	37.0	25.0	43.4
9 30	20.0	23.2	28.9	39.2	48.5	61.5	67.2	68.8	61.6	45.7	37.4	25.3	43.9
10	20.4	23.7	29.6	39.8	49.0	62.0	67.9	69.6	62.3	46.4	37.9	25.6	44.5
10 30	21.0	24.4	30.3	40.3	49.5	62.5	68.4	70.5	63.0	47.1	38.3	25.9	45.1
11	21.6	25.1	31.3	40.8	49.8	62.8	68.9	71.3	63.6	47.8	38.7	26.3	45.7
11 30	22.2	25.7	31.3	41.2	50.1	63.1	69.3	72.0	64.2	48.4	39.2	26.7	46.1

Thunder Bay Island.—Continued.

Hour.	Jan.	Feb.	Mar.	Apr.	May.	June.	July.	Aug.	Sept.	Oct.	Nov.	Dec.	Year.
Noon	22°.8	26°.2	31°.5	41°.4	50°.5	63°.5	69°.7	72°.6	64°.8	49°.1	39°.6	26°.9	46°.5
0 30	23.3	26.7	31.9	41.7	50.7	64.2	69.9	73.1	65.1	49.6	40.0	27.1	46.9
1	23.5	27.0	32.1	41.9	50.9	64.0	69.8	73.6	65.4	49.9	40.4	27.3	47.1
1 30	23.7	27.4	32.3	42.0	51.0	64.0	70.3	73.8	65.7	50.3	40.6	27.4	47.4
2	23.9	27.5	32.5	42.1	51.2	64.6	70.5	73.9	65.9	50.5	40.8	27.3	47.6
2 30	23.8	27.5	32.3	42.1	51.2	64.6	70.6	73.8	65.9	50.5	40.9	27.3	47.5
3	23.6	27.4	32.0	42.0	51.5	64.5	70.7	73.4	65.7	50.2	40.8	27.1	47.4
3 30	23.2	27.0	31.7	41.7	51.6	64.2	70.5	73.0	65.2	49.9	40.4	26.9	47.1
4	22.5	26.4	31.3	41.5	51.5	63.7	70.3	72.5	64.7	49.4	39.8	26.6	46.7
4 30	22.3	25.7	30.8	41.1	51.1	63.4	69.7	72.0	64.2	48.7	39.5	26.4	46.2
5	21.9	25.2	30.1	40.6	50.6	63.0	69.1	71.2	63.6	48.1	39.0	26.2	45.7
5 30	21.6	24.8	29.5	40.1	49.9	62.4	68.4	70.3	62.8	47.5	38.7	26.1	45.2
6	21.2	24.2	29.0	39.5	49.2	61.8	67.6	69.5	62.1	46.8	38.5	26.0	44.6
6 30	21.0	23.9	28.3	38.8	48.5	60.7	66.8	68.4	61.5	46.2	38.3	25.9	44.0
7	20.7	23.7	27.7	38.2	47.7	59.6	66.0	67.8	60.8	45.8	38.1	25.7	43.5
7 30	20.6	23.4	27.2	37.6	46.9	58.9	65.1	67.1	60.3	45.4	38.0	25.5	43.0
8	20.5	23.3	27.0	37.2	46.3	58.1	64.3	66.5	59.8	45.0	37.9	25.7	42.6
8 30	20.4	22.8	26.7	36.8	45.6	57.4	63.8	65.8	59.5	44.9	37.7	25.6	42.2
9	20.3	22.9	26.5	36.4	45.1	56.9	63.2	65.2	59.1	44.4	37.6	25.4	41.9
9 30	20.1	22.6	26.3	36.1	44.6	56.4	62.8	64.7	58.8	44.2	37.5	25.3	41.6
10	20.0	22.5	26.2	35.8	44.2	56.0	62.2	64.2	58.7	44.0	37.4	25.3	41.3
10 30	19.8	22.0	26.0	35.4	43.9	55.4	62.0	63.8	58.4	43.8	37.2	25.0	41.0
11	19.6	22.0	25.7	35.1	43.6	55.1	61.6	63.4	58.1	43.5	37.1	25.2	40.8
11 30	19.5	21.8	25.5	34.9	43.3	54.7	61.2	62.8	57.9	43.2	36.9	24.8	40.6
Mean	20.3	23.3	27.5	37.4	46.5	58.6	64.6	66.9	60.6	45.5	37.7	25.4	42.8

HOURLY MEANS OF TEMPERATURE.

Toronto, Canada West.[1] Lat. 43° 39′. Long. 79° 23′ W. of G.

Alt. 342 feet. Captains Riddell, Younghusband, and Lefroy, R. A. July, 1842, to July, 1848.

Hour.	Jan.	Feb.	Mar.	Apr.	May.	June.	July.	Aug.	Sept.	Oct.	Nov.	Dec.	Year.
Mdn't[2]	+23.80	21.45	27.33	39.37	47.88	55.37	59.45	60.30	53.63	40.95	34.42	26.53	40.87
1	23.33	21.07	26.85	38.62	47.02	54.68	58.58	59.65	53.02	40.35	34.13	25.95	40.27
2	23.25	20.73	26.47	37.95	46.18	53.98	58.02	58.97	52.43	40.03	33.85	25.58	39.79
3	23.10	20.30	26.18	37.75	45.47	53.20	57.30	58.30	51.97	39.87	33.53	25.45	39.37
4	23.00	20.00	25.80	37.32	45.00	52.63	56.67	57.92	51.38	39.57	33.37	25.42	39.01
5	22.82	19.65	25.28	36.95	45.05	52.82	56.62	57.73	50.75	39.40	33.48	25.40	38.83
6	23.55	19.08	25.00	37.08	47.50	55.47	59.83	59.18	51.43	39.62	33 75	24 98	39.71
7	23.45	18.95	25.87	39.37	50.48	58.28	63.50	62.15	53.98	40.37	33.75	24.82	41.25
8	23.68	19.97	27.85	41.62	52.70	60.62	66.10	65.42	56.73	42.62	34.80	25.25	43.11
9	24.65	22.27	30.02	43.60	55.02	62.50	68.30	67.92	59.15	45.30	36.33	26.43	45.12
10	25.88	24.28	31.75	45.12	56.72	64.17	70.00	69.90	61.12	47.23	37.77	27.88	46.82
11	27.05	25.87	32.98	46.50	57.85	65.45	71.55	71.35	62.55	48.60	38.78	29.12	48.14
Noon	27.83	27.07	34.00	47.53	58.80	66.55	72.85	72.30	63.52	49.50	39.57	29.93	49.12
1	28.33	27.93	34.65	48.47	59.72	67.28	73.77	73.07	64.12	49.93	39.97	30.65	49.82
2	28.60	28.33	35.22	48.85	60.07	67.70	74.62	73.65	64.52	50.28	40.05	30.80	50.22
3	28.57	28.32	35.02	48.92	60.13	68.08	74.82	74.00	64.55	50.05	39.88	30.55	50.24
4	28.05	27.77	34.55	48.53	60.08	68.32	74.83	73.85	64.33	49.32	38.98	29.90	49.88
5	27.05	26.57	33.80	47.80	59.70	67.72	74.37	73.30	63.37	47.57	37.77	28.95	49.00
6	26.23	25.12	32.12	46.00	57.95	66.42	72.93	71.40	60.70	45.52	36.95	28.25	47.47
7	25.70	24.13	30.65	43.47	55.08	63.68	69.45	67.42	58.00	44.42	36.38	27.92	45.52
8	25.38	23.28	29.68	41.88	52.37	60.38	65.25	64.50	56.72	43.68	36.07	27.53	43.89
9	25.18	22.63	28.68	40.80	50.62	58.22	62.88	62.92	55.68	42.92	35.78	27.28	42.80
10	24.80	22.08	28.03	40.03	49.65	56.88	61.65	61.90	54.62	42.17	35.43	26.98	42.02
11	24.48	21.57	27.38	39.53	48.73	55.92	60.47	61.10	53.98	41.50	35.08	26.87	41.38
Mean	25.32	23.27	29.80	42.63	52.91	60.68	65.99	65.76	57.59	44.20	36.24	27.44	44.32

1 Phil. Trans., Roy. Soc., Vol. 143, 1853.

2 The table given by Gen. Sabine commences with noon, it was changed to commence with midnight, for the sake of uniformity with the other tables.

Hourly Means of Temperature.

From self-registering instrument (Lewis's thermograph).

Mohawk, N. Y. Lat. 43° 00′. Long. 75° 02′ W. of G.

Alt. 435 ft. By Dr. James Lewis.

Hour.	January. 1861	1862	1863	1864	1867	1868	1869	Mean of 7 years.
	°	°	°	°	°	°	°	°
Mdn't	16.06	20.08	26.76	23.18	12.91	15.98	22.79	19.68
1	16.93	19.99	26.65	22.69	12.43	15.63	22.39	19.53
2	17.11	19.49	26.35	22.44	12.17	15.11	21.92	19.23
3	16.93	18.75	26.06	22.29	11.57	14.72	21.43	18.82
4	16.76	18.16	25.84	22.11	11.06	14.69	20.88	18.50
5	16.61	17.81	25.69	21.96	10.74	14.49	20.36	18.24
6	16.58	17.52	25.54	21.85	10.43	14.46	20.08	18.07
7	16.50	16.92	25.39	21.70	10.34	14.46	29.85	17.88
8	16.57	16.77	25.44	21.45	10.68	14.42	20.09	17.92
9	17.36	17.68	26.62	21.68	11.55	15.24	20.56	18.67
10	19.05	19.58	28.62	22.51	13.04	16.71	21.67	20.17
11	21.16	21.85	30.30	23.72	14.63	18.38	23.47	21.93
Noon	22.40	23.15	31.68	25.14	16.14	20.00	25.46	23.42
1	22.67	24.04	32.36	25.90	17.28	21.40	26.99	24.38
2	22.98	24.62	32.57	26.93	17.97	21.82	27.90	24.97
3	22.50	25.13	32.56	27.36	18.19	21.69	28.19	25.09
4	22.04	24.25	31.73	27.43	17.72	21.36	27.80	24.62
5	20.95	23.18	30.46	26.85	16.81	20.16	26.91	23.62
6	19.05	21.99	29.27	26.18	16.07	19.01	25.88	22.49
7	17.85	21.50	28.73	25.37	15.44	18.21	24.94	21.72
8	17.23	21.20	28.42	24.79	14.75	17.50	24.16	21.15
9	16.54	20.56	28.00	24.30	14.20	16.94	23.60	20.59
10	15.82	20.45	27.67	23.89	13.70	16.49	23.45	20.21
11	15.66	20.19	27.15	23.48	13.34	16.35	23.11	19.90
Mean	18.47	20.62	28.33	23.96	13.88	17.30	23.50	20.87

Hour.	February. 1861	1862	1863	1864	1867	1868	Mean of 6 years.
	°	°	°	°	°	°	°
Mdn't	24.03	18.81	19.63	25.46	26.87	11.21	21.00
1	22.85	18.18	18.98	25.21	26.07	10.74	20.34
2	22.57	17.49	18.75	24.98	25.91	10.03	19.96
3	22.31	16.90	18.67	24.66	25.71	9.40	19.61
4	22.08	16.20	18.61	24.43	25.84	8.68	19.31
5	22.03	16.66	18.21	24.20	25.60	8.01	19.12
6	21.64	16.45	17.97	23.89	25.74	7.27	18.83
7	21.08	16.28	17.53	23.56	25.22	6.74	18.40
8	21.26	16.88	18.03	23.29	25.58	6.69	18.62
9	22.87	18.80	19.59	23.47	26.77	7.70	19.87
10	26.30	21.29	21.52	24.36	27.94	9.88	21.88
11	27.81	23.29	23.46	25.68	29.55	12.55	23.72
Noon	29.41	25.50	25.24	26.73	30.98	15.14	25.50
1	29.85	26.51	26.51	28.15	31.59	17.37	26.66
2	30.80	26.52	27.15	28.92	31.92	19.14	27.41
3	30.79	26.57	27.39	29.20	31.82	20.27	27.67
4	30.13	25.56	27.04	29.20	31.21	20.36	27.25
5	28.83	24.07	26.41	28.66	30.59	19.57	26 36
6	27.09	22.41	24.92	27.95	29.86	18.44	25.11
7	26.33	21.34	23.53	27.32	29.18	17.04	24.12
8	25.70	20.51	22.56	26.64	28.74	15.89	23.34
9	25.03	20.01	21.71	26.16	28.25	15.09	22.71
10	24.53	19.67	20.91	26.07	27.62	13.66	22.08
11	24.26	19.69	20.04	25.48	27.18	12.33	21.50
Mean	25.40	20.65	21.84	[illegible]	[illegible]	[illegible]	22.51

Hour.	March. 1861	1862	1863	1864	1867	1868	Mean of 6 years.
Mdn't	25.73	27.53	22.13	30.59	26.82	27.85	26.77
1	25.39	26.46	21.18	29.60	26.05	26.11	25.80
2	24.90	26.28	20.50	29.14	25.71	25.51	25.34
3	24.24	25.75	20.09	28.55	25.07	25.06	24.79
4	23.77	25.40	19.38	28.03	24.71	24.67	24.33
5	23.60	24.78	18.81	27.59	24.33	24.35	23.91
6	23.33	24.18	18.17	27.30	23.93	24.10	23.50
7	23.55	24.70	17.97	26.97	23.79	24.26	23.54
8	24.95	26.54	20.10	27.11	25.22	25.42	24.89
9	27.25	28.32	22.65	28.52	27.07	27.20	26.83
10	28.93	30.52	25.13	30.54	28.63	29.39	28.86
11	29.89	32.43	27.46	32.21	29.93	31.65	30.59
Noon	31.07	33.98	29.06	33.69	31.41	33.73	32.16
1	31.99	34.59	30.24	35.05	32.34	35.61	33.30
2	32.68	35.83	30.90	35.99	32.97	36.98	34.22
3	32.68	35.45	31.30	36.70	33.14	38.10	34.56
4	32.64	34.58	31.31	36.80	33.19	38.82	34.56
5	32.16	33.56	30.61	36.37	32.62	38.95	34.05
6	30.73	32.34	29.23	35.36	31.31	37.07	32.67
7	28.91	30.94	27.69	34.17	29.96	34.82	31.08
8	27.90	30.20	26.59	33.31	29.01	32.95	29.99
9	27.49	29.40	25.53	32.60	28.29	31.29	29.10
10	27.44	28.78	24.27	31.99	27.69	29.86	28.34
11	26.83	28.39	23.07	31.32	27.24	28.88	27.62
Mean	27.84	29.62	24.72	31.65	28.36	30.53 *	28.78

Hour.	April. 1861	1862	1863	1864	1867	1868	Mean of 6 years.
Mdn't	38.63	38.08	43.36	41.56	39.04	35.61	39.38
1	37.51	36.85	41.83	40.48	37.99	34.45	38.18
2	36.92	36.52	40.93	39.81	37.63	33.89	37.62
3	36.43	36.08	40.36	39.22	37.16	33.39	37.11
4	35.96	35.50	39.85	38.70	36.74	32.68	36.57
5	35.96	34.95	39.22	38.18	36.82	32.09	36.20
6	35.97	34.71	38.50	37.65	36.96	31.63	35.90
7	37.22	35.30	38.28	37.51	37.89	32.42	36.44
8	40.50	37.86	39.50	38.09	39.43	34.04	38.23
9	43.50	40.87	41.46	39.76	41.01	36.16	40.46
10	45.89	43.52	43.75	41.54	42.61	38.43	42.62
11	47.75	45.16	45.91	43.27	44.37	40.42	44.48
Noon	49.11	46.78	47.98	44.66	46.14	42.42	46.18
1	49.71	47.85	49.72	46.11	47.43	44.21	47.51
2	50.26	49.04	51.22	47.52	48.44	45.28	48.63
3	49.88	49.15	52.62	48.75	49.54	45.78	49.29
4	49.45	48.76	53.23	49.26	50.21	46.80	49.62
5	49.23	48.12	53.19	48.74	49.97	46.62	49.31
6	48.19	47 18	52.32	48.28	48.38	44.85	48.20
7	46.09	44.63	50.74	47.05	45.85	42.80	46.19
8	43.55	41.79	48.70	45.41	43.65	40.62	43.95
9	41.82	40.08	47.18	44.20	41.83	38.74	42.31
10	40.37	39.46	45.75	43.21	40.82	37.45	41.18
11	39.39	38.83	44.41	42.28	39.97	36.42	40.22
Mean	42.90	41.56	45.42	42.97	42.50	38.63	42.33

Mohawk.—Continued.

Hour.	May.						Mean of 6 years.	June.						Mean of 6 years.
	1861	1862	1863	1864	1867	1868		1860	1861	1862	1863	1867	1868	
	°	°	°	°	°	°	°	°	°	°	°	°	°	°
Mdn't	46.27	48.65	56.90	58.23	46.11	51.89	51.34	59.83	58.97	56.63	60.96	62.35	60.78	60.25
1	45.12	47.70	55.23	56.77	45.65	50.92	50.23	58.86	57.52	55.46	59.60	60.23	58.78	58.41
2	44.37	46.76	54.05	55.93	44.90	50.03	49.34	57.89	56.76	54.76	58.70	59.39	57.68	57.53
3	43.71	45.77	53.01	55.20	44.19	49.12	48.50	57.06	55.53	54.38	57.96	58.99	56.70	56.77
4	43.15	44.86	52.08	54.55	43.14	48.31	47.68	56.26	54.57	53.77	57.27	58.58	55.93	56.06
5	42.88	44.37	51.19	53.99	42.96	47.77	47.19	55.64	54.16	53.21	56.67	58.19	55.60	55.58
6	43.08	44.67	50.50	53.62	43.39	47.86	47.19	56.48	54.98	54.07	56.29	59.33	56.21	56.23
7	44.31	48.05	50.94	54.65	44.83	49.01	48.63	57.99	57.55	57.12	56.90	61.65	57.96	58.20
8	46.90	52.60	52.87	55.52	46.75	51.00	50.94	60.69	61.27	61.00	58.67	64.73	60.69	61.17
9	49.67	56.31	55.62	57.54	48.50	52.81	53.41	63.11	64.58	63.75	60.91	67.89	63.63	63.98
10	52.54	59.19	58.17	59.65	50.20	54.59	55.72	65.77	67.18	66.13	63.38	70.86	66.21	66.59
11	54.44	61.46	60.81	61.88	51.90	56.67	57.86	67.72	69.21	68.49	65.52	73.23	68.43	68.77
Noon	56.09	63.17	63.07	63.89	53.50	58.20	59.65	69.14	70.61	70.11	67.50	75.30	70.76	70.57
1	56.53	64.44	64.94	65.49	54.99	59.52	60.99	69.89	71.63	70.30	69.18	77.05	72.77	71.80
2	57.37	64.93	66.84	67.27	55.78	60.47	62.11	71.06	72.39	71.11	70.95	78.16	74.56	73.04
3	57.31	65.08	68.11	68.35	56.29	60.69	62.64	71.81	72.61	70.97	72.13	77.97	76.02	73.58
4	57.26	64.66	68.74	68.84	56.36	61.59	62.91	71.28	72.60	70.40	72.30	78.31	76.82	73.62
5	56.62	64.09	68.67	68.56	56.03	61.78	62.62	70.43	71.78	69.47	72.15	77.78	76.63	73.04
6	55.96	62.27	67.80	67.66	54.93	61.23	61.64	68.65	70.21	68.44	71.25	76.66	75.14	71.72
7	53.74	58.94	66.15	65.84	52.95	59.40	59.50	67.25	67.80	66.19	69.63	73.68	72.17	69.45
8	50.50	54.46	63.80	64.03	50.86	57.01	56.78	65.35	64.71	62.59	67.83	69.48	68.96	66.49
9	48.34	51.97	61.68	62.08	49.22	55.75	54.84	63.39	62.33	60.30	65.52	66.42	66.29	64.04
10	46.99	50.93	59.91	60.62	47.88	54.19	53.42	62.03	60.72	59.40	63.74	64.92	64.17	62.50
11	46.56	49.79	58.35	59.42	46.87	53.00	52.33	60.88	59.75	57.64	62.26	63.45	62.37	61.06
Mean	49.99	54.78	59.56	60.81	49.51	54.70 *	54.89	63.70	63.73	62.28	64.06	68.11	65.64	64.59

Hour.	July.						Mean of 6 years.	August.						Mean of 6 years.
	1860	1861	1862	1863	1867	1868		1860	1861	1862	1863	1867	1868	
Mdn't	61.21	63.16	62.41	70.48	63.01	71.38	65.27	62.23	61.64	61.62	67.96	63.23	64.48	63.53
1	60.40	62.31	61.54	69.56	62.08	69.89	64.30	61.67	61.93	60.62	67.53	62.56	63.45	62.96
2	59.50	61.68	60.54	68.90	60.93	68.64	63.36	61.07	61.66	59.86	66.67	61.59	62.60	62.24
3	58.75	61.06	59.80	68.40	60.00	67.56	62.59	60.58	60.71	59.14	65.94	60.99	61.97	61.55
4	58.12	60.46	59.13	67.89	59.12	66.66	61.90	59.97	59.87	58.44	65.44	60.45	61.51	60.95
5	57.46	60.04	58.68	67.44	58.53	66.05	61.37	59.64	59.16	58.01	65.05	59.81	61.02	60.45
6	57.95	60.41	59.21	67.20	58.83	66.12	61.62	59.70	58.90	57.98	64.67	59.69	60.70	60.27
7	59.84	61.92	61.74	67.52	61.18	67.47	63.28	60.70	60.02	59.99	64.78	61.29	61.45	61.37
8	62.42	64.14	64.81	68.79	64.41	69.61	65.70	62.84	62.24	62.65	65.87	64.49	63.20	63.55
9	65.24	66.95	67.40	70.36	67.50	72.19	68.27	65.34	65.00	65.96	67.56	67.25	65.13	66.04
10	68.10	69.63	69.63	71.90	71.58	75.11	70.99	68.27	67.75	69.07	69.61	70.18	67.38	68.71
11	70.23	71.61	71.51	73.63	72.91	78.01	72.98	70.70	69.95	71.67	71.44	72.77	69.63	71.03
Noon	71.81	73.06	72.93	74.98	74.88	80.77	74.74	72.82	71.23	73.93	72.96	74.94	71.70	72.93
1	72.37	73.79	74.26	76.47	77.13	82.63	76.11	73.97	71.93	75.55	74.69	76.88	73.27	74.38
2	72.30	73.96	74.89	77.98	79.05	84.95	77.19	74.34	71.98	75.76	76.53	78.24	74.80	75.27
3	72.14	74.35	75.20	79.31	80.74	86.63	78.06	74.50	72.11	76.02	78.23	79.04	75.86	75.96
4	71.83	74.07	74.60	79.98	81.32	88.43	78.37	74.09	72.10	75.82	78.78	79.13	76.78	76.12
5	71.61	73.40	74.47	80.10	81.59	88.83	78.33	73.20	71.69	75.02	78.36	78.55	76.97	75.63
6	70.56	72.27	73.12	79.29	79.27	87.68	77.03	71.75	70.69	73.64	77.59	76.63	76.10	74.40
7	68.70	70.75	70.99	77.77	75.42	84.69	74.72	69.10	68.58	71.03	76.01	73.07	73.40	71.86
8	66.14	68.20	68.20	75.92	71.85	80.60	71.82	66.49	65.98	68.00	73.77	69.53	70.83	69.10
9	64.27	66.00	65.99	74.10	68.34	77.63	69.39	65.21	64.41	65.42	71.83	67.16	68.47	67.08
10	63.22	64.75	64.15	72.56	66.31	75.15	67.69	64.13	63.20	63.77	70.19	65.58	66.82	65.61
11	62.08	63.99	63.25	71.38	64.60	73.06	66.39	63.26	62.45	62.59	69.01	64.17	65.51	64.50
Mean	65.26	67.16	67.02	72.99 *	69.20 *	76.24 *	69.64	66.48	65.63	66.73	70.85	68.63	68.04 *	67.73

Mohawk.—Continued.

Hour.	September.						Mean of 6 years.	October.						Mean of 6 years.
	1860	1861	1862	1863	1867	1868		1860	1861	1862	1863	1867	1868	
	°	°	°	°	°	°	°	°	°	°	°	°	°	°
Mdn't	53.35	56.87	55.99	56.51	54.63	53.84	55.20	48.30	48.45	46.74	47.57	44.94	40.65	46.11
1	53.49	56.09	55.89	55.86	54.52	53.98	54.97	47.08	48.09	46.55	47.22	43.54	39.96	45.41
2	52.90	55.39	55.19	55.12	53.79	53.40	54.30	46.85	47.34	46.26	46.75	42.71	39.49	44.90
3	52.15	54.96	54.70	54.33	53.10	52.99	53.71	46.65	46.82	46.03	46.24	42.02	39.12	44.48
4	51.24	54.46	54.16	53.65	52.66	52.51	53.11	45.95	46.50	45.49	45.80	41.57	38.68	44.00
5	50.36	54.12	53.86	53.06	52.04	52.06	52.58	45.29	46.34	45.25	45.42	41.02	38.46	43.63
6	49.92	53.84	53.57	52.54	51.48	51.81	52.19	44.77	46.09	44.99	45.12	40.61	38.30	43.31
7	50.25	54.39	54.51	52.22	51.76	52.01	52.52	44.55	45.86	44.85	44.86	40.65	38.19	43.16
8	51.80	56.04	57.08	52.99	53.58	53.14	54.10	44.92	46.52	45.81	45.05	41.75	38.86	43.82
9	54.40	58.40	60.16	54.90	56.10	54.72	56.45	46.18	48.60	47.05	46.19	44.13	40.21	45.39
10	57.03	61.03	63.09	57.16	59.14	56.71	59.03	48.25	50.98	49.24	47.98	47.13	42.05	47.60
11	59.53	63.01	66.05	59.48	61.64	58.54	61.38	50.22	53.17	51.33	49.69	50.27	43.76	49.74
Noon	61.58	64.55	68.37	61.66	64.05	60.11	63.39	52.02	54.94	53.15	51.19	52.53	45.53	51.56
1	63.38	65.49	70.18	63.62	66.63	61.65	65.16	53.18	56.05	54.04	52.50	54.76	46.82	52.89
2	64.42	65.86	70.70	65.52	68.97	62.50	66.33	53.84	56.96	54.26	53.75	56.20	47.71	53.79
3	64.11	66.23	71.19	67.12	70.56	63.26	67.08	54.16	57.20	53.87	54.57	56.97	48.37	54.19
4	63.78	65.87	70.73	67.56	71.11	63.41	67.08	53.79	56.48	53.38	54.58	56.50	48.19	53.82
5	62.85	65.25	69.49	67.22	68.96	62.48	66.04	52.70	55.01	52.25	53.77	54.97	47.13	52.64
6	61.20	63.60	67.15	65.79	65.79	61.09	64.10	51.31	53.11	50.81	52.69	52.20	45.71	50.97
7	58.62	60.88	64.08	63.75	62.54	59.29	61.53	49.48	51.39	49.37	51.53	50.20	44.47	49.41
8	56.32	59.38	61.15	61.65	60.05	57.69	59.37	48.45	50.46	48.34	50.49	48.69	43.43	48.31
9	55.11	58.51	59.36	59.96	58.16	56.41	57.92	47.68	50.00	47.78	49.58	47.41	42.53	47.50
10	54.54	57.92	57.94	58.59	56.73	55.49	56.87	48.04	50.40	47.53	48.84	46.51	41.82	47.19
11	53.82	57.33	56.83	57.43	55.75	54.66	55.97	48.38	49.37	46.85	48.17	45.74	41.20	46.62
Mean	56.51	59.57	61.31	59.07	59.32	56.82	58.77	48.83	50.67	48.80	49.15	47.63	42.53	47.94

Hour.	November.						Mean of 6 years.	December.						Mean of 6 years.
	1860	1861	1862	1863	1867	1868		1860	1861	1862	1863	1867	1868	
Mdn't	37.72	35.02	34.45	39.17	34.38	32.54	35.54	21.00	25.81	25.47	23.32	17.62	19.87	22.18
1	38.53	35.06	34.69	39.80	34.80	33.49	36.06	21.41	25.54	25.80	22.85	16.70	19.38	21.95
2	38.48	34.65	34.23	39.26	34.19	33.11	35.65	21.22	25.06	25.54	22.51	16.22	19.03	21.60
3	38.27	34.09	33.74	39.08	33.82	32.63	35.27	20.90	24.44	25.41	22.22	15.82	18.57	21.23
4	38.20	33.74	33.43	38.78	33.52	32.34	35.00	20.68	24.10	25.10	21.97	15.44	18.30	20.93
5	38.01	33.32	33.10	38.53	32.87	32.21	34.67	20.67	23.84	24.95	21.81	15.34	18.23	20.81
6	37.95	32.94	32.88	38.32	32.28	32.04	34.40	20.61	23.57	24.85	21.69	14.97	18.07	20.63
7	37.59	32.42	32.24	38.04	32.15	32.01	34.07	20.41	23.77	24.68	21.59	14.47	17.96	20.48
8	37.47	32.52	33.09	37.92	32.40	32.12	34.25	19.93	23.99	24.93	21.54	14.34	18.17	20.50
9	37.89	33.74	34.55	38.11	33.73	32.63	35.11	20.90	25.02	26.08	21.88	15.38	18.73	21.33
10	38.96	35.74	36.38	39.10	35.27	33.66	36.52	22.38	27.00	27.09	22.56	16.61	20.13	22.63
11	40.51	37.52	38.16	40.18	37.07	34.66	38.02	23.97	28.89	28.42	23.75	18.50	21.16	24.11
Noon	41.70	39.05	39.42	41.31	38.33	35.74	39.26	24.98	30.65	29.42	25.08	20.17	22.59	25.48
1	42.40	40.11	40.01	42.20	39.00	36.54	40.04	25.52	31.54	30.31	26.18	21.44	23.52	26.42
2	42.69	40.46	40.41	42.70	39.38	26.93	40.43	25.36	31.62	30.35	26.87	22.19	24.18	26.76
3	42.72	40.66	40.54	42.96	39.31	37.17	40.56	24.96	31.05	30.30	27.21	22.35	24.00	26.65
4	42.07	39.65	40.24	42.69	38.72	36.94	40.05	24.49	29.66	29.97	26.87	22.06	23.51	26.09
5	41.14	38.14	39.15	42.24	37.71	36.31	39.11	23.42	27.98	29.02	26.44	21.36	22.69	25.15
6	40.11	37.02	37.93	41.48	37.02	35.46	38.17	22.63	27.10	28.27	25.87	20.79	21.81	24.41
7	39.17	36.20	37.05	40.83	36.20	34.76	37.37	22.28	26.20	27.62	25.35	20.44	21.18	23.84
8	38.31	35.77	36.95	40.46	35.75	34.20	36.91	21.93	25.73	27.11	24.86	19.69	20.93	23.38
9	37.91	35.19	36.25	39.96	35.45	33.71	36.41	21.57	25.76	26.42	24.36	19.22	20.63	22.99
10	37.76	35.01	35.68	39.58	35.21	33.40	36.11	21.19	26.28	26.00	24.10	18.87	20.26	22.78
11	37.76	34.98	35.01	39.35	35.03	32.91	35.84	21.14	25.97	25.71	23.79	18.48	20.04	22.52
Mean	39.31	35.96	36.24	40.08	35.57	34.06	36.88	22.24	26.69	27.03	23.94	18.27	20.54	23.12

Mohawk.—Continued.

N. B. In the following means the preceding months marked thus *, are omitted.

Hour.	Mar. 5 years.	May. 5 years.	July. 5 years.	Aug. 5 years.	Hour.	Mar. 5 years.	May. 5 years.	July. 5 years.	Aug. 5 years.
Mdn't	26°.56	51°.23	62°.26	63°.34	Noon	31°.84	59°.94	72°.60	73°.18
1	25.74	50.09	61.42	62.86	1	32.84	61.28	73.47	74.60
2	25.31	49.20	60.57	62.17	2	33.67	62.43	73.72	75.37
3	24.74	48.38	59.87	61.47	3	33.85	63.03	73.90	75.98
4	24.26	47.56	59.24	60.83	4	33.70	63.17	73.50	75.98
5	23.82	47.08	58.73	60.33	5	33.06	62.79	73.16	75.36
6	23.38	47.05	59.19	60.19	6	31.79	61.72	71.98	74.06
7	23.40	48.56	61.17	61.36	7	30.33	59.52	70.15	71.56
8	24.78	50.93	63.79	63.62	8	29.40	56.73	67.51	68.75
9	26.76	53.53	66.53	66.22	9	28.66	54.65	65.42	66.81
10	28.75	55.95	69.12	68.98	10	28.03	53.27	64.04	65.37
11	30.38	58.10	71.12	71.31	11	27.37	52.20	63.11	64.30
					Mean	28.44	54.93	66.48	67.66

N. B. The observer remarks that the indications of the instrument are absolutely correct, but that its exposure was not unexceptionable; the locality, though in the shade and on the north side of the house, being accessible to the influence of the sun between 2½ or 3 P. M., and sunset or to within half an hour previous to sunset. In 1865 the station was movable to avoid this influence, in 1866–7 it was tolerably free from disturbance, in the winter 1868–9 a screen was erected to the westward. I have omitted the results in all months marked *, considering the indications affected from the above cause. [S.]

Bi-hourly means of Temperature.

Cambridge,[1] Mass. Lat. 42° 23′. Long. 71° 07′ W. of G.

Alt. about 71 ft. Observer . . . . . Oct. 1841, to Dec. 1842, inclusive.

Hour.	Jan.	Feb.	Mar.	Apr.	May.	June.	July.	Aug.	Sept.	Oct.	Nov.	Dec.	Year.
0.6_m	27°.92	34°.21	33°.02	39°.41	46°.93	54°.65	66°.00	61°.20	49°.90	39°.66	33°.13	29°.22	42°.94
2.6	27.31	32.94	31.79	39.76	45.67	52.68	64.79	60.35	48.49	38.40	32.77	28.75	41.97
4.6	26.97	32.01	31.48	38.24	45.06	52.60	64.93	59.50	48.17	37.90	32.41	28.66	41.49
6.6	25.71	32.15	30.59	38.93	49.61	59.74	68.24	62.11	47.81	37.75	32.27	28.24	42.76
8.6	23.90	32.54	37.09	43.31	57.04	65.09	73.56	68.00	56.44	43.15	35.37	29.48	47.08
10.6	29.30	36.42	42.41	46.55	60.52	68.95	78.48	71.95	63.45	51.33	41.51	33.85	52.06
0.6_a	33.24	40.40	45.04	48.22	63.08	71.18	79.03	72.72	66.10	55.07	43.66	36.57	54.53
2.6	33.27	40.99	44.51	48.52	63.98	71.49	78.49	73.01	66.04	55.91	43.69	36.33	54.69
4.6	31.76	38.87	42.11	47.01	62.51	69.33	76.64	71.79	63.28	52.28	40.58	33.33	52.46
6.6	29.55	35.13	37.77	44.31	58.13	66.54	72.45	68.39	58.09	45.59	37.62	31.64	48.77
8.6	28.82	34.58	35.24	41.07	52.40	59.60	68.80	64.40	53.82	42.52	35.67	30.58	45.62
10.6	28.13	34.57	33.85	40.21	49.40	56.08	67.00	62.86	51.30	40.82	34.57	29.61	44.03
Mean	28.82	35.40	37.07	42.96	54.53	62.33	71.53	66.36	56.07	45.03	35.94	31.35	47.37
No. of days	13	10	14	15	14	11	10	11	11	15	30	23	

It is apparent that the small number of observations is the principal cause of certain anomalies presented in the above means.

[1] Memoirs Am. Acad., vol. ii, new series; also Trans. Conn. Acad. of Arts and Sci., vol. i, part 1, 1866.

HOURLY MEANS OF TEMPERATURE.

Amherst, Mass. Lat. 42° 22′. Long. 72° 34′ W. of G.

Alt. 267 feet. Prof. E. S. Snell. 1839.

Hour.	Jan.	Feb.	Mar.	Apr.	May.	June.	July.	Aug.	Sept.	Oct.	Nov.	Dec.	Year.
Mdn't	+20°.44	26°.87	29°.96	43°.62	52°.17	56°.12	66°.30	62°.92	54°.46	46°.37	32°.40	27.°30	43°.24
1	19.04	25.79	30.08	42.31	51.41	54.96	65.22	62.30	54.44	45.59	32.46	27.65	42.61
2	18.70	25.54	30.00	41.85	50.44	54.32	64.78	61.78	53.68	44.81	31.81	27.08	42.07
3	18.81	25.37	29.46	41.12	49.51	53.68	64.33	61.41	52.88	44.00	31.31	26.73	41.55
4	18.44	24.63	29.12	40.69	49.04	53.56	64.19	61.15	52.24	43.37	31.08	26.58	41.17
5	18.22	24.37	28.77	40.42	48.74	53.80	64.07	60.78	51.92	42.74	30.77	25.96	40.88
6	18.26	23.79	28.69	40.77	50.15	55.64	65.59	61.63	52.36	42.81	30.46	25.50	41.30
7	18.19	23.79	30.19	42.57	52.70	57.40	67.81	62.96	54.48	43.59	30.52	25.31	42.47
8	19.11	24.79	32.73	45.50	55.30	60.20	70.52	65.48	57.28	46.15	32.12	25.15	44.53
9	21.48	27.12	35.27	48.46	57.52	62.48	72.48	68.37	60.36	49.63	34.46	26.88	47.04
10	24.26	29.42	37.38	51.23	60.04	64.72	75.41	70.48	63.12	52.70	36.23	29.83	49.57
11	27.04	31.29	39.58	54.19	62.04	67.28	78.04	72.89	65.84	55.48	37.81	32.04	51.96
Noon	29.26	32.83	41.19	56.46	63.67	69.68	80.11	74.30	67.96	57.52	39.81	33.58	53.86
1	30.40	33.92	42.46	58.00	65.07	70.96	80.44	75.67	68.92	58.70	40.92	35.42	55.07
2	30.74	34.63	43.15	58.96	65.67	70.60	81.11	75.30	69.60	59.74	40.77	35.58	55.49
3	30.26	34.37	42.92	58.35	65.19	70.20	79.11	75.11	69.00	59.70	40.08	34.88	54.93
4	28.74	33.46	42.04	57.15	64.78	69.44	78.78	73.67	68.20	58.70	38.65	33.04	53.89
5	26.26	31.67	40.46	55.58	62.89	67.60	77.44	72.70	66.24	56.11	37.08	31.31	52.11
6	25.00	29.75	38.27	53.04	61.00	65.80	75.78	70.26	63.32	53.96	35.65	29.96	50.15
7	22.70	29.62	34.64	50.23	59.30	63.52	73.15	68.88	61.27	51.70	35.44	29.59	48.34
8	22.30	29.00	33.88	48.27	57.11	61.56	70.63	67.11	59.69	50.33	34.72	29.08	46.97
9	21.44	28.29	32.92	46.77	55.26	59.64	68.56	65.85	57.81	49.30	34.00	28.59	45.70
10	20.93	28.00	31.52	45.23	54.19	58.40	67.82	64.42	56.27	48.56	33.64	28.08	44.75
11	20.52	27.38	30.52	44.31	52.93	57.40	67.37	63.65	55.19	47.22	32.84	27.70	43.92
Mean	22.94	28.57	34.80	48.54	56.92	61.62	71.62	67.45	59.85	50.36	34.79	29.28	47.23

DERIVED HOURLY MEANS OF TEMPERATURE.

New Haven,[1] Conn. Lat. 41° 18′. Long. 72° 56′ W. of G.

Approx. Alt. 45 feet. Various observers. 1778 to 1865 inclusive.

Hour.	Jan.	Feb.	Mar.	Apr.	May.	June.	July.	Aug.	Sept.	Oct.	Nov.	Dec.	Year.
Mdn't	24.26	25.24	32.28	42.19	51.88	61.15	66.46	65.57	57.71	47.02	37.68	28.25	44.98
1	23.91	24.77	31.77	41.41	51.01	60.03	65.49	64.75	56.87	45.26	37.14	27.93	44.28
2	23.53	24.31	31.24	40.74	50.12	58.91	64.69	64.03	56.18	45.62	36.64	27.60	43.63
3	23.19	23.80	30.72	40.10	49.31	58.25	64.11	63.56	55.70	45.05	36.22	27.25	43.10
4	22.83	23.32	30.28	39.52	48.78	58.10	63.97	63.16	55.27	44.59	35.82	26.93	42.71
5	22.46	22.95	29.91	39.31	48.90	58.79	64.27	63.22	55.15	44.29	35.52	26.64	42.62
6	22.19	22.81	30.00	39.69	50.68	60.83	65.51	63.96	55.66	44.45	35.52	26 45	43.15
7	22.15	23.01	31.18	41.57	53.65	63.79	67.98	66.21	57.75	45.83	35.84	26.46	44.62
8	22.71	24.42	33.79	44.80	56.77	66.99	70.80	68.98	50.78	48.81	37.34	27.21	46.95
9	25.20	27.60	36.55	47.96	59.42	69.64	73.30	71.54	63.75	51.68	39.86	29.41	49.66
10	28.12	30.59	39.33	50.71	61.49	71.69	75.45	73.71	66.28	54.62	42.56	32.05	52.22
11	30.16	32.34	40.95	52.33	63.05	73.04	77.23	75.60	68.15	56.75	44.51	33.91	54.00

[1] Transactions of the Connecticut Academy of Arts and Sciences. Vol. I, Part. I. New Haven, 1866. Art. v. By E. Loomis and H. A. Newton.

The numbers of the tables are derived in part from 3 observations a day, during 86 years, and in part from 5 observations a day, during 9 years, with the assistance of the law of the diurnal fluctuation as found at Philadelphia, Amherst, and Cambridge.

Hour.	Jan.	Feb.	Mar.	April.	May.	June.	July.	Aug.	Sept.	Oct.	Nov.	Dec.	Year.
New Haven.—Continued.													
Noon	31°.72	33°.67	42°.23	53°.62	64°.26	74°.08	78°.37	76°.82	69°.39	58°.05	45°.95	35°.47	55°.30
1	32.60	34.70	43.12	54.58	65.21	74.89	79.12	77.62	70.17	58.85	46.69	36.27	56.15
2	32.87	35.06	43.56	55.16	65.79	75.28	79.47	78.01	70.54	59.18	46.89	36.54	56.53
3	32.41	34.87	43.43	55.19	65.81	75.21	79.37	77.94	70.39	58.81	46.51	35.95	56.32
4	31.26	33.89	42.69	54.67	65.30	74.59	78.85	77.38	69.65	57.70	44.95	34.44	55.45
5	29.37	31.92	40.83	53.44	64.07	73.44	77.79	76.21	68.30	55.57	43.20	32.51	53.89
6	27.92	30.12	38.63	50.89	62.00	71.27	75.84	74.26	66.47	53.86	41.88	31.42	52.05
7	26.84	28.73	36.97	48.31	58.93	69.12	73.69	72.24	64.38	52.28	40.82	30.63	50.24
8	26.04	27.67	35.52	46.23	56.66	66.88	71.77	70.31	62.42	50.88	39.95	29.93	48.69
9	25.42	26.88	34.43	44.86	55.05	65.14	70.01	68.67	60.81	49.64	39.25	29.38	47.46
10	24.98	26.27	33.69	43.87	53.81	63.68	68.78	67.53	59.65	48.68	38.73	28.96	46.55
11	24.58	25.73	33.04	43.04	52.83	62.36	67.55	66.46	58.63	47.82	38.20	28.60	45.74
Mean	26.53	28.11	36.09	46.84	57.28	66.96	71.66	70.32	62.50	51.10	40.32	30.42	49.01

HOURLY MEANS BETWEEN 4 A. M. AND 10 P. M.

Brooklyn Heights,[1] N. Y. Lat. 40° 41′. Long. 73° 59′ W. of G.

Alt. . . E. Merriam. Dec. 1847, to May, 1849, inclusive.

Hour.	Jan.	Feb.	Mar.	April.	May.	June.	July.	Aug.	Sept.	Oct.	Nov.	Dec.	Year.
Mdn't	..	..	..	..	..	..	..	..	..	..	..	..	..
1	..	..	..	..	..	..	..	..	..	..	..	..	..
2	..	..	..	..	..	..	..	..	..	..	..	..	..
3	..	..	..	..	..	..	..	..	..	..	..	..	..
4	27.7	24.5	31.9	42.9	53.8	62.8	67.6	67.2	56.9	48.5	36.6	36.8	46.4
5	27.5	24.4	32.4	43.2	53.8	63.3	67.6	67.2	56.8	50.0	36.6	36.8	46.6
6	27.5	24.5	32.4	43.3	54.5	64.4	67.6	67.6	57.1	51.3	37.2	37.0	47.0
7	27.5	24.5	33.1	44.9	56.7	67.7	68.3	68.5	58.0	51.3	37.0	37.2	47.9
8	27.8	25.5	34.9	48.5	58.8	70.7	69.6	69.9	59.3	52.8	38.4	37.3	49.4
9	28.8	27.5	36.8	50.4	60.3	72.9	71.0	71.8	61.3	54.6	40.2	38.2	51.1
10	30.3	29.5	39.1	52.1	62.2	73.9	72.1	74.0	63.8	56.2	42.2	39.5	52.9
11	32.0	30.8	41.1	54.2	64.3	75.7	73.8	75.5	66.5	57.8	43.8	40.8	54.7
Noon	33.1	32.0	42.0	55.8	65.7	77.1	74.7	77.1	67.3	58.9	44.6	41.8	55.8
1	33.7	32.9	42.7	56.9	65.9	77.7	75.6	78.0	67.3	59.4	45.4	42.3	56.5
2	34.0	33.0	43.5	57.2	65.9	78.0	75.6	76.7	67.2	59.9	45.6	42.6	56.6
3	33.5	32.9	43.6	56.9	65.2	77.9	75.7	76.6	67.0	59.6	45.4	42.3	56.4
4	33.0	32.4	42.6	55.3	64.7	77.0	75.6	75.7	66.2	58.5	44.1	41.5	55.5
5	31.9	31.6	41.3	53.7	63.5	75.3	74.8	74.8	65.1	57.1	41.8	40.6	54.3
6	31.2	30.3	39.7	51.8	61.9	73.4	73.5	73.5	63.8	56.3	41.0	39.8	53.0
7	30.7	29.6	38.6	50.0	60.3	71.5	72.3	72.7	62.8	55.0	40.2	39.2	51.9
8	30.1	29.1	37.8	48.7	59.2	69.6	71.5	71.6	61.9	53.9	39.9	38.9	51.0
9	29.8	28.5	37.3	47.7	58.2	68.5	70.6	70.8	61.1	53.5	39.6	38.3	50.3
10	29.5	28.1	35.9	46.0	57.5	66.0	70.0	70.0	60.3	53.1	39.6	37.8	49.5
11	..	..	..	..	..	..	..	..	..	..	..	..	..

Some of these observations do not appear to me altogether trustworthy. [S.]

By graphical interpolation the following quite reliable numbers were found to supply the missing observations:—

Hour.	Jan.	Feb.	Mar.	April.	May.	June.	July.	Aug.	Sept.	Oct.	Nov.	Dec.	Year.
11	29.1	27.5	34.2	45.0	56.6	64.6	69.2	69.4	59.5	52.0	38.9	37.5	48.6
Mdn't	28.8	26.8	33.3	44.2	55.8	63.6	68.8	68.7	58.8	51.0	38.4	37.2	47.9
1	28.5	26.2	32.7	43.6	55.1	63.0	68.4	68.1	58.2	50.1	37.8	37.0	47.4
2	28.2	25.5	32.3	43.2	54.5	62.8	68.0	67.6	57.6	49.3	37.3	36.9	46.9
3	27.9	24.9	32.1	43.0	54.1	62.7	67.8	67.3	57.2	48.9	36.8	36.8	46.6
Mean	30.1	28.4	37.1	49.1	59.5	70.0	71.2	71.7	61.7	54.1	40.4	38.9	51.0

[1] MS. in Smithsonian Coll.

HOURLY MEANS OF TEMPERATURE.

Philadelphia, Girard College,[1] Penn. Lat. 39° 58′. Long. 75° 10′ W. of G.

Alt. 114 feet. A. D. Bache. June, 1840, to June, 1845, inclusive.

Hour.	Jan.	Feb.	Mar.	Apr.	May.	June.	July.	Aug.	Sept.	Oct.	Nov.	Dec.	Year.
Mdn't	30°.90	30°.10	39°.25	46°.60	54°.16	63°.53	68°.06	67°.68	59°.76	47°.74	38°.46	31°.14	48°.11
1	30.35	29.67	38.60	45.76	53.54	62.82	67.32	67.08	59.50	47.36	38.32	30.72	47.59
2	30.20	29.28	38.05	44.96	52.82	62.25	66.76	66.60	59.10	46.78	37.94	30.36	47.09
3	29.92	28.73	37.75	44.60	52.14	61.60	66.26	66.44	58.64	46.36	37.66	30.06	46.68
4	29.72	28.45	37.58	44.18	51.48	61.13	65.82	65.88	58.32	45.88	37.18	29.78	46.28
5	29.50	28.22	36.78	44.08	51.60	61.60	66.04	65.78	58.10	45.46	36.90	29.46	46.12
6	29.22	27.95	36.77	44.54	53.04	63.03	67.10	66.36	58.08	45.12	36.64	29.22	46.42
7	29.10	28.08	37.42	46.08	55.16	65.45	69.40	68.20	59.94	46.50	36.96	29.52	47.65
8	29.52	29.63	39.40	48.12	57.44	67.85	71.66	70.48	62.40	48.96	38.20	30.02	49.47
9	30.80	31.55	41.40	50.10	59.64	69.78	73.62	72.40	64.54	51.38	40.10	31.40	51.39
10	32.32	33.60	43.25	52.08	61.22	71.45	75.24	74.22	66.62	53.54	41.82	32.94	53.19
11	33.65	35.32	45.27	53.86	62.70	72.95	76.74	75.86	68.30	55.20	43.28	34.46	54.80
Noon	34.88	36.70	46.75	55.46	63.86	74.35	77.96	77.16	69.64	56.70	44.48	35.54	56.12
1	35.87	37.83	47.80	56.70	64.90	75.37	78.80	77.94	70.56	57.76	45.46	36.28	57.10
2	36.53	38.47	48.55	57.68	65.80	76.25	79.54	78.84	71.38	58.54	46.14	36.88	57.88
3	36.60	38.73	49.10	57.94	66.26	76.54	79.82	79.08	71.48	58.46	45.88	36.66	58.04
4	36.37	38.50	49.00	58.00	66.46	76.67	79.76	78.98	71.40	58.20	45.40	36.28	57.92
5	35.05	37.35	47.85	57.14	66.00	75.77	79.10	77.94	70.00	56.34	43.88	35.06	56.79
6	34.23	35.70	45.98	55.74	64.44	74.43	77.76	76.52	67.80	54.14	42.54	34.36	55.30
7	33.42	34.50	44.85	53.10	61.86	71.93	75.62	74.44	65.60	52.48	41.50	33.62	53.57
8	32.75	33.23	43.80	51.08	59.22	68.93	73.04	71.98	63.36	51.00	40.66	33.00	51.83
9	32.17	32.47	41.35	49.70	57.64	67.28	71.32	70.60	62.12	49.98	40.00	32.60	50.60
10	31.58	31.68	41.00	48.46	56.28	65.93	70.04	69.46	60.92	48.82	39.50	32.16	49.65
11	31.12	31.10	40.28	47.40	55.06	64.63	69.08	68.64	60.34	48.06	39.02	31.70	48.86
Mean	32.32	32.79	42.41	50.56	58.86	68.81	72.74	72.02	64.08	51.28	40.75	32.63	51.60
No of years	4	4	4	5	5	6	5	5	5	5	5	5	

HOURLY MEANS BETWEEN 3 A. M. AND 9 P. M.

Jackson, Jackson Co., Ohio.[2] Lat. 39° 02′. Long. 82° 32′ W. of G.

Alt. 700 feet. G. L. Crookham. May, 1851, to June, 1852, inclusive.

Hour.	Jan.	Feb.	Mar.	Apr.	May.	June.	July.	Aug.	Sept.	Oct.	Nov.	Dec.	Year.
Mdn't	..	..	..	..	..	..	..	..	..	..	..	..	45.1
1	..	..	..	..	..	..	..	..	..	..	..	..	44.4
2	..	..	..	..	..	..	..	..	..	..	..	..	43.9
3	20.9	31.5	37.6	40.9	52.2	57.8	64.5	61.1	54.9	41.0	36.1	23.2	43.5
4	20.5	31.2	37.3	40.6	51.8	56.5	61.5	60.5	54.2	40.0	35.7	23.0	42.7
5	20.4	30.8	36.9	40.4	52.3	56.8	61.7	60.5	53.7	39.4	35.1	22.5	42.5
6	20.3	30.3	37.3	41.1	54.3	59.3	63.7	62.0	54.2	39.3	34.4	22.4	43.2
7	20.1	30.9	38.7	44.0	58.4	63.9	68.0	65.6	57.2	40.0	34.3	23.0	45.3
8	21.6	33.1	42.4	47.2	63.3	68.5	73.9	70.1	63.5	45.9	35.3	23.8	49.0
9	24.7	35.3	46.0	50.2	66.9	72.1	77.0	73.6	68.9	52.5	38.8	26.9	52.7
10	28.3	37.9	48.1	53.1	70.0	74.9	80.0	76.2	72.9	56.9	41.8	29.7	55.8
11	30.7	40.3	50.2	55.0	71.8	77.1	83.0	79.1	75.9	60.5	44.2	31.7	58.3

[1] The observations between June, 1840, and Dec. 1841, inclusive, were taken bi-hourly, and those between June, 1840, and Feb. 1841, inclusive, 25 minutes after the full hours; those between March, 1841, and Dec. 1841, inclusive, 15 minutes after the full hours. By *interpolation* the results were *changed* to refer to the full hours and for every hour. The means for each hour for the whole period of observations were then combined separately for each month. There is no record for Jan., Feb., and March, 1843. For record see "Observations at the magnetical and meteorological Observatory." Washington, D. C., 1847, four volumes.

[2] MS. in Sm. Coll.

The record begins with Jan. 1851, but is not sufficiently regular for use till May, 1851. Numbers interpolated at the following hours: 3 A. M. May, 1851; 9 A. M., 3 P. M., and 9 P. M. May, June, July, 1851. The annual means for 10, 11 P. M., 0, 1, and 2 A. M. are graphically interpolated.

There are many omissions in the record. Some scattering observations between the hours 10 P. M. and 3 A. M. cannot be utilized.

Hour.	Jan.	Feb.	Mar.	Apr.	May.	June.	July.	Aug.	Sept.	Oct.	Nov.	Dec.	Year.
Jackson.—Continued.													
Noon	32°.4	42°.0	51°.7	56°.4	74°.0	78°.3	85°.0	80°.8	78°.6	62°.6	45°.9	33°.6	60°.1
1	32.9	43.1	52.9	57.7	74.9	79.2	85.4	81.9	80.0	63.9	46.6	34.4	61.1
2	32.9	43.4	53.8	59.2	75.5	78.9	84.1	82.6	79.8	64.2	47.4	35.2	61.4
3	32.4	42.9	53.6	58.9	75.2	78.0	83.2	82.6	80.1	63.7	47.0	35.2	61.1
4	31.2	42.0	52.9	58.3	73.6	76.2	82.3	80.7	79.0	62.3	46.0	34.3	59.9
5	29.0	39.5	51.2	56.4	72.1	75.4	81.1	78.7	76.4	58.8	43.1	31.9	57.8
6	27.0	35.8	47.1	53.8	68.9	72 8	78.1	75.0	70.3	52.9	40.4	29.9	54.3
7	25.6	34.1	43.6	49.7	64.4	68.8	73.1	69.6	64.3	49.6	39.8	28.8	51.0
8	24.9	33.2	41.7	46.9	60.9	64.1	69.4	66.3	61.3	47.3	38.9	27.1	48.5
9	23.7	32.6	40.6	45.7	57.9	62.2	67.8	65.1	59.6	46.0	38.1	27.0	47.2
10	..	..	..	..	..	..	..	..	..	..	..	..	46.4
11	..	..	..	..	..	..	..	..	..	..	..	..	45.8
Mean													50.9

BI-HOURLY MEANS OF TEMPERATURE.

Washington City, Capitol Hill, D. C.[1] Lat. 38° 53′. Long. 77° 01′ W. of G.

Alt. 80 feet. Lieut. J. M. Gilliss, U. S. N. Jan. 1841, to June, 1842, inclusive.

Hour.	Jan.	Feb.	Mar.	Apr.	May.	June.	July.	Aug.	Sept.	Oct.	Nov.	Dec.	Year.
0.2$_{m}$	32.37	32.58	42.48	47.91	55.20	66.83	68.78	66.82	62.70	44.90	41.80	33.50	49.66
2.2	32.10	31.22	41.26	46.92	53.34	66.04	68.09	65.12	61.90	43.70	40.70	33.16	48.63
4.2	31.71	30.51	40.06	46.12	52.42	65.07	66.78	64.17	61.00	42.30	39.40	32.20	47.64
6.2	30.74	30.18	39.88	46.49	55.50	68.26	70.64	65.69	61.29	41.70	38.80	31.60	48.40
8.2	33.13	31.44	42.28	49.93	59.72	73.63	75.19	71.39	65.73	45.00	39.50	31.88	51.57
10.2	35.38	36.72	48.06	54.02	63.23	77.37	78.38	76.09	71.02	51.61	44.10	36.00	55.99
0.2$_{a}$	38.28	40.04	51.39	57.68	66.38	79.33	81.13	78.70	74.66	55.30	48.00	39.20	59.17
2.2	40.83	42.51	53.61	59.98	68.48	81.93	83.25	80.73	76.50	57.00	49.20	41.30	61.27
4.2	40.18	42.28	53.28	60.20	68.69	83.43	84.76	80.09	76.30	56.20	48.50	40.60	61.21
6.2	36.68	38.22	49.97	57.22	65.93	76.89	81.33	75.93	72.30	52.94	47.30	37.95	57.72
8.2	35.48	35.38	46.20	52.18	59.83	72.29	74.93	71.48	68.59	48.40	44.20	36.26	53.77
10.2	34.25	33.86	44.37	49.12	56.70	68.70	71.56	68.00	64.90	46.60	43.20	34.70	51.33
Mean	35.10	35.41	46.08	52.31	60.45	73.32	75.40	72.02	68.07	48.80	43.73	35.70	53.87

TRI-HOURLY MEANS OF TEMPERATURE.

Washington City, U. S. Naval Observatory. Lat. 38° 54′. Long. 77° 03′ W. of G.

Alt. 110 feet. Sup't U. S. N. O. Astro. and Met. Obs. for 1866–7–8–9. Jan. 1862, to Dec. 1869, inclusive.

Hour.	Jan.	Feb.	Mar.	Apr.	May.	June.	July.	Aug.	Sept.	Oct.	Nov.	Dec.	Year.
Mdn't	29.55	31.75	37.76	47.71	56.80	65.72	70.64	69.16	62.94	50.35	41.35	32.57	49.69
3	28.45	30.45	36.31	45.45	54.54	63.77	68.96	67.58	61.34	48.54	39.76	31.49	48.05
6	27.56	29.58	35.20	44.62	54.41	63.67	68.53	66.66	60.35	47.35	38.82	30.64	47.28
9	29.46	32.63	39.54	51.66	62.37	71.56	76.38	74.25	69.23	53.99	42.82	32.67	53.05
Noon	35.89	39.02	45.35	57.46	68.28	77.40	82.68	81.46	75.37	62.25	51.00	38.51	59.56
3	37.43	41.13	47.56	59.50	70.51	78.88	84.10	83.67	77.11	63.76	51.94	39.51	61.26
6	33.70	37.20	44.40	56.26	66.51	75.35	80.64	78.13	70.08	56.47	46.21	35.62	56.71
9	31.29	34.04	40.07	51.03	60.24	68.91	73.56	72.31	65.14	52.36	43.16	33.41	52.13
Mean	31.67	34.47	40.77	51.71	61.71	70.66	75.69	74.15	67.70	54.38	44.38	34.30	53.47

[1] Pub. Doc., 2d Session, 28th Congress, vol. x, No. 172. Washington, 1845.

Hourly Means of Temperature.

Fort Morgan, Mobile Point, Alabama.[1] Lat. 30° 14′. Long. 88° 01′ W. of G.

Alt. 20 feet. Observed by U. S. Coast Survey. June, 1848 and 1850.

Hour.	Jan.	Feb.	Mar.	Apr.	May.	June.	July.	Aug.	Sept.	Oct.	Nov.	Dec.	Year.
Mdn't	..	..	63°.55	66°.98	..	79°.10	83°.53	84°.44	81°.45	70°.93	60°.21	54°.95	68°.8
1	..	..	62.25	65.93	..	78.42	83.14	84.55	81.21	70.70	59.98	54.95	68.4
2	..	..	62.16	66.27	..	78.21	82.78	84.34	80.57	70.11	59.60	54.69	68.1
3	..	..	61.69	65.22	..	78.05	82.51	83.98	80.13	69.55	59.23	54.16	67.7
4	..	..	60.95	66.24	..	78.17	82.12	83.82	79.59	68.87	58.74	53.75	67.4
5	..	..	60.52	66.04	67°.39	77.97	82.00	83.68	79.10	68.47	58.35	53.42	67.1
6	56°.38	52°.28	60.05	65.98	67.45	78.30	82.49	84.01	78.80	68.18	57.76	53.27	67.0
7	55.89	51.88	60.30	67.24	68.42	79.34	83.53	84.68	79.50	68.74	57.51	52.99	67.5
8	57.05	53.03	61.46	68.25	69.58	80.62	84.46	85.87	80.86	69.18	58.30	53.65	68.5
9	58.12	54.79	62.84	69.43	70.75	81.76	85.53	86.99	82.25	70.52	59.28	54.48	69.7
10	59.45	55.77	63.80	70.73	71.76	82.86	86.66	88.33	83.73	71.78	60.32	55.74	70.9
11	60.55	57.03	64.96	71.82	72.56	83.40	88.16	89.49	84.96	72.85	61.44	56.72	71.9
Noon	61.28	58.01	65.91	72.98	73.43	83.75	88.55	90.15	85.75	73.95	62.56	57.38	72.8
1	61.73	58.74	66.34	73.44	74.56	84.08	89.38	90.85	86.56	74.74	63.43	58.14	73.5
2	62.04	59.19	66.70	73.61	75.18	84.21	89.65	90.77	86.97	75.56	64.35	58.89	73.9
3	62.13	58.95	67.06	73.68	75.37	84.17	88.96	90.09	87.31	75.73	64.74	59.14	73.9
4	61.71	58.54	66.96	73.56	74.93	83.76	88.35	89.75	86.99	75.54	64.44	58.67	73.5
5	60.70	57.87	66.27	72.18	73.70	82.79	87.27	88.89	86.27	74.56	63.46	57.74	72.6
6	60.06	56.86	65.04	70.85	72.61	81.94	86.34	87.74	84.78	73.25	62.41	57.04	71.5
7	59.63	56.12	64.22	69.83	71.76	80.89	85.38	86.45	83.74	72.68	62.08	56.61	70.7
8	59.21	55.79	63.87	69.39	71.31	80.27	84.76	85.67	83.19	72.39	61.58	56.33	70.3
9	59.07	55.27	63.61	68.98	71.00	79.93	84.45	85.16	82.92	72.13	61.17	56.08	70.0
10	58.61	55.09	63.28	68.58	..	79.35	84.20	84.91	82.26	71.91	60.83	55.95	69.6
11	..	..	62.93	66.74	..	79.29	83.94	84.67	81.89	71.54	60.50	55.54	69.1
Mean	58.96*	55.50*	63.61	69.33	71.04*	80.86	85.34	86.64	82.95	71.83	60.93	55.84	70.24

N. B. Some of the results are not altogether reliable, as the series is too short and broken.

* These values were found by means of graphical interpolation for the hours of no record, viz:—

Hour.	Jan.	Feb.	Mar.	Apr.	May.
10 P. M.	..	..	..	..	70.6
11	58.0	54.8	..	..	70.1
Mdn't	57.7	54.5	..	..	69.5
1	57.6	54.2	..	..	69.1
2	57.4	53.9	..	..	68.5
3	57.2	53.5	..	..	68.0
4	56.9	53.2	..	..	67.6
5 A. M.	56.6	52.7	..	..	

Hourly Means of Temperature.

Galveston, Texas.[1] Lat. 29° 18′. Long. 94° 47′ W. of G.

Alt. 20 ft. Obs'd by U. S. Coast Survey. June, Sept. Oct. Nov. Dec. 1851; Jan. Feb. Mar. 1852; Jan. Feb. 1853.

Hour.	Jan.	Feb.	Mar.	Apr.	May.	June.	July.	Aug.	Sept.	Oct.	Nov.	Dec.	Year.
Mdn't	48.2	56.5	65.3	..	..	..	..	..	78.5	70.4	58.0	52.2	..
1	47.9	55.9	64.9	..	..	..	..	..	78.7	70.0	58.7	52.3	..
2	47.7	55.8	64.5	..	..	..	..	..	78.7	69.6	58.2	51.8	..
3	47.5	55.6	64.2	..	..	..	..	..	78.3	69.2	57.8	51.6	..
4	47.1	53.3	63.8	..	..	..	..	..	77.8	68.8	57.4	51.2	..
5	46.7	55.2	63.6	..	..	75.7	..	..	77.7	69.0	57.1	50.7	..
6	46.6	55.5	64.0	..	..	77.1	..	..	77.7	70.7	57.2	50.4	..
7	46.7	55.5	65.1	..	..	79.7	..	..	79.7	74.1	58.2	50.3	..
8	47.7	57.0	68.0	..	..	81.3	..	..	82.2	76.2	61.3	51.1	..
9	48.6	59.1	71.1	..	..	82.4	..	..	83.9	77.2	62.7	53.4	..
10	51.2	60.5	73.1	..	..	81.8	..	..	84.8	77.2	63.3	54.7	..
11	51.8	61.3	73.6	..	..	83.3	..	..	84.7	76.9	62.5	54.7	..

[1] MS. in Sm. Coll.

Galveston.—Continued.

Hour.	Jan.	Feb.	Mar.	Apr.	May.	June.	July.	Aug.	Sept.	Oct.	Nov.	Dec.	Year.
Noon	51°.8	61°.1	72°.8	..	..	83°.0	..	..	84°.2	76°.9	61°.9	54°.8	..
1	51.8	61.0	71.8	..	..	83.3	..	..	84.1	76.8	61.7	54.9	..
2	51.6	60.8	71.7	..	..	83.8	..	..	83.6	76.3	61.7	54.9	..
3	51.5	60.4	70.9	..	..	84.8	..	..	83.2	75.6	61.6	54.9	..
4	51.5	60.0	70.5	..	..	86.0	..	..	82.8	74.4	61.4	54.6	..
5	50.8	59.0	69.5	..	..	84.3	..	..	82.0	73.6	60.7	54.1	..
6	50.1	58.4	68.3	..	..	81.0	..	..	81.4	72.6	60.2	53.7	..
7	49.6	58.0	67.4	..	..	79.1	..	..	80.4	72.1	59.5	53.3	..
8	49.2	57.5	66.8	..	..	..	..	..	79.6	71.7	58.9	52.9	..
9	48.7	57.1	66.3	..	..	..	..	..	79.3	71.1	58.6	52.7	..
10	48.6	56.9	65.8	..	..	..	..	..	79.1	70.9	58.2	52.3	..
11	48.4	56.7	65.7	..	..	..	..	..	78.7	70.8	58.1	52.2	..
Mean	49.2	57.8	67.9	..	..	80.4[1]	..	..	80.9	73.0	59.8	52.9	..

Hourly Means of Temperature.

Key West, Florida.[2] Lat. 24° 33′. Long. 81° 48′ W. of G.

Alt. 20 feet. Observed by the U. S. Coast Survey. June, 1851, to May, 1852, inclusive.

Hour.	Jan.	Feb.	Mar.	Apr.	May.	June.	July.	Aug.	Sept.	Oct.	Nov.	Dec.	Year.
Mdn't	63.32	69.64	74.06	75.67	79.79	81.70	82.87	83.54	..	79.03	..	70.74	..
1	63.34	69.09	74.02	75.40	79.45	81.68	83.02	83.35	..	78.74	..	70.81	..
2	63.27	69.12	74.06	75.38	79.50	81.35	82.77	83.09	..	78.79	..	70.85	..
3	63.16	68.74	73.89	75.32	79.34	81.26	82.58	82.84	..	78.79	..	70.66	..
4	63.00	68.62	73.74	75.30	79.16	81.00	82.29	82.71	..	78.71	..	70.48	..
5	62.56	68.12	73.31	74.92	78.60	80.93	82.00	82.35	..	78.39	..	69.97	..
6	62.55	68.10	73.19	74.98	78.97	81.23	82.19	82.48	..	78.34	..	69.32	..
7	62.48	68.17	73.85	75.97	81.18	82.18	83.76	83.42	..	78.90	..	69.15	..
8	63.02	69.33	75.53	77.48	83.26	83.38	85.43	85.00	..	80.08	..	69.63	..
9	64.66	71.17	77.11	78.58	84.53	84.68	86.47	85.77	..	80.97	..	70.61	..
10	65.74	72.52	78.18	79.28	85.02	85.71	87.23	86.39	..	81.60	..	71.26	..
11	66.63	73.34	78.76	79.57	85.27	85.81	87.53	86.81	..	81.98	..	71.82	..
Noon	67.08	73.84	78.97	79.78	85.16	86.16	87.76	86.84	..	82.10	..	72.10	..
1	67.71	73.93	79.21	80.30	85.27	86.36	88.32	87.35	..	82.48	..	72.08	..
2	67.89	74.05	79.39	80.50	85.37	86.18	88.15	87.42	..	82.52	..	72.21	..
3	68.16	74.48	79.29	80.57	85.19	86.30	88.11	87.39	..	82.44	..	72.37	..
4	68.23	74.84	79.15	80.28	85.08	86.28	87.70	87.29	..	82.29	..	72.39	..
5	67.71	74.50	78.53	80.17	84.69	85.83	87.65	87.03	..	81.79	..	71.89	..
6	66.26	73.14	77.32	79.85	84.53	85.11	86.43	86.42	..	80.77	..	70.97	..
7	65.06	71.76	75.79	77.92	82.18	83.68	85.15	85.42	..	80.16	..	70.44	..
8	64.58	71.03	75.11	76.98	81.34	82.64	84.47	84.84	..	79.97	..	70.40	..
9	64.34	70.69	74.98	76.67	80.92	82.10	84.00	84.39	..	79.77	..	70.60	..
10	63.94	70.28	74.52	76.22	80.42	81.76	83.38	83.97	..	79.47	..	70.79	..
11	63.53	69.93	74.23	75.92	79.97	81.76	83.03	83.81	..	79.26	..	70.84	..
Mean	64.92	71.18	76.09	77.62	82.25	83.54	85.09	84.99	..	80.30	..	70.93	..

N. B. No observations in Sept. and Nov. 1851.

[1] Obtained by interpolation for 3 A. M. and 9 P. M., by the hours 3, 9, 3, 9. The observations extend over too short a time to be relied on.

[2] MS. in Sm. Coll.; Gustavus Wurdemann, observer.

TABLES OF DIFFERENCES

OF

BI-HOURLY, HOURLY AND SEMI-HOURLY MEAN TEMPERATURES FROM THE MEAN OF THE DAY,

FOR

EACH MONTH AND THE YEAR.

AT VARIOUS PLACES IN AMERICA.

18 February, 1875.

TABLES OF DIFFERENCES OF MEAN TEMPERATURES AT DIFFERENT HOURS OF THE DAY FROM THE DAILY MEAN, FOR EACH MONTH AND THE YEAR.

INDEX TO STATIONS.

[Arranged according to latitudes.]

No.	Station	Years
1.	Van Rensselaer, North Greenland	1853–55
2.	Port Foulke, North Greenland	1860–61
3.	Melville Island, Arctic America	1819–20
4.	Port Kennedy, North Somerset	1858–59
5.	Boothia Felix, Arctic America	1829–30
6.	Sitka, Alaska Territory	1857–64
7.	Montreal, Canada East	1839–41
8.	Thunder Bay Island, Lake Huron, Mich.	1863–65
9.	Toronto, Canada West	1842–48
10.	Mohawk, N. Y.	1860–69
11.	Cambridge, Mass.	1841–42
12.	Amherst, Mass.	1839
13.	New Haven, Conn.	1779–1865
14.	Brooklyn Heights, N. Y.	1847–49
15.	Frankford Arsenal	1836–37
16.	Philadelphia, Girard College	1840–45
17.	Washington City, Capitol Hill, D. C.	1841–42
"	Washington City, U. S. Naval Observatory	1862–69
18.	Fort Morgan, Mobile Point, Ala.	1848–50
19.	Galveston, Texas	1851–53
20.	Key West, Florida	1851–52
21.	Rio Janeiro, Brazil	?

DIURNAL FLUCTUATION OF TEMPERATURE (Fah. scale).

Van Rensselaer Harbor, North Greenland. Lat. 78° 37′. Long. 70° 53′ W. of G.

Kane. Near sea level. Sept. 1853, to Jan. 1855, inclusive.

(Uncorrected for effect of annual fluctuation.)

Hour.	Jan.	Feb.	Mar.	Apr.	May.	June.	July.	Aug.	Sept.	Oct.	Nov.	Dec.	Year.
	°	°	°	°	°	°	°	°	°	°	°	°	°
Mdn't	—0.1	—0.9	—1.6	—3.7	—3.2	—1.9	—1.3	—2.0	—2.7	—1.1	—0.6	—0.3	—1.6
1	—0.1	—1.6	—2.0	—4.5	—4.4	—3.1	—1.6	—2.6	—2.2	+0.1	+0.7	—0.4	—1.8
2	—0.3	—1.6	—1.8	—4.5	—4.1	—3.0	—1.5	—2.3	—2.1	+0.1	+0.7	—0.2	—1.7
3	—0.4	—1.4	—2.0	—4.9	—3.4	—2.9	—1.4	—2.3	—1.9	+0.1	+0.7	—0.5	—1.7
4	—0.5	—0.8	—2.2	—4.4	—2.8	—2.5	—1.4	—2.0	—2.0	+0.2	+0.7	—0.7	—1.5
5	—0.5	—1.5	—2.1	—3.5	—1.6	—1.3	—1.3	—2.1	—2.0	+0.3	0.0	+0.2	—1.3
6	—0.5	—0.9	—1.9	—2.9	—0.7	—0.6	—0.6	—1.5	—1.4	+0.3	—0.2	+0.3	—0.9
7	—0.8	—0.5	—1.2	—1.8	+0.1	+0.3	—0.4	—0.8	—0.4	+0.4	0.0	+0.1	—0.4
8	—0.3	—0.2	—0.8	—0.7	+1.0	+1.5	+0.2	+0.1	+1.0	+0.4	—0.2	+0.1	+0.2
9	—0.4	+0.1	+0.5	+0.9	+1.0	+0.7	+1.2	+1.2	+1.8	+0.7	0.0	+0.4	+0.7
10	—0.1	+0.6	+1.1	+1.6	+1.7	+0.9	+1.4	+2.1	+2.4	+0.9	—0.1	+0.5	+1.1
11	+0.4	+0.3	+2.3	+2.6	+1.9	+1.3	+1.8	+2.2	+2.8	+0.8	+0.4	+0.6	+1.4
Noon	+0.9	+0.9	+2.8	+3.2	+2.5	+2.1	+1.8	+2.4	+3.0	+0.6	+0.6	+1.1	+1.8
1	+0.7	+1.4	+3.2	+3.7	+2.7	+2.2	+1.6	+2.4	+3.1	+0.6	+0.3	+1.0	+1.9
2	+0.6	+1.4	+3.6	+4.5	+3.0	+2.1	+1.5	+2.4	+2.7	+0.4	+0.2	+0.7	+1.9
3	+0.1	+1.3	+3.0	+4.6	+3.1	+1.8	+1.5	+2.0	+2.2	+0.5	+0.2	+0.3	+1.7
4	—0.1	+1.2	+1.9	+4.3	+3.3	+1.5	+1.4	+1.5	+1.6	+0.3	+0.1	0.0	+1.4
5	+0.2	+0.9	+1.2	+4.2	+2.8	+1.3	+0.7	+1.2	+1.0	+0.1	+0.2	—0.1	+1.1
6	+0.2	+1.0	+0.6	+3.3	+1.9	+1.1	+0.3	+0.7	+0.5	—0.3	0.0	—0.2	+0.8
7	+0.3	+1.1	+0.1	+1.9	+1.1	+0.7	0.0	+0.3	—0.3	—0.9	—0.2	—0.8	+0.3
8	+0.1	+0.9	—0.8	+1.0	+0.2	+0.5	—0.5	—0.1	—0.8	—1.0	—0.3	—0.7	—0.1
9	+0.1	+0.5	—0.9	—0.4	—0.6	—0.2	—1.0	—0.3	—1.2	—1.0	—0.8	—0.6	—0.5
10	+0.2	—0.6	—1.2	—1.9	—1.7	—0.6	—1.5	—1.0	—1.6	—1.0	—0.5	—0.6	—1.0
11	—0.4	—0.6	—1.4	—2.6	—2.7	—1.5	—1.4	—1.4	—2.3	—1.0	—0.7	—0.5	—1.4
Comb's													
10, 10	0.0	0.0	0.0	—0.1	0.0	+0.1	0.0	+0.5	+0.4	0.0	—0.3	0.0	0.0
6, 2, 9	+0.1	+0.3	+0.3	+0.4	+0.6	+0.4	0.0	+0.2	0.0	—0.3	—0.3	—0.1	+0.2
6, 2, 10	+0.1	0.0	+0.2	—0.1	+0.2	+0.3	—0.2	0.0	—0.1	—0.1	—0.2	+0.1	0.0
7, 2, 9	0.0	+0.5	+0.5	+0.8	+0.8	+0.7	0.0	+0.4	+0.4	—0.1	—0.2	+0.1	+0.3
7, 2, 9 bis	0.0	+0.5	+0.1	+0.5	+0.5	+0.5	—0.2	+0.2	0.0	—0.3	—0.3	—0.1	+0.1
3, 9, 3, 9	—0.1	+0.1	+0.1	0.0	0.0	—0.1	+0.1	+0.1	+0.2	+0.1	0.0	—0.1	+0.0

Port Foulke, North Greenland. Lat. 78° 18′. Long. 73° 00′ W. of G.

Hayes. Near sea level. Sept. 1860, to July, 1861, inclusive.

(Uncorrected for effect of annual fluctuation.)

Hour.	Jan.	Feb.	Mar.	Apr.	May.	June.	July.	Aug.	Sept.	Oct.	Nov.	Dec.	Year.
Mdn't	—0.2	—0.9	—2.4	—1.8	—3.0	—2.1	—2.1	—1.6	—1.1	—0.7	—0.5	+0.5	—1.32
2	—0.5	—2.0	—2.9	—2.3	—4.1	—2.9	—2.0	—1.3	—0.6	—0.9	—0.9	+1.2	—1.61
4	—0.2	—2.3	—3.6	—2.7	—2.2	—1.4	—1.7	—1.0	—0.3	—0.8	—1.0	—0.1	—1.45
6	—0.6	—1.0	—3.0	—1.4	—1.0	—0.5	—1.3	—0.7	—0.2	—1.0	—0.1	—0.3	—0.94
8	+0.3	+0.7	—0.7	+0.2	+1.3	0.0	+0.2	+0.2	0.0	—0.5	—0.2	—0.7	+0.06
10	+0.7	+0.8	0.0	+0.8	+2.1	+1.2	+1.0	+0.6	+0.1	+0.2	0.0	—0.1	+0.60
Noon	+0.8	+0.9	+1.7	+2.1	+2.6	+1.7	+0.8	+0.7	+0.6	+0.9	+0.2	0.0	+1.09
2	+0.2	+2.0	+5.4	+3.0	+2.3	+2.3	+2.2	+1.6	+0.9	+1.2	+0.3	+0.1	+1.77
4	—0.2	+0.8	+3.9	+2.0	+2.0	+1.8	+1.9	+1.4	+0.8	+1.1	+0.6	+1.0	+1.43
6	—0.1	+0.5	+1.6	+0.9	+1.7	+1.2	+0.9	+0.6	+0.2	+0.7	+0.9	—0.2	+0.73
8	+0.1	+0.2	+0.5	+0.3	—0.2	+0.2	+0.1	+0.1	0.0	+0.5	+0.5	—0.1	+0.19
10	—0.2	+0.4	—0.9	—1.3	—1.8	—1.2	—0.2	—0.2	—0.3	—0.4	+0.4	—0.8	—0.56
Comb's													
10, 10	+0.2	+0.6	—0.4	—0.2	+0.1	0.0	+0.4	+0.2	—0.1	—0.1	+0.2	—0.4	+0.02
6, 2, 10	—0.2	+0.5	+0.5	+0.1	—0.2	+0.2	+0.2	+0.2	+0.1	—0.1	+0.2	—0.3	+0.09

The values for August are interpolated.

Melville Island, Arctic America.[1] Lat. 74° 47′. Long. 110° 48′ W. of

Parry. At sea level. 1819 to 1820.

Hour.	Jan.	Feb.	Mar.	Apr.	May.	June.	July.	Aug.	Sept.	Oct.	Nov.	Dec.	Year.
	°	°	°	°	°	°	°	°	°	°	°	°	..
Mdn't	..	..	..	..	..	..	..	..	..	..	—0.56	0.00	..
1	—0.26	—0.22	—2.34	..	..	..	..	..	..	—0.09	..	..	..
2	..	..	..	..	..	..	..	..	..	..	+0.26	+0.20	..
3	—0.40	—0.11	—2.74	..	..	..	..	..	..	—0.26	..	..	..
4	..	..	..	..	..	..	..	..	..	..	+0.04	+0.13	..
5	—0.16	—0.56	—2.02	..	..	..	..	..	..	—0.54	..	..	..
6	..	..	..	..	..	..	..	..	..	..	0.00	—0 24	..
7	—0.24	—0.65	—1.28	..	..	..	..	..	..	—0.45	..	..	..
8	..	..	..	..	..	..	..	..	..	..	+0.49	—0.16	..
9	+0.29	+0.54	+0.65	..	..	..	..	..	..	+0.33	..	..	..
10	..	..	..	..	..	..	..	..	..	..	+0.85	—0.24	..
11	+0.78	+0.97	+2.99	..	..	..	..	..	..	+1.03	..	..	..
Noon	..	..	..	..	..	..	..	..	..	..	+0.92	—0.54	..
1	+0.49	+1.46	+3.86	..	..	..	..	..	..	+0.97	..	..	..
2	..	..	..	..	..	..	..	..	..	..	+0.61	—0.32	..
3	+0.56	+1.16	+2.25	..	..	..	..	..	..	—0.49	..	..	..
4	..	..	..	..	..	..	..	..	..	..	—0.36	0.00	..
5	—0.09	—0.09	+0.97	..	..	..	..	..	..	+0.54	..	..	..
6	..	..	..	..	..	..	..	..	..	..	—0.61	+0.26	..
7	—0.09	—0.54	—0.13	..	..	..	..	..	..	+0.22	..	..	..
8	..	..	..	..	..	..	..	..	..	..	—0.85	+0.58	..
9	—0.24	—0.78	—0.74	..	..	..	..	..	..	—0.24	..	..	..
10	..	..	..	..	..	..	..	..	..	..	—0.80	+0.26	..
11	—0.90	—1.10	—1.48	..	..	..	..	..	..	—0.97	..	..	..

Port Kennedy, North Somerset. Lat. 72° 01′. Long. 94° 14′ W. of G.

McClintock. Near sea level. Aug. 1858, to Aug. 1859, inclusive.

(Uncorrected for effect of annual fluctuation.)

Hour.	Jan.	Feb.	Mar.	Apr.	May.	June.	July.	Aug.	Sept.	Oct.	Nov.	Dec.	Year.
Mdn't	—0.2	—0.5	—2.9	—3.3	—3.9	—4.2	—3.1	—1.0	—0.7	—1.0	—1.3	—0.4	—1.9
2	—0.2	—0.6	—3.3	—2.9	—4.3	—5.1	—3.6	—1.3	—0.9	—0.5	—0.3	+0.4	—1.9
4	—0.7	—0.2	—3.3	—1.9	—2.0	—2.0	—2.9	—1.3	—1.2	0.0	+0.1	+0.5	—1.2
6	—0.4	—0.2	—3.8	—1.3	—1.0	—0.3	—0.9	—0.9	—1.3	—0.4	+0.7	+0.3	—0.8
8	—0.4	+0.1	—1.7	+0.2	+1.2	+2.8	+1.2	—0.1	—0.7	—0.2	+0.9	—0.4	+0.2
10	0.0	+0.2	+3.0	+2.2	+2.3	+4.5	+2.8	+0.7	+0.1	+0.7	+1.2	+0.2	+1.5
Noon	+0.3	+0.8	+5.8	+3.8	+3.5	+4.5	+3.4	+1.2	+1.1	+1.5	+1.0	+0.1	+2.2
2	0.0	+0.8	+5.7	+4.2	+3.7	+3.2	+2.2	+1.3	+1.6	+1.0	+0.2	+0.2	+2.0
4	+0.3	+0.3	+4.0	+3.1	+2.9	+1.6	+1.9	+1.1	+1.4	0.0	—0.3	—0.2	+1.3
6	+0.7	—0.2	—0.7	+0.6	+1.2	+0.1	+1.0	+0.8	+1.0	—0.2	—0.6	—0.3	+0.3
8	+0.5	0.0	—1.5	—1.6	—1.0	—1.4	—0.1	+0.3	+0.2	—0.3	—0.9	—0.4	—0.5
10	+0.5	+0.1	—1.8	—3.0	—2.7	—3.3	—1.5	—0.2	0.0	—0.4	—1.0	—0.5	—1.2
Comb's													
10, 10	+0.2	+0.1	+0.6	—0.4	—0.2	+0.6	+0.6	+0.2	0.0	+0.1	+0.1	—0.1	+0.1
6, 2, 9[2]	0.0	+0.2	0.0	+0.2	+0.3	+0.2	+0.2	+0.1	+0.1	+0.1	0.0	0.0	+0.1
6, 2, 10	0.0	+0.2	0.0	0.0	0.0	—0.1	—0.1	+0.1	+0.1	+0.1	0.0	0.0	0.0
7, 2, 9[2]	0.0	+0.3	+0.4	+0.4	+0.7	+0.7	+0.4	+0.3	+0.2	+0.1	0.0	—0.1	+0.3
7, 2, 9 bis[2]	+0.1	+0.2	—0.1	—0.2	0.0	0.0	+0.2	+0.2	+0.2	0.0	—0.2	—0.1	0.0
3, 9, 3, 9[2]	0.0	0.0	+0.1	0.0	0.0	+0.1	0.0	0.0	+0.1	0.0	0.0	0.0	0.0

[1] From Prof. Guyot's Meteorological and Physical Tables, Smithsonian Misc. Coll.; Washington, 1858. Reaumur's changed into Fahrenheit's scale. Table by Dove.

[2] By interpolation.

Boothia Felix, Arctic America.[1] Lat. 69° 59′. Long. 92° 01′ W. of G.

At sea level. Ross. [Table by Dove]. 1829 to 1830.

Hour.	Jan.	Feb.	Mar.	Apr.	May.	June.	July.	Aug.	Sept.	Oct.	Nov.	Dec.	Year.
	°	°	°	°	°	°	°	°	°	°	°	°	°
Mdn't	−0.11	−1.10	−3.10	−4.68	−5.17	−4.59	−3.57	−2.81	−1.14	−0.63	−0.33	−0.26	−2.29
1	−0.18	−0.94	−3.62	−4.88	−5.94	−5.35	−4.00	−3.01	−1.25	−0.67	−0.04	−0.26	−2.51
2	−0.22	−0.63	−4.16	−5.06	−6.18	−5.73	−4.00	−2.92	−1.39	−0.71	+0.40	−0.29	−2.58
3	−0.24	−0.56	−4.72	−5.17	−5.87	−5.51	−3.71	−2.63	−1.48	−0.74	+0.65	−0.22	−2.51
4	−0.24	−0.47	−5.17	−5.08	−5.02	−4.61	−3.03	−2.29	−1.48	−0.76	+0.69	−0.13	−2.29
5	−0.22	−0.49	−5.35	−4.54	−3.95	−3.12	−2.22	−1.93	−1.25	−0.71	+0.54	−0.04	−1.96
6	−0.22	−0.58	−5.02	−3.44	−2.29	−1.46	−1.37	−1.57	−1.03	−0.61	+0.29	+0.09	−1.44
7	−0.20	−0.65	−3.98	−1.82	−0.78	+0.09	−0.58	−1.12	−0.61	−0.38	+0.04	+0.16	−0.83
8	−0.18	−0.49	−2.20	+0.13	+0.71	+1.30	+0.07	−0.54	−0.11	−0.02	+0.02	+0.22	−0.09
9	−0.13	−0.11	+0.13	+2.20	+2.13	+2.22	+0.83	+0.22	+0.26	+0.45	+0.09	+0.22	+0.71
10	−0.04	+0.58	+2.75	+4.07	+3.46	+2.99	+1.57	+1.10	+0.97	+0.92	+0.32	+0.22	+1.57
11	+0.04	+1.30	+5.13	+5.51	+4.63	+3.73	+2.36	+1.93	+1.46	+1.32	+0.58	+0.24	+2.36
Noon	+0.11	+1.96	+6.86	+6.43	+5.53	+4.54	+3.22	+2.60	+1.84	+1.55	+0.71	+0.26	+2.96
1	+0.24	+2.29	+7.60	+6.82	+5.99	+5.24	+3.82	+3.01	+2.09	+1.53	+0.67	+0.32	+3.31
2	+0.32	+2.20	+7.33	+6.65	+5.97	+5.58	+4.18	+3.10	+2.11	+1.28	+0.42	+0.29	+3.28
3	+0.33	+1.75	+6.25	+6.01	+5.40	+5.26	+4.00	+2.96	+2.09	+0.85	+0.09	+0.22	+2.94
4	+0.32	+1.03	+4.63	+4.90	+4.45	+4.45	+3.50	+2.65	+1.53	+0.40	−0.13	+0.11	+2.32
5	+0.24	+0.32	+2.90	+3.37	+3.26	+3.05	+2.65	+2.27	+0.99	−0.02	−0.54	−0.02	+1.55
6	+0.20	−0.29	+1.28	+1.66	+1.98	+1.48	+1.75	+1.75	+0.38	−0.32	−0.69	−0.16	+0.76
7	+0.13	−0.71	−0.02	−1.13	+0.76	+0.02	+0.76	+1.12	−0.18	−0.49	−0.80	−0.22	+0.02
8	+0.11	−0.97	−0.99	−1.75	−0.45	−1.14	−0.16	+0.36	−0.58	−0.56	−0.85	−0.24	−0.61
9	+0.07	−1.12	−1.70	−3.03	−1.66	−2.06	−1.12	−0.54	−0.85	−0.58	−0.85	−0.22	−1.14
10	+0.04	−1.14	−2.22	−3.91	−2.88	−2.83	−2.02	−1.48	−0.99	−0.58	−0.78	−0.22	−1.59
11	−0.04	−1.16	−2.67	−4.38	−4.09	−3.67	−2.70	−2.27	−1.08	−0.58	−0.63	−0.20	−1.96
Comb's													
10, 10	0.00	−0.28	+0.26	+0.08	+0.29	+0.08	−0.22	−0.19	−0.01	+0.17	−0.23	0.00	0.00
6, 2, 9	+0.06	+0.17	+0.20	+0.06	+0.67	+0.69	+0.56	+0.33	+0.08	+0.03	−0.05	+0.05	+0.23
6, 2, 10	+0.05	+0.16	+0.03	−0.23	+0.27	+0.43	+0.26	+0.02	+0.03	+0.03	−0.02	+0.05	+0.08
7, 2, 9	+0.06	+0.14	+0.55	+0.60	+1.18	+1.20	+0.83	+0.48	+0.22	+0.11	−0.13	+0.08	+0.44
7, 2, 9, [illegible]	+0.06	−0.17	[illegible]	[illegible]	[illegible]	[illegible]	[illegible]	[illegible]	[illegible]	[illegible]	[illegible]	[illegible]	[illegible]
3, 9, 3, 9	These four hours appear to have been used for the daily means, the results of the combination being zero.												

Sitka, Alaska Ter'y.[1] Lat. 57° 03′. Long. 135° 20′ W. of G.

Alt. 20 feet. [Table by Dove.] From a 5 year series.

Hour.	Jan.	Feb.	Mar.	Apr.	May.	June.	July.	Aug.	Sept.	Oct.	Nov.	Dec.	Year.
Mdn't	−0.74	−1.30	−2.18	−3.39	−4.05	−4.07	−3.78	−3.01	−2.41	−2.67	−0.92	−0.63	−2.43
1	−0.76	−1.48	−2.45	−3.78	−4.59	−4.63	−4.23	−3.44	−2.65	−2.49	−1.03	−0.74	−2.70
2	−0.78	−1.61	−2.63	−4.07	−4.95	−5.06	−4.59	−3.73	−2.99	−2.65	−1.10	−0.74	−2.90
3	−1.14	−1.75	−3.05	−4.25	−5.47	−5.60	−4.85	−3.98	−2.79	−1.44	−1.08	−0.40	−2.99
4	−1.01	−1.93	−3.31	−4.54	−5.73	−5.78	−4.95	−4.09	−2.90	−1.53	−1.10	−0.40	−3.10
5	−1.01	−1.87	−3.53	−4.66	−5.37	−5.56	−6.63	−4.25	−2.99	−1.57	−1.10	−0.32	−3.24
6	−1.01	−1.89	−3.51	−4.25	−3.95	−3.98	−3.76	−3.64	−2.99	−1.75	−1.03	−0.40	−2.67
7	−1.16	−1.84	−3.08	−2.54	−2.15	−2.43	−2.15	−2.45	−2.36	−1.30	−0.90	−0.38	−1.91
8	−1.08	−1.70	−1.68	−0.69	0.00	−0.58	−0.58	−0.90	−1.06	−1.19	−0.74	−0.26	−0.87
9	−0.87	−1.10	+0.18	+1.42	+1.84	+1.16	+1.30	+0.58	+0.38	−0.26	−0.52	−0.22	+0.33
10	−0.35	+0.07	+1.55	+2.58	+3.03	+2.88	+2.86	+2.13	+1.64	+0.63	0.00	+0.24	+1.44
11	+0.42	+1.35	+2.90	+3.78	+3.93	+3.82	+4.43	+3.53	+2.88	+1.68	+0.78	+0.24	+2.49

[1] From Prof. Guyot's Meteorological and Physical Tables, Smithsonian Misc. Coll.; Washington, 1858. Reaumur's changed into Fahrenheit's scale.

Hour.	Jan.	Feb.	Mar.	Apr.	May.	June.	July.	Aug.	Sept.	Oct.	Nov.	Dec.	Year.
Sitka.—Continued.													
	°	°	°	°	°	°	°	°	°	°	°	°	°
Noon	+1.28	+2.36	+3.84	+4.79	+4.88	+4.74	+4.74	+4.59	+3.71	+2.56	+1.61	+0.71	+3.33
1	+1.87	+3.05	+3.91	+5.24	+5.33	+5.28	+5.06	+5.24	+3.50	+3.10	+1.89	+1.03	+3.71
2	+2.13	+3.24	+4.47	+5.13	+5.40	+5.44	+5.19	+4.85	+4.18	+3.19	+2.25	+1.12	+3.89
3	+2.13	+3.31	+4.36	+4.72	+5.13	+5.19	+4.79	+4.50	+3.86	+3.08	+2.11	+0.99	+3.69
4	+1.75	+2.70	+3.76	+4.29	+4.59	+4.70	+4.36	+3.95	+3.50	+2.54	+1.68	+0.71	+3.22
5	+1.12	+1.91	+2.58	+3.67	+3.89	+3.95	+3.71	+3.22	+2.79	+1.98	+1.01	+0.45	+2.54
6	+0.56	+1.01	+1.84	+2.54	+3.08	+3.33	+2.83	+2.29	+1.44	+1.12	+0.47	+0.22	+1.73
7	+0.33	+0.22	+0.65	+1.08	+1.70	+2.25	+1.82	+1.10	+0.63	+0.35	+0.09	+0.07	+0.85
8	+0.02	−0.24	−0.29	−0.33	+0.52	+0.92	+0.49	−0.26	−0.42	−0.13	−0.16	−0.02	0.00
9	−0.33	−0.67	−0.99	−1.57	−1.08	−0.61	−0.74	−1.49	−1.16	−0.47	−0.49	−0.26	−0.83
10	−0.52	−0.83	−1.44	−2.41	−2.29	−2.18	−2.22	−2.15	−1.70	−0.67	−0.65	−0.43	−0.46
11	−0.69	−1.08	−1.89	−2.88	−3.53	−3.28	−3.10	−2.67	−2.02	−2.13	−0.97	−0.49	−2.09
Comb's													
10, 10	−0.43	−0.38	+0.05	+0.08	+0.37	+0.35	+0.32	−0.01	−0.03	−0.02	−0.32	−0.33	−0.01
6, 2, 9	+0.26	+0.23	−0.01	−0.23	+0.12	+0.28	+0.23	−0.09	+0.01	+0.32	+0.24	+0.15	+0.13
6, 2, 10	+0.20	+0.17	−0.16	−0.91	−0.28	−0.24	−0.26	−0.31	−0.17	+0.26	+0.19	+0.10	−0.08
7, 2, 9	+0.21	+0.24	+0.13	+0.34	+0.72	+0.80	+0.77	+0.30	+0.22	+0.47	+0.29	+0.16	+0.38
7, 2, 9 bis	+0.08	+0.01	−0.15	−0.14	+0.27	+0.45	+0.39	−0.14	−0.12	+0.24	+0.09	+0.05	+0.08
3, 9, 3, 9	−0.05	−0.05	+0.12	+0.08	+0.10	+0.03	+0.12	−0.10	+0.07	+0.23	0.00	+0.03	+0.05
Sitka, Alaska Ter'y. Lat. 57° 03′. Long. 135° 20′ W. of G. Alt. 20 feet. Months of old style. From an 8 year series, 1857 to 1864.													
Mdn't	−0.85	−1.22	−2.34	−3.69	−4.45	−4.67	−3.86	−3.20	−2.49	−1.39	−0.83	−0.35	−2.44
1	−0.84	−1.39	−2.48	−4.01	−4.88	−5.12	−4.16	−3.50	−2.99	−1.49	−0.83	−0.36	−2.67
2	−0.82	−1.57	−2.59	−4.21	−5.08	−5.44	−4.46	−3.80	−3.35	−1.63	−0.80	−0.38	−2.84
3	−0.77	−1.71	−2.75	−4.23	−5.12	−5.60	−4.66	−3.94	−3.55	−1.73	−0.80	−0.40	−2.94
4	−0.72	−1.82	−2.98	−4.18	−4.93	−5.40	−4.52	−3.89	−3.58	−1.74	−0.83	−0.48	−2.92
5	−0.68	−1.89	−3.24	−3.92	−4.34	−4.34	−3.79	−3.63	−3.45	−1.65	−0.90	−0.64	−2.70
6	−0.66	−2.00	−3.24	−3.28	−2.77	−2.68	−2.61	−3.09	−3.24	−1.61	−1.15	−0.62	−2.24
7	−0.72	−2.20	−2.47	−1.56	−0.92	−1.51	−1.07	−1.52	−2.23	−1.45	−1.10	−0.69	−1.45
8	−0.77	−1.82	−0.92	+0.30	+0.75	+0.67	+0.41	−0.01	−0.75	−0.77	−1.04	−0.66	−0.38
9	−0.45	−0.65	+1.00	+1.93	+2.46	+2.34	+2.12	+1.60	+0.83	+0.30	−0.36	−0.50	+0.89
10	+0.28	+1.01	+2.52	+3.39	+3.85	+3.69	+3.31	+2.98	+2.34	+1.34	+0.49	+0.04	+2.11
11	+1.21	+2.65	+3.74	+4.53	+5.00	+4.79	+4.24	+4.17	+3.69	+2.26	+1.28	+0.75	+3.18
Noon	+2.02	+3.13	+4.24	+5.01	+5.45	+5.85	+5.00	+4.96	+4.61	+3.02	+2.16	+1.50	+3.92
1	+2.10	+3.42	+4.58	+5.64	+5.68	+5.85	+5.27	+4.94	+4.88	+3.02	+2.27	+1.63	+4.11
2	+2.06	+3.35	+4.39	+4.94	+5.45	+5.47	+5.04	+4.73	+4.57	+2.93	+2.07	+1.43	+3.87
3	+1.52	+2.87	+3.92	+4.60	+4.84	+5.02	+4.76	+4.21	+4.14	+2.48	+1.51	+0.93	+3.42
4	+0.78	+2.13	+3.32	+3.73	+4.19	+4.38	+3.63	+3.50	+3.39	+1.77	+0.92	+0.48	+2.69
5	+0.24	+1.08	+2.10	+2.73	+3.17	+3.58	+2.66	+2.46	+2.42	+0.94	+0.33	+0.08	+1.82
6	−0.05	+0.34	+0.72	+1.43	+1.89	+2.30	+1.49	+1.18	+1.12	+0.19	+0.02	−0.17	+0.87
7	−0.39	−0.24	−0.49	−0.08	+0.45	+0.88	+0.30	−0.01	−0.05	−0.39	−0.27	−0.21	−0.04
8	−0.41	−0.61	−1.21	−1.32	−1.14	−0.79	−0.96	−1.16	−0.90	−0.73	−0.34	−0.30	−0.82
9	−0.59	−0.91	−1.63	−1.84	−2.36	−2.11	−2.06	−1.79	−1.44	−1.07	−0.50	−0.43	−1.39
10	−0.77	−0.92	−1.98	−2.64	−3.24	−3.13	−2.78	−2.31	−1.82	−1.22	−0.67	−0.41	−1.82
11	−0.83	−1.07	−2.19	−3.19	−3.98	−3.97	−3.36	−2.80	−2.09	−1.30	−0.76	−0.38	−2.16
Comb's													
10, 10	−0.24	+0.04	+0.27	+0.37	+0.32	+0.28	+0.26	+0.34	+0.26	+0.06	−0.09	−0.18	+0.14
6, 2, 9	+0.27	+0.15	−0.16	−0.06	+0.11	+0.23	+0.12	−0.05	−0.04	+0.08	+0.14	+0.13	+0.08
6, 2, 10	+0.21	+0.14	−0.28	−0.33	−0.19	−0.11	−0.12	−0.22	−0.16	+0.09	+0.08	+0.13	−0.06
7, 2, 9	+0.25	+0.08	+0.10	+0.51	+0.72	+0.62	+0.64	+0.47	+0.30	+0.14	+0.16	+0.10	+0.34
7, 2, 9 bis	+0.05	−0.22	−0.45	−0.10	−0.06	−0.09	−0.05	−0.12	−0.18	−0.22	−0.01	−0.04	−0.12
3, 9, 3, 9	−0.07	−0.10	+0.13	+0.11	−0.04	−0.09	+0.04	+0.02	0.00	0.00	−0.04	−0.10	0.00

Montreal, Canada East.[1] Lat. 45° 30′. Long. 73° 33′ W. of G.

J. S. McCord. Alt. 57 feet. Aug. 1839, to July, 1841, inclusive.

Hour.	Jan.	Feb.	Mar.	Apr.	May.	June.	July.	Aug.	Sept.	Oct.	Nov.	Dec.	Year.
	°	°	°	°	°	°	°	°	°	°	°	°	°
Mdn't	—1.1	—1.3	—1.3	—2.5	—4.5	—5.2	—4.4	—4.0	—3.9	—2.8	—1.4	—1.7	—2.85
1	—1.4	—1.6	—4.4	—3.1	—4.8	—4.5	—5.1	—5.0	—4.9	—2.5	—1.2	—0.9	—3.30
2	—2.4	—2.7	—2.9	—4.4	—6.9	—7.4	—7.2	—5.4	—4.3	—4.0	—1.6	—1.0	—4.20
3	—1.3	—2.7	—5.2	—5.1	—6.5	—5.1	—6.8	—6.0	—5.2	—3.6	—1.6	—1.8	—4.25
4	—2.9	—3.4	—5.6	—7.1	—7.0	—7.2	—7.6	—6.3	—5.6	—4.8	—1.8	—1.4	—4.96
5	—1.9	—4.0	—6.8	—6.5	—6.6	—6.3	—7.7	—6.4	—5.4	—4.5	—2.1	—2.2	—5.05
6	—3.5	—3.9	—5.2	—5.6	—6.6	—5.5	—5.5	—6.0	—4.6	—4.8	—1.4	—1.3	—4.50
7	—2.0	—5.2	—7.1	—3.8	—3.6	—4.7	—3.0	—2.1	—3.5	—3.6	—2.0	—2.1	—3.56
8	—3.1	—3.2	—3.3	—3.4	—3.1	—0.9	—0.6	—2.8	—2.2	—2.5	—0.8	—0.9	—2.24
9	—1.2	—4.0	—3.0	—0.7	—0.5	0.0	—0.2	+0.6	—0.7	—0.8	—0.6	—1.1	—1.02
o	+0.2	+0.8	0.0	+0.8	+1.0	+1.7	+2.9	+1.7	+1.5	+1.0	+0.4	—0.2	+0.93
11	+1.1	+0.2	+2.5	+2.5	+2.8	+3.4	+3.2	+3.6	+2.2	+2.7	+1.4	+0.5	+2.17
Noon	+2.8	+3.5	+4.2	+5.0	+7.1	+5.2	+5.5	+5.6	+5.4	+4.2	+1.9	+1.2	+4.30
1	+1.5	+4.8	+7.4	+4.9	+5.8	+6.0	+6.1	+6.6	+5.1	+5.4	+3.5	+2.4	+4.95
2	+4.1	+5.4	+6.5	+6.0	+8.8	+7.7	+7.4	+7.9	+6.6	+7.0	+2.4	+2.5	+6.02
3	+2.4	+6.1	+9.0	+6.3	+6.5	+6.9	+8.0	+7.3	+6.7	+5.8	+3.2	+2.8	+5.91
4	+3.9	+3.6	+6.0	+5.8	+8.4	+7.0	+7.5	+7.7	+6.7	+5.6	+2.5	+3.2	+5.65
5	+0.6	+4.1	+6.5	+5.6	+6.6	+6.2	+6.5	+5.5	+5.8	+3.2	+1.2	+1.4	+4.43
6	+1.8	+1.5	+3.4	+3.9	+3.9	+5.0	+5.4	+5.6	+2.8	+2.8	+1.0	+1.3	+3.20
7	+0.6	+1.2	+2.4	+2.9	+3.5	+3.2	+2.9	+1.4	+0.6	+1.0	+0.4	+0.7	+1.74
8	+0.9	+0.6	+1.2	+0.8	+1.6	+1.1	+0.7	+0.7	—0.1	+0.2	0.0	0.0	+0.65
9	+0.7	+1.0	+0.7	—0.4	—0.6	—1.6	—1.2	—1.6	—1.3	—0.3	—0.1	+0.7	—0.34
10	—0.2	—0.2	+0.3	—0.6	—1.9	—2.5	—2.6	—2.0	—2.4	—1.4	—1.2	—0.9	—1.30
11	—0.6	—0.2	—1.8	—2.1	—2.5	—3.5	—3.4	—3.1	—3.0	—2.5	—1.5	—0.2	—2.02
Comb's													
10, 10	0.0	+0.3	+0.1	+0.1	—0.4	—0.4	+0.1	—0.1	—0.4	—0.2	—0.4	—0.5	—0.18
6, 2, 9	+0.4	+0.8	+0.7	0.0	+0.5	+0.2	+0.2	+0.1	+0.2	+0.4	+0.3	+0.6	+0.39
6, 2, 10	+0.1	+0.4	+0.5	—0.1	+0.1	—0.1	—0.2	0.0	—0.1	+0.3	—0.1	+0.1	+0.07
7, 2, 9	+0.9	+0.4	0.0	+0.6	+1.5	+0.5	+1.1	+1.4	+0.6	+1.0	+0.1	+0.4	+0.71
7, 2, 9 bis	+0.9	+0.5	+0.2	+0.3	+1.0	0.0	+0.5	+0.6	+0.1	+0.7	0.0	+0.4	+0.44
3, 9, 3, 9	+0.1	+0.1	+0.4	0.0	—0.3	0.0	0.0	+0.1	—0.1	+0.3	+0.2	+0.1	+0.07

Thunder Bay Island, Lake Huron, Mich. Lat. 45° 2′. Long. 83° 17′ W. of G.

Alt. 610 feet. Dec. 1863, to Dec. 1865.

Hour.	Jan.	Feb.	Mar.	Apr.	May.	June.	July.	Aug.	Sept.	Oct.	Nov.	Dec.	Year.
Mdn't	—0.9	—1.9	—2.2	—2.9	—3.4	—4.3	—3.8	—4.0	—2.9	—2.5	—0.8	—0.8	—2.52
0 30	—1.3	—1.8	—2.9	—3.4	—4.1	—4.7	—4.5	—4.3	—2.6	—2.3	—1.1	—1.0	—2.82
1	—1.6	—2.2	—3.2	—3.8	—4.4	—4.9	—4.9	—4.5	—2.8	—2.5	—1.4	—1.1	—3.10
1 30	—2.0	—2.5	—3.4	—4.0	—4.7	—5.3	—5.4	—4.8	—2.9	—2.7	—1.5	—1.2	—3.36
2	—2.3	—2.6	—3.7	—4.4	—5.0	—5.6	—5.8	—5.1	—3.1	—2.9	—1.6	—1.3	—3.60
2 30	—2.5	—2.8	—3.9	—4.6	—5.1	—5.9	—6.1	—5.2	—3.3	—3.0	—1.6	—1.4	—3.77
3	—2.6	—2.9	—4.0	—4.7	—5.2	—6.1	—6.4	—5.4	—3.4	—3.0	—1.8	—1.6	—3.91
3 30	—2.6	—2.9	—3.9	—4.6	—5.3	—5.9	—6.4	—5.4	—3.5	—3.1	—1.8	—1.5	—3.90
4	—2.5	—2.8	—3.8	—4.5	—5.2	—5.8	—6.3	—5.5	—3.6	—3.1	—1.9	—1.4	—3.86
4 30	—2.4	—2.8	—3.7	—4.4	—5.1	—5.8	—6.2	—5.5	—3.8	—3.2	—1.8	—1.4	—3.83
5	—2.3	—2.6	—3.6	—4.3	—4.9	—5.4	—6.0	—5.5	—3.8	—3.2	—1.9	—1.3	—3.72
5 30	—2.2	—2.5	—3.5	—4.0	—4.2	—4.9	—5.5	—5.3	—3.7	—3.1	—1.8	—1.2	—3.48
6	—2.1	—2.4	—3.3	—3.6	—3.3	—4.0	—4.7	—5.0	—3.7	—3.0	—1.8	—1.1	—3.16
6 30	—2.0	—2.3	—2.9	—2.9	—2.6	—2.7	—3.5	—4.2	—3.3	—2.9	—1.7	—1.1	—2.66
7	—2.0	—2.1	—2.5	—2.0	—1.5	—1.7	—1.9	—3.2	—2.8	—2.6	—1.8	—1.1	—2.09
7 30	—1.9	—1.9	—2.0	—1.1	—0.5	—0.5	—1.2	—1.9	—2.0	—2.2	—1.6	—0.9	—1.46
8	—1.5	—1.6	—1.0	—0.2	+0.4	+0.6	—0.1	—0.7	—1.1	—1.8	—1.5	—0.7	—0.76
8 30	—1.2	—1.2	—0.1	+0.6	+1.1	+1.5	+1.0	+0.4	—0.5	—1.2	—1.1	—0.6	—0.10
9	—0.9	—0.6	+0.5	+1.3	+1.7	+2.1	+1.9	+1.3	+0.4	—0.5	—0.8	—0.4	+0.51
9 30	—0.3	—0.1	+1.4	+1.8	+2.0	+2.9	+2.6	+1.9	+1.0	+0.2	—0.3	—0.1	+1.09
10	+0.1	+0.4	+2.1	+2.4	+2.5	+3.4	+3.3	+2.7	+1.7	+0.9	+0.1	+0.2	+1.66
10 30	+0.7	+1.1	+2.8	+2.9	+3.0	+3.9	+3.8	+3.6	+2.4	+1.6	+0.6	+0.5	+2.25
11	+1.3	+1.8	+3.8	+3.4	+3.3	+4.2	+4.3	+4.4	+3.0	+2.3	+0.9	+0.9	+2.81
11 30	+1.9	+2.4	+3.8	+3.8	+3.6	+4.5	+4.7	+5.1	+3.6	+2.9	+1.5	+1.3	+3.27

[1] From Prof. Guyot's Met. and Phys. Tables, Sm. Misc. Coll.; Wash., 1858. From Aug. 1839, to July, 1840, inclu. the observations were taken at the *even* hours; from Aug. 1840, to July, 1841, at the *odd* hours. [Sch.]

Hour.	Jan.	Feb.	Mar.	Apr.	May.	June.	July.	Aug.	Sept.	Oct.	Nov.	Dec.	Year.
Thunder Bay Island.—Continued.													
	°	°	°	°	°	°	°	°	°	°	°	°	°
Noon	+2.5	+2.9	+4.0	+4.0	+4.0	+4.9	+5.1	+5.7	+4.2	+3.6	+1.8	+1.5	+3.69
0 30	+3.0	+3.4	+4.4	+4.3	+4.2	+5.6	+5.3	+6.2	+4.5	+4.1	+2.3	+1.7	+4.09
1	+3.2	+3.7	+4.6	+4.5	+4.4	+5.4	+5.2	+6.7	+4.8	+4.4	+2.6	+1.9	+4.29
1 30	+3.4	+4.1	+4.8	+4.6	+4.5	+5.4	+5.7	+6.9	+5.1	+4.8	+2.9	+2.0	+4.52
2	+3.6	+4.2	+5.0	+4.7	+4.7	+6.0	+5.9	+7.0	+5.3	+5.0	+3.0	+1.9	+4.62
2 30	+3.5	+4.2	+4.8	+4.7	+4.7	+6.0	+6.0	+6.9	+5.3	+5.0	+3.2	+1.9	+4.69
3	+3.3	+4.1	+4.5	+4.6	+5.0	+5.9	+6.1	+6.5	+5.1	+4.7	+3.0	+1.7	+4.55
3 30	+2.9	+3.7	+4.2	+4.3	+5.1	+5.6	+5.9	+6.1	+4.6	+4.4	+2.7	+1.5	+4.26
4	+2.2	+3.1	+3.8	+4.1	+5.0	+5.1	+5.7	+5.6	+4.1	+3.9	+2.0	+1.2	+3.83
4 30	+2.0	+2.4	+3.3	+3.7	+4.6	+4.8	+5.1	+5.1	+3.6	+3.2	+1.8	+1.0	+3.39
5	+1.6	+1.9	+2.6	+3.2	+4.1	+4.4	+4.5	+4.3	+3.0	+2.6	+1.2	+0.8	+2.86
5 30	+1.3	+1.5	+2.0	+2.7	+3.4	+3.8	+3.8	+3.4	+2.2	+2.0	+1.0	+0.7	+2.33
6	+0.9	+0.9	+1.5	+2.1	+2.7	+3.2	+3.0	+2.6	+1.5	+1.3	+0.7	+0.6	+1.76
6 30	+0.7	+0.6	+0.8	+1.4	+2.0	+2.1	+2.2	+1.5	+0.9	+0.7	+0.6	+0.5	+1.17
7	+0.4	+0.4	+0.2	+0.8	+1.2	+1.0	+1.4	+0.9	+0.2	+0.3	+0.3	+0.3	+0.62
7 30	+0.3	+0.1	−0.3	+0.2	+0.4	+0.3	+0.5	+0.2	−0.3	−0.1	+0.3	+0.1	+0.15
8	+0.2	0.0	−0.5	−0.2	−0.2	−0.5	−0.3	−0.4	−0.8	−0.5	+0.1	+0.3	−0.22
8 30	+0.1	−0.5	−0.8	−0.6	−0.9	−1.2	−0.8	−1.1	−1.1	−0.6	0.0	+0.2	−0.60
9	0.0	−0.4	−1.0	−1.0	−1.4	−1.7	−1.4	−1.7	−1.5	−1.1	−0.2	0.0	−0.94
9 30	−0.2	−0.7	−1.2	−1.3	−1.9	−2.2	−1.8	−2.2	−1.8	−1.3	−0.2	−0.1	−1.23
10	−0.3	−0.8	−1.3	−1.6	−2.3	−2.6	−2.4	−2.7	−1.9	−1.5	−0.4	−0.1	−1.48
10 30	−0.5	−1.3	−1.5	−2.0	−2.6	−3.2	−2.6	−3.1	−2.2	−1.7	−0.5	−0.4	−1.79
11	−0.7	−1.3	−1.8	−2.3	−2.9	−3.5	−3.0	−3.5	−2.5	−2.0	−0.7	−0.2	−2.02
11 30	−0.8	−1.5	−2.0	−2.5	−3.2	−3.9	−3.4	−4.1	−2.7	−2.3	−0.8	−0.6	−2.31
Comb's													
10, 10	−0.1	−0.2	+0.4	+0.4	+0.1	+0.4	+0.4	0.0	−0.1	−0.3	−0.1	0.0	+0.08
6, 2, 9	+0.5	+0.5	+0.2	0.0	0.0	+0.1	−0.1	+0.1	0.0	+0.3	+0.3	+0.3	+0.16
6, 2, 10	+0.4	+0.3	+0.1	−0.2	−0.3	−0.2	−0.4	−0.2	−0.1	+0.2	+0.3	+0.2	−0.02
7, 2, 9	+0.5	+0.6	+0.5	+0.6	+0.6	+0.9	+0.9	+0.7	+0.3	+0.4	+0.3	+0.3	+0.52
7, 2, 9 bis	+0.4	+0.3	+0.1	+0.2	+0.1	+0.2	+0.3	+0.1	−0.1	0.0	+0.2	+0.2	+0.15
3, 9, 3, 9	0.0	0.0	0.0	0.0	0.0	0.0	0.0	+0.2	+0.1	0.0	0.0	−0.1	+0.04

N. B. The hours 6_m, 9_m, 3_a, 6_a were employed in the U. S. Lake Survey, prior to June, 1860, the differences for the means at these hours are as follows:—

6, 9, 3, 6	+0.3	+0.5	+0.8	+1.1	+1.5	+1.5	+1.6	+1.3	+0.8	+0.6	+0.3	+0.2	+0.90

The mean of 6_m, 9_m, 3_a, is about the same as 7_a.

Toronto, Canada West. Lat. 43° 39′. Long. 79° 23′ W. of G.

Alt. 342 feet. July, 1842, to July, 1848.

Hour.	Jan.	Feb.	Mar.	Apr.	May.	June.	July.	Aug.	Sept.	Oct.	Nov.	Dec.	Year.
Mdn't	−1.52	−1.82	−2.47	−3.26	−5.03	−5.31	−6.54	−5.46	−3.96	−3.25	−1.82	−0.91	−3.45
1	−1.99	−2.20	−2.95	−4.01	−5.89	−6.00	−7.41	−6.11	−4.57	−3.85	−2.11	−1.49	−4.05
2	−2.07	−2.54	−3.33	−4.68	−6.73	−6.70	−7.97	−6.79	−5.16	−4.17	−2.39	−1.86	−4.53
3	−2.22	−2.97	−3.62	−4.88	−7.44	−7.48	−8.69	−7.46	−5.62	−4.33	−2.71	−1.99	−4.95
4	−2.32	−3.27	−4.00	−5.31	−7.91	−8.05	−9.32	−7.84	−6.21	−4.63	−2.87	−2.02	−5.31
5	−2.50	−3.62	−4.52	−5.68	−7.86	−7.86	−9.37	−8.03	−6.84	−4.80	−2.76	−2.04	−5.49
6	−1.77	−4.19	−4.80	−5.55	−5.41	−5.21	−6.16	−6.58	−6.16	−4.58	−2.49	−2.46	−4.61
7	−1.87	−4.32	−3.93	−3.26	−2.43	−2.40	−2.49	−3.61	−3.61	−3.83	−2.49	−2.62	−3.07
8	−1.64	−3.30	−1.95	−1.01	−0.21	−0.06	+0.11	−0.34	−0.86	−1.58	−1.44	−2.19	−1.21
9	−0.67	−1.00	+0.22	+0.97	+2.11	+1.82	+2.31	+2.16	+1.56	+1.10	+0.09	−1.01	+0.80
10	+0.56	+1.01	+1.95	+2.49	+3.81	+3.49	+4.01	+4.14	+3.53	+3.03	+1.53	+0.44	+2.50
11	+1.73	+2.60	+3.18	+3.87	+4.94	+4.77	+5.56	+5.59	+4.96	+4.40	+2.54	+1.68	+3.82

Toronto.—Continued.

Hour.	Jan.	Feb.	Mar.	Apr.	May.	June.	July.	Aug.	Sept.	Oct.	Nov.	Dec.	Year.
	°	°	°	°	°	°	°	°	°	°	°	°	°
Noon	+2.51	+3.80	+4.20	+4.90	+5.89	+5.87	+6.86	+6.54	+5.93	+5.30	+3.33	+2.49	+4.80
1	+3.01	+4.66	+4.85	+5.84	+6.81	+6.60	+7.78	+7.31	+6.53	+5.73	+3.73	+3.21	+5.50
2	+3.28	+5.06	+5.42	+6.22	+7.16	+7.02	+8.63	+7.89	+6.93	+6.08	+3.81	+3.36	+5.90
3	+3.25	+5.05	+5.22	+6.29	+7.22	+7.40	+8.83	+8.24	+6.96	+5.85	+3.64	+3.11	+5.92
4	+2.73	+4.50	+4.75	+5.90	+7.17	+7.64	+8.84	+8.09	+6.74	+5.12	+2.74	+2.46	+5.56
5	+1.73	+3.30	+4.00	+5.17	+6.79	+7.04	+8.38	+7.54	+5.78	+3.37	+1.53	+1.51	+4.68
6	+0.91	+1.85	+2.32	+3.37	+5.04	+5.74	+6.94	+5.64	+3.11	+1.32	+0.71	+0.81	+3.15
7	+0.38	+0.86	+0.85	+0.84	+2.17	+3.00	+3.46	+1.66	+0.41	+0.22	+0.14	+0.48	+1.20
8	+0.06	+0.01	−0.12	−0.75	−0.54	−0.30	−0.74	−1.26	−0.87	−0.52	−0.17	+0.09	−0.43
9	−0.14	−0.64	−1.12	−1.83	−2.29	−2.46	−3.11	−2.84	−1.91	−1.28	−0.46	−0.16	−1.52
10	−0.52	−1.19	−1.77	−2.60	−3.26	−3.80	−4.34	−3.86	−2.97	−2.03	−0.81	−0.46	−2.30
11	−0.84	−1.70	−2.42	−3.10	−4.18	−4.76	−5.52	−4.66	−3.61	−2.70	−1.16	−0.57	−2.94
Comb's													
10, 10	+0.02	−0.09	+0.09	−0.05	+0.27	−0.15	−0.16	+0.14	+0.28	+0.50	+0.36	−0.01	+0.10
6, 2, 9	+0.46	+0.08	−0.17	−0.39	−0.18	−0.22	−0.21	−0.51	−0.38	+0.07	+0.29	+0.25	−0.08
6, 2, 10	+0.33	−0.11	−0.38	−0.64	−0.50	−0.66	−0.62	−0.85	−0.73	−0.18	+0.17	+0.15	−0.34
7, 2, 9	+0.42	+0.03	+0.12	+0.38	+0.81	+0.72	+1.01	+0.48	+0.37	+0.32	+0.29	+0.19	+0.44
7, 2, 9 bis	+0.28	−0.13	−0.19	−0.17	+0.04	−0.07	−0.02	−0.35	−0.12	−0.08	+0.10	+0.10	−0.05
3, 9, 3, 9	+0.05	+0.11	+0.17	+0.14	−0.10	−0.18	−0.16	+0.02	+0.25	+0.33	+0.14	−0.01	+0.06

Mohawk, N. Y. Lat. 43° 00′. Long. 75° 02′ W. of G.

Alt. 435 feet. June, 1860, to May, 1864, inclusive; and Jan. 1867, to Jan. 1869, inclusive.

Hour.	Jan.	Feb.	Mar.	Apr.	May.	June.	July.	Aug.	Sept.	Oct.	Nov.	Dec.	Year.
Mdn't	−1.19	−1.51	−1.88	−2.95	−3.70	−4.34	−4.22	−4.32	−3.57	−1.83	−1.34	−0.94	−2.65
1	−1.34	−2.17	−2.70	−4.15	−4.84	−6.18	−5.06	−4.80	−3.80	−2.53	−0.82	−1.17	−3.30
2	−1.64	−2.55	−3.13	−4.71	−5.73	−7.06	−5.91	−5.49	−4.47	−3.04	−1.23	−1.52	−3.88
3	−2.05	−2.90	−3.70	−5.22	−6.55	−7.82	−6.61	−6.19	−5.06	−3.46	−1.61	−1.89	−4.42
4	−2.37	−3.20	−4.18	−5.76	−7.37	−8.53	−7.24	−6.83	−5.66	−3.94	−1.88	−2.19	−4.93
5	−2.63	−3.39	−4.62	−6.13	−7.85	−9.01	−7.75	−7.33	−6.19	−4.31	−2.21	−2.31	−5.31
6	−2.80	−3.68	−5.06	−6.43	−7.88	−8.36	−7.29	−7.47	−6.58	−4.63	−2.48	−2.49	−5.43
7	−2.99	−4.11	−5.04	−5.89	−6.37	−6.39	−5.31	−6.30	−6.25	−4.78	−2.81	−2.64	−4.91
8	−2.95	−3.89	−3.66	−4.10	−4.00	−3.42	−2.69	−4.04	−4.67	−4.12	−2.63	−2.62	−3.56
9	−2.20	−2.64	−1.68	−1.87	−1.40	−0.61	+0.05	−1.44	−2.32	−2.55	−1.77	−1.79	−1.69
10	−0.70	−0.63	+0.31	+0.29	+1.02	+2.00	+2.64	+1.32	+0.26	−0.34	−0.36	−0.49	+0.44
11	+1.06	+1.21	+1.94	+2.15	+3.17	+4.18	+4.64	+3.65	+2.61	+1.80	+1.14	+0.99	+2.38
Noon	+2.55	+2.99	+3.40	+3.85	+5.01	+5.98	+6.12	+5.52	+4.62	+3.62	+2.38	+2.36	+4.03
1	+3.51	+4.15	+4.40	+5.18	+6.35	+7.21	+6.99	+6.94	+6.39	+4.95	+3.16	+3.30	+5.21
2	+4.10	+4.90	+5.23	+6.30	+7.50	+8.45	+7.24	+7.71	+7.56	+5.85	+3.55	+3.64	+6.00
3	+4.22	+5.16	+5.41	+6.96	+8.10	+8.99	+7.42	+8.32	+8.31	+6.25	+3.68	+3.53	+6.36
4	+3.75	+4.74	+5.26	+7.29	+8.24	+9.03	+7.02	+8.32	+8.31	+5.88	+3.17	+2.97	+6.17
5	+2.75	+3.85	+4.62	+6.98	+7.86	+8.45	+6.68	+7.70	+7.27	+4.70	+2.23	+2.03	+5.42
6	+1.62	+2.60	+3.35	+5.87	+6.79	+7.13	+5.50	+6.40	+5.33	+3.03	+1.29	+1.29	+4.19
7	+0.85	+1.61	+1.89	+3.86	+4.59	+4.86	+3.67	+3.90	+2.76	+1.47	+0.49	+0.72	+2.55
8	+0.28	+0.83	+0.96	+1.62	+1.80	+1.90	+1.03	+1.09	+0.60	+0.37	+0.03	+0.26	+0.90
9	−0.28	+0.20	+0.22	−0.02	−0.28	−0.55	−1.06	−0.85	−0.85	−0.44	−0.47	−0.13	−0.38
10	−0.66	−0.43	−0.41	−1.15	−1.66	−2.09	−2.44	−2.29	−1.90	−0.75	−0.77	−0.34	−1.24
11	−0.97	−1.01	−1.07	−2.11	−2.73	−3.53	−3.37	−3.36	−2.80	−1.32	−1.04	−0.60	−1.99
Comb's													
10, 10	−0.68	−0.53	−0.05	−0.43	−0.32	−0.04	+0.10	−0.48	−0.82	−0.54	−0.57	−0.42	−0.40
6, 2, 9	+0.34	+0.47	+0.13	−0.05	−0.22	−0.15	−0.37	−0.20	+0.04	+0.26	+0.20	+0.34	+0.06
6, 2, 10	+0.21	+0.26	−0.08	−0.43	−0.68	−0.67	−0.80	−0.68	−0.31	+0.16	+0.10	+0.27	−0.22
7, 2, 9	+0.28	+0.33	+0.14	+0.13	+0.28	+0.50	+0.29	+0.19	+0.15	+0.21	+0.09	+0.29	+0.24
7, 2, 9 bis	+0.14	+0.29	+0.16	−0.09	+0.14	+0.24	−0.05	−0.07	−0.10	+0.05	−0.05	+0.18	+0.08
3, 9, 3, 9	−0.08	−0.04	+0.06	−0.04	−0.03	0.00	−0.05	−0.04	+0.02	−0.05	−0.04	−0.06	−0.03

Cambridge, Mass. Lat. 42° 23′. Long. 71° 07′ W. of G.

Alt. about 71 feet. Oct. 1841, to Dec. 1842, inclusive.

Hour.	Jan.	Feb.	Mar.	April.	May.	June.	July.	Aug.	Sept.	Oct.	Nov.	Dec.	Year.
	°	°	°	°	°	°	°	°	°	°	°	°	°
0.6 A.M.	−0.90	−1.19	−4.05	−3.55	−7.60	−7.68	−5.53	−5.16	− 6.17	− 5.37	−3.81	−2.13	−4.43
2.6	−1.51	−2.46	−5.28	−3.20	−8.86	−9.65	−6.74	−6.01	− 7.58	− 6.63	−4.17	−2.60	−5.40
4.6	−1.85	−3.39	−5.59	−4.72	−9.47	−9.73	−6.60	−6.86	− 7.90	− 7.13	−4.53	−2.69	−5.88
6.6	−3.11	−3.25	−6.48	−4.03	−4.92	−2.59	−3.29	−4.25	− 8.26	− 7.28	−4.67	−3.11	−4.61
8.6	−4.92	−2.86	+0.02	+0.35	+2.51	+2.76	+2.03	+1.64	+ 0.37	− 1.88	−1.57	−1.87	−0.29
10.6	+0.48	+1.02	+5.34	+3.59	+5.99	+6.62	+6.95	+5.59	+ 7.38	+ 6.30	+4.57	+2.50	+4.69
0.6 P.M.	+4.42	+5.00	+7.97	+5.26	+8.55	+8.85	+7.50	+6.36	+10.03	+10.04	+6.72	+5.22	+7.16
2.6	+4.45	+5.59	+7.44	+5.56	+9.45	+9.16	+6.96	+6.65	+ 9.97	+10.88	+6.75	+4.98	+7.32
4.6	+2.94	+3.47	+5.04	+4.05	+7.98	+7.00	+5.11	+5.43	+ 7.21	+ 7.25	+3.64	+1.98	+5.09
6.6	+0.73	−0.27	+0.70	+1.35	+3.60	+4.21	+0.92	+2.03	+ 2.02	+ 0.56	+0.68	+0.29	+1.40
8.6	0.00	−0.82	−1.83	−1.89	−2.13	−2.73	−2.73	−1.96	− 2.25	− 2.51	−1.27	−0.77	−1.75
10.6	−0.69	−0.83	−3.22	−2.75	−5.13	−6.25	−4.53	−3.50	− 4.77	− 4.21	−2.37	−1.74	−3.34

The following values for certain combinations of hours were obtained by a process of graphical interpolation, the above monthly results having been plotted on a suitable scale for that purpose:—

Comb's	Jan.	Feb.	Mar.	April.	May.	June.	July.	Aug.	Sept.	Oct.	Nov.	Dec.	Year.
7, 2, 9	+0.3	+0.5	−0.2	+0.1	+0.9	+1.4	+0.5	+0.3	− 0.1	+ 0.4	+0.2	+0.3	+0.4
7, 2, 9 bis	+0.2	+0.1	−0.7	−0.4	−0.1	+0.2	−0.4	−0.3	− 0.7	− 0.4	−0.2	0.0	−0.2
3, 9, 3, 9	−0.5	−0.1	+0.2	+0.4	+0.2	−0.2	+0.1	+0.4	+ 0.5	+ 0.2	+0.4	0.0	+0.1

The above results are of comparatively little value on account of the small number of observations.

Amherst, Mass. Lat. 42° 22′. Long. 72° 34′ W. of G.

Alt. 267 feet. 1839.

Hour.	Jan.	Feb.	Mar.	April.	May.	June.	July.	Aug.	Sept.	Oct.	Nov.	Dec.	Year.
Mdn't	−2.50	−1.70	−4.84	− 4.92	−4.75	−5.50	−5.32	−4.53	−5.39	−3.99	−2.39	−1.98	−3.98
1	−3.90	−2.78	−4.72	− 6.23	−5.51	−6.66	−6.40	−5.15	−5.41	−4.77	−2.33	−1.63	−4.62
2	−4.24	−3.03	−4.80	− 6.69	−6.48	−7.30	−6.84	−5.67	−6.17	−5.55	−2.98	−2.20	−5.16
3	−4.13	−3.20	−5.34	− 7.42	−7.41	−7.94	−7.29	−6.04	−6.97	−6.36	−3.48	−2.55	−5.68
4	−4.50	−3.94	−5.68	− 7.85	−7.88	−8.06	−7.43	−6.30	−7.61	−6.99	−3.71	−2.70	−6.05
5	−4.72	−4.20	−6.03	− 8.12	−8.18	−7.82	−7.55	−6.67	−7.93	−7.62	−4.02	−3.32	−6.36
6	−4.68	−4.78	−6.11	− 7.77	−6.77	−5.98	−6.03	−5.82	−7.49	−7.55	−4.33	−3.78	−5.92
7	−4.75	−4.78	−4.61	− 5.97	−4.22	−4.22	−3.81	−4.49	−5.37	−6.77	−4.27	−3.97	−4.77
8	−3.83	−3.78	−2.07	− 3.04	−1.62	−1.42	−1.10	−1.97	−2.57	−4.21	−2.67	−4.13	−2.70
9	−1.46	−1.45	+0.47	− 0.08	+0.60	+0.86	+0.86	+0.92	+0.51	−0.73	−0.33	−2.40	−0.19
10	+1.32	+0.85	+2.58	+ 2.69	+3.12	+3.10	+3.79	+3.03	+3.27	+2.34	+1.44	+0.55	+2.34
11	+4.10	+2.72	+4.78	+ 5.65	+5.12	+5.66	+6.42	+5.44	+5.99	+5.12	+3.02	+2.76	+4.73
Noon	+6.32	+4.26	+6.39	+ 7.92	+6.75	+8.06	+8.49	+6.85	+8.11	+7.16	+5.02	+4.30	+6.64
1	+7.46	+5.35	+7.66	+ 9.46	+8.15	+9.34	+8.82	+8.22	+9.07	+8.34	+6.13	+6.14	+7.85
2	+7.80	+6.06	+8.35	+10.42	+8.75	+8.98	+9.49	+7.85	+9.75	+9.38	+5.98	+6.30	+8.26
3	+7.32	+5.80	+8.12	+ 9.81	+8.27	+8.58	+7.49	+7.66	+9.15	+9.34	+5.29	+5.60	+7.70
4	+5.80	+4.89	+7.24	+ 8.61	+7.86	+7.82	+7.16	+6.22	+8.35	+8.34	+3.86	+3.76	+6.66
5	+3.32	+3.10	+5.66	+ 7.04	+5.97	+5.98	+5.82	+5.25	+6.39	+5.75	+2.29	+2.03	+4.89
6	+2.06	+1.18	+3.47	+ 4.50	+4.08	+4.18	+4.16	+2.81	+3.47	+3.60	+0.86	+0.68	+2.93
7	−0.24	+1.05	−0.16	+ 1.69	+2.38	+1.90	+1.53	+1.43	+1.42	+1.34	+0.65	+0.31	+1.11
8	−0.64	+0.43	−0.92	− 0.27	+0.19	−0.06	−0.99	−0.34	−0.16	−0.03	−0.07	−0.20	−0.25
9	−1.50	−0.28	−1.88	− 1.77	−1.66	−1.98	−3.06	−1.60	−2.04	−1.06	−0.79	−0.69	−1.53
10	−2.01	−0.57	−3.28	− 3.31	−2.73	−3.22	−3.80	−3.02	−3.58	−1.80	−1.15	−1.20	−2.47
11	−2.42	−1.19	−4.28	− 4.23	−3.99	−4.22	−4.25	−3.80	−4.66	−3.14	−1.95	−1.58	−3.31
Comb's													
10, 10	−0.34	+0.14	−0.35	− 0.31	+0.19	−0.06	0.00	0.00	−0.19	+0.27	+0.24	−0.32	−0.06
6, 2, 9	+0.54	+0.33	+0.12	+ 0.29	+0.11	+0.34	+0.13	+0.14	+0.07	+0.26	+0.29	+0.61	+0.27
6, 2, 10	+0.37	+0.24	−0.35	− 0.22	−0.25	−0.07	−0.11	−0.33	−0.44	+0.01	+0.17	+0.44	−0.04
7, 2, 9	+0.52	+0.33	+0.62	+ 0.89	+0.96	+0.93	+0.87	+0.59	+0.78	+0.52	+0.31	+0.55	+0.65
7, 2, 9 bis	+0.01	+0.18	0.00	+ 0.23	+0.30	+0.20	−0.11	+0.04	+0.07	+0.12	+0.03	+0.24	+0.11
3, 9, 3, 9	+0.06	+0.22	+0.34	+ 0.13	−0.05	−0.12	−0.50	+0.23	+0.16	+0.30	+0.17	−0.01	+0.08

New Haven, Conn. Lat. 41° 18′. Long. 72° 56′ W. of G.

Alt. about 45 feet. Partly 1779 to 1865, partly 1838 to 1852, constructed from various hours of observation.

Hour.	Jan.	Feb.	Mar.	Apr.	May.	June.	July.	Aug.	Sept.	Oct.	Nov.	Dec.	Year.
	°	°	°	°	°	°	°	°	°	°	°	°	°
Mdn't	−2.27	−2.87	−3.71	−4.65	−5.40	−5.81	−5.20	−4.75	−4.79	−4.08	−2.64	−2.17	−4.03
1	−2.62	−3.34	−4.32	−5.43	−6.27	−6.93	−6.17	−5.57	−5.63	−4.84	−3.18	−2.49	−4.73
2	−3.00	−3.80	−4.85	−6.10	−7.16	−8.05	−6.97	−6.29	−6.32	−5.48	−3.68	−2.82	−5.38
3	−3.34	−4.31	−5.37	−6.74	−7.97	−8.71	−7.55	−6.76	−6.80	−6.05	−4.10	−3.17	−5.91
4	−3.70	−4.79	−5.81	−7.32	−8.50	−8.86	−7.69	−7.16	−7.23	−6.51	−4.50	−3.49	−6.30
5	−4.07	−5.16	−6.18	−7.53	−8.38	−8.17	−7.39	−7.10	−7.35	−6.81	−4.80	−3.78	−6.39
6	−4.34	−5.30	−6.09	−7.15	−6.60	−6.13	−6.15	−6.36	−6.84	−6.65	−4.80	−3.97	−5.86
7	−4.38	−5.10	−4.91	−5.27	−3.63	−3.17	−3.68	−4.11	−4.75	−5.27	−4.48	−3.96	−4.39
8	−3.82	−3.69	−2.30	−2.04	−0.51	+0.03	−0.86	−1.34	−1.72	−2.29	−2.98	−3.21	−2.06
9	−1.33	−0.51	+0.46	+1.12	+2.14	+2.68	+1.64	+1.22	+1.25	+0.58	−0.46	−1.01	+0.65
10	+1.59	+2.48	+3.24	+3.87	+4.21	+4.73	+3.79	+3.39	+3.78	+3.52	+2.24	+1.63	+3.21
11	+3.63	+4.23	+4.86	+5.49	+5.77	+6.08	+5.57	+5.28	+5.65	+5.65	+4.19	+3.49	+4.99
Noon	+5.19	+5.56	+6.14	+6.78	+6.98	+7.12	+5.71	+6.50	+6.89	+6.95	+5.63	+5.05	+6.29
1	+6.07	+6.59	+7.03	+7.74	+7.93	+7.93	+7.46	+7.30	+7.67	+7.75	+6.37	+5.85	+7.14
2	+6.34	+6.95	+7.47	+8.32	+8.51	+8.32	+7.81	+7.69	+8.04	+8.08	+6.57	+6.12	+7.52
3	+5.88	+6.76	+7.34	+8.35	+8.53	+8.25	+7.71	+7.62	+7.89	+7.71	+6.19	+5.53	+7.31
4	+4.73	+5.78	+6.60	+7.83	+8.02	+7.63	+7.19	+7.06	+7.15	+6.60	+4.63	+4.02	+6.44
5	+2.84	+3.81	+4.74	+6.60	+6.79	+6.48	+6.13	+5.89	+5.80	+4.47	+2.88	+2.09	+4.88
6	+1.39	+2.01	+2.54	+4.05	+4.72	+4.31	+4.18	+3.94	+3.97	+2.76	+1.56	+1.00	+3.04
7	+0.31	+0.62	+0.88	+1.47	+1.65	+2.16	+2.03	+1.92	+1.88	+1.18	+0.50	+0.21	+1.23
8	−0.49	−0.44	−0.57	−0.61	−0.62	−0.08	+0.11	−0.01	−0.08	−0.22	−0.37	−0.49	−0.32
9	−1.11	−1.23	−1.66	−1.98	−2.23	−1.82	−1.65	−1.65	−1.69	−1.46	−1.07	−1.04	−1.55
10	−1.55	−1.84	−2.40	−2.97	−3.47	−3.28	−2.88	−2.79	−2.85	−2.42	−1.59	−1.46	−2.46
11	−1.95	−2.38	−3.05	−3.80	−4.45	−4.60	−4.11	−3.86	−3.87	−3.28	−2.12	−1.82	−3.27
Comb's													
10, 10	+0.02	+0.32	+0.42	+0.45	+0.37	+0.72	+0.45	+0.30	+0.46	+0.55	+0.32	+0.08	+0.37
6, 2, 9	+0.30	+0.14	−0.09	−0.27	−0.11	+0.12	0.00	−0.11	−0.16	−0.01	+0.23	+0.37	+0.04
6, 2, 10	+0.15	−0.06	−0.34	−0.60	−0.52	−0.36	−0.41	−0.49	−0.55	−0.33	+0.06	+0.23	−0.27
7, 2, 9	+0.28	+0.21	+0.30	+0.36	+0.88	+1.11	+0.83	+0.64	+0.53	+0.45	+0.34	+0.37	+0.53
7, 2, 9 bis	−0.06	−0.15	−0.19	−0.23	+0.10	+0.38	+0.21	+0.07	−0.02	−0.03	−0.01	[illegible]	[illegible]
3, 9, 3, 9	+0.02	+0.18	+0.19	+0.19	+0.12	+0.10	+0.04	+0.11	+0.16	+0.19	+0.14	+0.08	+0.13

Brooklyn Heights, N. Y. Lat. 40° 41′. Long. 73° 59′ W. of G.

Alt. . . Dec. 1847, to May, 1849, inclusive.

Hour.	Jan.	Feb.	Mar.	Apr.	May.	June.	July.	Aug.	Sept.	Oct.	Nov.	Dec.	Year.
Mdn't	−1.3	−1.6	−3.8	−4.9	−3.7	−6.4	−2.4	−3.0	−2.9	−3.1	−2.0	−1.7	−3.1
1	−1.6	−2.2	−4.4	−5.5	−4.4	−7.0	−2.8	−3.6	−3.5	−4.0	−2.5	−1.9	−3.6
2	−1.9	−2.9	−4.8	−5.9	−5.0	−7.2	−3.2	−4.1	−4.1	−4.8	−3.1	−2.0	−4.1
3	−2.2	−3.5	−5.0	−6.1	−5.4	−7.3	−3.4	−4.4	−4.5	−5.2	−3.5	−2.1	−4.4
4	−2.4	−3.9	−5.2	−6.2	−5.7	−7.2	−3.6	−4.5	−4.8	−5.6	−3.8	−2.1	−4.6
5	−2.6	−4.0	−4.7	−5.9	−5.7	−6.7	−3.6	−4.5	−4.9	−4.1	−3.7	−2.1	−4.4
6	−2.6	−3.9	−4.7	−5.8	−5.0	−5.6	−3.6	−4.1	−4.6	−2.8	−3.2	−1.9	−4.0
7	−2.6	−3.9	−4.0	−4.2	−2.8	−2.3	−2.9	−3.2	−3.7	−2.8	−3.3	−1.7	−3.1
8	−2.3	−2.9	−2.2	−0.6	−0.7	+0.7	−1.6	−1.8	−2.4	−1.3	−2.0	−1.6	−1.6
9	−1.3	−0.9	−0.3	+1.3	+0.8	+2.9	−0.2	+0.1	−0.4	+0.5	−0.1	−0.7	+0.1
10	+0.2	+1.1	+2.0	+3.0	+2.7	+3.9	+0.9	+2.3	+2.1	+2.1	+1.8	+0.6	+1.9
11	+1.9	+2.4	+4.0	+5.1	+4.8	+5.7	+2.6	+3.8	+4.8	+3.7	+3.5	+1.9	+3.7

Brooklyn Heights.—Continued.

Hour.	Jan.	Feb.	Mar.	Apr.	May.	June.	July.	Aug.	Sept.	Oct.	Nov.	Dec.	Year.
Noon	+3.0°	+3.6°	+4.9°	+6.7°	+6.2°	+7.1°	+3.5°	+5.4°	+5.6°	+4.8°	+4.2°	+2.9°	+4.8°
1	+3.6	+4.5	+5.6	+7.8	+6.4	+7.7	+4.4	+6.3	+5.6	+5.3	+5.1	+3.4	+5.5
2	+3.9	+4.6	+6.4	+8.1	+6.4	+8.0	+4.4	+5.0	+5.5	+5.8	+5.2	+3.7	+5.6
3	+3.4	+4.5	+6.5	+7.8	+5.7	+7.9	+4.5	+4.9	+5.3	+5.5	+5.1	+3.4	+5.4
4	+2.9	+4.0	+5.5	+6.2	+5.2	+7.0	+4.4	+4.0	+4.5	+4.4	+3.7	+2.6	+4.5
5	+1.8	+3.2	+4.2	+4.6	+4.0	+5.3	+3.6	+3.1	+3.4	+3.0	+1.5	+1.7	+3.3
6	+1.1	+1.9	+2.6	+2.7	+2.4	+3.4	+2.3	+1.8	+2.1	+2.2	+0.6	+0.9	+2.0
7	+0.6	+1.2	+1.5	+0.9	+0.8	+1.5	+1.1	+1.0	+1.1	+0.9	−0.1	+0.3	+0.9
8	0.0	+0.7	+0.7	−0.4	−0.3	−0.4	+0.3	−0.1	+0.2	−0.2	−0.5	0.0	0.0
9	−0.3	+0.1	+0.2	−1.4	−1.3	−1.5	−0.6	−0.9	−0.6	−0.6	−0.7	−0.6	−0.7
10	−0.6	−0.3	−1.2	−3.1	−2.0	−4.0	−1.2	−1.7	−1.4	−1.0	−0.8	−1.1	−1.5
11	−1.0	−0.9	−2.9	−4.1	−2.9	−5.4	−2.0	−2.3	−2.2	−2.1	−1.4	−1.4	−2.4
Comb's													
10, 10	−0.2	+0.4	+0.4	0.0	+0.3	0.0	−0.1	+0.3	+0.3	+0.5	+0.5	−0.2	+0.2
6, 2, 9	+0.3	+0.3	+0.6	+0.3	0.0	+0.3	+0.1	0.0	+0.1	+0.8	+0.4	+0.4	+0.3
6, 2, 10	+0.2	+0.1	+0.2	−0.3	−0.2	−0.5	−0.1	−0.3	−0.2	+0.7	+0.4	+0.2	0.0
7, 2, 9	+0.3	+0.3	+0.9	+0.8	+0.8	+1.4	+0.3	+0.3	+0.4	+0.8	+0.4	+0.5	+0.6
7, 2, 9 bis	+0.2	+0.2	+0.7	+0.3	+0.2	+0.7	+0.1	0.0	+0.1	+0.4	+0.1	+0.2	+0.3
3, 9, 3, 9	−0.1	0.0	+0.3	+0.4	0.0	+0.5	+0.1	−0.1	0.0	0.0	+0.2	0.0	+0.1

The above results are not entitled to full confidence, either from insufficiency or irregularity of observation.

Frankford Arsenal, near Philadelphia,[1] Penn. Lat. 40° 00′. Long. 75° 04′ W. of G.

Alt. 24 feet. Captain Mordecay, U. S. A. 1836 and 1837.

Hour.	Jan.	Feb.	Mar.	Apr.	May.	June.	July.	Aug.	Sept.	Oct.	Nov.	Dec.	Year.
Mdn't	−2.68	−3.06	−3.33	−3.65	−4.52	−6.84	−5.92	−5.40	−5.29	−4.91	−2.59	−2.10	−4.23
1	−3.02	−3.29	−3.94	−4.21	−5.85	−7.67	−6.91	−6.05	−5.92	−5.40	−2.66	−3.02	−4.84
2	−3.40	−3.89	−4.79	−5.24	−6.86	−8.39	−7.90	−6.84	−6.86	−6.01	−2.86	−3.38	−5.54
3	−4.10	−4.46	−5.76	−6.48	−7.72	−8.82	−8.62	−7.47	−7.85	−6.62	−3.17	−3.74	−6.23
4	−4.79	−5.02	−6.53	−7.40	−8.03	−8.64	−8.64	−7.56	−8.39	−7.04	−3.40	−4.05	−6.62
5	−5.20	−5.54	−6.64	−7.45	−7.74	−7.56	−7.65	−6.73	−7.97	−7.02	−3.89	−4.21	−6.44
6	−5.06	−5.29	−5.90	−6.37	−5.96	−5.54	−5.67	−4.97	−6.39	−6.35	−3.11	−4.05	−5.38
7	−4.23	−4.52	−4.30	−4.37	−3.74	−2.84	−3.02	−2.59	−3.85	−4.93	−2.39	−3.42	−3.69
8	−2.75	−2.99	−2.12	−1.91	−1.28	+0.07	−0.18	−0.02	−0.81	−2.84	−1.31	−2.18	−1.53
9	−0.77	−0.68	+0.16	+0.45	+1.01	+2.70	+2.39	+2.25	+2.16	−0.27	+0.05	−0.41	+0.77
10	+1.40	+1.62	+2.25	+2.36	+2.90	+4.75	+4.41	+4.01	+4.64	+2.54	+1.58	+1.71	+2.86
11	+3.47	+3.98	+3.96	+3.80	+4.43	+6.17	+5.94	+5.27	+6.50	+5.24	+2.52	+3.83	+4.59
Noon	+5.18	+5.85	+5.22	+5.00	+5.29	+7.13	+7.11	+6.26	+7.81	+7.54	+4.41	+5.51	+6.03
1	+6.41	+6.77	+6.17	+6.12	+6.91	+7.90	+8.06	+7.11	+8.69	+9.11	+5.36	+6.46	+7.09
2	+6.80	+7.16	+6.77	+7.18	+7.92	+8.48	+8.71	+7.83	+9.16	+9.81	+5.72	+6.58	+7.67
3	+6.57	+6.59	+6.98	+7.94	+8.51	+8.75	+8.87	+8.12	+9.05	+9.50	+5.40	+5.72	+7.67
4	+5.69	+5.49	+6.64	+7.99	+8.33	+8.44	+8.26	+7.70	+8.17	+8.24	+4.41	+4.37	+6.98
5	+4.28	+4.21	+5.63	+7.00	+7.20	+7.27	+6.75	+6.32	+6.39	+6.19	+3.42	+2.77	+5.63
6	+2.57	+2.50	+4.01	+5.02	+5.20	+5.24	+4.50	+4.12	+3.87	+3.71	+1.26	+1.24	+3.60
7	+0.83	+1.04	+2.07	+2.45	+2.68	+2.61	+1.87	+1.51	+1.08	+1.22	−0.32	−0.02	+1.42
8	−0.65	−0.27	+0.14	−0.05	+0.23	−0.16	−0.63	−0.97	−1.49	−0.97	−1.55	−0.95	−0.61
9	−1.71	−1.48	−1.37	−1.91	−1.80	−2.63	−2.63	−2.90	−3.35	−2.63	−2.30	−1.60	−2.21
10	−2.30	−2.09	−2.36	−2.97	−3.22	−4.55	−4.03	−4.14	−4.41	−3.74	−2.59	−2.03	−3.20
11	−2.54	−2.66	−2.95	−3.38	−4.16	−5.87	−5.04	−4.84	−4.91	−4.41	−2.05	−2.39	−3.76
Comb's													
10, 10	−0.45	−0.25	−0.07	−0.29	−0.16	+0.11	+0.18	−0.07	+0.11	−0.59	−0.52	−0.16	−0.18
6, 2, 9	+0.01	+0.13	−0.17	−0.37	+0.05	+0.10	+0.14	−0.01	−0.19	+0.28	+0.10	+0.31	+0.03
6, 2, 10	−0.18	−0.07	−0.50	−0.72	−0.42	−0.54	−0.33	−0.43	−0.55	−0.09	+0.01	+0.17	−0.30
7, 2, 9	+0.29	+0.39	+0.37	+0.30	+0.79	+1.00	+1.02	+0.78	+0.65	+0.75	+0.34	+0.52	+0.59
7, 2, 9 bis	−0.21	−0.08	−0.07	−0.25	+0.14	+0.09	+0.11	−0.14	−0.35	−0.09	−0.32	−0.01	−0.11
3, 9, 3, 9	These four hours appear to have been employed for the daily means, the results of the combination being zero.												

[1] From Prof. A. Guyot's Meteorological and Physical Tables, Smithsonian Misc. Coll.; Washington, 1858. Table by Dove.

Philadelphia, Girard College, Penn. Lat. 39° 58′. Long. 75° 10′ W. of G.

Alt. 114 feet. June, 1840, to June, 1845, inclusive.

Hour.	Jan.	Feb.	Mar.	Apr.	May.	June.	July.	Aug.	Sept.	Oct.	Nov.	Dec.	Year.
	°	°	°	°	°	°	°	°	°	°	°	°	°
Mdn't	−1.42	−2.69	−3.16	−3.96	−4.70	−5.28	−4.68	−4.34	−4.32	−3.54	−2.29	−1.49	−3.49
1	−1.97	−3.11	−3.81	−4.80	−5.32	−5.99	−5.42	−4.94	−4.58	−3.92	−2.43	−1.91	−4.01
2	−2.12	−3.51	−4.36	−5.60	−6.04	−6.56	−5.98	−5.42	−4.98	−4.50	−2.81	−2.27	−4.51
3	−2.40	−4.05	−4.66	−5.96	−6.72	−7.21	−6.48	−5.58	−5.44	−4.92	−3.09	−2.57	−4.92
4	−2.60	−4.34	−4.83	−6.38	−7.38	−7.68	−6.92	−6.14	−5.76	−5.40	−3.57	−2.85	−5.32
5	−2.82	−4.56	−5.63	−6.48	−7.26	−7.21	−6.70	−6.24	−5.98	−5.82	−3.85	−3.17	−5.48
6	−3.10	−4.84	−5.64	−6.02	−5.82	−5.78	−5.64	−5.66	−6.00	−6.16	−4.11	−3.41	−5.18
7	−3.22	−4.70	−4.99	−4.48	−3.70	−3.36	−3.34	−3.82	−4.14	−4.78	−3.79	−3.11	−3.95
8	−2.80	−3.16	−3.01	−2.44	−1.42	−0.96	−1.08	−1.54	−1.68	−2.32	−2.55	−2.61	−2.13
9	−1.52	−1.23	−1.01	−0.46	+0.78	+0.97	+0.88	+0.38	+0.46	+0.10	−0.65	−1.23	−0.21
10	0.00	+0.81	+0.84	+1.52	+2.36	+2.64	+2.50	+2.20	+2.54	+2.26	+1.07	+0.31	+1.59
11	+1.33	+2.54	+2.86	+3.30	+3.84	+4.14	+4.00	+3.84	+4.22	+3.92	+2.53	+1.83	+3.20
Noon	+2.56	+3.91	+4.34	+4.90	+5.00	+5.54	+5.22	+5.14	+5.56	+5.42	+3.73	+2.91	+4.52
1	+3.55	+5.05	+5.39	+6.14	+6.04	+6.56	+6.06	+5.92	+6.48	+6.48	+4.71	+3.65	+5.50
2	+4.21	+5.68	+6.14	+7.12	+6.94	+7.44	+6.80	+6.82	+7.30	+7.26	+5.39	+4.25	+6.28
3	+4.28	+5.95	+6.69	+7.38	+7.40	+7.73	+7.08	+7.06	+7.40	+7.18	+5.13	+4.03	+6.44
4	+4.05	+5.71	+6.59	+7.44	+7.60	+7.86	+7.02	+6.96	+7.32	+6.92	+4.65	+3.65	+6.32
5	+2.73	+4.57	+5.44	+6.58	+7.14	+6.96	+6.36	+5.92	+5.92	+5.06	+3.13	+2.43	+5.19
6	+1.91	+2.91	+3.57	+5.18	+5.58	+5.62	+5.02	+4.50	+3.72	+2.86	+1.79	+1.73	+3.70
7	+1.10	+1.72	+2.44	+2.54	+3.00	+3.12	+2.88	+2.42	+1.52	+1.20	+0.75	+0.99	+1.97
8	+0.43	+0.44	+1.39	+0.52	+0.36	+0.12	+0.30	−0.04	−0.72	−0.28	−0.09	+0.37	+0.23
9	−0.15	−0.31	−1.06	−0.86	−1.22	−1.53	−1.42	−1.42	−1.96	−1.30	−0.75	−0.03	−1.00
10	−0.74	−1.11	−1.41	−2.10	−2.58	−2.88	−2.70	−2.56	−3.16	−2.46	−1.25	−0.47	−1.95
11	−1.20	−1.68	−2.13	−3.16	−3.80	−4.18	−3.66	−3.38	−3.74	−3.22	−1.73	−0.93	−2.74
Comb's													
10, 10	−0.37	−0.15	−0.28	−0.29	−0.11	−0.12	−0.10	−0.18	−0.31	−0.10	−0.09	−0.08	−0.18
6, 2, 9	+0.32	+0.18	−0.19	+0.08	−0.03	+0.04	−0.09	−0.09	−0.22	−0.07	+0.18	+0.27	+0.03
6, 2, 10	+0.12	−0.09	−0.30	−0.33	−0.49	−0.41	−0.51	−0.47	−0.62	−0.45	+0.01	+0.12	−0.28
7, 2, 9	+0.28	+0.22	+0.03	+0.59	+0.67	+0.85	+0.68	+0.53	+0.40	+0.39	+0.28	+0.37	+0.44
7, 2, 9 bis	+0.17	+0.09	−0.24	+0.23	+0.20	+0.25	+0.15	+0.04	−0.19	−0.03	+0.02	+0.27	+0.08
3, 9, 3, 9	+0.05	+0.09	−0.01	+0.02	+0.06	−0.01	+0.01	+0.11	+0.11	+0.26	+0.16	+0.05	+0.08

Washington City, Capitol Hill, D. C. Lat. 38° 53′. Long. 77° 01′ W. of G.

Alt. 80 feet. Lieut. J. M. Gilliss, U. S. N. Jan. 1841, to June, 1842, inclusive.

Hour.	Jan.	Feb.	Mar.	Apr.	May.	June.	July.	Aug.	Sept.	Oct.	Nov.	Dec.	Year.
0.2 A.M.	−2.73	−2.83	−3.60	−4.40	−5.25	− 6.49	−6.62	−5.20	−5.37	−3.90	−1.93	−2.20	−4.21
2.2	−3.00	−4.19	−4.82	−5.39	−7.11	− 7.28	−7.31	−6.90	−6.17	−5.10	−3.03	−2.54	−5.24
4.2	−3.39	−4.90	−6.02	−6.19	−8.03	− 8.25	−8.62	−7.85	−7.07	−6.50	−4.33	−3.50	−6.22
6.2	−4.36	−5.23	−6.20	−5.82	−4.95	− 5.06	−4.76	−6.33	−6.78	−7.10	−4.93	−4.10	−5.47
8.2	−1.97	−3.97	−3.80	−2.38	−0.73	+ 0.31	−0.21	−0.63	−2.34	−3.80	−4.23	−3.82	−2.30
10.2	+0.28	+1.31	+1.98	+1.71	+2.78	+ 4.05	+2.98	+4.07	+2.95	+2.81	+0.37	+0.30	+2.13
0.2 P.M.	+3.18	+4.63	+5.31	+5.37	+5.93	+ 6.01	+5.73	+6.68	+6.59	+6.50	+4.27	+3.50	+5.31
2.2	+5.73	+7.10	+7.53	+7.67	+8.03	+ 8.61	+7.85	+8.71	+8.43	+8.20	+5.47	+5.60	+7.41
4.2	+5.08	+6.87	+7.20	+7.89	+8.24	+10.11	+9.36	+8.07	+8.23	+7.40	+4.77	+4.90	+7.34
6.2	+1.58	+2.81	+3.89	+4.91	+5.48	+ 3.57	+5.93	+3.91	+4.23	+4.14	+3.57	+2.25	+3.86
8.2	+0.38	−0.03	+0.12	−0.13	−0.62	− 1.03	−0.47	−0.54	+0.52	−0.40	+0.47	+0.56	−0.10
10.2	−0.85	−1.55	−1.71	−3.19	−3.75	− 4.62	−3.84	−4.02	−3.17	−2.20	−0.51	−1.00	−2.53

By means of interpolation we find the diurnal ordinates for the full hours of combination, as follows:—

Comb's	Jan.	Feb.	Mar.	Apr.	May.	June.	July.	Aug.	Sept.	Oct.	Nov.	Dec.	Year.
10, 10	−0.4	−0.3	−0.1	−0.8	−0.5	− 0.3	−0.4	0.0	−0.2	+0.1	−0.2	−0.5	−0.3
6, 2, 9	+0.4	+0.4	+0.2	+0.1	+0.3	+ 0.2	+0.3	0.0	+0.2	0.0	+0.2	+0.4	+0.2
6, 2, 10	+0.2	+0.1	−0.1	−0.4	−0.3	− 0.4	−0.3	−0.5	−0.5	−0.3	0.0	+0.2	−0.2
7, 2, 9	+0.7	+0.5	+0.6	+0.6	+1.0	+ 1.0	+1.0	+0.9	+0.8	+0.5	+0.3	+0.5	+0.7
7, 2, 9 bis	+0.5	+0.3	+0.3	+0.2	+0.3	+ 0.2	+0.3	+0.2	+0.4	+0.1	+0.3	+0.3	+0.3
3, 9, 3, 9	+0.2	0.0	0.0	0.0	−0.1	+ 0.2	0.0	+0.1	+0.1	0.0	−0.1	+0.1	0.0

Hour.	Jan.	Feb.	Mar.	Apr.	May.	June.	July.	Aug.	Sept.	Oct.	Nov.	Dec.	Year.
Washington City, U. S. Naval Observatory.[1] Lat. 38° 54′. Long. 77° 03′ W. of G. Alt. 110 feet. Jan. 1862, to Dec. 1869, inclusive.													
	°	°	°	°	°	°	°	°	°	°	°	°	°
Mdn't	−2.12	−2.72	−3.01	−4.00	−4.91	−4.94	−5.02	−4.99	−4.76	−4.03	−3.03	−1.73	−3.77
3	−3.22	−4.02	−4.46	−6.26	−7.17	−6.89	−6.73	−6.57	−6.36	−5.84	−4.62	−2.81	−5.41
6	−4.11	−4.89	−5.57	−7.09	−7.30	−6.99	−7.16	−7.49	−7.35	−7.03	−5.56	−3.66	−6.18
9	−2.21	−1.84	−1.23	−0.05	+0.66	+0.90	+0.69	+0.10	+1.53	−0.39	−1.56	−1.63	−0.42
Noon	+4.22	+4.55	+4.58	+5.75	+6.57	+6.74	+6.99	+7.31	+7.67	+7.87	+6.62	+4.21	+6.09
3	+5.76	+6.66	+6.79	+7.79	+8.80	+8.22	+8.41	+9.52	+9.41	+9.38	+7.56	+5.21	+7.79
6	+2.03	+2.73	+3.63	+4.55	+4.80	+4.69	+4.95	+3.98	+2.38	+2.09	+1.83	+1.32	+3.25
9	−0.38	−0.43	−0.70	−0.68	−1.47	−1.75	−2.13	−1.84	−2.56	−2.02	−1.22	−0.89	−1.34
Comb's 3, 9, 3, 9	−0.01	+0.09	+0.10	+0.20	+0.20	+0.12	+0.06	+0.30	+0.50	+0.28	+0.04	−0.03	+0.15
Fort Morgan, Mobile Point, Alabama. Lat. 30° 14′. Long. 88° 01′ W. of G. Alt. 20 feet. 1851 to Feb. 1853, inclusive, June, 1848 to 1850.													
Mdn't	−1.3	−1.0	−0.1	−2.4	−1.7	−1.8	−1.8	−2.2	−1.5	−0.9	−0.7	−0.9	−1.4
1	−1.4	−1.3	−1.4	−3.4	−2.1	−2.4	−2.2	−2.1	−1.7	−1.1	−1.0	−0.9	−1.8
2	−1.6	−1.6	−1.5	−3.1	−2.7	−2.6	−2.6	−2.3	−2.4	−1.7	−1.3	−1.2	−2.1
3	−1.8	−2.0	−1.9	−4.1	−3.2	−2.8	−2.8	−2.7	−2.8	−2.3	−1.7	−1.7	−2.5
4	−2.1	−2.3	−2.7	−3.1	−3.5	−2.6	−3.2	−2.8	−3.4	−3.0	−2.2	−2.1	−2.8
5	−2.4	−2.8	−3.1	−3.3	−3.7	−2.9	−3.3	−3.0	−3.8	−3.4	−2.6	−2.4	−3.1
6	−2.6	−3.2	−3.6	−3.4	−3.6	−2.6	−2.8	−2.6	−4.1	−3.6	−3.2	−2.6	−3.2
7	−3.1	−3.6	−3.3	−2.1	−2.6	−1.5	−1.8	−2.0	−3.4	−3.1	−3.4	−2.9	−2.7
8	−1.9	−2.5	−2.2	−1.1	−1.5	−0.2	−0.9	−0.8	−2.1	−2.6	−2.6	−2.2	−1.7
9	−0.8	−0.7	−0.8	+0.1	−0.3	+0.9	+0.2	+0.3	−0.7	−1.3	−1.7	−1.4	−0.5
10	+0.5	+0.3	+0.2	+1.4	+0.7	+2.0	+1.3	+1.7	+0.8	0.0	−0.6	−0.1	+0.7
11	+1.6	+1.5	+1.3	+2.5	+1.5	+2.5	+2.8	+2.8	+2.0	+1.0	+0.5	+0.9	+1.7
Noon	+2.3	+2.5	+2.3	+3.6	+2.4	+2.9	+3.2	+3.5	+2.8	+2.1	+1.6	+1.5	+2.6
1	+2.8	+3.2	+2.7	+4.1	+3.5	+3.2	+4.0	+4.2	+3.6	+2.9	+2.5	+2.3	+3.3
2	+3.1	+3.7	+3.1	+4.3	+4.1	+3.4	+4.3	+4.1	+4.0	+3.7	+3.4	+3.0	+3.7
3	+3.1	+3.5	+3.4	+4.3	+4.3	+3.3	+3.6	+3.4	+4.4	+3.9	+3.8	+3.3	+3.7
4	+2.8	+3.0	+3.3	+4.2	+3.9	+2.9	+3.0	+3.1	+4.0	+3.7	+3.5	+2.8	+3.3
5	+1.7	+2.4	+2.7	+2.8	+2.7	+1.9	+1.9	+2.2	+3.3	+2.7	+2.5	+1.9	+2.4
6	+1.1	+1.4	+1.4	+1.5	+1.6	+1.1	+1.0	+1.1	+1.8	+1.4	+1.5	+1.2	+1.3
7	+0.7	+0.6	+0.6	+0.5	+0.7	0.0	0.0	−0.2	+0.8	+0.8	+1.1	+0.8	+0.5
8	+0.2	+0.3	+0.3	+0.1	+0.3	−0.6	−0.6	−1.0	+0.2	+0.6	+0.6	+0.5	+0.1
9	+0.1	−0.2	0.0	−0.3	0.0	−0.9	−0.9	−1.5	0.0	+0.3	+0.2	+0.2	−0.2
10	−0.3	−0.4	−0.3	−0.8	−0.6	−1.5	−1.1	−1.7	−0.7	+0.1	−0.1	+0.1	−0.6
11	−1.0	−0.7	−0.7	−2.6	−1.1	−1.6	−1.4	−2.0	−1.1	−0.3	−0.4	−0.3	−1.1
Comb's													
10, 10	+0.1	0.0	0.0	+0.3	0.0	+0.2	+0.1	0.0	0.0	0.0	−0.3	0.0	0.0
6, 2, 9	+0.2	+0.1	−0.2	+0.2	+0.2	0.0	+0.2	0.0	0.0	+0.1	+0.1	+0.2	+0.1
6, 2, 10	+0.1	0.0	−0.3	0.0	0.0	−0.2	+0.1	−0.1	−0.3	+0.1	0.0	+0.2	0.0
7, 2, 9	0.0	0.0	−0.1	+0.6	+0.5	+0.3	+0.5	+0.2	+0.2	+0.3	+0.1	+0.1	+0.3
7, 2, 9 bis	0.0	−0.1	0.0	+0.4	+0.4	0.0	+0.2	−0.2	+0.1	+0.3	+0.1	+0.1	+0.1
3, 9, 3, 9	+0.1	+0.1	+0.2	0.0	+0.2	+0.1	0.0	−0.1	+0.2	+0.1	+0.1	+0.1	+0.1

[1] The differences in this table depend on the assumption that the mean of 8 equidistant observations represents the daily mean, which is only an approximation to the truth.

Galveston, Texas. Lat. 29° 18′. Long. 94° 47′ W. of G.

Alt. 20 feet. June, 1851, to Feb. 1853, inclusive.

Hour.	Jan.	Feb.	Mar.	April.	May.	June.	July.	Aug.	Sept.	Oct.	Nov.	Dec.	Year.
	°	°	°	°	°	°	°	°	°	°	°	°	°
Mdn't	−1.0	−1.3	−2.6	..	..	..	..	..	−2.4	−2.6	−1.8	−0.7	..
1	−1.3	−1.9	−3.0	..	..	..	..	..	−2.2	−3.0	−1.1	−0.6	..
2	−1.5	−2.0	−3.4	..	..	..	..	..	−2.2	−3.4	−1.6	−1.1	..
3	−1.7	−2.2	−3.7	..	..	..	..	..	−2.6	−3.8	−2.0	−1.3	..
4	−2.1	−4.5	−4.1	..	..	..	..	..	−3.1	−4.2	−2.4	−1.7	..
5	−2.5	−2.6	−4.3	..	..	−5.1	..	..	−3.2	−4.0	−2.7	−2.2	..
6	−2.6	−2.3	−3.9	..	..	−3.7	..	..	−3.2	−2.3	−2.6	−2.5	..
7	−2.5	−2.3	−2.8	..	..	−1.1	..	..	−1.2	+1.1	−1.6	−2.6	..
8	−1.5	−0.8	+0.1	..	..	+0.5	..	..	+1.3	+3.2	+1.5	−1.8	..
9	−0.6	+1.3	+3.2	..	..	+1.6	..	..	+3.0	+4.2	+2.9	+0.5	..
10	+2.0	+2.7	+5.2	..	..	+1.0	..	..	+3.9	+4.2	+3.5	+1.8	..
11	+2.6	+3.5	+5.7	..	..	+2.5	..	..	+3.8	+3.9	+2.7	+1.8	..
Noon	+2.6	+3.3	+4.9	..	..	+2.2	..	..	+3.3	+3.9	+2.1	+1.9	..
1	+2.6	+3.2	+3.9	..	..	+2.5	..	..	+3.2	+3.8	+1.9	+2.0	..
2	+2.4	+3.0	+3.8	..	..	+3.0	..	..	+2.7	+3.3	+1.9	+2.0	..
3	+2.3	+2.6	+3.0	..	..	+4.0	..	..	+2.3	+2.6	+1.8	+2.0	..
4	+2.3	+2.2	+2.6	..	..	+5.2	..	..	+1.9	+1.4	+1.6	+1.7	..
5	+1.6	+1.2	+1.6	..	..	+3.5	..	..	+1.1	+0.6	+0.9	+1.2	..
6	+0.9	+0.6	+0.4	..	..	+0.2	..	..	+0.5	−0.4	+0.4	+0.8	..
7	+0.4	+0.2	−0.5	..	..	−1.7	..	..	−0.5	−0.9	−0.3	+0.4	..
8	0.0	−0.3	−1.1	..	..	..	..	..	−1.3	−1.3	−0.9	0.0	..
9	−0.5	−0.7	−1.6	..	..	..	..	..	−1.6	−1.9	−1.2	−0.2	..
10	−0.6	−0.9	−2.1	..	..	..	..	..	−1.8	−2.1	−1.6	−0.6	..
11	−0.8	−1.1	−2.2	..	..	..	..	..	−2.2	−2.2	−1.7	−0.7	..
Comb's													
7, 2, 9	−0.2	0.0	−0.2	..	..	..	..	..	0.0	+0.8	−0.3	−0.3	..
7, 2, 9 bis	−0.3	−0.2	−0.5	..	..	..	..	..	−0.4	+0.1	−0.5	−0.2	..
3, 9, 3, 9	−0.1	+0.2	+0.2	..	..	..	..	..	+0.3	+0.3	+0.4	+0.2	..

Key West, Florida. Lat. 24° 33′. Long. 81° 48′ W. of G.

Alt. 20 feet. June, July, Aug. Oct. Dec. 1851, Jan. to May, inclusive, 1852.

Hour.	Jan.	Feb.	Mar.	April.	May.	June.	July.	Aug.	Sept.	Oct.	Nov.	Dec.	Year.
Mdn't	−1.60	−1.54	−2.03	−1.95	−2.46	−1.84	−2.22	−1.45	[1] −1.36	−1.27	[1] −0.73	−0.19	−1.55
1	−1.58	−2.09	−2.07	−2.23	−2.80	−1.86	−2.07	−1.64	−1.60	−1.56	−0.84	−0.12	−1.70
2	−1.65	−2.06	−2.03	−2.24	−2.75	−2.19	−2.32	−1.90	−1.70	−1.51	−0.80	−0.08	−1.77
3	−1.76	−2.44	−2.20	−2.31	−2.91	−2.28	−2.51	−2.15	−1.83	−1.51	−0.89	−0.27	−1.92
4	−1.92	−2.56	−2.35	−2.32	−3.09	−2.54	−2.80	−2.28	−1.93	−1.59	−1.02	−0.45	−2.07
5	−2.36	−3.06	−2.78	−2.71	−3.65	−2.61	−3.09	−2.64	−2.27	−1.91	−1.44	−0.96	−2.46
6	−2.37	−3.08	−2.90	−2.64	−3.28	−2.31	−2.90	−2.51	−2.23	−1.96	−1.78	−1.61	−2.47
7	−2.44	−3.01	−2.24	−1.66	−1.07	−1.36	−1.33	−1.57	−1.48	−1.40	−1.59	−1.78	−1.74
8	−1.90	−1.85	−0.56	−0.14	+1.01	−0.16	+0.34	+0.01	−0.11	−0.22	−0.76	−1.30	−0.47
9	−0.26	−0.01	+1.02	+0.95	+2.28	+1.14	+1.38	+0.78	+0.72	+0.67	+0.18	−0.32	+0.71
10	+0.82	+1.34	+2.09	+1.66	+2.77	+2.17	+2.14	+1.40	+1.35	+1.30	+0.81	+0.33	+1.51
11	+1.71	+2.16	+2.67	+1.94	+3.02	+2.27	+2.44	+1.82	+1.75	+1.68	+1.28	+0.89	+1.97

[1] Interpolated values, the mean of Aug. and Oct. for Sept. and the mean of Oct. and Dec. for Nov.

Key West.—Continued.

Hour.	Jan.	Feb.	Mar.	Apr.	May.	June.	July.	Aug.	Sept.	Oct.	Nov.	Dec.	Year.
	°	°	°	°	°	°	°	°	°	°	°	°	°
Noon	+2.16	+2.66	+2.88	+2.16	+2.91	+2.62	+2.67	+1.85	+1.82	+1.80	+1.49	+1.17	+2.18
1	+2.79	+2.75	+3.12	+2.67	+3.02	+2.82	+3.23	+2.36	+2.27	+2.18	+1.67	+1.15	+2.50
2	+2.97	+2.87	+3.30	+2.88	+3.12	+2.64	+3.06	+2.43	+2.32	+2.22	+1.75	+1.28	+2.57
3	+3.24	+3.30	+3.20	+2.94	+2.94	+2.76	+3.02	+2.40	+2.27	+2.14	+1.79	+1.44	+2.62
4	+3.31	+3.66	+3.06	+2.66	+2.83	+2.74	+2.61	+2.30	+2.15	+1.99	+1.73	+1.46	+2.54
5	+2.79	+3.32	+2.44	+2.55	+2.44	+2.29	+2.56	+2.04	+1.76	+1.49	+1.23	+0.96	+2.16
6	+1.34	+1.96	+1.23	+2.22	+2.28	+1.57	+1.34	+1.43	+0.95	+0.47	+0.25	+0.04	+1.26
7	+0.14	+0.58	—0.30	+0.30	—0.07	+0.14	+0.06	+0.43	+0.15	—0.14	—0.32	—0.49	+0.04
8	—0.34	—0.15	—0.98	—0.65	—0.91	—0.90	—0.62	—0.15	—0.24	—0.33	—0.43	—0.53	—0.52
9	—0.58	—0.49	—1.11	—0.95	—1.33	—1.44	—1.09	—0.60	—0.57	—0.53	—0.43	—0.33	—0.79
10	—0.98	—0.90	—1.57	—1.41	—1.83	—1.78	—1.71	—1.02	—0.92	—0.83	—0.48	—0.14	—1.13
11	—1.39	—1.25	—1.86	—1.70	—2.28	—1.78	—2.06	—1.18	—1.11	—1.04	—0.56	—0.09	—1.36
Comb's													
10, 10	—0.08	+0.22	+0.26	+0.12	+0.47	+0.19	+0.21	+0.19	+0.21	+0.23	+0.16	+0.09	+0.19
6, 2, 9	+0.01	—0.23	—0.24	—0.24	—0.50	—0.37	—0.31	—0.23	—0.16	—0.09	—0.15	—0.22	—0.23
6, 2, 10	—0.13	—0.37	—0.39	—0.39	—0.66	—0.48	—0.52	—0.37	—0.28	—0.19	—0.17	—0.16	—0.34
7, 2, 9	—0.02	—0.21	—0.02	+0.09	+0.24	—0.05	+0.21	+0.09	+0.09	+0.10	—0.09	—0.28	+0.01
7, 2, 9 bis	—0.16	—0.28	—0.29	—0.17	—0.15	—0.40	—0.11	—0.08	—0.07	—0.06	—0.17	—0.29	—0.19
3, 9, 3, 9	+0.16	+0.09	+0.23	+0.16	+0.24	+0.04	+0.20	+0.11	+0.15	+0.19	+0.16	+0.13	+0.15

Rio Janeiro, Brazil, S. Am.[1] Lat. —22° 54′. Long. 43° 09′ W. of G.

Fort Villegagnon (Con. des Temps, 1870).

Hour.	Jan.	Feb.	Mar.	Apr.	May.	June.	July.	Aug.	Sept.	Oct.	Nov.	Dec.	Year.
Mdn't	0.00	—0.59	—1.06	—0.23	—0.14	+0.29	—0.92	—0.61	—0.38	—0.32	—1.15	—0.65	—0.47
1	—0.74	—1.51	—1.80	—0.90	—1.13	—0.56	—1.85	—1.31	—1.04	—0.97	—1.76	—1.31	—1.24
2	—1.64	—2.41	—2.48	—1.64	—2.12	—1.53	—2.75	—2.00	—1.69	—1.64	—2.32	—2.05	—2.03
3	—2.50	—3.11	—3.02	—2.32	—2.93	—2.43	—3.47	—2.66	—2.27	—2.21	—2.75	—2.66	—2.70
4	—3.08	—3.90	—3.24	—2.79	—3.38	—3.04	—3.87	—3.04	—2.59	—2.50	—2.93	—2.99	—3.06
5	—3.22	—3.29	—3.15	—2.90	—3.40	—3.29	—3.83	—3.08	—2.66	—2.52	—2.79	—2.99	—3.08
6	—2.93	—2.84	—2.75	—2.75	—3.06	—3.20	—3.47	—2.79	—2.41	—2.27	—2.32	—2.68	—2.79
7	—2.30	—2.21	—2.14	—2.30	—2.48	—2.84	—2.70	—2.25	—2.00	—1.82	—1.67	—2.12	—2.23
8	—1.49	—1.49	—1.40	—1.71	—1.85	—2.39	—1.96	—1.60	—1.46	—1.28	—0.90	—1.40	—1.58
9	—0.68	—0.72	—0.59	—1.04	—1.15	—1.82	—1.15	—0.90	—0.86	—0.68	—0.14	—0.59	—0.86
10	+0.07	+0.05	+0.23	—0.32	—0.50	—1.13	—0.32	—0.23	—0.18	—0.05	+0.56	+0.23	—0.14
11	+0.77	+0.86	+1.01	+0.45	+0.23	—0.32	+0.50	+0.50	+0.54	+0.59	+1.22	+1.04	+0.61
Noon	+1.40	+1.64	+1.71	+1.22	+0.99	+0.65	+1.31	+1.19	+1.26	+1.22	+1.80	+1.82	+1.35
1	+2.00	+2.30	+2.30	+1.94	+1.71	+1.67	+2.16	+1.91	+1.89	+1.78	+2.32	+2.43	+2.03
2	+2.41	+2.75	+2.66	+2.41	+2.30	+2.48	+2.88	+2.48	+2.34	+2.16	+2.66	+2.81	+2.52
3	+2.59	+2.88	+2.84	+2.66	+2.66	+2.99	+3.40	+2.84	+2.50	+2.27	+2.79	+2.86	+2.77
4	+2.45	+2.70	+2.77	+2.57	+2.75	+3.04	+3.60	+2.93	+2.36	+2.12	+2.66	+2.59	+2.70
5	+2.05	+2.30	+2.50	+2.21	+2.54	+2.75	+3.47	+2.68	+2.00	+1.78	+2.25	+2.09	+2.39
6	+1.51	+1.82	+2.12	+1.76	+2.21	+2.23	+3.04	+2.23	+1.55	+1.37	+1.67	+1.49	+1.91
7	+1.04	+1.40	+1.67	+1.28	+1.89	+1.76	+2.39	+1.67	+1.13	+1.04	+1.08	+0.99	+1.44
8	+0.72	+1.13	+1.22	+0.95	+1.67	+1.42	+1.85	+1.13	+0.83	+0.77	+0.59	+0.61	+1.08
9	+0.59	+0.92	+0.77	+0.72	+1.44	+1.26	+1.22	+0.70	+0.61	+0.61	+0.14	+0.38	+0.79
10	+0.56	+0.63	+0.25	+0.52	+1.13	+1.13	+0.59	+0.32	+0.41	+0.45	—0.23	+0.16	+0.50
11	+0.41	+0.14	—0.36	+0.25	+0.63	+0.86	—0.09	—0.09	+0.09	+0.16	—0.65	—0.14	—0.09
Comb's													
10, 10	+0.31	+0.34	+0.24	+0.10	+0.31	0.00	+0.13	+0.04	+0.11	+0.20	+0.16	+0.14	+0.18
6, 2, 9	+0.02	+0.28	+0.23	+0.13	+0.23	+0.18	+0.21	+0.13	+0.18	+0.17	+0.16	+0.17	+0.17
6, 2, 10	+0.01	+0.18	+0.05	+0.06	+0.12	+0.14	0.00	0.00	+0.11	+0.11	+0.04	+0.10	+0.08
7, 2, 9	+0.23	+0.49	+0.43	+0.28	+0.42	+0.30	+0.47	+0.31	+0.32	+0.32	+0.38	+0.36	+0.36
7, 2, 9 bis	+0.32	+0.59	+0.51	+0.39	+0.67	+0.54	+0.65	+0.41	+0.39	+0.39	+0.32	+0.36	+0.47
3, 9, 3, 9	These four hours appear to have been employed for the daily means, the result of the combination being zero.												

[1] From Prof. Guyot's Meteorological and Physical Tables, Smithsonian Misc. Coll.; Washington, 1858. Table by Dove.

For systematic comparison of the law of the diurnal fluctuation we present the resulting hourly numbers, on the yearly average as contained in the table of differences, in an analytical form, making use of Bessel's periodic function—[1]

$$t = A + B_1 \sin(\theta + C_1) + B_2 \sin(2\,\theta + C_2) + B_3 \sin(3\,\theta + C_3) + \text{etc.}$$

---

[1] See Bessel's paper in the Astronomische Nachrichten, No. 136 (May, 1828). His first publication on the subject is contained in the Literary Gazette of Jena, in 1814.

See also a memoir by M. A. Bravais in "Voyages en Scandinavie, en Laponie, au Spitzberg et aux Feroe, pendant les années 1838, 1839, et 1840, Météorologie." An extract is given by M. J. Haeghens in the "Annuaire Météorologique de la France pour 1850, p. 93.

See also Sir J. Herschel's Article, "Meteorology" in the Encyclopædia Britannica. Reprint, p. 144.

The general formulæ given in this article, when applied to the case of 24 equidistant observations in a cycle, change into the following expressions, which were employed for the numerical computations:

$$A = \tfrac{1}{24}(y_1 + y_2 + y_3 + \ldots\ldots + y_{24})$$

$$12\,a_1 = 0.966\,(y_1 - y_{11} - y_{13} + y_{23}) + 0.866\,(y_2 - y_{10} - y_{14} + y_{22}) + 0.707\,(y_3 - y_9 - y_{15} + y_{21})$$
$$+ 0.500\,(y_4 - y_8 - y_{16} + y_{20}) + 0.259\,(y_5 - y_7 - y_{17} + y_{19}) - y_{12} + y_{24}$$
$$12\,b_1 = 0.259\,(y_1 + y_{11} - y_{13} - y_{23}) + 0.500\,(y_2 + y_{10} - y_{14} - y_{22}) + 0.707\,(y_3 + y_9 - y_{15} - y_{21})$$
$$+ 0.866\,(y_4 + y_8 - y_{16} - y_{20}) + 0.966\,(y_5 + y_7 - y_{17} - y_{19}) + y_6 - y_{18}$$

$$B_1 = \sqrt{a_1^2 + b_1^2} \quad \text{and} \quad \tan C_1 = \frac{a_1}{b_1}$$

$$12\,a_2 = 0.866\,(y_1 - y_5 - y_7 + y_{11} + y_{13} - y_{17} - y_{19} + y_{23}) + 0.500\,(y_2 - y_4 - y_8 + y_{10} + y_{14} - y_{16} - y_{20} + y_{22})$$
$$- y_6 + y_{12} - y_{18} + y_{24}$$
$$12\,b_2 = 0.500(y_1 + y_5 - y_7 - y_{11} + y_{13} + y_{17} - y_{19} - y_{23}) + 0.866\,(y_2 + y_4 - y_8 - y_{10} + y_{14} + y_{16} - y_{20} - y_{22})$$
$$+ y_3 - y_9 + y_{15} - y_{21}$$

$$12\,a_3 = 0.707\,(y_1 - y_3 - y_5 + y_7 + y_9 - y_{11} - y_{13} + y_{15} + y_{17} - y_{19} - y_{21} + y_{23})$$
$$- y_4 + y_8 - y_{12} + y_{16} - y_{20} + y_{24}$$
$$12\,b_3 = 0.707\,(y_1 + y_3 - y_5 - y_7 + y_9 + y_{11} - y_{13} - y_{15} + y_{17} + y_{19} - y_{21} - y_{23})$$
$$+ y_2 - y_6 + y_{10} - y_{14} + y_{18} - y_{22}$$

$$12\,a_4 = 0.500\,(y_1 - y_2 - y_4 + y_5 + y_7 - y_8 - y_{10} + y_{11} + y_{13} - y_{14} - y_{16} + y_{17} + y_{19} - y_{20} - y_{22} + y_{23})$$
$$- y_3 + y_6 - y_9 + y_{12} - y_{15} + y_{18} - y_{21} + y_{24}$$
$$12\,b_4 = 0.866\,(y_1 + y_2 - y_4 - y_5 + y_7 + y_0 - y_{10} - y_{11} + y_{13} + y_{14} - y_{16} - y_{17} + y_{19} + y_{20} - y_{22} - y_{23})$$

etc.

The values $B_2\ B_3\ B_4$ . . and $C_2\ C_3\ C_4$ . . are found in a similar manner as B_1 and C_1.

For 12 equidistant observations in a cycle, as in our bi-hourly series, we use the formulæ:

$$A = \tfrac{1}{12}(y_1 + y_2 + y_3 + \ldots + y_{12})$$

$$6\,a_1 = 0.866\,(y_1 - y_5 - y_7 + y_{11}) + 0.500\,(y_2 - y_4 - y_8 + y_{10}) - y_6 + y_{12}$$
$$6\,b_1 = 0.500\,(y_1 + y_5 - y_7 - y_{11}) + 0.866\,(y_2 + y_4 - y_8 - y_{10}) + y_3 - y_9$$

$$6\,a_2 = 0.500\,(y_1 - y_2 - y_4 + y_5 + y_7 - y_8 - y_{10} + y_{11}) - y_3 + y_6 - y_9 + y_{12}$$
$$6\,b_2 = 0.866\,(y_1 + y_2 - y_4 - y_5 + y_7 + y_8 - y_{10} - y_{11})$$

$$6\,a_3 = -y_2 + y_4 - y_6 + y_8 - y_{10} + y_{12}$$
$$6\,b_3 = y_1 - y_3 + y_5 - y_7 + y_9 - y_{11}$$

$$6\,a_4 = 0.500\,(-y_1 - y_2 - y_4 - y_5 - y_7 - y_8 - y_{10} - y_{11}) + y_3 + y_6 + y_9 + y_{12}$$
$$6\,b_4 = 0.866\,(y_1 - y_2 + y_4 - y_5 + y_7 - y_8 + y_{10} - y_{11})$$

etc.

The values $B_1\ B_2\ B_3\ B_4$ . . and $C_1\ C_2\ C_3\ C_4$ . . are found as stated.

The above expressions, together with others, are given in Coast Survey Report of 1862, Appendix, No. 22 (with erratum in 1866 report).

We retain three periodic terms as generally sufficient for our purpose. The angle θ counts from midnight at the rate of 15° an hour; at those stations where the observations were not made at the full hours, the angles C_1, C_2, C_3 were changed in the expression for t in order to refer them to the same epoch. The table also contains the latitude (ϕ), the longitude (λ), the elevation (h) of the station, and the number of years (n) of observation. The column headed T contains the annual mean temperature or the mean of the twelve monthly averages.

Numerical quantities in Bessel's function for the DAILY *fluctuation of temperature, on the yearly average.*

	STATION.	ϕ	λ	h feet	n	T	B_1	C_1	B_2	C_2	B_3	C_3
1	Van Rensselaer Harbor . .	78°37′	70°53′	6	1	− 2°.47	1.86	243°19′	0.18	158°.6	0.03	301°
2	Port Foulke	78 18	73 00	6	1	+ 5.86	1.57	235 08	0.02	195.3	0.11	148
3	Port Kennedy	72 01	94 14	4	1	+ 1.89	1.98	254 04	0.19	81.0	0.15	264
4	Boothia Felix.	69 59	92 01	4	..	+ 3.68	2.82	247 24	0.40	58.5	0.09	194
5	Sitka	57 03	135 20	20	13	43.03	3.46	239 59	0.66	66.6	0.09	330
6	Montreal	45 31	73 34	57	2	44.73	5.19	221 54	0.94	42.8	0.12	104
7	Thunder Bay Island . . .	45 02	83 17	610	2	42.83	4.06	233 19	0.67	66.4	0.17	101
8	Toronto	43 39	79 23	342	6	44.18	5.61	232 04	0.84	59.2	0.48	41
9	Mohawk	43 00	75 02	435	6	44.84	5.63	216 20	1.19	33.7	0.24	357
10	Cambridge	42 23	71 07	71	1	47.37	6.57	236 07	1.52	62.1	0.26	5
11	Amherst	42 22	72 34	267	1	47.23	6.84	230 16	1.49	65.7	0.08	317
12	New Haven	41 18	72 57	45	..	49.01	6.75	231 50	1.39	65.8	0.29	22
13	Brooklyn	40 41	73 58	125	1	51.00	4.94	231 30	1.01	67.1	0.10	243
14	Frankford Arsenal	40 00	75 04	24	1	52.66	6.96	232 54	1.14	51.1	0.51	53
15	Philadelphia	39 58	75 10	114	5	51.35	5.77	224 50	0.93	40.9	0.34	34
16	Jackson	39 02	82 32	700	1	50.90	9.28	237 41	2.24	57.4	0.68	39
17	Washington, D. C.	38 53	77 03	110	9½	53.52	6.72	227 21	1.61	49.6	0.21	13
18	Fort Morgan	30 14	88 01	20	1	70.24	3.06	222 16	0.90	54.9	0.07	95
19	Key West	24 33	81 48	20	1	76.63	2.48	234 58	0.55	60.4	0.35	26
20	Rio Janeiro	—22 54	43 09	..	..	73.75	2.68	205 20	0.42	83.6	0.22	110

A better insight into the systematic character of the co-efficients and epochal angles, as far as they depend upon the latitude and local conditions, can be had by a combination of the results into groups. The hourly values for the stations forming a group were combined into mean values, and then submitted to the numerical process, which produced the following results:—

Types of the daily fluctuation of the temperature on the yearly average.

Group I. The four Arctic stations. $\phi_m = 74°.7$ $\lambda_m = 82°.5$. 4 years.

$$t = + 2°.23 + 2°.11 \sin(\theta + 243°.6) + 0°.14 \sin(2\theta + 66°.3) + 0.04 \sin(3\theta + 216°).$$

Group II. The Alaska station. $\phi = 57°.1$ $\lambda = 135°.3$. 13 years.

$$t = + 43°.03 + 3°.46 \sin(\theta + 240°.0) + 0°.66 \sin(2\theta + 66°.6) + 0.09 \sin(3\theta + 330°).$$

Group III. Four stations in Canada and Northern New York. $\phi_m = 44°.3$ $\lambda_m = 77°.8$. 16 years.

$$t = + 44°.14 + 5°.08 \sin(\theta + 225°.5) + 0°.89 \sin(2\theta + 48°.2) + 0.21 \sin(3\theta + 50°).$$

Group IV. Four stations in Mass., Conn., and N. Y. $\phi_m = 41°.7$ $\lambda_m = 72°.6$. More than 4 years.

$$t = +48°.65 + 6°.27 \sin(\theta + 232°.7) + 1°.38 \sin(2\theta + 61°.1) + 0.10 \sin(3\theta + 359°).$$

Group V. Three stations in Penn. and Dist. of Col. $\phi_m = 39°.6$ $\lambda_m = 75°.8$. 15 years.

$$t = +53°.38 + 6°.55 \sin(\theta + 228°.7) + 1°.27 \sin(2\theta + 48°.1) + 0.35 \sin(3\theta + 36°).$$

Group VI. Two Gulf stations. $\phi_m = 27°.4$ $\lambda_m = 84°.9$. 2 years.

$$t = +73°.44 + 2°.75 \sin(\theta + 227°.8) + 0°.70 \sin(2\theta + 57°.5) + 0.17 \sin(3\theta + 31°).$$

The hourly means from which these expressions were derived are contained in the following table:—

Observed Daily fluctuation of temperature, on the yearly average, for groups of stations.

HOUR.	I.	II.	III.	IV.	V.	VI.	HOUR.	I.	II.	III.	IV.	V.	VI.
	Van Rensselaer Har. Port Foulke. Port Kennedy. Boothia Felix.	Sitka.	Montreal. Thunder Bay Island. Toronto. Mohawk.	Cambridge. Amherst. New Haven. Brooklyn.	Frankford Arsenal. Philadelphia. Washington.	Fort Morgan. Key West.		Van Rensselaer Har. Port Foulke. Port Kennedy. Boothia Felix.	Sitka.	Montreal. Thunder Bay Island. Toronto. Mohawk.	Cambridge. Amherst. New Haven. Brooklyn.	Frankford Arsenal. Philadelphia. Washington.	Fort Morgan. Key West.
	°	°	°	°	°	°		°		°	°	°	°
Midn't	—1.8	—2.4	—2.9	—3.9	—3.8	—1.5	Noon	+2.0	+3.7	+4.2	+6.1	+5.6	+2.4
1	—1.9	—2.7	—3.4	—4.4	—4.4	—1.8	1	+2.2	+4.0	+5.0	+7.0	+6.7	+2.9
2	—2.0	—2.9	—4.0	—5.0	—4.9	—2.0	2	+2.3	+3.9	+5.6	+7.3	+7.4	+3.1
3	—1.8	—2.9	—4.4	—5.4	—5.5	—2.2	3	+2.0	+3.5	+5.7	+6.9	+7.4	+3.1
4	—1.6	—3.0	—4.8	—5.7	—6.0	—2.4	4	+1.6	+2.9	+5.3	+5.8	+6.8	+2.9
5	—1.4	—2.9	—4.9	—5.8	—6.2	—2.8	5	+1.2	+2.1	+4.3	+4.3	+5.4	+2.3
6	—1.0	—2.4	—4.4	—5.3	—5.7	—2.8	6	+0.7	+1.2	+3.1	+2.5	+3.5	+1.3
7	—0.5	—1.7	—3.1	—4.0	4.3	—2.2	7	+0.2	+0.3	+1.5	+0.9	+1.7	+0.3
8	+0.1	—0.6	—1.9	—2.0	—2.2	—1.1	8	—0.3	—0.5	+0.2	—0.4	—0.2	—0.2
9	+0.7	+0.7	—0.4	+0.4	0.0	+0.1	9	—0.7	—1.2	—0.8	—1.5	—1.5	—0.5
10	+1.2	+1.8	+1.4	+2.5	+2.2	+1.1	10	—1.1	—1.7	—1.6	—2.4	—2.5	—0.8
11	+1.6	+2.9	+2.8	+4.7	+4.1	+1.8	11	—1.5	—2.1	—2.2	—3.2	—3.3	—1.2

At several stations, interpolation, graphical or analytical, was required to complete the hourly values before they could be combined into groups. Frankford Arsenal and Philadelphia values were united into a mean and then combined with the Washington values.

By means of the equations we readily find the following times of greatest, least, and average heat of the day and of the daily range, on the yearly average.

	Max. at P. M.	Min. at A. M.	Mean at A. M.	Mean at P. M.	Range.
Group I . . .	1h 31m	1h 56m	8h 0m	7h 32m	4°.3
II . . .	1 20	3 43	8 28	7 24	7.2
III . . .	2 38	4 31	9 12	8 11	10.6
IV . . .	1 46	4 24	8 53	7 42	13.1
V . . .	2 28	4 28	9 01	7 54	13.6
VI . . .	2 12	4 54	9 04	7 49	5.9
Mean III, IV, V	2 17	4 28	9 02	7 56	12.4

The results of the daily fluctuation, as given above, may be summed up as follows:—

The daily range diminishes from about latitude 40° in either direction north or south. The precise latitude of maximum range cannot yet be given. Diagram A shows the extremely small ranges in latitude 75° and in latitude 27°, the former produced by the small range in the sun's altitude during the Arctic day, the latter by the equalizing effect of the aqueous vapor near the Gulf coast notwithstanding the sun's great daily range in altitude near the tropic of cancer. Diagram B shows the large daily range for the stations comprising groups IV and V, and the somewhat smaller one for group III.

DIAGRAM A.

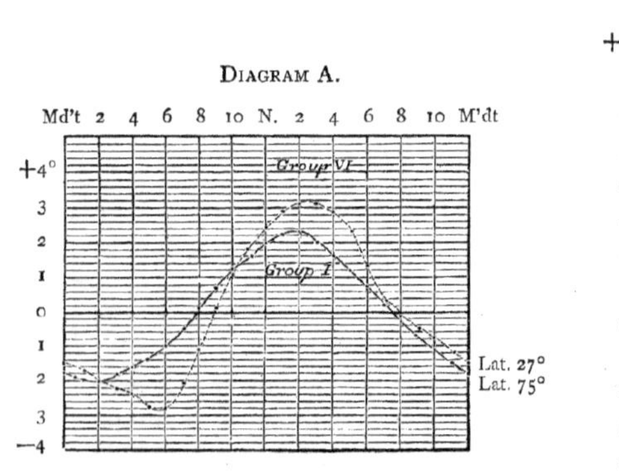

DIAGRAM B.

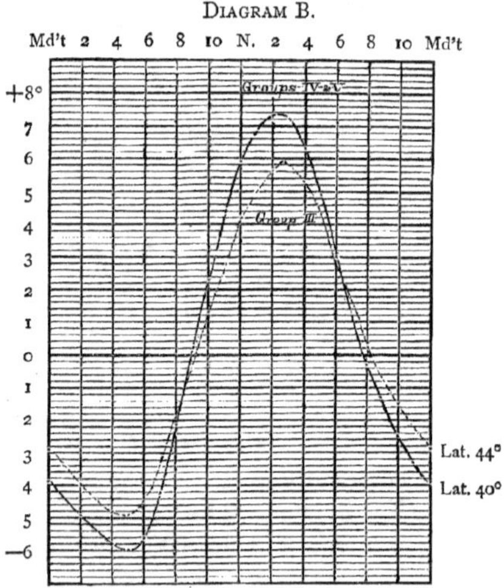

The greatest heat of the day is reached earlier in the high than in the low latitudes; with the mean annual temperature near or below the freezing point, the warmest time of the day is about 1½ P. M., in the middle and lower latitudes this epoch changes to 2¼ P. M. The greatest depression in the daily fluctuation occurs in the Arctic regions about two hours after midnight, in the temperate zone about

4½ A. M. or about one hour and a half *before* sunrise. The epochs of mean daily temperature are subject to less variations with respect to latitude than the epochs of the daily extremes. In the Arctic regions the mean temperature of the day is reached about 8 A. M., in the temperate regions about 9 A. M., and again about 7½ P. M. and about 8 P. M. respectively.

The material for the discussion of the daily fluctuation for stations in the Mississippi valley and in the western states and territories is yet wanting.

The annual variation in the range of the daily fluctuation is shown in the following table. From want of completeness in the records the tabular numbers, in many instances, are the result of interpolation, and they can only be considered as close approximations.

Monthly means of the RANGE *of the daily fluctuation.*

	Group I. Arctic Regions. 4 Stations.	Group II. Alaska. 1 Station.	Group III. Canada and N. New York. 4 Stations.	Groups IV & V.[1] Mass., Conn., Penn., D. of C. 6 Stations.	Group VI. Gulf Coast. 2 Stations.
	°	°	°	°	°
January	1.2	3.1	6.3	10.4	6.0
February	3.0	5.4	8.9	11.2	7.0
March	9.2	7.9	10.9	13.6	6.6
April	8.6	9.8	12.0	14.8	7.1
May	8.6	10.9	14.0	17.0	7.4
June	7.8	11.3	14.9	17.2	5.8
July	5.7	10.6	15.4	15.8	6.9
August	4.2	9.2	14.6	14.9	6.1
September	3.5	8.4	12.5	16.6	6.5
October	2.2	4.8	10.3	16.2	5.8
November	1.7	3.4	5.9	11.1	5.4
December	1.0	2.1	5.3	9.8	4.7

[1] Omitting Brooklyn as too irregular.

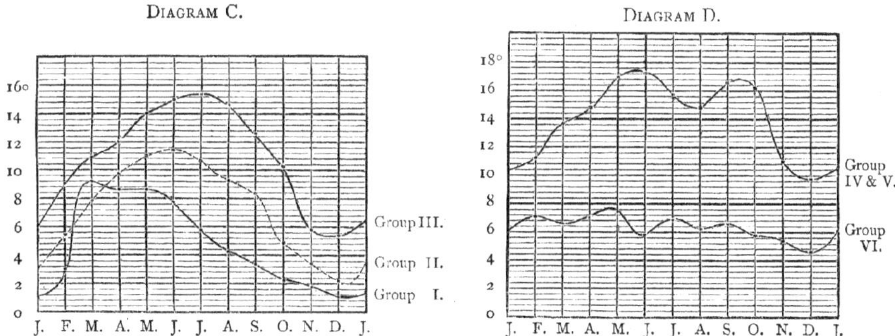

At all stations, of the above table, between the Gulf of Mexico and the Arctic Sea, the daily range is a minimum in December; this, however, is the only feature they have in common, as shown in diagrams C and D. In the first diagram the curves for the northern stations appear single-crested, in the second the curve of the middle latitude stations is double-crested and that of the Gulf stations exhibits three or more elevations and depressions, all ill-defined. The marked feature of the low latitude range is its great uniformity throughout the year. In the Arctic regions, with the returning day, the range suddenly rises to its maximum in March; in Canada and northern New York the range is greatest in July or about the time of greatest heat; along the coast from Massachusetts to the District of Columbia the range attains two maxima, one early in June the other late in September, with an intermediate depression of range during the hottest season. As our observations become more extended, other features in the march of the daily temperature will undoubtedly make their appearance, and those already recognized will become better defined. At San Francisco especially, it would be interesting to have a series of hourly observations, extending at least over one year, this locality being otherwise noted for anomalous temperature relations. According to Dr. Gibbons the coldest and warmest periods of the day are not far from sunrise and noon, and by taking the differences of the mean monthly temperatures at these times, as given in the Smithsonian report for 1854, p. 231 and foll. For the years 1851 to 1854, I obtain the following table of daily range of temperature at San Francisco.

Month	Range	Month	Range
January	12°.1	July	15°.7
February	14.0	August	12.8
March	15.3	September	14.9
April	16.5	October	16.1
May	14.9	November	13.7
June	16.2	December	11.5

These numbers are approximations only, yet they indicate a comparatively large range, a minimum range in December and two maxima—one in spring, the other in autumn.

The modification which the daily fluctuation undergoes in the course of a year can be advantageously brought out by a comparison of its value in December when near the least, with its value in June when not far from its greatest development.

The fluctuations observed at Van Rensselaer, Port Foulke, Port Kennedy, and Boothia Felix were united into a mean, those at Thunder Bay Island, Toronto, Mohawk, Amherst, and Philadelphia into another, and those at Fort Morgan, Key West, and Galveston into a third; these localities are designated, Arctic stations, Temperate stations, and Gulf stations respectively.

Before taking means, the record for Galveston, Texas, was made complete by interpolation.

Extremes of daily fluctuation in December and June.

	Arctic Stations (4).		Temperate Stations (5).		Gulf Stations (3).	
	Dec.	June.	Dec.	June.	Dec.	June.
	°	°	°	°	°	°
Md'nt	—0.2	—3.2	—1.5	—4.9	—1.3	—2.0
1	—0.2	—3.9	—2.2	—6.0	—1.4	—2.3
2	—0.3	—4.2	—2.5	—6.7	—1.6	—2.5
3	—0.3	—3.5	—2.7	—7.3	—1.8	—2.8
4	—0.4	—2.6	—2.9	—7.6	—2.0	—3.0
5	—0.4	—1.6	—3.0	—7.5	—2.4	—3.4
6	—0.4	—0.7	—2.9	—5.9	—2.5	—2.7
7	—0.4	+0.3	—2.9	—3.6	—2.7	—1.2
8	—0.2	+1.4	—2.5	—1.1	—1.8	+0.2
9	0.0	+1.8	—1.4	+1.0	—0.6	+1.3
10	+0.1	+2.4	+0.3	+2.9	+1.1	+1.9
11	+0.3	+2.8	+1.9	+4.6	+2.0	+2.6
Noon	+0.5	+3.2	+3.3	+6.1	+2.4	+2.7
1	+0.4	+3.3	+4.1	+7.0	+2.7	+3.0
2	+0.3	+3.3	+4.6	+7.6	+2.8	+3.1
3	+0.2	+2.9	+4.5	+7.7	+2.9	+3.5
4	+0.1	+2.4	+3.7	+7.5	+2.8	+3.7
5	+0.2	+1.7	+2.4	+6.6	+2.0	+2.7
6	+0.2	+1.0	+1.5	+5.2	+1.1	+1.1
7	+0.2	+0.2	+0.5	+2.8	+0.4	—0.4
8	+0.2	—0.5	+0.1	+0.2	0.0	—1.1
9	+0.1	—1.3	—0.4	—1.7	—0.3	—1.4
10	+0.1	—2.0	—0.8	—2.9	—0.6	—1.8
11	—0.1	—2.6	—1.2	—4.0	—1.1	—1.9

The above numbers are plotted on diagrams E, F, and G. These diagrams show plainly, in December the morning minimum later and the afternoon maximum earlier than in June; also the morning and afternoon epochs of mean daily temperature later in December (nearly two hours) than in June, but in the temperate latitudes the afternoon hour (8 o'clock) answers for the time of the winter as well as for the time of the summer solstice.

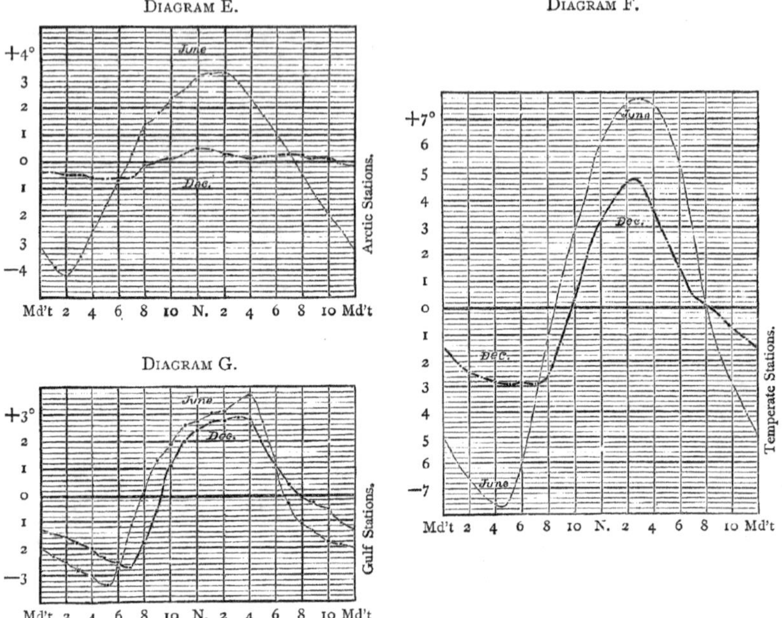

The vicinity of San Francisco, Cal., probably presents the greatest anomaly yet noticed. Dr. H. Gibbons remarks[1] that at San Francisco the warmest period of the day in winter is from 1 to 2 P. M., but in summer (May to August) it is an hour or two earlier owing to the sea breeze, which springs up about noon or soon after, instantly depressing the temperature. In the season of the westerly breezes the temperature is rapidly reduced and the change is effected long before sunset, after which time the thermometer shows but little variation till the following morning. Under the influence of this brisk sea breeze, the rays of a high sun fail to impart any appreciable heat to the air. These conditions are quite local and the attending phenomena respecting the daily and annual fluctuations are confined to the vicinity of the Bay of San Francisco, though traces of it appear at all stations along the western coast exposed to the immediate influence of the westerly winds from the Pacific ocean. Observations of the daily march of the temperature in these localities are specially desirable. For the study of the effect of height on the daily fluctuation no material is at present available, but our records show that under this condition it may become quite excessive; at elevated regions the air is comparatively dry and the sun's rays reach the ground but little impeded, while at night radiation is going on with great energy from the comparative absence of an absorbing medium. The great interior basin bounded on the east by the Rocky Mountains and the

[1] The climate of San Francisco; Smithsonian Annual Report for 1854, p. 231 and foll.

Sierra Madre, on the west by the Sierra Nevada and including the regions of the Colorado River, also the northern portion of the Rio Grande, furnishes many interesting examples of an excessively large daily range, the magnitude of which may, in a measure, be inferred from the following comparisons of the difference of temperature at the observing hours 7 A. M. and 2 P. M., or at the time of sunrise and 3 P. M., for a few selected places, located in New Mexico, Texas, Arizona, and California. With the exception of Fort Yuma, which is but 200 feet above the sea level, these stations are all at considerable elevations.

Average difference in the temperature, between sunrise and 3 P. M., or between 7 A. M. and 2 P. M., taken from the monthly means at these hours of observation. [Army Met. Regs. for 1855 and 1860.]

Name of Station, State, or Territo	Fort Thorn, N. M.	Albuquerque, N. M.	Fort Quitman, Tex.	Fort Defiance, Ariz.	Fort Buchanan, Ariz.	Fort Craig, N. M.	Fort Yuma, Cal.	Fort Chadburne, Tex.	Fort Crook, Cal.	Weighted Mean
Latitude . . .	32°40′	35°06′	30°45′	35°43′	31°40′	33°36′	32°46′	31°58′	41°07′	
Longitude . . .	107 09	106 38	105 00	109 10	110 55	107 00	114 44	100 15	121 29	
Altitude (feet) .	4500	5032	3710	6500	5330	4576	200	2120	3390	
No. of years of record . .	4	7	1	7	2	4	7	7	2	
January . . .	26°	27°	37°	24°	27°	26°	22°	23°	15°	24°
February . . .	31	26	35	23	28	28	25	24	13	25
March	30	31	41	25	32	27	24	26	16	27
April	34	31	30	25	29	29	24	26	24	28
May	30	34	29	24	25	22	22	19	20	25
June	34	29	21	27	23	22	22	20	21	25
July	27	25	13	19	13	20	20	20	25	21
August	25	26	17	19	15	17	20	20	29	21
September . . .	25	28	14	25	17	17	20	18	29	22
October . . .	32	27	17	28	22	21	21	21	31	25
November . . .	33	26	29	24	23	22	20	24	17	24
December . . .	25	22	30	22	21	23	18	23	12	21
Year	30	28	26	24	23	23	22	22	21	24

The mean daily range, for any month or for the year, at any of the above stations is necessarily several degrees higher than the corresponding tabular difference since the morning and afternoon extremes do not take place at the hours of observation; even the tabular numbers, when contrasted with the observed daily range in other parts of the United States, appear excessive, and imperfect as they must be owing to the short number of years and the great variability of the quantities themselves, the annual fluctuation of the differences given in the last column presents quite a regular double crested curve. The maximum daily range occurs in March and April, a second smaller maximum in October with minima in July and August, and again in December, the latter minimum being apparently a common feature within the boundaries of the United States. The great development of the daily fluctuation at Albuquerque, N. M., would recommend this station as a suitable locality for an extended hourly series (to be recorded with a self-registering instrument). Such observations would greatly assist in establishing corrections to the mean temperature derived from the ordinary hours of observation (7 A.M. and 2 and 9 P.M.) in order to refer them to the true daily mean.

A table of the daily fluctuation for this place would answer for most stations situated within the elevated and arid region generally known as the great interior basin, as well as for the regions of the upper Rio Grande and of western Texas.

In some instances the recorded mean monthly difference between the morning and afternoon temperatures rises to 40°, and if the observations are to be trusted to 45°; the corresponding daily incidental range is equally great and for the regions described above it is not uncommon to meet, in the morning, with a temperature below the freezing point and to experience in the afternoon of the same day a heat rising to 70 or 80° Fah.

Variability of the temperature at any hour of the day from the normal value of that hour.

To complete the investigation of the general laws of the daily fluctuation we have yet to inquire into the amount of digression of the monthly mean of any observed hourly temperature when compared with its normal value.

These irregular variations are most readily ascertained by a comparison of the *monthly means* for each hour of the day, given separately for a *series* of years, with the mean of the combined years for each hour. By this method we completely free our results from the effects of the annual fluctuation, and have the advantage of presenting the probable error to the hourly temperatures, as given in the first set of tables for each month, provided the particular table was derived from a *single year* of observations; if the tables are constructed from n years, the probable errors require a division by $\sqrt{n}$ in order to represent the probable uncertainties of their tabular numbers.

With a special view to this investigation the Mohawk table of hourly temperatures is given in full, from 1860 to 1868, only six years of hourly observations, however, could be utilized for the present purpose. At Philadelphia, the Girard College series furnished hourly means for nearly 5 years from 1840 to 1845. At Sitka a series of hourly observations (with omissions of 5 readings in each day) was taken from the records of the observatory, for 5 years, selecting 1847-8-9 and 1862-3-4. For Toronto, Can., the results are copied from Table VII[1] of the

[1] The following is, in part, a copy of the Toronto table.

Hour.	Jan.	Feb.	March.	April.	May.	June.	July.	August.	Sept.	Oct.	Nov.	Dec.	Oct. to March inclusive.	Apr. to Sept. inclusive.
	°	°	°	°	°	°	°	°	°	°	°	°	°	°
2 P. M.	3.49	2.47	2.43	1.94	2.38	2.20	2.36	1.66	1.95	1.69	1.45	3.12	2.44	2.08
4 "	3.31	2.54	2.59	1.76	2.36	2.13	2.09	1.37	1.71	1.46	1.30	3.10	2.38	1.90
10 "	3.53	3.52	2.69	1.56	1.82	1.76	1.36	1.10	1.21	1.54	1.26	3.02	2.59	1.47
Mdn't	3.67	3.85	2.76	1.52	1.76	1.88	1.33	1.14	1.07	1.56	1.30	3.04	2.70	1.45
6 A. M.	3.90	3.65	2.98	1.32	1.72	1.85	1.59	1.09	1.25	1.48	1.24	3.20	2.74	1.47
8 "	3.89	3.57	2.85	1.38	1.95	1.99	1.67	1.01	1.26	1.59	1.23	3.12	2.71	1.54
All hours	3.63	3.27	2.72	1.58	2.00	1.97	1.73	1.23	1.41	1.55	1.30	3.10	2.59	1.65

"Results of meteorological observations made at the magnetical observatory, during the years 1860-1-2." G. T. Kingston, Director. This table is headed "Probable variability of the monthly means of temperature at each of the 6 observation hours, in a single year, together with their half-yearly and yearly averages, from the years 1854 to 1862 inclusive," and the deduction from the results is stated as follows: The *warm* hours are most liable to disturbances of temperature in the *warm* months, and the *cold* hours in the *cold* months, and altogether the abnormal digressions are greater in the colder half year than in the warmer.

A series of hourly observations continued for 6 years is barely sufficient for the investigation and the results for the three winter months (Dec., Jan., Feb.) were contracted into a mean, also the results of the three summer months (June, July, Aug.); it was not deemed necessary to investigate the six remaining months, since the law is seen to change gradually from season to season, the variability of the temperature of any hour being nearly the same about or after the epochs of the equinoxes.

Probable error of the monthly mean temperature for any hour of the day, derived from a series of years.

Hours of day.	Winter.					Summer.				
	Toronto.	Mohawk.	Phila.	Sitka.		Toronto.	Mohawk.	Phila.	Sitka.	
Md't	±3.5°	±3.2°	±2.4°	±..°		±1.4°	±1.2°	±0.8°	±..°	
1	..	3.2	2.4	..		..	1.2	0.8	..	
2		[illegible]	[illegible]				1.2	0.9		
3	..	3.3	2.4	..		..	1.2	0.8	..	
4	..	3.3	2.4	2.4		..	1.2	0.8	0.8	
5	..	3.3	2.4	2.5		..	1.2	0.8	0.8	
6	3.6	3.3	2.4	2.5		1.5	1.2	0.8	1.0	
7	..	3.3	2.3	2.6		..	1.0	0.7	1.2	
8	3.5	3.4	2.3	2.5		1.5	1.0	0.7	1.3	
9	..	3.2	2.2	2.4		..	1.0	0.8	1.5	
10	..	3.1	2.3	2.2		..	1.0	0.9	1.4	
11		3.0	2.2	2.2		..	1.0	0.8	1.4	
Noon	..	2.9	2.1	2.0		..	1.1	0.9	1.4	
1	..	2.8	2.3	1.9		..	1.3	0.8	1.3	
2	3.0	2.8	2.4	1.9		2.1	1.6	1.0	1.1	
3	..	2.7	2.5	2.0		..	1.8	1.0	1.1	
4	3.0	2.8	2.5	2.1		1.9	2.0	1.0	1.0	
5	..	2.8	2.5	2.2		..	2.0	1.0	0.8	
6	..	2.9	2.4	2.3		..	2.0	1.1	0.9	
7	..	2.9	2.4	2.3		..	1.9	1.0	0.8	
8	..	3.0	2.4	2.4		..	1.8	1.1	0.9	
9	..	3.0	2.4	2.4		..	1.6	1.0	0.8	
10	3.3	3.1	2.5	2.3		1.4	1.4	1.1	0.8	
11	..	3.2	2.5	..		..	1.3	1.0	..	
Mean	±3.3	±3.1	±2.4	±2.3	±2.8°	±1.6	±1.4	±0.9	±1.0	±1.2°

The Toronto results are in the main confirmed by those at the other stations, and there is no doubt a much closer accordance would be obtained from longer series of records. In winter the maximum variability occurs a few hours after midnight, or about the period of the maximum cold of the day; in summer the reverse of this happens, the maximum variability then occurs about 3 P. M., or about the period of maximum heat. In winter the greatest constancy is noted about 2 P. M., but in summer the temperature is most steady some hours after midnight.

The progression of the tabular numbers from hour to hour is quite regular, particularly for Mohawk. The amount of variation is nearly the same at Toronto and Mohawk, but less at Philadelphia and Sitka. In general the variability in winter is more than double that of summer; this latter variation will be found further investigated under the head of the annual fluctuation.

In winter the maximum variability at any hour is to the minimum variability as 5 to 4, and in summer as 8 to 5.

Multiplying the above average probable errors $\pm$ 2°.8 in winter, and $\pm$ 1°.2 in summer by $\sqrt{30.4}$ or by 5.5 nearly, we have an approximation to the probable error of an observed temperature at any hour of the day at these seasons, with reference to the normal values of that hour, month, and season. These quantities are $\pm$ 15° and $\pm$ 7° respectively.

Any attempt to deduce, for any given time and place at the earth's surface, even approximately, the daily fluctuation of the temperature, as far as it depends upon the variations of the sun's altitude[1] and with consideration of the loss of heat by absorption while passing through various depths of atmosphere,[2] must lead to

---

[1] Let ζ = the sun's zenith distance, δ its declination, t the hour angle, then for the latitude ϕ

$$\cos\zeta = \sin\phi \sin\delta + \cos\phi \cos\delta \cos t,$$

from which expression the altitude or depression of the sun for any hour of the day may be computed.

[2] If we treat the *length* of the oblique path of a ray of heat passing through the atmosphere simply as a geometrical problem, it is given by

$$l = \sqrt{r^2 \cos^2\zeta + 2rh + h^2} - r\cos\zeta,$$

hence for the case of a horizontal ray (irrespective of refraction),

$$L = \sqrt{2rh + h^2},$$

where r = the earth's radius and h = the height of the atmosphere. Taking for instance h = 45 st. miles, at which elevation twilight yet indicates the presence of air capable of reflection, and r = 3956 miles, we find that horizontal ray must traverse nearly 600 miles of atmosphere or 13.3 times the vertical thickness, if h = 74 miles, which is the average height at which shooting stars become incandescent when coming in contact with the atmosphere, the length of path is about 770 miles or 10.4 times the vertical thickness. The decrease of heat of inclined rays is greater than that resulting from the inverse proportion of the length of tract, and is due to the density of the air increasing geometrically, while the depth increases arithmetically. The following measures of atmospheric tract and of calorific effect on a surface vertically exposed to the ray, is extracted from a table given in the Encyclopædia Britannica (8th edition), article, climate; it supposes that of one thousand rays, vertically incident on the outer boundary of the atmosphere, only 750 will be transmitted through it and received on the ground. The numbers in the column headed "H" are computed by the formula $(\frac{2}{3})^{\sec\zeta}$, given in the article meteorology, according to which only 667 rays reach the ground. The last two columns contain the number of rays incident on a horizontal surface, obtained by multiplying the numbers in the preceding columns by $\cos\zeta$.

Zenith distance. ζ	Length of atmospheric tract.	Rays transmitted. (L)	$(\frac{2}{3})^{\sec\zeta}$ (H)	$L\cos\zeta$	$H\cos\zeta$
0°	1.000	750	667	750	667
10	1.015	747	663	735	653
20	1.064	736	650	691	611
30	1.154	718	626	619	542
40	1.305	687	589	526	451
50	1.554	640	531	411	341
60	1.995	563	444	282	222
70	2.905	434	306	148	105
80	5.610	199	97	35	17
90	37.850	0	0	0	0

unsatisfactory results, for the reason that the distribution of heat passing into the atmosphere directly and indirectly through surface radiation, evection, and conduction, and the amount parted with by radiation during the night, as well as the modifying influence of the aqueous vapor, present far too complex phenomena to be accounted for numerically. We have already seen that the absolute amount of vapor and the relative humidity are among the causes sufficient to impress a totally different character upon the range of the daily fluctuation, from that we might otherwise have expected from the meridian altitude of the sun and the length of its diurnal arc.

DISCUSSION

OF THE

ANNUAL FLUCTUATION, OF THE MONTHLY AND ANNUAL EXTREMES AND OF THE SECULAR VARIATION OF THE ATMOSPHERIC TEMPERATURE,

WITH

TABLES OF RESULTING TEMPERATURES FOR EACH DAY IN THE YEAR, OF MONTHLY EXTREMES AND OF ANNUAL MEANS FOR A SUCCESSION OF YEARS.

SECTION III.

DISCUSSION OF THE ANNUAL FLUCTUATION, OF THE MONTHLY AND ANNUAL EXTREMES AND OF THE SECULAR VARIATION OF THE ATMOSPHERIC TEMPERATURE

WITH

TABLES OF RESULTING TEMPERATURES FOR EACH DAY OF THE YEAR, OF OBSERVED MONTHLY EXTREMES AND OF ANNUAL MEANS FOR A SUCCESSION OF YEARS.

The annual fluctuation of the temperature.—The annual fluctuation in the temperature of the lower atmosphere is exhibited in the progression of the successive monthly means, for a great number of stations in the General Temperature—Tables of Section I, but it may also be shown by the tabulation of the mean temperature, derived from a series of years, of every day of the year. The latter method, while more advantageous, is also more laborious than the first, but is indispensable in inquiries respecting certain suspected irregularities in the annual fluctuation.

In the application of Bessel's periodic function to the case of the annual fluctuation of the temperature as derived from the *monthly means*, corrections are required for the inequality in the *length* of the calendar months, and for *curvature* or difference in the *mean* monthly temperature, and the temperature for the *middle* of the month. The first correction, for unequal length, affects principally the mean annual temperature, and but slightly the periodic terms in the epochs; the second correction, for curvature, affects only the amplitude of the fluctuations. These corrections may be applied separately and for each month before the application of the periodic function, especially in the case where the temperature for each day is known. When we have to make many applications of the formula, it becomes desirable to reduce this labor as far as is possible, without sacrifice of accuracy. There is no need for introducing these small corrections to results from short series, and it suffices to state the rules for complete quadriennia, in which, consequently, the mean length of February equals 28.25 days, and the year 365.24 days nearly; the average or normal month comprises 30.44 days nearly.

The mean temperature for the months of normal length may readily be computed by means of the following epochs of the ending of each month—

Normal months:							
	January	ends	with	0.44	of the	31st	of Calendar month.
	February	"	"	0.62	" "	2d	" March.
	March	"	"	0.06	" "	2d	" April.
	April	"	"	0.50	" "	2d	" May.
	May	"	"	0.94	" "	1st	" June.
	June	"	"	0.37	" "	2d	" July.
	July	"	"	0.81	" "	1st	" August.
	August	"	"	0.25	" "	1st	" September.
	September	"	"	0.69	" "	1st	" October.
	October	"	"	0.13	" "	1st	" November.
	November	"	"	0.56	" "	1st	" December.
	December	"	"	with midnight of the 31st.			

To make use of these expressions we require to know the mean temperature of certain days near the beginning of each month; this may either be taken directly from the observations or may be computed from the monthly means. In Silliman's Journal of Science and Arts, May numbers of 1866 and of 1867, Mr. E. L. De Forest has presented the case in a different and very convenient form[1] by using the monthly means already computed and finding corrections thereto, employing the means of the months preceding and following. Practically the results by the two methods are identical. The general effect of the correction for inequality is to increase the annual means by a small fraction of a degree.

To exhibit the magnitude of the monthly corrections, the results for the New Haven series, extending over nearly 86 years, may serve as a sample. The second column contains the uncorrected or calendar means, the third and fourth the correction to reduce to months of mean length, according to first and second methods, the last column gives the corrected means.

---

[1] On page 316 of Sill. Journ., No. 129 (May, 1867), we find the expressions for the normal months, M, by means of the calendar months, m, as follows:—

$$
\begin{aligned}
M_1 &= m_1 + .0037\,m_1 + .0030\,m_{12} - .0067\,m_2 \\
M_2 &= m_2 - .0127\,m_2 - .0031\,m_1 + .0158\,m_3 \\
M_3 &= m_3 + .0028\,m_3 - .0249\,m_2 + .0221\,m_4 \\
M_4 &= m_4 - .0042\,m_4 - .0200\,m_3 + .0242\,m_5 \\
M_5 &= m_5 + .0016\,m_5 - .0218\,m_4 + .0202\,m_6 \\
M_6 &= m_6 - .0039\,m_6 - .0180\,m_5 + .0219\,m_7 \\
M_7 &= m_7 + .0026\,m_7 - .0200\,m_6 + .0174\,m_8 \\
M_8 &= m_8 + .0025\,m_8 - .0103\,m_7 + .0078\,m_9 \\
M_9 &= m_9 - .0027\,m_9 - .0067\,m_8 + .0094\,m_{10} \\
M_{10} &= m_{10} + .0030\,m_{10} - .0085\,m_9 + .0055\,m_{11} \\
M_{11} &= m_{11} - .0026\,m_{11} - .0046\,m_{10} + .0072\,m_{12} \\
M_{12} &= m_{12} + .0032\,m_{12} - .0064\,m_{11} + .0032\,m_1
\end{aligned}
$$

Mr. De Forest also remarks that the term $T = A + B_1 \sin(\theta + C_1)$ obtained on the supposition of calendar months will be very nearly corrected, for temperate climates, for the inequality of months by taking $T = A + .0041\,B_1 + B_1 \sin(\theta + C_1 + 46')$. The effect on the periodical terms involving multiples of θ is small and variable. They are preferred in the form $\pm A_n \sin n(\theta - e_n)$, as determined by $\sin(n\theta + E_n) = \sin n(\theta - \frac{1}{n}(360^\circ - E_n))$ or $-\sin n(\theta - \frac{1}{n}(180 - E_n))$ according to $E_n >$ or $<$ than 180°, the arc e_n indicates the position of the first intersection, and the ascending or descending wave is shown by the sign of the term. In the usual form the signs are all positive.

	Calendar Month. Mean.	Correction. I.	II.	Corr'd Mean.		Calendar Month. Mean.	Correction. I.	II.	Corr'd Mean.
January	26°.46	0°.00	0°.00	26°.46	July	71°.69	+0°.06	+0°.07	71°.76
February	28.08	+0.12	+0.12	28.20	August	70.24	—0.07	—0.07	70.17
March	36.03	+0.46	+0.43	36.47	September	62.49	—0.18	—0.16	62.32
April	46.96	+0.44	+0.47	47.42	October	51.06	—0.15	—0.16	50.90
May	57.28	+0.41	+0.42	57.70	November	40.28	—0.14	—0.11	40.16
June	66.96	+0.27	+0.28	67.24	December	30.42	—0.08	—0.08	30.34

Uncorrected annual mean	48°.996
Correction	+ 0.099
Corrected mean	49.095

The monthly corrections, beginning with January and continuing in regular progression, for two extreme cases are given below, viz., for Key West, Flo., with an annual range of about 14°.7, for New Haven, Conn., with about 46°.7 and for Fort Snelling, Minn., with about 61°.8.

	°	°	°	°	°	°	°	°	°	°	°	°
Key West	.00	+.04	+.11	+.14	+.13	+.09	+.02	—.01	—.04	—.05	—.04	—.03
New Haven	.00	+.12	+.44	+.46	+.42	+.28	+.07	—.07	—.17	—.16	—.12	—.08
Fort Snelling	.00	+.21	+.67	+.63	+.47	+.28	+.04	—.12	—.19	—.19	—.18	—.11

Expressed in parts of the half of the annual range or nearly as a multiplier of B_1, the correction to the mean temperature of the year derived from the mean temperature of the calendar months, in order to obtain the true mean derived from the daily means, has been determined for a number of stations as follows:—

Locality.	Approx. Value of Half Range.	Factor.
Fort Snelling, Min.	30°.9 Fah.	0.0043
Brunswick, Me.	24.2	41
St. Louis, Mo.	24.1	38
Fort Laramie, Wyo.	23.7	37
Albion Mines, Nov. Sco.	23.6	50
New Haven, Conn.	23.3	44
Toronto, Can.	22.8	45
Providence, R. I.	22.6	44
Marietta, Ohio	21.4	43
Austin, Tex.	16.0	34
Charleston, S. C.	15.9	34
Sitka, Alas.	12.3	39
San Diego, Cal.	9.5	36
Key West, Flo.	7.3	38
San Francisco, Cal.	4.9	23

The factor seems to diminish with a diminishing range, but is sufficiently constant and equal to 0.0043 for half ranges above 20°, and equal to 0.0036 for half ranges below 20°. The San Francisco value is known to be exceptional.

The effect or correction to the epochal angles, C_1 C_2 C_3, may be seen from the following selected expressions of typical stations:—

Station.	Extent of Series in Years.	Calendar or Mean Mo.	A	B_1	B_2	B_3	C_1	C_2	C_3
Fort Snelling, Min.	42	Cal.	44°.52	30°.03	1°.60	0°.65	238°58′	208°.8	184°.4 [1]
		Mean	44.65	30.03	1.71	0.69	239 46	209.4	182.7
New Haven, Conn.	86	Cal.	49.00	22.66	0.27	0.39	233 37	298.0	139.4
		Mean	49.10	22.66	0.26	0.41	234 25	283.2	140.2
Marietta, Ohio	49	Cal.	52.24	21.16	0.79	0.41	238 38	284.1	72.6
		Mean	52.33	21.16	0.80	0.42	239 25	279.7	77.6
San Diego, Cal.	20	Cal.	62.11	8.78	1.59	0.17	224 07	285.7	156.7
		Mean	62.14	8.78	1.58	0.19	224 50	285.8	161.7
Key West, Flo.	26	Cal.	77.05	7.23	0.29	0.20	228 49	235.7	243.6
		Mean	77.08	7.23	0.31	0.19	229 34	233.0	243.2

[1] Uncorrected for daily fluctuation.

The terms in B_4 and B_5 are of no practical consequence in the present inquiry. The difference in the angle C_1 for calendar and mean months is for Fort Snelling, Min., $+48'$; for New Haven, Conn., $+48'$; for Marietta, Ohio, $+47'$; also (Sill. Journ., May, 1866, p. 377–378) for St. Paul, Min.; New York; and Charleston, S. C., $+46'$, and for San Diego, Cal. $+43'$; for Key West, Flo., $+45'$. We can therefore correct our expressions derived from the calendar months, for their inequality in length, by *substituting* for stations having a range between the hottest and coldest months exceeding 40°,

$$A + 0.0043\ B_1 \text{ for } A \text{ and } C_1 + 47' \text{ for } C_1,$$

and for stations having a less range,

$$A + 0.0036\ B_1 \text{ for } A \text{ and } C_1 + 45' \text{ for } C_1.$$

The effect on C_2 and C_3 appears irregular, and may therefore be omitted as of little importance; the values of B_2 and B_3 are not sensibly affected.

The preceding five expressions for the annual fluctuation refer to the middle of December for their epoch; hence, in order to count the angle θ from the *first day of January*, we must increase C_1 by 15°, C_2 by twice 15°, and C_3 by thrice 15°.

The second correction is nearly zero in April and May, and again in Oct. and Nov., and reaches a maximum (a few tenths of a degree) in July or August, and again in January or February, the monthly amounts changing gradually, with opposite sign for the half year when the temperature is above, and the half year when it is below the mean. Since the mean monthly temperature is numerically less than the temperature corresponding to the middle of the month, the parameters of the fluctuations must be increased, and the correction for curvature is effected[1] by multiplying the parameters or values, $B_1\ B_2\ B_3 \ldots$, as found without regard to this, by the factors,

$$\frac{\frac{\pi}{12}}{\sin\frac{\pi}{12}},\quad \frac{\frac{2\pi}{12}}{\sin\frac{2\pi}{12}},\quad \frac{\frac{3\pi}{12}}{\sin\frac{3\pi}{12}} \quad \ldots\ldots$$

respectively. To allow, therefore, for curvature, we increase the co-efficients $B_1\ B_2\ B_3 \ldots$ as ordinarily obtained

[1] A. Bravais in "Voyages en Scandinavie, etc." Pendant les années 1838, 1839, 1840. Météorologie, Vol 2, pp. 291 and 325. Paris, 18 . .

by their $\frac{1}{88}$, $\frac{1}{21}$, $\frac{1}{9}$ . . . . part respectively. Inversely, if we wish to compare computed monthly means with observed means, the respective multipliers are

$$\frac{\sin\frac{\pi}{12}}{\frac{\pi}{12}}, \quad \frac{\sin\frac{2\pi}{12}}{\frac{2\pi}{12}}, \quad \frac{\sin\frac{3\pi}{12}}{\frac{3\pi}{12}} \quad \ldots .$$

In the case of incomplete monthly means, one or more being wanting, the function may still be employed by first finding, by interpolation, graphical or analytical, values for the terms omitted, and obtaining first an approximate, and by a second or third (if necessary) application an exact expression for T. For the supposition of one month being omitted in the observations or y_0 in the values, $y_1\,y_2\,y_3 \ldots y_{11}$, wanting, Mr. Bravais gives the formula:—

$$y_0 = \tfrac{2}{7}(y_1 + y_5 + y_7 + y_{11}) + \tfrac{1}{7}(y_2 - y_3 - y_4 + y_6 - y_8 - y_9 + y_{10}) + \tfrac{1}{7}\sqrt{3}\,(y_1 - y_5 - y_7 + y_{11})$$

The expressions for two or more adjacent ordinates are too complicated, and of too little use to be inserted here.

In connection with the use of the periodic function, a table giving the value of θ for each day (noon) is herewith appended.[1]

---

[1] Table, as given by Mr. De Forest—

Day.	Jan.	Feb.	Mar.	Apr.	May.	June.	July.	Aug.	Sept.	Oct.	Nov.	Dec.
1	0°30′	31° 3′	58°53′	89°26′	119° 1′	149°34′	179° 8′	209°41′	240°15′	269°49′	300°22′	329°56′
2	1 29	32 2	59 52	90 20	120 0	150 33	180 7	210 40	241 14	270 40	301 21	330 55
3	2 28	33 1	60 51	91 25	120 59	151 32	181 6	211 40	242 13	271 47	302 20	331 55
4	3 27	34 0	61 51	92 24	121 58	152 31	182 5	212 39	243 12	272 46	303 20	332 54
5	4 26	34 59	62 50	93 23	122 57	153 30	183 5	213 38	244 11	273 45	304 19	333 53
6	5 25	35 59	63 49	94 22	123 56	154 30	184 4	214 37	245 10	274 44	305 18	334 52
7	6 24	36 58	64 48	95 21	124 55	155 29	185 3	215 36	246 9	275 44	306 17	335 51
8	7 24	37 57	65 47	96 20	125 55	156 28	186 2	216 35	247 9	276 43	307 16	336 50
9	8 23	38 56	66 46	97 19	126 54	157 27	187 1	217 34	248 8	277 42	308 15	337 49
10	9 22	39 55	67 45	98 19	127 53	158 26	188 0	218 34	249 7	278 41	309 14	338 49
11	10 21	40 54	68 44	99 18	128 52	159 25	188 59	219 33	250 6	279 40	310 13	339 48
12	11 20	41 53	69 44	100 17	129 51	160 24	189 59	220 32	251 5	280 39	311 13	340 47
13	12 19	42 53	70 43	101 16	130 50	161 24	190 58	221 31	252 4	281 38	312 12	341 46
14	13 18	43 52	71 42	102 15	131 49	162 23	191 57	222 30	253 3	282 38	313 11	342 45
15	14 18	44 51	72 41	103 14	132 48	163 22	192 56	223 29	254 3	283 37	314 10	343 44
16	15 17	45 50	73 40	104 13	133 48	164 21	193 55	224 28	255 2	284 36	315 9	344 43
17	16 16	46 49	74 39	105 13	134 47	165 20	194 54	225 28	256 1	285 35	316 8	345 42
18	17 15	47 48	75 38	106 12	135 46	166 19	195 53	226 27	257 0	286 34	317 7	346 42
19	18 14	48 47	76 38	107 11	136 45	167 18	196 53	227 26	257 59	287 33	318 7	347 41
20	19 13	49 47	77 37	108 10	137 44	168 17	197 52	228 25	258 58	288 32	319 6	348 40
21	20 12	50 46	78 36	109 9	138 43	169 17	198 51	229 24	259 57	289 32	320 5	349 39
22	21 11	51 45	79 35	110 8	139 42	170 16	199 50	230 23	260 57	290 31	321 4	350 38
23	22 11	52 44	80 34	111 7	140 42	171 15	200 49	231 22	261 56	291 30	322 3	351 37
24	23 10	53 43	81 33	112 7	141 41	172 14	201 48	232 22	262 55	292 29	323 2	352 36
25	24 9	54 42	82 32	113 6	142 40	173 13	202 47	233 21	263 54	293 28	324 1	353 36
26	25 8	55 41	83 32	114 5	143 39	174 12	203 46	234 20	264 53	294 27	325 1	354 35
27	26 7	56 40	84 31	115 4	144 38	175 11	204 46	235 19	265 52	295 26	326 0	355 34
28	27 6	57 40	85 30	116 3	145 37	176 11	205 45	236 18	266 51	296 26	326 59	356 33
29	28 5	58 16	86 29	117 2	146 36	177 10	206 44	237 17	267 51	297 25	327 58	357 32
30	29 5		87 28	118 1	147 36	178 9	207 43	238 16	268 50	298 24	328 57	358 31
31	30 4		88 27		148 35		208 42	239 15		299 23		359 30

The arc from the beginning of the year to the middle of each calendar month is found in the above table opposite the 16th for months of 31 days, and by subtracting 30′, for months of 30 days; the arc to the middle of February is 44° 28′.

To exhibit the annual fluctuation in a concise form, suitable for comparisons and further deductions, a number of characteristic stations have been selected, representing various climatological features, and for which the numerical values of the several quantities entering in the expression—

$$T = A + B_1 \sin(\theta + C_1) + B_2 \sin(2\theta + C_2) + B_3 \sin(3\theta + C_3)$$

have been computed and tabulated. In preference, stations having long and reliable series of observations have been selected, and they comprise with some rough approximation to uniformity of distribution, the area of the United States, with a few representative stations in Arctic and British North America. The results are based on the monthly means presented in the general table of temperatures (Section I), they were first corrected for *daily* fluctuation[1] according to the hours of observation, whenever needed, those depending on $7_m\ 2_a\ 9_{a\ bis}$ receiving no correction. They were next corrected for *inequality* in length of months and for *curvature*, as explained. It was deemed sufficient for the present purpose to stop at the term involving $B_3\ C_3$, considering that this and any subsequent term represent rather local peculiarities and, moreover, are subject to considerable changes with the use of additional observations. The days of average epochs of maxima and minima were computed by the formula—

$$0 = B_1 \cos(\theta + C_1) + 2B_2 \cos(2\theta + C_2) + 3B_3 \cos(3\theta + C_3)$$

resulting from putting $\frac{dT}{d\theta} = 0$

The 46 stations are given in five groups, each arranged according to latitude.

---

[1] Excepting the results for Fort Franklin, to which no corrections whatever have been applied, it is a series of less than two years. The expressions for the Arctic stations, Van Rensselaer Harbor, Port Foulke, and Port Kennedy, were taken from my discussion of the Physical Observations in the Arctic Seas by Dr. I. I. Hayes; Smithsonian Contributions to Knowledge, No. 196, Washington, June, 1867, p. 180. To these a fourth term has now been added, and the parameters have been corrected for curvature. [On p. 180 B_1 for Van Rensselaer Harbor should have been 35.39.]

TABLE OF COMPUTED ANNUAL FLUCTUATION

OF THE

TEMPERATURE OF 46 STATIONS.

ANNUAL FLUCTUATION

[The angle θ counts from January 1,

No.	Locality.	Lat.	Long. W. of Gr.	Height.	Extent of Series.	A	B_1	C_1
	ARCTIC REGIONS.							
				feet.	yrs. mos.			
1	Polaris Bay, Hall Land	81°38′	61°14′	34	1 0	+4°.19	33.09	247°52′
2	Van Rensselaer Harbor, N. Greenland .	78 37	70 53	6	1 8	— 2.20	35.79	251 43
3	Port Foulke, North Greenland . . .	78 18	73 00	6	0 11	+ 6.06	33.49	242 14
4	Port Kennedy, North Somerset . . .	72 01	94 14	4	1 1	+ 2.02	39.46	249 05
	BRITISH NORTH AMERICA AND CANADA.							
5	Fort Franklin, Great Bear Lake . . .	65 12	122 45	230	1 9	+17.18	37.64	248 55
6	Fort Chipewyan, Athabasca Lake . .	58 43	111 15	700	3 6	+28.69	34.36	246 55
7	Nain, Labrador	57 10	61 50	...	9 6	+23.46	25.09	241 18
8	Toronto, Canada West	43 39	79 23	342	31 0	+44.26	22.37	246 11
	ALASKA.							
9	Sitka	57 03	135 20	20	16 11	+42.09	12.38	234 47
10	Illoolook, Unalaska Island	53 54	166 24	20	7 1	+37.56	10.08	235 51

1 Through the courtesy of Dr. E. Bessels, who had charge of the scientific observations in the Hall Polar expedition, I have received in advance of the publication, the monthly mean temperatures as observed at Polaris Bay, between Sept. 1871, and Aug. 1872, together with some other information bearing on the same.

These results are given in the table below, to which I have added a reduction to refer them to months of average length, also the results computed by the formula—

$$T = +4^\circ.19 + 33.09 \sin(\theta + 247^\circ\ 52') + 7.15 \sin(2\theta + 81^\circ.9) + 1.83 \sin(3\theta + 51^\circ) + 2.59 \sin(4\theta + 211^\circ).$$

For the fourth term the correction for curvature $\dfrac{\frac{4\pi}{12}}{\sin\frac{4\pi}{12}}$ amounts to nearly $\frac{1}{5}$ of B_4.

Polaris Bay, Hall Land.

	Observed Temp. Calendar Month.	Red'n.	Temp. for Average Month.	Comp'd.	Obs'd.—Com'd.
1872 January	—22°.42	—°.01	—22°.43	—22°.78	+°.35
February	—23.52	+.01	—23.51	—24.15	+ .64
March	—22.65	+.17	—22.48	—21.98	— .50
April	— 7.66	+.56	— 7.10	— 8.95	+1.85
May	+17.59	+.20	+17.79	+19.19	—1.40
June	+36.94	+.05	+36.99	+37.27	— .28
July	+39.28	—.01	+39.27	+39.24	+ .03
August	+35.88	+.05	+35.93	+37.21	—1.28
1871 September	+23.07	—.76	+22.31	+21.62	+ .69
October	— 1.59	—.03	— 1.62	— 1.11	— .51
November	— 8.76	—.22	— 8.98	—10.17	+1.19
December	—15.79	—.09	—15.88	—15.11	— .77

OF THE TEMPERATURE.

and T is expressed in degrees of Fahrenheit.

No.	B_2	C_2	B_3	C_3	B_4	C_4	Warmest Day. Average date.	Warmest Day. Temp.	Coldest Day. Average date.	Coldest Day. Temp.	Annual Range.	Yearly Means reached.	Notes.
							ARCTIC REGIONS.						
1	7.15	81°.9	1.83	51°	2.59	211°	July 10	+39°.4	Jan. 30	—24°.3	63°.7	May 2; Oct. 8	1
2	7.02	69.8	3.56	17	3.79	328	July 8	+39.3	Mar. 1	—28.6	67.9	Apr. 25; Oct. 12	2
3	6.62	119.0	0.82	318	4.80	250	July 15	+41.6	Feb. 16	—28.0	69.6	May 1; Oct. 31	2
4	0.84	256.9	1.18	275	1.16	79	July 15	+42.0	Jan. 22	—38.3	80.3	Apr. 23; Oct. 25	
						Mean:	July 12		Feb. 9			Apr. 28; Oct. 19	
							BRITISH NORTH AMERICA AND CANADA.						
5	0.91	213.0	1.24	32	..	..	July 22	+52.7	Jan. 23	—21.0	73.7	Apr. 22; Oct. 24	
6	3.06	147.1	1.10	259	..	..	July 13	+63.9	Jan. 28	— 7.1	71.0	Apr. 26; Oct. 28	a
7	2.81	245.2	1.91	200	..	..	Aug. 3	+48.1	Jan. 24	— 6.0	54.1	May 1; Oct. 26	a
8	0.70	48.4	0.53	151	..	..	July 28	+67.7	Jan. 28	+22.1	45.6	Apr. 26; Oct. 24	
							ALASKA.						
9	0.88	324.9	0.20	351	..	..	Aug. 13	+54.9	Jan. 30	+30.3	24.6	May 9; Nov. 4	} *
10	2.73	8.4	0.44	103	..	..	Aug. 12	+50.6	Feb. 9	+30.0	20.6	May 21(?); Oct. 26	b }

2 At Van Rensselaer Harbor and Port Foulke the epochs and amount of maxima and minima are those resulting from 3 variable terms, as preferable to those resulting from 4 terms. The dates are quite uncertain on account of the shortness of the series.

a Monthly means corrected for daily variation by the general table p. xiv.

* Expressions referred to new style, by subtracting 10° 51′ from C_1, 21°.7 from C_2, and 33° from C_3.

b Monthly means corrected for daily variation by the Sitka table; for Astoria allowance was made for change of style.

ANNUAL FLUCTUATION

No.	Locality.	Lat.	Long. W. of Gr.	Height.	Extent of Series.	A	B_1	C_1
	UNITED STATES EAST OF THE 98th MERIDIAN.							
				feet.	yrs. mos.			
11	Fort Brady, Michigan	46°30′	84°28′	600	32 1	40°.22	24.70	247°18
12	Fort Snelling (St. Paul), Minnesota	44 53	93 10	820	42 2	44.23	30.14	254 37
13	Dennysville, Maine	44 53	67 14	..	40 0	42.25	23.72	247 16
14	Burlington, Vermont	44 28	73 12	346	29 6	44.52	25.95	249 33
15	Brunswick, Maine	43 54	69 57	74	51 3	44.50	23.31	248 45
16	Milwaukee, Wisconsin	43 04	88 00	604	26 7	45.84	23.84	248 24
17	Penn Yan, New York	42 42	77 04	740	31 0	45.51	22.79	250 33
18	Detroit, Michigan	42 20	83 03	597	30 3	47.33	22.79	250 36
19	New Bedford, Massachusetts	41 39	70 56	90	58 1	48.30	21.16	245 20
20	Muscatine, Iowa	41 26	91 05	586	27 6	47.08	25.60	253 53
21	New Haven, Connecticut	41 18	72 57	45	86 0	49.10	22.90	249 25
22	Marietta, Ohio	39 28	81 26	670	49 10	52.33	21.40	254 25
23	Fort Leavenworth, Kansas	39 21	94 54	896	39 11	52.84	25.21	254 52
24	Fort McHenry, Baltimore, Maryland	39 16	76 35	36	36 0	54.59	22.39	249 57
25	Cincinnati, Ohio	39 06	84 30	540	36 8	54.80	22.79	254 12
26	St. Louis, Missouri	38 37	90 12	481	41 0	55.09	23.94	254 56
27	Chapel Hill, North Carolina	35 58	78 54	..	20 0	59.83	18.87	253 52
28	Fort Gibson, Indian Territory	35 48	95 20	560	29 10	60.56	21.48	254 55
29	Columbus, Mississippi	33 31	88 28	227	15 9	62.25	18.57	256 01
30	Fort Moultrie, Charleston, S. C.	32 45	79 51	25	32 11	66.43	16.15	250 54
31	Fort Barrancas, Pensacola, Florida	30 21	87 18	20	20 2	68.44	15.10	253 16
32	Austin, Texas	30 17	97 44	650	19 0	66.78	16.91	256 36
33	New Orleans, Louisiana	29 56	90 03	25	32 9	69.12	14.11	255 53
34	Fort Marion, St. Augustine, Florida	29 54	81 19	25	25 4	69.73	12.33	248 38
35	Fort Brown, Texas	25 50	97 37	50	13 5	73.74	12.04	255 22
36	Key West, Florida	24 33	81 48	10	26 6	77.08	7.31	244 34
	UNITED STATES WEST OF THE 98th MERIDIAN.							
37	Fort Stevenson, Dakota	47 36	101 10	..	2 11	41.84	33.82	253 33
38	Fort Shaw, Montana	47 30	111 42	6000	3 4	46.13	23.03	253 44
39	Astoria, Oregon	46 11	123 48	52	18 3	49.22	10.87	242 44
40	Fort Laramie, Wyoming	42 12	104 31	4472	17 9	49.22	23.63	252 37
41	Salt Lake City, Utah	40 46	111 54	4260	9 0	51.95	23.72	250 32
42	Presidio, San Francisco, California	37 47	122 28	150	19 0	54.80	4.22	234 55
43	Fort Garland, Colorado	37 32	105 40	8365	15 3	42.53	23.65	255 09
44	Fort Mojavé, Arizona	35 06	114 35	604	6 5	73.20	20.95	254 31
45	Fort Craig, New Mexico	33 36	107 00	4576	13 10	60.03	22.17	259 31
46	San Diego, California	32 42	117 14	150	20 10	62.14	8.88	239 50

a Monthly means corrected for daily variation by the general table p. xiv.

b Monthly means corrected for daily variation by the Sitka table; for Astoria allowance was made for change of style.

c Monthly means corrected for daily variation by the tables for Key West and Fort Morgan.

OF THE TEMPERATURE.—Continued.

No.	B_2	C_2	B_3	C_3	B_4	C_4	Warmest Day.		Coldest Day.		Annual Range.	Yearly Means reached.	Notes.
							Average date.	Temp.	Average date.	Temp.			
UNITED STATES EAST OF THE 98th MERIDIAN.													
11	0.64	171°.8	0.80	163°	..	..	July 26	+65°.2	Jan. 28	+14.4	50°.8	Apr. 22; Oct. 24	a
12	1.75	243.2	0.78	226	..	..	July 18	+73.4	Jan. 16	+11.6	61.8	Apr. 14; Oct. 20	a
13	0.62	238.6	0.86	225	..	..	July 23	+66.2	Jan. 21	+17.1	49.1	Apr. 24; Oct. 27	a
14	0.59	191.9	0.19	56	..	..	July 21	+69.8	Jan. 24	+18.3	51.5	Apr. 21; Oct. 23	a
15	0.92	258.0	0.88	225	..	..	July 24	+67.9	Jan. 18	+19.5	48.4	Apr. 20; Oct. 24	d
16	1.19	313.8	0.86	241	..	..	July 25	+70.3	Jan. 15	+21.0	49.3	Apr. 23; Oct. 24	
17	0.68	90.7	0.36	163	..	..	July 22	+69.1	Jan. 24	+22.9	46.2	Apr. 22; Oct. 20	a
18	0.34	36.5	0.49	168	..	..	July 24	+70.8	Jan. 23	+24.5	46.3	Apr. 22; Oct. 20	
19	0.40	13.3	0.42	222	..	..	July 27	+70.2	Jan. 23	+27.1	43.1	Apr. 28; Oct. 27	a
20	1.75	273.3	0.04	325	..	..	July 23	+71.3	Jan. 13	+19.9	51.4	Apr. 15; Oct. 15	
21	0.27	313.2	0.46	185	..	..	July 25	+72.4	Jan. 21	+25.7	46.7	Apr. 21; Oct. 22	
22	0.84	309.7	0.47	123	..	..	July 24	+73.6	Jan. 15	+30.7	42.9	Apr. 15; Oct. 16	
23	1.90	284.7	0.22	190	..	..	July 26	+77.0	Jan. 12	+26.1	50.9	Apr. 14; Oct. 20	a
24	0.62	317.0	0.15	170	..	..	July 26	+77.0	Jan. 19	+32.0	45.0	Apr. 21; Oct. 22	a
25	0.98	341.2	0.48	120	..	..	July 26	+77.9	Jan. 14	+32.3	45.6	Apr. 17; Oct. 16	
26	1.14	291.2	0.29	147	..	..	July 24	+78.5	Jan. 13	+30.3	48.2	Apr. 15; Oct. 19	
27	0.68	337.5	0.29	299	..	..	July 19	+78.9	Jan. 10	+40.9	38.0	Apr. 19; Oct. 18	
28	2.14	296.2	0.64	143	..	..	July 31	+81.7	Jan. 12	+37.7	44.0	Apr. 13; Oct. 18	
29	1.38	330.9	0.32	97	..	..	July 26	+81.0	Jan. 9	+43.7	37.3	Apr. 15; Oct. 15	
30	0.73	302.4	0.15	22	..	..	July 26	+82.2	Jan. 15	+50.1	32.1	Apr. 21; Oct. 21	e
31	1.08	287.0	0.39	45	..	..	July 28	+82.6	Jan. 12	+52.9	29.7	Apr. 16; Oct. 21	c
32	1.95	316.8	0.01	315	..	..	July 29	+81.7	Jan. 12	+37.7	44.0	Apr. 13; Oct. 17	
33	1.37	301.5	0.81	349	..	..	July 18	+82.8	Dec. 31	+54.1	28.7	Apr. 16; Oct. 20	
34	1.36	296.2	0.82	335	..	..	July 30	+81.0	Jan. 4	+56.7	24.3	Apr. 23; Oct. 27	c
35	1.24	270.0	0.30	247	..	..	July 22	+85.0	Jan. 12	+60.3	24.7	Apr. 11; Oct. 21	c
36	0.32	263.0	0.21	288	..	..	July 27	+84.2	Jan. 21	+69.5	14.7	Apr. 27; Oct. 29	
UNITED STATES WEST OF THE 98th MERIDIAN.													
37	2.30	198.0	2.21	211	..	..	July 16	+76.1	Jan. 21	+ 4.0	72.1	Apr. 14; Oct. 22	a
38	0.70	205.7	1.98	242	..	..	July 14	+70.6	Jan. 15	+20.8	49.8	Apr. 19; Oct. 21	a
39	1.25	280.9	0.38	168	..	..	Aug. 2	+59.2	Jan. 23	+37.4	21.8	Apr. 26; Oct. 31	b
40	3.24	9.7	0.58	252	..	..	July 25	+75.8	Jan. 4	+26.7	49.1	Apr. 26; Oct. 16	a
41	1.42	330.1	1.59	234	..	..	July 23	+77.4	Jan. 14	+25.8	51.6	Apr. 24; Oct. 22	
42	1.46	258.7	0.61	307	..	..	Sept. 23	+59.1	Jan. 9	+49.3	9.8	May 1; Nov. 13	
43	1.91	313.3	1.00	249	..	..	July 21	+66.6	Jan. 8	+17.1	49.5	Apr. 14; Oct. 19	a
44	1.91	330.0	0.71	239	..	..	July 22	+95.0	Jan. 8	+51.2	43.8	Apr. 18; Oct. 17	c
45	2.39	312.1	1.15	304	..	..	July 15	+81.6	Dec. 31	+35.5	46.1	Apr. 12; Oct. 16	a
46	1.66	315.8	0.21	207	..	..	Aug. 15	+72.0	Jan. 13	+52.9	19.1	May 6; Oct. 31	

d See Smithsonian Contributions to Knowledge, No. 204; Washington, June, 1867, p. 32. The expression is here corrected for curvature.

e Monthly means corrected for daily variation by one-half of the value given by the general table p. xiv.

The positions of the meteorological stations, embraced in the preceding table, are shown on the accompanying chart by dots, to which the tabular number has been attached.

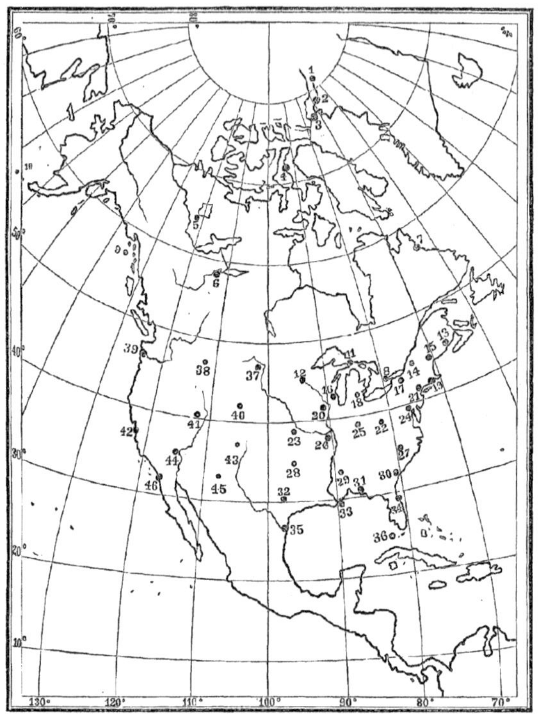

If we examine the variability of the respective dates, given in the columns of "warmest day," "coldest day," and "days of mean temperature," we shall find the latter confined to the narrowest limit; near these epochs the expression for T reaches its greatest daily change and consequently fixes them with comparative accuracy, whereas near the epochs of maxima and minima the daily change is least, in consequence of which greater uncertainty must attach to these dates.

The results for the 4 Arctic stations have been united into a mean for each epoch; even these means have less weight than corresponding values at any other station, since they are based upon less than 5 years of observation. The epoch when the mean of the year is reached, with a falling temperature, is the most constant for all the stations; its dates are comprised between October 8, at Polaris Bay, and November 13, at San Francisco, both stations being of an exceptional character; all the rest cluster closely around the 22d of October, which follows 30 days after the autumnal equinox. The average deviation from this date is 4 days, earlier or later.

The epochs of the mean value of the year, reached with rising temperature, are comprised, with the exception of Illoolook which is doubtful, between April 11, at Fort Brown, Texas, and May 9, at Sitka; the average date for all other stations being April 21, which is 32 days after the vernal equinox. The average deviation from this date is 5 days, earlier or later.

The dates for the maximum temperature, with the exception of that for San Francisco which is anomalous and delayed to Sept. 23, are comprised between the limits of July 8, at Van Rensselaer Harbor, and August 15, at San Diego; all the other stations cluster about July 24, which is 33 days after the summer solstice. The average deviation from this date is $4\frac{1}{2}$ days, earlier or later.

The dates for the minimum temperature vary between the limits of December 31, at New Orleans and at Fort Craig, and February 16, at Port Foulke; we have to except, however, the date for Van Rensselaer Harbor, which has the highly uncertain date March 1; the remainder of the stations cluster about January 18, which is 28 days after the winter solstice. The average deviation from this date is 6 days, earlier or later.

We thus see that the daily balance between the decreasing radiation and the increasing insolation at the midwinter extreme is struck earlier by 5 days than the opposite balance between the decreasing insolation and the increasing radiation at the midsummer extreme, as compared with the corresponding astronomical epochs.

Altogether, then, the curve expressive of the annual distribution of heat, for our stations, follows in epoch, on the average 31 days, or very nearly $\frac{1}{12}$ of a year, the corresponding astronomical epochs depending on the revolution of the earth around the sun.

Examining the dates of the four epochs with respect to geographical distribution of stations within the area of the United States, we find for the 9 Atlantic coast stations, Nos. 13, 15, 19, 21, 24, 27, 30, 34, 36, the average dates: July 25, January 17, for maximum and minimum, and April 23, October 24, for an average of the year in spring and autumn. Compared with the normal epochs, viz.:—

July 24, January 18, April 21, and October 22, they appear about 1 day later than the normals. No dependence on the latitude is indicated.

The 10 centrally located stations in the valley of the Mississippi and east of the foot of the Rocky Mountains, also including two Texas stations, viz.: Nos. 37, 12, 20, 23, 26, 28, 29, 32, 33, and 35, give the respective dates:—

July 23, January 12, April 14, and October 19, which are on the average 4 days earlier than the normal values. The latitude of the stations is apparently of no consequence in this inquiry. Similarly we find for the three Pacific coast stations, Nos. 9, 39, and 46 the respective dates: August 10, January 22, May 4, and November 1, which are on the average 15 days *later* than the respective normal values, while at San Francisco the dates for the maximum and for the autumnal mean are still later. With respect to the annual thermal epochs we thus notice the apparent effect on the coast stations by the Atlantic is to retard them by about

1 day and by the Pacific for about 15 days, the later effect being necessarily the greater, owing to the prevalence of westerly winds over the whole area under consideration. In the interior, on the contrary, the epochs appear about 4 days earlier than the average values. Our data are yet too scanty to allow of any precise estimate respecting the effect of elevation on these epochs, but they appear to occur earlier for greater elevation.

The result arrived at respecting the shifting of the epochs in different longitudes may also be stated as follows: The seasons occur 5 days earlier in the valley of the Mississippi and the western plains than on the Atlantic seacoast, and 19 days earlier than on the Pacific coast.

We may arrive at a tolerably fair estimate of the annual mean temperature at any place by observing for a few days the temperature about the two epochs when the mean is reached, and still better by observing in addition about the epochs of maximum and minimum. The least labor will be spent by observing only at 8 P. M. (8^h 05^m may still improve the result), an hour which has the advantage of convenience for the observer and which produces equally good results in *all months* of the year, the values will probably keep within a half degree, during any month, and within one-tenth of a degree, for the year, of the true value.

If we now turn our attention to the annual range, we find it to vary between the limits of 80°, nearly, at Port Kennedy (in approximate latitude 72°) and of 10°, nearly, at San Francisco. The next smallest annual range is attained at Key West, of about 15°, next follows San Diego with 19°, and Illoolook (approximate latitude 54°) with 20½°. The smaller ranges are due almost entirely to the proximity and equalizing effect of the sea.

The magnitude of the annual range depends principally on the latitude and the distance from the ocean, apparently less on the altitude of the station; it is greater in the higher latitudes and appears to reach its maximum value in the region about the Great Bear and the Great Slave Lakes; from the vicinity of Lake Athabasca high values extend towards Lake Winnipeg and even within the northern boundary of the United States. Our four Arctic stations in the average latitude of 77½° show an average amplitude of 70½°, at Peel River in latitude 67° 32′ the amplitude probably exceeds[1] 83°, Fort Simpson in latitude 62° 10′ has an annual amplitude probably greater than 75°, our stations Nos. 5 and 6 in the average latitude of 62° have an amplitude of nearly 72½°, Norway House in latitude 53° 50′ shows nearly 71°, while at Fort Stevenson, Dakota, in latitude 47° 36′ the observed amplitude is as high as 72°, and at Fort Pierre, Dakota, in latitude 44° 23′ a range above 70° is indicated; these last two stations exhibit a range of a truly arctic character.

The rigor of a climate may be supposed measurable by two factors, viz.: the mean annual temperature and its range, which latter is approximated by the value $2\,B_1$ (provided B_2 B_3 . . . are small in comparison). The values of A in our table fluctuate between the extreme limits of —2°.2 at Van Rensselaer Harbor, and of

[1] A still greater range of about 90° probably occurs at Fort Yukon, Alaska, in latitude 66° 34′, but our observations are too limited to give an exact value.

+77°.1 at Key West, Florida; their geographical distribution and relations within the limits of the United States are sufficiently shown on the chart of the mean annual isothermals.

Apparent interruptions in the regularity of the annual fluctuation.

While, for all general purposes of comparison, monthly means will be found quite sufficient for the elucidation of the character of the annual fluctuation, they will not be adequate in the case of a special and detailed examination, having for its object to ascertain the reality of certain anomalies in the otherwise regular progression.

It has been noticed, elsewhere, that at certain stations and at certain periods of the year, the regularity of the annual march of the temperature appears interrupted for a few days by interfering with the ordinary rising or falling of the temperature, as we should expect it, at these periods of the year. The phenomenon has been attributed to local as well as to cosmical influences; it would seem to be referable to the setting in of a particular wind at these times, causing the mean temperature to be more or less influenced.

Of such periods of apparent irregularities, pointed out by different meteorologists,[1] the following may be mentioned: About the beginning of December and the middle of May; about the 12th of February and between the first and second week in March; it cannot be said, however, that any such periods have been fully tested or confirmed for stations in the United States, but the subject demands further research. From observations at Geneva, N. Y., Dr. Wilson[2] suspects an arrest of the increasing warmth during about 16 days, commencing with May 25, and a retrocession of the increasing cold in autumn from October 28th to about November 10th.

To meet the requirements of such investigations the observed temperatures have, by some, been united into 5 day means or penthemers, while others have gone through the extremely laborious process of determining the mean temperature of every day, resulting from a long series of years. Owing to the great labor of preparation but few of such tables exist, and they extend yet over too limited a period to be conclusive in their results. In places where the annual range is small, a 15 year series is quite valuable, but in our temperate and higher latitudes a combination of observations embracing at least double this time is requisite to eliminate the greater irregularities in the daily means.

There is another use of tables of daily average temperatures; by their means we can ascertain for any given day (and in combination with the known daily fluctuation, for any given hour) how much the observed temperature will be in excess or defect of the normal (or tabular) temperature belonging to that day, a

---

[1] See report of British Association for Advancement of Science; Birmingham meeting, 1865; also Silliman's Journal, May, 1867, p. 290.

[2] Local Climatology, in the 20th annual report of the Regents of the University of the State of New York. Albany, 1868.

question to which an answer is often demanded in the study of the progress of certain unusually hot or cold terms or waves spreading themselves over large surfaces.

In the following series of tables of the average temperature of each day of the year, the observing hours as well as the corrections applied (if possible or necessary) to reduce to daily mean are added to each station.

Day of Month.	Jan.	Feb.	Mar.	Apr.	May.	June.	July.	Aug.	Sept.	Oct.	Nov.	Dec.
Albion Mines, Nova Scotia. Lat. 45° 34′. Long. 62° 42′ W. of G. Alt. 120 feet. 10 years of observation, between 1843 and 1852, inclusive. H. Poole. MS. in Smithsonian Coll.												
1	21°.8	13°.0	22°.0	33°.9	41°.8	50°.9	59°.3	70°.0	59°.9	50°.6	42°.8	26°.8
2	17.4	15.7	20.5	31.0	46.2	52.3	60.5	69.6	60.9	48.0	44.5	28.1
3	22.6	20.4	20.1	32.9	43.6	55.5	61.9	67.9	63.2	49.5	44.5	27.1
4	20.5	20.7	18.0	34.4	43.7	57.5	63.0	67.3	63.5	48.7	43.9	31.0
5	19.8	22.9	20.2	34.5	43.8	57.4	64.2	67.9	62.0	49.5	41.5	35.0
6	20.6	22.8	19.3	33.0	46.5	55.3	65.1	66.7	61.1	49.3	41.8	27.8
7	19.8	21.7	21.2	36.3	48.3	54.5	63.7	65.7	63.4	47.8	38.2	26.0
8	23.7	19.6	24.8	38.7	50.0	55.4	64.6	66.5	62.3	48.4	38.5	27.6
9	18.9	18.5	29.9	38.9	49.0	56.7	65.4	67.8	58.4	44.6	36.1	27.2
10	23.4	21.5	24.8	34.7	47.2	57.1	66.1	68.9	55.9	47.2	36.8	27.9
11	19.7	21.1	24.6	36.0	47.5	57.2	68.8	68.3	58.0	47.1	36.7	26.3
12	19.5	20.2	23.5	33.9	47.0	53.8	67.9	67.6	58.2	48.0	33.8	24.8
13	20.4	15.1	25.9	35.0	42.7	53.2	67.4	64.7	56.9	51.7	33.3	23.4
14	23.9	15.0	28.8	37.6	49.0	56.2	66.7	68.4	55.4	49.6	30.2	19.8
15	19.9	19.9	25.1	37.8	50.9	57.2	66.9	67.1	54.8	46.3	31.8	25.1
16	20.0	19.2	24.1	37.3	52.6	55.8	66.3	62.4	54.2	44.0	33.1	25.8
17	18.7	19.0	28.5	36.6	52.2	55.6	68.1	65.1	53.5	44.5	34.7	25.4
18	17.5	18.5	26.5	35.4	50.3	58.8	69.5	63.9	54.5	47.2	36.8	24.0
19	11.3	16.5	28.9	37.7	47.3	63.6	66.6	64.1	55.6	50.8	36.2	20.2
20	10.3	17.3	28.5	38.0	50.1	64.5	69.3	62.8	53.8	47.7	35.9	23.6
21	16.7	20.6	32.2	42.3	49.5	62.0	71.0	62.2	58.8	43.4	35.9	22.4
22	14.6	20.8	29.9	41.1	48.9	62.8	73.5	63.3	53.8	44.7	35.4	14.7
23	12.9	22.4	27.2	40.5	53.6	63.3	71.8	64.5	52.3	47.1	34.8	18.9
24	18.2	20.3	31.2	40.9	50.1	61.2	67.1	62.7	52.3	43.5	36.4	21.1
25	23.0	19.3	30.2	38.6	50.1	63.3	65.0	64.3	50.3	43.7	34.7	20.6
26	23.7	21.2	31.9	40.3	50.4	60.2	64.8	63.1	50.1	44.2	37.3	21.6
27	18.9	21.9	34.7	40.1	51.1	61.4	64.6	63.5	51.9	43.7	31.3	17.3
28	13.4	16.7	33.9	40.2	49.7	61.6	64.6	63.7	50.1	41.7	30.6	19.8
29	18.7	20.5	35.0	41.0	51.2	62.0	64.3	64.1	51.0	40.4	26.3	26.5
30	21.3		34.7	40.5	50.5	63.5	64.7	65.0	51.9	45.3	26.8	24.2
31	12.8		34.2		49.8		67.3	64.1		42.6		24.0

Observations at ⊙ rise, 9 A. M., 3 and 9 P. M. To the mean at these hours the correction for daily fluctuation is very small, throughout the year, and judging from the Montreal table probably does not exceed 0°.1; no correction was therefore applied.

Toronto, Canada West. Lat. 43° 39′. Long. 79° 23′ W. of G.
Alt. 342 feet. Observed temperature at Toronto, in groups of 10 and 30 years.
Communicated to the Smithsonian Institution by G. T. Kingston, Director of the Toronto observatory.

Day of Month.	January.				February.				March.			
	1840–9[1]	1850–9	1860–9	1840–69	1840–9	1850–9	1860–9	1840–69	1840–9	1850–9	1860–9	1840–69
1	25°.9	25°.2	23°.7	25°.0	20°.1	26°.7	22°.8	23°.0	28°.1	25°.2	29°.3	27°.2
2	21.4	24.2	20.3	21.8	27.8	18.9	21.7	22.6	24.9	24.2	28.5	24.9
3	21.5	25.6	21.3	22.9	25.2	20.7	17.3	21.4	26.9	25.6	27.1	25.7
4	21.1	27.0	18.3	21.9	23.7	21.9	21.3	22.2	28.2	25.1	20.2	24.6
5	23.6	23.7	23.7	23.6	25.1	18.1	23.9	22.3	29.7	27.3	22.6	26.4
6	26.7	23.8	21.5	24.2	24.5	16.9	24.9	22.3	28.6	22.5	25.7	25.7
7	29.3	20.2	18.2	22.1	22.9	22.3	17.8	21.0	31.0	26.6	28.6	28.7
8	23.4	18.1	20.4	20.6	23.0	20.9	20.9	21.6	32.3	25.3	29.2	28.8
9	23.7	23.8	23.7	23.7	19.9	22.3	22.9	21.7	29.9	27.6	29.4	29.1
10	20.5	21.5	23.4	21.8	23.8	18.6	18.4	20.6	28.8	24.2	26.6	26.5
11	20.3	26.1	18.0	21.7	18.7	19.1	23.9	20.7	27.3	29.8	26.3	27.9
12	25.6	25.4	19.5	23.6	19.2	17.5	28.5	21.5	29.8	28.4	26.3	28.1
13	26.3	25.6	21.7	24.7	19.0	23.5	25.7	22.9	30.7	32.1	26.1	29.5
14	28.6	25.8	22.0	25.3	21.6	24.2	21.3	22.4	28.7	32.4	28.3	29.7
15	29.6	22.8	21.7	24.8	20.3	26.1	22.0	22.7	23.4	33.4	28.4	28.6
16	23.2	26.4	19.6	22.8	19.8	25.2	21.0	22.1	27.4	34.1	29.3	31.3
17	21.2	19.9	15.3	18.8	21.4	23.1	20.4	21.7	29.2	35.4	30.6	31.8
18	20.8	23.8	19.8	21.4	25.3	21.3	22.5	22.9	29.5	33.1	22.9	28.4
19	19.5	20.6	22.4	20.8	28.2	20.2	25.4	24.6	33.5	28.9	23.7	28.5
20	25.9	25.2	25.1	25.5	28.6	24.8	25.2	26.1	34.5	26.2	28.6	29.9
21	27.1	23.0	23.3	24.4	29.8	26.4	22.1	26.1	30.7	31.9	27.3	29.8
22	20.2	17.8	20.2	19.4	28.9	25.6	27.3	27.3	31.1	32.4	28.2	30.6
23	27.2	16.9	28.2	24.4	21.5	22.5	28.8	24.2	33.1	33.4	32.7	33.0
24	24.6	21.1	28.1	24.1	23.7	25.8	21.3	24.3	33.8	31.8	30.2	32.0
25	23.5	23.6	22.0	23.0	24.2	26.5	22.9	24.6	35.5	30.8	31.1	32.4
26	22.4	23.0	21.6	23.3	27.0	25.4	26.0	26.1	36.6	32.4	29.0	32.7
27	23.8	22.0	20.0	22.1	26.9	24.4	26.6	26.0	34.3	30.3	33.4	32.7
28	28.3	23.7	22.5	24.7	29.4	25.2	27.3	27.3	37.5	29.4	32.7	33.2
29	28.2	23.1	24.7	25.4	36.3	25.9	23.9	28.4	36.0	34.2	30.5	33.6
30	23.3	19.5	23.2	22.1					33.6	36.1	38.3	36.0
31	19.3	25.5	21.3	22.2					34.6	35.0	38.1	36.[illegible]

Day of Month.	April.				May.				June.			
	1840–9	1850–9	1860–9	1840–69	1840–9	1850–9	1860–9	1840–69	1840–9	1850–9	1860–9	1840–69
1	32.7	35.1	34.2	34.0	48.0	45.3	40.7	44.5	54.6	56.8	57.2	56.2
2	38.7	29.3	34.4	33.7	47.5	45.1	41.4	44.5	56.9	59.3	56.8	57.7
3	39.7	36.2	35.9	37.4	46.5	46.5	42.4	45.1	58.0	59.0	58.2	58.4
4	40.7	36.6	36.9	38.0	47.3	49.2	47.3	47.9	59.5	53.6	57.2	56.8
5	35.6	37.0	40.0	37.6	46.1	49.1	49.1	48.0	56.5	57.3	57.4	57.1
6	39.2	25.2	38.4	37.7	49.2	48.7	48.2	48.7	53.4	58.9	57.9	56.8
7	38.8	34.5	34.8	36.1	48.1	50.2	48.4	49.0	57.0	59.3	59.5	58.6
8	38.5	37.2	34.2	36.7	49.4	49.0	50.6	49.7	58.2	57.2	59.3	58.3
9	39.6	39.1	36.2	38.2	47.6	48.1	52.7	49.6	62.0	56.3	57.9	58.8
10	43.0	36.7	38.3	39.5	50.1	48.7	49.8	49.5	58.5	57.0	59.5	58.3
11	42.5	36.0	41.0	39 9	50.5	46.1	49.7	48.9	58.8	55.9	59.4	58.0
12	42.0	39.5	42.6	41.3	52.6	50.9	53.0	52.1	58.0	58.0	63.2	59.8
13	40.1	36.8	38.1	38.4	51.8	53.1	49.2	51.5	58.8	61.9	61.7	60.8
14	37.6	40.5	38.7	39.0	52.2	51.3	51.6	51.7	56.7	63.4	61.2	60.6
15	41.5	38.4	44.0	41.2	52.1	53.7	51.4	52.4	60.8	64.9	63.7	63.0
16	40.0	40.0	45.0	41.7	52.4	53.8	53.7	53.3	59.7	61.8	61.7	61.0
17	41.0	40.1	43.7	41.7	53.2	52.0	52.6	52.6	60.3	61.4	63.9	61.8
18	40.1	41.8	41.6	41.1	55.3	49.4	50.8	51.9	63.3	63.2	62.4	62.9
19	39.6	43.5	43.8	42.3	54.3	50.4	52.6	52.4	63.5	64.9	62.2	63.5
20	42.7	43.1	44.6	43.5	53.1	48.9	52.6	51.5	63.4	64.7	62.9	63.6
21	46.2	45.1	46.3	45.8	50.8	52.5	52.6	52.0	63.9	65.3	63.0	64.2
22	48.3	45.7	43.5	45.9	52.9	52.6	53.2	52.9	64.3	64.1	64.2	64.2
23	48.5	40.3	40.0	42.9	54.7	54.0	52.2	53.6	65.4	63.1	63.8	64.1
24	47.8	44.2	42.1	44.6	54.8	54.5	54.2	54.5	66.1	62.4	64.3	64.3
25	46.4	45.6	41.0	44.2	57.9	56.7	58.0	57.6	65.2	64.3	67.2	65.6
26	45.7	44.9	44.0	44.9	56.4	56.0	56.6	56.3	67.1	69.1	67.0	67.7
27	42.0	41.8	43.5	42.4	58.6	56.4	55.9	57.0	66.1	65.7	64.8	65.5
28	46.2	44.3	46.3	45.6	59.4	56.7	52.9	56.2	65.1	69.8	62.9	66.1
29	44.6	45.0	45.0	44.8	56.5	54.2	55.5	55.4	67.2	70.0	64.9	67.3
30	49.1	47.1	47.4	47.8	53.5	52.1	56.7	54.2	66.6	66.9	66.6	66.7
31					51.0	53.2	57.8	54.0				

[1] Observations made 6 times each day, excluding Sundays, at the hours 6, 8 A. M. and 2, 4, 10, and 12 P. M.; their mean is sufficiently near the true daily mean.

Toronto.—Continued.

Day of Month.	July.				August.				September.			
	1840–9	1850–9	1860–9	1840–69	1840–9	1850–9	1860–9	1840–69	1840–9	1850–9	1860–9	1840–69
1	64°.0	62°.2	66°.0	63°.9	63°.0	69°.3	69°.9	67°.5	65°.1	63°.7	60°.9	63°.3
2	62.8	63.3	66.1	64.1	63.4	67.9	68.2	66.5	66.5	64.3	60.5	63.9
3	60.7	67.3	70.1	66.0	66.2	68.4	68.0	67.9	63.5	62.8	60.8	62.4
4	62.1	67.0	69.7	66.4	67.0	68.4	69.9	67.6	66.1	64.2	63.2	64.4
5	63.4	65.3	66.5	65.1	67.8	68.3	70.2	68.7	63.0	65.2	64.3	64.2
6	65.5	65.6	68.5	66.6	66.8	68.6	67.6	67.7	61.3	65.2	64.5	63.7
7	66.1	66.4	69.7	67.2	66.7	67.8	67.6	67.3	63.3	61.0	61.5	61.9
8	66.1	68.7	70.6	68.4	66.6	67.6	71.5	68.7	60.0	63.7	60.2	61.4
9	68.1	66.7	68.2	67.7	68.3	68.4	69.6	68.7	58.7	63.9	60.5	61.1
10	69.1	68.7	66.6	68.1	65.0	69.9	69.3	67.7	60.2	65.7	58.1	61.4
11	68.4	69.0	67.2	68.2	65.8	68.3	66.3	66.8	57.9	64.7	61.9	61.4
12	70.7	66.9	65.2	67.6	66.8	69.8	64.6	67.1	56.8	62.6	60.6	60.0
13	69.7	67.4	66.4	67.9	65.6	69.4	64.8	66.6	56.6	55.2	59.4	56.9
14	67.6	69.9	67.8	68.5	66.9	65.8	64.9	65.9	58.8	55.8	59.9	58.3
15	66.8	70.2	67.4	68.2	66.2	64.9	65.4	65.5	57.5	55.3	60.9	57.7
16	67.5	71.2	68.9	69.3	69.7	65.4	63.6	66.2	57.7	55.0	59.8	57.4
17	67.4	74.6	65.6	69.0	67.0	64.7	64.3	65.4	59.9	58.7	59.8	59.5
18	68.9	70.3	68.0	69.0	65.8	62.5	64.8	64.3	56.7	57.2	57.9	57.2
19	69.6	68.3	67.4	68.4	65.2	62.6	67.1	64.1	56.9	56.9	56.3	56.7
20	66.4	68.7	67.6	67.5	65.2	65.8	66.1	65.0	57.5	55.5	57.9	56.9
21	68.0	67.8	65.5	67.2	66.3	66.3	66.2	66.2	53.0	55.2	53.1	53.7
22	68.2	69.8	66.8	68.3	66.5	67.3	64.0	65.9	51.0	51.8	55.2	52.6
23	67.0	67.5	67.0	67.2	64.9	65.5	62.7	64.4	55.5	55.0	57.9	56.0
24	66.9	69.0	69.0	68.3	63.4	67.8	64.0	64.8	52.5	54.6	55.7	54.3
25	65.3	70.6	67.5	67.8	65.9	63.2	64.0	64.4	53.2	55.3	54.6	54.4
26	66.1	67.8	69.0	67.6	65.9	64.6	66.0	65.5	47.8	57.2	50.6	51.8
27	64.5	67.2	69.1	66.9	63.9	60.2	64.2	62.7	49.6	52.3	51.8	51.3
28	66.1	68.1	67.8	67.3	65.2	61.8	65.3	64.2	49.9	51.6	52.2	51.2
29	66.3	68.8	66.4	67.3	66.9	61.4	61.2	63.1	53.8	50.2	53.2	52.4
30	63.8	67.5	68.4	66.6	66.2	63.6	59.3	63.1	52.6	49.8	51.0	51.1
31	64.3	65.9	67.4	65.9	65.6	63.1	60.3	63.0				

Day of Month.	October.				November.				December.			
	1840–9	1850–9	1860–9	1840–69	1840–9	1850–9	1860–9	1840–69	1840–9	1850–9	1860–9	1840–69
1	48.6	51.1	51.3	50.4	43.2	45.2	45.8	44.7	27.5	32.3	29.3	29.7
2	50.2	51.0	54.4	51.9	42.5	42.3	42.0	42.3	29.8	28.6	28.5	29.4
3	50.0	50.4	50.8	50.4	41.9	39.3	40.0	40.4	29.5	28.8	29.2	29.2
4	48.9	53.1	50.9	51.1	40.0	40.4	40.5	40.3	31.1	28.7	31.9	30.6
5	50.6	52.0	49.2	50.6	42.6	40.9	39.2	40.8	26.5	28.6	28.7	28.0
6	50.2	50.4	48.2	49.7	38.7	42.2	35.1	38.5	28.2	33.0	28.9	30.1
7	51.0	48.8	53.2	50.9	41.0	40.2	35.9	38.9	30.7	28.5	31.0	30.1
8	51.7	48.7	50.4	50.2	38.0	39.3	38.8	38.8	33.9	26.7	26.6	29.2
9	50.1	53.3	52.7	51.2	39.1	38.5	40.5	39.4	33.0	28.1	25.8	29.1
10	47.8	49.7	51.2	49.7	39.3	35.9	35.9	37.1	30.4	27.0	26.7	27.9
11	47.3	50.7	48.6	48.9	38.2	35.6	36.8	36.9	27.5	27.0	26.6	27.0
12	47.1	47.2	44.2	46.1	41.4	40.3	36.6	39.4	24.6	24.8	23.4	24.2
13	43.6	48.6	43.2	45.2	38.2	35.7	38.3	37.5	30.2	26.1	21.4	25.9
14	44.0	44.9	46.2	45.0	36.6	35.4	38.6	35.5	31.9	31.1	20.1	27.6
15	43.0	42.6	45.6	43.8	35.7	36.2	34.0	35.3	29.1	28.7	23.3	27.2
16	45.4	42.5	47.8	45.3	37.7	35.1	36.9	36.6	26.3	26.8	27.5	26.8
17	41.2	45.8	48.2	45.2	38.7	35.2	41.5	38.4	23.7	21.8	28.0	24.5
18	42.2	47.4	49.2	46.3	35.5	36.5	34.7	35.6	23.4	16.8	26.0	22.5
19	41.6	44.5	47.6	44.6	34.2	35.3	37.4	35.7	26.3	19.0	25.9	23.8
20	41.1	45.0	45.3	43.7	36.2	32.3	36.7	35.1	22.9	24.7	20.3	22.7
21	39.5	44.6	44.1	42.7	34.4	34.7	34.4	34.6	23.8	25.7	23.2	24.2
22	40.0	45.4	44.9	43.6	37.6	35.3	32.8	35.2	19.6	22.1	21.9	21.2
23	40.7	43.2	40.3	41.3	37.3	34.7	33.6	35.2	23.2	19.7	19.8	20.9
24	42.7	40.6	40.4	41.2	36.0	29.1	30.8	32.0	24.1	18.4	23.1	21.8
25	40.8	40.3	40.6	40.6	29.7	31.4	26.6	32.4	[1]	[1]	[1]	[1]
26	38.6	39.8	40.3	39.6	27.5	33.6	34.6	32.3	25.2	20.6	29.9	25.7
27	38.1	41.4	38.7	39.4	25.1	34.8	35.4	31.7	26.0	24.0	31.4	27.0
28	38.9	43.4	40.0	40.8	27.6	34.3	35.9	32.8	27.8	20.5	27.1	25.3
29	42.4	42.1	43.4	42.6	26.2	33.5	37.8	32.6	30.2	18.5	28.4	25.6
30	41.3	45.8	43.8	43.6	28.4	33.7	31.7	31.2	28.4	23.7	24.7	25.6
31	38.2	42.2	44.6	41.8					26.7	22.0	24.5	28.2

[1] No observations made on this day.

Portland, Maine. Lat. 43° 39′. Long. 70° 15′ W. of G.

Alt. 87 feet. 37 years of observation; from 1816 to 1852, inclusive. Moody.
MS. in Smithsonian Coll.

Day of Month.	Jan.	Feb.	Mar.	Apr.	May.	June.	July.	Aug.	Sept.	Oct.	Nov.	Dec.
	°	°	°	°	°	°	°	°	°	°	°	°
1	21.0	16.4	24.7	36.0	46.7	55.0	64.8	64.7	61.1	51.2	41.9	28.2
2	20.1	16.1	23.8	36.1	46.9	56.4	65.7	66.2	61.6	51.9	42.1	29.3
3	18.4	19.2	23.3	36.1	46.8	57.0	63.8	66.3	61.8	52.0	40.1	28.9
4	18.5	18.3	24.5	36.5	46.4	57.6	64.5	66.6	62.7	50.3	40.5	29.3
5	18.0	14.7	26.8	36.4	45.7	58.5	65.0	66.2	62.6	50.3	40.6	29.0
6	18.8	17.7	28.1	37.6	46.4	58.7	66.3	65.0	62.8	51.8	39.3	26.0
7	20.3	19.2	28.1	38.8	48.2	58.4	66.9	65.9	60.5	49.6	39.4	27.1
8	20.0	19.2	28.1	38.7	48.6	59.8	66.0	66.4	60.0	49.3	39.8	28.5
9	21.1	17.2	29.2	38.9	48.8	59.8	66.8	65.6	60.1	50.7	38.6	28.8
10	22.0	20.0	28.7	38.9	47.7	60.3	67.0	66.4	60.2	49.5	37.9	27.1
11	18.0	21.2	28.6	37.8	48.8	59.9	67.1	65.7	59.3	48.2	37.3	24.1
12	20.4	18.5	29.4	37.9	50.1	59.4	67.5	66.2	58.0	47.8	37.4	24.1
13	18.3	17.9	31.1	38.7	49.3	59.1	67.8	66.5	57.5	47.6	35.2	23.1
14	17.9	17.8	29.1	38.4	49.4	60.0	66.6	65.8	57.1	46.1	36.1	25.3
15	19.3	18.3	28.6	39.0	50.2	59.6	67.5	65.1	57.4	45.2	35.7	24.8
16	21.1	19.8	28.3	38.2	51.2	60.5	66.7	64.0	55.7	46.4	35.7	22.4
17	20.6	19.0	29.2	40.2	52.7	60.6	67.6	64.1	55.8	46.4	36.2	22.5
18	19.8	20.9	28.9	39.6	52.6	60.3	66.8	64.2	58.0	47 3	36.3	22.1
19	17.5	21.5	29.7	40.6	51.6	62.7	67.4	63.9	58.2	48.5	34.5	21.6
20	18.8	24.9	30.9	41.3	51.5	61.7	67.5	64.2	59.1	45.3	33.7	22.2
21	19.9	26.6	30.8	41.3	54.2	62.0	68.0	63.6	56.1	43.5	33.6	21.6
22	17.8	27.3	29.7	43.9	51.9	61.8	68.3	63.8	53.7	43.3	33.4	16.1
23	17.1	25.3	32.0	43.0	53.5	61.3	67.4	64.3	53.9	43.7	33.4	16.2
24	16.9	22.0	34.0	42.7	52.9	62.5	66.1	63.9	53.5	44.9	31.2	21.5
25	18.8	22.4	33.7	41.3	53.4	61.7	65.8	64.2	53.5	41.9	30.2	23.9
26	21.1	24.3	33.1	44.4	53.2	62.7	64.7	63.4	53.2	41.5	30.2	20.1
27	20.8	24.8	33.2	44.5	53.0	62.8	65.4	62.8	52.8	41.2	29.2	19.6
28	20.1	24.4	33.9	43.6	55.1	63.3	65.6	62.0	53.1	41.3	27.3	22.1
29	19.3	26.0	33.6	45.5	53.7	63.2	66.2	62.0	51.9	41.8	28.9	21.6
30	18.6		33.2	45.6	52.8	61.3	66.0	63.1	52.3	42.0	29.9	20.8
31	16.7		34.9		54.5		65.7	62.9		39.8		21.8

Observations at ⊙ rise, noon, and 8 P. M. Means uncorrected.

Using the tables for Montreal and Amherst, the correction to mean deduced from observations at ⊙ rise, noon, and 8 P. M., to refer to mean of day is very small, for 6 months it is nearly 0, and probably does not rise to 0.2 or 0.3 in any one month.

Salem, Mass. Lat. 42° 31′. Long. 70° 53′ W. of G.

Alt. 30 feet.[1] 43 years of observation; from 1786 to 1828, inclusive. Dr Holyoke.
MS. in Smithsonian Coll.

Day of Month.	Jan.	Feb.	Mar.	Apr.	May.	June.	July.	Aug.	Sept.	Oct.	Nov.	Dec.
1	28.0	23.5	31.9	41.3	54.8	62.7	73.5	73.1	67.2	55.4	41.5	35.0
2	28.2	24.9	30.6	41.7	53.5	63.2	73.1	72.6	68.8	56.7	41.6	34.2
3	24.9	26.5	31.3	41.2	52.2	65.1	72.8	71.5	68.4	56.6	42.8	32.3
4	26.9	27.1	30.7	42.8	54.5	64.1	72.0	72.1	68.0	56.5	42.9	33.7
5	24.6	22.8	30.2	44.2	53.7	64.9	72.7	73.7	66.2	56.1	43.9	31.6
6	25.2	24.2	32.5	43.2	52.6	65.7	72.9	71.4	65.4	57.2	43.4	33.0
7	25.6	28.2	31.1	43.8	52.7	65.3	72.9	72.2	63.6	52.1	42.4	33.3
8	26.3	28.3	31.3	43.9	52.7	65.8	72.9	73.6	64.9	52.2	41.5	33.0
9	25.6	27.2	30.9	43.2	53.7	65.0	72.8	73.4	64.7	52.5	41.5	32.1
10	26.3	25.1	32.0	41.8	54.7	66.7	73.6	73.4	65.0	54.4	43.2	30.4
11	25.1	26.4	34.5	43.0	54.4	66.6	73.0	72.9	65.3	52.6	41.3	30.0
12	26.5	28.6	35.7	43.1	54.4	66.6	73.9	72.6	65.1	53.6	39.3	29.0
13	24.6	27.2	35.2	44.5	55.4	68.1	73.3	72.3	64.5	53.2	38.6	30.8
14	23.9	27.8	34.1	45.7	56.3	66.8	72.0	71.0	64.9	52.2	38.8	31.6
15	26.5	26.4	34.8	45.6	55.9	67.4	73.6	70.7	65.0	53.4	39.1	30.1
16	26.0	25.0	35.8	45.8	55.9	66.8	72.9	71.1	63.6	51.1	39.3	28.7
17	26.7	26.5	36.3	47.1	55.3	68.9	73.1	71.1	62.7	50.4	38.4	28.6
18	24.8	29.7	36.2	47.8	56.7	67.7	73.5	71.0	62.6	47.4	38.1	28.7
19	23.0	27.1	36.9	48.1	56.7	69.6	72.1	70.6	62.5	47.4	36.4	30.3
20	25.2	30.2	36.4	48.9	57.9	68.7	73.0	71.1	60.3	46.0	35.7	29.0

[1] Given as 75 feet in the general table.

Salem.—Continued.

Day of Month.	Jan.	Feb.	Mar.	Apr.	May.	June.	July.	Aug.	Sept.	Oct.	Nov.	Dec.
	°	°	°	°	°	°	°	°	°	°	°	°
21	25.3	31.0	37.3	47.7	58.8	68.4	71.9	69.6	60.8	48.6	37.5	27.9
22	23.8	30.4	36.5	46.3	60.4	68.6	72.6	69.5	58.1	47.7	36.3	26.3
23	23.4	27.7	38.3	48.1	61.1	70.6	74.0	68.8	58.7	44.9	35.7	26.6
24	24.6	29.8	38.4	47.8	62.4	71.7	74.2	68.4	58.5	45.2	35.8	28.5
25	23.1	28.8	38.9	48.4	61.1	71.5	73.5	69.3	58.7	43.7	34.3	26.3
26	24.4	29.1	38.1	50.4	61.4	69.2	72.2	68.9	57.5	46.8	33.2	26.8
27	25.4	30.0	38.0	50.2	60.2	70.3	72.4	68.6	57.2	44.1	35.7	28.4
28	27.5	30.9	39.1	49.6	61.6	71.8	72.5	68.3	56.8	45.6	35.0	29.5
29	26.0	30.5	38.4	50.5	62.9	72.6	73.1	69.3	56.4	44.9	35.7	31.0
30	24.7		38.5	52.3	63.1	72.4	72.9	68.7	56.5	43.5	36.0	28.5
31	24.1		39.9		61.5		74.0	67.4		41.7		29.9

Observations at 8 A. M. Tabular numbers corrected for daily fluctuation.

To correct the table of temperatures observed at 8 A. M., for daily fluctuation, two sets of corrections were applied; first, the observed means were referred to the means from observations at 8 A. M., Noon, sunset, and 10 P. M., taken at Salem from a 10 year series between 1819 and 1828, inclusive; secondly, the means so corrected were referred to the daily mean by means of the Amherst table. The two sets of corrections and their sum are as follows:—

	I.	II.	I & II.		I.	II.	I & II.
	°	°	°		°	°	°
January	+4.52	—0.89	+3.63	July	+2.26	—0.96	+1.30
February	+4.48	—0.47	+4.01	August	+2.51	—0.82	+1.69
March	+3.52	—0.91	+2.61	September	+3.49	—1.25	+2.24
April	+2.49	—1.03	+1.46	October	+4.54	—1.62	+2.92
May	+1.94	—0.98	+0.96	November	+3.57	—1.03	+2.54
June	+1.70	—0.99	+0.71	December	+4.16	—0.46	—3.70

The above corrections refer to the middle of each month, and by interpolation they were found for each day.

Williamstown, Mass. Lat. 42° 43′. Long. 73° 13′ W. of G.

Alt. 721 feet. 23 years of observation; from 1816 to 1838, inclusive. Prof. C. Dewey and Prof. E. Kellogg. MS. in Smithsonian Coll.

Day of Month.	Jan.	Feb.	Mar.	Apr.	May.	June.	July.	Aug.	Sept.	Oct.	Nov.	Dec.
1	25.8	16.1	26.2	38.6	54.9	63.9	70.4	69.9	62.5	53.5	40.7	31.6
2	22.8	18.9	24.8	38.6	53.9	64.5	70.4	69.3	62.8	54.8	40.5	30.8
3	22.0	20.7	23.9	39.8	54.4	63.3	68.8	69.5	63.6	52.9	39.7	29.3
4	22.1	19.5	25.5	39.2	52.9	65.1	69.7	68.4	64.6	50.4	41.4	28.5
5	23.2	14.8	29.6	40.3	51.6	65.4	70.3	67.7	64.4	52.9	41.3	28.0
6	22.9	17.6	30.8	40.6	54.1	63.4	70.7	67.4	63.6	52.0	37.9	28.5
7	21.5	21.7	28.6	42.0	52.3	67.4	72.0	69.3	61.7	50.7	40.1	29.8
8	22.7	21.2	28.3	42.8	51.6	65.7	71.1	69.6	61.4	50.0	40.1	30.0
9	23.9	21.3	29.2	41.5	49.3	66.0	70.3	68.0	62.0	52.0	39.1	29.0
10	23.1	24.5	31.0	41.4	51.7	64.7	70.0	69.0	61.2	50.5	40.0	25.9
11	19.4	22.5	31.9	41.3	53.3	66.6	70.9	70.0	61.5	49.5	39.3	27.3
12	22.4	21.7	33.1	41.0	56.0	66.8	70.5	70.9	59.8	47.9	39.0	27.1
13	24.0	21.2	33.6	41.6	55.0	66.0	69.0	69.1	59.5	47.8	34.3	25.4
14	18.8	20.3	30.3	43.9	54.3	65.9	69.1	68.5	59.7	46.7	35.8	26.7
15	21.4	21.7	29.8	43.5	55.6	65.9	69.2	67.4	58.6	46.4	35.2	25.5
16	22.5	22.4	30.1	44.6	56.2	66.8	69.1	66.6	57.7	48.2	36.4	19.4
17	24.3	22.9	29.0	43.9	57.4	66.7	68.6	66.7	58.4	47.0	38.2	22.8
18	24.9	23.9	29.7	43.5	59.3	66.3	69.2	67.1	59.2	48.0	36.3	26.9
19	23.2	23.3	30.1	44.7	58.6	65.9	70.3	66.9	58.1	46.7	35.3	26.7
20	20.5	27.9	33.8	46.8	59.0	63.9	70.8	66.9	57.9	46.9	35.4	26.0
21	20.3	30.6	31.8	47.1	61.0	66.2	69.5	66.7	56.7	44.9	35.0	22.7
22	20.7	29.0	32.2	44.1	61.2	66.2	69.6	66.2	55.3	43.4	35.0	17.8
23	18.7	26.5	35.4	46.2	59.3	66.4	70.8	69.7	55.0	46.3	33.7	17.5
24	17.9	23.7	37.9	43.3	59.7	67.1	70.3	63.8	55.2	45.0	29.9	24.4
25	18.1	24.8	37.7	46.2	59.6	66.4	69.2	63.6	55.4	40.3	29.1	26.7
26	23.0	24.6	35.3	48.9	58.1	67.0	68.0	64.7	54.0	40.9	30.0	24.0
27	23.3	27.5	35.5	46.8	60.1	67.1	68.9	63.8	55.6	41.9	29.3	22.2
28	24.0	24.4	36.7	47.5	62.7	67.3	69.6	62.7	54.2	40.3	30.0	23.0
29	20.6	26.7	34.5	51.6	60.7	67.3	70.5	62.6	63.0	39.9	31.4	25.2
30	19.8		35.5	51.5	60.5	70.0	71.3	69.3	51.8	39.9	32.0	22.1
31	20.8		37.7		62.5		70.5	64.9		39.7		28.0

Observing hours 7_m, 2_a, 9_a. Tabular quantities uncorrected for daily fluctuation.

Day of Month.	Jan. (29)	Feb. (29)	Mar. (29)	April. (29)	May. (29)	June.	July.	Aug.	Sept.	Oct.	Nov.	Dec. (29)

Providence, Rhode Island. Lat. 41° 50′. Long. 71° 24′ W. of G.

Alt. 155 feet. 28½ years of observation; Dec. 1831, to May, 1860, inclusive. Prof. A. Caswell, observer.

Smithsonian Cont. to Knowl. Washington, 1860.

Day of Month.	Jan.	Feb.	Mar.	April.	May.	June.	July.	Aug.	Sept.	Oct.	Nov.	Dec.
	°	°	°	°	°	°	°	°	°	°	°	°
1	28.3	24.6	29.8	41.0	51.7	59.5	69.7	70.4	65.4	56.5	44.7	33.5
2	25.9	24.6	29.0	39.5	51.6	62.4	69.7	70.4	65.6	57.6	46.6	33.1
3	25.3	24.8	27.5	41.6	52.1	63.9	69.0	70.0	67.2	54.5	45.8	34.1
4	26.2	23.8	29.2	42.6	52.0	63.2	69.9	69.9	67.7	53.7	45.8	33.3
5	26.4	24.7	30.4	42.4	51.3	62.3	70.4	71.1	67.8	53.6	45.2	32.2
6	26.4	24.7	32.5	43.4	53.4	62.2	67.6	71.0	67.2	54.6	43.3	31.2
7	28.1	25.8	32.1	43.6	53.5	61.9	67.5	70.7	65.9	52.9	42.8	32.4
8	27.1	26.0	34.0	44.5	53.1	63.1	71.3	70.8	64.5	54.0	44.1	32.7
9	27.3	26.0	34.8	45.5	53.7	64.3	71.2	71.2	65.6	54.2	44.3	32.3
10	27.7	25.4	33.6	44.6	52.9	65.2	71.3	69.7	63.7	52.7	41.6	33.0
11	27.5	25.9	32.7	44.3	53.7	63.9	71.2	69.7	65.0	52.2	40.6	31.3
12	27.5	23.9	33.3	45.9	56.3	63.2	71.2	71.2	63.0	54.0	42.4	29.4
13	27.4	24.0	36.4	44.9	55.8	64.5	71.9	72.1	60.7	53.5	42.4	28.6
14	28.2	26.4	34.3	42.4	55.5	65.8	72.1	71.8	59.4	50.1	40.3	30.7
15	29.4	27.1	34.5	42.7	55.7	65.6	71.9	69.5	61.3	48.7	38.3	30.9
16	29.5	28.0	34.4	43.0	57.5	65.6	70.0	68.5	60.3	50.7	39.7	28.3
17	29.6	25.5	36.1	43.8	58.2	65.6	71.6	68.3	60.5	52.0	40.2	28.9
18	25.5	25.5	36.2	44.2	58.1	65.8	72.7	68.3	63.4	53.9	42.1	26.4
19	23.3	27.4	35.5	45.5	58.5	67.1	72.8	68.1	62.7	52.8	40.2	26.4
20	26.3	30.2	37.0	45.8	57.0	67.0	72.2	67.4	63.2	49.5	37.3	27.6
21	29.6	31.1	38.1	47.3	57.1	67.9	72.3	67.9	61.6	47.5	37.2	26.9
22	25.2	32.5	34.8	49.0	56.4	67.0	72.3	68.8	57.6	48.9	39.4	25.4
23	23.9	32.3	35.0	48.4	58.2	67.8	71.9	68.4	57.0	49.1	39.5	25.5
24	26.2	28.7	37.0	48.5	58.2	68.0	72.2	68.8	57.6	49.3	36.6	26.7
25	28.5	27.8	37.2	47.5	57.4	68.3	72.1	67.9	58.0	46.9	34.2	27.7
26	29.6	28.4	37.7	50.1	58.4	68.5	72.1	66.7	57.4	44.3	34.2	26.8
27	26.8	29.6	39.7	49.9	58.3	69.0	70.8	67.4	57.4	45.8	32.7	24.9
28	26.5	29.6	39.7	49.1	60.8	69.7	70.3	66.4	57.4	45.3	32.6	27.5
29	27.7	32.4	39.1	50.7	59.0	70.4	70.7	66.1	55.4	46.6	33.0	27.4
30	29.1		39.7	51.1	56.8	70.3	71.0	66.7	55.4	47.5	34.0	26.4
31	26.5		40.9		56.4		71.0	67.3		44.8		27.7

Observing hours various, generally $\odot_r$, 1_a or 2_a, 10_a, from Oct. to March, inclusive, and 6_m, 1_a or 2_a, 10_a, in the remaining months. The tabular quantities are corrected for daily fluctuation.

To correct the observed daily means resulting from three observations a day, taken at various hours, the following table was prepared and used:—

		°		°		°		°
January	7, 1, 9	—0.2	⊙, 1, 10	—0.1	⊙, 2, 10	—0.2		
February	7, 1, 10	+0.1	⊙, 1, 10	+0.1	⊙, 2, 10	0.0		
March	6, 1, 10	+0.5	⊙, 1, 10	+0.4	6, 2, 10	+0.3	⊙, 2, 10	+0.2
April	⊙, 1, 9	+0.5	⊙, 1, 10	+0.8	6, 1, 10	+0.8	6, 2, 10 } ⊙, 2, 10 }	+0.6 } +0.6 }
May	⊙, 1, 10	+1.2	6, 1, 10	+0.7	6, 2, 10	+0.5		
June	6, 1, 10	+0.5	5, 1, 10 } ⊙, 1, 10 }	+1.2 } +1.3 }	6, 2, 10	+0.3		
July	⊙, 1, 10	+1.0	5, 1, 10	+0.9	6, 1, 10	+0.5	6, 2, 10	+0.4
August	⊙, 1, 10	+0.9	6, 1, 10	+0.6	5, 1, 10	+0.5	6, 2, 10	+0.5
September	⊙, 1, 10	+0.7	6, 1, 10	+0.7	6, 2, 10	+0.5		
October	⊙, 1, 10	+0.4	6, 1, 10	+0.4	⊙, 2, 10	+0.3		
November	⊙, 1, 10	—0 1			⊙, 2, 10	—0.1		
December	⊙, 1, 10	—0.2	7, 1, 9	—0.3	⊙, 2, 10	—0.3		

The above corrections apply to the middle of each month, and were interpolated for every day.

Day of Month.	Jan.	Feb.	Mar.	Apr.	May.	June.	July.	Aug.	Sept.	Oct.	Nov.	Dec.

Albany, New York. Lat. 42° 39′. Long. 73° 44′ W. of G.

Alt. 130 feet. 21 years of observation; including the years 1820 to 1829, inclusive.

MS. in Smithsonian Coll.

Day of Month.	Jan.	Feb.	Mar.	Apr.	May.	June.	July.	Aug.	Sept.	Oct.	Nov.	Dec.
	°	°	°	°	°	°	°	°	°	°	°	°
1	25.4	18.4	27.2	42.6	53.3	64.5	73.3	71.6	64.3	55.7	43.6	35.8
2	23.4	22.7	29.5	43.1	54.7	66.6	71.2	71.4	67.2	57.0	43.3	34.2
3	22.8	23.4	28.0	43.4	57.0	66.6	70.8	73.4	65.2	56.3	43.4	32.8
4	19.8	19.9	29.3	43.3	55.9	68.6	71.4	71.4	66.7	56.0	44.0	31.7
5	22.1	20.1	33.3	43.9	55.1	68.8	72.0	71.6	65.0	56.3	42.9	31.0
6	23.0	22.7	31.6	45.7	57.4	68.7	72.5	72.8	64.9	53.8	41.1	32.3
7	24.3	24.4	30.6	45.9	55.2	70.0	73.5	74.2	62.2	53.8	42.8	34.7
8	23.3	24.1	32.2	45.7	55.6	68.6	73.1	73.0	61.9	53.7	42.4	32.9
9	24.3	23.6	33.9	45.7	54.6	67.5	72.0	71.3	62.5	55.1	42.0	31.4
10	22.8	27.2	35.1	48.6	54.9	66.3	72.3	72.0	62.6	53.6	42.0	29.8
11	21.4	25.9	35.8	46.6	57.1	68.9	70.6	73.2	63.3	51.0	40.8	30.5
12	24.8	23.3	36.9	47.1	59.4	69.5	70.3	72.2	61.2	50.5	38.7	28.1
13	24.3	25.2	33.7	46.6	58.5	69.4	69.4	71.3	62.2	52.3	37.6	29.2
14	23.7	23.8	31.5	49.8	59.8	68.2	72.2	71.3	61.9	49.6	38.0	30.3
15	23.7	26.2	34.0	50.4	58.7	70.0	72.3	69.8	61.3	50.0	36.0	28.9
16	24.4	28.2	32.3	48.7	58.6	70.4	72.3	70.1	62.3	49.5	38.4	28.9
17	24.9	30.0	32.8	48.6	62.3	68.8	72.1	71.6	60.5	50.6	39.0	25.9
18	24.7	29.1	33.5	49.9	63.7	68.8	71.9	68.5	60.0	51.5	37.1	27.6
19	25.6	28.5	35.3	51.9	62.5	69.1	73.1	68.5	60.7	48.5	37.0	28.0
20	23.0	30.1	37.4	53.5	63.8	67.7	71.3	69.7	61.0	47.5	36.6	29.9
21	20.6	30.7	33.5	50.9	61.7	68.3	73.6	68.7	60.2	45.7	36.7	28.9
22	22.8	29.5	35.7	50.5	61.7	67.9	73.3	69.1	57.3	44.6	36.7	26.0
23	21.1	27.9	37.5	50.7	64.3	68.2	72.6	68.9	57.9	48.9	37.0	21.7
24	17.9	26.3	40.0	47.5	62.9	69.0	72.9	69.1	57.6	46.6	34.4	28.9
25	21.3	26.6	38.5	48.9	63.2	69.5	72.4	68.5	57.9	46.6	35.7	26.7
26	25.0	30.4	39.1	51.8	63.1	70.7	71.6	67.6	55.9	45.3	34.8	24.2
27	25.6	28.1	42.4	52.7	65.1	73.4	72.3	66.6	56.9	45.7	34.1	25.9
28	25.9	27.4	40.9	51.0	67.0	70.4	71.7	66.3	55.3	44.7	34.3	27.5
29	22.6	24.7	40.3	53.9	64.2	71.3	72.2	67.3	54.9	45.3	33.8	27.6
30	21.0		40.4	53.5	64.2	73.3	73.1	68.9	55.5	44.2	34.3	27.7
31	20.8		41.8		64.3		73.6	69.6		42.6		28.3

Observations at 3 P. M. for 2 years, at 9 P. M. for 10 years, and at 7 A. M., 2 and 9 P. M. for 9 years. Tabular numbers corrected for daily fluctuation.

In computing the original table, the observations at 3 P. M. were used for two of the years, those at 9 P. M. for ten, and the daily means at 7 A. M., 2 and 9 P. M. for the remaining nine. When combined they afford a tolerable approximation to the true mean, as may be seen from the following statement, which shows the correction for daily fluctuation at 2 and 9 P. M. deduced from the observations of ten years of this series, from 1820 to 1829, inclusive, and the reduction from 2 P. M. to 3 P. M. from the Mohawk table of daily fluctuation:—

	Corr'n at 2 P. M.	Refer'd to 3 P. M.	Corr'n at 3 P. M.	Corr'n at 9 P. M.	Corr'n to $7_m, 2_a, 9_a$		Corr'n at 2 P. M.	Refer'd to 3 P. M.	Corr'n at 3 P. M.	Corr'n at 9 P. M.	Corr'n to $7_m, 2_a, 9_a$
	°		°	°	°		°		°	°	°
January	—4.4	—.1	—4.5	+0.7	—0.3	July	—7.7	—.3	—8.0	+1.9	—0.3
February	—5.4	—.2	—5.6	+0.6	—0.3	August	—8.3	—.6	—8.9	+1.7	—0.2
March	—6.6	—.3	—6.9	+1.0	—0.1	September	—7.3	—.6	—7.9	+1.4	—0.2
April	—8.3	—.6	—8.9	+2.2	—0.1	October	—6.8	—.3	—7.1	+1.3	—0.2
May	—8.4	—.5	—8.9	+1.7	—0.3	November	—4.3	—.1	—4.4	+0.9	—0.1
June	—7.9	—.5	—8.4	+1.8	—0.5	December	—3.8	+.1	—3.7	+0.7	—0.3

The correction to mean of 7, 2, 9 is from the Mohawk table; now twice the correction 3 P. M. + ten times that at 9 P. M. + nine times that at 7, 2, 9, divided by 21, gives the following table of corrections:—

	°		°		°		°
January	—0.2	April	+0.1	July	0.0	October	—0.1
February	—0.4	May	—0.1	August	—0.1	November	0.0
March	—0.2	June	—0.1	September	—0.1	December	—0.1

These small corrections were applied, they answer to the middle of each month, and were interpolated for any other day.

Geneva, New York. Lat. 42° 53′. Long. 77° 01′ W. of G.

Alt. 567 feet. From 12 years of observation; from 1854 to 1865, inclusive. Dr. W. D. Wilson.
In the 20th Annual Report of the Regents of the University of the State of New York, Albany, 1868.

Day of Month.	Jan.	Feb.	Mar.	Apr.	May.	June.	July.	Aug.	Sept.	Oct.	Nov.	Dec.
	°	°	°	°	°	°	°	°	°	°	°	°
1	24.73	27.81	29.29	33.32	49.19	62.00	68.19	73.29	63.93	54.13	48.25	34.98
2	23.31	21.45	28.72	38.45	48.98	62.92	68.21	73.12	62.72	55.45	47.92	32.01
3	26.19	19.09	31.81	41.44	48.14	62.40	69.68	71.64	63.76	58.94	44.75	30.26
4	27.22	19.41	30.84	41.42	50.38	60.15	64.54	70.93	63.65	58.54	44.23	29.84
5	24.82	23.10	29.26	41.29	53.12	60.49	68.67	71.34	65.38	56.87	43.42	31.30
6	25.34	23.34	28.26	37.80	52.17	60.89	70.62	71.15	65.17	54.51	41.32	32.17
7	24.74	26.11	27.82	41.98	51.63	61.55	71.98	70.78	65.01	54.60	43.38	32.03
8	19.09	24.19	29.78	34.92	55.31	60.34	71.47	71.44	65.12	52.82	43.13	28.35
9	22.54	24.43	29.66	41.81	55.18	61.68	71.36	71.94	64.45	50.12	41.69	30.43
10	25.00	19.93	26.30	40.23	53.66	61.10	71.43	72.40	66.94	50.59	40.58	30.70
11	23.57	21.28	30.62	42.63	51.63	60.81	70.09	71.53	66.56	52.41	40.85	29.84
12	28.11	23.68	29.53	44.63	54.31	63.13	69.35	70.03	63.03	50.65	42.37	28.25
13	27.32	25.05	29.50	42.17	51.71	61.94	69.02	70.59	59.39	49.48	39.98	33.63
14	27.52	25.00	35.16	42.79	56.27	63.72	70.52	63.35	61.38	48.48	36.82	35.69
15	28.29	27.54	35.31	41.92	58.22	66.04	72.35	67.88	62.71	45.73	34.87	31.06
16	26.10	27.15	36.71	43.64	58.17	61.53	71.57	67.99	60.37	48.62	38.84	33.08
17	24.21	25.16	35.67	43.72	55.92	64.49	72.24	67.87	63.69	48.74	38.61	27.96
18	22.42	29.12	33.06	46.54	56.23	67.75	72.41	68.23	61.03	51.74	39.70	25.01
19	25.57	22.78	30.24	45.46	55.76	66.45	74.32	66.90	58.21	49.06	38.87	27.31
20	27.10	26.59	30.76	44.02	55.82	66.00	71.38	68.45	58.89	46.37	35.03	26.22
21	25.89	26.93	32.52	47.07	58.29	67.12	67.79	69.29	59.20	47.30	35.30	25.96
22	24.19	30.51	32.82	49.16	56.71	69.89	68.26	68.53	55.54	47.62	35.51	23.48
23	26.49	29.71	35.65	45.88	59.91	65.48	68.32	65.88	56.94	45.14	36.32	24.25
24	26.28	27.86	32.96	45.25	63.29	66.61	70.12	68.00	57.90	45.07	31.40	21.87
25	27.62	27.04	33.62	45.94	60.84	70.17	71.79	66.86	55.84	43.09	34.05	24.26
26	25.55	27.72	33.00	47.70	60.65	72.25	72.53	67.55	57.18	41.29	34.27	30.61
27	24.34	31.02	33.10	47.68	60.25	69.88	71.66	65.39	57.64	41.54	36.13	28.73
28	27.32	29.92	32.70	46.76	57.32	72.35	72.12	65.38	56.53	45.17	35.75	27.38
29	26.08	33.37	37.22	49.30	57.57	72.88	71.37	63.77	55.37	47.85	34.62	25.22
30	25.22		37.82	49.70	57.65	69.48	70.96	61.55	52.88	49.68	36.22	27.82
31	22.18		40.00		62.31		71.46	62.41		48.66		22.85

Value of April 8 doubtful. Observing hours, 7_m, 2_a, 9_a. Tabular quantities uncorrected for daily fluctuation.

Marietta, Ohio. Lat. 39° 28′. Long. 81° 26′ W. of G.

Alt. 580 feet.[1] 32 years; between 1818–1823 and 1829–1859. J. Wood and Dr. S. P. Hildreth.
Smithsonian Cont. to Knowl. No. 120. Washington, June, 1867.

Day of Month.	Jan.	Feb.	Mar.	Apr.	May.	June.	July.	Aug.	Sept.	Oct.	Nov.	Dec.
				(31 yr's)	(31 yr's)							[2]
1	33.2	30.2	38.6	47.3	60.8	65.0	72.6	71.4	68.9	59.6	47.1	37.2
2	31.1	31.5	35.7	47.2	59.8	66.8	72.3	71.5	68.6	59.0	48.0	36.9
3	30.0	31.4	34.8	49.4	60.0	67.3	70.8	73.0	68.7	57.4	47.9	36.3
4	31.1	30.1	37.2	50.4	60.6	67.1	68.9	72.5	69.0	55.8	47.7	36.0
5	30.4	29.2	37.5	49.3	61.1	67.2	71.6	71.9	69.6	54.9	46.3	35.6
6	32.7	30.2	38.4	49.1	59.2	67.0	72.5	72.7	68.7	54.8	46.0	35.7
7	33.9	30.0	42.0	53.1	60.2	68.4	73.6	72.5	68.7	54.4	46.3	35.7
8	30.9	30.7	41.6	51.2	59.5	68.4	73.8	72.6	69.0	56.2	45.6	35.4
9	30.9	31.6	41.4	50.7	59.4	69.2	73.3	72.4	68.6	56.4	44.6	34.7
10	30.4	31.6	41.3	52.5	58.9	68.9	73.0	72.7	68.3	55.1	44.1	33.4
11	31.4	31.9	41.8	53.0	61.1	68.5	72.4	72.9	65.7	54.5	45.6	33.8
12	30.6	33.0	43.3	53.0	60.5	69.1	72.5	72.7	63.5	53.4	45.5	32.4
13	31.0	32.4	42.7	53.2	60.7	69.4	73.5	73.7	63.3	51.6	41.3	33.8
14	33.6	33.6	41.6	51.5	62.0	70.0	73.2	74.3	64.3	50.3	41.0	35.1
15	34.7	33.7	40.9	50.6	60.6	70.0	72.0	73.3	64.2	49.8	40.2	32.9
16	32.6	32.7	41.5	51.6	62.3	70.3	71.8	72.8	63.3	52.7	40.8	32.4
17	32.8	30.9	41.8	52.6	62.8	70.7	72.9	72.3	63.4	52.8	43.0	31.6
18	31.9	33.6	40.9	50.6	61.9	70.6	73.2	71.9	63.8	52.6	42.2	31.4
19	29.8	36.1	40.1	52.1	60.8	70.0	74.3	71.8	64.1	50.5	39.4	33.4
20	33.4	36.5	41.1	54.5	60.7	70.0	73.6	70.5	64.5	49.6	40.0	32.3

[1] Stated to be 670 feet in the general table.

[2] After 16th 30 years.

Marrietta.—Continued.

Day of Month.	Jan.	Feb.	Mar.	Apr.	May.	June.	July.	Aug.	Sept.	Oct.	Nov.	Dec.
21	33.1°	37.3°	42.9°	56.5°	62.0°	69.3°	74.0°	70.9°	62.2°	48.5°	41.7°	30.8°
22	30.3	37.9	42.0	58.6	63.6	70.3	73.6	70.6	60.5	48.9	42.5	29.9
23	28.7	36.6	43.5	57.9	64.3	70.1	74.5	68.6	59.7	51.4	40.9	29.4
24	30.1	35.4	45.0	57.8	63.1	70.2	74.3	69.7	61.5	48.1	38.1	32.0
25	31.3	35.7	44.7	58.2	62.8	70.5	74.1	69.8	61.5	47.8	36.4	33.3
26	32.1	36.8	47.1	57.6	63.8	72.0	74.0	69.7	60.1	47.5	35.9	32.3
27	31.1	36.4	46.1	56.0	64.7	73.0	73.4	69.5	60.2	47.4	33.8	30.8
28	31.9	36.4	46.6	58.1	65.5	72.5	74.1	69.0	58.3	46.2	36.6	32.2
29	33.4	39.0	47.1	59.1	66.5	72.7	75.0	68.9	58.5	45.8	37.9	32.4
30	33.7		45.9	61.3	65.6	72.4	74.7	69.3	58.1	46.3	37.6	33.0
31	32.2		48.6		64.3		72.7	69.6		46.9		31.6

Hours of observations various: During 5 years $\odot_r$, 2_a, $\odot_s$, during the remaining years generally 6_m, 2_a, 9_a in summer, and 7_m, 2_a, 9_a in winter; the tabular numbers are corrected for daily fluctuation; see table on p. 16 of the Smithsonian Cont. to Knowl., No. 120. Washington, 1867.

MEAN TEMPERATURE OF EACH DAY OF THE YEAR.

Washington, Arkansas. Lat. 33° 44′. Long. 93° 41′ W. of G.

Alt. 660 feet. From 20 years of observations; from 1840 to 1859, inclusive. Dr. N. D. Smith.

Smithsonian Cont. to Knowl. Washington, 1860.

Day of Month.	Jan.	Feb.	Mar.	Apr.	May.	June.	July.	Aug.	Sept.	Oct.	Nov.	Dec.
1	40.57	46.02	50.60	57.50	66.52	73.40	77.82	77.48	75.97	66.37	58.60	48.27
2	42.97	45.57	50.17	60.70	67.65	74.58	77.57	77.80	75.80	65.62	59.00	47.42
3	42.25	42.22	47.80	62.00	66.97	75.11	77.37	77.83	76.27	65.12	59.67	43.87
4	41.90	43.37	50.85	62.77	66.27	74.82	78.30	78.80	76.80	66.27	58.05	44.57
5	46.65	44.60	53.50	59.35	66.00	74.98	78.20	78.60	76.10	66.32	57.55	45.47
6	46.62	46.27	54.90	58.95	66.58	74.47	79.32	78.90	75.90	65.17	53.92	43.42
7	41.30	45.90	53.65	61.22	66.98	75.53	79.75	79.50	76.67	65.05	54.17	44.35
8	42.00	44.90	55.47	61.82	66.79	75.66	80.12	79.10	76.10	64.37	52.32	44.17
9	40.12	44.32	54.45	63.50	66.63	75.56	79.85	79.55	75.72	63.82	52.47	44.50
10	40.00	43.42	52.17	64.70	67.90	73.92	79.97	78.68	74.57	65.72	52.35	43.65
11	41.85	45.25	51.87	62.97	68.21	73.63	78.90	79.28	74.72	66.27	54.40	42.10
12	42.75	48.20	50.85	61.87	69.50	74.28	79.57	79.00	74.50	64.00	49.90	43.77
13	43.87	50.17	50.95	62.85	70.61	75.53	79.95	79.98	74.07	61.70	47.85	44.63
14	44.25	46.55	55.00	61.45	69.95	75.92	80.37	79.92	74.67	62.45	49.30	44.85
15	47.37	45.77	53.22	61.32	70.00	75.40	81.17	79.58	74.37	60.32	51.12	45.12
16	45.77	46.87	54.72	62.92	70.29	77.27	81.10	79.23	73.57	61.22	54.07	45.30
17	40.42	47.95	55.77	62.55	69.61	78.34	80.85	80.00	74.82	59.92	51.17	40.00
18	37.72	50.22	54.95	62.35	68.79	77.24	79.87	79.65	73.82	58.95	46.65	40.52
19	39.07	51.60	54.55	62.95	69.92	77.42	79.92	79.43	71.80	58.32	44.70	45.00
20	43.90	50.00	54.77	63.12	70.82	77.50	79.37	78.83	70.32	58.75	48.15	42.82
21	40.20	49.67	56.57	65.20	70.84	76.16	79.52	79.30	67.55	60.37	51.57	40.67
22	40.07	50.82	55.30	66.70	72.24	76.61	79.47	79.30	67.90	58.20	47.85	41.70
23	41.45	49.72	54.70	65.71	72.19	75.85	79.82	77.95	68.35	58.97	49.37	41.42
24	46.70	50.27	57.87	66.72	72.82	75.37	79.97	77.50	69.62	59.77	47.20	42.07
25	48.27	49.13	56.87	65.55	72.19	75.77	80.00	78.18	69.60	55.45	47.50	44.75
26	48.82	51.89	57.79	67.08	72.37	76.87	79.92	77.43	69.60	56.27	46.82	44.52
27	48.57	52.65	57.17	62.95	73.13	78.37	79.82	77.38	67.80	55.97	48.60	47.47
28	46.42	54.50	58.05	63.27	73.74	79.32	80.45	76.58	67.85	55.70	47.32	47.10
29	45.80	56.20	58.22	64.70	72.65	78.85	80.27	76.03	67.47	55.10	47.67	46.50
30	44.45		59.60	67.65	73.13	79.67	79.27	76.73	65.69	55.90	48.32	43.16
31	43.80		57.62		73.12		78.78	76.50		56.55		42.06

Two observations a day; $\odot_r$ and 2_a, Nov. to April, inclusive; $\odot_r$ and 3_a, May to Oct. inclusive. Means uncorrected for daily fluctuation.

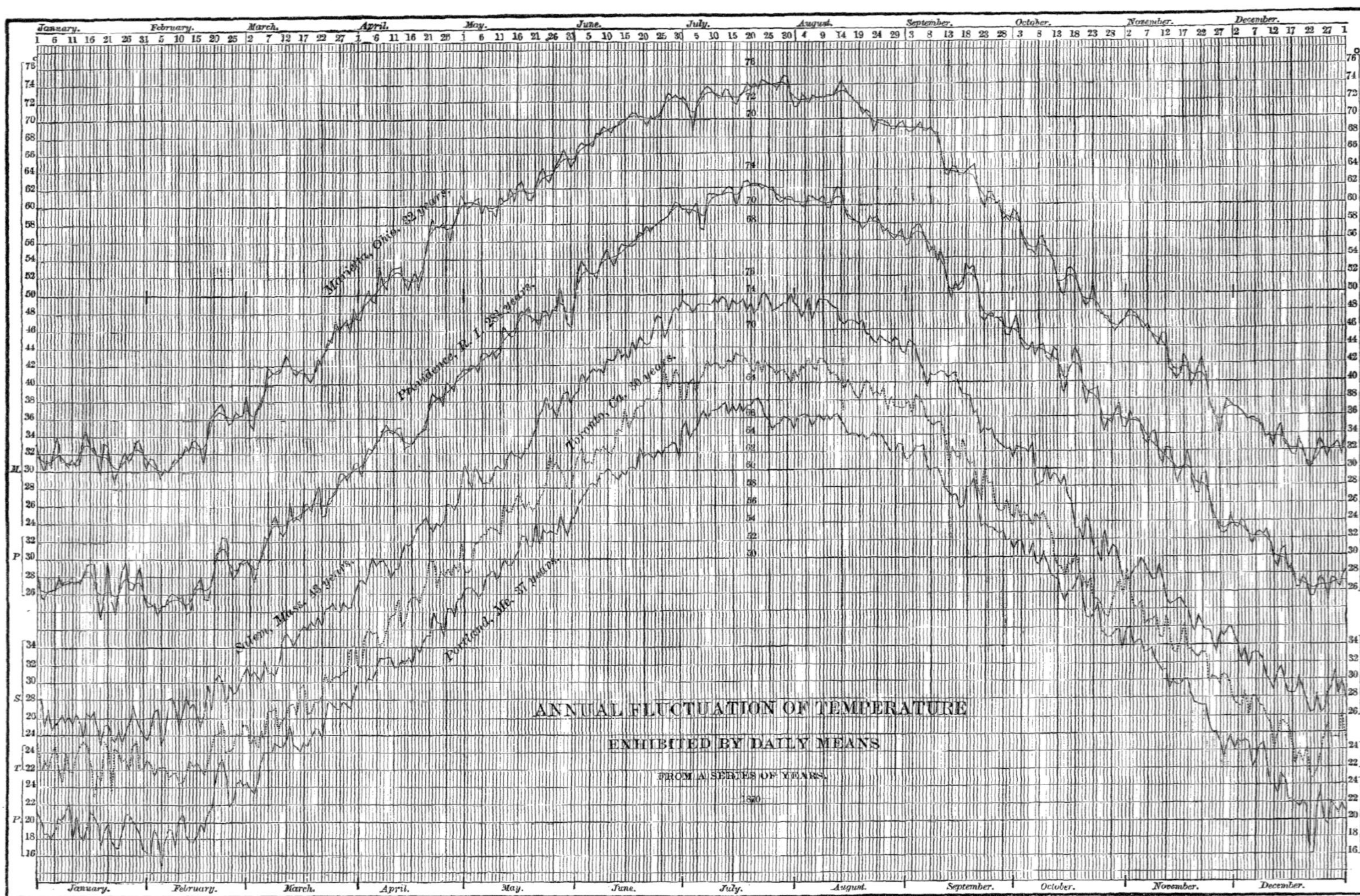

ANNUAL FLUCTUATION OF TEMPERATURE
EXHIBITED BY DAILY MEANS
FROM A SERIES OF YEARS.
1870
Marietta, Ohio. 32 years.
Providence, R. I. 28 years.
Toronto, Ca. 30 years.
Salem, Mass. 48 years.
Portland, Me. 37 years.
January.
February.
March.
April.
May.
June.
July.
August.
September.
October.
November.
December.
H. Chandler, Engraver, Buffalo.

The tabular numbers for five stations, having the longest series of observations, are graphically represented on the accompanying plate.

The greater irregularity for the shorter series is sufficiently well marked, and the zigzag lines of the Salem temperature, derived from a 43 year series, are yet inconveniently large for the purposes of comparison.

The Marietta and Providence daily temperatures show many coincidences in the zigzag lines or in the differences from their respective mean values and particularly so in the *winter season;* the Portland temperatures, also, frequently conform to the same fluctuations. From this we infer that changes from the normal temperatures extend, especially in the winter season, over large tracts of country, and there are also indications of the occurrence of the same phase about one day later in Rhode Island than in Ohio, showing that the normal state of the weather has a tendency (especially in the winter) to an easterly progression, the same as recognized in the case of storms or unusual thermal disturbances of the atmosphere. About the 20th of February, all stations indicate a rapid rise of temperature, this epoch, therefore, deserves further attention; there are also fainter indications of an unusual depression about May 31, of a constancy between September 13 and 18, and of a rapid decline about Nov. 26.

The temperatures recorded at the above stations refer nearly to the *same* period of time, and consequently exhibit many coincidences of departures from regularity which only belong to this period, but as soon as we compare with recorded temperatures covering *another* period, these coincidences disappear, and it is only by such comparisons of different epochs that we can assure ourselves of the reality or non-reality of any suspected deviation from the regular annual progression. The character of the Salem line is essentially different from that of any of the other lines, its period terminating about the time of the beginning of the others. This is the only station where the record extends, in part, to the past century.

Examining now, specially, the suspected periods of irregularity they will possess a strong probability of existence if exhibited alike for two independent epochs, for instance, those of the Salem and Providence series. About the beginning of December the march of temperature, at all the stations given, appears to be normal, though there is a remarkable depression about November 26, 27, 28, which latter feature seems to demand further attention. There is no thermal anomaly about the middle of May,[1] and the progression about February 12th and in the first and second week of March appears regular enough; at this season, however, the accidental irregularities are very great, and may hide any smaller fixed deviation. The suspected arrest of increasing temperature after May 25 is not supported by the Marietta and Salem observations, and the rise or constancy of temperature noted

[1] In an Article on the Variations of Temperature at Toronto, Canada (Phil. Trans. Roy. Soc., 1853, Vol. 143, part 1), Col. Sabine remarks: "On a reference to Table IV, it is seen that on the average of the twelve years from 1841 to 1852 the 11th of May was 0°.1 *below* and on the 12th and 13th of May respectively 3°.1 and 2°.4 *above* the general mean of the temperature. The meteorological observations at Toronto during these twelve years do not, therefore, support the supposition that the depression of temperature on the 11th, 12th, and 13th of May observed at Berlin (from a series of 86 years of observations) is a general and periodically recurring phenomenon over the whole globe."

at Marietta and Providence between October 27, and November 2, is contradicted by the ordinary fall of temperature observed at Salem during this period, but appears supported by Toronto.

The smooth curves, given in the Marietta and Providence diagrams, which cut off the zigzags, equally, above and below, are obtained by the method of successive means, and in this instance represent the sixth order of means.[1] This process facilitates comparison and enables us to construct tables of daily temperature, the values of which have thus become more consistent by the removal of the greater accidental irregularities.

In the tables which follow, the annual fluctuation is given either directly by the daily ordinates or by those of smooth curves, obtained by the process just explained, or by means of Bessel's periodic function with constants supplied by observation, as stated at the top of each table.

The director of the Toronto observatory noticed the curious fact, that the daily means or normals of temperature made out by General Sabine for the epoch 1841 to 1852 had now become totally inapplicable, in consequence of which a new set of normals was prepared, employing the series of observations from 1859 to 1868, and calculating the table with the help of Bessel's periodic function as had been done before.

The two sets of tables given for Toronto will, therefore, represent the variability of the annual fluctuation for two epochs not very remote from those when the extreme values obtain, as has been found from a further study of this phenomenon of the shifting of the epoch of maximum cold and of apparent changes in the curve of the annual fluctuation.[2]

On account of this variability of the annual fluctuation, the years of observation from which the daily means were deduced, are stated at the head of each table.

---

[1] Supposing $y_1\, y_2\, y_3\, y_4\, y_5\, y_6\, y_7$ to represent consecutive values of the daily temperature, the resulting mean of the sixth order and corresponding in point of time to the middle ordinate y_4 will be given by

$$\tfrac{1}{64}\,\{y_1 + 6y_2 + 15y_3 + 20y_4 + 15y_5 + 6y_6 + y_7\}$$

and in general for $n + 1$ ordinates, the co-efficients are those of the *nth* power of a binomial and the divisor equals their sum.

No precise rule can be given prescribing the limiting number of successive means, but as the values converge towards a constant, at first rapidly and afterwards more slowly, it will soon be found that after repeating the process a few times very little impression can be made on the results by continuing it, which sufficiently indicates that we have arrived at a practical limit. We may either compute directly by means of the formula, or we may set down *each* series of consecutive means; the latter process offers the advantage of a partial check in the regularity of progression of the numbers standing in the same horizontal line. It will also be convenient to stop at an order of an *even* number, in which case the resulting means refer, in point of time, to noon, whereas odd numbers (which may be written between the line) refer to midnight.

[2] Referring the reader to a subsequent part of this paper for the analyzation of the results connected with this inequality, it may be stated that it probably exists over the greater part of the United States east of the Mississippi River, and, perhaps with some modification, also in other parts of the country; allied with it, but not necessarily connected, there appears also an inequality in the amount of greatest cold and heat extending over a number of years, which, however, leaves the annual range almost undisturbed. These inequalities are necessarily of a periodic nature, and consequently our daily means, in order to become truly normals, must comprise at least one full period (or at least half a period if the curve be regular and just includes the maximum and minimum).

Toronto, Canada West.

[General Sabine, Phil. Trans. 1853, vol. 143, part i.]

Resulting annual fluctuation from a series of 12 years of observations between 1841 and 1852, or mean temperature of every day derived from computation by Bessel's periodic function,

$$T = 44^\circ.23 - 21^\circ.81 \sin(\theta + 81^\circ\ 27') + 1^\circ.06 \sin(2\theta + 71^\circ\ 32') - 0^\circ.80 \sin(3\theta + 347^\circ\ 42') + 0^\circ.22 \sin(4\theta + 37^\circ\ 27') + 0^\circ.88 \sin(5\theta + 50^\circ\ 41') + 0^\circ.325 \cos 6\,\theta,$$ the angle θ reckoning from Jan. 15.

Day of Month.	Jan.	Feb.	Mar.	Apr.	May.	June.	July.	Aug.	Sept.	Oct.	Nov.	Dec.
1	25°.2	23°.9	25°.4	36°.3	46°.4	56°.9	64°.7	66°.9	63°.1	50°.5	40°.5	30°.8
2	25.2	23.9	25.6	36.7	46.7	57.2	64.9	66.8	62.8	50.0	40.3	30.5
3	25.1	23.8	25.9	37.1	47.0	57.5	65.1	66.8	62.5	49.6	40.0	30.1
4	25.1	23.7	26.2	37.4	47.4	57.8	65.2	66.8	62.2	49.1	39.8	29.8
5	25.1	23.6	26.4	37.8	47.7	58.1	65.3	66.8	61.9	48.7	39.5	29.4
6	25.1	23.6	26.7	38.1	48.0	58.4	65.5	66.8	61.5	48.3	39.2	29.1
7	25.1	23.5	27.0	38.5	48.4	58.7	65.6	66.7	61.2	47.9	39.0	28.7
8	25.1	23.5	27.4	38.8	48.7	59.0	65.7	66.7	60.8	47.5	38.7	28.5
9	25.1	23.4	27.7	39.1	49.1	59.4	65.9	66.6	60.4	47.1	38.4	28.2
10	25.1	23.4	28.0	39.5	49.4	59.7	66.0	66.6	60.1	46.7	38.1	27.9
11	25.0	23.4	28.4	39.8	49.8	59.9	66.1	66.5	59.7	46.3	37.8	27.7
12	25.0	[23.4]	28.7	40.2	50.1	60.2	66.2	66.4	59.3	46.0	37.5	27.4
13	25.0	23.4	29.1	40.5	50.5	60.5	66.3	66.3	58.9	45.6	37.2	27.2
14	25.0	23.4	29.5	40.8	50.8	60.8	66.3	66.3	58.4	45.3	36.9	27.0
15	25.0	23.4	29.9	41.1	51.2	61.1	66.4	66.2	58.0	44.9	36.5	26.8
16	24.9	23.5	30.2	41.5	51.5	61.3	66.5	66.1	57.6	44.6	36.2	26.6
17	24.9	23.5	30.6	41.8	51.9	61.6	66.6	66.0	57.1	44.3	35.8	26.4
18	24.9	23.6	31.0	42.1	52.2	61.9	66.6	65.9	56.7	44.1	35.5	26.2
19	24.8	23.7	31.4	42.4	52.5	62.1	66.7	65.8	56.2	43.8	35.1	26.1
20	24.8	23.8	31.8	42.8	52.9	62.4	66.7	65.6	52.7	43.6	34.8	25.9
21	24.7	23.9	32.2	43.1	53.2	62.6	66.7	65.5	55.2	43.3	34.4	25.8
22	24.7	24.0	32.6	43.4	53.6	62.9	66.8	65.4	54.7	43.0	34.1	25.7
23	24.6	24.1	32.9	43.7	53.9	63.1	66.8	65.2	54.3	42.8	33.7	25.6
24	24.5	24.3	33.3	44.0	54.2	63.3	66.8	65.0	53.8	42.5	33.3	25.5
25	24.5	24.5	33.7	44.4	54.6	63.5	66.9	64.8	53.3	42.3	33.0	25.4
26	24.4	24.7	34.1	44.7	54.9	63.8	66.9	64.6	52.8	42.0	32.6	25.3
27	24.3	24.9	34.5	45.0	55.2	64.0	66.9	64.4	52.3	41.8	32.2	25.3
28	24.3	25.1	34.8	45.4	55.6	64.2	[66.9]	64.2	51.9	41.5	31.9	[illegible]
[illegible]	[illegible]		[illegible]	[illegible]	[illegible]	[illegible]	[illegible]	[illegible]	51.4	41.3	31.5	25.2
30	24.1		35.6	46.0	56.2	64.5	66.9	63.7	50.9	41.0	31.1	25.2
31	24.0		36.0		56.5		66.9	63.4		40.8		25.2

Toronto, Canada West.

[Received from G. T. Kingston, Director of the Toronto Mag. Observatory, May 23, 1870.]

Resulting annual fluctuation from a series of 10 years of observation between 1859 and 1868, or mean temperature of every day derived from computation by Bessel's periodic function.

Day of Month.	Jan.	Feb.	Mar.	Apr.	May.	June.	July.	Aug.	Sept.	Oct.	Nov.	Dec.
1	21.3	22.5	25.6	35.6	46.8	57.5	66.4	68.1	62.5	51.0	42.2	30.5
2	21.3	22.6	25.8	36.0	47.2	57.8	66.5	68.0	62.3	50.6	41.9	30.0
3	21.3	22.7	26.0	36.4	47.6	58.1	66.7	67.9	62.0	50.2	41.7	29.6
4	21.2	22.7	26.2	36.8	47.9	58.5	66.9	67.8	61.7	49.9	41.4	29.1
5	21.2	22.8	26.5	37.1	48.3	58.8	67.1	67.8	61.4	49.5	41.2	28.6
6	21.2	22.8	26.7	37.6	48.6	59.1	67.2	67.7	61.1	49.2	40.9	28.2
7	[21.2]	22.9	27.0	37.9	49.0	59.3	67.4	67.6	60.7	48.8	40.6	27.7
8	21.2	23.0	27.3	38.4	49.3	59.7	67.5	67.4	60.4	48.5	40.3	27.3
9	21.2	23.0	27.5	38.7	49.7	60.0	67.7	67.3	60.0	48.1	40.0	26.8
10	21.3	23.1	27.9	39.0	50.0	60.4	67.8	67.2	59.6	47.8	39.7	26.4
11	21.3	23.1	28.1	39.4	50.4	60.7	67.9	67.0	59.2	47.5	39.3	26.0
12	21.4	23.2	28.5	39.8	50.7	61.0	68.0	66.9	58.8	47.2	39.0	25.6
13	21.4	23.3	28.8	40.2	51.1	61.3	68.1	66.7	58.4	46.9	38.6	25.3
14	21.5	23.4	29.1	40.6	51.4	61.7	68.2	66.6	58.0	46.6	38.2	24.9
15	21.5	23.5	29.4	40.9	51.8	62.0	68.2	66.4	57.6	46.3	37.8	24.5
16	21.6	23.6	29.7	41.3	52.2	62.3	68.3	66.2	57.2	46.1	37.4	24.2
17	21.6	23.7	30.1	41.7	52.5	62.6	68.3	66.1	56.8	45.8	37.0	23.9
18	21.7	23.8	30.4	42.1	52.8	62.9	68.4	65.9	56.4	45.5	36.6	23.6
19	21.8	23.9	30.8	42.4	53.2	63.2	68.4	65.7	56.0	45.3	36.2	23.3
20	21.8	24.0	31.1	42.8	53.5	63.5	68.4	65.5	55.5	45.0	35.7	23.1
21	21.9	24.2	31.4	43.2	53.9	63.8	68.5	65.3	55.1	44.8	35.3	22.8
22	21.9	24.3	31.8	43.5	54.2	64.1	[68.5]	65.1	54.7	44.5	34.8	22.6
23	22.0	24.5	32.3	43.9	54.5	64.4	68.4	64.8	54.3	44.3	34.4	22.4
24	22.1	24.6	32.6	44.3	54.9	64.6	68.4	64.6	53.8	44.1	33.9	22.2
25	22.1	24.8	32.9	44.7	55.2	64.9	68.4	64.4	53.4	43.8	33.4	22.0
26	22.2	25.0	33.3	45.0	55.6	65.1	68.4	64.1	53.0	43.6	32.9	21.9
27	22.3	25.2	33.7	45.4	55.9	65.3	68.3	63.8	52.6	43.3	32.5	21.7
28	22.3	25.4	34.1	45.8	56.2	65.6	68.3	63.6	52.2	43.1	32.0	21.6
29	22.4	25.5	34.5	46.1	56.5	65.9	68.2	63.3	51.8	42.9	31.5	21.5
30	22.4		34.8	46.5	56.9	66.1	68.2	63.1	51.4	42.6	31.0	21.4
31	22.5		35.2		57.2		68.1	62.8		42.4		21.4

Providence, Rhode Island.

Resulting annual fluctuation from a series of $28\frac{1}{2}$ years, 1831–1860, or mean temperature of every day, derived from the 6th order of successive means.

Day of Month.	Jan.	Feb.	Mar.	Apr.	May.	June.	July.	Aug.	Sept.	Oct.	Nov.	Dec.
1	27°.1	25°.6	30°.0	40°.5	51°.3	59°.5	69°.8	70°.6	66°.2	56°.1	45°.6	33°.6
2	26.6	24.8	29.3	40.8	51.6	61.3	69.8	70.5	66.2	55.9	45.7	33.5
3	26.2	24.6	29.0	41.3	51.8	62.5	69.7	70.4	66.7	55.1	45.7	33.4
4	26.2	24.5	29.4	42.0	52.0	62.8	69.6	70.4	67.2	54.3	45.4	33.0
5	26.4	24.6	30.4	42.2	52.2	62.7	69.3	70.5	67.2	54.0	44.7	32.6
6	26.8	24.9	31.6	43.2	52.6	62.5	69.0	70.7	66.7	53.9	44.0	32.2
7	27.1	25.3	32.6	43.8	53.0	62.6	68.9	70.8	66.0	53.8	43.6	32.2
8	27.3	25.6	33.4	44.3	53.2	63.2	69.9	70.7	65.3	53.7	43.4	32.3
9	27.4	25.6	33.8	44.6	53.3	63.8	70.7	70.5	64.7	53.6	43.0	32.3
10	27.4	25.5	33.7	44.7	53.6	64.1	71.1	70.3	64.3	53.2	42.4	32.0
11	27.5	25.2	33.7	44.7	54.2	64.1	71.2	70.4	63.7	53.1	41.9	31.1
12	27.6	24.9	34.0	44.5	55.0	64.2	71.3	70.8	62.6	52.8	41.6	30.2
13	27.7	25.1	34.5	44.0	55.5	64.5	71.5	71.1	61.4	52.0	41.2	29.8
14	28.3	25.9	34.7	43.4	55.7	65.0	71.6	70.7	60.7	50.8	40.4	29.8
15	28.8	26.6	34.7	43.1	56.1	65.4	71.5	69.8	60.6	50.2	39.8	29.7
16	28.8	26.7	35.0	43.2	56.9	65.5	71.4	69.0	60.8	50.7	39.8	29.0
17	27.7	26.5	35.5	43.6	57.7	65.7	71.6	68.5	61.3	51.7	40.1	28.1
18	26.5	26.8	35.9	44.1	58.0	66.2	72.1	68.3	61.9	52.2	40.3	27.3
19	25.8	27.8	36.2	44.9	57.8	66.6	72.3	68.0	62.3	51.7	39.7	27.0
20	26.1	29.4	36.5	45.8	57.5	67.1	72.4	67.9	61.9	50.3	38.7	26.8
21	26.4	30.7	36.4	47.0	57.3	67.2	72.4	68.0	60.6	49.1	38.3	26.6
22	26.1	31.3	36.1	47.9	57.2	67.4	72.3	68.2	58.9	48.7	38.3	26.3
23	25.9	30.8	36.0	48.2	57.5	67.6	72.2	68.2	57.9	48.6	37.9	26.3
24	26.5	29.7	36.5	48.3	57.8	67.9	72.1	68.2	57.6	48.0	36.7	26.5
25	27.4	28.9	37.3	48.6	58.0	68.2	71.9	67.8	57.6	47.4	35.1	26.7
26	27.9	28.8	38.1	49.1	58.3	68.6	71.6	67.3	57.5	45.9	34.0	26.6
27	27.7	29.3	38.8	49.5	58.8	69.1	71.2	67.0	57.2	45.5	33.3	26.6
28	27.5	30.0	39.2	49.8	59.0	69.5	70.9	66.7	56.7	45.8	33.2	26.7
29	27.5	30.3	39.5	50.3	58.6	69.9	70.7	66.6	56.2	46.1	33.3	26.9
30	27.3		39.9	50.9	58.0	69.9	70.7	66.6	56.1	46.1	33.6	27.1
31	26.6		40.3		58.1		70.7	66.5		45.8		27.3

New Haven, Conn.

[Conn. Acad. vol. i, part 1, 1866.]

Resulting annual fluctuation from a series of 86 years of observations between 1778 and 1865, or mean temperature of every day derived from computation by Bessel's periodic function,

$$T' = 49^\circ.11 + 22^\circ.92 \sin(\theta + 263^\circ\ 38') + 0^\circ.29 \sin(2\theta + 345^\circ\ 24') + 0^\circ.45 \sin(3\theta + 229^\circ\ 50')$$
$$+ 0^\circ.02 \sin(4\theta + 150^\circ) + 0^\circ.38 \sin(5\theta + 54^\circ\ 31') - 0.08 \cos 6\theta,$$ where θ counts from Jan. 15.

Day of Month.	Jan.	Feb.	Mar.	Apr.	May.	June.	July.	Aug.	Sept.	Oct.	Nov.	Dec.
1	27.4	26.4	31.1	41.8	52.1	62.8	70.5	71.9	67.4	56.5	45.5	34.6
2	27.3	26.5	31.4	42.1	52.5	63.1	70.6	71.9	67.1	56.1	45.2	34.3
3	27.2	26.5	31.7	42.5	52.8	63.4	70.8	71.8	66.8	55.7	44.8	33.9
4	27.1	26.6	32.0	42.9	53.1	63.8	70.9	71.7	66.5	55.3	44.5	33.6
5	27.0	26.7	32.3	43.2	53.4	64.1	71.0	71.7	66.2	55.0	44.1	33.3
6	26.9	26.8	32.6	43.6	53.8	64.4	71.1	71.6	65.9	54.6	43.8	32.9
7	26.8	26.9	32.9	43.9	54.1	64.7	71.2	71.5	65.6	54.3	43.4	32.6
8	26.7	27.0	33.2	44.3	54.5	65.1	71.3	71.5	65.3	53.9	43.1	32.3
9	26.6	27.1	33.6	44.6	54.8	65.4	71.4	71.4	65.0	53.5	42.7	32.0
10	26.6	27.2	33.9	45.0	55.2	65.7	71.5	71.3	64.6	53.2	42.3	31.7
11	26.5	27.3	34.2	45.3	55.5	66.0	71.6	71.2	64.3	52.8	42.0	31.4
12	26.5	27.4	34.6	45.7	55.9	66.2	71.7	71.1	64.0	52.5	41.6	31.1
13	26.4	27.6	34.9	46.0	56.2	66.5	71.7	71.0	63.6	52.1	41.3	30.9
14	26.4	27.7	35.3	46.4	56.6	66.8	71.8	70.9	63.3	51.8	40.9	30.6
15	26.3	27.9	35.6	46.7	56.9	67.1	71.8	70.8	62.9	51.4	40.5	30.3
16	26.3	28.0	36.0	47.1	57.3	67.3	71.9	70.6	62.5	51.1	40.2	30.1
17	26.3	28.2	36.3	47.4	57.6	67.6	71.9	70.5	62.1	50.7	39.8	29.8
18	26.3	28.4	36.7	47.8	58.0	67.8	72.0	70.3	61.8	50.4	39.4	29.6
19	26.3	28.6	37.1	48.1	58.3	68.1	72.0	70.2	61.4	50.0	39.1	29.4
20	26.2	28.8	37.4	48.4	58.7	68.3	72.0	70.0	61.0	49.7	38.7	29.2
21	26.2	29.0	37.8	48.7	59.0	68.5	72.1	69.8	60.6	49.3	38.3	29.0
22	26.2	29.2	38.2	49.1	59.4	68.8	72.1	69.6	60.2	49.0	38.0	28.8
23	26.3	29.5	38.5	49.4	59.8	69.0	72.1	69.5	59.8	48.6	37.6	28.6
24	26.3	29.7	38.9	49.7	60.1	69.2	72.1	69.3	59.4	48.3	37.2	28.4
25	26.3	29.9	39.3	50.1	60.4	69.4	72.1	69.1	59.0	47.9	36.8	28.2
26	26.3	30.2	39.6	50.4	60.8	69.6	72.1	68.9	58.6	47.6	36.5	28.1
27	26.3	30.5	40.0	50.7	61.1	69.8	72.1	68.6	58.1	47.2	36.1	27.9
28	26.3	30.8	40.4	51.1	61.4	70.0	72.0	68.4	57.7	46.9	35.8	27.8
29	26.4		40.7	51.4	61.8	70.1	72.0	68.2	57.3	46.6	35.4	27.7
30	26.4		41.1	51.8	62.1	70.3	72.0	67.9	56.9	46.2	35.0	27.6
31	26.4		41.4		62.5		71.9	67.7		45.9		27.5

Marietta, Ohio.

Resulting annual fluctuation from a series of 32 years, 1818–1859, or mean temperature of every day, derived from the 6th order of successive means.

Day of Month.	Jan.	Feb.	Mar.	Apr.	May.	June.	July.	Aug.	Sept.	Oct.	Nov.	Dec.
	°	°	°	°	°	°	°	°	°	°	°	°
1	31.8	31.3	37.3	47.7	60.3	65.6	72.3	72.3	69.0	58.6	47.1	37.1
2	31.4	31.0	36.6	48.1	60.3	66.3	71.8	72.1	69.0	58.3	47.4	36.8
3	31.0	30.7	36.4	48.8	60.3	66.8	71.1	72.2	68.9	57.4	47.4	36.4
4	30.9	30.3	36.8	49.4	60.3	67.0	70.8	72.3	68.9	56.3	47.2	36.1
5	31.1	30.0	37.9	49.8	60.2	67.2	71.4	72.4	68.9	55.3	46.7	35.8
6	31.5	30.0	39.2	50.3	60.1	67.5	72.2	72.4	68.9	55.0	46.3	35.6
7	31.9	30.3	40.4	50.9	60.0	68.0	72.9	72.4	68.8	55.2	45.9	35.5
8	31.7	30.7	41.2	51.3	59.8	68.4	73.2	72.5	68.7	55.4	45.4	35.2
9	31.1	31.2	41.4	51.5	59.7	68.7	73.2	72.6	68.2	55.5	45.0	34.6
10	30.9	31.6	41.6	52.0	59.9	68.8	73.0	72.7	67.3	55.0	44.8	33.9
11	31.0	32.0	42.0	52.5	60.2	68.9	72.9	72.8	65.9	54.2	44.5	33.5
12	31.2	32.5	42.2	52.6	60.6	69.1	72.8	73.0	64.6	53.1	43.8	33.5
13	31.9	32.8	42.1	52.4	60.9	69.4	72.8	73.3	64.0	52.0	42.5	33.6
14	32.7	33.0	41.8	51.9	61.1	69.6	72.7	73.5	63.8	51.2	41.4	33.6
15	33.2	33.0	41.5	51.6	61.5	69.9	72.5	73.3	63.7	51.2	41.1	33.3
16	33.0	32.7	41.4	51.6	61.8	70.2	72.5	72.9	63.6	51.7	41.3	32.6
17	32.4	32.8	41.3	51.7	61.9	70.3	72.8	72.4	63.6	52.0	41.5	32.2
18	31.9	33.7	41.1	52.0	61.7	70.3	73.2	71.9	63.7	51.7	41.3	32.2
19	31.9	35.1	41.1	52.8	61.4	70.2	73.6	71.5	63.7	50.7	40.8	32.2
20	31.9	36.2	41.4	54.3	61.5	70.1	73.7	71.1	63.2	49.7	40.7	31.8
21	31.6	36.9	42.0	56.1	62.1	70.0	73.8	70.6	62.3	49.4	41.0	31.0
22	30.8	36.9	42.8	57.3	62.9	70.1	73.9	70.1	61.3	49.3	41.0	30.4
23	30.3	36.6	43.6	57.8	63.3	70.1	74.0	69.8	60.8	49.2	40.0	30.6
24	30.3	36.2	44.4	57.9	63.4	70.4	74.1	69.7	60.8	48.7	38.4	31.3
25	30.9	36.1	45.3	57.8	63.5	70.9	74.0	69.6	60.7	48.0	36.8	32.0
26	31.4	36.2	46.0	57.6	63.9	71.6	74.0	69.5	60.3	47.5	35.8	32.0
27	31.8	36.5	46.4	57.5	64.5	72.2	74.0	69.5	59.7	47.0	35.7	31.9
28	32.2	37.1	46.5	58.1	65.2	72.5	74.1	69.4	59.0	46.6	36.2	32.0
29	32.6	37.6	46.7	59.2	65.5	72.5	74.2	69.3	58.6	46.3	36.9	32.2
30	32.6		46.9	60.0	65.4	72.4	73.8	69.2	58.6	46.3	37.2	[illegible]
31	[illegible]		[illegible]		[illegible]		73.0	69.1		46.8		32.2

Variability in the mean temperature of any one day, in a succession of years.

The fact that the amount of departure of the observed temperature of any day of the year from the normal value assigned to that day from a series of years, is variable at different periods of the year may be verified at a glance by an examination of the accompanying diagram of the annual fluctuation showing the progression of the temperature from day to day. The zigzag lines or irregularities are evidently much greater in winter than in summer.

To obtain a measure of this irregularity we deduce the probable error of each normal, and thus secure the advantage of comparative numbers of the amount of this irregularity, as well as a knowledge of the degree of reliability of our normal temperatures.

Let n = number of years from which the mean temperature of any one day is deduced.

Δ = difference from this mean and any observed temperature.

e = probable error of a single value observed, or the probable amount of ordinary departure from the mean or normal value.

ε = probable error of normal value; then, with sufficient accuracy for our purpose,

$$e = 0.845 \frac{\Sigma\Delta}{\sqrt{n(n-1)}} \qquad \text{and} \qquad \varepsilon = \frac{e}{\sqrt{n}}.$$

To shorten the labor, I shall here only present the values of e and ε for four epochs of the annual fluctuation, and for three days in each case, viz.: for January 20, 21, 22, for April 21, 22, 23, for July 22, 23, 24, for October 21, 22, 23; epochs which correspond respectively nearly to the times of maximum cold, of average temperature, of maximum heat, and again of average temperature.

Selecting a station near the Atlantic sea-board, one on the western slope of the Alleghanies, and one near the Red River, we have the following results:—

Probable error (e) of the mean temperature of any day about the periods of maximum cold and heat—

	January.				July.			
	20th.	21st.	22d.	Mean.	22d.	23d.	24th.	Mean.
Providence, R. I. . .	7°.0	6°.1	7°.9	±7°.0	3°.4	3°.9	3°.2	±3°.5
Marietta, Ohio . . .	7.0	6.9	7.2	±7.0	3.4	3.1	2.8	±3.1
Washington, Ark. . .	9.8	8.0	7.9	±8.6	1.6	1.9	1.4	±1.6

and about the periods of average temperature—

	April.				October.			
	21st.	22d.	23d.	Mean.	21st.	22d.	23d.	Mean.
Providence, R. I. . .	4°.4	4°.2	3°.9	±4°.2	5°.9	6°.3	4°.7	±5°.6
Marietta, Ohio . . .	5.7	5.8	6.6	±6.0	6.2	6.4	5.3	±6.0
Washington, Ark. . .	5.2	4.6	5.2	±5.0	5.2	5.5	7.0	±5.9

We have also the probable error (ε) of our daily normals as given in the preceding tables for Providence (from a series of 28½ years), for Marietta (from a series of 32 years), and for Washington, Ark. (from a series of 20 years).

	Providence.	Marietta.	Washington, Ark.
January 20–22	±1°.3	±1°.2	±1°.9
April 21–23	±0.8	±1.0	±1.1
July 22–24	±0.6	±0.5	±0.4
October 21–23	±1.0	±1.0	±1.3

In midwinter the mean temperature of any day will, therefore, fluctuate, in different years, from 2 to 5 times as much as in midsummer, and the fluctuation for days in that part of the year where its mean temperature is reached, are intermediate between the maxima and minima values.

In our annual curve of the temperature at Providence, the daily means for any two adjacent days in midwinter, will, therefore, ordinarily differ by $\varepsilon \sqrt{2}$ or by $\pm$ 1°.8, and in midsummer by $\pm$ 0°.8, and at the intermediate times by $\pm$ 1°.3, and *may* differ by three times these amounts, or even more, before positively indicating any abnormal influence in the annual fluctuation. In a series of observations comprehending 100 years, the probable error of the resulting average temperature of any day, in the colder half of the year, would still be $\pm$ 0°.6, and in the warmer half $\pm$ 0°.4, and on the average, the normals for two consecutive days will differ $\pm$ 0°.7, thus showing the difficulty of clearly making out small deviations at certain suspected periods of the year. If a series of observations can be had long enough to be divided into two or more parts, and the same apparent deviations are noted in each, the probability of their being real and not accidental would be much strengthened.

At Providence, for any day in the winter, a deviation of 20° (or of three times the probable error [e] assigned), either in excess or defect of the normal temperature of that day, is a limit which is but rarely surpassed, and for any day in summer this limit becomes 10°. At Washington, Arkansas, these limits must be changed to 25° in winter, and to 6° in summer.

As a specimen of a table exhibiting the extreme heat and cold experienced, during a number of years, on the same calendar day, the following table is given from Dr. Wilson's paper, 20th Annual Report of the Regents of the University, State of New York (Albany), for 1868.

Geneva, New York. Lat. 42° 52′. Long. 77° 02′ W. of G.

Alt. 567 feet. From 12 years of observations; 1854 to 1865, inclusive.

Day of Month.	Jan.		Feb.		Mar.		Apr.		May.		June.		July.		Aug.		Sept.		Oct.		Nov.		Dec.	
1	51°	5°	50°	−2°	53°	13°	61°	11°	69°	39°	75°	46°	86°	55°	90°	56°	83°	50°	69°	40°	73°	34°	59°	12
2	41	−2	41	3	53	7	65	21	69	31	84	50	84	49	89	59	81	46	68	39	68	31	54	14
3	41	6	35	−5	57	5	65	25	68	36	80	50	88	49	86	57	82	46	80	44	62	34	59	12
4	52	7	36	−6	57	6	61	28	67	34	87	38	84	32	92	62	82	47	79	42	69	23	54	11
5	53	6	42	−1	57	−1	68	23	78	40	84	44	87	52	84	61	87	50	82	40	72	20	48	8
6	42	7	53	−19	41	10	54	22	80	33	86	48	88	54	84	62	81	49	74	36	62	24	53	12
7	46	5	55	−12	58	4	61	27	84	31	86	47	88	55	90	57	88	56	79	36	58	22	53	8
8	42	−1	39	−9	51	5	63	25	81	35	78	49	87	57	88	58	89	52	85	35	58	22	61	4
9	41	−8	46	11	48	−4	68	26	73	40	82	46	89	58	89	58	88	47	75	34	65	29	51	14
10	46	−16	44	4	49	−5	55	31	77	41	85	47	90	62	90	59	87	47	74	38	58	28	64	11
11	53	5	51	3	54	13	72	29	69	30	86	41	90	57	90	58	86	53	76	41	50	27	[illegible]	[illegible]
12	65	2	51	−2	53	10	66	32	78	36	83	46	[illegible]	56	86	[illegible]	[illegible]	44	68	37	58	26	47	9
13	43	6	47	−6	61	0	63	22	75	39	79	50	90	55	92	58	84	50	63	33	55	22	47	12
14	42	5	42	−1	54	15	62	27	74	39	79	54	89	59	90	55	77	46	65	34	57	20	58	7
15	44	6	56	5	56	4	62	26	82	46	87	54	88	60	82	56	86	37	70	29	50	22	54	5
16	46	0	46	8	60	16	67	32	84	39	80	46	90	58	84	55	82	52	66	30	48	27	58	15
17	40	1	56	−1	59	8	75	30	84	36	81	50	97	56	84	54	85	48	77	35	58	26	45	8
18	39	−15	47	2	60	8	74	31	82	37	89	48	91	58	86	52	90	48	73	37	56	29	49	−5
19	42	2	46	−1	54	6	64	35	68	44	87	53	91	63	85	50	78	41	74	31	63	28	46	6
20	54	0	44	12	63	11	67	32	75	41	88	54	92	61	88	54	86	37	70	30	45	20	45	5
21	51	10	48	9	72	10	64	34	82	43	87	55	89	56	85	57	76	48	70	29	48	23	40	14
22	43	−8	49	4	50	15	79	34	84	44	88	55	82	56	86	53	78	41	63	33	52	24	37	1
23	51	−1	52	7	52	15	66	32	85	45	86	54	84	58	79	50	78	40	57	36	50	23	44	7
24	48	6	59	8	49	12	77	32	85	42	85	57	85	54	06	52	75	45	65	32	57	19	40	9
25	50	1	45	7	56	16	70	31	85	43	91	55	90	60	82	53	74	42	65	32	47	10	52	12
26	52	5	49	10	51	19	72	32	84	44	88	62	91	62	86	52	74	41	63	28	44	20	50	10
27	54	3	60	10	52	19	76	30	80	48	86	60	87	57	75	51	79	41	69	28	47	20	44	0
28	40	6	51	11	61	13	78	30	82	44	89	54	88	61	80	53	76	45	66	30	46	23	44	−2
29	39	17	50	15	59	17	69	33	83	40	94	56	87	62	78	55	71	34	71	34	59	18	46	−5
30	41	7			68	18	68	37	80	39	90	52	86	56	80	48	74	34	72	33	60	20	38	10
31	38	−8			70	16			82	40			91	53	76	48			72	32			39	3

Inequality in the epoch of the annual fluctuation of the temperature.

A secular inequality in the law of the annual distribution of the temperature has lately been noticed by Mr. Kingston, director of the Toronto observatory, who stated that about the end of 1868, it was noticed that the normals given in General Sabine's paper (Phil. Trans. vol. 143, 1853), derived from 12 years of observations at Toronto, between 1841 and 1852, were wholly inapplicable to observations of recent years, and that a new set of normals had been prepared in consequence, using the records for ten years between 1859 and 1868 and Bessel's interpolation formula.

He further communicated two tables,[1] showing by five-year means that January was warmer than February in 1841–5, and has since become gradually colder, and that by forming two groups of years, whose centres were distant about 20 years, the temperature of winter and spring (1841–50) had now (1861–8) become lower, and the temperature of summer and autumn higher, and suggests an examination of the larger series of places in the United States with a view of learning whether the progressive change is general or confined to special localities.

In taking up the study of this subject the existence of such an inequality was confirmed for a number of places, and its geographical range and epochs were approximately determined. Selecting, from our general tables of monthly temperatures, such stations as appeared to me best suited for the purpose, on account of their location and length of record, the differences (J.—F.) of the monthly means of January and February, as well as the differences (J.—A.) of the monthly means of July and August, were formed for each year, and the results were united into means of five years:—

Table of differences (J.—F.): a + sign indicates February colder than January, a — sign the reverse.

Epochs.	Quebec, Can., and Windsor, N. S.	Brunswick, Me.	Montreal, Can.	Salem, Mass.	Cambridge, Mass.	New Haven, Conn.	Toronto, Can.	Philadelphia, Penn.	Charleston, S. C.	Savannah, Ga.	Marietta, Ohio.	Forts Snelling and Ridgeley, Minn.	Fort Leavenworth, Kan.
	°	°	°	°	°	°	°	°	°	°	°	°	°
1781–85	..	..	..	..	..	—1.9	..	..	..	..	..	..	..
1786–90	..	..	..	+2.1	..	0.0	..	..	..	..	..	..	..
1791–95	..	..	..	—1.8	—0.8	—0.5	..	..	..	..	..	..	..
1796–1800	—1.8	..	..	—2.5	—1.6	—1.4	..	..	..	..	..	..	..
1801–05	—4.1	..	..	—2.3	—2.4	—2.2	..	..	..	..	..	..	..
1806–10	—2.3	—4.6	..	—3.4	—4.2	—4.5	..	—4.5	..	..	..	..	..
1811–15	—4.6	—4.0	..	—2.9	—5.4	—2.5	..	—2.0	..	..	..	..	..
1816–20	..	—2.9	..	—1.9	..	—1.2	..	—3.6	..	..	..	..	..
1821–25	..	—4.2	..	—2.7	..	—2.4	..	—2.7	..	..	—2.9	—3.3	..
1826–30	..	—3.5	..	—2.1	..	—2.8	..	—2.1	..	..	—4.0	—3.6	..
1831–35	..	—1.2	—3.2	..	..	—0.3	+1.6	—1.7	—3.1	—4.6	—3.0	—1.1	+0.3
1836–40	..	—2.8	—3.3	..	..	—1.3	+1.4	—0.1	..	—2.9	—1.1	—3.3	—3.2
1841–45	..	—0.1	+0.1	..	—0.7	+0.3	+2.6	[+2.1]	[+1.7]	[+0.3]	[+0.5]	[—1.7]	—0.2
1846–50	..	[+0.1]	[+1.2]	..	+[2.3]	[+1.6]	[+2.6]	+1.5	+0.5	+0.2	—0.1	—4.0	—3.3
1851–55	..	—4.9	..	..	..	—1.1	+0.8	—2.0	—4.2	—6.5	—3.8	—6.0	—6.6
1856–60	..	—5.8	..	..	..	—3.4	—0.4	—2.6	—5.1	..	—4.4	—3.9	—5.3
1861–65	..	..	..	..	..	—2.9	—1.6	—2.6	—3.7	..	..	—4.2	—5.6
1866–69	..	..	..	..	..	..	—2.1	—3.9	..	..	..	..	..

[1] Comparison of means of Jan. and Feb. in groups of five years, from observations at Toronto:—

1841–45 Jan. *warmer* than Feb. 2°.6	1856–60 Jan. *colder* than Feb. 0°.3
1846–50 " " " " 2.6	1861–65 " " " " 1.5
1851–55 " " " " 0.9	1866–69 " " " " 2.1

Comparison of seasons in two groups of years:—

	Winter.	Spring.	Summmer.	Autumn.
1841–50	25°.1	41°.0	64°.7	46°.4
1861–68	23.4	40.3	65.6	47.4
Difference	—1.7	—0.7	+0.9	+1.0

In General Sabine's paper, the coldest day is Feb. 14, the warmest July 28.
In 1849–68 " " " " Jan. 6, " " " 22.

(Letter to the Secretary of the Smithsonian Institution of Jan. 25, 1870.)

In a few instances the means are derived only from 3 or 4 years, and to complete the table means from a station adjacent to that heading the column were introduced; upon the whole, the table required the use of monthly records for an aggregate of 540 years. Notwithstanding the incidental irregularities in the successive values of this table, they appear to point conclusively to an epoch between 1841 and 1850 when the positive values reached a maximum, in other words, when the mean temperature of February was the lower (or when the lowest temperature of the year fell in that month). They also indicate, though with less certainty, a preceding epoch about the beginning of the century, when the coldest epoch of the year fell early in January, in which month it is again found at the present time. Such a shifting in the epoch of greatest annual cold can only be of a periodic nature, and we may, therefore, look forward in the course of a few years to a return motion.

To elucidate the point, whether the epoch of maximum annual heat was accompanied by a corresponding movement, a similar table was prepared containing the differences (J.—A.), a + sign indicating July warmer than August, a — sign would indicate the reverse. The successive annual values of which this table is made up were found to be much more irregular than the corresponding values for the cold period, though the individual differences are *smaller*, a fact which might have been anticipated from our knowledge of the greater variability of temperature in winter when compared with that of summer. The parallelism of the movement over large areas, also, is less distinctly pronounced in summer than in winter.

Table of differences (J.—A.) for supposed change in epoch of the greatest annual heat.

Epochs.	Quebec, Can., and Windsor, N. S.	Brunswick, Me.	Montreal, Can.	Salem, Mass.	Cambridge, Mass.	New Haven, Conn	Toronto, Can.	Philadelphia, Penn	Charleston, S. C.	Savannah, Ga.	Marietta, Ohio.	Forts Snelling and Ridgeley, Minn.	Fort Leavenworth, Kan.
	°	°	°	°	°	°	°	°	°	°	°	°	°
1781–85	..	..	..	..	..	—0.2	..	..	..	..	..	..	..
1786–90	..	..	..	—1.7	..	+1.2	..	..	..	..	..	..	..
1791–95	..	..	..	0.0	+2.8	+0.6	..	..	..	..	..	..	.
1796–1800	+1.1	..	..	+1.9	+1.9	+1.3	..	..	..	..	..	..	.
1801–05	+0.1	..	..	+1.2	+1.8	+0.9	..	..	..	..	..	..	.
1806–10	+0.2	—0.5	..	+0.8	+1.2	+1.2	..	+0.6	..	..	..	..	..
1811–15	+1.8	+1.2	..	+2.5	—0.7	+1.4	..	+2.9	..	..	..	..	..
1816–20	+1.7	+1.8	..	+2.5	..	+2.5	..	+1.2	..	..	+1.7	..	..
1821–25	..	+2.8	..	+2.4	..	+2.2	..	+1.2	+0.9	..	..	+1.7	..
1826–30	..	+2.1	+1.2	+2.4	..	+0.6	..	+2.8	+0.7	..	+0.1	+4.0	..
1831–35	..	+1.7	+3.0	+2.2	..	+1.5	..	+2.3	+0.7	+0.6	+2.2	+4.0	+1.5
1836–40	..	+2.7	+4.3	..	..	+3.0	..	+2.9	..	+2.2	+2.0	+3.9	+2.0
1841–45	..	—0.4	—1.4	..	+1.5	+0.5	—0.5	+1.2	+1.8	+1.0	+2.0	+3.4	+3.5
1846–50	..	+1.4	+3.9	..	+2.8	+2.0	+0.6	+0.7	+0.8	—1.2	+1.2	+3.0	+2.0
1851–55	..	+4.1	..	..	..	+3.3	+1.4	+3.5	+0.6	+1.7	+2.3	+4.0	+1.1
1856–60	..	+2.9	..	..	..	+1.9	+1.6	+3.4	+0.5	..	+3.2	+5.7	+4.7
1861–65	..	..	..	..	..	+1.5	+0.1	0.0	+0.3	..	..	+3.1	+0.5
1866–69	..	..	..	..	..	..	+6.1	+4.6	..	..	..	..	..

There appears to be no regular progression in any of the figures of this table that could be ascribed as accompanying the singular anomaly of values between 1841–50, and even when means are taken for each five-year combination, the result remains inconclusive. If there is any variation in the epoch of maximum heat, it must be confined within much narrower limits than the variation in the epoch of maximum cold.

On the western coast the records of three stations were examined (San Diego, San Francisco, and Sitka), but, owing to the shortness of the record, only a glimpse of the existence of an inequality could be obtained with an indication of the occurrence of the extreme shift in winter later than in 1844.

Taking means of the values for the different stations, for winter and summer, we obtain the following results:—

Epochs.	Cold Season.		Warm Season.		Epochs.	Cold Season.		Warm Season.	
	No. of Stations.	Mean of Jan.—Feb.	No. of Stations.	Mean of July—Aug.		No. of Stations.	Mean of Jan.—Feb.	No. of Stations.	Mean of July—Aug.
		°		°			°		°
1786–90	2	+1.0	2	+1.5	1831–35	10	—1.6	10	+2.0
1791–95	3	—1.0	3	+1.1	1836–40	9	—1.8	8	+2.9
1796–1800	4	—1.8	4	+1.5	1841–45	10	[+0.6]	10	+1.1
1801–05	4	—2.7	4	+1.0	1846–50	10	0.0	10	+1.4
1806–10	6	[—3.9]	6	[+0.6]	1851–55	9	—3.4	9	+2.4
1811–15	6	—3.6	6	+1.5	1856–60	8	—3.9	8	+3.0
1816–20	4	—2.4	6	+1.9	1861–65	..	..	..	..
1821–25	6	—3.0	6	+1.9	1866–69	..	..	..	..
1826–30	6	—3.0	8	+1.8					

Extreme values are indicated by being contained within brackets, and they point approximately to the epochs 1809 and 1844, when the greatest cold fell on the average early in January and about the middle of February, respectively. Respecting the epoch of greatest heat, the figures leave us in no doubt, though the probability would seem to be in favor of a *corresponding* lateness about 1808 and an earlier occurrence in the position of the maximum at some rather undefined later epoch.

If the preceding result could be considered as well established, the cycle of the shifting of these dates of maximum cold (and heat) would be about twice 35 years.

Tables of observed extremes of temperature, for every month, for a series of years.

To complete our information respecting the annual fluctuation of the temperature, it is necessary to examine the extreme variations from the normal values; with this view the following table of monthly extremes has been prepared for a number of selected stations. They comprise nearly all the longer series, for which maxima and minima have been tabulated; the extreme values given are those found in the record, entered at the regular hours of observation, as adopted by the respective observers, the cases of maxima and minima thermometers being very restricted. They do not, therefore, exhibit the absolute extremes, but only approximations to them; besides, the intervals of time over which the series extend are far too restricted to entitle the extremes to be regarded as anything more than approximations. For the geographical position, and the actual duration of each series, after the deduction of breaks, the reader will have to consult the general tables of mean temperatures, given in Section I. Observations of a later date than 1870 are included in our table.

The tabular values are taken from a large manuscript collection, which embraces the observed monthly extremes for every year separately; in this form the table was found far too bulky to conform to the plan of this paper, and only an abstract of the manuscript is here presented.

The headings to the table give all the explanation needed. To render it easy to refer to the general tables for any further information, the table of extremes is arranged alphabetically, by States or Territories, and the stations in each are also given in alphabetical order.

TABLES OF OBSERVED EXTREMES OF TEMPERATURE

FOR EVERY MONTH, FROM A SERIES OF YEARS.

PRINCIPALLY FOR STATIONS WITHIN THE UNITED STATES.

ALL VALUES ARE EXPRESSED IN DEGREES OF THE FAHRENHEIT SCALE.

BRITISH NORTH AMERICA AND CANADA.

Name of Station.	Height.	Series. Begins.	Ends.	Highest Temperature Jan.	Feb.	Mar.	Apr.	May.	June.
1. Caledonia Coal Mine, N. S.	60	Jan. 1867;	Dec. 1869	51°	50°	46°	62°	72°	81°
2. Chambly, C. E.	...	Jan. 1820;	Dec. 1826	49	51	61	75	91	89
3. Fort Simpson	300	June, 1848;	Apr. 1862	40	38	51	61	83	102
4. Halifax, N. S.	8	Jan. 1861;	Dec. 1869	54	53	56	70	79	92
5. Montreal, C. E.	60	Mar. 1845;	June, 1863	48	48	64	79	87	95
6. Peel River	...	Feb. 1863;	Dec. 1865	18	16	32	57	63	87
7. Rigolet, Lab.	...	July, 1860;	June, 1863	30	39	55	48	68	76
8. St. John, N. B.	135	Dec. 1863;	Dec. 1870	44	47	50	60	73	86
9. St. John's, N. F.	170	Jan. 1834;	Feb. 1869	49	51	55	61	66	80
10. Stanbridge, C. E.	222	Feb. 1860;	Dec. 1870	44	48	63	71	84	90
11. Toronto, C. W.	342	Jan. 1840;	Dec. 1870	55	52	67	90	82	93
12. Wolfville, N. S.	80	Jan. 1861;	Dec. 1870	55	54	57	79	83	92

ALABAMA.

Name of Station.	Height.	Series. Begins.	Ends.	Jan.	Feb.	Mar.	Apr.	May.	June.
1. Huntsville	600	Jan. 1831;	Dec. 1839	75	75	84	86	90	92
2. Mobile	15	Apr. 1840;	Sept. 1873	78	79	80	85	92	96
3. Mt. Vernon Arsenal	200	Jan. 1843;	June, 1874	80	84	90	95	102	100

ALASKA.

Name of Station.	Height.	Series. Begins.	Ends.	Jan.	Feb.	Mar.	Apr.	May.	June.
1. Fort Tongass	20	June, 1868;	Sept. 1870	47	45	59	60	70	75
2. Fort Wrangel	...	May, 1868;	Sept. 1870	42	54	54	69	78	86
3. Illoolook	...	July, 1829;	Mar. 1867	43	52	64	53	61	67
4. Sitka	20	Jan. 1833;	June, 1874	55	55	64	70	75	82

ARIZONA.

Name of Station.	Height.	Series. Begins.	Ends.	Jan.	Feb.	Mar.	Apr.	May.	June.
1. Camp Bowie	...	Aug. 1867;	June, 1874	68	74	87	87	100	105
2. Camp Colorado	...	Jan. 1869;	Dec. 1870	75	81	87	93	105	107
3. Camp Crittenden	...	Mar. 1866;	Dec. 1870	67	72	76	94	92	105
4. Camp Date Creek	3726	Aug. 1867;	Dec. 1870	73	84	86	92	101	108
5. Camp Goodwin	...	Jan. 1866;	May, 1870	74	83	86	96	100	106
6. Camp Grant	...	1861;	June, 1874	85	90	93	100	108	111
7. Camp Lowell Tucson	...	Nov. 1866;	Dec. 1870	76	82	93	98	102	111
8. Camp McDowell	...	Sept. 1866;	June, 1874	90	82	95	100	105	114
9. Camp Verde	...	Dec. 1868;	June, 1874	70	79	89	94	111	112
10. Camp Wallen	...	Nov. 1866;	Sept. 1869	68	73	79	87	89	102
11. Fort Buchanan	5330	Aug. 1857;	Dec. 1859	71	76	91	91	95	103
12. Fort Canby	6500	Dec. 1851;	Nov. 1863	63	61	76	80	89	98
13. Fort Mojavé	604	Jan. 1860;	June, 1864	78	83	92	100	110	117
14. Fort Whipple	5700	Jan. 1865;	June, 1874	82	78	76	94	98	110

ARKANSAS.

Name of Station.	Height.	Series. Begins.	Ends.	Jan.	Feb.	Mar.	Apr.	May.	June.
1. Fort Smith	460	Jan. 1840;	Mar. 1861	80	87	90	96	93	99
2. Little Rock	...	Jan. 1840;	Dec. 1867	71	78	80	84	87	95
3. Washington, near	660	Jan. 1840;	Sept. 1867	76	80	90	92	94	95

BRITISH NORTH AMERICA AND CANADA.

	During Each Month.						Year of Extreme Heat.	Lowest Temperature during Each Month.												Year of Extreme Cold.
	July.	Aug.	Sept.	Oct.	Nov.	Dec.		Jan.	Feb.	Mar.	Apr.	May.	June.	July.	Aug.	Sept.	Oct.	Nov.	Dec.	
	°	°	°	°	°	°		°	°	°	°	°	°	°	°	°	°	°	°	
1	89	85	78	75	63	55	1868	—10	—13	— 4	10	22	32	36	42	36	22	15	— 4	1868
2	92	90	90	80	63	54	1825	—36	—29	—12	13	30	58	62	55	30	23	— 5	—22	1822
3	104	80	70	68	30	46	1855	—53	—54	—46	—49	22	31	41	35	29	— 7	—54	—55	1851
4	87	89	82	75	67	54	1864	—15	—14	— 5	10	22	32	46	41	34	19	13	— 7	1866
5	101	94	93	81	64	51	1847	—20	—32	— 9	8	25	40	47	47	30	18	— 2	—18	1861
6	88	74	56	34	33	28	1864	—54	—55	—53	—20	— 3	28	35	30	19	—15	—51	—56	1865
7	88	86	72	56	50	28	1861	—31	—35	—21	—14	19	30	28	29	28	7	— 8	—24	1863
8	83	77	76	70	56	50	1866	—21	—11	— 3	10	29	39	45	46	36	22	10	—14	1866
9	86	81	77	71	61	47	1861[1]	—11	—14	—15	12	18	27	30	33	30	21	12	2	1863
10	95	90	85	83	69	52	1868	—33	—36	—34	11	25	38	52	45	32	16	2	—19	1865
11	98	99	94	76	64	55	1854	—27	—25	—16	6	13	28	39	40	28	16	— 4	—15	1859
12	88	82	82	82	67	63	1866	— 9	—13	— 3	12	26	41	55	49	39	26	17	— 7	1861

ALABAMA.

	July.	Aug.	Sept.	Oct.	Nov.	Dec.	Year of Extreme Heat.	Jan.	Feb.	Mar.	Apr.	May.	June.	July.	Aug.	Sept.	Oct.	Nov.	Dec.	Year of Extreme Cold.
1	95	96	91	86	78	68	1838	— 9	— 7	11	31	40	50	51	54	39	29	13	— 7	1836[2]
2	98	96	96	94	85	76	1873	19	33	31	44	55	51	68	70	60	42	36	27	1873
3	100	104	98	96	88	84	1860	9	13	23	33	48	58	61	57	46	32	24	14	1852

ALASKA.

	July.	Aug.	Sept.	Oct.	Nov.	Dec.	Year of Extreme Heat.	Jan.	Feb.	Mar.	Apr.	May.	June.	July.	Aug.	Sept.	Oct.	Nov.	Dec.	Year of Extreme Cold.
1	92	81	67	58	51	46	1870	6	23	— 2	33	38	43	52	47	38	37	32	24	1870
2	78	80	68	58	48	42	1868	0	16	—10	32	36	38	47	47	38	32	28	20	1870
3	76	77	59	55	55	47	1832[3]	3	— 1	0	16	27	34	39	38	26	21	6	5	1830
4	82	80	70	62	57	53	1833[4]	— 4	2	0	10	28	30	31	30	28	19	4	2	1871

ARIZONA.

	July.	Aug.	Sept.	Oct.	Nov.	Dec.	Year of Extreme Heat.	Jan.	Feb.	Mar.	Apr.	May.	June.	July.	Aug.	Sept.	Oct.	Nov.	Dec.	Year of Extreme Cold.
1	103	97	99	96	85	80	1873	0	20	32	32	47	55	62	57	56	31	22	20	1873
2	106	108	104	101	90	68	1869	30	33	31	49	54	61	80	74	63	52	43	31	1869
3	105	94	92	89	76	69	1868	25	23	29	40	49	56	61	59	57	39	27	17	1869
4	111	105	106	97	86	84	1870	20	22	25	38	45	48	65	58	52	32	27	16	1869
5	111	102	98	98	83	72	1869	10	20	30	34	54	59	71	70	50	34	27	14	1866
6	116	106	106	100	98	88	1871	19	16	27	24	30	50	58	55	53	35	26	21	1874
7	112	102	101	96	98	78	1869	22	22	27	36	52	53	72	70	62	40	31	20	1869
8	114	108	110	108	99	89	1869[5]	16	18	30	29	43	49	62	65	51	20	17	21	1874
9	113	105	101	99	89	75	1873	5	12	19	27	34	43	48	50	36	16	6	6	1874
10	100	91	94	90	82	76	1867	23	3	30	36	49	50	64	61	52	35	17	16	1867
11	102	98	95	93	75	78	1858	14	24	13	28	42	57	60	56	55	28	24	15	1858
12	99	96	87	79	72	65	1855	—20	—12	— 1	12	19	30	36	43	30	17	0	—25	1855
13	118	116	109	105	90	81	1870[6]	21	14	36	40	47	39	47	52	45	27	20	23	1873
14	105	91	92	93	88	83	1865	—10	10	11	13	31	36	31	48	32	12	— 1	— 9	1866

ARKANSAS.

	July.	Aug.	Sept.	Oct.	Nov.	Dec.	Year of Extreme Heat.	Jan.	Feb.	Mar.	Apr.	May.	June.	July.	Aug.	Sept.	Oct.	Nov.	Dec.	Year of Extreme Cold.
1	105	102	101	91	87	76	1860	2	— 4	— 3	24	37	47	54	49	32	26	6	0	1840
2	94	96	88	90	76	86	1840	16	17	12	40	50	58	64	65	51	36	19	23	1867
3	108	102	98	90	82	78	1860	3	6	6	24	38	48	54	52	36	24	15	— 6	1845

[1] Also in 1834. [2] Also in 1832. [3] Also in 1830.
[4] Also in 1870. [5] Also in 1874. [6] Also in 1873.

CALIFORNIA.

Name of Station.	Height.	Series. Begins.	Ends.	Highest Temperature Jan.	Feb.	Mar.	Apr.	May.	June.
1. Alcatraz Island	...	Feb. 1860;	June, 1874	78°	70°	78°	82°	86°	88°
2. Angel Island	30	Dec. 1867;	June, 1874	72	75	76	83	93	88
3. Benicia Barracks	64	Nov. 1849;	June, 1874	70	78	82	98	95	103
4. Camp Bidwell	4680	Nov. 1863;	June, 1874	72	77	82	85	90	97
5. Camp Cady	3000	Jan. 1868;	Dec. 1870	71	76	90	98	104	114
6. Camp Gaston	...	Sept. 1861;	June, 1874	66	69	83	89	103	108
7. Camp Independence	4800	Nov. 1862;	June, 1874	73	78	86	95	95	105
8. Camp Lincoln	...	Sept. 1866;	May, 1869	62	70	70	77	86	75
9. Camp Wright	...	July, 1864;	June, 1874	77	81	89	91	102	108
10. Drum Barracks	32	May, 1864;	Nov. 1870	81	80	85	95	101	99
11. Fort Bragg	...	Dec. 1860;	Sept. 1864	64	65	70	75	72	72
12. Fort Crook	3390	Jan. 1858;	Apr. 1869	53	68	76	84	89	99
13. Fort Humboldt	50	Jan. 1854;	Dec. 1869	66	70	72	75	73	78
14. Fort Jones	2570	Jan. 1853;	June, 1858	60	70	82	92	98	99
15. Fort Miller	402	Aug. 1851;	Aug. 1864	70	74	88	101	113	121
16. Fort Point	27	Jan. 1860;	Dec. 1870	65	74	70	77	83	76
17. Fort Reading	674	Apr. 1852;	Mar. 1856	72	80	89	89	95	106
18. Fort Tijon	3240	Mar. 1855;	Aug. 1864	72	73	83	84	90	100
19. Fort Ter-Waw	...	Apr. 1859;	Oct. 1861	58	67	80	82	78	84
20. Fort Yuma	200	Dec. 1850;	June, 1874	83	86	94	106	108	117
21. Monterey	40	May, 1847;	Dec. 1869	76	74	86	85	85	92
22. Point San José	...	Mar. 1866;	June, 1874	65	75	78	90	81	87
23. Presidio	150	Oct. 1847;	June, 1874	72	74	82	82	86	89
24. Sacramento	52	July, 1849;	Dec. 1866	63	73	89	94	91	101
25. San Diego	150	July, 1849;	Apr. 1866	80	83	90	93	96	102
26. Union Ranche	...	Jan. 1861;	Dec. 1862	64	70	80	87	92	102
27. Yerba Buena Island	...	Feb. 1869;	Oct. 1873	70	74	83	80	88	90

COLORADO.

Name of Station.	Height.	Series. Begins.	Ends.	Jan.	Feb.	Mar.	Apr.	May.	June.
1. Fort Garland	8365	Sept. 1852;	June, 1874	59	64	70	80	93	93
2. Fort Lyon	4000	Jan. 1861;	June, 1874	72	75	81	98	98	107

CONNECTICUT.

Name of Station.	Height.	Series. Begins.	Ends.	Jan.	Feb.	Mar.	Apr.	May.	June.
1. Colebrook	1210	Jan. 1861;	Nov. 1870	53	56	72	81	87	91
2. Columbia	...	Jan. 1861;	Dec. 1870	70	64	78	82	92	96
3. Fort Trumbull	23	Jan. 1827;	June, 1874	62	61	69	82	92	93
4. Middletown	175	Jan. 1860;	Dec. 1870	56	63	78	85	86	95
5. New Haven	45	July, 1778;	Oct. 1865	64	68	76	85	93	102
6. Pomfret	587	Jan. 1861;	Dec. 1868	56	57	69	80	87	89

DAKOTA.

Name of Station.	Height.	Series. Begins.	Ends.	Jan.	Feb.	Mar.	Apr.	May.	June.
1. Fort Abercrombie	...	Feb. 1859;	June, 1874	43	44	58	83	102	99
2. Fort Buford	1900	Sept. 1866;	June, 1874	52	51	78	88	99	106
3. Fort Randall	1245	Jan. 1860;	June, 1874	65	68	79	95	101	105
4. Fort Ransom	..	Dec. 1868;	Dec. 1870	34	39	63	82	85	97
5. Fort Sully	...	Jan. 1866;	June, 1874	61	64	71	98	101	108
6. Fort Wadsworth	...	Sept. 1866;	June, 1874	40	42	54	84	93	96

DELAWARE.

Name of Station.	Height.	Series. Begins.	Ends.	Jan.	Feb.	Mar.	Apr.	May.	June.
1. Fort Delaware	10	Jan. 1826;	Sept. 1870	62	65	80	85	91	97

[1] Also in 1874. [2] Also in 1870. [3] Also in 1873. [4] Also in 1857.

CALIFORNIA.

	[Highest Temperature] during Each Month.						Year of Extreme Heat.	Lowest Temperature during Each Month.												Year of Extreme Cold.
	July.	Aug.	Sept.	Oct.	Nov.	Dec.		Jan.	Feb.	Mar.	Apr.	May.	June.	July.	Aug.	Sept.	Oct.	Nov.	Dec.	
	°	°	°	°	°	°		°	°	°	°	°	°	°	°	°	°	°	°	
1	69	75	90	89	84	87	1872	37	42	39	20	43	46	46	48	48	45	43	38	1870
2	93	85	88	85	74	71	1870[1]	34	34	35	37	45	46	37	49	48	44	38	36	1873[1]
3	102	105	97	96	84	68	1857	19	21	26	36	40	47	47	46	46	44	27	25	1854
4	96	99	90	79	82	61	1870	—18	—18	0	9	22	31	39	38	24	12	9	—10	1868
5	118	112	109	101	80	77	1868	15	22	30	40	51	56	72	68	52	34	28	12	1869
6	110	114	100	92	77	70	1870	23	25	23	31	39	45	47	48	41	30	21	19	1872
7	107	107	100	90	80	73	1867[2]	13	1	14	21	29	38	48	31	37	21	12	— 2	1873
8	88	82	94	93	71	68	1867	27	30	30	35	38	44	48	49	42	39	35	33	1868
9	110	110	108	103	86	76	1870[3]	18	15	16	26	33	32	35	39	34	25	18	16	1867
10	98	102	97	100	103	86	1869	35	31	33	45	49	55	58	55	50	43	35	28	1869
11	78	78	75	72	70	66	1863	29	18	31	31	39	45	46	44	42	39	31	30	1861
12	103	100	96	85	71	60	1858	—20	4	2	18	31	40	48	46	30	20	10	0	1859
13	80	73	78	89	75	66	1862	16	29	30	29	32	40	41	46	42	33	30	20	1854
14	103	106	91	88	72	60	1856	—17	11	20	27	25	32	42	41	18	24	16	—17	1855[4]
15	118	113	114	98	88	72	1853	23	32	29	38	41	51	59	54	50	41	28	28	1854
16	80	74	82	82	72	68	1865	31	35	36	44	46	50	50	50	50	47	40	36	1862
17	110	107	108	98	87	71	1854	15	30	29	36	44	51	53	51	39	35	31	11	1855
18	97	98	98	89	76	68	1859	24	28	28	30	30	46	57	56	48	29	27	22	1855
19	73	88	91	80	68	62	1860	31	31	32	35	41	48	48	52	46	41	31	30	1359[5]
20	116	115	111	105	88	84	1859	26	19	32	46	46	59	70	60	59	35	34	15	1850
21	92	86	95	90	82	75	1867	30	29	32	38	40	45	46	44	43	36	33	27	1869
22	87	80	80	90	71	71	1871[6]	23	32	35	36	34	34	39	32	34	30	33	29	1871
23	95	84	91	92	78	70	1872	27	33	35	38	40	40	46	41	47	45	39	34	1854
24	102	102	100	94	74	68	1849[7]	29	31	35	43	41	55	52	50	45	44	34	28	1849
25	99	99	101	103	84	78	1859	27	27	31	40	39	48	56	56	62	38	34	26	1854
26	109	104	101	90	77	64	1861	20	30	32	37	44	54	63	60	58	41	34	30	1862
27	90	78	90	92	73	66	1870	38	40	40	40	42	46	48	50	50	44	41	34	1872
COLORADO.																				
1	97	96	89	80	76	70	1871	—40	—23	— 1	0	14	30	35	39	24	3	—35	—30	1873
2	108	108	99	92	82	73	1868[8]	—25	—22	— 7	11	22	34	41	40	29	13	— 3	—23	1870
CONNECTICUT.																				
1	94	92	87	84	71	59	1868	—25	—28	—10	15	25	46	52	47	31	20	9	—11	1861
2	100	96	94	88	80	78	1866	—20	—18	— 6	23	35	46	53	48	34	22	16	— 6	1866
3	98	94	90	77	67	60	1872	—15	— 8	— 3	15	25	33	44	44	32	24	11	— 7	1866
4	95	97	89	85	75	61	1870	—14	—17	— 4	19	32	46	51	48	33	23	14	—18	1860
5	101	98	92	83	74	68	1864	—24	—16	— 9	11	27	35	44	39	27	19	2	—11	1835
6	91	90	84	81	69	55	1866	—19	—20	— 3	10	30	45	51	50	37	21	14	— 5	1861
DAKOTA.																				
1	104	102	94	82	78	50	1871	—35	—40	—40	— 7	19	35	34	32	20	7	—22	—32	1861[8]
2	106	102	99	96	78	60	1868[2]	—38	—36	—40	5	15	32	37	29	8	4	—33	—35	1867
3	107	108	106	92	80	67	1863	—32	—30	—19	0	10	37	42	34	19	2	—14	—30	1873
4	103	102	87	81	70	54	1869	—25	—29	—24	11	37	42	45	39	32	2	— 7	—24	1870
5	114	107	101	93	80	64	1871	—30	—26	—12	0	19	37	42	36	24	— 3	—12	—27	1871
6	102	100	93	85	74	55	1871	—32	—32	—24	4	28	37	43	40	22	— 9	—24	—35	1872
DELAWARE.																				
1	101	101	90	88	75	65	1865	— 5	0	5	24	38	49	53	51	47	32	20	9	1866

[5] Also in 1860. [6] Also in 1872. [7] Also in 1863. [8] Also in 1869.

Name of Station.	Height.	Series. Begins.	Series. Ends.	Highest Temperature Jan.	Feb.	Mar.	Apr.	May.	June.
DISTRICT OF COLUMBIA.									
1. Washington	110	Jan. 1822;	Dec. 1870	° 74	° 72	° 84	° 91	° 96	° 99
FLORIDA.									
1. Fort Barrancas	20	Jan. 1822;	June, 1874	78	78	86	85	93	104
2. Fort Brooke	20	Jan. 1825;	July, 1869	88	89	88	91	92	96
3. Fort Dallas	20	Apr. 1850;	May, 1858	89	83	85	86	90	88
4. Fort Jefferson	11	Feb. 1861;	Nov. 1873	85	84	88	91	95	95
5. Fort King	50	Jan. 1833;	Feb. 1843	85	86	93	94	98	106
6. Fort Marion	25	Jan. 1825;	May, 1866	84	86	88	92	97	103
7. Fort Meade	80	May, 1851;	Nov. 1854	81	87	88	92	95	96
8. Fort Myers	50	Jan. 1851;	June, 1858	84	86	90	94	94	98
9. Fort Pierce	30	Oct. 1851;	May, 1858	83	87	89	90	98	96
10. Indian Key	...	Jan. 1836;	Dec. 1838	81	85	83	86	88	88
11. Key West	10	Jan. 1831;	June, 1874	88	88	90	91	95	97
GEORGIA.									
1. Atlanta	1050	July, 1870;	June, 1874	72	75	79	89	94	95
2. Augusta Arsenal	350	Jan. 1826;	June, 1874	77	97	86	94	96	100
3. Oglethorpe Barracks	40	Jan. 1834;	Mar. 1870	80	87	86	93	96	102
4. Savannah	42	June, 1837;	June, 1874	78	85	88	94	97	102
IDAHO.									
1. Fort Boisé	...	Feb. 1864;	June, 1874	60	69	83	83	95	106
2. Fort Hall	...	Jan. 1871;	June, 1874	54	53	70	78	92	99
3. Fort Lapwai	...	Jan. 1864;	June, 1874	65	61	69	85	101	105
ILLINOIS.									
1. Augusta	500	Jan. 1861;	Dec. 1870	66	69	79	83	87	99
2. Chicago	600	Jan. 1833;	Dec. 1870	64	64	84	84	98	102
3. Fort Armstrong	528	Jan. 1827;	Dec. 1835	64	60	74	87	96	96
4. Galesburg	795	Jan. 1862;	Dec. 1870	67	63	79	85	87	96
5. Highland	620	Jan. 1841;	Dec. 1852	68	74	82	88	94	100
6. Manchester	683	Jan. 1860;	Dec. 1870	68	70	80	86	92	99
7. Pleasant Ridge Nursery	550	Jan. 1864;	Dec. 1869	60	62	77	86	92	99
8. Rock Island Arsenal	528	Feb. 1866;	June, 1874	64	66	75	89	94	102
9. Sandwich	575	Jan. 1860;	Dec. 1869	65	68	74	86	90	96
10. Springfield	550	Jan. 1865;	Dec. 1869	52	70	75	88	92	94
11. Winnebago	900	Jan. 1860;	Dec. 1870	48	58	73	85	91	99
INDIANA.									
1. New Harmony	350	Jan. 1860;	Dec. 1870	68	66	78	86	91	96
2. Spiceland	1025	Jan. 1864;	Dec. 1870	64	66	74	84	94	97
3. Vevay	525	Jan. 1865;	Dec. 1870	69	70	82	97	98	100

DISTRICT OF COLUMBIA.

	during Each Month.						Year of Extreme Heat.	Lowest Temperature during Each Month.												Year of Extreme Cold.
	July.	Aug.	Sept.	Oct.	Nov.	Dec.		Jan.	Feb.	Mar.	Apr.	May.	June.	July.	Aug.	Sept.	Oct.	Nov.	Dec.	
	°	°	°	°	°	°		°	°	°	°	°	°	°	°	°	°	°	°	
1	103	101	95	90	75	72	1838	−14	− 5	− 5	24	33	45	50	49	33	22	12	−10	1835

FLORIDA.

	July.	Aug.	Sept.	Oct.	Nov.	Dec.	Year of Extreme Heat.	Jan.	Feb.	Mar.	Apr.	May.	June.	July.	Aug.	Sept.	Oct.	Nov.	Dec.	Year of Extreme Cold.
1	100	102	98	92	86	87	1854	10	11	28	30	36	51	67	58	47	28	19	15	1852
2	94	98	94	90	88	86	1848	26	30	34	40	52	59	64	55	59	45	29	28	1857[1]
3	92	95	93	87	88	87	1850	30	35	42	50	63	68	71	73	72	55	50	35	1857
4	97	98	100	90	89	85	1871	48	55	50	58	59	72	70	72	71	65	56	42	1868
5	103	106	100	99	88	88	1833	23	11	27	44	44	60	64	55	54	31	28	27	1835
6	96	96	93	89	86	82	1837	21	26	32	30	48	58	70	65	57	43	33	23	1831
7	95	96	93	90	86	83	1851[2]	24	34	39	44	56	65	68	68	58	49	36	30	1852
8	95	95	99	93	89	85	1856	31	33	38	49	61	69	71	73	66	52	42	32	1852
9	97	95	95	89	86	88	1852	29	30	38	48	64	70	67	70	70	46	40	29	1851[3]
10	88	89	88	87	84	82	1836	49	47	56	62	64	71	73	72	73	62	58	54	1836
11	96	98	98	93	89	86	1861[4]	44	45	49	50	60	63	72	73	66	65	52	48	1857

GEORGIA.

	July.	Aug.	Sept.	Oct.	Nov.	Dec.	Year of Extreme Heat.	Jan.	Feb.	Mar.	Apr.	May.	June.	July.	Aug.	Sept.	Oct.	Nov.	Dec.	Year of Extreme Cold.
1	96	97	96	92	81	78	1873	3	15	12	33	44	59	65	56	46	21	10	6	1873
2	103	100	98	92	80	79	1845	8	− 2	15	33	46	56	56	58	43	26	11	10	1835
3	99	96	99	89	82	78	1845	22	16	28	38	52	54	64	59	48	32	31	20	1835
4	100	98	97	88	81	80	1839[5]	18	32	27	41	53	60	68	69	49	36	27	15	1870[5]

IDAHO.

	July.	Aug.	Sept.	Oct.	Nov.	Dec.	Year of Extreme Heat.	Jan.	Feb.	Mar.	Apr.	May.	June.	July.	Aug.	Sept.	Oct.	Nov.	Dec.	Year of Extreme Cold.
1	113	121	97	95	75	67	1871	− 9	−10	5	27	35	41	50	47	31	20	7	−14	1865
2	102	101	97	90	68	60	1871	−12	−11	− 1	12	25	33	40	30	18	7	−12	− 6	1872[6]
3	110	103	95	86	72	64	1864	− 3	0	1	24	29	38	39	40	20	17	0	−15	1865

ILLINOIS.

	July.	Aug.	Sept.	Oct.	Nov.	Dec.	Year of Extreme Heat.	Jan.	Feb.	Mar.	Apr.	May.	June.	July.	Aug.	Sept.	Oct.	Nov.	Dec.	Year of Extreme Cold.
1	96	97	100	87	75	70	1864	−26	−17	− 5	23	35	49	55	50	34	16	−12	−19	1864
2	106	102	97	90	74	78	1868	−25	−22	−12	13	29	38	46	42	30	16	− 4	−20	1864
3	98	95	90	88	74	68	1830	−24	−24	−14	20	38	46	50	51	36	20	0	−16	1830[7]
4	96	95	94	86	69	69	1868[4]	−29	−22	− 7	20	32	38	41	39	33	14	− 6	−22	1864
5	100	99	100	87	80	68	1841[8]	−15	− 4	2	20	34	38	48	47	34	17	3	− 7	1852
6	101	101	102	90	78	69	1864	−24	−14	− 3	20	33	48	53	44	34	11	0	−15	1864
7	102	94	94	80	70	58	1868	−24	−19	− 7	18	34	42	50	48	33	17	3	−14	1864
8	100	102	94	87	68	66	1870[6]	−29	−21	−14	16	34	39	51	38	31	12	− 7	−26	1873
9	97	98	98	85	70	64	1860[9]	−26	−25	− 8	16	29	43	50	46	32	12	− 3	−22	1860[10]
10	103	98	95	84	80	64	1868	− 9	−12	− 2	26	34	46	56	51	40	20	2	−18	1868
11	97	95	90	85	68	60	1870	−28	−26	− 9	14	30	45	50	46	31	15	− 6	−20	1864

INDIANA.

	July.	Aug.	Sept.	Oct.	Nov.	Dec.	Year of Extreme Heat.	Jan.	Feb.	Mar.	Apr.	May.	June.	July.	Aug.	Sept.	Oct.	Nov.	Dec.	Year of Extreme Cold.
1	99	99	93	86	75	70	1868	−15	− 2	7	28	34	48	56	48	38	20	10	− 2	1864
2	100	97	94	82	71	61	1864	−19	−21	0	25	34	49	55	48	39	15	4	−11	1866
3	100	98	99	96	78	76	1865[11]	− 4	−10	6	23	35	50	58	50	42	21	10	− 9	1867

[1] Also in 1827. [2] Also in 1852. [3] Also in 1857. [4] Also in 1870.
[5] Also in 1845. [6] Also in 1873. [7] Also in 1835. [8] Also in 1843.
[9] Also in 1861. [10] Also in 1864. [11] Also in 1865 and 1866.

INDIAN TERRITORY.

Name of Station.	Height.	Series. Begins.	Ends.	Highest Temperature Jan.	Feb.	Mar.	Apr.	May.	June.
				°	°	°	°	°	°
1. Fort Arbuckle	1000	Oct. 1850;	Aug. 1870	75	84	94	92	100	100
2. Fort Gibson	560	Jan. 1828;	June, 1874	83	80	95	95	99	103
3. Fort Sill	...	July, 1870;	June, 1874	77	80	90	97	98	103
4. Fort Towson	300	Jan. 1833;	Apr. 1854	78	82	89	92	99	98
5. Fort Washita	645	Jan. 1843;	Mar. 1861	79	86	92	94	95	99

IOWA.

Name of Station.	Height.	Series. Begins.	Ends.	Jan.	Feb.	Mar.	Apr.	May.	June.
1. Algona	1500	Jan. 1862;	Dec. 1870	44	48	68	80	92	98
2. Brookside	...	Jan. 1864;	Dec. 1868	48	55	76	88	93	100
3. Davenport	737	Jan. 1862;	Dec. 1869	53	60	71	81	86	90
4. Bubuque	680	Jan. 1860;	Dec. 1870	51	71	74	84	91	102
5. Fort Atkinson	700	Jan. 1842;	May, 1846	53	53	82	88	84	90
6. Fort Dodge	944	Aug. 1851;	Dec. 1868	52	55	74	71	89	98
7. Fort Madison, near	600	Jan. 1860;	Dec. 1870	60	68	76	85	91	100
8. Guttenberg	690	Jan. 1867;	Dec. 1870	46	56	74	88	91	103
9. Independence	850	Jan. 1864;	Dec. 1870	49	53	63	87	91	102
10. Iowa City	621	Jan. 1861;	Dec. 1870	55	68	72	90	90	99
11. Monticello	880	Jan. 1866;	Dec. 1870	45	61	77	89	90	102
12. Mount Vernon	...	Jan. 1864;	Dec. 1870	45	60	75	90	93	98
13. Muscatine	586	Jan. 1839;	Dec. 1865	60	71	84	86	90	96
14. Spring Grove	...	Jan. 1864;	Dec. 1869	45	50	66	80	87	90
15. Vawter's Grove	1500	Jan. 1867;	Dec. 1870	48	58	82	87	91	97
16. Waterloo	666	Jan. 1865;	Dec. 1869	46	52	77	82	87	96

KANSAS.

Name of Station.	Height.	Series. Begins.	Ends.	Jan.	Feb.	Mar.	Apr.	May.	June.
1. Atchison	1000	Jan. 1867;	Dec. 1870	58	68	70	90	90	101
2. Baxter Springs	...	Jan. 1868;	Dec. 1870	68	78	84	86	96	103
3. Council Grove	1480	Jan. 1866;	Dec. 1870	62	75	92	89	91	100
4. Fort Atkinson	2330	Nov. 1850;	Sept. 1853	68	69	85	88	92	93
5. Fort Dodge	...	Nov. 1867;	Feb. 1871	71	82	86	91	90	101
6. Fort Hays	2107	Aug. 1867;	June, 1874	80	74	86	92	91	106
7. Fort Larned	1932	Sept. 1860;	June, 1874	67	81	86	96	99	105
8. Fort Leavenworth	896	Jan. 1831;	June, 1874	69	78	89	102	94	103
9. Fort Riley	1300	Nov. 1853;	June, 1874	69	77	88	95	99	104
10. Fort Scott	1000	Jan. 1843;	Mar. 1853	75	77	87	87	90	92
11. Holton	1172	Jan. 1868;	Dec. 1870	60	67	91	91	91	106
12. Lawrence	850	Jan. 1868;	Dec. 1870	64	72	93	89	91	101
13. Leavenworth City	896	Jan. 1861;	Dec. 1870	65	70	95	90	98	102
14. Manhattan	1000	Jan. 1861;	Dec. 1870	61	70	87	93	93	102
15. Olatha	...	Jan. 1866;	Dec. 1870	60	70	91	89	97	100

KENTUCKY.

Name of Station.	Height.	Series. Begins.	Ends.	Jan.	Feb.	Mar.	Apr.	May.	June.
1. Chilesburg	900	Jan. 1867;	Dec. 1870	62	66	76	82	90	92
2. Newport Barracks	500	July, 1847;	June, 1874	70	69	80	89	90	96

LOUISIANA.

Name of Station.	Height.	Series. Begins.	Ends.	Jan.	Feb.	Mar.	Apr.	May.	June.
1. Baton Rouge	41	Jan. 1822;	June, 1874	82	90	92	96	99	98
2. Fort Jesup	80	Jan. 1823;	Dec. 1845	84	86	90	98	98	98
3. Fort Wood	20	Jan. 1833;	Apr. 1846	81	78	84	88	95	98
4. Fort Pike	10	Jan. 1827;	Apr. 1870	80	86	87	94	93	96
5. New Orleans	25	Jan. 1820;	Dec. 1870	82	84	90	91	96	98

[1] Also in 1857. [2] Also in 1838, 1841, 1845. [3] Also in 1856. [4] Also in 1843. [5] Also in 1869.

INDIAN TERRITORY.

	...during Each Month.						Year of Extreme Heat.	Lowest Temperature during Each Month.												Year of Extreme Cold.
	July.	Aug.	Sept.	Oct.	Nov.	Dec.		Jan.	Feb.	Mar.	Apr.	May.	June.	July.	Aug.	Sept.	Oct.	Nov.	Dec.	
	°	°	°	°	°	°		°	°	°	°	°	°	°	°	°	°	°	°	
1	109	107	99	94	83	75	1856	—4	—4	12	25	35	51	54	56	38	26	12	—1	1856[1]
2	106	116	103	95	86	91	1834	—20	—12	7	28	32	50	54	37	30	18	0	—8	1857
3	109	109	103	96	84	75	1871	—20	5	20	27	39	54	50	59	46	21	8	—11	1873
4	102	101	100	88	82	78	1845	0	0	10	30	38	52	54	56	35	24	10	0	1835[2]
5	106	106	100	92	84	78	1845[3]	—4	—1	10	28	38	52	61	58	42	29	17	1	1857

IOWA.

	July.	Aug.	Sept.	Oct.	Nov.	Dec.	Year of Extreme Heat.	Jan.	Feb.	Mar.	Apr.	May.	June.	July.	Aug.	Sept.	Oct.	Nov.	Dec.	Year of Extreme Cold.
1	97	96	89	86	72	58	1864	—29	—26	—25	13	30	45	55	43	30	10	—6	—18	1862
2	105	98	97	86	68	51	1868	—26	—35	—11	10	33	47	50	44	29	10	—1	—27	1868
3	95	91	88	82	69	56	1868	—22	—24	—8	19	32	32	51	51	35	19	3	—17	1868
4	100	98	91	85	67	58	1870	—29	—20	—7	13	36	50	53	46	34	19	—6	—23	1864
5	99	92	92	84	78	46	1844	—19	—22	—16	4	29	40	44	44	22	2	—12	—22	1842[4]
6	99	93	90	82	70	58	1868	—28	—25	—19	16	31	51	57	50	34	18	—1	—18	1852
7	105	103	97	85	72	66	1870	—33	—20	—12	18	33	44	40	41	29	16	—2	—20	1864
8	99	99	87	82	68	52	1870	—30	—37	—20	16	27	41	50	42	26	8	—4	—22	1868
9	99	97	88	81	69	52	1870	—30	—21	—16	17	34	47	58	48	34	12	—5	—16	1864
10	100	99	92	86	72	62	1870	—26	—25	—13	20	31	42	46	43	33	16	0	—17	1864
11	101	98	90	82	68	55	1870	—22	—30	—10	22	33	35	59	48	34	16	2	—18	1868
12	99	95	90	80	76	53	1868	—24	—20	—15	11	30	43	52	49	30	16	—1	—18	1864
13	98	101	96	87	75	70	1861	—26	—25	—10	5	23	33	42	36	30	8	—11	—22	1860
14	92	94	86	78	68	47	1867[5]	—29	—14	—19	10	30	34	50	42	30	19	—5	—13	1864
15	103	97	89	81	71	58	1868	—18	—16	—12	17	36	49	33	47	33	13	—2	—21	1868
16	100	96	88	80	68	48	1868	—18	—28	—20	15	32	46	50	40	30	14	0	—19	1868

KANSAS.

	July.	Aug.	Sept.	Oct.	Nov.	Dec.	Year of Extreme Heat.	Jan.	Feb.	Mar.	Apr.	May.	June.	July.	Aug.	Sept.	Oct.	Nov.	Dec.	Year of Extreme Cold.
1	100	101	96	90	76	62	1870	—6	—6	—14	23	34	52	61	53	39	12	4	—7	1867
2	106	100	95	86	79	70	1868	—2	—7	6	32	46	54	70	62	46	24	22	—10	1870
3	106	102	96	93	78	67	1868	—12	—6	—17	24	36	50	58	48	33	24	6	—15	1867
4	96	102	94	86	68	60	1853	—6	2	9	22	43	45	64	56	40	30	10	—12	1850
5	103	102	93	90	82	69	1868	—5	—1	4	31	42	52	60	50	38	10	6	—10	1869[6]
6	110	104	102	97	96	82	1868	—15	—15	4	23	30	49	57	46	30	5	—7	—15	1872[7]
7	115	105	104	98	82	79	1871	—22	—9	4	11	31	49	54	47	34	11	1	—13	1861
8	105	105	104	93	78	71	1860[8]	—30	—26	—9	13	21	43	50	48	30	11	—14	—19	1834
9	111	108	108	97	81	71	1860	—29	—18	—20	10	34	45	50	48	28	9	—6	—16	1862
10	98	104	98	95	80	69	1850	—9	—12	—10	22	31	46	47	48	31	21	—10	—14	1848
11	111	102	93	83	77	66	1868	—11	—10	—2	22	40	52	61	52	32	11	14	—19	1868
12	101	98	93	82	73	64	1868[6]	—7	—5	—1	18	35	37	47	53	29	15	17	—16	1868
13	109	103	97	90	80	69	1868	—12	—16	—18	19	30	42	55	41	26	12	5	—19	1868
14	103	101	97	94	96	68	1862	—12	—9	—9	19	41	46	56	52	34	14	7	—16	1868
15	108	102	94	89	77	66	1868	—12	—14	—8	22	37	51	60	51	30	21	4	—20	1868

KENTUCKY.

	July.	Aug.	Sept.	Oct.	Nov.	Dec.	Year of Extreme Heat.	Jan.	Feb.	Mar.	Apr.	May.	June.	July.	Aug.	Sept.	Oct.	Nov.	Dec.	Year of Extreme Cold.
1	98	96	96	88	74	66	....	—2	—2	8	22	40	48	54	50	36	17	10	—6	1870
2	98	96	96	85	78	70	....	—15	—20	3	21	31	46	55	47	38	23	4	—8	....

LOUISIANA.

	July.	Aug.	Sept.	Oct.	Nov.	Dec.	Year of Extreme Heat.	Jan.	Feb.	Mar.	Apr.	May.	June.	July.	Aug.	Sept.	Oct.	Nov.	Dec.	Year of Extreme Cold.
1	99	102	97	91	90	82	1860	8	10	26	34	49	57	63	63	47	32	26	18	1852
2	101	100	100	91	88	86	1824	11	7	16	34	44	54	50	58	36	23	17	14	1823[9]
3	98	100	97	90	86	76	1835[10]	30	14	28	46	62	62	68	69	51	43	31	30	1835
4	98	100	94	89	83	82	1870	21	23	26	42	54	64	70	66	48	38	30	22	1832
5	100	100	94	96	90	86	1840[11]	17	26	29	38	48	58	70	70	62	40	29	19	1852

[6] Also in 1870. [7] Also in 1873. [8] Also in 1834. [9] Also in 1838. [10] Also in 1845. [11] Also in 1841.

MAINE.

Name of Station.	Height.	Series. Begins.	Series. Ends.	Highest Temperature Jan.	Feb.	Mar.	Apr.	May.	June.
				°	°	°	°	°	°
1. Brunswick	74	Jan. 1807;	Nov. 1859	56	61	76	85	98	98
2. Castine	50	Jan. 1810;	Dec. 1849	52	55	64	74	90	90
3. Fort Preble	31	Jan. 1822;	June, 1874	51	52	63	90	92	92
4. Fort Sullivan	70	Jan. 1822;	Sept. 1873	54	60	60	82	90	92
5. Gardiner	76	Jan. 1837;	Dec. 1870	52	55	65	86	90	94
6. Hancock Barracks	620	Jan. 1829;	Aug. 1845	57	58	86	85	91	98
7. Portland	50	Dec. 1815;	Dec. 1852	50	49	63	80	93	92

MARYLAND.

Name of Station.	Height.	Series. Begins.	Series. Ends.	Jan.	Feb.	Mar.	Apr.	May.	June.
1. Annapolis	20	Jan. 1861;	Dec. 1870	69	67	79	84	90	100
2. Baltimore	80	Jan. 1817;	Oct. 1853	68	73	77	88	90	97
3. Fort Foote	...	July, 1871;	June, 1874	68	72	69	87	90	97
4. Fort McHenry	36	Jan. 1831;	June, 1874	66	74	76	89	93	100
5. Fort Severn	20	Jan. 1822;	July, 1845	68	72	76	88	90	96
6. Fort Washington	60	Jan. 1833;	Sept. 1870	68	70	79	93	97	105
7. Mount Saint Mary's College	498	Jan. 1867;	Dec. 1870	60	64	66	83	84	92

MASSACHUSETTS.

Name of Station.	Height.	Series. Begins.	Series. Ends.	Jan.	Feb.	Mar.	Apr.	May.	June.
1. Amherst	267	Sept. 1837;	Dec. 1870	56	56	73	84	88	94
2. Fort Independence	50	Jan. 1831;	June, 1874	56	65	66	82	90	99
3. Fort Warren	...	Oct. 1862;	June, 1874	56	58	61	76	94	92
4. Lawrence	143	Jan. 1861;	Dec. 1869	48	58	69	82	87	91
5. Lunenburg	450	Jan. 1847;	Dec. 1870	59	60	70	82	88	97
6. Mendon	...	Jan. 1860;	Dec. 1870	58	56	74	80	90	94
7. Nantucket	30	Jan. 1847;	Dec. 1860	54	57	58	63	81	92
8. New Bedford	90	Oct. 1812;	Dec. 1870	64	63	73	80	90	95
9. North Billerica	135	Jan. 1867;	Dec. 1870	59	56	58	80	87	95
10. Topsfield	...	Jan. 1861;	Dec. 1869	51	66	72	81	87	93
11. Watertown Arsenal	100	Jan. 1837;	Nov. 1844	55	64	66	85	92	95
12. Williamstown	686	Jan. 1816;	Dec. 1870	61	61	71	87	95	95
13. Worcester	528	Jan. 1861;	Dec. 1870	55	58	71	79	85	92

MICHIGAN.

Name of Station.	Height.	Series. Begins.	Series. Ends.	Jan.	Feb.	Mar.	Apr.	May.	June.
1. Detroit	597	Jan. 1840;	June, 1874	63	64	78	90	94	95
2. Fort Brady	600	Jan. 1823;	June, 1874	52	62	72	80	92	96
3. Fort Gratiot	598	Jan. 1831;	May, 1852	60	63	75	94	93	95
4. Fort Mackinac	728	Jan. 1826;	Apr. 1860	50	46	63	80	76	90
5. Grand Haven	588	Aug. 1859;	July, 1863	65	52	63	76	88	88
6. Lansing	895	Jan. 1864;	Dec. 1869	55	60	68	78	84	95
7. Marquette	710	July, 1859;	Dec. 1867	51	53	63	74	93	101
8. Monroe	551	July, 1859;	Dec. 1869	73	69	75	78	92	101
9. Ontonagon	620	Aug. 1859;	Dec. 1870	45	48	61	79	94	97
10. Tawas City	583	Jan. 1859;	Dec. 1867	50	57	56	61	81	90
11. Thunderbay Island	610	Jan. 1859;	Dec. 1870	47	47	51	62	76	90

MAINE.

	…during Each Month.						Year of Extreme Heat.	Lowest Temperature during Each Month.												Year of Extreme Cold.
	July.	Aug.	Sept.	Oct.	Nov.	Dec.		Jan.	Feb.	Mar.	Apr.	May.	June.	July.	Aug.	Sept.	Oct.	Nov.	Dec.	
	°	°	°	°	°	°		°	°	°	°	°	°	°	°	°	°	°	°	
1	102	98	96	88	72	61	1808	—32	—28	—19	10	21	27	27	35	23	9	— 3	—22	1859
2	94	93	86	78	65	58	1849	—20	—21	—13	10	25	34	41	43	30	19	2	—16	1824
3	96	96	88	74	70	58	1822[1]	—16	—12	— 5	13	31	33	45	45	32	21	1	—10	1830
4	98	91	85	87	66	56	1826	—24	—20	—15	12	30	35	42	45	33	24	— 5	—20	1826
5	96	94	89	77	72	58	1841	—31	—25	—20	5	15	33	44	42	28	16	3	—24	1844
6	99	97	90	81	73	55	1836	—24	—23	—15	2	16	32	42	34	27	16	— 6	—23	1829[2]
7	96	90	94	77	70	56	1846[3]	—19	—24	—13	13	24	34	45	42	31	18	— 2	—13	1826

MARYLAND.

	July.	Aug.	Sept.	Oct.	Nov.	Dec.	Year of Extreme Heat.	Jan.	Feb.	Mar.	Apr.	May.	June.	July.	Aug.	Sept.	Oct.	Nov.	Dec.	Year of Extreme Cold.
1	98	95	92	86	74	69	1864	— 5	— 1	6	26	39	56	58	54	42	31	21	6	1866[4]
2	98	98	98	85	76	76	1819[5]	— 9	— 4	9	18	35	41	52	48	36	26	12	4	1852
3	100	95	94	76	67	67	1872	— 5	— 2	4	23	38	44	55	55	37	26	15	— 2	1873
4	100	100	94	89	78	73	1834[6]	—15	— 4	0	20	31	45	54	50	38	25	11	— 1	1873
5	96	99	92	80	72	60	1834	1	8	9	27	42	46	62	58	45	34	19	2	1832
6	102	100	99	92	76	64	1853	— 4	11	10	32	34	48	58	52	42	31	22	5	1852
7	95	94	85	77	72	60	1868	4	2	2	22	37	50	54	48	44	27	19	3	1868

MASSACHUSETTS.

	July.	Aug.	Sept.	Oct.	Nov.	Dec.	Year of Extreme Heat.	Jan.	Feb.	Mar.	Apr.	May.	June.	July.	Aug.	Sept.	Oct.	Nov.	Dec.	Year of Extreme Cold.
1	95	98	89	83	70	59	1864	—22	—20	— 9	5	27	34	40	38	26	15	3	—15	1844
2	99	92	89	83	69	60	1854[7]	—13	—10	— 6	18	31	35	35	40	34	24	5	—10	1857
3	100	95	100	73	65	58	1872	—10	— 8	— 2	16	35	39	50	50	41	30	9	— 8	1866[8]
4	95	97	85	75	66	55	1864	—15	—16	— 7	22	32	44	54	48	33	23	13	— 8	1861
5	98	96	89	83	71	66	1868	—29	—26	— 6	10	26	42	50	44	[illegible]	[illegible]	8	—16	18[illegible]
6	[illegible]	[illegible]	[illegible]	[illegible]	[illegible]	[illegible]	[illegible]	—17	—17	— 8	19	30	46	50	49	30	22	11	— 5	1861[9]
7	89	88	83	76	70	60	1849	—12	— 5	3	17	40	46	53	44	36	25	15	— 2	1859
8	96	91	88	83	71	64	1818	—11	—16	0	18	26	38	55	44	33	23	6	—10	1861
9	97	90	88	78	70	51	1868	—14	—22	—11	22	32	48	50	43	34	16	12	— 9	1868
10	97	96	90	87	72	61	1861[10]	—16	—24	— 8	18	29	42	54	50	34	18	16	— 3	1861
11	97	94	91	82	72	49	1840	—12	—11	0	17	27	30	42	42	29	24	5	— 3	1839[11]
12	97	96	95	85	72	59	1820[12]	—30	—26	—12	17	28	35	43	39	25	13	— 3	—19	1835
13	94	89	85	85	70	60	1866	—15	—19	— 2	21	33	44	53	51	39	25	12	— 3	1861

MICHIGAN.

	July.	Aug.	Sept.	Oct.	Nov.	Dec.	Year of Extreme Heat.	Jan.	Feb.	Mar.	Apr.	May.	June.	July.	Aug.	Sept.	Oct.	Nov.	Dec.	Year of Extreme Cold.
1	96	98	91	86	80	78	1861	—19	—14	— 5	11	24	32	41	37	31	15	2	—13	1864
2	96	96	98	82	72	60	1854	—42	—47	—29	—4	16	24	33	37	29	10	— 9	—41	1873
3	98	94	91	78	74	72	1834	—15	—18	— 7	2	22	33	40	39	30	19	1	—16	1836
4	88	86	82	70	62	51	1835	—27	—24	—19	6	21	32	41	41	30	17	— 4	—16	1851
5	90	91	81	75	62	57	1861	— 5	—16	1	8	27	28	33	48	28	17	9	0	1861
6	96	99	89	81	71	52	1864	—22	—15	— 2	20	30	44	52	38	22	18	4	—17	1864
7	103	100	93	85	69	61	1862	—31	—33	—19	3	16	30	33	38	23	15	— 4	—19	1861
8	103	99	98	89	71	59	1866	—17	—21	— 8	19	29	38	41	34	27	20	5	—13	1868
9	98	98	91	89	69	53	1864[4]	—34	—37	—22	—5	18	30	30	33	20	4	— 3	—16	1861
10	86	87	85	75	59	60	1864	—25	—25	—10	9	17	27	34	31	28	23	11	— 6	1861[9]
11	90	93	81	73	61	51	1864	—17	—25	—12	8	25	35	41	40	33	26	8	— 5	1861

[1] Also in 1834 and 1835.
[2] Also in 1833 and 1839.
[3] Also in 1849.
[4] Also in 1868.
[5] Also in 1820, 1850, and 1851.
[6] Also in 1849 and 1872.
[7] Also in 1872.
[8] Also in 1873.
[9] Also in 1866.
[10] Also in 1866 and 1868.
[11] Also in 1840.
[12] Also in 1825 and 1826.

MINNESOTA.

Name of Station.	Height.	Series. Begins.	Ends.	Highest Temperature Jan.	Feb.	Mar.	Apr.	May.	June.
				°	°	°	°	°	°
1. Beaver Bay	1270	Jan. 1861;	Dec. 1870	46	49	65	74	84	96
2. Fort Ridgeley	1230	July, 1853;	Dec. 1864	53	54	78	90	91	95
3. Fort Ripley	1130	Jan. 1860;	June, 1874	53	53	70	83	101	96
4. Fort Snelling	820	Jan. 1820;	June, 1874	59	60	79	88	92	96
5. Minneapolis	856	Jan. 1865;	Dec. 1870	42	46	67	84	91	96
6. New Ulm	821	Jan. 1865;	Dec. 1870	41	43	71	85	92	98
7. Saint Paul	800	Jan. 1864;	Dec. 1870	49	50	70	83	89	99
8. Sibley	...	Jan. 1866;	Dec. 1870	41	47	67	82	88	93

MISSISSIPPI.

Name of Station.	Height.	Series. Begins.	Ends.	Jan.	Feb.	Mar.	Apr.	May.	June.
1. Columbus	227	Jan. 1861;	Dec. 1870	78	79	84	86	93	98
2. Natchez	264	Jan. 1861;	June, 1870	80	83	80	85	89	92
3. Vicksburg	350	Sept. 1866;	May, 1870	80	81	83	85	95	97

MISSOURI.

Name of Station.	Height.	Series. Begins.	Ends.	Jan.	Feb.	Mar.	Apr.	May.	June.
1. Allenton	...	Jan. 1867;	Dec. 1870	67	77	88	93	96	101
2. Harrisonville	...	Jan. 1865;	Dec. 1870	62	66	78	84	88	94
3. Jefferson Barracks	472	Jan. 1827;	July, 1862	72	81	98	94	92	100
4. Oregon	1100	Jan. 1867;	Dec. 1870	62	69	69	88	89	98
5. Rolla, near	950	Jan. 1868;	Dec. 1870	67	76	87	89	91	96
6. Saint Louis	481	Mar. 1833;	Dec. 1870	71	81	86	93	97	100

MONTANA.

Name of Station.	Height.	Series. Begins.	Ends.	Jan.	Feb.	Mar.	Apr.	May.	June.
1. Camp Baker	...	Nov. 1870;	June, 1874	52	63	65	83	91	85
2. Deer Lodge City	4240	Jan. 1869;	Dec. 1870	51	55	62	76	85	98
3. Fort Benton	2730	Nov. 1869;	June, 1874	60	60	65	83	94	104
4. Fort Ellis	4800	Aug. 1868;	June, 1874	60	54	68	78	87	95
5. Fort Shaw	6000	Sept. 1867;	June, 1874	67	71	81	93	98	101

NEBRASKA.

Name of Station.	Height.	Series. Begins.	Ends.	Jan.	Feb.	Mar.	Apr.	May.	June.
1. Bellevue	...	Jan. 1860;	Dec. 1870	58	65	76	88	92	96
2. De Soto	1100	Jan. 1868;	Dec. 1869	43	57	86	78	89	93
3. Fort Calhoun	1327	Jan. 1822;	Dec. 1826	67	68	80	90	98	102
4. Fort Kearney	2360	Jan. 1849;	Jan. 1868	70	68	82	92	94	101
5. Fort McPherson	...	Nov. 1866;	June, 1874	78	82	86	96	96	104
6. Glendale	1010	Jan. 1867;	Dec. 1868	52	66	92	89	89	92
7. Omaha	1300	July, 1870;	Sept. 1873	58	60	69	96	91	96
8. Omaha Agency	...	Jan. 1869;	Dec. 1870	50	67	68	84	91	95
9. Richland	1350	Jan. 1861;	Dec. 1869	49	65	85	90	95	101

NEVADA.

Name of Station.	Height.	Series. Begins.	Ends.	Jan.	Feb.	Mar.	Apr.	May.	June.
1. Camp Halleck	5600	Oct. 1867;	June, 1874	56	57	69	84	104	111
2. Camp McDermit	4700	Dec. 1865;	Nov. 1873	56	65	72	85	90	100
3. Camp McGarry	6000	Nov. 1865;	Nov. 1868	48	54	57	75	77	85
4. Camp Winfield Scott	...	Dec. 1866;	July, 1870	49	54	64	86	91	94
5. Fort Churchill	4284	Oct. 1860;	May, 1869	59	68	68	83	89	98
6. Fort Ruby	5922	Jan. 1863;	Oct. 1868	72	82	80	80	88	95

MINNESOTA.

	During Each Month.						Year of Extreme Heat.	Lowest Temperature during Each Month.												Year of Extreme Cold.
	July.	Aug.	Sept.	Oct.	Nov.	Dec.		Jan.	Feb.	Mar.	Apr.	May.	June.	July.	Aug.	Sept.	Oct.	Nov.	Dec.	
	°	°	°	°	°	°		°	°	°	°	°	°	°	°	°	°	°	°	
1	94	89	84	80	64	45	1864	—35	—34	—26	3	25	37	45	41	30	15	—14	—21	1864
2	101	102	92	87	70	52	1861	—30	—31	—11	10	30	39	49	42	22	9	— 8	—26	1862
3	103	97	92	80	64	50	1871	—44	—43	—37	—5	21	28	26	28	12	8	—30	—40	1860
4	100	97	92	90	74	53	1838	—37	—35	—24	1	23	34	41	39	28	8	—23	—34	1840
5	101	91	88	86	67	53	1868	—40	—31	—27	8	28	47	52	46	25	12	— 6	—33	1868
6	100	100	91	87	71	55	1870	—30	—28	—20	10	29	46	55	46	31	16	— 8	—22	1868
7	97	99	87	83	65	52	1870	—39	—29	—26	8	30	46	51	45	23	16	— 6	—26	1868
8	98	94	87	86	68	53	1866[1]	—36	—37	—26	7	29	37	47	41	18	11	—11	—22	1866

MISSISSIPPI.

	July.	Aug.	Sept.	Oct.	Nov.	Dec.	Year of Extreme Heat.	Jan.	Feb.	Mar.	Apr.	May.	June.	July.	Aug.	Sept.	Oct.	Nov.	Dec.	Year of Extreme Cold.
1	100	99	94	89	80	76	1862	10	14	20	37	47	59	72	56	47	29	22	15	1864
2	94	92	90	86	80	79	1860	16	20	22	37	45	63	60	60	46	36	22	16	1860[1]
3	96	96	95	90	85	91	1868	18	25	25	37	53	64	69	67	50	35	26	17	1868

MISSOURI.

	July.	Aug.	Sept.	Oct.	Nov.	Dec.	Year of Extreme Heat.	Jan.	Feb.	Mar.	Apr.	May.	June.	July.	Aug.	Sept.	Oct.	Nov.	Dec.	Year of Extreme Cold.
1	109	103	100	100	84	73	1868	— 7	— 5	0	26	36	48	54	53	35	14	— 5	—16	1870
2	105	95	90	86	76	64	1868	— 8	— 8	—12	26	36	50	58	52	34	20	8	—14	1868
3	103	102	99	93	78	69	1860	—14	—18	0	17	32	44	52	35	37	22	— 2	—15	1835
4	105	96	93	91	78	72	1868	—12	—10	— 7	20	38	48	57	50	34	15	3	—16	1868
5	97	93	91	81	77	68	1870	0	— 3	10	23	39	44	61	58	39	18	15	—23	1870
6	103	108	98	95	81	74	1834	—19	—25	— 6	23	31	37	54	49	35	22	— 1	— 7	1835

MONTANA.

	July.	Aug.	Sept.	Oct.	Nov.	Dec.	Year of Extreme Heat.	Jan.	Feb.	Mar.	Apr.	May.	June.	July.	Aug.	Sept.	Oct.	Nov.	Dec.	Year of Extreme Cold.
1	92	93	82	82	69	56	1873	—32	—43	—12	14	30	32	40	43	19	0	—42	—53	1871
2	92	95	85	81	68	56	1870	—36	—33	—28	16	32	35	45	32	26	0	8	—16	1870
3	105	101	92	85	70	62	1870	—38	—35	—23	11	27	29	40	28	9	—4	—36	—51	1871
4	102	100	93	75	71	60	1869	—53	—53	—36	10	25	28	30	28	18	—3	—19	—45	1872
5	112	102	94	91	80	74	1872	—43	—31	—25	10	24	30	34	24	17	—5	—37	—37	1870

NEBRASKA.

	July.	Aug.	Sept.	Oct.	Nov.	Dec.	Year of Extreme Heat.	Jan.	Feb.	Mar.	Apr.	May.	June.	July.	Aug.	Sept.	Oct.	Nov.	Dec.	Year of Extreme Cold.
1	102	103	99	84	76	63	1861	—22	—13	—15	19	32	49	60	50	36	6	1	—14	1860
2	104	95	86	81	70	52	1868	—19	—17	— 9	19	41	42	56	53	33	10	9	—19	1868
3	108	104	94	96	87	63	1862	—21	—16	3	13	30	48	54	50	40	13	— 6	—17	1864
4	102	100	97	91	77	68	1857	—28	—22	— 4	10	26	39	45	37	27	8	1	—23	1852
5	115	110	102	102	81	76	1870	—20	—24	— 3	10	28	35	35	40	19	6	— 4	—18	1874
6	106	97	95	87	78	68	1868	—26	—22	—20	22	35	51	57	52	30	22	— 7	—30	1868
7	100	101	93	88	78	65	1873	—21	—16	— 1	16	28	24	54	46	34	24	— 7	—20	1873
8	102	98	91	78	72	70	1870	—10	—14	— 5	18	40	48	59	50	40	20	9	—15	1870
9	105	104	99	87	76	61	1862	—22	—20	—15	17	34	49	56	50	32	11	1	—21	1864

NEVADA.

	July.	Aug.	Sept.	Oct.	Nov.	Dec.	Year of Extreme Heat.	Jan.	Feb.	Mar.	Apr.	May.	June.	July.	Aug.	Sept.	Oct.	Nov.	Dec.	Year of Extreme Cold.
1	107	100	88	93	68	60	1871	—22	—18	— 8	7	13	25	23	24	19	3	—12	—13	1868
2	100	104	95	88	73	58	1870	— 9	— 9	3	11	23	29	40	35	24	11	5	— 4	1868
3	90	88	86	76	71	47	1867[1]	—18	—10	— 6	15	20	32	40	48	32	16	9	—13	1868
4	98	99	93	80	64	59	1868	—15	—12	— 2	29	35	27	51	49	39	25	15	10	1868
5	100	97	92	85	71	65	1863	— 9	0	17	25	27	42	57	59	43	16	13	— 1	1866
6	100	99	94	101	88	78	1863	—23	—19	2	19	32	34	48	47	25	8	— 2	—15	1864

[1] Also in 1868.

NEW HAMPSHIRE.

Name of Station.	Height.	Series. Begins.	Ends.	Highest Temperature Jan.	Feb.	Mar.	Apr.	May.	June.
				°	°	°	°	°	°
1. Claremont	536	Jan. 1860;	Dec. 1867	52	54	60	79	90	94
2. Concord	374	Jan. 1828;	Dec. 1835	56	60	69	88	89	94
3. Dartmouth College	...	Jan. 1835;	Dec. 1852	52	68	71	86	90	93
4. Fort Constitution	40	Jan. 1820;	Sept. 1853	60	59	68	85	87	96
5. Portsmouth	38	Jan. 1839;	July, 1842	52	58	66	80	88	92
6. Stratford	1000	Jan. 1860;	Dec. 1870	42	51	62	72	86	95

NEW JERSEY.

Name of Station.	Height.	Begins.	Ends.	Jan.	Feb.	Mar.	Apr.	May.	June.
1. Greenwich	30	Jan. 1864;	Dec. 1870	62	63	76	82	87	98
2. Haddonfield	50	Jan. 1864;	Dec. 1870	67	61	75	84	85	96
3. Newark	35	Jan. 1861;	Dec. 1870	57	62	75	84	88	95
4. Paterson	60	Jan. 1865;	Dec. 1870	55	58	72	85	90	95

NEW MEXICO.

Name of Station.	Height.	Begins.	Ends.	Jan.	Feb.	Mar.	Apr.	May.	June.
1. Albuquerque	5032	Sept. 1849;	July, 1867	66	78	83	98	100	114
2. Cebolleta	6200	Dec. 1849;	Feb. 1852	60	70	73	83	87	96
3. Fort Bascom	...	Feb. 1864;	Oct. 1870	69	85	84	95	98	104
4. Fort Bayard	4450	Mar. 1867;	June, 1874	64	70	76	86	92	100
5. Fort Conrad	4576	Oct. 1851;	Mar. 1854	70	69	87	91	93	98
6. Fort Craig	4576	Apr. 1854;	June, 1874	77	84	94	104	108	110
7. Fort Cummings	...	Mar. 1869;	July, 1873	95	83	100	90	102	107
8. Fort Fillmore	3937	Sept. 1851;	Apr. 1861	95	85	92	99	102	107
9. Fort McRae	4500	Mar. 1864;	June, 1874	79	71	88	100	109	120
10. Fort Selden	...	Nov. 1865;	June, 1874	72	80	86	98	106	105
11. Fort Stanton	...	Aug. 1855;	Oct. 1872	65	68	76	83	93	100
12. Fort Sumner	...	Apr. 1864;	July, 1869	74	75	85	90	100	97
13. Fort Thorn	4500	Jan. 1854;	Jan. 1859	75	78	89	99	105	113
14. Fort Union	6670	Aug. 1851;	June, 1874	74	70	79	85	94	100
15. Fort Wingate	...	Nov. 1862;	June, 1874	62	66	75	82	95	96
16. Santa Fé	6846	Jan. 1849;	July, 1873	65	66	77	91	92	98

NEW YORK.

Name of Station.	Height.	Begins.	Ends.	Jan.	Feb.	Mar.	Apr.	May.	June.
1. Albany	130	Jan. 1795;	Dec. 1849	60	60	73	88	93	94
2. Auburn	650	Jan. 1827;	Dec. 1865	62	64	78	83	92	96
3. Belleville	300	Jan. 1830;	Dec. 1844	59	58	72	80	88	95
4. Beverly	180	Jan. 1867;	Dec. 1870	58	57	61	79	86	92
5. Bridgewater	1286	Jan. 1833;	Dec. 1837	64	58	66	83	89	93
6. Buffalo	623	Jan. 1841;	Dec. 1870	56	59	74	82	87	96
7. Cambridge	500	Jan. 1827;	Dec. 1841	60	60	74	85	91	98
8. Canajoharie	284	Jan. 1830;	Dec. 1835	52	52	64	86	88	92
9. Canandaigua	590	Jan. 1829;	Dec. 1838	66	59	70	88	90	91
10. Cazenovia	1260	Jan. 1830;	Dec. 1870	61	59	76	90	95	93
11. Charlotte	273	July, 1859;	Dec. 1867	64	58	66	77	84	93
12. Cherry Valley Academy	1335	Jan. 1827;	Dec. 1845	62	57	78	85	90	96
13. East Hampton	16	Jan. 1827;	Dec. 1843	64	61	68	78	86	95
14. Fairfield	1185	Jan. 1827;	Dec. 1849	53	55	70	85	88	93
15. Flatbush	54	Jan. 1826;	Dec. 1869	64	64	74	85	92	96
16. Fort Columbus	23	Jan. 1822;	June, 1874	60	68	78	84	92	98
17. Fort Hamilton	25	Jan. 1843;	June, 1874	62	70	76	84	90	106
18. Fort Niagara	263	Jan. 1829;	June, 1874	62	60	84	94	94	94
19. Fort Ontario	295	Jan. 1843;	June, 1874	64	58	76	80	89	94

NEW HAMPSHIRE.

	during Each Month.						Year of Extreme Heat.	Lowest Temperature during Each Month.												Year of Extreme Cold.
	July.	Aug.	Sept.	Oct.	Nov.	Dec.		Jan.	Feb.	Mar.	Apr.	May.	June.	July.	Aug.	Sept.	Oct.	Nov.	Dec.	
	°	°	°	°	°	°		°	°	°	°	°	°	°	°	°	°	°	°	
1	92	92	90	80	73	57	1866	—22	—30	—18	16	30	41	50	42	30	21	4	—16	1861
2	98	93	91	80	68	57	1834	—32	—20	— 9	18	29	38	43	40	27	14	— 5	—16	1835
3	96	96	92	79	69	58	1843[1]	—34	—33	—23	0	22	26	40	27	20	12	— 9	—29	1848
4	96	94	90	76	68	59	1850[2]	—12	—10	— 7	16	30	36	47	48	32	26	9	—10	1821[3]
5	99	97	87	70	68	50	1840	—11	— 3	— 2	14	28	36	48	46	36	24	15	0	1839
6	100	90	86	79	70	50	1868	—33	—37	—22	2	20	36	43	40	28	10	2	—24	1861

NEW JERSEY.

	July.	Aug.	Sept.	Oct.	Nov.	Dec.	Year of Extreme Heat.	Jan.	Feb.	Mar.	Apr.	May.	June.	July.	Aug.	Sept.	Oct.	Nov.	Dec.	Year of Extreme Cold.
1	95	93	86	79	73	67	1864	— 9	2	7	30	40	53	55	53	45	29	19	5	1866
2	102	94	90	78	72	62	1866	—12	3	16	30	32	45	46	51	42	31	19	1	1866
3	92	92	86	83	70	66	1864	— 5	— 7	2	21	31	44	52	49	39	28	19	— 1	1861
4	99	95	90	81	70	60	1866	—13	— 5	0	22	37	50	38	48	42	26	16	— 1	1866

NEW MEXICO.

	July.	Aug.	Sept.	Oct.	Nov.	Dec.	Year of Extreme Heat.	Jan.	Feb.	Mar.	Apr.	May.	June.	July.	Aug.	Sept.	Oct.	Nov.	Dec.	Year of Extreme Cold.
1	110	105	98	96	86	66	1857	— 4	0	12	22	28	38	50	44	40	20	8	— 5	1850
2	100	99	90	86	68	65	1850	9	2	20	25	31	44	50	53	50	38	11	3	1851
3	109	108	99	93	78	76	1870	0	10	10	28	48	54	56	59	46	25	24	—18	1869
4	96	97	89	85	71	68	1871	— 8	— 1	12	9	29	35	50	50	40	12	3	8	1873
5	101	100	95	90	81	67	1852	4	11	17	27	31	45	55	60	41	25	14	11	1852
6	112	105	103	96	84	81	1857	— 3	8	16	20	36	45	57	54	42	25	10	— 2	1874
7	102	101	102	106	90	94	1871	— 5	13	23	10	36	45	56	54	47	23	3	20	1873
8	107	106	100	99	86	80	1852[4]	0	20	14	26	40	50	50	58	50	30	14	15	1859
9	116	107	103	90	78	81	1873	3	9	12	22	37	46	55	59	44	20	22	4	1871
10	104	105	99	94	79	74	1872	—12	11	15	27	33	52	49	52	39	18	4	9	1873
11	93	98	90	87	75	65	1867	— 2	1	9	21	32	44	50	50	29	22	2	0	1856
12	98	97	98	84	75	75	1865	1	6	8	28	40	57	60	58	46	26	2	1	1865[5]
13	110	107	95	95	79	76	1854	7	0	5	25	30	39	51	50	41	19	10	4	1854
14	101	96	90	89	87	72	1871	—13	— 7	— 4	15	20	25	40	32	28	9	5	—28	1855
15	99	102	97	95	89	68	1870	—16	3	4	18	30	38	51	50	30	18	— 3	— 8	1864
16	99	100	91	82	78	68	1850	— 9	— 2	8	19	28	39	50	49	34	3	3	—11	1850

NEW YORK.

	July.	Aug.	Sept.	Oct.	Nov.	Dec.	Year of Extreme Heat.	Jan.	Feb.	Mar.	Apr.	May.	June.	July.	Aug.	Sept.	Oct.	Nov.	Dec.	Year of Extreme Cold.
1	97	96	89	80	70	62	1830[6]	—23	—16	—12	6	28	40	50	31	30	21	1	—13	1835[7]
2	98	110	90	85	70	63	1861	—14	—16	— 6	6	14	28	44	42	30	18	0	— 6	1861[8]
3	98	98	90	78	65	57	1834	—28	—34	—22	14	23	23	39	30	19	14	— 1	—36	1835
4	96	95	88	78	70	53	1868	0	—10	2	25	34	50	57	52	40	25	18	— 2	1868
5	94	93	88	76	68	52	1834	—31	—18	—16	15	17	30	38	33	21	17	— 4	—23	1835
6	98	97	91	80	73	60	1868	—11	—15	—11	13	22	36	44	41	32	23	10	— 6	1861
7	96	96	90	78	74	60	1831	—36	—32	—20	12	23	37	41	36	23	14	— 6	—29	1835
8	97	96	94	80	69	50	1830	—36	—16	— 6	22	28	43	48	38	26	22	4	—18	1835
9	94	93	84	79	70	61	1834	—10	—11	— 8	22	27	42	50	41	32	20	4	— 9	1832
10	97	92	93	83	70	59	1838	—28	—22	—19	11	17	27	37	32	25	10	— 6	—21	1840
11	98	96	92	84	73	66	1866	—15	—20	— 3	7	13	32	38	35	26	17	4	—22	1866
12	98	90	88	83	67	57	1834	—30	—30	—12	4	21	31	34	36	26	17	1	—19	1835[9]
13	93	92	88	78	68	60	1841	— 8	— 1	— 2	20	25	32	47	42	30	20	10	— 2	1835
14	94	96	90	78	69	60	1838	—21	—22	— 8	—1	23	26	32	30	22	14	—10	—26	1835
15	96	96	92	81	72	68	1827[10]	— 6	— 6	3	24	28	39	53	48	32	22	12	4	1835[11]
16	104	99	92	86	71	69	1825	—12	— 7	2	17	31	42	54	49	39	29	12	— 3	1866
17	99	96	90	84	76	65	1864	—10	— 7	0	18	34	40	47	50	37	29	13	— 2	1866
18	98	95	94	82	72	63	1830	— 9	15	1	14	18	37	48	46	33	25	12	— 8	1861
19	96	98	96	82	73	67	1870	—20	—16	—21	2	26	35	43	41	31	26	1	—20	1872

[1] Also in 1845. [2] Also in 1852. [3] Also in 1851. [4] Also in 1860.
[5] Also in 1867. [6] Also in 1845 and 1846. [7] Also in 1840. [8] Also in 1865.
[9] Also in 1836. [10] Also in 1849 and 1864. [11] Also in 1861.

NEW YORK.—Continued.

Name of Station.	Height.	Series. Begins.	Ends.	Highest Temperature Jan.	Feb.	Mar.	Apr.	May.	June.
20. Fort Porter	660	Dec. 1865;	Dec. 1870	50°	45°	58°	68°	80°	85°
21. Fredonia	715	Jan. 1830;	Dec. 1848	70	65	76	86	90	96
22. Gaines	427	Jan. 1839;	Dec. 1842	59	64	65	83	89	91
23. Goshen	425	Jan. 1835;	Dec. 1849	60	65	78	84	98	96
24. Gouverneur	400	Jan. 1831;	Dec. 1870	64	59	74	85	94	95
25. Hamilton	1127	Jan. 1826;	Dec. 1849	63	64	78	90	92	96
26. Hartwick	1100	Jan. 1826;	Dec. 1850	59	63	76	82	92	92
27. Homer	1096	Jan. 1832;	Dec. 1850	67	60	75	89	93	91
28. Hudson	150	Jan. 1827;	Dec. 1849	62	64	73	87	94	99
29. Ithaca	417	Jan. 1827;	Dec. 1848	71	60	76	98	89	96
30. Jamaica	30	Jan. 1826;	Dec. 1850	67	62	79	86	93	98
31. Johnstown	...	Jan. 1828;	Dec. 1845	52	60	75	93	92	96
32. Kinderhook	125	Jan. 1830;	Dec. 1846	65	68	76	88	91	96
33. Kingston	188	Jan. 1829;	Dec. 1849	69	64	78	86	96	97
34. Lansingburgh	30	Jan. 1826;	Dec. 1846	61	66	78	90	96	99
35. Ledyard	447	Jan. 1830;	Dec. 1850	62	65	76	85	89	96
36. Lewiston	280	Jan. 1831;	Dec. 1849	62	66	77	82	96	96
37. Lowville	847	Jan. 1827;	Dec. 1848	60	60	78	86	91	99
38. Madison Barracks	262	Jan. 1827;	June, 1874	65	58	70	79	88	90
39. Malone	703	Jan. 1839;	Dec. 1842	54	68	68	88	88	89
40. Mexico	331	Jan. 1837;	Dec. 1849	66	60	72	87	90	94
41. Middlebury	800	Jan. 1826;	Dec. 1848	65	70	84	88	96	97
42. Millville	600	Jan. 1840;	Dec. 1847	58	64	80	86	91	91
43. Mohawk	435	June, 1860;	Dec. 1868	50	52	60	75	85	94
44. Montgomery	300	Jan. 1828;	Dec. 1842	70	68	79	92	97	100
45. Moriches	13	Jan. 1865;	Dec. 1870	60	58	71	81	85	102
46. Mount Pleasant	125	Jan. 1831;	Dec. 1844	57	67	71	81	93	95
47. Newburg	74	Jan. 1828;	Dec. 1867	68	66	78	92	98	102
48. New York	25	Jan. 1844;	Dec. 1870	62	62	74	84	89	97
49. Nichols	800	Jan. 1860;	Dec. 1870	60	62	76	86	90	97
50. North Granville	250	Jan. 1835;	Dec. 1849	60	55	69	86	90	97
51. North Salem	361	Jan. 1829;	Dec. 1850	66	72	76	88	92	95
52. Oneida	500	Jan. 1861;	Dec. 1869	56	54	71	78	87	92
53. Onondaga	1260	Jan. 1826;	Dec. 1844	64	60	80	90	94	99
54. Oswego	232	Jan. 1861;	Dec. 1870	57	49	72	79	81	88
55. Oxford	961	Jan. 1829;	Dec. 1845	64	60	74	84	94	98
56. Palermo	327	Jan. 1860;	Dec. 1870	56	52	68	84	86	95
57. Penn Yan	740	Jan. 1829;	Dec. 1844	66	65	74	88	93	95
58. Plattsburg	186	Jan. 1829;	Dec. 1870	56	60	72	83	96	95
59. Pompey	1300	Jan. 1826;	Dec. 1843	59	56	72	83	88	90
60. Potsdam	394	Jan. 1828;	Dec. 1848	57	67	76	84	94	95
61. Poughkeepsie	...	Jan. 1829;	Dec. 1849	65	65	78	88	94	102
62. Redhook	...	Jan. 1830;	Dec. 1842	65	65	72	90	92	97
63. Rochester	506	Jan. 1830;	Dec. 1869	64	62	76	88	89	97
64. Sackett's Harbor	266	July, 1859;	Dec. 1867	58	52	69	73	81	88
65. Salem	...	Jan. 1828;	Dec. 1847	57	60	73	85	97	96
66. Schenectady	300	Jan. 1829;	Dec. 1864	53	49	59	74	91	92
67. Springville	500	Jan. 1834;	Dec. 1850	58	64	70	80	88	91
68. Troy	58	Jan. 1861;	Dec. 1868	46	61	66	82	83	92
69. Utica	473	Jan. 1826;	Dec. 1848	75	68	79	90	90	97
70. Watervliet Arsenal	50	Jan. 1831;	Dec. 1854	59	64	73	83	94	99
71. West Point	167	Jan. 1827;	June, 1874	68	67	82	89	93	99
72. Whitestone	824	Jan. 1834;	Dec. 1840	53	56	61	81	90	95

NORTH CAROLINA.

Name of Station.	Height.	Series. Begins.	Ends.	Jan.	Feb.	Mar.	Apr.	May.	June.
1. Fort Johnson	...	Jan. 1820;	June, 1874	76	72	80	88	92	99
2. Fort Macon	...	Jan. 1834;	Aug. 1849	68	72	78	86	93	96

NEW YORK.—Continued.

	During Each Month.						Year of Extreme Heat.	Lowest Temperature during Each Month.												Year of Extreme Cold.
	July.	Aug.	Sept.	Oct.	Nov.	Dec.		Jan.	Feb.	Mar.	Apr.	May.	June.	July.	Aug.	Sept.	Oct.	Nov.	Dec.	
	°	°	°	°	°	°		°	°	°	°	°	°	°	°	°	°	°	°	
20	92	89	83	73	67	54	1868	-7	-3	-10	20	24	37	51	44	33	22	11	-10	1866[1]
21	97	94	94	83	73	64	1830	-7	-12	-6	18	25	34	42	41	32	20	9	2	1832
22	94	92	90	78	62	56	1841[2]	-7	-7	-4	19	30	39	46	40	30	20	4	5	1839
23	96	91	88	82	78	62	1839	-30	-16	-5	10	26	36	42	36	32	14	4	-10	1835
24	100	99	93	81	73	58	1842	-38	-32	-30	10	22	33	37	32	22	10	-17	-40	1835
25	96	96	90	82	70	64	1831[3]	-34	-28	-15	4	20	28	38	33	19	11	-4	-20	1835
26	96	91	89	80	74	64	1826	-30	-24	-12	6	20	32	40	36	27	16	-2	-10	1831
27	95	93	88	82	70	63	1845	-28	-26	-19	0	16	28	40	34	28	17	-7	-14	1836
28	99	98	92	80	68	67	1827[4]	-24	-10	-2	12	28	33	48	44	30	18	7	-16	1835
29	99	98	94	86	75	66	1847	-18	-12	-10	15	20	37	43	37	28	19	1	-5	1836
30	100	95	93	85	76	70	1830	-7	-7	5	16	26	37	46	45	29	22	7	1	1836[4]
31	93	94	92	78	74	56	1828[5]	-30	-22	-8	6	24	30	42	38	25	15	-4	-25	1835[6]
32	102	97	95	89	73	57	1845	-30	-18	-10	9	24	33	41	38	26	16	0	-17	1840
33	100	93	91	88	83	64	1845	-30	-22	-5	10	27	40	47	41	30	16	6	-12	1835
34	101	104	98	82	75	57	1845	-28	-25	-13	4	25	34	42	42	25	17	4	-14	1835
35	96	96	90	86	72	57	1843[7]	-6	-10	-4	14	27	40	50	42	31	19	6	2	1841
36	97	93	95	82	76	70	1840	-6	-6	0	16	25	38	49	44	33	22	5	-1	1832[8]
37	100	96	88	80	75	60	1842	-35	-32	-17	10	20	30	37	33	16	10	-2	-40	1835
38	94	95	90	80	70	60	1872	-25	-30	-36	7	21	34	45	38	28	18	-6	-44	1871
39	94	94	84	74	64	45	1840	-24	-15	-12	11	25	30	38	40	23	20	6	-14	1840
40	99	92	92	92	72	58	1838	-24	-24	-15	2	18	31	40	42	28	20	8	-11	1837[4]
41	100	99	90	88	78	75	1826	-15	-20	-17	4	17	25	40	32	24	14	7	-17	1832
42	95	96	91	79	78	55	1845	-6	-5	-12	12	26	32	40	42	28	18	5	3	1841
43	102	92	96	82	70	56	1868	-22	-30	-12	11	23	34	44	41	29	18	11	-20	1861
44	104	99	98	87	79	62	1830	-33	-25	-6	4	20	40	38	38	25	17	-6	-10	1835
45	105	98	96	85	71	62	1868	-14	-15	0	28	37	51	58	51	44	30	16	-4	1868
46	100	97	85	78	70	57	1838	-8	-2	5	15	27	37	48	49	34	27	9	-4	1835[9]
47	105	98	97	80	76	69	1849	-27	-14	-2	16	27	32	48	43	30	20	8	-15	1835
48	99	96	90	85	72	69	1866	-13	-3	5	24	34	46	56	53	40	31	20	2	1866
49	101	99	92	86	72	64	1868	-18	-21	-11	17	28	43	49	44	30	21	6	-24	1866
50	102	94	90	81	80	64	1849	-31	-25	-14	-4	24	34	42	31	26	14	0	-22	1844
51	102	98	94	81	74	64	1841	-31	-15	-7	15	24	30	42	37	22	17	-1	-17	1835
52	97	98	88	84	70	61	1864	-16	-28	-9	12	27	38	50	44	35	24	8	-6	1865
53	99	95	93	81	70	69	1826[10]	-18	-22	-10	0	23	34	42	40	30	16	2	-18	1826
54	90	94	87	75	66	59	1863	-11	-14	0	16	28	43	51	44	37	26	15	-15	1866
55	96	93	91	81	68	62	1829	-36	-33	-19	9	20	28	40	32	17	14	2	-21	1836
56	99	97	93	87	73	58	1868	-23	-24	-8	15	30	39	40	45	29	20	5	-22	1861
57	96	94	90	84	75	63	1830[11]	-12	-13	-10	10	26	32	44	34	25	16	7	-7	1836
58	98	94	96	78	69	60	1840[4]	-19	-20	-14	12	25	35	42	34	26	12	4	-8	1849
59	91	89	84	76	70	60	1837	-18	-16	-8	10	20	29	45	40	28	16	-3	-18	1835[12]
60	96	95	89	86	71	59	1838	-34	-32	-28	-1	20	32	40	34	23	12	-10	-26	1840
61	105	98	100	95	76	68	1849	-30	-20	-4	2	32	30	46	36	28	16	4	-22	1835
62	98	93	91	82	78	60	1835[11]	-28	-16	-1	19	15	42	44	40	30	23	6	-8	1835
63	102	98	94	83	74	62	1844	-9	-13	-4	11	25	35	34	44	28	21	7	-9	1861
64	91	93	88	82	73	61	1863	-36	-46	-34	7	25	36	48	43	28	23	8	-30	1861
65	100	102	94	78	75	63	1840	-40	-26	-12	2	30	35	41	41	27	13	1	-23	1840
66	94	96	87	73	72	54	1864	-12	-16	-10	18	32	42	51	46	33	21	3	-10	1836
67	95	91	87	83	70	60	1834	-20	-11	-14	9	20	28	38	34	25	18	-8	-14	1849
68	100	94	85	87	67	56	1868	-22	-28	-1	19	32	43	55	50	39	26	19	-5	1861
69	95	96	89	79	71	57	1826	-26	-27	-16	9	20	32	41	37	30	0	2	-16	1836
70	98	99	92	79	70	66	1834[13]	-32	-28	-20	4	26	40	47	47	30	16	3	-18	1835
71	101	101	99	87	73	70	1827	-30	-10	-6	14	27	40	51	46	36	24	6	-11	1873
72	97	98	88	81	70	49	1840	-33	-32	-26	11	6	35	41	34	23	16	-2	-18	1835

NORTH CAROLINA.

	July.	Aug.	Sept.	Oct.	Nov.	Dec.	Year of Extreme Heat.	Jan.	Feb.	Mar.	Apr.	May.	June.	July.	Aug.	Sept.	Oct.	Nov.	Dec.	Year of Extreme Cold.
1	102	100	98	90	84	74	1831	15	3	14	31	43	52	63	57	46	28	9	9	1835
2	95	95	92	85	74	68	1834	19	20	25	39	48	61	64	68	56	42	31	28	1844

[1] Also in 1868. [2] Also in 1842. [3] Also in 1843. [4] Also in 1849.
[5] Also in 1831. [6] Also in 1844. [7] Also in 1846 and 1850. [8] Also in 1837.
[9] Also in 1839. [10] Also in 1828. [11] Also in 1841. [12] Also in 1840.
[13] Also in 1852.

OHIO.

Name of Station.	Height.	Series. Begins.	Series. Ends.	Highest Temperature Jan.	Feb.	Mar.	Apr.	May.	June.
1. Bethel	555	Jan. 1864;	Dec. 1870	66°	67°	74°	88°	91°	95°
2. Cincinnati	540	Jan. 1835;	Dec. 1870	70	75	86	93	95	99
3. Cleveland	643	June, 1859;	Dec. 1870	65	71	76	84	89	95
4. College Hill	800	Jan. 1814;	Dec. 1870	67	77	82	89	93	98
5. Granville	995	Jan. 1837;	Apr. 1852	66	68	78	85	89	93
6. Hillsborough	1150	Jan. 1836;	Dec. 1870	66	68	79	83	88	94
7. Hudson	1137	Jan. 1838;	Dec. 1859	62	69	78	84	88	90
8. Kelly's Island	587	Jan. 1860;	Dec. 1870	54	56	63	75	84	93
9. Marietta	670	June, 1818;	Dec. 1871	70	76	85	90	94	99
10. Marion	1077	Jan. 1866;	Dec. 1870	59	65	69	80	87	93
11. New Lisbon	961	Jan. 1861;	Dec. 1868	62	68	76	86	90	98
12. Norwalk	...	Jan. 1861;	Dec. 1868	64	70	72	81	87	94
13. Toledo	604	Jan. 1860;	Dec. 1869	68	68	72	82	90	98
14. Urbana	1015	Jan. 1862;	Dec. 1870	64	66	74	84	89	05
15. Witchfield	1205	Jan. 1861;	Dec. 1865	58	67	70	79	87	95

OREGON.

Name of Station.	Height.	Series. Begins.	Series. Ends.	Jan.	Feb.	Mar.	Apr.	May.	June.
1. Astoria	...	Aug. 1850;	Dec. 1870	56	69	64	82	80	84
2. Block House	...	Mar. 1858;	Dec. 1862	59	60	70	75	77	94
3. Camp Harney	...	Jan. 1868;	Dec. 1873	50	57	69	80	85	100
4. Camp Warner	...	Jan. 1868;	June, 1874	57	68	65	70	81	85
5. Fort Dalles	...	Sept. 1850;	Mar. 1866	62	83	86	90	96	104
6. Fort Haskins	...	Nov. 1856;	Mar. 1865	67	70	80	90	95	102
7. Fort Oxford	...	June, 1852;	July, 1856	71	70	75	68	80	77
8. Fort Stevens	...	Nov. 1865;	June, 1874	54	55	66	73	78	84
9. Fort Umpqua	...	Aug. 1856;	May, 1862	64	61	73	72	81	82
10. Fort Yamhill	...	Oct. 1856;	Apr. 1866	60	59	64	81	91	98

PENNSYLVANIA.

Name of Station.	Height.	Series. Begins.	Series. Ends.	Jan.	Feb.	Mar.	Apr.	May.	June.
1. Allegheny Arsenal	704	Jan. 1836;	Apr. 1867	67	75	83	86	96	96
2. Carlisle Barracks	600	Jan. 1840;	June, 1874	66	68	76	88	92	100
3. Fallsington	30	Jan. 1860;	Dec. 1870	65	68	78	81	87	95
4. Fayette Tannery	...	Jan. 1865;	Dec. 1870	67	68	76	88	88	98
5. Fleming	780	Jan. 1861;	Dec. 1866	62	64	76	85	93	95
6. Fort Mifflin	20	Jan. 1823;	Oct. 1853	62	68	76	80	89	99
7. Frankford Arsenal	30	Jan. 1836;	Dec. 1843	66	70	77	84	94	95
8. Germantown	100	Jan. 1820;	Nov. 1870	68	64	78	85	93	99
9. Harrisburg	375	Jan. 1860;	Dec. 1868	58	64	76	85	89	96
10. Lewisburg	...	Jan. 1865;	Dec. 1870	54	53	74	82	88	93
11. Mooreland	250	Jan. 1865;	Dec. 1870	63	65	80	80	89	91
12. Mount Joy	...	Jan. 1860;	Dec. 1869	63	69	82	88	97	100
13. North Whitehall	...	Jan. 1860;	Dec. 1869	57	59	70	84	90	96
14. Pennsville, near	1400	Jan. 1865;	Dec. 1870	60	58	78	85	90	92
15. Philadelphia	36	Jan. 1758;	Dec. 1870	65	70	79	88	90	98
16. Pocopson	218	Jan. 1861;	Dec. 1870	65	65	76	86	88	97

RHODE ISLAND.

Name of Station.	Height.	Series. Begins.	Series. Ends.	Jan.	Feb.	Mar.	Apr.	May.	June.
1. Fort Adams	40	Jan. 1842;	June, 1874	51	54	60	69	81	92
2. Fort Wolcott	20	Jan. 1822;	Dec. 1835	58	58	61	74	83	87
3. Newport	25	Jan. 1866;	Dec. 1870	52	56	64	68	78	86
4. Providence	155	Dec. 1831;	Dec. 1866	63	68	75	82	91	97

	during Each Month.						Year of Extreme Heat.	Lowest Temperature during Each Month.												Year of Extreme Cold.
	July.	Aug.	Sept.	Oct.	Nov.	Dec.		Jan.	Feb.	Mar.	Apr.	May.	June.	July.	Aug.	Sept.	Oct.	Nov.	Dec.	
OHIO.																				
1	98°	95°	93°	85°	72°	71°	1864	—8°	—8°	3°	20°	33°	37°	50°	42°	36°	20°	8°	—8°	1864[1]
2	101	100	99	90	80	73	1868	—12	—17	—4	20	27	38	48	46	31	19	2	—7	1835
3	96	93	88	85	75	68	1866	—11	—13	—5	17	29	42	48	43	35	24	5	—9	1866
4	99	97	97	89	78	70	1868	—12	—10	—10	14	27	39	37	38	26	16	—2	—10	1864
5	96	98	89	81	74	67	1838	—20	—14	—14	20	28	32	47	41	34	19	4	—12	1850
6	97	92	90	80	72	68	1864	—14	—22	—10	18	27	40	50	44	30	20	2	—12	1838
7	93	91	89	76	69	61	1841	—10	—8	—4	20	27	32	44	45	34	22	6	—6	1841
8	93	91	89	79	70	58	1866[2]	—12	—13	—5	17	35	50	56	52	42	29	10	0	1866
9	102	96	95	88	82	71	1859	—22	—18	—10	7	28	33	42	43	32	19	10	—11	1852
10	94	93	89	78	76	61	1868[2]	—17	—14	—11	19	37	44	56	40	36	19	12	—9	1867
11	100	100	95	88	90	68	1861[3]	—18	—14	—12	20	30	45	48	45	34	20	10	—13	1867
12	94	93	92	84	72	67	1864[4]	—12	—14	—6	16	32	48	52	50	37	26	14	—3	1868
13	100	96	90	88	70	67	1868	—10	—16	—6	13	34	42	48	48	36	19	6	—5	1866
14	96	95	92	86	74	64	1868	—16	—12	0	22	32	47	54	48	36	20	8	—12	1864
15	93	94	89	82	69	64	1864	—13	—12	5	17	30	43	52	47	37	27	12	2	1864
OREGON.																				
1	89	84	84	82	74	59	1870	15	19	19	32	38	45	44	47	43	36	25	15	1855[5]
2	80	98	88	81	68	59	1860	4	16	27	30	35	43	48	44	38	32	27	10	1862
3	100	100	93	83	70	53	1869[6]	—15	—16	—3	10	21	25	30	33	18	9	4	—6	1868
4	89	90	81	79	64	57	1869[2]	—14	—3	1	18	22	27	38	36	20	8	5	3	1868
5	105	104	94	100	79	64	1853	—23	1	3	32	31	41	42	47	40	25	4	—6	1862
6	101	103	98	89	75	67	1860	0	6	14	29	33	41	42	40	33	26	21	8	1857[7]
7	80	78	92	79	74	66	1852	32	31	30	31	38	45	45	45	40	39	33	30	1853[8]
8	82	86	84	72	62	59	1873	19	28	27	34	31	44	44	48	37	35	31	21	1868
9	74	81	84	77	67	59	1860[9]	16	28	34	36	42	50	50	49	49	38	35	20	1862
10	95	94	95	76	63	56	1859	9	13	13	29	37	35	46	42	39	28	[illegible]	[illegible]	[illegible]
PENNSYLVANIA.																				
1	100	96	96	84	77	68	1854	—18	—22	—4	10	28	33	48	40	30	17	4	—6	1856
2	105	98	97	89	75	70	1868	—28	—11	—6	23	31	30	48	43	32	17	10	—14	1873
3	98	99	88	84	76	62	1865	—9	—6	0	25	37	50	55	55	43	30	17	4	1866
4	98	97	92	80	71	70	1868[2]	—10	—16	—7	20	32	44	50	48	35	20	10	—9	1865
5	99	100	93	87	72	65	1861	—26	—21	7	22	30	38	40	42	33	20	17	—19	1861
6	98	93	98	86	83	59	1849[10]	4	5	12	24	34	36	52	50	38	28	19	9	1849
7	98	92	88	86	72	63	1841	2	—7	7	25	32	42	56	49	35	29	18	10	1836
8	101	100	93	83	70	64	1866	—13	—4	8	21	33	46	55	53	33	26	18	0	1866
9	96	96	89	87	75	60	1861[11]	—2	1	6	25	39	55	61	55	45	30	16	4	1866
10	98	94	87	79	72	58	1866[4]	—13	—23	—11	22	35	48	51	46	38	20	17	—23	1865[12]
11	96	94	88	80	71	62	1866	—12	—4	2	26	38	45	58	53	43	27	18	0	1866
12	103	105	93	90	86	65	1869	—13	—12	14	13	36	48	58	52	39	21	13	7	1861
13	96	94	87	80	78	56	1864[4]	—13	—11	—2	17	30	42	46	43	33	23	12	—12	1866
14	102	90	87	77	66	60	1868	—14	—17	—14	10	28	38	44	42	30	12	4	—8	1865
15	101	97	93	88	80	72	1866	—9	—2	5	22	31	42	50	50	37	17	12	3	1866
16	101	99	93	85	70	65	1866	—10	—10	0	28	35	52	55	54	43	27	20	1	1866[4]
RHODE ISLAND.																				
1	102	92	89	76	64	61	1867	—13	—15	—6	18	33	44	53	47	37	22	8	0	1873
2	92	89	84	76	66	62	1834	—2	—1	3	21	33	45	52	50	36	30	18	—6	1835
3	90	86	88	79	66	55	1866	—6	4	4	26	35	48	53	52	40	24	15	2	1866
4	99	95	90	85	74	65	1866	—17	—16	—4	15	28	37	49	45	33	22	4	—12	1866

[1] Also in 1866 and 1870. [2] Also in 1870. [3] Also in 1867 and 1868. [4] Also in 1868.
[5] Also in 1859 and 1862. [6] Also in 1871. [7] Also in 1862. [8] Also in 1855.
[9] Also in 1856. [10] Also in 1852. [11] Also in 1862, 1866, and 1868. [12] Also in 1867.

SOUTH CAROLINA.

Name of Station.	Height.	Series. Begins.	Series. Ends.	Highest Temperature Jan.	Feb.	Mar.	Apr.	May.	June.
				°	°	°	°	°	°
1. Charleston	20	Jan. 1750;	Dec. 1854	77	79	83	88	94	96
2. Fort Moultrie	25	Jan. 1823;	Dec. 1860	72	77	88	89	92	96

TENNESSEE.

Name of Station.	Height.	Series. Begins.	Series. Ends.	Jan.	Feb.	Mar.	Apr.	May.	June.
1. Glenwood Cottage	481	Jan. 1860;	Dec. 1870	73	73	80	89	88	91
2. Humboldt	...	July, 1870;	June, 1874	70	77	82	89	98	104

TEXAS.

Name of Station.	Height.	Series. Begins.	Series. Ends.	Jan.	Feb.	Mar.	Apr.	May.	June.
1. Austin	650	Apr. 1851;	June, 1874	87	87	96	102	103	104
2. Camp Colorado	...	Nov. 1856;	Jan. 1861	78	85	92	92	102	108
3. Camp Stockton	...	June, 1859;	June, 1874	88	88	98	105	111	112
4. Camp Verde	1400	Dec. 1856;	Feb. 1869	82	87	90	95	100	98
5. Fort Belknap	1600	July, 1851;	Jan. 1859	78	87	94	95	99	104
6. Fort Bliss	3830	July, 1854;	June, 1871	78	86	89	98	107	112
7. Fort Brown	50	Sept. 1849;	June, 1874	87	90	93	99	98	102
8. Fort Chadbourne	2120	May, 1852;	Mar. 1861	80	83	94	99	106	106
9. Fort Clarke	1000	Aug. 1852;	July, 1873	83	92	98	99	106	107
10. Fort Croghan	1000	June, 1849;	Aug. 1853	84	94	95	96	94	98
11. Fort Davis	4700	Nov. 1854;	Dec. 1873	81	83	90	96	100	107
12. Fort Duncan	1460	Oct. 1849;	June, 1874	91	94	100	104	106	112
13. Fort Graham	900	Mar. 1850;	Aug. 1853	80	80	96	92	98	100
14. Fort Griffin	...	July, 1870;	June, 1874	80	86	92	100	99	105
15. Fort Inge	845	Sept. 1849;	Jan. 1868	88	90	96	101	103	105
16. Fort Lancaster	2350	May, 1856;	Feb. 1860	73	85	95	98	107	110
17. Fort McIntosh	806	July, 1849;	June, 1874	90	101	105	108	110	106
18. Fort McKavett	2060	Apr. 1852;	June, 1874	80	89	92	100	102	103
19. Fort Mason	1200	Apr. 1852;	Feb. 1861	83	85	92	101	105	107
20. Fort Richardson	...	Apr. 1868;	June, 1874	78	86	84	94	97	101
21. Fort Worth	1100	Nov. 1849;	Aug. 1853	76	86	95	92	93	100
22. Gilmer, near	950	Jan. 1860;	Dec. 1870	86	82	87	94	98	98
23. Ringgold Barracks	521	Sept. 1849;	June, 1874	90	100	100	104	109	108
24. San Antonio	600	Jan. 1846;	July, 1873	82	93	94	98	107	108

UTAH.

Name of Station.	Height.	Series. Begins.	Series. Ends.	Jan.	Feb.	Mar.	Apr.	May.	June.
1. Camp Douglas	4800	Dec. 1862;	June, 1874	62	64	70	82	91	98
2. Fort Crittenden	4860	July, 1858;	July, 1861	49	52	67	85	90	103
3. Great Salt Lake City	4260	Jan. 1864;	Dec. 1866	46	58	68	80	88	90

VERMONT.

Name of Station.	Height.	Series. Begins.	Series. Ends.	Jan.	Feb.	Mar.	Apr.	May.	June.
1. Craftsbury	1100	Jan. 1862;	Dec. 1870	45	54	58	69	83	90
2. Lunenburg	1124	Jan. 1862;	Dec. 1870	42	65	78	78	88	98
3. Middlebury	398	Jan. 1865;	Dec. 1869	44	58	66	76	79	85
4. Randolph	700	Jan. 1866;	Dec. 1870	47	49	60	77	86	95

VIRGINIA.

Name of Station.	Height.	Series. Begins.	Series. Ends.	Jan.	Feb.	Mar.	Apr.	May.	June.
1. Alexandria	56	Jan. 1853;	Feb. 1864	70	70	79	92	96	96
2. Fortress Monroe	8	Jan. 1826;	June, 1874	72	72	78	91	91	97

[1] Also in 1874. [2] Also in 1872. [3] Also in 1871. [4] Also in 1852.

	DURING EACH MONTH.						Year of Extreme Heat.	LOWEST TEMPERATURE DURING EACH MONTH.												Year of Extreme Cold.
	July.	Aug.	Sept.	Oct.	Nov.	Dec.		Jan.	Feb.	Mar.	Apr.	May.	June.	July.	Aug.	Sept.	Oct.	Nov.	Dec.	
	SOUTH CAROLINA.																			
1	101°	96°	92°	89°	85°	78°	1752	16°	22°	31°	32°	46°	53°	62°	61°	49°	33°	28°	20°	1852
2	99	96	93	88	82	79	1851	14	6	25	35	45	52	64	59	52	38	27	19	1835
	TENNESSEE.																			
1	99	98	91	87	79	74	1860	— 8	— 4	11	30	40	52	57	51	33	24	13	0	1864
2	98	104	97	88	75	72	1871[1]	— 8	11	11	29	39	54	58	50	40	20	9	— 3	1873
	TEXAS.																			
1	107	106	104	98	91	86	1860	6	19	21	28	44	61	66	65	49	29	18	10	1864
2	107	104	97	92	87	76	1857	7	17	22	28	46	58	70	64	55	41	21	9	1860
3	111	108	109	102	88	88	1873	— 3	15	24	22	32	54	49	58	44	24	14	— 9	1859
4	102	102	97	98	85	86	1857	10	9	16	29	45	57	61	63	43	37	14	12	1857
5	108	110	101	96	84	80	1855	2	11	23	31	42	52	62	57	46	32	10	1	1855
6	109	107	103	99	85	78	1871	11	12	18	28	41	54	58	56	51	25	11	11	1869[2]
7	102	100	96	98	91	89	1860[3]	20	28	36	44	48	63	63	67	51	44	31	22	1873
8	109	110	100	99	89	90	1855	— 1	9	20	28	36	55	48	61	44	26	15	3	1860
9	109	113	103	98	88	82	1871	1	20	29	30	51	59	68	68	50	40	10	12	1873
10	99	103	101	92	88	83	1851	8	15	25	32	40	50	62	60	50	40	28	9	1852
11	101	98	96	98	85	78	1873	—15	17	9	—2	38	45	56	45	30	21	10	7	1873
12	108	109	104	99	94	85	1860	12	19	24	36	43	62	63	67	54	38	27	12	1850[4]
13	112	112	105	96	87	82	1852	15	20	25	36	40	56	68	64	49	32	27	5	1850
14	106	108	101	96	88	82	1871	— 4	10	14	27	39	55	48	50	38	16	9	— 7	1870
15	106	106	101	92	93	84	1859	11	20	26	33	48	57	65	63	49	36	22	19	1868
16	[illegible]	106	97	94	95	79	1850	5	10	25	31	44	53	64	62	49	31	14	16	1857
17	108	109	106	104	97	93	1871	19	23	28	37	48	62	68	69	48	38	23	17	1850
18	105	104	100	91	85	81	1873	6	8	20	27	39	55	50	63	19	31	19	7	1873
19	114	103	96	91	86	83	1860	11	20	24	30	44	59	66	52	51	41	27	20	1860
20	109	107	102	94	85	74	1868	—10	10	23	9	40	45	55	50	48	30	8	2	1873
21	104	107	103	96	86	75	1850	5	16	25	34	44	60	62	61	44	30	26	7	1852
22	108	102	98	90	90	79	1860	10	16	22	38	40	62	71	63	47	31	21	17	1868
23	107	105	105	98	95	90	1871	20	26	32	30	49	63	69	70	56	40	22	18	1850
24	108	109	102	98	90	89	1871	14	25	29	32	46	62	60	60	55	36	27	14	1852[5]
	UTAH.																			
1	103	105	89	99	71	68	1871	— 4	0	0	15	19	34	38	44	31	21	11	4	1864
2	96	95	90	86	69	60	1859	—15	— 6	— 2	20	21	43	58	56	30	12	8	—22	1859
3	95	95	85	83	72	52	1864[6]	— 8	— 3	4	22	38	45	56	60	35	30	22	6	1864
	VERMONT.																			
1	101	92	85	80	64	64	1868	—25	—18	—17	13	28	36	47	42	28	11	3	—18	1866
2	97	100	90	83	70	48	1864	—25	—25	—23	4	25	32	38	43	25	15	5	—30	1868
3	90	82	82	70	65	49	1868	—21	—16	—20	13	31	43	54	48	34	23	7	—13	1866[7]
4	102	97	88	77	63	48	1868	—22	—31	—27	4	28	37	49	42	30	15	1	—24	1868
	VIRGINIA.																			
1	100	104	96	80	72	65	1863	7	3	16	23	35	41	52	47	42	25	22	12	1855
2	102	96	97	89	82	69	1837	2	4	13	31	43	50	61	60	40	30	15	17	1857

[5] Also in 1870. [6] Also in 1865. [7] Also in 1867 and 1868.

WASHINGTON.

Name of Station.	Height.	Series. Begins.	Ends.	Highest Temperature Jan.	Feb.	Mar.	Apr.	May.	June.
				°	°	°	°	°	°
1. Camp Steele	150	Jan. 1860;	Dec. 1870	56	55	67	76	78	89
2. Cape Disappointment	30	Aug. 1864;	June, 1874	55	58	70	75	93	92
3. Fort Colville	1963	Jan. 1860;	June, 1874	48	51	68	78	91	90
4. Fort Steilacoom	250	Nov. 1849;	Mar. 1868	60	64	76	78	92	93
5. Fort Townshend	135	Jan. 1859;	June, 1874	57	55	63	72	79	85
6. Fort Vancouver	50	Dec. 1849;	July, 1868	61	64	82	82	98	98
7. Fort Walla-Walla	...	Jan. 1857;	May, 1867	68	61	76	96	99	104

WISCONSIN.

Name of Station.	Height.	Series. Begins.	Ends.	Jan.	Feb.	Mar.	Apr.	May.	June.
1. Beloit	750	Jan. 1860;	Dec. 1866	48	51	70	82	90	93
2. Embarrass	...	Jan. 1864;	Dec. 1870	53	56	66	82	98	98
3. Fort Crawford	642	Jan. 1820;	Aug. 1845	66	60	84	91	96	96
4. Fort Howard	620	Jan. 1822;	May, 1852	59	54	85	87	97	100
5. Fort Winnebago	770	Jan. 1831;	Aug. 1845	53	61	80	87	96	98
6. Manitowoc	658	Jan. 1860;	Dec. 1870	49	56	70	77	92	97
7. Milwaukee	604	Aug. 1859;	Dec. 1870	49	56	70	80	91	100
8. Superior City	680	Aug. 1859;	Dec. 1862	53	55	70	70	92	96
9. Waupaca	900	Jan. 1864;	Dec. 1869	54	50	71	77	95	98

WYOMING.

Name of Station.	Height.	Series. Begins.	Ends.	Jan.	Feb.	Mar.	Apr.	May.	June.
1. Fort Bridger	6656	July, 1858;	June, 1874	53	58	75	75	82	90
2. Fort D. A. Russell	...	Dec. 1869;	June, 1874	61	63	70	79	88	97
3. Fort Fetterman	...	Nov. 1868;	June, 1874	63	59	70	81	91	99
4. Fort Fred. Steele	...	Jan. 1860;	June, 1874	56	55	61	75	93	104
5. Fort Laramie	4472	Sept. 1849;	June, 1874	68	70	83	89	98	102
6. Fort Sanders	7161	Sept. 1866;	June, 1874	57	60	70	70	83	89

MEXICO.

Name of Station.	Height.	Series. Begins.	Ends.	Jan.	Feb.	Mar.	Apr.	May.	June.
1. Cordova	860	Jan. 1862;	Dec. 1864	76	78	84	86	82	81
2. Mirador	3600	Jan. 1861;	Dec. 1870	85	86	91	90	95	91

COSTA RICA.

Name of Station.	Height.	Series. Begins.	Ends.	Jan.	Feb.	Mar.	Apr.	May.	June.
1. San José	3772	Jan. 1865;	Dec. 1866	81	85	85	85	82	81

CUBA.

Name of Station.	Height.	Series. Begins.	Ends.	Jan.	Feb.	Mar.	Apr.	May.	June.
1. Havana	50	Jan. 1859;	Nov. 1870	85	90	93	98	96	103

NEW GRANADA.

Name of Station.	Height.	Series. Begins.	Ends.	Jan.	Feb.	Mar.	Apr.	May.	June.
1. Aspinwall	6	Jan. 1865;	Dec. 1870	84	83	84	90	93	87

WASHINGTON.

	…during Each Month.						Year of Extreme Heat.	Lowest Temperature during Each Month.												Year of Extreme Cold.
	July.	Aug.	Sept.	Oct.	Nov.	Dec.		Jan.	Feb.	Mar.	Apr.	May.	June.	July.	Aug.	Sept.	Oct.	Nov.	Dec.	
	°	°	°	°	°	°		°	°	°	°	°	°	°	°	°	°	°	°	
1	95	88	85	67	59	56	1870	10	15	10	34	43	48	44	49	42	32	30	19	1862[1]
2	104	85	86	81	75	59	1865	20	26	20	33	38	38	49	46	40	36	30	17	1871
3	103	96	89	76	63	59	1872	—30	—20	—20	15	20	30	30	35	12	9	— 8	—22	1862
4	94	97	87	80	66	69	1860	— 8	2	12	25	35	41	44	13	28	28	17	0	1862
5	95	88	76	67	56	54	1870	18	19	26	32	35	38	41	40	35	32	19	—22	1872
6	96	98	94	82	68	59	1852[2]	—10	2	15	31	39	44	50	43	40	28	21	— 1	1862
7	107	107	98	88	78	63	1859[3]	—24	— 2	3	30	40	48	54	52	35	29	8	— 6	1862

WISCONSIN.

	July.	Aug.	Sept.	Oct.	Nov.	Dec.	Year of Extreme Heat.	Jan.	Feb.	Mar.	Apr.	May.	June.	July.	Aug.	Sept.	Oct.	Nov.	Dec.	Year of Extreme Cold.
1	94	96	86	82	61	50	1864	—29	—27	— 4	19	30	45	52	48	32	19	— 2	—20	1864
2	104	98	90	84	62	54	1866	—36	—25	—17	11	23	32	40	40	27	14	— 8	—18	1864
3	100	98	90	86	76	56	1839	—28	—32	—23	4	26	26	48	44	30	6	—12	—22	1832
4	100	100	98	84	76	54	1823[4]	—30	—38	—21	5	22	32	42	38	24	16	— 8	—25	1823
5	104	94	91	82	68	57	1838	—29	—33	—20	8	19	32	40	39	24	8	—13	—24	1832
6	96	94	86	80	63	56	1870	—26	—17	— 6	18	30	42	48	44	34	20	— 3	—16	1864
7	97	97	91	81	69	59	1870	—30	—18	— 7	16	27	39	44	43	33	20	— 3	—19	1864
8	99	97	88	84	66	49	1866	—37	—38	—24	—5	15	29	35	33	21	15	—19	—32	1863
9	97	98	90	83	64	49	1864	—30	—27	—17	10	30	45	52	45	35	18	— 6	—20	1864

WYOMING.

	July.	Aug.	Sept.	Oct.	Nov.	Dec.	Year of Extreme Heat.	Jan.	Feb.	Mar.	Apr.	May.	June.	July.	Aug.	Sept.	Oct.	Nov.	Dec.	Year of Extreme Cold.
1	91	92	85	79	69	57	1873	—33	—22	—29	0	17	24	32	26	15	—13	—27	—28	1873
2	103	97	99	85	71	62	1871	—23	—26	—21	1	14	25	38	30	20	0	—14	—29	1870
3	100	107	90	85	76	59	1869	—30	—40	—22	12	21	29	40	28	3	— 6	—22	[illegible]	[illegible]
4	102	100	97	80	64	57	1871	—38	—22	[illegible]	[illegible]	[illegible]	[illegible]	34	33	18	— 8	—20	—22	1873
5	105	105	[illegible]	[illegible]	[illegible]	[illegible]	[illegible]	[illegible]	—35	— 6	5	17	31	37	34	11	— 1	—18	—33	1864
6	96	97	87	90	73	60	1869	—50	—30	—21	—6	12	23	29	31	16	—25	—32	—36	1873

MEXICO.

	July.	Aug.	Sept.	Oct.	Nov.	Dec.	Year of Extreme Heat.	Jan.	Feb.	Mar.	Apr.	May.	June.	July.	Aug.	Sept.	Oct.	Nov.	Dec.	Year of Extreme Cold.
1	78	80	79	77	77	77	1862	53	53	58	60	67	68	68	68	68	60	57	58	1863
2	85	84	81	80	80	81	1868	41	43	48	50	59	63	63	64	61	52	49	46	1864

COSTA RICA.

	July.	Aug.	Sept.	Oct.	Nov.	Dec.	Year of Extreme Heat.	Jan.	Feb.	Mar.	Apr.	May.	June.	July.	Aug.	Sept.	Oct.	Nov.	Dec.	Year of Extreme Cold.
1	79	79	79	79	79	80	1865	59	57	60	60	64	63	61	62	60	60	60	60	1866

CUBA.

	July.	Aug.	Sept.	Oct.	Nov.	Dec.	Year of Extreme Heat.	Jan.	Feb.	Mar.	Apr.	May.	June.	July.	Aug.	Sept.	Oct.	Nov.	Dec.	Year of Extreme Cold.
1	100	99	99	95	89	86	1869	54	52	51	60	66	73	73	73	73	64	59	52	1869

NEW GRANADA.

	July.	Aug.	Sept.	Oct.	Nov.	Dec.	Year of Extreme Heat.	Jan.	Feb.	Mar.	Apr.	May.	June.	July.	Aug.	Sept.	Oct.	Nov.	Dec.	Year of Extreme Cold.
1	86	86	86	86	86	86	1865	72	70	72	71	74	75	72	74	74	73	73	74	1865

1 Also in 1870.
2 Also in 1857, 1858, and 1860.
3 Also in 1860.
4 Also in 1824, 1825, 1826, and 1830.
5 Also in 1871.

Although the contents of the tables of observed extremes of temperature can readily be scanned by simple inspection, there are a few prominent features which deserve to be specially noticed.

With respect to extreme heat, perhaps the most remarkable contrast is presented in the case of Fort Simpson, in latitude 62° 10′, having a greater recorded maximum (104°) than even stations on the Gulf of Mexico; as for instance, New Orleans (100°) and Key West (98°). This arises on the one hand from the prolonged insolation and consequent accumulation of heat and from the dryness of the air at the northern station, and, on the other hand, mainly from the presence of a large amount of moisture at the southern stations. The difference of latitude is not less than 37½°. Of places showing high extremes in all months, Forts Fillmore and Cummings, New Mexico, are prominent examples; at these stations the heat in January rises to 95° but only to 107° in June. The former fort has an altitude of 3937 feet. Other stations of high January heat are Fort Duncan, Texas, with 91°, and Camp McDowell, Arizona, Fort McIntosh and Ringgold Barracks, Texas, with 90° each.

If we regard 110° Fah. as an exceptionally high temperature we shall find it exceeded in the following states or territories and stations, according to our limited table:—

Arizona	Fort Mojavé . .	118°
California . . .	Fort Miller . . .	121, also Camp Cady 118°, elevation 3000 feet.
Dakota	Fort Sully . . .	114
Idaho	Fort Boisé . . .	121
Indian Territory	Fort Gibson . .	116
Kansas	Fort Larned . .	115, elevation 1932 feet.
Montana	Fort Shaw . . .	112, elevation 6000 feet.
Nebraska	Fort McPherson .	115
Nevada	Camp Halleck . .	111, elevation 5600 feet.
New Mexico . . .	Fort McRae . .	120, elevation 4500 feet, also
	Albuquerque . .	114, elevation 5032 feet.
Texas	Fort Mason . . .	114.

These stations are all in the western part of the United States, and many of them at considerable elevations.

Exceptionally depressed heat, in *January*, we find noted at: Fort Ransom 34° and Fort Wadsworth 40° in Dakota; at New Ulm and Sibley, Minn., 41°, and at Lunenburg, Vt., Stratford, N. H., and Fort Wrangel, Alaska, of 42°.

With respect to extreme cold its geographical distribution depends mostly on the latitude, and not like the extreme heat, as we have seen, mostly on the longitude. Outside the boundaries of the United States, we have at Van Rensselaer Harbor the lowest temperature recorded —66°.4. At Peel River we find —56° recorded, at Fort Simpson —55°. The temperature sinks below that at which mercury congeals, which is —39° Fah. ±1°, in the following States and places, according to our limited table:—

Colorado	Fort Garland	—40°, elevation 8365 feet.
Dakota	Fort Abercrombie	—40
	Fort Buford	—40
Michigan	Fort Brady	—47
Minnesota	Fort Ripley	—44
	Minneapolis	—40
Montana	Camp Baker	—53
	Fort Benton	—51
	Fort Ellis	—53
	Fort Shaw	—43
New York	Gouverneur	—40
	Lowville	—40
	Madison Barracks	—44
	Sackett's Harbor	—46
	Salem	—40
Wyoming	Fort Fetterman	—40
	Fort Laramie	—40
	Fort Sanders	—50, elevation 7160 feet.

(Dakota through Montana:) The region in the vicinity of these stations is one frequently visited by the most excessive cold reached within the limits of the United States.

To the above would certainly have been added the States of Iowa, Maine, New Hampshire, Vermont, and Wisconsin, and most probably others bordering on these to the southward, but for our limited collection both in number of stations and in length of interval of time.

In the warmest month in the year, that is, for July, the temperature is recorded to have sunk to the freezing point of water (32°) or *below* it, in Arizona, Maine (at Brunswick, 27°), Michigan, Minnesota, Montana, Nevada, New York, Oregon, Washington Territory, and Wyoming.

Subtracting the lowest from the highest temperature recorded at any one station we obtain the *extreme range* of recorded variability, of which the following selected values may serve as examples: Extreme ranges at one or more stations equaling or exceeding 140°. British North America (Fort Simpson) 159°. Dakota 146°, Iowa 140°, Kansas 140°, Michigan 140°, Minnesota 147°, Montana 156°, New York 142°, Wisconsin 140°, and Wyoming 147°.

The least annual extreme range is recorded at Indian Key,[1] Florida, 42°, and very small ranges at Key West, Florida, 54°, at Fort Point, Golden Gate, California, 52°, and at Alcatraz Island, Harbor of San Francisco, of 53°. The ratio of the highest to the lowest range within the limits of the United States (excepting Alaska) is as 3.7 to 1.

If we investigate the extreme range for *each month separately* we find, for instance, from the 72 stations in our table for the State of New York, the average values:—

Averages.	Jan.	Feb.	Mar.	Apr.	May.	June.	July.	Aug.	Sept.	Oct.	Nov.	Dec.
	°	°	°	°	°	°	°	°	°	°	°	°
Highest temperature	61	61	73	85	91	95	98	96	91	82	72	61
Lowest temperature	—21	—19	—10	11	24	35	45	40	29	19	4	—14
Absolute monthly range	82	80	83	74	67	60	53	56	62	63	68	75
Ratio, the average being 69	1.2	1.2	1.2	1.1	1.0	0.9	0.8	0.8	0.9	0.9	1.0	1.1

[1] A very short series.

The monthly absolute range is least in summer and greatest in winter, a result which has already been reached in a different way in reference to variations in the monthly means, and the ratios indicate a regular progression in the yearly period; the January variability in the temperature is one and a half times as great as the July variability.

The 11 stations given in the table for Florida yield the following results:—

Averages.	Jan.	Feb.	Mar.	Apr.	May.	June.	July.	Aug.	Sept.	Oct.	Nov.	Dec.
	°	°	°	°	°	°	°	°	°	°	°	°
Highest temperature . . .	84.2	85.4	88.0	90.2	94.1	97.0	95.7	97.1	95.5	90.8	87.2	85.4
Lowest temperature . . .	30.4	32.4	39.3	45.9	55.1	64.1	68.8	66.7	63.0	49.1	40.2	33.0
Absolute monthly range . .	53.8	53.0	48.7	44.3	39.0	32.9	26.9	30.4	32.5	41.7	47.0	52.4
Ratio, the average being 41.9	1.3	1.3	1.2	1.1	0.9	0.8	0.6	0.7	0.8	1.0	1.1	1.2

We have the same regularity in the law of the annual progression, but the ratio of the variability in January to that of July is as 2 to 1. The average variability during the year in the latitude of New York is to the variability in the latitude of Florida as 69 to 42.

Tabulation of the Mean Annual Temperature in the United States, and at some places in British North America, for a succession of years, from the earliest records to the close of the year 1870.

The object of this tabulation was to furnish, in a convenient form, a basis for discussions relating to the study of the variations of our climate—as far as the same depends on temperature—during long intervals, involving questions of permanency, of periodic variations, of irregular fluctuations, and other relations. The tables will, therefore, be of permanent value, since they furnish the earliest material available, and they have consequently been made as complete as possible, at least within the area of the United States. The arrangement is that by States and Territories and by stations in each, the whole in alphabetical order.

In conformity with previous investigation the annual means have been corrected, as far as that could be done now, for daily variation, excepting those few cases where the hours of observation were unknown, as indicated by foot notes. To give to the tables the fullest extent compatible with accuracy, broken records (extending over less than one year) have been completed by interpolation, but only when observations were found recorded during at least 9 months of the calendar year. This interpolation for 1, 2, or 3 months (as the case may be) was effected as follows: comparison by differences was made with *records* complete during the period *at an adjacent station or at near places* for some months preceding and following the lacuna, and the average difference was applied to the record to furnish the interpolated value for the incomplete station. If no suitable adjacent station for comparison could be found, the general mean from the whole series for the particular months or month was substituted in the place of the blank record. The first method of interpolation is quite perfect, the second is less satisfactory, yet it is not apprehended that the annual mean could in the worst case be vitiated or in general rendered uncertain by more than $\pm$ 0°.5. In all cases where such limited interpolation had to be resorted to the *fact* is indicated in the tables by an asterisk affixed.

It should also be understood that all tabular annual means were found by dividing by 12, the sum of the monthly means belonging to the *calendar months;* the small correction for inequality of months (previously referred to) is nearly *constant*, and would not affect any conclusions we may deduce from the tables; of the same nature are index errors to the thermometers and reductions for difference of elevation or different exposures of stations at no great distance apart, as for instance within the limits of a city.

The bottom line of the tables contains the resulting mean temperatures for the respective stations; they are in general the mean of all the annual means in their respective columns, but they are made up from the *separate* monthly means, and include consequently all monthly means whether they belong to complete or incomplete years, in fact we might have a resulting annual mean from observations scattered over all the months but in different years and yet no single year complete. This explains the occasional differences of the resultant temperature from the simple mean of the individual complete years, and has nothing to do with interpolation.

In conformity with custom the mean temperatures are given to two places of decimals, but the hundredths of a degree have very little real value, and that only differentially.

TABLES OF THE MEAN ANNUAL TEMPERATURE IN THE UNITED STATES AND BRITISH NORTH AMERICA

FOR A SUCCESSION OF YEARS.

ALL NUMBERS ARE EXPRESSED IN DEGREES AND FRACTIONS OF THE FAHRENHEIT SCALE.

GREENLAND.		BRITISH NORTH AMERICA.														
Year.	Van Rensselaer Harbor.	Peel River, Arctic Region.	Abbittibe.	Fort Churchill.	Fort Simpson.	Little Whale River.	Moose Factory.	Red River Settlement.	Rigolet, Labrador.	Winnipeg.	St. John's, New Foundland.	St. John's, New Foundland.	St. John's, New Foundland.	Albion Mines, Nova Scotia.	Caledonia Mine, Nova Scotia.	Halifax, Nova Scotia.
	°	°	°	°	°	°	°	°	°	°	°	°	°	°	°	°
1769	...	...	...	19.75	...	...	...	...	...	...	...	...	...	...	...	...
1834	...	...	...	...	...	...	...	...	...	...	37.40	...	...	...	...	...
1835	...	...	...	...	...	...	...	...	...	...	38.90	...	...	...	...	...
1836	...	...	...	...	...	...	...	...	...	...	37.81	...	...	...	...	...
1837	...	...	...	...	...	...	...	...	...	...	37.87	...	...	...	...	...
1838	...	...	...	...	...	...	...	...	...	...	37.65	...	...	...	...	...
1843	...	...	...	...	...	...	...	...	...	...	...	...	...	41.57	...	...
1844	...	...	...	...	...	...	...	33.8*	...	...	...	...	...	...	...	...
1854	—4.2	...	...	...	...	...	...	...	...	...	...	...	...	...	...	43.15
1855	...	...	...	...	...	...	...	...	...	...	...	40.9	...	...	...	44.77
1856	...	...	...	...	...	...	...	...	...	...	...	41.5	...	...	...	...
1857	...	...	...	...	...	...	...	...	...	...	...	...	41.82	...	...	...
1858	...	...	...	...	...	...	26.15	33.70*	...	...	...	40.0	39.91	...	...	...
1859	...	...	...	...	...	...	...	31.90	...	...	...	...	44.11	...	...	...
1860	...	...	...	...	...	...	...	...	...	...	...	...	...	...	...	...
1861	...	...	...	...	24.0*	...	29.03	...	27.61	...	...	...	41.84	...	...	...
1862	...	...	...	...	...	21.7*	...	...	27.51*	...	...	...	...	...	...	...
1863	...	...	...	...	...	...	...	...	...	...	...	...	...	...	...	...
1864	...	12.5*	...	...	...	...	...	...	...	...	...	...	...	...	...	...
1865	...	13.1	...	...	...	...	...	...	...	...	...	...	...	...	...	...
1866	...	...	...	...	...	...	...	...	...	...	...	...	...	...	...	...
1867	...	...	...	...	...	...	...	...	...	...	...	...	...	...	39.66	...
1868	...	...	31.88*	...	...	...	...	...	...	...	...	...	...	...	38.80	...
1869	...	...	...	...	...	...	...	...	...	37.1*	...	...	...	...	40.42	...
	—2.47	13.15	31.18	19.75[1]	...	22.36	...	...	26.75	37.17	37.93	40.80[1]	41.20	42.19	39.62	43.35

1 Hours of observation unknown.

BRITISH NORTH AMERICA.—Continued.

Year.	Halifax, Nova Scotia.	Halifax, Nova Scotia.	Halifax, Nova Scotia.	Windsor, Nova Scotia.	Windsor, Nova Scotia.	Wolfville, Nova Scotia.	St. John, New Brunswick.	Year.	Fort Coulonge, Prov. of Quebec.	Is'd of St. Helen, Prov. of Quebec.	Montreal, Prov. of Quebec.	Montreal, Prov. of Quebec.	Montreal, Prov. of Quebec.	Montreal, Prov. of Quebec.	Year.	Montreal, Prov. of Quebec.
	°	°	°	°	°	°	°		°	°	°	°	°	°		°
1794	...	...	...	52.44	...	...	...	...	...	...	...	...	...	...	...	...
1795	...	...	...	51.76	...	...	...	...	...	...	...	...	...	...	...	...
1796	...	...	...	50.48	...	...	...	...	...	...	...	...	...	...	...	...
1797	...	...	...	48.72	...	...	...	...	...	...	...	...	...	...	...	...
1798	...	...	...	51.93	...	...	...	1824	41.0	...	...	...	...	...	...	...
1799	...	...	...	49.16	...	...	...	1825	42.5	...	...	...	...	...	...	...
1800	...	...	...	52.72	...	...	...	1826	40.3	...	45.9	...	...	...	...	...
1801	...	...	...	52.31	...	...	...	1827	40.0	...	43.5	...	...	...	...	...
1802	...	...	...	51.38*	...	...	...	1828	42.4	...	46.1	...	...	...	...	...
1803	...	...	...	50.95	...	...	...	1829	42.3	...	44.8	...	...	...	...	...
1804	...	...	...	49.10	...	...	...	1830	40.4	...	46.6	...	...	...	...	...
1805	...	...	...	51.80	...	...	...	1831	40.7	...	45.6	...	...	...	...	...
1806	...	...	...	50.61	...	...	...	1832	...	...	43.5	...	...	...	...	...
1807	...	...	...	52.09	...	...	...	1833	...	...	43.6	...	...	...	...	...
1808	...	...	...	...	...	...	...	1834	...	...	43.8	...	...	...	...	...
1809	...	...	...	52.54	...	...	...	1835	...	...	41.7	...	...	...	...	...
1810	...	...	...	52.50	...	...	...	1836	...	...	39.5	40.05	...	...	...	...
1811	...	...	...	53.20	...	...	...	1837	...	...	40.8	40.84	...	...	...	...
								1838	...	...	41.3	41.20	...	...	...	...
1856	...	...	...	...	...	43.32*	...	1839	...	...	43.8	43.69	...	...	...	...
1857	...	...	...	...	...	45.48	...	1840	...	42.54	42.8	43.91	...	...	...	...
1858	...	...	...	...	41.71	43.02*	...	1841	...	...	43.2	...	...	...	...	...
1859	...	...	...	...	43.15	44.04*	...	1842	...	...	42.7	...	...	...	...	...
1860	43.5	...	...	...	...	...	...	1843	...	...	42.5	...	...	...	...	...
1861	42.7	...	...	...	...	...	...	1844	...	...	42.2	...	...	...	...	...
1862	43.0	...	...		...	43.07*	...	1845	...	...	43.3	...	42.75	...	...	...
1863	44.5	43.4	...	...	...	...	...	1846	...	...	45.4	...	44.39	42.9	...	...
1864	...	42.7	...	...	...	43.97*	40.45	1847	...	...	43.1	...	42.07	41.0	1856	42.99
1865	...	42.8	...	...	...	43.65*	40.92	1848	...	...	44.0	...	42.88	44.0	1857	42.86
1866	...	42.4	...	...	...	43.54*	40.21	1849	...	...	43.1	...	42.45	42.1	1858	41.95
1867	...	...	41.98	...	...	42.80*	39.72	1850	...	...	43.4	...	42.56	43.8	1859	42.22*
1868	...	...	42.05	...	...	41.72*	38.60	1851	...	...	42.2	...	41.70	...	1860	...
1869	...	...	43.20	...	...	44.17*	41.31	1852	...	...	43.4	...	42.93	...	1861	44.41
1870	...	...	...	...	...	...	41.56*	1853	...	...	...	...	43.15	...	1862	43.99
	43.65[1]	42.83[2]	42.41	51.43[1]	42.95	43.75	40.39		41.18	42.12	43.44	44.48	42.75	42.77[1]		43.11

[1] Hours of observation unknown.

[2] Three observations daily; hours not stated.

BRITISH NORTH AMERICA.—Continued.

Year.	Montreal, Prov. of Quebec.	Nicolet, Prov. of Quebec.	Quebec, Prov. of Quebec.	St. Martin, Prov. of Quebec.	Year.	Stanbridge, Prov. of Quebec.	Ancaster, Prov. of Ontario.	Brantford, Prov. of Ontario.	Hamilton, Prov. of Ontario.	Kingston, Prov. of Ontario.	Kingston, Prov. of Ontario.	Michipicoten, Prov. of Ontario.	Michipicoten, Prov. of Ontario.	Toronto, Prov. of Ontario.
	°	°	°	°		°	°	°	°	°	°	°	°	°
...	...	...	...	...	1835	...	43.93	...	...	...	...	...	...	...
...	...	...	...	...	1836	...	44.01	...	...	...	...	...	...	...
...	...	...	...	...	1837	...	44.85	49.2	...	...	...	...	...	...
...	...	...	...	...	1838	...	45.81	49.0	...	...	...	...	...	...
1809	...	...	39.35	...	1839	...	48.23	51.7	...	...	...	...	...	...
1810	...	...	41.50	...	1840	...	48.42	51.7	...	...	...	...	...	43.62
1811	...	...	42.94	...	1841	...	48.03	50.7	...	...	...	...	...	43.92
1812	...	...	40.20	...	1842	...	48.01	49.7	...	...	...	...	...	43.96
1813	...	...	41.07	...	1843	...	49.42	49.7	...	...	...	...	...	42.35
1814	...	...	41.12	...	1844	...	48.67	52.5	...	...	...	...	...	44.48
1815	...	...	39.75	...	1845	...	48.65	...	...	...	...	...	...	44.58
1816	...	...	38.12	...	1846	...	...	...	50.82	...	...	...	...	46.36
1817	...	...	38.62	...	1847	...	...	...	48.77	...	...	38.59	...	43.70
1818	...	...	40.49	...	1848	...	...	...	49.91	...	...	...	...	45.08
					1849	...	...	...	48.72	...	...	...	...	44.09
1838	...	40.3	...	...	1850	...	...	...	49.34	...	...	...	...	44.45
1839	...	41.4	...	...	1851	...	...	...	49.37	...	...	...	...	43.98
1840	...	41.5	...	...	1852	...	...	...	48.86	...	...	...	...	43.84
1841	...	41.2	...	...	1853	...	...	...	50.08	...	...	...	...	44.80
1842	...	40.2	...	...	1854	...	...	...	49.61	...	...	...	...	45.23
1843	...	40.3	...	...	1855	...	...	...	...	...	...	...	...	43.98
1844	...	39.8	...	...	1856	...	...	...	44.66	40.55	41.5	...	...	42.18
1845	...	40.8	...	...	1857	41.93	...	...	46.48	41.08	43.7	...	...	42.75
1846	...	42.3	...	...	1858	41.10	...	...	48.77	41.96	43.1	...	...	44.76
					1859	41.43	...	...	47.49	40.75	...	...	...	44.21
1851	...	...	...	42.09	1860	42.68*	...	...	...	42.16	...	...	...	44.34
1852	...	...	...	42.82	1861	41.42	...	...	...	39.20	...	...	35.76*	44.24
1853	...	...	...	42.56	1862	41.23	...	...	...	...	...	...	...	44.37
1854	...	...	...	41.52	1863	41.35*	...	...	...	...	...	...	...	44.59
1855	...	...	...	41.63	1864	43.89	...	...	...	...	...	...	...	44.70
1856	...	...	...	39.91	1865	...	...	...	...	...	...	...	...	44.92
1857	40.58	...	...	40.93	1866	...	...	...	...	...	...	...	...	43.51
1858	40.06	...	...	40.35	1867	...	...	...	...	...	...	...	...	43.84
1859	...	...	...	41.58	1868	40.59	...	...	...	...	...	...	...	43.33
1860	43.42	...	...	...	1869	41.20	...	...	...	...	...	...	...	43.13
1861	41.72	...	...	42.96	1870	44.41	...	...	...	...	...	...	...	45.94
	41.45[1]	40.84	40.31[1]	41.62		41.89	47.09	50.54[1]	48.64	40.95	42.77[1]	38.59	35.01	44.17

[1] Hours of observation unknown.

ALABAMA.

Year.	Ashville.	Auburn.	Carlowville.	Coatopa.	Elyton (near).	Florence.	Fort Morgan.	Greene Springs.	Greensboro'.	Mobile.	Moulton.	Mt. Vernon Arsenal.	Opelika (near).	Prairie Bluff.	Selma.	Springhill.
	°	°	°	°	°	°	°	°	°	°	°	°	°	°	°	°
1835	...	...	...	...	...	...	66.20*	...	...	...	...	...	...	...	...	...
1840	...	...	...	...	...	...	...	...	...	70.05*	...	...	...	...	...	...
1841	...	...	...	...	...	...	...	...	...	68.41	...	...	...	...	...	70.01
1842	...	...	...	...	...	...	66.56*	...	...	69.74	...	65.01*	...	...	...	...
1843	...	...	...	...	...	...	...	...	...	...	...	65.48	...	...	...	...
1844	...	...	...	...	...	...	...	...	...	...	...	...	...	...	...	...
1845	...	...	...	...	...	...	...	...	...	...	...	65.03	...	...	...	...
1846	...	...	...	...	...	...	...	...	...	...	...	65.85	...	...	...	...
1847	...	...	...	...	...	...	...	...	...	...	...	64.68	...	...	...	...
1848	...	...	...	...	...	...	...	...	...	...	...	65.68	...	...	...	...
1849	...	...	...	...	...	62.52	...	...	...	...	...	65.87	...	...	...	...
1850	...	...	...	...	...	...	...	...	...	...	...	66.82	...	...	...	...
1851	...	...	...	...	...	...	...	...	...	...	...	66.57	...	...	...	...
1852	...	...	...	...	...	...	...	...	...	...	...	68.16	...	...	...	...
1853	...	...	...	...	...	...	...	...	...	...	...	66.49	...	...	...	...
1854	...	...	...	...	...	...	...	...	...	...	...	66.67	...	...	...	...
1855	...	64.36*	...	...	...	...	...	65.24*	...	...	...	66.61	...	...	...	...
1856	...	62.48	...	...	...	...	...	62.99*	...	...	...	65.18	...	...	...	...
1857	56.45	61.96	62.89	...	...	...	...	60.80	60.64*	...	...	64.58	...	...	...	...
1858	...	...	63.95*	...	...	...	...	62.40	62.65*	...	...	66.32	...	...	63.81*	...
1859	...	...	65.62*	...	...	...	...	63.06	62.64*	...	...	66.22	...	...	64.29*	...
1860	...	...	...	...	...	...	...	...	...	...	...	69.25*	...	...	...	...
1861	...	...	...	...	...	...	...	...	64.56*	...	...	...	...	...	...	...
1867	...	...	66.35*	...	...	...	...	63.65	...	...	60.66*	...	64.36*	66.43*	...	...
1868	...	...	64.61	...	...	...	...	61.93	61.80	...	59.32	...	62.30	...	...	...
1869	[illegible]	[illegible]	64.[illegible]		...	...	...	61.14	61.85*	...	58.63	...	62.74*	...	...	...
1870	...	...	64.58	61.71*	61.28*	...	...	61.76	...	...	...	...	...	...	...	...
	56.45	63.18	64.72	...	61.28	62.52[1]	67.59	62.57	62.73	68.75	59.83	66.15	63.13	66.43	64.10	70.01

[1] Hours of observation unknown.

Year.	ALASKA. Fort Kadiak.	Fort Tongass.	Fort Wrangel.	Illoolook.	Sitka.	Sitka.	ARIZONA. Camp Bowie.	Camp Colorado.	Camp Crittenden.	Camp Date Creek.	Camp Goodwin.	Camp Grant.	Camp Lowell Tucson.	Camp McDowell.	Camp Reno.	Camp Verde.
	°	°	°	°	°	°	°	°	°	°	°	°	°	°	°	°
1828	...	...	...	38.96	...	...	...	...	...	...	...	...	...	...	...	...
1829	...	...	...	37.43	...	...	...	...	...	...	...	...	...	...	...	...
1830	...	...	...	34.97	...	...	...	...	...	...	...	...	...	...	...	...
1831	...	...	...	35.20	...	...	...	...	...	...	...	...	...	...	...	...
1832	...	...	...	38.37	...	...	...	...	...	...	...	...	...	...	...	...
1833	...	...	...	37.67	...	...	...	...	...	...	...	...	...	...	...	...
1848	...	...	...	...	41.77	...	...	...	...	...	...	...	...	...	...	...
1849	...	...	...	...	40.37*	...	...	...	...	...	...	...	...	...	...	...
1850	...	...	...	...	40.27	...	...	...	...	...	...	...	...	...	...	...
1851	...	...	...	...	43.67	...	...	...	...	...	...	...	...	...	...	...
1852	...	...	...	...	42.26	...	...	...	...	...	...	...	...	...	...	...
1853	...	...	...	...	40.87	...	...	...	...	...	...	...	...	...	...	...
1854	...	...	...	...	41.81	...	...	...	...	...	...	...	...	...	...	...
1855	...	...	...	...	...	...	...	...	...	...	...	...	...	...	...	...
1856	...	...	...	...	43.36	...	...	...	...	...	...	...	...	...	...	...
1857	...	...	...	...	43.05	...	...	...	...	...	...	...	...	...	...	...
1858	...	...	...	...	41.32	...	...	...	...	...	...	...	...	...	...	...
1859	...	...	...	...	40.84	...	...	...	...	...	...	...	...	...	...	...
1860	...	...	...	...	43.23	...	...	...	...	...	...	...	...	...	...	...
1861	...	...	...	...	42.55	...	...	...	...	...	...	...	...	...	...	...
1862	...	...	...	...	41.28	...	...	...	...	...	...	...	...	...	...	...
1863	...	...	...	...	42.34	...	...	...	...	...	...	...	...	...	...	...
1864	...	...	...	...	43.31	...	...	...	...	...	...	...	...	...	...	...
1867	...	...	...	...	...	...	...	...	...	...	66.33	68.00*	69.39*	72.12	...	...
1868	...	...	...	...	...	44.74	62.79	...	...	61.79	63.93	67.28	68.87	68.88*	...	...
1869	42.17*	47.37	43.30*	...	...	46.39	61.87	72.04	59.26	63.01	65.34	67.91	67.24	71.16	69.75	62.38
1870	...	45.38*	43.16*	...	...	44.58	63.81	72.13	60.35	64.04	...	66.84	67.15	70.92	...	62.89
	41.66	46.19	43.48	37.51[1]	42.05[1]	45.14	63.09	72.09	60.58	62.91	65.78	67.25	68.27	70.67	69.90	62.79

[1] Old style.

ARIZONA.—Continued.							ARKANSAS.					CALIFORNIA.				
Year.	Camp Wallen.	Camp Willow Grove.	Fort Buchanan.	Fort Canby.	Fort Mojavé.	Fort Whipple.	Fort Smith.	Fort Wayne.	Helena (near).	Little Rock.	Washington (near).	Alcatraz Island.	Angel Island.	Benicia Barracks.	Calto.	Camp Babbitt.
	°	°	°	°	°	°	°	°	°	°	°	°	°	°	°	°
1840	...	...	...	...	...	...	60.03	59.67	...	62.28	60.29	...	...	...	...	...
1841	...	...	...	...	...	...	...	...	...	...	58.81	...	...	...	...	...
1842	...	...	...	...	...	...	59.35	...	...	...	59.88	...	...	...	...	...
1843	...	...	...	...	...	...	56.93	...	...	...	57.54	...	...	...	...	...
1844	...	...	...	...	...	...	59.71	...	...	...	61.15	...	...	...	...	...
1845	...	...	...	...	...	...	60.25	...	...	...	60.62	...	...	...	...	...
1846	...	...	...	...	...	...	61.16	...	...	...	60.57	...	...	...	...	...
1847	...	...	...	...	...	...	59.00	...	...	...	58.74	...	...	...	...	...
1848	...	...	...	...	...	...	59.93	...	...	...	61.06*	...	...	...	...	...
1849	...	...	...	...	...	...	61.00	...	...	...	63.10	...	...	...	...	...
1850	...	...	...	...	...	...	...	...	...	...	62.00	...	...	58.63*	...	...
1851	...	...	...	...	...	...	...	...	...	...	63.06	...	...	59.58	...	...
1852	...	...	...	...	...	...	62.23	...	...	...	62.94	...	...	58.88	...	...
1853	...	...	...	47.60	...	...	60.05	...	...	...	62.76	...	...	58.24	...	...
1854	...	...	...	47.11	...	...	61.62	...	...	...	64.05	...	...	56.39	...	...
1855	...	...	...	46.99*	...	...	60.82	...	...	...	62.90	...	...	58.67*	...	...
1856	...	...	...	44.44	...	...	58.15	...	...	...	61.36	...	...	58.30	...	...
1857	...	...	...	48.84	...	...	58.20	...	...	...	61.50	...	...	60.05	...	...
1858	...	...	57.50	46.23	...	...	...	...	...	...	62.78	...	...	59.27	...	...
1859	...	...	57.85	46.64*	...	...	60.65*	...	...	...	63.42	...	...	56.54	...	...
1860	...	...	60.39	49.20*	72.74	...	62.21*	...	...	...	63.89	...	...	57.83*	...	...
1861	...	...	...	...	...	...	...	...	...	...	...	54.46	...	59.17	...	...
1862	...	...	...	...	...	...	...	...	...	...	...	54.61	...	58.08*	...	...
1863	...	...	...	...	...	...	...	...	...	...	...	55.09	...	58.43	...	...
1864	...	...	...	...	...	...	...	...	...	...	...	...	...	60.48	...	64.04*
1865	...	...	...	...	...	53.74*	...	...	...	...	...	...	...	...	...	...
1866	...	...	...	...	...	...	...	...	62.10	...	...	...	...	...	...	...
1867	61.01*	...	...	...	...	57.00*	...	...	...	63.61*	...	56.33	...	...	...	...
1868	61.39	53.97*	...	...	72.91	51.38*	...	...	...	...	...	55.10	57.15	...	...	...
1869	61.50	55.67*	...	...	72.69	...	...	...	...	...	...	59.44	58.03	...	...	...
1870	...	...	...	...	72.54	53.60	...	...	61.26	...	...	57.83	58.41	...	58.16	...
	61.33	54.82	59.15	47.26	72.82	54.03	60.12	59.67	61.15	62.30	61.56	56.27	57.94	58.36	58.16	...

CALIFORNIA.—Continued.

Year.	Camp Bidwell.	Camp Cady.	Camp Far West.	Camp Gaston.	Camp Independence.	Camp Lincoln.	Camp Wright.	Chico.	Drum Barracks.	Fort Bragg.	Fort Crook.	Fort Humboldt.	Fort Jones.	Fort Miller.	Fort Point.	Fort Reading.
	°	°	°	°	°	°	°	°	°	°	°	°	°	°	°	°
1851	...	...	60.72	...	...	...	...	...	...	...	...	...	...	...	...	...
1852	...	...	...	...	...	...	...	...	...	...	...	...	...	67.17*	...	...
1853	...	...	...	...	...	...	...	...	...	...	...	...	51.89*	66.64	...	62.72
1854	...	...	...	...	...	...	...	...	...	...	...	51.64	49.75	64.71*	...	61.55
1855	...	...	...	...	...	...	...	...	...	...	...	53.84*	50.76	66.85	...	63.18*
1856	...	...	...	...	...	...	...	...	...	...	...	53.66	52.63	65.58	...	...
1857	...	...	...	...	...	...	...	...	...	...	...	53.44*	52.98*	66.06	...	...
1858	...	...	...	...	...	...	...	...	...	...	49.27	51.74	...	...	...	...
1859	...	...	...	...	...	...	...	...	...	...	47.98	51.91	...	...	...	...
1860	...	...	...	...	...	...	...	...	...	...	48.04	51.20	...	...	54.23	...
1861	...	...	...	...	...	...	...	...	...	51.97*	51.29*	51.77*	...	...	54.17	...
1862	...	...	...	59.33	...	...	...	...	...	51.50*	48.93	...	...	...	53.60	...
1863	...	...	...	61.86	...	...	...	...	...	53.36	50.64	52.44	...	...	53.89	...
1864	...	...	...	57.27	...	...	...	...	...	...	52.93	53.70*	...	...	55.86	...
1865	...	...	...	55.10	...	...	56.17	...	60.65	...	50.67*	51.87	...	...	54.26	...
1866	...	...	...	...	...	...	...	...	...	...	...	...	...	...	54.94	...
1867	49.48	...	...	...	59.96*	52.47*	57.22*	...	64.28*	...	50.36*	...	...	...	55.16	...
1868	45.57	68.23	...	54.17	57.73	52.54	57.27	...	66.52*	...	51.30*	...	...	...	55.01	...
1869	50.87	67.71	...	56.85	58.42	...	58.85	...	62.10	...	...	...	...	...	56.50*	...
1870	49.56	65.70	...	56.73	57.81*	...	57.50	62.79	62.06*	...	...	...	...	...	57.41	...
	50.39	67.22	60.65	57.37	58.33	53.47	57.39	62.89	63.16	52.44	50.31	52.46	51.85	66.15	55.00	62.44

CALIFORNIA.—Continued.

Year.	Fort Ross.	Fort Tejon.	Fort Ter-Waw.	Fort Yuma.	Marysville.	Meadow Valley.	Montere.	Murphy's.	New San Diego.	Point San José.	Presidio.	Ranche de Jurupa.	Sacramento.	San Diego.	San Francisco.	Stockton.
1837	51.43	...	...	...	...	...	...	...	...	...	...	...	...	...	...	...
1838	50.16	...	...	...	...	...	...	...	...	...	...	...	...	...	...	...
1839	51.18	...	...	...	...	...	...	...	...	...	...	...	...	...	...	...
1840	50.79	...	...	...	...	...	...	...	...	...	...	...	...	...	...	...
1850	...	...	...	...	...	...	54.40	...	...	...	...	...	...	60.72	...	...
1851	...	...	...	...	...	...	...	...	...	...	56.59	...	...	...	...	...
1852	...	...	...	...	...	...	...	...	...	...	...	...	...	61.95	...	...
1853	...	...	...	75.41	...	...	...	...	...	...	55.28	64.64	62.41*	63.39	...	...
1854	...	...	...	73.85	...	...	...	...	...	...	54.76	...	59.51	61.97	56.00	60.14
1855	...	56.22*	...	74.96*	...	...	...	...	...	...	55.87	...	59.29	62.50	...	...
1856	...	58.12	...	73.84	...	...	...	...	...	...	54.42	...	59.62	60.97	...	...
1857	...	59.99	...	74.98*	...	...	...	...	...	...	54.75	...	59.60	61.85	57.02	...
1858	...	56.67	...	74.79	62.91	...	...	...	...	...	53.80	...	59.17	61.11	55.82	...
1859	...	57.38*	52.67*	73.60	...	...	...	...	...	...	52.98	...	58.33	61.09	54.94*	...
1860	...	56.48*	52.52*	74.74	...	...	54.27*	...	...	...	53.80	...	58.76	61.30	...	...
1861	...	...	...	76.44	...	49.54*	...	...	...	...	53.48*	...	60.00	63.32	55.92	...
1862	...	...	...	73.85*	59.91	...	...	...	...	...	...	...	60.03	62.46	55.02	...
1863	...	...	...	...	...	...	...	...	...	...	54.55*	...	60.64*	61.60	54.49*	...
1864	...	...	...	...	...	49.65	56.31	...	...	...	54.55	...	61.42*	63.41	55.66	...
1865	...	...	...	...	...	48.05	54.84	...	61.24	...	53.41	...	60.77	62.08	53.82	...
1866	...	..	...	...	...	...	56.42	...	...	55.83*	54.46*	...	61.59	62.98	54.10	...
1867	...	...	...	76.46	...	...	56.21	...	...	...	54.74*	...	...	63.77*	...	...
1868	...	...	...	74.46	...	...	54.70	55.51*	...	...	53.51	...	...	63.08	53.92*	...
1869	...	...	...	72.39	...	...	55.50	...	...	...	55.27	...	...	62.17	...	...
1870	...	...	...	72.18	...	...	55.71*	...	...	...	54.93	...	...	61.20	...	...
	50.89	57.62	52.71	74.36	61.55	48.72	55.45	...	62.08	...	54.38	63.81	60.00	62.11	55.23	60.35

	CALIFORNIA.—Continued.					COLORADO.						CONNECTICUT.				
Year.	Union Ranche.	Vacaville.	Visalia.	Watsonville.	Yerba Buena Island.	Denver.	Fort Garland.	Fort Lyon.	Fort Morgan.	Fort Reynolds.	Fort Sedgwick.	Brookfield.	Canton.	Colebrook.	Columbia.	Fort Trumbull.
	°	°	°		°	°	°	°	°	°	°	°	°	°	°	°
1827	...	...	...	...	...	...	...	...	...	...	...	...	...	...	...	52.69
1828	...	...	...	...	...	...	...	...	...	...	...	...	...	...	...	56.40
1831	...	...	...	...	...	...	...	...	...	...	...	...	...	...	...	53.60
1832	...	...	...	...	...	...	...	...	...	...	...	...	...	...	...	54.34
1833	...	...	...	...	...	...	...	...	...	...	...	...	...	...	...	52.59
1834	...	...	...	...	...	...	...	...	...	...	...	...	...	...	...	50.11
1835	...	...	...	...	...	...	...	...	...	...	...	...	...	...	...	48.76
1843	...	...	...	...	...	...	...	...	...	...	...	...	...	...	...	46.57
1844	...	...	...	...	...	...	...	...	...	...	...	...	...	...	...	47.64
1845	...	...	...	...	...	...	...	...	...	...	...	...	..	...	...	49.70
1850	...	...	...	...	...	...	...	...	...	...	...	...	...	...	...	50.38
1851	...	...	...	...	...	...	...	...	...	...	...	...	...	...	...	50.17
1852	...	...	...	...	...	...	...	...	...	...	...	...	...	...	...	50.10
1853	...	...	...	...	...	...	40.39*	...	...	...	...	...	...	...	...	51.22*
1854	...	...	...	...	...	...	...	...	...	...	...	...	...	...	...	...
1855	...	...	...	...	...	...	40.71*	...	...	...	...	...	...	...	...	...
1856	...	...	...	...	...	...	39.20	...	...	...	...	...	...	...	...	...
1857	...	...	...	...	...	...	40.38	...	...	...	...	...	...	...	46.28	...
1858	...	...	...	...	...	...	39.86*	...	...	...	...	...	...	...	46.92	...
1859	...	...	...	...	...	...	39.79	...	...	...	...	...	...	...	46.54	...
1860	60.54*	...	...	...	...	...	42.05	...	...	...	...	...	...	...	...	...
1861	63.28	...	...	...	...	...	45.48	53.22	...	...	...	...	...	45.12	47.18	...
1862	60.98	...	...	...	...	...	44.24	...	...	...	...	...	44.58	44.97	49.96	49.36*
1863	...	...	...	...	...	...	43.24	...	...	...	...	...	...	45.96	48.96	50.81
1864	...	...	...	...	...	...	...	...	...	...	...	...	...	...	50.34	50.91
1865	...	...	...	...	...	...	...	...	...	...	...	...	...	45.83	51.13	52.14
1866	...	...	...	...	...	...	...	...	...	...	...	...	...	44.57	49.43	49.09
1867	...	...	...	...	...	...	47.71	55.09	51.03*	...	...	...	...	44.12	47.52	49.25
1868	...	...	...	...	...	...	44.52	50.95	...	...	50.05	...	...	43.12	46.99	48.45
1869	...	63.85*	...	58.85*	56.37*	...	43.62	48.43*	...	51.16	47.43*	48.30*	...	44.06	48.45	49.39
1870	...	...	61.47	58.34*	56.53	48.23	44.94	51.07	...	53.26	50.01	51.45	...	46.92*	50.99	51.52
	61.71	62.91	61.47	58.60	56.45	48.13	42.45	51.61	...	52.29	49.51	49.57	45.63	44.91	48.26	50.64

CONNECTICUT.—Continued.

Year.	Georgetown.	Goshen.	Hartford.	Lynde Point Light-House.	Year.	Middletown.	Year.	New Haven.	Year.	New Haven.	Year.	New Haven.	New London.	Norwich.	Plymouth.	Pomfret.
	°	°	°	°		°		°		°		°	°	°	°	°
1807	...	...	47.71	...	...	...	...	...	...	...	...	...	...	...	...	...
					...	...	...	...	...	...	...	...	...	...	...	...
1829	...	48.74	...	...	...	...	...	...	...	...	...	...	...	...	...	...
1830	...	50.85	...	...	...	...	...	...	...	...	1838	48.17	...	...	...	...
1831	...	49.40	...	...	...	...	...	...	...	...	1839	49.17	...	...	...	...
1832	...	47.61	...	...	...	...	1780	49.73*	1809	49.25	1840	49.04	...	...	...	...
1833	...	48.42	...	...	...	...	1781	50.36	1810	49.95	1841	49.54	...	...	...	...
1834	...	48.86	...	...	...	...	1782	49.06	1811	49.70	1842	49.86	...	...	...	...
1835	...	46.69	...	...	...	...	1783	48.39	1812	46.90	1843	47.38	...	...	...	...
1836	...	45.26	...	...	...	...	1784	47.27	1813	49.04	1844	50.24	...	...	...	...
1837	...	45.97	44.75	...	...	...	1785	47.70	1814	48.60	1845	50.16	...	...	...	...
1838	...	47.34	46.11	...	...	...	1786	48.51	1815	47.27	1846	50.10	...	...	...	...
1839	...	47.96	47.31	...	...	...	1787	48.47	1816	46.61	1847	49.44	...	...	...	...
1840	...	47.72	47.06	...	...	...	1788	49.72	1817	46.45	1848	49.22	...	...	...	...
1841	...	48.82	46.88	...	...	...	1789	49.50	1818	46.77	1849	48.29	...	...	...	...
1842	...	48.12	47.34	...	...	...	1790	49.46	1819	49.01	1850	48.75	...	...	...	...
1843	...	47.80	45.80	...	...	...	1791	49.50	1820	47.92	1851	49.00	...	...	...	...
1844	...	48.22	47.68	...	...	...	1792	48.15	1821	47.56	1852	48.78	...	...	...	...
1845	...	48.90	48.23	...	...	...	1793	50.35	1822	49.70	1853	49.60	...	...	...	...
1846	...	49.11	47.26	...	...	...	1794	50.17	1823	48.10	1854	49.30	49.97*	...	...	46.11
1847	...	48.41	45.68	...	...	...	1795	...	1824	49.86	1855	48.96	49.90*	...	...	45.71
1848	...	48.33	47.92	...	...	...	1796	48.36	1825	50.75	1856	46.98	47.00	47.21*	...	44.28
1849	...	47.89	45.92	...	1859	47.91	1797	48.11	1826	49.70	1857	47.53	47.79	47.96	...	44.63
1850	...	48.11	46.32	...	1860	47.11	1798	49.32	1827	48.87	1858	48.26	...	...	...	44.93
1851	...	...	45.53	...	1861	47.34	1799	48.41	1828	51.82	1859	48.01	...	...	...	44.99
1852	...	...	...	...	1862	47.25	1800	50.16	1829	48.67	1860	48.55	...	...	...	45.30*
1853	...	...	...	...	1863	48.03*	1801	50.96	1830	50.83	1861	50.10	...	...	...	45.43
1854	...	...	...	48.76*	1864	48.94*	1802	51.34	1831	49.24	1862	49.50	...	...	...	45.43
1855	...	...	...	48.36*	1865	49.88*	1803	50.77	1832	47.66	1863	50.00	...	...	45.50	46.01
1856	45.18*	...	...	47.47	1866	49.01*	1804	49.83	1833	48.29	1864	49.86	...	...	...	46.18
1857	...	...	...	47.03	1867	48.01	1805	51.72	1834	48.92	1865	49.97*	...	...	...	47.03
1858	...	...	...	48.27	1868	45.95	1806	49.71	1835	46.56	1866	...	...	...	...	45.73
1859	...	...	...	48.10	1869	47.42	1807	49.25	1836	45.18	1867	...	...	...	...	45.52
1860	...	...	...	49.00*	1870	50.01	1808	50.29	1837	46.41	1868	...	...	...	...	43.48
	...	48.16	46.61	48.07		48.09						49.00	49.14	48.18	45.74	46.01

CONNECTICUT.—Continued.

Year.	Salisbury.	Sharon.	Southington.	Wallingford.	Warren Center.	Waterbury.	West Cornwall.
	°	°	°	°	°	°	°
1816	...	45.82*	...	...	...	...	...
1817	...	45.51	...	...	...	...	...
1818	...	45.73	...	...	...	...	...
1819	...	48.68	...	...	...	...	...
1820	...	47.42	...	...	...	...	...
1821	...	45.20	...	...	...	...	...
1822	...	48.47	...	...	...	...	...
1823	...	45.31	...	...	...	...	...
1824	...	46.61	...	...	...	...	...
1825	...	48.00	...	...	...	...	...
1826	...	48.21	...	...	...	...	...
1827	...	46.47	...	...	...	...	...
1828	...	49.51	...	...	...	...	...
1829	...	45.85	...	...	...	...	...
1830	...	48.09	...	...	...	...	...
1831	...	46.83	...	...	...	...	...
1832	...	46.30	...	...	...	...	...
1833	...	46.31	...	...	...	...	...
1834	...	46.95	...	...	...	...	...
1835	...	44.75	...	...	...	...	...
1836	...	43.45	...	...	...	...	...
1849	...	...	...	...	45.84	...	...
1854	47.01	...	...	...	...	...	45.97
1856	...	...	...	45.85*	...	...	...
1857	...	...	...	46.04	...	...	...
1858	...	...	...	46.83	...	...	...
18[illegible]				[illegible]			
1860	...	...	...	47.17	...	...	...
1861	...	...	...	47.65	...	...	...
1867	...	...	...	...	...	48.36*	...
1868	...	...	...	...	...	45.29*	...
1870	...	...	49.99*	...	...	...	...
	47.33	46.61	49.99	46.98	45.84[1]	46.49	45.97

DAKOTA.

Year.	Fort Abercrombie.	Fort Buford.	Fort Pierre.	Fort Randall.	Fort Ransom.	Fort Rice.	Fort Stevenson.	Fort Sully.
	°	°	°	°	°	°	°	°
...	...	...	...	...	...	...	...	...
...	...	...	...	...	...	...	...	...
...	...	...	...	...	...	...	...	...
...	...	...	...	...	...	...	...	...
...	...	...	...	...	...	...	...	...
...	...	...	...	...	...	...	...	...
...	...	...	...	...	...	...	...	...
...	...	...	...	...	...	...	...	...
...	...	...	...	...	...	...	...	...
...	...	...	...	...	...	...	...	...
...	...	...	...	...	...	...	...	...
...	...	...	...	...	...	...	...	...
...	...	...	...	...	...	...	...	...
...	...	...	...	...	...	...	...	...
...	...	...	...	...	...	...	...	...
...	...	...	...	...	...	...	...	...
...	...	...	...	...	...	...	...	...
...	...	...	...	...	...	...	...	...
...	...	...	...	...	...	...	...	...
...	...	...	...	...	...	...	...	...
...	...	...	...	...	...	...	...	...
...	...	...	...	...	...	...	...	...
1856	...	...	45.56	...	...	...	...	...
1857	...	...	...	47.29	...	...	...	...
1858	...	...	...	46.92	...	...	...	...
1859	...	...	...	46.39	...	...	...	...
1860	...	...	...	48.68	...	...	...	...
1861	40.20	...	...	47.25	...	...	...	...
1862	39.23	...	...	46.33	...	...	...	...
186[illegible]	[illegible]			[illegible]				...
1864	41.50	...	...	48.85*	...	...	...	...
1865	41.73*	...	...	...	...	...	...	...
1866	...	...	...	...	...	...	...	...
1867	39.17	39.19*	...	45.66*	...	...	...	...
1868	38.51	41.23	...	46.80	...	...	40.73	...
1869	38.02	40.90	...	47.52*	38.20	42.14*	...	44.15
1870	41.58	40.78	...	49.56	40.46	42.91*	41.26*	48.34
	39.93	40.64	45.43	46.56	39.27	42.23	41.70	45.44

[1] Hours of observation unknown.

DAKOTA.—Cont'd.				DELAWARE.					DIST. OF COLUMBIA.					FLORIDA.		
Year.	Fort Totten.	Fort Wadsworth.	Yankton Indian Ag'y.	Fort Delaware.	Georgetown.	Milford.	Newark.	Wilmington.	Georgetown.	Year.	Washington.	Year.	Washington.	Belair.	Cedar Keys.	Fairview.
	°	°	°	°	°	°	°	°	°		°		°	°	°	°
...	...	...	...	...	...	...	...	...	...	1820	54.57	...	...	...	...	...
...	...	...	...	...	...	...	...	...	...	1821	53.41	...	...	...	...	...
...	...	...	...	...	...	...	...	...	...	1822	...	...	...	...	...	...
...	...	...	...	...	...	...	...	...	...	1823	56.56	...	...	...	...	...
...	...	...	...	...	...	...	...	...	...	1824	55.58	...	...	...	...	...
...	...	...	...	...	...	...	...	...	...	1825	56.63	...	...	...	...	...
...	...	...	...	...	...	...	...	...	...	1826	57.60	...	...	...	...	...
...	...	...	...	...	...	...	...	...	...	1827	57.43	...	...	...	...	...
1825	...	...	...	55.56*	...	...	...	...	...	1828	57.29	...	...	...	...	...
1826	...	...	...	56.30	...	...	...	...	...	1829	54.25	...	...	...	...	...
1827	...	...	...	57.11*	...	...	...	...	...	1830	56.72	...	...	...	...	...
1828	...	...	...	58.54	...	...	...	...	...	1831	52.59	1841	...	...	69.99	...
1829	...	...	...	52.66	...	...	...	...	...	1832	...	1842	...	...	69.09	...
1830	...	...	...	54.38	...	...	...	...	...	1833	55.33	——				
——										1834	55.34	1854	...	...	71.03	...
1855	...	...	...	52.97	...	...	...	...	...	1835	53.22	1855	...	...	69.73	...
1856	...	...	...	50.96	...	...	...	...	...	——		1856	...	...	68.87	...
1857	...	...	...	52.46	...	...	52.26	...	...	1839	53.63	1857	...	65.85	68.64	...
1858	...	...	...	53.52	55.66	...	...	...	...	1840	53.55	1858	...	69.03	70.51	...
1859	...	...	...	...	...	...	...	...	...	1841	52.87	1859	54.99	68.64	69.57*	...
1860	...	...	49.72	...	...	...	...	...	56.16	——		1860	...	...	...	...
1861	...	...	...	...	...	...	...	...	57.03*	1846	56.77	1861	...	...	...	...
1862	...	...	...	53.18*	...	...	...	...	54.92	1847	55.17	1862	54.09	...	...	...
1863	...	...	...	52.81*	...	...	...	...	...	1848	55.37	1863	53.65	...	...	...
1864	...	...	...	54.51	...	...	...	53.00	...	1849	55.82	1864	54.17	...	...	...
1865	...	...	...	56.06	...	...	...	52.82*	...	——		1865	55.00	...	...	...
1866	...	...	...	54.53*	...	...	...	...	...	1854	55.59*	1866	54.45	...	...	...
1867	...	37.44*	...	54.39*	...	...	...	...	...	1855	54.42	1867	53.03	...	...	...
1868	...	...	...	53.50	...	...	...	...	...	1856	51.67	1868	52.36	...	...	...
1869	...	38.16	...	52.54	...	...	...	...	...	1857	52.01*	1869	53.58	...	...	68.41*
1870	39.51	40.26	...	54.89*	...	54 95	...	...	...	1858	54.83	1870	55.13	...	...	69.55*
	38.40	38.73	48.22	54.28	55.52	55.06	51.82	52.91	56.00				54.91	68.10	70 05	68.98

FLORIDA.—Continued.

Year.	Fort Barrancas.	Fort Brooke.	Fort Dallas.	Fort Deynaud.	Fort Fanning.	Fort Gamble.	Fort Heiloman.	Fort Henderson.
	°	°	°	°	°	°	°	°
...	...	...	...	...	...	...	...	...
...	...	...	...	...	...	...	...	...
...	...	...	...	...	...	...	...	...
...	...	...	...	...	...	...	...	...
...	...	...	...	...	...	...	...	...
...	...	...	...	...	...	...	...	...
...	...	...	...	...	...	...	...	...
...	...	...	...	...	...	...	...	...
1822	68.56	...	...	...	...	...	...	...
1823	67.85	...	...	...	...	...	...	...
1824	68.70	...	...	...	...	...	...	...
1825	...	71.98	...	...	...	...	...	...
1826	69.51	72.91	...	...	...	...	...	...
1827	69.87	73.78	...	...	...	...	...	...
1828	69.86	73.47	...	...	...	...	...	...
1829	68.57	71.16*	...	...	...	...	...	...
1830	...	72.58	...	...	...	...	...	...
1831	...	71.01	...	...	...	...	...	...
1838	...	70.06	...	...	...	...	...	...
1839	...	71.64	74.71*	...	...	...	67.08	68.38*
1840	...	70.46	74.91	...	...	...	68.90*	...
1841	...	71.18	74.56*	...	71.15	...	...	...
1842	...	71.16	...	...	69.48	69.56	...	...
1843	68.54	70.33	...	...	...	...	...	...
1844	69.24	70.40	...	...	...	...	...	...
1845	67.57*	70.60	...	...	...	...	...	...
1846	68.26*	71.59	...	...	...	...	...	...
1847	...	71.66	...	...	...	...	...	...
1848		70.80*						
1849	...	74.36	...	...	...	...	...	...
1850	...	73.47*	78.09*	...	...	...	...	...
1851	68.38*	71.33	...	...	...	...	...	...
1852	...	71.98	...	...	...	...	...	...
1853	67.73*	72.99	...	...	...	...	...	...
1854	68.73	71.54	...	...	...	...	...	...
1855	67.82	70.94*	74.38	72.91*	...	...	...	...
1856	65.95	70.70	75.59	...	...	...	...	...
1857	...	70.52*	75.87	...	...	...	...	...
1858	...	...	...	...	...	...	...	...
1859	67.75	...	...	...	...	...	...	...
1860	67.67	...	...	...	...	...	...	...
	68.08	71.51	74.90	72.44	69.80	69.16	68.29	68.39

Year.	Fort Jefferson.	Fort King.	Fort Marion.	Fort Meade.	Fort Micanopy.	Fort Myers.	Fort Pierce.
	°	°	°	°	°	°	°
1825	...	...	71.80	...	...	...	...
1826	...	...	72.12*	...	...	...	...
1827	...	...	71.27*	...	...	...	...
1828	...	...	72.91	...	...	...	...
1829	...	...	68.62*	...	...	...	...
1830	...	...	70.80	...	...	...	...
1831	...	...	68.32	...	...	...	...
1832	...	...	70.19	...	...	...	...
1833	...	72.00	70.16	...	...	...	...
1834	...	72.49	69.93*	...	...	...	...
1835	...	68.15	...	...	...	...	...
1837	...	...	67.29	...	...	...	...
1838	...	...	66.22	...	...	...	...
1839	...	...	66.58	...	70.55	...	...
1840	...	...	...	...	69.93	...	71.97
1841	...	67.90	66.74	...	68.48	...	...
1842	...	68.45	68.01	...	69.61	...	...
1843	...	...	68.68	...	...	...	...
1844	...	...	69.18	...	...	...	...
1845	...	...	69.51*	...	...	...	...
1851	...	...	70.39	...	...	74.90	...
1852	...	...	...	71.91	...	76.14	73.30
1853	...	...	...	71.06	...	75.28	75.07
1854	...	...	...	72.15*	...	74.37	74.64
1855	...	...	...	...	...	73.37	74.58*
1856	...	...	...	...	...	73.53	73.44
1857	...	...	69.04	...	...	72.53	73.33
1858	...	...	71.42*	...	...	...	...
1859	...	...	71.20	...	...	...	...
1861	78.01*	...	...	...	...	...	...
1862	78.12	...	...	...	...	...	...
1863	76.30*	...	...	...	...	...	...
1864	75.88	...	...	...	...	...	...
1865	78.42*	...	...	...	...	...	...
1867	79.53	...	...	...	...	...	...
1868	78.17	...	...	...	...	...	...
1870	77.02	...	...	...	...	...	...
	77.67	69.65	69.39	71.51	69.71	74.04	73.26

31 May, 1875.

FLORIDA.—Continued.

Year.	Fort Russell.	Fort Shannon.	Fort Wacahootee.	Fort Waccassassa.	Gainesville.	Jacksonville.	Key West.	Knoxhill.	Lake City.	Manatee.	Micanopy.	New Smyrna.	Ocala.	Picolata.	Port Orange.	Seville
	°	°	°	°	°	°	°	°	°	°	°	°	°	°	°	°
1830	...	...	...	...	...	...	77.74	...	...	...	...	...	...	...	...	...
1831	...	...	...	...	...	...	76.22	...	...	...	...	...	...	...	...	...
1832	...	...	...	...	...	...	76.30	...	...	...	...	...	...	...	...	...
1833	...	...	...	...	...	...	...	...	...	...	...	...	...	...	...	...
1834	...	...	...	...	...	...	75.37	...	...	...	...	...	...	...	...	...
1835	...	...	...	...	...	...	75.49*	...	...	...	...	...	...	...	...	...
1836	...	...	...	...	...	...	...	...	...	...	...	...	...	...	...	...
1837	...	...	...	...	...	...	75.64	...	...	...	...	...	...	...	...	...
1838	...	...	...	...	...	...	75.69	...	...	...	...	...	...	...	...	...
1840	...	71.47	...	...	...	...	...	...	...	...	...	71.61	...	...	...	...
1841	70.58	70.54*	67.95	69.40	...	...	...	...	...	...	...	71.43*	...	69.65*	...	...
1842	...	69.15	...	68.10	...	...	...	...	...	...	...	...	...	...	...	...
1843	...	...	...	...	...	...	77.60*	...	...	...	...	...	...	...	...	...
1844	...	...	...	...	...	...	77.04	...	...	...	...	...	...	...	...	...
1845	...	...	...	...	...	...	...	...	...	...	...	...	...	...	...	...
1849	...	...	...	...	...	...	...	...	...	...	...	...	...	...	...	...
1850	...	...	...	...	...	...	...	...	...	...	...	...	...	...	...	...
1851	...	...	...	...	...	69.33	78.22	...	...	...	...	...	...	...	...	...
1852	...	...	...	...	...	...	77.45	...	...	...	...	...	...	...	...	...
1853	...	...	...	...	...	...	76.32	...	...	...	...	71.10*	...	...	...	...
1854	...	...	...	...	...	69.21	76.69	67.13*	...	...	...	...	...	...	...	...
1855	...	...	...	...	...	68.83	76.12	66.23*	...	...	...	...	...	...	...	...
1856	...	...	...	...	66.61*	68.08	76.23	...	...	...	...	...	...	...	...	...
1857	...	...	...	...	66.87	67.48*	75.98	...	66.83*	...	...	...	...	...	...	...
1858	...	...	...	...	68.29	69.36	77.71	...	68.83	...	...	...	...	...	...	...
1859	...	...	...	...	68.21*	69.85	77.08	...	68.77	...	69.15	...	...	...	...	66.97*
1860	...	...	...	...	68.19*	69.84	77.67*	...	...	...	...	...	...	...	...	...
1861	...	...	...	...	...	...	78.55	...	...	...	...	...	...	...	...	...
1862	...	...	...	...	...	...	78.29	...	...	...	...	...	...	...	...	...
1863	...	...	...	...	...	...	77.69	...	...	...	...	...	...	...	...	...
1864	...	...	...	...	...	...	77.14	...	...	...	...	...	...	...	...	...
1865	...	...	...	...	...	...	78.10	...	...	...	...	...	...	...	...	...
1866	...	...	...	...	...	...	...	...	...	...	...	...	...	...	...	...
1867	...	...	...	...	...	69.73*	...	...	...	...	...	...	...	...	72.36	...
1868	...	...	...	...	...	69.44	...	...	...	...	...	...	...	...	...	...
1869	...	...	...	...	...	68.29	...	...	...	73.39	...	...	70.58*	...	69.12	...
1870	...	...	...	...	...	68.56	78.88	...	...	...	...	...	...	...	...	...
	70.31	70.10	68.03	68.66	67.48	68 98	77.05	66.68	68.44	73.17	69.63	71.29	69.73	69.84	70.23	66.97

FLA.—Continued.		GEORGIA.												IDAHO.		
Year.	Warrington.	Athens.	Atlanta.	Augusta.	Augusta Arsenal.	Berne.	Oglethorpe Barracks.	Penfield.	Savannah.	Sparta.	The Rock.	Whitemarsh Island.	Zebulon.	Year.	Fort Boisé.	Fort Lapwai.
	°	°	°	°	°	°	°	°	°	°	°	°	°		°	°
1819	...	...	...	...	...	...	...	...	64.60*	...	...	...	...	...	...	...
—														...	...	...
1826	...	...	...	...	67.10	...	...	...	...	...	...	...	...	...	...	...
1827	...	...	...	...	66.41	...	...	...	...	...	...	...	...	...	...	...
1828	...	...	...	...	67.40	...	...	...	...	...	...	...	...	...	...	...
1829	...	...	...	...	61.22	...	...	...	...	...	...	...	...	...	...	...
1830	...	...	...	...	65.64	...	...	...	...	...	...	...	...	...	...	...
1831	...	...	...	...	61.78	...	...	...	...	...	...	...	...	...	...	...
1832	...	...	...	...	64.23	...	66.35*	...	...	...	...	...	...	...	...	...
1833	...	...	...	...	65.72	...	...	...	67.64	...	...	...	...	...	...	...
1834	...	...	...	...	64.99	...	69.64	...	...	...	...	...	...	...	...	...
1835	...	...	...	...	61.93	...	65.71	...	...	...	...	...	...	...	...	...
1836	...	...	...	...	62.09*	...	...	...	...	...	...	...	...	...	...	...
1837	...	...	...	...	62.36*	...	...	...	62.20	...	...	...	...	...	...	...
1838	...	...	...	...	62.21*	...	...	...	61.96	...	...	...	...	...	...	...
1839	...	...	...	64.00	61.64	...	...	...	63.62	...	...	...	...	...	...	...
1840	...	...	...	61.42	61.24	...	...	...	67.06	...	61.71	...	...	...	...	...
1841	...	...	...	61.09	61.58	...	...	...	68.32	...	61.11*	...	...	...	...	...
1842	...	...	...	62.61	62.58	...	...	...	66.45	...	62.35*	...	...	...	...	...
1843	...	...	...	61.97	64.61	...	67.22	...	66.13	...	...	...	...	...	...	...
1844	...	...	...	...	65.14	...	66.41	...	65.36	...	...	...	...	...	...	...
1845	...	...	...	...	65.44	...	66.94	...	62.09	...	...	...	...	...	...	...
1846	...	...	...	...	...	...	66.96*	...	64.27	...	...	...	...	...	...	...
1847	...	...	...	...	...	...	...	...	65.51	...	...	...	...	...	...	...
1848	...	...	...	...	...	...	...	...	66.63	...	...	...	...	...	...	...
1849	...	...	...	...	...	...	67.46*	...	66.34	...	...	...	...	...	...	...
1850	...	...	...	...	...	...	...	...	67.41	...	...	...	...	...	...	...
1851	...	...	...	...	...	...	...	...	65.80	...	...	...	...	...	...	...
1852	...	...	...	...	...	...	...	...	66.09	...	...					
1853	...	...	...	...	...	...	...	...	65.45	...	...	...	...	...	...	...
1854	69.42	...	...	...	...	...	...	...	66.37	63.24	...	64.71	...	...	...	...
1855	68.23	...	...	...	...	...	...	...	65.83	61.97	59.37	65.13	...	...	...	...
1856	69.07	...	...	...	...	...	...	...	64.42	60.78	...	63.49	63.01	...	...	...
1857	68.69	...	...	...	...	...	...	...	63.87	61.31	61.00	63.48*	62.53	...	...	...
1858	...	59.47*	...	...	...	...	...	...	66.27	62.74	...	65.80	...	...	...	...
1859	69.60*	60.73*	59.44	66.46*	...	...	...	...	65.84*	60.77*	...	66.01	...	...	...	...
1860	68.82	...	...	...	...	...	...	...	...	61.32*	...	65.93*	...	...	...	...
—														1864	51.43*	53.55
1866	...	...	57.60*	...	...	...	...	...	...	...	...	...	...	1865	51.39	51.82*
1867	...	...	...	...	...	...	65.87	...	...	...	...	...	...	—		
1868	...	...	56.85	...	...	...	65.74	...	...	...	...	...	...	1868	49.97	51.44
1869	...	...	56.98*	...	63.83	...	66.12	61.22	...	...	...	...	...	1869	54.16	53.73
1870	...	...	60.21*	...	63.67	63.49	65.64*	61.36	...	...	...	...	...	1870	52.11	52.54
	69.18	60.93	58.36	63.30	63.77	63.04	66.70	61.33	65.40	61.98	61.33	64.92	63.49		52.05	52.45

ILLINOIS.

Year.	Alto.	Andalusia	Athens.	Augusta.	Aurora.	Batavia.	Belleville.	Belvidere.	Brighton.	Carthage.	Charleston.	Chicago.	Coloma (near).	Decatur.	Elgin.	Elmira.
	°	°	°	°	°	°	°	°	°	°	°	°	°	°	°	°
1833	...	...	...	...	...	...	...	...	...	...	...	49.25	...	...	...	...
1834	...	...	...	55.31	...	...	...	...	...	...	...	47.62	...	...	...	...
1835	...	...	...	53.12	...	...	...	...	...	...	...	44.00	...	...	...	...
1836	...	...	...	52.11	...	...	...	...	...	...	...	42.93	...	...	...	...
1837	...	...	...	49.47	...	...	...	...	...	...	...	...	...	...	...	...
1838	...	...	...	49.12	...	...	...	...	...	...	...	...	...	...	...	...
1839	...	...	...	54.43	...	...	...	...	...	...	...	...	...	...	...	...
1850	...	...	...	50.53	...	...	...	...	...	...	...	...	...	...	...	...
1851	...	...	53.17	50.80	...	...	...	...	...	...	...	...	...	...	...	...
1852	...	...	...	49.66	...	...	...	...	...	...	...	...	...	...	...	...
1853	...	...	...	50.82	...	...	...	...	...	...	...	...	...	...	...	...
1854	...	...	54.89	52.79	...	...	...	...	...	...	...	...	...	...	...	...
1855	...	...	52.21	50.19	...	...	...	...	...	...	...	...	...	...	...	...
1856	...	...	50.51	47.41	...	...	...	...	...	...	...	...	...	...	...	...
1857	...	45.56*	48.00*	47.66	...	45.90*	...	...	51.44	...	...	44.15*	...	...	...	...
1858	...	49.13	51.55	50.30	48.33	46.91	...	...	54.21	...	...	...	...	...	46.61	...
1859	...	48.67	...	49.52	46.92	46.77	...	...	...	49.97*	...	...	...	...	46.07	...
1860	...	50.14*	...	...	46.88*	...	...	...	...	...	...	44.86	...	...	46.13	...
1861	...	...	...	50.97	...	...	...	...	...	...	...	45.41	...	...	46.74*	...
1862	...	...	...	49.63	...	...	57.11	...	...	...	...	45.14	...	...	...	...
1863	...	...	...	49.60*	...	...	...	...	...	...	...	44.29*	...	...	...	...
1864	...	...	...	49.34	...	...	...	...	...	...	...	42.48	...	...	...	...
1865	...	...	...	50.83	...	...	...	...	...	...	...	44.33	...	...	...	49.93*
1866	...	49.87	...	51.39	46.07	...	...	...	...	...	...	46.18	48.81	...	...	47.96
1867	46.48	49.68*	...	52.25	45.89	...	...	...	...	...	...	49.45	51.38*	...	...	48.70
1868	44.75	49.16	...	51.66	44.80*	...	...	44.16*	...	...	...	47.90	48.95	...	...	48.13
1869	45.47	48.68	...	49.91	...	...	...	44.19	...	...	...	47.21	52.83	...	...	46.18*
1870	47.63*	51.29	...	52.36	48.22	...	...	47.75	...	...	51.65*	50.73	54.75*	51.92	...	...
	46.15	49.07	51.92	50.87	47.15	46.90	57.13	45.36	52.43	50.37	51.65	45.85	51.53	51.19	46.15	48.41

ILLINOIS.—Continued.

Year.	Evanston.	Farm Ridge.	Fort Armstrong.	Fremont Center.	Galesburg.	Golconda.	Hennepin.	Highland.	Hoyleton.	Jacksonville.	Lebanon.	Loami.	Louisville.	Manchester.	Marengo.	Mattoon.
	°	°	°	°	°	°	°	°	°	°	°	°	°	°	°	°
1824	...	...	49.33	...	...	...	...	...	...	...	...	...	...	...	...	...
1825	...	...	52.18	...	...	...	...	...	...	...	...	...	...	...	...	...
1826	...	...	50.19	...	...	...	...	...	...	...	...	...	...	...	...	...
1827	...	...	51.42	...	...	...	...	...	...	...	...	...	...	...	...	...
1828	...	...	51.25	...	...	...	...	...	...	...	...	...	...	...	...	...
1829	...	...	49.07	...	...	...	...	...	...	...	...	...	...	...	...	...
1830	...	...	52.89	...	...	...	...	...	...	...	...	...	...	...	...	...
1831	...	...	45.46	...	...	...	...	...	...	...	...	...	...	...	...	...
1832	...	...	...	...	...	...	...	...	...	...	...	...	...	...	...	...
1833	...	...	50.51	...	...	...	...	...	...	...	...	...	...	...	...	...
1834	...	...	49.71	...	...	...	...	...	...	...	...	...	...	...	...	...
1835	...	...	46.22	...	...	...	...	...	...	...	...	...	...	...	...	...
1841	...	...	...	...	...	...	...	53.69	...	...	...	...	...	...	...	...
1842	...	...	...	...	...	...	...	54.45	...	...	...	...	...	...	...	...
1843	...	...	...	...	...	...	...	50.44	...	...	...	...	...	...	...	...
1844	...	...	...	...	...	...	...	54.43	...	...	...	...	...	...	...	...
1845	...	...	...	...	...	...	...	54.37	...	...	...	...	...	...	...	...
1846	...	...	...	...	...	...	...	55.82	...	...	...	...	...	...	...	...
1847	...	...	...	...	...	...	...	55.08	...	...	...	...	...	...	...	...
1848	...	...	...	...	...	...	...	55.85	...	...	...	...	...	...	...	...
1849	...	...	...	...	...	...	...	55.88	...	...	...	...	...	...	...	...
1850	...	...	...	...	...	...	...	56.68	...	...	...	...	...	...	...	...
1851	...	...	...	...	...	...	...	56.97	...	...	...	...	...	...	...	...
1852	...	...	...	...	...	...	...	56.10	...	...	...	...	...	...	...	...
1853	...	...	...	...	...	...	...	...	...	...	...	...	...	...	...	...
1854	...	...	...	...	...	...	...	...	...	...	...	...	...	...	...	...
1855	...	...	...	...	...	...	...	...	...	...	...	...	...	51.26	...	...
1856	...	...	...	...	...	...	...	...	...	...	...	...	...	48.82	45.69*	...
1857	...	...	...	45.13	...	...	...	...	...	...	...	...	...	48.59	45.23	...
1858	...	...	...	...	...	...	...	...	...	53.22*	...	...	...	51.88	48.47	...
1859	...	...	...	...	...	...	...	...	...	...	...	...	...	51.24	45.97	...
1860	...	46.58*	...	...	...	...	...	...	...	...	...	...	...	53.69	44.96	...
1861	...	...	...	...	48.71*	...	...	55.65*	...	53.21	56.30	...	...	52.95	45.81	...
1862	...	...	...	...	47.42	...	...	53.43	...	...	...	...	...	51.59	45.02	...
1863	...	...	...	...	48.62*	...	...	52.84*	...	...	...	...	...	50.87*	...	...
1864	...	...	...	...	47.53	...	...	...	52.46*	...	...	...	...	51.38	...	...
1865	48.54	...	...	...	49.45	...	...	...	...	...	...	...	...	...	...	...
1866	...	...	...	...	47.20	59.03	...	...	...	...	...	49.97	...	52.31	...	...
1867	...	...	...	...	48.38	57.04	...	...	...	...	...	51.05*	...	52.16	...	...
1868	...	...	...	...	48.24	58.65	...	...	...	...	...	...	...	52.05	44.89	...
1869	46.71	...	...	...	47.52	57.82	...	...	...	...	...	50.08*	52.74*	51.33	...	...
1870	49.02	...	...	...	51.62*	57.85*	52.48	...	...	...	...	...	55.13	53.63	...	53.09
	47.67	46.58	49.82	46.19	48.48	58.08	52.48	54.73	...	52.82	55.79	50.34	53.93	51.60	46.04	52.62

ILLINOIS.—Continued.

Year.	Milford.	Mt. Sterling.	Orchard Farm.	Osceola.	Ottawa.	Pana.	Pekin.	Peoria.	Pleasant Ridge Nursery.	Riley.	Rock Island Arsenal.	Sandwich.	South Pass, near.	Springfield.	Upper Alton.	Warsaw, near.
	°	°	°	°	°	°	°	°	°	°	°	°	°	°	°	°
1850	...	...	...	...	...	...	...	...	...	...	...	...	...	...	...	49.27
1851	...	...	...	...	...	...	...	...	...	...	...	...	...	...	...	50.37
1852	...	...	...	...	...	...	...	...	...	...	...	...	...	...	...	50.07*
1853	...	...	...	...	...	...	...	...	...	...	...	...	...	...	...	...
1854	49.42	...	...	...	51.28	...	...	...	...	...	...	...	...	...	55.41*	...
1855	...	...	...	...	48.84*	...	48.77	...	...	...	...	...	...	...	52.51	48.56*
1856	...	...	...	...	47.60	...	46.47	50.22*	...	44.15*	...	...	...	...	50.32*	46.23
1857	...	...	...	...	45.47	...	46.82	46.31	...	42.73	...	...	...	...	...	49.18
1858	...	...	...	...	48.60	...	49.68	52.05	...	45.86	...	...	...	...	...	...
1859	...	...	...	...	47.96	...	49.98	51.81	...	45.60	...	48.08	...	...	52.28*	...
1860	...	...	50.47	50.12	48.94*	...	...	52.80	...	45.32*	...	49.14	...	...	...	...
1861	...	...	50.04*	...	48.68	...	...	52.96	...	44.42	...	49.14	...	...	...	...
1862	...	...	48.68	...	48.32	...	...	51.78	...	44.04	...	48.33*	...	...	...	...
1863	...	...	50.29*	...	48.37*	...	...	51.97*	...	44.12*	...	49.21*	57.04*	...	...	...
1864	...	...	...	...	47.17	...	50.50	51.57	48.32	44.27	...	46.58	58.74*	...	...	...
1865	...	...	...	...	49.12*	...	51.63*	52.35	50.15	45.85*	...	48.22	...	54.28	...	...
1866	...	51.89	...	...	48.30*	...	...	50.40	48.17	43.67*	...	45.42	...	49.59	...	...
1867	...	52.85	...	...	49.82	...	...	50.81	48.00	...	48.97	46.22	...	49.71	...	...
1868	...	52.48	...	...	48.88*	...	...	50.44	47.84	...	49.03	45.40	...	48.83	...	...
1869	...	49.89	...	...	49.15*	...	...	50.09	47.83	...	47.94	45.27	54.90*	49.71	...	50.13
1870	...	54.15*	...	...	52.39*	52.84	...	53.48	...	47.86	51.83*	...	...	...	...	52.69
	49.42[1]	52.25	49.81	49.54	48.92	52.09	49.09	51.36	48.37	44.76	49.40	46.94	56.62	49.74	51.10	50.49

	ILLINOIS.—Continued.									INDIANA.						
Year.	Waterloo.	Waverly.	Waynesville.	West Salem.	West Urbana.	Wheaton.	Winnebago.	Wyanet, near.	York Neck.	Aurora.	Bloomington.	Cadiz, near.	Cannelton.	Columbia City.	Evansville.	Harveysburg.
1855	...	...	...	...	...	...	...	...	...	...	...	45.41	...	...	...	...
1856	...	...	...	52.15*	...	...	...	...	...	...	...	42.40	...	...	...	...
1857	...	...	...	52.88	47.82*	...	...	...	...	...	...	43.80	...	...	54.06*	...
1858	...	...	50.25	55.76	51.70	47.19	47.35	...	...	..	...	47.44*	54.04*	...	57.42*	...
1859	...	...	...	55.73	51.14	46.72	46.00	...	...	55.55	...	45.99*	55.47	...	...	...
1860	...	...	...	...	...	...	45.86	...	...	...	...	48.43	...	...	...	...
1861	...	...	...	...	...	...	44.70	...	...	...	...	50.36	55.58	...	...	...
1862	...	52.85*	...	...	...	...	44.84*	...	...	...	...	...	...	...	...	...
1863	...	50.08*	...	...	...	...	45.96*	...	...	...	...	50.62*	...	...	...	...
1864	...	50.84	...	...	...	...	45.07	...	50.47	...	...	50.04	...	...	...	...
1865	...	51.69	...	...	...	...	46.86	49.59	51.94	...	...	...	...	...	...	...
1866	...	...	...	...	...	...	44.37	48.01	...	52.90*	...	...	...	46.97	...	...
1867	56.12	...	...	...	...	...	45.10	48.66	...	52.17	...	...	...	48.14	...	...
1868	56.53*	...	...	...	...	...	44.22	48.14*	...	52.30*	51.02*	...	...	47.76*	...	...
1869	...	...	...	...	...	...	43.96	47.78	...	51.51	...	...	...	48.08*	...	50.14
1870	...	...	...	...	...	...	47.55	49.16*	...	54.27	...	...	...	52.18*	...	...
	56.31	51.37	50.58	54.46	50.18	47.07	45.53	48.61	51.20[1]	53.09	51.38	47.32	54.86	48.79	55.74	49.91

[1] Hours of observation unknown.

INDIANA.—Continued.

Year.	Indianapolis.	Jeffersonville.	Kentland.	Laconia.	Laporte.	Laporte, near.	Logansport.	Madison.	Merom.	Michigan City.	Milton.	Mt. Carmel.	Mt. Hope.	Muncie.	New Albany.	New Harmony.
	°	°	°	°	°	°	°	°	°	°	°	°	°	°	°	°
1819	...	60.17	...	...	...	...	...	...	...	...	...	...	...	...	...	...
1851	...	...	...	...	43.41	...	...	...	...	...	...	...	...	...	...	...
1852	...	...	...	...	...	...	...	...	...	...	...	...	...	...	...	...
1853	...	...	...	...	...	...	...	...	...	...	51.38	...	...	...	...	...
1854	...	...	...	...	...	...	...	...	...	...	52.95	...	...	...	...	57.72
1855	...	...	...	...	...	...	...	...	...	...	50.80	...	...	...	...	55.21
1856	...	...	...	...	...	...	47.82	...	...	...	...	...	...	...	...	52.86
1857	...	...	...	...	...	...	47.64	...	...	45.73	...	...	...	...	...	52.85
1858	...	...	...	...	...	...	52.38	52.85	...	48.50*	...	...	...	...	...	56.10
1859	...	...	...	...	...	...	52.37	...	...	...	...	...	...	...	...	55.32
1860	...	...	...	...	...	...	...	...	...	...	...	...	...	...	...	56.33
1861	...	...	...	...	...	...	...	...	...	...	...	...	...	...	...	56.35
1862	...	...	...	...	...	...	...	...	...	...	...	...	...	...	...	55.81
1863	...	...	...	...	...	...	...	...	...	...	...	...	...	...	...	54.72*
1864	50.67	...	...	...	...	...	...	...	...	...	...	...	...	...	52.82*	54.19*
1865	51.84	...	...	...	...	...	...	...	...	...	...	...	...	...	54.96	56.31
1866	...	...	...	...	...	...	...	...	...	...	...	...	...	...	...	55.49
1867	50.42*	...	...	...	...	...	...	...	51.83	...	...	...	...	49.79	...	55.05
1868	49.65	...	...	...	...	...	...	...	53.11	...	...	...	...	49.36	...	55.04
1869	50.04	...	48.27*	...	...	...	...	...	51.77	...	...	...	50.01	49.57	...	54.60
1870	52.07	...	...	54.87	...	51.03	...	...	55.39*	...	...	52.63	52.98	...	...	56.03
	50.66	60.17	48.22	54.20	43.41[1]	49.39	50.66	54.63	52.81	47.66	51.62	52.05	51.32	49.90	53.41	55.22

[1] Hours of observation unknown.

Year.	INDIANA.—Continued.							INDIAN TERRITORY.					IOWA.			
	Rensselaer.	Richmond.	Rockville, near.	Rockville.	South Bend.	Spiceland.	Vevay.	Caney.	Fort Arbuckle.	Fort Gibson.	Fort Towson.	Fort Washita.	Algona.	Algona, near.	Bellevue.	Boonesboro.
	°	°	°	°	°	°	°	°	°	°	°	°	°	°	°	°
1828	...	...	...	...	...	...	...	...	...	63.00	...	...	...	...	...	...
1829	...	...	...	...	...	...	...	...	...	60.85	...	...	...	...	...	...
1830	...	...	...	...	...	...	...	...	...	64.65	...	...	...	...	...	...
1831	...	...	...	...	...	...	...	...	...	57.71	...	...	...	...	...	...
1832	...	...	...	...	...	...	...	...	...	61.32	...	...	...	...	...	...
1833	...	...	...	...	...	...	...	...	...	61.67	61.58	...	...	...	...	...
1834	...	...	...	...	...	...	...	...	...	62.75	61.60	...	...	...	...	...
1835	...	...	...	...	...	...	...	...	...	55.78	58.59	...	...	...	...	...
1836	...	...	...	...	...	...	...	...	...	59.49	59.69	...	...	...	...	...
1837	...	...	...	...	...	...	...	...	...	61.06	61.72	...	...	...	...	...
1838	...	...	...	...	...	...	...	...	...	58.03	59.32	...	...	...	...	...
1839	...	...	...	...	...	...	...	...	...	62.18	62.83	...	...	...	...	...
1840	...	...	...	...	...	...	...	...	...	59.66	62.49	...	...	...	...	...
1841	...	...	...	...	...	...	...	...	...	59.79	59.59	...	...	...	...	...
1842	...	...	...	...	...	...	...	...	...	60.69	63.67	...	...	...	...	...
1843	...	...	...	...	...	...	...	...	...	58.94	61.19	60.82	...	...	...	...
1844	...	...	...	...	...	...	...	...	...	60.64	63.00	63.94	...	...	...	...
1845	...	...	...	...	...	...	...	...	...	61.58	62.19	63.41	...	...	...	...
1846	...	...	...	...	...	...	...	...	...	61.03	...	64.02	...	...	...	...
1847	...	...	...	...	...	...	...	...	...	58.91	...	61.23	...	...	...	...
1848	...	...	...	...	...	...	...	...	...	59.37	...	61.66	...	...	...	...
1849	...	...	...	...	...	...	...	...	...	59.20	...	61.70	...	...	...	...
1850	...	...	...	...	...	...	...	...	...	60.24	61.95	62.13	...	...	...	...
1851	...	...	...	...	...	...	...	...	61.14	61.22	62.92	63.08	...	...	...	...
1852	...	...	...	...	...	...	...	...	59.58	59.54	...	60.42	...	...	...	...
1853	...	...	...	...	...	...	...	...	61.18	60.53	61.69	61.24	...	...	...	...
1854	...	52.63*	...	...	...	...	...	...	62.55	62.22	...	63.28	...	...	...	...
1855	...	...	...	...	...	...	...	...	61.91	59.98	...	62.73	...	...	...	...
1856	...	...	...	...	...	...	...	...	58.70	58.34	...	60.45	...	...	43.76*	...
1857	...	48.11	...	...	...	...	...	...	58.46	...	...	60.60	...	...	44.16	...
1858	...	51.75	...	...	...	...	...	...	...	...	...	...	...	...	47.39	...
1859	...	52.40	...	...	...	...	...	...	62.31	...	...	...	...	...	47.13	...
1860	...	53.02*	...	...	...	...	...	59.01*	64.01	...	...	...	...	...	...	...
1861	...	...	...	...	...	...	...	...	...	...	...	...	...	...	...	...
1862	...	...	50.40	...	...	...	...	...	...	...	...	...	41.94	...	...	...
1863	...	...	50.40	50.13*	47.62*	...	...	...	...	...	...	...	43.08*	...	...	...
1864	...	...	50.20	...	47.99	49.77	...	...	...	...	...	...	43.55	...	...	...
1865	49.02*	50.13*	51.30	...	...	51.34	55.40	...	...	...	...	...	...	...	...	...
1866	...	48.17	50.00	...	...	49.54	55.55	...	...	...	...	...	...	...	...	...
1867	...	48.58	...	...	...	50.22	55.70	...	...	...	...	...	43.06*	41.10	...	...
1868	48.37*	...	...	...	...	49.74	54.99	...	...	...	...	...	42.71	42.26*	...	44.65*
1869	...	...	...	...	...	49.69	...	...	59.64	...	...	...	42.63	41.89	...	...
1870	50.81*	...	...	...	...	52.16	54.96	...	...	...	...	...	45.49	...	...	46.69
	48.70	50.78	50.11[1]	49.71	48.78	50.27	54.68	59.01	61.05	60.48	61.50	62.18	43.29	41.86	46.00	45.75

[1] Hours of observation unknown.

IOWA.—Continued.

Year.	Border Plains.	Bowen's Prairie.	Burlington.	Brookside.	Ceres.	Clinton.	Council Bluffs.	Dakota.	Davenport.	Des Moines.	Bubuque.	Fairfield.	Fairfield.	Fayette Village.	Forrestville.	Fort Atkinson.
	°	°	°	°	°	°	°	°	°	°	°	°	°	°	°	°
1820	...	...	...	...	...	...	48.19	...	...	...	...	...	...	...	...	...
1821	...	...	...	...	...	...	47.12	...	...	...	...	...	...	...	...	...
1822	...	...	...	...	...	...	50.25	...	...	...	...	...	...	...	...	...
1823	...	...	...	...	...	...	51.28	...	...	...	...	...	...	...	...	...
1824	...	...	...	...	...	...	48.25	...	...	...	...	...	...	...	...	...
1825	...	...	...	...	...	...	52.21	...	...	...	...	...	...	...	...	...
1842	...	...	...	...	...	...	...	...	...	...	...	...	...	...	...	46.87
1843	...	...	...	...	...	...	...	...	...	...	...	...	...	...	...	41.76
1844	...	...	...	...	...	...	...	...	...	49.54	...	...	...	...	...	45.36
1845	...	...	...	...	...	...	...	...	...	50.20*	...	...	...	...	...	46.21
1854	...	...	...	...	...	...	...	...	...	...	50.18	...	...	...	...	...
1855	...	...	...	...	...	...	...	...	...	...	47.80	50.08	...	...	...	...
1856	...	...	...	...	...	...	...	...	...	...	...	...	...	...	...	...
1857	44.31	...	...	...	...	...	...	...	...	...	...	...	47.20	...	...	...
1858	47.48	...	...	...	...	...	...	...	...	...	47.98	...	49.49	...	...	...
1859	47.97*	...	51.31*	...	...	...	...	...	...	...	47.62	...	48.91	...	...	...
1860	...	...	...	...	...	...	...	...	...	...	49.72	...	...	45.23*	45.64*	...
1861	...	...	...	...	...	47.14	...	...	47.59*	...	47.65	...	...	...	44.86	...
1862	...	...	...	45.85*	...	46.28	...	...	46.24	...	46.65	...	...	...	...	...
1863	...	...	...	46.74*	...	47.02*	...	...	...	...	47.96	...	...	...	...	...
1864	...	...	...	45.32	...	47.41*	...	...	46.60	...	46.92	...	...	...	...	...
1865	...	...	...	45.18	...	49.08	...	...	48.45	...	48.31	...	...	...	...	...
1866	...	...	...	43.19	43.62	47.24	...	...	46.91	46.82	45.76	...	...	...	...	...
1867	...	...	...	43.47*	46.33	48.76*	...	41.33*	47.32	...	47.10	...	...	...	...	...
1868	...	...	...	43.57	...	48.37	...	...	46.86	...	46.09	...	...	...	...	...
1869	...	44.45	...	43.55*	...	46.01	...	...	46.51	...	46.15	...	...	...	...	...
1870	...	48.17	...	47.37*	...	48.75	...	...	...	...	49.54	...	...	...	...	...
	46.45	46.28	51.36	44.94	45.35	47.65	49.55	42.63	47.33	48.94	47.69	50.08[1]	49.00	...	44.83	45.29

[1] Hours of observation unknown.

IOWA.—Continued.

Year.	Fort Croghan.	Fort Dodge.	Fort Madison, near.	Franklin.	Grant City.	Guttenberg.	Harris Grove.	Independence.	Iowa City.	Iowa Falls.	Manchester.	Monticello.	Mt. Vernon.	Muscatine.	Mt. Pleasant.	North Union, near.
	°	°	°	°	°	°	°	°	°	°	°	°	°	°	°	°
1839	...	...	...	...	...	...	...	...	...	...	...	...	...	51.32	...	...
1840	...	...	...	...	...	...	...	...	...	...	...	...	...	49.09	...	...
1841	...	...	...	...	...	...	...	...	...	...	...	...	...	46.49	...	...
1842	...	...	...	...	...	...	...	...	...	...	...	...	...	47.29	...	...
1843	45.65*	...	...	...	...	...	...	...	...	...	...	...	...	43.71	...	...
1844	...	...	...	...	...	...	...	...	...	...	...	...	...	47.75	...	...
1845	...	...	...	...	...	...	...	...	...	...	...	...	...	47.33	...	...
1846	...	...	...	...	...	...	...	...	...	...	...	...	...	48.64	...	...
1847	...	...	...	...	...	...	...	...	...	...	...	...	...	43.19	...	...
1848	...	...	50.57*	...	...	...	...	...	...	...	...	...	...	43.91	...	...
1849	...	...	49.09	...	...	...	...	...	...	...	...	...	...	45.32	...	...
1850	...	...	50.34	...	...	...	...	...	...	...	...	...	...	47.00	...	...
1851	...	48.26	51.00	...	...	...	...	...	...	...	...	...	...	47.66	...	...
1852	...	...	50.03	...	...	...	...	...	...	...	...	...	...	46.90	...	...
1853	...	...	...	...	...	...	...	...	...	...	...	...	...	47.79	...	...
1854	...	...	54.82	...	...	...	...	...	...	...	...	...	...	49.53	...	...
1855	...	...	50.64	...	...	...	...	...	...	...	...	...	...	47.14	...	...
1856	...	...	48.08	...	...	...	...	...	...	...	...	...	...	43.84	...	...
1857	...	...	47.38	43.08	...	...	...	...	...	...	...	...	...	44.11	...	...
1858	...	...	50.16	47.38*	...	...	...	...	48.17	...	...	...	...	47.40	...	...
1859	...	...	49.57	...	...	...	...	...	...	...	...	...	...	46.63	...	...
1860	...	...	51.17	...	...	...	...	...	...	...	...	...	...	48.06	...	...
1861	...	...	50.95	47.38	...	...	...	...	45.77	...	...	...	46.24	48.96	...	...
1862	...	...	49.32	...	...	...	...	...	44.60	...	...	...	45.24*	47.35	...	...
1863	...	...	50.31	...	...	...	...	...	46.07*	...	...	...	46.65*	...	...	...
1864	...	...	49.56	...	...	...	...	45.69	47.44	44.85	...	...	45.63	47.18*	48.19*	...
1865	...	...	50.81	...	...	45.79*	...	46.30*	49.79	45.78	...	...	47.55	48.27	...	...
1866	...	...	49.27	...	...	42.48*	...	44.51	47.34	45.21	43.09*	44.60	45.61	...	...	...
1867	...	43.78	49.55	...	...	42.79	46.26	44.84	47.56	44.06	...	45.43	45.42	...	...	...
1868	...	44.45	49.42	...	...	42.41	46.78*	43.04*	47.52*	46.37*	...	45.83	45.70	...	...	...
1869	...	...	48.92	...	44.73	42.86	45.72	43.53	46.98	46.80	...	44.69	45.17	...	...	45.49
1870	...	...	52.12	...	47.94*	45.96	48.78	47.72	49.80	...	...	48.55	48.30	...	...	48.74
	45.65	45.94	50.13	45.33	46.34	43.75	46.87	45.29	47.45	45.93	43.55	45.54	46.03	46.98	48.52	47.11

IOWA.—Continued. / KANSAS.

Year.	Pella.	Pleasant Plain.	Poultney.	Quasqueton.	Rolfe.	Rossville.	Sioux City.	Vawter's Grove.	Waterloo.	Webster City.	Whiteboro'.	Woodbine.	Woodlands, The	Atchison. (KANSAS)	Baxter Springs. (KANSAS)	Burlingame. (KANSAS)
1854	...	...	46.60	48.23*	...	...	...	...	...	...	...	...	...	...	...	...
1855	45.63	...	45.04	45.51*	...	...	...	...	...	...	...	...	...	...	...	...
1856	...	45.72	...	...	...	...	...	...	...	...	...	...	...	...	...	...
1857	...	46.11	...	...	...	...	...	...	...	...	...	...	...	...	...	...
1858	...	49.31	...	...	...	44.45*	45.55*	...	...	...	...	...	...	...	...	52.30
1859	...	48.28	...	...	...	44.09	...	...	...	...	...	...	...	...	...	52.49
1860	...	49.50	...	...	...	...	...	...	...	...	...	...	...	...	...	56.56
1861	...	48.98	...	...	...	...	44.07*	...	...	...	...	...	...	...	...	...
1862	...	49.12	...	...	...	...	44.29*	...	...	...	...	...	...	...	...	...
1863	...	49.16*	...	...	...	...	...	...	...	...	...	...	...	...	...	...
1864	...	48.60	...	...	...	...	...	...	...	...	...	...	...	...	...	...
1865	...	...	...	...	...	...	...	...	47.08	...	...	...	...	...	...	...
1866	...	...	...	...	...	...	...	...	44.57	...	...	...	...	...	...	...
1867	...	...	...	...	...	...	...	45.79	44.27	...	...	...	...	50.54	...	...
1868	...	...	...	...	43.19*	...	...	46.41	44.87	...	45.15*	...	...	51.17*	57.32	...
1869	...	...	...	...	43.52	...	...	46.06	44.15	...	...	45.31*	44.44	50.64	57.04	...
1870	...	...	...	...	...	...	...	49.26	...	46.51*	...	47.51*	48.19	53.31	58.62	...
	46.71	48.35	44.82	46.16	43.53	44.57	45.22	46.83	45.38	46.51	45.51	46.41	46.31	51.35	58.00	53.66

KANSAS.—Continued.

Year.	Council Grove.	Fort Atkinson.	Fort Dodge.	Fort Harker.	Fort Hays.	Fort Larned.	Fort Leavenworth.	Fort Riley.	Fort Scott.	Holton.	Lawrence.	Leavenworth.	Le Roy, near.	Manhattan.	Neosho Falls.	Olatha.
	°	°	°	°	°	°	°	°	°	°	°	°	°	°	°	°
1830	...	...	...	...	...	...	56.56	...	...	...	...	...	...	...	...	...
1831	...	...	...	...	...	...	49.78	...	...	...	...	...	...	...	...	...
1832	...	...	...	...	...	...	53.39	...	...	...	...	...	...	...	...	...
1833	...	...	...	...	...	...	55.54	...	...	...	...	...	...	...	...	...
1834	...	...	...	...	...	...	52.40	...	...	...	...	...	...	...	...	...
1835	...	...	...	...	...	...	51.65*	...	...	...	...	...	...	...	...	...
1836	...	...	...	...	...	...	48.73	...	...	...	...	...	...	...	...	...
1837	...	...	...	...	...	...	52.89	...	...	...	...	...	...	...	...	...
1838	...	...	...	...	...	...	51.14	...	...	...	...	...	...	...	...	...
1839	...	...	...	...	...	...	53.64	...	...	...	...	...	...	...	...	...
1840	...	...	...	...	...	...	51.36	...	...	...	...	...	...	...	...	...
1841	...	...	...	...	...	...	51.20	...	...	...	...	...	...	...	...	...
1842	...	...	...	...	...	...	52.85	...	...	...	...	...	...	...	...	...
1843	...	...	...	...	...	...	49.01	...	52.58	...	...	...	...	...	...	...
1844	...	...	...	...	...	...	52.67	...	55.00	...	...	...	...	...	...	...
1845	...	...	...	...	...	...	54.79	...	55.85	...	...	...	...	...	...	...
1846	...	...	...	...	...	...	55.31	...	55.95	...	...	...	...	...	...	...
1847	...	...	...	...	...	...	49.79	...	52.65	...	...	...	...	...	...	...
1848	...	...	...	...	...	...	...	...	54.00	...	...	...	...	...	...	...
1849	...	...	...	...	...	...	52.22	...	53.67	...	...	...	...	...	...	...
1850	...	...	...	...	...	...	52.04	...	55.12	...	...	...	...	...	...	...
1851	...	55.44	...	...	...	...	53.19	...	56.05	...	...	...	...	...	...	...
1852	...	53.04	...	...	...	...	51.54	...	54.85	...	...	...	...	...	...	...
1853	...	55.34*	...	...	...	...	53.12	...	...	...	...	...	...	...	...	...
1854	...	...	...	...	...	...	55.94	57.40	...	...	...	...	...	...	...	...
1855	...	...	...	...	...	...	54.30	54.59	...	...	...	...	...	...	...	...
1856	...	...	...	...	...	...	49.98	52.08	...	...	...	...	...	...	...	...
1857	...	...	...	...	...	...	52.19	51.14	...	...	...	...	...	53.71	...	...
1858	...	...	...	...	...	...	55.35	53.93	...	...	54.10	53.28*	...	...	...	...
1859	...	...	...	...			[illegible]	54.30			...	...	...	53.92	54.19*	...
1860	...	...	...	...	...	...	56.04	58.46	...	...	...	...	...	...	58.35	...
1861	...	...	...	...	...	54.50	54.01	52.61	...	...	55.05*	54.72	...	53.98	55.46*	...
1862	...	...	...	...	...	54.41	52.72	54.88	...	...	...	...	...	52.38	...	...
1863	...	...	...	...	...	54.20	52.95	55.04	...	...	54.01*	...	...	53.87*	...	...
1864	...	...	...	...	...	52.66	51.99	55.91	...	...	...	...	...	53.05*	...	51.25*
1865	53.50*	...	...	...	...	53.77	53.53	54.57	...	...	...	...	...	...	...	51.30*
1866	53.50	...	...	...	...	...	...	...	...	...	...	50.44	...	...	...	50.97
1867	52.96	...	...	51.06*	...	54.72	52.00	52.89	...	...	...	50.21	...	51.39	...	50.42
1868	54.15	...	51.62		53.89	57.62*	52.87	52.32	...	52.05	52.81	50.51	...	50.96	...	51.59
1869	53.67	...	54.63	...	52.92	...	50.82	51.09	...	51.30	49.59	49.71	53.66	49.21	50.14*	50.27*
1870	55.54	...	56.38	53.24*	54.42	53.71	53.72	53.73	...	53.62	53.70	52.25	...	53.76	...	53.11
	53.88	54.77	55.32	51.81	54.44	53.91	52.75	54.21	54.58	52.51	53.49	51.45	53.26	52.89	54.27	51.27

KAN.—Continued.		KENTUCKY.											LOUISIANA.			
Year.	Paola.	Arcadia.	Ballardsville.	Bardstown.	Chilesburg.	Danville.	Louisville.	Millersberg.	Newport Barracks.	Nicholasville.	Paris.	Springdale.	Baton Rouge.	Benton.	Black River Plantation.	Fort Jackson.
	°	°	°	°	°	°	°	°	°	°	°	°	°	°	°	°
1822	...	..	...	...	...	...	...	...	...	...	...	...	67.87	...	...	69.95
1829	...	...	...	...	...	...	...	...	...	...	...	...	66.97	...	...	...
1830	...	...	...	...	...	...	...	...	...	...	...	...	68.77	...	...	...
1831	...	...	...	...	...	...	...	...	...	...	...	...	64.56	...	...	67.51*
1832	...	...	...	...	...	...	...	...	...	...	...	...	68.22	...	...	73.50
1833	...	...	...	...	...	...	...	...	...	...	...	...	68.74	...	...	...
1834	...	...	...	...	...	...	...	...	...	...	...	...	68.80	...	...	71.04*
1835	...	...	...	...	...	...	...	...	...	...	...	...	65.96	...	...	...
1837	...	...	...	...	...	...	...	...	...	...	...	...	69.54*	...	...	...
1838	...	...	...	...	...	...	...	...	...	...	...	...	68.05*	...	...	...
1839	...	...	...	...	...	...	...	...	...	...	...	...	68.02	...	...	...
1840	...	...	...	...	...	...	...	...	...	...	...	...	70.88*	...	...	...
1842	...	...	...	...	...	...	...	...	...	...	...	51.55	...	...	...	...
1843	...	...	...	...	...	...	...	...	...	...	...	50.65	68.43	...	...	...
1844	...	...	...	...	...	...	...	...	...	...	...	54.39	69.26	...	...	...
1845	...	...	...	...	...	...	...	...	...	...	...	52.76	67.18	...	...	...
1846	...	...	...	...	...	...	...	...	...	...	...	55.32	68.55	...	...	...
1847	...	...	...	...	...	...	...	...	...	...	...	52.78	...	...	...	...
1848	...	...	...	...	...	...	...	...	55.58	...	...	53.46	...	...	...	...
1849	...	...	...	...	...	...	...	...	55.36	...	...	53.03	70.10*	...	...	...
1850	...	...	...	...	...	...	...	...	50.12*	...	...	53.00	69.85*	...	...	...
1851	...	...	...	...	...	...	...	...	56.08	...	...	53.68	66.86	...	...	...
1852	...	...	...	...	...	...	...	...	55.55	...	...	53.55	66.85	...	...	...
1853	...	...	...	...	...	59.23*	...	...	54.64	...	...	...	66.01*	...	...	...
1854	...	...	57.21	...	...	59.73	...	56.30*	56.47	...	...	56.18	68.01	...	...	...
1855	...	...	...	...	...	58.32*	...	54.16*	54.69	...	...	55.02*	67.71	...	...	...
1856	...	...	52.36	...	...	...	...	...	51.14	...	50.49	52.51	66.05	...	...	...
1857	...	...	...	...	...	54.64*	...	...	51.44	...	50.08	51.80	66.29	...	65.13	...
1858	...	...	...	55.81	...	...	55.99*	...	55.06	...	53.83	55.11	67.58*	...	66.96*	...
1859	...	...	...	55.66	...	57.55*	...	...	54.57	...	53.68	54.23	68.46	...	...	...
1860	...	...	...	...	...	57.33*	...	...	54.42	...	...	...	...	...	...	...
1861	...	...	55.43	56.10*	...	57.23*	56.09*	55.80	54.71	54.47*	...	54.87	...	...	...	...
1862	...	...	...	...	...	...	55.49	...	54.39*	56.35	...	55.26	...	...	...	...
1863	...	...	...	...	...	...	...	...	54.51	...	...	53.29*	...	...	...	...
1864	...	...	...	...	...	...	...	...	53.33	...	...	52.57	...	...	...	...
1865	...	...	...	...	54.99*	56.32	...	...	54.61	...	...	55.00	...	...	...	...
1866	...	...	...	...	53.82*	...	...	...	...	...	...	53.59	...	...	...	...
1867	...	...	...	...	54.00	...	...	...	54.08	...	...	54.16	...	...	...	...
1868	...	...	...	...	52.42	...	...	...	53.27	...	...	53.81	...	64.43	...	...
1869	...	...	...	...	52.93	56.82*	...	...	53.38	...	...	53.53*	...	...	...	...
1870	54.38	54.79*	...	...	53.77	57.08*	...	...	55.19	...	...	55.49	...	65.74*	...	...
	53.46	54.00	55.15	55.87	53.65	57.07	55.70	54.36	54.37	55.34	52.04	53.71	68.03	65.25	66.35	70.91

LOUISIANA.—Continued.							**MAINE.**								
Year.	Fort Jesup.	Fort Pike.	Fort Wood.	New Orleans.	New Orleans.	New Orleans.	Blake.	Belfast.	Bethel.	Biddeford.	Year.	Brunswick.	Year.	Brunswick.	Carmel.
	°	°	°	°	°	°	°	°	°	°		°		°	°
1823	67.33	...	...	...	...	...	...	...	...	...	...	...	...	...	...
1824	69.16	...	...	...	...	...	...	...	...	...	...	...	...	...	...
1825	67.74	70.26*	...	69.17	...	...	...	...	...	...	...	...	...	...	...
1826	68.91	...	...	72.16	...	...	...	...	...	...	...	...	...	...	...
1827	69.10	70.67	...	71.11*	...	...	...	...	...	...	...	...	...	...	...
1828	68.13	72.59	...	...	...	...	...	...	...	...	...	...	...	...	...
1829	65.08	69.16	...	...	...	...	...	...	...	...	...	...	...	...	...
1830	66.41	72.26	...	...	...	...	...	...	...	...	...	...	...	...	...
1831	62.57	67.80	...	...	...	...	...	...	...	...	...	...	...	...	...
1832	66.04	70.63	...	...	...	...	42.97	...	...	...	...	...	...	...	...
1833	67.15	70.37	68.91	...	...	...	42.87	...	...	...	...	...	...	...	...
1834	67.54	70.10	...	...	...	...	43.57	...	...	...	...	...	...	...	...
1835	63.95	68.71*	68.16	...	...	...	42.37	...	...	...	...	...	...	...	...
1836	63.69	...	...	...	66.17	...	41.27	...	...	...	1807	43.66*	...	...	...
1837	65.12	...	...	...	...	...	41.37	...	...	...	1808	43.43	...	...	...
1838	64.18	70.14*	...	67.49	...	...	42.97	...	...	...	1809	42.14	...	...	...
1839	67.30	...	...	69.28	...	...	44.97	...	...	...	1810	43.57	1835	44.42	...
1840	67.80	...	...	71.95	...	...	46.17	...	...	...	1811	44.71	1836	43.00	...
1841	65.05	...	...	70.33	...	...	45.47	...	...	...	1812	40.94	1837†	49.60	...
1842	66.41	...	...	68.12	...	...	...	...	...	...	1813	43.18	1838†	50.69	...
1843	64.29	67.84	68.19	68.98*	...	...	...	...	...	...	1814	43.29	1839†	51.45	...
1844	66.26	69.64	70.06	71.32*	...	...	...	...	...	...	1815	42.87	1840†	51.60	...
1845	65.71*	...	69.45*	...	...	...	...	...	...	...	1816	42.09	1841	46.58	...
—											1817	41.64	1842	45.84	...
1847	...	...	...	69.39	...	...	...	...	...	...	1818	44.78	1843	43.87	...
1848	...	...	...	70.45	...	...	...	...	...	44.60	1819	45.46	1844	42.32	...
1849	...	...	...	...	...	68.96	...	...	...	44.28	1820	44.03	1845	43.27	...
1850	...	...	...	68.60*	...	...	...	...	...	46.57	1821	43.91	1846	44.01	...
1851	...	...	...	...	...	...	...	...	...	45.76*	1822	43.06	1847	43.98	...
—											1823	41.03	1848	43.70	...
1854	...	...	...	67.74	...	...	...	...	...	...	1824	43.86*	1849	43.00	...
1855	...	...	...	68.35	...	...	...	...	...	...	1825	45.73	1850	43.37	...
1856	...	...	...	68.97	...	...	...	...	...	...	1826	45.46	1851	42.60	...
1857	...	...	...	69.24	...	...	...	...	...	...	1827	43.87	1852	43.91	...
1858	...	...	...	71.40	...	...	...	...	...	...	1828	46.94	1853	44.53	...
1859	...	...	...	71.07	...	...	...	...	...	...	1829	46.19	1854	42.73	45.06
1860	...	...	...	72.23*	...	...	...	43.21	...	...	1830	47.50	1855	42.95*	41.44*
1861	...	...	...	...	...	...	...	41.75	41.91	...	1831	47.66	1856	41.78	40.54*
1862	...	...	...	...	...	...	...	40.75*	...	...	1832	45.17	1857	43.62	...
—											1833	45.61	1858	43.75	...
1870	...	...	...	65.70	...	...	...	...	...	...	1834	45.36	1859	40.31	...
	66.32	69.88	69.32	69.06	66.17[1]	68.96[1]	43.58	41.72	41.68	45.57				44.40	41.46

[1] Hours of observation unknown.

† Values for 1837–8–9–40 doubtful, about 6.40 too high.

MAINE.—Continued.

Year.	Castine.	Year.	Castine.	Cornish.	Year.	Dennysville.	Year.	Dennysville.	Dexter.	Eastport.	Fort Fairfield.	Fort Kent.	Fort Preble.	Fort Sullivan.	Year.	Gardiner.
	°		°	°		°		°	°	°	°	°	°	°		°
...	...	...	...	...	...	...	1822	...	...	...	...	...	...	42.20	...	...
...	...	...	...	...	...	...	1823	...	...	...	...	...	...	40.90	...	...
...	...	...	...	...	...	...	1824	...	...	...	...	...	45.46	41.54	...	...
...	...	...	...	...	...	...	1825	...	...	...	...	...	46.87	43.98	...	...
...	...	...	...	...	...	...	1826	...	...	...	...	...	46.67	44.55	...	...
...	...	...	...	...	...	...	1827	...	...	...	...	...	45.52	44.29*	...	...
...	...	...	...	...	...	...	1828	...	...	...	...	...	48.18	43.38	...	...
...	...	...	...	...	...	...	1829	...	...	...	...	...	45.03	42.22	1837	40.68
...	...	...	...	...	...	...	1830	...	...	...	...	...	46.34	43.10	1838	42.74
...	...	...	...	...	...	...	1831	...	...	...	...	...	46.63	44.21	1839	44.09
...	...	...	...	...	...	...	1832	...	...	...	...	...	44.13*	40.98	1840	45.04
...	...	...	...	...	...	...	1833	...	...	41.48	...	...	45.10	42.52	1841	45.52
1810	43.08	1838	43.07	...	1816	40.43	1834	...	...	42.64	...	...	45.60	42.74	1842	43.88
1811	44.88	1839	43.36	...	1817	40.63	1835	...	...	...	...	...	44.05	41.23	1843	42.57
1812	41.48	1840	43.65	...	1818	41.23	——								1844	40.54
1813	43.57	1841	43.91	...	1819	43.23	1841	...	...	...	...	...	43.81	43.14	1845	41.74
1814	44.00	1842	44.10	...	1820	41.13	1842	...	...	...	37.50	36.26	43.87	42.08	1846	44.47
1815	42.44	1843	43.68	...	1821	41.03	1843	...	...	...	...	...	43.53*	42.86	1847	44.26
1816	41.85	1844	42.94	...	1822	41.73	1844	42.03	...	...	...	...	43.05	43.49	1848	43.82
1817	41.95	1845	45.19	...	1823	40.73	1845	42.53	...	...	...	...	44.55*	...	1849	43.38
1818	42.81	1846	48.40	...	1824	42.23	1846	42.73	...	...	...	...	...	...	1850	44.19
1819	44.73	1847	45.02	...	1825	43.43	1847	43.33	...	...	...	...	...	...	1851	43.98
1820	43.50	1848	45.01	...	1826	43.73	1848	44.03	...	...	...	...	...	...	1852	44.71
1821	42.83	1849	44.02	...	1827	41.53	1849	42.33	...	...	...	...	...	...	——	
1822	44.51	——			1828	44.13	1850	43.83	...	...	...	...	44.97	43.17	1855	45.18
1823	42.97	1856	...	...	1829	41.73	1851	41.93	...	...	...	...	44.31	42.79	1856	43.53
1824	44.97	1857	...	42.12	1830	42.73	1852	43.33	...	...	...	...	44.63	43.56	1857	44.36
1825	46.34	1858	...	42.06	1831	43.33	1853	43.93	...	...	...	...	...	...	1858	42.42
1826	46.56	1859	...	42.43	1832	40.13	1854	43.13	...	...	...	...	...	...	1859	41.43
1827	43.98	1860	...	43.84	1833	40.83	1855	43.13	...	...	...	...	...	...	——	
1828	47.46	1861	...	42.64	1834	40.13	——								1861	43.10
1829	44.46	1862	...	42.39	1835	40.63	1861	...	41.56	...	...	...	...	...	1862	42.89
1830	44.65	1863	...	43.17	1836	40.33	1862	...	43.07	...	...	...	...	...	1863	43.14*
1831	44.95	1864	...	43.29	1837	40.23	——							...	1864	44.56
1832	42.08	1865	...	44.99	1838	40.93	1865	...	...	...	...	...	48.37*	...	1865	44.47
1833	42.02	1866	...	44.04	1839	42.33	——								1866	43.61
1834	43.03	1867	...	42.53	1840	42.33	1867	...	...	...	...	...	44.94	...	1867	42.52
1835	42.61	1868	...	42.00	1841	42.73	1868	...	...	...	...	...	42.49	...	1868	42.38
1836	40.86	1869	...	44.14	1842	42.23	1869	...	...	...	...	...	43.87*	...	1869	43.79
1837	41.20	1870	...	46.46	1843	41.93	1870	...	...	...	...	...	45.51	...	1870	46.09
			43.79[1]	43.30				42.13	42.65	42.06[1]	37.73	36.87	45.26	42.83		43.53

[1] Hours of observation unknown.

MAINE.—Continued.

Year.	Hancock Barracks.	Hiram.	Lee.	Lisbon.	North Bridgeton.	Oldtown.	Oxford.	Perry.	Year.	Portland.	Saco.	Standish.	Steuben.	Vassalboro.	West Waterville.	Williamsburg.
	°	°	°	°	°	°	°	°		°	°	°	°	°	°	°
...	...	...	...	...	...	...	...	...	1820	42.98	...	...	...	...	...	...
...	...	...	...	...	...	...	...	...	1821	42.73	...	...	...	...	...	...
...	...	...	...	...	...	...	...	...	1822	43.64	...	...	...	...	...	...
...	...	...	...	...	...	...	...	...	1823	41.64	...	...	...	...	...	...
...	...	...	...	...	...	...	...	...	1824	43.23	...	...	...	...	...	...
...	...	...	...	...	...	...	...	...	1825	45.23	...	...	...	...	...	...
...	...	...	...	...	...	...	...	...	1826	44.98	...	...	...	...	...	...
...	...	...	...	...	...	...	...	...	1827	43.23	...	...	...	...	...	...
...	...	...	...	...	...	...	...	...	1828	45.39	...	...	...	...	...	...
1829	39.47	...	...	...	...	...	...	...	1829	43.23	...	...	...	...	...	...
1830	41.87	...	...	...	...	...	...	...	1830	44.48	...	...	...	...	...	...
1831	42.24	42.83	...	...	...	...	...	...	1831	44.23	...	...	...	...	...	...
1832	39.26	41.03	...	...	...	...	...	...	1832	41.98	...	...	...	...	...	...
1833	39.54	41.33	...	...	...	...	...	...	1833	42.23	...	...	...	...	...	...
1834	40.11	41.13	...	...	...	...	...	...	1834	42.73	...	...	...	...	...	...
1835	38.31	40.63	...	...	...	...	...	...	1835	41.89	...	...	...	...	...	...
1836	39.29	39.43	...	...	...	...	...	...	1836	40.23	...	...	...	...	...	...
1837	39.68	39.13	...	...	...	...	...	...	1837	40.23	...	...	...	...	...	...
1838	40.82	39.33	...	...	...	...	...	...	1838	42.03	...	...	...	...	...	...
1839	41.58	41.93	...	...	...	...	...	...	1839	43.06	...	...	...	...	...	...
1840	41.36	42.33	...	...	...	...	...	...	1840	43.23	...	...	...	...	...	...
1841	41.13	42.03	...	...	...	...	...	...	1841	43.06	...	...	...	...	...	...
1842	40.12	42.13	...	...	...	...	...	...	1842	43.06	...	...	...	...	...	...
1843	40.13	41.43	...	...	...	...	...	...	1843	42.05	...	...	...	...	...	...
1844	39.09	42.03	...	...	...	...	...	...	1844	42.73	42.24	...	...	...	...	...
1845	...	41.73	...	...	...	...	...	...	1845	43.31	44.24	...	...	...	...	...
1846	...	43.03	...	...	...	...	...	...	1846	44.39	46.14	...	...	...	...	...
1847	...	41.93	...	..	...	...	...	...	1847	43.06	44.74	...	...	...	...	...
1848	...	42.73	...	...	...	...	...	...	1848	44.56	...	...	...	...	...	...
1849	...	41.93	...	...	...	...	...	...	1849	43.64	...	...	...	...	...	...
1850	...	41.53	...	...	...	...	...	...	1850	44.39	...	...	...	...	...	...
1851	...	40.43	...	...	...	...	...	...	1851	43.11	...	...	...	...	...	...
1852	...	42.53	...	...	...	...	...	...	1852	43.65	...	...	...	...	...	...
1853	...	42.53	...	...	...	...	...	...	1853	...	...	...	...	...	...	...
1854	...	40.53	...	...	...	...	...	42.35*	1854	...	...	...	...	...	...	...
1855	...	41.93	...	...	...	...	...	40.93	1855	...	...	...	42.07	...	...	...
1856	...	40.53	...	...	...	...	...	40.22	1856	44.30	...	...	40.63	...	...	...
1857	...	41.33	...	...	...	...	...	41.38	1857	44.35	...	...	41.86	...	...	...
1858	...	40.13	...	...	...	...	...	40.06	1858	43.48	...	...	40.53	...	...	...
1859	...	40.93	...	43.18*	...	...	...	40.79	1859	42.96	...	...	41.47	...	...	...
1860	...	42.23	...	45.35	...	...	42.97*	...	1860	...	...	...	42.47	44.22*	...	...
1861	...	40.83	...	44.69	43.03	...	...	40.97	1861	...	...	...	42.10	42.13*	...	...
1862	...	41.73	...	44.94	...	...	...	40.52	1862	...	...	...	41.30	42.84*	...	...
1863	...	42.13	...	45.38*	...	...	...	...	1863	...	...	...	42.08	...	...	...
1864	...	42.33	...	44.09*	...	...	...	41.77	1864	...	...	...	42.40	...	44.82	...
1865	...	...	42.82	...	...	...	...	...	1865	...	...	...	42.83	...	44.61	...
1866	...	...	42.65*	43.01	...	...	...	...	1866	...	...	...	42.22	...	44.18	...
——									1867	...	...	43.40*	40.83	...	42.88	...
1868	...	...	...	...	...	...	40.84	...	1868	...	...	42.25	39.56	...	42.01	...
1869	41.82*	...	...	...	...	...	42.55	...	1869	...	...	...	42.24	...	44.35	38.72*
1870	43.89*	...	...	45.67	...	43.76	45.25	...	1870	...	...	...	...	...	46.58	41.13*
	40.48	41.45	42.53	44.32	43.03	40.57	42.81	41.57		43.23	44.14	44.03	41.72	42.94	44.21	40.15

MARYLAND.

Year.	Agricultural College.	Annapolis.	Baltimore.	Bladensburg.	Catonsville.	Chestertown.	Cumberland.	Emmettsburg.	Eyrie House.
	°	°	°	°	°	°	°	°	°
...	...	...	...	...	...	...	...	...	...
...	...	...	...	...	...	...	...	...	...
...	...	...	...	...	...	...	...	...	...
...	...	...	...	...	...	...	...	...	...
...	...	...	...	...	...	...	...	...	...
...	...	...	...	...	...	...	...	...	...
...	...	...	...	...	...	...	...	...	...
...	...	...	...	...	...	...	...	...	...
...	...	...	...	...	...	...	...	...	...
...	...	...	...	...	...	...	...	...	...
...	...	...	...	...	...	...	...	...	...
...	...	...	...	...	...	...	...	...	...
...	...	...	...	...	...	...	...	...	...
...	...	...	...	...	...	...	...	...	...
1817	...	...	52.68	...	...	...	...	...	...
1818	...	...	51.89	...	...	...	...	...	...
1819	...	...	54.04	...	...	...	...	...	...
1820	...	...	52.30	...	...	...	...	...	...
1821	...	...	52.86	...	...	...	...	...	...
1822	...	...	56.08	...	...	...	...	...	...
1823	...	...	53.76	...	...	...	...	...	...
1824	...	...	54.64	...	...	...	...	...	...
1846	...	...	54.04	...	...	...	...	...	51.41*
1847	...	...	52.89	...	...	...	...	...	...
1848	...	...	53.47	...	...	...	...	...	...
1849	...	...	52.27	...	...	...	...	...	...
1850	...	...	53.08	...	...	...	...	...	...
1851	...	...	53.93	...	...	...	...	...	...
1852	...	...	52.56	...	...	...	...	...	...
1853	...	...	54.04*	...	...	...	...	...	...
1855	...	...	...	53.23*	...	...	...	...	...
1856	...	50.89*	...	50.14	...	...	...	...	...
1857	...	53.02	...	51.85*	...	...	...	...	...
1858	...	55.10	54.42	52.77	...	53.85	...	...	...
1859	...	54.89	...	53.36	...	53.16	52.14	...	...
1860	...	...	...	...	...	...	52.53	...	...
1861	56.97*	55.80	...	43.08*	...	55.18	53.18	...	...
1862	...	55.33*	...	...	...	54.02	51.45	...	...
1863	...	55.87*	...	53.50*	...	...	51.44*	...	...
1864	...	55.61	...	54.92	...	...	51.63	...	...
1865	...	56.68	...	...	...	...	52.25	...	...
1866	...	55.62	...	...	51.59	...	50.65*	...	...
1867	...	55.80	...	...	51.12*	...	49.94*	50.41	...
1868	...	55.38	...	...	...	...	50.44*	49.27	...
1869	...	56.95	...	...	...	...	51.06*	50.50	...
1870	...	58.12	...	...	...	...	52.43	52.34	...
	56.60	55.38	53.46	53.02	50.93	54.04	51.59	50.67	51.41

Year.	Fort McHenry.	Fort Severn.	Fort Washington.	Frederick.	Leitersburg.	Leonardtown.
	°	°	°	°	°	°
1822	...	57.02	...	...	...	...
1824	...	...	57.74	...	...	...
1825	...	...	58.92	...	...	...
1826	...	...	59.68	...	...	...
1827	...	...	58.50*	...	...	...
1829	...	...	56.24	...	...	...
1830	...	...	59.25	...	...	...
1831	53.73	53.41	56.92*	...	...	...
1832	55.45	55.49	57.87*	...	...	...
1833	55.69	55.93	58.66	...	...	...
1834	55.28	54.91	57.34	...	...	...
1835	52.59	...	54.90*	...	...	...
1836	51.17	...	...	...	...	...
1837	52.69	...	...	...	...	...
1838	52.71	...	...	...	...	...
1839	54.15	...	...	...	...	...
1840	52.51	...	...	...	...	...
1841	52.03	...	...	...	...	...
1842	53.46	...	...	...	...	...
1843	53.04	53.27*	...	...	...	...
1844	53.45	55.57	...	...	...	...
1845	54.30	...	...	...	...	...
1846	53.82	...	...	...	...	...
1847	54.71	...	...	...	...	...
1848	56.31	...	...	...	...	...
1849	55.35	...	...	...	...	...
1850	56.56	...	...	...	...	...
1851	56.29	...	...	...	...	...
1852	53.97	...	55.71	...	...	...
1853	55.45	...	57.30*	...	...	...
1854	55.70	...	...	54.45	...	...
1855	55.69	...	...	52.89	...	...
1856	52.68	...	...	50.76	...	...
1857	53.56	...	...	50.82	...	...
1858	55.37	...	...	52.92	...	...
1859	...	...	...	52.83	51.44	55.17*
1860	...	...	...	52.79	50.92*	...
1861	55.25*	...	...	52.99	51.42	...
1862	...	...	...	52.39	...	...
1864	55.86	...	...	...	...	...
1865	56.75	...	...	...	...	...
1866	...	...	...	52.20*	...	...
1867	54.25	...	...	...	...	...
1868	53.92	...	...	...	...	...
1869	55.05	...	...	...	...	...
1870	57.12	...	...	...	...	...
	54.50	55.27	57.17	53.09	51.10	55.30

MD.—Continued.				MASSACHUSETTS.											
Year.	St. Mary's.	Shellman Hills.	Woodlawn.	Amherst.	Year.	Andover.	Baldwinsville.	Boston.	Bradford.	Bridgewater.	Year.	Cambridge.	Cambridge.	Chelsea.	Deerfield.
	°	°	°	°		°	°	°	°	°		°	°	°	°
...	...	...	...	...	...	...	...	...	...	...	1781	49.81*	...	...	...
...	...	...	...	...	...	...	...	...	...	...					
...	...	...	...	...	...	...	...	...	...	...	1783	50.00	...	...	...
...	...	...	...	...	...	...	...	...	...	...					
...	...	...	...	...	...	...	...	...	...	...	1790	...	48.72	...	...
...	...	...	...	...	...	...	...	...	...	...	1791	...	49.71	...	...
...	...	...	...	...	...	...	...	...	...	...	1792	...	48.01	...	...
...	...	...	...	...	...	...	...	...	...	...	1793	...	50.67	...	...
...	...	...	...	...	1772	...	...	...	48.88	...	1794	...	51.53	...	...
...	...	...	...	...							1795	...	49.79	...	...
...	...	...	...	...	1798	48.87	...	...	...	...	1796	...	47.01	...	...
...	...	...	...	...	1799	47.97	...	...	...	...	1797	...	46.82	...	...
...	...	...	...	...	1800	48.87	...	...	...	...	1798	...	47.85	...	...
...	...	...	...	...	1801	49.87	...	...	...	...	1799	...	46.76	...	...
...	...	...	...	...	1802	49.87	...	...	...	...	1800	...	48.52	...	...
...	...	...	...	...	1803	49.57	...	...	...	...	1801	...	49.32	...	...
...	...	...	...	...	1804	47.37	...	...	...	...	1802	...	49.68	...	...
...	...	...	...	...	1805	50.37	...	...	...	...	1803	...	48.57	...	...
...	...	...	...	...	1806	47.37	...	...	...	...	1804	...	47.01	...	...
...	...	...	...	...	1807	43.27	...	...	...	...	1805	...	49.47	...	...
...	...	...	...	...	1808	44.17	...	...	...	...	1806	...	46.80	...	47.13*
...	...	...	...	...							1807	...	46.66	...	46.43*
...	...	...	...	...	1820	...	...	47.95	...	...	1808	...	47.52	...	...
...	...	...	...	...	1821	...	...	47.63	...	...	1809	...	46.14	...	...
...	...	...	...	...	1822	...	...	49.40	...	...	1810	...	47.94	...	...
1836	...	...	...	41.12	1823	...	...	46.90	...	...	1811	...	48.80	...	...
1837	...	...	...	40.66	1824	...	...	48.82	...	...	1812	...	44.40	...	...
1838	...	...	...	42.35	1825	...	...	51.01	...	...	1813	...	47.20	...	...
1839	...	...	...	42.81	1826	...	...	50.30	...	...					
1840	...	...	...	45.62	1827	...	...	48.71	...	...	1816	...	46.17	...	...
1841	...	...	...	45.16	1828	...	...	51.72	...	...	1817	...	45.00	...	...
1842	...	...	...	45.95	1829	...	...	48.30	...	...					
1843	...	...	...	44.67	1830	...	...	49.85	...	...	1841	...	46.75	...	...
1844	...	...	...	45.26	1831	...	...	49.16	...	...	1842	...	46.73	...	...
1845	...	...	...	46.69	1832	...	...	48.12	...	...	1843	...	45.47	...	...
1846	...	53.64	...	47.39	1833	...	...	48.42	...	...	1844	...	46.15	...	...
1847	...	52.80	...	46.67	1834	...	...	48.30	...	...	1845	...	48.87	...	...
1848	...	52.77*	...	46.36	1835	...	...	47.27	...	...	1846	...	49.06	...	...
1849	...	51.55	...	45.56	1836	...	...	45.63	...	...	1847	...	47.74	...	...
1850	...	53.23*	...	46.06	1837	...	...	46.16	...	...	1848	...	47.83	...	...
1851	...	53.20	...	45.74	1838	...	...	47.81	...	...	1849	...	47.02	...	...
1852	...	52.64	...	46.57*	1839	...	...	48.96	...	...	1850	...	47.38	...	...
1853	...	53.63	...	46.52*	1840	...	...	49.79	...	...	1851	...	47.39	...	...
1854	...	54.32	...	46.38	1841	...	...	49.11	...	...	1852	...	47.69	...	...
1855	...	52.08	...	46.09	1842	...	...	49.95	...	...	1853	...	47.77	...	...
1856	...	48.83	...	44.56	1843	...	...	48.62	...	...	1854	...	47.47	...	...
1857	...	50.24	...	45.79	1844	...	...	49.30	...	...	1855	...	47.19	...	...
1858	...	52.35	...	46.18*	1845	...	...	50.36	...	...	1856	...	45.66	...	...
1859	...	52.27	...	45.73	1846	...	...	50.57	...	...	1857	...	47.07	...	...
1860	...	51.44	...	46.23	1847	...	...	50.28	...	...	1858	...	46.77	...	...
1861	...	52.10	...	45.98	1848	...	...	50.04	...	...	1859	...	46.86	...	...
1862	56.82*	50.77	...	45.98	1849	...	...	49.21	...	...					
1863	...	50.70*	...	46.52*							1861	...	...	50.00	...
1864	56.13*	51.47	...	46.98	1855	...	...	49.53*	...	...	1862	...	...	49.07*	...
1865	57.59*	52.09*	54.10*	47.51	1856	...	...	46.07*	...	46.05*					
1866	...	...	52.86	46.37							1864	...	...	47.50	...
1867	...	...	51.79	45.78	1858	...	...	...	...	46.59*					
1868	54.03*	...	50.04*	44.90							1868	...	46.94	...	...
1869	...	...	51.71	46.41	1864	...	44.05*	...	...	...	1869	...	48.40	...	...
1870	...	...	53.35	48.87	1865	...	44.91*	...	...	...	1870	...	51.41	...	...
	55.98	52.15	52.30	45.64		47.94	44.39	48.35	48.88	46.83		50.01[1]	47.54	49.03	45.61

[1] Hours of observation unknown.

MASSACHUSETTS.—Continued.

Year.	Fitchburg.	Fort Independence.	Fort Warren.	Georgetown.	Hinsdale.	Kingston.	Lawrence.	Lowell.	Lunenburg.	Medfield.	Mendon.	Milton.	Nantucket.	Nantucket.	Year.	New Bedford.
	°	°	°	°	°	°	°	°	°	°	°	°	°	°		°
...	...	...	...	...	...	...	...	...	...	...	...	...	...	...	1813	48.25
...	...	...	...	...	...	...	...	...	...	...	...	...	...	...	1814	48.35
...	...	...	...	...	...	...	...	...	...	...	...	...	...	...	1815	47.35
...	...	...	...	...	...	...	...	...	...	...	...	...	...	...	1816	46.65
...	...	...	...	...	...	...	...	...	...	...	...	...	...	...	1817	47.25
...	...	...	...	...	...	...	...	...	...	...	...	...	...	...	1818	47.95
...	...	...	...	...	...	...	...	...	...	...	...	...	...	...	1819	49.35
...	...	...	...	...	...	...	...	...	...	...	...	...	...	...	1820	48.55
...	...	...	...	...	...	...	...	...	...	...	...	...	...	...	1821	47.95
...	...	...	...	...	...	...	...	...	...	...	...	...	...	...	1822	50.05
...	...	...	...	...	...	...	...	...	...	...	...	...	...	...	1823	47.45
1824	...	48.71	...	...	...	...	...	...	...	...	...	...	...	...	1824	49.35
1825	...	50.67	...	...	...	...	...	...	...	...	...	...	...	...	1825	50.85
1826	...	49.62	...	...	...	...	...	...	...	...	...	...	...	...	1826	50.65
1827	...	47.95*	...	...	...	...	...	...	...	...	...	...	49.60*	...	1827	48.75
1828	...	50.64	...	...	...	...	...	...	...	...	...	...	52.03	...	1828	50.45
1829	...	47.70*	...	...	...	...	...	...	...	...	...	...	...	...	1829	47.05
1830	...	50.44	...	...	...	...	...	...	...	...	...	...	...	...	1830	49.55
1831	...	49.26	...	...	...	...	...	...	...	47.02	...	...	...	...	1831	48.65
1832	...	48.41	...	...	...	...	...	...	...	45.84	...	...	...	...	1832	47.46
1833	...	49.07*	...	...	...	...	...	...	...	...	47.76	...	...	...	1833	48.18
1834	...	47.79	...	...	...	...	...	...	...	...	47.36	...	...	...	1834	48.17
1835	...	...	...	...	...	...	...	...	...	...	45.06	...	...	...	1835	46.65
1836	...	45.93	...	...	...	...	...	...	...	...	43.26	...	...	...	1836	44.90
1837	...	...	...	...	...	...	...	...	...	...	44.56	...	...	...	1837	45.72
1838	...	...	...	...	...	...	...	...	46.57	...	45.76	...	...	...	1838	47.09
1839	...	...	...	...	...	...	...	...	47.43	...	46.76	...	...	...	1839	47.70
1840	...	...	...	...	...	...	...	...	47.90	...	46.26	...	...	...	1840	47.47
1841	...	...	...	...	...	...	...	...	47.41	...	45.66	...	...	...	1841	46.63
1842	...	...	...	...	...	...	...	...	48.59	...	46.76	...	...	...	1842	47.24
1843	...	...	...	...	...	...	...	...	46.84	...	43.86	...	...	...	1843	47.17
1844	...	...	...	...	...	...	...	...	47.54	...	45.80	...	...	...	1844	48.47
1845	...	...	...	...	...	...	...	...	47.67	...	47.10	...	...	...	1845	49.13
1846	...	...	...	...	...	...	...	48.13	47.75	...	47.30	...	...	...	1846	49.33
1847	...	...	...	...	...	...	...	47.03	49.80	...	46.30	...	50.33	...	1847	49.13
1848	...	...	...	...	...	...	...	46.73	49.25	...	46.70	...	51.42	...	1848	49.20
1849	...	...	...	...	...	...	...	46.53	45.33	...	46.20	...	51.75	...	1849	48.52
1850	...	...	...	...	...	...	...	46.63	48.42	...	46.49	...	52.13	...	1850	48.41
1851	...	...	...	...	...	...	...	46.33	49.75	...	...	...	51.95	...	1851	48.08
1852	...	48.23	...	...	...	...	...	47.53	48.38	...	...	...	50.04	...	1852	48.36
1853	...	49.49	...	...	...	...	...	...	48.16	...	...	...	49.86	...	1853	46.10
1854	...	48.81	...	...	...	...	...	...	47.50	...	46.18	...	...	49.95	1854	48.53
1855	...	48.88	...	...	...	...	...	...	46.99	...	46.71	...	...	50.25	1855	48.06
1856	...	47.01*	...	...	...	...	43.61	...	42.15	...	44.93	...	...	49.02	1856	46.71
1857	...	48.01	...	...	...	...	45.80	...	46.34	...	46.29	...	...	49.45	1857	47.23
1858	...	48.22	...	...	...	...	45.39	...	45.73	...	46.39	...	...	49.45	1858	47.65
1859	...	47.42	...	...	...	...	45.48	...	45.80	...	46.47	...	...	50.37	1859	47.68
1860	...	49.31	...	...	...	...	46.21	...	46.86	...	47.25	...	...	...	1860	48.51
1861	47.87*	...	...	...	...	...	46.06	...	46.45	...	47.21	...	...	...	1861	49.25
1862	...	...	...	...	...	...	45.52*	...	46.90	...	46.78	...	...	...	1862	49.33
1863	...	...	47.94	...	...	...	45.72*	...	47.24	...	47.17	...	...	...	1863	49.61*
1864	...	...	47.76*	...	...	...	45.81	...	48.12	...	47.17	...	...	...	1864	48.19
1865	...	...	49.39	47.04*	...	...	...	...	47.69	...	48.73	...	...	...	1865	50.34
1866	...	...	...	...	...	...	46.17	...	46.43	...	46.94	...	...	...	1866	47.91
1867	...	48.77	47.36*	45.34*	...	46.30	45.44	...	45.30	...	45.19	...	...	...	1867	47.83
1868	...	45.64	45.47	44.01*	...	47.28	44.49	...	44.74	...	43.90	44.15	...	...	1868	46.32
1869	...	48.14	46.82	...	42.80	47.64	46.37	...	46.46	...	46.12	49.15	...	...	1869	47.95
1870	...	49.31	49.69	...	44.78*	49.04	48.37*	...	48.77	...	48.26	51.10	...	...	1870	49.00
	47.87	48.35	47.84	46.05	43.61	47.65	45.77	46.86	46.91	46.86	46.32	47.60	51.02[1]	49.74		48.21

[1] Hours of observation unknown.

MASSACHUSETTS.—Continued.

Year.	Newbury.	Newburyport.	North Attleboro.	North Billerica.	Princeton.	Richmond.	Roxbury.	Year.	Salem.	Year.	Sandwich.	Springfield.	Topsfield.	Watertown Arsenal.	Westfield.	Weymouth.
	°	°	°	°	°	°	°		°		°	°	°	°	°	°
...	...	...	...	...	...	...	...	1786	47.70	...	...	...	...	...	...	...
...	...	...	...	...	...	...	...	1787	47.02	...	...	...	...	...	...	...
...	...	...	...	...	...	...	...	1788	47.01	...	...	...	...	...	...	...
...	...	...	...	...	...	...	...	1789	46.83	...	...	...	...	...	...	...
...	...	...	...	...	...	...	...	1790	45.97	...	...	...	...	...	...	...
...	...	...	...	...	...	...	...	1791	48.04	...	...	...	...	...	...	...
...	...	...	...	...	...	...	...	1792	47.71	...	...	...	...	...	...	...
...	...	...	...	...	...	...	...	1793	50.13	...	...	...	...	...	...	...
...	...	...	...	...	...	...	...	1794	49.93	...	...	...	...	...	...	...
...	...	...	...	...	...	...	...	1795	49.34	...	...	...	...	...	...	...
...	...	...	...	...	...	...	...	1796	47.84	...	...	...	...	...	...	...
...	...	...	...	...	...	...	...	1797	47.30	...	...	...	...	...	...	...
...	...	...	...	...	...	...	...	1798	48.64	...	...	...	...	...	...	...
...	...	...	...	...	...	...	...	1799	48.63	...	...	...	...	...	...	...
...	...	...	...	...	...	...	...	1800	49.16	...	...	...	...	...	...	...
...	...	...	...	...	...	...	...	1801	49.60	...	...	...	...	...	...	...
...	...	...	...	...	...	...	...	1802	49.96	...	...	...	...	...	...	...
...	...	...	...	...	...	...	...	1803	49.41	1837	...	...	...	45.51	...	...
...	...	...	...	...	...	...	...	1804	47.49	1838	...	...	...	46.92	...	...
...	...	...	...	...	...	...	...	1805	49.96	1839	...	...	...	48.02	...	...
...	...	...	...	...	...	...	...	1806	47.15	1840	...	...	...	48.10	...	...
...	...	...	...	...	...	...	...	1807	47.30	1841	...	...	...	47.87*	...	...
...	...	...	...	...	...	...	...	1808	48.65							
...	...	...	...	...	...	...	...	1809	47.09	1843	...	...	...	46.25	...	...
...	...	...	...	...	...	...	...	1810	48.17	1844	...	...	...	46.40*	...	...
1849	...	...	...	...	...	...	49.41*	1811	49.24							
								1812	44.45	1854	...	47.33	...	...	...	...
1854	...	46.71	47.08	...	43.61	45.14*	...	1813	46.77	1855	...	47.82	...	...	45.54	...
1855	...	46.25	45.61	...	43.49	45.79*	...	1814	47.44	1856	...	...	...	...	44.41	...
1856	...	44.16	45.02	...	41.87	44.12	...	1815	46.77	1857	...	...	...	...	45.27	47.85
1857	...	46.88	...	...	...	45.01*	...	1816	46.28	1858	...	...	...	...	43.67	...
1858	...	46.11*	...	...	...	45.67*	...	1817	46.44	1859	...	...	...	...	45.13	...
1859	...	...	...	...	...	45.65*	...	1818	47.17	1860	...	...	46.07*	...	...	...
1860	...	...	...	...	...	46.12*	...	1819	49.87	1861	...	...	46.20	...	46.11	...
1861	...	...	...	...	...	47.07	...	1820	48.01	1862	...	...	...	...	46.06	...
1862	...	...	...	...	...	46.68*	...	1821	47.28	1863	...	...	...	...	46.23*	...
								1822	48.97	1864	48.11	49.89*	48.15*	...	46.98	...
1865	47.49*	...	...	...	...	48.08*	...	1823	46.73	1865	...	...	50.40	...	47.48	...
1866	46.36	...	...	47.39*	...	46.77*	...	1824	48.42	1866	...	...	49.83	...	...	...
1867	45.46	...	...	46.41	...	46.96*	...	1825	50.16	1867	...	...	48.50	47.77*	...	...
1868	43.37*	...	...	45.22	...	...	...	1826	49.46	1868	...	...	43.42	46.64*	...	...
1869	...	...	...	47.32	...	46.12*	...	1827	47.57	1869	...	...	45.64	48.87	...	...
1870	...	...	...	49.48	...	49.12*	...	1828	50.28	1870	...	...	47.59*	51.52*	...	...
	46.15	46.00	47.78	47.16	43.25	46.30	49.41		48.08		48.25	48.71	47.20	47.61	46.39	47.27

	MASS.—Cont'd.		MICHIGAN.													
Year.	Williams-town.	Worcester.	Ann Arbor.	Battle Creek.	Central Mine.	Coldwater.	Cooper.	Copper Falls Mine.	Dearborn-ville.	Detroit.	Eagle River.	Eureka Valley.	Flint.	Fort Brady.	Fort Gratiot.	Fort Mackinac.
	°	°	°	°	°	°	°	°	°	°	°	°	°	°	°	°
1816	43.94	...	...	...	...	...	...	...	...	...	...	...	...	...	...	...
1817	43.38	...	...	...	...	...	...	...	...	...	...	...	...	...	...	...
1818	43.78	...	...	...	...	...	...	...	...	...	...	...	...	...	...	...
1819	46.20	...	...	...	...	...	...	...	...	...	...	...	...	...	...	...
1820	45.55	...	...	...	...	...	...	...	...	...	...	...	...	...	...	...
1821	45.06	...	...	...	...	...	...	...	...	...	...	...	...	...	...	...
1822	46.32	...	...	...	...	...	...	...	...	...	...	...	...	...	...	...
1823	44.33	...	...	...	...	...	...	...	...	...	...	...	...	39.27	...	...
1824	45.46	...	...	...	...	...	...	...	...	...	...	...	...	40.54	...	...
1825	47.63	...	...	...	...	...	...	...	...	...	...	...	...	43.05	...	...
1826	47.72	...	...	...	...	...	...	...	...	...	...	...	...	40.89*	...	41.25
1827	45.42	...	...	...	...	...	...	...	...	...	...	...	...	41.05	...	...
1828	48.36	...	...	...	...	...	...	...	...	...	...	...	...	42.22	...	41.26
1829	44.91	...	...	...	...	...	...	...	...	...	...	...	...	40.48*	...	41.06
1830	46.70	...	...	...	...	...	...	...	...	...	...	...	...	42.97	48.56*	42.81
1831	45.63	...	...	...	...	...	...	...	...	...	...	...	...	41.04	46.17	40.15
1832	45.51	...	...	...	...	...	...	...	...	...	...	...	...	41.52	47.47	39.73
1833	45.19	...	...	...	...	...	...	...	...	...	...	...	...	40.93	47.70	40.74
1834	46.00	...	...	...	...	...	...	...	...	...	...	...	...	40.75	48.40	40.34
1835	43.73	...	...	...	...	...	...	...	...	...	...	...	...	39.67	46.46	38.69
1836	42.14	...	...	...	...	...	...	...	42.76*	...	...	...	...	36.62	42.28	36.71
1837	42.24	...	...	...	...	...	...	...	43.92	...	...	...	...	36.04	...	...
1838	43.54	...	...	...	...	...	...	...	45.30	...	...	...	...	37.49	...	...
1839	...	...	...	...	...	...	...	...	47.92	...	...	...	...	41.21	...	...
1840	...	47.26	...	...	...	...	...	...	...	48.70	...	...	...	40.68	45.94	...
1841	...	46.12	...	...	...	...	...	...	...	48.31	...	...	...	39.55	45.73	...
1842	...	47.45	...	...	...	...	...	...	...	49.05	...	...	...	38.26	46.04	41.91
1843	...	46.14	...	...	...	...	...	...	...	46.43	...	...	...	37.65	43.78	39.44
1844	...	46.80	...	...	...	...	...	...	...	49.62	...	...	...	38.76	46.90	41.43
1845	...	47.38	...	...	...	...	...	...	...	49.41	...	...	...	39.80	46.67	41.27
1846	...	47.84	...	...	...	...	...	...	...	50.27	...	...	...	44.24*	...	43.46
1847	...	47.21	...	...	...	...	...	...	...	41.91	...	...	...	39.34	...	38.26
1848	...	47.21	...	...	...	...	...	...	...	45.99	...	...	...	...	...	...
1849	...	47.59	...	...	...	...	...	...	...	48.71	...	...	...	...	...	39.87
1850	...	46.67	...	...	...	...	...	...	...	49.71	...	...	...	42.06	46.39	42.67
1851	...	46.91	...	...	...	...	...	...	...	49.18	...	...	...	39.53	46.03	41.47
1852	...	47.71	...	...	...	...	...	...	...	49.24	...	...	...	40.23	...	40.67*
1853	...	47.31	...	...	...	...	...	...	...	51.71	...	...	...	40.76	...	41.46
1854	...	47.35	48.13	51.22	...	...	...	...	...	49.43	...	...	48.46	39.14	...	41.27
1855	44.22	46.37	45.93	48.03	...	...	47.22*	...	...	47.56	...	...	45.88	38.33*	...	39.84
1856	42.40	45.70	...	45.48*	...	...	43.45	36.46	...	45.26*	38.59	...	...	38.11*	...	38.08*
1857	44.22*	46.67	...	45.91	...	...	44.56	...	...	...	...	...	...	...	...	...
1858	43.94	47.11	...	49.20	...	...	49.33	...	...	50.56*	...	...	...	...	...	...
1859	43.59*	47.21	...	48.20	...	...	...	...	...	49.72	...	...	...	...	...	40.71
1860	...	47.09	...	...	...	...	...	...	...	48.04	...	...	...	...	...	41.10
1861	44.49	47.53	...	...	...	...	48.38	...	...	48.56	...	...	...	...	...	...
1862	...	47.39	...	...	...	...	47.02*	...	...	48.44	...	40.35*	...	...	...	...
1863	...	...	...	...	...	...	...	...	...	48.23	...	...	...	...	...	...
1864	45.58	...	...	...	...	...	...	...	...	47.63	...	...	...	...	...	...
1865	46.06*	49.38	...	...	...	...	...	...	...	49.12	...	...	...	...	...	...
1866	44.72	47.74	...	...	...	...	...	...	...	45.55	...	...	...	...	...	...
1867	44.32	46.80	...	...	...	...	...	...	...	46.55	...	...	...	...	...	...
1868	43.54	45.13	...	...	36.82	...	...	...	...	...	...	...	...	...	...	...
1869	44.45*	46.92	...	...	36.67	45.25	...	...	...	...	...	...	...	...	...	...
1870	46.94	48.59	...	...	39.95	48.11	...	...	...	48.54*	...	...	...	...	...	...
	44.92	47.20	46.94	48.10	37.75	47.32	46.84	35.79	44.97	48.28	38.68	40.06	47.17	40.11	46.08	40.61

MICHIGAN.—Continued.

Year.	Fort Wilkins.	Grand Haven.	Grand Rapids.	Holland.	Homestead.	Lansing.	Laphamsville.	Litchfield.	Marquette.	Mill Point.	Monroe.	Muskegan.	New Buffalo.	Northport.	Ontonagon.	Otsego.
	°	°	°	°	°	°	°	°	°	°	°	°	°	°	°	°
1845	40.34	...	...	...	...	...	...	...	...	...	...	...	...	...	...	...
1851	...	...	...	...	...	...	47.78*	...	...	...	...	...	...	...	...	...
1854	...	...	49.58*	...	...	...	...	...	...	...	...	...	...	...	...	...
1855	...	...	45.62	...	...	...	...	...	...	...	...	...	...	...	...	...
1856	...	...	43.58	...	...	...	...	...	...	...	...	...	...	...	...	...
1857	...	...	44.71	...	...	...	...	...	...	...	...	...	...	...	...	...
1858	...	...	47.73	...	...	...	...	...	40.73	...	...	...	48.76	...	...	...
1859	...	...	47.49*	...	...	...	...	...	39.46	...	...	...	47.78*	...	...	...
1860	...	46.89	...	45.57*	...	...	...	...	40.61	44.75	48.08	...	...	...	39.94	...
1861	...	46.99	...	45.95	...	...	...	...	40.32	...	46.04	...	...	...	40.13	...
1862	...	46.79	...	45.77*	...	...	...	...	39.51	...	48.42	...	...	...	38.23	...
1863	...	...	...	45.36*	...	...	...	...	41.42	...	48.86	...	...	...	39.83	...
1864	...	...	...	...	...	46.76	...	...	42.39	...	48.66	...	...	...	40.20	...
1865	...	...	...	...	44.77	47.28	...	...	43.33	...	49.66	...	...	...	40.68	...
1866	...	...	45.59*	45.33*	42.50	45.20	...	...	40.34	...	48.26	...	...	...	39.15	...
1867	...	...	47.15	46.75*	...	46.25	...	45.95	41.48	...	49.76	...	...	43.48	39.02	48.20*
1868	...	...	46.56	46.11	...	45.23*	...	44.62	...	...	45.09	...	...	42.86	40.53	44.21
1869	...	...	46.70	...	...	45.34	...	45.11	...	...	47.19	49.58*	...	42.34	41.27	48.61
1870	...	...	50.01	48.37*	...	47.52*	...	47.76	...	...	52.05*	...	...	45.71	43.78	51.62*
	41.10	46.95	46.90	46.37	43.99	46.55	47.82[1]	45.77	40.88	43.63	48.17	50.34	48.31	43.43	40.03	48.16

[1] Hours of observation unknown.

	MICHIGAN.—Continued.									MINNESOTA.						
Year.	Pleasanton.	Pontiac.	Port Huron.	Romeo.	St. James.	Saugatuck.	Tawas City.	Thunder Bay Island.	Ypsilanti.	Afton.	Beaver Bay.	Burlington.	Forest City.	Fort Ridgeley.	Fort Ripley.	Fort Snelling.
	°	°	°	°	°	°	°	°	°	°	°	°	°	°	°	°
1820	...	...	...	...	...	...	...	...	...	...	...	...	...	...	...	43.00*
1821	...	...	...	...	...	...	...	...	...	...	...	...	...	...	...	42.86
1822	...	...	...	...	...	...	...	...	...	...	...	...	...	...	...	43.71
1823	...	...	...	...	...	...	...	...	...	...	...	...	...	...	...	43.38
1824	...	...	...	...	...	...	...	...	...	...	...	...	...	...	...	42.76
1825	...	...	...	...	...	...	...	...	...	...	...	...	...	...	...	47.07
1826	...	...	...	...	...	...	...	...	...	...	...	...	...	...	...	44.45
1827	...	...	...	...	...	...	...	...	...	...	...	...	...	...	...	45.69
1828	...	...	...	...	...	...	...	...	...	...	...	...	...	...	...	45.96
1829	...	...	...	...	...	...	...	...	...	...	...	...	...	...	...	45.30
1830	...	...	...	...	...	...	...	...	...	...	...	...	...	...	...	47.95
1831	...	...	...	...	...	...	...	...	...	...	...	...	...	...	...	42.44
1832	...	...	...	...	...	...	...	...	...	...	...	...	...	...	...	45.44
1833	...	...	...	...	...	...	...	...	...	...	...	...	...	...	...	47.54
1834	...	...	...	...	...	...	...	...	...	...	...	...	...	...	...	46.68
1835	...	...	...	...	...	...	...	...	...	...	...	...	...	...	...	43.00
1836	...	...	...	...	...	...	...	...	...	...	...	...	...	...	...	42.54
1837	...	...	...	...	...	...	...	...	...	...	...	...	...	...	...	43.65
1838	...	...	...	...	...	...	...	...	...	...	...	...	...	...	...	41.34
1839	...	...	...	...	...	...	...	...	...	...	...	...	...	...	...	46.79
1840	...	...	...	...	...	...	...	...	...	...	...	...	...	...	...	44.41
1841	...	...	...	...	...	...	...	...	...	...	...	...	...	...	...	43.89
1842	...	...	...	...	...	...	...	...	...	...	...	...	...	...	...	42.83
1843	...	...	...	...	...	...	...	...	...	...	...	...	...	...	...	39.93
1844	...	...	...	...	...	...	...	...	...	...	...	...	...	...	...	42.72
1845	...	...	...	...	...	...	...	...	...	...	...	...	...	...	...	45.80
1846	...	...	...	...	...	...	...	...	...	...	...	...	...	...	...	48.33
1847	...	...	...	...	...	...	...	...	...	...	...	...	...	...	...	41.93
1848	...	...	...	...	...	...	...	...	...	...	...	...	...	...	...	42.56
1849	...	...	...	...	...	...	...	...	...	...	...	...	...	...	...	42.26
1850	...	...	...	...	...	...	...	...	...	...	...	...	...	...	38.15	43.73
1851	...	...	...	...	...	...	...	...	...	...	...	...	...	...	39.11*	46.74
1852	...	...	...	...	...	...	...	...	...	...	...	...	...	...	39.21	43.79
1853	...	...	...	...	...	...	...	...	...	...	...	...	...	...	39.43	42.34
1854	...	...	...	...	42.68*	49.96*	...	...	...	...	...	...	...	47.96	40.35	44.82
1855	...	...	...	...	42.60	49.36*	...	...	...	...	...	...	...	42.51	38.61	43.18
1856	...	...	...	43.53	...	...	...	...	...	...	...	...	...	40.93	37.89	42.42
1857	...	...	...	...	...	...	...	...	...	...	...	...	...	39.84	...	41.09
1858	...	...	47.37	...	...	...	...	...	...	...	...	39.00	...	43.41	41.65	...
1859	...	...	...	...	...	...	43.24	40.14	47.51	...	36.21	36.56	40.08	42.46	39.39	...
1860	...	...	...	...	...	...	44.06	41.29	46.52*	...	...	...	42.63*	45.24	40.82	...
1861	...	...	...	...	...	...	44.09	42.19	47.90*	...	37.63	...	41.92	43.02	40.41	...
1862	...	...	...	...	...	...	43.49	42.49	46.82	...	37.16*	...	...	40.96	38.76	...
1863	...	...	...	...	...	...	43.69	42.49	...	...	37.35*	...	43.21*	43.75	41.00	...
1864	...	46.24*	...	...	...	...	43.89	43.20	...	...	38.58	...	...	44.29	40.76	...
1865	...	...	...	...	...	...	44.29	43.80	...	...	39.78	...	...	44.95*	41.48*	...
1866	...	...	...	...	...	...	42.99	...	...	40.91*	37.92	...	...	...	...	...
1867	...	...	...	...	...	...	44.19	...	...	...	36.84	...	...	...	38.16	44.56*
1868	...	...	...	...	...	...	...	...	...	...	36.95	...	...	...	38.58	43.94
1869	41.17*	...	...	...	...	...	...	41.53*	...	40.80	38.12	...	...	...	...	42.62
1870	...	...	...	...	...	...	...	44.41	...	...	40.37	...	...	...	41.23*	46.65
	42.35	46.17	47.10	43.85	42.12	48.67	43.92	42.30	47.13	41.49	37.84	38.10	42.06	43.07	39.77	44.11

Year.	MINNESOTA.—Continued.											MISSISSIPPI.				
	Hazelwood.	Hennepin Co.	Koniska.	Madelia.	Minneapolis.	New Ulm.	Princeton.	St. Anthony's Falls.	St. Joseph.	St. Paul.	Sibley.	Brookhaven.	Columbus.	Enterprise.	Fayette.	Garlandsville.
	o	o	o	o	o	o	o	o	o	o	o	o	o	o	o	o
1853	...	...	...	...	...	...	...	45.47*	...	...	...	...	...	...	...	...
1854	...	...	...	...	...	...	...	44.57*	37.83*	...	...	...	...	...	...	68.55
1855	41.94*	...	...	...	...	...	...	...	...	...	...	...	63.84	...	...	...
1856	39.56*	...	...	...	...	...	...	...	...	...	...	...	60.37	...	...	...
1857	39.12*	...	...	...	...	...	39.20	...	...	...	...	...	60.13	...	...	...
1858	42.65	...	...	...	...	...	43.99*	...	...	...	...	...	62.63	...	...	...
1859	40.89	...	...	...	...	...	42.47	...	...	...	...	...	62.42	...	...	...
1860	...	...	...	...	...	...	...	...	...	...	...	...	63.17*	...	...	...
1861	42.39*	...	...	...	...	...	...	...	...	...	...	...	63.73	...	...	...
1862	...	...	...	...	...	...	...	...	...	...	...	...	64.46	...	...	...
1863	...	...	...	...	...	...	...	...	...	42.22*	...	...	61.70	...	...	...
1864	...	...	...	...	...	44.87*	...	...	...	42.76	...	...	60.73	...	...	...
1865	...	43.61	...	...	43.92	45.62	...	...	...	43.22	...	...	63.35	...	...	...
1866	...	...	...	...	41.17	43.77	...	...	...	40.43	41.06*	...	61.86	...	...	...
1867	...	...	...	...	40.11	42.78	...	...	...	39.91	40.77	...	63.13	...	61.49	...
1868	...	...	...	...	40.78	43.37	...	...	...	41.67	41.08	63.93	62.43	...	...	...
1869	...	...	38.68*	42.25	40.71	42.51	...	...	...	42.38	41.12	64.68	61.15	...	...	...
1870	...	...	42.12*	45.40	43.84	45.62	...	...	...	45.99	44.47	63.26	62.19	64.90*	...	...
	41.24	43.61	40.40	43.83	41.67	44.08	41.63	44.63	37.94	42.32	42.01	63.94	62.19	64.90	61.64	68.25

Year.	MISSISSIPPI.—Continued.							MISSOURI.								
	Grenada.	Marion Court-House.	Natchez.	Oxford.	Paulding.	Philadelphia.	Vicksburg.	Allenton, near.	Athens.	Bolivar.	Brunswick.	Cape Girardeau.	Cassville.	East Prairie.	Easton.	Hannibal.
1799	...	...	64.89*	...	...	...	...	...	...	...	...	...	...	...	...	...
1800	...	...	65.05	...	...	...	...	...	...	...	...	...	...	...	...	...
1801	...	...	67.54	...	...	...	...	...	...	...	...	...	...	...	...	...
1802	...	...	65.70*	...	...	...	...	...	...	...	...	...	...	...	...	...
1803	...	...	67.58	...	...	...	...	...	...	...	...	...	...	...	...	...
1836	...	...	65.03	...	...	...	...	...	...	...	...	...	...	...	...	...
1837	...	...	66.64	...	...	...	...	...	...	...	...	...	...	...	...	...
1838	...	...	63.85	...	...	...	...	...	...	...	...	...	...	...	...	...
1839	...	...	67.21	...	...	...	...	...	...	...	...	...	...	...	...	...
1840	...	...	66.76	...	...	...	...	...	...	...	...	...	...	...	...	...
1841	...	...	67.63	...	...	...	67.35	...	...	...	...	...	...	...	...	...
1842	...	...	67.62	...	...	...	66.60*	...	...	...	...	...	...	...	...	...
1843	...	...	66.61	...	...	...	...	...	...	...	...	...	...	...	...	...
1844	...	...	67.97	...	...	...	...	...	...	...	...	...	...	...	...	...
1845	...	...	66.79	...	...	...	...	...	...	...	56.76	...	...	...	...	...
1846	...	...	67.56	...	...	...	...	...	...	...	...	...	...	...	...	...
1847	...	...	66.40	...	...	...	...	...	...	...	...	...	...	...	...	...
1848	...	...	...	...	...	...	...	...	...	...	...	...	...	...	...	...
1849	...	...	66.07*	...	...	...	...	...	...	...	...	...	...	...	...	...
1850	...	...	65.34	...	...	...	...	...	...	...	...	...	...	...	...	...
1851	...	...	...	...	...	...	...	...	...	...	...	...	...	...	...	...
1854	...	...	...	...	...	...	...	...	...	...	...	...	...	...	...	54.72*
1855	...	...	...	61.44*	...	...	...	...	...	...	...	...	...	...	...	...
1856	...	...	...	...	...	...	...	...	...	...	...	...	...	...	...	...
1857	...	...	...	...	...	...	...	...	...	...	...	53.14*	...	...	...	...
1858	...	...	66.27*	...	66.87*	...	...	...	...	...	...	...	...	...	...	...
1859	...	...	65.30	...	67.37*	...	...	...	...	...	...	...	...	...	...	...
1860	...	...	66.39	...	...	...	...	...	...	...	...	...	58.01*	...	...	...
1861	...	...	65.92	...	65.59*	...	...	...	...	...	...	...	...	...	...	...
1862	...	...	66.57*	...	...	...	...	...	...	...	...	...	...	...	...	...
1864	...	...	...	...	...	...	...	51.71*	...	...	...	...	...	...	...	...
1865	...	...	65.06	...	...	...	...	...	53.74*	...	...	...	...	...	53.41*	...
1866	...	...	64.37*	...	...	...	...	50.46*	...	...	...	...	...	...	...	...
1869	62.35*	...	65.24*	...	...	...	66.52	52.29	...	...	...	...	...	...	...	...
1868	62.86*	...	63.68	...	...	...	64.64	52.23	...	...	...	...	...	55.86	...	...
1869	63.06	63.67	63.52	...	...	...	64.53	51.88	...	56.59	...	...	...	55.56	...	...
1870	63.40	...	...	...	...	61.99*	...	53.60	...	...	...	...	...	55.26	...	...
	62.55	64.08	66.01	...	66.43	61.99	65.45	52.01	54.44	56.18	56.76	53.68	57.54	55.55	52.39	54.68

MISSOURI.—Continued.

Year.	Harrisonville.	Hematite.	Hermitage.	Hornersville.	Jefferson Barracks.	Jefferson City.	Kansas City.	Oregon.	Paris, near.	Rolla, near.	St. Joseph.	St. Louis.	Tower Grove.	Union.	Warrenton.	Wyaconda Prairie.
	°	°	°	°	°	°	°	°	°	°	°	°	°	°	°	°
1827	...	...	...	...	58.86	...	...	...	...	...	...	...	...	...	...	...
1828	...	...	...	...	58.84	...	...	...	...	...	...	...	...	...	...	...
1829	...	...	...	...	55.12	...	...	...	...	...	...	...	...	...	...	...
1830	...	...	...	...	58.13	...	...	...	...	...	...	...	...	...	...	...
1831	...	...	...	...	50.74*	...	...	...	...	...	...	...	...	...	...	...
1832	...	...	...	...	55.66	...	...	...	...	...	...	...	...	...	...	...
1833	...	...	...	...	57.02	...	...	...	...	...	...	...	...	...	...	...
1834	...	...	...	...	55.81	...	...	...	...	...	...	...	...	...	...	...
1835	...	...	...	...	52.89	...	...	...	...	...	...	...	...	...	...	...
1836	...	...	...	...	...	...	...	...	...	...	...	53.19	...	...	...	...
1837	...	...	...	...	53.67*	...	...	...	...	...	...	54.58	...	...	...	...
1838	...	...	...	...	52.09*	...	...	...	...	...	...	53.29	...	...	...	...
1839	...	...	...	...	54.07	...	...	...	...	...	...	55.26	...	...	...	...
1840	...	...	...	...	53.31*	...	...	...	...	...	...	55.56	...	...	...	...
1841	...	...	...	...	54.37	...	...	..	...	...	...	55.48	...	...	...	...
1842	...	...	...	...	56.54	...	...	...	...	...	...	56.06	...	...	...	...
1843	...	...	...	...	52.33	...	...	...	...	...	...	53.56	...	...	...	...
1844	...	...	...	...	55.24	...	...	...	...	...	...	56.59	...	...	...	...
1845	...	...	...	...	57.30	...	...	...	...	...	...	56.33	...	...	...	...
1846	...	...	...	...	56.86	...	...	...	...	...	...	56.64	...	...	...	...
1847	...	...	...	...	...	...	...	...	...	...	...	53.79	...	...	...	...
1848	...	...	...	...	54.69	...	...	...	...	...	...	54.15	...	...	...	...
1849	...	...	...	...	54.47	...	...	...	...	...	...	53.73	...	...	...	...
1850	...	...	...	...	55.58	...	...	...	...	...	...	54.99	...	...	...	...
1851	...	...	...	...	56.11	...	...	...	...	...	...	55.15	...	...	...	...
1852	...	...	...	...	55.51	...	...	...	...	...	...	54.66	...	...	...	...
1853	...	...	...	...	56.57	...	...	...	...	...	...	54.91	...	...	...	...
1854	...	...	...	...	58.61	...	...	...	...	...	...	57.31	...	...	...	...
1855	...	...	...	...	55.63*	...	...	...	...	...	...	54.07	...	...	...	...
1856	...	...	...	...	...	...	...	...	...	...	...	52.40	...	...	...	...
1857	...	...	...	...	53.70	...	...	...	...	...	...	53.00	...	...	...	...
1858	...	...	...	...	56.07	...	...	...	...	...	...	56.28	...	...	...	...
1859	...	...	...	...	55.83	...	...	...	...	...	...	54.37	...	...	...	...
1860	...	...	...	62.21*	56.17	...	...	...	...	...	...	56.52	..	...	54.76	...
1861	...	...	...	...	56.41	...	...	...	51.85*	...	...	56.56	54.19	...	54.49	...
1862	...	...	...	...	...	...	...	...	...	...	...	55.61	53.19	...	52.98	50.50*
1863*	...	...	...	...	...	...	...	...	...	...	...	54.45	...	...	...	50.38*
1864	53.20*	...	...	...	...	...	...	...	...	...	...	54.77	...	...	...	49.56
1865	53.08	...	...	...	...	...	...	...	...	...	...	56.36	...	...	...	51.38
1866	52.49	...	...	...	...	...	...	...	...	...	...	55.21	...	53.45*	...	...
1867	51.65	...	...	...	...	...	...	51.42	...	...	...	55.27	...	...	...	...
1868	50.80*	55.11*	52.79*	...	...	53.45*	.:.	49.96*	...	52.91	...	54.32	...	...	...	50.36*
1869	51.25	54.61	50.82	...	...	52.76*	...	50.25	...	52.67	53.47*	54.06	...	...	...	...
1870	53.80*	56.42	...	...	...	55.84*	54.82*	53.01	...	55.39	...	55.88	...	...	...	...
	52.36	55.38	52.53	62.01	55.38	54.02	54.82	51.16	52.40	53.81	53.24	55.00	53.49	53.05	53.85	50.40

	MONTANA.							NEBRASKA.								
Year.	Camp Cooke.	Deer Lodge City.	Fort Benton.	Fort C. F. Smith.	Fort Ellis.	Fort Shaw.	Helena City.	Bellevue.	De Soto.	Fontanelle.	Fort Calhoun.	Fort Kearney.	Fort McPherson.	Glendale, near.	Nebraska City.	Omaha.
	°	°	°	°	°	°	°	°	°	°	°	°	°	°	°	°
1820	...	...	...	...	...	...	...	...	...	...	48.19	...	...	...	...	...
1821	...	...	...	...	...	...	...	...	...	...	47.12	...	...	...	...	...
1822	...	...	...	...	...	...	...	...	...	...	50.25	...	...	...	...	...
1823	...	...	...	...	...	...	...	...	...	...	51.28	...	...	...	...	...
1824	...	...	...	...	...	...	...	...	...	...	48.25	...	...	...	...	...
1825	...	...	...	...	...	...	...	...	...	...	52.20	...	...	...	...	...
1826	...	...	...	...	...	...	...	...	...	...	51.40	...	...	...	...	...
1849	...	...	...	...	...	...	...	...	...	...	...	45.30	...	...	...	...
1850	...	...	...	...	...	...	...	...	...	...	...	46.53	...	...	...	...
1851	...	...	...	...	...	...	...	...	...	...	...	48.97	...	...	...	...
1852	...	...	...	...	...	...	...	...	...	...	...	46.48	...	...	...	...
1853	...	...	...	...	...	...	...	...	...	...	...	48.40	...	...	...	...
1854	...	...	...	...	...	...	...	...	...	...	...	50.57	...	...	...	...
1855	...	...	...	...	...	...	...	...	...	...	...	48.70*	...	...	...	...
1856	...	...	...	...	...	...	...	...	...	...	...	45.83	...	...	...	...
1857	...	...	...	...	...	...	...	...	...	...	...	45.25	...	...	...	...
1858	...	...	...	...	...	...	...	48.73	...	...	...	48.10	...	...	...	...
1859	...	...	...	...	...	...	...	48.50	...	...	...	49.19	...	...	...	47.31
1860	...	...	...	...	...	...	...	51.78	...	...	...	51.30	...	...	...	...
1861	...	...	...	...	...	...	...	50.50*	...	48.17*	...	50.17	...	...	...	...
1862	...	...	...	...	...	...	...	48.91	...	...	...	49.09*	...	...	...	...
1863	...	...	...	...	...	...	...	...	...	...	...	...	...	...	...	...
1864	...	...	...	...	...	...	...	48.41	...	...	...	...	...	...	...	...
1865	...	...	...	...	...	...	...	50.14	...	...	...	...	...	...	...	...
1866	...	...	...	...	...	...	43.42	49.17	...	...	...	43.66*	...	46.76*	...	...
1867	41.99	...	...	47.56	...	...	...	...	45.66*	...	...	44.28*	...	45.83	...	...
1868	45.48	...	...	...	...	45.06	...	49.70*	46.65	...	...	...	51.60	46.90	...	...
1869	46.67	41.84	...	...	45.35	46.26	...	49.23	46.01	...	...	...	51.11	46.72*	50.00*	47.56*
1870	...	[illegible]	[illegible]		[illegible]	[illegible]	...	51.57	48.66*	...	...	...	52.76	...	51.39	51.24
	44.85	41.49	47.02	48.39	44.80	46.06	43.04	49.53	46.74	46.24	49.82	47.12	51.86	46.60	50.81	48.87

	NEB.—Cont'd.		NEVADA.						NEW HAMPSHIRE.							
Year.	Omaha Agency.	Richland.	Camp Halleck.	Camp McDermit.	Camp McGarry.	Camp Winfield Scott.	Fort Churchill.	Fort Ruby.	Claremont.	Concord.	Dover.	Dunbarton.	Exeter.	Farmouth.	Fort Constitution.	Francestown.
	°	°	°	°	°	°	°	°	°	°	°	°	°	°	°	°
1822	...	...	...	...	...	...	...	...	...	...	...	...	...	...	47.49	...
1825	...	...	...	...	...	...	...	...	...	...	...	...	...	...	47.77	...
1826	...	...	...	...	...	...	...	...	...	...	...	...	...	...	48.07	...
1827	...	...	...	...	...	...	...	...	...	...	...	...	...	...	45.81	...
1828	...	...	...	...	...	...	...	...	...	47.52	...	...	...	...	49.11	...
1829	...	...	...	...	...	...	...	...	...	44.42	...	...	...	...	45.59	...
1830	...	...	...	...	...	...	...	...	...	46.42	...	...	...	...	46.98	...
1831	...	...	...	...	...	...	...	...	...	45.72	...	...	...	...	46.32	...
1832	...	...	...	...	...	...	...	...	...	44.02	...	...	...	...	44.84	...
1833	...	...	...	...	...	...	...	...	...	44.12	44.87	...	...	...	45.31	...
1834	...	...	...	...	...	...	...	...	...	45.82	45.86	...	...	...	45.39	...
1835	...	...	...	...	...	...	...	...	...	43.12	43.66	...	...	...	44.23	...
1836	...	...	...	...	...	...	...	...	...	42.72	43.39	...	...	...	42.45	...
1837	...	...	...	...	...	...	...	...	...	42.92	43.88	...	...	...	42.78	...
1838	...	...	...	...	...	...	...	...	...	...	45.90	...	...	...	44.17	...
1839	...	...	...	...	...	...	...	...	...	...	47.43	...	...	...	45.12	...
1840	...	...	...	...	...	...	...	...	...	...	47.36	...	...	...	45.62*	...
1841	...	...	...	...	...	...	...	...	...	...	47.38	...	...	...	...	...
1842	...	...	...	...	...	...	...	...	...	...	47.58	...	...	...	45.70	...
1843	...	...	...	...	...	...	...	...	...	...	...	...	...	...	46.25	...
1844	...	...	...	...	...	...	...	...	...	...	...	...	...	...	45.31	...
1845	...	...	...	...	...	...	...	...	...	...	...	...	...	...	...	...
1849	...	...	...	...	...	...	...	...	...	46.20*	...	...	...	...	...	...
1850	...	...	...	...	...	...	...	...	...	45.80	...	...	...	...	45.62	...
1851	...	...	...	...	...	...	...	...	...	45.60	...	...	...	...	44.97	...
1852	...	...	...	...	...	...	...	...	...	45.70	...	...	...	...	45.06	...
1853	...	...	...	...	...	...	...	...	...	47.03	...	...	...	...	45.46*	...
1854	...	...	...	...	...	...	...	...	...	45.24	46.03	...	43.69	...	...	...
1855	...	...	...	...	...	...	...	...	...	45.28	...	...	43.57	...	...	...
1856	...	...	...	...	...	...	...	...	...	44.49*	...	...	...	...	...	...
1857	...	...	...	...	...	...	...	...	...	45.49*	...	...	...	...	...	44.05
1858	...	...	...	...	...	...	...	...	...	45.33*	...	...	...	...	...	...
1859	...	47.24	...	...	...	...	...	...	...	...	...	...	...	...	...	...
1860	...	49.15*	...	...	...	...	...	...	45.23	...	...	...	...	...	...	...
1861	...	47.56	...	...	...	...	54.53	...	44.93	...	...	...	46.17*	...	...	...
1862	...	46.78	...	...	...	...	51.48	...	44.56	...	...	...	46.47	...	...	...
1863	...	...	...	...	...	...	54.27*	51.71*	45.37	...	...	...	...	...	...	...
1864	...	47.54	...	...	...	...	55.37*	52.10	46.13	...	...	...	47.16	...	...	...
1865	...	48.26	...	...	...	...	54.07*	51.79	44.94	...	...	...	...	...	...	...
1866	...	47.50	...	...	45.18*	...	...	...	44.45	...	...	...	...	...	...	...
1867	...	45.54	...	48.11	42.80	50.88	54.62*	47.42*	43.63	...	...	...	...	...	...	...
1868	48.94*	47.07	44.40	46.81*	40.26*	46.80	50.34*	45.67*	43.70*	...	...	46.99*	...	...	...	...
1869	48.77	47.01	48.74	49.87	...	52.03*	...	...	...	...	...	45.30	...	...	...	...
1870	50.92	...	47.29*	48.93	...	...	...	...	...	...	...	48.31	...	45.12	...	...
	49.77	47.26	46.80	48.59	42.59	50.28	53.72	49.31	44.74	45.24	45.60	46.87	45.08	45.03	45.68	44.49

	NEW HAMPSHIRE.—Continued.											NEW JERSEY.				
Year.	Hanover.	Littleton.	Londonderry.	London Ridge.	Manchester.	North Barnstead.	Portsmouth.	Shelburne.	Stratford.	West Enfield.	Whitefield.	Bloomfield.	Burlington.	Chester.	Dover.	Elwood.
	°	°	°	°	°	°	°	°	°	°	°	°	°	°	°	°
1806	...	...	...	...	...	...	46.87*	...	...	...	...	...	...	...	...	...
1835	40.97	...	...	...	...	...	...	...	...	...	...	...	...	...	...	...
1836	39.97	...	...	...	...	...	...	...	...	...	...	...	...	...	...	...
1837	40.15*	...	...	...	...	...	...	...	...	...	...	...	...	...	...	...
1839	...	...	...	...	...	...	46.09	...	...	...	...	...	...	...	...	...
1840	...	...	...	...	...	...	45.99	...	...	...	...	...	...	...	...	...
1841	...	...	...	...	...	...	45.07	...	...	...	...	...	...	...	...	...
1845	...	...	...	...	47.16	...	...	...	...	...	...	...	...	...	...	...
1846	...	...	...	...	48.17	...	...	...	...	...	...	...	...	...	...	...
1847	...	...	...	...	46.98	...	...	...	...	...	...	...	...	...	...	...
1848	...	...	...	...	47.50	...	...	...	...	...	...	...	...	...	...	...
1849	...	...	...	...	46.96	...	...	...	...	...	...	...	...	...	...	...
1850	...	...	...	...	47.17	...	...	...	...	...	...	...	...	...	...	...
1851	...	...	...	...	47.58	...	...	...	...	...	...	...	...	...	...	...
1852	...	...	...	...	47.67	...	...	...	...	...	...	...	...	...	...	...
1853	43.70	...	...	...	47.53	...	...	...	...	...	...	...	...	...	...	...
1854	41.88	...	45.71*	...	46.58	...	...	...	...	...	...	51.29	52.64	...	...	...
1855	...	...	45.79*	...	46.16*	...	...	...	...	...	...	50.17	52.11	...	...	...
1856	...	...	...	...	45.21*	...	...	...	39.57*	...	...	48.34	50.42	...	...	...
1857	...	...	...	...	45.89	...	...	44.72*	...	42.44*	...	49.66	50.33	...	...	...
1858	...	...	...	...	...	...	...	42.91	39.15*	41.45	...	50.80*	...	...	...	...
1859	...	...	...	...	...	...	...	...	39.70	...	...	...	...	...	...	...
1860	...	...	...	...	46.94*	45.86*	...	...	40.75	...	...	...	...	...	...	...
1861	...	...	...	...	...	46.11	...	...	39.28	...	...	...	...	...	...	...
1862	...	...	...	51.28*	...	45.29	...	...	39.14	...	...	50.04	...	...	...	...
1863	...	42.53*	...	...	...	46.36*	...	...	40.05*	...	...	...	...	...	...	...
1864				...	...	46.20*	...	42.12*	40.89	...	...	...	50.50*	51.30	...	...
1865	...	...	...	...	...	47.47	...	42.95*	40.41	...	...	...	51.47	52.03	...	...
1866	...	...	...	...	...	46.11*	...	...	39.45	...	...	...	51.47	51.48	...	...
1867	...	...	...	...	...	44.65	45.65*	...	38.61	...	...	...	51.60	50.36*	49.02	...
1868	...	...	...	...	...	...	...	...	38.94	...	...	...	...	49.03*	47.69	49.91*
1869	...	...	...	...	...	...	...	...	39.89	...	...	...	...	50.81	...	...
1870	...	...	...	...	...	...	...	...	42.69	...	43.38	...	...	52.88	...	...
	42.79	43.06	46.47	51.67	47.50	45.81	45.86	42.01	39.92	42.22	42.39	50.46	51.94	51.49	49.19	50.01

	NEW JERSEY.—Continued.															N. M.
Year.	Freehold.	Greenwich.	Haddonfield.	Lamberts-ville.	Mt. Holly.	Newark.	New Brunswick.	Newfield.	New German-town.	Paterson.	Rio Grande.	Seaville.	Sergeants-ville.	Trenton.	Vineland.	Albuquerque.
	°	°	°	°	°	°	°	°	°	°	°	°	°	°	°	°
1840	...	...	...	...	...	...	...	...	...	...	...	...	...	49.63	...	...
1841	...	...	...	...	...	...	...	...	...	...	...	...	...	51.08*	...	...
1842	...	...	...	...	...	...	...	...	...	...	...	...	...	52.50	...	...
1843	...	...	...	49.10	...	...	...	...	...	...	...	...	...	51.67	...	...
1844	...	...	...	49.45	...	50.34	...	...	...	...	...	...	...	52.92	...	...
1845	...	...	...	50.13	...	51.00	...	...	...	...	...	...	...	53.66	...	...
1846	...	...	...	50.18	...	51.46	...	...	...	...	...	...	...	...	...	...
1847	...	...	...	51.45	...	50.23	...	...	...	...	...	...	...	...	...	...
1848	...	...	...	52.73	...	50.80	...	...	...	...	...	...	...	...	...	...
1849	...	...	...	51.08	...	50.52	...	...	...	...	...	...	...	...	...	...
1850	...	...	...	51.52	...	52.52	...	...	...	...	...	...	...	...	...	53.81
1851	...	...	...	51.27	...	51.39	...	...	...	...	...	...	...	...	...	...
1852	...	...	...	50.85	...	50.20	...	...	...	...	...	...	...	...	...	...
1853	...	...	...	52.43	...	52.38	...	...	...	...	...	...	...	...	...	58.41*
1854	...	...	...	52.36	...	50.76	...	...	...	...	...	...	...	...	...	57.29
1855	...	...	...	50.82	...	50.31	...	...	...	...	...	...	...	...	...	...
1856	...	...	...	48.85	...	47.75	...	...	...	...	...	...	...	...	...	56.28
1857	49.96*	...	...	49.75	...	48.02	...	...	...	...	...	...	52.19*	...	...	56.15
1858	51.12*	...	...	51.14	...	50.14	...	...	...	...	...	...	...	...	...	53.39
1859	50.88	...	...	50.82	...	49.74	...	...	...	...	...	...	...	...	...	51.84
1860	52.01*	...	...	...	...	49.63	...	...	...	...	...	...	...	...	...	55.54
1861	51.81	...	...	...	53.58	50.42	...	...	...	...	...	...	...	...	...	54.59*
1862	...	...	...	...	52.22	49.81	...	...	...	...	...	...	...	...	...	...
1863	...	...	...	...	52.00*	49.93	50.10*	...	...	...	...	...	...	...	...	55.67
1864	...	53.08	52.21	...	52.41	50.75	...	...	...	...	...	...	...	...	...	54.47
1865	...	53.48	52.60	...	52.86	50.99	51.39*	...	...	52.01	...	...	...	...	...	56.91*
1866	...	52.83	51.99	...	52.12	50.28	50.38	...	...	49.75	...	...	...	52.71*	...	...
1867	...	52.38	50.75	...	51.27	49.36	49.42	...	...	49.39	...	51.94*	...	52.50	...	...
1868	...	51.42	50.11*	...	...	48.26	48.17	50.90	...	48.01	...	...	...	50.80	50.98	...
1869	...	52.73	51.14*	...	...	50.04	...	51.85	49.32	49.64	51.96*	...	...	54.77	52.83	...
1870	...	54.76	52.86	...	...	52.30	...	...	51.41	52.43	53.92	...	...	57.28	54.19	...
	50.97	52.95	51.67	50.81	52.22	50.41	50.22	52.64	50.27	50.22	52.91	52.21	52.71	52.76	52.67	55.52

NEW MEXICO.—Continued.

Year.	Cantonment Burgwin.	Cebolleta.	Fort Bascom.	Fort Bayard.	Fort Conrad.	Fort Craig.	Fort Cummings.	Fort Fillmore.	Fort McRae.	Fort Selden.	Fort Stanton.	Fort Sumner.	Fort Thorn.	Fort Union.	Fort Webster.	Fort Wingate.
1850	...	54.02	...	...	...	...	...	...	...	...	...	...	...	...	...	...
1851	...	54.27*	...	...	...	...	...	...	...	...	...	...	...	...	...	...
1852	...	...	...	...	57.94	...	...	60.14	...	...	...	...	...	48.47	52.17*	...
1853	...	...	...	...	58.78	...	...	64.83	...	...	...	...	...	49.16	56.97	...
1854	...	...	...	...	...	60.20*	...	65.78	...	...	...	...	58.48	49.18	...	...
1855	46.54	...	...	...	...	61.21	...	65.28*	...	...	...	...	60.95	48.02	...	...
1856	43.60	...	...	...	...	60.98	...	64.71	...	...	52.53	...	57.67	46.56	...	...
1857	45.70	...	...	...	...	59.80	...	64.59	...	...	48.92	...	57.48*	48.27	...	...
1858	43.11	...	...	...	...	58.04	...	62.26	...	...	46.98	...	57.01	48.39	...	...
1859	45.23	...	...	...	...	58.28	...	61.41	...	...	52.38	...	...	48.07	...	...
1860	...	...	...	...	...	59.73*	...	62.89	...	...	53.50	...	...	49.78	...	...
1861	...	...	...	...	...	60.38	...	...	...	...	...	...	...	52.23	...	...
1862	...	...	...	...	...	61.46*	...	...	...	...	...	...	...	51.15	...	...
1863	...	...	...	...	...	...	...	...	...	...	...	...	...	51.35*	...	50.32
1864	...	...	59.09*	...	...	...	...	...	...	...	...	57.82*	...	...	...	52.33*
1865	...	...	61.46	...	...	60.11*	...	...	...	...	...	57.14	...	...	...	51.55
1866	...	...	...	...	...	61.65*	...	...	...	...	...	...	...	...	...	...
1867	...	...	...	55.47*	...	...	...	...	...	65.63	54.01*	60.24	...	55.39	...	53.72
1868	...	...	...	53.95	...	58.72	...	...	...	63.09	52.08	58.50	...	52.35*	...	50.49*
1869	...	...	57.19*	51.14	...	58.19	63.45*	...	59.65	62.96	51.56	...	...	50.56	...	51.73
1870	...	...	55.80*	54.26	...	57.98	64.82*	...	59.53*	60.66	52.74	...	...	52.42	...	50.72
	44.88	54.35	58.63	53.71	58.24	59.96	64.14	63.48	59.82	63.07	51.77	58.39	58.34	50.22	54.58	51.83

NEW MEXICO.—Cont'd.					NEW YORK.											
Year.	Las Vegas.	Los Pinos.	Santa Fé.	Socorro.	Albany.	Amenia.	Angelica.	Auburn.	Baldwinsville.	Beaver Brook.	Belleville.	Bellport.	Beverly.	Blackwell's Island.	Blooming-dale.	Bridgewater.
	°	°	°	°	°	°	°	°	°	°	°	°	°	°	°	°
1795	...	...	...	...	49.55	...	...	...	...	...	...	...	...	...	...	...
1796	...	...	...	...	46.61*	...	...	...	...	...	...	...	...	...	...	...
1813	...	...	...	...	47.92	...	...	...	...	...	...	...	...	...	...	...
1814	...	...	...	...	49.41	...	...	...	...	...	...	...	...	...	...	...
1820	...	...	...	...	48.57	...	...	...	...	...	...	...	...	...	...	...
1821	...	...	...	...	47.68	...	...	...	...	...	...	...	...	...	...	...
1822	...	...	...	...	48.77	...	...	...	...	...	...	...	...	...	...	...
1823	...	...	...	...	46.90	...	...	...	...	...	...	...	...	...	...	...
1824	...	...	...	...	47.47	...	...	...	...	...	...	...	...	...	...	...
1825	...	...	...	...	50.05	...	...	...	...	...	...	...	...	...	...	...
1826	...	...	...	...	50.59	...	...	...	...	...	...	...	...	...	...	...
1827	...	...	...	...	48.14	...	...	47.76	...	...	...	...	...	...	...	...
1828	...	...	...	...	50.88	...	...	48.48	...	...	...	...	...	...	...	...
1829	...	...	...	...	47.72	...	...	45.88	...	...	...	...	...	...	...	...
1830	...	...	...	...	50.17	...	...	46.89	...	...	44.63	...	...	...	...	...
1831	...	...	...	...	48.67	...	...	...	...	...	45.67	...	...	...	...	...
1832	...	...	...	...	47.62	...	...	46.44	...	...	...	...	...	...	...	...
1833	...	...	...	...	47.14	...	...	47.32	...	...	45.00	...	...	...	...	43.37
1834	...	...	...	...	48.05	...	...	48.45	...	...	46.04	...	...	...	...	42.31
1835	...	...	...	...	45.69	...	...	46.06	...	...	44.64	...	...	...	...	40.66
1836	...	...	...	...	44.25	...	...	44.27	...	...	42.63	...	...	...	...	...
1837	...	...	...	...	45.31	...	...	43.92	...	...	...	...	...	...	...	42.39
1838	...	...	...	...	46.67	...	...	44.63	...	...	...	...	...	...	...	...
1839	...	...	...	...	47.72	...	...	46.77	...	...	...	...	...	...	...	...
1840	...	...	...	...	48.22	...	...	47.07	...	...	...	...	...	...	...	...
1841	...	...	...	...	47.70	...	...	45.92	...	...	...	...	...	...	...	...
1842	...	...	...	...	47.98	...	...	46.65	...	...	45.71	...	...	...	...	...
1843	...	...	...	...	46.40	...	...	45.04	...	...	49.50	...	...	...	...	...
1844	...	...	...	...	47.68	...	...	47.84	...	...	49.65	...	...	...	...	...
1845	...	...	...	...	49.10	...	...	44.65	...	...	...	...	...	...	...	...
1846	...	...	...	...	49.91	...	...	48.28	...	...	...	...	...	...	51.95	...
1847	...	...	...	...	48.65	...	...	44.36	...	...	...	...	...	...	...	...
1848	...	...	...	...	49.35	...	...	44.83	...	...	...	...	...	...	...	...
1849	...	...	51.67*	...	47.32	45.98	...	44.16	...	...	...	...	...	...	...	...
1850	49.00	...	...	57.61	48.02	...	...	...	...	...	...	...	...	...	...	...
1851	...	...	...	...	47.65	...	...	...	...	...	...	...	...	...	...	...
1852	...	...	...	...	48.06	...	...	...	...	...	...	...	...	...	...	...
1853	...	...	49.80	...	...	...	...	...	...	...	...	...	...	...	...	...
1854	...	...	50.57	...	...	...	...	...	45.89	48.18*	...	...	49.50	...	...	...
1855	...	...	50.44	...	...	...	44.14	...	44.76	...	...	...	48.26	...	...	...
1856	...	...	49.12	...	...	...	42.47	...	43.31	...	...	...	46.77	49.66	...	...
1857	...	...	50.03	...	...	...	...	...	44.25	...	...	...	47.97*	50.40*	...	...
1858	...	...	48.65	...	...	...	...	...	...	...	...	48.83	...	...	...	...
1859	...	...	47.31	...	...	...	...	...	...	...	...	48.94	47.36	...	...	...
1860	...	...	50.28	...	...	...	...	48.01	45.74*	...	...	49.36	47.79*	...	...	...
1861	...	...	52.08	...	...	...	...	47.64	45.76	...	...	50.12	48.72*	...	...	...
1862	...	...	...	...	46.35	...	...	47.74	45.75	...	...	...	...	...	...	...
1863	...	57.67	50.66	...	46.65	...	...	48.34	44.62*	...	...	...	...	...	...	...
1864	...	...	49.51	...	47.99	...	...	50.09	45.79	...	...	...	48.98	...	...	...
1865	...	55.15*	48.98	...	49.27	...	...	49.72	45.47	...	...	...	49.95*	...	...	...
1866	...	...	...	...	48.41	...	...	...	44.07	...	...	...	48.19	...	...	...
1867	...	...	...	...	46.99	...	...	...	...	...	...	...	48.49	...	...	...
1868	...	...	48.97	...	45.76	...	...	...	...	...	...	...	47.20	...	...	...
1869	...	...	48.12	...	47.01	...	...	...	...	...	...	...	49.08	...	...	...
1870	...	...	52.44	...	50.06	...	...	...	...	...	...	...	50.77	...	...	...
	49.06	55.40	50.13	57.92	47.95	45.86	43 65	46.80	45.28	48.18	45.94	49.33	48.66	50.03	51.95	42.19

NEW YORK.—Continued.

Year.	Buffalo.	Cambridge.	Canajoharie.	Canandaigua.	Canton.	Cazenovia.	Charlotte.	Cherry Valley.	Clinton.	Clyde, near.	Cooperstown.	Dansville.	Delhi.	Depauville, near.	East Hampton.	Eden.
	°	°	°	°	°	°	°	°	°	°	°	°	°	°	°	°
1827	...	44.62	...	...	...	...	...	43.53	...	...	...	...	...	...	48.83	...
1828	...	48.52	...	...	...	...	...	46.60	...	...	...	...	46.41	...	50.81	...
1829	...	45.41	...	45.74	...	...	...	43.85	...	...	...	...	...	...	47.71	...
1830	...	47.44	46.05	47.08	...	44.89	...	44.69	...	...	...	...	...	...	49.34	...
1831	46.30	46.31	...	45.80	...	43.00	...	44.40	...	...	...	...	...	...	48.30	...
1832	45.03	45.13	...	46.68	...	43.88	...	44.30	...	...	...	...	...	...	47.52	...
1833	...	44.57	46.00	46.82	...	43.96	...	44.07	...	...	...	...	...	...	48.61	...
1834	...	45.72	...	46.44	...	44.49	...	44.74	...	...	...	...	...	...	48.90	...
1835	...	43.09	43.83	43.95	...	42.55	...	42.96	...	...	...	...	...	...	46.12	...
1836	...	42.20	...	43.30	...	41.10	...	40.77	...	...	...	...	...	...	46.44	...
1837	...	42.21	...	42.44	...	41.68	...	...	...	...	...	...	45.97	...	45.72	...
1838	...	43.73	...	43.72	...	42.49	...	...	...	...	...	...	...	...	46.51	...
1839	...	44.04	...	...	...	43.55	...	...	...	...	...	...	...	...	48.77	...
1840	...	...	...	...	...	42.21	...	...	...	...	...	...	...	...	48.98	...
1841	44.38	45.38	...	...	...	42.79	...	42.49	...	...	...	...	...	...	49.17	...
1842	46.72	...	...	...	...	43.69	...	43.80	...	...	...	...	...	...	50.42	...
1843	45.28	...	...	...	...	41.91	...	41.88	...	...	...	...	...	...	48.32	...
1844	47.21	...	...	...	...	43.32	...	43.63	...	...	...	...	...	...	...	...
1845	...	...	...	...	...	43.32	...	45.19	...	...	...	...	...	...	...	...
1846	...	...	...	...	...	43.67	...	...	...	...	...	...	...	...	...	...
1847	...	...	...	...	...	42.94	...	...	...	...	...	...	...	...	...	...
1848	...	...	...	...	...	43.42	...	...	...	...	...	...	...	...	...	...
1849	...	...	...	...	...	42.25	...	...	...	...	...	...	...	...	...	...
1850	...	...	...	...	...	...	...	...	...	...	...	...	...	...	...	...
1851	...	...	...	...	...	...	...	...	...	...	...	...	...	...	...	...
1852	...	...	...	...	...	...	...	...	...	...	...	...	44.45	...	...	...
1853	...	...	...	...	...	...	...	...	...	...	...	...	...	...	...	...
1854	46.68*	...	...	...	44.33	...	...	...	...	...	...	...	...	...	...	...
1855	...	...	...	...	44.21	...	...	...	...	...	...	...	...	...	...	...
1856	...	...	...	...	...	...	...	...	43.23*	...	...	...	...	...	...	...
1857	...	...	...	...	...	41.55	...	...	45.55	...	...	...	...	...	...	45.52*
1858	47.81	...	...	...	...	...	...	...	47.18	...	...	...	...	...	...	...
1859	47.33	...	...	...	...	...	...	...	...	...	...	...	...	...	...	...
1860	47.16	...	...	...	...	...	46.79	...	...	...	...	...	...	...	...	...
1861	47.25	...	...	...	...	43.63	46.89	...	...	46.46	...	47.94*	...	...	...	...
1862	47.29	...	...	...	...	43.39	47.39	...	47.54	...	...	...	...	...	...	...
1863	47.19	...	...	...	...	...	47.99	...	48.50*	...	...	...	...	...	...	...
1864	46.63	...	...	...	...	...	48.39	...	49.50	...	...	...	...	...	...	...
1865	47.31	...	...	...	...	...	48.89	...	...	...	...	...	...	46.18*	...	...
1866	45.29	...	...	...	...	...	47.19	...	...	...	...	...	...	43.75	...	...
1867	46.04	...	...	...	...	44.37	47.89	...	...	...	...	...	...	43.90	...	...
1868	45.63	...	...	...	...	43.25	...	...	...	...	...	...	...	43.09	...	...
1869	45.76	...	...	...	...	44.04	...	...	...	...	...	...	...	43.10	...	...
1870	48.44	...	...	...	...	46.56	...	...	...	...	46.92	...	...	46.19	...	...
	46.55	44.88	45.29	45.20	44.06	43.40	47.52	43.82	46.82	46.30	46.61	48.20	45.50	44.37	48.37	45.73

NEW YORK.—Continued.

Year.	Elmira.	Fairfield.	Fishkill, L.	Flatbush.	Flushing.	Fort Ann.	Fort Columbus.	Fort Edward.	Fort Hamilton.	Fort Niagara.	Fort Ontario.	Fort Porter.	Fredonia.	Friendship.	Gaines.	Geneva.
	°	°	°	°	°	°	°	°	°	°	°	°	°	°	°	°
1822	...	...	...	...	...	...	53.79	...	...	...	...	...	...	...	...	...
1823	...	...	...	...	...	...	50.21	...	...	...	...	...	...	...	...	...
1824	...	...	...	...	...	...	51.66	...	...	...	...	...	...	...	...	...
1825	...	...	...	...	...	...	54.00	...	...	...	...	...	...	...	...	...
1826	...	...	...	53.48	...	...	52.07	...	...	...	...	...	...	...	...	...
1827	...	42.70	...	51.18	...	...	51.36	...	...	...	...	...	...	...	...	...
1828	...	46.53	...	53.20	...	...	53.61	...	...	...	...	...	...	...	...	...
1829	...	43.07*	...	50.02	...	...	52.13	...	...	49.04	...	...	47.37*	...	...	...
1830	...	46.00*	...	52.05	...		54.42	...	...	...	...	...	49.09	...	...	...
1831	...	44.38	...	50.80	...	...	51.24	...	...	49.37	...	...	47.35	...	...	...
1832	...	44.40	...	51.06	...	...	51.13	...	...	...	...	...	48.75	...	...	...
1833	...	45.25	...	51.35	...	...	51.13	...	...	...	...	...	...	...	...	...
1834	...	...	...	50.88	...	...	50.63	...	...	...	...	...	49.96	...	...	...
1835	...	42.51	...	49.01	...	...	49.18	...	...	...	...	...	46.73	...	...	...
1836	...	42.00	...	47.25	...	...	46.82	...	...	...	...	...	44.06	...	...	...
1837	...	40.43	...	48.91	...	...	48.74	...	...	...	...	...	45.54	...	...	...
1838	...	40.38	...	50.01	...	...	49.94	...	...	...	...	...	45.15	...	...	...
1839	...	43.81	...	50.85	...	...	50.79	...	...	...	...	...	46.27	...	46.02	...
1840	...	42.69	...	50.86	...	...	50.77	...	...	46.94	...	...	47.56	...	46.64	...
1841	...	42.26	...	50.63	...	...	51.32	...	...	...	...	...	47.92	...	46.28	...
1842	...	43.46	...	51.57	...	...	52.87	...	...	46.83	...	...	49.46	...	46.32	...
1843	...	41.44	...	50.67	...	...	51.50	...	51.33	45.57	44.45	...	48.69	...	...	...
1844	...	41.90	...	51.33	...	...	52.13	...	51.25	46.90	45.81	...	49.60	...	...	...
1845	...	42.92	...	52.61	...	...	53.36	...	52.93	48.24	45.85	...	50.74	...	...	...
1846	...	...	...	52.57	...	...	52.38	...	52.33	...	...	...	50.60	...	...	...
1847	...	42.53	...	53.83	...	...	52.42	...	51.70	...	...	...	48.67	...	...	...
1848	...	42.45	...	52.40	...	...	52.28	...	51.98	...	...	...	46.08	...	...	...
1849	...	42.31	...	50.78	...	...	50.32	...	50.60	...	46.38	...	...	...	...	...
1850	...	...	...	50.74*	...	...	51.11	...	52.14	47.75	46.24	...	...	...	...	...
1851	...	...	...	50.96	...	...	52.25	...	52.57	47.03	46.21	...	46.84	...	...	...
[illegible]	[illegible]			[illegible]		...	[illegible]	...	[illegible]	[illegible]	[illegible]	...	[illegible]	...	...	[illegible]
1853	...	...	...	...	...	...	52.34	...	52.26	48.39	...	...	...	...	...	...
1854	...	...	52.03	...	...	...	50.82	...	51.85	47.37*	...	...	...	...	...	...
1855	...	...	...	...	...	...	50.26	...	51.64	...	44.40	...	...	...	...	...
1856	...	...	...	48.18	...	...	49.50	...	50.03	...	44.71*	...	...	...	...	44.83*
1857	...	...	...	48.68	...	...	49.89	...	48.75	...	...	...	...	...	...	...
1858	...	...	49.33	49.83	...	...	50.60	44.67	50.36	...	...	...	...	...	...	...
1859	...	...	...	49.50	...	...	51.63	...	49.80	...	...	...	...	...	...	...
1860	...	...	48.96	...	...	...	51.45	...	49.96	45.49	...	...	...	...	...	...
1861	...	...	49.35	50.71	...	...	52.18	...	50.89	46.09	...	...	...	...	...	...
1862	...	...	48.88	...	...	...	51.36*	...	50.37	46.59	...	...	...	...	...	...
1863	...	...	48.89*	...	...	...	51.82	...	51.37	46.09	...	...	...	...	...	...
1864	...	...	50.12	50.41	...	54.83*	52.57	...	50.84	46.49	...	...	...	...	...	47.59
1865	...	...	50.05	51.19	...	...	53.19	...	52.29	46.59	...	...	...	...	...	47.62
1866	...	...	49.16*	50.10*	...	...	...	...	...	45.99	...	...	...	...	...	46.21
1867	...	...	...	49.73*	...	...	50.99	...	51.17	45.79	...	46.20	...	43.67*	...	46.58
1868	...	...	...	47.92	...	...	49.52	...	49.75	...	...	45.55	...	...	...	...
1869	...	...	...	50.66	...	...	50.91	...	49.97	...	...	45.40	...	...	...	...
1870	...	...	...	52.69*	52.70	...	52.38*	...	...	...	48.63	48.25	...	...	...	...
	45.73	43.06	49.47	50.83	51.72	53.46	51.41	46.64	51.19	47.19	45.81	46.55	47.93	43.72	46.33	46.73

NEW YORK.—Continued.

Year.	Glasco.	Goshen.	Gouverneur.	Greenville.	Hamilton.	Hartwick.	Henrietta.	Hermitage.	Homer.	Houseville.	Hudson.	Ithaca.	Jamaica.	Jamestown.	Johnstown.	Kinderhook.
	°	°	°	°	°	°	°	°	°	°	°	°	°	°	°	°
1826	...	...	...	47.58	...	46.12	...	...	...	...	...	...	51.71	...	...	...
1827	...	...	...	...	41.22	44.92	...	...	...	...	48.71	49.52	50.47	...	...	...
1828	...	...	...	...	46.98	46.46	...	...	...	...	52.36	50.87*	51.57	...	47.41	...
1829	...	...	...	...	44.00	45.01	...	...	43.01*	...	48.57	49.53*	48.03	...	45.54	...
1830	...	...	...	...	45.39	46.20	...	...	...	...	49.60*	49.19	50.37	...	46.79*	47.76
1831	...	...	43.00	...	45.27	43.48	...	...	...	...	50.77	...	49.03	...	45.52	54.42
1832	...	...	43.18	...	...	45.41	...	...	45.11	...	48.77	...	48.72	...	45.42	46.00
1833	...	...	44.21	...	44.51	...	...	...	45.20	...	48.15	47.80	50.86	...	43.97*	46.07
1834	...	...	44.92	...	44.01	...	...	...	...	...	47.43	47.42*	49.62	...	44.95	46.60
1835	...	45.31	41.77	...	43.35	44.91	...	...	42.69	...	44.14	45.83	46.36	...	42.16	44.24
1836	...	...	...	...	39.97	...	...	...	41.56	...	...	43.80	46.04	...	41.83	43.33
1837	...	...	...	...	...	43.17	...	...	42.22	...	...	44.36	46.75	...	42.95	43.62
1838	...	46.52	40.14	...	...	...	...	...	42.82	...	...	44.48	47.84	...	44.11	44.60
1839	...	48.10	41.03	...	43.57	44.71	...	...	43.52	...	...	45.23	48.83	...	...	44.19
1840	...	49.03	44.06*	...	...	...	...	...	44.91	...	...	47.47	49.43	...	...	46.96
1841	...	46.40	43.87	...	...	...	...	...	44.07	...	49.17	...	49.70	...	45.90	46.29
1842	...	47.05	45.77	...	44.03	...	...	...	44.88	...	48.02	48.41	49.56	...	46.07	46.66
1843	...	...	45.61	...	43.88	...	...	...	44.54	...	45.21	46.89	47.59	...	41.92	45.32
1844	...	46.29	44.70	...	44.23	...	...	...	43.33	...	46.65	48.58	48.54	...	44.47	45.77
1845	...	47.81	43.39	...	45.25	50.58	...	...	45.09	...	47.52	48.70	49.23	...	43.84	48.51
1846	...	48.06	45.63*	...	45.88	51.58	...	...	45.70	...	47.61	49.94	49.14	...	...	48.45
1847	...	47.11	42.55*	...	44.99	47.94	...	...	44.18	...	46.42	49.02	49.01	...	...	...
1848	...	...	44.11	...	45.93	46.39	...	...	45.11	...	47.20	49.68	52.51	...	...	...
1849	...	46.20	...	...	45.62	44.83	...	...	44.15	...	46.49	...	49.64	...	...	...
1850	...	...	...	...	...	45.36	...	...	46.38	...	...	...	50.57	...	...	...
1851	...	...	...	...	...	...	...	...	42.30	...	...	48.07	...	...	...	...
1852	...	...	...	...	...	...	...	...	42.62	...	48.25	48.89	...	46.07	...	...
1854	...	...	44.55	...	...	...	...	...	...	...	...	...	...	...	...	...
1855	...	...	45.30	...	...	...	...	...	...	...	...	...	...	...	...	...
1858	...	...	...	...	...	...	...	...	...	42.63*	...	...	...	...	...	...
1860	...	...	...	...	...	...	49.99*	...	...	...	...	...	...	...	...	...
1861	...	..	41.35	...	...	...	51.62	42.78	...	...	...	...	...	...	...	...
1862	...	...	40.74	...	...	...	...	43.27	...	...	...	...	...	...	...	...
1863	...	...	42.36*	...	...	...	...	43.03	...	...	...	...	...	...	...	...
1864	...	...	44.44	...	...	...	...	...	...	...	...	...	...	45.90	...	...
1865	...	...	43.46	...	...	...	...	...	...	...	...	...	...	46.94	...	...
1866	...	...	43.02*	...	...	...	...	...	...	...	...	...	...	...	...	...
1867	...	...	41.98	...	...	...	...	...	...	42.29	...	...	...	...	...	...
1868	...	...	41.46	...	...	...	...	...	...	41.72	...	...	...	...	...	...
1869	...	...	42.28*	...	...	...	...	...	...	42.22	...	...	...	...	...	...
1870	48.66*	...	44.35	...	...	...	...	...	...	45.02*	...	...	...	...	...	...
	48.66	46.90	43.26	47.58	44.66	46.01	48.40	43.16	43.72	43.30	47.96	47.81	49.27	46.18	44.56	46.10

NEW YORK.—Continued.

Year.	Kingston.	La Farge-ville.	Lansingburgh	Ledyard.	Lewiston.	Leyden.	Liberty.	Little Genesee.	Lockport.	Lodi.	Lowville.	Lyons.	McGrawville.	Madison Barracks.	Madrid.	Malone.
	°	°	°	°	°	°	°	°	°	°	°	°	°	°	°	°
1824	...	...	..	...	...	...	...	...	...	...	...	...	...	46.33	...	...
1825	...	...	...	...	...	...	...	...	...	...	...	...	...	48.37*	...	...
1826	...	...	49.20	...	...	...	...	...	...	...	...	...	...	48.51	...	...
1827	...	...	47.64	...	...	...	...	...	...	...	43.29	...	...	...	...	...
1828	...	...	50.27	...	...	...	...	...	...	...	46.47	...	...	...	...	...
1829	47.95	...	47.22	...	...	...	...	...	...	...	42.90	...	...	47.11	...	...
1830	50.99	...	49.16	48.99	...	...	...	...	...	...	44.12	...	...	49.01	...	...
1831	50.58	...	47.15	48.00	49.04	...	...	...	...	...	43.49	...	...	48.56	...	...
1832	50.02	...	46.88	47.62	48.81	...	...	...	...	...	43.67	...	...	...	...	...
1833	50.92	...	47.63	...	49.21	...	...	...	...	...	43.54	...	...	...	...	...
1834	49.62	...	48.16	47.60	50.22	...	...	...	...	...	45.55	...	...	...	...	...
1835	47.77	...	47.62	...	47.88	...	...	...	...	...	42.06	...	...	...	...	...
1836	45.46	...	47.34	...	43.06	...	...	...	...	...	...	...	...	...	...	...
1837	46.64	...	48.07	...	44.03	...	...	...	...	...	41.19	...	...	...	...	...
1838	48.09	...	...	47.57	...	...	...	...	...	...	...	...	...	...	...	...
1839	50.01	...	46.98	...	46.43	...	...	...	...	...	44.62	...	...	46.49*	...	42.74
1840	48.92	...	46.68	49.14	48.46	...	...	...	...	...	44.39	...	...	...	...	44.42
1841	47.83	...	46.43	50.03	48.37	...	...	...	...	...	43.23	...	...	...	...	...
1842	51.03	...	45.74	51.14	47.39	...	...	...	...	...	43.60	...	...	44.75	...	41.63
1843	...	...	44.75	48.03	46.29	...	...	...	...	...	41.38	...	...	43.50	...	...
1844	...	...	45.12	47.04	47.28	...	...	...	...	...	42.25	...	...	44.15	...	...
1845	49.84	...	48.06	48.45	47.19	...	...	...	...	...	39.24	...	...	44.45	...	...
1846	45.69	...	48.76	49.96	50.24	...	...	...	...	...	44.88	...	...	...	...	...
1847	48.77	...	...	...	48.01	...	...	...	...	...	43.30	...	...	...	...	...
1848	48.68	...	...	...	49.33	...	...	...	...	...	43.82	...	...	...	...	...
1849	50.26	...	...	...	48.05	...	...	...	47.11*	...	...	...	...	46.95*	...	...
1850	...	...	...	49.28	...	...	...	...	46.26*	...	...	...	...	45.81	...	...
1851	...	46.49	...	...	...	...	...	...	...	...	43.86	...	...	45.18	...	...
1852	...	...	...	...	...	...	43.09*	...	...	...	...	...	...	...	...	...
1853	...	...	...	...	...	...	...	...	...	...	...	...	...	...	...	...
1854	...	...	...	...	...	...	...	...	...	47.88	...	...	...	...	43.41*	...
1855	...	...	...	...	...	...	...	...	...	45.24	...	...	...	...	...	...
1856	...	...	...	...	...	...	...	...	...	43.82	...	...	...	...	...	...
1857	...	...	...	...	...	...	...	...	...	44.97*	41.25	...	43.04*	...	...	...
1858	...	...	...	...	...	...	...	...	...	...	...	...	...	...	...	...
1859	...	...	...	...	...	...	...	...	...	...	...	...	...	...	...	...
1860	...	...	...	...	...	...	...	...	...	...	...	46.49	...	...	...	...
1861	...	...	...	...	...	...	...	...	...	...	...	45.87	...	...	...	...
1862	...	...	...	...	...	...	...	...	...	...	...	...	...	...	...	...
1863	...	...	...	...	...	...	...	...	...	...	...	...	...	...	...	...
1864	...	...	...	...	...	...	...	...	...	...	...	...	...	...	...	...
1865	...	...	...	...	...	...	...	...	...	...	...	...	...	...	...	...
1866	...	...	...	...	...	...	...	44.31*	...	...	...	...	...	...	...	...
1867	...	...	...	...	...	...	...	44.76	...	...	...	...	...	...	...	...
1868	...	...	...	...	...	...	...	43.82	...	...	...	...	...	...	...	...
1869	...	...	...	...	...	40.52*	...	43.58	...	...	...	...	...	...	...	...
1870	...	...	...	...	...	...	...	45.68	...	...	...	...	...	46.51	...	...
	49.16	46.49	47.29	48.68	47.86	41.14	43.09	44.43	47.39	46.21	43.33	45.95	43.12	46.15	43.94	42.93

NEW YORK.—Continued.

Year.	Mexico.	Middlebury.	Milo.	Millville.	Minaville.	Mohawk.	Montgomery.	Moriches.	Morrisania.	Mt. Pleasant.	Newark Valley.	Newburg.	New York.	Nichols.	North Granville.	North Hammond.
	°	°	°	°	°	°	°	°	°	°	°	°	°	°	°	°
1826	...	47.23	...	...	...	...	...	...	...	...	...	...	...	...	...	...
1827	...	45.75	...	...	...	...	...	...	...	...	...	...	...	...	...	...
1828	...	49.51	...	...	...	...	51.70	...	...	...	...	51.52	...	...	...	...
1829	...	45.87	...	...	...	...	48.55	...	...	...	...	48.18	...	...	...	...
1830	...	47.34	...	...	...	...	51.55	...	...	...	...	49.77	...	...	...	...
1831	...	45.87	...	...	...	...	48.98	...	...	48.21	...	...	...	...	...	...
1832	...	47.35	...	...	...	...	48.88	...	...	48.85	...	50.23	...	...	...	...
1833	...	48.30	...	...	...	...	49.42	...	...	...	...	49.48	...	...	...	...
1834	...	48.60	...	...	...	...	47.68	...	...	49.57	...	49.72	...	...	...	...
1835	...	45.27	...	...	...	...	47.08	...	...	48.50	...	47.69	...	...	43.28	...
1836	...	...	...	...	...	...	43.77	...	...	...	...	45.25	...	...	45.40	...
1837	43.97	...	...	...	...	...	44.96	...	...	44.79	...	47.34	...	...	...	...
1838	43.65	...	...	...	...	...	47.41	...	...	49.92	...	48.34	...	...	43.82	...
1839	...	46.56	...	...	...	...	...	...	...	50.35	...	46.09	...	...	44.11	...
1840	43.55	45.18	...	44.33	...	...	47.90	...	...	50.40	...	47.01	...	...	45.70	...
1841	43.26	41.65	...	44.54	...	...	...	...	...	49.40	...	...	...	...	47.61	...
1842	46.38	44.29	...	45.46	...	...	48.38	...	...	48.98	...	49.64	...	...	45.78	...
1843	42.47	43.89	...	44.56	...	...	...	...	...	47.41	...	48.31	...	...	42.13	...
1844	42.83	46.69	...	46.21	...	...	...	...	...	49.00	...	48.71	51.13	...	43.11	...
1845	43.77	44.78	...	47.90	...	...	...	...	...	...	...	45.64	...	...	44.50	...
1846	43.25	48.32	...	45.81	...	...	...	...	...	...	...	51.60	50.09	...	46.22	...
1847	...	...	...	46.27	...	...	...	...	...	...	...	50.18	50.15	...	45.10	...
1848	43.84	47.37	...	...	...	...	...	...	...	...	...	51.48	50.51	...	46.02	...
1849	42.58	...	...	...	...	...	...	...	...	...	...	49.92	49.42	...	45.02	...
1850	...	...	...	...	...	...	...	...	...	...	...	...	52.10	...	...	...
1851	...	...	...	...	...	...	...	...	...	...	...	49.84	...	...	...	...
1852	44.39	...	...	...	...	...	...	...	...	...	...	...	...	...	...	...
1853	...	...	...	...	...	...	...	...	...	...	...	...	...	...	...	...
1854	...	...	...	...	...	...	...	...	...	...	...	...	51.87	...	...	...
1855	...	...	...	...	...	...	...	...	...	...	...	...	50.50	...	...	...
1856	44.68*	...	...	...	...	...	...	...	...	...	...	...	50.14	...	...	...
1857	...	...	...	...	...	...	...	...	50.46	...	...	...	51.67	43.85	...	...
1858	...	...	...	...	...	...	...	...	...	...	...	...	...	46.90	...	...
1859	...	...	...	...	...	...	...	...	...	...	...	...	...	47.22	...	...
1860	...	...	...	...	...	...	...	...	...	...	...	...	52.13*	46.64	...	...
1861	...	...	...	...	...	44.49	...	...	...	...	...	...	52.71	46.97	...	...
1862	...	...	...	...	...	44.73	...	...	...	...	...	...	51.99	46.59	...	...
1863	...	...	...	...	...	46.23	...	...	...	...	...	...	53.90	46.70	...	...
1864	...	...	...	...	...	...	...	52.39*	...	...	...	...	53.26	47.58	...	...
1865	...	...	...	...	...	...	...	53.90	...	...	...	50.86*	53.28	47.55	...	...
1866	...	...	...	...	...	...	...	53.00	...	...	...	49.59	51.47	46.29	...	...
1867	...	...	...	...	...	44.10	...	52.13	...	...	...	51.43	50.44	45.95	...	43.18
1868	...	...	...	...	42.05	43.17	...	50.89	...	...	42.39*	48.80*	49.29	45.20	...	45.35
1869	...	...	...	...	45.10	...	...	52.34	...	...	44.39*	50.33*	51.45	45.94	...	45.74
1870	...	...	46.52	...	48.05	...	...	50.40	...	...	47.34*	53.66*	54.79	47.84	...	49.54
	43.83	46.29	45.59	45.93	44.80	44.79	48.18	52.15	50.77	49.14	44.71	49.51	51.66	46.57	44.90	45.52

NEW YORK.—Continued.

Year.	North Salem.	North Volney.	Ogdensburg.	Oneida.	Onondaga.	Oswego.	Ovid.	Oxford.	Oyster Bay.	Palermo.	Palmyra.	Penn Yan.	Plattsburg.	Pompey.	Potsdam.	Poughkeepsie.
	°	°	°	°	°	°	°	°	°	°	°	°	°	°	°	°
1826	...	...	...	...	50.23	...	...	...	...	...	...	...	...	44.16	...	...
1827	...	...	...	...	47.79	...	...	...	...	...	...	...	...	43.02	...	...
1828	...	...	...	...	50.42	...	...	44.17*	...	...	...	...	...	46.85	45.53	55.39*
1829	50.16	...	...	...	47.33	...	...	44.51	...	...	...	46.36	...	42.75	43.58	51.34
1830	49.48	...	...	...	...	...	...	46.07	...	...	...	47.29	...	44.20	44.20	52.25
1831	48.17	...	...	...	...	...	...	45.68	...	...	...	44.45	...	42.44	43.00	50.12
1832	48.49	...	...	...	48.07	...	...	44.51*	...	...	...	47.26	...	42.92	42.36	49.09
1833	47.60	...	...	...	47.33	...	...	43.74	...	...	...	46.85	...	43.14	40.09	49.45
1834	47.48	...	...	...	...	...	...	45.35	51.37	...	...	47.42	...	43.27*	41.98	49.94
1835	45.74	...	...	...	46.36	...	...	43.84	...	...	44.85	45.27	...	42.00	42.09	48.47
1836	...	...	...	...	44.68	...	...	42.32	...	...	...	44.36	...	39.70	40.30	46.84
1837	...	...	...	...	44.76	...	...	43.29	49.79	...	...	44.95	...	39.54	40.88	45.75*
1838	44.91	...	43.01	...	45.58	...	...	42.97	...	...	...	44.34	...	39.79	43.62	...
1839	...	...	...	...	46.48	...	...	45.31	...	...	...	44.99	45.33	41.93	44.92	...
1840	45.83	...	...	...	47.15	...	...	45.47	...	...	...	47.04	44.45	42.17	43.78	...
1841	47.01	...	...	...	46.41	...	...	44.76	...	...	...	45.40	43.10	41.65	42.75	49.34
1842	47.96	...	...	...	44.71	...	...	44.34	...	...	...	46.42	43.49	41.81	42.10	49.70
1843	46.42	...	...	...	43.52	...	...	42.36	...	...	...	44.21	45.89	41.24	42.79	48.54
1844	47.43	...	...	...	44.69	...	...	43.94	...	...	...	44.87	42.18	...	43.05	49.80
1845	48.51	...	...	...	...	...	...	44.19	...	...	...	44.79	43.08	...	44.04	49.66
1846	48.76	...	...	...	...	...	...	46.64	...	...	...	45.57	...	...	45.30	50.67
1847	47.91	...	...	...	...	...	...	46.96	...	...	...	44.32	45.90	...	43.67	49.42
1848	47.69	...	...	...	...	...	...	...	...	...	...	45.35	45.90	...	45.20	...
1849	46.92	...	...	...	...	...	...	...	...	...	...	44.36	44.39	...	...	49.20
1850	47.52	...	44.36*	...	...	...	...	...	...	...	...	44.43	43.91	42.91	...	...
1851	...	...	...	...	...	...	...	44.22	...	...	...	44.85	43.62	42.46	...	...
1852	47.59	...	43.50	...	...	...	...	44.54	...	...	...	44.59	44.11	42.73*	...	...
1853	...	...	...	...	...	...	...	...	...	...	...	45.99	...	...	...	...
1854	...	...	...	...	...	...	...	...	...	...	...	46.80	...	...	...	...
1855	...	...	...	...	...	45.49*	...	...	...	...	...	44.94	...	...	...	...
1856	45.83*	...	...	...	...	43.35	44.48	...	...	...	...	43.92	...	...	...	...
1857	...	...	...	...	...	45.15	45.43	...	...	...	...	44.59	...	...	...	...
1858	...	...	...	...	...	...	...	...	...	...	...	46.24	...	...	...	...
1859	...	...	...	...	...	46.01	...	...	...	...	...	45.38	...	...	...	...
1860	...	...	...	...	...	...	...	...	...	45.64	...	...	...	...	...	...
1861	...	...	...	...	...	45.63	...	...	...	45.26	...	...	...	...	...	...
1862	...	...	...	45.23	...	45.44*	...	...	...	45.89	...	...	...	...	...	...
1863	...	...	...	45.35	...	45.66	...	...	...	44.85	...	...	...	...	...	...
1864	...	...	...	47.28	...	46.18	...	...	...	44.66	...	...	...	...	...	...
1865	...	...	...	47.31	...	46.02	...	...	...	44.31	47.87‖	...	...	...	...	...
1866	...	...	...	45.92*	...	44.73	...	...	...	42.80	...	...	...	...	...	...
1867	...	...	...	45.61*	...	45.08	...	...	...	43.28*	...	...	...	...	...	...
1868	...	...	...	45.42	...	44.02	...	...	...	42.47	...	...	...	...	...	...
1869	...	...	...	45.96	...	44.84	...	...	...	43.26	...	...	42.01	...	...	...
1870	...	47.90	...	48.75*	...	47.62	...	...	...	46.35	...	...	45.97	...	...	...
	47.51	46.45	43.96	46.31	46.59	46.35	45.47	44.64	50.58	44.43	47.33	45.41	44.14	42.37	43.12	49.69

NEW YORK.—Continued.

Year.	Prattsburg.	Red Hook.	Rochester.	Rouse's Point.	Sackett's Harbor.	Sag Harbor.	Salem.	Saratoga.	Schenectady.	Seneca Falls.	Skaneateles.	Smithville.	South Hartford.	South Trenton.	Spencertown.	Springville.
	°	°	°	°	°	°	°	°	°	°	°	°	°	°	°	°
1828	...	...	...	...	...	...	48.15	...	...	...	...	...	...	...	...	...
1829	44.13	...	...	...	...	...	44.04	...	46.29	...	...	...	...	...	...	...
1830	45.90	48.62	48.82	...	...	...	45.54	...	...	...	...	...	...	...	...	...
1831	...	48.83	48.45	...	...	...	...	...	...	...	...	...	...	...	...	...
1832	...	47.38	50.22	...	...	...	...	...	...	...	...	...	...	...	...	...
1833	...	45.22	49.60	...	...	...	...	...	...	...	...	...	...	...	...	...
1834	...	48.20	50.16	...	...	...	...	...	...	...	...	...	...	...	...	48.42
1835	...	46.26	48.11	...	...	...	...	...	...	...	...	...	...	...	...	...
1836	...	45.63	44.11	...	...	...	...	...	44.18	...	...	...	...	...	...	...
1837	...	45.93	45.76	...	...	...	...	...	45.57	...	...	...	...	...	...	...
1838	...	...	44.60	...	...	...	...	...	...	...	...	...	...	...	...	...
1839	43.64	48.28	47.17	...	...	...	...	...	...	...	...	...	...	...	...	45.76
1840	44.80	51.67	46.29	...	...	...	45.99	...	...	...	...	...	...	...	...	...
1841	44.01	48.87	45.37	...	...	...	45.59	...	...	...	...	...	...	...	...	...
1842	44.00	49.67	46.36	...	...	...	...	...	...	...	...	...	...	...	...	41.39
1843	43.62	...	44.80	...	...	...	44.69	...	...	...	...	...	...	...	...	41.93
1844	45.19	...	47.18	...	...	...	47.32	...	...	...	...	...	...	...	...	...
1845	46.47	...	46.99	43.34*	...	...	46.27	...	...	...	...	...	...	...	...	...
1846	46.01	...	48.40	45.34	...	...	46.42	...	...	...	...	...	...	...	...	...
1847	...	...	46.07	43.48	...	...	45.94	...	...	...	...	...	...	...	...	45.06
1848	...	...	47.94	44.68	...	...	...	...	...	...	...	...	...	...	...	...
1849	...	...	46.32	42.94	...	...	...	...	...	...	...	...	...	...	...	45.10
1850	...	...	47.08	43.55	...	...	...	...	...	...	...	...	...	...	...	46.24
1851	...	...	47.05	42.54	...	...	...	...	...	...	...	...	...	...	...	...
1852	...	...	46.99	42.80	...	...	...	...	...	46.99	...	...	...	...	...	...
1853	...	...	...	...	...	...	...	...	...	...	...	...	...	...	...	...
1854	...	...	...	...	...	50.79	...	...	...	...	...	...	...	...	...	...
1855	...	...	...	...	...	51.30*	...	...	...	...	...	43 90	...	...	45.01	...
1856	...	...	45.72	...	...	49.18*	...	...	...	...	...	...	...	...	42.77	...
1857	...	...	46.75	...	...	49.98	...	45.46	...	...	...	...	...	...	44.78	...
1858	...	...	48.04	...	...	51.17	...	...	...	...	...	...	...	...	...	...
1859	...	...	47.94	...	...	...	...	...	...	...	...	...	...	...	...	...
1860	...	...	46.72	...	45.59	...	...	...	...	...	...	...	...	...	...	...
1861	...	...	46.99	...	44.59	...	...	...	...	...	45.80	...	...	...	...	...
1862	...	...	46.55	...	45.39	...	...	...	...	...	45.64*	...	...	...	...	...
1863	...	...	46.58	...	46.69	...	...	...	...	...	46.29*	...	...	...	...	...
1864	...	...	47.41	...	47.99	...	...	...	47.60	...	44.87	...	49.37	...	...	...
1865	...	...	47.79	...	47.99	...	...	...	...	...	45.21*	...	48.88	44.75*	...	...
1866	...	...	46.12	...	46.49*	...	...	...	...	...	44.52*	...	48.21	43.43	...	...
1867	...	...	45.44	...	44.69	...	...	...	...	...	...	...	47.29	43.31	...	...
1868	...	...	45.41	...	...	...	...	...	...	...	...	...	46.19*	41.11*	...	...
1869	...	...	46.06	...	...	...	...	...	...	...	...	...	47.46*	41.98	...	...
1870	...	...	48.54*	...	...	...	...	...	...	...	...	...	50.66	45.63	...	...
	44.67	47.89	47.06	43.64	46.04	50.62	46.08	45.92	45.90	46.73	45.39	44.41	48.31	43.37	44.84	44.79

	NEW YORK.—Continued.															N. C.
Year.	Syracuse.	Theresa.	Throgg's Neck.	Troy.	Utica.	Wampsville.	Waterbury.	Waterford.	Watertown.	Watervliet Arsenal.	Wellsville.	West Point.	White Plains.	Whitestone.	Wilson.	Ashville.
	°	°	°	°	°	°	°	°	°	°	°	°	°	°	°	°
1824	...	...	...	...	...	...	...	...	...	49.51	...	52.75	...	...	...	...
1825	...	...	...	...	...	...	...	...	...	50.48	...	...	...	...	...	...
1826	...	...	...	...	48.10	...	...	...	...	50.32	...	52.53	...	...	...	...
1827	...	...	...	...	46.64	...	...	...	...	47.85	...	51.28	...	...	...	...
1828	...	...	...	...	49.92	...	...	...	...	51.28	...	54.55	...	...	...	...
1829	...	...	...	...	44.03	...	...	...	...	47.81	...	50.25	...	...	...	...
1830	...	...	...	...	45.97	...	...	...	...	48.34	...	52.25	...	...	...	...
1831	...	...	...	...	44.77	...	...	...	...	47.83	...	51.42	...	...	...	...
1832	...	...	...	...	43.52	...	...	...	...	46.83	...	50.86	...	...	...	...
1833	...	...	...	...	43.81	...	...	...	...	46.27*	...	51.24	...	...	...	...
1834	...	...	...	...	44.43	...	...	...	...	48.60	...	51.13	...	44.69	...	...
1835	...	...	...	...	42.12	...	...	...	...	45.61	...	49.39	...	43.28	...	...
1836	...	...	...	...	40.42	...	...	...	...	43.91	...	47.41	...	43.83	...	...
1837	...	...	...	...	43.43	...	...	...	...	45.14	...	47.84	...	42.45	...	...
1838	...	...	...	...	45.37	...	...	...	...	46.35	...	50.41	...	43.88	...	...
1839	...	...	...	...	45.45	...	...	...	...	47.37	...	50.99	...	43.99	...	...
1840	...	...	...	...	46.63	...	...	...	...	47.82	...	51.01	...	48.35	...	...
1841	...	...	...	...	46.14	...	...	...	...	48.17	...	50.18	...	...	...	...
1842	...	...	...	...	46.40	...	...	...	...	48.67	...	52.99	...	...	...	...
1843	46.83	...	...	...	44.88	...	...	...	...	47.15	...	49.05	...	...	...	...
1844	...	...	...	...	46.43	...	...	...	...	47.36	...	48.86	...	...	...	...
1845	...	...	...	...	46.82	...	...	...	...	48.03	...	50.23	...	...	...	...
1846	...	...	...	...	47.73	...	...	...	...	47.21	...	50.69	...	...	...	...
1847	...	...	...	...	45.70	...	...	...	...	48.13	...	50.13	...	...	...	...
1848	...	...	...	...	45.05	...	...	...	...	48.93	...	50.28	...	...	...	...
1849	...	...	...	...	...	...	...	...	...	46.49	...	48.86	...	...	...	...
1850	...	...	...	...	...	...	...	...	...	46.11	...	49.11	...	...	...	...
1851	...	...	...	...	46.20	...	...	...	...	47.62	...	49.37	...	...	...	...
1852	47.49	...	...	...	46.27	...	...	...	...	49.39	...	48.87	...	...	...	...
1853	...	...	...	...	...	...	...	...	...	48.36	...	50.50	...	...	...	...
1854	...	...	...	...	...	46.82	...	...	...	46.06	...	50.14	...	...	...	...
1855	...	...	...	...	...	46.35	...	...	...	...	...	50.18	...	...	...	...
1856	...	...	...	...	...	44.91	...	45.12*	43.60	...	...	50.15	...	...	...	...
1857	...	...	...	...	...	45.80	...	46.09	...	...	43.99*	50.92	...	...	...	...
1858	...	...	...	...	...	...	...	47.03	...	...	...	52.77	...	...	...	...
1859	...	...	...	...	...	44.95	...	47.36	...	...	...	53.20	...	...	...	...
1860	...	...	...	...	...	45.44*	...	...	...	...	...	52.59	...	...	...	...
1861	...	42.54*	...	47.35	...	44.77	...	47.61	...	...	...	52.17	...	...	47.01	...
1862	...	42.92	...	47.68	...	...	...	47.19	...	...	...	51.98	...	...	47.27	...
1863	...	42.69*	...	47.61*	...	...	...	...	...	...	...	51.57	...	...	46.93*	...
1864	...	44.71	51.39*	...	...	...	...	...	...	...	...	52.25	50.62*	...	47.39	...
1865	...	44.18	...	...	...	...	...	...	...	...	...	53.35	50.72*	...	...	...
1866	...	...	49.68	...	...	...	...	...	...	...	...	51.42*	48.23*	...	...	...
1867	...	...	50.09	47.32*	...	...	...	...	...	...	...	50.94	48.98*	...	...	...
1868	...	...	48.67	46.64	...	...	...	...	...	...	...	49.98	47.94	...	...	53.41
1869	...	...	50.07*	...	...	...	43.31	...	...	...	...	54.51	49.41	...	...	53.27
1870	...	...	52.83	...	49.04	...	45.54*	...	...	...	...	54.69	51.92	...	...	53.84
	47.28	43.37	50.50	47.93	45.54	45.60	44.43	46.77	43.60	47.73	45.04	51.06	49.46	44.18	47.13	53.83

NORTH CAROLINA.—Continued.

Year.	Attaway Hill.	Beaufort.	Bethmont.	Chapel Hill.	Davidson College.	Fort Johnson.	Fort Macon.	Gaston.	Goldsboro.	Kenansville.	Murfreesboro.	Oxford.	Raleigh.	Statesville, near.	Thornburg.	Warrenton.
	°	°	°	°	°	°	°	°	°	°	°	°	°	°	°	°
1822	...	...	...	...	...	67.46	...	...	...	...	...	...	...	...	...	...
1823	...	...	...	...	...	65.27	...	...	...	...	...	...	...	...	...	...
1824	...	...	...	...	...	66.55	...	...	...	...	...	...	...	...	...	...
1825	...	...	...	...	...	65.77	...	...	...	...	...	...	...	...	...	...
1826	...	...	...	...	...	67.66	...	...	...	...	...	...	...	...	...	...
1827	...	...	...	...	...	...	...	...	...	...	...	...	...	...	...	...
1828	...	...	...	...	...	68.17	...	...	...	...	...	...	...	...	...	...
1829	...	...	...	...	...	64.37*	...	...	...	...	...	...	...	...	...	...
1830	...	...	...	...	...	65.76*	...	...	...	...	...	...	...	...	...	...
1831	...	...	...	...	...	63.25	...	...	...	...	...	...	...	...	...	...
1832	...	...	...	...	...	65.82	...	...	...	...	...	...	...	...	...	...
1833	...	...	...	...	...	64.48	...	...	...	...	...	...	...	...	...	...
1834	...	...	...	...	...	64.24	64.52	...	...	...	...	...	...	...	...	...
1835	...	...	...	...	...	62.74	61.29	...	...	...	...	...	...	...	...	...
1836	...	...	...	...	...	...	...	...	...	...	...	...	...	...	...	...
1837	...	...	...	...	...	...	...	...	...	...	...	...	...	...	...	...
1838	...	...	...	...	...	...	...	...	...	...	...	...	...	...	...	...
1839	...	...	...	...	...	...	...	...	...	...	...	...	...	...	...	...
1840	...	...	...	...	...	...	...	...	...	...	...	...	...	...	...	...
1841	...	...	...	...	...	...	...	...	...	...	...	...	...	...	...	...
1842	...	...	...	...	...	...	...	...	...	...	...	...	...	...	...	...
1843	...	...	...	...	...	64.23	61.98	...	...	...	...	...	...	...	...	...
1844	...	...	...	...	...	64.41	61.79*	...	...	...	...	...	...	...	...	...
1845	...	...	...	61.45	...	...	...	...	...	...	...	...	...	...	...	...
1846	...	...	...	60.39	...	...	...	...	...	...	...	...	...	...	...	...
1847	...	...	...	58.82	...	...	...	...	...	...	...	...	...	...	...	...
1848	...	...	...	59.93	...	...	...	...	...	...	...	...	...	...	...	...
1849	...	...	...	58.82	...	...	...	...	...	...	...	...	...	...	...	...
1850	...	...	59.20	59.32	...	...	...	...	...	...	...	...	...	...	...	...
1851	...	...	...	59.36	...	...	...	...	...	...	...	...	...	...	...	...
1852	...	...	...	59.14	...	...	...	...	...	...	...	...	...	...	...	...
1853	...	...	...	59.71	...	...	...	...	...	...	...	...	...	...	...	...
1854	...	...	...	60.21	...	...	...	...	...	...	...	...	...	...	59.39*	...
1855	...	...	...	59.36	...	...	...	...	...	...	...	...	...	...	...	...
1856	...	...	...	57.22	...	...	...	...	58.71*	...	...	...	...	...	...	...
1857	...	...	...	57.61	...	...	...	59.58	...	...	56.25	...	...	...	...	...
1858	...	...	...	58.89	58.68*	...	...	57.59	...	...	59.12	...	...	...	...	...
1859	...	...	...	59.41*	...	...	...	57.76	...	...	59.66	...	...	...	...	...
1860	...	...	...	...	...	...	...	56.89	60.81*	...	...	...	...	...	...	...
1861	...	...	...	...	...	...	...	...	...	...	...	...	...	...	...	...
1862	...	...	...	...	...	...	...	...	...	...	...	...	...	...	...	...
1863	...	...	...	...	...	...	...	...	...	...	...	...	...	...	...	...
1864	...	61.79	...	...	...	...	...	...	...	...	...	...	...	...	...	...
1865	...	...	...	...	...	...	...	...	...	...	...	...	...	...	...	...
1866	...	...	...	...	...	...	...	...	...	...	...	...	...	...	...	...
1867	57.69	...	...	...	...	...	...	...	61.12	...	...	58.04*	58.04	54.32*	...	...
1868	56.12	...	...	...	...	...	...	...	60.41	...	...	56.22	58.23	53.50	...	...
1869	56.41	...	...	63.16*	...	...	...	...	62.54*	62.85*	...	57.97*	...	53.79*	...	...
1870	57.58	...	...	...	...	...	...	...	63.44	...	...	56.85*	...	52.92*	...	56.61
	57.04	62.07	59.20	59.76	57.92	65.35	61.98	56.95	61.10	62.52	58.45	57.56	58.52	53.92	58.77	56.91

N. C.—Continued.		OHIO.									
Year.	Wilson.	Athens.	Austinburg.	Avon.	Bellefontaine.	Bethel.	Bowling Green.	Chillicothe.	Cincinnati.	Cincinnati.	Cleveland.
	°	°	°	°	°	°	°	°	°	°	°
...	...	...	...	...	...	...	...	...	...	...	...
...	...	...	...	...	...	...	...	...	...	...	...
...	...	...	...	...	...	...	...	...	...	...	...
...	...	...	...	...	...	...	...	...	...	...	...
...	...	...	...	...	...	...	...	...	...	...	...
...	...	...	...	...	...	...	...	...	...	...	...
1806	...	...	...	...	...	...	...	...	54.1	...	...
1807	...	...	...	...	...	...	...	...	54.4	...	...
1808	...	...	...	...	...	...	...	...	56.4	...	...
1809	...	...	...	...	...	...	...	...	54.4	...	...
1810	...	...	...	...	...	...	...	...	52.8	...	...
1811	...	...	...	...	...	...	...	...	56.6	...	...
1812	...	...	...	...	...	...	...	...	52.6	...	...
1813	...	...	...	...	...	...	...	...	52.7	...	...
1819	...	...	...	...	...	...	...	58.34	56.8	...	...
1835	...	...	...	...	...	...	...	...	...	50.93	...
1836	...	...	...	...	...	...	...	...	...	51.17	...
1837	...	...	...	...	...	...	...	...	...	53.00	...
1838	...	...	...	...	...	...	...	...	...	51.80	...
1839	...	...	...	...	...	...	...	...	...	54.10	...
1840	...	...	...	...	...	...	...	...	...	53.41	46.12
1841	...	...	...	...	...	...	...	...	...	53.93	45.73
1842	...	...	...	...	...	...	...	...	...	53.52	46.27
1843	...	...	...	...	...	...	...	...	...	51.39	44.78
1844	...	...	...	...	...	...	...	...	...	54.43	47.01
1845	...	...	...	...	...	...	...	...	...	53.08	47.08
1846	...	...	...	...	...	...	...	...	...	54.93	48.98
1847	...	...	...	...	...	...	...	...	...	52.62	...
1848	...	...	...	...	...	...	...	...	...	54.00	...
1849	...	...	...	...	...	...	...	...	...	53.61	...
1850	...	...	...	...	...	...	...	...	...	54.12	...
1851	...	...	...	...	...	...	...	...	...	54.89	...
1852	...	51.64	...	...	...	...	...	...	...	54.25	...
1853	...	...	...	...	...	...	...	...	...	54.12	...
1854	...	...	...	...	...	...	...	...	...	56.15	...
1855	...	...	...	...	...	...	...	...	...	55.10*	...
1856	...	...	44.50*	...	...	...	...	...	...	52.78	45.87
1857	...	...	...	...	...	...	...	...	...	53.43	46.99
1858	...	...	51.85	...	51.51	...	50.71	...	...	57.17	49.57
1859	...	...	...	50.00	49.57	...	50.30	...	...	56.27	49.50*
1860	...	...	...	...	...	51.52*	...	...	...	56.12	49.10
1861	...	...	...	...	...	...	50.55	...	...	55.87	50.32
1862	...	...	...	...	...	...	50.60*	...	...	56.28	49.63
1863	...	...	46.75*	...	...	49.56*	50.60*	...	...	55.39*	49.88
1864	...	...	47.31	...	...	49.58	...	...	...	53.88	49.77
1865	...	...	47.68	...	...	51.43	...	...	...	56.40	50.38
1866	60.54*	...	...	...	...	48.48	49.83	...	...	54.75	48.65
1867	...	...	...	...	...	49.68	48.80	...	...	55.77	49.41
1868	...	...	...	...	...	49.57	48.95	...	...	54.33	47.10
1869	...	...	...	...	...	50.69	49.09	...	...	55.39	47.47
1870	...	...	...	...	...	52.44	52.43	...	...	55.82	48.89
	60.54	52.29	47.96	50.21	49.50	50.37	50.22	58.34	53.73[1]	54.29	48.14

OHIO.				
Year.	College Hill.	Columbus.	Croton.	Dayton.
	°	°	°	°
1814	52.0	...	...	...
1815	51.7	...	...	...
1816	51.0	...	...	...
1817	50.4	...	...	...
1818	50.4	...	...	...
1819	53.7	...	...	...
1820	52.1	...	...	...
1821	51.0	...	...	...
1822	52.2	...	...	...
1823	51.7	...	...	...
1824	52.5	...	...	...
1825	53.6	...	...	...
1826	53.1	...	...	...
1827	52.9	...	...	...
1828	54.0	...	...	...
1829	50.8	...	...	...
1830	53.5	...	...	...
1831	48.0	...	...	...
1832	51.8	...	...	...
1833	52.5	...	...	...
1834	52.6	...	...	...
1835	49.2	...	...	...
1836	49.0	...	...	...
1837	50.3	...	...	...
1838	49.5	...	...	...
1839	52.8	...	...	...
1840	52.3	...	...	...
1841	52.0	...	...	...
1842	52.7	...	...	...
1843	48.8	...	...	...
1844	53.0	...	...	...
1845	52.6	...	...	...
1846	54.0	...	...	...
1847	52.0	...	...	...
1848	52.6	...	...	...
1854	55.9*	...	...	...
1856	...	...	...	48.55*
1857	...	...	...	...
1858	...	...	...	...
1859	52.8*	...	...	...
1860	...	...	49.75*	...
1861	52.9*	...	51.74	...
1862	53.1*	...	50.67*	...
1863	52.4*	...	...	...
1864	52.1	53.42*	...	...
1865	53.5*	...	...	...
1866	51.1	...	...	...
1867	52.7	...	...	...
1868	50.8	...	...	...
1869	52.3	...	...	...
1870	54.6	...	...	...
	51.91	53.29	50.42	50.07

[1] Hours of observation unknown.

OHIO.—Continued.

Year.	East Fairfield.	Edinburg.	Freedom.	Gallipolis.	Germantown.	Gilmore.	Granville.	Hillsboro.	Hiram.	Hudson.	Jackson (Jackson Co.)	Jackson (Monroe Co.)	Jacksonburg.	Kelly's Isl'd.	Kenton.	Kingston.
	°	°	°	°	°	°	°	°	°	°	°	°	°	°	°	°
1836	...	...	...	...	...	...	...	47.01	...	...	...	...	...	...	...	...
1837	...	...	...	...	...	...	49.51	48.21	...	...	...	...	...	...	...	...
1838	...	...	...	...	...	...	44.08	47.59	...	47.19*	...	...	...	...	...	...
1839	...	...	...	...	...	...	46.17	50.21	...	49.30	...	...	...	...	...	...
1840	...	...	...	...	...	...	43.87	51.87*	...	49.40	...	...	...	...	...	...
1841	...	...	...	...	...	...	43.54	50.06	...	48.80	...	...	...	...	...	...
1842	...	...	...	...	...	...	45.54	49.80	...	49.90	...	...	...	...	...	...
1843	...	...	...	...	...	...	42.33	48.67	...	47.89*	...	...	...	...	...	...
1844	...	...	...	...	...	...	45.41	52.10*	...	...	...	...	...	...	...	...
1845	...	...	...	...	...	...	46.50	52.35*	...	...	...	...	...	...	...	...
1846	...	...	...	...	...	...	46.71	53.67	...	...	...	...	...	...	...	...
1847	...	...	...	...	...	...	47.09	50.43	...	...	...	...	...	...	...	...
1848	...	...	...	...	...	...	45.09	51.45	...	...	...	...	...	...	...	...
1849	...	...	...	...	...	...	44.66	49.84	...	...	...	...	...	...	...	...
1850	...	...	...	...	...	...	44.33	51.51	...	...	...	...	...	...	...	...
1851	...	...	...	...	...	...	45.17	50.94	...	...	54.05	...	...	...	...	...
1852	...	...	...	...	...	...	...	52.82	...	...	...	...	...	...	...	...
1853	...	...	...	...	...	...	...	51.67	...	...	...	...	...	...	...	...
1854	...	...	...	56.86*	50.83	...	52.86*	53.32	...	...	54.56*	...	...	...	...	...
1855	...	...	...	55.19	50.39	...	50.82	50.69	...	...	53.64*	...	...	...	...	...
1856	...	...	...	...	47.60	...	47.50	49.68	45.51	...	...	...	...	...	...	...
1857	...	46.77*	...	50.88*	...	...	...	48.48	46.22	...	...	...	...	...	...	...
1858	...	49.18	...	...	...	...	...	51.78	49.16	...	...	52.40	...	...	...	...
1859	...	...	...	...	...	...	...	50.97	...	48.42	...	51.98	...	48.33*	...	...
1860	...	...	...	...	...	...	...	51.77	...	...	...	...	...	49.25	...	...
1861	49.04*	...	50.49*	...	...	...	...	...	...	50.24	...	...	...	49.92	...	...
1862	49.69	...	...	...	...	...	...	...	...	49.63	...	...	...	49.27	...	...
1863	49.07*	...	...	...	...	...	...	...	...	...	...	...	...	49.35	...	...
1864	48.35	...	...	...	...	...	...	51.11	...	...	...	...	...	49.65	...	51.83
1865	49.44	...	...	54.02*	...	...	...	52.00	...	...	...	...	...	51.12	...	52.40
1866	47.86	...	...	52.74*	...	...	...	50.45	...	...	...	...	...	49.31	...	51.23
1867	...	...	...	...	...	...	...	50.90	...	...	...	...	...	49.54	52.60	...
1868	...	...	...	...	...	...	...	49.90	...	...	...	...	...	48.51	50.37*	...
1869	...	...	...	...	...	50.35*	...	49.97	...	...	...	...	51.26	48.18	53.23*	...
1870	...	...	. .	...	...	...	...	52.23	...	...	...	...	53.86	51.91	53.37	...
	48.69	48.17	49.15	53.53	50.40	50.96	46.58	50.65	47.32	49.09	52.85	52.19	52.11	49.64	51.68	51.60

OHIO.—Continued.

Year.	Lancaster.	Little Mountain.	Madison.	Margaretta.	Year.	Marietta.	Year.	Marietta.	Marion.	Montville.	Mt. Auburn.	Newark.	New Birmingham.	New Lisbon.	New Westfield.	North Base Island.
	°	°	°	°		°		°	°	°	°	°	°	°	°	°
...	...	...	...	...	1818	53.45*	...	...	...	...	...	...	...	...	...	...
...	...	...	...	...	1819	54.07	...	...	...	...	...	...	...	...	...	...
...	...	...	...	...	1820	53.07	...	...	...	...	...	...	...	...	...	...
...	...	...	...	...	1821	31.61	1846	54.03	...	...	...	...	...	...	...	...
...	...	...	...	...	1822	54.09	1847	51.62	...	...	...	...	...	...	...	...
...	...	...	...	...	1823	51.86*	1848	53.28	...	...	...	...	...	...	...	...
...	...	...	...	...	1824	...	1849	51.85	...	...	...	...	...	...	...	...
...	...	...	...	...	1825	...	1850	52.07	...	...	...	...	...	...	...	...
...	...	...	...	...	1826	54.07	1851	52.33	...	...	...	...	...	...	...	...
...	...	...	...	...	1827	54.25	1852	52.20	...	...	...	...	...	...	...	...
...	...	...	...	...	1828	55.38	1853	52.61	...	...	...	...	...	...	...	...
...	...	...	...	...	1829	52.33	1854	53.96	...	...	...	...	...	...	...	...
1855	...	...	48.01*	...	1830	54.67	1855	52.84	...	...	...	...	...	47.94	...	...
1856	...	...	44.95	...	1831	50.36	1856	49.71	...	...	51.33*	...	...	45.11	...	...
1857	...	...	46.80	...	1832	52.66	1857	50.84	...	46.57*	...	...	...	51.40	...	...
1858	51.81*	...	49.15	...	1833	53.04	1858	53.44	...	49.37	...	...	...	55.38	...	...
1859	...	...	49.18	...	1834	53.39	1859	52.93	...	48.64	...	...	...	52.56	...	...
1860	...	...	47.83	...	1835	50.54	1860	52.42	...	48.30	...	49.24	...	...	...	...
1861	...	...	48.98	...	1836	50.43	1861	52.54	...	49.16	54.28	51.85*	...	50.83	...	...
1862	...	...	48.60	...	1837	51.28	1862	52.42	...	49.02	54.37	52.49*	...	50.21	51.63*	...
1863	...	...	...	...	1838	50.57	1863	51.50	...	...	...	...	...	49.53*	...	...
1864	...	...	...	...	1839	52.42	1864	50.59	...	...	...	...	47.84*	49.53	...	...
1865	...	...	...	...	1840	52.27	1865	52.32	49.46*	...	...	...	49.05*	50.86*	...	...
1866	...	...	...	...	1841	52.05	1866	50.33	47.00	...	...	...	47.65*	49.28	...	...
1867	...	47.81*	...	...	1842	52.39	1867	50.45	48.22	...	...	...	...	49.30	...	...
1868	...	...	...	47.77	1843	50.38	1868	50.21	47.30	...	...	...	47.93*	49.72	...	...
1869	...	47.20*	...	49.04	1844	52.84	1869	50.32	47.64	...	55.62	...	47.59*	...	...	...
1870	...	49.64	...	51.36	1845	52.16	1870	51.91	50.18	...	55.29	...	...	...	...	51.39
	51.14	47.70	47.98	49.39				52.24	48.46	48.79	54.34	51.07	48.23	50.09	51.78	50.20

OHIO.—Continued.

Year.	North Bend.	North Fairfield.	Norwalk.	Oberlin.	Oxford.	Perrysburg.	Portsmouth.	Ripley (Brown Co.)	Ripley (Huron Co.)	Rockport.	Salem.	Savannah.	Saybrook.	Seville.	Steubenville.	Tarlton.
	°	°	°	°	°	°	°	°	°	°	°	°	°	°	°	°
1824	...	...	...	...	...	...	55.28*	...	...	...	...	...	...	...	...	...
1825	...	...	...	...	...	...	55.13	...	...	...	...	...	...	...	...	...
1826	...	...	...	...	...	...	55.73	...	...	...	...	...	...	...	...	...
1827	...	...	...	...	...	...	55.83	...	...	...	...	...	...	...	...	...
1828	...	...	...	...	...	...	57.43	...	...	...	...	...	...	...	...	...
1829	...	...	...	...	...	...	53.93	...	...	...	...	...	...	...	...	...
1830	...	...	...	...	...	...	55.63	...	...	...	...	...	...	...	...	...
1831	...	...	...	...	...	...	...	...	...	...	...	...	...	...	51.20	...
1832	...	...	...	...	...	...	...	...	...	...	...	...	...	...	51.32	...
1833	...	...	...	...	...	...	...	...	...	...	...	...	...	...	50.85	...
1834	...	...	...	...	...	...	...	...	...	...	...	...	...	...	51.26	...
1835	...	...	...	...	...	...	...	...	...	...	...	...	...	...	48.59	...
1836	...	...	...	...	...	...	...	...	...	...	...	...	...	...	48.19	...
1837	...	...	...	...	...	...	...	...	...	...	...	...	...	...	49.01	...
1838	...	...	...	...	...	...	...	...	...	...	...	...	...	...	48.59	...
1839	...	...	...	...	...	...	...	...	...	...	...	...	...	...	50.39	...
1840	...	...	...	...	...	...	...	...	...	...	...	...	...	...	50.90	...
1841	...	...	...	...	...	...	...	...	...	...	...	...	...	...	49.84	...
1842	...	...	...	...	...	...	...	...	...	...	...	...	...	...	50.69	...
1843	...	...	...	...	...	...	...	...	...	...	...	...	...	...	49.12	...
1844	...	...	...	...	...	...	...	...	...	...	...	...	...	...	51.33	...
1845	...	...	...	...	...	...	...	...	...	...	...	...	...	...	51.14	...
1846	...	...	...	...	...	...	...	...	...	...	...	...	...	...	52.61	...
1847	...	...	..	...	...	...	...	...	...	...	...	...	...	...	50 81	...
1848	...	...	...	...	...	...	...	...	...	...	...	...	...	...	51.27	...
1849	...	...	...	...	...	...	...	...	...	...	...	...	...	...	51.46	...
1850	...	...	...	...	...	...	...	...	...	...	...	...	...	...	51.37	...
1851	...	...	...	...	...	...	...	...	...	...	...	...	...	...	51.97	...
1852	...	...	...	...	...	...	...	...	...	...	...	...	...	...	51.26	...
1853	...	...	...	...	...	...	...	...	...	...	...	...	...	...	51.78	...
1854	...	...	...	50.65	...	53.16*	...	...	...	50.69	...	52.94*	...	...	53.63	...
1855	...	...	...	49.21	...	51.83	...	..	...	52.69	...	49.67*	...	...	50.44	...
1856	...	...	...	46.67*	...	48.92	52.47*	...	...	49.69	...	45.32	...	...	47.71	...
1857	...	...	...	...	...	49.68	...	...	...	51.69	...	47.82	...	...	48.56	...
1858	...	...	...	...	...	...	...	54.01	...	53.69	...	50.81	...	...	51.35	...
1859	...	...	...	...	...	...	55.30	...	...	52.64	...	50.62	...	...	50.01	...
1860	53.28	...	...	...	...	...	...	56.85*	...	52.35	...	49.47	...	...	50.34	...
1861	53.05	...	49.28	...	...	...	55.20	...	...	53.28	...	50.00	...	49.81*	51.12	...
1862	53.38*	...	48.51	...	...	...	56.24*	...	...	52.65	...	48.25	...	...	51.72	...
1863	...	...	48.72*	...	...	...	...	...	...	52.30*	...	...	...	...	51.28	...
1864	...	...	48.06	...	51.48	...	54.18	53.85*	...	...	...	...	...	...	50.52	...
1865	...	...	49.30	...	52.13	...	...	56.21*	...	...	...	...	48.03	...	52.22	...
1866	...	...	47.64*	...	50.61*	...	...	...	...	...	...	...	...	...	51.08	...
1867	...	50.71*	48.54	...	51.04	...	...	...	50.50*	...	...	...	...	...	52.10	...
1868	...	48.41	47.34	...	50.56	...	...	...	...	...	...	...	...	...	50.41*	...
1869	...	49.12	...	...	50.97	...	...	...	...	...	...	...	...	...	51.11	...
1870	...	51.23	...	...	52.97*	...	...	...	...	...	51.14	...	...	...	52.74	54.73
	53.21	50.02	48.53	48.64	51.35	50.88	54.98	54.66	49.79	52.49	51.14	49.55	47.89	49.08	50.78	55.24

	OHIO.—Continued.								OREGON.							
Year.	Toledo.	Troy.	Urbana.	Welchfield.	Westerville.	Windham.	Wooster.	Zanesville.	Astoria.	Block House.	Camp Harney.	Camp Lyons.	Camp Three Forks.	Camp Warner.	Camp Watson.	Eola.
	°	°	°	°	°	°	°	°	°	°	°	°	°	°	°	°
1851	...	...	...	...	...	...	...	...	51.92*	...	...	...	...	...	...	...
1852	...	...	...	...	...	...	...	...	...	...	...	...	...	...	...	...
1853	...	...	...	...	...	...	...	...	...	...	...	...	...	...	...	...
1854	...	...	52.30*	...	...	...	...	...	48.67*	...	...	...	...	...	...	...
1855	...	...	49.59	...	...	...	...	51.47*	49.76*	...	...	...	...	...	...	...
1856	...	...	46.43	...	...	...	...	...	49.79*	...	...	...	...	...	...	...
1857	47.07	...	47.27	46.54*	...	46.57*	...	...	50.30	...	...	...	...	...	...	...
1858	50.00*	...	50.52	49.37	52.03	48.90	...	...	48.99	50.64*	...	...	...	...	...	...
1859	50.01	51.75	49.79	48.78	51.64	48.63	...	...	48.25	49.30*	...	...	...	...	...	...
1860	49.24	52.65	...	47.99*	51.23	...	...	...	49.81	50.71*	...	...	...	...	...	...
1861	50.01	52.05	...	48.80	51.71	...	...	...	48.49	...	...	...	...	...	...	...
1862	50.52	51.70	50.52	48.39	50.92	...	...	...	47.34	47.81	...	...	...	...	...	...
1863	50.81	...	50.72	47.87	48.85*	...	...	...	48.81	...	...	...	...	...	...	...
1864	49.56	...	49.19	47.59	49.71*	...	48.65*	...	49.13	...	...	...	...	...	...	...
1865	50.07	...	50.69	49.17	51.18*	...	50.08	...	47.46	...	...	...	...	...	...	...
1866	47.84	...	49.19	...	50.55	...	...	...	48.06	...	...	...	...	...	...	...
1867	48.43	...	50.17	...	...	...	50.63*	...	48.62	...	...	...	...	...	45.68*	...
1868	47.41	...	48.99	...	48.51*	...	50.71	...	47.94	...	45.90	48.01*	46.69	42.95	42.55	...
1869	48.19	...	49.12	...	49.45	...	50.32*	...	50.16	...	50.59	...	48.99	46.17	...	...
1870	...	...	51.46	...	52.06	...	...	...	49.48	...	49.57	...	...	46.62	...	49.24
	49.20	51.95	50.26	48.17	50.74	48.23	50.21	53.35	48.95	49.89	48.69	47.63	47.84	45.36	44.48	49.24

	OREGON.—Continued.											PENNSYLVANIA.				
Year.	Fort Dalles.	Fort Hoskins.	Fort Klamath.	Fort Lane.	Fort Oxford.	Fort Stevens.	Fort Umpqua.	Fort Yamhill.	Oregon City.	Portland.	Salem.	Abington.	Allegheny Arsenal.	Avondell.	Beaver Seminary.	Bedford.
	°	°	°	°	°	°	°	°	°	°	°	°	°	°	°	°
1825	...	...	...	...	...	...	...	...	...	...	...	...	52.75	...	...	...
1826	...	...	...	...	...	...	...	...	...	...	...	...	53.51*	...	...	...
1827	...	...	...	...	...	...	...	...	...	...	...	...	54.28	...	...	...
1828	...	...	...	...	...	...	...	...	...	...	...	...	...	...	...	...
1829	...	...	...	...	...	...	...	...	...	...	...	...	...	...	...	...
1830	...	...	...	...	...	...	...	...	...	...	...	...	...	...	...	...
1831	...	...	...	...	...	...	...	...	...	...	...	...	...	...	...	...
1832	...	...	...	...	...	...	...	...	...	...	...	...	...	...	...	...
1833	...	...	...	...	...	...	...	...	...	...	...	...	...	...	...	...
1834	...	...	...	...	...	...	...	...	...	...	...	...	...	...	...	...
1835	...	...	...	...	...	...	...	...	...	...	...	...	...	...	...	...
1836	...	...	...	...	...	...	...	...	...	...	...	...	47.84	...	...	...
1837	...	...	...	...	...	...	...	...	...	...	...	...	46.50	...	...	...
1838	...	...	...	...	...	...	...	...	...	...	...	...	49.61	...	...	...
1839	...	...	...	...	...	...	...	...	...	...	...	...	50.58	...	...	...
1840	...	...	...	...	...	...	...	...	...	...	...	...	50.15	...	...	...
1841	...	...	...	...	...	...	...	...	...	...	...	...	49.23	...	...	...
1842	...	...	...	...	...	...	...	...	...	...	...	...	50.42	...	...	...
1843	...	...	...	...	...	...	...	...	...	...	...	...	49.01	...	...	...
1844	...	...	...	...	...	...	...	...	...	...	...	...	50.91	...	...	...
1845	...	...	...	...	...	...	...	...	...	...	...	...	50.02	...	...	...
1846	...	...	...	...	...	...	...	...	...	...	...	...	52.94	...	...	...
1847	...	...	...	...	...	...	...	...	...	...	...	...	50.70	...	...	...
1848	...	...	...	...	...	...	...	...	...	...	...	...	50.92	...	...	...
1849	...	...	...	...	...	...	...	...	52.4	...	...	...	50.37	...	...	...
1850	...	...	...	...	...	...	...	...	53.8*	...	...	...	50.48	...	...	...
1851	...	...	...	...	...	...	...	...	54.1	...	...	...	50.94	...	...	...
1852	...	...	...	...	...	...	...	...	...	...	...	...	50.46	...	...	...
1853	53.54	...	...	...	...	...	...	...	...	...	...	...	51.54	...	...	...
1854	52.10	...	...	...	...	...	...	...	...	...	...	...	52.67	...	...	52.16
1855	54.94*	...	...	54.51*	53.16*	...	...	...	...	...	...	...	49.78	...	...	49.40*
1856	...	...	...	...	...	...	...	...	...	...	...	...	47.38	...	...	48.30
1857	53.71	52.49	...	...	...	...	53.96	50.98	...	...	55.41*	...	49.48	...	...	49.02
1858	52.92	51.90	...	...	...	...	52.88	48.63	...	...	...	...	52.05	...	...	51.38*
1859	50.88	49.72	...	...	...	...	50.97	47.78	...	...	...	...	51.30*	...	...	50.83*
1860	53.89	51.58	...	...	...	...	52.64	49.89	...	...	...	...	52.41	...	...	50.91
1861	53.54	50.83*	...	...	...	...	52.44	49.63*	...	...	...	...	51.25*	...	...	51.66
1862	49.26	49.03	...	...	...	...	...	45.46	...	...	...	...	52.04	...	...	...
1863	54.62	51.24	...	...	...	...	...	49.46*	...	...	...	...	51.55*	...	...	...
1864	53.54*	51.66*	42.02	...	...	...	...	50.03	...	...	...	46.18	51.65	...	...	...
1865	52.02	...	38.21	...	...	...	...	...	...	...	...	46.74	53.04	...	...	...
1866	...	...	...	...	...	50.73*	...	...	...	...	...	45.72	...	...	...	...
1867	...	...	...	...	...	51.20	...	...	...	...	...	45.29	...	...	...	...
1868	...	...	...	...	...	50.16*	...	...	...	...	...	44.59	...	47.58	50.13	...
1869	...	...	...	...	...	...	...	...	...	...	...	45.42	...	...	49.91	...
1870	...	...	...	...	...	...	...	...	...	54.25	...	47.81	...	...	51.86	...
	52.82	50.96	40.06	54.37	53.46	50.52	52.16	48.90	53.45	53.23	55.41[1]	45.96	50.78	48.64	50.74	50.54

[1] Hours of observation unknown.

PENNSYLVANIA.—Continued.

Year.	Berwick.	Blairsville.	Blooming-grove.	Brownsville.	Byberry.	Canonsburg.	Carlisle.	Ceres.	Chambers-burg.	Chromedale.	Dyberry.	Easton.	Ephrata.	Fallsington.	Fayette Tannery.	Fleming.
	°	°	°	°	°	°	°	°	°	°	°	°	°	°	°	°
1836	...	...	...	...	...	...	...	43.92	...	...	...	...	...	...	...	...
1837	...	...	...	...	...	...	...	...	...	...	...	...	...	...	...	...
1838	...	...	...	...	...	...	...	...	...	...	...	...	...	...	...	...
1839	...	...	...	...	...	...	...	...	...	...	...		...	...	...	...
1840	...	...	...	...	...	...	49.48	...	...	...	...		...	...	...	...
1841	...	...	...	...	...	...	49.06	...	...	...	...	...	...	...	...	...
1842	...	...	...	...	...	...	49.29	...	...	...	...	...	...	...	...	...
1843	...	...	...	...	...	...	49.76	...	...	...	...	...	...	...	...	...
1844	...	...	...	...	...	...	53.27	...	...	...	...	...	...	...	...	...
1845	...	...	...	...	...	...	55.75	47.24*	...	...	...	...	...	...	...	...
1846	...	...	...	...	...	...	...	45.79*	...	...	...	...	...	...	...	...
1847	...	...	...	...	...	...	49.04	46.03*	...	...	...	...	...	...	...	...
1848	...	...	...	...	...	...	50.22	46.20*	...	...	...	...	...	...	...	...
1849	...	...	...	...	...	...	50.35	45.76	...	51.21	...	...	...	...	...	...
1850	...	...	...	...	...	...	50.66	44.27	...	51.12	...	...	...	...	...	...
1851	...	...	...	...	...	...	50.49*	45.08	...	51.34	...	...	...	...	...	...
1852	...	...	...	...	...	...	50.03	46.23	...	50.28	...	...	...	...	...	...
1853	...	...	...	...	...	...	51.48*	...	...	51.30	...	...	...	...	...	...
1854	...	...	...	...	...	...	...	...	...	51.62	...	...	...	...	...	...
1855	...	...	...	...	...	...	50.38*	...	...	50.83	...	50.60	...	...	...	46.01*
1856	...	...	...	...	...	45.82*	47.84	...	...	49.08	...	48.64	...	...	...	46.01*
1857	49.24*	...	...	...	...	48.37	49.34	...	...	49.69	...	47.66	...	...	...	47.33
1858	50.85	...	...	...	...	51.93	51.54	...	...	...	...	49.14	...	...	...	49.49
1859	50.72	...	...	...	...	51.57	51.34*	...	52.60	...	...	49.16	...	...	...	49.85
1860	50.32	...	...	...	...	...	50.66	...	...	...	...	...	...	50.77	...	48.61*
1861	50.49*	...	...	...	53.15	49.83	51.78	...	53.28*	...	...	...	...	52.00	...	48.97
1862	...	42.12*	...	...	52.17*	...	50.98	...	...	...	...	...	...	51.34	50.54	48.82
1863	...	...	...	...	52.49*	48.45*	50.94*	...	...	...	...	...	...	51.64	50.04*	48.57
1864	...	45.63*	...	...	...	49.26	50.93	...	...	...	...	...	...	51.87	49.22	48.40
1865	...	...	...	...	...	49.18	52.03	...	...	...	42.81	...	...	52.79	50.61	48.22
1866	...	...	44.67*	...	...	48.52*	...	...	...	...	43.25*	...	51.71	52.00	49.01	46.80
1867	...	...	44.12	...	...	48.82*	50.43	...	...	...	43.60	...	52.42	50.88	49.07	...
1868	...	...	43.64	...	...	49.22	49.74	...	...	...	44.24	...	...	49.91	48.83	...
1869	...	...	44.37	...	...	49.53	50.69	...	...	...	44.90	...	53.65	51.57	48.57	...
1870	...	...	46.39*	55.33*	...	51.45	52.46	...	...	...	...	...	53.03	53.62	51.35	...
	50.15	44.51	44.48	55.36	51.94	50.23	50.83	45.48	53.07	50.86	44.05	48.91	52.59	51.67	49.80	48.38

PENNSYLVANIA.—Continued.

Year.	Fountaindale.	Franklin.	Fort Mifflin.	Germantown.	Gettysburg.	Harrisburg.	Haverford College.	Hollidays-burg.	Johnstown.	Lancaster Colliery.	Lehigh University.	Lewisburg.	Lewistown.	Meadville.	Mooreland.
	°	°	°	°	°	°	°	°	°	°	°	°	°	°	°
1820	...	...	...	49.94	...	...	...	...	...	...	...	...	...	...	...
1821	...	...	...	48.98	...	...	...	...	...	...	...	...	...	...	...
1822	...	...	52.95	51.78	...	...	...	...	...	...	...	...	...	...	...
1823	...	...	54.81	49.86	...	...	...	...	...	...	...	...	...	...	...
1824	...	...	54.94	51.76	...	...	...	...	...	...	...	...	...	...	...
1825	...	...	...	53.58	...	...	...	...	...	...	...	...	...	...	...
1826	...	...	...	53.83	...	...	...	...	...	...	...	...	...	...	...
1827	...	...	...	53.46	...	...	...	...	...	...	...	...	...	...	...
1828	...	...	...	...	...	...	...	...	...	...	...	...	...	...	...
1829	...	...	...	...	...	...	...	...	...	...	...	...	...	...	...
1830	...	...	...	...	...	...	...	...	...	...	...	...	...	...	...
1831	...	...	...	...	...	...	...	...	...	...	...	...	...	...	...
1832	...	...	...	...	...	...	...	...	...	...	...	...	...	...	...
1833	...	...	...	...	...	...	...	...	...	...	...	...	...	...	...
1834	...	...	...	...	...	...	...	...	...	...	...	...	...	...	...
1835	...	...	...	...	...	...	...	...	...	...	...	...	...	...	...
1836	...	...	...	...	...	...	...	...	...	...	...	...	...	...	...
1837	...	...	...	...	...	...	...	...	...	...	...	...	...	...	...
1838	...	...	...	...	...	...	...	...	...	...	...	...	...	...	...
1839	...	...	...	...	49.37	...	...	...	...	...	...	...	53.04*	...	...
1840	...	...	...	...	49.80	...	...	...	...	...	...	...	...	...	...
1841	...	...	...	...	50.00	53.32	...	...	...	...	...	...	...	...	...
1842	...	...	...	...	51.77	53.43*	...	...	...	...	...	...	...	...	...
1843	...	...	51.87	...	49.11	52.12*	...	...	...	...	...	...	...	...	...
1844	...	...	52.98	...	50.45	53.52	...	...	...	...	...	...	...	...	...
1845	...	...	53.94	...	51.58	53.83	...	...	...	...	...	...	...	...	...
1846	...	...	...	...	51.52	54.26	...	...	...	...	...	...	...	...	...
1847	...	...	...	...	50.13	53.52	...	...	...	...	...	...	...	...	...
1848	...	...	...	...	50.35	55.06	...	...	...	...	...	...	...	...	...
1849	...	...	53.03	...	49.66	54.38	...	...	...	...	...	...	...	...	...
1850	...	...	54.18*	...	51.19	53.86	...	...	...	...	...	...	...	...	...
1851	...	...	55.29	...	51.90	53.93	...	...	...	...	...	...	...	...	...
1852	...	...	53.99	...	50.10	53.06	...	...	...	...	...	...	...	...	...
1853	...	...	54.17*	...	52.23	55.48	...	50.40	...	...	...	...	...	...	...
1854	...	...	...	...	52.50	55.26	53.41	...	...	...	...	...	...	...	...
1855	...	...	...	...	50.78	53.35	50.74	...	...	...	...	...	...	...	...
1856	...	...	...	...	50.96	51.88	50.75	...	...	...	...	46.47	...	44.68*	...
1857	...	...	...	...	49.32	51.37	51.54*	...	...	46.53	...	47.60	...	45.79	...
1858	...	...	...	...	51.64	53.27	52.66*	...	...	48.06	...	49.48	...	48.28*	...
1859	...	...	...	...	51.15	53.36	52.14	...	...	47.81	...	49.42	...	...	...
1860	...	...	...	...	...	54.56	...	...	...	...	...	49.03*	...	...	...
1861	...	...	...	...	51.60	54.45	50.50*	...	...	...	...	...	...	...	...
1862	...	...	...	...	50.78	53.44	51.97*	...	...	...	...	...	...	...	...
1863	...	...	...	...	...	53.24*	...	...	...	...	...	...	...	...	...
1864	...	...	...	53.00	...	53.83	...	...	...	...	...	...	...	...	...
1865	...	...	...	52.37*	...	54.93	...	...	...	...	...	48.76	...	...	51.29
1866	...	...	...	51.62	...	54.01	...	...	...	...	...	48.14	...	...	50.61
1867	...	...	...	51.09*	...	52.60	...	...	...	...	...	47.72	...	...	49.62
1868	49.06*	45.64	...	49.98*	...	51.04	...	...	45.78*	...	47.23*	46.52	...	...	48.97
1869	50.39	46.70*	...	51.74	...	52.66*	...	...	47.12	...	...	47.82	...	...	50.65
1870	52.73	48.84	...	53.95	...	...	...	...	49.61	...	...	50.19	...	...	52.44
	51.26	47.28	53.77	51.86	50.63	53.73	51.85	50.40	47.70	47.40	47.41	48.21	53.04	47.80	50.55

PENNSYLVANIA.—Continued.

Year.	Morrisville.	Year.	Morrisville.	Mossgrove.	Mt. Joy.	Murrysville.	Nazareth.	Newcastle.	Newtown.	Norristown.	Paradise.	Pennsville.	Year.	Philadelphia.	Philadelphia.	Philadelphia.
	°		°	°	°	°	°	°	°	°	°	°		°	°	°
1790	52.7	...	...	...	...	...	...	...	...	...	...	...	...	...	...	...
1791	53.6	...	...	...	...	...	...	...	...	...	...	...	...	...	...	...
1792	51.9	...	...	...	...	...	...	...	...	...	...	...	...	...	...	...
1793	54.3	...	...	...	...	...	...	...	...	...	...	...	...	...	...	...
1794	50.5	...	...	...	...	...	...	...	...	...	...	...	...	...	...	...
1795	51.8	...	...	...	...	...	...	...	...	...	...	...	...	...	...	...
1796	52.1	...	...	...	...	...	...	...	...	...	...	...	1758	53.60	...	...
1797	51.6	...	...	...	...	...	...	...	...	...	...	...	1759	52.73	...	...
1798	52.1	...	...	...	...	...	...	...	...	...	...	...	1760	...	...	...
1799	51.5	...	...	...	...	...	...	...	...	...	...	...	1761	...	...	...
1800	51.8	...	...	...	...	...	...	...	...	...	...	...	1762	...	...	...
1801	52.4	...	...	...	...	...	...	...	...	...	...	...	1763	...	...	...
1802	54.2	...	...	...	...	...	...	...	...	...	...	...	1764	...	...	...
1803	52.2	1787	...	...	...	...	50.85	...	...	...	...	...	1765	...	...	...
1804	51.6	1788	...	...	...	...	49.13	...	...	...	...	...	1766	...	...	...
1805	52.0	1789	...	...	...	...	49.58	...	...	...	...	...	1767	53.25	...	...
1806	51.9	1790	...	...	...	...	48.85	...	...	...	...	...	1768	51.50	...	...
1807	52.4	1791	...	...	...	...	49.24	...	...	...	...	...	1769	51.83	...	...
1808	52.6	1792	...	...	...	...	47.42	...	...	...	...	...	1770	52.00	...	...
1809	51.6												1771	51.83	...	...
1810	51.4	1835	...	...	...	...	...	...	...	...	50.7	...	1772	52.50	...	...
1811	52.5	1836	...	...	...	...	...	...	...	...	51.4	...	1773	54.70	...	...
1812	51.4	1837	...	...	...	...	...	...	48.32*	...	50.9	...	1774	52.90	...	...
1813	50.9	1838	...	...	...	...	...	...	50.73	...	52.7	...	1775	54.40	...	...
1814	51.4	1839	...	...	...	...	...	...	52.76	...	53.3	...	1776	53.47	...	...
1815	51.7	1840	...	...	...	...	...	...	51.38	...	52.2	...	1777	50.96	...	...
1816	49.2	1841	...	...	...	...	...	...	48.80	...	53.6	...				
1817	53.1	1842	...	...	...	...	...	...	50.49	...	51.5	...	1798	...	54.9	...
1818	53.2	1843	...	...	...	...	...	...	...	...	52.9	...	1799	...	53.1	...
1819	51.6	1844	...	...	...	...	...	...	...	...	55.2	...	1800	...	53.4	...
1820	52.1	1845	...	...							[illegible]		1801		[illegible]	
1821	51.9	1846	53.9	...	...	...	...	...	...	...	54.4	...	1802	...	54.9	...
1822	53.6	1847	...	...	...	...	...	...	...	...	54.3	...	1803	...	54.1	...
1823	53.9	1848	...	...	...	...	...	...	...	...	52.0	...	1804	...	54.5	...
1824	54.0	1849	51.2*	...	...	...	...	...	...	...	53.5	...	1805	...	...	...
1825	54.4	1850	52.2	...	...	...	...	...	...	...	54.0	...	1806	...	...	...
1826	53.4	1851	51.3	...	...	...	...	...	...	...	52.6	...	1807	...	...	54.5
1827	50.7	1852	50.4	...	...	...	...	...	...	...	52.9	...	1808	...	...	59.4
1828	56.7	1853	52.3	...	...	...	...	...	...	...	53.2	...	1809	...	...	57.2
1829	53.4	1854	51.0	47.63*	...	...	...	...	...	52.29	53.2	...	1810	...	...	58.2
1830	52.9	1855	50.1	46.83*	...	...	...	...	...	50.11	48.7	...	1811	...	...	59.2
1831	53.4	1856	48.9	43.26*	...	...	46.95	...	...	49.26	51.6	...	1812	...	...	57.4
1832	50.6	1857	49.2	...	...	47.82*	46.91	...	...	49.16	51.1	...	1813	...	...	58.3
1833	53.0	1858	51.1	...	54.29	49.93	...	...	...	50.87	52.8	...	1814	...	...	58.5
1834	52.8	1859	50.2	...	54.46	...	...	...	...	50.94	...	...	1815	...	...	58.5
1835	52.6	1860	...	...	53.25	...	...	...	...	50.66	...	...	1816	...	...	57.5
1836	50.6	1861	...	...	54.12	...	49.41*	...	...	51.09	...	...	1817	...	...	57.0
1837	52.7	1862	...	...	53.85*	...	...	...	...	50.26	...	...	1818	...	...	57.1
1838	52.7	1863	...	...	53.40*	...	...	...	...	...	...	...	1819	...	...	59.2
1839	52.4	1864	...	...	54.08	...	50.94	...	...	...	...	...	1820	...	...	58.0
1840	52.7	1865	...	...	55.99	...	50.67*	...	...	...	...	46.68	1821	...	...	58.3
1841	52.1	1866	...	...	52.97	...	49.79*	50.09	...	...	...	45.00	1822	...	...	60.9
1842	53.2	1867	...	...	51.77*	...	...	49.50	...	...	...	43.92	1843	...	...	57.7
1843	52.0	1868	...	...	50.93*	...	...	49.87	...	...	...	42.64	1824	...	...	58.5
1844	53.5	1869	...	...	52.46	...	...	49.95	...	...	...	42.69	1825	...	...	61.1
1845	54.3	1870	...	...	54.94*	...	...	52.00	...	...	...	45.27	1826	...	...	60.8
			52.19	46.79	53.52	48.93	49.15	50.28	50.32	51.61	52.61[1]	44.47		52.75[1]	54.2[1]	58.6[1]

[1] Hours of observation unknown.

PENNSYLVANIA.—Continued.

Year.	Philadelphia.	Philadelphia.	Pittsburg.	Pocopson.	Pottsville	Plymouth Meeting.	Reading.	St. Vincent's College.	Shamokin.	Silver Spring.	Sewickley-ville.	Somerset.	Tarentum.	Tioga.	Westchester.	Westtown.
	°	°	°	°	°	°	°	°	°	°	°	°	°	°	°	°
1829	50.6	...	...	...	...	...	...	...	...	...	...	...	...	...	...	...
1830	53.4	...	...	...	...	...	...	...	...	...	...	...	...	...	...	...
1831	51.3	51.06	...	...	...	...	...	...	...	...	...	...	...	...	...	...
1832	51.5	51.39	...	...	...	...	...	...	...	...	...	...	...	...	...	...
1833	52.0	50.82	...	...	...	...	...	...	...	...	...	...	...	...	...	...
1834	53.6	51.60	...	...	...	...	...	...	...	...	...	...	...	...	...	...
1835	50.8	49.54	...	...	...	...	...	...	...	...	...	...	...	...	...	...
1836	48.0	48.77	...	...	...	...	...	...	...	...	...	...	...	...	...	...
1837	50.3	50.69	...	...	...	...	...	...	...	...	...	...	...	...	...	...
1838	52.6	51.48	...	...	...	...	...	...	...	...	...	...	...	...	...	...
1839	...	52.91	...	...	...	...	...	...	...	...	...	...	...	...	...	...
1840	...	52.80	...	...	...	...	...	...	...	...	...	47.39	...	...	...	...
1841	...	51.89	...	...	...	...	...	...	...	...	...	47.19*	...	...	...	...
1842	...	53.22	...	...	...	...	...	...	...	...	...	...	...	...	...	...
1843	...	51.72	...	...	...	...	...	...	...	...	...	...	...	...	...	...
1844	...	52.61	...	...	...	...	...	...	...	...	...	46.79	...	...	...	...
1845	...	53.88	...	...	...	...	...	...	...	...	...	46.39*	...	...	...	...
1846	...	53.93	...	...	...	...	...	...	...	...	...	47.29	...	...	...	...
1847	...	53.38	...	...	...	...	...	...	...	...	...	...	...	...	...	...
1848	...	53.54	...	...	...	...	...	...	...	...	...	45.99	...	...	...	...
1849	...	52.64	...	...	...	...	...	...	...	...	...	44.99	...	...	...	...
1850	...	53.58	...	...	...	...	...	...	...	...	...	...	...	...	...	...
1851	...	54.00	...	...	...	...	...	...	...	...	...	...	...	...	...	...
1852	...	53.12	...	...	...	...	...	...	...	...	...	...	...	...	...	...
1853	...	54.63	...	54.28	...	...	...	...	...	...	...	42.29	...	...	...	...
1854	...	54.61	52.88	53.63	...	...	...	...	...	...	...	46.19	...	...	...	...
1855	...	53.65	50.41	52.57	48.20	...	...	...	...	...	...	44.49*	...	...	51.72*	...
1856	...	51.54	47.14	49.71	...	...	...	...	...	...	...	43.36	...	...	49.30	...
1857	...	52.09	48.62*	50.28	...	...	...	...	...	...	...	45.03	49.00	...	50.35	...
1858	...	53.77	52.43	52.35	...	...	...	...	...	...	...	48.79	50.91	...	51.24	50.87
1859	...	53.30	51.88	51.91	...	...	...	...	...	...	...	48.62	50.05*	...	50.87	...
1860	...	52.55	...	51.54*	...	...	...	...	49.94*	...	...	...	...	...	51.08	...
1861	...	53.13	...	52.18	...	...	...	51.53	52.05	...	48.63	48.68	...	...	51.72	...
1862	...	52.25	...	51.50	...	...	...	...	50.79	...	...	...	...	...	50.56	...
1863	...	53.80	...	51.61*	...	...	...	...	...	50.47*	...	...	...	...	51.09	...
1864	...	53.89	...	51.73	...	...	...	...	...	51.20*	...	...	...	48.38*	51.56	...
1865	...	56.84	...	52.42	...	...	...	...	...	51.61	...	...	...	48.60	51.88	...
1866	...	55.68	51.85	51.68	...	...	...	...	...	...	...	...	...	46.58	51.10	...
1867	...	54.95	...	50.88	...	...	51.47	...	...	...	...	...	...	46.98*	51.15	...
1868	...	52.63	...	49.87	...	49.57*	50.75	...	...	...	...	...	...	45.41	49.91	...
1869	...	54.32	...	51.54	...	51.09	52.20	...	...	...	...	...	...	42.85	50.89*	...
1870	...	55.39	52.62*	53.51	...	52.85	54.97	...	...	...	...	...	...	48.21	52.74	...
	51.4[1]	52.94	51.94	51.79	49.09	51.43	51.35	51.41	51.35	50.74	48.22	46.16	50.06	46.79	51.28	51.50

[1] Hours of observation unknown.

PENNSYLVANIA.—Cont'd.			RHODE ISLAND.					
Year.	Whitehall.	Worthington, near.	Fort Adams.	Fort Wolcott.	Newport.	North Scituate.	Year.	Providence.
	°	°	°	°	°	°		°
1822	...	...	..	51.54	...	..	...	...
1823	...	...	...	48.58	...	...	...	...
1824	...	...	...	50.51	...	...	...	...
1825	...	...	...	51.58	...	...	...	...
1826	...	...	...	50.98	...	...	...	...
1827	...	...	...	49.40	...	...	...	...
1828	...	...	...	52.09	...	...	...	...
1829	...	...	...	47.57	...	...	...	...
1830	...	...	...	49.40	...	...	...	...
1831	...	...	...	48.77	...	...	...	...
1832	...	...	...	47.59	...	...	1832	47.4
1833	...	...	...	48.18	...	...	1833	48.5
1834	...	...	...	48.22	...	...	1834	48.3
1835	...	...	...	47.50	...	...	1835	46.5
							1836	45.0
1842	...	...	49.68	...	...	...	1837	45.8
1843	...	...	49.02	...	...	...	1838	47.4
1844	...	...	49.82	...	...	...	1839	48.3
1845	...	...	49.99	...	...	...	1840	48.7
1846	...	...	49.67*	...	...	...	1841	48.2
1847	...	...	...	...	...	...	1842	49.5
1848	...	...	...	...	...	...	1843	47.7
1849	...	...	50.00	...	...	...	1844	48.5
1850	...	...	50.44	...	...	...	1845	48.1
1851	...	...	50.37	...	...	...	1846	48.2
1852	...	...	49.94	...	...	...	1847	49.6
1853	...	...	50.90*	...	...	46.66	1848	50.0
1854	...	...	...	...	...	...	1849	48.8
1855	...	...	...	...	...	...	1850	49.0
1856	47.21	...	...	...	...	...	1851	48.7
[illegible]	[illegible]	...	...	...	...	...	[illegible]	[illegible]
1858	50.47	...	48.43*	...	...	...	1853	49.2
1859	49.89	49.83	48.56*	...	...	...	1854	48.1
1860	49.75	49.79*	...	...	...	...	1855	48.5
1861	50.48	49.90	...	...	...	...	1856	46.8
1862	49.44*	...	...	...	...	...	1857	47.7
1863	49.62	...	51.51*	...	...	...	1858	48.6
1864	50.34	...	51.46*	...	...	...	1859	48.1
1865	50.45	...	52.37*	...	...	...	1860	48.5*
1866	48.91	...	...	...	47.71	...	1861	47.5
1867	48.49	...	47.91	...	46.62	...	1862	47.4
1868	47.93	...	47.93	...	45.92	...	1863	48.3
1869	49.34	...	47.67	...	48.70	...	1864	48.1
1870	52.22	...	48.87	...	50.88	...	1866	47.7
	49.55	49.43	49.73	49.43	48.12	45.77		47.91

SOUTH CAROLINA.

Year.	Aiken.	All Saints.	Beaufort.	Bluffton.	Camden.	Charleston.	Columbia.	Edisto Island.	Fort Moultrie.	Gowdysville.	Greenville.	Hilton Head.	Nightingale Hall.	Robertville.	St. Johns.	Wilkinsville.
	°	°	°	°	°	°	°	°	°	°	°	°	°	°	°	°
1738	...	...	...	...	...	66.03	...	...	...	...	...	...	...	...	...	...
1739	...	...	...	...	...	64.83	...	...	...	...	...	...	...	...	...	...
1740	...	...	...	...	...	63.93	...	...	...	...	...	...	...	...	...	...
1742	...	...	...	...	...	64.73	...	...	...	...	...	...	...	...	...	...
1750	...	...	...	...	...	64.63	...	...	...	...	...	...	...	...	...	...
1751	...	...	...	...	...	66.33	...	...	...	...	...	...	...	...	...	...
1752	...	...	...	...	...	66.93	...	...	...	...	...	...	...	...	...	...
1753	...	...	...	...	...	66.43	...	...	...	...	...	...	...	...	...	...
1754	...	...	...	...	...	67.43	...	...	...	...	...	...	...	...	...	...
1755	...	...	...	...	...	63.23	...	...	...	...	...	...	...	...	...	...
1756	...	...	...	...	...	66.63	...	...	...	...	...	...	...	...	...	...
1757	...	...	...	...	...	65.33	...	...	...	...	...	...	...	...	...	...
1758	...	...	...	...	...	63.93	...	...	...	...	...	...	...	...	...	...
1759	...	...	...	...	...	64.73	...	...	...	...	...	...	...	...	...	...
1823	...	...	...	...	...	...	...	...	64.31	...	...	...	...	...	...	...
1824	...	...	...	...	...	...	...	...	66.47	...	...	...	...	...	...	...
1825	...	...	...	...	...	...	...	...	66.80*	...	...	...	...	...	...	...
1826	...	...	...	...	...	...	...	...	67.95*	...	...	...	...	...	...	...
1827	...	...	...	...	...	...	...	...	67.03*	...	...	...	...	...	...	...
1828	...	...	...	...	...	...	...	...	70.73	...	...	...	...	...	...	...
1829	...	...	...	...	...	...	...	...	65.53*	...	...	...	...	...	...	...
1830	...	...	...	...	...	...	...	...	69.75	...	...	...	...	...	...	...
1831	...	...	...	...	...	...	...	...	65.44	...	...	...	...	...	...	...
1832	...	...	...	...	...	...	...	...	65.85	...	...	...	...	...	...	...
1833	...	...	...	...	...	...	...	...	65.66	...	...	...	...	...	...	...
1834	...	...	...	...	...	...	...	...	66.33	...	...	...	...	...	...	...
1835	...	...	...	...	...	...	...	...	63.78	...	...	...	...	...	...	...
1838	...	...	...	...	59.98	...	...	...	...	...	...	...	...	...	...	...
1840	...	...	...	...	...	66.57	...	...	65.59	...	...	...	...	...	...	...
1841	...	...	...	...	...	65.79	...	...	65.41	...	...	...	...	...	...	...
1842	...	...	...	...	...	...	...	...	64.83	...	...	...	...	...	...	...
1843	...	...	...	...	...	...	...	...	65.82	...	...	...	...	61.33	...	...
1844	...	...	...	...	...	65.17	...	...	67.10	...	60.12*	...	...	...	...	...
1845	...	...	...	...	...	...	...	...	66.35	...	60.84*	...	...	...	...	...
1846	...	...	...	...	...	...	...	...	67.18*	...	...	...	...	...	64.05*	...
1847	...	...	...	...	...	64.82	...	...	66.47	...	...	...	...	...	63.36	...
1848	...	...	...	...	...	...	63.23*	...	66.75*	...	...	...	...	...	64.04	...
1849	...	...	...	...	...	...	64.12	...	66.29	...	...	...	64.43*	...	64.00	...
1850	...	...	...	...	...	...	...	...	66.72	...	...	...	...	...	65.09	...
1851	...	...	...	...	...	65.85	...	...	66.71	...	...	...	...	...	63.73	...
1852	...	...	...	...	...	...	...	...	66.08	...	...	...	...	...	64.22	...
1853	...	...	...	...	...	...	...	...	66.78	...	...	...	...	...	63.26	...
1854	...	...	...	...	62.85	...	...	...	66.50	...	...	...	...	...	63.00	...
1855	...	63.42	...	...	62.38	65.56	...	...	65.67	...	...	...	...	..	62.37	...
1856	60.79*	61.84	...	...	59.90	64.00	...	63.96*	63.69	...	...	...	...	...	60.91	...
1857	61.70	61.92	...	...	59.54	64.16	...	...	63.67	...	...	...	...	...	60.16	...
1858	61.62	63.77	...	...	...	65.83	...	...	65.66	...	...	...	...	...	63.23*	...
1859	61.54	63.49	...	...	...	65.76	...	...	65.48	...	...	...	...	...	62.92	...
1860	...	63.75*	...	...	...	...	...	...	...	...	...	...	...	...	62.70	...
1861	...	...	...	...	...	65.92*	...	...	...	...	...	...	...	...	...	...
1864	...	...	64.89*	...	...	...	...	...	...	...	...	67.75*	...	...	...	...
1865	...	...	...	...	...	...	...	...	...	...	...	66.59*	...	...	...	...
1866	...	...	...	...	...	...	...	...	...	...	...	64.49*	...	...	...	...
1867	61.67	...	...	...	...	...	...	...	...	...	...	66.12	...	...	...	...
1868	61.11	...	...	...	...	...	...	...	...	...	...	...	...	...	...	59.98*
1869	61.97	...	...	...	...	...	...	...	...	62.43*	...	...	...	...	...	...
1870	62.35*	...	...	67.09	...	...	...	...	...	62.33*	...	...	...	...	...	...
	61.61	63.02	64.69	67.09	61.75	65.53	61.62	63.96	66.16	62.38	60.83	66.11	64.43	61.33	63.22	59.86

Year.	TENNESSEE. Austin.	Dixon's Springs.	Elizabethton.	Fort Humboldt.	Gallatin.	Glenwood.	Knoxville.	Lookout Mt.	Memphis.	Pomona.	Trenton.	University Place.	TEXAS. Austin.	Blue Branch.	Burkeville.	Camp Colorado.
1819	°	°	°	°	°	°	°	°	°	°	°	°	°	°	°	°
	...	...	...	...	60.6*	...	...	...	...	...	...	...	...	...	...	...
1852	...	58.63*	...	...	...	...	...	...	...	...	...	...	...	...	...	...
1853	...	...	...	...	...	...	...	...	...	...	...	...	...	...	...	...
1854	...	...	...	...	...	59.14	57.28	...	62.16*	...	...	...	66.02	...	...	...
1855	...	...	...	...	...	57.02	...	...	...	...	...	...	65.43	...	...	...
1856	...	...	...	...	...	53.82	...	...	...	...	...	...	64.23	...	...	...
1857	...	...	...	...	...	54.13	...	...	59.20*	...	...	...	65.44	...	...	63.67
1858	...	...	...	...	...	56.71	...	...	61.03	...	...	...	67.36	...	...	65.00*
1859	...	...	...	...	...	56.21	...	...	60.52*	...	...	...	67.35	...	...	66.00
1860	...	...	...	...	...	57.92*	...	...	61.55*	55.82	...	57.09	67.07	...	64.96	65.09
1861	...	...	...	...	...	57.26	...	...	...	...	...	...	67.17	...	...	...
1862	...	...	...	...	...	57.19	...	...	...	...	...	...	67.25	...	...	...
1863	...	...	...	...	...	55.43	...	...	...	...	...	...	67.16	...	...	...
1864	...	...	...	...	...	54.59	...	...	...	...	...	...	65.88	...	...	...
1865	...	...	...	...	...	57.19	...	...	...	...	...	...	66.20	...	...	...
1866	...	...	...	...	...	56.30	...	...	...	...	...	...	66.93	...	...	...
1867	...	...	...	...	...	56.25	...	59.12	...	...	...	...	68.21	...	...	...
1868	58.57	...	51.64	...	...	55.41	...	58.28*	59.43	...	...	...	66.41	...	...	...
1869	...	...	54.46	...	...	55.10	...	58.62*	58.25	...	59.11*	...	65.21	65.13	...	...
1870	57.35*	...	55.79	61.90*	...	56.44*	56.29*	59.08	...	...	60.46*	..	66.57	67.15	...	...
	58.09	58.63	54.96	61.90	60.6	56.53	56.74	58.92	60.71	56.16	59.76	56.98	66.72	66.14	65 00	64.83

TEXAS.—Continued.

Year.	Camp Concordia.	Camp Cooper.	Camp Hudson.	Camp Stockton.	Camp Verde.	Cedar Grove Plantation.	Clinton.	Corpus Christi.	Cross Roads.	Fort Belknap.	Fort Bliss.	Fort Brown.	Fort Chadbourne.	Fort Clark.	Fort Croghan.	Fort Davis.
1846	...	...	...	...	...	...	...	70.47*	...	...	...	...	...	...	...	...
1847	...	...	...	...	...	...	...	...	...	...	...	74.57	...	...	...	...
1848	...	...	...	...	...	...	...	...	...	...	...	...	...	...	...	...
1849	...	...	...	...	...	...	...	...	...	...	...	...	...	...	...	...
1850	...	...	...	...	...	...	...	...	...	...	...	73.70	...	...	65.62	...
1851	...	...	...	...	...	...	...	71.52*	...	...	...	72.72	...	...	66.36	...
1852	...	...	...	...	...	...	...	...	...	62.13	...	73.92	...	...	66.50	...
1853	...	...	...	...	...	...	...	...	...	64.18	...	72.99	60.45	66.30	...	...
1854	...	...	...	...	...	...	...	...	...	65.58	...	74.01	63.80	68.85	...	...
1855	...	...	...	...	...	...	...	...	...	65.27	67.12*	73.12	63.66*	66.50	...	63.39
1856	...	...	...	...	...	...	...	...	...	63.65	62.76	71.88	61.78	68.23	...	60.10
1857	...	62.05*	...	...	62.70	...	...	...	...	62.96	63.01*	72.54	61.47	68.69*	...	61.35*
1858	...	...	...	...	62.14*	...	...	...	...	...	63.15	73.22	63.28	69.54	...	62.03
1859	...	...	69.23	...	66.29	...	...	...	...	...	63.62	...	64.40	70.21	...	62.33
1860	...	...	69.98	65.63	66.87	...	...	...	68.86*	...	65.41	...	64.89	70.06	...	63.19
1861	...	...	...	...	...	...	...	...	...	...	...	...	...	...	...	...
1862	...	...	...	...	...	...	...	...	...	...	...	...	...	...	...	...
1863	...	...	...	...	...	...	...	...	...	...	...	...	...	...	...	...
1864	...	...	...	...	...	...	...	...	...	...	...	...	...	...	...	...
1865	...	...	...	...	...	...	...	...	...	...	...	...	...	...	...	...
1866	...	...	...	...	...	...	...	...	...	...	...	...	...	...	...	...
1867	...	...	...	...	69.26*	70.25*	...	...	...	...	65.94	...	...	...	...	...
1868	66.33*	...	...	...	64.65	68.11	...	...	...	...	...	...	...	...	...	...
1869	...	...	...	...	...	...	67.95*	...	...	...	64.62*	...	...	...	...	...
1870	...	...	...	65.82	...	...	68.33	...	...	...	...	72.04	...	67.82	...	60.95*
	66.33	62.73	69.01	65.67	64.70	68.67	68.18	70.20	68.54	63.91	64.78	73.40	62.90	68.28	65.84	61.73

TEXAS.—Continued.

Year.	Fort Duncan.	Fort Ewell.	Fort Gates.	Fort Graham.	Fort Griffin.	Fort Houston.	Fort Inge.	Fort Lancaster.	Fort Lincoln.	Fort McIntosh.	Fort McKavett.	Fort Martin Scott.	Fort Mason.	Fort Merrill.	Fort Quitman.	Fort Richardson.
	°	°	°	°	°	°	°	°	°	°	°	°	°	°	°	°
1842	...	...	...	...	...	73.03	...	...	...	...	...	...	...	...	...	...
1849	...	...	...	...	...	...	...	...	...	...	...	...	...	...	...	...
1850	71.14	...	65.51	65.61*	...	...	67.39	...	68.21*	73.11	...	62.32	...	...	...	...
1851	72.41	...	65.92	66.63	...	...	68.34*	...	...	73.29	...	62.68	...	70.40*	...	...
1852	71.76	...	...	65.99	...	...	67.31	...	...	74.86	63.57*	...	65.37*	...	...	...
1853	69.48	71.59	...	...	...	...	67.19	...	...	73.20	...	...	65.10*	...	...	...
1854	70.7[illegible]	70.28*	...	...	...	...	68.76	...	...	72.98	64.08	...	...	72.82	...	...
1855	69.37	...	...	...	...	...	...	...	...	72.80	62.79	...	...	70.37*	...	...
1856	70.02	...	...	...	...	...	...	...	...	71.69	64.04	...	65.19*	...	...	...
1857	70.62	...	...	...	...	...	...	63.48	...	73.28	63.28	...	64.75	...	...	...
1858	72.97	...	...	...	...	...	...	64.79	...	73.50	63.70	...	67.11	...	...	...
1859	...	...	...	...	...	...	70.70	67.46	...	...	...	...	...	...	61.65	...
1860	...	...	...	...	...	...	70.58*	68.11	...	...	...	...	68.12*	...	62.75*	...
1861	...	...	...	...	...	...	...	...	...	...	...	...	...	...	...	...
1862	...	...	...	...	...	...	...	...	...	...	...	...	...	...	...	...
1863	...	...	...	...	...	...	...	...	...	...	...	...	...	...	...	...
1864	...	...	...	...	...	...	...	...	...	...	...	...	...	...	...	...
1865	...	...	...	...	...	...	...	...	...	...	...	...	...	...	...	...
1866	...	...	...	...	...	...	...	...	...	...	...	...	...	...	...	...
1867	...	...	...	...	...	...	...	...	...	...	...	...	...	...	...	...
1868	...	...	...	...	...	...	...	...	...	...	...	...	...	...	...	64.43*
1869	...	...	...	...	...	...	...	...	...	...	...	...	...	...	...	64.27
1870	...	...	...	...	62.93*	...	...	...	...	72.40*	...	...	...	...	63.26	...
	71.51	71.40	65.95	65.87	63.17	73.03[1]	68.65	65.67	67.63	72.98	63.69	62.48	66.40	71.32	62.54	64.31

TEXAS.—Continued.

Year.	Fort Terrett.	Fort Worth.	Galveston.	Gilmer, near.	Goliad.	Gonzales.	Houston.	Jefferson.	Larissa.	Lavaca.	New Braunfels.	Oakland.	Pin Oak.	Phantom Hill.	Ringgold Barracks.	Round Top.
1848	...	...	...	...	...	71.36*	...	...	...	...	...	...	...	...	...	...
1849	...	...	...	...	...	72.18	...	...	...	...	...	...	...	...	...	...
1850	...	64.29	..	...	...	...	...	...	...	...	...	...	...	...	75.22	...
1851	...	64.00	...	...	...	...	...	...	...	...	...	...	...	...	75.47	...
1852	64.40*	63.35	...	...	...	...	...	...	...	...	...	...	...	63.19	75.31	...
1853	63.29	...	...	...	...	...	...	...	...	...	...	...	...	64.26	73.88	...
1854	...	...	...	...	...	...	...	...	...	...	64.20	...	...	...	73.39	...
1855	...	...	...	...	...	...	...	...	...	...	68.44	...	...	...	72.11*	...
1856	...	...	...	...	...	...	...	...	...	...	68.48	...	64.29	...	71.32	...
1857	...	...	...	...	...	...	...	...	...	...	69.33*	...	...	...	72.44	...
1858	...	...	...	...	68.63	...	...	...	65.50	...	...	...	...	...	73.41	...
1859	...	...	...	...	...	..	...	...	66.38	...	69.66	...	...	...	...	69.76
1860	...	...	...	65.51	...	...	...	...	...	...	...	...	...	...	...	69.16
1861	...	...	...	...	...	...	...	...	...	...	...	...	...	...	...	...
1862	...	...	...	...	...	...	...	...	...	...	...	...	...	...	...	...
1863	...	...	...	...	...	...	...	...	...	...	...	...	...	...	...	...
1864	...	...	...	...	...	...	...	...	...	...	...	...	...	...	...	...
1865	...	...	...	...	...	...	...	...	...	...	...	...	...	...	...	...
1866	...	...	...	...	...	...	...	...	...	...	...	...	...	...	...	...
1867	...	...	...	...	...	...	...	...	...	...	...	...	...	...	...	...
1868	...	...	70.44	64.77	...	...	67.16*	...	...	...	...	...	...	...	...	...
1869	...	...	68.78	63.92	...	...	...	...	...	68.05*	...	...	...	...	...	...
1870	...	...	...	66.52*	...	...	...	67.09	...	...	...	69.28*	...	...	...	...
	63.74	63.81	69.38	65.22	69.93	71.36	67.26	66.45	65.94	68.17	68.49	69.28	64.29	63.83	73.78	69.29

[1] Hours of observation unknown.

	TEXAS.—Continued.						UTAH.							VERMONT.		
Year.	San Antonio.	Sisterdale.	Union Hill.	Waco.	Washington.	Weberville.	Camp Douglas.	Coalville.	Camp Crittenden.	Great Salt Lake City.	Heberville.	St. Mary's.	Wanship.	Brandon.	Burlington.	Castleton.
	°	°	°	°	°	°	°	°	°	°	°	°	°	°	°	°
1828	...	...	...	...	...	...	...	...	...	...	...	...	...	...	47.92	...
1829	...	...	...	...	...	...	...	...	...	...	...	...	...	...	...	...
1830	...	...	...	...	...	...	...	...	...	...	...	...	...	...	...	...
1831	...	...	...	...	...	...	...	...	...	...	...	...	...	...	...	...
1832	...	...	...	...	...	...	...	...	...	...	...	...	...	...	44.09	...
1833	...	...	...	...	...	...	...	...	...	...	...	...	...	...	43.64	...
1834	...	...	...	...	...	...	...	...	...	...	...	...	...	...	...	...
1835	...	...	...	...	...	...	...	...	...	...	...	...	...	...	...	...
1836	...	...	...	...	...	...	...	...	...	...	...	...	...	...	...	...
1837	...	...	...	...	...	...	...	...	...	...	...	...	...	...	40.96*	...
1838	...	...	...	...	...	...	...	...	...	...	...	...	...	...	43.95	...
1839	...	...	...	...	...	...	...	...	...	...	...	...	...	...	45.82	...
1840	...	...	...	...	...	...	...	...	...	...	...	...	...	...	46.02	...
1841	...	...	...	...	...	...	...	...	...	...	...	...	...	...	45.09	...
1842	...	...	...	...	...	...	...	...	...	...	...	...	...	...	45.92	...
1843	...	...	...	...	...	...	...	...	...	...	...	...	...	...	43.57	...
1844	...	...	...	...	...	...	...	...	...	...	...	...	...	...	44.72	...
1845	...	...	...	...	...	...	...	...	...	...	...	...	...	...	45.74	...
1846	...	...	...	...	...	...	...	...	...	...	...	...	...	...	46.47	...
1847	...	...	...	...	...	...	...	...	...	...	...	...	...	...	44.78	...
1848	...	...	...	...	...	...	...	...	...	...	...	...	...	...	45.71	...
1849	...	...	...	...	...	...	...	...	...	...	...	...	...	...	44.72	...
1850	69.88	...	...	...	...	...	...	...	...	...	...	...	...	...	45.46	...
1851	67.47	...	...	...	...	...	...	...	...	...	...	...	...	...	44.86	...
1852	71.33*	...	...	...	...	...	...	...	...	...	...	...	...	...	45.11	...
1853	...	...	...	...	...	...	...	...	...	...	...	...	...	...	45.55	...
1854	...	...	...	...	...	...	...	...	...	...	...	...	...	44.05	45.28	45.87
1855	...	...	...	...	...	...	...	...	...	...	...	...	...	44.20	45.28	...
1856	...	...	...	...	...	...	...	...	...	...	...	...	...	41.63	42.35	...
1857	...	...	...	...	66.76	...	...	...	...	...	...	...	...	42.55	...	...
1858	67.42		67.80				...	...	...	...	...	...	...	43.02	42.22	...
1859	69.91	66.12	66.45	...	66.98	69.67*	...	...	48.24	51.28*	...	...	...	43.81	42.43	...
1860	71.80	...	67.77*	...	...	...	...	...	48.60	...	...	...	...	44.35*	...	...
1861	...	...	...	...	...	...	...	...	...	51.23*	...	...	...	43.85	42.92	...
1862	...	...	...	...	...	...	...	...	...	...	...	...	...	44.45*	42.17*	...
1863	...	...	...	...	...	...	52.42	...	...	...	...	...	...	45.65	42.12*	...
1864	...	...	...	...	...	...	52.22	...	...	52.41	...	...	...	...	43.38*	...
1865	...	...	...	...	...	...	50.96	...	...	50.54	61.80*	...	...	...	...	...
1866	...	...	...	...	...	...	52.39*	...	...	51.85	...	44.3*	...	45.21*	...	...
1867	...	...	...	...	...	...	51.78	...	...	...	...	...	45.97*	...	...	...
1868	...	...	...	65.91	...	...	50.46	...	...	...	...	...	...	...	...	...
1869	...	...	...	...	...	...	51.76*	...	...	...	...	...	...	...	...	...
1870	67.35	...	...	...	...	...	50.00	44.72*	...	...	..	...	...	...	...	47.06
	69.22	66.12	66.15	66.22	67.29	69.34	51.49	45.14	48.45	51.86	61.37	43 87	45.48	44.12	44.44	45.76

VERMONT.—Continued.

Year.	Craftsbury.	Fayetteville.	Ferrisburg.	Lunenburg.	Middlebury.	Montpelier.	Newbury.	Newport.	Norwich.	Randolph.	Rupert.	Rutland.	St. Johnsbury.	Shelburn.	Springfield.	West Charlotte.
	°	°	°	°	°	°	°	°	°	°	°	°	°	°	°	°
1789	...	...	...	...	...	...	...	...	...	...	...	43.62	...	...	...	...
1827	...	43.87	...	...	...	...	...	...	...	...	...	...	...	...	...	...
1828	...	46.96	...	...	...	...	...	...	...	...	...	...	...	...	...	...
1829	...	42.75	...	...	...	...	...	...	...	...	...	...	...	...	...	...
1830	...	45.09	...	...	...	...	...	...	...	...	...	...	...	...	...	...
1831	...	43.98	...	...	...	...	...	...	...	...	...	...	...	...	...	...
1832	...	42.75	...	...	...	...	...	...	...	...	...	...	...	...	...	...
1833	...	42.14	...	...	...	...	...	...	...	...	...	...	...	...	...	...
1834	...	43.41	...	...	...	...	...	...	...	...	...	...	...	...	...	...
1835	...	...	...	...	...	...	...	...	...	...	...	...	...	...	...	...
1836	...	...	...	...	...	...	39.55	...	...	...	...	...	...	...	...	...
1840	...	...	...	...	...	...	43.21	...	...	...	...	...	...	...	...	...
1841	...	...	...	...	...	...	43.32	...	...	...	...	...	...	...	...	...
1842	...	...	...	...	...	...	42.72	...	...	...	...	...	...	...	...	...
1843	...	...	...	...	...	...	42.10	...	...	...	...	...	...	...	...	...
1844	...	...	...	...	...	...	42.05	...	...	...	...	...	...	...	...	...
1845	...	...	...	...	...	...	42.39	...	...	...	...	...	...	...	...	...
1846	...	...	...	...	...	...	44.38	...	...	...	...	...	...	...	...	...
1847	...	...	...	...	...	...	43.40	...	...	...	...	...	...	...	...	...
1848	...	...	...	...	...	...	43.77	...	...	...	...	...	...	...	...	...
1849	...	...	...	...	...	...	42.69	...	...	...	...	...	...	...	...	...
1853	...	...	...	...	...	...	...	...	...	...	...	...	42.44	...	...	...
1854	40.72	...	...	...	...	...	...	...	...	...	...	...	41.55	...	...	...
1855	39.33	...	...	...	...	41.93	...	...	...	...	...	...	...	...	...	...
1856	39.05	...	...	...	...	...	...	...	...	...	...	...	...	41.81*	...	...
1857	39.55	...	...	...	...	...	...	...	43.13*	...	46.85	...	41.03	42.68	...	...
1858	39.49	...	...	...	...	...	...	...	...	...	47.99	...	39.30	...	...	...
1859	40.28	...	...	...	...	...	...	...	...	...	47.37	...	39.59	...	...	...
1860	41.19*	...	...	43.40*	...	...	...	...	...	...	47.86	...	...	...	...	...
1861	39.52*	...	...	41.98*	...	...	...	...	...	...	...	...	...	...	42.99	...
1862	39.38	...	...	42.21	...	...	...	...	...	...	47.17	...	...	...	43.65*	...
1863	39.36*	...	...	42.59*	...	...	...	...	...	...	...	...	...	...	...	...
1864	40.76	...	...	44.52	46.91*	...	...	...	...	...	...	...	...	...	...	...
1865	40.28	...	...	41.98	45.57	...	...	...	...	...	...	...	...	...	...	...
1866	39.58	...	...	42.13*	43.97	...	...	...	...	42.64	...	...	...	...	...	...
1867	39.44	...	...	40.20*	42.83	...	...	...	...	41.39	...	...	...	...	...	...
1868	39.78	...	...	39.70	42.24	...	...	...	...	41.00	...	...	...	...	...	...
1869	38.78	...	...	41.61	43.95	...	...	...	...	42.38	...	...	...	...	...	45.48
1870	40.99	...	47.00	43.92	...	...	...	44.28*	...	45.08	...	...	...	...	...	48.50
	39.89	44.26	46.65	41.41	44.57	42.14	42.46	44.20	42.78	42.61	47.44	43.62[1]	40.37	42.28	43.44	46.81

[1] Hours of observation unknown.

	VERMONT.—Continued.				VIRGINIA.											
Year.	West Fairlee.	Williams-town.	Windsor.	Woodstock.	Alexandria.	Bellona Arsenal.	Berryville	Cape Charles Light.	Cottage Home.	Crichton's Store.	Fortress Monroe.	Garrysville.	Glasgow, near.	Hampton.	Lewinsville.	Lexington.
	°	°	°	°	°	°	°	°	°	°	°	°	°	°	°	°
1806	...	...	44.92	...	...	...	...	...	...	...	...	...	...	...	...	...
1824	...	...	...	...	...	56.39*	...	...	...	...	...	...	...	...	...	...
1825	...	...	...	...	...	...	...	...	...	...	61.95	...	...	...	...	...
1826	...	...	...	...	...	...	...	...	...	...	61.66	...	...	...	...	...
1827	...	...	...	...	...	60.16*	...	...	...	...	59.96	...	...	...	...	...
1828	...	...	...	...	...	61.74	...	...	...	...	63.18	...	...	...	..	...
1829	...	39.2*	...	...	...	57.41	...	...	...	...	59.07	...	...	...	...	...
1830	...	41.0	...	...	...	59.43	...	...	...	...	60.71	...	...	...	...	...
1831	...	39.7	...	...	...	...	...	...	...	...	57.26	...	...	...	...	...
1832	...	39.9*	...	...	...	59.26	...	...	...	...	54.10	...	...	...	...	...
1833	...	39.8	...	...	...	60.48*	...	...	...	...	57.18	...	...	...	...	...
1834	...	40.5	...	...	...	...	...	...	...	...	60.30	...	...	...	...	...
1835	...	39.1	...	...	...	...	...	...	...	...	58.19	...	...	...	...	...
1836	...	38.0	...	...	...	...	...	...	...	...	55.65	...	...	...	...	...
1837	...	37.8	...	...	...	...	...	...	...	...	58.33	...	...	...	...	...
1838	...	39.4	...	...	...	...	...	...	...	...	58.09	...	...	...	...	...
1839	...	40.5	...	...	...	...	...	...	...	...	58.49	...	...	...	...	...
1840	...	40.2	...	...	...	...	...	...	...	...	59.71	...	...	...	...	...
1841	...	40.3	...	...	...	...	...	...	...	...	59.03	...	...	...	...	...
1842	...	...	...	...	...	...	...	...	...	...	59.93	...	...	...	...	...
1843	...	...	...	...	...	...	...	...	...	...	57.77	...	...	...	...	...
1844	...	...	...	...	...	...	...	...	...	...	59.06	...	...	...	...	...
1845	...	...	...	...	...	...	...	...	...	...	59.76	...	...	...	...	...
1846	...	...	...	...	...	...	...	...	...	...	60.51	...	...	...	...	...
1847	...	...	...	...	...	...	...	...	...	...	58.19	...	...	...	...	...
1848	...	...	...	...	...	...	...	...	...	...	58.83	...	...	...	...	...
1849	...	...	...	...	...	...	...	...	...	...	57.82	...	...	...	...	...
1850	...	...	...	...	...	...	...	...	...	...	58.92	...	...	...	...	...
1851	...	...	...	...	...	...	...	...	...	...	58.84	...	...	...	...	...
1852	...	...	...	...	...	...	...	...	...	...	58.48	...	...	...	...	...
1853	...	...	...	...	...	...	...	...	...	...	59.36	...	...	...	...	...
1854	...	...	...	...	56.06	...	...	...	...	61.02	61.24	...	...	...	...	...
1855	...	...	...	...	53.68	...	...	...	...	59.93*	59.58*	...	...	...	...	...
1856	...	...	...	...	52.45	...	51.37*	...	...	57.43	57.17	52.78	...	...	...	...
1857	43.35	...	...	...	54.18	...	50.43	...	...	58.07	57.68	...	...	...	...	...
1858	...	...	...	...	...	...	...	...	...	59.73	59.53	...	...	...	...	...
1859	...	...	...	...	...	...	...	...	...	59.83	59.97*	...	...	...	55.69*	...
1860	...	...	...	...	...	...	...	...	...	59.39*	59.70	...	...	...	...	...
1861	...	...	...	...	...	...	...	...	...	...	60.89	...	...	...	...	...
1862	...	...	...	...	...	...	...	...	...	...	59.71	...	...	...	...	...
1863	...	...	...	...	54.86*	...	...	...	...	...	58.26	...	...	...	...	...
1864	...	...	...	...	...	...	...	...	...	...	58.30	...	...	...	...	...
1865	...	...	...	...	...	...	...	...	...	...	59.55	...	...	...	...	...
1866	...	...	...	...	...	...	...	...	...	...	...	...	...	...	...	...
1867	...	...	...	...	...	...	...	56.56*	...	...	57.56	...	55.77	...	...	...
1868	...	...	...	39.01*	...	...	...	...	58.05	...	57.21	...	55.00*	...	...	...
1869	...	...	...	40.16	...	...	...	...	59.40	...	57.24	...	...	57.66	...	55.64
1870	...	...	...	42.86	...	...	...	...	60.27*	...	58.64	...	...	58.98	...	55.32
	42.90	39.68	44.92	40.65	54.45	59.21	50.45	56.02	59.41	59.49	59.11	52.78	55.30[1]	58.32	56.17	55.27

[1] Hours of observation unknown.

VIRGINIA.—Continued.

Year.	Lynchburg, near.	Meadow Dale.	Mechanicsville.	Montrose.	Mossy Creek.	Mt. Solon.	Mt. View.	Mulberry Hill.	Norfolk.	Peachlawn.	Piedmont, near.	Portsmouth.	Powhatan Hill.	Prospect Hill.	Richmond.	Rougemont.
	°	°	°	°	°	°	°	°	°	°	°	°	°	°	°	°
1822	...	...	...	...	...	...	...	...	63.05	...	...	...	...	...	...	...
1852	...	...	...	...	...	...	...	...	...	...	...	...	...	...	57.43	...
1853	...	...	...	...	...	...	...	...	...	...	...	...	...	...	58.09	...
1854	...	...	...	...	...	...	...	...	...	...	...	...	...	...	...	...
1855	...	...	...	...	...	...	...	...	...	...	...	...	...	...	...	...
1856	...	...	...	...	...	...	...	...	...	...	...	58.96*	...	...	...	54.88
1857	...	46.41	...	...	49.35*	...	...	...	...	...	...	56.87	...	...	...	54.85
1858	...	48.83	...	55.59*	...	...	...	...	...	55.86	...	58.87	...	...	...	56.97*
1859	...	...	...	54.19*	...	...	55.54*	...	...	56.52	...	58.32	...	...	...	56.90
1860	...	...	...	...	...	...	55.58*	...	...	55.83	...	58.29	...	...	...	...
1861	...	...	...	...	...	...	...	...	...	...	...	...	...	...	...	...
1862	...	...	...	...	...	...	...	...	...	...	...	...	...	...	...	...
1863	...	...	...	...	...	...	...	...	...	...	...	...	...	...	...	...
1864	...	...	...	...	...	...	...	...	...	...	...	...	...	...	...	...
1865	...	...	...	...	...	...	...	...	...	...	...	60.42*	...	...	...	...
1866	...	...	...	...	...	...	...	...	...	...	...	60.09	...	...	...	...
1867	58.80*	...	...	...	...	...	...	...	...	...	...	59.48	...	...	...	...
1868	56.51*	...	...	...	...	54.72*	...	...	...	...	...	...	55.15*	55.62*	...	...
1869	57.67*	...	...	...	...	...	...	58.32*	...	...	...	57.57*	56.27	56.01	...	...
1870	58.42	...	53.22	...	...	...	...	...	...	...	53.85	...	57.59	57.51	...	...
	57.18	47.74	53.27	54.31	50.05	56.22	55.29	58.48	63.05	56.08	53.68	59.24	56.61	56.66	56.91	56.18

	VIRGINIA.—Continued.								WASHINGTON TERRITORY.							
Year.	Ruthven.	Smithfield.	Snowville.	Staunton.	Vienna, near.	Westwood.	Wytheville, near.	Winchester.	Camp Simiahmoo.	Camp Steele.	Cape Disappointment.	Fort Bellingham.	Fort Cascades.	Fort Colville.	Fort Simcoe.	Fort Steilacoom.
1850	...	...	...	...	...	...	...	...	...	...	...	...	...	...	...	49.59
1851	...	...	...	...	...	...	...	...	...	...	...	...	...	...	...	51.65
1852	...	...	...	...	...	...	...	...	...	...	...	...	...	...	...	50.58
1853	...	...	...	...	...	...	...	...	...	...	...	...	...	...	...	51.68
1854	...	...	...	...	...	...	...	55.42*	...	...	...	...	...	...	...	50.69
1855	...	56.96	...	...	...	...	...	53.59*	...	...	...	...	...	...	...	51.26*
1856	...	54.22	...	...	...	...	...	51.86*	...	...	...	...	...	...	...	51.30
1857	54.62*	55.78	...	...	...	...	...	51.54*	...	...	...	51.68*	...	...	50.70*	49.47
1858	...	57.29	...	...	...	...	...	54.22*	47.8	...	...	49.39	...	...	53.11	49.08
1859	...	56.66	...	...	...	57.31	...	53.94*	48.6	...	...	...	49.27	...	...	47.88
1860	...	56.20	...	...	...	...	...	...	...	50.84*	...	...	52.06	44.81	...	51.82
1861	...	...	...	...	...	...	...	...	...	48.98	...	...	...	43.72	...	51.91*
1862	...	...	...	...	...	...	...	...	...	48.02	...	...	...	41.64	...	48.13
1863	...	...	...	...	...	...	...	...	...	50.11*	...	...	...	44.16	...	51.10
1864	...	...	...	...	...	...	...	...	...	49.58	...	...	...	...	...	51.44
1865	...	...	...	...	...	...	...	...	...	...	52.02*	...	...	...	...	49.82*
1866	...	...	...	...	...	...	...	...	...	...	...	...	...	...	...	...
1867	...	...	...	...	...	...	...	...	...	49.36	51.30	...	...	43.98	...	50.21*
1868	...	...	50.05	...	...	...	50.72*	...	...	49.61	51.50	...	...	44.52	...	...
1869	...	...	50.18	53.53	...	...	51.29	...	...	51.96	...	...	...	46.49	...	...
1870	...	...	...	53.79*	54.79	...	52.12	...	...	50.56	...	...	...	45.96	...	...
	55.89	56.33	50.74	53.79	54.93	57.54	52.11	53.65	48.55	49.78	52.35	50.11	51.08	44.55	50.90	50.40

Year.	WASHINGTON TER.—Cont'd. Fort Vancouver.	Fort Vancouver.	Fort Walla-Walla.	Nee-ah Bay.	Tatoosh Isl'd Light-house.	WEST VIRGINIA. Ashland.	Ashland.	Buffalo.	Crack Whip.	Cross Creek.	Grafton.	Kanawah.	Kanawah.	Lewisburg.	Poplar Grove.	Romney.
	°	°	°	°	°	°	°	°	°	°	°	°	°	°	°	°
1829	...	...	...	...	...	...	...	...	...	...	...	53.2	...	...	...	...
1830	...	...	...	...	...	...	...	...	...	...	...	55.7	...	...	...	...
1831	...	...	...	...	...	...	...	...	...	...	...	52.0	...	...	...	...
1832	...	...	...	...	...	...	...	...	...	...	...	53.8*	...	...	...	...
1833	51.87*	...	...	...	...	...	...	...	...	...	...	...	...	...	...	...
1836	...	...	...	...	...	...	...	...	...	...	...	52.2	...	...	...	...
1840	...	...	...	...	...	...	...	...	...	...	...	53.7	...	...	...	...
1850	...	52.01	...	...	...	...	...	...	...	...	...	...	...	...	...	...
1851	...	...	...	...	...	...	...	...	...	...	...	...	...	...	...	...
1852	...	52.06*	...	...	...	...	...	54.29	...	...	...	...	...	...	...	...
1853	...	53.40	...	...	...	...	...	...	...	...	...	...	...	...	...	...
1854	...	51.95*	...	...	...	57.65	...	...	...	...	...	...	...	54.96	...	...
1855	...	52.42*	...	...	...	54.10*	...	...	...	...	...	...	...	53.48	...	...
1856	...	52.12	...	...	...	...	...	...	46.88*	...	...	...	51.96	50.17	...	...
1857	...	53.19*	53.56*	...	...	50.88*	...	...	...	...	...	...	...	47.53	52.62*	...
1858	...	51.86	52.60	...	...	...	...	...	...	...	...	...	...	51.90*	55.52	...
1859	...	50.32	53.20	...	...	...	...	...	...	49.15	...	...	...	53.42	54.78	...
1860	...	52.61	53.78	...	...	...	...	...	...	...	...	...	...	50.64	54.85*	...
1861	...	51.93	54.17	...	...	...	...	...	...	...	...	...	...	...	...	...
1862	...	48.51	49.24*	...	...	...	...	...	...	...	...	...	...	...	...	...
1863	...	52.92	54.40*	...	...	...	...	...	...	...	...	...	...	...	...	...
1864	...	52.71	54.89	47.32*	...	...	...	...	...	...	...	...	...	...	...	...
1865	...	51.19*	53.30*	45.96*	...	...	55.14*	...	...	...	...	...	...	...	...	...
1866	...	...	...	...	...	...	53.57*	...	...	...	...	...	...	...	...	...
1867	...	51.40	...	...	...	...	55.06	...	...	...	55.04*	...	...	...	...	...
1868	...	...	...	...	...	...	...	...	...	...	...	...	...	...	...	51.57*
1869	...	...	...	...	51.07*	...	52.82	...	...	...	...	...	...	...	...	...
1870	...	...	...	...	51.19	...	...	...	...	...	...				...	...
	51.87	51.83	53.22	47.64	51.13	53.83	54.18	54.29	47.50	49.49	54.99	53.65	52.50	51.81	54.31	51.95

W. V.—Continued.		WISCONSIN.														
Year.	Wirt Court House.	Appleton.	Baraboo.	Bay City.	Bayfield.	Bellefontaine.	Beloit College.	Bloomfield.	Dartford.	Delafield.	Delavan.	Edgerton.	Embarrass.	Fort Crawford.	Fort Howard.	Fort Winnebago.
	°	°	°	°	°	°	°	°	°	°	°	°	°	°	°	°
1822	...	...	...	...	...	...	...	...	...	...	...	...	...	45.09	43.64	...
1823	...	...	...	...	...	...	...	...	...	...	...	...	...	...	41.97	...
1824	...	...	...	...	...	...	...	...	...	...	...	...	...	46.27	43.96	...
1825	...	...	...	...	...	...	...	...	...	...	...	...	...	...	46.32	...
1826	...	...	...	...	...	...	...	...	...	...	...	...	...	...	44.72	...
1827	...	...	...	...	...	...	...	...	...	...	...	...	...	...	45.19	...
1828	...	...	...	...	...	...	...	...	...	...	...	...	...	...	45.40	...
1829	...	...	...	...	...	...	...	...	...	...	...	...	...	...	42.98	47.08
1830	...	...	...	...	...	...	...	...	...	...	...	...	...	51.42	46.36	52.05
1831	...	...	...	...	...	...	...	...	...	...	...	...	...	44.89	41.22	46.34
1832	...	...	...	...	...	...	...	...	...	...	...	...	...	45.58	44.31*	49.91
1833	...	...	...	...	...	...	...	...	...	...	...	...	...	51.43	46.28	...
1834	...	...	...	...	...	...	...	...	...	...	...	...	...	47.78	46.48	...
1835	...	...	...	...	...	...	...	...	...	...	...	...	...	45.65	43.55	41.30
1836	...	...	...	...	...	...	...	...	...	...	...	...	...	44.32	42.38	39.73
1837	...	...	...	...	...	...	...	...	...	...	...	...	...	45.55	43.14	41.13
1838	...	...	...	...	...	...	...	...	...	...	...	...	...	45.75	42.17	40.16
1839	...	...	...	...	...	...	...	...	...	...	...	...	...	50.80	45.68	43.89
1840	...	...	...	...	...	...	...	...	...	...	...	...	...	48.03	44.42	42.26
1841	...	...	...	...	...	...	...	...	...	...	...	...	...	47.61	...	41.96
1842	...	...	...	...	...	...	...	...	...	...	...	...	...	48.07	...	43.23
1843	...	...	...	...	...	...	...	...	...	...	...	...	...	43.06	...	41.84
1844	...	...	...	...	...	...	...	...	...	...	...	...	...	47.71	...	45.58*
1845	...	...	...	...	...	...	...	...	...	46.92	...	...	...	...	...	...
1846	...	...	...	...	...	...	...	...	...	48.99	...	...	...	...	...	...
1847	...	...	...	...	...	...	...	...	...	...	...	...	...	...	...	...
1848	...	...	...	...	...	...	...	...	...	44.71	...	...	...	...	...	...
1849	...	...	...	...	...	...	...	...	...	44.61	...	...	...	...	...	...
1850	...	...	...	...	...	...	...	...	...	45.51	...	...	...	...	...	...
1851	...	...	...	...	...	...	...	...	...	44.70	...	...	...	...	...	...
1852	...	...	...	...	...	...	...	...	...	44.24	...	...	...	...	...	...
1853	...	...	...	...	...	...	...	...	...	...	...	...	...	...	...	...
1854	...	...	...	...	...	47.22*	48.85	...	...	...	...	...	...	...	...	...
1855	...	...	...	...	...	...	45.48	...	...	...	...	...	...	...	...	...
1856	...	42.24	...	...	...	...	45.10	...	...	...	...	...	...	...	...	...
1857	49.02	42.17	...	36.25	...	...	43.70	...	...	...	...	...	40.69	...	...	...
1858	53.09	45.45	...	38.54	...	...	47.35	...	...	...	...	...	...	...	...	...
1859	...	44.18	...	35.21	...	...	46.58	...	...	...	...	...	...	...	...	...
1860	...	44.40	...	36.64*	...	...	46.15	...	...	...	...	...	...	...	...	...
1861	...	44.00	...	36.38*	...	...	46.68*	...	46.26*	45.03	...	...	...	...	...	...
1862	...	...	...	33.62	...	...	46.74	...	...	43.27*	...	...	...	...	...	...
1863	...	...	...	...	...	...	46.76*	...	...	...	...	...	...	...	...	...
1864	...	...	...	...	...	...	45.15	44.34*	...	...	...	...	42.97	...	...	...
1865	...	...	47.86	...	...	...	46.07	45.18*	...	...	45.29	...	44.40*	...	...	...
1866	...	...	46.61	...	...	...	44.50	...	...	...	43.73*	...	41.90	...	...	...
1867	...	...	46.87*	...	...	...	...	...	...	...	44.31	...	41.62	...	...	...
1868	...	...	...	...	38.33*	...	...	44.79*	...	...	...	44.98	41.95	...	...	...
1869	...	44.45*	43.13	...	38.82*	...	...	43.73*	...	...	...	44.85	41.71	...	...	...
1870	...	...	47.97	...	41.50	...	...	47.28	...	...	...	50.28	44.90	...	...	...
	51.21	44.20	46.20	37.13	39.73	47.22	46.39	45.16	45.25	45.27	44.14	46.78	42.67	47.32	44.12	44.46

WISCONSIN.—Continued.

Year.	Green Bay.	Green Lake.	Holland.	Janesville.	Kenosha.	Lowell.	Madison.	Manitowoc.	Milwaukee.	Mosinee.	New Danemore.	New Lisbon.	Norway.	Parfreyville.	Platteville.	Plymouth.
	°	°	°	°	°	°	°	°	°	°	°	°	°	°	°	°
1844	...	...	...	...	...	...	...	...	47.65	...	...	...	...	...	...	...
1845	...	...	...	...	...	...	...	...	49.21	...	...	...	...	...	...	...
1846	...	...	...	...	...	...	...	...	51.01	...	...	...	...	...	...	...
1847	...	...	...	...	...	...	...	...	46.44	...	...	...	...	...	...	...
1848	...	...	...	...	...	...	...	...	47.41	...	...	...	...	...	...	...
1849	...	...	...	...	...	...	...	...	44.65*	...	...	...	...	...	...	...
1850	...	45.63	...	...	...	...	...	...	46.86	...	...	...	...	...	...	...
1851	...	...	...	...	...	...	...	...	47.03	...	...	...	...	...	...	...
1852	...	...	...	...	...	...	...	45.19	45.84	...	...	...	...	...	...	...
1853	...	...	...	45.83	...	...	45.77	45.80	...	...	...	...	...	...	...	...
1854	...	...	...	47.19	...	...	46.80*	46.25	47.45*	...	...	...	...	...	48.48	...
1855	...	...	...	44.96	...	...	...	44.32	43.34	...	...	...	...	...	47.74	...
1856	...	...	...	42.95	43.15	...	...	42.23	42.00	...	...	...	43.77*	...	45.00	...
1857	...	...	...	44.66	43.74	42.93	43.16	43.01	42.13	...	...	...	...	...	44.83	...
1858	...	...	...	47.27*	46.93	...	45.97*	45.83	45.84	...	43.94*	...	...	...	48.29	...
1859	...	...	...	...	46.67	...	...	44.56	45.76	...	...	...	...	...	46.28	...
1860	...	...	...	47.04	...	...	...	45.11	46.12	...	...	...	...	...	...	...
1861	...	...	...	45.11*	46.84	...	44.47*	44.79	46.06	...	...	...	...	46.05*	...	...
1862	...	...	...	...	46.25	...	...	44.46	45.38	...	...	...	...	...	...	...
1863	...	...	...	...	...	...	...	44.93	46.28	...	...	...	...	...	...	...
1864	42.85	...	...	...	...	...	...	44.11	44.62	...	...	...	...	...	...	...
1865	43.61*	...	...	...	...	...	...	45.17	45.67	...	...	...	...	...	...	...
1866	...	...	...	...	...	...	...	42.97	43.80	...	...	...	...	...	...	42.13
1867	...	...	...	...	...	...	...	44.10	45.34	...	...	...	...	...	...	43.82
1868	...	...	...	...	...	...	...	43.15	43.90	...	...	...	...	...	...	41.89
1869	...	...	43.00	...	...	...	43.23*	42.96	44.16	...	...	43.70	...	...	...	42.24
1870	...	...	46.97*	...	...	...	47.31	46.65	47.29	42.03	...	...	...	...	...	...
	43.65	45.16	44.20	45.66	45.64	42.93[1]	45.40	44.48	45.75	42.33	43.06	44.85	44.33	45.91	46.81	42.71

WISCONSIN.—Continued. / WYOMING.

Year.	Racine.	Rocky Run.	Sturgeon Bay.	Superior.	Waukesha.	Waupaca.	Wausau.	Weyauwega.	Fort Bridger.	Fort D. A. Russell.	Fort Fetterman.	Fort F. Steele.	Fort Halleck.	Fort Laramie.	Fort P. Kearney.	Fort Sanders.
	Wisconsin								*Wyoming*							
1850	...	...	...	...	...	...	...	...	...	...	...	...	...	49.69	...	...
1851	...	...	...	...	...	...	...	...	...	...	...	...	...	50.64	...	...
1852	...	...	...	...	...	...	...	...	...	...	...	...	...	46.97	..	...
1853	...	...	...	...	...	...	...	...	...	...	...	...	...	50.00	...	...
1854	...	...	...	...	...	...	...	...	...	...	...	...	...	52.76	...	...
1855	...	...	...	...	...	...	...	...	...	...	...	...	...	50.83	...	...
1856	41.98*	...	...	38.07	43.26*	...	...	...	...	...	...	...	...	48.78	...	...
1857	...	...	...	...	43.98*	...	...	...	...	...	...	..	...	48.90	...	...
1858	...	...	...	...	47.44*	...	...	...	...	...	...	...	...	48.08	...	...
1859	...	...	...	...	...	...	42.69	...	38.81*	...	...	...	...	48.90	...	...
1860	...	45.45*	...	38.74	...	...	...	...	41.35	...	...	...	...	49.31	...	...
1861	...	45.09	...	38.13	...	...	...	...	...	...	...	...	...	50.44*	...	...
1862	...	44.47	...	37.16	...	...	...	42.20	...	...	...	...	...	49.31	...	...
1863	...	45.76*	...	38.71	...	...	...	45.56*	41.78	...	...	...	43.12	50.02	...	...
1864	...	44.89	...	38.39	...	45.68	...	...	41.30	...	...	...	...	50.59	...	...
1865	...	45.71	...	38.89	...	46.92	...	...	38.86	...	...	...	40.81*	...	...	...
1866	...	43.65*	...	36.99	...	44.63	...	...	42.44*	...	...	...	...	...	...	...
1867	...	44.80	...	37.09	...	44.59	...	...	40.92	...	...	...	...	...	42.90	...
1868	...	43.57*	...	...	...	44.30	...	...	39.42	...	...	...	...	...	...	40.94*
1869	...	43.72*	...	...	...	44.04	...	...	41.48*	...	43.47*	42.38	...	44.43	...	41.26
1870	...	47.46	45.20*	...	...	47.47*	...	...	41.63	42.88	44.34*	44.66	...	47.46	...	41.70
	43.83	44.96	45.20	37.74	45.28	45.31	42.90	44.27	40.86	42.94	43.77	43.52	42.20	49.15	45.92	41.47

[1] Hours of observation unknown.

	Mexico.					Costa Rica.		Guatemala.	British Honduras.	Bahama Islands.	Bermuda Islands.		Caribbean Islands.			
Year.	Cordova.	Mazatlan.	Mexico.	Mirador.	Vera Cruz.	Heredia.	San José.	Guatemala.	Belize.	Nassau.	Bermuda.	St. George.	Antigua.	Barbadoes.	St. Thomas.	Sombrero Island.
	°	°	°	°	°	°	°	°	°	°	°	°	°	°	°	°
1833	...	...	...	...	...	...	...	...	...	...	...	...	...	...	81.82	...
1834	...	...	...	...	...	...	...	...	...	...	...	...	79.38*	...	...	...
1836	...	...	...	...	...	...	...	...	...	...	...	...	79.68	...	...	...
1841	...	...	...	...	...	...	...	...	...	78.25	...	...	...	...	...	...
1844	...	...	...	...	...	...	...	...	...	...	...	...	...	80.93	...	...
1848	...	...	...	...	...	...	...	...	...	...	68.24	...	...	...	...	...
1849	...	...	...	...	...	...	...	...	...	...	68.50*	...	...	...	...	...
1850	...	...	...	...	...	...	...	...	...	...	68.87	...	...	...	...	...
1851	...	...	...	...	...	...	...	...	...	...	69.28	...	...	...	...	...
1852	...	...	...	...	...	...	...	...	...	...	68.27	...	...	...	...	...
1853	...	...	...	...	...	...	...	...	...	...	...	...	...	...	...	...
1854	...	...	...	67.19	...	...	...	...	...	...	...	...	...	...	...	...
1855	...	...	...	65.81	...	...	...	...	...	...	...	...	...	...	...	...
1856	...	...	61.00*	...	...	...	...	...	...	...	...	...	...	...	...	...
1857	...	...	...	...	...	...	...	64.89	...	...	...	69.04*	...	...	...	...
1858	68.76	...	...	67.83	78.16	...	...	65.57	...	...	...	...	...	...	...	...
1859	69.50	...	...	68.18	...	...	...	65.57	...	...	...	...	...	...	...	...
1860	...	...	...	...	...	...	...	...	...	...	...	...	...	...	...	...
1861	68.89	...	...	66.77	...	...	...	...	...	...	...	...	...	...	...	...
1862	69.96	...	...	67.25	...	...	67.30*	...	...	...	...	...	...	...	...	...
1863	68.54	...	...	66.38	...	...	...	...	79.90	...	...	...	...	...	...	78.62*
1864	68.61	...	...	66.75	...	...	...	...	...	...	...	...	...	...	...	...
1865	...	...	...	67.43	...	...	68.86	...	...	...	...	...	...	...	...	...
1866	...	...	...	67.56	...	...	67.92	...	...	...	...	...	...	...	...	...
1867	...	...	...	68.30	...	...	...	...	...	...	...	...	...	...	...	...
1868	...	79.43	...	67.22	...	69.59	...	...	...	...	...	...	...	...	...	...
1869	...	...	...	67.65	...	...	...	...	...	...	...	...	...	...	...	...
1870	...	...	...	66.30	...	...	...	...	...	...	...	...	...	...	...	...
	69.04	79.43	61.10	67.19	77.72	69.59	69.28	66.26	79.90	79.59	69.46	69.10	79.53[1]	80.93	81.82	78.74

[1] Hours of observation unknown.

	Cuba.			Jamaica.	Hayti.	Dutch Guiana.		New Granada.	Venezuela.	Brazil.	
Year.	Havana.	Havana.	Havana.	Kingston.	Tivoli.	Catharina Sophia.	Rustenburg.	Aspinwall.	Colonia Tovar.	Pernambuco.	Rio de Janeiro.
	°	°	°	°	°	°	°	°	°	°	°
1779	...	...	...	...	73.72	...	...	...	...	...	...
1794	81.80	...	...	...	...	...	...	...	...	...	...
1832	...	...	...	78.77	...	...	...	...	...	...	75.89
1833	...	...	...	...	...	...	...	...	...	...	78.11
1834	...	...	...	...	...	...	...	...	...	...	76.11
1835	...	...	...	...	...	...	...	...	...	...	75.35
1836	...	...	...	...	...	...	...	...	...	...	75.51
1837	...	...	...	...	...	...	...	...	...	...	74.15
1838	...	...	...	...	...	...	...	...	...	...	75.40
1839	...	...	...	...	...	...	...	...	...	...	74.68
1840	...	...	...	...	...	...	...	...	...	...	76.41
1841	...	...	...	...	...	...	...	...	...	...	75.66
1842	...	79.69	...	...	...	...	...	...	...	78.95	76.49
1843	...	...	...	...	...	...	...	...	...	...	76.19
1854	...	...	...	...	...	...	...	...	62.40*	...	...
1855	...	...	...	...	...	...	...	...	...	...	...
1856	...	...	...	...	...	80.33*	...	...	...	...	...
1857	...	...	...	...	...	80.31*	...	...	...	...	...
1858	...	...	...	...	...	79.49	...	...	...	...	...
1859	...	...	77.96	...	...	79.64	...	...	...	...	...
1860	...	...	78.42*	...	...	...	...	...	...	...	...
1861	...	...	77.88*	...	...	...	...	...	...	...	...
1862	...	...	78.03	...	...	...	78.75	...	...	...	...
1863	...	...	77.72*	...	...	...	77.52*	77.69*	...	...	...
1864	...	...	78.24*	...	...	...	...	78.54*	...	...	...
1865	...	...	78.72	...	...	...	...	79.39	...	...	...
1866	...	...	78.53		...	...	...	78.93	...	...	...
1867	...	...	79.37	...	...	...	...	78.47*	...	...	...
1868	...	...	78.83	...	...	...	...	80.22*	...	...	...
1869	...	...	79.35	...	...	...	...	...	...	...	...
1870	...	...	78.30*	...	...	...	...	...	...	...	...
	81.80[1]	79.36	78.44	78.77[1]	73.72[1]	79.88	77.77	78.66	61.44	78.95[1]	75.83

[1] Hours of observation unknown.

Investigation of the Secular Variation.—The following discussion, which is based upon the preceding tabular numbers,[1] will be limited to the examination of the secular variations of the temperature for places within the United States or for adjacent stations. To ascertain in general the character of these variations a number of stations were selected possessing the requisite length of series or from which, by proper combination from several stations at no great distance apart, such a series could be produced having as few interruptions as possible. These separate or combined series were plotted (see accompanying illustration); this could be done either by plotting directly the annual means, as in the case of New Haven (see isolated dots), or by smooth curves, as shown for all the stations which resulted from the application of the process of successive means (to the 4th order) which has been explained before. This process, while it preserves all the characteristic features of any systematic progression of temperature during a succession of years, also relieves us in a great degree from the embarrassing presence of the accidental and minor irregularities. The 4th order of means was found quite sufficient; the 8th is given for New Haven.

Further, the process of combination of the results from several adjacent stations, either for the purpose of producing a more extended series, or for filling up gaps, must be such as to preserve exactly any feature or features *common* to all the stations, whether of a progressive or a periodic character as might be produced by a disturbing influence of a general or cosmical nature. This will be done by the method of differences, as will be explained further on. If we examine any of the numerical and graphical results, for instance those for New Haven, we recognize in the first place certain apparently altogether irregular fluctuations in the annual means, their influence will be greatly reduced or destroyed by successive means and by combination of series (since they are equally liable to + and — deviations, which will tend to cancel themselves); in the second place, we notice certain systematic changes or undulations of irregular epochs and extent which will be subjected to further study with respect to their character and geographical distribution. If all the series, proposed for combination to a normal series, were of equal extent and complete, the simple mean for each year would be all that is needed, but for indirectly connected, overlapping, or defective series, the combination is more laborious, as we must take account of all possible differences or combinations,[2] which can only be done by application of the method of least squares. After the series have all been rendered homogeneous, by application to each of the corrections indicated with consideration of all possible combinations and their weights, the means for each year can be taken as before. A full example of the method is given below,[3] and the same is intended to show also the amount of local variation in the annual means after they have been reduced to a uniform series.

[1] The tables contain altogether about 1210 stations with an aggregate of about 8500 annual means. The general tables are estimated to represent nearly $11\frac{1}{2}$ millions of individual observations.

[2] The number of combinations of n elements by *twos* is expressed by $\frac{n(n-1)}{2}$.

[3] Suppose it be proposed to combine to a uniform system the results of the mean annual temperature of the 49-year series at Brunswick, the 37-year series at Portland, the 31-year series at Gardiner, the 40-year series at Castine, and the 14-year series at Cornish, all in the State of Maine, for which

The series of annual means thus obtained, after undergoing the process of successive means, are given in the following table. A combination series is indicated

---

see preceding tables. Designating these series in the order named by $A\ B\ C\ D\ E$, we proceed to find the differences $A - B$ from each year from the 33 years common to the two series; this gives the mean value $A - B = +0^\circ.8$ with the weight 33; in like manner we form the other differences designated by $V_1\ V_2\ V_3\ .\ .\ .$ subject to the small corrections $v_1\ v_2\ v_3\ .\ .\ .$ as follows.

V_1	$A - B = +0.8$	$+ v_1$	weight 33
V_2	$A - C = -0.1$	$+ v_2$	17
V_3	$A - D = +0.3$	$+ v_3$	36
V_4	$A - E = +0.4$	$+ v_4$	3
V_5	$B - C = -0.1$	$+ v_5$	20
V_6	$B - D = -1.6$	$+ v_6$	30
V_7	$B - E = +1.4$	$+ v_7$	3
V_8	$C - D = -0.8$	$+ v_8$	13
V_9	$C - E = +0.3$	$+ v_9$	13
	($D - E$ does not exist.)		

By means of the relation $V_2 - V_1 - V_5 = 0$ and similarly in the other four cases we establish the conditional equations:—

$$\begin{cases} 0 = -0.8 - v_1 + v_2 - v_5 \\ 0 = +0.5 - v_1 + v_3 - v_6 \\ 0 = -1.8 - v_1 + v_4 - v_7 \\ 0 = +1.2 - v_2 + v_3 - v_8 \\ 0 = +0.2 - v_2 + v_4 - v_9 \end{cases}$$

whence the equations of correlatives and the normal equations—

	$\frac{100}{p}$	C_1	C_2	C_3	C_4	C_5
v_1	9	−1	−1	−1		
v_2	18	+1			−1	−1
v_3	8		+1		+1	
v_4	100			+1		+1
v_5	15	−1				
v_6	10		−1			
v_7	100			−1		
v_8	23				−1	
v_9	23					−1

	C_1	C_2	C_3	C_4	C_5
$0 = -0.8$	+42	+ 9	+ 9	−18	− 18
$0 = +0.5$	+ 9	+27	+ 9	+ 8	
$0 = -1.8$	+ 9	+ 9	+209		+100
$0 = +1.2$	−18	+ 8		+49	+ 18
$0 = +0.2$	−13		+100	+18	+141

hence:

$C_1 = +0.0127$	$v_1 = +0.02$	$A - B = +0^\circ.8$
$C_2 = -0.0228$	$v_2 = +0.60$	$A - C = +0.5$
$C_3 = +0.0123$	$v_3 = -0.29$	$A - D = \ \ 0.0$
$C_4 = -0.0136$	$v_4 = +0.55$	$A - E = +1.0$
$C_5 = -0.0098$		

and applying these differences to the respective series—the Brunswick series remaining unchanged—they become as follows:—

Year.	Brunswick. A	Portland. B	Gardiner. C	Castine. D	Cornish. E	Brunswick. (C. V.)	Successive means, 4th order.
	°					°	
1807	43.7	...	...	...	...	43.7	...
1808	43.4	...	...	...	...	43.4	(43.1)
1809	42.1	...	...	...	...	42.1	43.1
1810	43.6	...	...	43.1	...	43.3	43.2
1811	44.7	...	...	44.9	...	44.8	43.2
1812	40.9	...	...	41.5	...	41.2	43.0
1813	43.2	...	...	43.6	...	43.4	43.0
1814	43.3	...	...	44.0	...	43.6	43.0
1815	42.9	...	...	42.4	...	42.7	42.7
1816	42.1	...	...	41.9	...	42.0	42.4
1817	41.6	...	...	42.0	...	41.8	42.7
1818	44 8	...	...	42.8	...	43.8	43.5
1819	45.5	...	...	44.7	...	45.1	44.1
1820	44.0	43.8	...	43.5	...	43.8	44.0
1821	43.9	43.5	...	42.8	...	43.4	43.7
1822	43.1	44.4	...	44.5	...	44.0	43.5
1823	41.0	42.4	...	43.0	...	42.1	43.5
1824	43.9	44.0	...	45.0	...	44.3	44.2
1825	45.7	46.0	...	46.3	...	46.0	45.2
1826	45.5	45.8	...	46.6	...	46.0	45.4
1827	43.9	44.0	...	44.0	...	44.0	45.4
1828	46.9	46.2	...	47.5	...	46.9	45.5

Year.	Brunswick. A	Portland. B	Gardiner. C	Castine. D	Cornish. E	Brunswick. (C. V.)	Successive means, 4th order.
	°					°	
1829	46.2	44.0	...	44.5	...	44.9	45.6
1830	47.5	45.3	...	44.6	...	45.8	45.5
1831	47.7	45.0	...	45.0	...	45.9	45.0
1832	45.2	42.8	...	42.1	...	43.4	44.2
1833	45.6	43.0	...	42.0	...	43.5	43.7
1834	45.4	43.5	...	43.0	...	44.0	43.4
1835	44.4	42.7	...	42.6	...	43.2	42.9
1836	43.0	41.0	...	40.9	...	41.6	42.2
1837	...	41.0	41.5	41.2	...	41.2	42.1
1838	...	42.8	43.2	43.1	...	43.0	42.8
1839	...	43.9	44.6	43.4	...	44.0	43.7
1840	...	44.0	45.5	43.6	...	44.4	44.3
1841	46.6	43.9	46.0	43.9	...	45.1	44.5
1842	45.8	43.9	44.4	44.1	...	44.5	44.2
1843	43.9	42.9	43.1	43.7	...	43.4	43.5
1844	42.3	43.5	41.0	42.9	...	42.4	43.3
1845	43.3	44.1	42.2	45.2	...	43.7	43.8
1846	44.0	45.2	45.0	48.4	...	45.6	44.4
1847	43.1	43.9	44.8	45.0	...	44.2	44.5
1848	43.7	45.4	44.3	45.0	...	44.6	44.3
1849	43.0	44.4	43.9	44.0	...	43.8	44.2
1850	43.4	45.2	44.7		...	44.4	44.1

Year.	Brunswick. A	Portland. B	Gardiner. C	Castine. D	Cornish. E	Brunswick. (C. V.)	Successive means, 4th order.
	°					°	
1851	42.6	43.9	44.5	...	...	43.7	44.1
1852	43.9	44.5	45.2	...	...	44.5	44.1
1853	44.5	...	...	...	...	44.5	43.9
1854	42.7	...	...	...	...	42.7	43.8
1855	42.9	...	45.7	...	...	44.3	43.8
1856	41.8	45.1	44.0	...	...	43.6	43.8
1857	43.6	45.1	44.9	...	43.1	44.2	43.7
1858	43.8	44.3	42.9	...	43.1	43.5	43.5
1859	40.3	43.8	41.8	...	43.4	42.3	43.4
1860	...	...	...	...	44.8	44.8	43.6
1861	...	...	43.6	...	43.6	43.6	43.7
1862	...	...	43.4	...	43.4	43.4	43.7
1863	...	...	43.6	...	44.2	43.9	44.0
1864	...	...	45.1	...	44.3	44.7	44.5
1865	...	...	45.0	...	46.0	45.5	44.8
1866	...	...	44.1	...	45.0	44.5	44.4
1867	...	...	43.0	...	43.5	43.3	43.8
1868	...	...	42.9	...	43.0	43.0	43.5
1869	...	...	45.3	...	45.1	45.2	(45.1)
1870	...	...	46.6	...	47 5	47.0	...

by having the letter *C* and a Roman numeral expressing the number of individual series attached to the name of the principal station. These combinations are as follows:—

Combination	Series	Length	Reduction
Brunswick, Me.	Brunswick	49 years.	
	Portland	37 "	Constant Reduction +0°.8
	Gardiner	31 "	" " +0.5
	Castine	40 "	" " 0.0
	Cornish	14 "	" " +1.0
Salem, Mass.	Salem	43 years.	
	New Bedford	58 "	Constant Reduction —0°.5
	Cambridge	50 "	+0.4
	Boston	32 "	—1.1
	Fort Independence	25 "	—0.7
	Providence	34 "	—0.6
Montreal, Can.	Montreal	27 years.	
	Second series	5 "	Constant Reduction —0°.3
	Third "	9 "	+0.7
	Fourth "	5 "	+0.9
	Fifth "	6 "	—1.1
	Sixth "	4 "	+1.2
	St. Martin	10 "	+0.6
New Haven, Conn.	New Haven	85 years.	
Toronto, Can.	Toronto	31 years.	
New York, N. Y.	Flatbush	39 years.	
	Fort Columbus	48 "	Constant Reduction —0°.6
	Fort Hamilton	26 "	—0.3
	New York	21 "	—0.7
Philadelphia, Penn.	Philadelphia, series Nos. 80, 81, 83 of general table	30 years.	
	Philadelphia, series No. 82 of gen'l table	20 "	Constant Reduction —5°.8
	Philadelphia, series No. 87 of gen'l table	40 "	" " +0.5
	Morrisville, series No. 65 of general table to 1847	57 "	" " +0.1
	Morrisville, series No. 65 of general table, 1849 to 1870	11 "	" " +3.3
	Germantown, series No. 40 of gen'l table	15 "	" " +2.2
	West Chester, series No. 119 of gen'l table	16 "	" " +3.0
Charleston, S. C.	Charleston	25 years.	
	Fort Moultrie	33 "	Constant Reduction —0°.1
	St. Johns	15 "	" " +2.7

Central station	Series	Years	Constant Reduction
Savannah, Ga. . .	Savannah	25 years.	
	Augusta Arsenal . .	22 "	Constant Reduction +2°.3
	Augusta	6 "	" " +2.7
	Oglethorpe Barracks	12 "	" " —0.9
Fort Brooke, Fla. .	Fort Brooke . . .	27 years.	
Cincinnati, Ohio .	Cincinnati . . .	45 years.	
	Marietta	46 "	Constant Reduction +2°.1
	College Hill . . .	47 "	" " +2.3
	Portsmouth . . .	12 "	" " —0.1
Fort Snelling, Minn.	Fort Snelling . . .	42 years.	
	St. Paul	8 "	Constant Reduction +1°.9
Muscatine, Iowa .	Muscatine	26 years.	
	Fort Madison . .	22 "	Constant Reduction —3°.4
St. Louis, Mo. . .	St. Louis	35 years.	
	Jefferson Barracks .	32 "	Constant Reduction —0°.1
Ft. Leavenworth, Kan.	Fort Leavenworth .	40 years.	
	Leavenworth City .	5 "	Constant Reduction +1°.6
Fort Gibson, Indian Territory . . .	Fort Gibson . . .	29 years.	
	Fort Towson . . .	16 "	Constant Reduction —1°.2
	Fort Washita . . .	15 "	" " —1.9
Fort Jesup, La. . .	Fort Jesup . . .	23 years.	
San Francisco, Cal.	Alcatraz Island . .	7 years.	
	Angel Island . . .	3 "	Constant Reduction —1°.0
	Fort Point . . .	11 "	" " +0.9
	Presidio	18 "	" " +1.0
	San Francisco . .	11 "	" " 0.0

On the whole the constant reduction deduced by a rigorous method and applied to each separate series to refer to the central station, answered well enough, yet there were indications, when the several series were thus brought *side by side*, of deviations from constant reduction for some consecutive years, which imperfections may have been produced by a change of thermometer, a change in the location of the instrument, or a change of observing hours; in the latter case, it would indicate an imperfect correction for daily variation.

Year.	Brunswick, Me.		Salem, Mass.		Montreal, Can.		New Haven, Con.		Toronto, Can.		New York, N. Y.		Philadelphia, Pa.	
	C. V.	4th or.	C. VI.	4th or.	C. VII.	4th or.	C. I.	8th or.	C. I.	4th or.	C. IV.	4th or.	C. VII.	4th or.
	°	°	°	°	°	°	°	°	°	°	°	°	°	°
1750	...	...	...	...	...	...	...	...	...	...	...	...	...	...
1751	...	...	...	...	...	...	...	...	...	...	...	...	...	...
1752	...	...	...	...	...	...	...	...	...	...	...	...	...	...
1753	...	...	...	...	...	...	...	...	...	...	...	...	...	...
1754	...	...	...	...	...	...	...	...	...	...	...	...	...	...
1755	...	...	...	...	...	...	...	...	...	...	...	...	...	...
1756	...	...	...	...	...	...	...	...	...	...	...	...	...	...
1757	...	...	...	...	...	...	...	...	...	...	...	...	...	...
1758	...	...	...	...	...	...	...	...	...	...	...	...	53.6	- - -
1759	...	...	...	...	...	...	...	...	...	...	...	...	52.7	- - -
1760	...	...	...	...	...	...	...	...	...	...	...	...	...	...
1761	...	...	...	...	...	...	...	...	...	...	...	...	...	...
1762	...	...	...	...	...	...	...	...	...	...	...	...	...	...
1763	...	...	...	...	...	...	...	...	...	...	...	...	...	...
1764	...	...	...	...	...	...	...	...	...	...	...	...	...	...
1765	...	...	...	...	...	...	...	...	...	...	...	...	...	...
1766	...	...	...	...	...	...	...	...	...	...	...	...	...	...
1767	...	...	...	...	...	...	...	...	...	...	...	...	53.3	- - -
1768	...	...	...	...	...	...	...	...	...	...	...	...	51.5	52.1
1769	...	...	...	...	...	...	...	...	...	...	...	...	51.8	52.0
1770	...	...	...	...	...	...	...	...	...	...	...	...	52.0	52.0
1771	...	...	...	...	...	...	...	...	...	...	...	...	51.8	52.2
1772	...	...	...	...	...	...	...	...	...	...	...	...	52.5	52.9
1773	...	...	...	...	...	...	...	...	...	...	...	...	54.7	53.5
1774	...	...	...	...	...	...	...	...	...	...	...	...	52.9	53.7
1775	...	...	...	...	...	...	...	...	...	...	...	...	54.4	53.6
1776	...	...	...	...	...	...	...	...	...	...	...	...	53.5	53.2
1777	...	...	...	...	...	...	...	...	...	...	...	...	51.0	- - -
1778	...	...	...	...	...	...	...	...	...	...	...	...	...	...
1779	...	...	...	...	...	...	...	...	...	...	...	...	...	...
1780	...	...	...	...	...	...	49.7	- - -	...	...	...	...	...	...
1781	...	...	50.2	- - -	...	...	50.4	49.9	...	...	...	...	...	...
1782	...	...	- - -	- - -	...	...	49.1	49.1	...	...	...	...	...	...
1783	...	...	50.4	- - -	...	...	48.4	48.5	...	...	...	...	...	...
1784	...	...	- - -	- - -	...	...	47.3	48.1	...	...	...	...	...	...
1785	...	...	- - -	- - -	...	...	47.7	48.0	...	...	...	...	...	...
1786	...	...	47.7	- - -	...	...	48.5	48.3	...	...	...	...	...	...
1787	...	...	47.0	47.1	...	...	48.5	48.7	...	...	...	...	...	...
1788	...	...	47.0	47.1	...	...	49.7	49.0	...	...	...	...	...	...
1789	...	...	46.8	47.3	...	...	49.5	49.2	...	...	...	...	...	...
1790	...	...	47.6	47.8	...	...	49.5	49.3	...	...	...	...	52.8	- - -
1791	...	...	49.0	48.4	...	...	49.5	49.3	...	...	...	...	53.7	53.0
1792	...	...	48.1	49.1	...	...	48.2	49.3	...	...	...	...	52.0	52.9
1793	...	...	50.6	49.8	...	...	50.3	49.3	...	...	...	...	54.4	52.6
1794	...	...	50.9	50.1	...	...	50.2	49.3	...	...	...	...	50.6	52.1
1795	...	...	49.7	49.4	...	...	- - -	49.1	...	...	...	...	51.9	51.9
1796	...	...	47.6	48.3	...	...	48.4	48.7	...	...	...	...	52.2	52.0
1797	...	...	47.3	47.8	...	...	48.1	48.6	...	...	...	...	51.7	52.3
1798	...	...	48.4	48.0	...	...	49.3	48.8	...	...	...	...	53.5	52.6
1799	...	...	47.9	48.3	...	...	48.4	49.2	...	...	...	...	52.4	52.7
1800	...	...	49.1	48.9	...	...	50.2	49.8	...	...	...	...	52.6	52.9
1801	...	...	49.6	49.4	...	...	51.0	50.3	...	...	...	...	52.9	53.2
1802	...	...	50.0	49.4	...	...	51.3	50.5	...	...	...	...	54.6	53.6
1803	...	...	49.2	49.0	...	...	50.8	50.5	...	...	...	...	53.2	53.4
1804	...	...	47.5	48.6	...	...	49.8	50.4	...	...	...	...	53.1	52.9
1805	...	...	49.9	48.4	...	...	51.7	50.3	...	...	...	...	52.1	52.3
1806	...	...	47.2	48.0	...	...	49.7	50.1	...	...	...	...	52.0	51.9
1807	43.7	- - -	47.2	47.7	...	...	49.2	49.9	...	...	...	...	50.6	51.8
1808	43.4	43.1	48.2	47.6	...	...	50.3	49.7	...	...	...	...	53.1	51.9
1809	42.1	43.1	46.8	47.7	...	...	49.3	49.6	...	...	...	...	51.6	52.0
1810	43.3	43.2	48.3	47.8	...	...	50.0	49.4	...	...	...	...	51.9	52.1
1811	44.8	43.2	49.2	47.5	...	...	49.7	49.1	...	...	...	...	53.0	52.1
1812	41.2	43.0	44.7	46.9	...	...	46.9	48.7	...	...	...	...	51.6	52.0
1813	43.4	43.0	47.4	46.8	...	...	49.0	48.3	...	...	...	...	51.8	51.9
1814	43.6	43.0	47.6	47.0	...	...	48.6	48.0	...	...	...	...	52.1	51.9
1815	42.7	42.7	46.8	46.8	...	...	47.3	47.5	...	...	...	...	52.2	51.7
1816	42.0	42.4	46.3	46.6	...	...	46.6	47.2	...	...	...	...	50.5	51.6
1817	41.8	42.7	46.2	46.8	...	...	46.5	47.1	...	...	...	...	52.2	51.8
1818	43.8	43.5	47.3	47.4	...	...	46.8	47.3	...	...	...	...	52.3	52.1
1819	45.1	44.1	49.4	48.0	...	...	49.0	47.7	...	...	...	...	52.5	52.3

Year.	Brunswick, Me.		Salem, Mass.		Montreal, Can.		New Haven, Con.		Toronto, Can.		New York, N. Y.		Philadelphia, Pa.	
	C. V.	4th or.	C. VI.	4th or.	C. VII.	4th or.	C. I.	8th or.	C. I.	4th or.	C. IV.	4th or.	C. VII.	4th or.
	°	°	°	°	°	°	°	°	°	°	°	°	°	°
1820	43.8	44.0	47.6	47.9	...	...	47.9	48.0	...	...	...	...	52.2	52.4
1821	43.4	43.7	47.1	47.8	...	...	47.6	48.3	...	...	...	...	51.9	52.7
1822	44.0	43.5	48.9	47.7	...	...	49.7	48.6	...	...	53.2	- - -	54.3	53.3
1823	42.1	43.5	46.5	47.7	...	...	48.1	49.0	...	...	49.6	50.9	53.6	53.8
1824	44.3	44.2	48.3	48.2	...	...	49.9	49.4	...	...	51.1	51.5	53.6	54.1
1825	46.0	45.2	49.6	48.9	...	...	50.7	49.7	...	...	53.4	52.1	55.2	54.4
1826	46.0	45.4	49.7	49.1	45.9	- - -	49.7	49.8	...	...	52.5	52.2	54.8	54.5
1827	44.0	45.4	48.1	48.9	43.5	44.8	48.9	49.9	...	...	51.0	52.0	53.2	54.5
1828	46.9	45.5	49.5	48.7	46.1	45.2	51.8	49.8	...	...	53.1	51.9	56.8	54.3
1829	44.9	45.6	47.9	48.4	44.8	45.5	48.7	49.7	...	...	50.8	51.8	52.1	53.6
1830	45.8	45.5	48.3	48.2	46.6	45.6	50.8	49.5	...	...	52.9	51.7	53.2	52.7
1831	45.9	45.0	48.6	48.1	45.6	45.1	49.2	49.0	...	...	50.7	51.3	52.1	52.2
1832	43.4	44.2	47.4	47.9	43.5	44.2	47.7	48.5	...	...	50.8	50.8	51.4	52.0
1833	43.5	43.7	47.6	47.5	43.6	43.6	48.3	48.2	...	...	50.9	50.5	52.1	52.0
1834	44.0	43.4	47.7	47.0	43.8	42.9	48.9	47.7	...	...	50.4	49.9	52.9	51.8
1835	43.2	42.9	46.3	46.2	41.7	41.7	46.6	47.0	...	...	48.8	48.8	51.2	51.2
1836	41.6	42.2	44.6	45.6	39.6	40.8	45.2	46.6	...	...	46.7	48.1	49.3	50.7
1837	41.1	42.1	45.2	45.7	40.7	40.8	46.4	46.9	...	...	48.5	48.4	51.4	51.2
1838	43.0	42.8	46.7	46.5	41.1	41.7	48.2	47.6	...	...	49.7	49.4	52.5	52.1
1839	44.0	43.7	47.6	47.2	43.6	42.6	49.2	48.5	...	...	50.5	50.2	52.9	52.6
1840	44.4	44.3	47.9	47.5	43.2	43.0	49.0	49.0	43.6	- - -	50.5	50.6	53.0	52.3
1841	45.1	44.5	47.2	47.6	43.2	43.0	49.5	49.1	43.9	43.8	50.6	51.0	52.3	52.8
1842	44.5	44.2	47.9	47.5	42.7	42.8	49.9	49.1	40.0	43.6	51.9	51.2	53.5	52.8
1843	43.4	43.5	46.8	47.5	42.5	42.6	47.4	49.1	42.4	43.6	50.9	51.3	52.2	53.0
1844	42.4	43.3	47.7	47.8	42.2	42.8	50.2	49.4	44.5	44.1	51.1	51.5	53.4	53.4
1845	43.7	43.8	48.7	48.3	43.4	43.3	50.2	49.6	44.6	44.8	52.7	51.8	54.4	53.9
1846	45.6	44.4	48.9	48.6	44.8	43.6	50.1	49.6	46.4	45.0	51.5	51.8	54.2	54.1
1847	44.2	44.5	48.7	48.6	42.6	43.6	49.4	49.4	43.7	44.8	51.6	51.5	53.9	54.0
1848	44.6	44.3	48.8	48.4	44.2	43.5	49.2	49.1	45.1	44.6	51.4	51.0	54.0	54.0
1849	43.8	44.2	47.9	48.2	43.1	43.4	48.3	48.9	44.1	44.4	49.9	50.8	53.8	54.1
1850	44.4	44.1	48.0	48.1	43.8	43.3	48.8	48.8	44.5	44.3	51.1	51.0	54.8	54.2
1851	43.7	44.1	47.8	48.0	42.4	43.2	49.0	48.8	44.0	44.2	51.6	51.2	54.5	54.3
1852	44.5	44.1	48.0	48.1	43.5	43.1	48.8	48.9	43.8	44.2	51.3	51.3	53.7	54.4
1853	44.5	43.9	48.5	48.1	43.5	42.9	49.6	49.0	44.8	44.5	51.8	51.3	55.3	54.6
1854	42.7	43.8	47.9	47.9	42.1	42.5	49.3	48.0	[illegible]	[illegible]	[illegible]	[illegible]	54.7	54.4
1855	44.3	43.8	47.9	47.5	42.2	42.0	49.0	48.5	44.0	43.8	50.3	50.2	54.1	53.7
1856	43.6	43.8	46.4	47.1	41.2	41.7	47.0	48.1	42.2	43.2	49.0	49.6	52.2	53.1
1857	44.2	43.7	47.1	47.1	41.7	41.5	47.5	47.9	42.8	43.3	49.3	49.5	52.8	53.1
1858	43.5	43.5	47.4	47.2	41.0	41.6	48.3	48.0	44.8	43.9	50.0	49.7	54.3	53.5
1859	42.3	43.4	47.2	47.4	41.6	42.3	48.0	48.3	44.2	44.2	50.0	50.1	53.7	53.7
1860	44.8	43.6	48.2	47.7	44.4	43.2	48.6	48.7	44.3	44.3	50.7	50.5	53.5	53.7
1861	43.6	43.7	47.8	47.8	43.6	43.6	50.1	49.1	44.2	44.3	51.2	50.9	54.1	53.7
1862	43.4	43.7	47.8	47.9	42.9	- - -	49.5	49.6	44.4	44.4	50.7	51.1	53.2	53.8
1863	43.9	44.0	48.4	48.0	...	...	50.0	49.8	44.6	44.5	51.8	51.3	54.2	54.1
1864	44.7	44.5	47.8	48.2	...	...	49.9	50.0	44.7	44.6	51.4	51.5	54.7	54.6
1865	45.5	44.8	49.8	48.3	...	...	50.0	- - -	44.9	44.4	52.1	51.3	55.6	54.9
1866	44.5	44.4	47.3	47.9	...	...	...	...	43.5	44.0	50.5	50.7	54.7	54.6
1867	43.3	43.8	47.7	47.4	...	...	...	...	43.8	43.7	50.2	50.1	54.2	53.9
1868	43.0	43.5	46.0	47.3	...	...	...	...	43.3	43.6	48.7	50.0	52.7	53.7
1869	45.2	45.1	47.9	47.8	...	...	...	...	43.1	43.8	50.4	50.6	54.2	54.2
1870	47.0	- - -	49.6	- - -	...	...	...	...	45.9	- - -	52.9	- - -	55.9	- - -

Year.	Charleston, S. C.		Savannah, Ga.		Fort Brooke, Fla.		Cincinnati, Ohio.		Fort Snelling, Minn.		Muscatine, Iowa.		St. Louis, Mo.	
	C. III.	4th or.	C. IV.	4th or.	C. I.	4th or.	C. IV.	4th or.	C. II.	4th or.	C. II.	4th or.	C. II.	4th or.
	°	°	°	°	°	°	°	°	°	°	°	°	°	°
1730	...	...	...	...	...	...	...	...	...	...	...	...	...	...
1731	...	...	...	...	...	...	...	...	...	...	...	...	...	...
1732	...	...	...	...	...	...	...	...	...	...	...	...	...	...
1733	...	...	...	...	...	...	...	...	...	...	...	...	...	...
1734	...	...	...	...	...	...	...	...	...	...	...	...	...	...
1735	...	...	...	...	...	...	...	...	...	...	...	...	...	...
1736	...	...	...	...	...	...	...	...	...	...	...	...	...	...
1737	...	...	...	...	...	...	...	...	...	...	...	...	...	...
1738	66.0	- - -	...	...	...	...	...	...	...	...	...	...	...	...
1739	64.8	64.9	...	...	...	...	...	...	...	...	...	...	...	...
1740	63.9	- - -	...	...	...	...	...	...	...	...	...	...	...	...
1741	- - -	- - -	...	...	...	...	...	...	...	...	...	...	...	...
1742	64.7	- - -	...	...	...	...	...	...	...	...	...	...	...	...
1743	- - -	...	...	...	...	...	...	...	...	...	...	...	...	...
1744	- - -	...	...	...	...	...	...	...	...	...	...	...	...	...
1745	- - -	...	...	...	...	...	...	...	...	...	...	...	...	...
1746	- - -	...	...	...	...	...	...	...	...	...	...	...	...	...
1747	- - -	...	...	...	...	...	...	...	...	...	...	...	...	...
1748	- - -	...	...	...	...	...	...	...	...	...	...	...	...	...
1749	- - -	...	...	...	...	...	...	...	...	...	...	...	...	...
1750	64.6	- - -	...	...	...	..	...	...	...	...	...	...	...	...
1751	66.3	66.0	...	...	...	...	...	...	...	...	...	...	...	...
1752	66.9	66.5	...	...	...	...	...	...	...	...	...	...	...	...
1753	66.4	66.5	...	...	...	...	...	...	...	...	...	...	...	...
1754	67.4	66.0	...	...	...	...	...	...	...	...	...	...	...	...
1755	63.2	65.5	...	...	...	...	...	...	...	...	...	...	...	...
1756	66.6	65.3	...	...	...	...	...	...	...	...	...	...	...	...
1757	65.3	65.1	...	...	...	...	...	...	...	...	...	...	...	...
1758	63.9	64.5	...	...	...	...	...	...	...	...	...	...	...	...
1759	64.7	- - -	...	...	...	...	...	...	...	...	...	...	...	...
1760	...	...	...	...	...	...	...	...	...	...	...	...	...	...
1761	...	...	...	...	...	...	...	...	...	...	...	...	...	...
1762	...	...	...	...	...	...	...	...	...	...	...	...	...	...
1763	...	...	...	...	...	...	...	...	...	...	...	...	...	...
1764	...	...	...	...	...	...	...	...	...	...	...	...	...	...
1765	...	...	...	...	...	...	...	...	...	...	...	...	...	...
1766	...	...	...	...	...	...	...	...	...	...	...	...	...	...
1767	...	...	...	...	...	...	...	...	...	...	...	...	...	...
1768	...	...	...	...	...	...	...	...	...	...	...	...	...	...
1769	...	...	...	...	...	...	...	...	...	...	...	...	...	...
1770	...	...	...	...	...	...	...	...	...	...	...	...	...	...
1771	...	...	...	...	...	...	...	...	...	...	...	...	...	...
1772	...	...	...	...	...	...	...	...	...	...	...	...	...	...
1773	...	...	...	...	...	...	...	...	...	...	...	...	...	...
1774	...	...	...	...	...	...	...	...	...	...	...	...	...	...
1775	...	...	...	...	...	...	...	...	...	...	...	...	...	...
1776	...	...	...	...	...	...	...	...	...	...	...	...	...	...
1777	...	...	...	...	...	...	...	...	...	...	...	...	...	...
1778	...	...	...	...	...	...	...	...	...	...	...	...	...	...
1779	...	...	...	...	...	...	...	...	...	...	...	...	...	...
1780	...	...	...	...	...	...	...	...	...	...	...	...	...	...
1781	...	...	...	...	...	...	...	...	...	...	...	...	...	...
1782	...	...	...	...	...	...	...	...	...	...	...	...	...	...
1783	...	...	...	...	...	...	...	...	...	...	...	...	...	...
1784	...	...	...	...	...	...	...	...	...	...	...	...	...	...
1785	...	...	...	...	...	...	...	...	...	...	...	...	...	...
1786	...	...	...	...	...	...	...	...	...	...	...	...	...	...
1787	...	...	...	...	...	...	...	...	...	...	...	...	...	...
1788	...	...	...	...	...	...	...	...	...	...	...	...	...	...
1789	...	...	...	...	...	...	...	...	...	...	...	...	...	...
1790	...	...	...	...	...	...	...	...	...	...	...	...	...	...
1791	...	...	...	...	...	...	...	...	...	...	...	...	...	...
1792	...	...	...	...	...	...	...	...	...	...	...	...	...	...
1793	...	...	...	...	...	...	...	...	...	...	...	...	...	...
1794	...	...	...	...	...	...	...	...	...	...	...	...	...	...
1795	...	...	...	...	...	...	...	...	...	...	...	...	...	...
1796	...	...	...	...	...	...	...	...	...	...	...	...	...	...
1797	...	...	...	...	...	...	...	...	...	...	...	...	...	...
1798	...	...	...	...	...	...	...	...	...	...	...	...	...	...
1799	...	...	...	...	...	...	...	...	...	...	...	...	...	...

Year.	Charleston, S. C.		Savannah, Ga.		Fort Brooke, Fla.		Cincinnati, Ohio.		Fort Snelling, Minn.		Muscatine, Iowa.		St. Louis, Mo.	
	C. III.	4th or.	C. IV.	4th or.	C. I.	4th or.	C. IV.	4th or.	C. II.	4th or.	C. II.	4th or.	C. II.	4th or.
	°	°	°	°	°	°	°	°	°	°	°	°	°	°
1800	...	...	...	...	...	...	...	...	...	...	...	...	...	...
1801	...	...	...	...	...	...	...	...	...	...	...	...	...	...
1802	...	...	...	...	...	...	...	...	...	...	...	...	...	...
1803	...	...	...	...	...	...	...	...	...	...	...	...	...	...
1804	...	...	...	...	...	...	...	...	...	...	...	...	...	...
1805	...	...	...	...	...	...	...	...	...	...	...	...	...	...
1806	...	...	...	...	...	...	54.1	- - -	...	...	...	...	...	...
1807	...	...	...	...	...	...	54.4	54.8	...	...	...	...	...	...
1808	...	...	...	...	...	...	56.4	55.1	...	...	...	...	...	...
1809	...	...	...	...	...	...	54.4	54.7	...	...	...	...	...	...
1810	...	...	...	...	...	...	52.8	54.4	...	...	...	...	...	...
1811	...	...	...	...	...	...	56.6	54.3	...	...	...	...	...	...
1812	...	...	...	...	...	...	52.6	53.8	...	...	...	...	...	...
1813	...	...	...	...	...	...	52.7	53.5	...	...	...	...	...	...
1814	...	...	...	...	...	...	54.3	53.7	...	...	...	...	...	...
1815	...	...	...	...	...	...	54.0	53.7	...	...	...	...	...	...
1816	...	...	...	...	...	...	53.3	53.4	...	...	...	...	...	...
1817	...	...	...	...	...	...	52.7	53.5	...	...	...	...	...	...
1818	...	...	...	...	...	...	54.1	54.2	...	...	...	...	...	...
1819	...	...	64.6	- - -	...	...	56.3	54.9	...	...	...	...	...	...
1820	...	...	- - -	- - -	...	...	54.8	54.8	43.0	- - -	...	...	...	...
1821	...	...	- - -	- - -	...	...	53.5	54.5	42.9	43.2	...	...	...	...
1822	...	...	- - -	- - -	...	...	55.3	54.5	43.7	43.3	...	...	...	...
1823	64.2	- - -	- - -	- - -	...	...	54.0	54.6	43.4	43.5	...	...	...	...
1824	66.4	65.9	- - -	- - -	...	...	55.0	54.9	42.8	44.2	...	...	...	...
1825	66.7	66.8	- - -	- - -	72.0	- - -	55.4	55.2	47.1	45.0	...	...	...	...
1826	67.9	67.5	69.4	- - -	72.9	72.9	55.7	55.6	44.4	45.3	...	...	...	...
1827	66.9	67.9	68.7	69.1	73.8	73.1	55.8	55.8	45.7	45.5	...	...	58.8	- - -
1828	70.6	68.1	69.7	67.7	73.5	72.9	57.0	55.7	46.0	45.7	...	...	58.7	57.8
1829	65.4	67.9	63.5	66.5	71.2	72.4	53.8	55.0	45.3	45.8	...	...	55.0	56.6
1830	69.7	67.3	67.9	65.8	72.6	71.9	55.7	54.1	47.9	45.6	...	...	58.0	55.3
1831	65.3	66.5	64.1	65.8	71.0	- - -	51.4	53.6	42.4	45.1	...	...	50.6	54.4
1832	65.7	65.8	66.0	66.3	- - -	...	54.4	53.9	45.4	45.3	...	...	55.6	54.8
1833	65.6	65.6	67.8	66.9	- - -	...	54.9	54.4	47.5	46.1	...	...	56.9	55.5
1834	66.0	65.5	68.0	66.6		...	55.4	53.9	46.7	45.5	...	...	55.7	55.0
1835	63.7	- - -	64.5	65.4	- - -	...	51.7	52.8	43.0	44.1	...	...	52.8	53.9
1836	- - -	- - -	64.4	64.4	- - -	...	51.7	52.2	42.5	43.1	...	...	53.2	53.4
1837	- - -	- - -	63.5	63.9	- - -	...	53.0	52.4	43.6	43.0	...	...	54.1	53.5
1838	- - -	- - -	63.3	63.9	70.1	- - -	52.1	52.9	41.3	43.5	...	...	52.7	53.7
1839	- - -	- - -	64.7	64.4	71.6	70.9	54.6	53.6	46.8	44.4	51.3	- - -	54.6	54.1
1840	66.0	- - -	64.9	64.9	70.5	70.9	54.1	54.0	44.4	44.6	49.1	49.0	54.4	54.5
1841	65.6	65.5	65.3	65.2	71.2	70.9	54.1	54.0	43.9	44.0	46.5	47.5	54.9	54.9
1842	64.7	65.4	65.5	65.5	71.2	70.8	54.3	53.6	42.8	42.7	47.3	46.3	56.2	54.9
1843	65.7	65.6	66.0	65.7	70.3	70.7	51.7	53.5	39.9	42.0	43.7	46.0	52.9	54.8
1844	66.1	66.0	66.1	65.7	70.4	70.7	54.9	53.9	42.7	43.1	47.7	46.6	55.8	55.3
1845	66.2	66.2	65.3	65.6	70.6	70.9	54.1	54.5	45.8	44.9	47.3	47.2	56.7	56.0
1846	66.9	66.3	65.2	65.5	71.6	71.3	55.8	54.6	48.3	45.3	48.6	46.6	56.7	55.8
1847	65.8	66.3	65.5	65.8	71.7	72.0	53.5	54.4	41.9	43.9	43.2	45.5	53.8	54.9
1848	66.6	66.4	66.6	66.1	72.8	72.8	54.4	54.2	42.6	42.8	45.5	45.2	54.4	54.5
1849	66.4	66.6	66.3	66.4	74.4	73.4	53.8	54.2	42.3	43.0	45.5	45.8	54.1	54.6
1850	67.2	66.6	67.0	66.4	73.5	73.1	54.2	54.2	43.7	44.0	47.0	46.6	55.2	55.0
1851	66.3	66.5	65.8	66.1	71.3	72.4	54.6	54.3	46.7	44.6	47.6	47.1	55.5	55.2
1852	66.4	66.4	66.1	65.9	72.0	72.1	54.3	54.6	43.8	44.2	46.7	47.5	55.1	55.5
1853	66.3	66.2	65.4	65.9	73.0	72.1	54.4	55.0	42.3	43.6	47.8	48.2	55.7	56.0
1854	66.1	65.9	66.4	65.8	71.5	71.7	56.8	55.2	44.8	43.5	50.5	48.3	57.9	56.0
1855	65.4	65.1	65.8	65.4	70.9	71.2	55.0	54.6	43.2	43.2	47.2	47.1	54.8	55.0
1856	63.7	64.4	64.4	64.9	70.7	70.7	52.3	53.8	42.4	42.3	45.2	45.6	52.4	53.8
1857	63.6	64.4	63.9	65.0	70.5	- - -	53.1	54.0	41.1	- - -	44.1	45.3	53.3	54.0
1858	65.8	65.0	66.3	66.0	...	...	56.3	54.9	- - -	...	47.1	46.0	56.1	54.9
1859	65.6	65.5	67.5	- - -	...	...	55.4	55.4	- - -	...	46.4	47.0	55.1	55.6
1860	65.4	65.6	- - -	...	...	...	55.3	55.4	- - -	...	48.0	47.4	56.3	55.9
1861	65.9	- - -	- - -	...	...	...	55.2	55.3	- - -	...	48.3	47.5	56.5	55.9
1862	- - -	...	- - -	...	...	...	55.6	55.2	- - -	...	46.6	47.1	55.6	55.5
1863	- - -	...	- - -	...	...	...	55.1	55.0	44.1	- - -	46.9	46.9	54.4	55.1
1864	- - -	...	- - -	...	...	...	54.1	55.0	44.7	44.6	46.7	46.9	54.8	55.2
1865	- - -	...	- - -	...	...	...	56.1	55.0	45.1	44.1	47.8	46.8	56.4	55.5
1866	- - -	...	- - -	...	...	...	54.1	54.8	42.3	43.5	45.9	46.5	55.2	55.4
1867	- - -	...	65.0	- - -	...	...	55.4	54.5	43.2	43.2	46.2	46.2	55.3	55.0
1868	- - -	...	64.8	65.0	...	...	53.2	54.2	43.7	43.5	46.0	46.2	54.3	54.7
1869	- - -	...	65.6	65.3	...	...	54.1	54.2	43.1	44.2	45.5	46.4	54.1	54.6
1870	- - -	...	65.4	- - -	...	...	55.6	- - -	47.2	- - -	48.7	- - -	55.9	- - -

Year.	Fort Leavenworth, Kan.		Fort Gibson, Indian Ter.		Fort Jesup, La.		San Francisco, Cal.	
	C. II.	4th or.	C. III.	4th or.	C. I.	4th or.	C. V.	4th or.
	°	°	°	°	°	°	°	°
1820	...	...	...	...	...	...	...	...
1821	...	...	...	...	...	...	...	...
1822	...	...	...	...	...	...	...	...
1823	...	...	...	...	67.3	- - -	...	...
1824	...	...	...	...	69.2	68.4	...	...
1825	...	...	...	...	67.7	68.5	...	...
1826	...	...	...	...	68.9	68.6	...	...
1827	...	...	...	...	69.1	68.4	...	...
1828	...	...	63.0	- - -	68.1	67.6	...	...
1829	...	...	60.9	62.3	65.1	66.2	...	...
1830	56.6	- - -	64.6	61.6	66.4	65.1	...	...
1831	49.8	52.4	57.7	60.7	62.6	64.8	...	...
1832	53.4	53.1	61.3	60.5	66.0	65.5	...	...
1833	55.5	53.6	61.1	60.7	67.1	66.4	...	...
1834	52.4	52.8	61.5	60.3	67.5	66.1	...	...
1835	51.7	51.5	58.1	59.6	64.0	65.0	...	...
1836	48.7	51.0	59.0	59.5	63.7	64.4	...	...
1837	52.9	51.4	60.8	59.7	65.1	64.6	...	...
1838	51.1	52.0	58.1	60.0	64.2	65.4	...	...
1839	53.6	52.2	61.9	60.3	67.3	66.4	...	...
1840	51.4	52.0	60.5	60.4	67.8	66.6	...	...
1841	51.2	51.6	59.1	60.3	65.1	66.1	...	...
1842	52.8	51.4	61.6	60.3	66.4	65.7	...	...
1843	49.0	51.4	59.3	60.5	64.3	65.5	...	...
1844	52.7	52.3	61.5	60.8	66.3	65.7	...	...
1845	54.8	53.6	61.4	61.1	65.7	- - -	...	...
1846	55.3	53.3	61.5	60.7	...	...	...	...
1847	49.8	52.1	59.1	60.0	...	...	...	...
1848	51.7	51.7	59.6	59.6	...	...	...	...
1849	52.2	51.9	59.5	59.9	...	...	...	...
1850	52.0	52.2	60.4	60.2	...	...	...	...
1851	53.2	52.3	61.4	60.3	...	...	58.5	- - -
1852	51.5	53.0	59.0	60.1	...	...	- - -	57.8
1853	53.1	53.9	60.1	60.3	...	...	57.2	57.7
1854	55.9	54.1	61.8	60.6	...	...	56.3	57.3
1855	54.3	53.4	60.4	60.1	...	...	57.8	56.8
1856	50.0	52.4	58.4	59.0	...	...	56.3	56.6
1857	52.2	52.6	58.7	- - -	...	...	56.8	56.2
1858	55.3	53.6	...	...	...	...	55.7	55.7
1859	52.9	54.3	...	...	...	...	54.9	55.4
1860	56.0	54.4	...	...	...	...	55.4	55.2
1861	54.0	54.0	...	...	...	...	55.5	55.2
1862	52.7	53.1	...	...	...	...	54.7	55.2
1863	52.9	52.7	...	...	...	...	55.2	55.3
1864	52.0	52.6	...	...	...	...	56.3	55.4
1865	53.5	52.5	...	...	...	...	54.8	55.5
1866	52.0	52.3	...	...	...	...	55.4	55.6
1867	51.8	52.0	...	...	...	...	56.3	55.9
1868	52.1	52.0	...	...	...	...	55.3	56.3
1869	51.3	52.2	...	...	...	...	58.0	57.2
1870	54.1	- - -	...	...	...	...	57.6	- - -

The character of the secular variation in the mean annual temperature, as exhibited on the accompanying plate, is that of a series of irregular waves representing a succession of warmer and colder periods, during which, however, the mean temperature deviates only about one or two degrees, in excess or defect, from its normal value. Irrespective of the minor irregularities, which have to some extent been eliminated, some of the single progressions appear quite systematic; thus, for instance, at New Haven, the temperature steadily declined from 1802 to 1817, it then increased till 1827, after which it again decreased, reaching a decided minimum in 1836. These undulations, when compared for a number of stations exposed to similar climatological conditions, approach to parallelism over large tracts of country, and exhibit considerable uniformity in their general character;

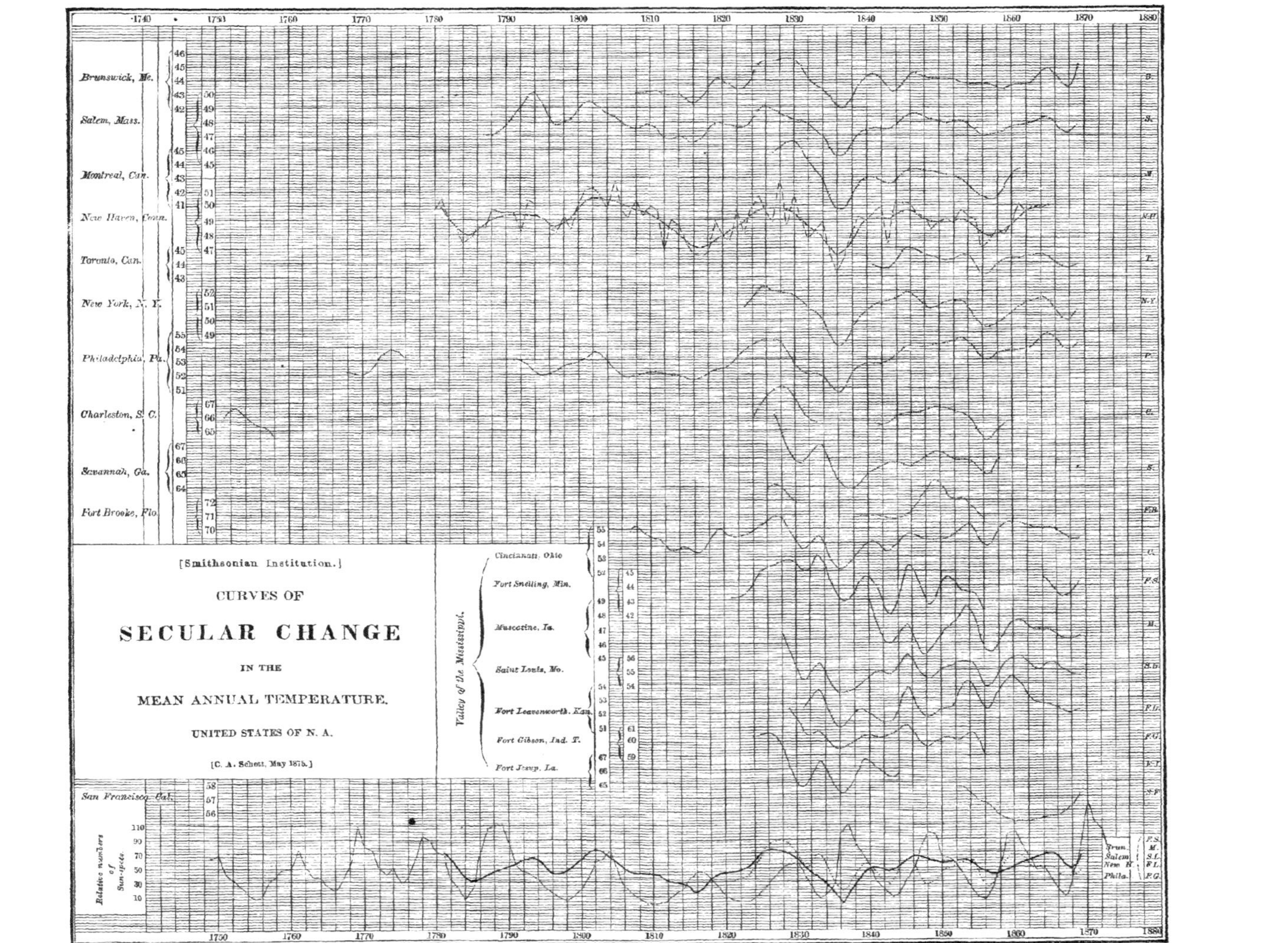

[Smithsonian Institution.]
CURVES OF
SECULAR CHANGE
IN THE
MEAN ANNUAL TEMPERATURE.
UNITED STATES OF N. A.
[C. A. Schott, May 1875.]
Brunswick, Me.
Salem, Mass.
Montreal, Can.
New Haven, Conn.
Toronto, Can.
New York, N. Y.
Philadelphia, Pa.
Charleston, S. C.
Savannah, Ga.
Fort Brooke, Fla.
Valley of the Mississippi.
Cincinnati, Ohio
Fort Snelling, Min.
Muscatine, Ia.
Saint Louis, Mo.
Fort Leavenworth, Kan.
Fort Gibson, Ind. T.
Fort Jesup, La.
San Francisco, Cal.
Relative numbers of Sun-spots.

thus from Maine to Georgia these waves are of a broad and well-defined shape, as at New Haven, but they become somewhat changed in their appearance over the vast area watered by the Mississippi and its tributaries; here the undulations become more narrow and numerous, as at Fort Snelling. The change from one form into the other is very gradual, and with an increase of the geographical distances some of the old features become obliterated and new ones make their appearance. The curve for Cincinnati, for instance, partakes of an intermediate character between the eastern or Atlantic type and that of the Mississippi basin. On our western coast, as might have been expected, a new feature is developed, subject perhaps to less irregularities than in any other part of the country, and for this reason well suited for the study of the proximate causes which determine its laws. The curve for San Francisco is presented as a type for the Pacific coast.

The remarkably cold epoch about 1837 with cold years preceding and following is common to all stations represented between the Atlantic coast and the eastern flank of the Rocky Mountains, and the exceptionally warm period about 1827 perhaps extended likewise over a very large area.

There is nothing in these curves to countenance the idea of any permanent change in the climate having taken place, or being about to take place; in the last 90 years of thermometric records, the mean temperatures showing no indication whatever of a sustained rise or fall. The same conclusion was reached in the discussion of the secular change in the Rain-Fall, which appears also to have remained permanent in amount as well as in annual distribution.

The degree of parallelism of the curves is sufficiently close to warrant an additional consolidation of results for a few characteristic stations, for further study; one typical curve will be given for the Atlantic coast and another for the Mississippi valley.

The first is composed of the long series of mean annual temperatures at Brunswick, Me., Salem, Mass., New Haven, Conn., and Philadelphia, Penn., to represent during 91 years the type of the secular change for those eastern States which are situated between the Atlantic and the Alleghany Mountains. These four series are unbroken between 1807 and 1865, and for these 59 years the individual means are set down, as in the table below; to reduce those values which lie outside of these limits to uniformity, the 59 differences for each series from the mean series were formed, and the respective mean difference applied as reductions; they are, for Brunswick +4°.5, for Salem +0°.6, for New Haven —0°.4, and for Philadelphia —4°.7. After this the means were taken for each of these years, except for the years 1780, 1783, 1784, and 1785, which are covered by one series only.

Table of consolidated mean annual temperatures at Brunswick, Salem, New Haven, and Philadelphia.

	0	1	2	3	4	5	6	7	8	9
1780	49°.3	50.4	48.7	49.5	46.9	47.3	48.2	47.9	48.5	48.3
1790	48.5	49.2	47.9	50.3	49.1	48.7	47.9	47.5	48.9	48.1
1800	49.1	49.7	50.5	49.6	48.6	49.7	48.1	47.7	48.7	47.5
1810	48.4	49.2	46.1	47.9	48.0	47.2	46.4	46.7	47.8	49.0
1820	47.9	47.5	49.2	47.6	49.0	50.4	50.0	48.6	51.2	48.4
1830	49.5	48.9	47.5	47.9	48.4	46.8	45.2	46.0	47.6	48.4
1840	48.6	48.5	48.9	47.5	48.4	49.3	49.7	49.0	49.2	48.5
1850	49.0	48.8	48.8	49.5	48.7	48.8	47.3	47.9	48.4	47.8
1860	48.8	48.9	48.5	49.1	49.2	50.2	49.0	48.5	47.4	49.2
1870	51.0									
General mean, 48.52.										

From the preceding table we form the successive means of the 4th order, as follows:—

	0	1	2	3	4	5	6	7	8	9
1780	- - -	(49.6)	49.2	48.5	47.8	47.6	47.7	48.0	48.2	48.4
1790	48.6	48.7	49.0	49.2	49.1	48.6	48.1	48.1	48.3	48.6
1800	49.1	49.5	49.8	49.6	49.2	48.9	48.5	48.2	48.1	48.1
1810	48.1	48.0	47.6	47.5	47.4	47.2	46.8	47.1	47.7	48.1
1820	48.1	48.2	48.3	48.5	49.0	49.6	49.8	49.7	49.6	49.4
1830	49.1	48.6	48.1	47.8	47.5	46.8	46.2	46.4	47.3	48.1
1840	48.4	48.5	48.4	48.3	48.6	49.0	49.3	49.2	49.0	48.9
1850	48.8	48.8	48.9	49.0	48.8	48.4	48.1	48.0	48.1	48.3
1860	48.5	48.7	48.9	49.1	49.3	49.4	49.1	48.5	48.4	(49.2)
1870	- - -									

Also the following table of differences from the mean 48°.5, a + sign indicating a warmer, a — sign a colder year than the normal one.

	0	1	2	3	4	5	6	7	8	9
1780	- - -	+1.1	+0.7	0.0	—0.7	—0.9	—0.8	—0.5	—0.3	—0.1
1790	+0.1	+0.2	+0.5	+0.7	+0.6	+0.1	—0.4	—0.4	—0.2	+0.1
1800	+0.6	+1.0	+1.3	+1.1	+0.7	+0.4	0.0	—0.3	—0.4	—0.4
1810	—0.4	—0.5	—0.9	—1.0	—1.1	—1.3	—1.7	—1.4	—0.8	—0.4
1820	—0.4	—0.3	—0.2	0.0	+0.5	+1.1	+1.3	+1.2	+1.1	+0.9
1830	+0.6	+0.1	—0.4	—0.7	—1.0	—1.7	—2.3	—2.1	—1.2	—0.4
1840	—0.1	0.0	—0.1	—0.2	+0.1	+0.5	+0.8	+0.7	+0.5	+0.4
1850	+0.3	+0.3	+0.4	+0.5	+0.3	—0.1	—0.4	—0.5	—0.4	—0.2
1860	0.0	+0.2	+0.4	+0.6	+0.8	+0.9	+0.6	0.0	—0.1	(+0.7)
1870	- - -									

The use of this table for obtaining the normal annual temperature from a single year or from a few years of observation is obvious; we have only to apply the tabular quantity with its sign reversed as a correction to the mean (observed) temperature of each year

The second type-curve is made up from the stations: Fort Snelling, Minn., Muscatine, Iowa, St. Louis, Mo., Fort Leavenworth, Kan., and Fort Gibson, Indian Ter. These series have 19 years in common (1839 to 1857 inclusive), for each of which the means from the five values were set down, the observed annual temperatures for years before and after were first referred to the same mean series by the reductions +7°.9, +4°.7, —3°.2, —0°.8, and —8°.6 to the stations respectively (these numbers were deduced from comparisons of each series with every other). We have the following tables:—

Table of consolidated mean annual temperatures at Fort Snelling, Muscatine, St. Louis, Fort Leavenworth, and Fort Gibson.

	0	1	2	3	4	5	6	7	8	9
1820	50.9	50.8	51.6	51.3	50.7	55.0	52.3	54.6	54.6	52.4
1830	55.6	48.9	52.7	54.1	53.1	50.2	49.7	51.7	49.6	53.6
1840	52.0	51.1	52.1	49.0	52.1	53.2	54.1	49.6	50.8	50.7
1850	51.7	52.9	51.2	51.8	54.2	52.0	49.5	49.9	53.1	51.7
1860	53.7	53.2	51.9	51.7	51.7	52.8	51.0	51.3	51.4	50.6
1870	53.6									
General mean, 51.95.										

From the above table we derive the following successive means of the 4th order:—

	0	1	2	3	4	5	6	7	8	9
1820	- - -	(51.1)	51.3	51.4	52.0	53.0	53.6	53.9	53.9	53.6
1830	52.9	52.1	52.3	52.9	52.3	51.1	50.5	50.7	51.4	52.1
1840	52.1	51.6	51.1	51.0	51.8	52.6	52.4	51.3	50.8	51.0
1850	51.6	51.9	52.1	52.3	52.5	51.8	50.7	50.8	51.8	52.5
1860	52.8	52.7	52.2	51.9	51.9	51.9	51.5	51.3	51.3	(51.6)
1870	- - -									

Table of differences from the mean 52°.0.

	0	1	2	3	4	5	6	7	8	9
1820	- - -	(—0.9)	—0.7	—0.6	0.0	+1.0	+1.6	+1.9	+1.9	+1.6
1830	+0.9	+0.1	+0.3	+0.9	+0.3	—0.9	—1.5	—1.3	—0.6	+0.1
1840	+0.1	—0.4	—0.9	—1.0	—0.2	+0.6	+0.4	—0.7	—1.2	—1.0
1850	—0.4	—0.1	+0.1	+0.3	+0.5	—0.2	—1.3	—1.2	—0.2	+0.5
1860	+0.8	+0.7	+0.2	—0.1	—0.1	—0.1	—0.5	—0.7	—0.7	(—0.4)
1870	- - -									

[This table can be used to obtain normal temperatures at places in the Mississippi valley, as explained above.]

These differences from the normal values have been thrown into curves, and are given, together with the exhibit of the relative frequency and amount of solar spots, in the bottom line of the accompanying plate; the Atlantic type-curve is shown heavy, the Mississippi type-curve dotted, and the sun-spot curve by a zigzag line, according to Prof. R. Wolf's numbers.[1]

The distinguishing features, as described above, of these two type-curves appear well marked, the longer waves of the Atlantic stations show:

Principal maxima in 1802 1826 1846 1865
and principal minima in 1785 1816 1836 1857

the average interval being about 22 years; the shorter waves of the interior states show:—

Principal maxima in 1827 1833 1839 1845 1854 1860
and principal minima in 1831 1836 1843 1848 1856 1867

the average interval being about 7 years. These undulations, however, are not sufficiently regular nor sufficiently distinct, being mixed with subordinate fluctuations, to serve as a basis of prediction; all that can be claimed for them is a general exponent of the character of the secular change.

Comparison of the secular variation of the temperature with the variations in the frequency of the solar spots.—It is evident, from the preceding statements respecting the average duration of successions of warmer and colder years, that no intimate relation appears to exist between the two phenomena—they seem to have no feature in common, the sun-spot period of about 11 years is not systematically followed by any of the temperature waves; the chief characteristic of connection, that of equality of average periods, being wanting, we necessarily have coincidence, viz., greater development of sun-spots corresponding to greater *cold*, as for the years between 1810 and 1822, as well as opposition, viz., a greater development of sun-spots during a time of increased *heat*, as for the years 1799 to 1806, and in general we have phases of the two curves presented in all possible combinations. If we consider the small difference in the radiating energy of the surface of a spot and of the unbroken surface of the sun, as well as the comparatively small collective area of

[1] Prof. Wolf's relative numbers of sun-spots; from Astronomische Nachrichten, Nos. 1978 (March, 1874) and No. 2014 (Nov. 1874), those prior to 1759 from his "Mittheilungen."

	0	1	2	3	4	5	6	7	8	9
1740										63.8
1750	68.2	40.9	33.2	23.1	13.8	6.0	8.8	30.4	38.3	48.6
1760	48.9	75.0	50.6	37.4	34.5	23.0	17.5	33.6	52.2	108.3
1770	79.4	73.2	49.2	39.8	47.6	27.5	35.2	63.0	94.8	90.2
1780	72.6	67.7	33.2	22.5	5.0	21.2	68.6	104.8	107.8	110.7
1790	84.4	53.4	47.5	40.2	34.3	22.3	15.1	7.8	4.4	10.2
1800	18.5	38.6	57.8	65.0	75.0	50.0	25.0	15.0	7.2	3.4
1810	0.0	1.2	5.4	13.7	20.0	35.0	45.5	43.5	34.1	22.5
1820	8.9	4.3	2.9	1.3	6.7	17.4	29.4	39.9	52.5	53.5
1830	59.1	38.8	22.5	7.5	11.4	45.5	96.7	111.0	82.6	68.5
1840	51.8	29.7	19.5	8.6	13.0	37.0	47.0	79.4	100.4	95.6
1850	64.5	61.9	52.2	37.7	19.2	6.9	4.2	21.6	50.9	96.4
1860	98.6	77.4	59.1	44.0	46.9	30.5	16.3	7.3	37.3	73.9
1870	139.1	111.2	101.7	66.3						

the spotted surface as contrasted with the whole sun, the failure in the detection of any close relationship between the annual changes of spots and of terrestrial temperature (as examined by the comparatively crude process of annual means) should not be surprising, unless there should be connected with these solar disturbances some other less direct cause producing changes of radiation. Still it is very desirable to follow up the subject by further comparisons of the American results with those obtained on the Eastern Continent, and especially with results from stations in the Southern Hemisphere.[1]

Comparison of the secular variation in the temperature and the rain-fall, in the United States.—The data for the annual rain-fall are taken from p. 154 of my memoir on the Rain-Fall (Smithsonian Contributions to Knowledge, No. 222; Washington, May, 1872), from which groups I and IV have been selected as representative stations of the same climatological conditions to which the temperature types I and II refer. The fourth order of successive means are tabulated below; these proportional numbers have already been charted on p. 157 of the Rain-Fall Memoir. The average annual amount of rain deduced from the whole series is put equal to 100.

Secular variation in the Rain-Fall, sea-coast, Maine to Virginia.

	0	1	2	3	4	5	6	7	8	9
1800	- - -	- - -	- - -	- - -	- - -	(94)	96	102	106	101
1810	94	96	101	104	103	97	92	90	87	87
1820	93	94	96	97	91	[illegible]	91	90	102	108
1830	111	108	104	99	94	91	90	90	93	98
1840	103	105	106	103	98	96	100	102	99	100
1850	105	106	105	105	102	98	98	102	106	108
1860	108	108	111	110	106	104	(107)			

Secular change in the Rain-Fall, Ohio Valley, Ohio, Indiana, Illinois, Kentucky, and part of Missouri.

	0	1	2	3	4	5	6	7	8	9
1810	- - -	- - -	- - -	- - -	- - -	- - -	- - -	- - -	- - -	(96)
1820	95	100	105	107	106	104	103	103	102	97
1830	95	101	102	97	93	93	93	89	84	86
1840	92	95	98	99	100	104	110	114	113	110
1850	106	102	97	93	93	94	93	99	109	109
1860	103	101	99	95	93	97	(103)			

[1] To mention but one case of evidence, supposed to be in favor of a correspondence of the sun-spot and temperature periods, the reader may consult: The London, Edinburgh, and Dublin Phil. Mag., vol. xlii, July to Dec. 1871. "On the approximate decennial variation of the temperature at the Observatory at the Cape of Good Hope, between the years 1841 and 1870, viewed in connection with the variation of the solar-spots." By E. J. Stone, F.R.S, Astron. Roy. at the Cape of Good Hope. Here it is believed that the same cause which leads to an excess of mean annual temperature leads equally to a dissipation of the solar spots.

On the annexed diagram, the upper pair of curves refer to stations on the Atlantic coast, the lower pair to stations in the Mississippi valley; the heavy lines represent the secular change in the temperature, the light ones that of the rain-fall. Though the connection between the changes of temperature and rain-fall is not, in detail, any way conclusive, yet in general following out the larger waves, there seems to be some ground for concluding that years with a mean temperature above the normal have a rain-fall above the normal or average amount, and years deficient in the mean temperature present also a deficiency in the rain-fall.

That this apparent law is not expressive in the minor undulations may be explained by the small number of stations contributing information to both temperature and rain-fall, and thus admitting the presence to some extent of local peculiarities; yet it cannot be overlooked that there is some similarity in the general character of the two phenomena; further comparisons, however, are desirable.

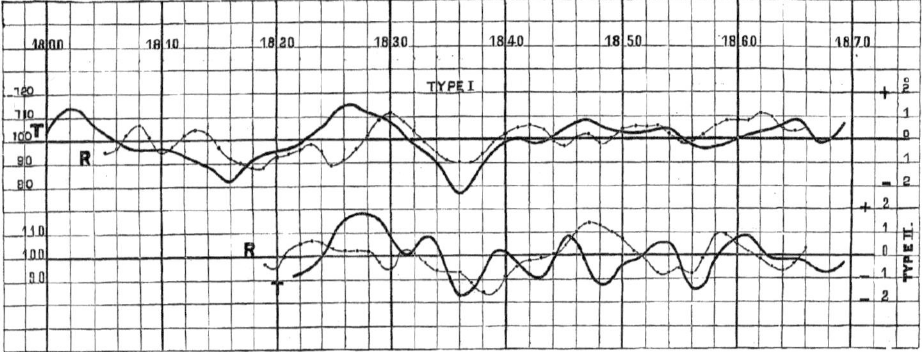

In explanation it may be remarked, that the greater the heat of the air, the greater the amount of vapor it can hold, hence the greater the capacity for precipitation as well as for evaporation.

Comparison of the secular variation in the temperature with the average annual direction of the wind.—The following numbers have been extracted from p. 42 of my discussion of the Meteorological Observations[1] at Brunswick, Maine, made by Prof. P. Cleaveland; they give the deflections in degrees, + to the north (increasing azimuth), — to the south (decreasing azimuth), from the mean assumed direction of the wind $x = 101°$, counted like azimuths from the south around by west to 360°.

	0	1	2	3	4	5	6	7	8	9
1800	- - -	- - -	- - -	- - -	- - -	- - -	- - -	- - -	- - -	+ 3°
1810	+ 5	+ 6	0	— 6	— 7	— 6	— 8	— 8	+ 4	+20
1820	+28	+25	+13	+ 8	+16	+22	+19	+13	+ 9	+11
1830	+ 5	— 5	— 2	+ 3	+ 4	+ 6	+ 1	— 6	— 9	—15
1840	—18	—14	— 9	—12	—12	—12	—10	—11	— 7	— 5
1850	— 7	— 9	—11	—15	—15	—10	—11	—13	—10	- - -

[1] Smithsonian Contributions to Knowledge, No. 204; Washington, June, 1867.

The table below contains the deflections from the normal direction of the wind $x = 68°$ at Marietta, Ohio, taken from p. 36 of my discussion of the Meteorological Observations[1] at Marietta, made by Dr. S. P. Hildreth.

	0	1	2	3	4	5	6	7	8	9
1830	+18	+11	+11	+20	+20	+13	+14	+21	+19	+ 2
1840	0	+ 8	0	—10	—11	—12	—23	—35	—34	—25
1850	—22	- - -	—20	— 1	+ 7	- - -	- - -	- - -	- - -	- - -

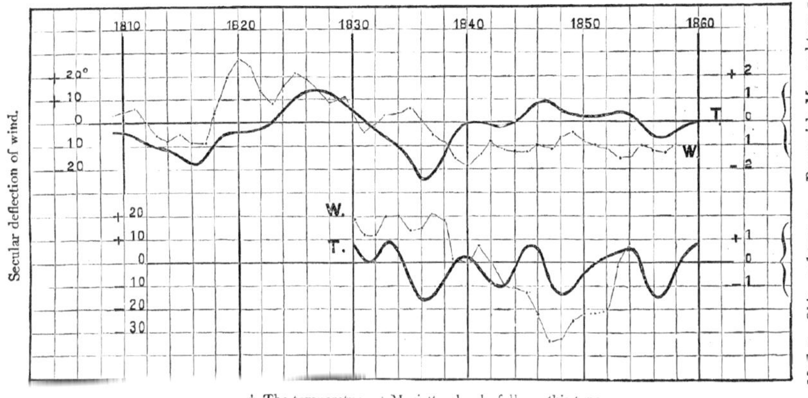

† The temperature at Marietta closely follows this type.

To interpret the above diagrams correctly, the true relation between the secular change, as shown by a succession of annual means, of the direction of the wind and of the temperature, will appear with sufficient distinctness by considering the zero line or axis of abscissæ, not as a straight line but as a curve, drawn midway between the two curves; in other words, either the normal direction of the wind is imperfectly made out (through insufficiency or imperfection of observations), or the relation of the mean direction of the wind to the mean temperature of the air is not constant; I incline to the former alternative. So far as our evidence goes, for years of northerly (+) deflections of the winds, the temperature appears to be lower, and for southerly deflections higher than the normal value. This subject also demands further investigation.

Enough has been shown to make it evident that for final explanation the secular variations in the temperature, in the rain-fall, and in the direction of the wind must be studied together, and it will probably be found that the former depend directly on the latter, though, ultimately, the deflections in the resulting direction of the wind must be referred to effects of solar radiation; the discussion must take a wider range so as to include long series of records at stations representing all parts of the globe.

---

[1] Smithsonian Contributions to Knowledge, No. 120; Washington, June, 1868.

Range of variability in the secular variation of the annual temperature.—If we consider the deviations of the annual means from the normal temperature of the place as fortuitous, we may employ a simple formula for the mean deviation as a measure of the amount of variability, and deduce also a value for the *probable* uncertainty to which the normal temperature, or the mean of the whole series, may be liable.

Let $\varepsilon =$ the mean deviation of any yearly value,
$\Delta =$ the difference of any annual mean from the normal temperature,
$\Sigma\Delta =$ their sum, irrespective of sign,
$n =$ number of yearly values,

then, with sufficient precision for our comparison,

$$\varepsilon = \pm 1.253 \frac{\Sigma\Delta}{n},$$

which expression supposes the positive and negative Δ's to balance. The probable uncertainty attaching to the mean of the series is given by

$$r_0 = \pm 0.845 \frac{\Sigma\Delta}{n\sqrt{n}}.$$

Applying these expressions to a few of our larger and systematic series, we deduce the following results:—

Stations.	Normal T	n	ε	r_0	Lowest and Highest value.	Difference from normal.	Range.
Brunswick, Me.[1] . . .	43.9	49	±1°.78	±0°.15	40.3 47.7	—3.6 +3.8	7°.4
Salem, Mass.	48.1	43	1.48	.15	44.5 50.3	—3.6 +2.2	5.8
New Bedford, Mass. . .	48.2	58	1.15	.10	44.9 50.9	—3.3 +2.7	6.0
New Haven, Conn. . .	49.0	85	1.25	.09	45.2 51.8	—3.8 +2.8	6.6
Marietta, Ohio	52.4	46	1.24	.12	49.7 55.4	—2.7 +3.0	5.7
Fort Snelling, Minn. . .	44.1	42	2.07	.21	41.3 48.3	—2.8 +4.2	7.0
Fort Leavenworth, Kan. .	52.7	40	1.83	.20	48.7 56.6	—4.0 +3.9	7.9
Fort Brooke, Fla. . . .	71.7	27	1.21	.16	70.1 74.4	—1.6 +2.7	4.3

[1] The annual means for 1837–8–9–40 are omitted, as defective.

The weighted average value of the mean annual ,direction ε is $\pm$ 1°.44, hence means derived from series of 25, 50, and 100 years are uncertain by a probable amount of $r_0 = \frac{0.6745\,\varepsilon}{\sqrt{n}} = \pm 0°.19, \pm 0°.14$, and $\pm 0°.10$ respectively. To these values any errors that may exist in the graduation of the instruments would have to be added.

Secular variation in the annual maxima and minima, compared with the variation in the annual means.—In conclusion of this section of the paper, it is still desirable to inquire into the changes of the maxima and minima, and to ascertain how far these partake of the character of the secular change of the mean annual temperature. For this purpose it will suffice to examine the two typical series at New Haven and Marietta. Since the minima fall generally in January and February, and the maxima in July and August, the respective mean temperatures of these months were formed and compared with the corresponding annual means. To eliminate irregularities, the fourth order means were employed and tabulated; comparing each value with the mean from the whole series, the differences were formed, a + sign indicating higher temperature, a — sign lower temperature than the mean—they are as follows:—

New Haven series.

	½ (J. & F.) 4th order.	½ (J. & A.) 4th order.	$\frac{1}{12}$ (J. to D.) 4th order.	Differences from Mean. Jan. and Feb.	July and Aug.	Year.		½ (J. & F.) 4th order.	½ (J. & A.) 4th order.	$\frac{1}{12}$ (J. to D.) 4th order.	Differences from Mean. Jan. and Feb.	July and Aug.	Year.
	°	°	°	°	°	°		°	°	°	°	°	°
1780	(29.6)	74.3	(49.9)	+2.4	+3.6	+1.0	1825	29.5	71.2	49.9	+2.3	+0.5	+0.9
1781	29.5	73.3	49.7	+2.3	+2.6	+0.7	1826	29.0	71.0	49.9	+1.8	+0.3	+1.0
1782	28.1	72.0	49.2	+0.9	+1.3	+0.3	1827	29.1	70.7	49.9	+1.9	0.0	+0.9
1783	26.0	71.3	48.5	—1.2	+0.6	—0.5	1828	29.1	71.0	50.0	+1.9	+0.3	+1.1
1784	24.5	71.1	48.0	—2.7	+0.4	—0.9	1829	27.5	71.4	49.9	+0.3	+0.7	+0.9
1785	24.7	70.7	47.9	—2.5	0.0	—1.0	1830	25.5	71.7	49.6	—1.7	+1.0	+0.7
1786	26.0	70.3	48.2	—1.2	—0.4	—0.7	1831	25.3	71.6	49.0	—1.9	+0.9	0.0
1787	26.5	70.6	48.8	—0.7	—0.1	—0.2	1832	26.5	70.6	48.5	—0.7	—0.1	—0.4
[illegible]	[illegible]	[illegible]	[illegible]	[illegible]	+1.0	+0.3	1833	27.7	69.9	48.2	+0.5	—0.8	—0.8
1789	27.1	72.2	49.4	—0.1	+1.5	+0.4	1834	27.3	69.8	47.8	+0.1	—0.9	—1.1
1790	27.8	71.7	49.4	+0.6	+1.0	+0.5	1835	25.0	69.8	46.8	—2.2	—0.9	—2.2
1791	27.1	70.9	49.2	—0.1	+0.2	+0.2	1836	23.5	68.8	46.3	—3.7	—1.9	—2.6
1792	26.5	70.7	49.2	—0.7	0.0	+0.3	1837	24.5	68.8	46.7	—2.7	—1.9	—2.3
1793	27.3	70.9	49.5	+0.1	+0.2	+0.5	1838	26.5	69.3	47.8	—0.7	—1.4	—1.1
1794	27.8	71.0	49.6	+0.6	+0.3	+0.7	1839	27.3	69.6	48.7	+0.1	—1.1	—0.3
1795	27.5	71.1	49.1	+0.3	+0.4	+0.1	1840	27.8	69.8	49.1	+0.6	—0.9	+0.2
1796	27.3	71.6	48.6	+0.1	+0.9	—0.3	1841	29.1	69.8	49.3	+1.9	—0.9	+0.3
1797	27.0	72.5	48.5	—0.2	+1.8	—0.5	1842	29.6	69.3	49.1	+2.4	—1.4	+0.2
1798	26.5	73.0	48.7	—0.7	+2.3	—0.2	1843	28.1	68.8	49.0	+0.9	—1.9	0.0
1799	26.4	72.9	49.2	—0.8	+2.2	+0.2	1844	27.1	69.3	49.4	—0.1	—1.4	+0.5
1800	27.3	72.5	49.9	+0.1	+1.8	+1.0	1845	27.4	70.3	49.9	+0.2	—0.4	+0.9
1801	28.9	72.5	50.6	+1.7	+1.8	+1.6	1846	27.7	71.2	49.9	+0.5	+0.5	+1.0
1802	29.8	72.7	50.8	+2.6	+2.0	+1.9	1847	27.7	71.4	49.4	+0.5	+0.7	+0.4
1803	29.3	72.7	50.7	+2.1	+2.0	+1.7	1848	27.1	71.0	49.0	—0.1	+0.3	+0.1
1804	28.3	72.6	50.6	+1.1	+1.9	+1.7	1849	27.1	70.6	48.7	—0.1	—0.1	—0.3
1805	28.2	72.3	50.5	+1.0	+1.6	+1.5	1850	28.4	70.3	48.7	+1.2	—0.4	—0.2
1806	28.6	71.8	50.1	+1.4	+1.1	+1.2	1851	29.1	70.[illegible]	48.9	+1.9	—0.7	—0.1
1807	28.4	71.2	49.8	+1.2	+0.5	+0.8	1852	28.7	69.8	49.1	+1.5	—0.9	+0.2
1808	27.9	70.3	49.7	+0.7	—0.4	+0.8	1853	28.6	70.0	49.2	+1.4	—0.7	+0.2
1809	27.7	69.6	49.7	+0.5	—1.1	+0.7	1854	27.9	70.4	49.1	+0.7	—0.3	+0.2
1810	27.8	69.4	49.5	+0.6	—1.3	+0.6	1855	26.1	70.4	48.5	—1.1	—0.3	—0.5
1811	27.2	69.5	49.1	0.0	—1.2	+0.1	1856	24.6	69.8	47.9	—2.6	—0.9	—1.0
1812	26.2	69.8	48.5	—1.0	—0.9	—0.4	1857	25.5	69.1	47.7	—1.7	—1.6	—1.3
1813	25.9	70.2	48.3	—1.3	—0.5	—0.7	1858	27.4	68.7	47.9	+0.2	—2.0	—1.0
1814	25.8	70.0	48.2	—1.4	—0.7	—0.7	1859	28.1	68.7	48.3	+0.9	—2.0	—0.7
1815	25.4	69.0	47.6	—1.8	—1.7	—1.4	1860	28.1	69.4	48.8	+0.9	—1.3	—0.1
1816	24.5	68.3	47.0	—2.7	—2.4	—1.9	1861	28.1	70.4	49.3	+0.9	—0.3	+0.3
1817	24.0	68.5	46.8	—3.2	—2.2	—2.2	1862	28.5	71.6	49.6	+1.3	+0.9	+0.7
1818	25.1	69.4	47.3	—2.1	—1.3	—1.6	1863	28.9	72.5	49.7	+1.7	+1.8	+0.7
1819	26.8	70.2	47.9	—0.4	—0.5	—1.1	1864	(28.5)	(72.7)	(49.7)	+1.3	+2.0	+0.8
1820	27.0	70.3	48.1	—0.2	—0.4	—0.8							
1821	25.9	70.2	48.2	—1.3	—0.5	—0.8							
1822	25.7	70.2	48.6	—1.5	—0.5	—0.3							
1823	27.0	70.5	49.1	—0.2	—0.2	+0.1	Mean of 85 years.	27.24	70.69	48.93			
1824	28.7	71.0	49.6	+1.5	+0.3	+0.7							

Marietta series.

	½ (J. & F.) 4th order.	½ (J. & A.) 4th order.	$\frac{1}{12}$ (J. to D.) 4th order.	Differences from Mean. Jan. and Feb.	Differences from Mean. July and Aug.	Differences from Mean. Year.		½ (J. & F.) 4th order.	½ (J. & A.) 4th order.	$\frac{1}{12}$ (J. to D.) 4th order.	Differences from Mean. Jan. and Feb.	Differences from Mean. July and Aug.	Differences from Mean. Year.
	°	°	°	°	°	°		°	°	°	°	°	°
1819		(75.2)	(53.7)		+3.0	+1.5	1847	33.6	70.9	52.5	+0.9	−1.3	+0.3
1820	(34.8)	74.5	53.1	+2.1	+2.3	+0.9	1848	33.3	70.7	52.1	+0.6	−1.5	−0.1
1821	32.0	74.1	52.8	−0.7	+1.9	+0.6	1849	33.2	71.3	52.1	+0.5	−0.9	−0.1
1822	31.0	73.5	52.8	−1.7	+1.3	+0.6	1850	33.4	72.0	52.1	+0.7	−0.2	−0.1
1823	32.0	72.9	52.8	−0.7	+0.7	+0.6	1851	34.1	71.9	52.2	+1.4	−0.3	0.0
1824	(34.3)	(72.9)	(53.2)	+1.6	+0.7	+1.0	1852	33.2	71.9	52.4	+0.5	−0.3	+0.2
1825	(35.3)	(73.2)	(54.1)	+2.6	+1.0	+1.9	1853	32.8	72.6	52.6	+0.1	+0.4	+0.4
1826	35.2	73.3	54.4	+2.5	+1.1	+2.2	1854	32.0	73.7	52.9	−0.7	+1.5	+0.7
1827	36.0	73.2	54.3	+3.3	+1.0	+2.1	1855	29.4	74.0	52.2	−3.3	+1.8	0.0
1828	36.0	72.8	54.2	+3.3	+0.6	+2.0	1856	27.8	73.5	51.3	−4.9	+1.3	−0.9
1829	33.8	72.6	53.6	+1.1	+0.4	+1.4	1857	29.6	73.1	51.4	−3.1	+0.9	−0.8
1830	31.2	72.3	52.9	−1.5	+0.1	+0.7	1858	32.6	72.9	52.2	−0.1	+0.7	0.0
1831	30.8	71.6	52.3	−1.9	−0.6	+0.1	1859	34.0	72.5	52.7	+1.3	+0.3	+0.5
1832	32.4	71.1	52.4	−0.3	−1.1	+0.2	1860	34.4	71.7	52.6	+1.7	−0.5	+0.4
1833	33.9	71.6	52.7	+1.2	−0.6	+0.5	1861	34.6	71.1	52.4	+1.9	−1.1	+0.2
1834	33.1	71.7	52.3	+0.4	−0.5	+0.1	1862	34.5	71.5	52.1	+1.8	−0.7	−0.1
1835	31.0	71.0	51.4	−1.7	−1.2	−0.8	1863	33.3	72.2	51.7	+0.6	0.0	−0.5
1836	29.8	70.8	50.8	−2.9	−1.4	−1.4	1864	31.1	72.0	51.4	−1.6	−0.2	−0.8
1837	29.9	71.8	50.9	−2.8	−0.4	−1.3	1865	29.6	71.1	51.2	−3.1	−1.1	−1.0
1838	30.8	72.6	51.3	−1.9	+0.4	−0.9	1866	29.2	70.8	50.9	−3.5	−1.4	−1.3
1839	32.2	72.0	51.8	−0.5	−0.2	−0.4	1867	29.3	71.5	50.5	−3.4	−0.7	−1.7
1840	33.0	71.2	52.1	+0.3	−1.0	−0.1	1868	30.4	72.4	50.5	−2.3	+0.2	−1.7
1841	33.6	70.6	52.1	+0.9	−1.6	−0.1	1869	(32.6)	(72.8)	(50.7)	−0.1	+0.6	−1.5
1842	34.8	70.5	51.8	+2.1	−1.7	−0.4							
1843	35.2	71.0	51.8	+2.5	−1.2	−0.4							
1844	34.9	71.8	52.1	+2.2	−0.4	−0.1	Mean						
1845	34.5	72.1	52.6	+1.8	−0.1	+0.4	of 49	32.67	72.19	52.24			
1846	33.9	71.7	52.8	+1.2	−0.5	+0.6	years.						

Note.—Values in parenthesis are imperfect.

If we examine, by means of the successive signs of the tabular differences, whether or not a cold winter is followed by a cold summer, and whether the average temperature of the year is below or above the normal, we find, from the New Haven series, by comparisons of the signs for the cold months with those for the year, the following results: an accord, a + sign being followed by a + sign, or a — sign by a — sign, in 64 cases; and a discord, a + sign being followed by a — sign, or the reverse, in 18 cases; there are 3 indifferent cases, one of the differences being zero; in all, 85 cases. Comparing the signs of the warmest months with those of the year, we find 61 accords, 19 discords, and 5 indifferent cases; and comparing directly the coldest and warmest months there are 50 accords, 31 discords, and 4 indifferent cases. Altogether strongly favoring the conclusion that the changes which constitute the secular variation are generally exhibited in winter as well as in summer; in other words, the causes of these variations are alike, active at all seasons of the year. In the case of Marietta, we have likewise for winter and year 30 accords, 17 contradictions, and 3 neutral cases; for summer and year 32 accords, 15 contradictions, and 4 neutral cases, and for winter and summer 19 accords, 30 contradictions, and 1 neutral case. Here the evidence is somewhat weaker, probably owing to the greater number and shorter secular undulations, due to the more western position of the station.

LIST OF STATIONS.

LIST OF OBSERVERS.

INDEX.

ERRATA.

Page 15, (California) Station 54, *read* Frombes.
" 18, Florida " 2, " Atsena.
" 18, Florida " 4, " Pilatka.
" 21, Georgia " 13, " McAfee.
" 23, Illinois " 12, " Eldredge.
" 23, Illinois " 18, " Brookes.
" 23, Illinois " 18, " J. G. Langguth.
" 25, Illinois " 31, " Eldredge.
" 25, Illinois " 30, " Livingston.
" 27, Illinois " 82, " Jozöfé.
" 27, Indiana " 26, " Berthoud.
" 27, Indiana " 26, " Helm.
" 27, Indiana " 21, " Crosier.
" 29, Indiana " 35, " Crosier.
" 29, Indiana " 37, " Chappelsmith.
" 31, Iowa " 44, " Collin.
" 38, Maryland " 11, " Emmittsburg.
" 39, Maryland " 17, " Hanshew.
" 43, Michigan " 24, " Streng.
" 45, Minnesota " 7, " Hibbard.
" 46, Minnesota " 49, " Lapham.
" 48, Missouri " 22, " Keytesville.
" 50, Nebraska " 5, " De Soto.
" 53, New Jersey " 2, " Readington.
" 57, New York " 66, " Sias.
" 59, New York " 86, " Hibbard.
" 61, New York " 145, " Partrick.
" 61, New York " 150, " Malcolm.
" 62, New York " 193, " Throg's.
" 63, New York " 178, " Maurice.
" 63, New York " 193, " E. Morris.
" 65, N. Carolina " 1, " F. J. Kron
" 65, N. Carolina " 10, " Morelle.

Page 65, N. Carolina Station 23, *read* Morelle.
" 65, Ohio " 11, " J. H. Phillips.
" 67, Ohio " 38, " Samms.
" 67, Ohio " 45, " Owsley.
" 69, Ohio " 100, " Clung.
" 71, Oregon " 3, " Ironside.
" 71, Pennsylvania " 14, " Grathwohl.
" 71, Pennsylvania " 15, " Deering.
" 73, Pennsylvania " 31, " Spera.
" 73, Pennsylvania " 32, " Hance.
" 73, Pennsylvania " 40, " Meehan.
" 76, S. Carolina " 26, " Wickinsville.
" 77, S. Carolina " 2, " Ravenel.
" 77, S. Carolina " 25, " Ravenel.
" 78, Tennessee " 7, " Elizabethton.
" 79, Tennessee " 20, " J. M. Parker.
" 79, Texas " 3, " S. K. Jennings.
" 80, Texas " 65, " Pin Oak.
" 81, Texas " 61, " Ervendberg.
" 82, Vermont " 15, " Lunenburg.
" 83, Vermont " 16, " Sheldon.
" 85, Virginia " 4, " Kounslar.
" 85, Virginia " 5, " Principal.
" 85, Virginia " 39, " Mettauer.
" 85, Virginia " 41, " Appleyard.
" 91, Wisconsin " 37, " Dunegan.
" 91, Mexico " 1, " Laszlo.
" 91, Mexico " 3, " Laszlo.
" 214, Nebraska " 4, " Kearney.
" 220, Oregon " 6, " Hoskins.
" 257, Maryland, column 2, " Schellman.
" 296, Virginia, " 5, " Montross.
" 305, Georgia, line 4, " Oglethorpe

www.ingramcontent.com/pod-product-compliance
Lightning Source LLC
LaVergne TN
LVHW010143110826
845151LV00002B/413

9781425539078